HOME IMPROVEMENT 1-2-3

EXPERT ADVICE FROM THE HOME DEPOT

Meredith®

Meredith Publishing Group
Ray Wolf, Project Director
Benjamin W. Allen, Editor
Christopher Cavanaugh, Managing Editor
Ernie Shelton, Cover Design
Doug Johnston, Production Manager
Book Development Team:
Bill Jones
Barry Benecke
Paul Currie
Bill Nelson
Steve Meyer
J. Keith Moore
Sandy Graff

The Home Depot
Dick Hammill, Senior VP, Marketing
Rob Hallam, Project Director

First Edition. Printing number and year: 16 15 14 02 01 00
ISBN: 0-696-20168-2 Library of Congress Catalog Number: 95-76225

Distributed by Meredith Corp.

Note to the Reader: Due to differing conditions, tools, and individual skills, Meredith Publishing Group and The Home Depot assume no responsibility for any damages, injuries suffered, or losses incurred as a result of following the information published in this book. Before beginning any project, review the plans and instructions carefully, and if any doubts or questions remain, consult local experts or authorities. Because local codes and regulations vary greatly, you should always check with local authorities to ensure that your project complies with all applicable local codes and regulations. Always read and observe all of the safety precautions provided by any tool or equipment manufacturer and follow all accepted safety procedures.

The editors of Home Improvement 1-2-3 are dedicated to providing accurate, helpful, do-it-yourself information. We welcome your comments about improving this book and ideas for other books we might offer home improvement enthusiasts. Contact us by any of the methods listed below.

Leave a voice message at: 800/678-2093

Write to: Meredith Books, Home Improvement 1-2-3
1716 Locust St.
Des Moines, IA 50309

Send e-mail to: hi123@dsm.mdp.com

Fax us at: 515/284-2320

CONTENTS

One of many *experts' round tables* held to scrutinize the pages of this book.

Welcome to Home Improvement 1-2-3

We challenge you to find a more innovative and comprehensive home improvement book!

Go ahead, thumb through the pages and see for yourself. What you have here are the combined efforts of a partnership between two of the home improvement industry's finest players–Better Homes and Gardens® and The Home Depot.

To create this one-of-a-kind book for homeowners, the editors of Better Homes and Gardens® Books combined their publishing and home improvement expertise with the day-to-day *Wisdom of the Aisles* of thousands of Home Depot employees across North America.

Here's how it all happened.

Weeks 1-8: Together we survey over 2000 Home Depot department heads across the country to determine what questions they most commonly receive from customers and what home improvement projects customers most actively pursue.

Weeks 9-19: Everyone agrees. Customers need a problem-solving book. The end-all, be-all home improvement book. People come to us when they have a problem, so why not make our wisdom readily available in one place?

Armed with a rough table of contents for the book, we return to Home Depot stores all across the country. This time we talk to customers. Our table of contents is designed with one thing in mind: "What do homeowners need to know to get the job done right?"

Weeks 20-40: We design two sample books, each based on our research, but each using a completely different approach to layout and design. These books are shown to panels of homeowners and Home Depot customers to find out which approach works best.

Weeks 41-44: The customer is always right. Homeowners tell us they want their information clearly illustrated and easy to understand. They want additional information and advice with each project.

Our challenge is to pack this book with information, make it highly visual, but most of all, keep it easy to use. Our goal is to keep every single block of text (with the exception of this introduction) under 250 words. The result is the dynamic, visual design used for this book. (See pages 4 and 5 for a list of the features and *Before You Use This Book.*)

Weeks 45-84: The hard work begins. We feel we have a handle on what people want and how they want it presented, so we set to work on the actual pages.

To make this book even better, we create a rigorous review process. As each project, or solution, is developed, it is sent to selected former professional tradespeople who are now Home Depot employees for review. Based on this *Wisdom of the Aisles* from The Home Depot employees, each project in the book is written, illustrated, and edited by the very best journalists and illustrators in the field.

Finished chapters are then subjected to an *experts' round table* for final review. Every page of the book is sent to a group of the most experienced Home Depot employees–known as *Homers*–for both an accuracy and reality check. After they study the pages, we meet with them to go over each and every page. These *Homer round tables* result in more than 700 changes to the pages of this book.

Weeks 85-90: After all suggestions and corrections from the *round tables* are made, pages are sent to senior Home Depot staff for final approval. Only then do we consider the pages to be complete.

Today, we firmly believe this unique and thorough review and approval process resulted in a book that not only is extremely accurate, but also reflects the best advice possible.

We also know, however, this book does not address every problem or contingency. Differences in regional construction practices, differences in materials, and differences in local code issues make it impossible to cover every contingency a homeowner may face. We also know *Murphy's 2nd Law of Publishing* dictates that minor errors are likely to occur in the production of a book of this size and scope. For that reason we caution you to make sure you have a complete and thorough understanding of any project before you begin. Make sure you know the safety and legal issues surrounding your project, and don't attempt a project that is too far above your skill level.

We believe this book is the tool that can best prepare you for your next home improvement project. For that, we thank the employees of The Home Depot—they were instrumental in shaping this book, and you'll find their names on the inside back cover.

We wish you success and enjoyment in all your home improvement projects.

Ray Wolf
Project Director
Meredith Books

Rob Hallam
Project Director
The Home Depot

BEFORE YOU USE THIS BOOK

We've tried to make this a very hardworking book, one that has additional information, ideas, and tips on every page. Take a minute and read through the different types of features we've included, so you'll have a better idea of what to expect.

Finally, we've included our thoughts on both safety and building and zoning codes. We ask that you read these two sections carefully, and that you make your home improvements in a legal fashion. Above all else, work safely.

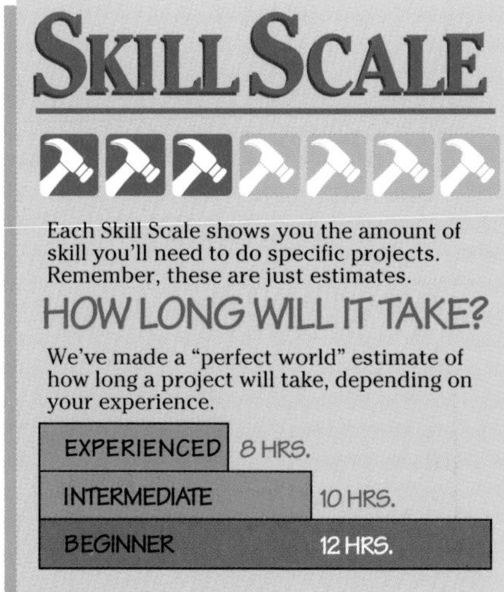

Sometimes brawn is definitely not the way to go. Work Smarter shows you the intelligent way to go about your repairs or improvements.

USING TOOL TIPS

When a job requires specialized tools, Tool Tips tells you what you need to know to produce the best results.

STUFF YOU'LL NEED:

- ☐ Every set of similar projects includes Stuff You'll Need: the **Tools** and **Materials** you'll need to get the job done right.

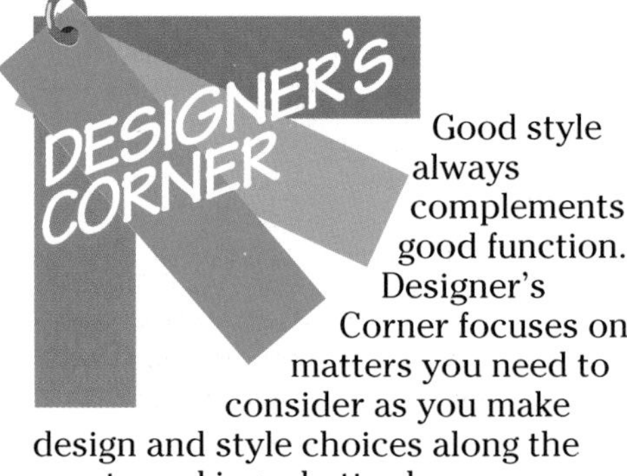

Good style always complements good function. Designer's Corner focuses on matters you need to consider as you make design and style choices along the way to making a better home.

THE RED TAPE OF HOME IMPROVEMENTS

Just about every local government has its own zoning regulations and building codes. In some regions homeowners are free to do most anything they like within the exterior walls of their home; in other locales, homeowners' options are more tightly regulated.

Basically, zoning codes regulate the types of construction you may undertake on your lot, while building codes regulate the way construction and repairs must be done. Your projects must comply with both sets of regulations.

Although there are several national codes that serve as models for local building codes, we can't tell you what you can and cannot do to your home in your locality. What we can tell you with absolute certainty is that you must check with local authorities before you begin any project.

You should have a clear understanding of what your local ordinances will and will not allow before you even begin to plan your project. Your local home improvement retailer can give you good advice and direction about local codes, but if you have the slightest doubt about what is or isn't allowed, check it out with local authorities! The consequences of violating zoning and building codes can be severe–in some cases requiring you to have the work professionally checked, in other cases requiring you to tear down the work completely and start over.

In short, do not try to short circuit your local ordinances. Know what they will let you do, and what they will not. Know when you need a permit, and always get a permit before you begin work.

A simple tip can save you hours of time going to and from the store.

SAFETY

If any project in the book includes a potentially dangerous situation, we display it prominently in red so you know exactly what you're getting into.

ALERT

BUYER'$ GUIDE

Buyer's Guide not only helps you get the right part for the right price but also offers advice on how to get the best value.

PROTECTING LIFE AND LIMB

Working on your home can be fun, it certainly has economic rewards, and many people even find it personally satisfying. Above all else, however, you must remember that it can also be dangerous.

Throughout this book we give safety warnings where most needed and show sound practices. However, you should add a good dose of common sense every time you reach for a power tool, climb a ladder, or start a new project.

Do-it-yourself work involves sharp and often powerful tools. Keeping yourself out of harm's way should be your top priority. Before operating any power tool, carefully read the owner's manual for safety information. The manufacturer's instructions are your best guide.

Cutting and shaping various materials invariably involves working with materials that can and do splinter, chip, and break. Your eyes and skin are little match for these sharp materials. Wear protective gloves whenever they will not hinder your handling of tools; whenever in doubt, wear protective eye wear.

Materials can be heavy. You may hate to admit it, but you're not as strong as you may think. Handling heavy materials can put you in awkward positions that will subject your body to stress. Your body, especially your back, must last a lifetime. Get help when moving heavy materials and learn to lift properly.

It should go without saying that working with electricity can be a life-and-death matter. Double-check to make sure the power is off at the breaker box before you start working with wiring. Once the power is off, mark the breaker box so someone else will not turn it on while you are working with wiring.

Falls are the most common cause of injury in the home. Extreme care must be used when working with ladders. Check that your ladder is properly erected, that it's on a firm and level surface, and that you won't be exceeding its recommended uses.

Above all else, know your limits–technical, physical and intellectual–and do not try to do more than you think you are capable of doing.

ENVIRONMENTAL IMPROVEMENT

MAKE THE ULTIMATE HOME IMPROVEMENT

From the basic materials we use to create our homes, to energy resources we use for heating and cooling, to the products we select to maintain and enhance our lifestyles–the home has a powerful effect on the environment.

We have a tremendous opportunity to choose products for our homes that minimize environmental burdens. You don't have to search far and wide for "green" products. Products with positive environmental features and benefits are all around us.

LUMBER & BUILDING MATERIALS

1 **Pressure-Treated Lumber** – Chemical preservatives help prolong wood life. Remember to cut this wood outside, wash hands after handling, and do not burn.

2 **Engineered Lumber** – Maximizes wood resources.

3 **Steel Studs** – Alternative building material with recycled content.

4 **Roof Windows/Skylights** – Natural light saves on lighting costs; roof windows provide ventilation.

5 **High-Efficiency Fireplace Inserts** – The most efficient indoor air quality and heating alternative to wood, wax, or gas logs.

6 **Hardboard or Simulated Rain Forest Wood Doors** – High performance alternatives that maximize wood resources.

7 **Whole House Attic Fans** – Energy saver that also increases comfort. Power Attic Ventilators and Fans—Energy savers that also increase comfort.

8 **High R-Value Attic Insulation** – Energy saver that increases comfort. The higher the R-Value, the greater the insulating performance.

9 **Low U-factor Windows** – Look for this measure of glass performance. The lower the U-factor, the greater the heat transmission savings.

10 **Light Colored Roof Shingles** – Energy saver in most climates.

11 **Poly-Wrapped Insulation** – Decreases air infiltration – increases handling comfort.

12 **Cellulose Insulation** – Alternative with high content of recycled paper.

13 **Reinforced Gypsum/ Cellulose Underlayment** – Dimensionally stable, recycled content, tropical wood alternative features smooth surface, no paper to delaminate, no swelling, and no bleeding from wood fibers.

FLOOR & WALL COVERINGS

14 **Cedar Closet Liners** – Naturally repels insects.

15 **Marble Tiles** – Natural, indoor air quality flooring alternative.

16 **Wood Flooring** – Natural, indoor air quality flooring alternative. Combine with Area Rugs, which can be removed from home for cleaning.

17 **Ceramic Tile** – Natural, indoor air quality flooring alternative.

18 **Recycled Rubber Doormats** – High performance product that helps recycle tires (national recycling rate for tires is only 5%).

19 **Carpet** – When selecting carpet, look for the Carpet and Rug Institute environmental label to assure the carpet meets indoor air quality standards.

PAINT/SEALERS

20 **Duct Tape/Mastic** – Leaky air ducts can account for up to 30% of your home energy costs.

21 **Water-Based Sealers** – Causes less air pollution.

22 **Low or No-Odor Paints** – New formulations enhance user friendliness and indoor air quality.

23 **Caulk** – Helps stop air infiltration and increases energy savings.

24 **Lead Testers** – Helps determine presence of lead-based paint, lead solder, or lead in other household items like dishes.

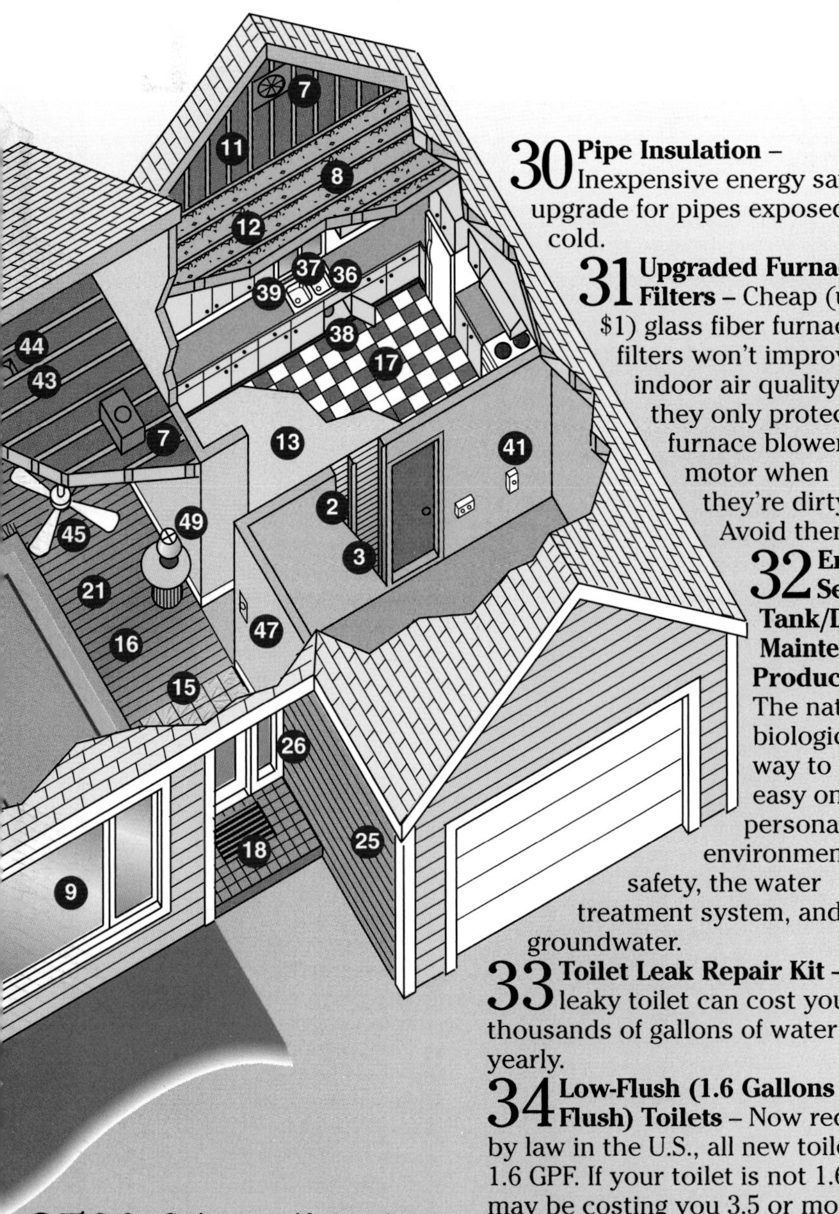

25 **Safer Stripper** – Alternative to faster, riskier chemicals. Takes a little longer, but worth the wait.

26 **Weather stripping** – Like caulking, an energy saver.

PLUMBING, KITCHEN & BATH

27 **Whole-House Water Filters** – For better water quality.

28 **Water Heater and Blanket** – Select the most energy efficient water heater you can afford, considering operating costs on the yellow energy label. A water heater blanket and setting the thermostat to 120° will help save energy.

29 **Lead-Free Plumbing Solder** – Always use only lead-free solder on drinking water lines.

30 **Pipe Insulation** – Inexpensive energy savings upgrade for pipes exposed to cold.

31 **Upgraded Furnace Filters** – Cheap (under $1) glass fiber furnace filters won't improve indoor air quality and they only protect the furnace blower motor when they're dirty. Avoid them.

32 **Enzyme Septic Tank/Drain Maintenance Products** – The natural biological way to go easy on your personal environmental safety, the water treatment system, and groundwater.

33 **Toilet Leak Repair Kit** – A leaky toilet can cost you thousands of gallons of water yearly.

34 **Low-Flush (1.6 Gallons Per Flush) Toilets** – Now required by law in the U.S., all new toilets are 1.6 GPF. If your toilet is not 1.6, it may be costing you 3.5 or more gallons each time you flush.

35 **Low-Flow Showerhead (2.5 Gallons Per M Minute)** – Now required by law for all newly manufactured showerheads.

36 **No-Lead or Low-Lead Faucet** – Faucets with cast brass passageways can contain up to 8% lead in the brass, which is why you should always run only cold water through them for a minute or two before drinking or cooking. There are no-lead and low-lead alternatives on the market.

37 **Faucet Aerator** – Another inexpensive water saver.

38 **Food Waste Disposal** – Used in addition to compost bins to create a total home food waste management system.

39 **Point-of-Use Water Filter** – Filtering at the tap ensures removal of impurities from your home's plumbing lines and fixtures.

40 **Enzyme Drain Opener** – Biological alternative for enhanced personal environmental safety and groundwater/water treatment system friendliness.

ELECTRICAL/LIGHTING

41 **Occupancy Sensor** – Energy saver that automatically lights only when room is in use.

42 **Programmable Thermostat** – Energy saver that allows automatic time and temperature control of heating and cooling.

43 **Smoke Detector** – Inexpensive environmental safety product. Test your detectors today, and make sure that you have one per floor; fires still cause about 7,000 deaths per year, and manufacturers recommend detector replacement every 10 years.

44 **Carbon Monoxide Detector** – Carbon Monoxide injures about 10,000 people per year. Have your home and heating appliances inspected regularly to prevent this leading cause of poisoning.

45 **Ceiling Fans** – Can reduce energy use by up to 8% in summer by making you feel cooler.

46 **Night Lights** – Environmental safety product especially useful on stairs, where falls cause about 4,000 deaths per year. Newer night lights are more energy efficient.

47 **Light Dimmer** – Simple device can help you save on lighting cost. For example, an incandescent light dimmed by 25% can save 10% on energy use and extend bulb life.

48 **Electric Timer** – Simple energy savings and security product.

49 **Compact Fluorescent Lighting** – Energy saver. Lighting accounts for about 5 to 7% of home energy costs. To save on energy costs when purchasing lighting, first select the amount of "lumens," or light output, then select the light with the lowest wattage, or energy usage.

Planning Primer

Home improvement projects fall into three basic categories: general spruce-up, room redo, and whole-house redo. Before you begin your project, you'll need to spend some time determining which decorating style best fits your family's personal tastes and habits.

Once you've decided on the style for your home or room, the next step is to create a master plan, which will provide the framework and schedule for the entire project. The more adventuresome your plans, the greater the need for a schedule and some help.

Your plan should have information from a variety of sources including: your style preferences gathered from books and magazines; advice from friends and relatives; subject specific advice from experts such as tile representatives or electricians and carpenters; specialized advice from professional planners regarding ergonomics and layout; and assistance from a professional project coordinator, or interior decorator.

Often you don't have to spend a bundle to design a pleasing room. Here are some tips on how to squeeze the most from your decorating dollar without compromising style.

Invest in high quality hardware and decorative trim. Money spent on solidly built curtain rods, interesting drawer pulls, and decorative drapes and fringes will pay off with a home that has one-of-a-kind appeal and the finished look a professional decorator brings.

Bone up on faux-finishing basics. Marbled floors, sponged walls, and painted furniture add instant pizzazz.

Steps to a Design Plan

1. FIND SOURCES OF INFORMATION

FRIENDS & RELATIVES | BOOKS & MAGAZINES | PROJECT COORDINATORS | SUBJECT SPECIFIC ADVICE | SPECIALIZED ADVICE

2. DETERMINE YOUR TASTES AND HABITS

YOUR TASTES | YOUR HABITS

3. DETERMINE THE EXTENT OF THE PROJECT

SIMPLE SPRUCE-UP | WHOLE HOUSE | ROOM REDO

WHAT STYLE IS IT ?

• **TRADITIONAL** style has the look of some historic period other than your own and features antiques or reproductions of period pieces as key elements. Subsets of traditional style include colonial or craftsman styles among many others. Many furniture manufacturers will have complete lines of reproductions, and whole books are written on single styles.

• **COUNTRY** looks typically have well-worn, simple, or primitive furniture and folk-art motifs. A country-styled room abounds with natural textures: wood, brick, tile, earthenware, and hand-loomed fabrics all contribute to an informal, comfortable atmosphere.

• **CONTEMPORARY** styling is clean, uncluttered, and sophisticated. It's the art of understatement. Furnishings and accessories are few, but their effect is powerful. This simple elegance is generally built around a focal element–a beautiful piece of furniture, striking artwork, or a dramatic floor covering.

• **ECLECTIC** styles reflect a combination of all three styles above. Sometimes designers will use pieces from other cultures to create an attractive collection and enhance the contrast between the styles within a room. Don't be fooled; this is not a haphazard hodgepodge that you can just throw together and call eclectic–it's often the most difficult style to master.

Ideas of decorating style can come from many sources, including books, magazines, family, friends and decorating professionals. Sort through your collected ideas and you'll arrive at the style that suits you best. The result can be elegant or eccentric, as long as it pleases you. The bath above shows a simple contemporary style with hints of Oriental influences.

Sources of Information

FRIENDS & RELATIVES

The most important thing at this point is to collect as many ideas and as much information as you can. The source of your information can make a difference. Advice from Uncle Leo may not be your best bet—especially if he thinks dress socks, plaid shorts, and T-shirts are appropriate summer attire!

BOOKS & MAGAZINES

Browsing through books, brochures, and magazines will give you ideas about materials and style. Most of the information is inexpensive, and best of all, nobody's feelings will be hurt if you don't follow their advice.

Don't limit yourself to publications specifically about decorating. Some of your best ideas may come from home and garden magazines; architectural, furniture, and art magazines; department store catalogs; manufacturers' brochures—the list goes on and on.

When possible, cut out the ideas you like and assemble them in a scrapbook. Include paint and wallpaper swatches with notes about where you found them. That way, when you want to refer back to an idea, you'll be able to find it.

PROJECT COORDINATORS

If your remodeling is limited to a single room, you may be able to get all the information and help you need from specialized advisors, books, and magazines. But if your project involves several rooms—and especially if you are going to have to deal with subcontractors, inspectors and furnishing sales representatives—consider using a professional project coordinator to represent your interests. Project coordinators are also known as interior designers.

Subject specific advice will help you choose flooring, fixtures and wallcoverings that all go together as shown in the photograph above.

Available from in-store planning departments of home improvement retailers, or from private interior designers, a project coordinator will work with you to establish a style.

Project coordination is typically a paid service, and unless you are experienced with the complexities and headaches of dealing with contractors and inspectors, the service is well worth the fee. **Whole–house** decorating projects can be complex. You have to juggle contractors, subcontractors, suppliers, schedules, and keep everything on track to produce the look you're after. As your advocate, a project coordinator can help you find the best contractors, negotiate the best prices, and most importantly, protect you from overcharging and unnecessary stress. In many cases, home improvement retailers also offer installation of purchased items by subcontractors.

Interior designers don't get involved with the permit process, but they'll work as a liaison between you and the vendors to assure that your project stays on schedule and on budget. A good project coordinator will help you plan your project so that the new decor fits into the style of the rest of your home.

SUBJECT SPECIFIC ADVICE

Subject specific advice is the practical, sometimes technical information you need to make smart choices about your design materials. Your subject specific advisors will most often be found at the place where your decorating materials are sold. Sales representatives, the answer-booth staff, or manufacturers' representatives can supply valuable information about their products and which might be most suitable for your application.

Let each advisor make recommendations regarding the materials in their area of expertise.

These kinds of sources of ideas are often the best when you're considering a room **spruce-up**.

SPECIALIZED ADVICE

Where subject specific advice may help you choose a single type of product or decorating material, specialized advice is concerned with integrating all the elements to produce a well-designed functional room. If you're considering a total **room redo**, then you should consider getting specialized advice.

Rooms that have clearly defined purposes, such as kitchens and baths, need specialized advice that looks beyond appearance to assure functional efficiency.

A design specialist offers a more sophisticated level of decorating advice than product representatives because the specialist considers the whole room, not merely its parts. Drawing upon both experience and training, they can help you apply the principles of good design.

DESIGN BASICS

Color is the key to successful decorating. It underlies all the other decorating choices you make.

Choosing a single color may be quite simple. On the other hand, assembling a color family for a decorating scheme may be a little trickier. (Your ultimate color choices should be based on very personal criteria. Working with color favorites is a good place to begin.) Color schemes succeed if you learn to speak color's language.

In interior design, colors are most often "bundled" in harmonious color families. Within a color family, a single color may occur in any number of shades or tints. Sometimes, for purposes of contrast, colors are grouped with their complements (their opposites on the color wheel).

In the same way, texture and pattern, horizontal and vertical elements, and objects of large and small scale are balanced against each other until a satisfying variety and rhythm is achieved.

Repetition is not enough to tie a room together. A professional designer will identify an element—a color, pattern, texture or object—that can be modified, echoed, or reintroduced to achieve a sense of unity without becoming predictable or boring.

The use of texture in room design connects the sense of touch to the sense of sight. The same or similar colors expressed in different textures provides interesting variations to a common theme.

Finally, for a living space to be truly satisfactory, careful attention must be given to its sense of proportion and scale. Proper scale is accomplished by a variety of small intimate objects contrasted by larger pieces of furniture. Good design can enhance a well-proportioned room and also help correct the faults of an ill-proportioned room. Color, for example, can alter how large a room appears. To make a small room look larger, use a light color on walls and ceiling.

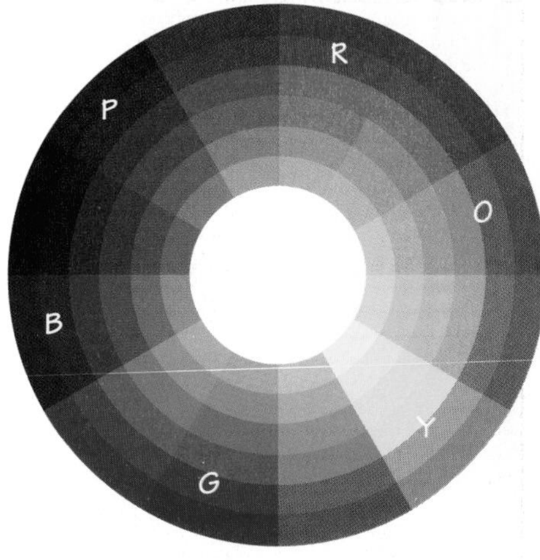

The Color Wheel

The color wheel represents the relationship between the primary colors (**R**, **Y**, **B**), the secondary colors (**O**, **G**, **P**), and the tertiary hues (the ones between the primary and secondary colors). The lighter values toward the center of the wheel are called tints. The darker ones toward the outside are shades. Colors that fall directly opposite each other on the wheel are complementary.

Primary Colors

Primary colors—specifically red, yellow, and blue—are colors in their most basic form. No other colors can be mixed together to make primary colors.

The simplicity of primary colors gives any decorating scheme an open, vibrant, and youthful appearance. Because primary colors are so elementary, they are perceived as lacking in depth and sophistication unless accented with complex colors, a mix of texture, or the addition of pattern.

A primary color scheme is most effective when one of the three colors is predominant, either alone or in a family of related values. Use the other two primaries as vivid accent colors.

Primary colors can be very bold and energetic (right). In this mock-up room, the fully saturated hues are kept in check by liberal use of black and white.

Secondary colors—green, orange, and purple—are blends of two primary colors, mixed in equal parts. This makes secondary colors more complex and versatile than primaries. Secondary colors work well when used with each other or in combination with primaries. Because of their intensity, secondary colors are often used as accents, especially with neutral colors.

Subdued color schemes are used most often in home decorating. Subdued colors include multicolor blends, hues plus their complement, tints, and shades. Hues plus their complement are responsible for browns and muted, earthy tones. Shades are colors or color mixtures to which black has been added. Tints are the result of combining color with white. When working with color, remember that color sets a visual temperature. Reds, yellows, and oranges are considered warm colors. Blues, greens, and violets are cool hues.

Balancing Color, Texture, & Pattern

To please the eye, an interior design must provide both variety and structure. While a mix of textures, colors, and patterns is stimulating, an underlying theme prevents chaos. However, an *even* balance of contrast is usually unsatisfactory; the effect goes unnoticed.

The driving principle of effective design may be expressed as: "A lot of one element mixed with some of its opposite." The primary design element can be a color family, a shape, a texture, a pattern. The predominance of this element sets the scheme. Add excitement by placing a few items that contrast sharply with the predominant element.

As a rule, use your dominant element in large areas such as walls and floors. Distribute that element evenly around the room in furniture, window treatments, and accessories. Finally, add contrasting accents. Trust your eye. If the result doesn't look right, move things around, or add and subtract elements one at a time.

A monochromatic palette (different shades of the same color) is invigorated by accessories of different textures. The key is the calculated interplay of surface finishes. Soft, filmy fabrics mix with nubby yarn. The wooden table is set beside a plush chair, plump with pillows. The sleek, glass-enclosed artwork contrasts with the lush flower arrangements.

Eclectic and informal collections of fragments and forms contribute an intriguing twist to any room. This sitting room, for example, is filled with fascinating shapes, from the collection on the wall to the graceful iron table frame.

Rough textures evoke a casual atmosphere. In this room, rough-textured flooring, wicker chairs, and unembellished wood inspire a comfortable, informal atmosphere. The refined antique elegance of the table is the room's counterpoint. The rich variety of surfaces and the attention to decorative detail keep this space visually compelling.

A good pattern is worth repeating. Lines, both straight and ziggy, add zest and wit to the room (left). The design is especially compelling because the pattern is expressed in a variety of ways. For example: the couch, the standing lamp, the chair. Don't be afraid to be bold. Areas of intensity make the overall design more interesting.

A distinctive architectural feature may suggest a form that can be reflected in other areas. In this bedroom (above), the sunburst cap to the window begins a rhythmic line that shows up again in the slats of the shutter, the ribs of the lampshade, and the meandering lines of the furniture covers. The very limited spectrum of colors helps call attention to the repeating pattern.

Deep, rich colors give an expansive space (above) warmth and weight. Standing lamps that cast small pools of light prevent the large space from becoming overwhelming. Thoughtful placement of furniture creates cozy conversational groupings. Focal points of intricate detail also contribute to the comfortable sense of scale.

Details make or break a design. Keep your eyes open for accessories that work with your decorating scheme–and each other–in surprising ways (left).

Extending Your Design To the Window

Window treatments serve a variety of purposes. Because windows provide the visual transition between outside and inside environments, their selection will be determined in part by the nature of the room and in part by the view presented.

Where the view complements the room design, window treatments may serve as a frame to dramatize the vistas—both inside and out. Tailored drapery folds or graceful billows of curtain pleasantly soften otherwise rigid architectural lines.

Sheers, on the other hand, are used to screen the outside view without impeding the natural light. When the exterior aspect does not flatter the interior, sheer draperies can be a satisfactory solution.

If you need draperies or blinds that can be easily opened for light or shut for privacy, your best choices will come from ready-made products with specially designed mechanisms. Ready-made window treatments are equal in every way to custom-made ones, but size and color choices are more limited.

If, on the other hand, your window treatments are primarily decorative, the sky's the limit. Your window solutions are free to be as whimsical or stylized as you wish them to be.

Shutters flatter their surroundings without competing with them. They easily adjust to changing light conditions and provide total privacy when closed. Shutters are extremely versatile—equally at home in several style settings, from country to contemporary.

Fabric knots anchor each corner of this fancifully draped swag. The richly colored fabric treatment accents the view and relieves the severe lines of a kitchen.

Simple but dramatic swathes of fabric strongly outline a window bay, creating the room's focal point. In a predominantly horizontal room arrangement, their sharp, vertical formality adds a welcome contrast.

A gossamer sheer curtain brings softness and a sense of grace to this room. A scalloped valance is the perfect finishing touch.

Painted wooden shutters are a sophisticated way to unify a ribbon of windows in this office setting.

This lushly gathered drape enhances a richly romantic ambience, while shrubbery supplies the privacy. The billowing swag provides counterpoint to the narrowness of the space.

Formal rooms need not be restricted to traditional heavy draperies. The gathered swag maintains the restrained mood of the room, but offers refreshing curves to an otherwise angular setting.

Considering Floorcovering In Your Design Plans

Floorcoverings are available in as many different types, colors, and pattern variations as there are personal tastes. Although the floor is a functional element that's often covered with furnishings, it is the foundation of your room and deserves full attention. The type and style of floorcovering you choose can help set the decorative mood for your room or section of house. Basic flooring materials such as ceramic tile, slate, hardwood, vinyl, or carpeting can stand alone and be visually spectacular. They also can be accentuated by a stylish inlay, throw rug, or woven accent rug.

Hardwood flooring combined with area rugs create a sense of warmth and elegance. The rugs spark the color scheme. The contrasting textures enhance both the wood and the rug (above and left).

Ceramic floor tile offers a durable, easy-to-maintain surface. Tile is available in a vast selection of colors and sizes. Here, tile creates a classic checked pattern in a contemporary kitchen (right).

Painted floorcoverings such as this tile-patterned canvas (right) are stylish yet surprisingly economical.

Patterned carpeting or rugs are classic ways to tie a room together. Patterns can be floral, abstract, geometric, or a combination of any of these (above).

Wide-plank softwood flooring adapts beautifully, whether the decor is country, traditional, or contemporary (above).

Standard hardwood floors lend a handsome, mellow warmth to family rooms and sitting areas (left).

Tile floors work well in bathrooms and kitchens. Patterns and choice of grout color can enhance the tile's visual effect (above and right). Often, vinyl sheet flooring appears similar to tile. It's economical and forms a water resistant floor.

Quarry tile flooring is reminiscent of old-world settings. Earthy and organic in appearance, it is nearly indestructible (above).

Enhancing Room Design With Architectural Details

Decorative structural details such as archways, sunbursts, cove molding, panel molding, curved walls, stepped ceilings and floors, ornamental plaster, and glass block walls can add drama and sophistication to an otherwise forgettable room.

Some architectural details are available ready-made or are relatively simple for do-it-yourselfers to manufacture. Others will require the services of skilled and experienced professionals in order to achieve the desired finished quality.

Wide, massive door casing with decorative rosettes (above) lend a sense of permanence and stability to a room. Elaborate cove molding (left) adds grace and distinction.

Bold room dividers demand attention, especially when they are as forcefully presented as this breakfast counter. Sometimes the merest suggestion of a division is enough to set a space apart.

Glass block partition walls are stylishly contemporary (above). Their bulk is offset by their airy light-transmitting qualities.

Decorative molding on a wall can be used like a frame to highlight artwork (left).

A classically derived end counter combined with custom wall caps and newel post top detailing transform this otherwise simple, contemporary kitchen.

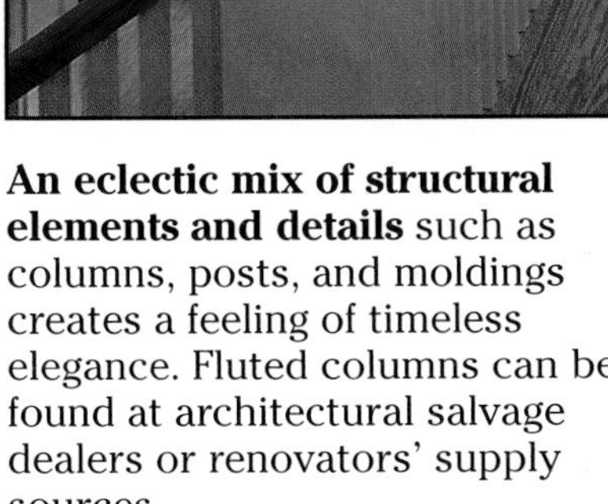

An eclectic mix of structural elements and details such as columns, posts, and moldings creates a feeling of timeless elegance. Fluted columns can be found at architectural salvage dealers or renovators' supply sources.

Generous use of ceiling coves, half columns, and a richly detailed mantel give this living room substance and character.

Accenting With Light

Artificial light is certainly the most flexible and popular way to change the mood, atmosphere, or feeling of a room. You can exaggerate space or diminish faults at the flick of a switch or the turn of a dimmer. Create dramatic light-and-shadow scenes on a wall by standing a canister light beneath a plant.

Natural light is another light source that can be easily and economically accentuated to provide spectacular effects. Wispy or lacy fabric at a window diffuses natural light, giving the room a softer, more mellow feel than that of direct sunlight or artificial light.

Be aware that extraneous lighting can make an otherwise impeccable room look dreary, whereas creative lighting can give the simplest space a special quality (See pages 202-207).

Manipulating accent light for pictures, objects, or textures is quite an art in itself. Getting the right amount of light and the correct positioning is crucial. When you are successful, however, the balance of light and shade and glow and drama that you can infuse into a room can be spectacular.

Incandescent lighting by special fixtures provides a glamorous feel to a bathroom and cosmetic center (above).

Pendant fixtures spotlight specific activity areas in the kitchen and family room (left and below).

Natural, ambient light produces a mellow atmosphere. These large windows capture lots of indirect light as well as a view.

Detailing with Accessories

Display the things you love. Personal collections used as accessories reflect your personality.

Accessories "soften" the stark utility of a room, lending it a feel that is, or should be, a reflection of your personality.

Unless you are one of those rare people who can artfully combine unrelated objects, it's best to strive for some degree of visual unity. All items, whether they are personal treasures or objects chosen for special effect, should fit compatibly into your decorating scheme.

Finishing touches such as plant and flower arrangements, shelves, collectibles, and art make a room memorable.

Use pillows to soften the angular lines of furniture. In addition to contributing color and pattern, pillows add the look of comfort to a room. As a bonus benefit, they are easy and inexpensive to change or replace.

Room accessories should be chosen to consistently reinforce your particular decorating scheme.

You may prefer the eclectic look where diversity reigns. Don't be fooled. The style is not haphazard. Success takes careful planning.

PAINTING BASICS

A color scheme can dramatically change a room or your entire home. Even without changing expensive furniture or carpeting, a fresh infusion of new paint color can transform the most ordinary room into an inviting living space.

Since color is a very personal choice, start your painting scheme with colors you enjoy: colors such as those found in your existing or new furnishings and artwork. Look for ideas in magazines and browse decorating centers for color scheme ideas.

Look at paint samples in your own home during the day in natural light and at night under incandescent lighting. You may be surprised at the change in color due to the different lighting.

Paint color can be light or dark, creating warm or cool, bright or subdued moods. The particular color scheme will set the mood for the entire room, so be sure to choose colors that capture the feeling you want to convey.

PAINT FINISHES

Range of sheens, from left: Gloss, a highly reflective finish for areas where high washability is important. Semi-gloss paint is also highly washable with a slightly less reflective finish. Gloss paints tend to show surface flaws. Eggshell, or satin, combines soft finish with washability. Flat provides a soft finish that hides surface irregularities better than gloss or satin paints but is not as washable.

Paint is available in a variety of finishes, ranging from flat latex to gloss enamel. Gloss enamels dry to a shiny, reflective surface and are used for surfaces that will be washed often like bathrooms and kitchens. Flat paints are most commonly used for wall and ceiling applications in family rooms and bedrooms.

The two main types of paints are oil-based and water-based, or "latex." Oil-based is a very durable paint but requires solvents for cleanup. New developments in latex paints have made them as durable as oil-based paints. Latex paints clean up with soap and water.

High washability is a feature of quality paint, whether it be oil or water-based. The pigments in bargain paints may "chalk" and wash away with mild scrubbing.

Paint coverage listed on the label of quality paint should be about 330 square feet per gallon. Bargain paints may initially cost less but sometimes require 2 or even 3 coats to cover the same area as a slightly more expensive quality paint.

SELECTING THE RIGHT PAINT

ROOM	Plaster Walls and Ceilings	Wallboard Walls and Ceilings	Wood Trim and Cabinets	Metal Trim
Living Room Dining Room Bedroom	Use oil-based primer, then flat latex for final coat	Use latex primer if unpainted, or oil-based primer if painted; finish with flat latex coat	Use varnish or oil-based primer; finish with oil-based final coat	Metal primer or oil-based primer; finish with a latex coat
Kitchen Bathroom	Use oil-based paints for primer. Use latex for final coat			Use metal primer; and oil-based finish coat
	Concrete Floors and Walls			
Basement Garage	Use sealer or exterior primer, then finish with latex paint		Varnish or oil-based primer, then oil-based final coat	Metal primer, then latex final coat

CALCULATING PAINT COVERAGE

1.) Length of Wall or Ceiling................................ ________

2.) Height of Wall or Ceiling................................ X ________

3.) Surface Area... = ________

4.) Coverage Per Gallon of Chosen Paint.................. ÷ ________

5.) Gallons of Paint Needed................................ = ________

Tools for Painting

Most painting jobs can be done with a few quality tools. It is a good idea to purchase two or three premium brushes, a sturdy paint pan that can be attached to a stepladder, and one or two good rollers. With proper maintenance and cleanup, these tools will last for years and perform better than the cheaper alternatives.

All-purpose brushes blend polyester, nylon, and animal bristles that perform well with a variety of paints. Choose a 3" straight-edged wall brush, a 2" straight-edged trim brush, and a tapered sash brush for the most common applications.

Rollers should have a wire frame with nylon bearings, a comfortable handle, and a threaded end for attaching extensions when painting walls and ceilings. Quality covers perform well and will not leave fibers behind on the freshly painted surface!

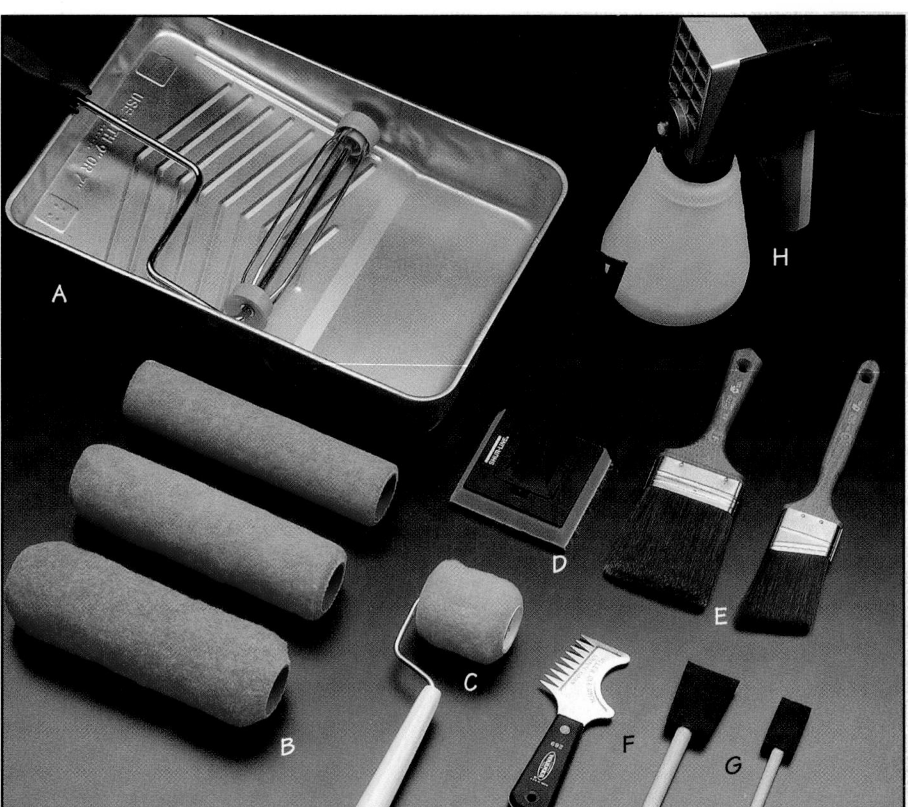

Specialty tools make difficult painting situations easier. Paint roller and pan (A) and roller covers (B) simplify painting large areas. Trim roller (C) and paint pad (D) are used for trim. Quality brushes (E) are a traditional alternative to pads and roller. Cleaning tool (F) eases brush and roller cleanup. Disposable foam brushes (G) work well with latex paints and airless paint sprayers (H) simplify painting odd-shaped and intricate areas.

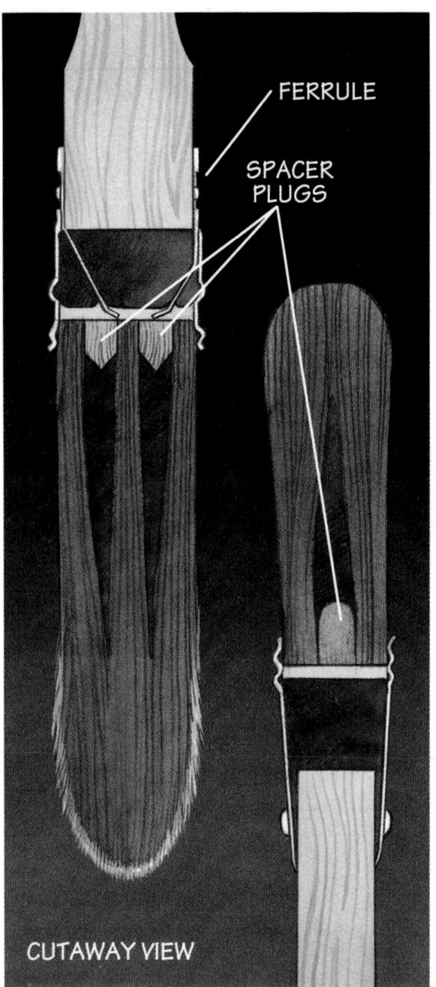

BUYER'$ GUIDE

Choosing the Right Brush

A quality brush, on the left, has a shaped hardwood handle and a sturdy reinforced ferrule made of non-corrosive metal. Multiple spacer plugs separate the bristles. The quality brush also has flagged (split) bristles and a chiseled end for precise edging. The cheaper brush will have a blunt end, unflagged bristles, and a cardboard spacer that will soften when it gets wet.

A 3" straight-edged brush, on the right, is a good choice for cutting in paint lines at ceilings and in corners. For painting woodwork, a 2" trim brush works well. Choose brushes with chiseled tips for painting in corners. A tapered sash brush may help when painting corners or window sashes.

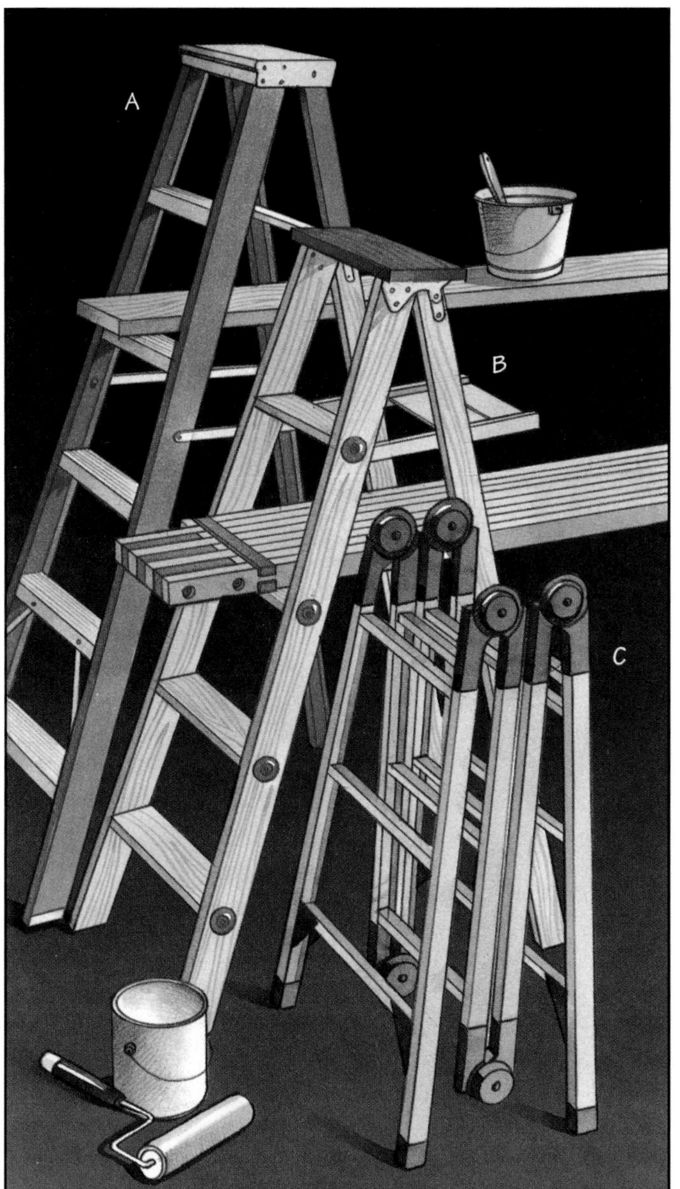

Ladders & Scaffolds

Fiberglass ladders (A) are very strong and yet non-conductive which makes them ideal when working with electricity. **Wooden ladders (B)** are less expensive and lighter, which makes them preferable in situations when the ladder needs to be moved frequently. **Adjustable ladders (C)** are good for situations when positioning is difficult due to an uneven surface.

For ceilings and high spots on walls, make a simple scaffold by running an extension plank through the steps of 2 stepladders. Planks should be no more than 12 ft. long and thick enough to support your weight without flexing. Ladders should be placed with the steps toward each other and with the braces down and locked.

For stairs, run an extension plank through the step of a ladder, and place the other end on a stairway step. Make sure the ladder is steady and check that the plank is level. Keep the plank close to the wall, if possible, and never overreach.

An adjustable ladder adapts to many different work needs. It can be used as a straight ladder, folded over for use as a stepladder, or used as a base for a scaffold plank.

WORK SMARTER

Tips for Using Ladders & Scaffolds

- Legs of the ladder should be level and steady against the ground.
- Always center your weight on the ladder.
- Move the ladder often and don't overreach.
- Keep the ladder in front of you when working.
- Lean your body against the ladder for balance.
- Don't stand on the top step, top brace or on the utility shelf of a stepladder.
- Be sure to tighten the step braces periodically.
- Never move a ladder with paint on it.
- Metal ladders should have rubber tips on the legs so they grip the floor.

Planning Your Attack

When the entire house is washed, scraped, sanded, filled, and caulked, you're ready to paint. One simple rule to follow is to always paint on the shaded side of the house. This is not only easier on you, but it will also keep the paint from drying too quickly which can cause it to peel and blister later.

Determining the proper order in which to proceed will save you time and aggravation. Generally, paint a house in the following order: soffits, the main body, then trim. In the example shown, right, the first step is to paint the soffit (**1**) for the side of the house that you are starting. Next paint the fascia (**2**) then proceed to the siding (**3**). Start by priming all the bare wood spots, then paint the siding, working across the house horizontally. Next do the window and door trim (**4**) and then the doors along with any posts (**5**) and balusters. If you intend to paint the entry steps or porch (**6**), do them last.

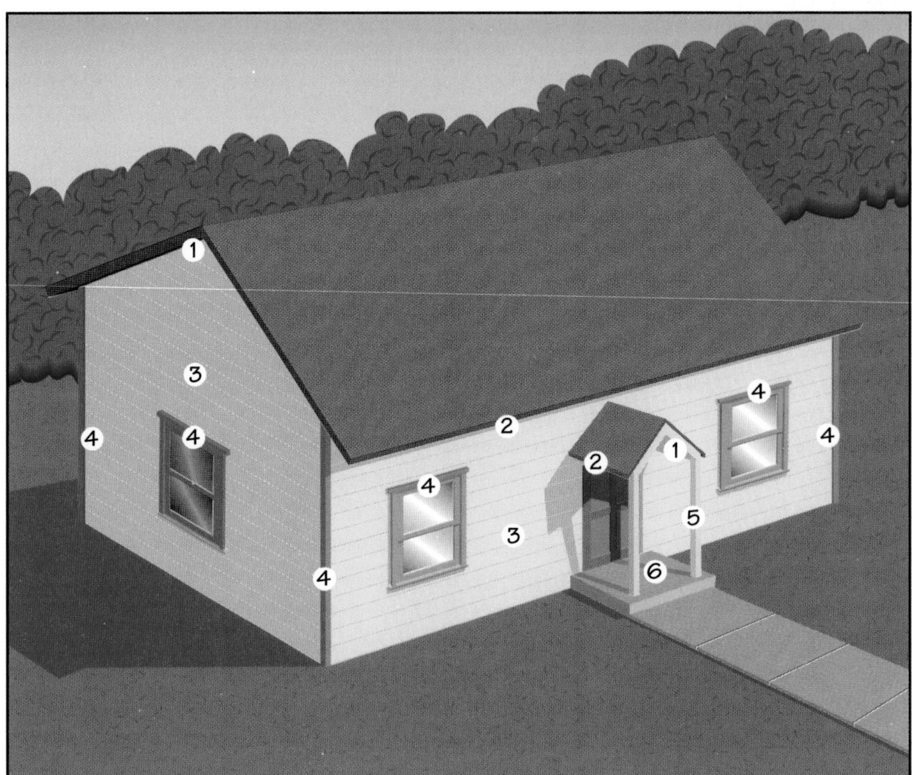

PAINTING A ROOM

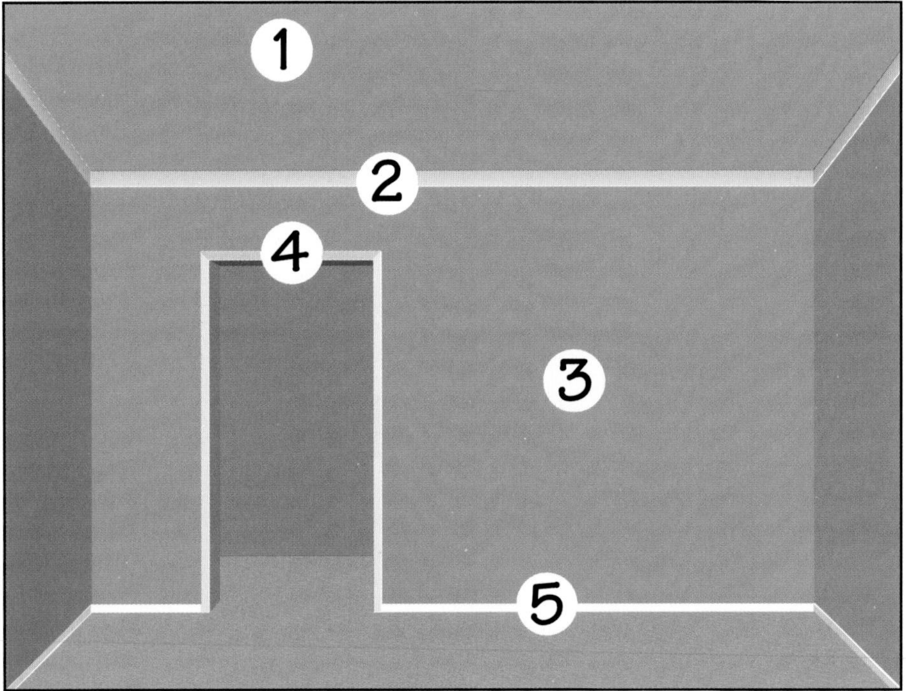

Once the interior walls and ceilings are prepped, painting the room in the proper sequence will make the job go much smoother. Start with the ceiling (**1**) and then proceed with any crown or cove molding (**2**). Next paint the walls (**3**) then the door trim (**4**) and door (if the room has one). Finish the room by completing the baseboard trim (**5**).

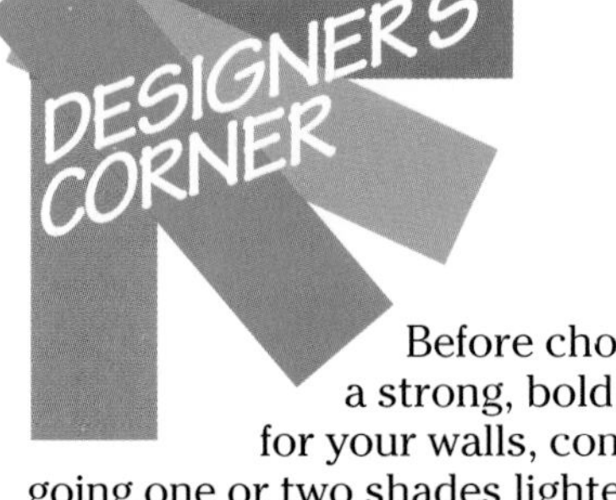

Before choosing a strong, bold color for your walls, consider going one or two shades lighter. Because walls are much larger than a paint swatch, you will find the color selected seems to darken and intensify as you spread it over the area. If you select a color that's too strong, you may end up with more color than you really wanted.

You can change the physical perspective of a room with your color choices. If you want a long, narrow room to look wider, paint one or both of the short walls a bright or dark color and the other walls a pale color.

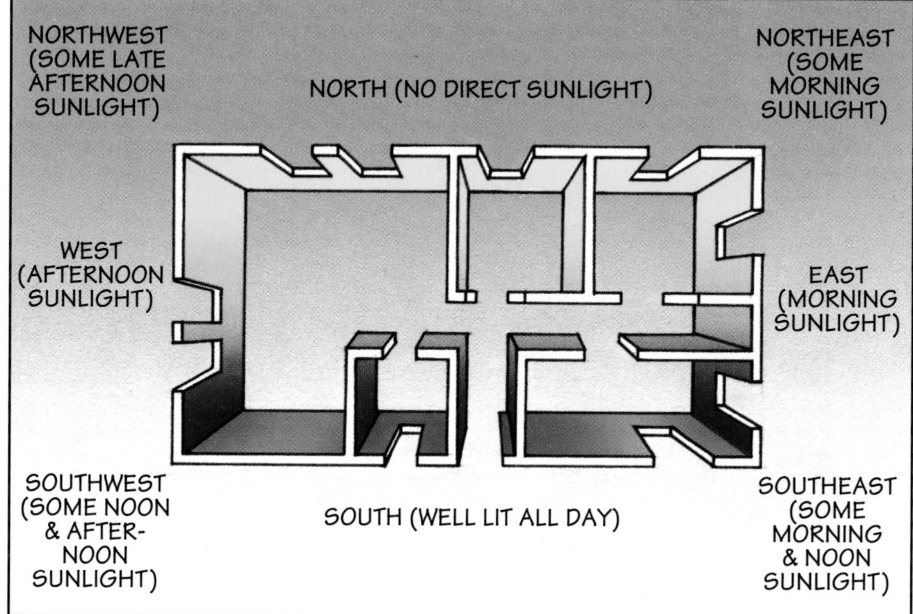

Rooms that face north, northeast, or northwest receive little or no sunshine during the day, making them relatively dark and uninviting. You can lend some cheer to these rooms by choosing from a palette of warm colors such as yellow, red, orange, and brown. Likewise, you can make sunny rooms seem a little cooler with blues, greens, grays, and lavenders. But beware of those cool colors if you live in a cold climate. Psychological research shows that people feel colder in rooms with cool colors. If you are set on using off-white, choose either a warm or a cool tint of that neutral color.

HOMER'S HINDSIGHT

Paint materials and solvents are becoming more and more friendly toward users and good old Mother Earth, but there are still many that need to be used with extreme caution and disposed of with great care.

Instead of throwing away leftover paint, put an extra coat on a little area . Let empty paint cans sit open until the solvent evaporates and the inside dries out. Then, tightly cover the can and dispose according to your local disposal guidelines.

The safest type of scaffolding is a steel pipe system, which is available from most rental outlets. It gives a stable support and a wide, safe work platform because the aluminum planks lock into the scaffolding frame. Most systems utilize casters for level terrain or adjustable base-plates for uneven ground.

Choose an exterior color scheme to create your desired effect. Light and warm colors seem to make a house stand out from its surroundings. Dark and cool colors make the house seem less obtrusive. If your house is small, you can make it seem larger by using an accent that is lighter than the main color. It is usually best to stay away from the bold contrast of a light main color and dark accent color. Pick out an accent color for any features that you would like to stand out, such as the front door and the window shutters. This accent color is usually lighter than the main color with a moderate contrast.

BASIC PAINTING TECHNIQUES

For a professional-looking paint job, the paint must be spread evenly onto the surfaces without running, dripping, or lapping onto other areas. If you load up too much paint, it will run on the surface and drip onto woodwork and floors. On the other hand, if you apply too little, you will leave lap marks and bare spots resulting in incomplete coverage.

Painting with brushes and rollers is a three-step process. The paint is applied, distributed evenly, and smoothed out for an even finish.

With a little practice, you can get a finish any professional would be proud of. Only your wallet will know the difference.

THE RIGHT WAY TO USE A PAINTBRUSH

1 Dip the brush to about one-third of the bristle length. Tap the bristles against the side of the can to remove excess paint. Dipping the brush deeper will overload the brush. Dragging the brush against the lip of the can causes the bristles to wear excessively.

2 Cut in the edges using the narrow edge of brush, pressing just hard enough to flex the bristles. Keep an eye on the paint edge, and paint with long, slow strokes. Always paint from dry area back into the wet paint to avoid lap marks.

3 Brush wall corners using the wide edge of the brush. Paint all open areas and cut in before the paint dries to avoid lap marks.

4 To paint large areas with a brush, apply paint with 2 or 3 diagonal strokes. Hold the brush at about a 45° angle to the work surface, pressing just enough to flex bristles. Distribute the paint evenly with horizontal strokes.

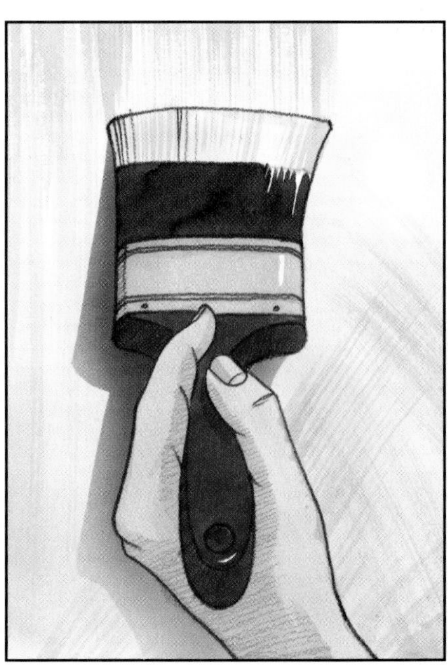

5 Smooth off the surface by drawing the brush vertically from top to bottom of the painted area. Use light strokes and lift the brush from the surface at the end of each stroke. This method is best for oil-based paints, which dry slowly.

USING A PAINT ROLLER

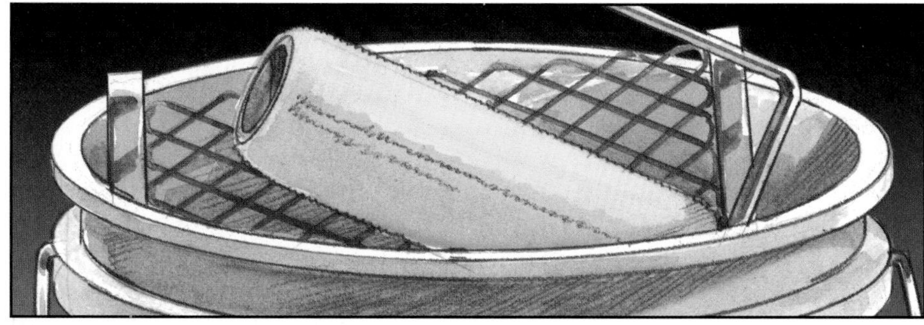

Use a five-gallon paint container and a paint screen to speed the painting of large areas. Load the paint roller straight from the bucket, using a roller extension handle. Don't try to balance the pail on a stepladder shelf; keep it on the floor or other flat, stable surface.

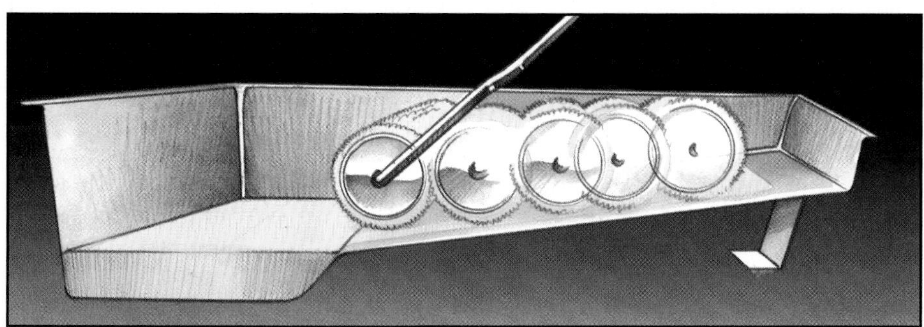

Use a paint tray when painting smaller areas. Fill the paint tray reservoir and dip the roller fully into the reservoir. Lift the roller and roll it on the textured part of the paint pan to distribute the paint evenly on the nap. The roller should be full but not dripping when lifted from the paint pan.

If using multiple containers of paint, "box" the paint before you apply it to the house. This entails pouring paint from several containers together in order to blend the paint and even out slight color variations between different paint batches. Mix by pouring from one five-gallon bucket to another.

1 With the loaded roller, make a sweep in the shape of a "W" about 4' long on the surface. On walls, roll upward on the first stroke to avoid spilling paint. Use slow roller strokes to avoid splattering.

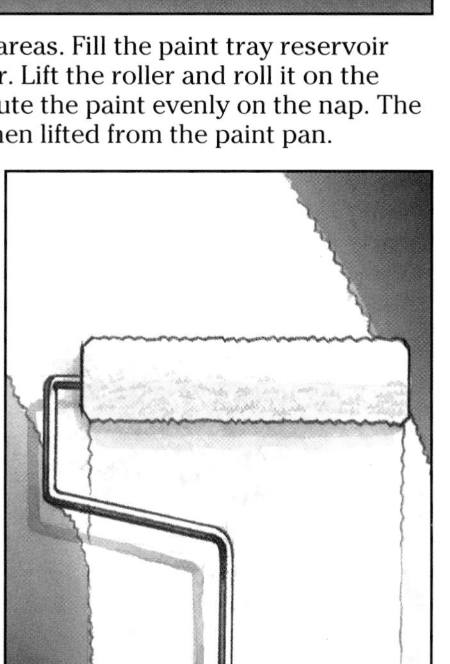

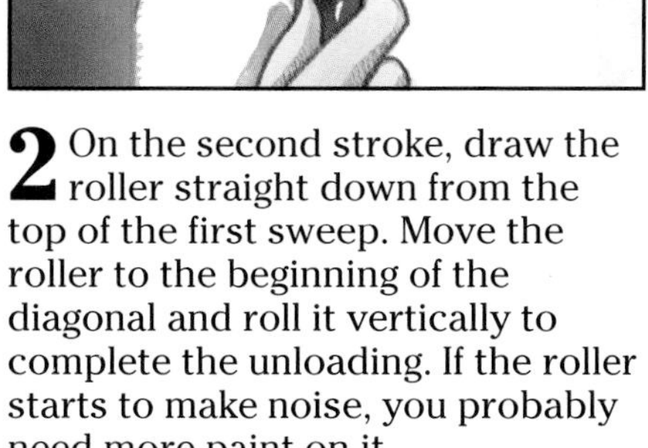

2 On the second stroke, draw the roller straight down from the top of the first sweep. Move the roller to the beginning of the diagonal and roll it vertically to complete the unloading. If the roller starts to make noise, you probably need more paint on it.

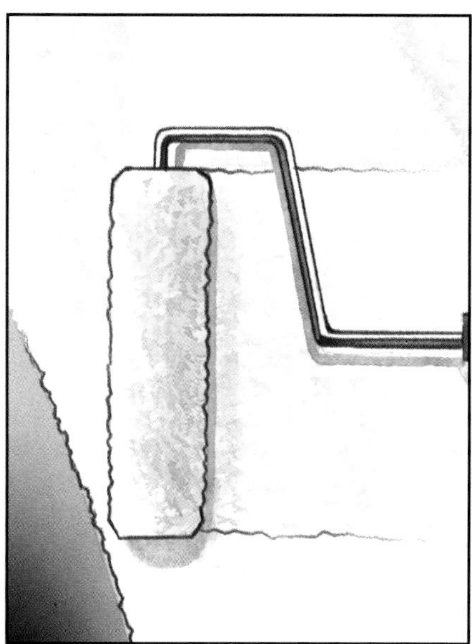

3 Distribute the paint over the area with horizontal back-and-forth strokes. Smooth off the area by lightly drawing the roller vertically from top to bottom of the painted area. Lift the roller and return it to the top of the area after each stroke.

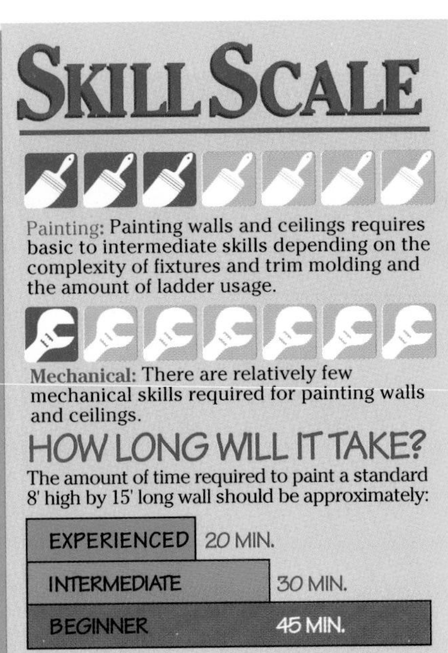

STUFF YOU'LL NEED:

- ☐**Tools:** Paint roller, roller cover, extension handle, paintbrush, foam brush or pad.
- ☐**Materials:** Wall paint, ceiling paint.

If you can, cut in the corners of the room while the paint you applied with the roller is still wet. Because surfaces painted with brushes and those painted with rollers look slightly different when dry, cutting in the corners while the walls are still wet gives you a chance to blend textures produced by the roller and brush. In the end, you have a seamless, smooth finish.

Painting Ceilings & Walls

For a smooth finish on large wall and ceiling areas, it is best to paint them in small sections. First, roll the section, then immediately use a paintbrush to cut in the edge before moving on. If rolled areas are left to dry before the edges are brushed, visible marks will be left on the finished surface where you ended rolling out the paint.

When you are painting an entire room, the ceiling is the first area to be painted. Plan your painting process so you will be facing the light as you work. This way it will be easier to see areas that were missed or just lightly covered. Working in natural light, whenever possible, also makes it easier to spot these areas. If your ceiling is covered with acoustic tiles you're facing a special case. Before you begin you should consult with a professional where you buy your paint.

Quality paint and tools will make the job go smoother and give you better results. Work with a full brush or roller to avoid lap marks and to ensure full coverage. Keep the roller speed slow to minimize the likelihood of splattering.

If necessary, set up a scaffold of a plank between two stepladders, making sure the plank is trustworthy and the stepladder footings are stable and secure. Any miscellaneous details and chores such as masking and draping should be done from a stepladder prior to setting up the scaffold since the scaffold is cumbersome to move.

SAFETY ALERT

Always wear safety glasses for protection from splatters when painting ceilings.

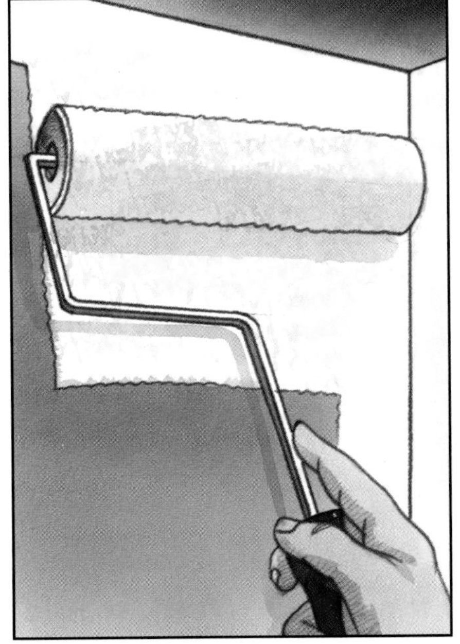

Minimize roller marks by cutting in the corners as soon as possible after rolling, since brushed areas dry to a different finish than rolled paint. With two painters, let one roll large areas while the other cuts in with a brush.

TOOLTIPS

Pressurized power rollers and pads can simplify painting walls and ceilings by reducing annoying drips from conventional painting tools.

Some are designed with a plunger type mechanism that draws paint out of the can and stores it in the handle. A simple press of the trigger releases a consistent, controlled paint flow to the roller or pad, practically eliminating the occurrence of overflow.

Other designs include rollers that attach to airless sprayers in place of the spray gun. These rollers have a control knob that is adjusted for the desired amount of paint flow.

HOW TO PAINT CEILINGS & WALLS

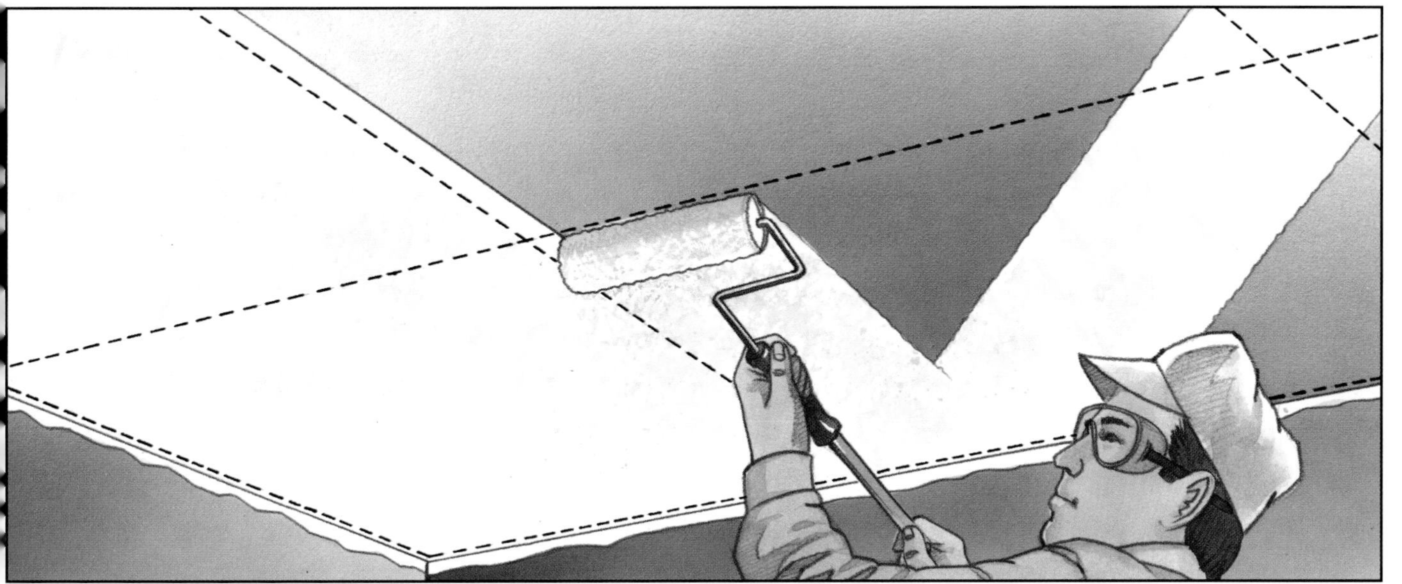

Paint ceilings with a roller handle extension and always use eye protection while painting overhead. Start at the corner farthest from the entry door, then paint the ceiling along the narrow end in 3' x 3' sections, cutting in the edges of the section with a brush before rolling. Apply paint with diagonal strokes, and be sure to distribute the paint evenly with back-and-forth strokes. Be careful not to press too hard when rolling or you will squeeze reserve paint from the roller cover. For the final smoothing strokes, roll each section toward the entry wall, lifting the roller at the end of each sweep.

Paint walls in 2' x 4' sections, starting in an upper corner. Cut in the ceiling and wall corners with a brush, then roll in the section. Make an initial diagonal stroke with the roller from the bottom of the section upward to avoid dripping any paint. Many painters use a large "W" shape to spread the paint initially. Distribute the paint evenly with horizontal strokes, then finish with downward sweeps of the roller. Next, cut in and roll the section directly underneath. Continue with adjacent areas, cutting in and rolling top sections before bottom. All finish strokes should be rolled toward the floor.

It is always a good practice to dress appropriately for the work you will be doing. Coveralls and a cap will save hours of cleanup time and replacement costs for damaged clothing. Gloves can sometimes be more cumbersome than beneficial but are usually selected by personal preference.

With many of the latex paints in use today, cleanup of hands and fingers is fairly simple with water and a mild detergent. Clothing should be scrubbed with soap and water as soon as possible to reduce the risk of permanent paint stains.

Exterior Paint Preparation

Exterior paint preparation, like that for interior painting, involves thoroughly cleaning the surface and restoring it to its original condition. This usually requires reconstruction with similar material, patching with some sort of fiberglass filler, caulking with a quality exterior caulk, and cleaning the entire surface with a trisodium phosphate mixture or a phosphate free TSP substitute. **Good preparation is probably the most important step to a good paint job**.

Where exterior preparation differs from interior is in the equipment used and the potential hazards that exist when working at extreme elevations. Caution always should be used when performing repairs and painting at the varying "altitudes" on the exterior of your home.

Falling ladders may be funny in the cartoons but they are very serious in real life. Be sure to get assistance whenever possible.

STUFF YOU'LL NEED:

- ☐ **Tools:** Putty knife, broadknife, grinder, sander, wire brush, broom, caulk gun, hammer, screwdriver, garden hose.
- ☐ **Materials:** Drop cloth, tape, caulk, TSP/bleach solution (or a phosphate free cleaner), wood filler.

TOOLTIPS

Working with tall ladders can be tricky and sometimes dangerous unless you follow a few simple guidelines. Place the ladder so the feet are away from the building at a distance equal to one-fourth the height of the ladder.

Make sure the legs are on a level surface; on uneven surfaces, use wood shims to level them.

1/4

If the surface slopes away from the house, place a 2x4 across the base of the ladder and drive two 2x4 stakes into the ground to secure the ladder base.

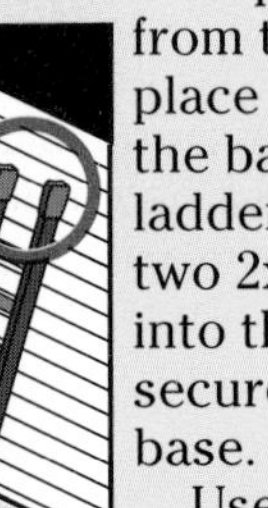

Use ladder boots or wrap a cloth around the top of the ladder legs to keep them from slipping and also from damaging the siding.

Remember, always be careful and be sure to get help when you need it.

GETTING READY TO PAINT

1 Tie back or trim bushes and limbs that will interfere with your work. Cover plants in the work area with drop cloths or tarps. Turn off air conditioning and exhaust fans. Cover and seal air conditioning units and exhaust vents with plastic and tape as needed.

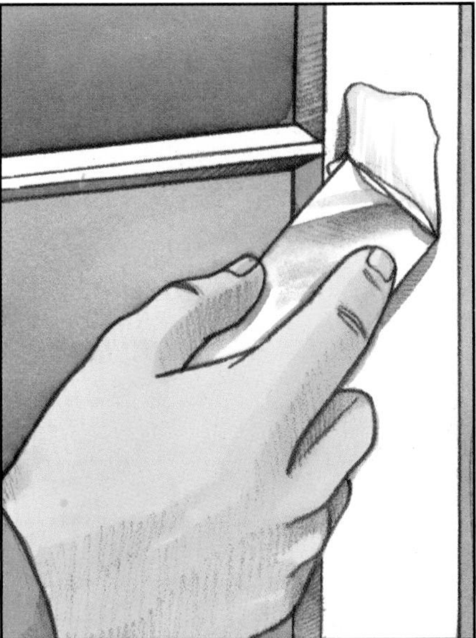

2 Remove shutters and hardware and close storm windows. Make repairs to siding and trim as necessary and fill rotted or insect-damaged areas with wood filler.

3 Reglaze windows as needed. Remove the old putty with a chisel or stiff putty knife; apply new glazing compound. When removing old putty be careful not to break the glass.

4 Starting at the top of the walls, scrape any loose paint from the siding and trim.

5 Use a power sander to remove remaining paint particles from smooth-surfaced wood or hardboard siding. The sander cuts through the paint quickly, so be careful not to damage the siding. A rotary sander, as shown, should have a speed of 10,000 to 12,000 rpm so it doesn't leave swirl marks.

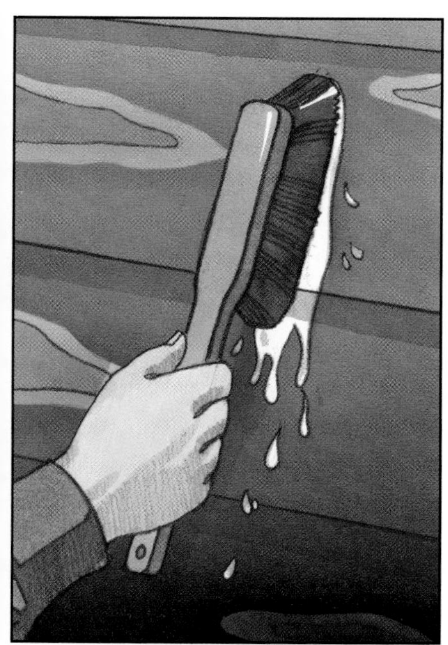

6 Using a brush or broom to scrub the surfaces, wash the siding and trim with a trisodium phosphate bleach solution or a phosphate free TSP substitute. Pressure washers can be rented for a faster, thorough washing.

7 Rinse the entire house with a garden hose and water until the runoff water is clear. If you used TSP to clean the house, rinse twice to ensure the solution is completely gone. Let the siding and trim dry completely, usually 2 days, before painting.

Your local rental center has a wide variety of equipment available that will make your exterior painting project go much smoother. Items such as scaffolding, planking, extension ladders, ladder jacks, and hydraulic lifts are available to make your elevated tasks not only easier, but also much safer.

When it comes to scraping and washing the siding and trim, you may want to consider the rental of a high-pressure washer that will actually blast the old, peeling paint right off the siding. These are real time-savers but can be dangerous, so be sure to follow the manufacturers' instructions and warnings.

Painting Exterior Walls

Painting exterior walls is quite different from painting interior walls because of the variety of siding types available and the equipment needed for working at higher elevations.

Siding material ranges from cedar lap, board and bat, and slate, to masonite, stucco, and masonry. Each requires slight technique variations, but all follow the same basic principles discussed in this section. The type of siding may dictate what you use to apply paint. Brushes, rollers, and sprayers all have advantages and disadvantages.

Be sure you have quality ladders and scaffolds in proper working condition to make your painting go as smoothly as possible. Remember, you are trusting your life to this equipment, so buy or rent the best available.

STUFF YOU'LL NEED:

- **Tools:** Paintbrush, trim brush, foam pad, extension ladder, stepladder, edge roller.
- **Materials:** Exterior house paint, exterior trim paint.

EXTERIOR PAINTING TECHNIQUES

1 Wait until the surface is dry and check to make sure there is no rain in the weather forecast. Apply primer to any bare siding. For best results, allow primer to dry according to the manufacturer's recommendation. Although a brush is shown, a sprayer or roller could be used to speed the process.

2 Masonry surfaces always should be primed, especially if problems such as water stains are present or if glossy paint is to be top-coated. Cedar and redwood contain resins that bleed through water-based paints, so use oil-based primers on woods.

3 Paint the roof trim and soffits before the walls if they will be different colors. This prevents trim paint from dripping onto the newly painted walls.

4 Paint the inside corners and around the trim. Use a corner roller or trim brush to cut in these areas.

5 On clapboard or shingle siding, cut in the lip (bottom edges) of the siding before painting the face.

6 Roll or brush, starting at the top of the wall. Work from as far as you can reach to your left, pulling the roller or brush toward you. Finish the stroke directly in front of you. Repeat until the block of siding you can reach is painted, then use the same technique for the right side.

7 Start each stroke to the right by feathering the brush or roller. Feathering means placing the surface of the brush or roller against the siding gradually, instead of abruptly. This eliminates a definite start line and makes it easier to blend the next block of strokes into the present block.

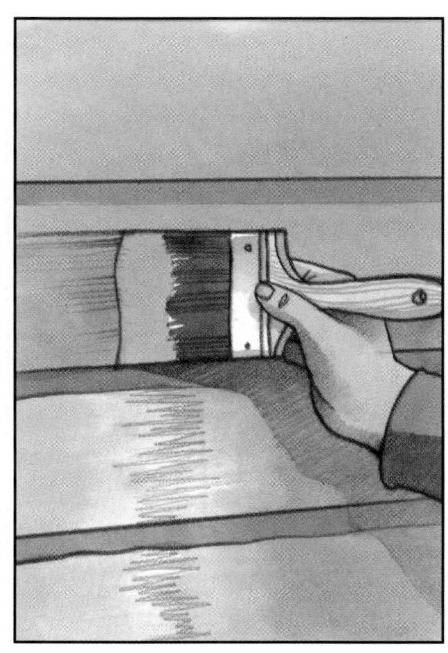

8 Blend the two strokes together where they meet in front of you. Work quickly. It is important to blend the new stroke into the completed stroke while the paint is still wet to avoid lap marks. Never stop in the middle of a section. Paint to the corner of the house so the paint color is consistent.

9 Move the ladder so you can just reach the completed block of siding. To eliminate lap marks, rewet the feathered edges of the previously painted block with your brush or roller just before you start each stroke. Repeat the process until the top area is completed; complete the lower sections.

Speed up the painting process by renting or buying a paint sprayer. A variety of sprayers is available. Before you start spraying, ask your paint sprayer supplier exactly how the sprayer operates, what masking will be required, and the appropriate methods to clean the sprayer. Choose a calm day to spray your house. A windy day can make spraying difficult. Regardless of how you paint the house, let the paint dry and then touch up any missed areas. You may need to correct drips or sags with a razor blade or sanding block.

Painting Exterior Windows

When painting exterior windows and trim, be sure to use a quality trim paint. Trim paint is formulated with a more durable finish that will keep your windows looking better longer. Don't be afraid if you get a little paint on the glass; it will easily clean off with a razor scraper. If you wish, you can use masking tape to protect the window, but chances are you'll still have to clean the window from the adhesive residue left from the tape.

Some basic window terminology as illustrated at right is: (1) window rail, (2) window stile, (3) window sill, (4) window frame or trim, (5) upper sash, (6) lower sash, and (7) head jamb.

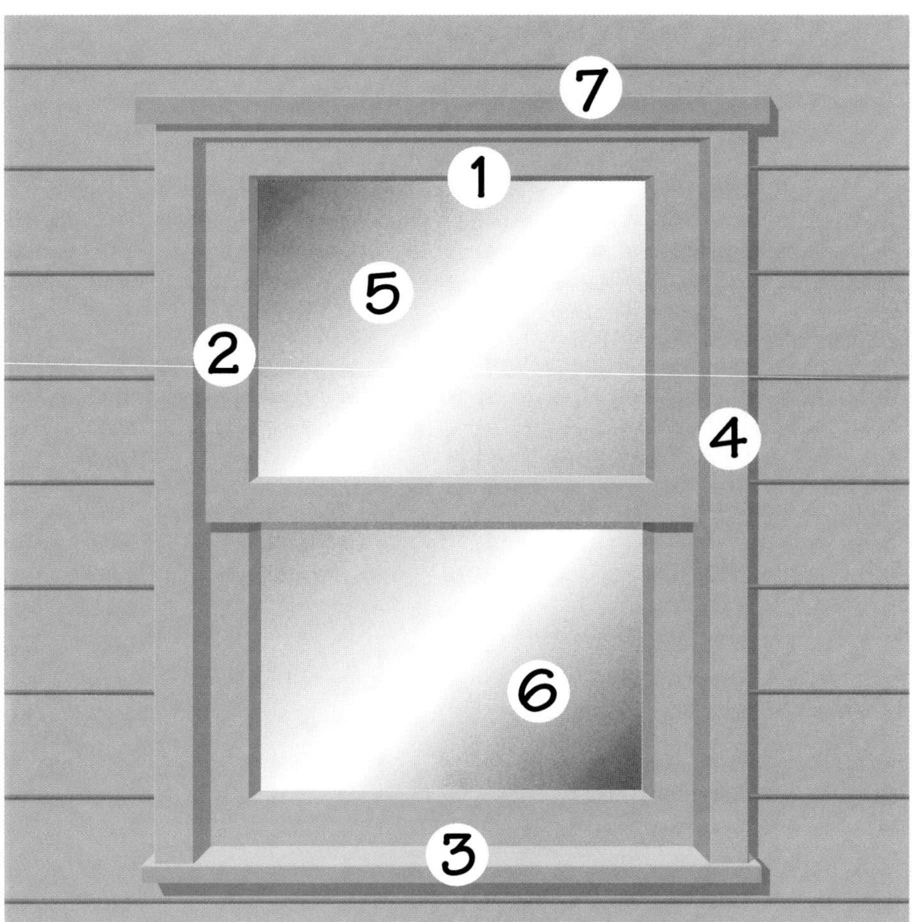

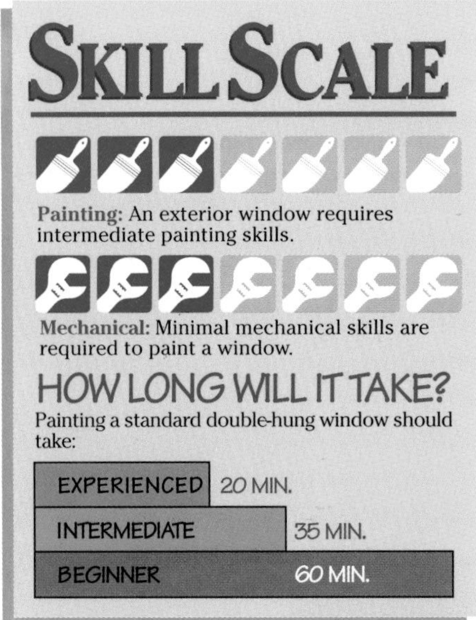

STUFF YOU'LL NEED:

- ☐ **Tools:** Tapered sash brush, putty knife.
- ☐ **Materials:** Trim paint.

PAINTING WINDOWS THE RIGHT WAY

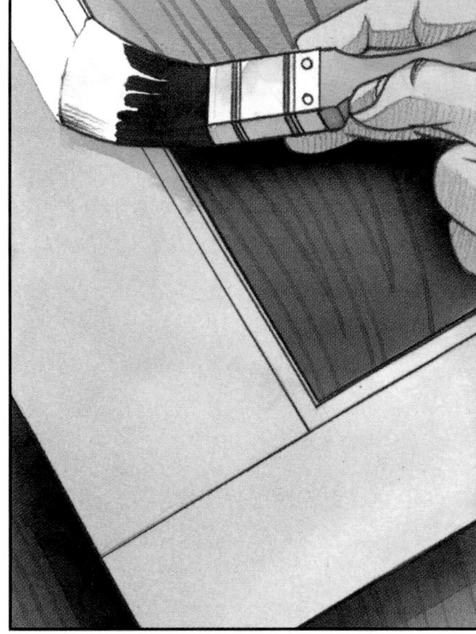

1 When painting double-hung windows, start with the upper sash (shown removed from window casing). Paint the sides of the stiles (vertical members) first. Using a small trim brush with a small amount of paint, apply paint to the entire length of the stile.

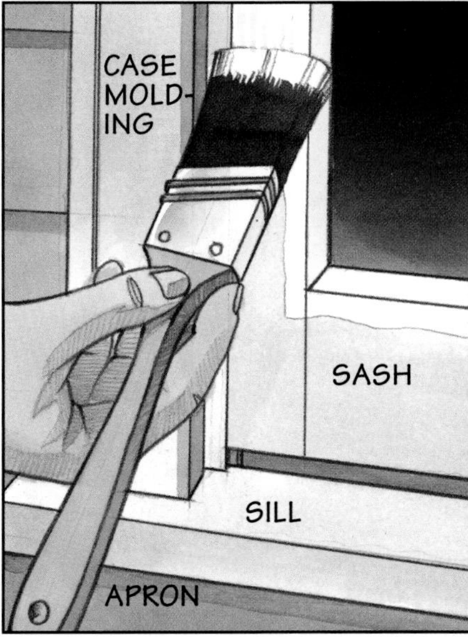

2 Start in the upper left corner, continuing downward until you reach a muntin (cross-grid member) or the bottom of the sash. Lift up on the brush at the end of the stroke. Continue until the sides of all the vertical members are completed.

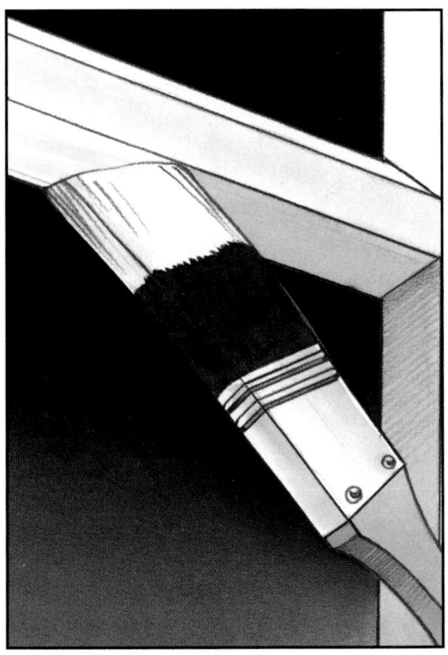

3 Paint both sides of any vertical and horizontal muntins in the sash. You can use a razor blade to remove any paint you get on the glass. It's much easier when the paint is still wet.

4 Now paint both sides of the rails (horizontal members) on the upper sash.

5 Paint the faces of the muntins, rails, and stiles on the upper sash. When completed, repeat the process for the lower sash.

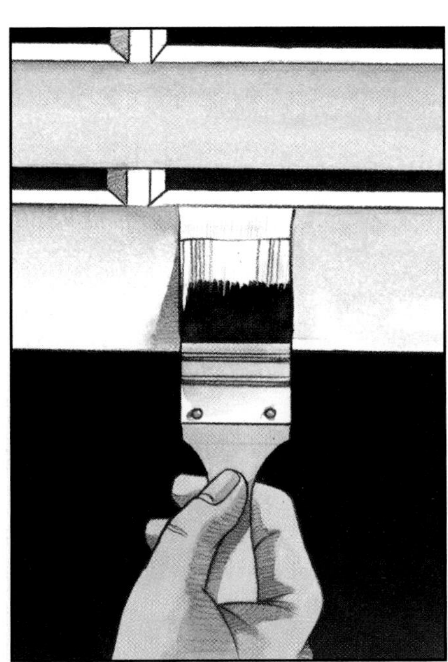

6 When painting double-hung windows still in the jamb, lower the upper sash and raise the lower sash to paint the surfaces that contact each other when closed. Let the paint dry completely before closing the window. Don't paint the bottom of the sash.

7 Return the sashes to their normal position and paint the stops and jambs.

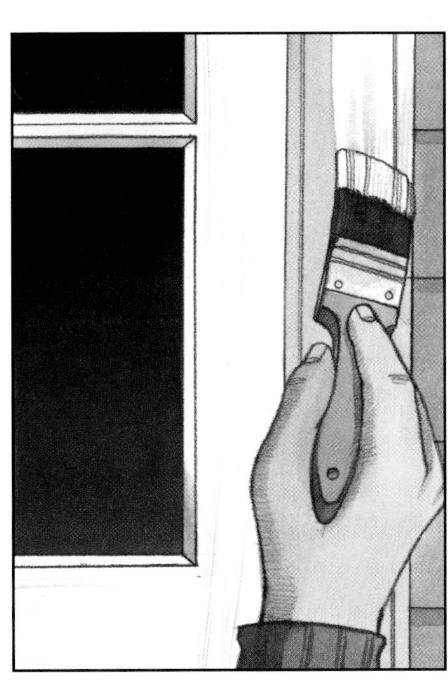

8 Paint the sides of the casing, then the faces of the casing, and continue to the sill. Use masking tape or a paint shield to keep trim paint off the siding. If you use tape, be sure to remove it as soon as the paint is dry to the touch.

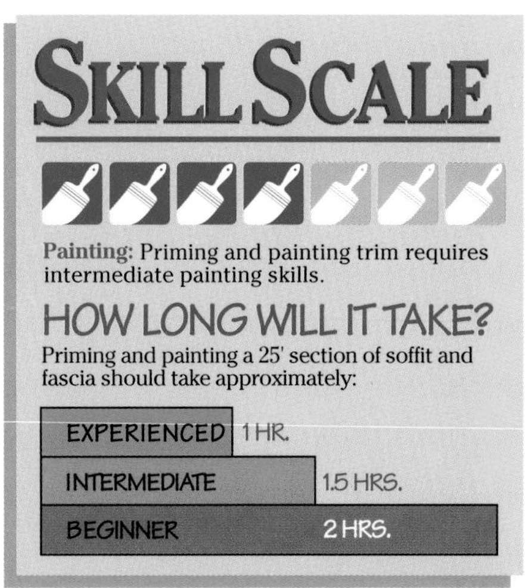

Priming & Painting Trim

Once the trim has been prepared and is ready to paint, be sure to brush and wipe the trim just before applying primer. When the primer has dried thoroughly, paint the trim as soon as possible but no later than three days after priming. The longer you wait to paint, the greater the chances for chemical deposits and dirt to affect the surface.

Trim paint is specially formulated to withstand the extreme exposure and high traffic areas of roof trim, porches, railings, doors, and window trim. Trim paint is available in most popular finishes and can be custom blended for your specific color requirements.

STUFF YOU'LL NEED:

- ☐ **Tools:** 4" brush, 2" tapered sash brush, wire brush, corner roller.
- ☐ **Materials:** Trim paint, primer for the appropriate surface.

Use the right primer. Most general purpose latex primers can be used on any surface. For best results on metal, use a metal primer with a rust inhibitor. Masonry primers are specially formulated to adhere to chalky surfaces.

WEAR GLOVES WHEN PREPPING METAL SURFACES TO PROTECT YOUR HANDS FROM METAL SLIVERS.

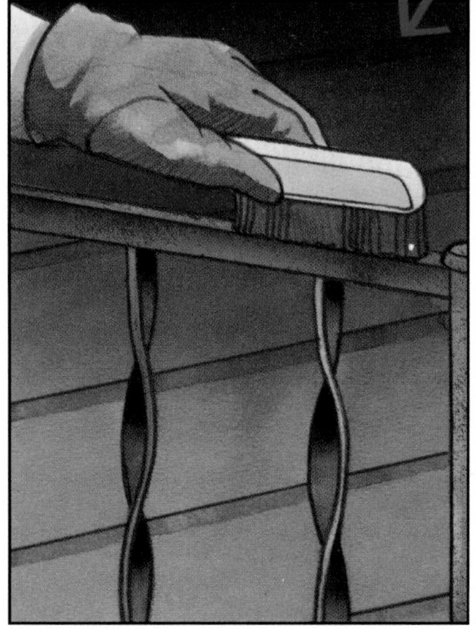

Remove loose paint from metal railing and trim with a wire brush. Rust can be brushed from the iron or steel but must be primed right away to prevent further rusting. Use an enamel paint to ensure a long-lasting protective finish.

Prime and paint wood stairs and porch floors after all other surfaces have been primed and painted. This prevents the need to touch up drips on the horizontal surfaces. Make sure to use specially formulated enamel floor paint that resists high volumes of traffic.

After the walls and trim are painted, you may want to prime and paint the foundation walls. Paint them the same color as the siding or choose an accent color. Paint around windows and doors first with a sash brush, then paint the broad areas with a 4" brush, working paint into the mortar lines.

PAINTING SOFFITS AND FASCIA

1 Paint the soffit trim and the edges of the soffit panels with a corner roller or sash brush. Always paint horizontal surfaces before vertical ones. Minor mistakes won't be as noticeable that way. After the edges are painted, paint the soffit panels with a 4" brush, blending in at the edges.

2 Using a corner roller or a sash brush, paint the bottom edges of the soffit trim before you paint the broad faces.

3 Paint the fascia next, then the gutters and downspout outlets (begin at the back and work around to the fronts of gutter, blending in around the corners). Also paint the back sides of fascia and trim for better protection and to ensure even expansion and contraction.

PAINTING JAMBS, CASINGS, AND TRIM

1 Paint windows and doors with a trim brush. Wedge the doors and windows open so they are held steady for painting. Mask the floors underneath the doors. Paint the bottoms of doors to seal and protect them. Apply paint to the bottoms of doors by sliding a foam brush along their underside. See pg. 52 for the proper door painting sequence.

2 After the door or window is dry, paint the jamb. Start at the top on the inside with a moderate load of paint on a beveled trim brush. Paint the stop, then work outward. After the top, move to the inside edge (hinge side on doors and casement windows), saving the outside edge for last.

3 Paint the casings while the jambs are still wet. Mask the siding along the outside edges or cut in with a brush. Feather the paint into the mitered joints from the rails and follow the miter line when painting the stiles. Paint thresholds after the jambs and casings have dried.

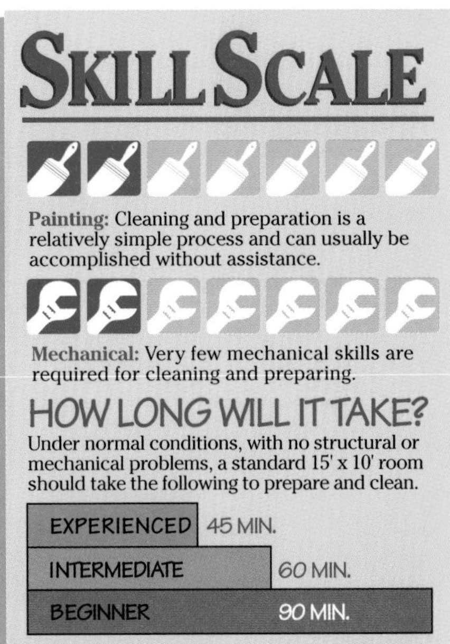

STUFF YOU'LL NEED:

- ☐ **Tools:** Sponge, wallboard knife, sanding block.
- ☐ **Materials:** TSP solution, stain remover, pigmented shellac.

SAFETY
Always wear safety glasses and a dust mask or respirator when sanding and removing wallboard and plaster.
ALERT

Water or rust stains may indicate water damage. Check for leaking pipes and soft wallboard in the area. Be sure to make any necessary repairs before applying stain sealer and proceeding with paint or wallpaper.

Getting a Wall Surface Ready

Careful preparation is the best way to ensure a durable paint job. Before you start, take a good look around to assess the preparation needed. Water or rust stains may indicate water damage. Make repairs before you start painting and let the repairs dry thoroughly.

Thoroughly wash, rinse, and sand your walls before priming and painting to guarantee a long-lasting finish. Clean walls with a TSP (trisodium phosphate) solution or newer phosphate free cleaners.

Carefully check your walls and ceilings for damage and repair the wallboard or plaster as needed. Priming the problem areas after you patch them will ensure that the patched areas will not absorb more paint than the surrounding areas.

Pregummed fiberglass repair tapes and premixed patching compounds reduce drying time and let you patch and paint a wall the same day. These compounds also dry quickly on your patching tools, so be sure to clean up your tools as soon as you finish with them.

Wash and sand before repainting. Use a TSP (trisodium phosphate) solution, or a phosphate free substitute, and a sponge to wash the wall. Wear rubber gloves and wash walls from the bottom up with a damp sponge to avoid streaks. Rinse thoroughly with clean water. After drying, sand surfaces lightly and wipe off remaining dust.

REMOVING STAINS

1 Apply stain remover to a clean, dry cloth and rub lightly to remove the stain.

2 Seal all stain areas with white pigmented shellac or a stain blocker. Pigmented shellac and stain blockers prevent stains from bleeding through the new paint.

REMOVING MILDEW

1 Test stains by washing with water and detergent. Mildew stains will not wash out. If the stains don't wash out, sand the stain out and then repair the wall by priming and then patching.

2 Wearing rubber gloves and eye protection, wash the walls with bleach, which kills mildew spores. After bleach treatment, wash mildew away with TSP solution or a phosphate free substitute and rinse with clear water. Allow the wall to completely dry.

PATCHING PEELING PAINT

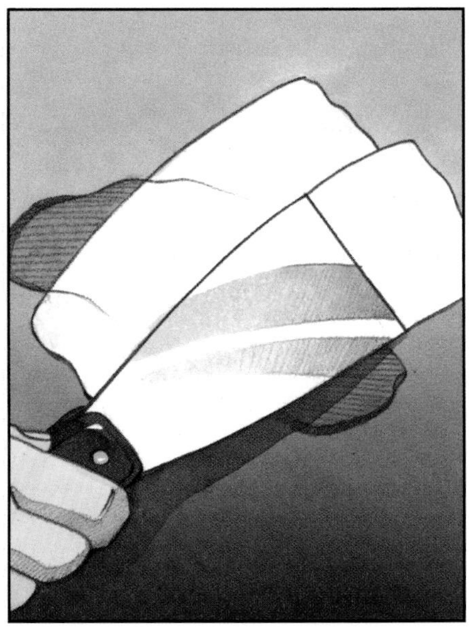

1 Scrape away loose paint with a putty knife or paint scraper. Apply spackle to the edges of chipped paint with a putty knife or flexible wallboard knife.

2 Sand the patch area with 150-grit production sandpaper. Patch area should feel smooth to the touch. If the walls have a textured surface you need to texture the patched areas to match.

Check all surfaces to be painted with a strong side-light. Patch any rough spots with spackle and then sand them smooth. If you notice any additional rough spots after priming, repatch and reprime before painting.

STUFF YOU'LL NEED:

- ☐**Tools:** Wallboard knife, bucket, perforation tool, sprayer, sponge.
- ☐**Materials:** Wallpaper remover solution, water.

Removing Wallpaper

Newer vinyl wallpaper can often be peeled off by hand. Non-peelable wallpaper requires the use of remover solutions to penetrate the paper and soften the adhesive. When using remover solutions, give them a chance to work.

Wallpaper remover fluids contain wetting agents that dissolve the old adhesive while the wallpaper is still on the wall. Remover fluid is useful in washing away adhesive left on the wall after removing the paper.

Sometimes wallpaper was hung over unsealed wallboard and is virtually impossible to remove without damaging the wallboard. You may be able to hang new wallpaper over the old wallpaper, but the surface should be smooth.

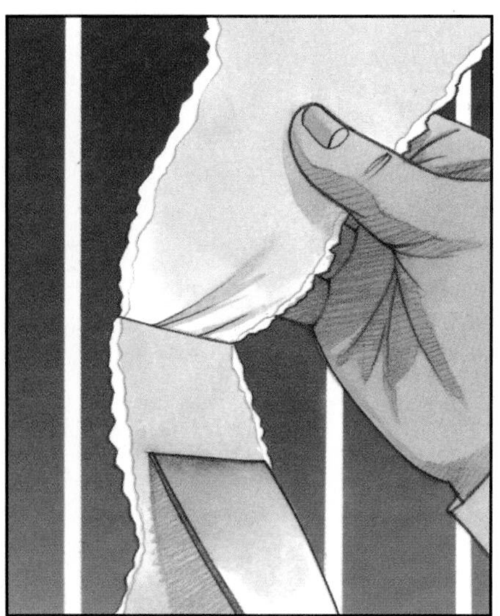

1 Find a loose edge and begin to strip the wallpaper. Vinyls often peel away easily, but you may need the assistance of a wallboard knife.

2 If the wallpaper won't strip by hand, cover the floor with layers of newspaper or a drop cloth. Add wallpaper remover to hot water as directed by manufacturer.

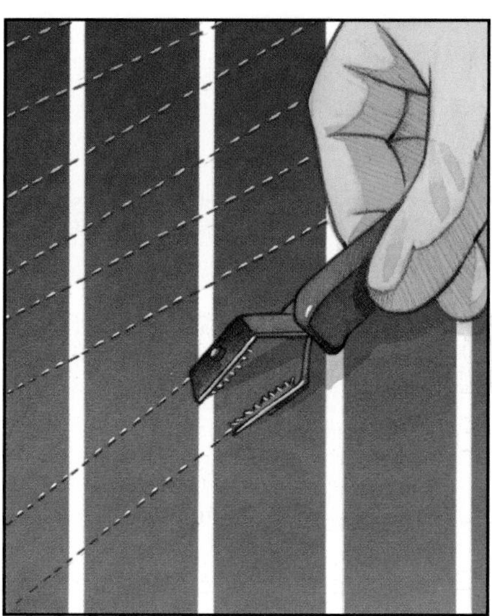

3 Pierce the surface of the wallpaper with a perforation tool. This allows the remover solution to enter and soften the adhesive.

4 Use a sprayer, paint roller, or sponge to apply the remover solution. Let the solution soak into the wallpaper according to the manufacturer's directions.

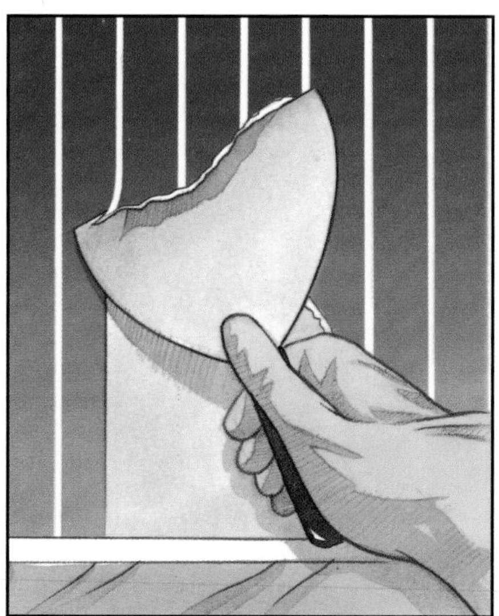

5 Once you've loosened the wallpaper, peel it away with a 6" broadknife. Be careful not to damage the plaster or wallboard. Completely remove all of the backing paper.

6 Rinse the adhesive residue from the wall with remover solution. Rinse with clear water and let the walls dry completely.

Patching & Preparing Woodwork

For the best results, woodwork should be cleaned, patched, and sanded before it is repainted. Liquid deglossers help to dull shiny surfaces so the paint will bond with the surface, but pay careful attention to the length of time the manufacturer recommends the deglosser should be left on the woodwork. If you wait too long the deglosser won't provide a good surface for the paint to adhere to.

If new hardware is to be installed, check that the new pieces will fit the old screw holes. If new screw holes must be drilled, fill the old holes with wood patch or putty. Any color wood putty will work if you're going to paint over it. For surfaces to be stained, buy a stainable putty, or better yet, wait until after staining and match the putty color to the stained wood.

To renew varnished wood, clean the surfaces with mineral spirits or furniture refinisher. Patch any holes, sand the wood smooth, and apply one or two coats of varnish.

STUFF YOU'LL NEED:

- ☐ **Tools:** 150-grit sandpaper, putty knife, tapered sash brush.
- ☐ **Materials:** Latex wood patch, TSP solution, clean cloth.

Roughen gloss surfaces with fine sandpaper, then prime to provide good bonding between the new and old paint. Primers provide "tooth" for the new coat of paint.

USE A FINISHING SANDER TO SPEED UP YOUR REPAIR WORK.

PREPARING WOODWORK FOR PAINTING

1 Wash woodwork with TSP solution or a phosphate free substitute and rinse thoroughly. Scrape away any peeling or loose paint. Badly chipped woodwork should be stripped and sanded.

2 Use a putty knife to apply latex wood patch or spackle to any nail holes, dents, or other damaged areas. Colored wood patch material also can be used. It is less likely to be noticeable through your new paint job.

3 Sand surfaces with 150-grit sandpaper until they are smooth to the touch. Wipe woodwork with a tack cloth before priming and painting.

BUYER'$ GUIDE

Choosing the Right Stripper or Solvent

There are two types of finish strippers: chemical or solvent. The type to use depends on the finish you are removing. Talk to your local supplier about the type to buy.

Solvents such as mineral spirits, denatured alcohol, and lacquer thinner work immediately to dissolve the finish so you can remove the softened material without waiting.

Chemical strippers must stay in contact with the surface of the wood for a period of time to dissolve the finish, but they should not be left so long that they dry, requiring the process to be repeated.

Many strippers on the market are water based for easy cleanup and to alleviate environmental concerns. They are still potentially harmful chemicals and should be treated as such. Whenever you use strippers or solvents make sure you dispose of them in accordance with local guidelines.

Using Chemical Strippers

Chemical strippers and solvents are liquid or semi-paste chemicals that can be applied to wood surfaces of all shapes and sizes. They soften and loosen finish materials such as polyurethane, paint, varnish, lacquer, and shellac, so the finish may be scraped or brushed from the wood. When all traces of the strippers and solvents have been removed, the wood is ready for sanding and finishing.

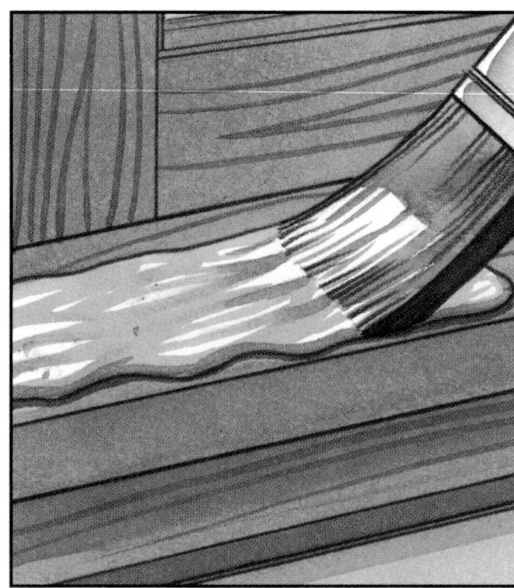

1 Pour a small amount of stripper into a convenient glass or metal container and apply as specified on the label. Let it set undisturbed for the recommended time. Strip your project starting at the top and working your way down.

2 Sprinkle a light coating of sawdust over the stripper just before removal. The sawdust thickens the stripper, making removal and disposal easier.

3 Reapply the stripper to detailed or problem areas and use specialty scrapers to remove the softened material. Use light pressure on the scrapers to keep from tearing or gouging the wood. If you can't find a contoured scraper, use the corner of a putty knife.

4 Scrub the entire project with brushes or abrasive pads to remove all traces of the old finish and stripper sludge.

5 Rinse the project with denatured alcohol or a solvent recommended by the stripper manufacturer. This will dissolve and remove the sludge left by the stripper so further sanding, staining, and finishing will not be hindered.

Using a Heat Gun

Heat guns are an effective method of removing multiple layers of paint and old finish material. When the finished surfaces are exposed to the heat, the paint or varnish softens and peels away from the surface immediately with a scraper. Using a heat gun followed by scraping or chemical strippers will result in a very thorough removal job.

Because of the high temperatures involved with heat guns, take the necessary precautions: Keep a fire extinguisher nearby, make sure to turn off the tool when not in use, wear long sleeves to keep the hot paint away from your skin, and wear safety glasses and respirators designed for heat removal procedures.

Be sure to use an extension cord with sufficient wire size for the power of the particular model of heat gun being used.

Make a protective heat shield by covering a piece of cardboard with heavy-duty aluminum foil. Use this shield to prevent the heat gun from stripping painted areas you don't want to strip. Leave a 2" border around the entire removal area, then use chemical strippers to remove the finish in the border.

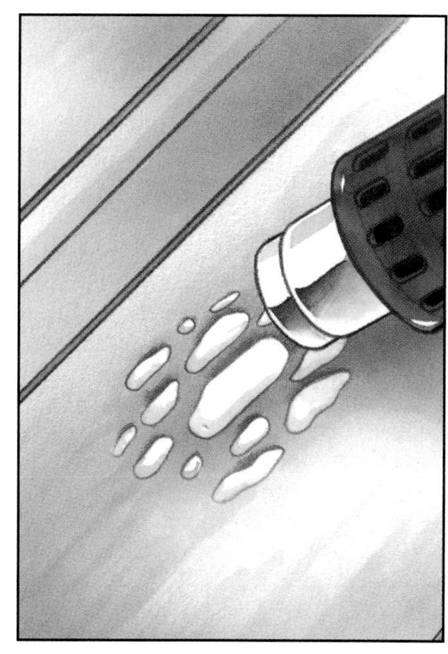

1 Beginning with the flat surfaces, point the heat gun nozzle toward the removal area, keeping it about 2" away. Move the gun back and forth across the surface. Watch the paint release from the surface as it reaches the optimal removal temperature.

2 Use the scraper like a plow, holding it at a 30° angle to the surface, and push the paint away. Avoid gouging the wood softened by the heat. Keep the scraper clean by depositing paint sludge into a coffee can as you work. Special paint scrapers with angled blades work better than most ordinary scrapers.

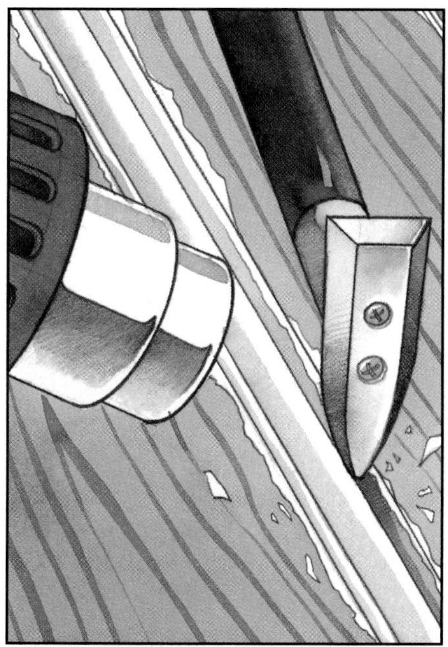

3 Go back over detailed areas with the heat gun, using a contoured scraper to match the area being stripped. Leave a space between the edges of the area being stripped and adjacent areas that will not be stripped.

4 Dry scrape the entire surface to remove any remaining paint, then wash the surface with denatured alcohol or mineral spirits. Avoid using water because it will raise the wood grain.

Masking & Draping

For fast, mess-free painting, it is necessary to protect any surfaces that could get splattered. If you are painting only the ceiling, drape the walls and woodwork. When painting the walls, mask the baseboards and the window and door casings.

Remove any lightweight furniture, and move heavier pieces to the center of the room and cover with plastic. Be sure to leave an alley so you can reach the entire ceiling. Cover the floors with canvas drop cloths. They will absorb paint splatters and are not as slippery as plastic drop cloths.

Masking and draping materials, clockwise from top left: plastic and canvas drop cloths, self-adhesive plastic, masking tape, pregummed masking papers. Plastic-paper laminates are also available.

STUFF YOU'LL NEED:

- ☐**Tools:** Putty knife, hammer, screwdriver, vacuum.
- ☐**Materials:** Masking tape, plastic tarp, canvas drop cloth.

MASKING WOOD TRIM

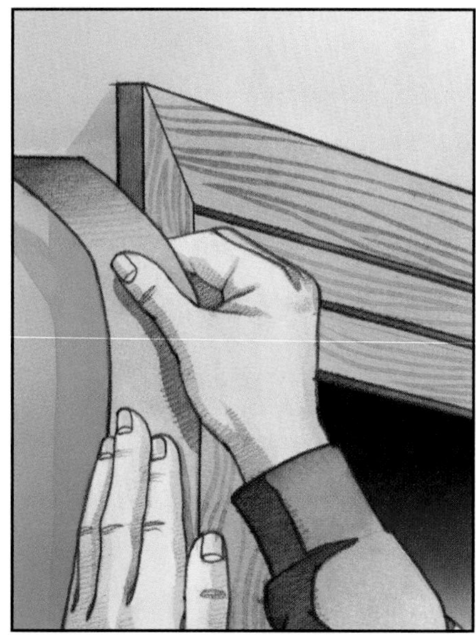

1 Use pregummed paper or wide masking tape to protect wood moldings from paint splatters. Leave outside edge of masking tape loose.

2 After applying tape, run the tip of a putty knife along inside edge of tape to seal against seeping paint. Remove material as soon as paint is too dry to run.

PREPARING THE ROOM FOR DRAPING

1 Use a vacuum cleaner to pick up the dust from window sills, window tracks, baseboards, and casements.

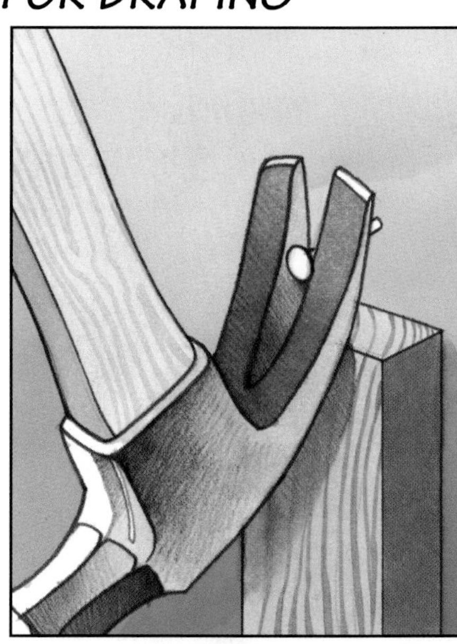

2 Remove all nails, screws, picture hangers, and other hardware from the surfaces to be painted. To prevent damage to the plaster or wallboard, use a block of wood or broadknife under the head of the hammer.

3 Remove covers from heating and air-conditioning ducts to protect them from splatters. Remove thermostats or use masking tape to protect them against paint drips.

4 Turn off electricity. Drop light fixtures away from electrical boxes, or remove the fixtures. Cover hanging fixtures with plastic bags. Remove coverplates from outlets and switches. Return cover screws to screw holes.

5 Wipe dust from woodwork with a damp rag or with a clean cloth and liquid deglosser. Be sure to apply paint within 30 to 60 minutes after deglossing.

DRAPING WALLS

1 Press top half of 2" masking tape along ceiling-wall corners. Leave bottom half of tape loose. Use a safe releasing tape rather than masking tape if you're going to leave the tape up more than twelve hours.

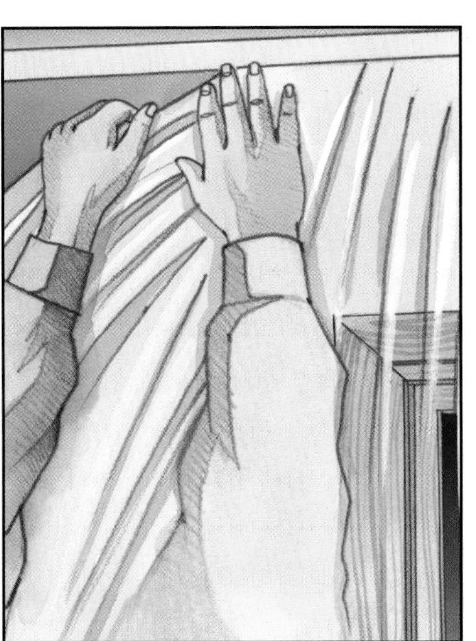

2 Hang sheet plastic under masking tape, draping walls and baseboards. Remove loose edge as soon as the paint is too dry to run.

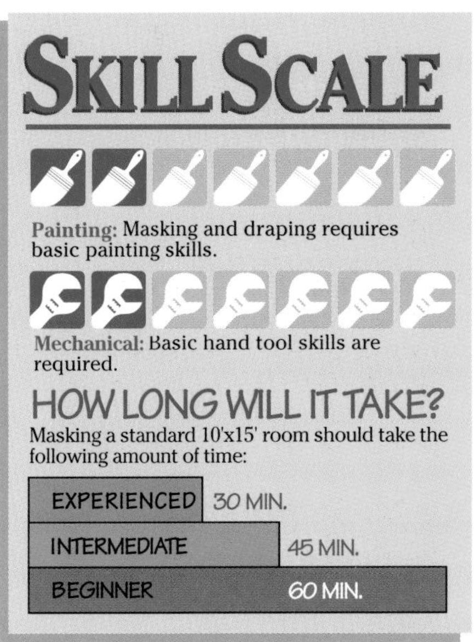

Decorative Paint Techniques

Decorative painting is a creative way to express your style and to give walls and ceilings a customized finish. Choose from a variety of paint finishes that can be used on plaster, wood, and wallboard.

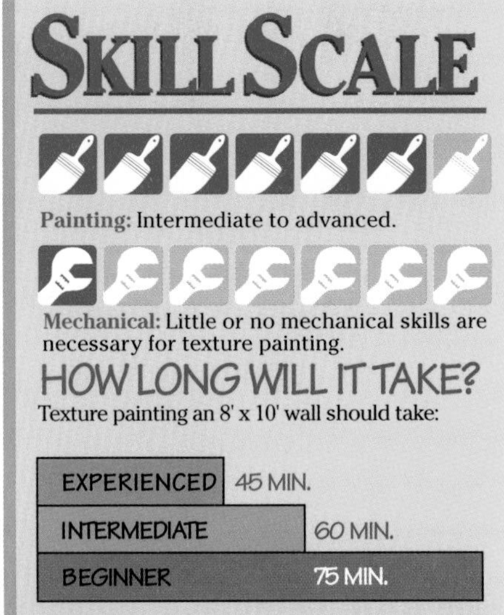

STUFF YOU'LL NEED:

- ☐**Tools:** Roller, paintbrush, whisk broom, cellulose sponge, cement trowel, sea sponge, foam brush, feather.
- ☐**Materials:** Texture paint, acrylic paint, paint thickener, paint extender, acrylic sealer.

Rag Rolling

Rag rolling is a painting technique that gives a rich, textural look with an overall mottled effect. It works well for walls and can be used on flat surfaces, such as dresser tops, drawers and shelves. Test the technique and the colors you intend to use on a large piece of cardboard before you start the project.

APPLYING A RAG-ROLLED FINISH

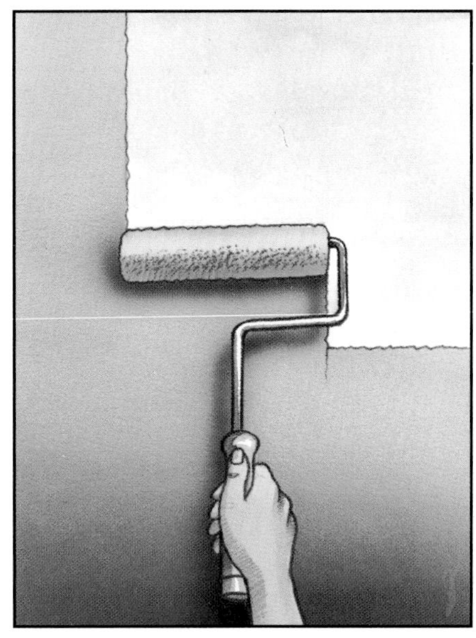

1 Apply a base coat of low-luster latex enamel, using a paintbrush or paint roller, then allow it to dry.

2 Mix the basic glaze and pour it into a paint tray. Apply the glaze over the base coat, using a paint roller or paint pad.

3 Roll up a lint-free rag irregularly and fold it in half to the width of both of your hands. Roll the rag through the wet glaze, working upward at varying angles.

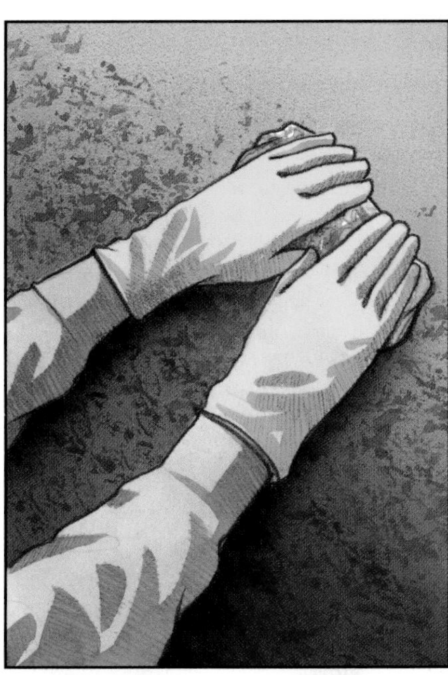

Variation: To use the ragging-on method, mix the basic glaze in a pail. Saturate a lint-free rag in the glaze and wring it out well. Roll up the rag irregularly, then fold it in half. Roll the rag upward over the wall surface. Rewet as necessary and wring out.

Sponging Paint

Sponge painting produces a soft, mottled effect and is one of the easiest techniques to use. To achieve this paint finish, use either a natural sea sponge or a modified synthetic sponge to dab the paint onto a surface. Cellulose or synthetic sponges must be modified to be used. Pull little pieces out of the square, synthetic sponges to give them a rough, irregular surface.

The sponged look can be varied, depending on the number of paint colors applied, the sequence in which you apply the colors, and the distance between the sponge impressions. You can use semi-gloss, low-luster, or flat latex paint for the base coat and the sponging. For a translucent finish, use a paint glaze that consists of paint, paint conditioner, and water.

The first color you put down will be the predominant color of the finished wall after you've applied accent colors by sponge painting. Choose the base-coat color carefully. The decorating issues you consider when using a solid color should also be considered when sponge painting. Make sure your base coat and subsequent accent coats produce an effect that enhances your furnishings, or that the colors won't make the room appear smaller.

For the most dramatic effect, choose a darker color as your base coat and then sponge on one or more lighter colors.

APPLYING A SPONGED FINISH

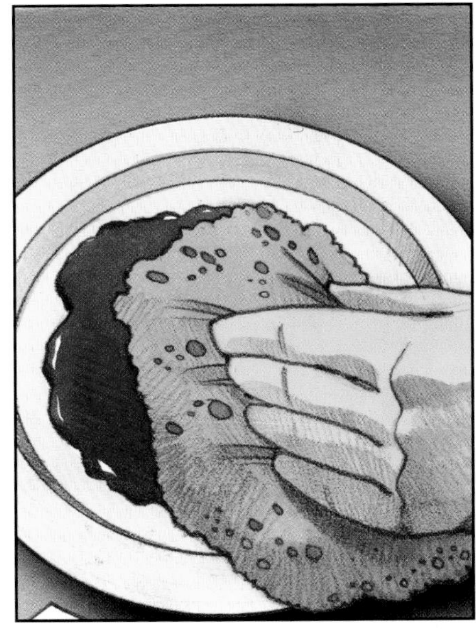

1 Once the base coat has dried, soften your sea sponge in water and then squeeze out the water. Using a paper plate to hold the paint, dip the sponge into the paint and blot it lightly on a paper towel.

2 Press the sponge repeatedly onto the surface using a wet sea sponge in your other hand to blot the paint, causing a softened, blended look. Continue to apply the first paint color to the entire project, continually blotting it with the moist sponge.

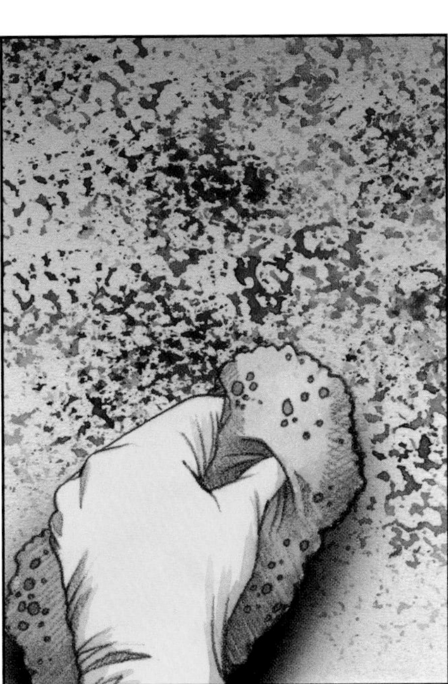

3 Repeat the steps with one or more accent colors. Be sure to allow each color to dry completely before applying the next.

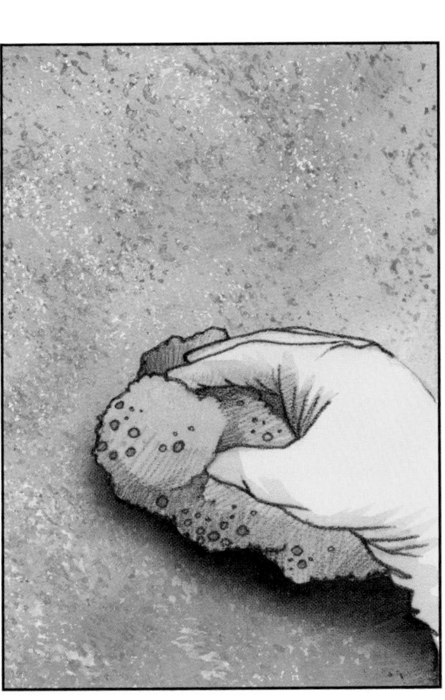

4 Apply the accent color to the entire project, continually blotting it with the moist sponge to even out and soften the effect. Use masking tape and paper to create sponged border and panel effects with the various accent colors.

Faux Marble

The look of marble can be readily duplicated in your paint finish by using a technique called *veining* combined with other techniques such as sponge painting.

To create the veined appearance, acrylic extender and acrylic thickener are used alongside the paint to create veins that fluctuate from opaque to translucent. A feather is used in an irregular, trembling motion to apply the veins.

Creating marble finishes can be accomplished with a variety of color combinations. Before applying a faux marble finish, test the paint colors on a large piece of scrap cardboard. This will help you develop confidence and become familiar with the materials and techniques. Develop a pattern you like by trying different effects as you practice. Be sure to ask at your decorating center about the appropriate colors to use for your desired effect. This should reduce your trial-and-error process.

APPLYING A FAUX MARBLE FINISH

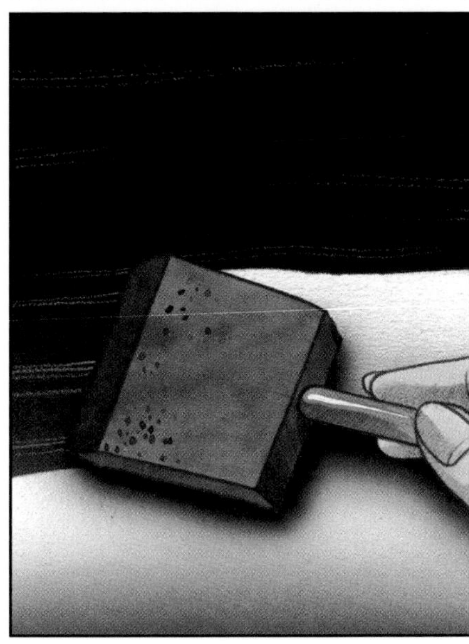

1 Apply the base coat of black acrylic or flat latex paint and allow it to dry. Place dark hunter green, medium green, and light blue-green paints in random spiraling lines onto a disposable plate, overlapping the paint colors.

2 To help keep the colors separate, place spiraling lines of thickener and extender, over the paints and then tilt the plate so the colors mingle and marbleize. Dip your dampened sea sponge into the marbleized paint and blot it lightly onto a paper towel to remove the excess paint.

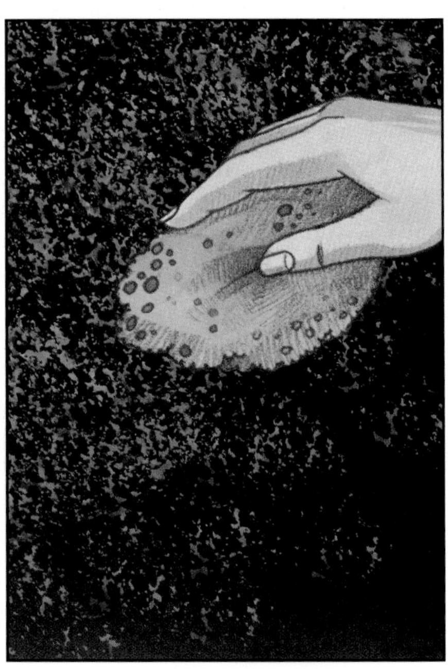

3 Dab the sponge lightly and repeatedly onto the black base coat in an up-and-down stippling motion, turning the sponge for a random pattern. Allow some base coat to show, and be careful not to mix the paint colors together completely.

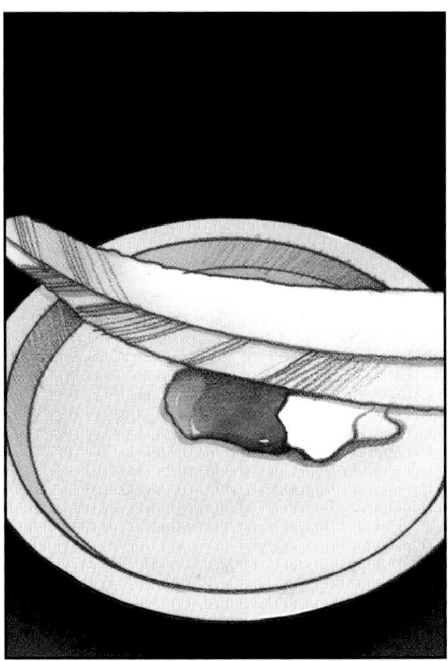

4 Pour long pools of white and medium green paint onto another disposable plate. Apply a pool of thickener on one side of the paints, and extender on the other. Run the edge of the feather through the pools, picking up some thickener, paints, and extender on the feather.

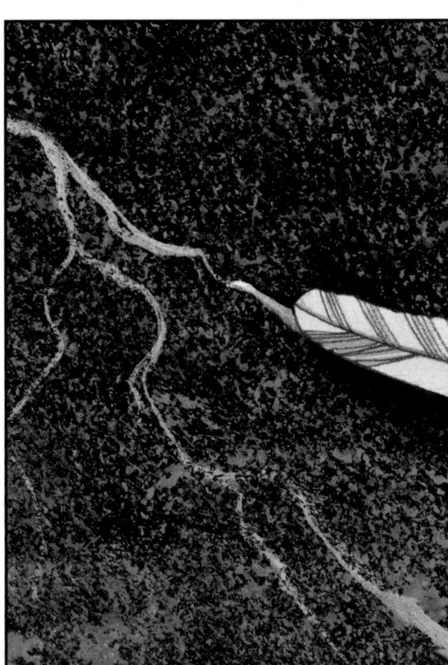

5 Place the tip of the feather onto the surface and drag the feather along, turning it slightly to create a veinlike appearance. Apply the veins in a diagonal direction, criss-crossing them as desired. Allow the paint to dry completely, then apply several light coats of high-gloss aerosol acrylic sealer.

Creating Texture Effects

Texture paints offer a decorating alternative to either flat paints or wallcoverings. The variety of possible effects you can achieve is limited only by your imagination. Texture paints are available in either premixed latex formulations or in dry powder form. Premixed latex texture paints are fine for producing light stipple patterns, and powder textures are usually a good choice for creating heavier adobe or stucco finishes. Powder textures must be mixed with water using a paint mixer bit and power drill. Some premixed adobe or stucco finishes now rival the powdered forms. Ask the local supplier about availability.

Practice different textures on heavy cardboard until you get the pattern you want. Remember, the depth of the texture depends on the stiffness of the texture paint, the amount applied to the surface, and the type of tool used to create the texture.

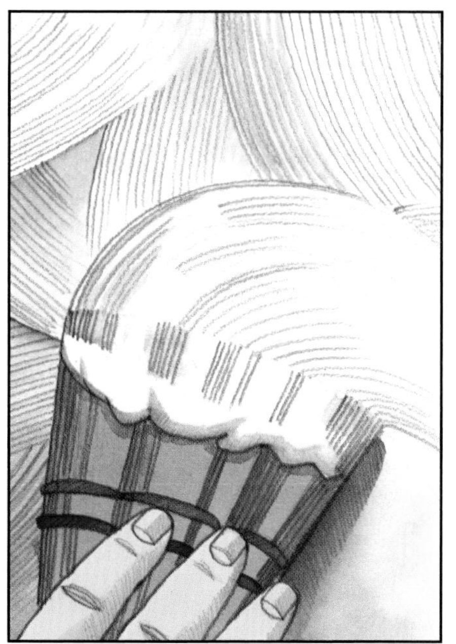

Create a swirl pattern with a whisk broom. Apply the texture paint with a roller, then use broom to achieve the design wanted.

Dab, drag, or swirl a sponge through texture paint to create an endless variety of texture patterns. Or let the first coat dry, then sponge another color on top for a two-toned stucco effect.

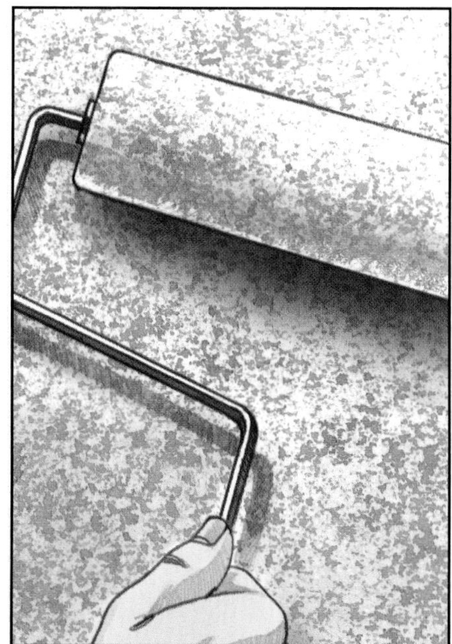

Use long-nap roller to make this stipple texture effect. For different patterns, vary the pressure on the roller and amount of texture paint on the surface.

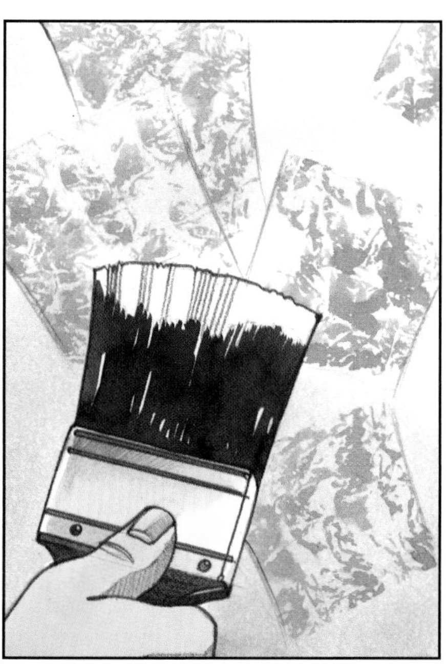

Create a crowsfoot design by applying texture paint with a roller, brushing it out level, then randomly striking the surface with the flat of the brush.

Trowel over the texture pattern when the paint has partially dried to flatten peaks and achieve a brocade design. Clean trowel between strokes with a wet brush or sponge.

STUFF YOU'LL NEED:

- **Tools:** Paintbrush, roller and cover, slotted screwdriver, hammer, broadknife.
- **Materials:** Interior latex or exterior enamel paint.

HOMER'S HINDSIGHT

There I was thinking I was so clever. I had waited for a nice fall day to paint my front door. A time when the flying insects would be gone for the season. The day started out nice and mild, but with the shorter days, it began to cool quickly. Consequently, the door wasn't completely dry when I had to close it to keep from freezing. Boy, was I surprised when I couldn't get out of the house the next morning because the paint had dried the door shut.

Painting Doors & Trim

The painting process for exterior doors is very similar to that of interior doors with just a few differences.

Exterior doors, by nature, are generally not removed for painting and therefore must be painted in place. When painting a door in the vertical position, it is a little more difficult to control drips and runs that may occur. One simple method is to carefully monitor the amount of paint you load onto the roller or brush and then work quickly to even out the coverage.

Another difference is the type of paint you use. Both latex and oil-based paints can be used for an exterior door and both provide excellent protection and are durable and washable. Latex-based paints have the advantage of being far easier to clean up than an oil-based paint.

PAINTING FLAT DOORS

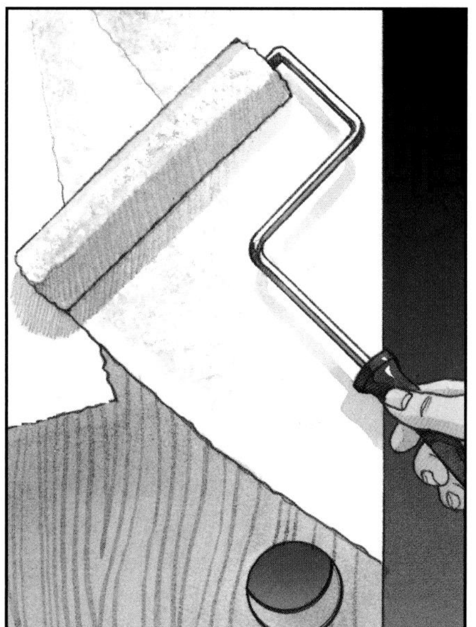

If the door is a simple flat style, after removing the door knob, you can brush or roll it with the same steps as you paint a wall. Finish the edges with a brush or roller and be sure to take extra care on the edges to eliminate runs and drips.

DOOR PAINTING SEQUENCE AT A GLANCE

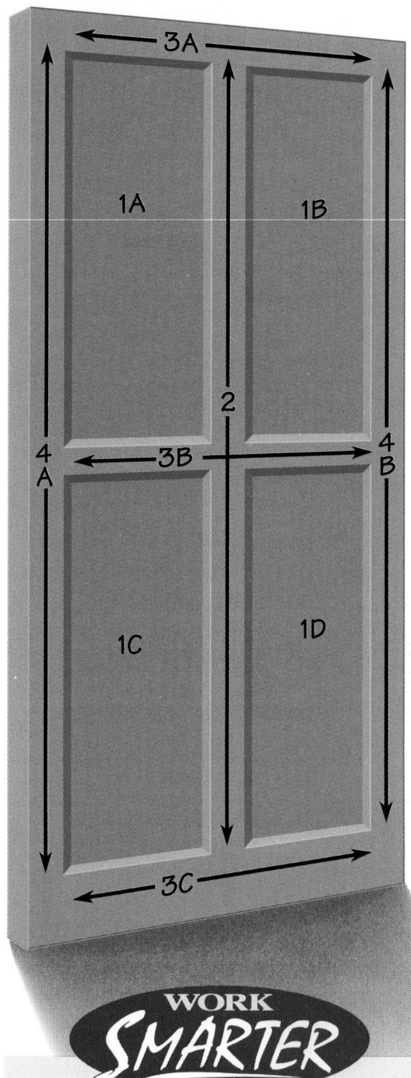

WORK SMARTER

You can check to see what sort of finish is on a door by rubbing with a cloth dampened with denatured alcohol. If the finish rubs off then you know it's a water based finish.

Make sure you prep the wood of the door well before painting (see pg. 43). If you've got a lot of panel doors to paint, you may want to try taking them off their hinges, laying them flat, and using a short nap roller and then cleaning up with a brush after painting the major surfaces with the roller. This will definitely speed up the process.

PAINTING DOORS

1 Apply paint to the inside of the top panels (1A, 1B). Smooth out the paint working with the grain doing the recessed areas first, then the faces of the panels. Repeat the process for the remaining panels (1C, 1D).

2 If the door has a center stile (vertical member #2), paint this next, then blend in the brush marks from the center stile when you paint the rails (3A, 3B, 3C).

3 Paint the rails (horizontal framing members), starting with the top rail (3A) and working your way to the bottom.

4 Paint the remaining stiles (4A, 4B), starting on the left. Feather the brush marks from the rails while they are still wet. Keep the line as straight as possible along the edge where the stiles meet the rails. Brush or roll the edges, but be careful not to get any runs on the face of the door.

THIS IS A GOOD TIME TO LUBRICATE THE HINGE PINS AND REPAIR LOOSE HINGES.

PAINTING INTERIOR DOORS

1 Remove the door by driving the lower hinge pin out with a screwdriver and hammer. Have a helper hold the door in place as you drive out the upper hinge pin.

2 Place the door flat on sawhorses to paint. On paneled doors, paint in the following order: (1) recessed panels, (2) horizontal rails, and (3) vertical stiles to avoid leaving any unnecessary brush marks.

3 Let the door dry completely. If a second coat of paint is needed, sand the door lightly and then wipe it with a tack cloth before repainting.

4 Seal the unpainted edges of the door with clear wood sealer to prevent moisture from entering the wood. Any water will cause the wood to warp and swell and result in a door that will not close properly.

HOMER'S HINDSIGHT

Save yourself some time and effort by replacing that old door hardware when you have the door removed for painting. This is an excellent opportunity not only to give that old beauty a facelift, but also to check for any structural problems and make the necessary corrections, leaving you with practically a brand new door! If you've always had problems with the latch not latching, or find yourself with a sore shoulder or squashed nose from the door sticking, now's your chance to get even. Warping is a common cause of latch and sticking problems. If the door is warped, straighten it by placing it bowed side up on a pair of sawhorses. Place heavy weights, like cement blocks, on the bowed section and let it sit for a couple of days until the door is straightened. Check it with a straightedge, then seal and/or paint all of the edges and faces.

TRIP SAVER

Take your old door hardware with you when you go to buy new hinges and latches. You will need to match the length of the latchbolt shaft and you'll want to get hinges at least the same size as the old ones. If you get bigger hinges, you can enlarge the mortise to fit, but you can't make the mortise smaller!

SPECIAL TIPS FOR PAINTING TRIM

Protect wall and floor surfaces with a wide broadknife or a plastic shielding tool.

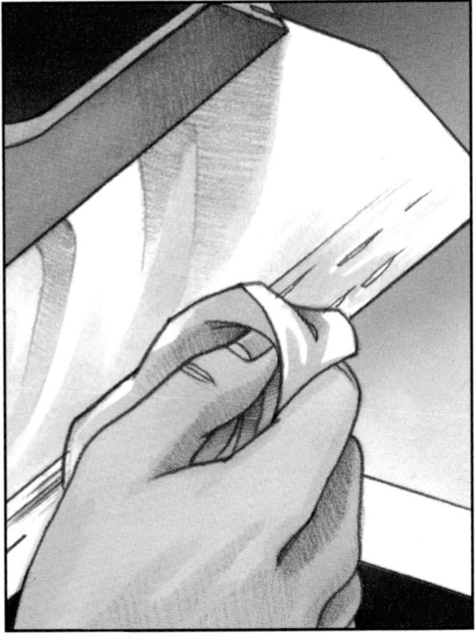

Wipe paint off broadknife or shielding tool each time it is moved to keep from getting paint on the trim and surrounding areas.

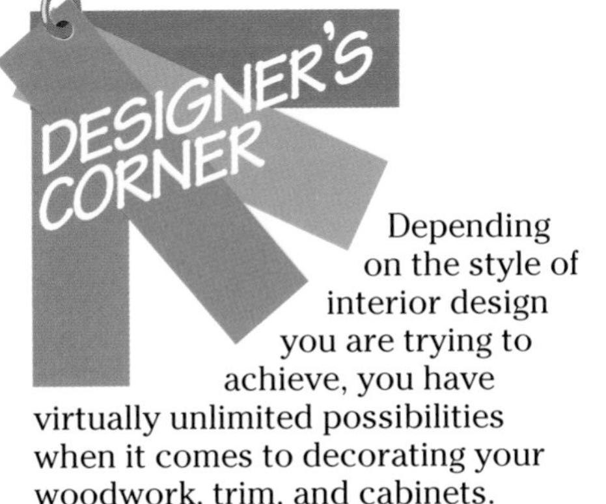

Depending on the style of interior design you are trying to achieve, you have virtually unlimited possibilities when it comes to decorating your woodwork, trim, and cabinets. Once primarily stained and varnished, woodwork today can use many decorative paint color combinations that will liven up any room and make it something special. Stenciling, sponge painting, and faux finishes are just a few of many decorating specialties you can use to make your projects unique.

Paint both sides of cabinet doors. This provides an even moisture seal and prevents warping.

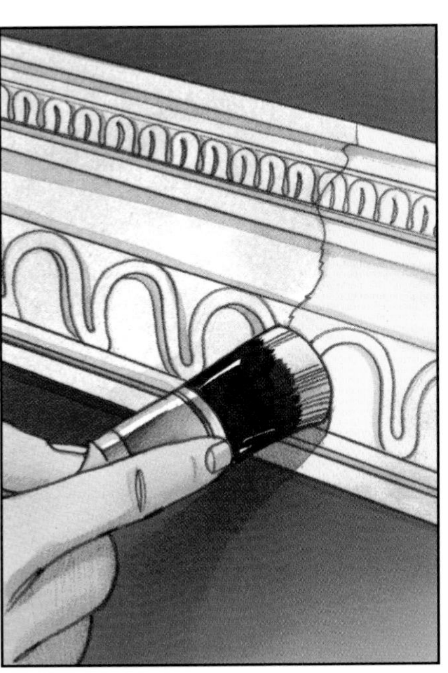

Paint deep-patterned surfaces with a stiff-bristled brush, like a stenciling brush. Use small circular strokes to penetrate recesses.

If you cannot remove them, interior doors can be painted while hanging on their hinges; however, you will find that the quality of finish and ease of application is much better if you can lay the doors flat.

Even if you think the door is manageable by yourself, it is a good idea to get assistance in removing it. This will help prevent damage to the door and nearby walls if it unexpectedly drops off the hinges when you remove the hinge pins. Best of all, a helper can lessen the likelihood of pinched fingers.

PAINTING A WINDOW FRAME

1 To paint double-hung windows, remove them from their frames if possible. Newer, spring-mounted windows are released by pushing against the frame. If you have an older window, consider painting it in place.

2 Drill holes and insert 2 nails into the legs of wooden stepladder, and mount the window easel-style for easy painting. Or, lay window flat on bench or sawhorses. Do not paint sides or bottom of sashes.

3 Using a tapered sash brush, begin by painting the wood next to the glass. Use the narrow edge of brush and overlap paint onto the glass to create a weathertight seal.

4 Clean excess paint off the glass with a putty knife wrapped in a clean cloth. Rewrap the knife often so that you always wipe with clean fabric. Leave 1/16" paint overlap from sash onto glass.

5 Paint the flat portions of the sashes, then the case moldings, sill, and apron. Use slow brush strokes, and avoid getting paint between sash and frame. For casement windows, open them completely and paint them in the same manner allowing them to dry completely before closing.

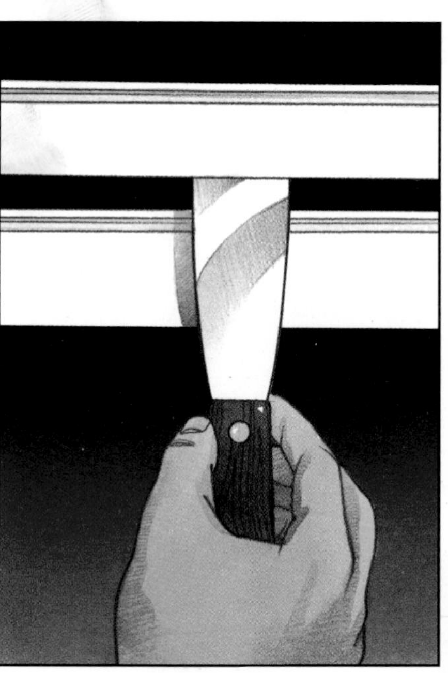

6 If you must paint windows in place, move the painted windows up and down several times during the drying period to keep them from sticking. Use a putty knife to avoid touching the painted surfaces.

Applying Stain

Wipe-on staining is the most common method of coloring woodwork and offers a wide variety of color choices. Stains today are available in either traditional liquid form (both water-based and oil-based) or in a newer gel-type form.

Whether you choose a liquid or gel, you will have better control over color if you apply the stain in two or more thin coats instead of one heavy coat. For consistent color, you need to seal the grain with a sanding sealer before finish-sanding. Sealing prior to staining is a must for consistent color on soft woods because they are more absorbent and will end up with a blotchy stain finish if not sealed.

Liquid stains are a good choice for surfaces where you have better control over their coverage. Gel stains are good for simulated wood construction like some new doors are made from.

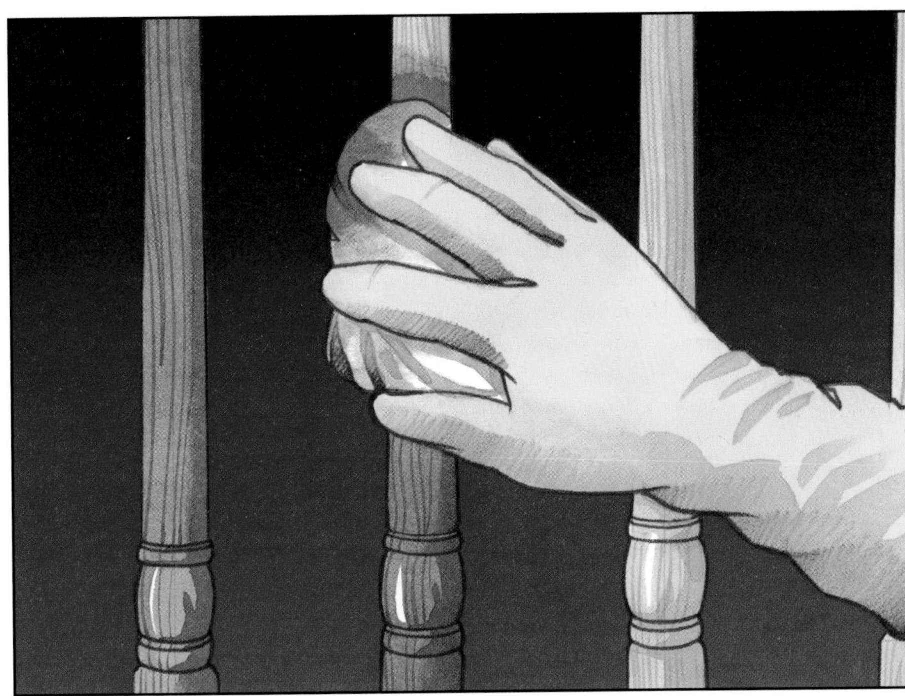

When staining a flat, horizontal surface you can use a brush to apply the stain. However, if you are staining a vertical surface, like the balusters above, use a rag to apply the stain so it doesn't drip or run.

STUFF YOU'LL NEED:

- ☐**Tools:** Paint brush, rubber gloves, staining cloth, abrasive pad.
- ☐**Materials:** Stain, thinner.

APPLYING LIQUID STAIN

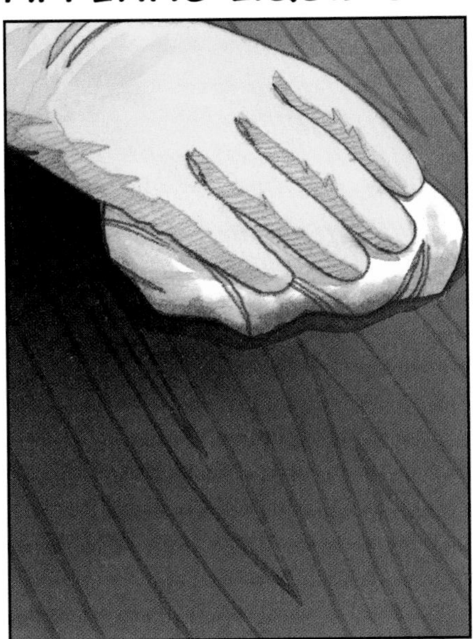

1 Stir the stain thoroughly, then apply a thin coat of stain with a brush or cloth. Stir the stain occasionally to keep the pigments from settling while you work. Wipe off any excess stain with a clean cloth, first against the grain, then with the grain.

2 Reapply thin layers of stain until the desired color tone is achieved. It's very hard to modify stain color so make sure to test the stain on a piece of scrap wood first, before you start and realize it's not the right color.

APPLYING GEL STAIN

1 Work the stain into the surfaces of the workpiece with a staining cloth using a circular motion.

2 Cover as much of the workpiece as you can reach with the staining cloth, recoating any areas that dry out as you work. Gel stain penetrates better if it is worked into the wood with a rag or brush rather than simply wiped onto the surface.

3 Use a stiff-bristled brush to apply gel stain into hard-to-reach areas where it is difficult to use a staining cloth.

4 Let the stain soak in (see the manufacturer's directions). Wipe off the excess with a clean rag using a polishing motion. Buff the stained surface with the wood grain using a soft, clean cloth.

5 Apply additional coats of stain until the workpiece has reached the desired color tone. Gel stain manufacturers usually recommend at least three coats to provide a thick stain layer that helps protect the wood against scratches and other surface flaws.

6 Let the stain dry, then buff with a fine abrasive pad before applying a topcoat.

Applying Polyurethane

SKILL SCALE

Painting: On normal pieces of woodwork, applying polyurethane requires average painting skills.

HOW LONG WILL IT TAKE?

Applying polyurethane to the trim in a standard 10'x15' room, excluding floors, should take the following:

EXPERIENCED	60 MIN.
INTERMEDIATE	75 MIN.
BEGINNER	90 MIN.

STUFF YOU'LL NEED:

☐**Tools:** Clean cloth, fine-bristled brush, fine paint pad.

☐**Materials:** #00 abrasive pad, mineral spirits, polyurethane, tack cloth.

Topcoat finishes are designed to seal the wood, protect the finish from scratches and other wear, and increase the visual appeal of the wood. Although there are many different types of topcoat material, the most commonly used for interior trim and woodwork is a polyurethane finish.

Polyurethane is a hard, durable topcoat material commonly used on floors, railings, baseboards, doors, and other heavy-use surfaces. It should never require waxing.

Available in both water-based and oil-based forms, polyurethane is a complex mixture of plastic resins and solvents that dries to a tough, light amber finish. Because polyurethane is difficult to retouch, be careful when applying it. Before it dries, it seemingly attracts any dust in the room. Cleaning up before applying it is always a good idea.

Polyurethane topcoats are available in gloss, semi-gloss, and satin finishes, although semi-gloss and satin are used the most. Select a gloss that best meets your needs.

HOMER'S HINDSIGHT

I wanted a perfectly smooth finish for my project so I made extra certain my polyurethane was mixed well by shaking it vigorously. What a mistake! I wound up with a polyurethane finish with hundreds of tiny bubbles. Now I know that you should never shake polyurethane. It's very important to mix it well, but you should stir it gently—or your bath won't be the only place where you'll wind up with bubbles.

FINISHING INTERIOR TRIM

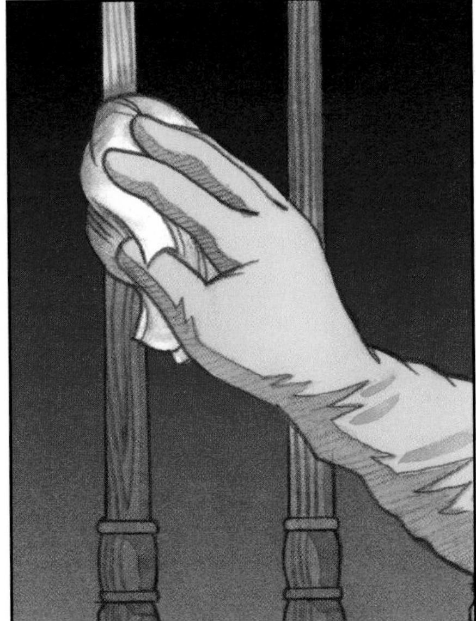

1 On bare wood, use a manufacturer's recommended solvent to dilute the varnish. Apply this diluted mixture with a clean cloth to seal the wood grain. Don't seal wood that is already stained or finished with penetrating oil.

2 Lightly sand the dried surface with extrafine wet/dry sandpaper. Wipe the surface with a tack cloth to remove any dust particles. Apply a thin coat of polyurethane using a fine-bristled brush. Elements in polyurethane can settle toward the bottom of the can. It's best to stir it continuously while you're using it.

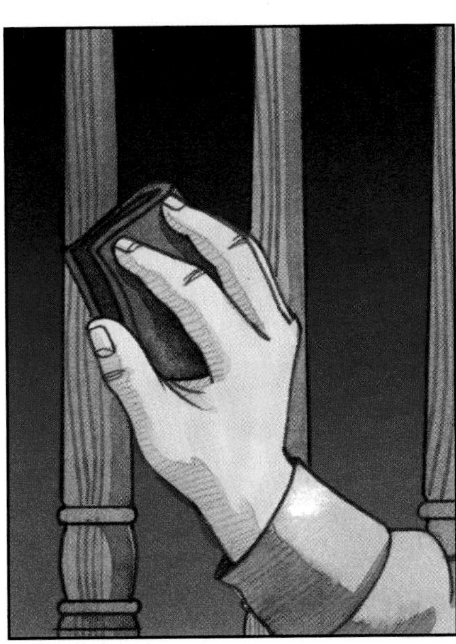

3 Lightly sand the dried finish with an extrafine-grit abrasive pad dipped in lemon furniture oil to smooth out the surface, remove dust particles, and create an attractive matte finish. Apply an extra coat of polyurethane to surfaces that receive heavy use.

WALLPAPERING BASICS

Wallpaper is an age-old term given to materials that are more typically included in the category of wallcoverings. Very few modern "wallpapers" are actually made of paper anymore. Today's wallpapers are made of vinyl, vinyl-coated paper or cloth, fabric, and textiles, natural grasses, foil or Mylar.

Vinyl or coated vinyl coverings are the easiest to hang, clean, and remove. Other types of wallpapers such as foil, burlap, cork, and hemp can give a room a unique look but will require special handling. They are more difficult to work with and demand more of your decorating budget.

Your choice of wallpaper depends on the needs of the room and on your confidence and ability.

Types of wallpaper: (A) Fabric wallpaper is made of woven textiles and is easy to hang because there is no pattern to match but the material can be difficult to work with and it may be difficult to clean. (B) Embossed has a stamped relief pattern that gives an elegant look. (C) Grasscloth uses natural plant fibers and softens the feeling in a room. It is a good choice for flawed walls. (D) Foil is highly reflective and adds brightness to any room but will reveal flaws in the wall on which it is applied. (E & F) Vinyl is a durable covering that is easy to apply, clean, and remove. It is available with repeat and free-form patterns and comes with a preapplied adhesive.

TIPS FOR CHOOSING WALLPAPER

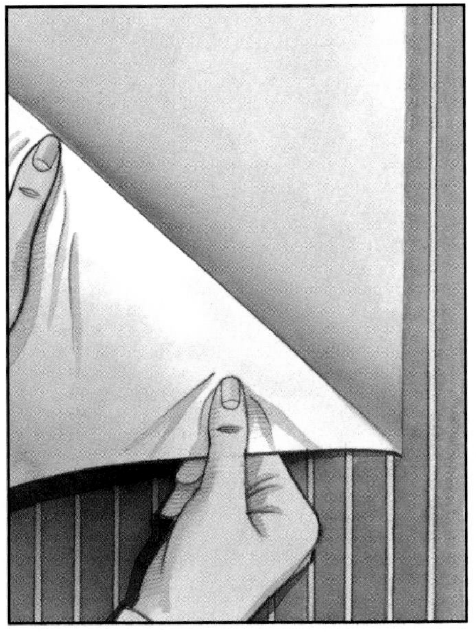

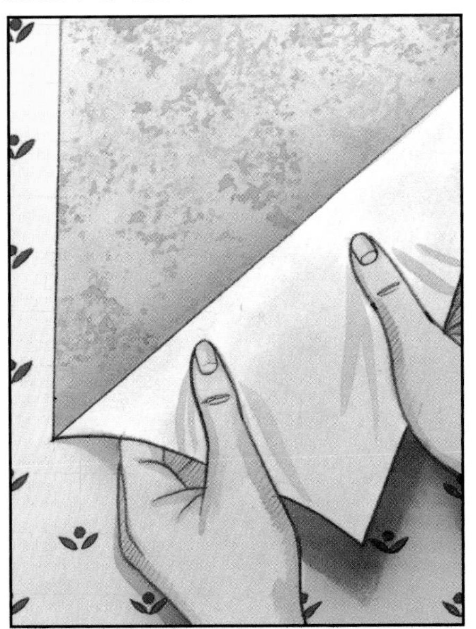

Removability: Strippable wallpapers (left) can be pulled away from the wall by hand leaving little or no film or residue. Peelable wallpapers (right) can be removed, but may leave a thin paper layer on the wall, which can usually be removed with soap and hot water. Check the back of the sample or the wallpaper package for its stripability rating. Choose a strippable product to make future redecorating easier.

Dye lot: Jot down dye-lot numbers for reference. If you need additional rolls, order from the same dye lot to avoid slight color differences.

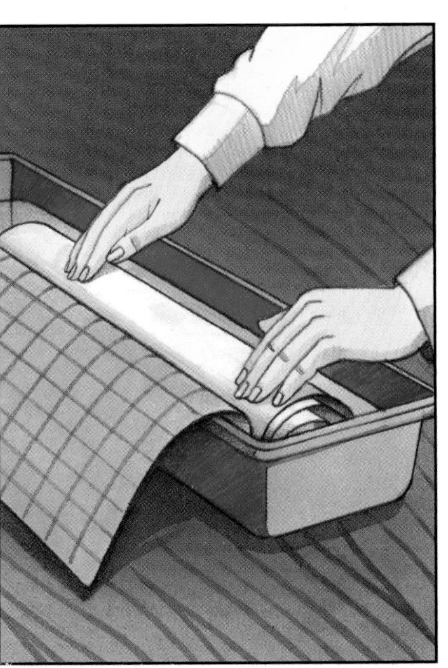

Patterns: There is generally more waste with large patterns. A wallpaper with a large drop pattern can be more expensive than one with a smaller repeat because you waste paper matching the pattern from one strip to the next. With large designs it may be difficult to avoid obvious pattern interruptions at baseboards or corners.

Application: Prepasted wallpapers (left) are factory-coated with a water-based adhesive that is activated when the wallpaper is inserted in a water tray. Today's prepasted products hold up just as well as those requiring an adhesive coat and are easier to prepare. Prepasted activators can be added to the water to ensure the adhesive bonds well with the wall and should be available at any wallpaper store. Unpasted wallpapers (right) must be coated with an adhesive for hanging.

Tools for Wallpapering

Many of the tools for hanging wallpaper are common items you may already have. Keep a supply of #2 pencils and a pencil sharpener handy for precise marking when laying out and cutting wallpaper. Never use an ink marker or ballpoint pen because the ink might bleed through the wet wallpaper.

Use a bubblestick or carpenter's level for establishing plumb lines and as a straightedge for cutting. Don't use a chalk line because the chalk can smear the new wallpaper or ooze through the seams. Trim the wallpaper with a razor knife that has breakaway blades; this will simplify the process of always using a sharp tool. Use a new section of blade every one or two cuts to prevent snagging and tearing the wallpaper.

Be sure to use non-corrosive pails for wash water and a high-quality sponge to avoid damaging the wallpaper.

As with most projects, the right tools make wallpapering go smoothly, yield better results, and produce a lot less gray hair. Be sure to use the best tools that your budget will allow and, if possible, have someone help you with the project.

Although wallpapering has been known to strenuously test the solidarity of many marriages, you will readily appreciate the help that an extra pair of hands will provide. No matter what the relationship, in the end you both will be better off.

Wallpaper tray (A) holds water for wetting prepasted wallpaper strips. Smoothing brushes (B) come in various nap lengths–short for smoothing out vinyl wallpapers and long for fragile wallpapers like flocks. Check with your supplier for flexible plastic smoothers. They are often less expensive and work well. A wide broadknife and wallpaper trimming tool (C) hold the wallpaper while trimming. Paste brush (D) and paint roller (F) are used for applying adhesive. Wallpaper scissors (E) and razor knife with breakaway blade (H) are used for trimming. Seam roller (I) presses down the seams where wallpaper strips meet. Wallpaper table (J) provides a flat working surface. You can rent a table or make one with plywood and sawhorses. A bubble stick (G) or level is used to check plumb lines and as a straight edge.

Measuring & Estimating Wallpaper

With a few room measurements and the information listed on the wallcovering package, you can estimate the correct amount of wallpaper to buy. The chart on this page will help you calculate the square footage of your walls and ceilings and show you how to find the per-roll coverage of the wallpaper.

Because of normal trimming waste, the per-roll coverage of wallpaper will be at least 15% less than the coverage listed on the package. The waste percentage can be higher depending on how much space it takes for the wallpaper pattern to repeat itself.

This "pattern repeat" measurement is listed on the wallpaper package. You can compensate for this extra waste factor by adding the pattern repeat measurement to the wall height measurement of the room.

MEASURING UNUSUAL ANGLES

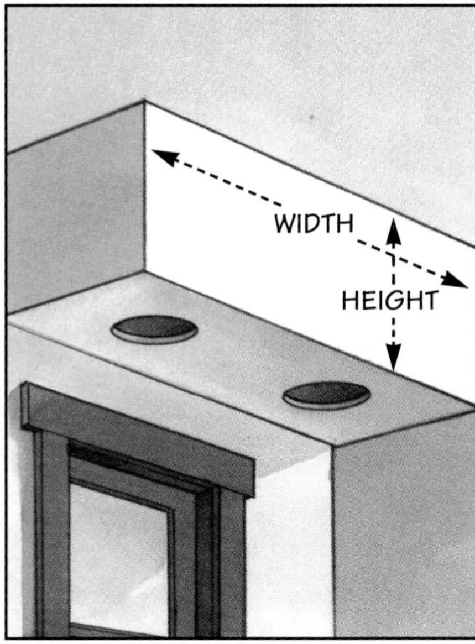

Soffits: If covering all sides of a soffit, add the **width** and **height** into the wall or ceiling measurement.

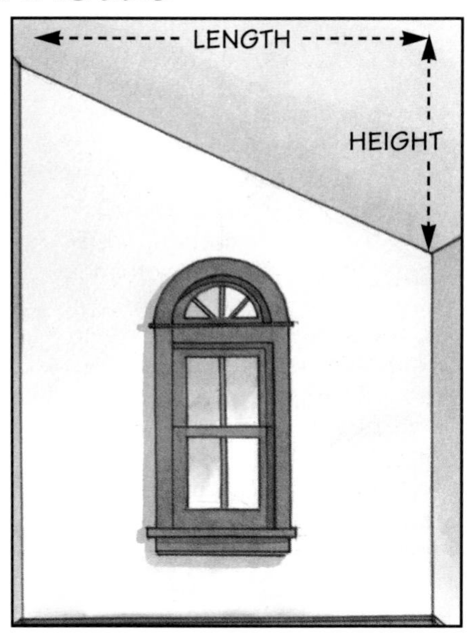

Triangular walls: Measure as though the surface were square: take the length times the height to get the correct amount.

ESTIMATING HOW MUCH WALLPAPER YOU'LL NEED

How to Determine the Actual Per-Roll Coverage

① Total per-roll coverage (square feet) ______

② Adjust for waste factor x .85

③ Actual Per-roll Coverage (square feet) ______

DROP-MATCH WALLPAPER

Drop-match waste

Wall Height

Drop-match waste

Wallpaper with diagonally repeating patterns are generally known as "drop-match." When hanging drop-match wallpaper, label one roll "A" and one "B." Then alternate which roll you cut from. That way you'll avoid wasting paper each time you trim for the drop-match waste.

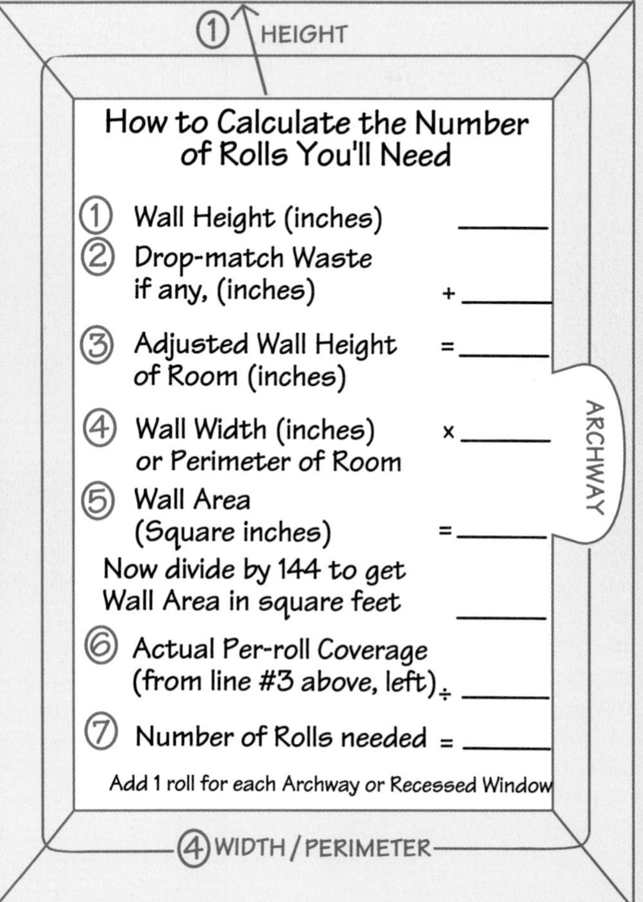

How to Calculate the Number of Rolls You'll Need

① Wall Height (inches) ______

② Drop-match Waste if any, (inches) + ______

③ Adjusted Wall Height of Room (inches) = ______

④ Wall Width (inches) or Perimeter of Room x ______

⑤ Wall Area (Square inches) = ______

Now divide by 144 to get Wall Area in square feet ______

⑥ Actual Per-roll Coverage (from line #3 above, left) ÷ ______

⑦ Number of Rolls needed = ______

Add 1 roll for each Archway or Recessed Window

Planning Your Attack

When hanging any patterned wallpaper, there will be one seam where a full strip meets a partial strip. The pattern will usually mismatch at this point. Plan this mismatched seam to fall in an inconspicuous spot, like behind a door or above an entrance.

Sketch out seam lines before you begin. Avoid placing seams that will be difficult to handle. A seam that falls close to the edge of a window or fireplace complicates the job. At corners, wallpaper should always overlap slightly onto the opposite wall. If one or more seams fall in a bad spot, adjust your plumb line a few inches to compensate.

USE A PENCIL FOR MARKING. INK PENS AND MARKERS MAY BLEED THROUGH WALLPAPER.

TOOLTIPS

In its simplest form, a plumb bob is just a weight on the end of a string. The kind you should buy has a center hole on top where the string enters so the plumb bob hangs straight up and down.

When wallpapering, a plumb bob is used to draw "plumb lines," perfectly vertical lines on walls. To use a plumb bob place a small nail or tack near the ceiling on the wall you wish to draw a vertical line on and tie the plumb bob and string to the nail so it hangs, nearly touching the floor. Once it has stopped swinging (you can steady it to slow it down quickly), mark the wall along the string's length. Then align your first strip of wallpaper with the line.

Start at the focal point, like a fireplace or large window. Center a "plumb line" (a perfectly vertical line, see Tool Tip, left), on the focal point, then sketch a wall covering plan in both directions from the center line.

Plan the mismatch. If the room has no obvious focal point, start at the corner farthest from the entry. Measure out a distance equal to the wallpaper width minus 1/2", and mark a point. Work in both directions, marking out points where the seams will fall.

Adjust for corners that fall exactly on seam lines. Make sure you have at least a 1/2" overlap on inside corners and 1" on outside corners.

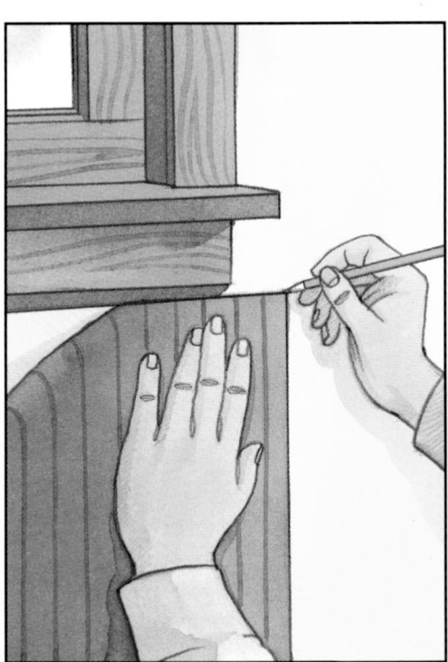

Adjust for seams that fall in difficult locations, like near the edge of windows or doors. Shift your starting point so that the seams leave you with workable widths of wallpaper around obstacles.

Basic Wallpapering Techniques

For durability and easy application, choose a quality prepasted vinyl wallpaper whenever possible. Clear the room of all furniture that can be easily removed and layer newspapers or drop cloths next to the walls.

For easy handling, rent a wallcoverer's table or use any flat, elevated surface. Shut off the electricity and cover the outlet receptacle slots with masking tape to keep out water and adhesive.

Work during daylight hours for best visibility and make sure each strip is perfectly positioned before going on to the next section. Get assistance from another person whenever possible, especially when covering ceilings.

Wallpaper Categories

Most patterned wallpapers fall into one of two categories: straight-match and drop-match. Sometimes these designations are stamped on the back of the paper. Be sure to determine which type you have before cutting any wallpaper.

If the pattern elements of the same design are directly opposite each other on the left and right edges of the strip, the paper is a straight-match and the pattern should repeat horizontally from strip to strip.

All others are drop-match patterns. Their elements begin near the edge of one sheet and are completed on the next sheet with a design that repeats diagonally on the wall. You'll spend a little more for drop-match paper because you'll use more to get the patterns to match up correctly. When hanging drop-match paper designate one roll as "A" and one as "B". Then alternate cutting from the rolls. This way you'll waste less paper. Always cut the next strip before you hang the previous one. It's easier to make sure the patterns line up without one glued to the wall.

1 Hold the wallpaper against the wall. Make sure there is a full pattern at the ceiling line, and that the wallpaper overlaps ceiling and baseboard by about 2". Cut the strip with a wallpaper scissors.

2 For the next strips, find the pattern match with the previously hung strip, then measure and cut a new strip with about 2" of excess at each end.

WETTING PREPASTED STRIPS

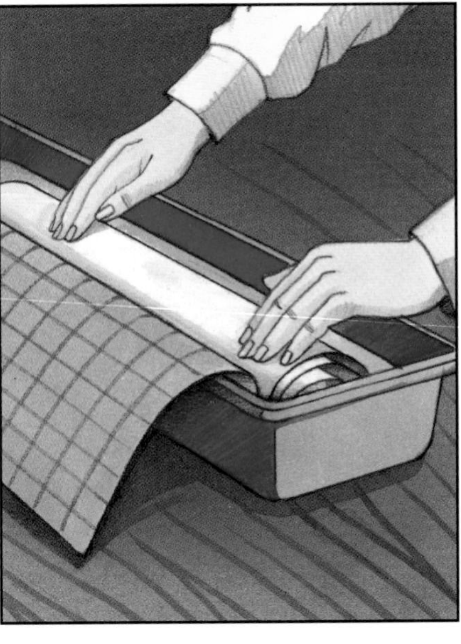

1 Fill the wallpaper water tray half full of lukewarm water. Roll the cut strip loosely with pattern side in. Wet roll in tray as directed by manufacturer, usually about 1 minute.

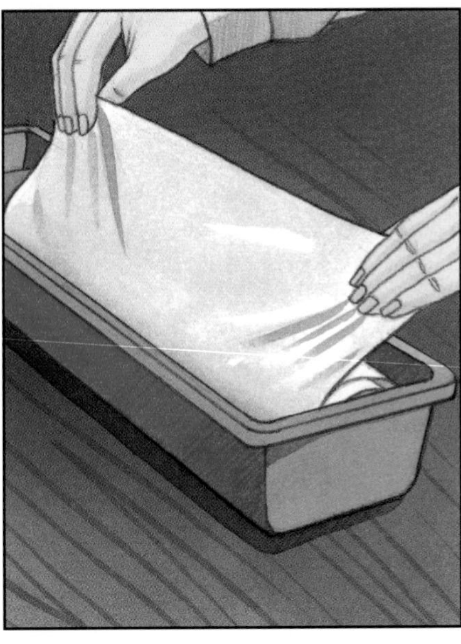

2 Holding one edge of the strip with both hands, lift wallpaper from the water. Inspect the pasted side to make sure the strip is evenly wetted. Book the strip as indicated below.

For unpasted wallpaper, lay the strip, pattern side down, on the wallpaperer's table or a flat surface. Apply the adhesive evenly to the strip, using a paint roller. Wipe any adhesive completely from the table before preparing the next strip.

HOMER'S HINDSIGHT

Remember, a wallpapering job is only as good as the wall you hang it on. Do good prep work first, and your wallpaper will stay put. The best thing you can do is paint with a wallpaper primer before you start. Not only will it make a surface the wallpaper will adhere to well, it will make it easier to take the wallpaper down five years from now when you want to remodel. Doing this again may be the last thing on your mind, but trust me, it'll be worth it.

BOOKING WALLPAPER

"Book" wallpaper by folding both ends of the strip to the center, with pasted side in. Do not crease the folds. Let the strip stand (cure) for about three to six minutes. Some wallpapers should not be booked, so be sure to follow the manufacturer's directions.

For ceiling strips or wallpaper borders, use an "accordion" book. Fold strip back and forth with pasted side in for easy handling. Let the strip stand (cure) from about three to six minutes or the length of time the manufacturer recommends.

POSITIONING WALLPAPER

Unfold the booked strip, and position it with the edge butted against plumb line or previous strip. Beginning at the top, smooth the wallpaper out from the center using a smoothing tool or brush. Check for bubbles. Seams should be butted properly. Pull the strip away and reposition if necessary.

TOOLTIPS

Traditionally, a wide brush has been used to smooth the wallpaper. Now flexible plastic smoother tools are available in a wide variety of sizes and shapes. Ask where you buy your wallpaper what kind of smoothing tool you should use, either brush or plastic.

Choosing the right tool will depend on the type of wallpaper you're hanging. Also consider if the tool fits your hand comfortably or if it is too heavy. What may seem like a light tool in the store will seem heavy after you've been holding it above your head for a couple of hours to smooth the wallpaper near the ceiling.

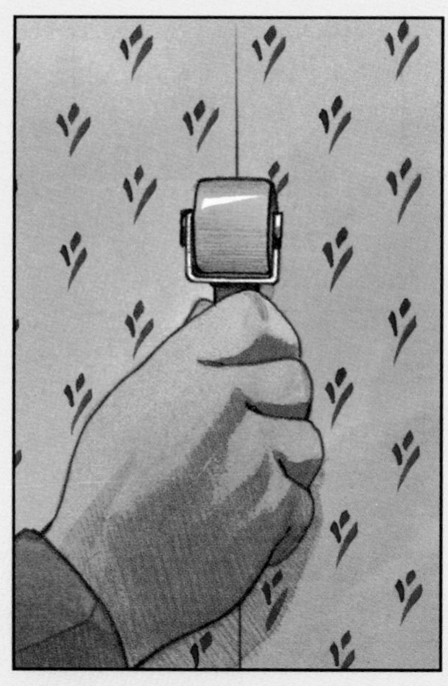

Let the strips stand for about half an hour. Roll the seam gently with seam roller. Do not squeeze out the adhesive. Do not roll seams on flocks, foils, fabrics, or embossed wallpapers. For these specialty wallpapers, tap the seams gently with a smoothing brush.

TRIMMING WALLPAPER

1 Hold the wallpaper against the molding or ceiling with a wide broadknife. Cut away the excess with a sharp razor knife. Keep the knife blade in place while changing position of the broadknife.

2 With a wallpapered ceiling, crease the wall strips with a broadknife then cut along the crease with wallpaper scissors. Cutting with a razor knife may puncture the ceiling strip.

Use clear water and a sponge to rinse the adhesive from surfaces. Change the water after every 3 or 4 strips. Do not let the water run along the seams. Do not use water on grasscloths, flocks, and fabrics.

WALLPAPERING WALLS

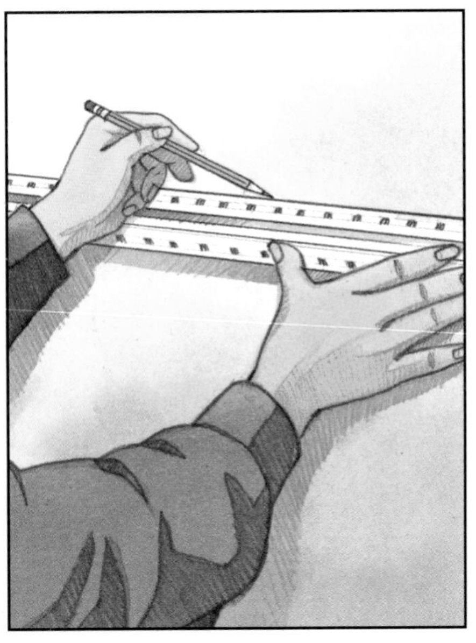

1 Measure from the corner a distance equal to the wallpaper width minus $\frac{1}{2}$", and mark a point. Sketch out the seam locations and adjust if necessary (see Planning Your Attack, page 64).

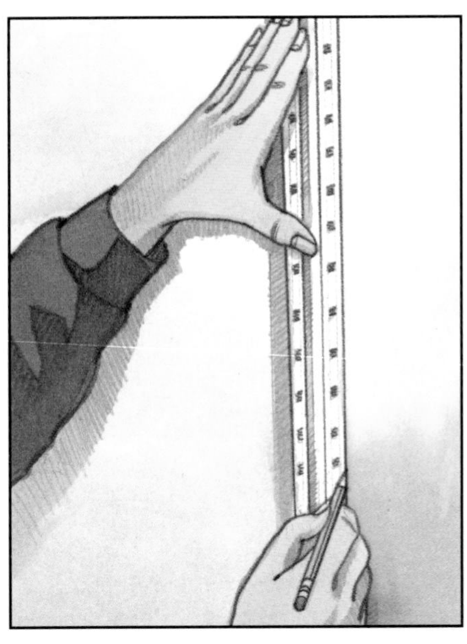

2 Draw a plumb line at the marked point using a bubblestick. For a wall that must match the pattern of a wallpapered ceiling, draw the plumb line straight down from the first ceiling seam.

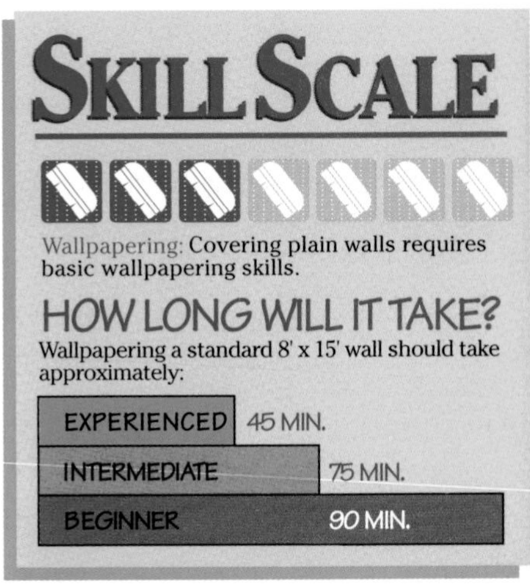

STUFF YOU'LL NEED:

- ☐ **Tools:** Bubblestick, pencil, smoothing brush, broadknife, razor knife, sponge, scissors.
- ☐ **Materials:** Wallpaper, adhesive (if needed), prepasted activators.

3 Cut and prepare the first strip. First unfold the top portion of the booked strip. Position the strip against the plumb line so that the strip overlaps onto the ceiling by about 2" and that there is a full pattern beginning at the ceiling line.

4 Using your smoothing brush, stroke the paper flat against the top of the wall. Then smooth the paper with downward strokes, working out from the center toward the sides.

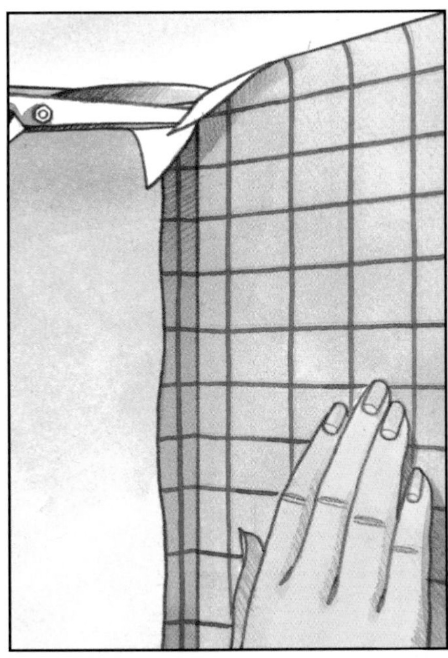

5 Snip the top corner of the strip so that the wallpaper wraps around the corner with no wrinkles. Use open palms to slide the strip into position with the edge butted against the plumb line. Press the strip flat with a smoothing brush.

TOOL TIPS

Vertical and horizontal marking lines can be determined with either a carpenter's level or a bubblestick. The bubblestick is the better tool for most wallpapering tasks because it is not as heavy and cumbersome as the level. It also has measurement marks for accurately marking your desired dimensions on the walls, ceilings, and wallpaper strips.

Trimming wallpaper will permanently affect the strip. Be sure to match patterns and align seams before any extra wallpaper is trimmed off.

6 Unfold the bottom of the strip, and use your palms flat to position the strip against the plumb line. Press the strip flat with a smoothing brush. Be sure to check for bubbles.

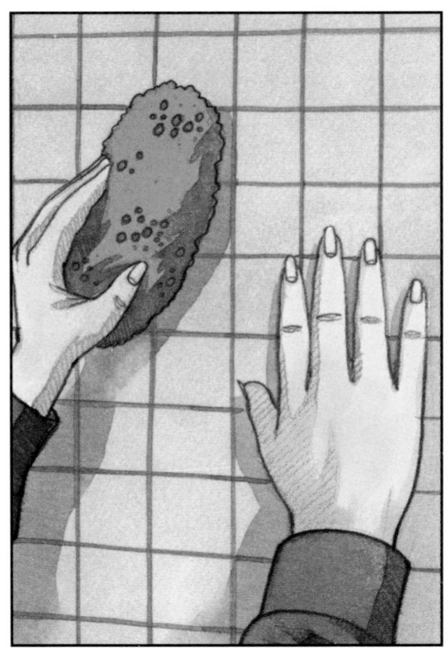

7 Working from the center to the edges, smooth the entire strip with a damp sponge to remove flecks of paste and air bubbles. Wait to trim the paper until you have hung the second strip.

SAFETY ALERT

Always turn the power off to outlets and switches before removing coverplates.

8 Hang any additional strips, butting the edges to align the pattern. Let the strips stand for about half an hour, then use a seam roller to lightly roll the seam. On flocks or fabrics, tap the seams gently with a smoothing brush.

9 Trim the excess wallpaper with a sharp razor knife. If the ceiling is wallpapered, crease the edge of the wall strip with a broadknife, then trim along the crease with wallpaper scissors to avoid punctures. Rinse the adhesive off the surfaces.

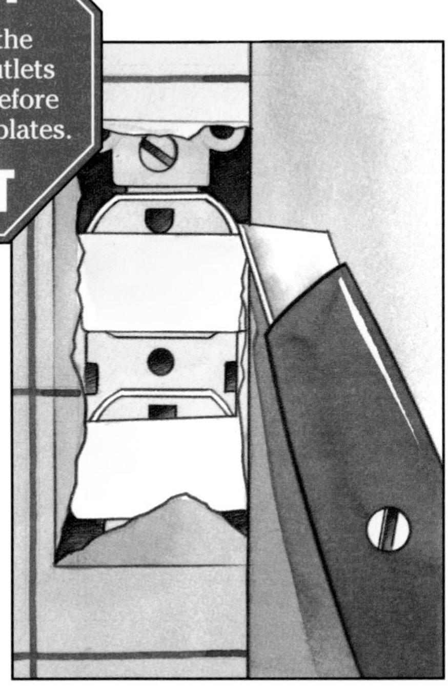

10 With the power turned off, hang the wallpaper over the outlets and switches. Make small diagonal cuts to expose the outlet. Trim the wallpaper back to the edges of the opening with a razor knife and broadknife.

WALLPAPERING INSIDE CORNERS

1 Cut and book a full strip. While the strip cures, measure from the edge of the previous strip to the corner at the top, middle, and bottom of the wall. Add $\frac{1}{2}$" to the longest of these measurements.

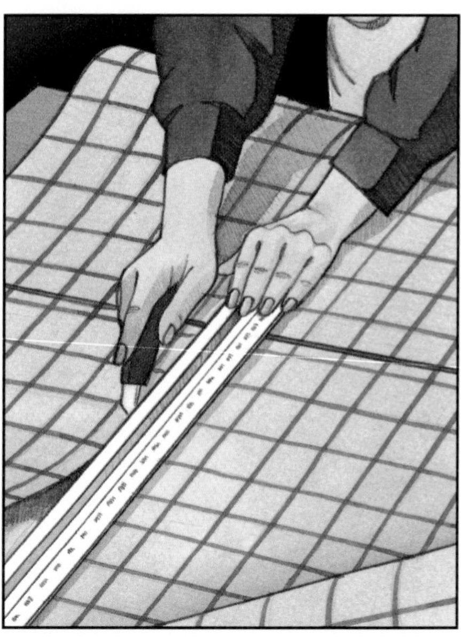

2 Align the edges of the booked strip. From the edge, measure at 2 points a distance equal to the measurement found in Step 1. Hold a straightedge that spans the booked strip against the 2 marked points and cut the wallpaper strip using a sharp razor knife.

3 Position the strip on the wall with the pattern matching the previous strip, overlapping the ceiling by about 2".

4 Using open palms, carefully butt the edges of the strips. The strip will overlap slightly onto the uncovered wall.

5 Make small corner slits at the top and bottom of the strip to wrap the overlap around the corner without any wrinkles.

6 Flatten the strip with a smoothing brush, then trim the excess at the ceiling and baseboard.

7 Measure the width of the next strip. Mark this distance from the corner onto the new uncovered wall and mark with pencil. Draw a plumb line from ceiling to floor on the new wall, using a bubblestick.

8 Position the strip on the wall with the cut edge toward the corner and the factory edge against the new plumb line. Press the strip flat with a smoothing brush. Trim at the ceiling and baseboard.

9 If using vinyl wallpaper, peel the back edge and apply the vinyl-to-vinyl adhesive to the lap seam. Press the seam area flat. Let the strips stand for half an hour, then roll the seams. Rinse using a damp sponge.

WALLPAPERING OUTSIDE CORNERS

1 Measure the distance from the previous strip to the corner at the top, middle, and bottom of the wall. Add 1" to this measurement for the wrap around the corner. If you're using fairly stiff wallpaper, you may want to add 4" - 6" for an overlap to ensure good adhesion.

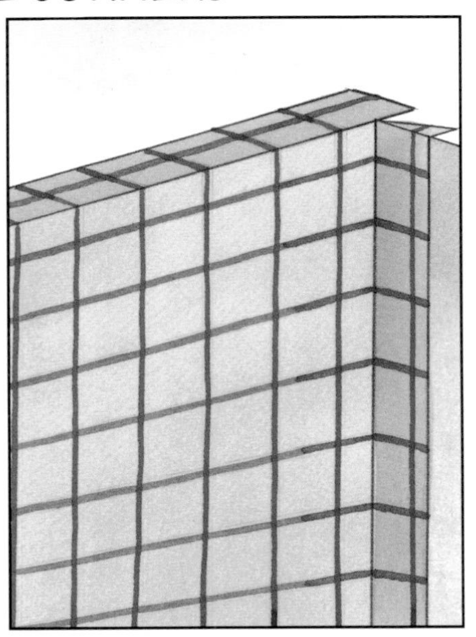

2 If the corner is not plumb, you will need to add more than 1" to the Step 1 measurement to allow for a wider wrap. Smooth the strip into place and cut the top and bottom slits exactly at the ceiling and baseboard corners. Fold the strip around the corner and trim the top and bottom excess.

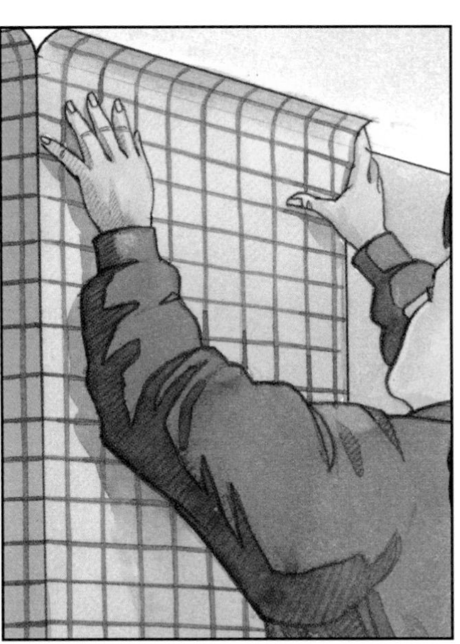

3 Measure the width of the next strip and add 1/4". Measure that distance from the corner along the new wall and draw a plumb line. Hang the next strip, lining it vertically with the plumb line and matching patterns with the overlap as much as possible.

Wallpapering Around Windows & Doors

A common mistake made when hanging wallpaper is to precut the strips to "fit" the shape of the windows and doors. This practice inevitably leads to redoing the entire area, since you can never measure and cut the precise dimensions without the strip applied to the wall. Think of window and door openings as simply larger electrical outlets that need to be wallpapered around.

The best method is to hang the strip as you normally would, right over the window or door casing. Then use a smoothing brush to smooth the strip before trimming the edges. To avoid damaging the wood, use scissors instead of a razor knife to trim the wallpaper and wipe any excess adhesive off the casing with a wet sponge.

Wallpapering around doors and windows requires basic to intermediate skills.

If you're hanging short strips directly above and below an opening, make sure these strips are hung exactly vertical to ensure a good pattern match with the next full strip. Remember, once you trim the strip, your option of adjusting it to better match the adjoining strips is greatly limited or possibly eliminated. Be sure not to trim the short strips until the full strips have been hung in place so you have the flexibility to make minor adjustments as necessary.

WALLPAPERING AROUND OPENINGS

1 Position the strip on the wall, directly over the window casing. Butt the seam carefully against the edge of the previous strip.

2 Smooth the flat areas of wallpaper with a smoothing brush. Press the strip tightly against the ceiling.

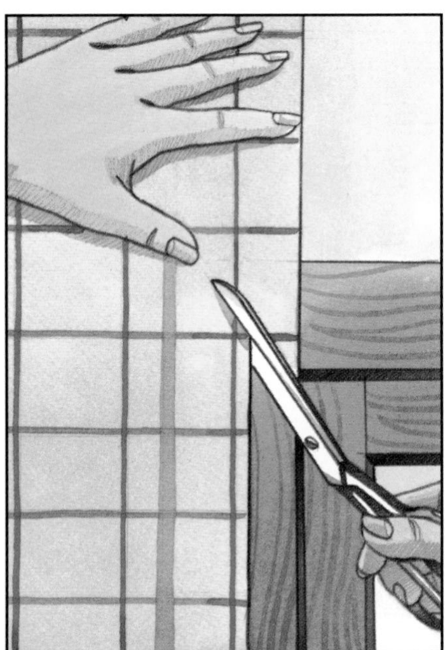

3 Use wallpaper scissors to cut diagonally from the edge of the strip to the corner of the casing. If hanging around a window, make a similar cut in the bottom of the corner.

4 Use wallpaper scissors to trim away any excess wallpaper to about 1" around the inside of the window frame. Smooth the wallpaper and any bubbles as you work.

5 Hold the wallpaper against the casing with a broadknife and trim the excess with a sharp razor knife. Trim the overlaps at the ceiling and baseboard and then rinse the wallpaper and casings with a damp sponge.

6 Cut short wallpaper strips for the sections above and below the window. You may find scraps that will match the pattern and fit these spaces. Make sure the small strips are hung exactly vertical to ensure that the pattern matches with the next full strip.

7 Cut and prepare the next full strip. Position it on the wall with the edge butting the previous strip so that the pattern matches.

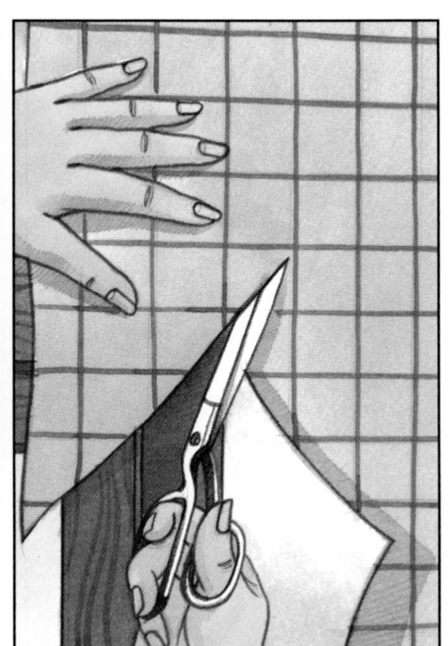

8 Snip the top and bottom corners diagonally from the edge to the corners of the casing. Trim away any excess wallpaper to about 1" around the inside of the window or door frame.

9 Match the seam on the bottom half of the strip. Trim any excess wallpaper to about 1" with wallpaper scissors. Flatten the strip with a smoothing brush.

10 Hold the wallpaper against the casing with a broadknife and cut the excess with a razor knife. Trim the overlaps at the ceiling and baseboard. Rinse the wallpaper and casings with a damp sponge.

WALLPAPERING A RECESSED WINDOW

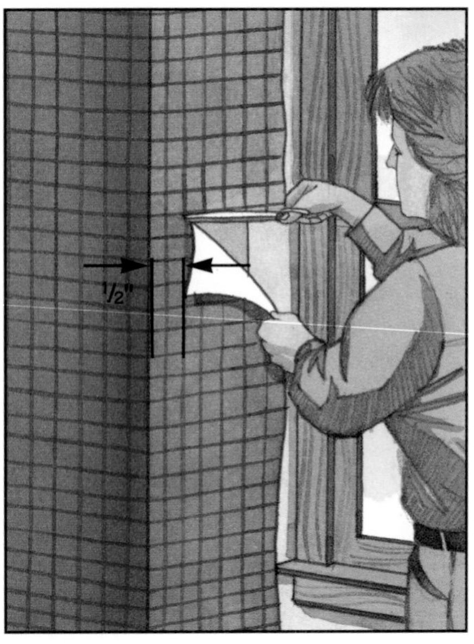

1 Hang the wallpaper strips so they overlap the recess. Smooth the strips and trim the excess at the baseboard and ceiling. To wrap the top and bottom of the recess, make a horizontal cut at the halfway point to within 1/2" of the wall.

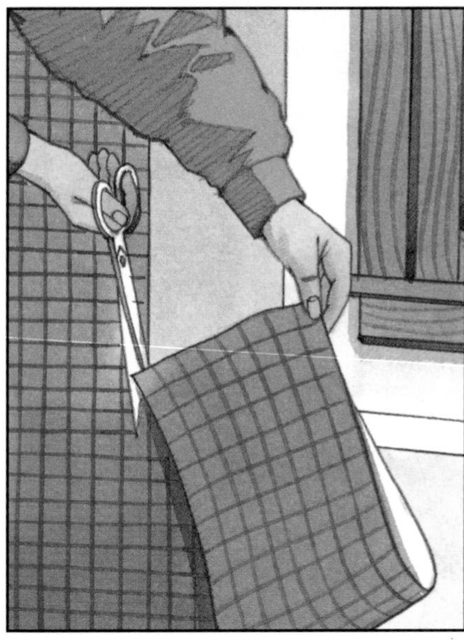

2 From the horizontal cut (Step 1), make vertical cuts to the top and bottom of the recess. Make small diagonal cuts to the corners of the recess.

3 Fold the upper and lower flaps of the wallpaper onto the recessed surfaces. Smooth the strips and trim at the back edge. Wrap the vertical edge around the corner. Hang wallpaper around window, if needed (pages 72–73).

4 Measure, cut, and prepare a matching piece of wallpaper to cover the side of the recess. Side pieces should slightly overlap the top and bottom of recess and the wrapped vertical edge. Use vinyl-to-vinyl adhesive to glue the overlapped seams.

With most windows and especially recessed ones, you can make your job easier by avoiding wallpaper with complicated patterns and long vertical repeats. Don't try to precut the paper to go around the window. It is easiest to trim when it is on the wall next to the obstacle to be cut around. If you have lots of recessed windows and a complex wallpaper pattern, consider calling a professional.

If you have difficulty papering around an obstacle, above all, don't panic! Stay calm, take a step back and rethink what you're doing. Remember that until the wallpaper has dried, it can almost always be adjusted. So relax and have fun!

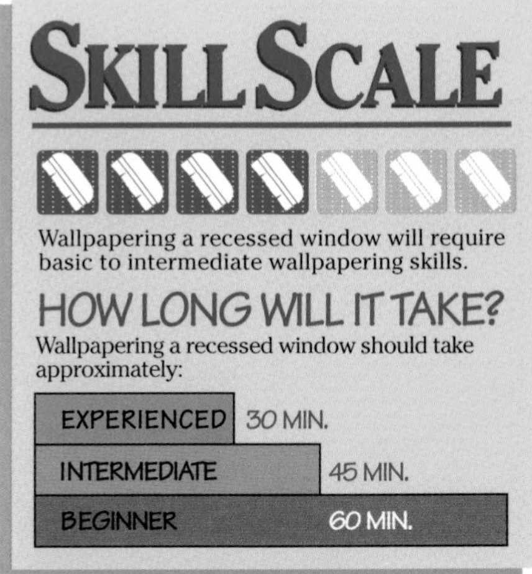

SKILL SCALE

Wallpapering a recessed window will require basic to intermediate wallpapering skills.

HOW LONG WILL IT TAKE?

Wallpapering a recessed window should take approximately:

EXPERIENCED	30 MIN.
INTERMEDIATE	45 MIN.
BEGINNER	60 MIN.

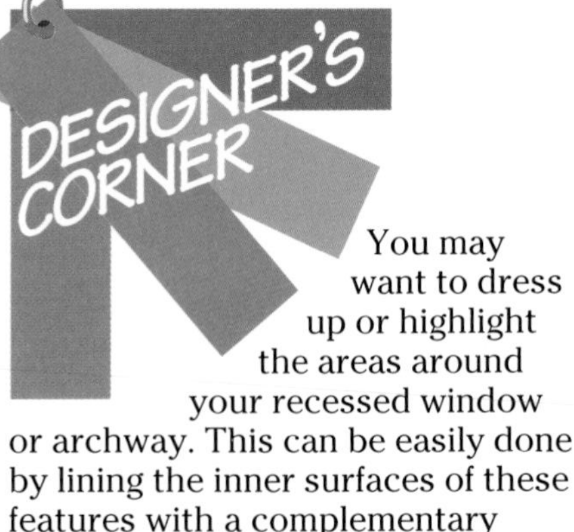

You may want to dress up or highlight the areas around your recessed window or archway. This can be easily done by lining the inner surfaces of these features with a complementary colored and patterned wallpaper. This contrasting design will help to accent the special area.

WALLPAPERING INSIDE AN ARCHWAY

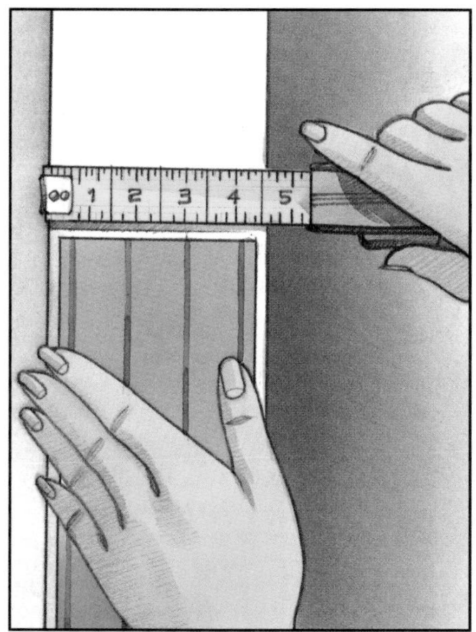

1 Some wallpapers are available with matching borders that can be used to cover the inside of an archway. Otherwise, measure the inside of the archway and cut an archway strip from your standard wallpaper. The strip should be 1/4" narrower than the inside surface of the archway.

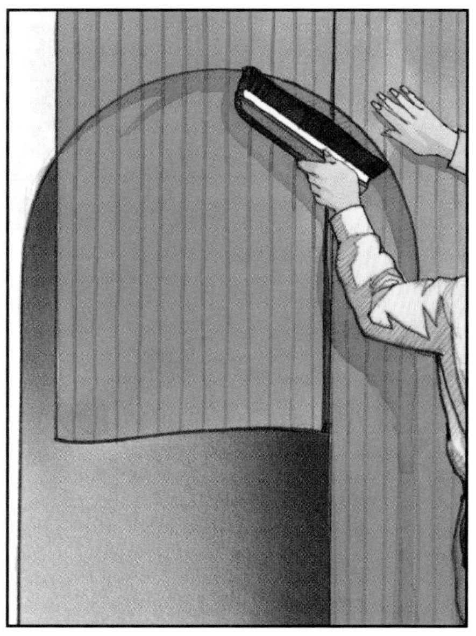

2 Hang the wallpaper on both sides of the archway with strips overlapping the archway opening. Smooth the strips and trim the excess at the ceiling and baseboard.

3 Use wallpaper scissors to trim the overlapping wallpaper in the archway, leaving about 1" excess.

4 Make small slits in the wallpaper along the curved portion of the archway, cutting as close as possible to wall edge.

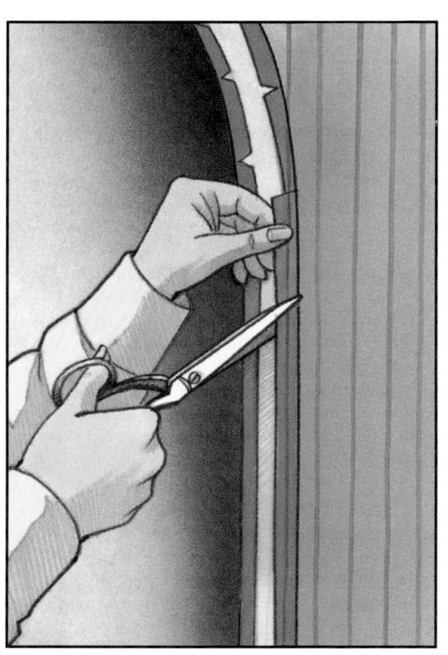

5 Wrap the cut edges inside the archway and press flat. If the adjacent room is to be wallpapered, wrap the wallpaper around the edge of the archway from both sides.

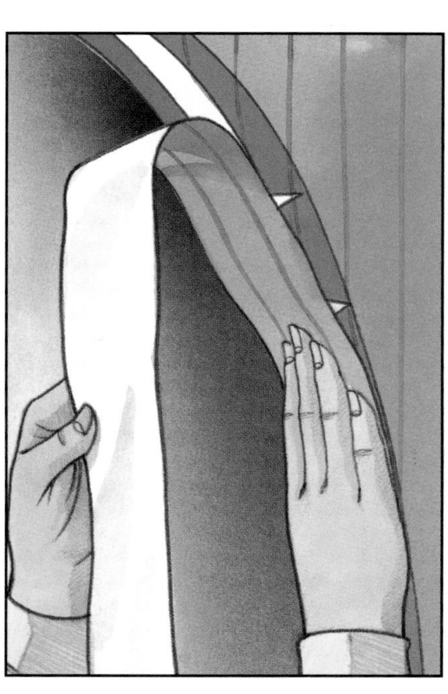

6 Coat the back of the archway strip with vinyl-to-vinyl adhesive. Position the strip along the inside of the archway with a 1/8" space on each edge of strip. Smooth the strip with a smoothing brush. Rinse the strip using a damp sponge.

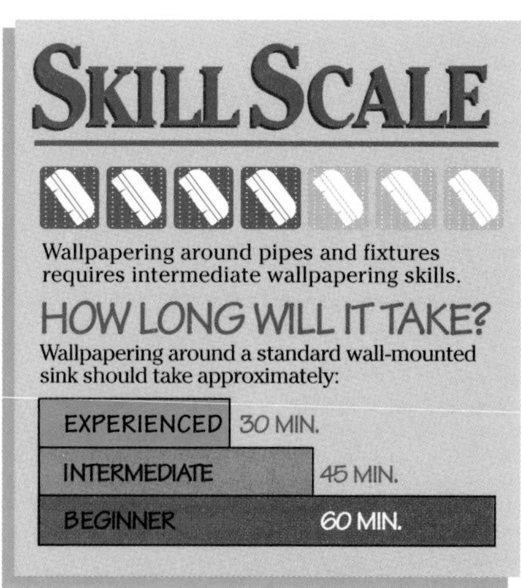

STUFF YOU'LL NEED:

- ☐ **Tools:** Smoothing brush, razor knife, yardstick.
- ☐ **Materials:** Wallpaper strips.

Wallpapering Around Pipes, Fixtures, & Obstacles

Hanging wallpaper around sinks, pipes, and other obstacles requires careful cutting into the body of the wallpaper strips. Hold the strip so the patterns match and cut from the edge closest to the fixture.

If possible, cut along a pattern line to hide the slit. At the end of the slit, cut an opening to fit around the fixture, cutting as close as possible to the fixture without damaging it.

On wall-mounted sinks, tuck the small ends of the wallpaper overlaps behind the sink rather than cutting flush with the edge of the sink. This will provide a more professional and finished look.

Wallpaper Durability

Be sure to use the type of wallpaper that is best suited for the specific area in which it will be used. Washability is a main consideration for certain areas.

Washable wallpaper can be cleaned with mild soap and water and a sponge. Scrubbable wallpaper is durable enough to be scrubbed more frequently with a soft brush.

Choose scrubbable wallpaper for heavy-use areas or where there is the possibility of heavy soiling such as in mud rooms or service entries. Washable wallpaper is good for bathrooms or laundry rooms where walls will probably be splashed with water or need light washing.

WALLPAPERING AROUND A PIPE

1 Pull out the escutcheon from the wall. Hold the wallpaper strip against the wall so that the pattern matches the previous strip. From the closest edge of the strip, cut a slit to reach the pipe.

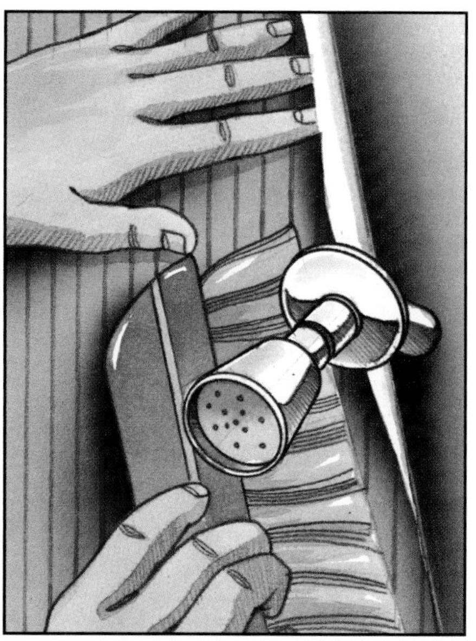

2 Press the strip flat up to the pipe with a smoothing brush.

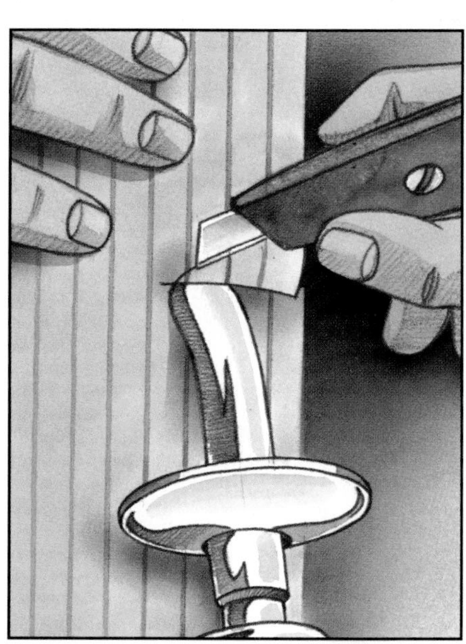

3 Cut a hole at the end of the slit to fit around the pipe. Butt the edges of slit and brush smooth.

WALLPAPERING AROUND A WALL-MOUNTED SINK

1 Brush the wallpaper strip up to the edge of the sink. Cut horizontal slits in the wallpaper, leaving $2^1/_4$" overlap at the top and the bottom of the sink.

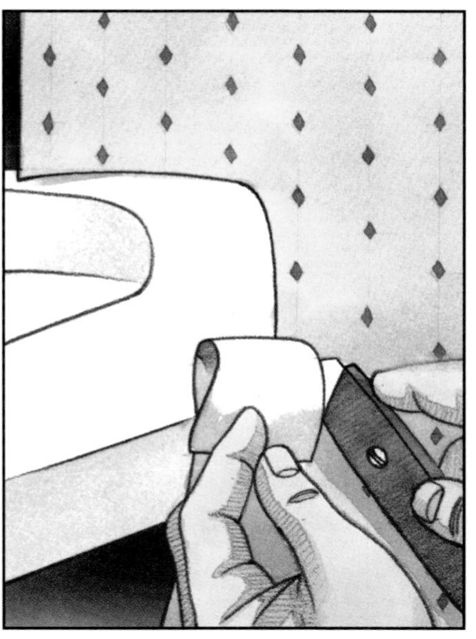

2 Trim the wallpaper around the side of the sink, leaving a slight overlap. Be careful not to scratch the sink fixture.

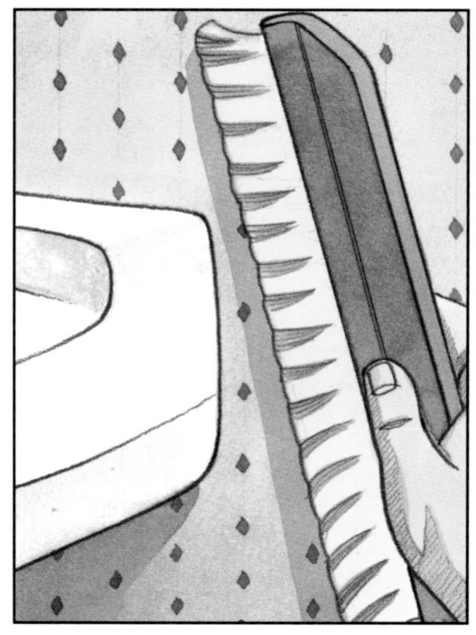

3 Smooth the wallpaper with a brush. Tuck the excess wallpaper into the crack between the sink and the wall, if possible; otherwise, trim the overlap.

BE CAREFUL WHEN WORKING AROUND HOT FIXTURES LIKE RADIATORS AND BASEBOARD HEATERS.

WALLPAPERING BEHIND A RADIATOR

1 Unfold the entire strip and position it on the wall. Smooth the strip from the ceiling to the top of the radiator. Use a flat wooden yardstick to lightly smooth the strip down behind the radiator. Crease the wallpaper along the baseboard with the yardstick.

2 Pull the bottom of the strip up from behind the radiator. Trim the excess wallpaper along crease line. Smooth paper back down behind radiator with yardstick.

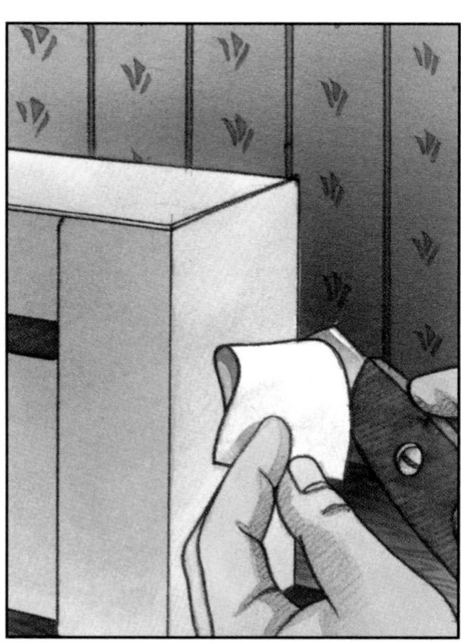

Electric baseboard heaters should be wallpapered with the same technique as other wall-mounted fixtures. Brush the strip up to the edge of the heater. Trim the wallpaper around the heater, leaving a slight overlap which you can tuck behind.

Wallpapering Ceilings

If there ever was a time to collect a favor, it will be when you wallpaper your ceiling. If you try it alone, you will not only end up looking like a mummy, you will either ruin the wallpaper or worse, injure yourself.

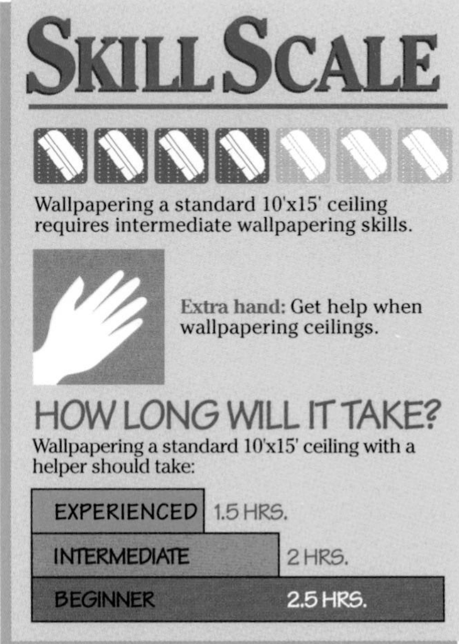

WALLPAPERING A CEILING

1 Measure the width of the wallpaper strip and subtract 1/2". Near the corner, measure this distance away from the wall at several points and mark them on the ceiling. Plan the ceiling so strips that require their pattern trimmed in order to fit the size of the ceiling end up on the wall of the entryway.

2 Using the marks, draw a guideline along the length of the ceiling with a pencil and a straightedge. Cut and prepare the first wallpaper strip (page 66).

3 Working in small sections, position the strip against the guideline. Overlap the side wall by 1/2" and the end wall by 2". Flatten the strip with a smoothing brush as you work. Trim each strip after it is smoothed.

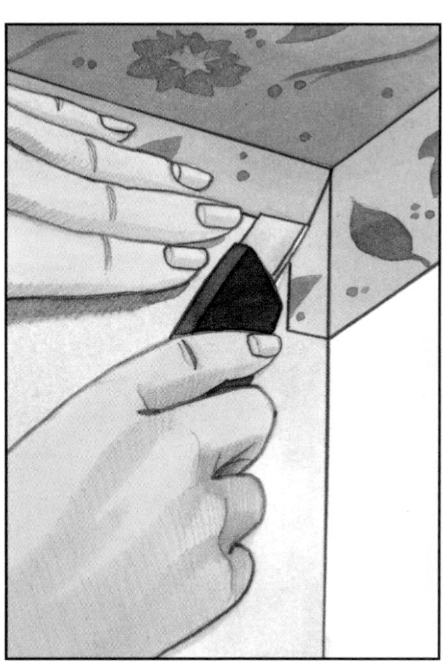

4 Cut out a small wedge of wallpaper in the corner so that the strip will lie smooth. Press the wallpaper into the corner with a broadknife.

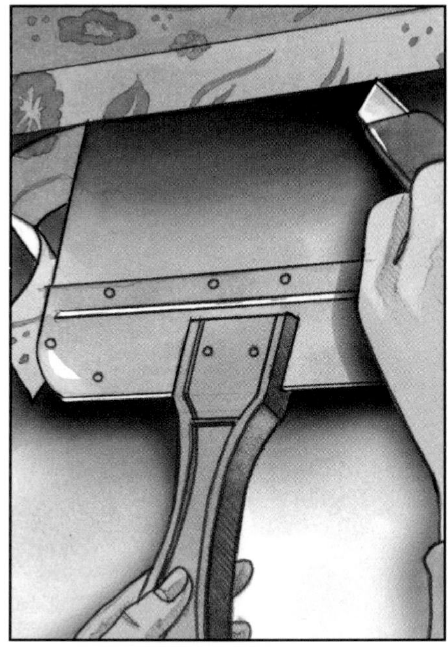

5 If the walls will be covered with matching wallpaper, trim the ceiling wallpaper so it overlaps the wall by 1/2". On walls that will not be covered, trim the excess by holding a broadknife against the corner and cutting with a sharp razor knife.

Special Handling for Specialty Wallpapers

Specialty wallpapers can add new interest to a room but most require special handling techniques. Reflective wallpapers, such as foils and Mylars, can lighten up even the darkest rooms, but the walls must be perfectly smooth before hanging. Fabric or grasscloth wallpaper can soften and hide flaws in irregular walls though they are difficult to keep clean.

HANDLE FOILS CAREFULLY! THEY'RE EASILY DAMAGED.

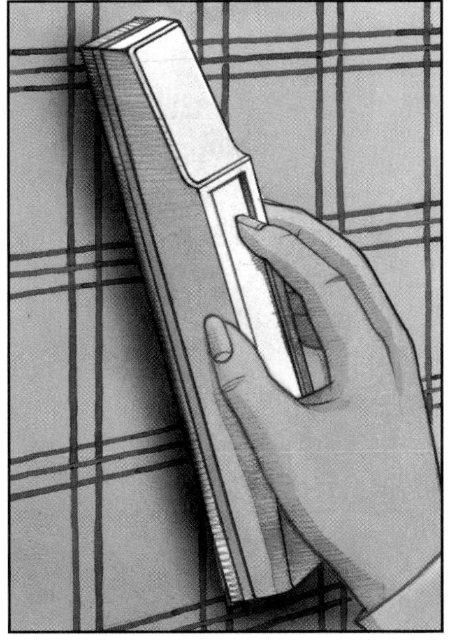

Use a soft smoothing brush on foils to avoid scratching or burnishing the reflective surface. Do not roll the seams: tap them gently with a smoothing brush to bond the seams. Be sure to flatten out all bubbles immediately when hanging.

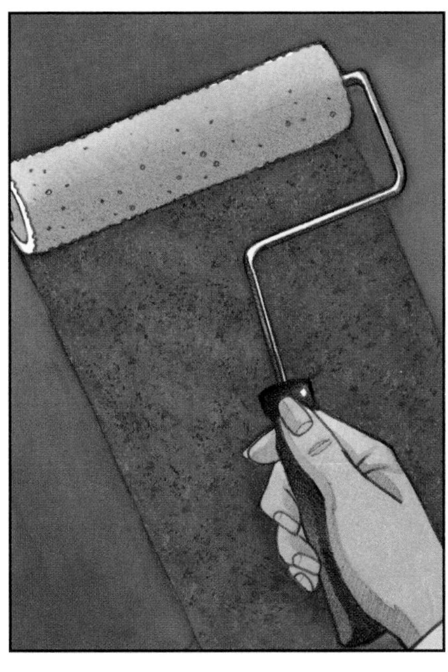

Use clear adhesive or traditional wheat paste as directed by the manufacturer. Clear adhesive will not bleed through and stain the fabric surfaces. Some wallpapers may direct you to apply adhesive to the walls instead of the strips.

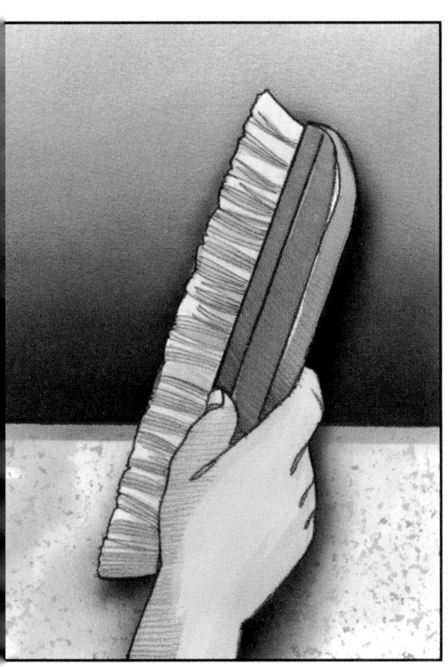

Apply liner paper underneath foils to create a smooth base for wallpaper over rough or uneven surface, such as paneled, textured, or masonry walls. Liner paper should be hung horizontally so its seams never line up with the wallpaper's seams.

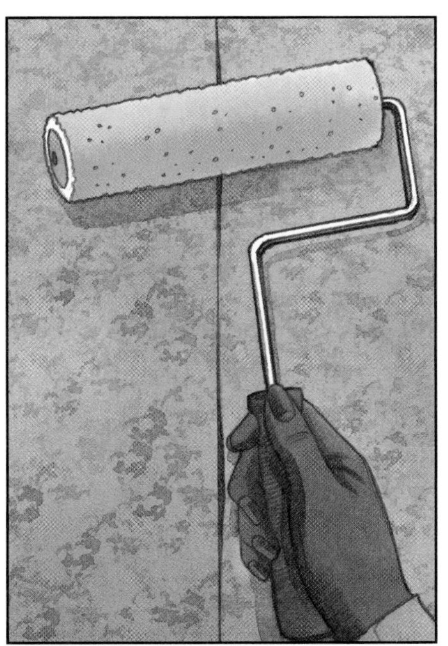

Use a dry paint roller with a soft nap or a soft brush with natural bristles to smooth flocks and fabrics and to keep from damaging the wallpaper. Keep adhesives off the face of flocks or fabrics. Remove wet adhesive, when necessary, with a slightly damp sponge.

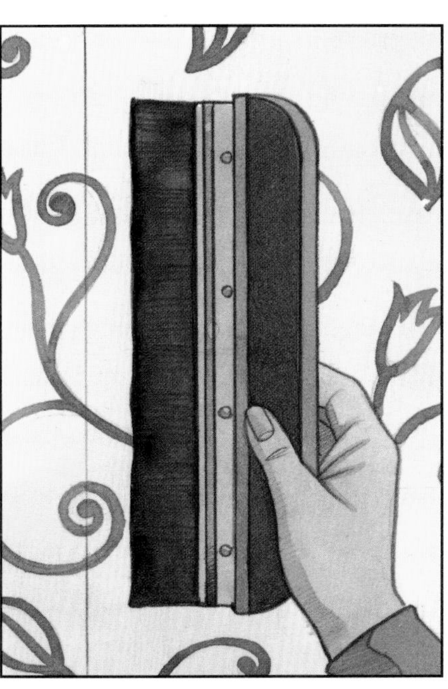

Tap seams with a smoothing brush or your fingers to bond the seams. Do not use a seam roller on flocks, fabrics, or other specialty wallpapers.

Finishing Touches

After you have finished wallpapering a room, check for final touch-ups while the job is still fresh. Pay special attention to the seams. If you rolled the seams too hard or rolled them before the adhesive set, you may have squeezed too much adhesive from under the edges of the covering. These edges will look tight while they are wet but will bubble after the wallpaper is dry.

Standing close to the wall, look down its length, against the light, to check for imperfections. You can also use a strong sidelight to see any bubbles or loose spots in the coverage in order to make the necessary corrections.

MATCHING SWITCH & OUTLET COVERS

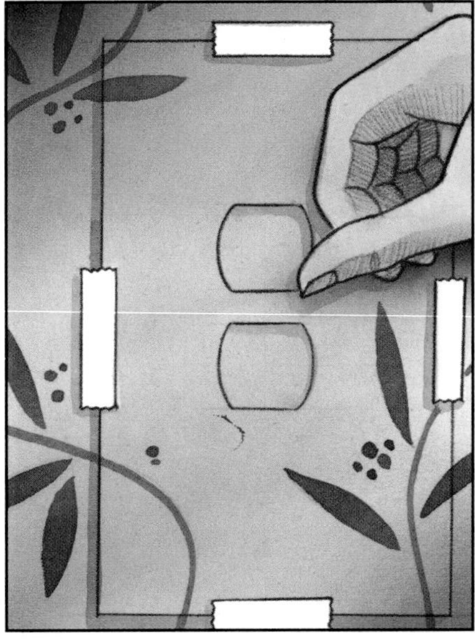

1 Remove cover plate and reinsert screws. Place wallpaper over fixture so the patterns match. Rub the surface of the wallpaper to emboss the outline of the fixture.

2 Lay the cover plate face down on the wallpaper, aligning it with the embossed marks. Mark the corners of the cover plate with a pencil. Trim the wallpaper $^1/_2$" wider than the cover plate on all sides. Trim the corners, cutting just outside the corner marks.

3 Apply vinyl-on-vinyl adhesive to the cover plate and wallpaper. Attach the cover plate to the wallpaper and smooth out bubbles. Wrap overlap around the cover plate and tape the edges in place. Cut out the cover plate openings with a razor knife and mount in place.

A shortcut for matching outlets and switches is to purchase new clear plastic coverplates. Cut the wallpaper to fit into the coverplates, and then cut openings for the switch levers and receptacle faces.

FIXING SEAMS

Dampen the wallpaper to make it easier to place back in position. Lift the wallpaper edge, and insert the tip of the glue applicator. Squirt vinyl-to-vinyl adhesive onto the wall and gently press the seam flat. Let it stand for half an hour, smooth lightly with a roller, and wipe the seam lightly with a damp sponge.

FIXING A BUBBLE

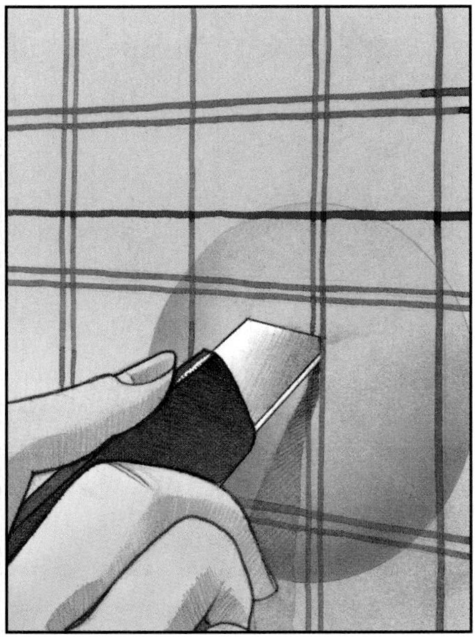

1 Cut a slit through the bubble using a sharp razor knife. If there is a pattern in the wallpaper, cut along a pattern line to hide the slit.

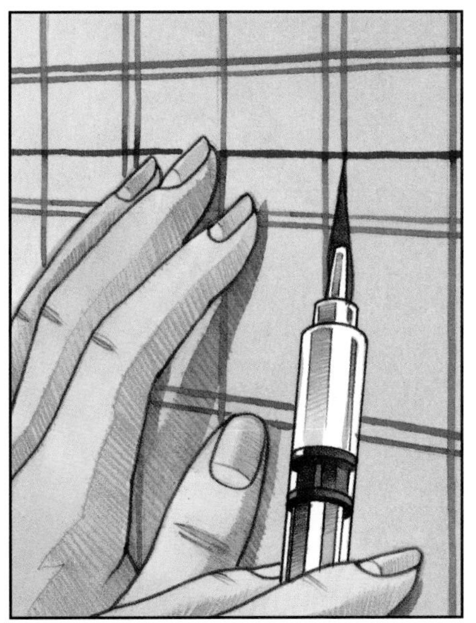

2 Insert the tip of the glue applicator through the slit and apply adhesive sparingly to the wall under the wallpaper.

3 Press the wallpaper gently to rebond it. Use a clean damp sponge to press the flap down and wipe away any excess glue.

PATCHING WALLPAPER

1 Fasten a scrap of matching wallpaper over the damaged portion with drafting tape, aligning the scrap so that the patterns match.

2 Holding a razor knife at a 90° angle to the wall, cut through both layers of wallpaper. If the wallpaper has strong pattern lines, cut along the lines to hide the seams. With less definite patterns, you can cut irregular lines.

3 Remove the scrap and patch. Peel away the damaged wallpaper. Apply adhesive to the back of the patch and position it in the hole so that the pattern matches. Rinse the patch area with a damp sponge.

Hanging Wallpaper Borders

Wallpaper borders add an elegant accent to either painted or wallpapered walls. Hang a border as a crown molding around a ceiling or as a frame around windows, doors, or fireplaces.

You can also use a border along the top of wainscoting or as an attractive chair rail on painted walls. Wallpaper borders can also be used to frame a favorite art piece.

Many wallpaper designs have complementary borders which are sold by the linear yard. Or you can create your own border by cutting narrow strips from full-size wallpaper pieces.

When attaching wallpaper borders it's best to use vinyl-to-vinyl adhesive.

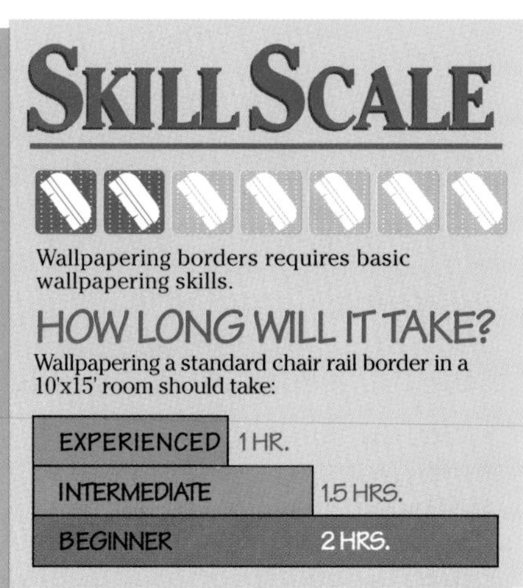

HANGING BORDERS

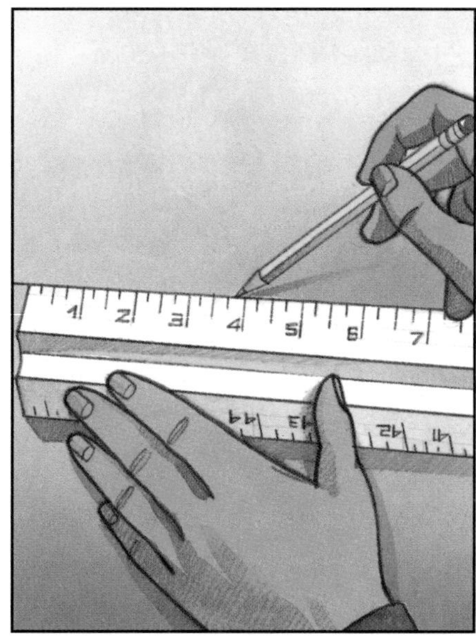

1 Plan the starting point so that the mismatch seam of the border will fall in an inconspicuous area. For chair rail borders, use a level and draw a light pencil line around room at the desired height.

2 Cut and prepare the first strip. Begin at a corner, and overlap the border onto the adjacent wall $^1/_4$". Have a helper hold the accordion-booked border while you apply and brush it.

3 For seams that fall in the middle of walls, overlap the border strips so that the patterns match. Double-cut the seam by cutting through both layers with a razor knife. Peel back the border and remove the cut ends. Press the border flat.

4 To cut in flush with wallpaper, overlap the border onto the wallpaper. Use a straightedge and razor knife to cut though the underlying wallpaper along the border edge.

5 Pull up the border and remove the cut wallpaper. Press the border flat with your hand and finish it with a smoothing brush.

MITERING BORDER CORNERS

1 Apply horizontal border strips so that they run past the corners with an overlap greater than the border width. Apply vertical border strips along the side casings, overlapping the top and bottom border strips.

2 Check the position of the border strip to make sure important pattern designs will remain intact at diagonal cuts. Remove and adjust the strips if necessary.

3 Holding a straightedge at a 45° angle from the casing corner, double-cut both wallpaper layers with a razor knife.

4 Peel back the ends of the border, and remove the cut pieces.

5 Press the border back in place, and let it stand for half an hour. Lightly roll the seams and rinse the border with damp sponge.

PLUMBING BASICS

Plumbing is nothing more than a matter of containing and controlling the water supply as it flows through your home. The idea of water moving through a pipe is certainly easy to grasp. And most plumbing fixtures are direct and basic.

On the other hand, plumbing components are aggravatingly unstandardized. Where electrical components by different manufacturers are so standardized as to be nearly identical, plumbing parts often vary widely. Whenever possible, take the old fittings with you when you buy new ones.

Some of the plumbing projects covered in this book are very quick repairs, requiring minimal tools and no experience. The more difficult projects will involve basic tools, specialized tools, and some acquired skill. Nothing in this book is beyond your capability. Just take your time.

Before plunging into a project, read through all the steps carefully. If you are uncertain about your ability in any area, practice that procedure on scrap material. Above all, use good judgment, care, and appropriate safety equipment when attempting any of these projects.

These instructions conform to national standards but codes may vary widely in different states, cities, and counties. Be sure you check with your local Building Department for information on building permits, codes, and other laws as they might apply to your plumbing project.

HOMER'S HINDSIGHT

Plumbing is a lot like life—one thing inevitably leads to another. Except in plumbing it's almost never good news!

Once a plumbing repair I started on Sunday afternoon hit a serious snag just about the time the stores closed. Talk about frustrating...

Allow for the unexpected. Start your plumbing projects when supplies are available and you have plenty of time to complete the job.

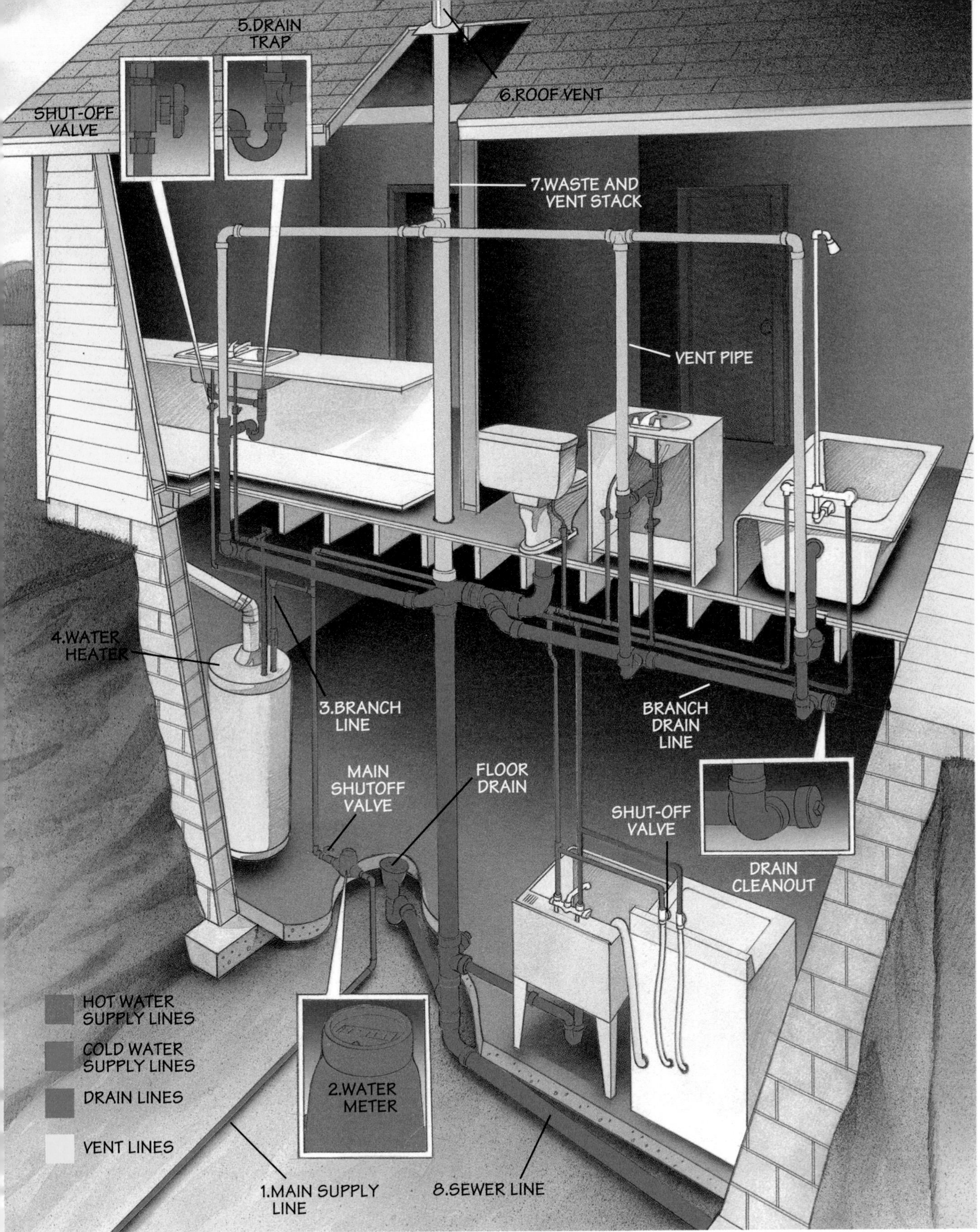

Understanding your home's plumbing: Water enters your house through a main supply line (1). It passes through a water meter (2) and a portion of the incoming water is then branched (3) off to enter a water heater (4). The heated water and the remaining cold water are then piped to fixtures throughout the house. Toilets need only cold water. Waste water travels by gravity, but first it must pass through a trap (5) located below each fixture. Traps allow water to flow through, but prevent sewer gas from drifting up the drain. Vents on the roof (6) let in air. This allows waste water to flow freely to the waste and vent stack (7) and out through the sewer line (8).

Tool Box

BASIC PLUMBING TOOLS:

Prepare yourself for most of the plumbing projects and repairs you are likely to encounter by assembling this basic tool kit.

A. Flanged Plunger: clears drain clogs.
B. Hacksaw: cuts metal supply pipes and plastic drain pipes.
C. Pipe Wrenches: pairs used to tighten and loosen pipes and large fittings.
D. Files–Round and Flat: smooth metal, wood or plastic.
E. Water Pump Pliers (also called Channel-Type): adjustable jaws for large and small objects.
F. Screwdrivers–Slotted and Phillips Type: include one or more of each.
G. Adjustable Wrench: movable jaw fits a variety of bolt heads and nuts.
H. Ratchet Wrench and Sockets: tightens and loosens bolts and nuts. Some projects may require special deep-set plumber's sockets.
I. Level: checks the slope of drain pipes and exhaust ducts.
J. Ball Peen Hammer: intended for striking metallic objects.
K. Cold Chisel: use with ball peen hammer to cut hardened metal, ceramic tile, mortar.
L. Small Wire Brush: cleans metals.
M. Putty Knife: scrapes putty and caulk from fixtures.
N. Utility Knife: trims plastic pipes; cuts through caulking.
O. Allen Wrenches–Assorted Sizes: tighten and loosen set screws.
P. Tape Measure: pick one at least 16 feet long with retractable steel blade.

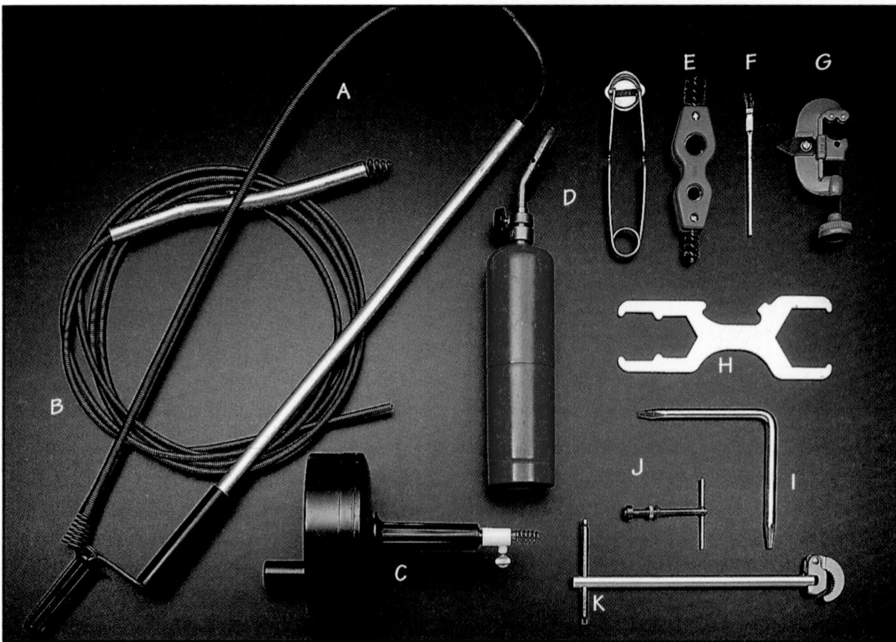

SPECIAL-PURPOSE TOOLS:

A. Closet Snake: clears toilet clogs.
B. Drain Snake: also called an auger.
C. Hand Snake: clears clogs in drain lines.
D. Propane Torch and Spark Lighter: solders copper pipe and fittings.
E. Wire Combination Brush: cleans inside and outside of ½" and ¾" copper pipe and pipe fittings.
F. Flux Brush: used for applying flux.
G. Tubing Cutter: makes straight, smooth cuts in copper or plastic pipe.
H. Spud Wrench: removes or tightens very large (2-4") nuts.
I. Seat Wrench: tightens or removes valve seats.
J. Seat-Dressing Tool: resurfaces rough or worn valve seats.
K. Basin Wrench: tightens or removes hard-to-reach faucet mounting and coupling nuts.

Materials

BASIC PLUMBING MATERIALS:

A. Penetrating Oil: eases "frozen" nuts and threaded pipes.

B. Heat-Resistant Grease: lubricates faucet and valve assemblies.

C. Pipe Joint Compound: used on threaded joints to ensure a perfect seal.

D. & E. Lead-free Flux & Lead-free Solder: used to join all water supply copper pipes.

F. Teflon Tape: replaces pipe joint compound; wrap clockwise around threaded ends.

G. Plumber's Putty: provides a watertight seal.

REPLACEMENT PARTS FOR TOILETS:

H. Assorted Washers: provide a watertight seal.

I. Ballcock Seal or Cone Washer: seals ballcock at seat.

J. Plunger Valve Ballcock Kit: reconditions plunger valve ballcock.

K. Diaphragm Ballcock Repair Kit: reconditions diaphragm ballcock.

L. Flapper: fits against flush valve to seal the tank.

REPLACEMENT PARTS FOR FAUCETS:

M. Spout Aerator Kit: reconditions spout aerators.

N. Faucet Cartridges: exact replacements for original cartridges.

O. Ball-type Faucet Repair Kits: recondition ball-type faucets.

P. Assorted Washers: replacement seat washers for compression-type faucets.

Q. Valve Seats: restore smooth seat in compression-type faucets.

PIPES AND FITTINGS:

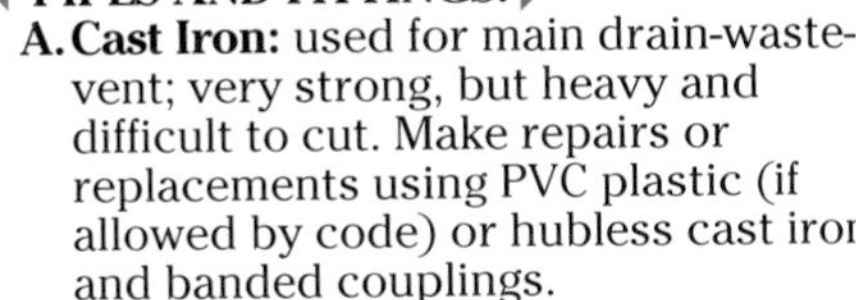

A. Cast Iron: used for main drain-waste-vent; very strong, but heavy and difficult to cut. Make repairs or replacements using PVC plastic (if allowed by code) or hubless cast iron and banded couplings.

B. Copper: best for water supply; smooth and corrosion resistant; join with lead-free solder.

C. Chromed Copper Tubing and Shut-off Valves: exposed water supply applications; join with compression fittings.

D. Traps: chromed brass or plastic; choose a style and diameter to fit application; join with compression fittings.

E. ABS: rigid plastic for drain-waste-vent; strong, but light and easy to cut. Join with solvent glue. Restricted in some areas.

F. Banded Couplings: adjustable stainless steel and neoprene bands join hubless cast iron or iron to plastic.

G. PVC: rigid plastic for drain-waste-vent; highly resistant to damage from heat or chemicals; superior to ABS; join with solvent glue.

H. Solvent Glue and Primer: joins rigid plastic pipe; use a solvent glue specific to the type of plastic you are joining.

I. PB (Polybutylene) Flexible Plastic: bendable hot and cold water supply; restricted by code in some areas; join with plastic grip fittings.

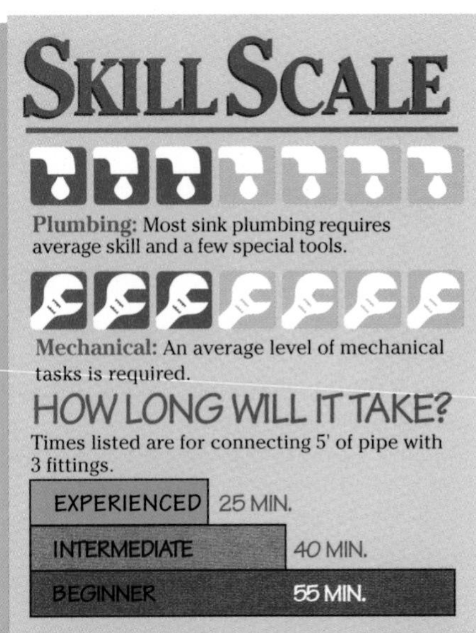

Working with Rigid Plastic Pipe

Rigid plastic pipe is used for DWV (drain-waste-vent) systems. It is available, with fittings, in $1^1/_4$, $1^1/_2$, 2, 3, and 4" inside diameters. One and one-fourth inch and $1^1/_2$" pipe is used for drain traps for sinks and lavatories; $1^1/_2$ and 2" for tubs and showers; 4" for toilet drains; and 2, 3, and 4" for drain lines and vents. No matter how you cut the pipe (see below), your cuts must be straight–this will make it easier to attach the fittings and will ensure watertight joints.

STUFF YOU'LL NEED:

- ☐ **Tools:** Tubing cutter or hacksaw; tape measure; utility knife.
- ☐ **Materials:** Plastic pipe, fittings, emery cloth, plastic pipe primer, solvent glue, a clean rag, petroleum jelly.

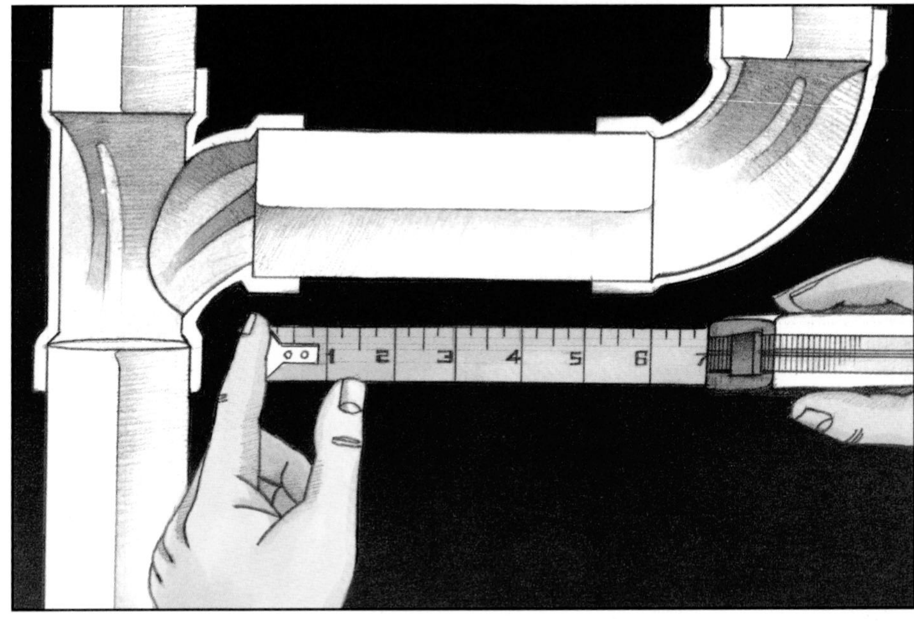

Find length of plastic pipe needed by measuring between the bottoms of the fitting sockets (fittings shown in cutaway). Mark the length on the pipe with a felt-tipped pen.

HOW TO CUT RIGID PLASTIC PIPE

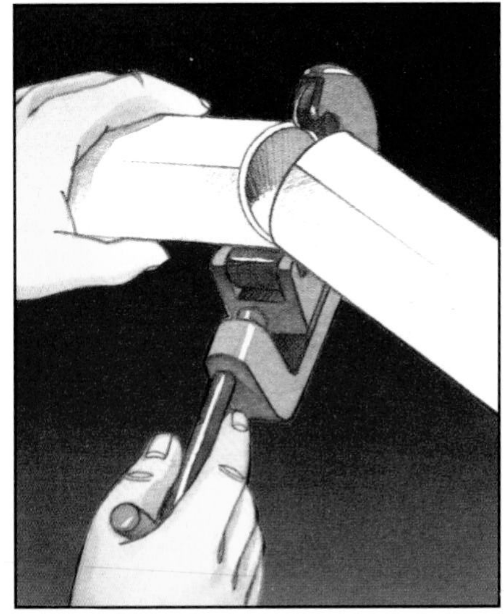

Tubing cutter: Tighten the cutter around the pipe so that the cutting wheel is on the marked line (see page 92). Rotate the cutter around the pipe, tightening the screw every two rotations, until the pipe snaps.

Hacksaw: Clamp the pipe in a portable gripping bench or a vise. Be sure to keep the hacksaw blade straight while you saw.

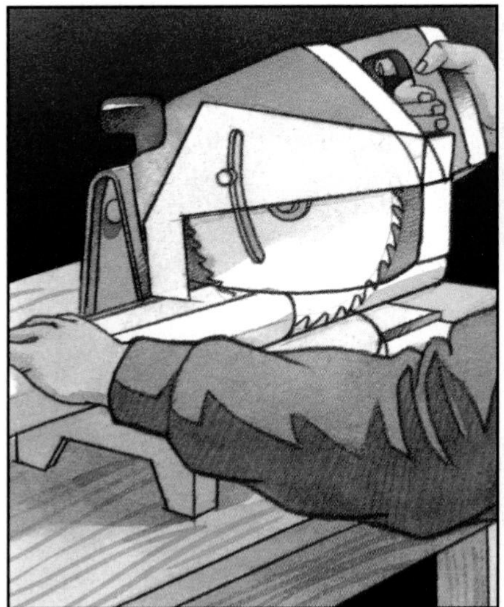

Miter box: Use a power or hand miter box to make straight cuts on all types of plastic pipe. Blades with a high number of teeth per inch (TPI) make cleaner cuts in rigid plastic pipes.

JOINING RIGID PLASTIC PIPE

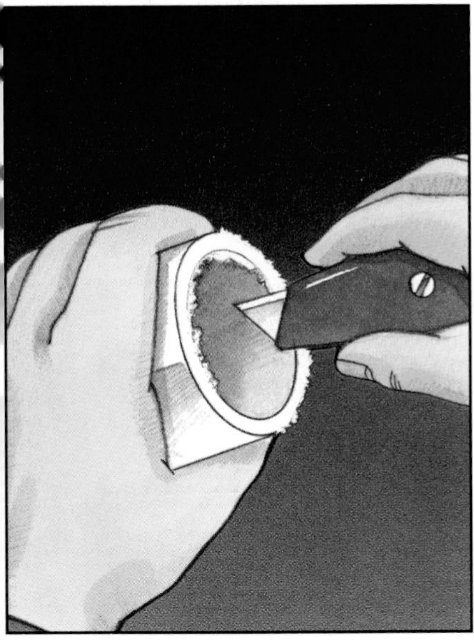

1 Using a utility knife, carefully smooth off the rough burrs on the cut ends of the pipe.

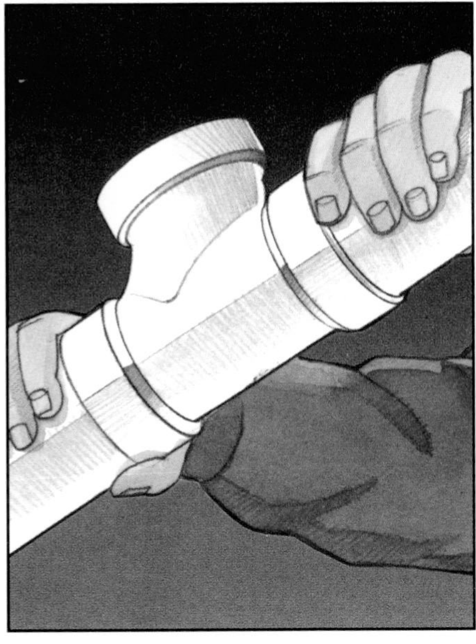

2 Test-fit all pipes and fittings. Your pipes should fit tightly against the bottom of the fitting sockets.

STRAIGHT CUTS ARE CRUCIAL FOR THE JOINT TO FIT PROPERLY

Cut, mark, and fit the entire run of rigid pipe you are making before you do any solvent gluing. It is a lot easier to adjust and trim for fit without having to cut apart glued-up sections. And while you're at the store, pick up a few extra fittings. It beats having to run out for more in the middle of a job, and you can usually return any leftovers.

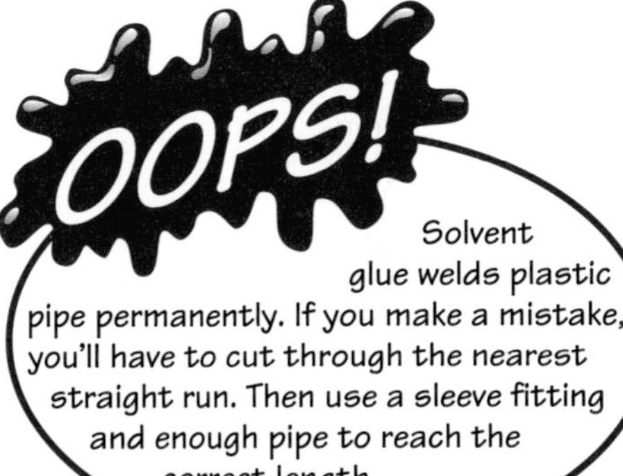

Solvent glue welds plastic pipe permanently. If you make a mistake, you'll have to cut through the nearest straight run. Then use a sleeve fitting and enough pipe to reach the correct length.

Plumbing

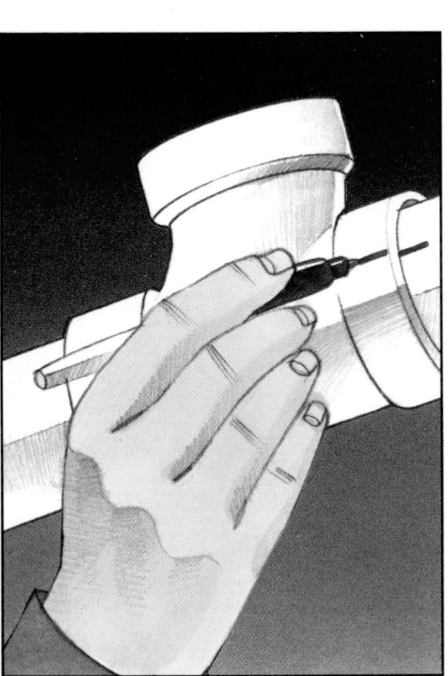

3 Make alignment marks across each joint with a felt-tipped pen.

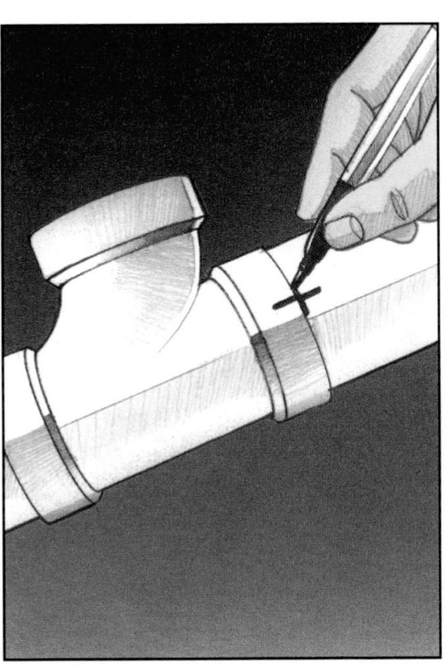

4 Mark the depth of the fitting sockets on the pipes. Take the pipes apart.

5 Emery cloth should be used only to scrape large burrs from the lip of the pipe. Leave the surface as smooth as possible for the plastic pipe primer.

JOINING RIGID PLASTIC PIPE (continued)

SAFETY ALERT

Solvent cleaner and glue emit harsh volatile fumes. Work only in well-ventilated areas.

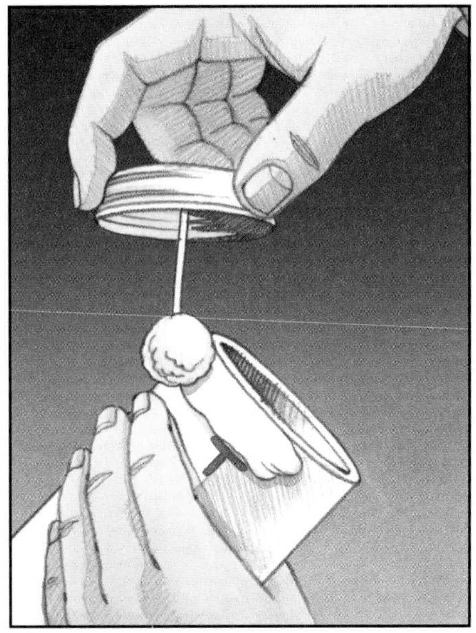

6 Apply plastic pipe primer to the ends of the pipes. This dulls the glossy surfaces and ensures a good seal.

7 Apply plastic pipe primer to the insides of the fitting sockets.

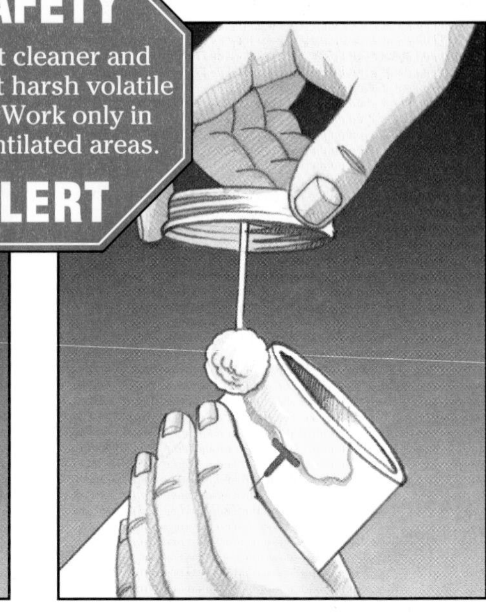

8 Apply a thick coat of the solvent glue to the end of the pipe and a thin coat to the inside surface of the fitting socket. Work quickly: this stuff hardens in about 30 seconds.

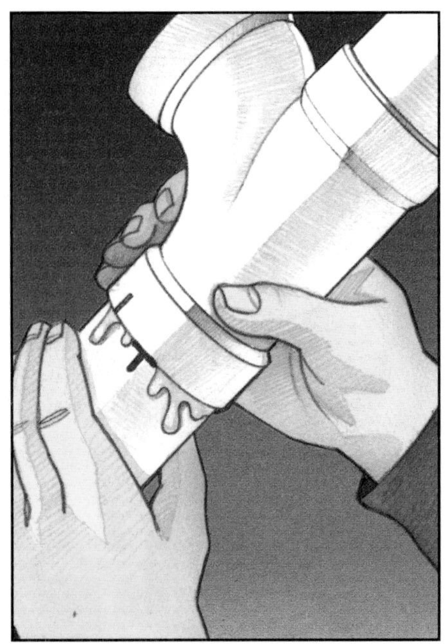

9 Still in your quick-but-steady mode, position the pipe and fitting so that the alignment marks are offset by about 2 inches. Then force the pipe into the fitting until the end fits flush against the bottom of the socket.

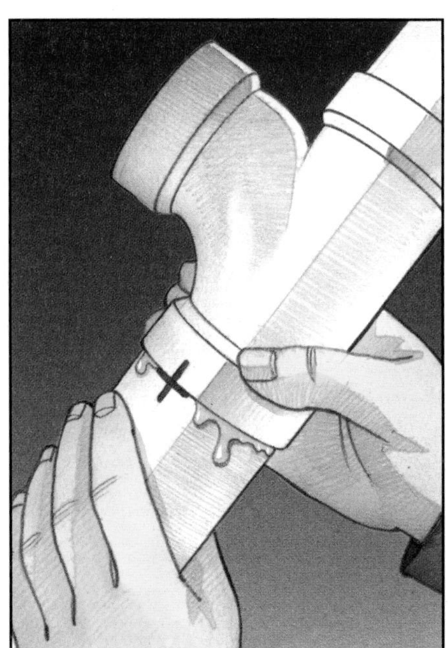

10 Spread the glue by twisting the pipe until the marks are aligned. Hold the pipe in place for 20 seconds to prevent slippage.

11 Wipe away excess glue with a rag. Don't disturb the joint for 30 seconds after gluing.

Working with Flexible Plastic Pipe

Flexible plastic pipe, sometimes called "PB pipe," is used for water supply lines. It comes in 3/8, 1/2, and 3/4" diameters. This pipe is easier to work with than copper pipe: it fits together with compression fittings so the only tools you need are a plastic tubing cutter and water pump pliers. Its flexibility allows you to maneuver around many obstacles without having to constantly cut pipe and insert fittings. Not all local Building Codes accept its use yet, so before you plan on using it, check with your building inspector. You can also use small-diameter rigid plastic pipe (CPVC) for water supply that is generally accepted by Codes. This pipe works just like large-diameter rigid plastic pipe (see pages 88-90). Both of these types of plastic pipe have fittings that connect to copper pipe, allowing you to add new supply lines even if you don't want to solder copper pipe.

JOINING FLEXIBLE PLASTIC PIPE

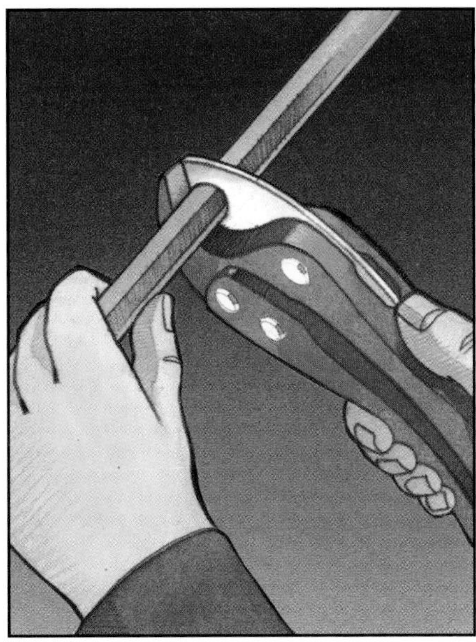

1 Cut flexible PB pipe with a plastic tubing cutter, or miter box and sharp knife. Remove any rough burrs with a utility knife.

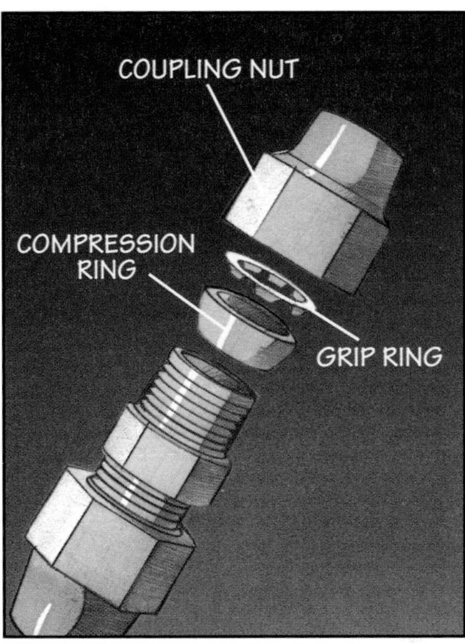

2 Take apart each grip fitting and make sure that the grip ring and the compression ring, or "O-ring," are positioned properly. Loosely re-assemble the fitting.

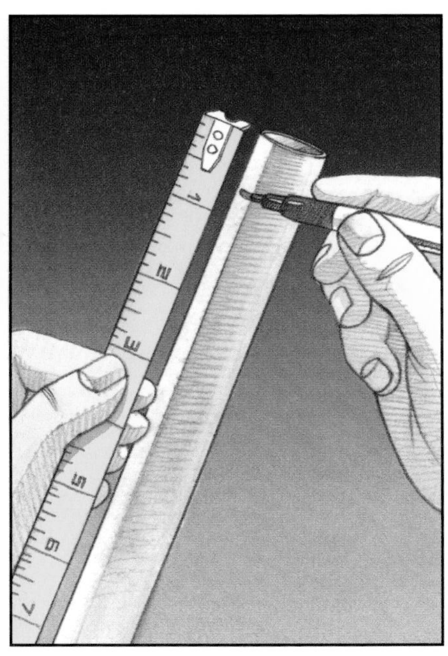

3 With a felt-tipped pen, mark the pipe showing the depth of the fitting socket. Round off the pipe's edges with an emery cloth.

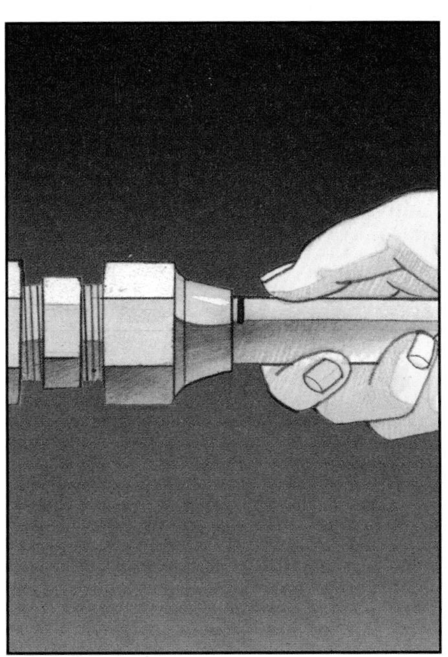

4 Lubricate the end of the pipe with petroleum jelly so it'll be easier to insert the pipe into the grip fittings. Force the end of the pipe into the fitting up to the mark on the pipe.

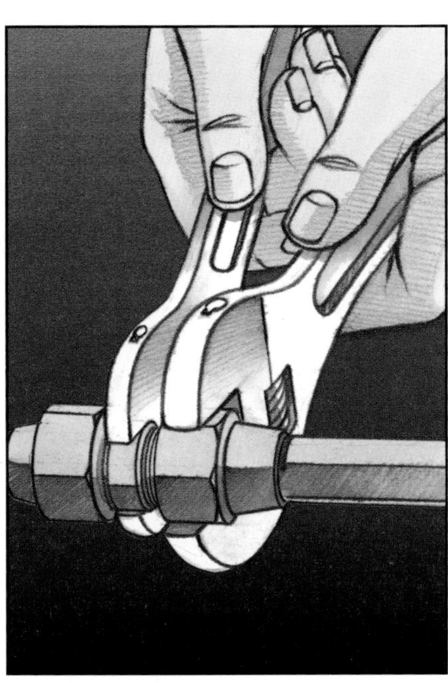

5 Hand-tighten the coupling nut; then use adjustable wrenches to tighten another 1/4 turn.

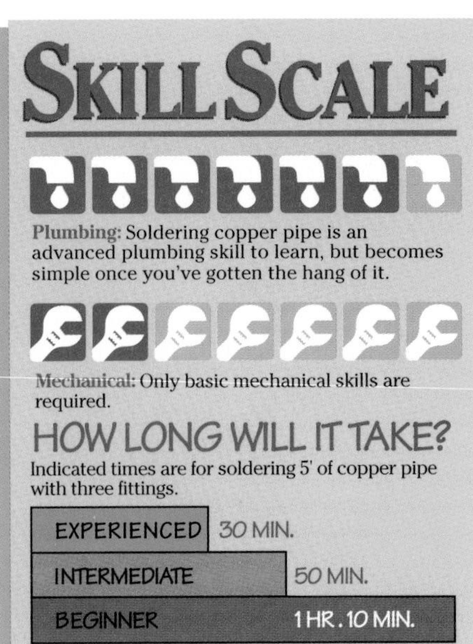

Plumbing

Working with Copper Pipe

With a little extra effort, you, too, can learn to plumb with copper pipe. The completed job will be more professional-looking and, perhaps for that reason alone, more satisfying.

STUFF YOU'LL NEED:

- ☐**Tools:** Basic plumbing tool kit (page 86), propane torch and spark lighter, round wire brush, flux brush, tubing cutter.
- ☐**Materials:** Copper pipe, copper fittings, emery cloth, lead-free flux (soldering paste), lead-free solder, rag.

SPLURGE ON A GOOD-QUALITY PIPE CUTTER. IT WORKS BETTER AND WILL LAST A LIFETIME.

Before you begin soldering, cut, flux, and assemble the entire pipe run to make sure it all fits and looks nice. Then start soldering at the highest point and work your way down to the lowest point.

TOOLTIPS

USING A TUBING CUTTER

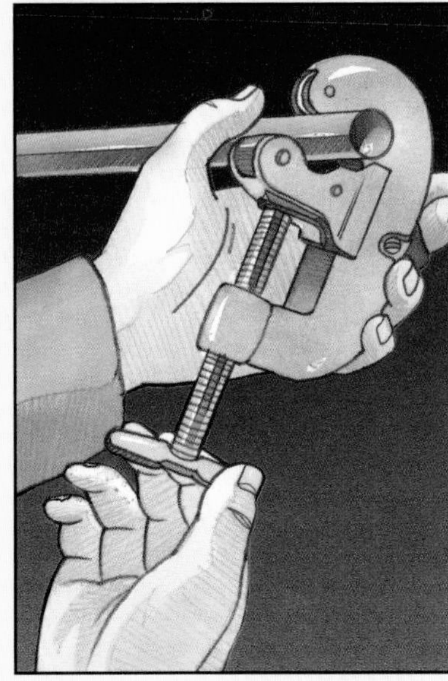

1 Place the tubing cutter over the pipe and tighten the handle until the pipe rests on both rollers and the cutting wheel is on the marked line.

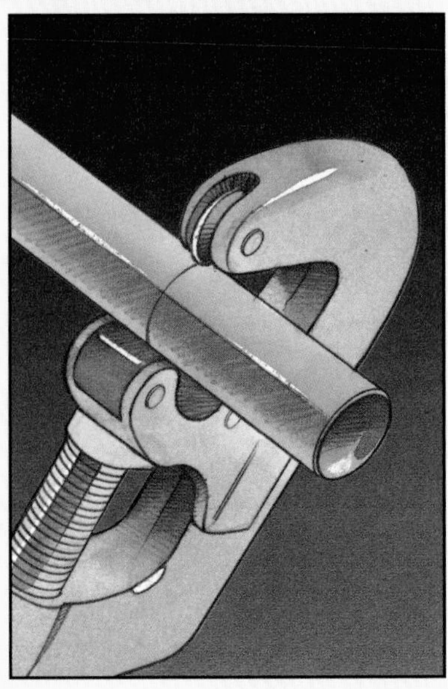

2 Turn the cutter one rotation so that the cutting wheel scores a continuous straight line around the pipe.

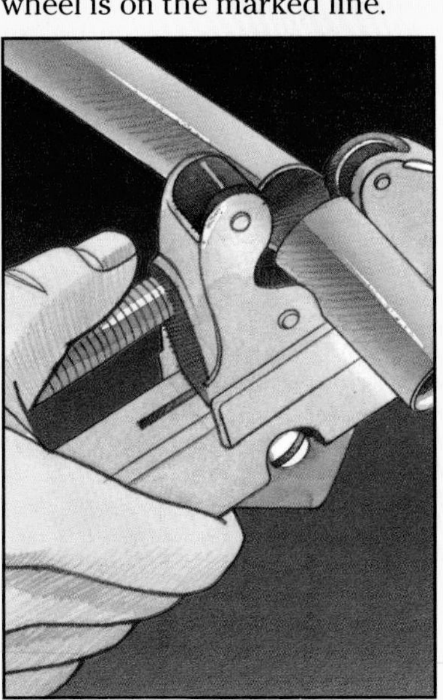

3 Rotate the cutter in the opposite direction, tightening the handle slightly after every two rotations, until the cut is complete.

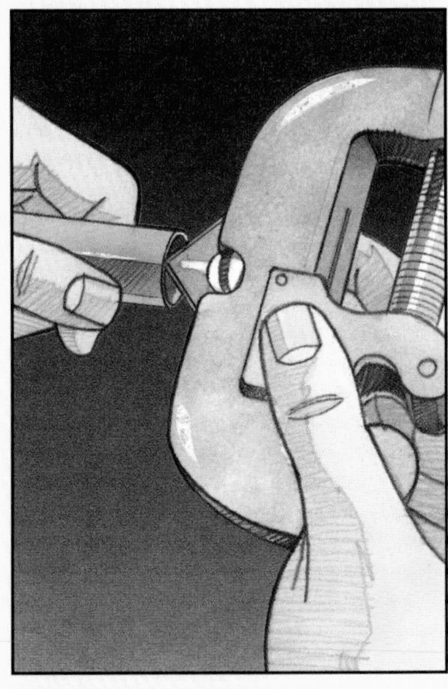

4 Use the tubing cutter's reaming point or a round file to smooth any sharp metal burrs from the inside edge of the cut pipe.

HOMER'S
HINDSIGHT

You can rush through a soldering job in record time as long as you aren't planning to put water through the pipe! The first time I tried sweating copper, I didn't get it clean enough and it leaked. I had to drain the whole line and then start over.

If your time is valuable, this is a good place to spend some. Take your time. Make sure all of the water is drained from the pipe. Sand all the parts clean and bright and flux them immediately. Then, when you solder, you'll get a good seal on your first try, and the water will stay where you put it.

SOLDERING COPPER PIPE

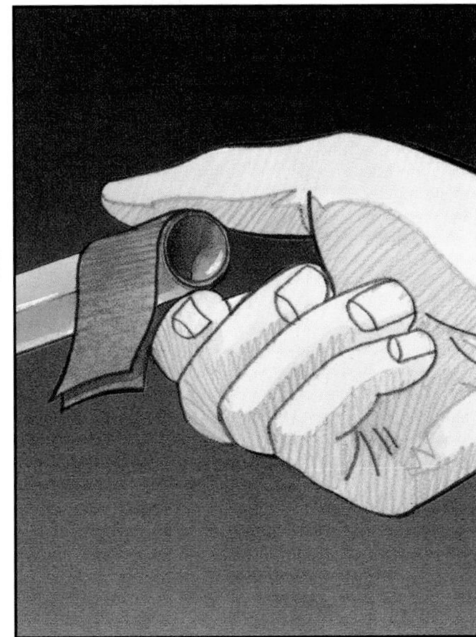

1 Sand the end of each pipe with emery cloth or steel wool. The ends must be really clean and grease-free to ensure a good seal.

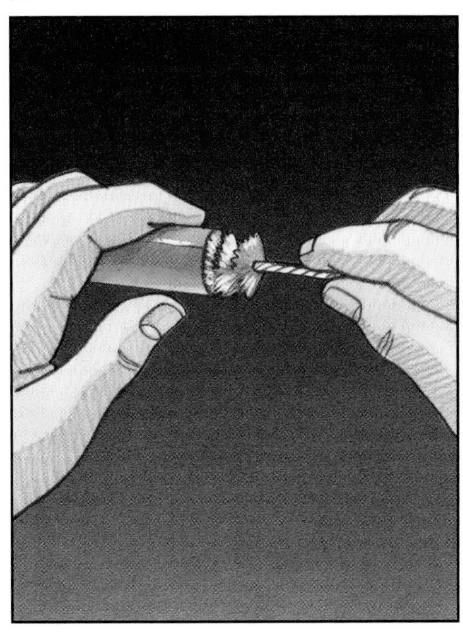

2 Scour the inside of each fitting with a wire brush or emery cloth.

ALWAYS USE LEAD-FREE SOLDER FOR PLUMBING PROJECTS.

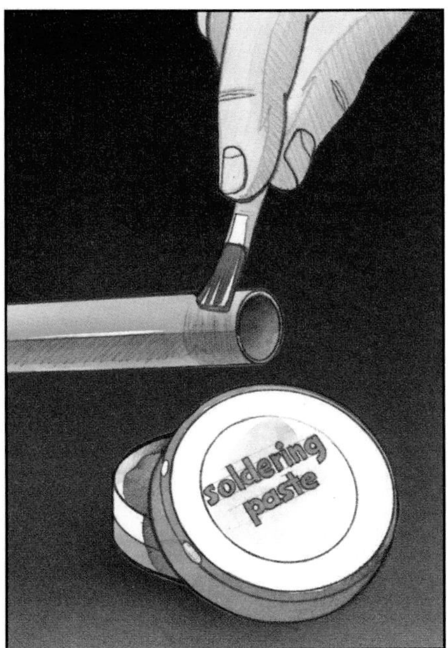

3 Apply a thin layer of lead-free soldering paste (flux) to the end of each pipe, using a flux brush. The paste should cover about 1 inch of pipe.

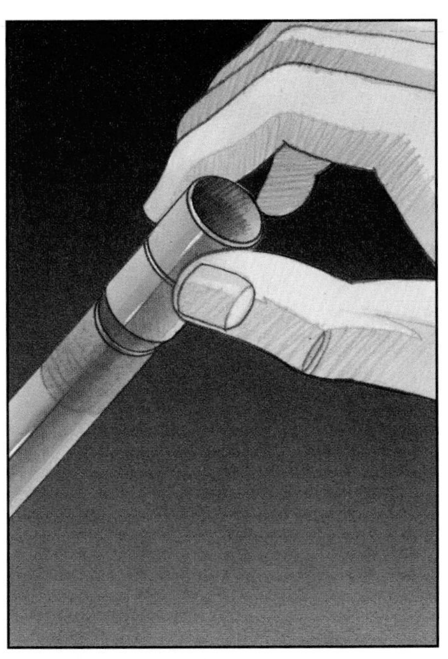

4 Insert the pipe into the fitting so that it's tight against the bottom of the fitting sockets. Slightly twist each fitting to spread the soldering paste.

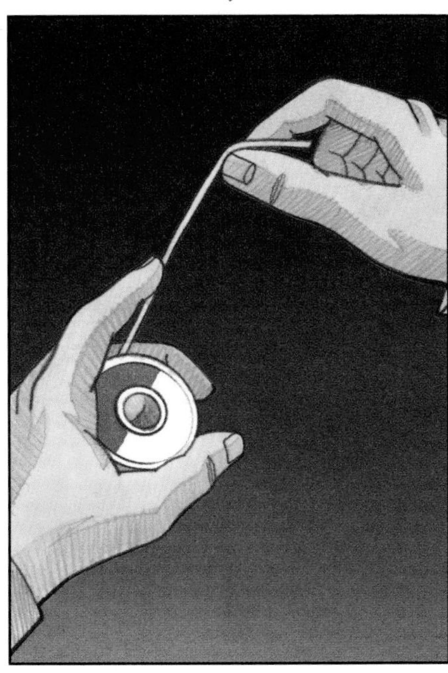

5 Prepare the wire solder by unwinding 8 to 10 inches of wire from the spool. Bend the first 2 inches of wire to a 90° angle.

SOLDERING COPPER PIPE (continued)

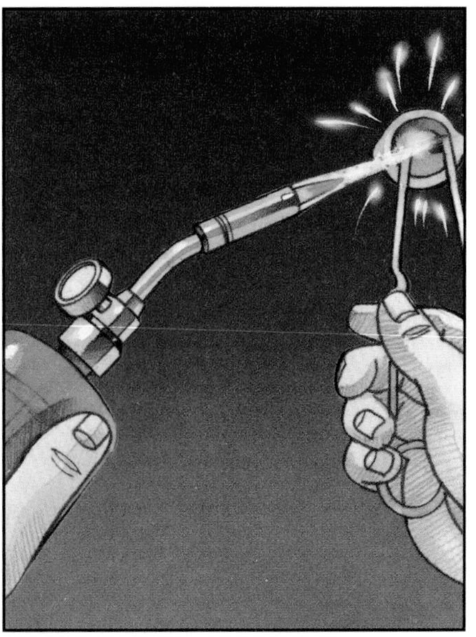

6 Light the propane torch by opening the valve and striking a spark lighter or a match next to the nozzle until the gas ignites.

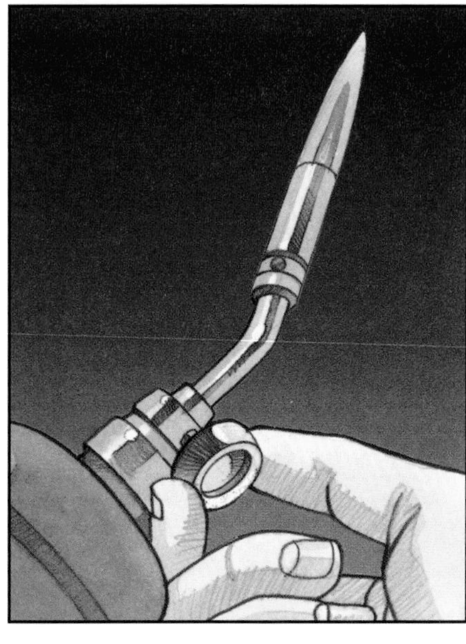

7 Adjust the torch valve until the blue portion of the flame is 1 to 2 inches long.

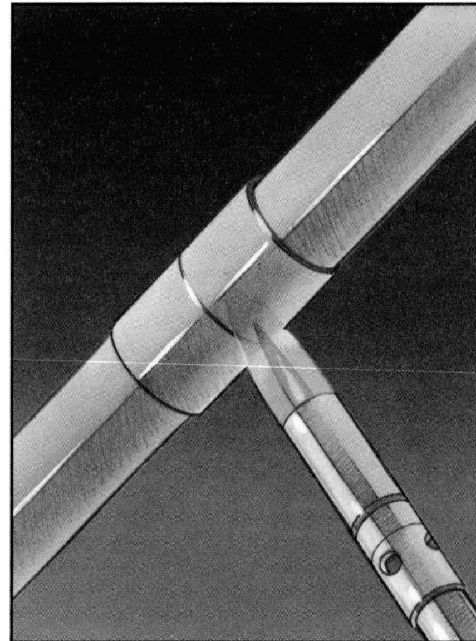

8 Hold the flame tip against the middle of the fitting for 4 to 5 seconds, until the soldering paste begins to sizzle.

USE A SHEET METAL SHIELD IF YOU ARE SOLDERING NEAR FLAMMABLE MATERIALS LIKE WOOD STUDS.

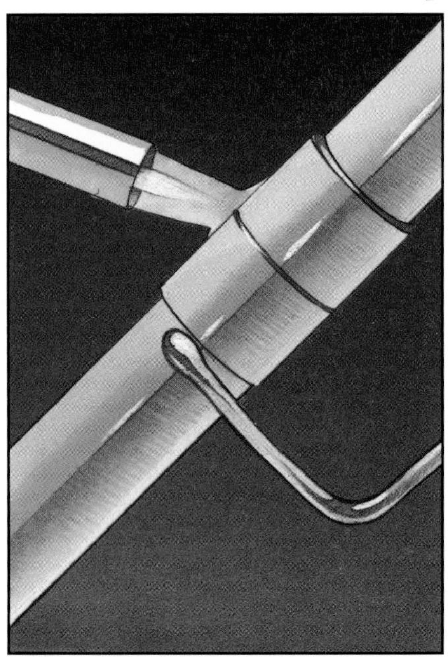

9 Heat the other side of the copper fitting to ensure that the heat is distributed evenly. Touch the solder to the pipe. If the solder melts, the pipe is ready to be soldered.

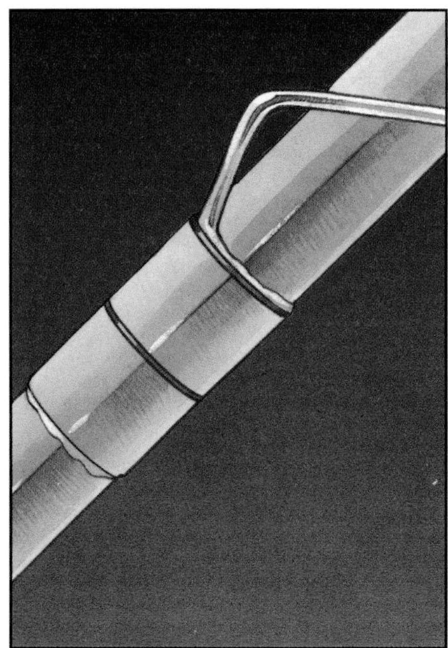

10 When the pipe is hot enough to melt the solder, remove the torch and quickly insert $^1/_2$ inch to $^3/_4$ inch of solder into each joint. Capillary action fills the joint with liquid solder. A correctly soldered joint should show a thin bead of solder around the lip of the fitting.

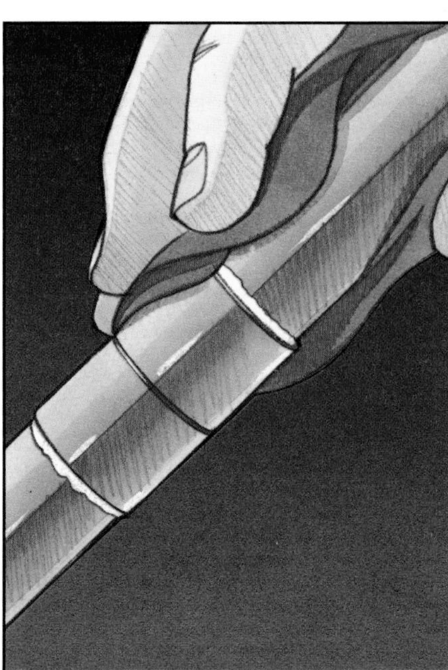

11 Wipe away the excess solder with a dry rag. **Be careful, though, because the pipes will be hot.** When all the joints have cooled, turn on the water and check for leaks. If the joint leaks, take apart the assembly (page 95, steps 1-4), and resolder it.

WORK SMARTER

Soldering Brass Valves

1 Remove the valve stem with an adjustable wrench. This prevents heat damage to the rubber or plastic stem parts while you're soldering. If you're soldering a ball valve and the stem can't be removed, open the valve all the way to reduce the possibility of heat damage. Drain water, prepare the copper pipes, and assemble the joints.

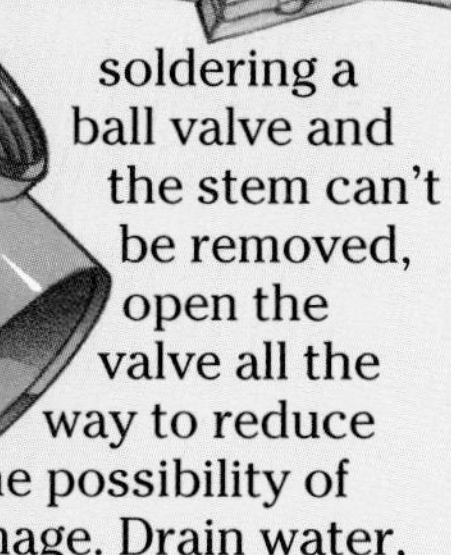

2 Light the propane torch. Heat the body of the valve, moving the flame so that you'll distribute heat evenly. Remember that brass is denser than copper, so it requires more heating time before the joints will draw solder. Apply the solder (see page 94). After the metal cools, reassemble the valve.

SAFETY ALERT
Always shut off your propane torch immediately after soldering. Be careful of pipes and fittings: they're hot!

TAKING APART SOLDERED JOINTS

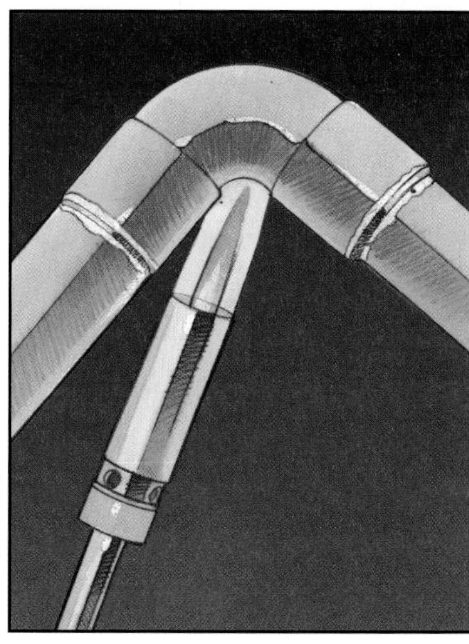

1 Turn off the water, and drain the pipes by turning on the highest and lowest faucets in the house. Light the propane torch. Hold the flame tip to the fitting until the solder becomes shiny and starts to melt.

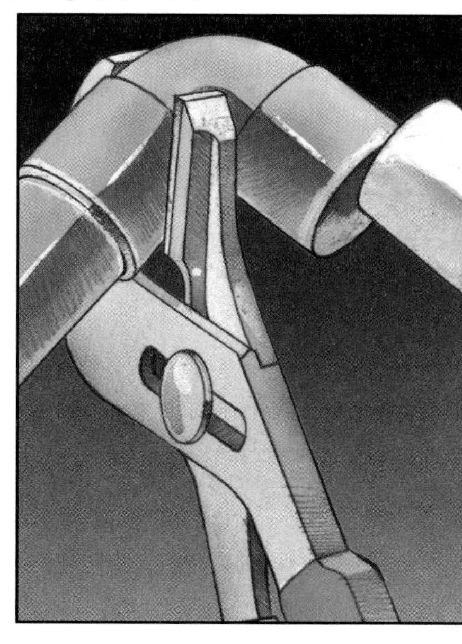

2 Use water-pump pliers to separate the pipes from the fitting. Be careful not to squeeze too tightly, though, because you may damage the fitting or the pipes.

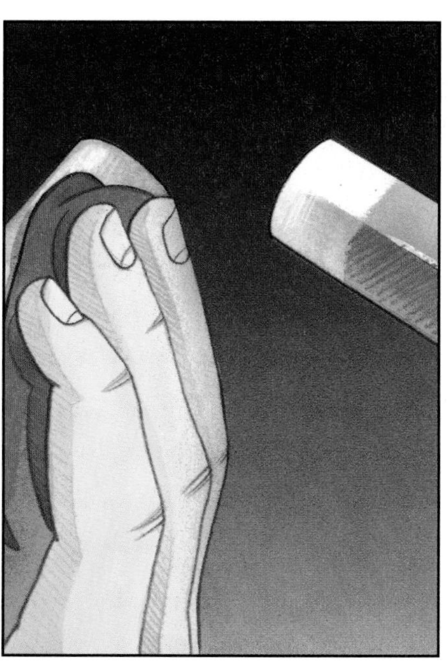

3 Remove the old solder by heating the ends of the pipe with a propane torch. Use a dry rag to wipe away melted solder. Do it quickly but be very careful: the pipes will be hot.

4 Use an emery cloth to polish the ends of the pipe down to bare metal. Another word of advice: never reuse old fittings.

Putting in Shutoff Valves & Supply Tubes

Worn-out shutoff valves or supply tubes can cause water leaks under a sink or plumbing fixture. First try tightening the fittings with an adjustable wrench, but if this doesn't work, replace the shutoff valves and supply tubes. You can get shutoff valves in several types: For copper pipes, valves with compression-type fittings are easiest to install. For plastic pipes, use grip-type valves. Most older plumbing systems don't have shutoff valves. So if your house doesn't have them, you may want to install them when you're repairing or replacing old plumbing fixtures.

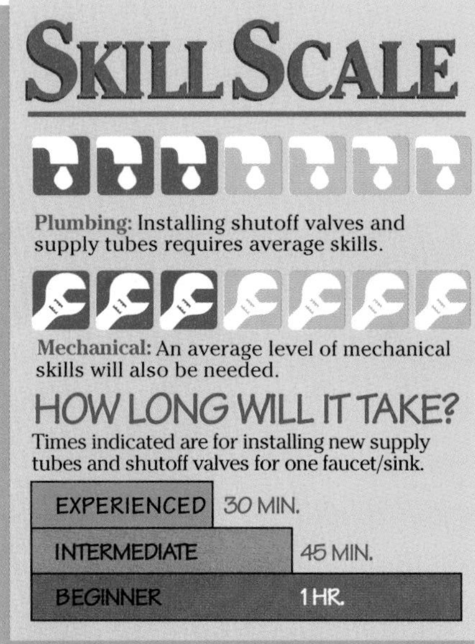

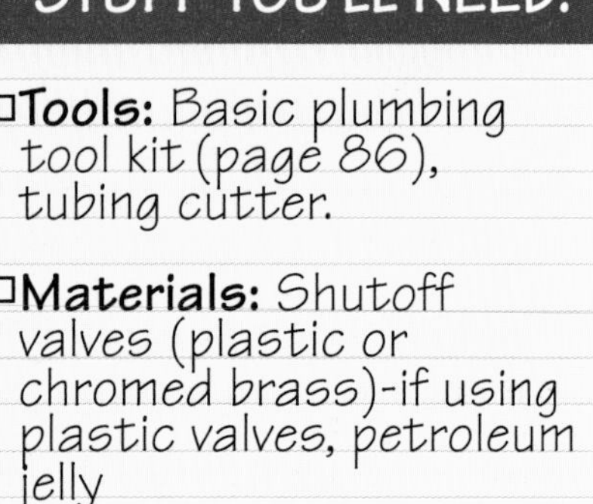

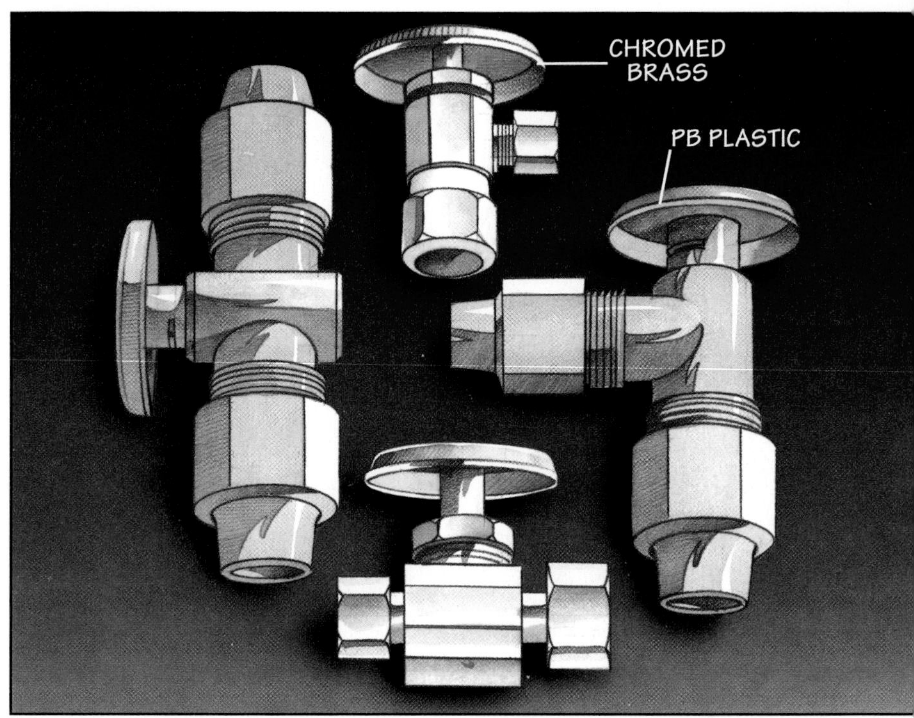

Shutoff valves allow you to shut off the water to an individual fixture so it can be repaired, without having to do so at the main shutoff, which would deprive your whole house of water for as long as it takes to make the repair. They can be made from durable chromed brass or lightweight plastic. These valves come in $^3/_8$, $^1/_2$, and $^3/_4$" diameters to match common water supply pipe sizes.

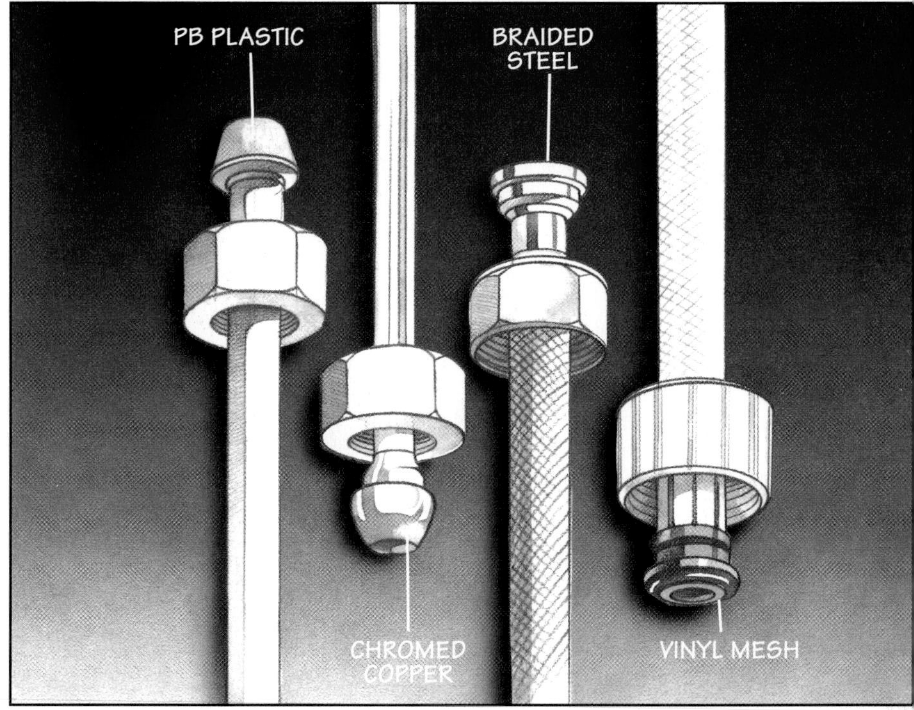

Supply tubes are used to connect water supply pipes to faucets, toilets, and other fixtures. They come in a variety of lengths–plastic and chromed copper tubes can be cut to the exact length you need. You have to be careful bending the chromed pipes when fitting them so you don't crimp them. Plastic, braided steel, and vinyl mesh tubes are easy to install, since they are flexible.

PUTTING IN SHUTOFF VALVES & SUPPLY TUBES

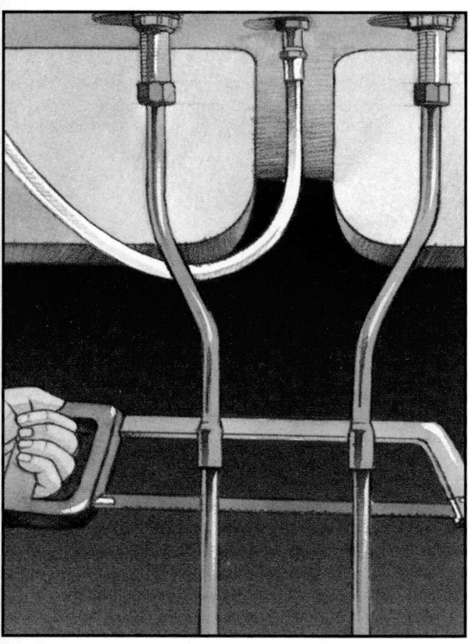

1 Turn off the water at the main shutoff valve. Remove the old supply pipes. If the pipes are soldered copper, cut them off just below the soldered joint, using a fine-toothed hacksaw or tubing cutter. Make sure the cuts are straight. Unscrew the coupling nuts and discard the old pipes.

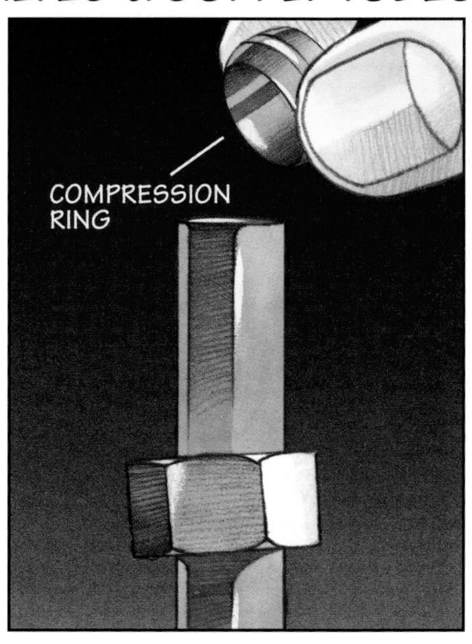

2 Slide a compression nut and compression ring over the copper water pipe. The threads of the nut should face the end of the pipe.

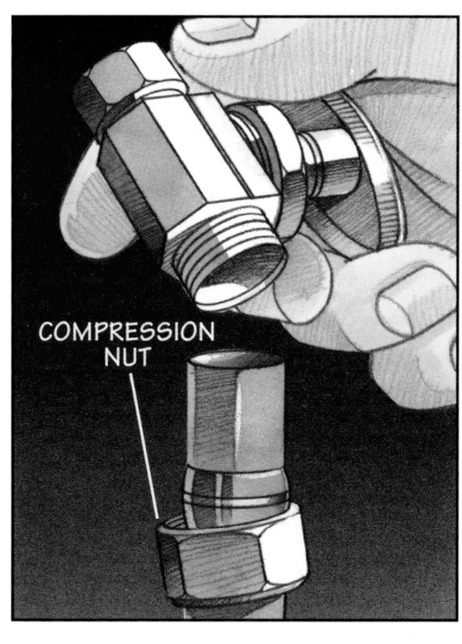

3 Slide a shutoff valve onto the pipe. Apply a layer of pipe joint compound to the compression ring. Screw the compression nut onto the shutoff valve and tighten with an adjustable wrench.

Plumbing

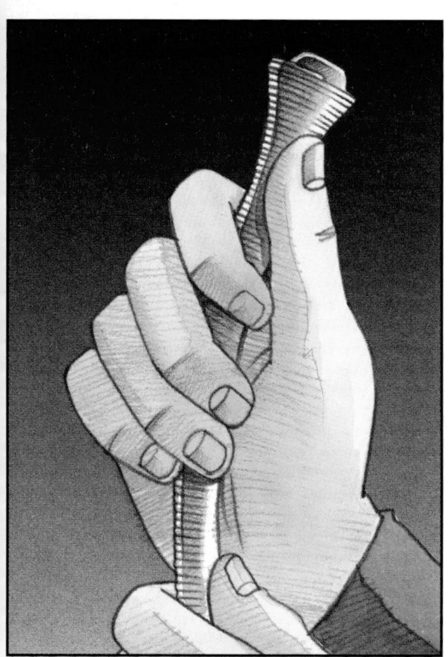

4 Bend the chromed copper supply tube to reach from the tailpiece of the fixture to the shutoff valve using a special tool called a "tubing bender." Using a tubing bender and bending the tube slowly will help avoid crimping the metal.

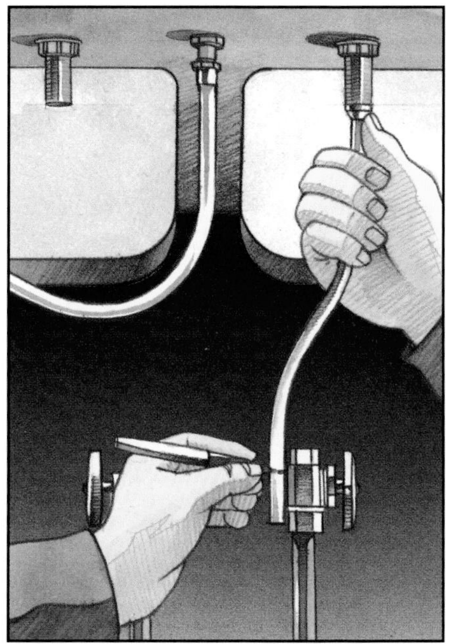

5 Position the supply tube between the fixture tailpiece and shutoff valve and mark the tube to length. Cut the supply tube with a tubing cutter (page 92).

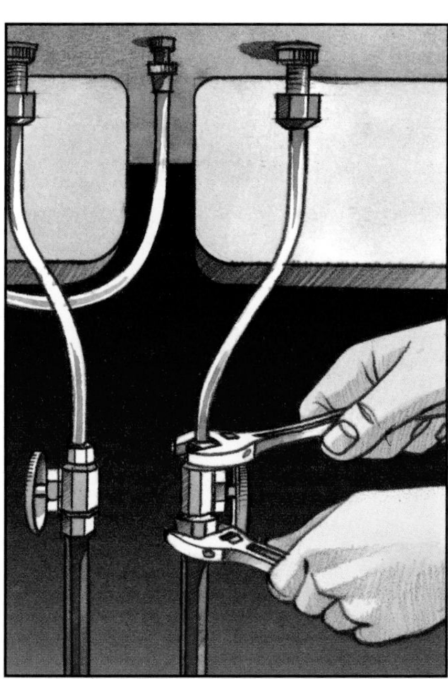

6 Attach the bell-shaped end of the supply tube to the fixture tailpiece with a coupling nut, then attach the other end to the shutoff valve with a compression ring and nut. Tighten all fittings with adjustable wrenches.

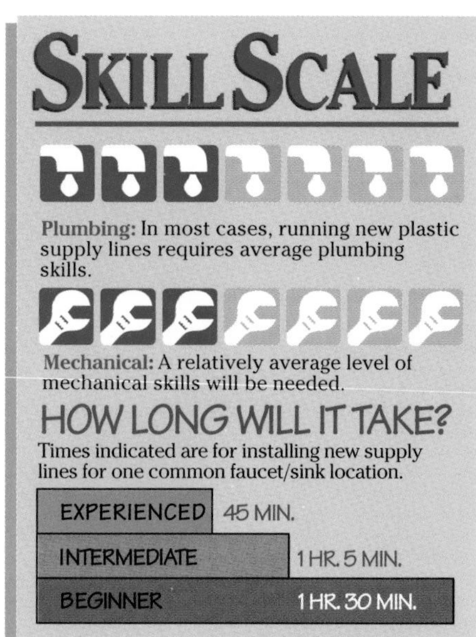

Running New Supply Line

Replacing an existing sink or other fixture is straightforward–the supply and drain hookups are in place and waiting for you. But it may come to pass, someday, that you'll want a fixture where no fixture has gone before. In that event, you'll need to think about extending supply lines to reach it.

Before you cut into anything, take stock of your situation. Obviously, you want to tap into the hot and cold water lines at some reasonably nearby location, but not necessarily at the point nearest to your new addition. Consider whether another point, even though not as close, might be more accessible with less damage. This is especially important if you are working around finished walls. Remember, pipe is cheap.

Typically, your new supply lines should be arranged to bracket the drain stub-out. Until you get the actual fixture in place, terminate the supply lines with shutoff valves (and be certain they are shut off).

The procedures shown here are for rigid plastic (CPVC) pipe, but the same principles would apply to copper pipe. See pages 92–95 for copper pipe cutting and joining techniques.

STUFF YOU'LL NEED:

- ☐ **Tools:** Basic plumbing tool kit (page 86).
- ☐ **Materials:** Pipe joint compound, pipe straps, solvent glue, plastic supply pipe and fittings.

PLAN YOUR PIPE ROUTE CAREFULLY TO GET PAST EXISTING PIPES.

INSTALLING WATER SUPPLY PIPES

1 Mark the location of new water supply pipes on the wall studs, using masking tape. Water supply stub-outs generally are centered around the drain outlet, spaced about 8" apart. The stub-out for the hot water line should be on the left side of the drain stub-out, and the cold water line should be on the right. Shut off main water supply, and run faucets to drain plumbing lines.

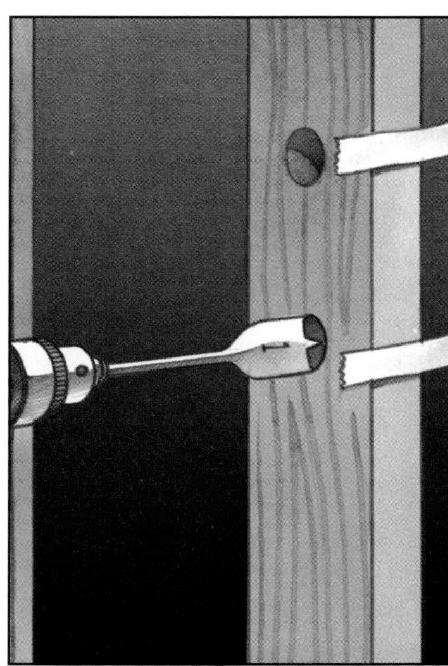

2 Drill holes through the centers of framing members to hold new plastic water supply pipes. New pipes must not be larger in diameter than the existing water supply pipes.

3 Cut out sections of existing supply pipes using a pipe cutter, and install T-fittings for connecting new plastic pipes.

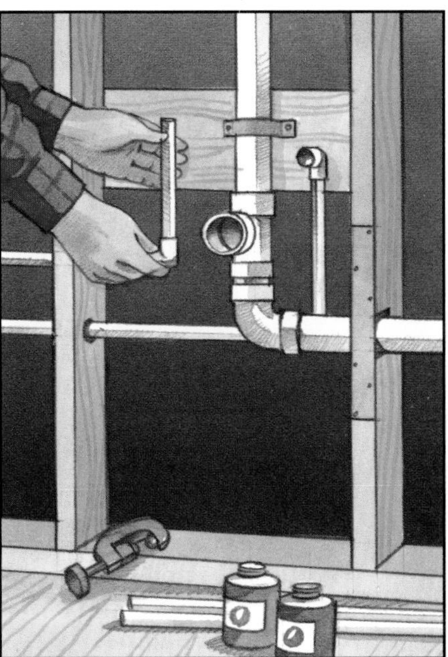

4 Cut and test-fit plastic supply pipes and fittings. When you are satisfied with the pipe layout, solvent-glue the pieces together.

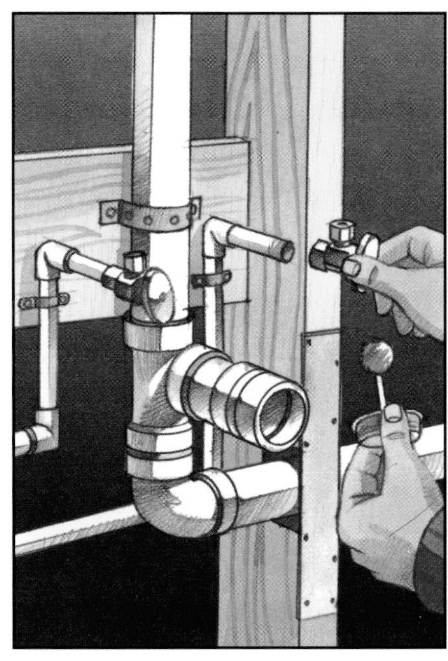

5 Attach the new pipes to the cross brace, using pipe straps, then attach shutoff valves to the ends of the pipes. (Some shutoff valves are solvent-glued, others use compression fittings.)

Replacing a Water Heater

Removing your old water heater and installing a new one is a job you can do if the replacement unit is similar to the old one. You must turn off the power source (either gas or electric) and disconnect the water heater, including the exhaust duct if it is a gas unit. Working with the water supply lines is like working with any supply lines (see steps at right). To install the new unit, you simply reconnect the power source exactly as it was attached to the old unit, following the manufacturer's directions.

If you need to change from a gas water heater to an electric one, or vice versa, call a professional to do the work. Most Building Codes require a licensed installer to remove or install gas lines.

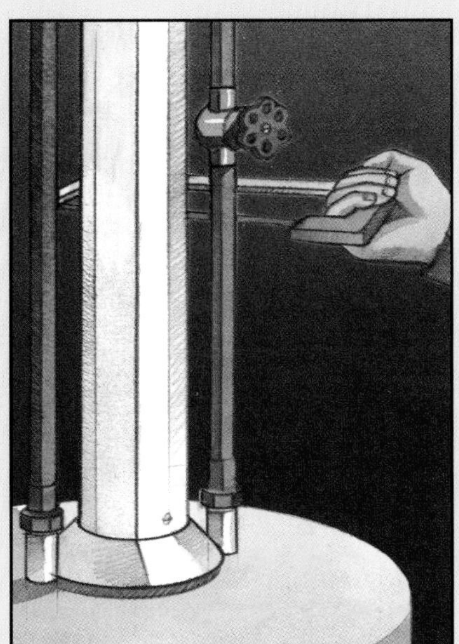

1 After shutting off and disconnecting the power source and shutting off the incoming water valve, make straight cuts through the pipes below the level of the shutoff valve. See pages 92-95 for working with copper pipe, or page 91 for plastic. Drain the heater and remove it using an appliance dolly.

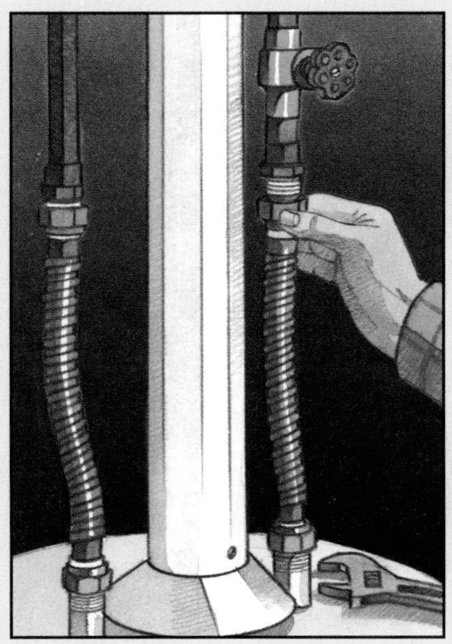

2 You will need to attach a threaded fitting onto the end of each pipe so that you can connect the new water heater with supply lines. Reinstall the exhaust duct if the heater uses gas. Follow the manufacturer's directions for starting the new unit.

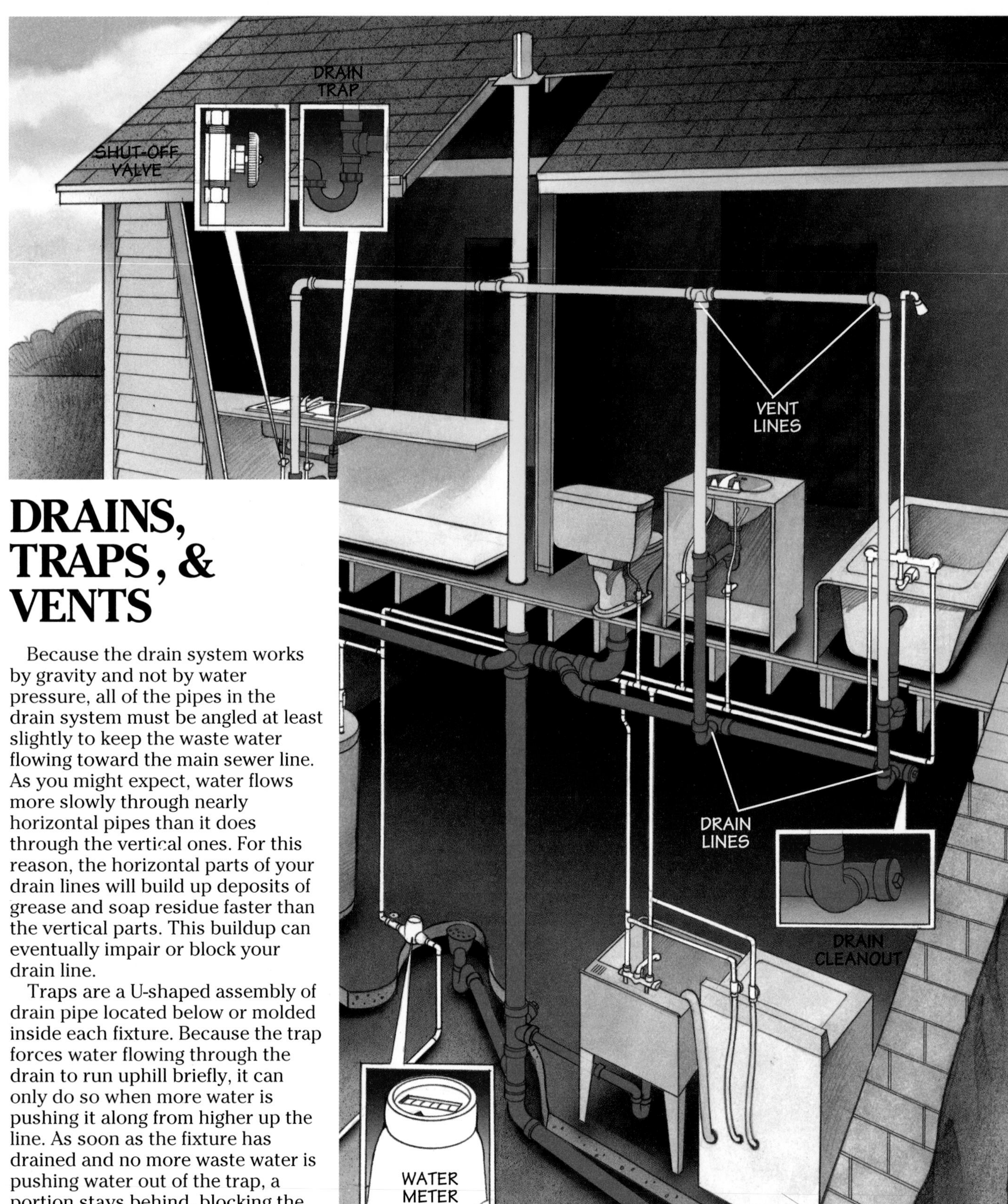

DRAINS, TRAPS, & VENTS

Because the drain system works by gravity and not by water pressure, all of the pipes in the drain system must be angled at least slightly to keep the waste water flowing toward the main sewer line. As you might expect, water flows more slowly through nearly horizontal pipes than it does through the vertical ones. For this reason, the horizontal parts of your drain lines will build up deposits of grease and soap residue faster than the vertical parts. This buildup can eventually impair or block your drain line.

Traps are a U-shaped assembly of drain pipe located below or molded inside each fixture. Because the trap forces water flowing through the drain to run uphill briefly, it can only do so when more water is pushing it along from higher up the line. As soon as the fixture has drained and no more waste water is pushing water out of the trap, a portion stays behind, blocking the pipe so that sewer gas can't seep up the drain line and into your house. Rooftop vents let air into the drain-waste-vent system. This helps waste water flow freely into the sewer line. Sometimes apparent drain problems turn out to be vent problems.

Replacing Drain Traps

Replace leaky or seriously corroded traps with nice new ones. If the traps won't show, plastic ones are just fine. Choose chromed brass traps for sinks with exposed plumbing. Traps come in $1^1/_4$" and $1^1/_2$" inside diameter (ID)–be sure you get the right size replacement.

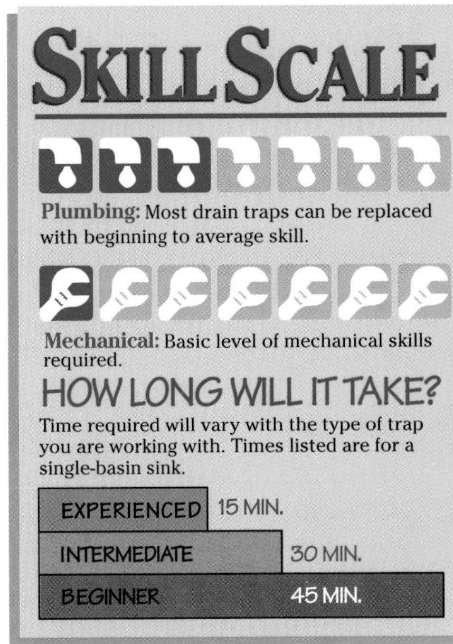

Plumbing

STUFF YOU'LL NEED:

- ☐ **Tools:** Basic plumbing tool kit (page 86).
- ☐ **Materials:** New plastic or chromed brass trap pipes.

REPLACING A DRAIN TRAP

1 Remove the drain trap assembly completely. Don't try to salvage any parts–it's not worth the aggravation. Replace them all with new ones.

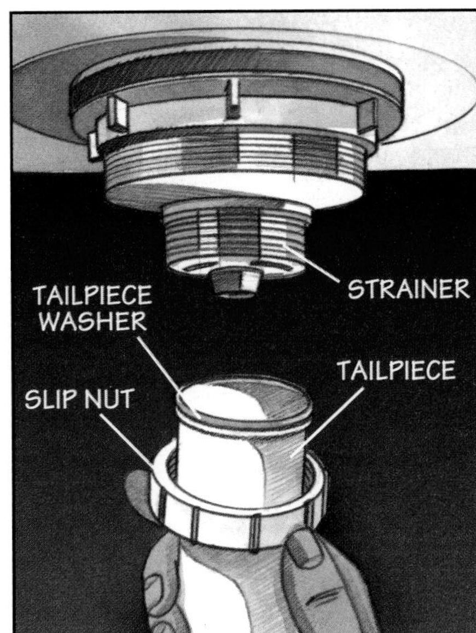

2 Place the tailpiece washer in the flared end of the tailpiece, then attach the tailpiece by screwing the slip nut onto the sink strainer. If necessary, the tailpiece can be cut to fit with a hacksaw.

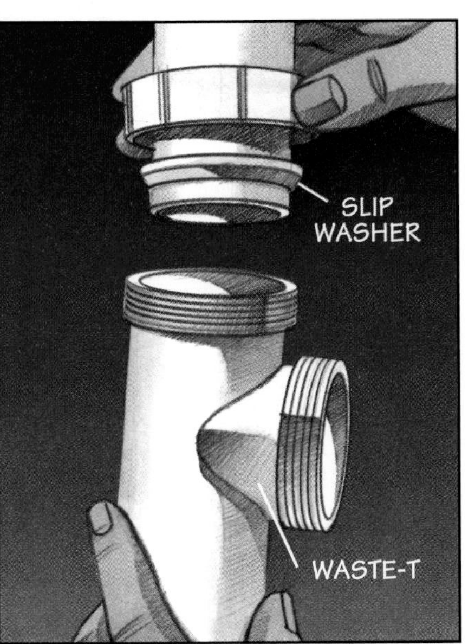

3 On sinks with two basins, use a continuous waste-T-fitting to join the tailpieces. Attach the fitting with slip washers and nuts. Beveled sides of washers face threaded portion of pipes. Pipe lubricant on the slip washer will ease installation and ensure a tight fit.

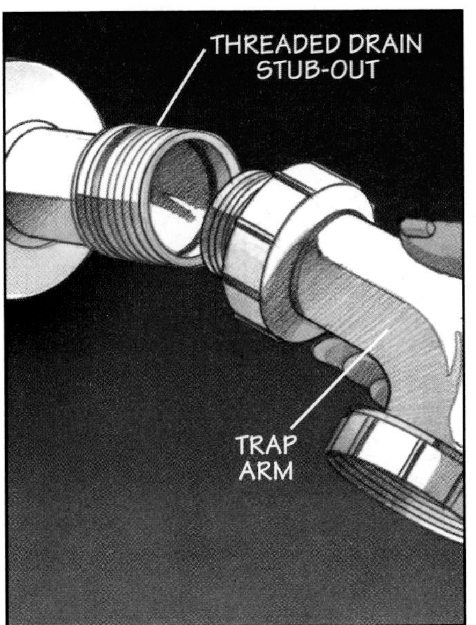

4 Attach the trap arm to the drain stub-out, using a slip nut and washer. Beveled side of washer should face threaded drain stub-out. If necessary, the trap arm can be cut to fit with hacksaw.

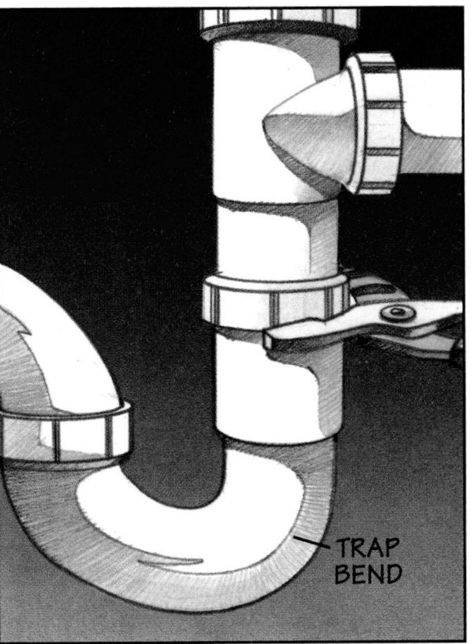

5 Attach the trap bend to the trap arm, using slip nuts and washers. Beveled side of washers should face trap bend. Tighten all nuts with water-pump pliers. Never use teflon tape on white plastic pipe threads and fittings.

Unclogging & Fixing Sink Drains

Clogged sinks usually occur when soap and hair build up in the drain trap or fixture drain line. First try that old standby, the plunger. If that doesn't work, disconnect and clean the trap (page 104), or use a snake.

Many sinks hold water with a mechanical plug called a pop-up stopper. If the sink won't hold standing water, or if the water drains too slowly, the stopper must be cleaned and adjusted (page 106).

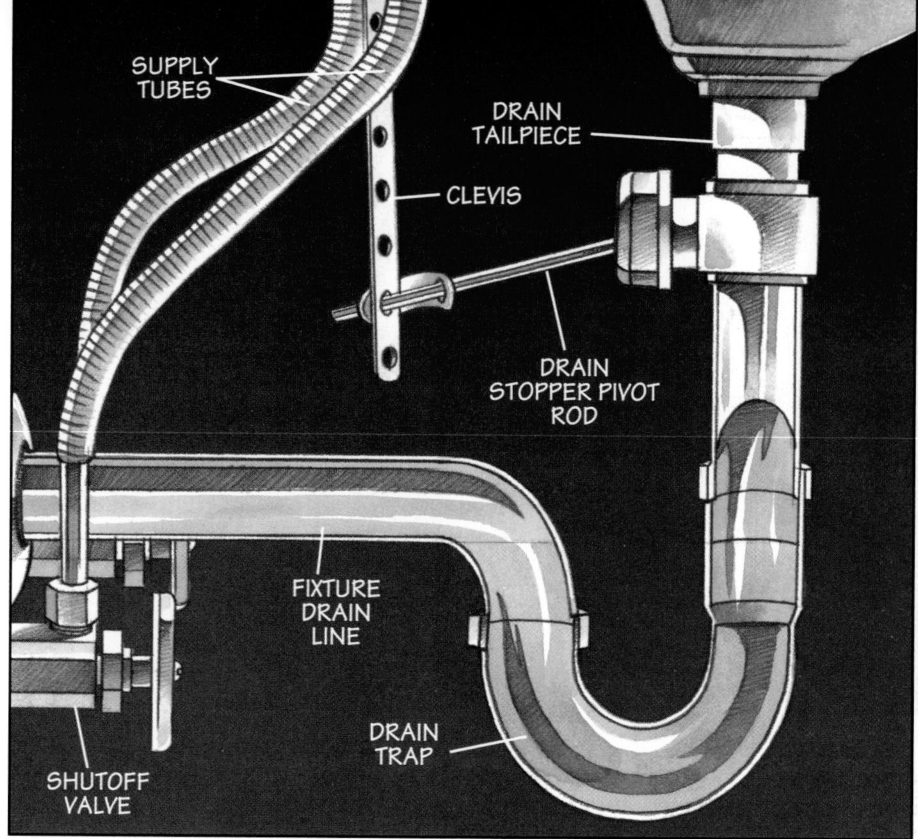

The drain trap holds water that seals the drain line and prevents sewer gases from entering the home. Each time a drain is used, the standing trap water is flushed away and replaced by new water. The shape of the trap and fixture drain line may resemble the letter "P," and sink traps sometimes are called P-traps.

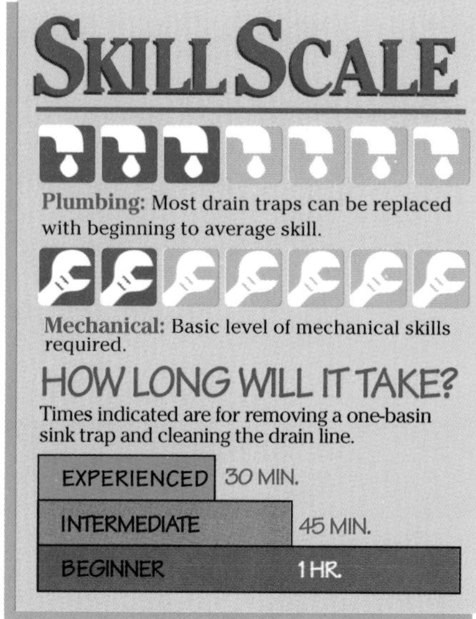

STUFF YOU'LL NEED:

- ☐ **Tools:** Basic plumbing tool kit (page 86), drain or hand auger, spud wrench, snake.
- ☐ **Materials:** Plumber's putty.

CLEARING SINK DRAINS WITH A PLUNGER

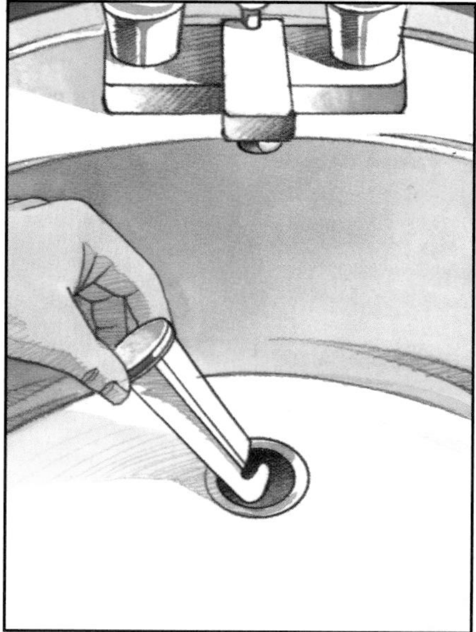

1 Remove the stopper. Some pop-up stoppers lift out directly; others turn counterclockwise. You may encounter an old stopper whose pivot rod must be removed before you can take the stopper out.

2 Stuff a wet rag in the sink overflow opening. This prevents air from breaking the suction created by the plunger. Place the plunger cup over the drain and run enough water to cover the rubber cup. Move the plunger up and down rapidly to clear the clog.

FIXING LEAKY SINK STRAINERS

The sink strainer assembly connects the sink to the drain line. Leaks may occur where the strainer body meets the lip of the drain opening or anywhere along the assembly. You'll need to take it all apart.

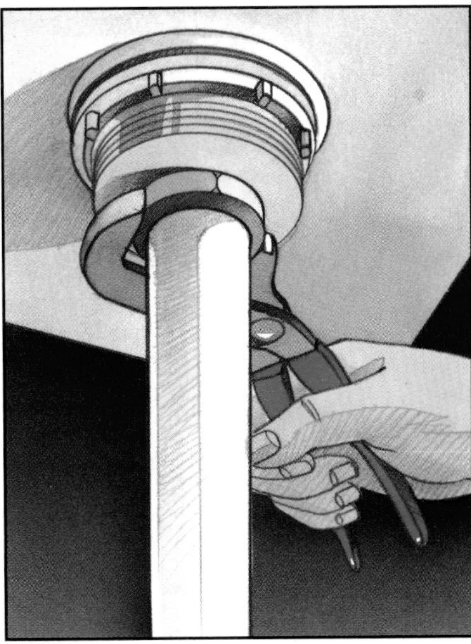

1 Unscrew the slip nuts from both ends of the tailpiece with water-pump pliers. Disconnect and remove the tailpiece from the strainer body and trap.

2 Remove the locknut with a spud wrench. Stubborn nuts may be removed by tapping on the lugs with a hammer. Unscrew the locknut and remove the strainer assembly.

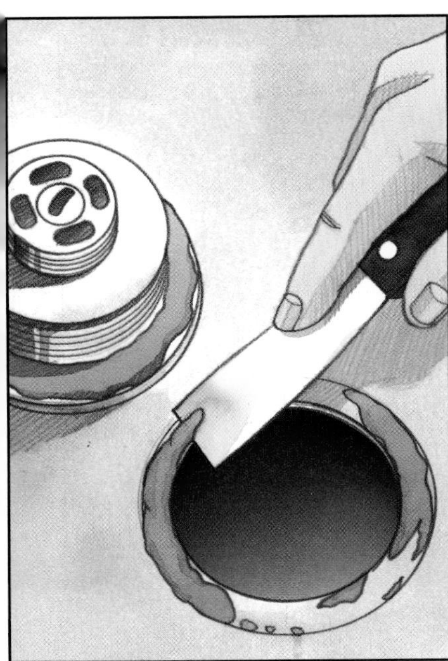

3 Remove old putty from the drain opening with a putty knife. If you're reusing the old strainer body, clean off the old putty from under the flange. You should also replace old gaskets and washers.

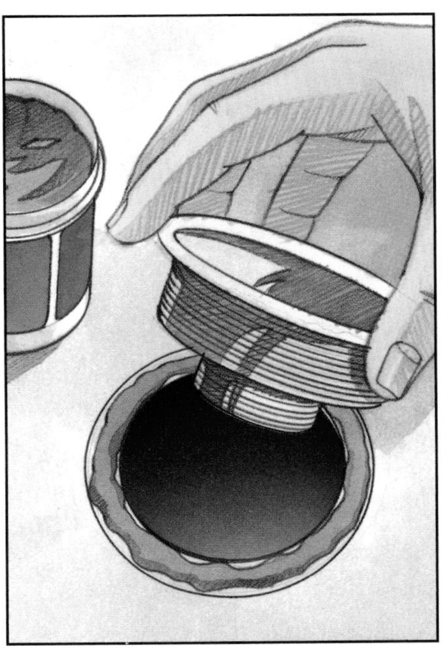

4 Apply a bead of plumber's putty to the lip of the drain opening. Press the strainer body into the opening. From under the sink, place a rubber gasket, then a metal or fiber friction ring, over the strainer. Reinstall the locknut and tighten. Reinstall the tailpiece.

Many potential drain problems can be averted with a little regular care. Kitchen drains, which typically receive most of the greasy and gooey stuff, should be thoroughly flushed with hot water once a week. Shower and tub drains benefit from an occasional dose of liquid bleach. And if your washing machine empties into a laundry tub, tie an old nylon stocking over the end of the rubber drain hose. The lint in your wash water can build up in drain pipes and eventually plug them.

Plumbing

BUYER'S GUIDE

Choosing the Right Drain Cleaner

Contrary to what those television ads have been telling you, plumbers don't hate drain cleaners. Not at all. As long as people keep using drain cleaners to eat away stubborn clogs, plumbers' jobs will be secure.

It's true that caustic, acid-based chemical drain cleaners will sometimes dissolve clogs – at the same time they are dissolving your pipes. It's a race.

You should never have to use caustic drain cleaners. A little regular maintenance will keep drains working nicely. Flush drains once each week with hot tap water to clear away soap and grease. Then once every six months or so, treat your drains with a non-caustic (copper sulfide- or sodium hydroxide-based) drain cleaner. A non-caustic cleaner will not hurt your pipes.

UNCLOGGING A SINK DRAIN TRAP

1 Put a bucket under the trap to catch water and debris. Loosen the slip nuts on the trap with water-pump pliers. Unscrew the nuts by hand and slide them away from the connections.

2 Dump out the debris. Clean the trap with a small wire brush. Inspect the slip nut washers for wear and replace them if necessary. Reinstall the trap and tighten the slip nuts. Oftentimes, clogs occur at the first fitting after the p-trap. If this is the case, follow the instructions below.

CLEARING A FIXTURE DRAIN LINE

1 Remove the trap. Push the end of the snake into the drain line opening until you meet resistance. This usually means the end of the snake has reached a bend in the drain pipe.

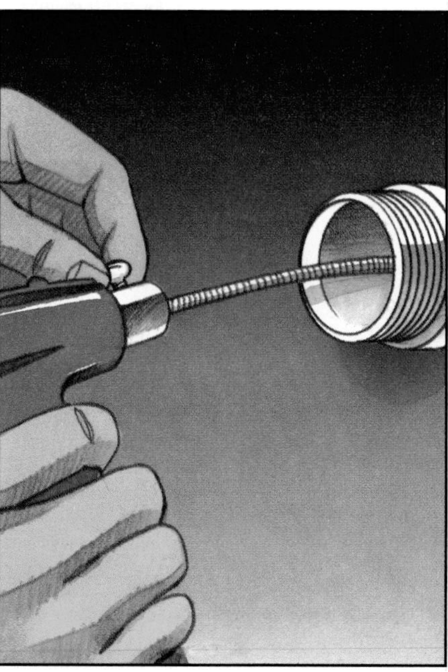

2 Set the snake lock so that at least 6 inches of cable extends from the opening. Crank the snake handle clockwise to move the end of the cable past the bend, pushing forward as you do.

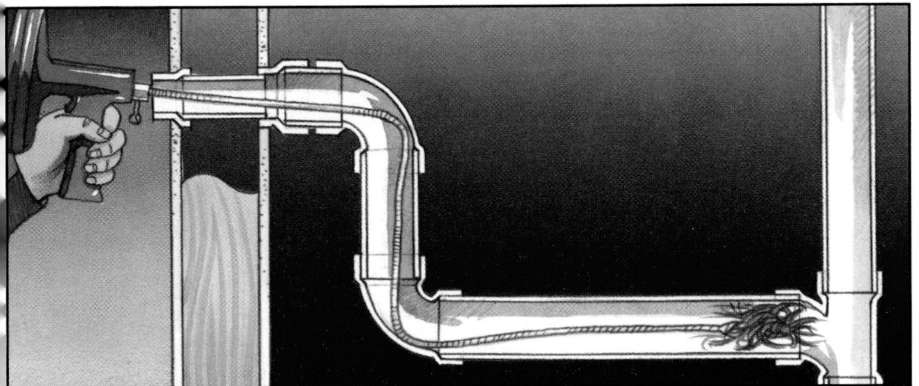

3 Release the lock and continue pushing the cable into the opening until you feel firm resistance. Set the snake lock and crank the handle clockwise. Solid resistance that prevents the cable from advancing indicates there's a clog. Some clogs, such as a sponge or accumulation of hair, can be snagged and retrieved (step 4). If you can advance the cable slowly, you probably have a soap clog (step 5).

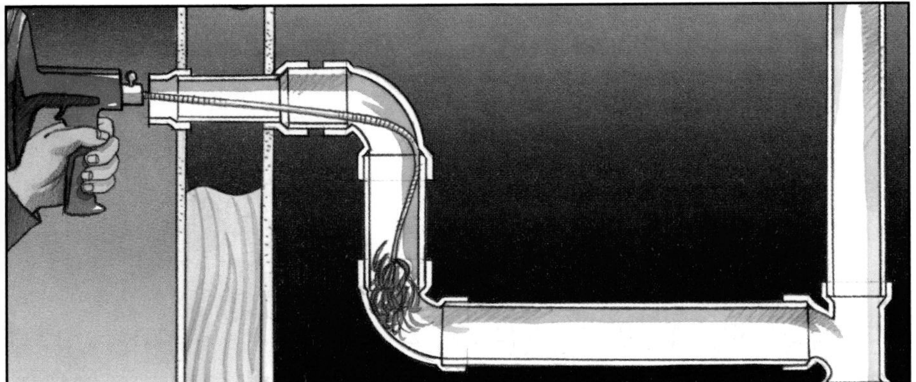

4 Pull any obstruction out of the line by releasing the snake lock and cranking the handle clockwise. If no object can be retrieved, reconnect the trap and use the snake to clear the nearest branch drain line or main waste and vent stack.

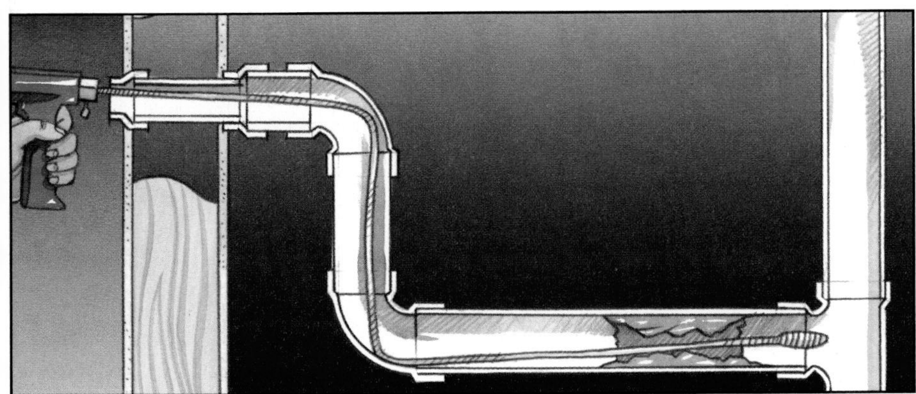

5 Bore through the soap clog by cranking the snake handle clockwise while applying steady pressure on the hand grip. Repeat the procedure several times, then retrieve the cable. Reconnect the trap and flush the system with hot water to remove debris.

TOOLTIPS

Snakes

Including a couple of special-purpose snakes (sometimes called "drain augers") in your kit of basic plumbing tools will let you take action when clogs occur.

Closet snakes are specially designed to clear toilet clogs. A bend in the tube allows the snake to be positioned in the bottom of the toilet bowl. The bend is usually covered by a rubber sleeve to protect the toilet. A crank handle turns the cable.

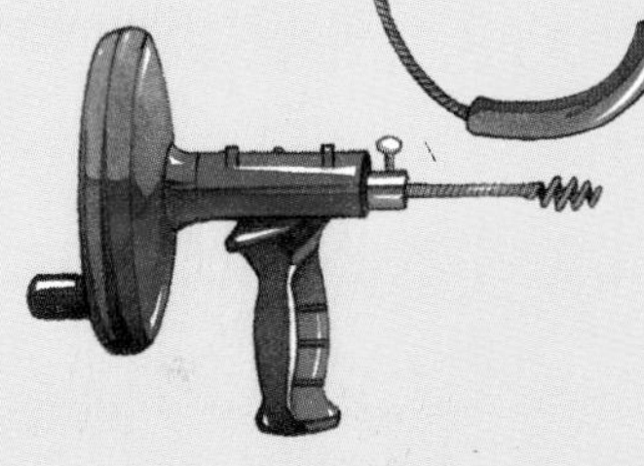

Hand snakes, sometimes called "augers," are used to clear clogs in drain lines. The pistol-grip style hand snake stores its flexible steel cable in a disk-shaped crank. The pistol-grip handle makes it easy to apply pressure on the cable.

Coiled drain snakes, another style of hand snake, have the advantage of being inexpensive. An offset snake handle locks to the cable with a wing screw.

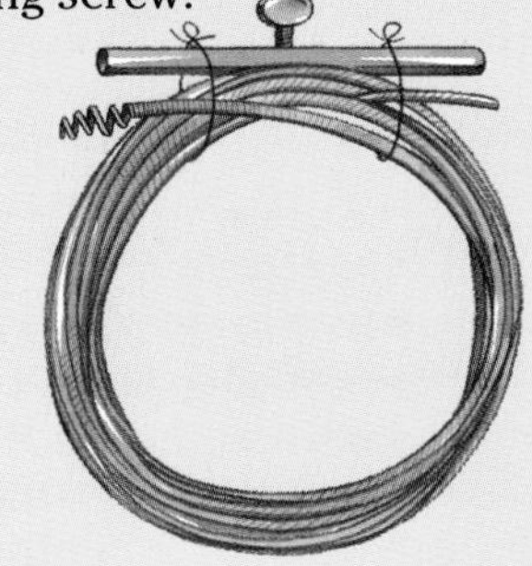

CLEANING & ADJUSTING A POP-UP SINK DRAIN STOPPER

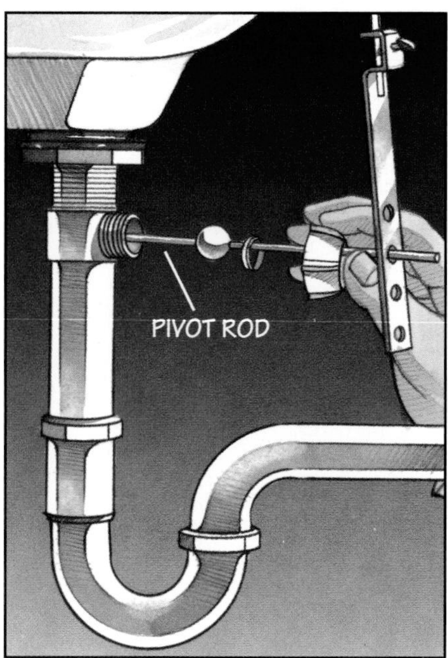

1 Raise the stopper lever to the full upright (closed) position. Unscrew the retaining nut that holds the pivot rod in position. Pull the pivot rod out of the drain pipe to release the stopper.

2 Remove the stopper. Clean debris from it with a small wire brush. Inspect the gasket for wear and damage and replace it if necessary. Reinstall the stopper.

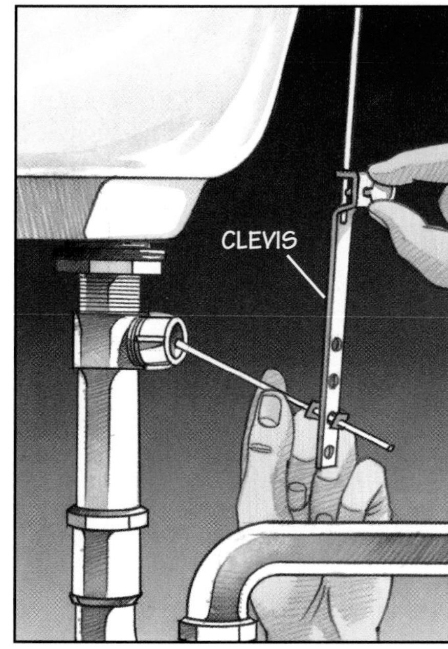

3 If the sink doesn't drain properly, adjust the clevis by loosening the clevis screw and sliding the clevis up or down on the stopper rod. Then tighten the clevis screw.

Unclogging Tub Drains

When your tub drains slowly–or worse, not at all–you'll have to remove and inspect the drain assembly. Tub drain mechanisms can be divided into two types: plunger and pop-up.

Take a look at your tub drain. If your tub uses a movable metal stopper to seal off the drain, you've got yourself a pop-up type. Plunger-type drains look open all the time, but a brass plug in the overflow tube moves up and down to block the drain line.

Both plunger and pop-up drain mechanisms catch hair and other debris that cause clogs.

If removing the drain mechanism doesn't work, the drain line is probably clogged. You'll want to try to clear the line with a plunger or a snake. Stuff a wet rag into the overflow opening so you'll get good suction on the drain with the plunger. When you use a snake, always insert the cable through the overflow drain opening.

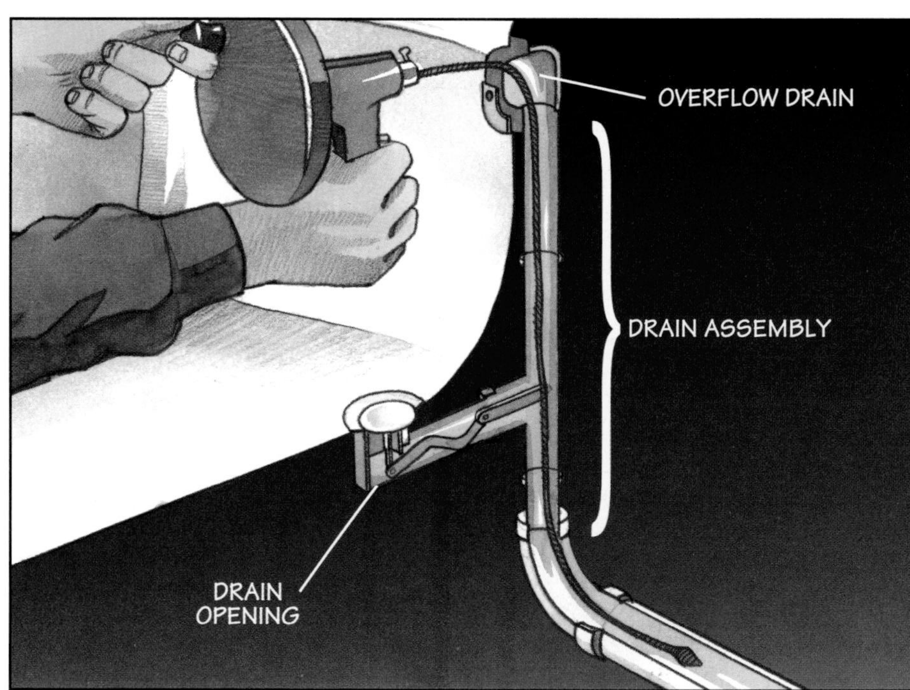

Clear a tub drain by running the snake cable through the overflow opening. First, remove the coverplate and carefully lift out the drain linkage (page opposite). Push snake cable into the opening until resistance is felt. After using the snake, replace drain linkage. Open drain and run hot water through the drain to flush out any debris.

CLEANING & ADJUSTING A PLUNGER-TYPE TUB DRAIN

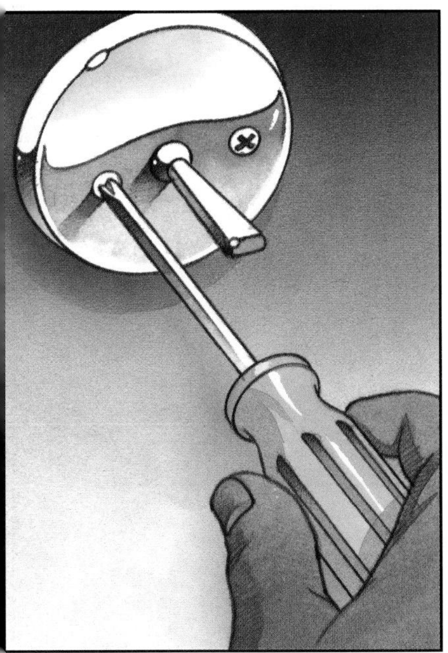

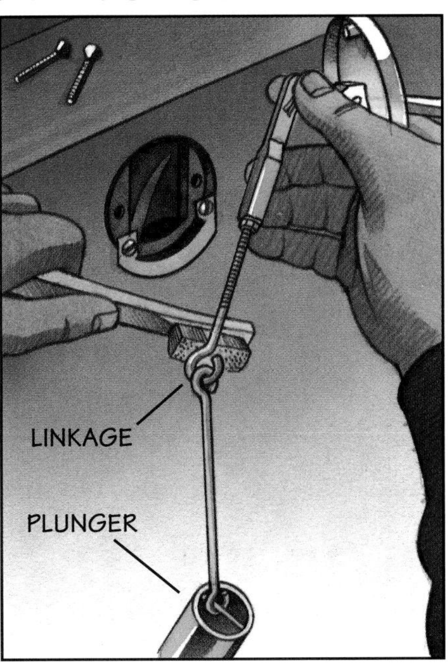

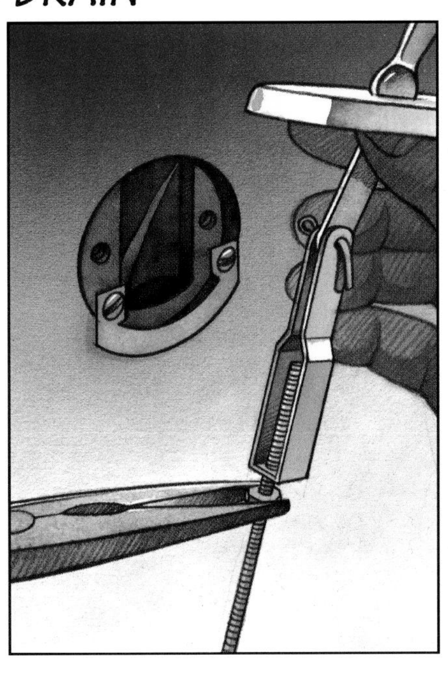

1 Remove the screws on the coverplate and carefully pull the coverplate, linkage, and plunger from the overflow drain opening.

2 Clean the linkage and plunger with a small wire brush dipped in vinegar. Lubricate the assembly with heatproof grease.

3 Adjust the drain flow and fix leaks by adjusting the linkage. To do this, unscrew the locknut on the threaded lift rod using needlenose pliers. Screw the rod down about $^1/_8$ inch. Then tighten the locknut and reinstall the whole works.

CLEANING & ADJUSTING A POP-UP TUB DRAIN

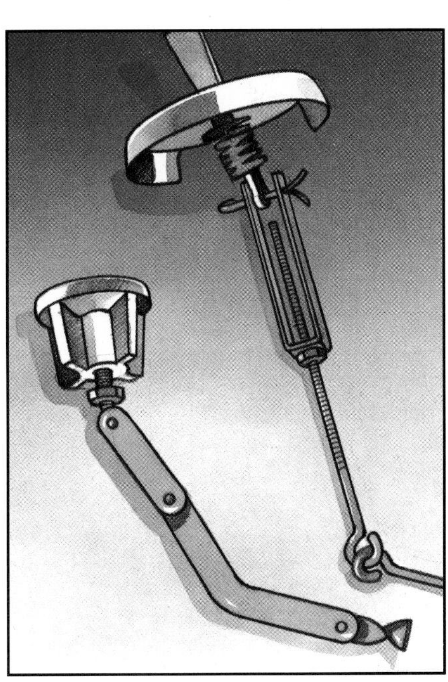

1 Flip the lever to the full open position and carefully pull the stopper and rocker arm assembly from the drain opening. Use a small wire brush to clean off the debris you find.

2 Remove the screws from the coverplate and pull it, the trip lever, and linkage from the overflow drain. Remove hair and debris, and remove any corrosion with a small wire brush and vinegar. Lubricate the linkage with heatproof grease.

3 Adjust the drain flow and fix any leaks by adjusting the linkage. To do this, loosen the locknut on the threaded lift rod and screw the lift rod up about $^1/_8$ inch. Tighten the locknut and reinstall everything, in reverse order.

Unclogging Shower Drains

The shower drain system has a sloped floor, a drain opening, a trap, and a drain line that connects to a branch drain line or waste and vent stack. Shower drain clogs usually are caused by an accumulation of hair in the drain line. Remove the strainer cover with a screwdriver, and look for clogs in the drain opening with a flashlight. Use a stiff wire brush or a piece of stiff wire to remove clogs if you can.

If that doesn't do the trick, you may need a plunger. Put the rubber cup over the drain opening and run enough water into the shower stall to cover the lip of the cup. Move the plunger up and down rapidly. If that fails, clear stubborn clogs with a snake.

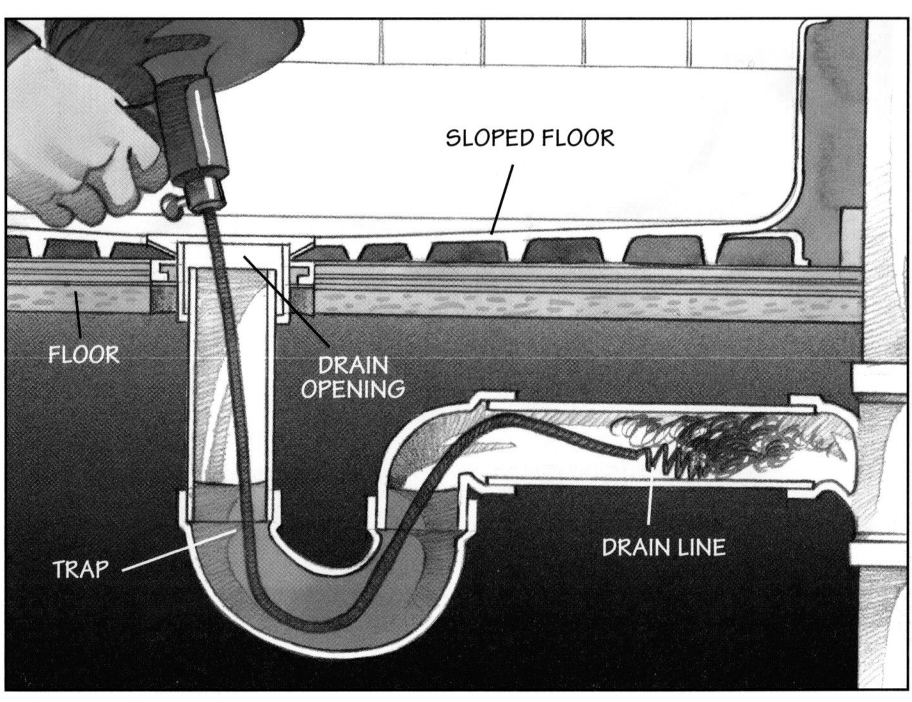

Clearing clogged showers: The shower drain system has a sloped floor, a drain opening, a trap, and a drain line that connects to a branch drain line or waste and vent stack.

UNCLOGGING A SHOWER DRAIN

Checking for clogs: Remove the strainer cover using a screwdriver. Use a flashlight to look for hair clogs in the drain opening. Use a stiff wire to clear shower drain of hair or to snag any obstructions.

Using a plunger: Clear most shower drain clogs by placing the rubber cup over the drain opening. Pour enough water into the shower stall to cover the lip of the cup. Move plunger handle up and down rapidly.

Clearing stubborn clogs: If the plunger didn't work try a hand snake. Use the snake as shown on pages 104-105.

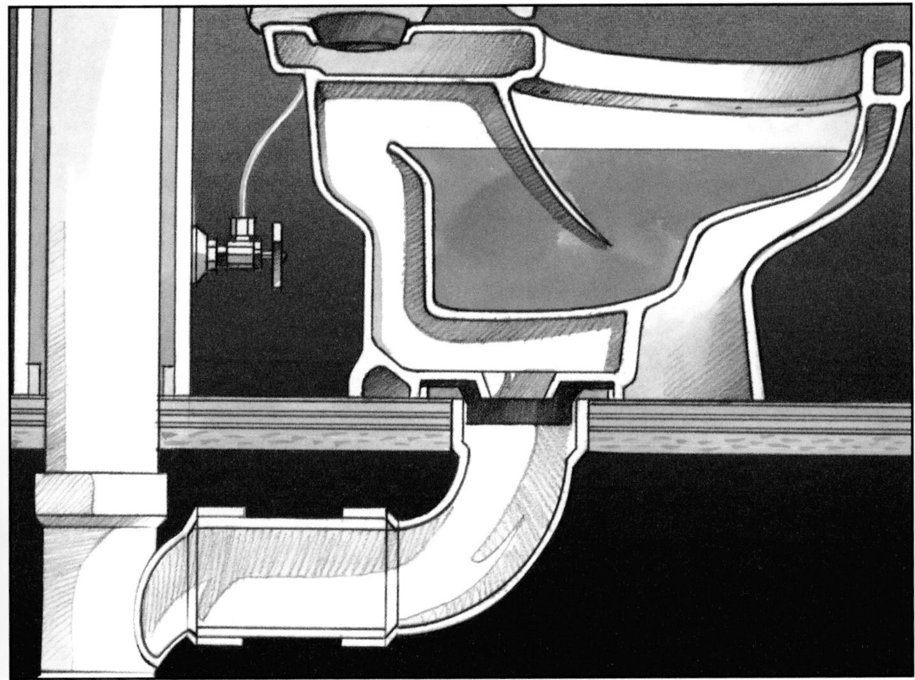

Clearing clogged toilets: The toilet drain system has a drain outlet at the bottom of the bowl and a built-in trap. The toilet drain is connected to a drain line and a main waste and vent stack.

Unclogging Toilet Drains

A clogged toilet is one of the most common plumbing problems, which is why we tell you to have a plunger and closet snake as part of your basic plumbing tool kit. If your toilet overflows or flushes poorly, try to clear the clog first with the easy-to-use plunger. The air pressure forced into the drain is quite powerful, yet it can't damage the toilet, so it should always be the first choice for trying to clear a clog. If that doesn't do the trick, then use the closet snake.

Toilet drain lines are large, usually formed with 4"-diameter pipe, but the built-in toilet trap is difficult to get through, even with the closet snake, which is specially designed to do so. It takes a little experience to "feel" the difference between the clog and a bend in the trap.

If you can't reach or clear the clog with the closet snake, then you'll need to remove the toilet (pages 138-139), which will make it easy to run a hand snake into the 4"-diameter drain line. After clearing the clog, replace the toilet (pages 140-141). If you couldn't find a clog to clear and the toilet still isn't working right, the clog may be in the main waste and vent stack. At this point it is best to call in a professional, since clogs in the stack are often beyond the reach of hand snakes.

UNCLOGGING A TOILET

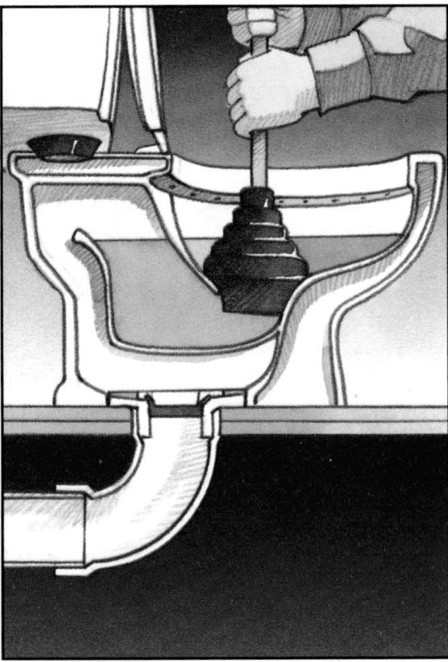

Clearing a toilet with a plunger: Place the plunger over the hole in the toilet. Plunge up and down rapidly, keeping the plunger under water and lifting it only an inch or so on every upstroke. Keep doing this for a minute or two. If it doesn't clear, use a closet snake.

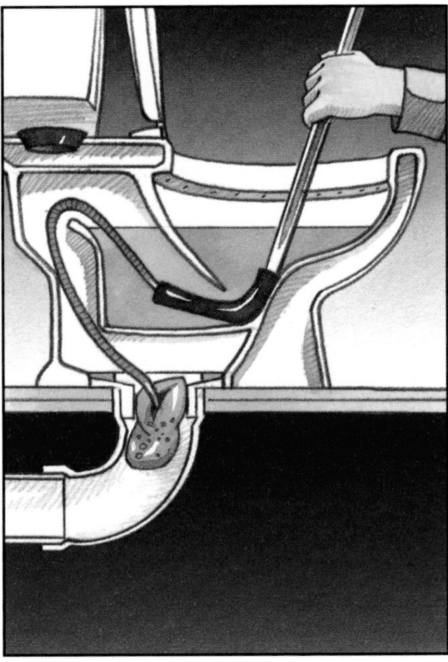

Clearing a toilet with a closet snake: Feed the end of the cable into the toilet, taking care not to scratch the bowl. Crank the handle clockwise to snag the obstruction. Continue cranking while pulling the obstruction out.

HOMER'S HINDSIGHT

It began as a simple clog and ended as a heap of broken china! That toilet may look big and strong, but don't use the closet snake like a battering ram. You can crack or even break the bowl, especially on inexpensive toilets. And there is no way to repair a cracked toilet—you'll have to replace the whole thing.

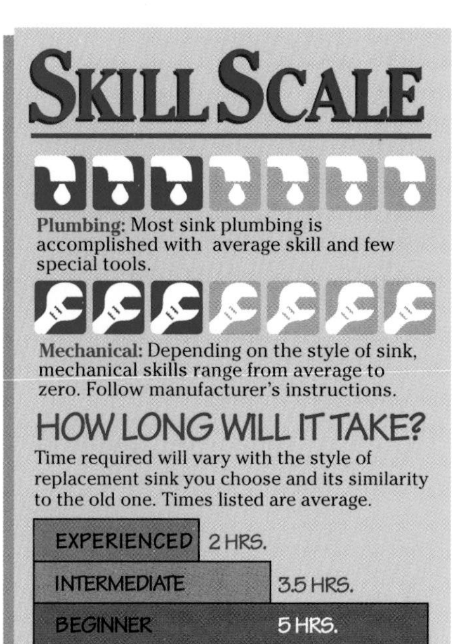

Plumbing

Removing & Replacing Sinks

STUFF YOU'LL NEED:

- ☐**Tools:** Basic plumbing tool kit (page 86), basin wrench.
- ☐**Materials:** Silicone caulk, bucket, plumber's putty, new supply tubes and shutoff valves, if necessary.

Unless there's an obvious problem, why replace your sink? There are more entertaining ways to spend a Saturday, after all. Still, replacing the sink, or a sink and countertop unit, is a relatively quick and inexpensive way to make a big improvement. And it's one you can easily handle.

Obviously, it's a good idea to have your new sink standing by before tearing the old one apart. If the new sink is similar in style to the old one, replacement should be straightforward. If you are contemplating a dramatic style change, you may be facing some additional work, either in making necessary plumbing modifications, or in repair to wall areas hidden by the original sink.

BE SURE TO HAVE A BUCKET READY; YOUR TRAP WILL HAVE WATER IN IT.

REMOVING A SINK

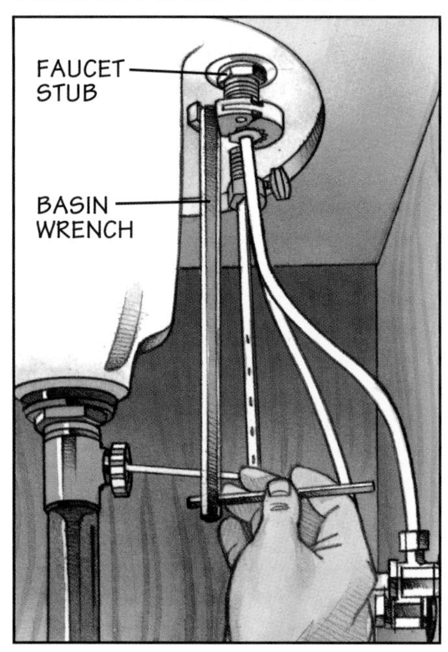

1 Turn off the shutoff valves, then remove the coupling nuts that connect the supply tube to the faucet tailpieces using a basin wrench. If supply tubes are soldered, cut them above the shutoff valves.

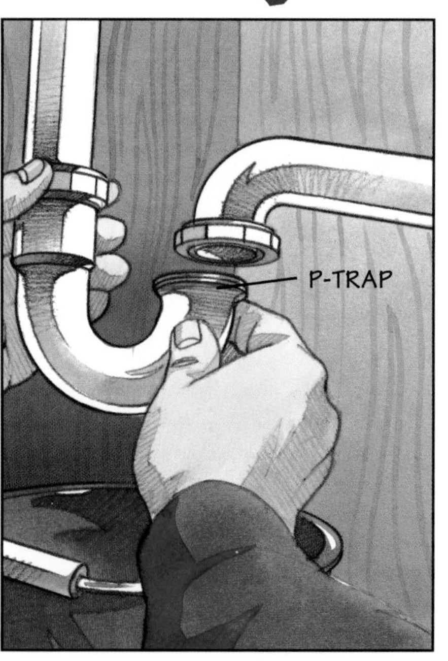

2 With bucket beneath, remove P-trap by loosening slip nuts at both ends. If the nuts will not turn, cut out the drain trap with a hacksaw. When prying or cutting, take care to avoid damaging the trap arm that runs into the wall.

Variations:

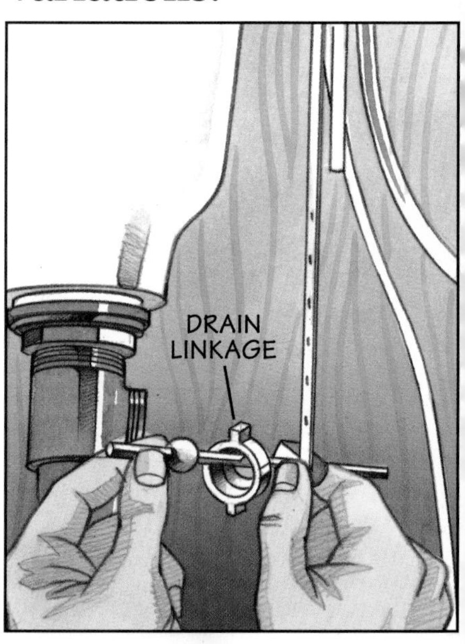

Sink with faucet mounted on the countertop: Disconnect pop-up drain linkage from the tailpiece of the sink drain by unscrewing the retaining nut.

Self-rimming sink: Disconnect the plumbing, then slice through any caulking or sealant between the sink rim and the countertop with a utility knife. Lift the sink off the countertop.

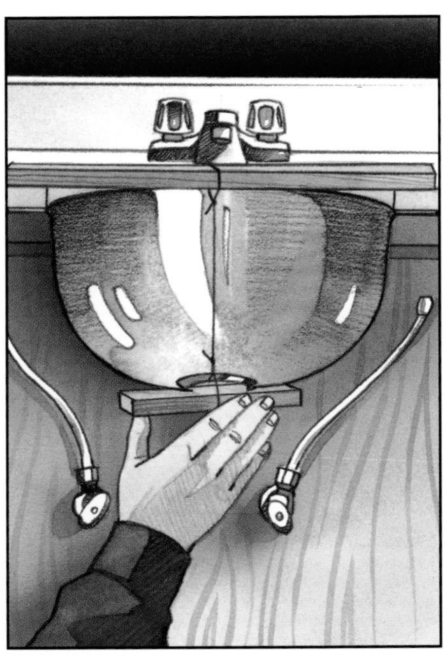

Rimless sink: Disconnect the plumbing; support the sink with wire and wood scraps, as shown. Twist the wire until it's taut, then detach the mounting clips. Slice the caulking, slowly loosen the wire, and remove the sink.

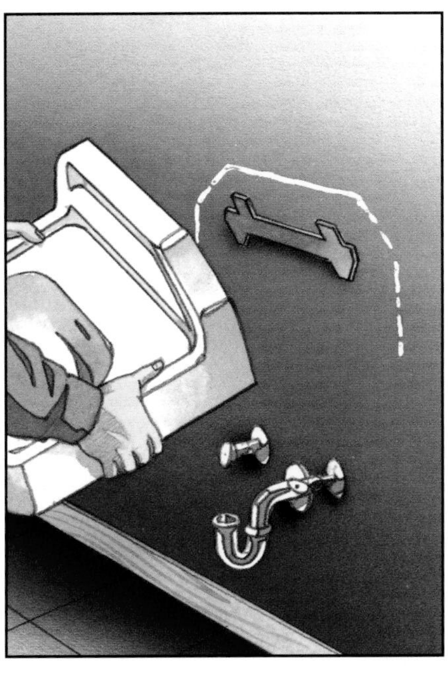

Wall-mounted sink: Disconnect the plumbing and slice through any caulking or sealant. Lift the sink off the wall brackets. (If it's attached to the wall with lag screws, wedge 2x4s between the sink and the floor. This supports the sink while you remove the screws.)

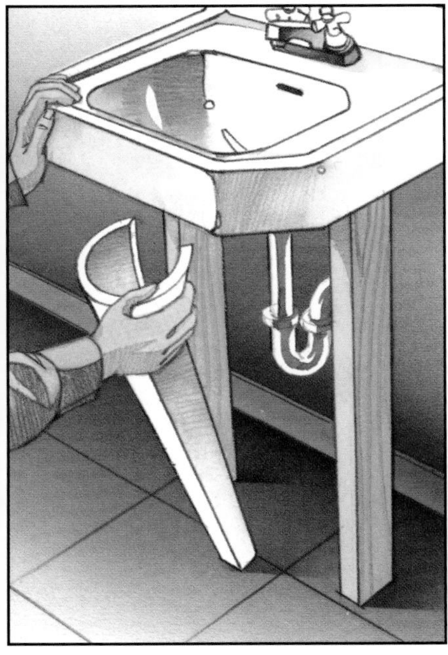

Pedestal sink: Disconnect the plumbing. If the sink and pedestal are bolted together, disconnect them. Remove the pedestal first, supporting the sink from below with 2x4s. Lift the sink off the wall brackets.

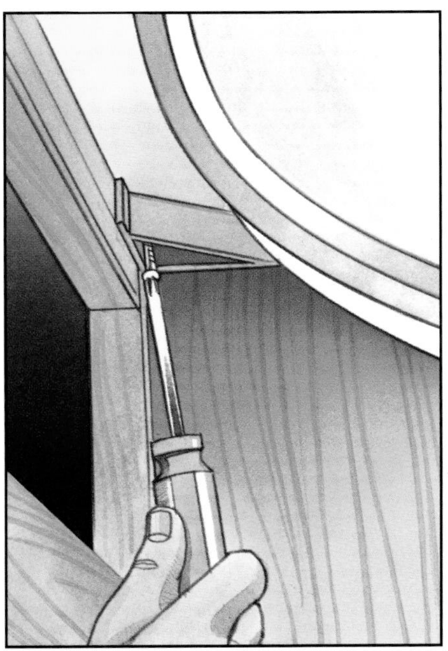

Integral sink-countertop: Disconnect the plumbing, then detach the mounting hardware under the countertop. Slice through the caulk or sealant between the countertop and the wall and between the countertop and the vanity. Now lift the sink-countertop unit off the vanity.

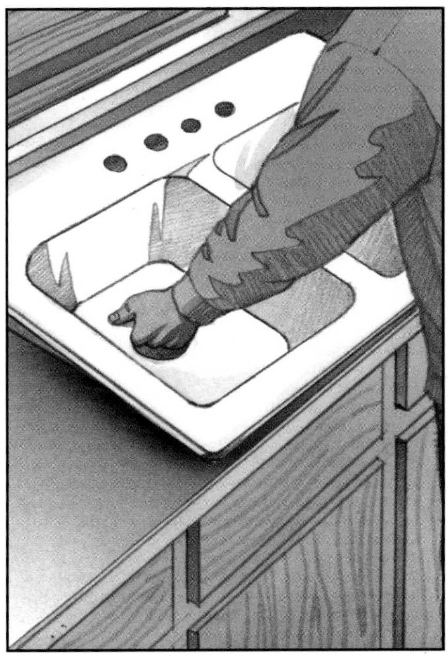

Kitchen sink: Similar to self-rimming sink (above). If sink is connected to a disposal unit or dishwasher, disconnecting the plumbing will be a little more complicated and time-consuming. If access to the underside of the sink is limited, install the faucet before reinstalling the sink.

INSTALLING AN INTEGRAL SINK-COUNTERTOP

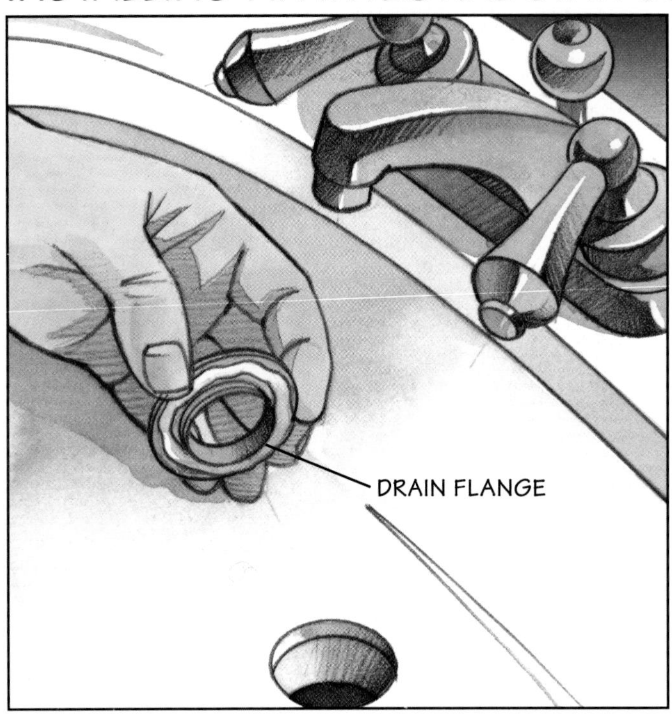

1 Set the sink-countertop on top of sawhorses. Attach the faucet and slip the drain lever through the faucet body. Place a ring of plumber's putty around the drain flange, then insert the flange in the drain opening. Use silicone caulk for the drain flange if your sink is made of cultured marble.

2 Thread the locknut and sealing gasket onto the drain tailpiece. Insert the tailpiece into the drain opening and screw it onto the drain flange. Tighten the locknut securely. Attach the tailpiece extension. Insert the pop-up stopper linkage.

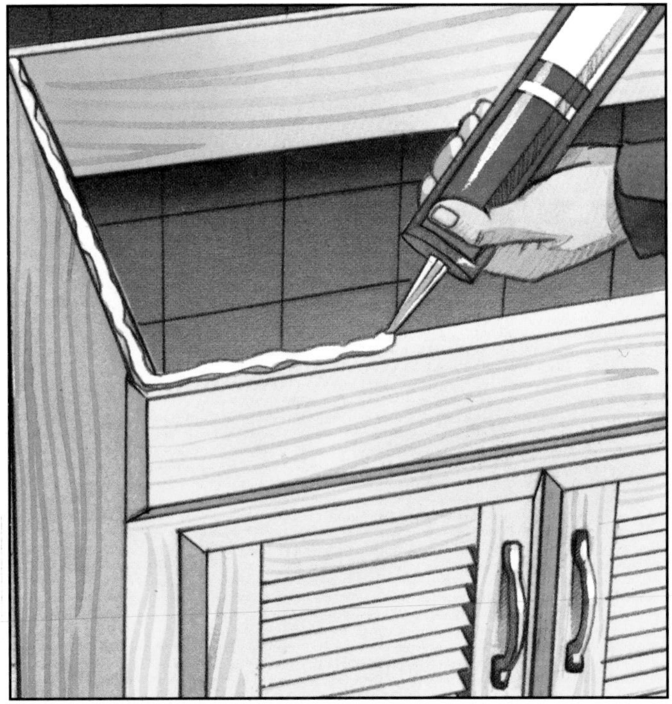

3 Apply a layer of tub and tile caulk (or an adhesive, if specified by the countertop manufacturer) to the top edges of the vanity and to any corner braces.

4 Center the sink-countertop unit over the vanity so that the overhang is equal on both sides and the backsplash of the countertop is flush with the wall. Press the countertop evenly into the caulk.

Variation:

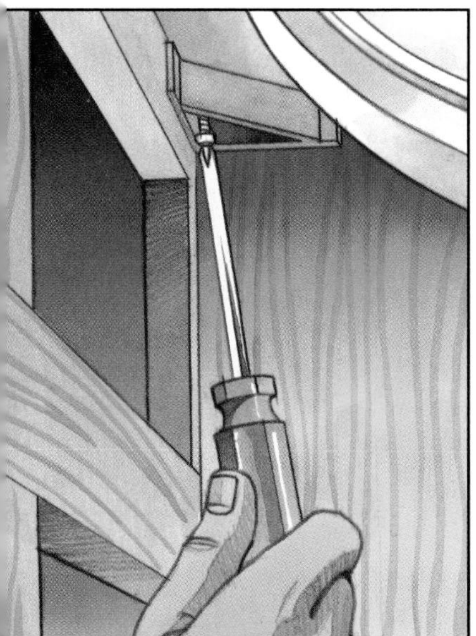

Cabinets with corner braces: Secure the countertop to the cabinet by driving a mounting screw through each corner brace and up into the countertop.

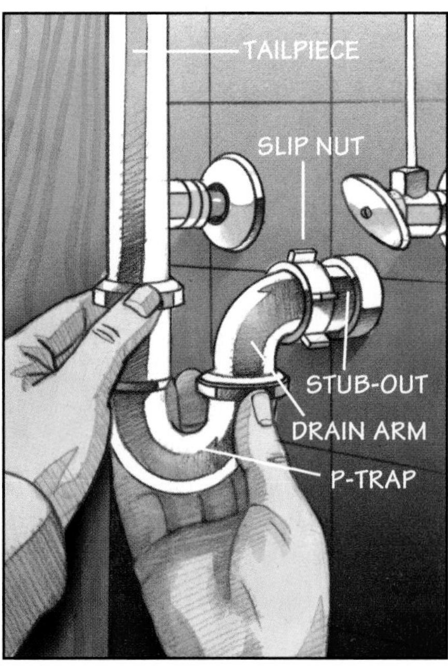

5 Attach the drain arm to the drain stub-out with a slip nut. Attach one end of the P-trap to the drain arm and the other to the tailpiece of the sink drain using slip nuts. Connect the supply tubes to the faucet tailpieces.

6 Seal the gap between the backsplash and the wall with tub and tile caulk.

Plumbing

USE A HIGH-QUALITY CAULK TO ENSURE LONG-TERM PROTECTION.

INSTALLING A DROP-IN SINK

1 Use a template ½ inch narrower than the sink rim to mark the countertop cutout. Drill a ³⁄₈" starter hole, then use a jigsaw to make the cutout. (For countertop-mounted faucets, drill faucet tailpiece holes according to the faucet manufacturer's directions.)

2 Apply a bead of silicone caulk around the sink cutout. Before you set the sink in place, attach the faucet body to the sink or countertop (pages 118-119), then attach the drainpiece and drain flange and the pop-up drain assembly.

3 Set the sink into the cutout area and gently press the rim of the sink into the silicone caulk. Hook up the drain and supply fittings, then caulk around the sink rim.

Installing a Pedestal Sink

1 Install 2x4 blocking between wall studs, behind the planned sink location. Cover the studs with water-resistant wallboard.

2 Set the basin and pedestal in position, bracing the basin with 2x4s. Outline the top of the basin on the wall, and mark the base of the pedestal on the floor. Mark reference points on the wall and floor through the mounting holes found on the back of the sink and bottom of the pedestal.

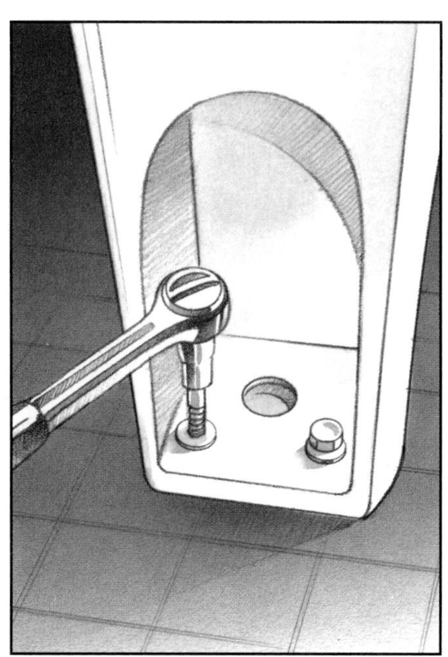

3 Set aside the basin and pedestal. Drill pilot holes in the wall and floor at reference points, then reposition the pedestal. Anchor the pedestal to the floor with lag screws. Do not over-tighten the screws.

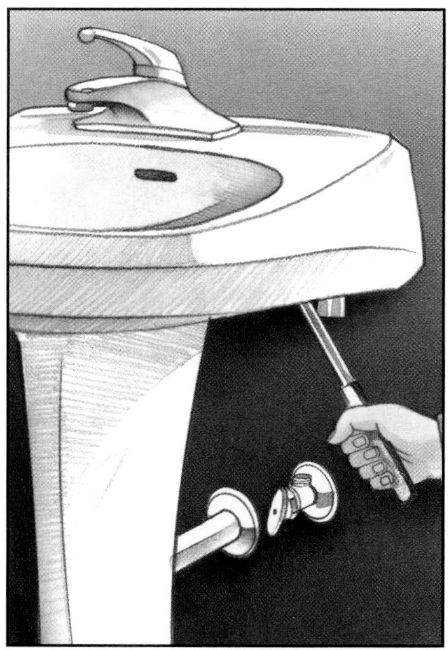

4 Attach the faucet (pages 118-119), then set the sink on the pedestal. Align the holes in the back of the sink with the pilot holes drilled in the wall, then drive lag screws and washers into the wall brace, using a ratchet wrench. Do not overtighten.

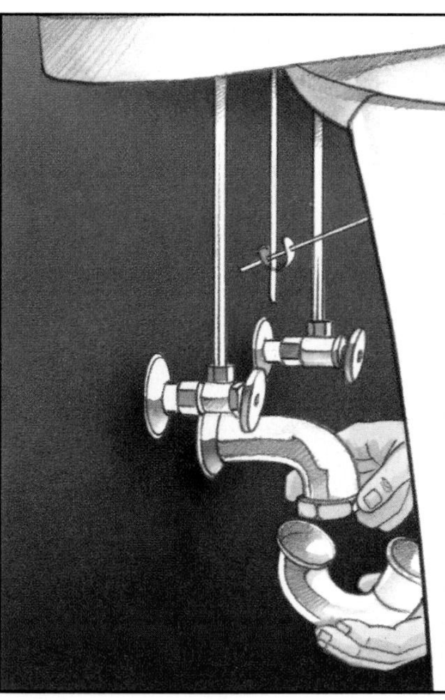

5 Hook up the drain and supply fittings (see pages 97 to 101). Caulk between the back of the sink and the wall when installation is finished (page 113).

Installing a Kitchen Sink

When, after a few years of daily use, your kitchen sink has gained a thoroughly disreputable patina, nothing will freshen the look and feel of your kitchen as immediately as a new sink. Fortunately, replacing a kitchen sink is not difficult.

Kitchen sinks are made from cast iron coated with enamel, enameled steel, and stainless steel. Some bargain-priced sinks are made with flimsy lightweight steel that will flex and dent with use. Avoid them.

Determine how much use and abuse the sink will receive. Kids aren't always the easiest on them with flying silverware and piles of dirty pots, pans and dishes. Choose one with durable construction and a high quality finish.

CAST-IRON SINKS ARE HEAVY; GET HELP TO SET THEM IN PLACE.

INSTALLING A FRAMELESS KITCHEN SINK

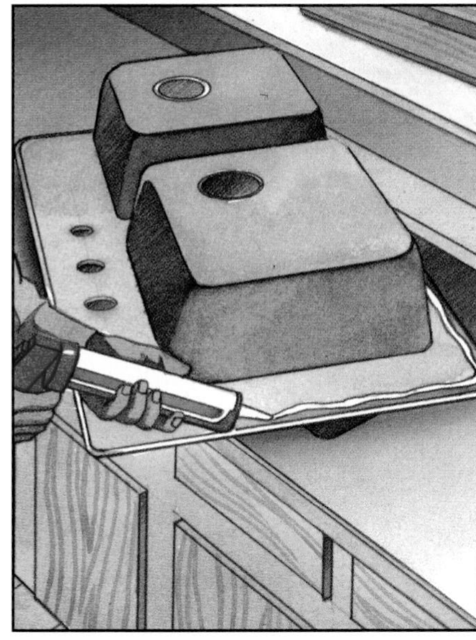

1 After making countertop cutout, lay the sink upside down. Apply a 1/4 inch bead of silicone caulk or plumber's putty around the underside of sink flange.

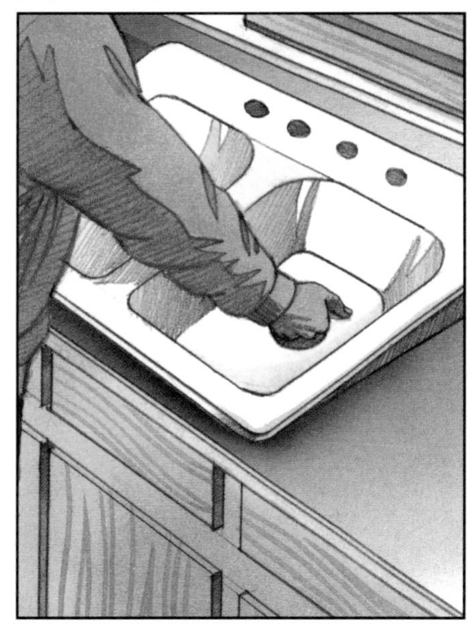

2 Position the sink's front in the countertop cutout by holding the sink from the drain openings. Carefully lower the sink into position. Press down to create a tight seal, then wipe away excess caulk.

Plumbing

INSTALLING A FRAMED KITCHEN SINK

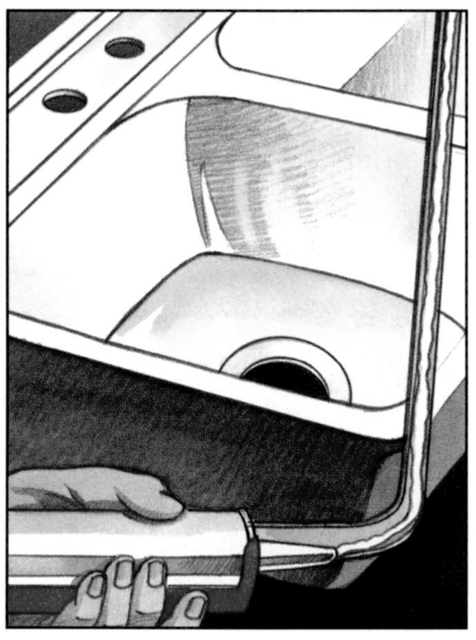

1 Turn the sink frame upside down. Apply a 1/4 inch bead of silicone caulk or plumber's putty around both sides of the vertical flange.

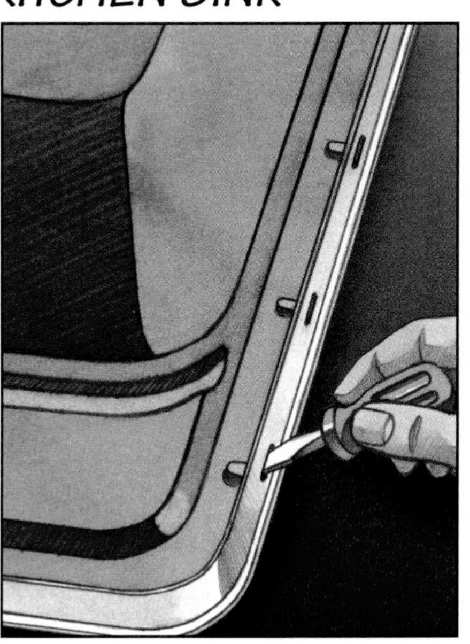

2 Set the sink upside down inside the frame. Bend frame tabs to hold the sink. Carefully set the sink into the cutout opening, and press down to create a tight seal.

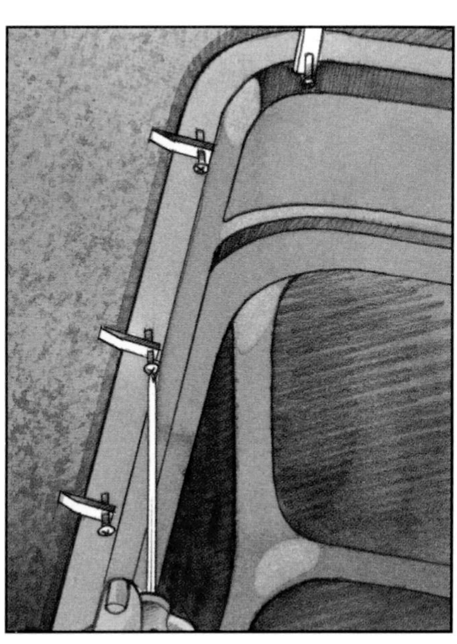

3 Hook mounting clips every 6 to 8 inches around the frame from underneath countertop. Tighten mounting screws. Wipe away excess caulk from the frame.

Repairing & Replacing Faucets

Installing a new faucet is an easy project that, under normal circumstances, should take about an hour. Before buying a new faucet, first do some measuring: find the diameter of the sink openings and also measure the distance between the tailpieces (measured on-center). Make sure the new faucet's tailpieces match the sink openings.

Buy a faucet made by a reputable manufacturer, which may not be the least expensive choice, but will make it easier to find replacement parts when the time comes. Better faucets have solid brass bodies. They're easier to install and provide years of trouble-free service. Some washerless models have lifetime warranties.

Always install new supply tubes when replacing a faucet, because they can wear out too and you'll have the most difficult part done just by removing the faucet. Besides, you'll want to minimize the number of times you have to crawl into that cramped little space under the sink! And if the water pipes under the sink don't have shutoff valves (page 97), you'll definitely want to install some at this time.

BUYER'$ GUIDE

Choosing the Right Faucet

Besides price, what's the difference between the high end and the low end of faucet selection? Some would say "style," but that, of course, is a matter of taste. The biggest difference is quality. Expensive faucets have durable brass bodies and leakproof cartridges. Cheap faucets are plastic and practically disposable. The one you choose will depend on where it's used, and how often.

ANATOMY OF A FAUCET (view from behind sink)

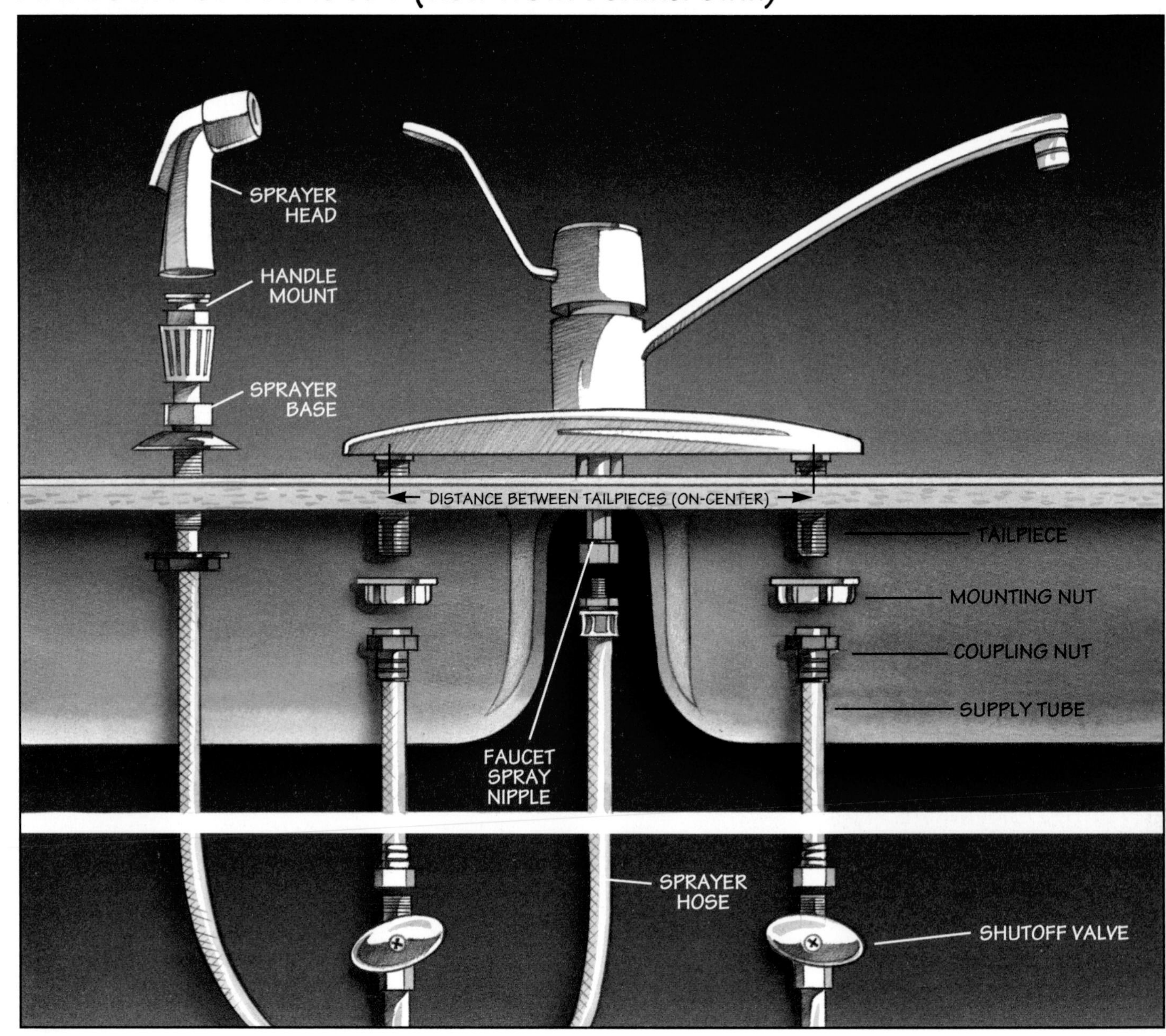

HOW TO REMOVE AN OLD SINK FAUCET

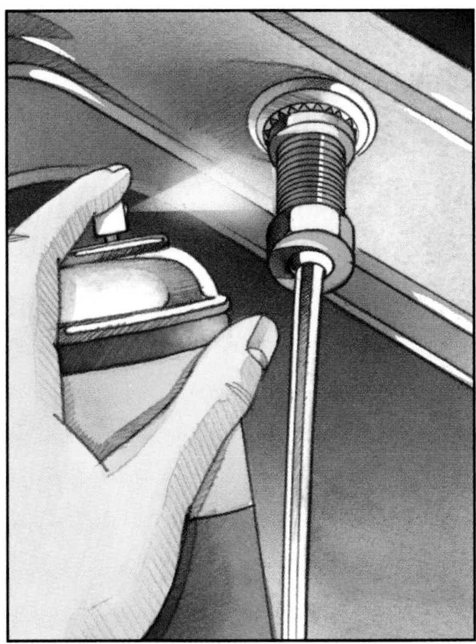

1 Apply penetrating oil to the tailpiece mounting nuts and the supply-tube coupling nuts. Remove the coupling nuts with a basin wrench or water-pump pliers.

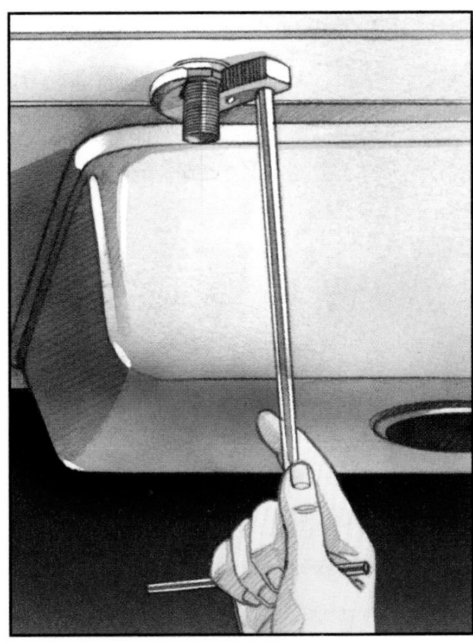

2 Remove the tailpiece mounting nuts the same way (a basin wrench has a long handle that makes it easier to use in tight areas).

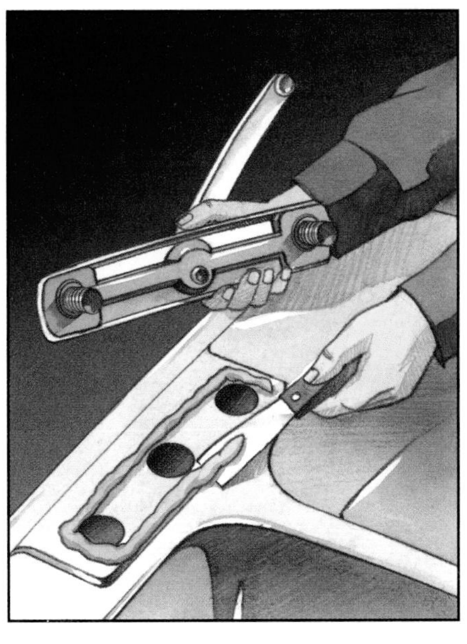

3 Remove the faucet. Use a putty knife to clean away old putty from the sink surface.

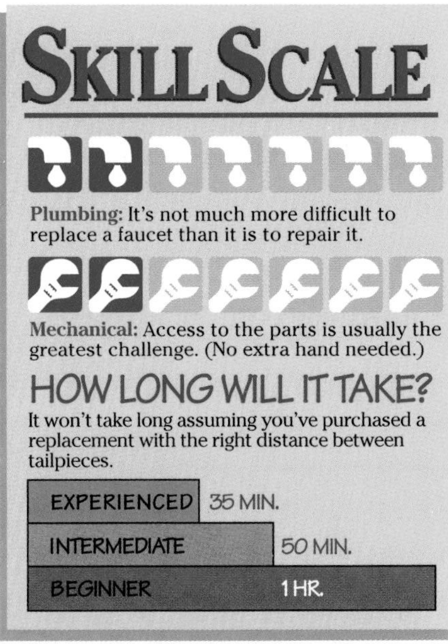

STUFF YOU'LL NEED:

- **Tools:** Basic plumbing tool kit (page 86).
- **Materials:** Plumber's putty.

FAUCET HOOKUP VARIATIONS

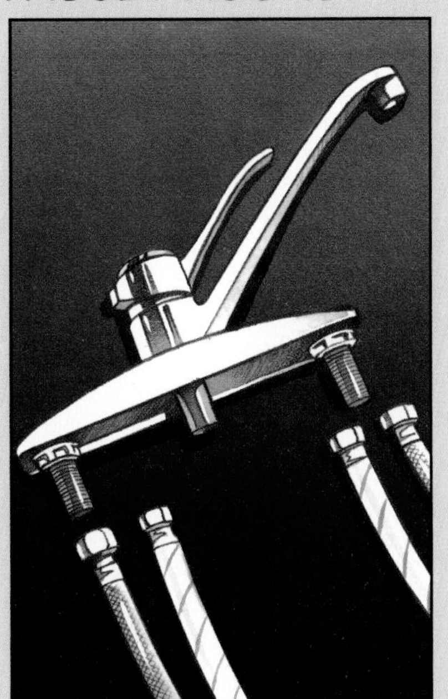

New faucet without supply tubes: Buy two supply tubes. They're available in braided steel, vinyl mesh, PB plastic or chromed copper. The more flexible the tube, the easier it is to install.

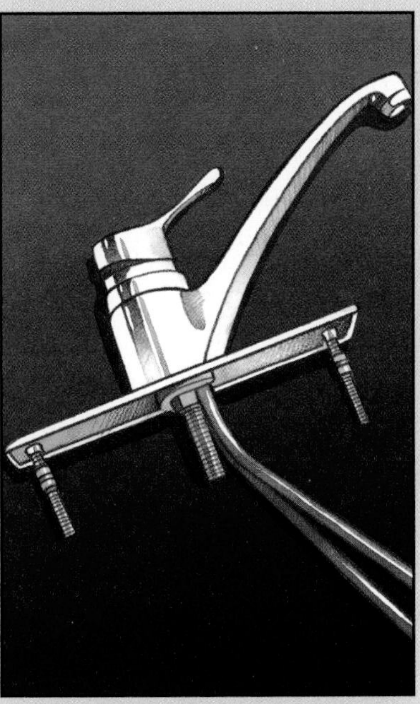

New faucet with pre-attached copper supply tubing: Make water connections by attaching the supply tubing directly to the shutoff valves with compression fittings. Extra tubing may be needed to reach the supply lines.

Installing a New Faucet

Faucets, like just about everything else, go in and out of style. If yours are hopelessly out of fashion–and that bothers you–you might consider replacing them. Keep in mind, too, that the older your faucets are, the harder it might be to find replacement parts.

Whether you are putting in a new faucet in your bathroom or your kitchen, the procedure is essentially the same, and these steps apply. Of course, in a kitchen sink you may have to also deal with a sink sprayer and in a bathroom sink you'll probably be looking at a pop-up drain assembly to attach, but it's nothing you can't handle.

This is a good time to read the manufacturer's suggestions regarding installation. That way, you'll know about any little quirks you might encounter before you encounter them.

MOUNTING A FAUCET

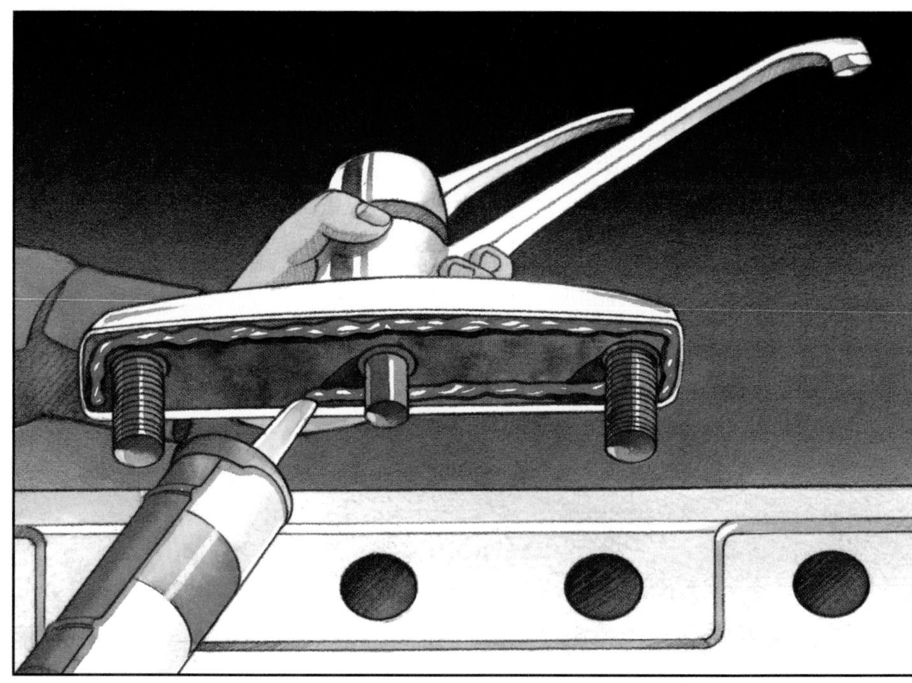

1 Apply a 1/4" bead of plumber's putty (or silicone caulk, if you're using cultured marble) around the base of the faucet. Insert the faucet tailpieces into the sink openings. Position the faucet so that the base is parallel to the back of the sink. Press the faucet down to make sure the putty forms a good seal.

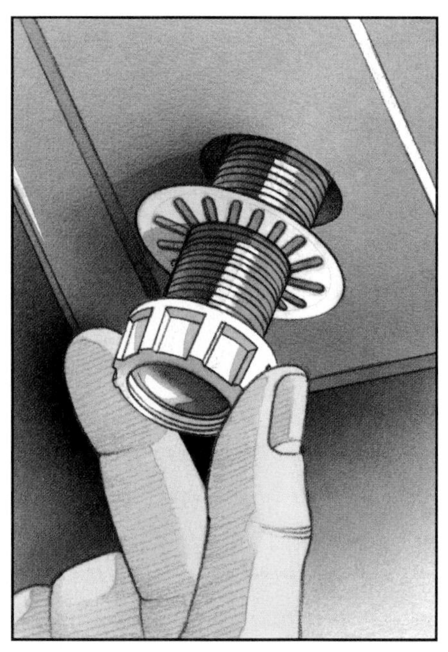

2 Screw the metal friction washers and the mounting nuts onto the tailpieces, then tighten them with a basin wrench or water-pump pliers. Wipe away excess putty around the base of the faucet.

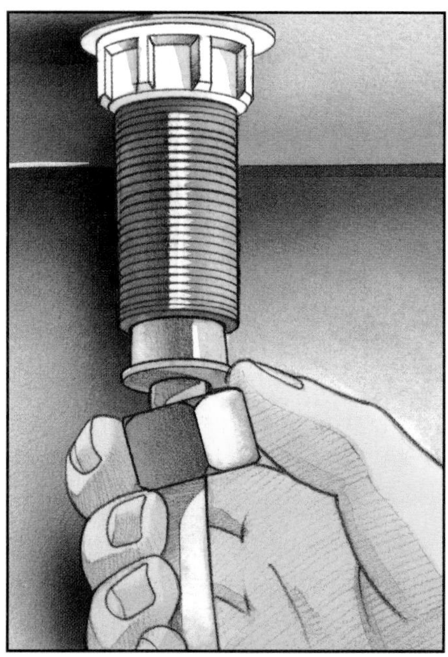

3 Connect the flexible supply tubes to the faucet tailpieces. Tighten the coupling nuts with a basin wrench or water-pump pliers.

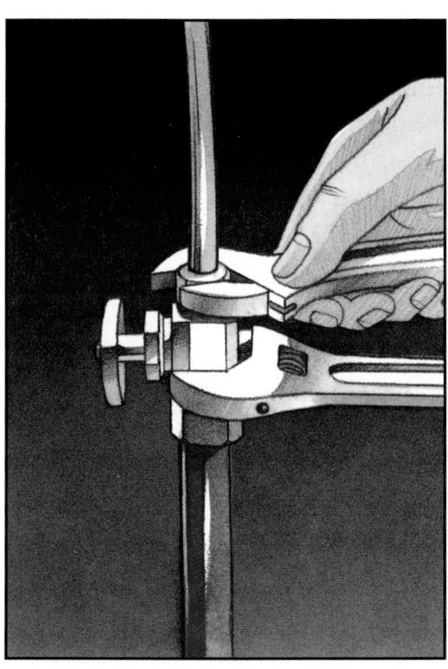

4 Attach the supply tubes to the shutoff valves. Hand-tighten the nuts, then give them an extra quarter-turn with an adjustable wrench. (If necessary, hold the valve with another wrench while you tighten them.)

CONNECTING A FAUCET WITH PRE-ATTACHED SUPPLY TUBING

1 Attach the faucet to the sink by placing a rubber gasket, retainer ring, and locknut onto the threaded tailpiece. Tighten the locknut with a basin wrench or water-pump pliers.

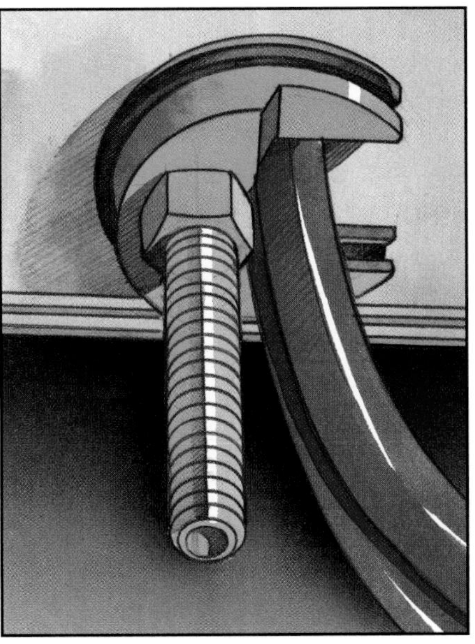

2 Some center-mounted faucets have a decorative coverplate. Secure the coverplate from below with washers and locknuts screwed onto the coverplate bolts.

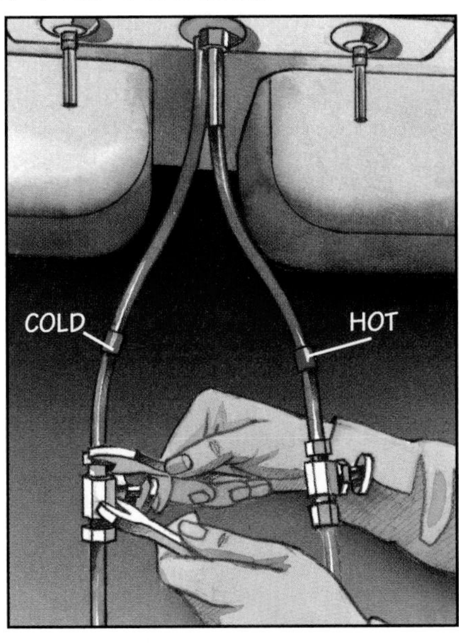

3 Connect the pre-attached supply tubing to the shutoff valves with compression fittings. The red-coded tube should be attached to the hot-water pipe, blue-coded to the cold.

Plumbing

ATTACHING A SINK SPRAYER

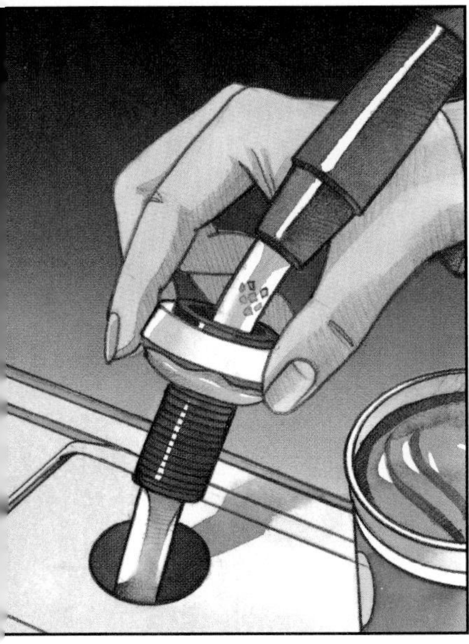

1 Apply a quarter-inch bead of plumber's putty to the bottom edge of the sprayer base. Insert the tailpiece of the sprayer base into the sink opening.

2 Place a friction washer over the tailpiece. Screw the mounting nut onto the tailpiece and tighten it with a basin wrench or water-pump pliers. Wipe away excess putty around the base.

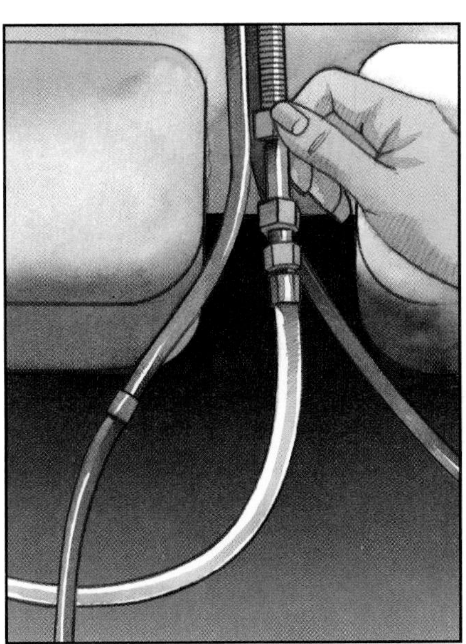

3 Screw the sprayer hose onto the hose nipple on the bottom of the faucet. Tighten a quarter-turn, using a basin wrench or water-pump pliers.

Fixing Your Faucets

Few escape, at least once in life, the "drip, drip, drip" of a leaky faucet. Comfort yourself with this thought: it's one of the easiest plumbing problems to fix. Even if your first repair attempt–replacing the washer, O-ring, or seals–only reduces your problem to a still-pesky "drip (pause) drip," replacing the whole thing shouldn't take you more than an hour.

First determine which faucet type you have: cartridge (either disc-type or sleeve-type), ball-type, or compression. This is important, because the repairs and parts are different for each one. If you can, find out what brand and even the model number of the faucet. Many stores will carry complete repair kits for specific faucet manufacturers.

Skill Scale

Plumbing: Most faucet repairs require beginning plumbing skills.

Mechanical: Basic mechanical skills are required for most faucet repairs.

How Long Will It Take?

Time required will vary with the style of faucet you're repairing. Times listed are average.

EXPERIENCED	20 MIN.
INTERMEDIATE	40 MIN.
BEGINNER	1 HR.

Stuff You'll Need:

- **Tools:** Basic plumbing tool kit (page 86).
- **Materials:** Plumber's putty.

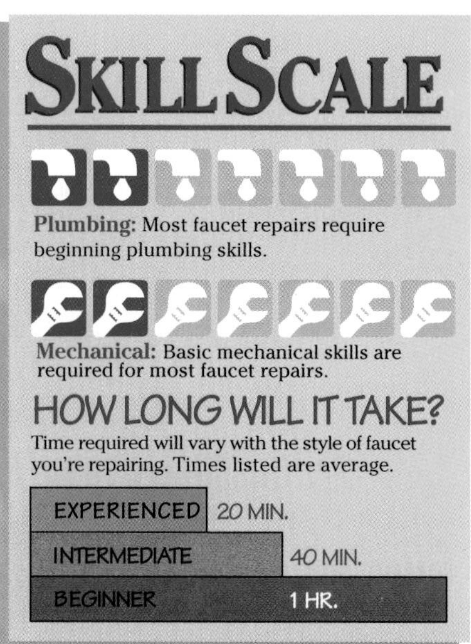

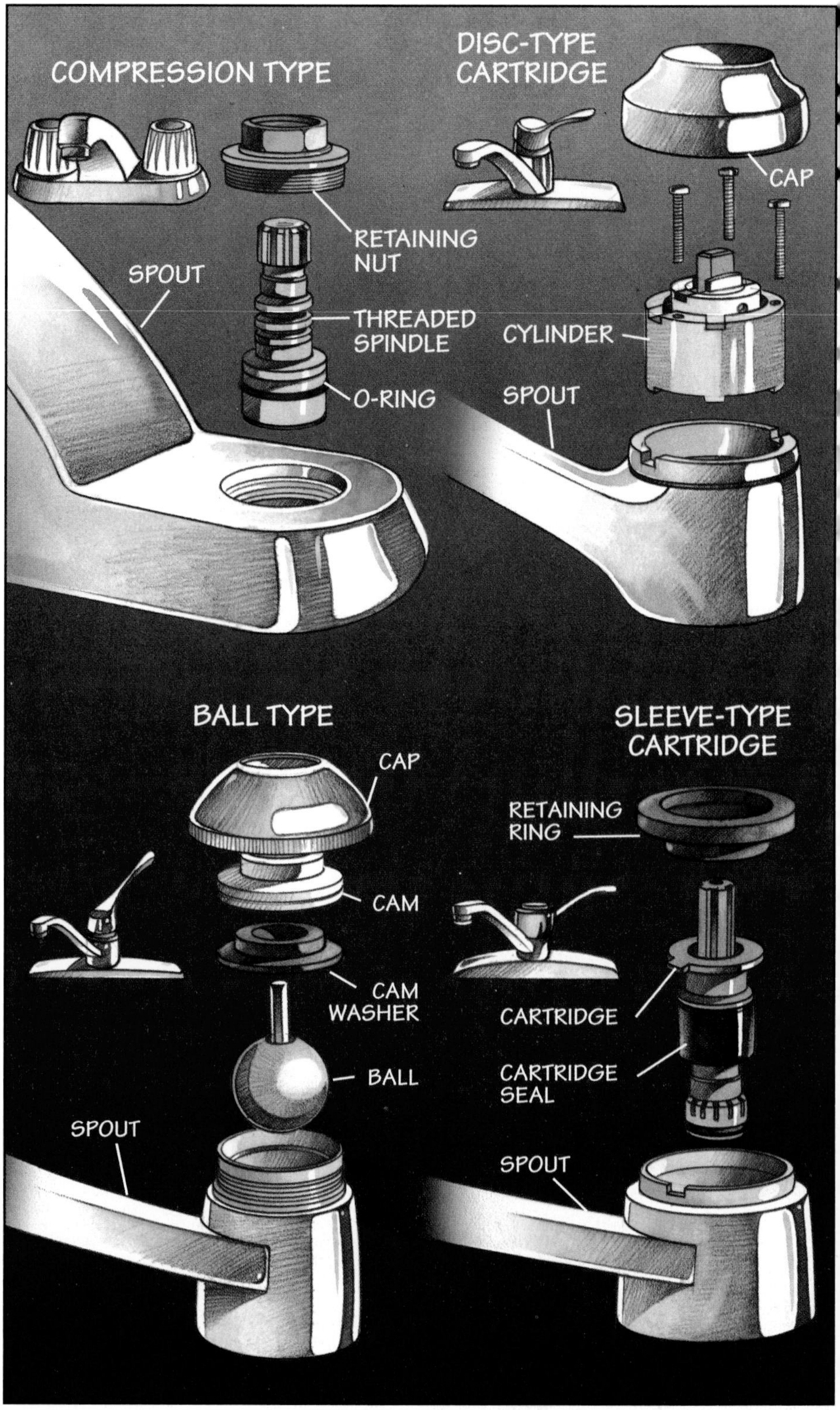

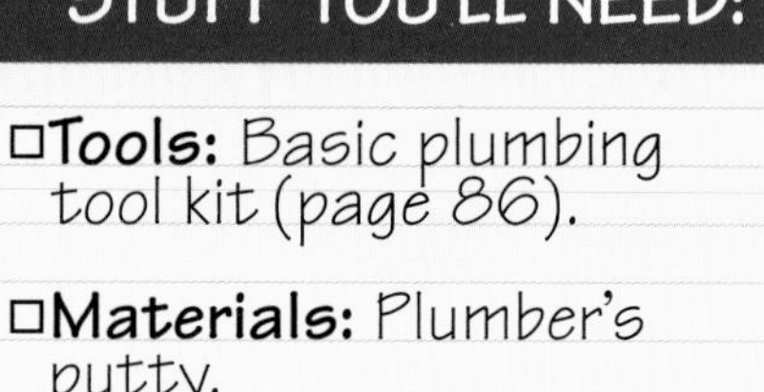

Identify your faucet type: Faucets can be grouped into four distinct types. The repair procedure varies with each type. **Compression faucets** usually have separate hot and cold handles. Repair often entails replacing worn or cracked washers. **Disc-type cartridge faucets** have a single handle that lifts and rotates. Repair usually means replacing the cartridge. **Ball-type faucets** have a single handle over a dome-shaped cap. Replacement parts are available in repair kits. **Sleeve-type cartridge faucets** can be single- or double-handled, but are washerless. Repair with replacement cartridges.

Cleaning a Clogged Aerator

If your faucet doesn't have an even stream of water, or its pressure seems low, unscrew the aerator sleeve, separate all the

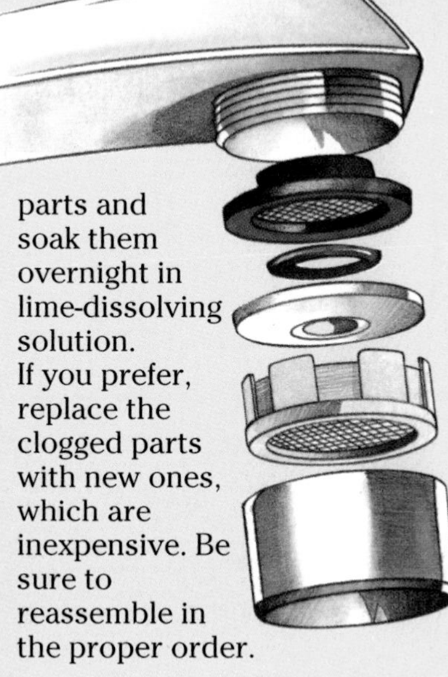

parts and soak them overnight in lime-dissolving solution. If you prefer, replace the clogged parts with new ones, which are inexpensive. Be sure to reassemble in the proper order.

FIXING A COMPRESSION FAUCET

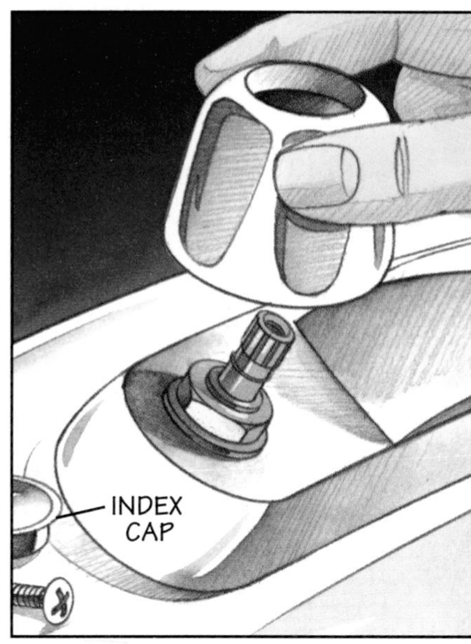

1 Remove index cap from top of faucet handle, and remove handle screw. Remove handle by pulling straight up. If necessary, use a handle puller to remove handle (page 122).

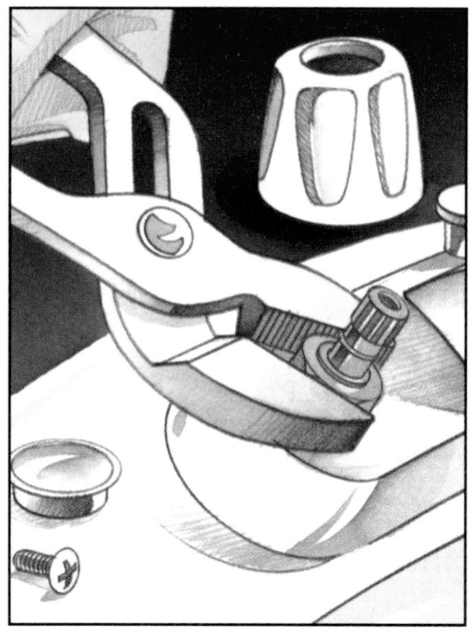

2 Unscrew the stem assembly from body of faucet, using water-pump pliers. Inspect valve seat for wear, and replace or resurface as needed (page 122). If faucet body or stems are badly worn, it usually is best to replace the faucet (pages 116-119).

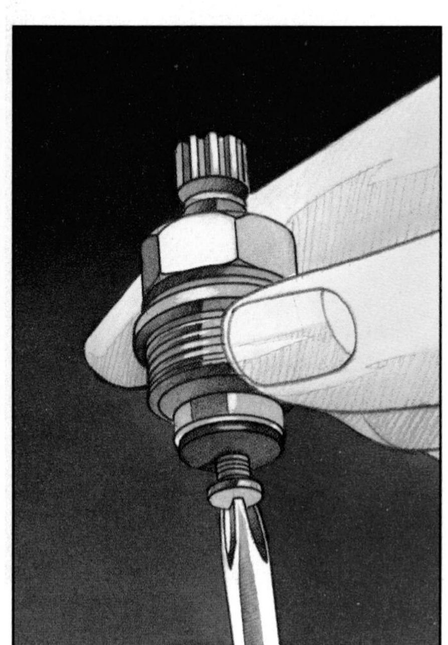

3 Remove the brass stem screw from the stem assembly. Remove worn stem washer.

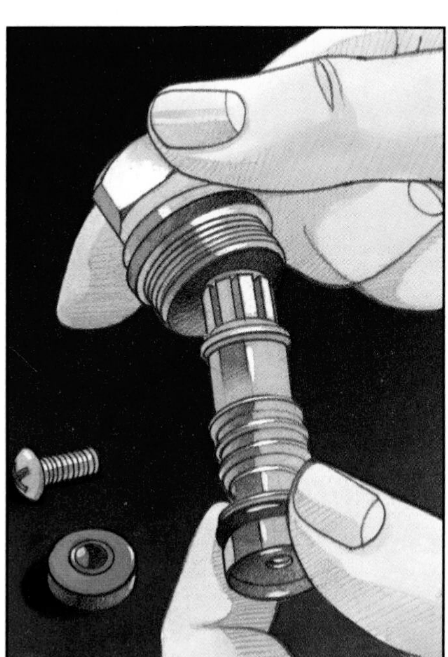

4 Unscrew the threaded spindle from the retaining nut.

5 Cut off O-ring and replace with an exact duplicate. Install new washer and stem screw. Coat all parts with heatproof grease, then reassemble the faucet.

UNLESS YOU WANT A SHOWER, ALWAYS TURN OFF THE WATER AT THE SUPPLY TUBES BEFORE DISASSEMBLING YOUR FAUCET.

REPLACING WORN VALVE SEATS

1 Feel around the rim of the seat for any damage; if it feels rough in there, replace the seat if it has flat edges. A round seat isn't replaceable. Double-check by looking into the valve with a flashlight.

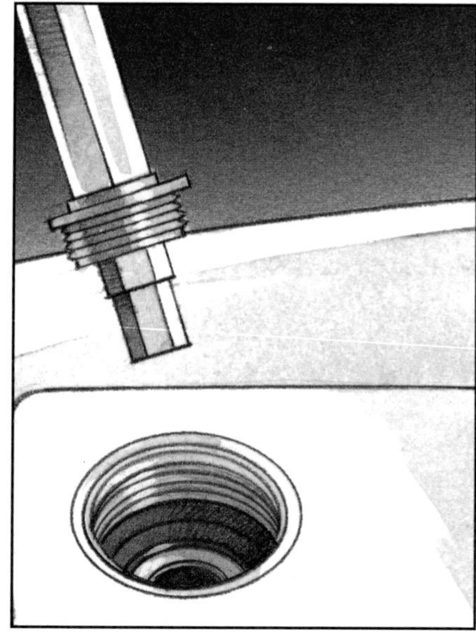

2 Insert the end of the seat wrench which fits the seat into the valve and turn it counter-clockwise to remove the seat. Then install a new seat, an exact duplicate. Lubricate the threads of the seat before inserting it. If the seat can't be removed, resurface it with a seat-dressing tool.

RESURFACING VALVE SEATS

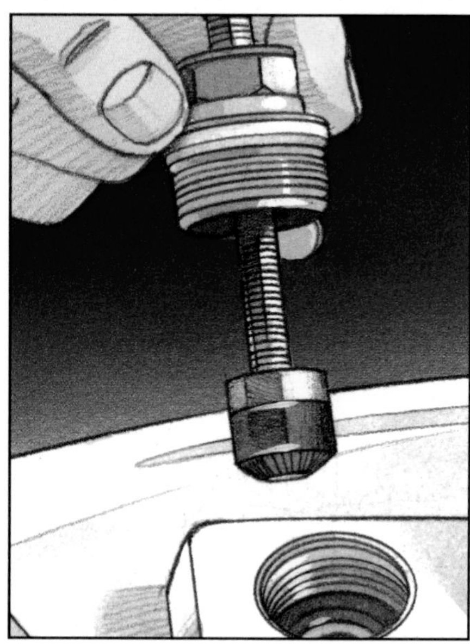

1 Select cutter head to fit the inside diameter of retaining nut. Slide retaining nut over threaded shaft of seat-dressing tool, then attach the locknut and cutter head to the shaft.

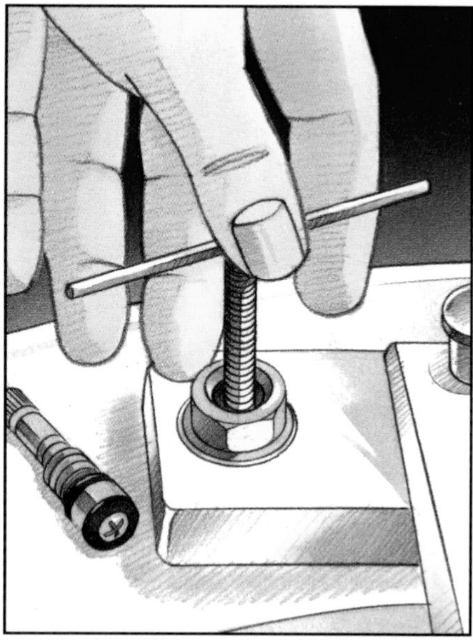

2 Screw retaining nut loosely into faucet body. Press the tool down lightly and turn tool handle clockwise two or three rotations. Reassemble valve.

IF VALVE SEAT IS SERIOUSLY NICKED OR ROUGH, IT CANNOT BE RESURFACED.

TOOLTIPS

Specialty Tools for Faucets: Along with your basic plumbing tools, a few special-purpose tools may come in handy some day. When you need them, nothing else will work as well, but you may not need them for years. So, unless you're really eager, you might want to postpone buying them until the situation comes up. Then try to borrow them first.

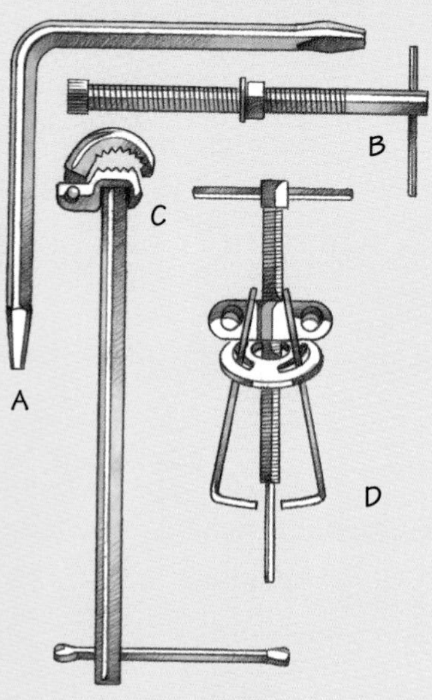

A) A **seat wrench** is used to reach into the faucet stem socket to remove or tighten removable seats.
(B) A **seat-dressing** tool smooths and resurfaces non-removable valve seats.
(C) A **basin wrench** makes it easier to reach and turn faucet mounting nuts.
(D) A **handle puller** removes stubborn handles without damaging them.

FIXING YOUR CERAMIC DISC FAUCET

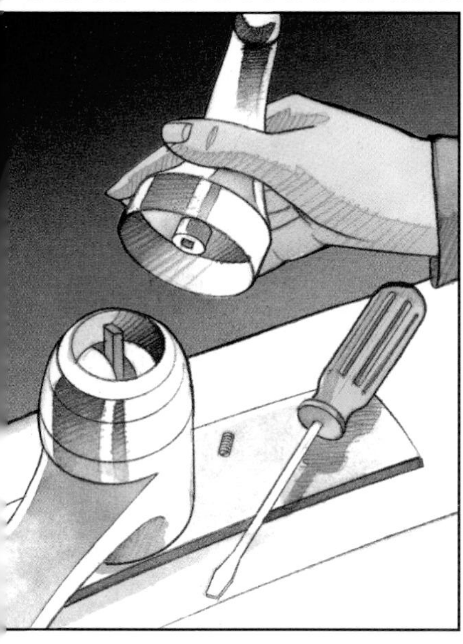

1 Rotate the faucet spout to the side and raise the handle. Remove the setscrew and lift off the handle.

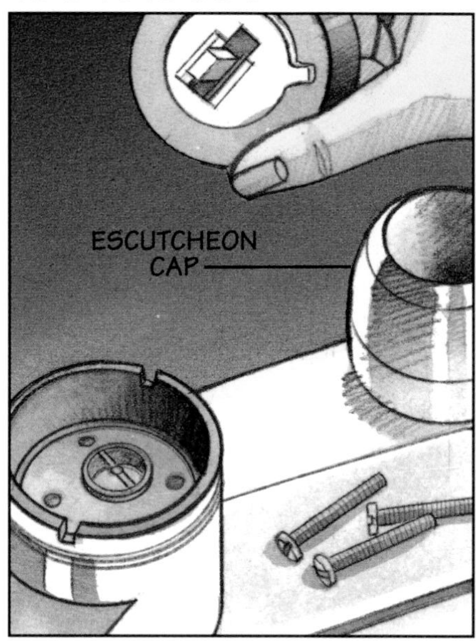

2 Remove the escutcheon cap, then take out the cartridge mounting screws and lift out the cylinder.

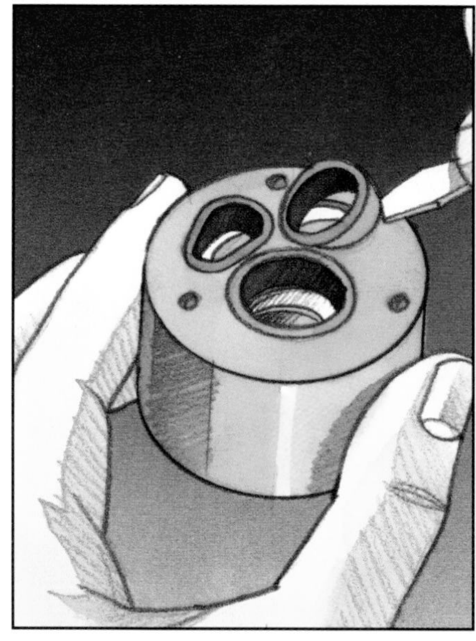

3 Remove the neoprene seals from the cylinder openings.

CLOSE YOUR DRAIN BEFORE DISASSEMBLING THE FAUCET SO YOU DON'T HAVE TO GO "FISHING" FOR PARTS IN THE TRAP!

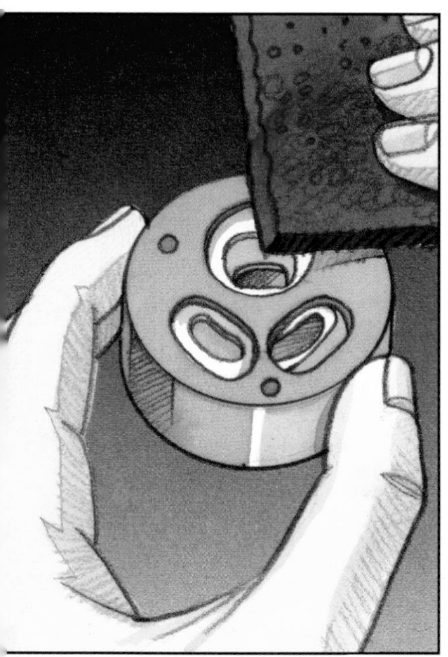

4 Clean the cylinder openings and the neoprene seals with a scouring pad. Rinse the cylinder with clear water.

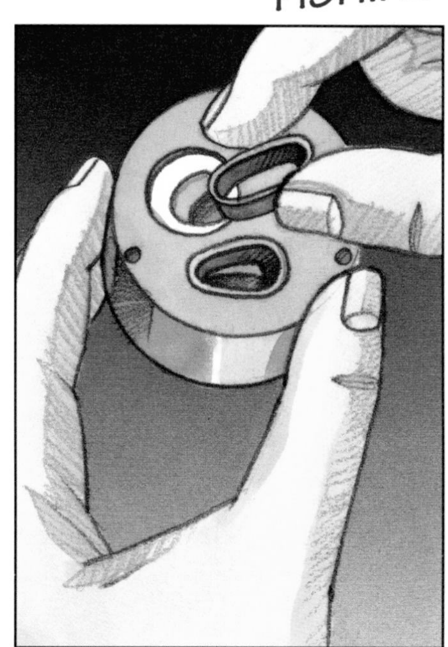

5 Return the seals to the cylinder openings and reassemble the faucet. Move the handle to the ON position and then SLOWLY open the shutoff valves. When the water runs steadily, close the faucet.

Install a new cylinder only if the faucet continues to leak after cleaning.

FIXING YOUR CARTRIDGE FAUCET

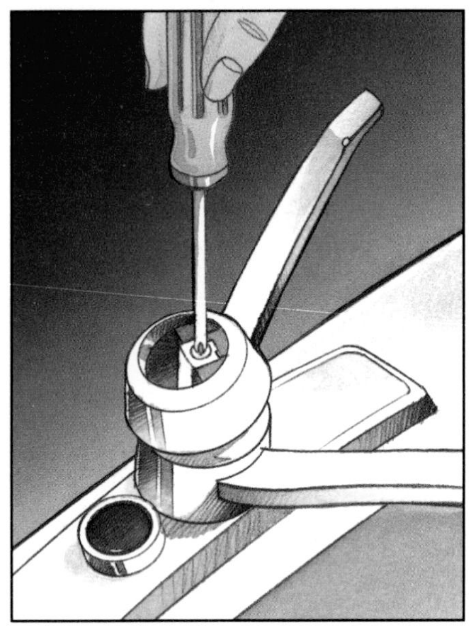

1 Pry off the index cap on the top of the faucet, and remove the handle screw underneath the cap.

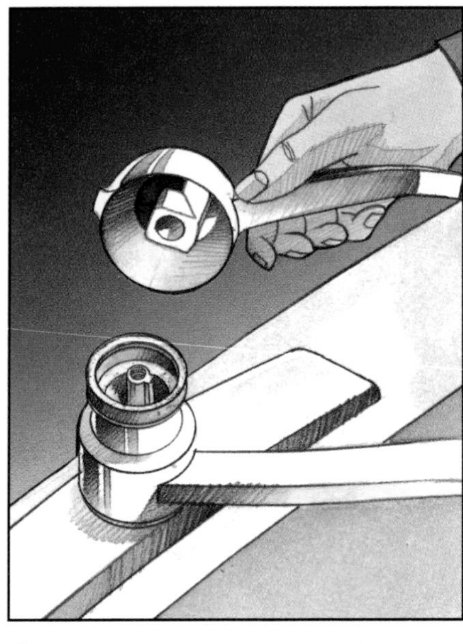

2 Remove the faucet handle by lifting it up and then tilting it backwards.

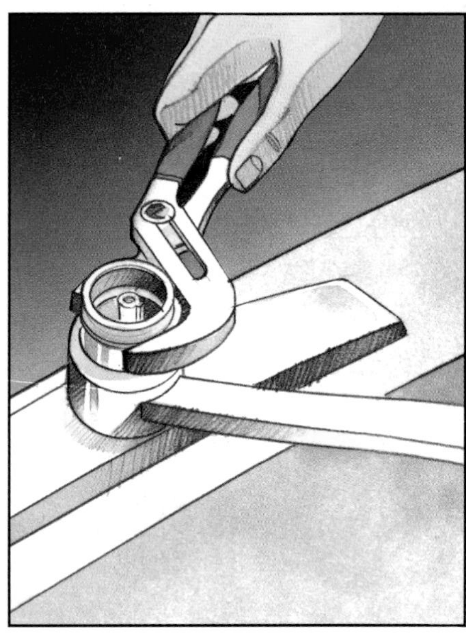

3 Remove the threaded retaining ring with water-pump pliers. Remove any retaining clip holding the cartridge in place.

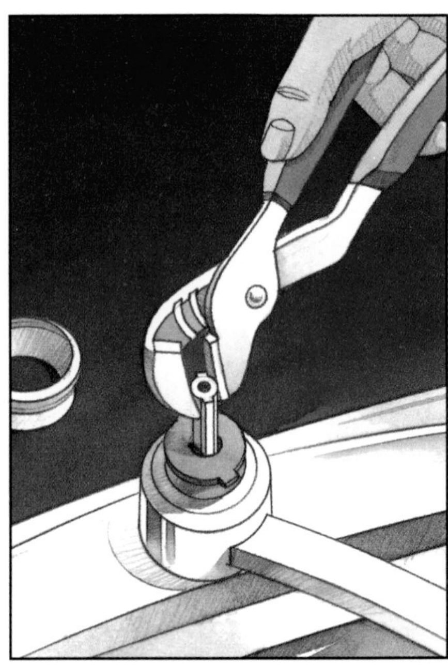

4 Grip the top of the cartridge with pliers. Pull straight up to remove the cartridge. Install the replacement cartridge so that the tab on the cartridge faces forward.

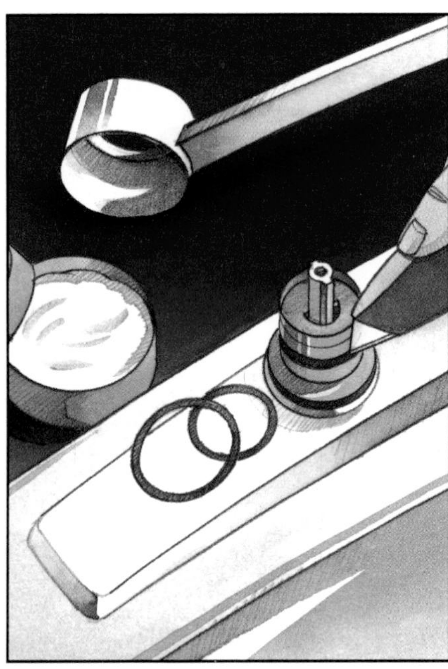

5 Remove the spout by pulling up and twisting, then cut off old O-rings with a utility knife. Coat new O-rings with heatproof grease and install.

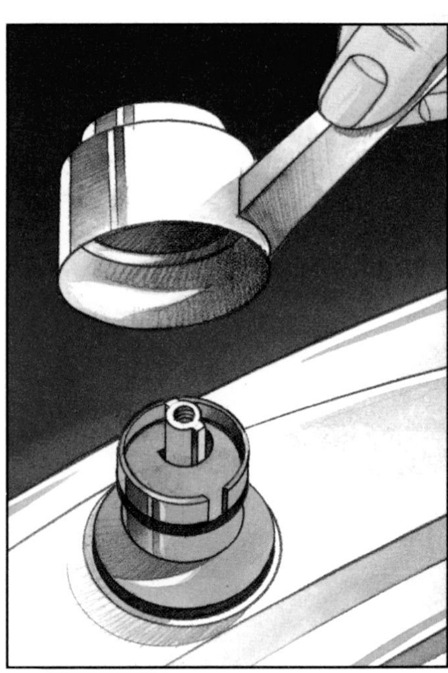

6 Reattach the spout. Screw the retaining ring onto the faucet, and tighten with water-pump pliers. Attach the handle, handle screw, and index cap.

FIXING YOUR BALL-TYPE FAUCET

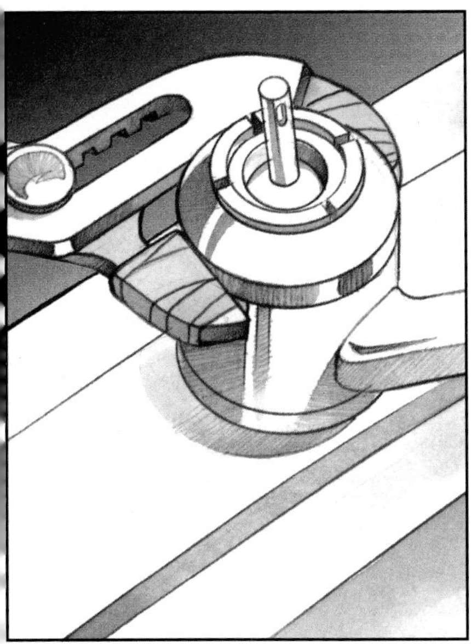

1 Loosen the handle setscrew and remove the handle to expose the faucet cap. Remove the cap with water-pump pliers. Be sure to wrap the pliers' jaws with masking tape or cloth to protect the cap from scratches or gouges.

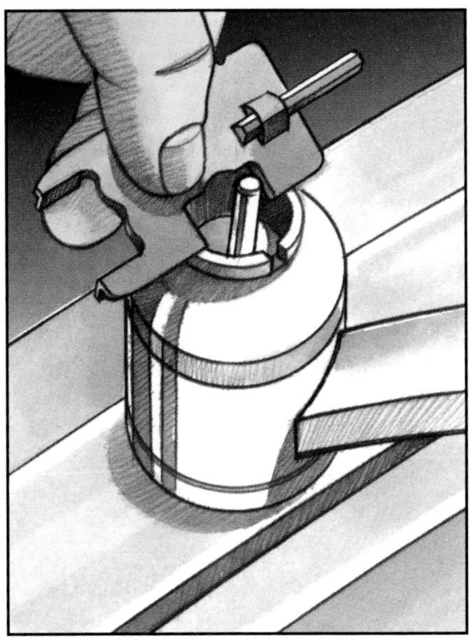

2 Using the special cam tool included in the faucet repair kit, loosen the faucet cam.

3 Lift out the faucet cam, cam washer, and the rotating ball. Check the ball for signs of wear.

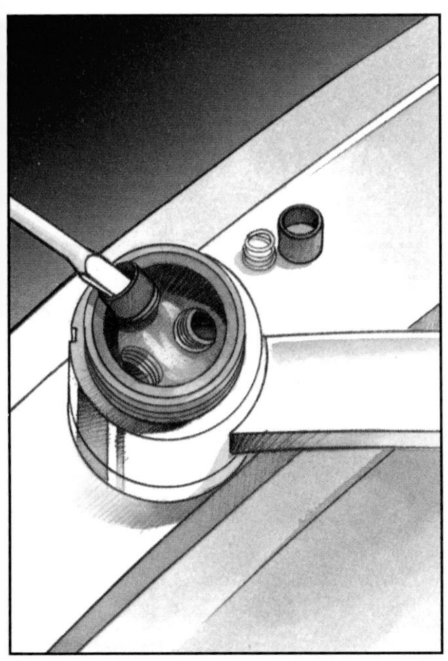

4 Reach into the faucet with a screwdriver and remove the springs and neoprene valve seats. Remove the spout by twisting it upward.

5 Cut off the old O-rings. Coat the new O-rings with heatproof grease and install. Reattach the spout, pressing downward until the collar rests on the plastic slip ring. Install new springs and valve seats.

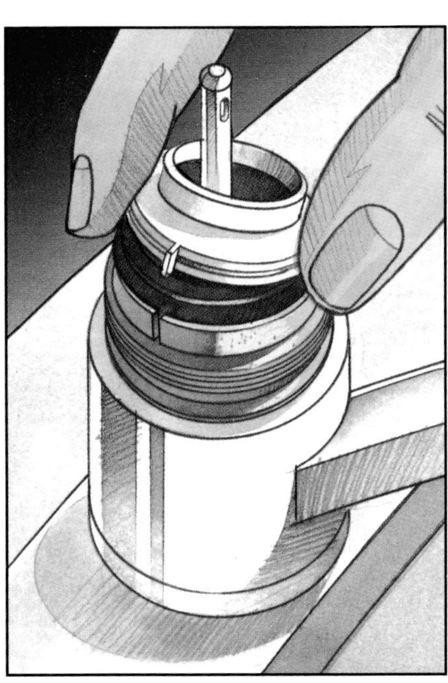

6 Insert the ball, new cam washer, and cam. The small lug on the cam should fit into the notch on the faucet body. Screw the cap onto the faucet and attach the handle.

Removing & Replacing Tubs

If nobody has mentioned it yet, here it is in black and white: removing a bathtub is a big deal.

You've probably observed that bathtubs are large, perhaps even concluded that they may be heavy. You'd be right. In older homes, they are typically cast iron.

And then, of course, they need to be disconnected from the water supply and drain systems. Since bathrooms are not known for their spaciousness, plan on removing the sink and toilet to buy yourself some elbow room while you cut open the wall and tear up the floor to set the old tub free. In other words, this is not a project to undertake unless your family life is exceptionally secure.

Once you get the silly thing out, your bathtub immediately becomes a disposal problem. You didn't want it–chances are, nobody else does, either. Fiberglass and polymer tubs can be cut into disposable pieces with a reciprocating saw. To break apart a cast iron tub, cover it with a heavy tarp and use a sledgehammer.

STUFF YOU'LL NEED:

- ☐**Tools:** Basic plumbing tool kit (page 86), grout saw, grout float, power drill & bit.
- ☐**Materials:** Caulk, grout, sponge, clean cloth.

Replacing a bathtub is a difficult job. In this instance, it doesn't hold true to think that by breaking it down into two smaller jobs, removing the old tub, then installing the new one, the overall job will be easier. You just end up with two difficult jobs! Since you're not talked out of it, here's what you'll need to do to get started.

Start off by cutting away at least 6" of wallboard above the tub on all sides, but first be sure to remove faucet handles, water spout, and the drain. Next, remove screws or nails that hold the tub flange to the studs. You may find a galvanized strip along the tub flange. Use a flat bar to remove this flange and to pry the bathtub loose. Now lift up the front edge of the tub with a pry bar and slip a pair of 1x4 boards beneath the tub. Pull the tub away from the wall using the 1x4s as skids. Always get help if you're removing a cast-iron tub. Back injuries will be with you a lot longer than that new tub will. Finally, cut or break the bathtub into small pieces for easy disposal. This is your chance to get even!

The following instructions are for tub surrounds that are more than one piece. Single piece surrounds vary by manufacturer and come with installation instructions.

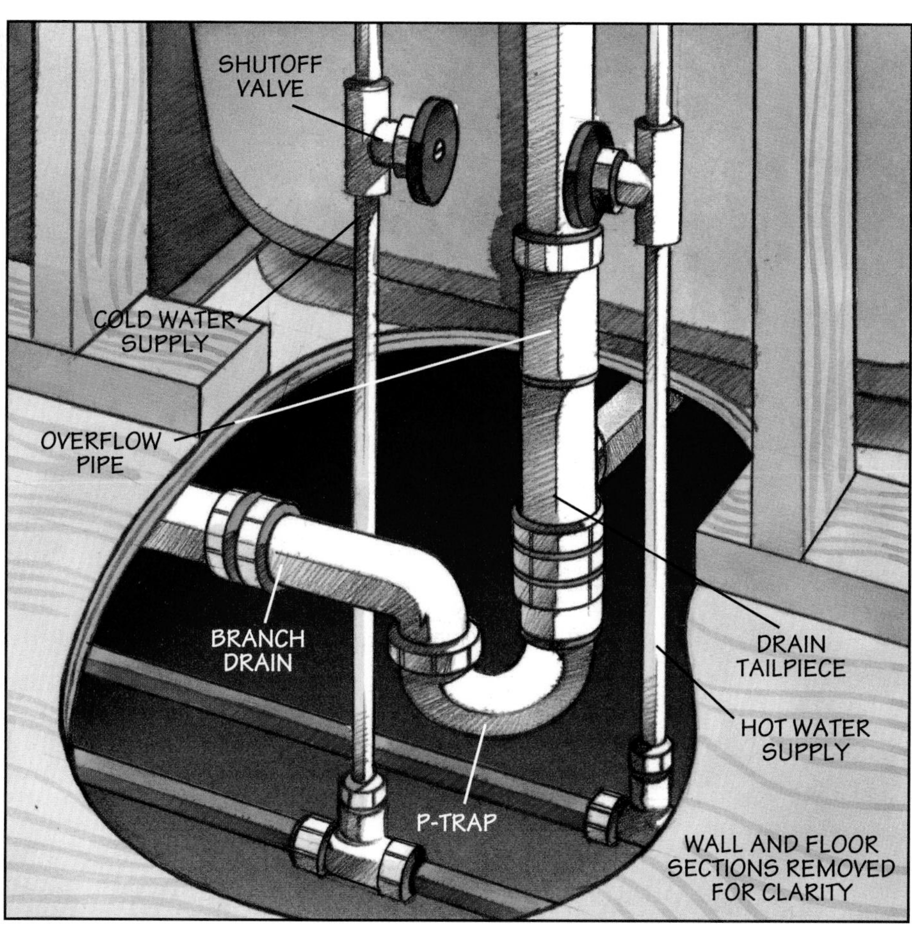

The supply system includes hot and cold supply pipes, usually made of copper or polybutylene plastic, with shutoff valves. These supply connections are roughed-in before the tub is installed, but be sure you measure accurately so that the fittings don't get damaged when you install the fixtures. The hot and cold lines run in tandem to all parts of the house. Usually, the supply pipes run inside wall cavities or are strapped to the undersides of floor joists. Faucets, faucet handles, and tub spouts are usually installed after the tub is in place.

The drain-waste-overflow system includes the overflow pipe, drain tee, P-trap, and branch drain. A drain-waste overflow kit with stopper mechanism must be purchased separately and attached to the tub before it is installed. Available in both brass and plastic types, most kits include an overflow coverplate, an overflow pipe that can be adjusted to different heights, a drain-tee fitting, an adjustable drain tailpiece, and a drain coverplate that screws into the tailpiece.

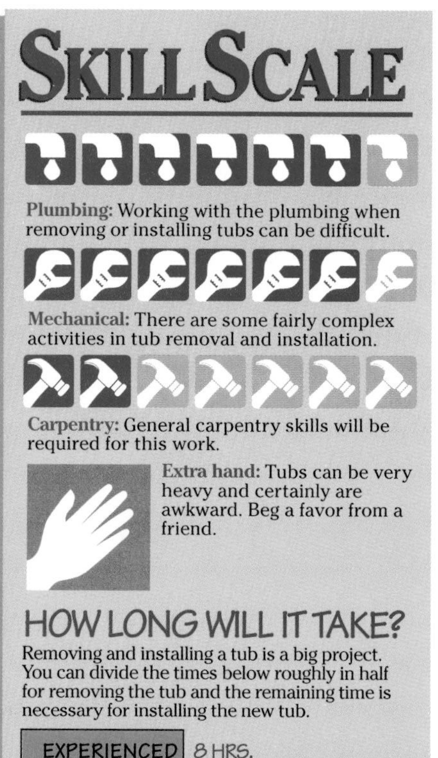

Plumbing: Working with the plumbing when removing or installing tubs can be difficult.

Mechanical: There are some fairly complex activities in tub removal and installation.

Carpentry: General carpentry skills will be required for this work.

Extra hand: Tubs can be very heavy and certainly are awkward. Beg a favor from a friend.

HOW LONG WILL IT TAKE?

Removing and installing a tub is a big project. You can divide the times below roughly in half for removing the tub and the remaining time is necessary for installing the new tub.

EXPERIENCED	8 HRS.
INTERMEDIATE	11 HRS.
BEGINNER	14 HRS.

INSTALLING A BATHTUB IN AN ALCOVE

1 Attach the faucet body and shower head to the water supply pipes, and attach the assembly to 1x4 cross braces before installing the tub. Trim the drain pipe to the height specified by the drain-waste-overflow kit manufacturer.

2 Place a tub-bottom protector, which can be cut from the shipping carton, into the tub. Test-fit the tub by sliding it into the alcove so it rests on the subfloor, flush against the wall studs.

INSTALLING A BATHTUB IN AN ALCOVE (continued)

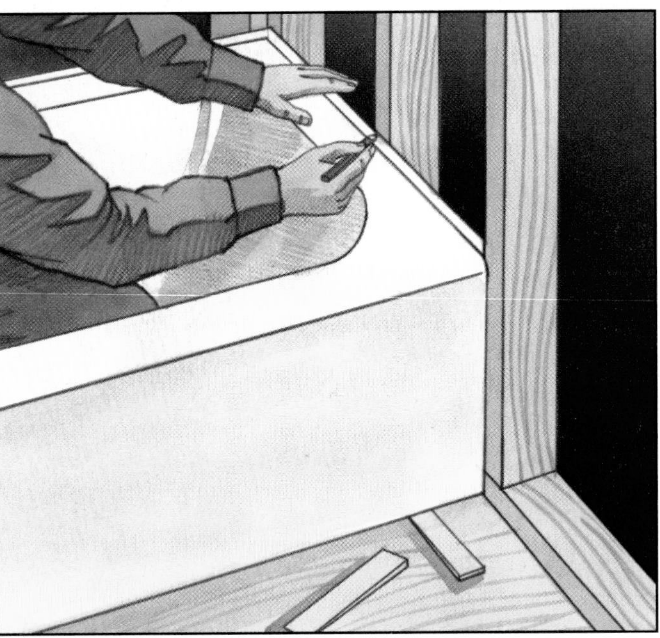

3 Check the tub rim with a carpenter's level, and shim below the tub to make it level. Mark the top of the nailing flange at each stud.

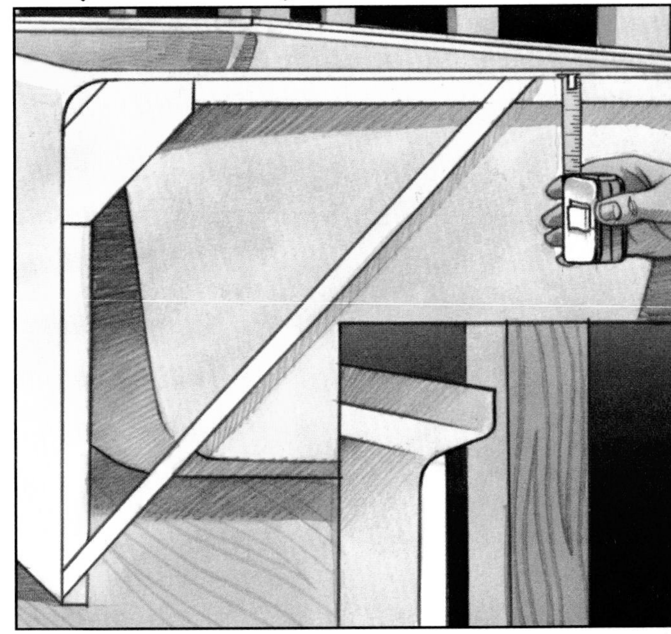

4 Measure the distance from the top of the nailing flange to the underside of the tub rim (inset), and subtract that amount (usually about 1") from the marks on the wall stud.

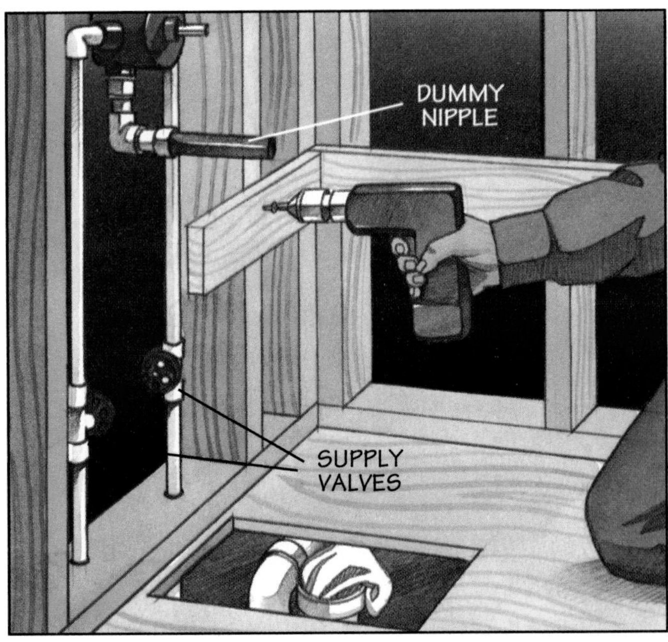

5 Cut ledger board strips, and attach them to the wall studs just below the mark for the underside of the tub rim (step 4). You may have to install the boards in sections to make room for any structural braces at the ends of the tub.

6 Adjust the drain-waste-overflow assembly (usually sold as a separate kit) to fit the drain and overflow openings. Attach gaskets and washers as directed by the manufacturer, then position the assembly against the tub drain and overflow openings.

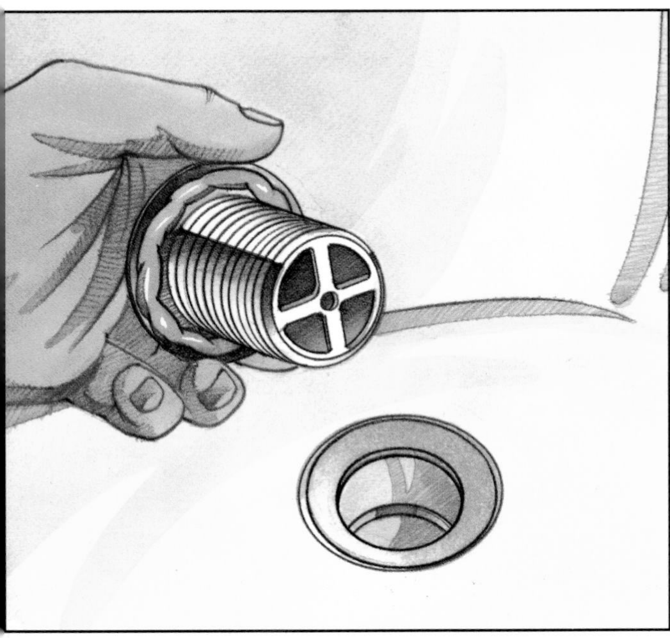

7 Apply a ring of plumber's putty to the bottom of the drain piece flange, then insert the drain piece through the drain hole in the bathtub. Screw the drain piece into the drain tailpiece, and tighten until snug.

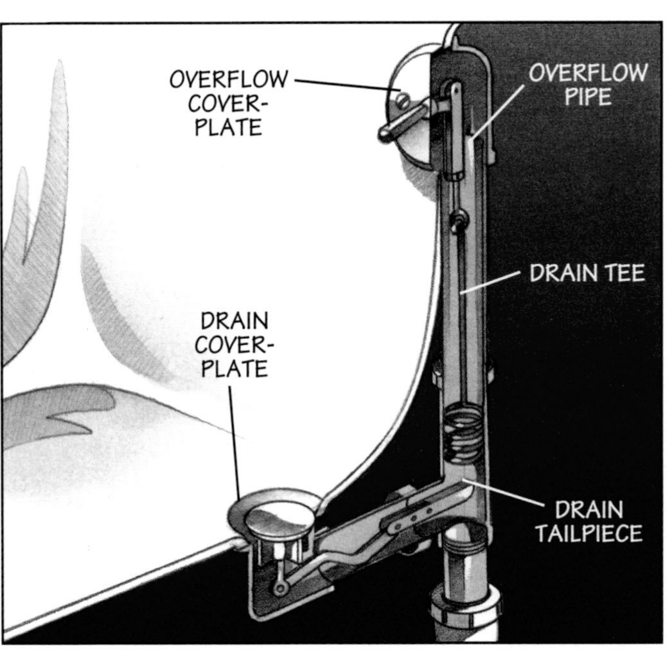

8 Insert drain plug linkage into the overflow opening, and attach the overflow coverplate with long screws driven into the mounting flange on the overflow pipe. Adjust drain plug linkage as directed by manufacturer.

Plumbing

9 Apply a ½"-thick layer of dry-set mortar to the subfloor, covering the entire area where the tub will rest. No mortar is needed if you are installing a metal tub.

10 Lay soaped 1x4 runners across the alcove so they rest on the far sill plate. The runners will allow you to slide the tub into the alcove without disturbing the mortar base. Slide the tub over the runners and into position; then remove the runners, allowing the tub to settle into the mortar. Press down evenly on the tub rims until they touch the ledger boards.

INSTALLING A BATHTUB IN AN ALCOVE (continued)

11 Before the mortar sets, nail the tub rim flanges to the wall studs. Attach the rim flange by nailing through the flange's pre-drilled holes into the wall studs with galvanized roofing nails.

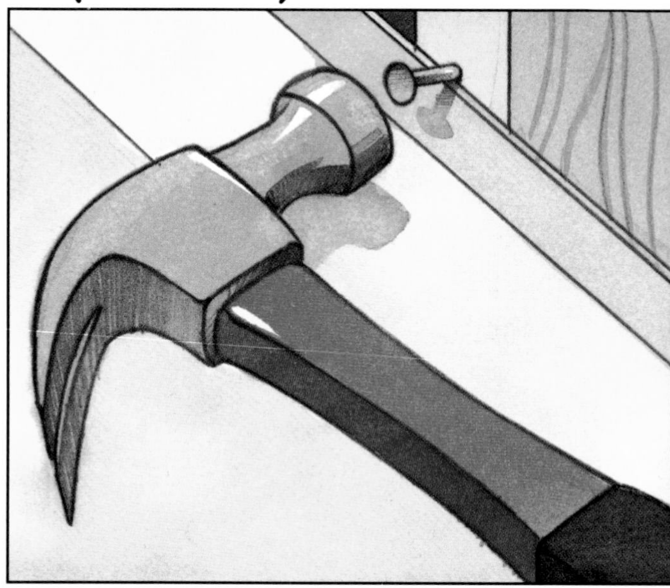

12 If the flange doesn't have pre-drilled holes, drive galvanized roofing nails into the wall studs so the head of the nail covers the rim flange. After the rim flanges are secured, allow the mortar to dry for 6 to 8 hours.

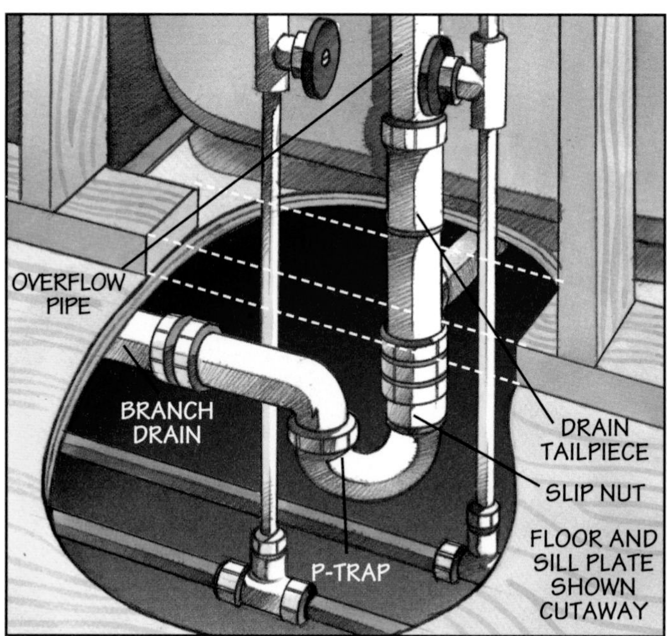

13 Adjust the drain tailpiece so it will fit into the P-trap (you may have to trim it with a hacksaw).

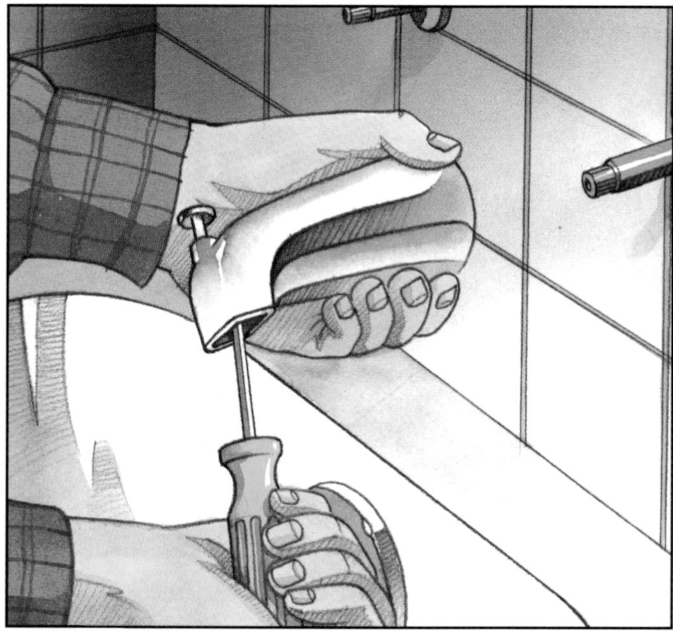

14 Then install the faucet handles and the tub spout. Finally, caulk all around the bathtub top, ends, and bottom edges with a good-quality tub and tile caulk.

INSTALLING A TUB SURROUND

1 Mark a cardboard template for the plumbing cutouts, then tape it to the tub surround panel that will cover the plumbing wall. Make the cutouts in the panel with a hole saw or a jigsaw.

2 Test-fit surround panels according to manufacturer's suggested installation sequence, and tape them in place. Draw lines along the tops of all the panels, at the outside edges of side panels, and on the tub rim, along the bottoms of panels.

3 Remove panels in reverse order, one at a time. As they are exposed, outline the inside edges of each panel on the surface of the wall.

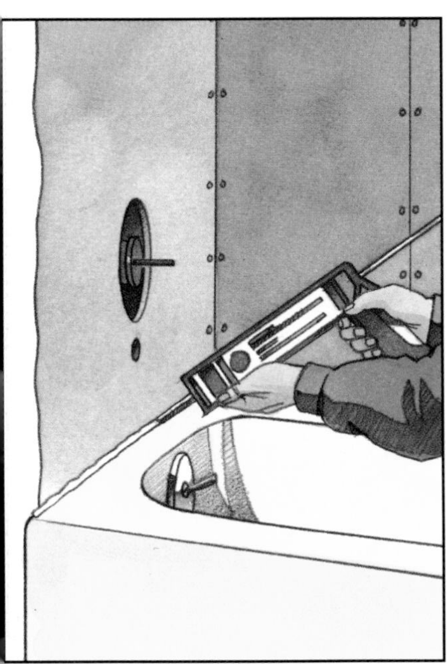

4 Apply a heavy bead of tub & tile caulk to the tub rim; follow marks made where the panels will rest.

5 Apply a panel adhesive recommended by the manufacturer to the wall in the outline area for the first panel. Carefully press the panel in place.

6 Install the rest of the panels in the proper sequence, following the manufacturer's directions for connecting panels and sealing the seams. Press all the panels in place, then brace for drying.

Tub & Shower Maintenance

Caulking seams, sealing tile and grout, and hanging towel rods and mirrors are a few of the small ongoing maintenance projects that will keep you busy on those boring weekends when you have absolutely nothing else to do.

It is best to use tub & tile caulk for most of your bathroom sealing projects. Most tub & tile caulk is a blend of silicone and latex that provides you with the best features of both. Silicone is extremely durable and expands and contracts with the tub and shower, while latex is easy to apply in smooth, neat beads and holds paint well.

For heavy mildew areas and high concentration of mineral deposits and scale, use a quality cleaner and mineral dissolver on a weekly basis. This will not only preserve the fixtures but will make the cleanup process quicker and easier.

APPLYING TUB & TILE CAULK

1 Scrape out old grout or caulk with an awl or can opener. Wipe away soap scum from joint with rubbing alcohol and a clean cloth.

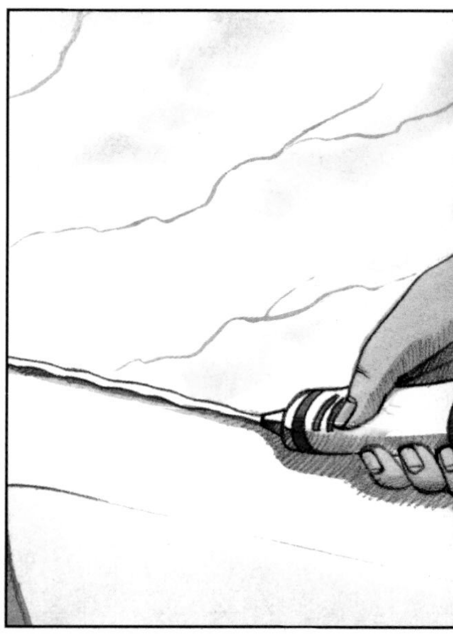

2 Fill tub with water so it will be heavy enough to pull tub away from the tile. Fill joint with a silicone or latex caulk that will not become brittle.

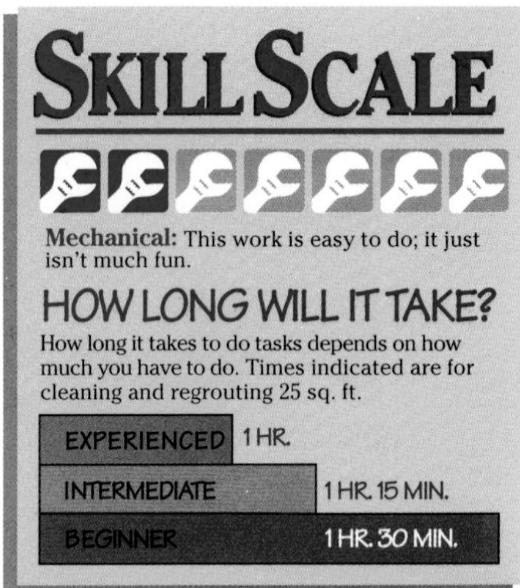

STUFF YOU'LL NEED:

- ☐ **Tools:** Basic plumbing tool kit (page 86), grout saw, grout float, power drill & bit.
- ☐ **Materials:** Caulk, grout, sponge, clean cloth.

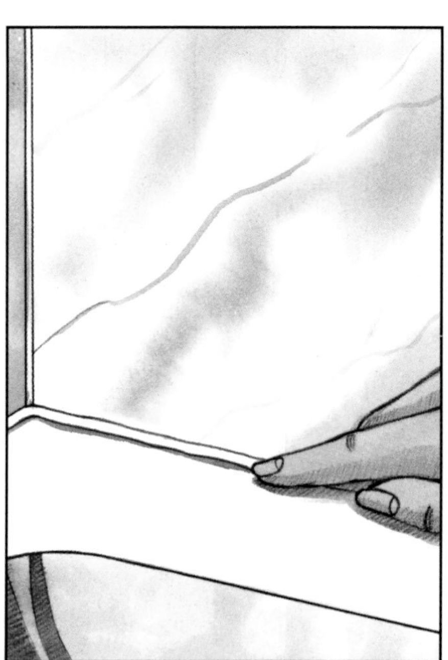

3 Wet your fingertip with cold water so the caulk will not stick to your finger, and smooth the caulk into a cove shape. Let caulk harden, and trim any excess away with a utility knife.

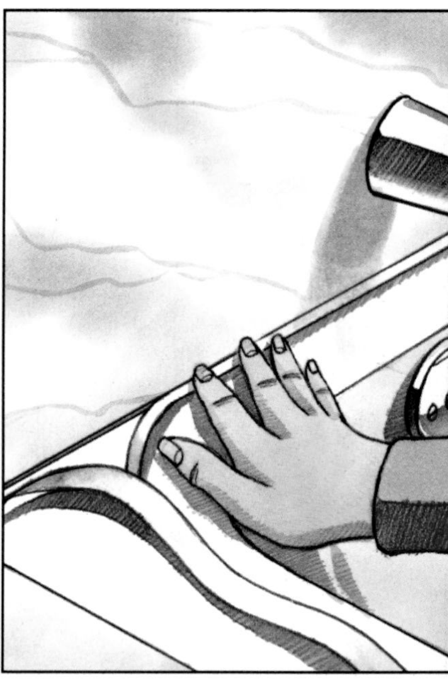

Peel-and-stick tub & tile caulks are pre-formed, reducing the work of cleaning the joint and cleaning up the new caulk. Peel the backing off and press the new caulk into place.

REGROUTING CERAMIC TILE

1 Scrape out old grout with an awl or utility knife to leave a clean bed for the new grout. Remove and replace any broken tiles.

2 Clean and rinse the grout joints with a sponge. Choose premixed grout that is resistant to mildew and stains.

3 Use a foam grout float or a sponge to spread grout over entire tile surface. Work grout well into joints. Let grout set slightly, until firm, then wipe away the excess with a damp cloth.

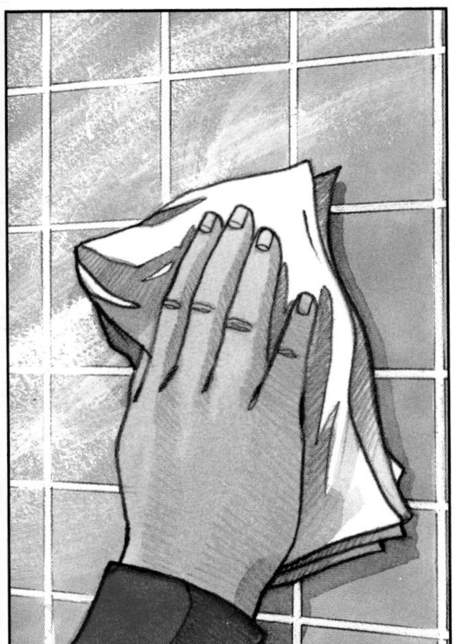

4 Let grout dry completely. Wipe away powdery residue and polish the tile with a dry soft cloth. Apply caulk around bathtub or shower stall (opposite). Do not use tub or shower for 24 hours.

INSERTING MASONRY ANCHORS IN CERAMIC

1 Place masking tape over the spot where you want to drill. Drill hole for anchor using a carbide masonry bit and 3/8" variable -speed drill. Drill bit should be same size as anchor. Use low drill speed to ensure that bit does not skip on tile.

2 Tap a plastic or lead masonry anchor plug into the hole and use a screw to attach the fixture. Be careful not to chip the tile.

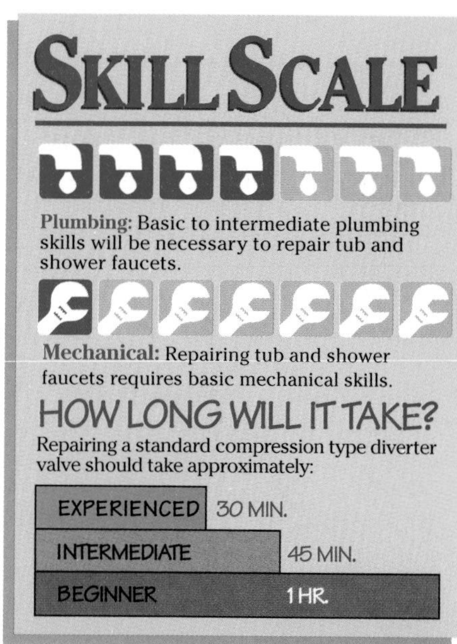

STUFF YOU'LL NEED:

- ☐**Tools:** *Basic plumbing tool kit (page 86).*
- ☐**Materials:** *Pipe-joint compound, heat-proof grease, vinegar.*

Fixing Shower Problems

Tub and shower faucets have the same basic designs as sink faucets, and the techniques for repairing leaks are basically the same as those for sink faucets. When a tub and shower are combined, the shower head and the tub spout share the same hot and cold water supply lines and handles. Combination faucets are commonly available in two-handle and single-handle styles.

With combination faucets, either a diverter valve (on three-handled faucets) or a gate diverter (on two-handle and single-handle faucets) is used to direct water flow to the tub spout or the shower head. On three-handled faucets, the middle handle controls the diverter valve, and on two-handled and single-handled faucets, the gate diverter is on the tub spout.

While gate diverters rarely need repair, diverter valves usually do from normal wear and mineral deposits. Shower heads sometimes need repair from mineral deposits in the spray outlets and worn out O-rings.

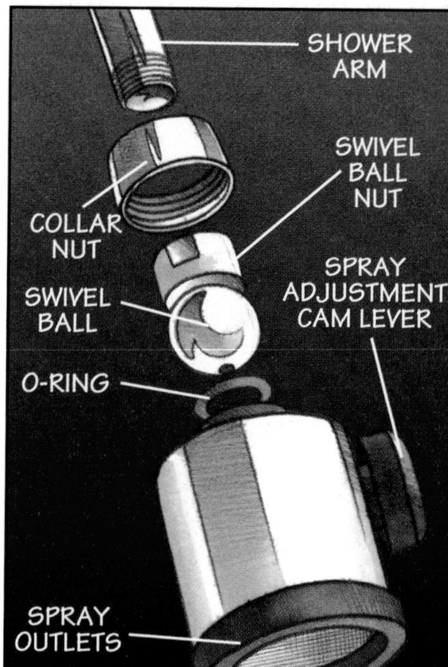

A typical shower head can be disassembled easily for cleaning and repair. Some shower heads include a spray adjustment cam lever that is used to change the force of the spray.

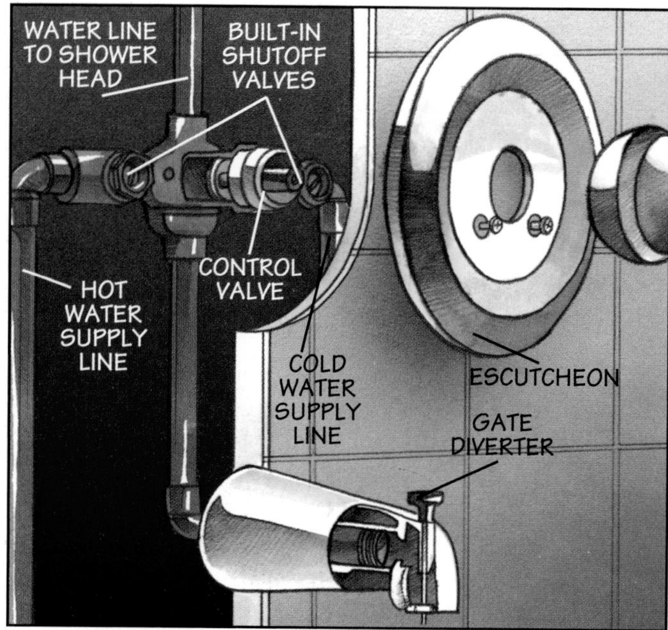

Single-handle faucets are similar to two-handle faucets which use a gate diverter to direct water to the shower head or to the tub spout. Instead of having a separate handle for hot water and a separate handle for cold water, the single-handle faucet has built-in shutoff valves that allow supply water to flow to the control valve which selects the proper blend of hot and cold water for the desired water temperature.

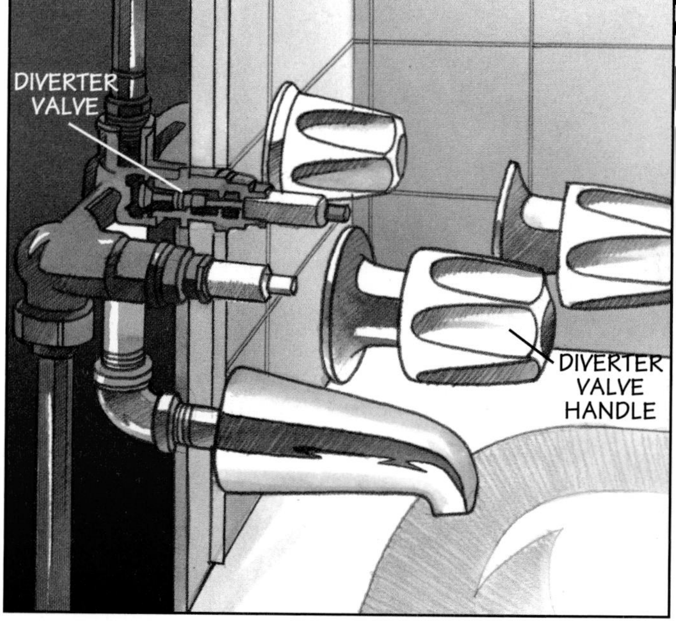

Three-handle faucets have handles to control hot and cold water, and a third handle to control the diverter valve. The separate hot and cold handles indicate that the faucet type is either cartridge or compression type. Most diverter valves are similar to either compression or cartridge faucet valves. Compression-type diverters can be repaired, but cartridge types should be replaced.

REPAIRING A DIVERTER VALVE

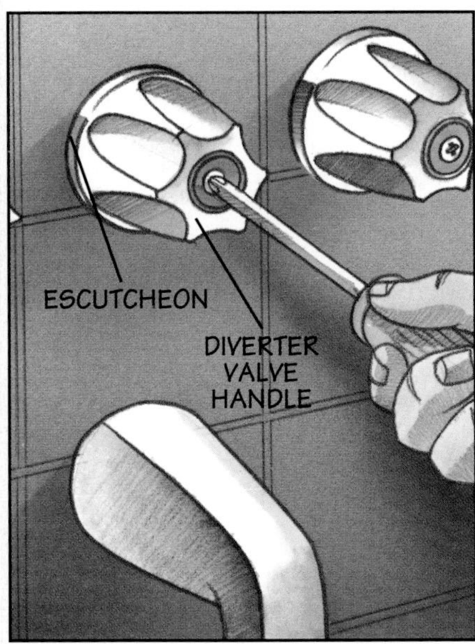

1 Remove the diverter valve index cap, being careful not to scratch the handle. Next, with a screwdriver, remove the diverter valve handle and then unscrew and remove the escutcheon.

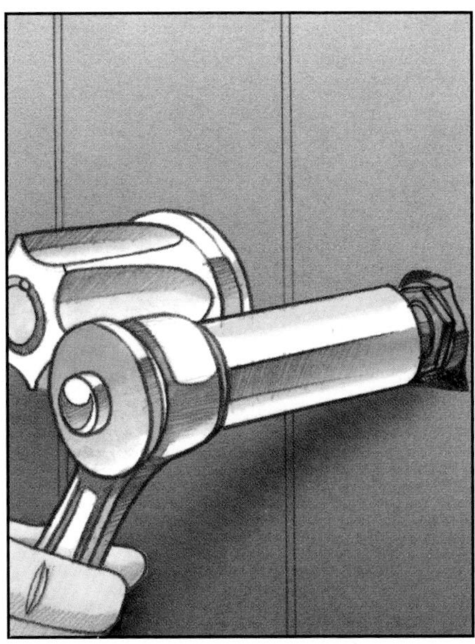

2 Remove the bonnet nut with an adjustable wrench, water-pump pliers or deep-set socket and ratchet wrench. Be careful on nuts that are seized up. If you pound on them too much, you can loosen not only the nut but also the solder joints on the supply lines.

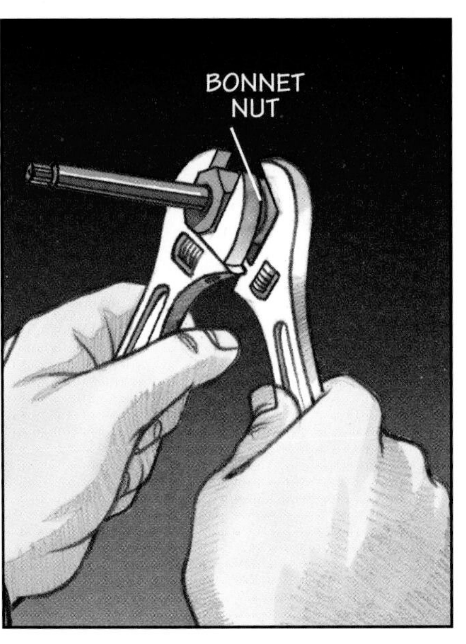

3 Unscrew the stem assembly from the bonnet nut, using adjustable wrenches.

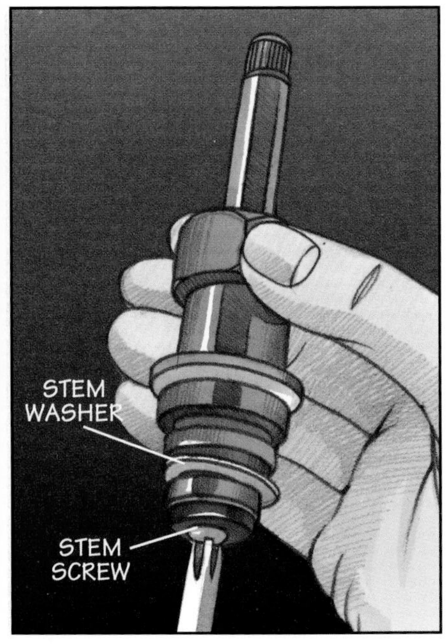

4 Remove the brass stem screw. Replace the stem washer with an exact duplicate and if the stem screw is worn, replace it also.

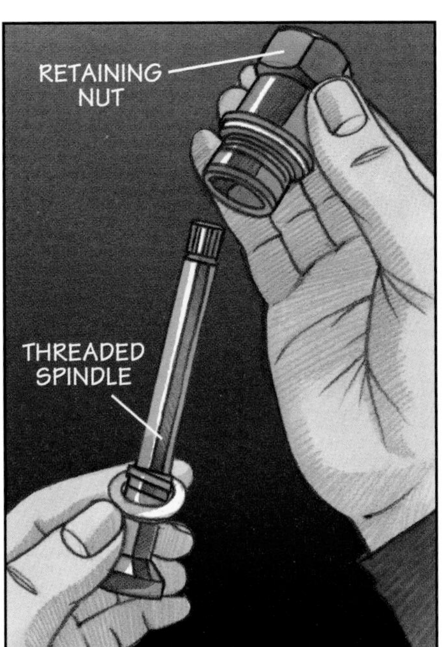

5 Unscrew the threaded spindle and remove it from the retaining nut.

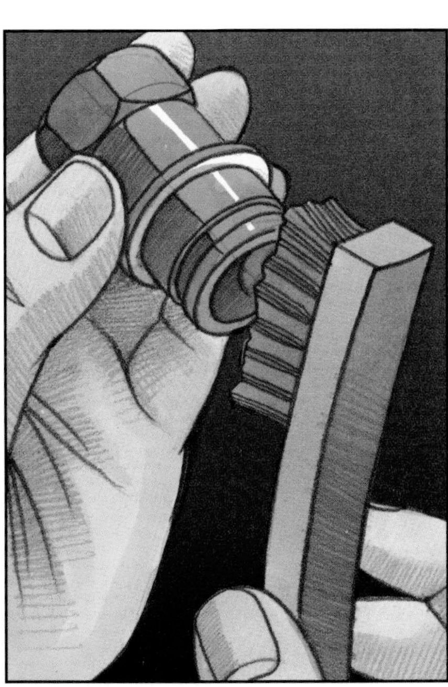

6 Clean any sediment and lime buildup from the nut, using a small wire brush dipped in vinegar. Coat all parts with heatproof grease and reassemble the diverter valve.

CLEANING AND REPAIRING A SHOWER HEAD

1 Unscrew the swivel ball nut, using an adjustable wrench or channel-type pliers. Wrap the jaws of the tool with masking tape to prevent marring the finish. Unscrew the collar nut from the shower head.

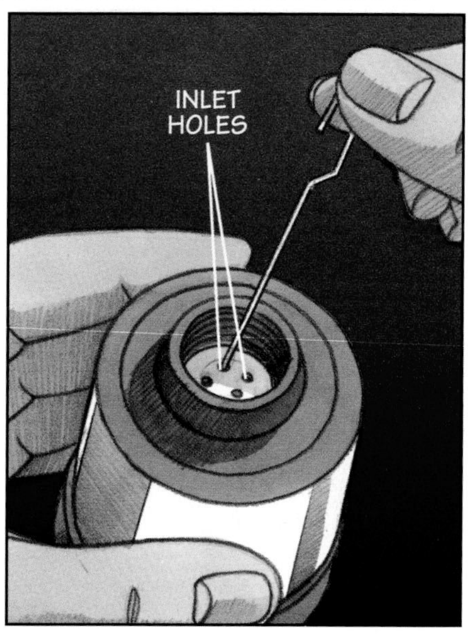

2 Clean the outlet and inlet holes of the shower head with a thin wire. Flush the head with clean water.

3 Replace the O-ring, if necessary. Lubricate the new O-ring with heatproof grease before installing into the shower head.

REPLACING A TUB SPOUT AND GATE DIVERTER

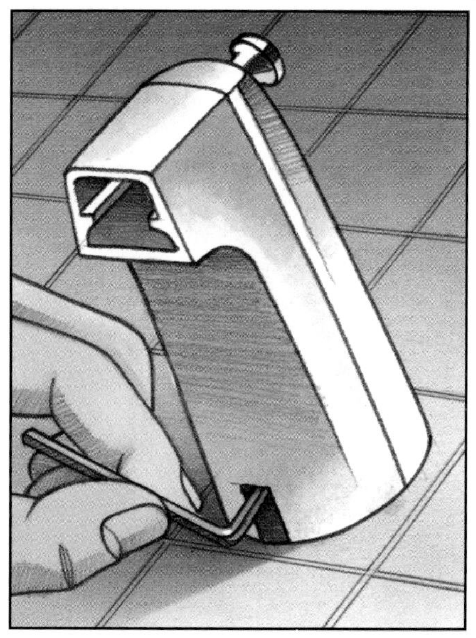

Check underneath the tub spout for a small access slot. The slot indicates the spout is held in place with an allen screw. Remove the screw using an allen wrench and remove the spout by sliding it off the spout nipple.

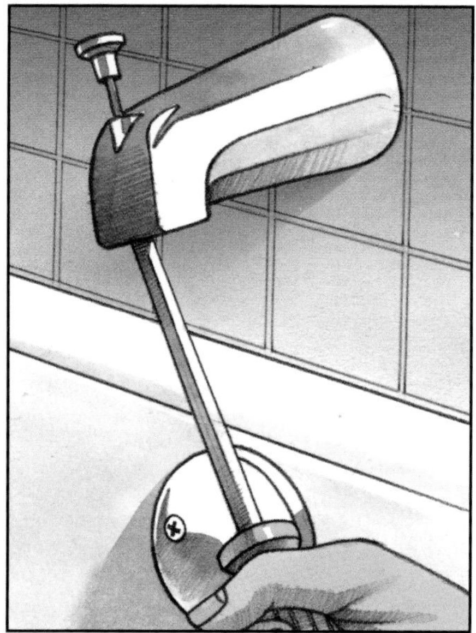

Tub spouts that are threaded onto the spout nipple will need to be unscrewed in order to be removed. Use a pipe wrench or insert a large screwdriver or hammer handle into the spout opening and turn spout counterclockwise.

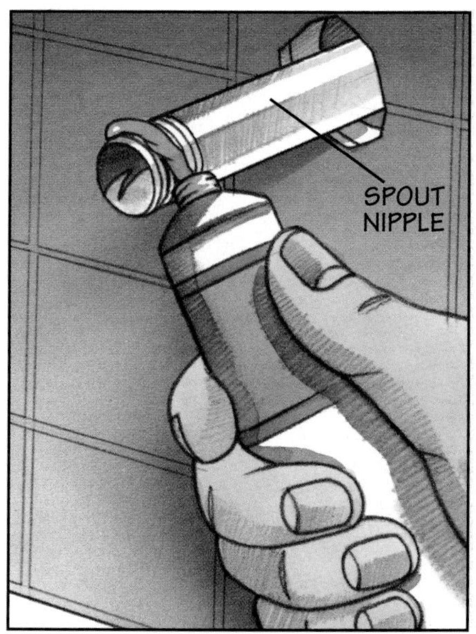

Spread pipe joint compound on the threads of the spout nipple before replacing the spout to ensure a leak-free connection.

REPAIRING A SINGLE-HANDLE CARTRIDGE SHOWER FAUCET

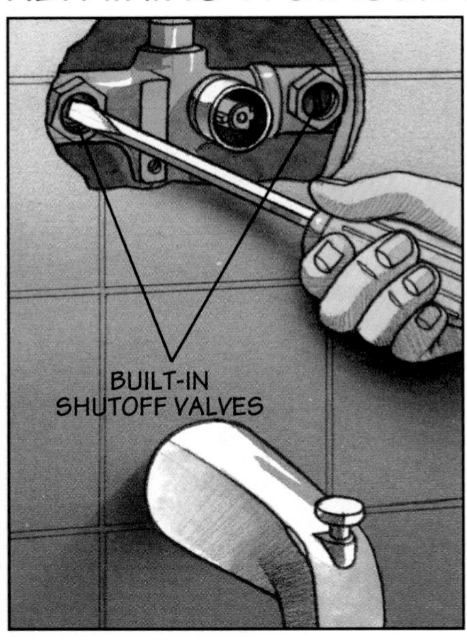

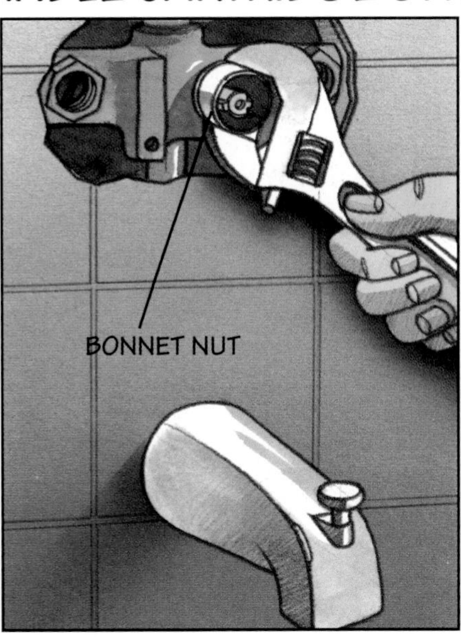

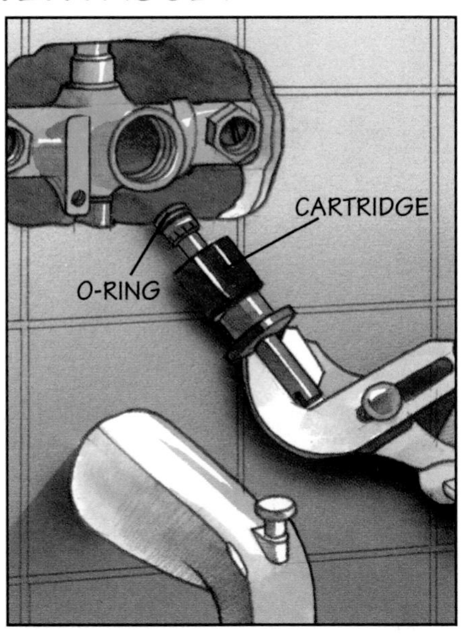

1 Use a screwdriver to remove the handle and the escutcheon. Turn off the water supply at the built-in shutoff valves or at the main shutoff valve.

2 Unscrew and remove the retaining ring or bonnet nut, using an adjustable wrench.

3 Remove the cartridge assembly by grasping the end of the valve with water-pump pliers and pulling gently. Flush the valve body with clean water to remove any sediment. Replace any worn O-rings then reinstall the cartridge and test the valve. If the faucet fails to work properly, replace the cartridge.

Plumbing

REMOVING A DEEP-SET FAUCET VALVE

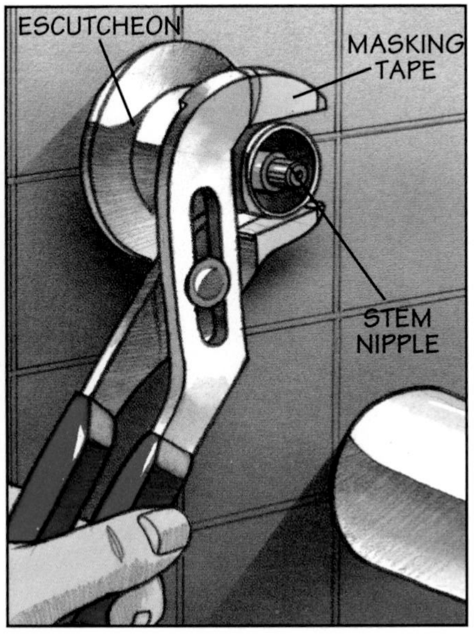

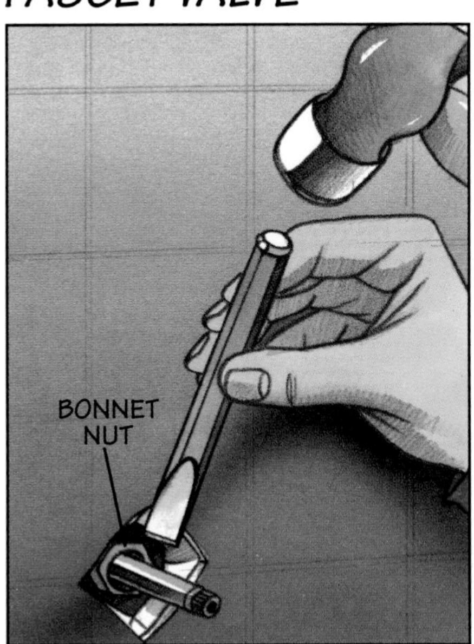

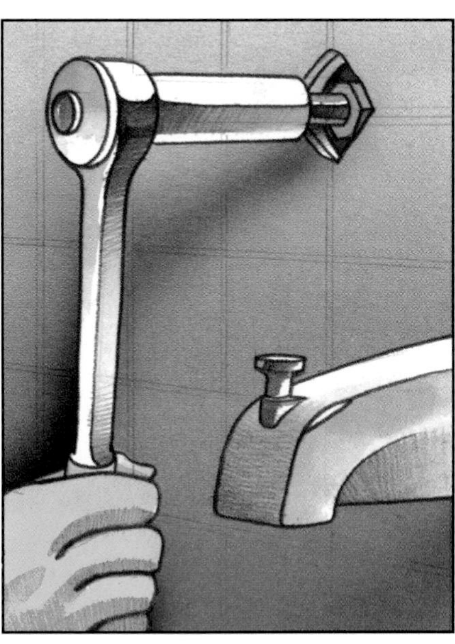

1 Remove the handle, and unscrew the escutcheon with water-pump pliers. Be sure to pad the jaws of the pliers with masking tape to prevent scratching the escutcheon.

2 Chip away any mortar surrounding the bonnet nut, using a ball peen hammer and a small cold chisel.

3 Unscrew the bonnet nut with a deep-set socket and ratchet wrench. Remove the packing nut and then remove the stem from the faucet body.

Replacing & Repairing Toilets

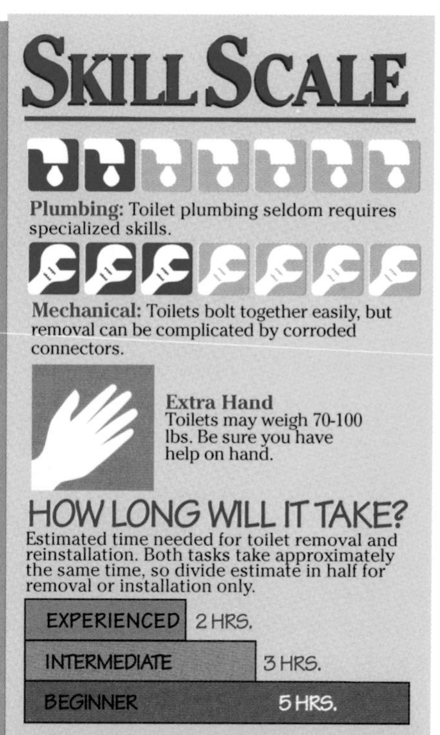

STUFF YOU'LL NEED:

- **Tools:** Basic plumbing tool kit (page 86); possibly: tubing cutter, nut splitter.
- **Specialty tools that will come in handy:** Basin wrench, nut splitter, spud wrench, tubing cutter.
- **Materials:** Rag, bucket, plastic tarp, tape, wax ring and sleeve, plumber's putty, floor bolts and mounting nuts, flush valve, supply shutoff and tube.

Some toilets are more "standard" than others. So, unless you want to move the drain pipes, measure the distance from the floor bolts to the wall (not the baseboard) before you go shopping. Make sure the new one fits those measurements. If the distance isn't one foot, you probably have a toilet that is non-standard.

Toilets get no respect. For appliances that are used daily by each member of every household, they receive little attention or appreciation. This is not all bad, of course. Rapt fascination with one's toilets quickly becomes unseemly. And toilets get more than their share of attention eventually–when they break down.

Unless it cracks, the main body of your toilet–the bowl and tank–will never wear out. It's just dumb, inert porcelain. But all of the working parts, most of them submerged in water and subject to continual use, will need to be replaced periodically.

Even if your toilet isn't actually broken, you may wish to remove and replace it. Sometimes in the course of remodeling, it's necessary to get the thing out of the way for awhile. You may even decide to discard your dowdy old white W.C. in favor of a sleeker, more stylish one (toilets are considered a decorator item in some circles).

Toilet swapping isn't as tricky as it may seem. The toughest part is likely to be loosening the rusted or corroded nuts and bolts that hold your toilet to the floor, and if they give you too much trouble you can just cut them off. Everything you are likely to need to know is covered in the instructions that follow.

Part of what makes do-it-yourself plumbing so darned exciting is that element of the unexpected. If you discover rotten flooring under the toilet, or really bizarre plumbing, it may be a good time to call in professional help. Don't overreach your abilities.

And before you disconnect the plumbing, you might want to resolve these important questions:

1. Do you have another toilet to use while this one is out of commission?
2. Are you certain you can handle it yourself? (It's heavy.) Can you get help if you need it?
3. How are you planning to dispose of the old one? Will your trash collector take it? As lawn ornaments, toilets are a fashion no–no.

REMOVING A TOILET

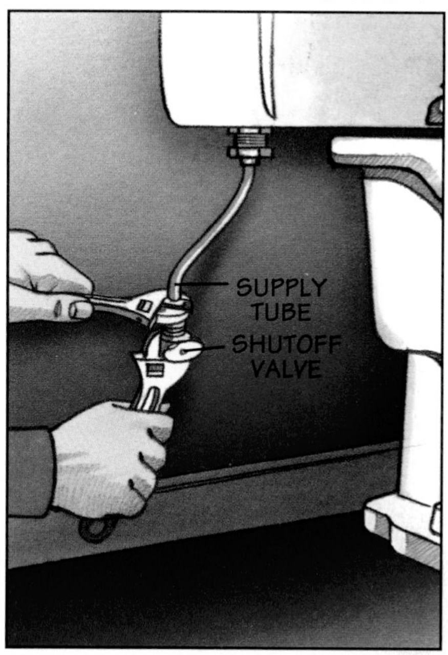

1 Turn off the shutoff valve on the water supply line. Flush the toilet – that empties the tank and bowl. Then sponge them both dry. Disconnect both ends of the water supply tube at the shutoff valve and the toilet tank.

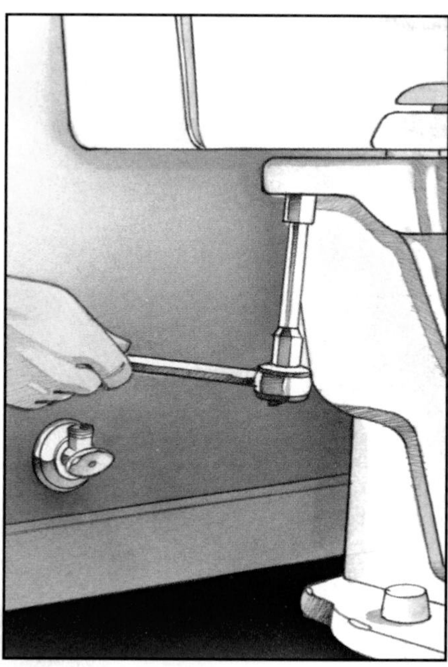

2 Use a ratchet wrench or basin wrench to remove the nuts from the bolts that hold the tank onto the bowl. Carefully lift the tank off the bowl and set it where it won't be in the way.

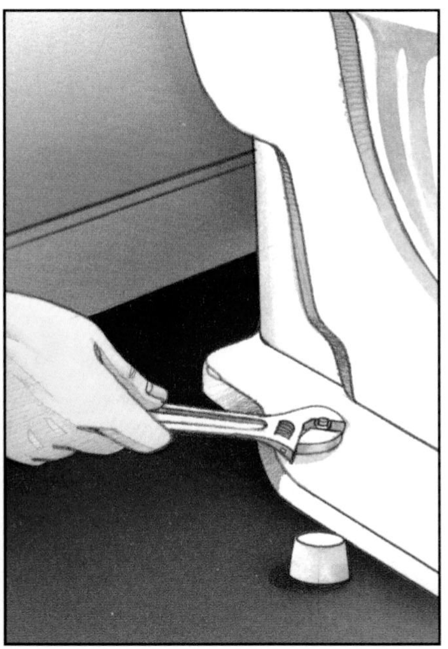

3 If you still have trim caps on the floor bolts, pry them off and then remove the nuts from the floor bolts with an adjustable wrench. If the nuts won't budge, see "If the nuts won't budge…"

IF THE NUTS WON'T BUDGE…

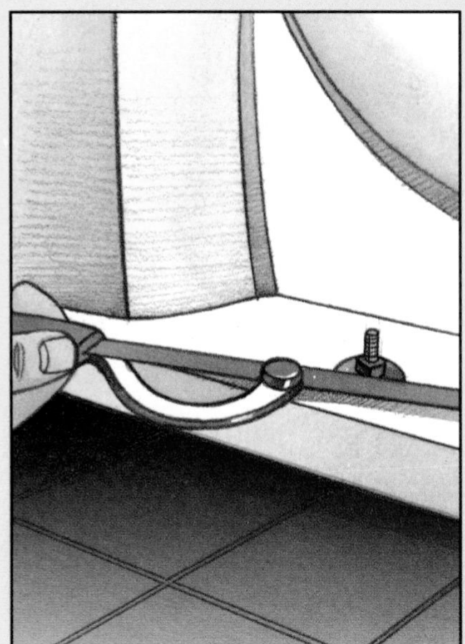

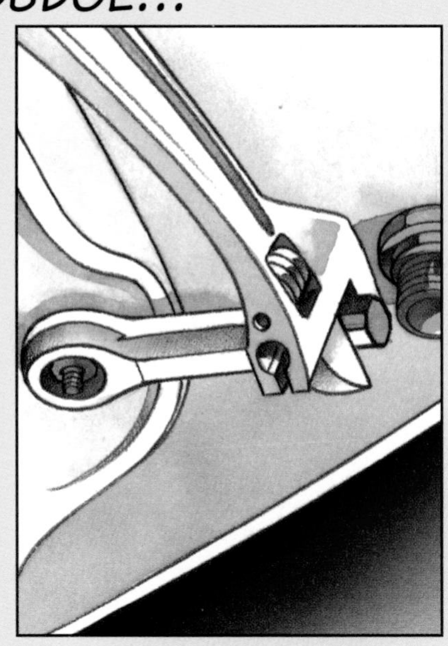

For obvious reasons, the nuts and bolts on toilets corrode in a hurry (it's best not to think about this too much). You could spend the day working on them with every wrench you own or can borrow. It's a great way to add to your vocabulary. If you're lucky enough to have a nut splitter among your car tools, use it. Otherwise, go at the stubborn little devils with a hacksaw blade and use the time you save to improve your vocabulary in other ways.

4 There's a wax ring that seals the bottom of the bowl to the toilet flange (underneath the toilet). To break the seal, you'll have to straddle the toilet and gently rock it. Lift off the bowl, then lay it on its side nearby (but out of the way).

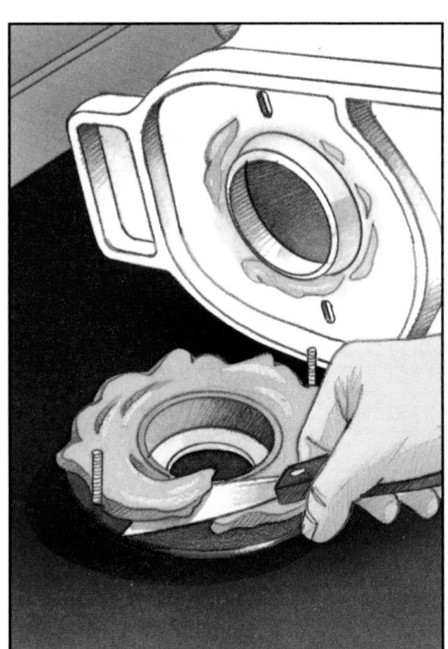

5 Use a putty knife to scrape away the old wax from the toilet flange and horn (you'll know them when you see them) and then clean them with a stiff wire brush. Use a strong bleach solution to disinfect the flange.

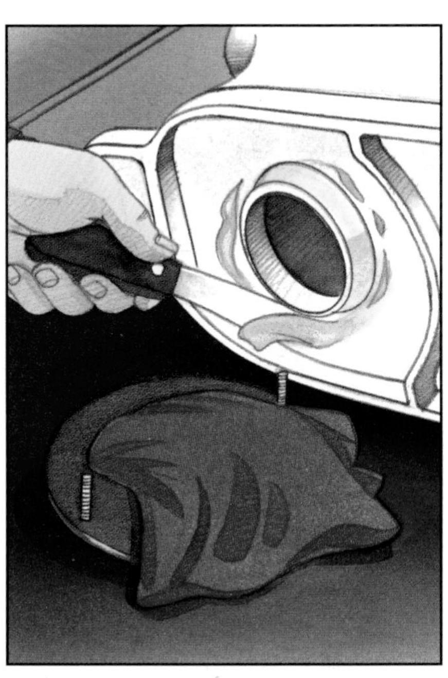

6 You'll probably be smelling something pretty strong and much less pleasant than the bleach (it's sewer gas), so you'll want to cut that off by stuffing a rag into the hole. Cover the flange and rag with an inverted bucket for the time being.

BUYER'$ GUIDE

You can't imagine how many types and colors of toilets there are until you try to decide which model you want to install. The price range can be dizzying too. Some thoughts to consider: (a) you get what you pay for; (b) many Building Codes now call for water-saver toilets; and (c) one-piece toilets are sleeker, easier to clean, more leakproof, and more expensive.

TWO-PIECE STANDARD TOILET

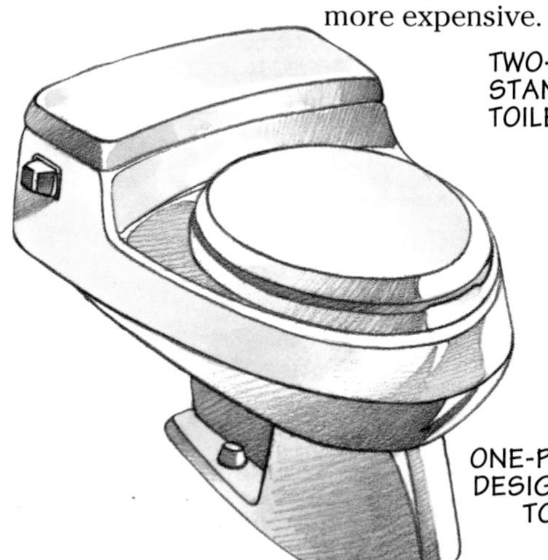

ONE-PIECE DESIGNER TOILET

DESIGNER'S CORNER

You might be living with this toilet for a long time, so while aqua and fire-engine red may look snazzy in a showroom, think neutral colors. Save the bright, trendy colors for bathroom accessories, like towels. Towels are far easier and cheaper t replace if you want to change the color scheme.

OOPS!

You think you're done and then you notice a slight leak. Turn off the shut-off valve. If the leak is along the supply line, tighten the nuts another quarter of a turn. If the leak is from the bottom of the tank, shut off the water and drain the tank. Then check the washers in the tank to make sure they are seated properly, and if so, tighten the bolts an additional quarter turn.

INSTALLING A TOILET

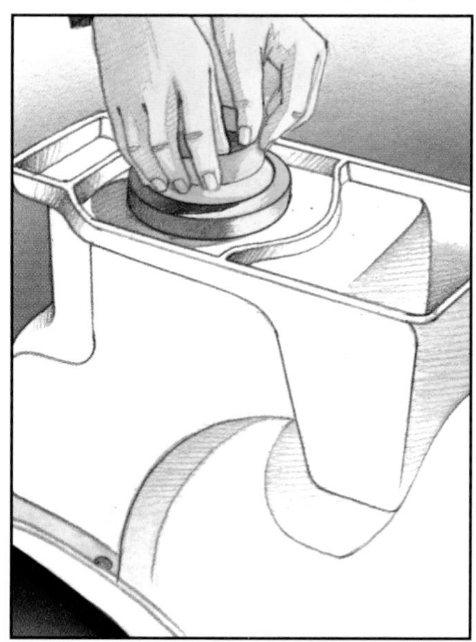

1 If you're reinstalling the old toilet, clean the wax and any other foreign materials off the bottom. Then, old or new, turn the bowl upside-down, put a new wax ring and sleeve over the drain horn.

2 Make sure the toilet flange is clean and the floor bolts point straight up. (Don't forget to take out that rag!) Then carefully position the toilet over the flange and fit the holes in the toilet base right over the floor bolts. If the floor is uneven apply a thin layer of plaster of Paris to the bottom of the toilet bowl.

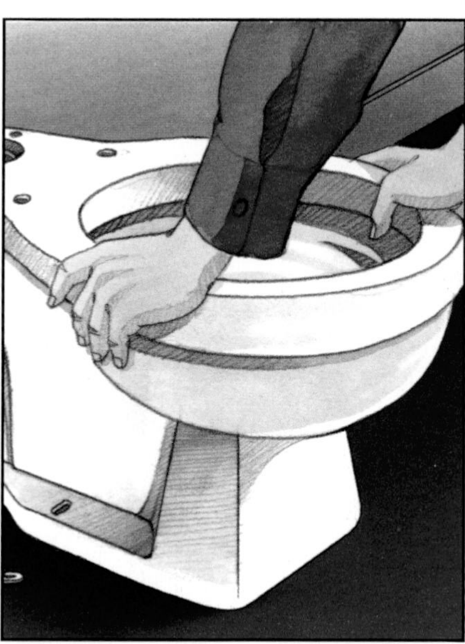

3 Press down on the toilet bowl to compress the wax ring, making a tight seal. Attach washers and nuts to the floor bolts and tighten with an adjustable wrench. (Note: Don't over- tighten; you could crack the base!) Attach trim caps.

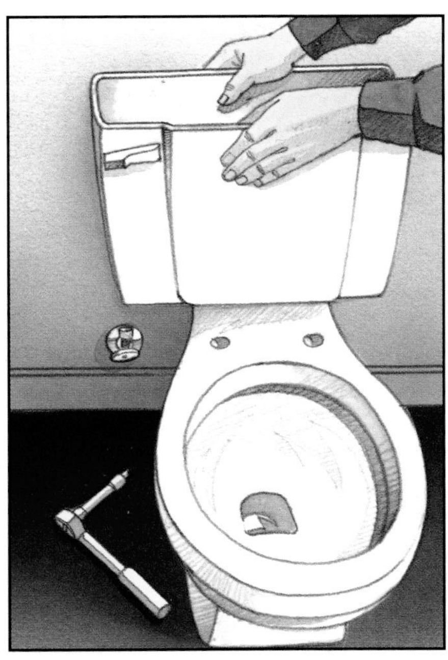

4 You're halfway there! Now for the tank. On some tanks, you'll have to install the handle, ballcock, and flush valve. Then turn the tank upside down and set the spud washer over the tailpiece of the flush valve.

5 Turn the tank back over and position it on the toilet bowl, centering the spud washer over the water inlet opening near the back edge of the bowl.

6 There are two holes in the bottom of the tank that you need to line up with two holes on the top of the bowl. Shift the tank gently until your mission is accomplished; then put a rubber washer on each of the tank bolts and set the bolts through the matching holes.

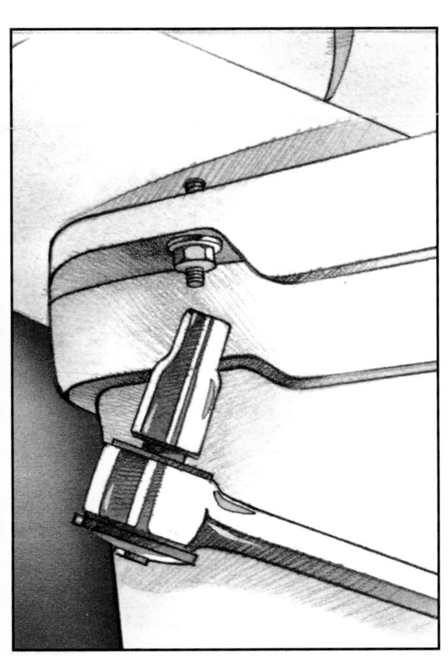

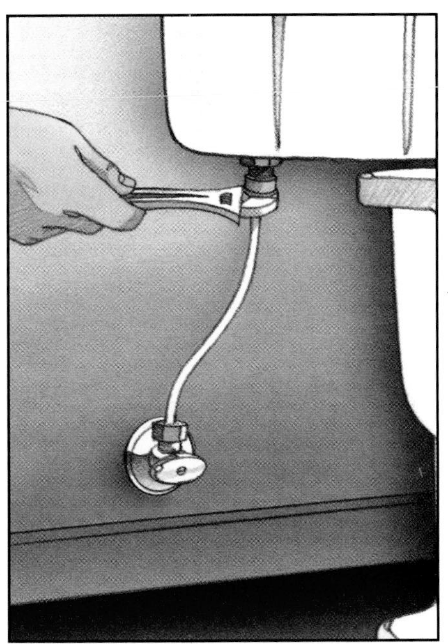

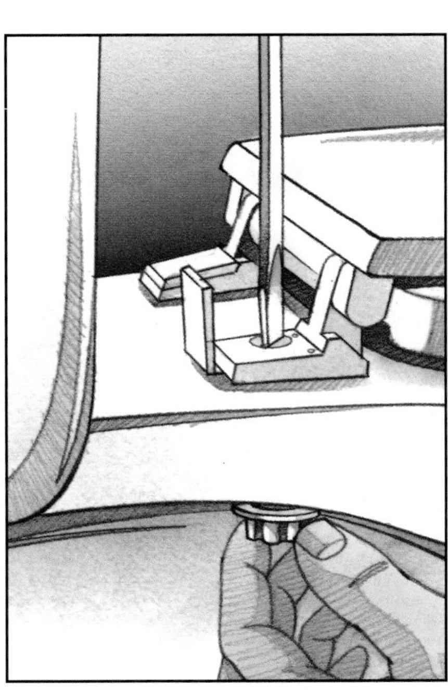

7 Attach washers and nuts to these bolts where they come through under the bowl edge and tighten with a ratchet wrench or basin wrench until snug. (Remember again, don't over-tighten!)

8 Cut a piece of supply tube to fit between the shutoff valve and the toilet tank. Attach the line to the valve first, then to the ballcock tailpiece. Tighten coupling nuts with adjustable wrenches until snug. Hold the ballcock while tightening the coupling nut (see page 144). Turn on the valve. The tank should fill.

9 Last is the toilet seat. Set the seat bolts into the toilet's mounting holes, screw the mounting nuts onto the seat bolts, and tighten.

Repairing Toilets

Late some night, when you're lying in bed listening to the gurgle of your running toilet, you can comfort yourself with the assurance that you probably can fix it. Or you can kick yourself for not having done it sooner. Consider it an insight into your character.

Toilets run because water is either leaking in or leaking out. Figure out which and you're halfway there.

Take the cover off the tank and take a look at the overflow tube (see diagram). If water is running into the overflow, your toilet is overfilling because water is leaking in, or the water level is set too high. Your problem is with the ballcock or the float ball.

If the overflow tube looks okay, then water is leaking out and your problem is with the lift chain or wire, or with the tank ball or flapper.

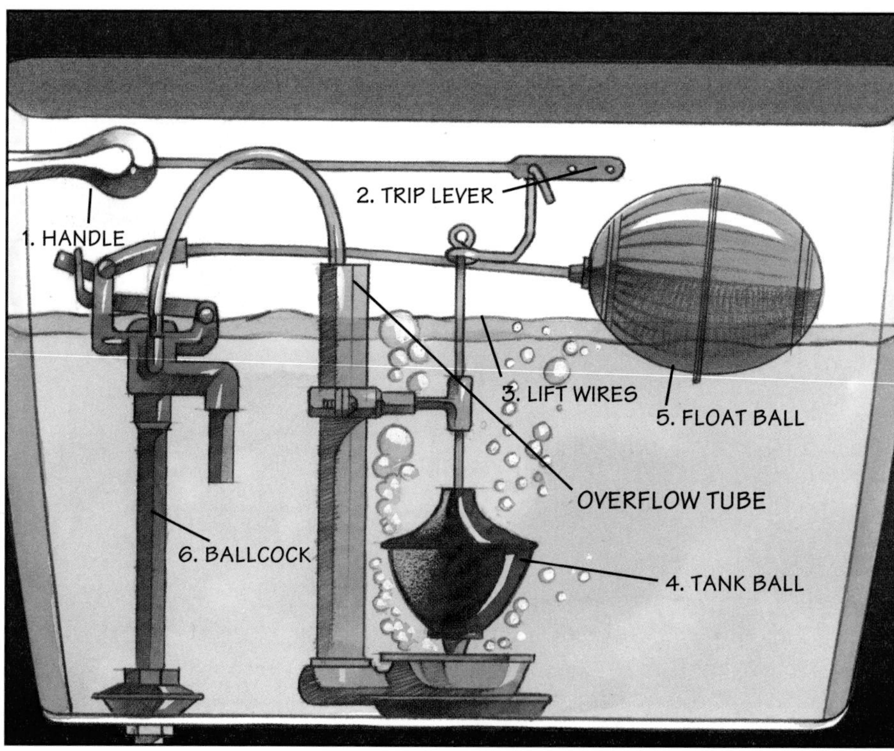

All tank toilets work the same way. When you push the handle (1), the trip lever (2) attached to the lift chain or lift wires (3) raises the tank ball (4) or flapper at the bottom of the tank. Fresh water rushes down into the toilet bowl. As the water level in the tank drops, a float ball (5) opens the ballcock (6) to let in fresh water which fills up the bowl and tank and raises the float ball to close the ballcock.

MAKING MINOR ADJUSTMENTS

1 Clean and adjust the handle mounting nut so the handle operates smoothly. The mounting nut has reversed threads. Loosen the nut by turning it clockwise; tighten it by turning counterclockwise.

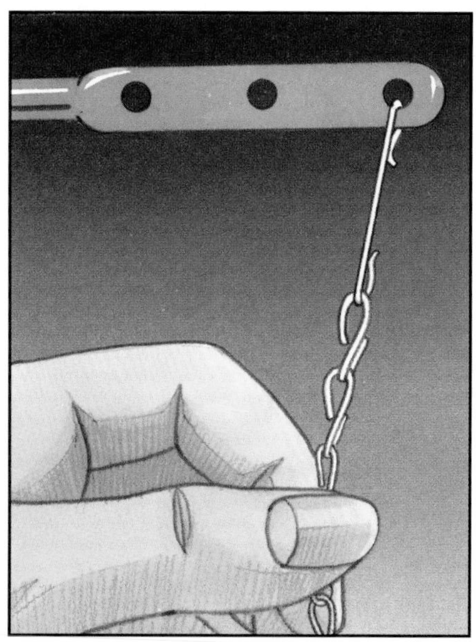

2 Adjust the lift chain so it hangs straight from the handle lever with about ½ inch of slack. Remove excess slack in the chain by hooking it in a different hole in the handle lever or by removing links. Adjust so the tank ball operates properly.

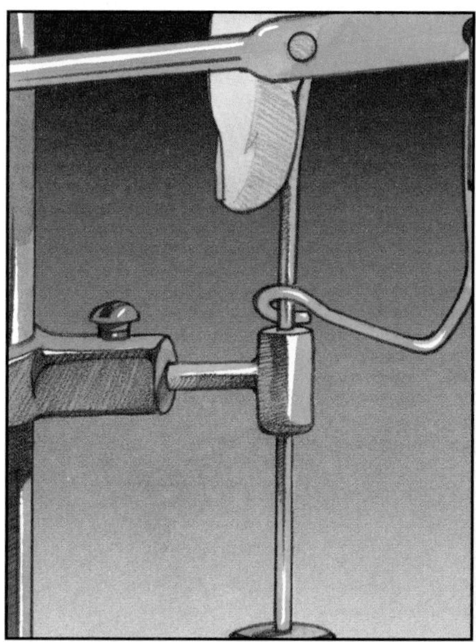

3 Adjust the lift wires (found on toilets without lift chains) so that the wires are straight and operate smoothly when the handle is pushed. A sticky handle often can be fixed by straightening bent lift wires.

SKILL SCALE

Plumbing: The simplest toilet repairs are mostly mechanical adjustments. The plumbing skills necessary are basic.

Mechanical: The mechanics of toilets are easy to tinker with. Just your usual nuts and bolts stuff.

HOW LONG WILL IT TAKE?

Allow an hour. If you haven't solved the problem by then, it probably means you'll have to drain and remove the tank to replace parts. Then you'll need an afternoon.

EXPERIENCED	10 MIN.
INTERMEDIATE	20 MIN.
BEGINNER	30 MIN.

STUFF YOU'LL NEED:

- ☐ **Tools:** Basic plumbing tool kit (page 86), basin wrench, spud wrench.
- ☐ **Materials:** Bucket, replacement parts as necessary.

HOMER'S HINDSIGHT

The sound of the toilet running didn't bother me at all– it was like having a little fountain. Then I got the water bill. Now all I can hear is money going down the drain.

SETTING WATER LEVEL

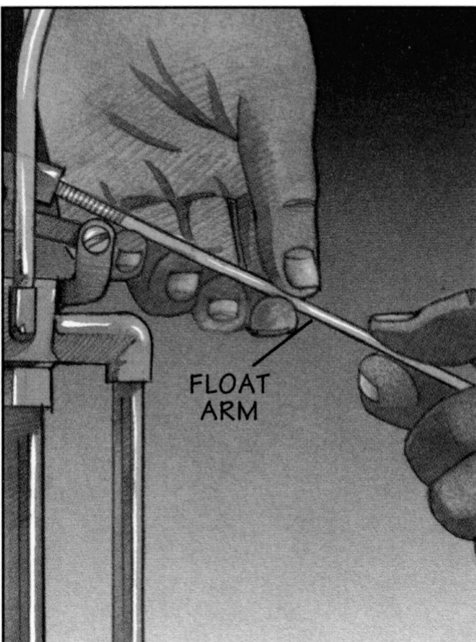

Traditional plunger-valve ballcocks are made of brass. The water flow is controlled by a plunger attached to the float arm and ball. To lower the water level, bend the float arm down slightly. Raise the level by bending the arm up.

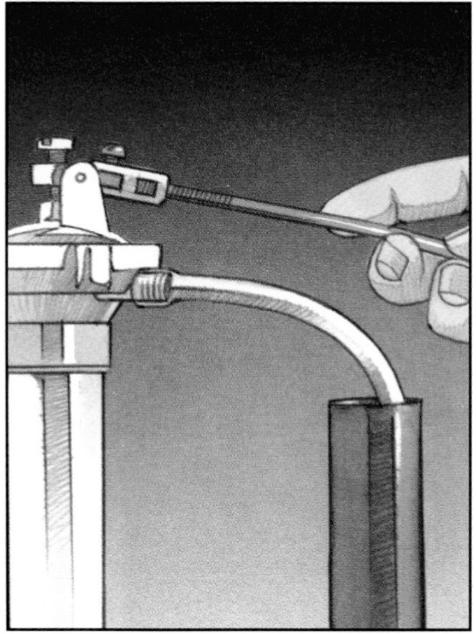

Diaphragm ballcocks usually are made of plastic and have a wide bonnet that contains a rubber diaphragm. Lower the water level by bending the float arm slightly downward; raise the level by bending the arm up.

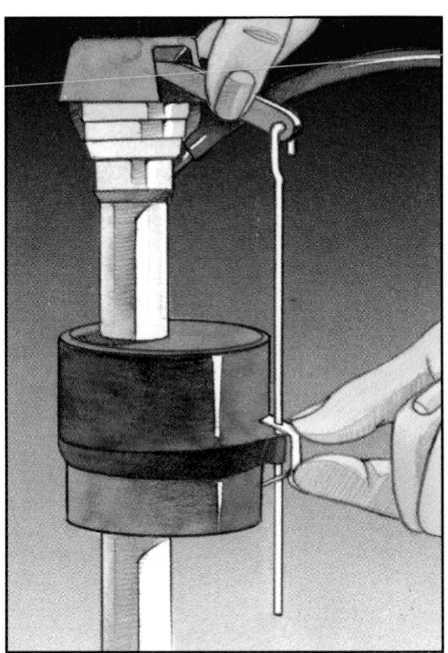

Float cup ballcocks are made of plastic and are easy to adjust. Lower the water level by pinching a spring clip on the pull rod and moving the float cup downward on the ballcock shank. You can raise it by moving the cup up.

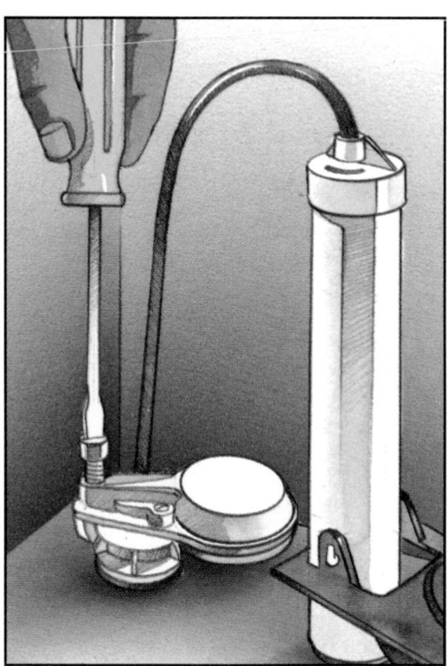

Floatless ballcocks control the water level with a pressure-sensing device. Lower the water level by turning the adjustment screw counterclockwise, half a turn at a time. Raise the water level by turning the screw clockwise.

FIXING A LEAKY PLUNGER-VALVE BALLCOCK

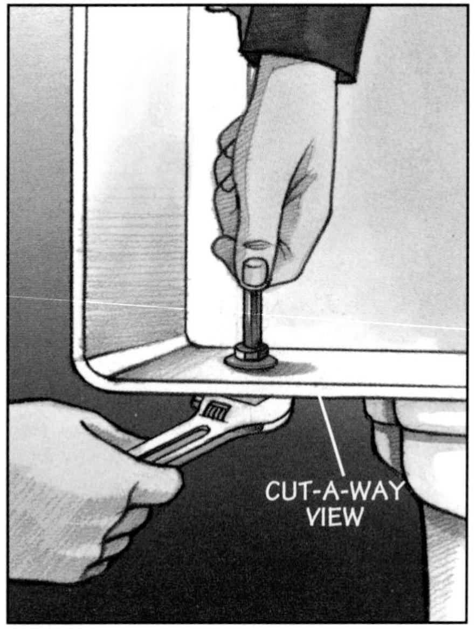

1 Shut off the water and flush the toilet to empty the tank. Loosen the ballcock retaining nut with an adjustable wrench and remove the old ballcock assembly.

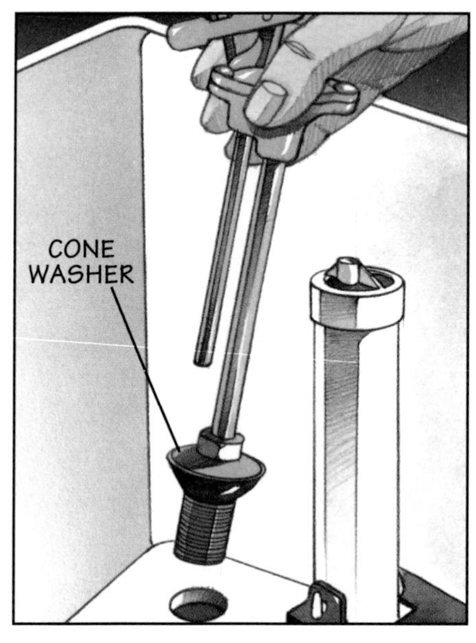

2 Attach the cone washer to the new ballcock tailpiece and insert the tailpiece into the tank opening.

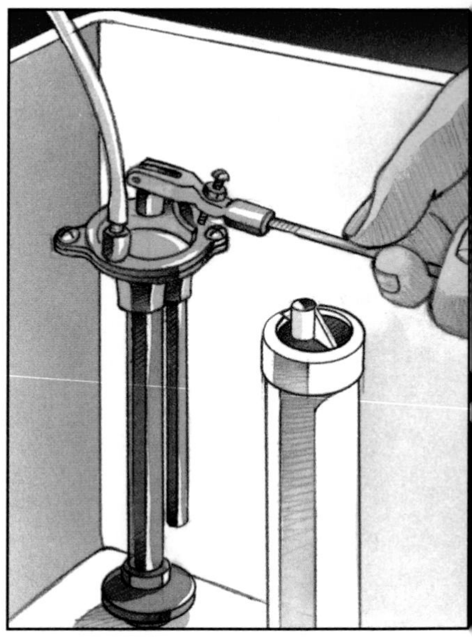

3 Align the float arm socket so that float arm will pass behind overflow pipe. Screw float arm onto ballcock. Screw float ball onto float arm.

FIXING A LEAKY DIAPHRAGM BALLCOCK

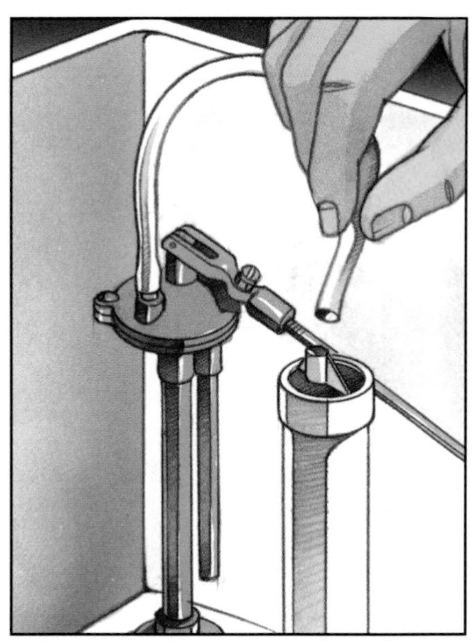

1 Bend or clip refill tube so tip is inside overflow pipe.

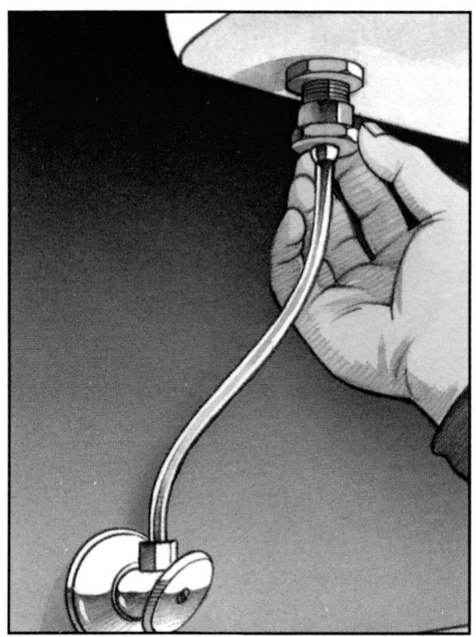

2 Screw the mounting nut and supply-type coupling nut onto the ballcock tailpiece and tighten with an adjustable wrench. Turn on the water and check for leaks.

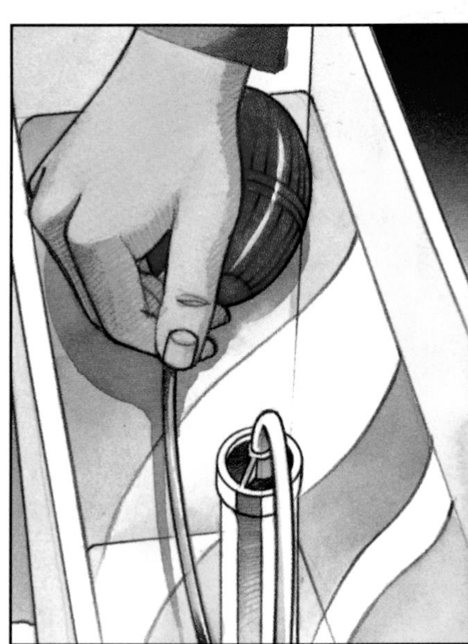

3 Adjust the water level in the tank so it is about $^1/_2$ inch below the top of the overflow pipe (page 143).

FIXING A LEAKY FLOATCUP ASSEMBLY

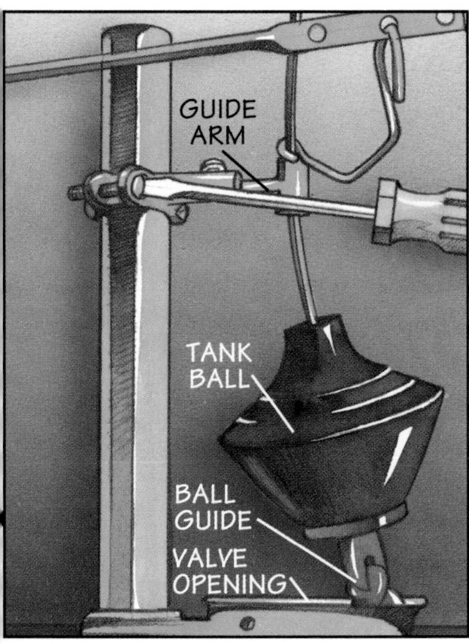

Adjust tank ball (or flapper) so it is directly over flush valve. Tank ball has a guide arm that can be loosened so that tank ball can be repositioned. (Some tank balls have a ball guide that helps seat the tank ball into the flush valve.)

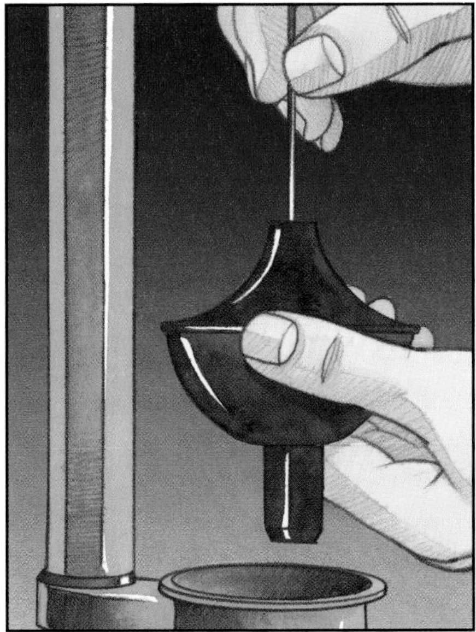

Replace the tank ball if it is cracked or worn. Tank balls have a threaded fitting that screws onto the lift wire. Clean opening of the flush valve using emery cloth (for brass valves) or a scrub pad (for plastic valves).

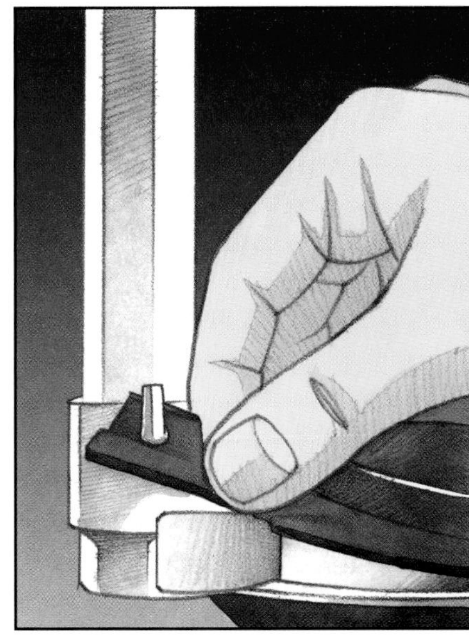

Replace flapper if it is worn. Flappers are attached to small lugs on the sides of overflow pipe.

Plumbing

INSTALLING A NEW FLUSH VALVE

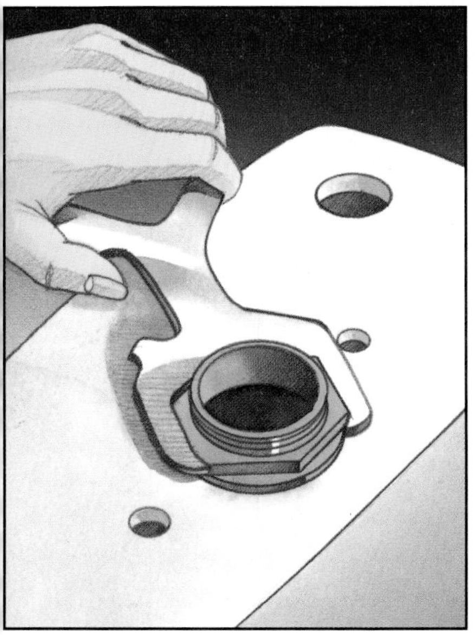

1 Shut off water, disconnect the ballcock (opposite, step 1), and remove toilet tank (page 138, steps 1 and 2). Remove the old flush valve by unscrewing the spud nut with a spud wrench or water-pump pliers.

2 Slide the cone washer onto the tailpiece of the new flush valve. Beveled side of the cone washer should face the end of tailpiece. Insert the flush valve into the tank opening so that the overflow pipe faces the ballcock.

3 Screw the spud nut onto the tailpiece of the flush valve, and tighten with a spud wrench or water-pump pliers. Place soft spud washer over tailpiece, and reinstall toilet tank (page 140).

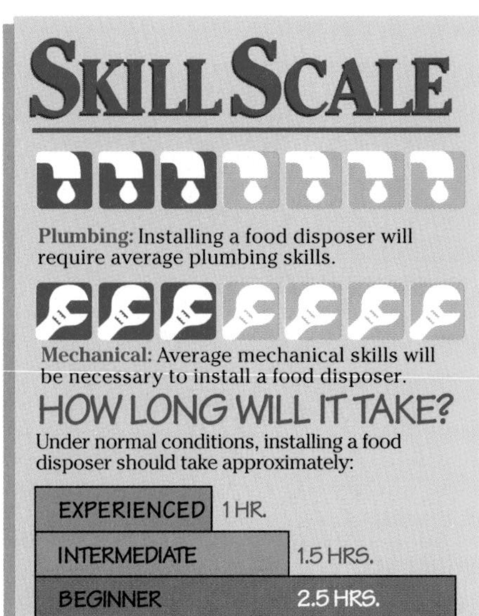

Plumbing

Installing a Food Disposer

A food disposer is designed to grind food waste so it can be flushed away. You may have to remind yourself of this when you get carried away and try to use it as an industrial grinder on those steak and chicken bones and end up with a jammed or damaged disposer.

When you're shopping for a disposer, be sure to look for one with at least a ½ horsepower rating and a self-reversing motor that will unclog any jams if they occur. Other features to look for include foam sound insulation, a cast-iron grinding ring, and overload protection that will let you reset the motor if it overheats. Most quality disposers will carry a 5-year manufacturer's warranty.

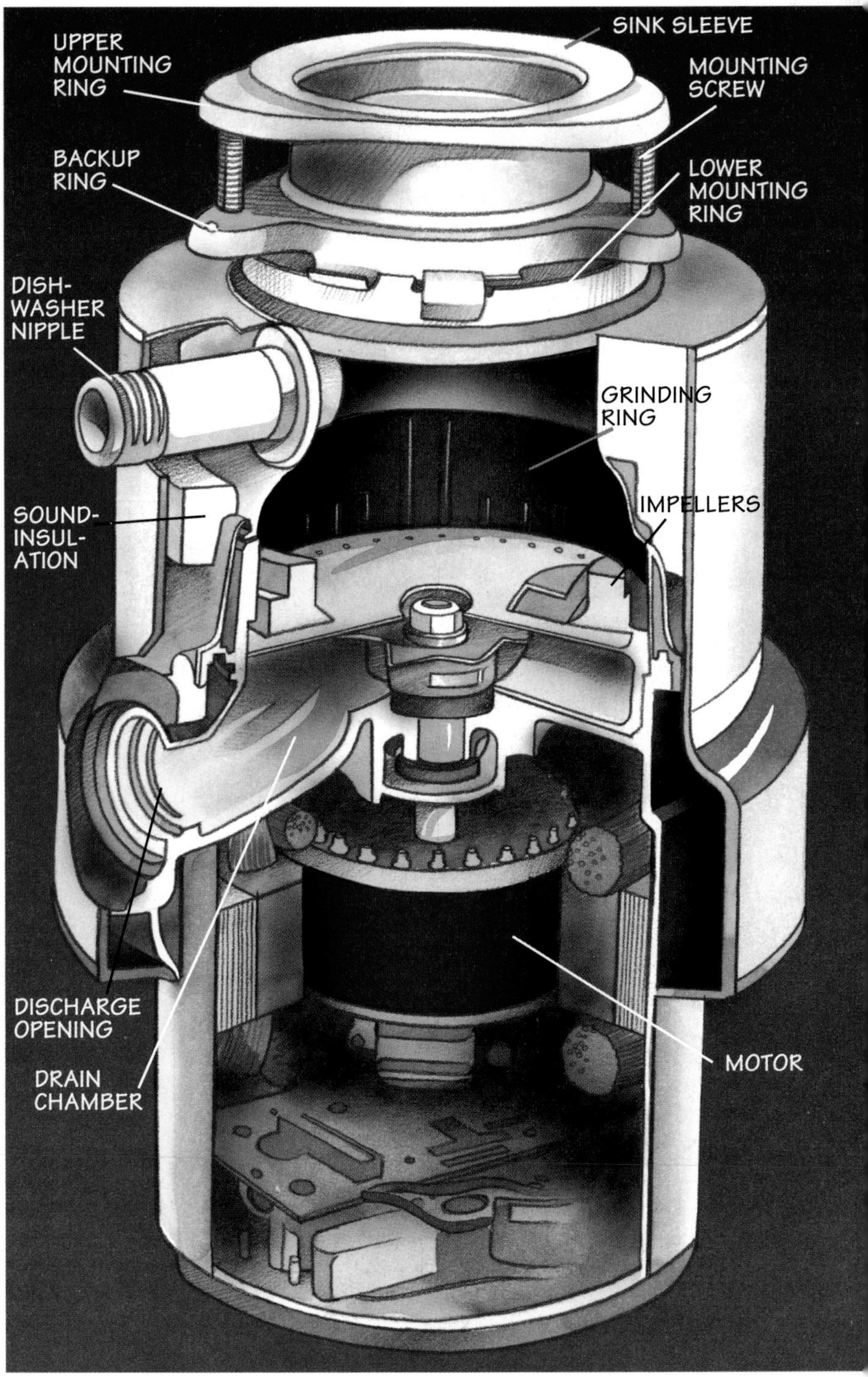

SINK SLEEVE
UPPER MOUNTING RING
MOUNTING SCREW
BACKUP RING
LOWER MOUNTING RING
DISH-WASHER NIPPLE
GRINDING RING
IMPELLERS
SOUND-INSUL-ATION
DISCHARGE OPENING
DRAIN CHAMBER
MOTOR

STUFF YOU'LL NEED:

- **Tools:** Basic plumbing tool kit (page 86).
- **Materials:** Plumber's putty, hose clamps.

ELECTRICAL HOOKUP

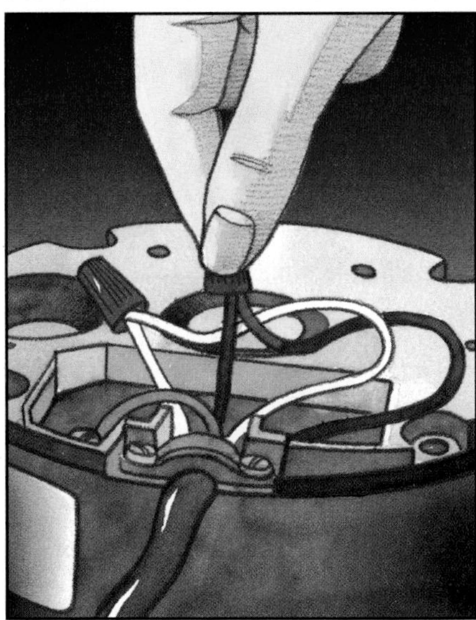

Remove the disposer's bottom. Use a combination tool to strip ½ inch of insulation from each wire in the appliance cord. Connect the white wires with a wire connector, then connect the black wires. Attach the green insulated wire to the green grounding screw. Gently push the wires in and replace the bottom plate.

MOUNTING & PLUMBING A FOOD DISPOSER

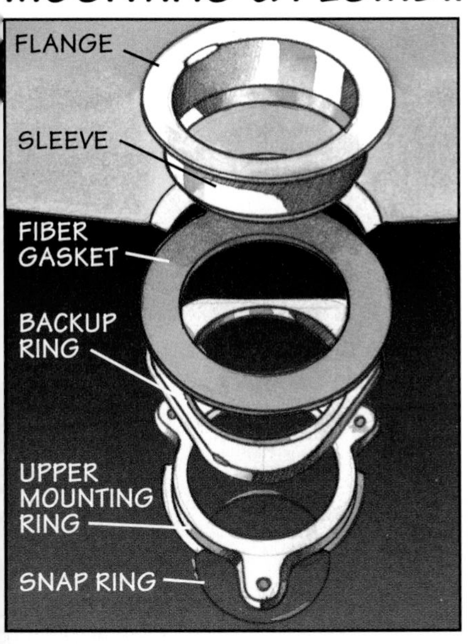

1 Apply a 1/4 inch bead of plumber's putty under the flange of the disposer sink sleeve. Insert the sleeve in the drain opening and slip the fiber gasket and the backup ring onto the sleeve. Place the upper mounting ring on the sleeve and slide the snap ring into the groove.

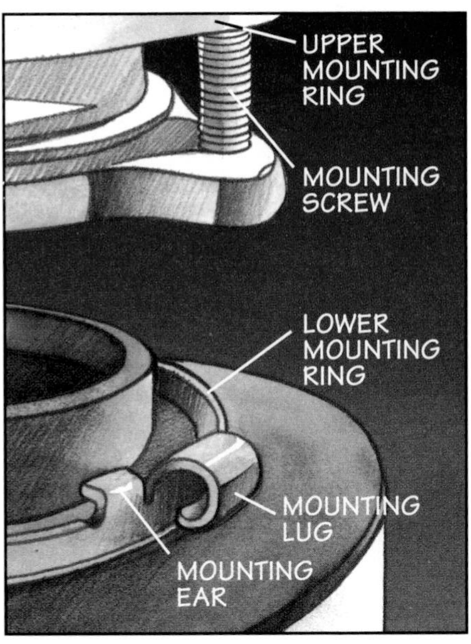

2 Tighten the three mounting screws. Hold the disposer against the upper mounting ring so that the mounting lugs on the lower mounting ring are directly under the mounting screws. Turn the lower mounting ring clockwise until the disposer is supported by the mounting assembly.

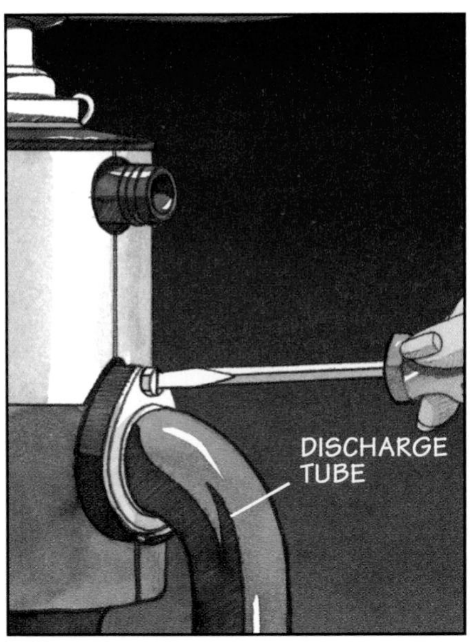

3 Attach the discharge tube to the discharge opening on the side of the disposer using the rubber washer and metal flange.

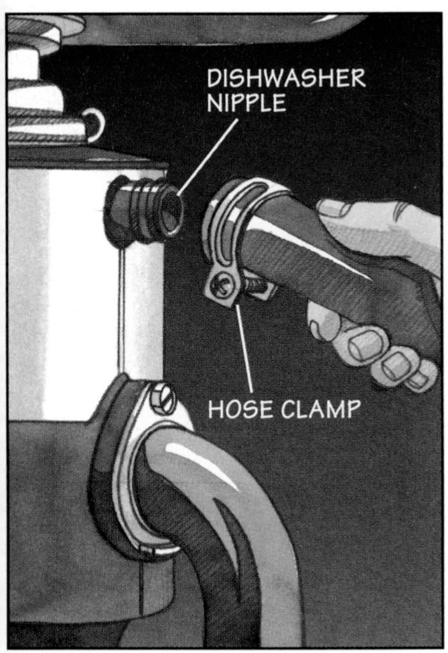

4 If a dishwasher will be attached, knock out the plug in the dishwasher nipple using a screwdriver. Attach the dishwasher drain hose to the nipple with a hose clamp.

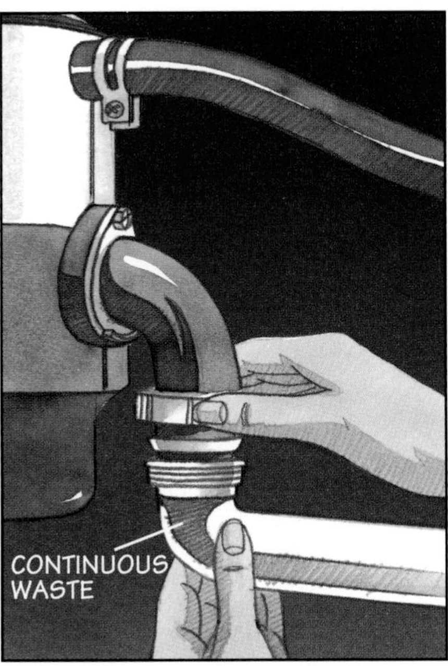

5 Attach the discharge tube to the continuous waste pipe with a slip washer and nut. If the discharge tube is too long, cut it with a hacksaw or tubing cutter.

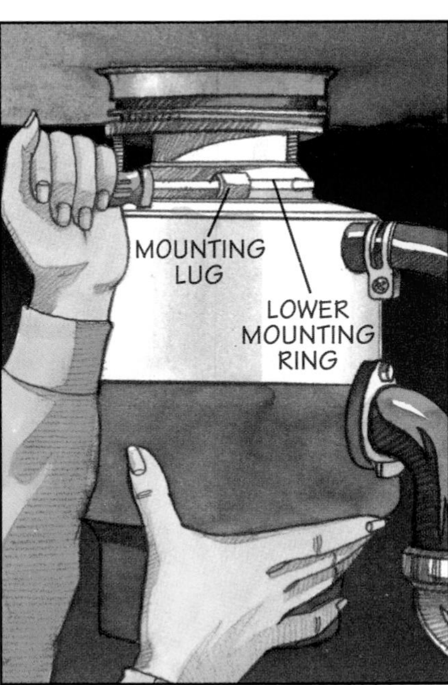

6 Lock the disposer into place. Insert a screwdriver or disposer wrench into a mounting lug on the lower mounting ring, and turn clockwise until the mounting ears are locked. Tighten all drain slip nuts with water-pump pliers.

Installing a Dishwasher

A dishwasher, as you know, will clean dishes, cooking utensils, and glasses, etc., but you may also realize that it cleans countertops too! By eliminating the piles of dirty dishes that overflow the kitchen sink, the dishwasher is a valuable helper in your daily housecleaning.

All it takes to install one of these beauties is simply a hot water supply connection, a drain connection, and an electrical hookup. These connections are easiest to make when the dishwasher is located next to the kitchen sink.

Many dishwashers are designed to drain directly into the disposer, while others are designed to drain by looping the dishwasher drain hose up through an air gap mounted on the sink or countertop. This air gap will help prevent a clogged drain from backing water up into the dishwasher.

PLUMBING & WIRING A DISHWASHER

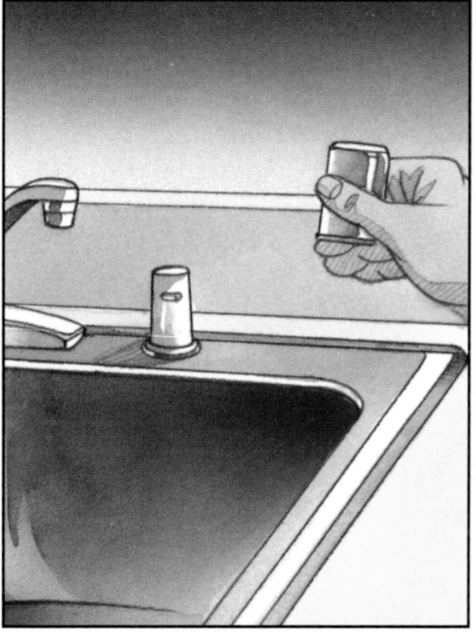

1 Mount the air gap using one of the predrilled sink openings. Or, bore a hole in the countertop with a drill and hole saw. Attach the air gap by tightening the mounting nut over the tailpiece with water-pump pliers.

2 Cut openings in the side of the sink base cabinet for electrical and plumbing lines using a drill and hole saw. Dishwasher instructions specify the size and location of the openings. Slide the dishwasher into place, feeding the rubber drain hose through the hole in the cabinet. Level the dishwasher.

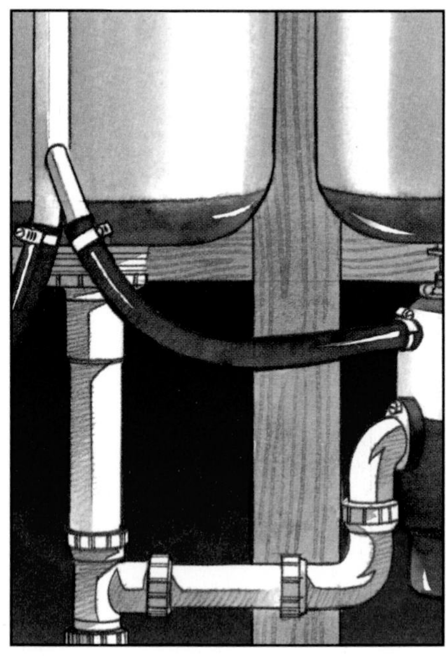

3 Attach the dishwasher drain hose to the smaller straight nipple on the air gap using a hose clamp. If the hose is too long, cut it to the correct length. Cut another length of rubber hose and attach one end to the larger, angled nipple on the food disposer and the other end to the air gap.

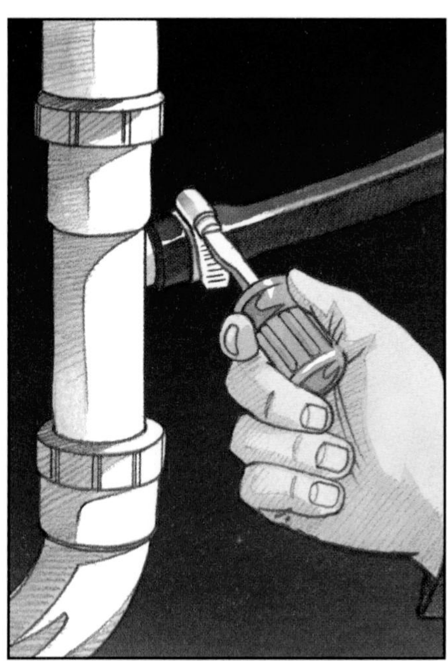

On sinks without a food disposer, attach a special waste-T sink tailpiece to the sink strainer. Attach the drain hose to the waste-T nipple with a hose clamp.

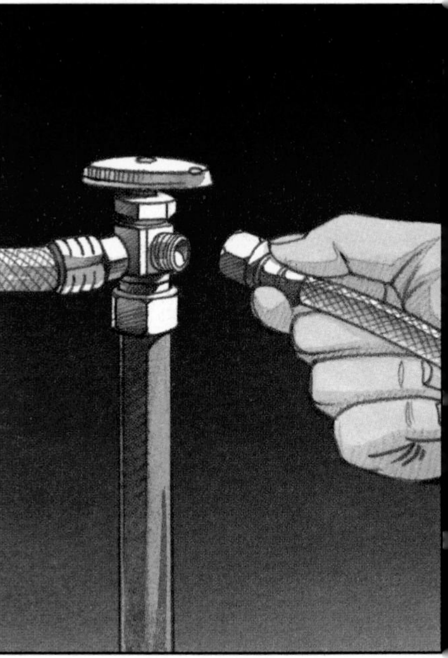

4 Connect the dishwasher supply tube to the hot water shutoff using pipe-joint compound and water-pump pliers. This connection is easiest with a multiple-outlet shutoff valve or a brass T-fitting. You could also use two valves after installing a T-fitting on the end of the hot water supply pipe.

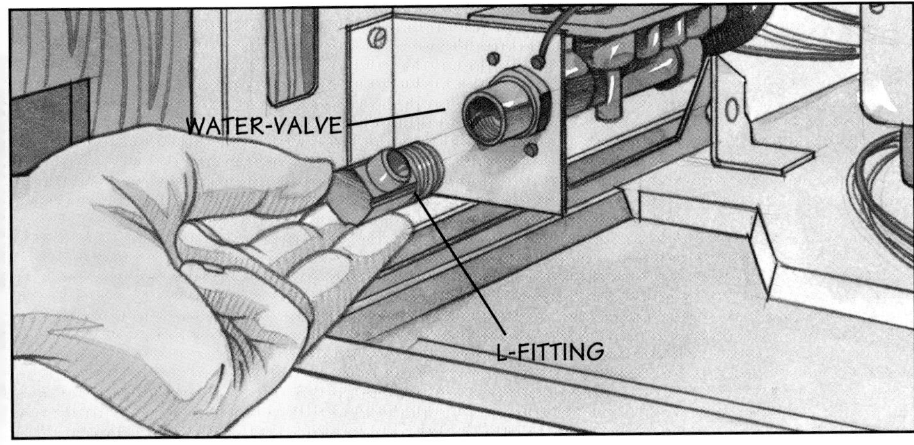

5 Remove the access panel on the front of the dishwasher. Connect a brass L-fitting to the threaded opening on the dishwasher water valve using pipe-joint compound and tighten with water-pump pliers.

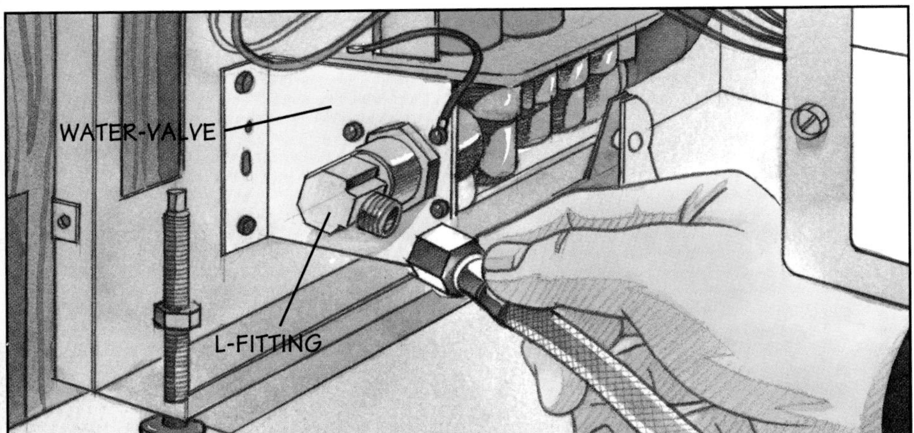

6 Run the braided steel supply tube from the hot water pipe to the dishwasher water valve. Attach the supply tube to the L-fitting, using pipe-joint compound and an adjustable wrench or water-pump pliers.

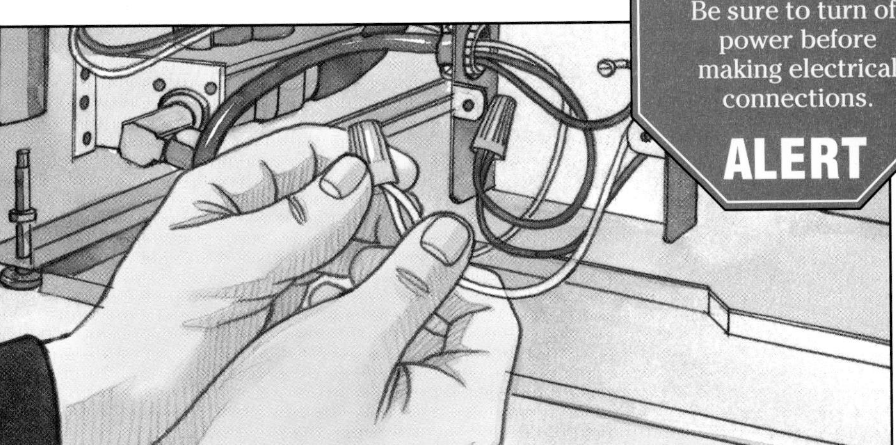

7 Remove the cover on the electrical box. Run the power cord from the outlet to electrical box. Strip about $^{1}/_{2}$ inch of insulation from each cord wire using a combination tool. Connect the red wires using a wire connector. Connect the white wires with a wire connector, then connect the green insulated wire to the grounding screw. Replace the cover and access panel.

SAFETY ALERT

Be sure to turn off power before making electrical connections.

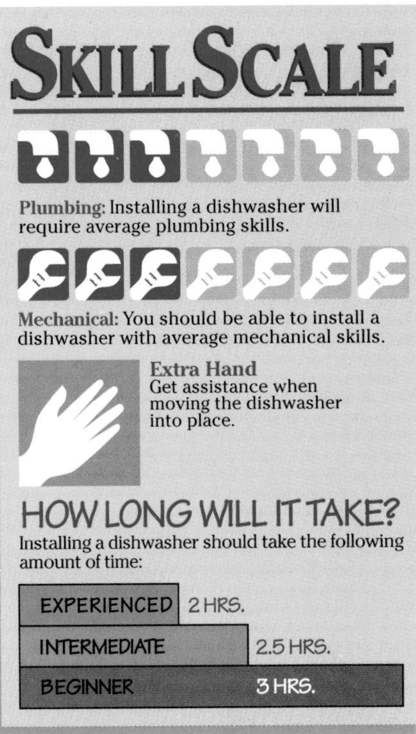

Plumbing

STUFF YOU'LL NEED:

- ☐ **Tools:** Basic plumbing tool kit (page 86).
- ☐ **Materials:** Pipe-joint compound, braided steel supply tube, hose clamps.

OOPS!

If you don't remove the plug in the dishwasher nipple of the disposer you'll get a dishwasher full of drain water and a tidal wave when you open the door. The only thing to do is to mop up and sponge the dishwasher dry, then disconnect the washer to get at the drain plug. Once you've taken out the drain plug, reconnect it as before.

ELECTRICAL BASICS

You may never have thought of it like this before, but a household electrical system is comparable to a home's plumbing system. Electrical current flows in wires in much the same way that water flows in pipes. Both electricity and water enter the home, are distributed throughout the house, do their "work," and then exit.

In plumbing, water first flows through the pressurized water supply system. In electricity, current first flows along hot wires. Current flowing along hot wires also is pressurized. The pressure of electrical current is called voltage.

Large pipes can carry a greater volume of water than small pipes. Likewise, large electrical wires carry more current than small wires. This current-carrying capacity of wires is called "amperage."

Water is made available for use through the faucets, spigots, and shower heads in a home. Electricity is made available through receptacles, switches, and fixtures.

Water finally leaves the home through a drain system which is not pressurized. Similarly, electrical current flows back through neutral wires. The current in neutral wires is not pressurized and is said to be at "zero voltage."

Safety should be the primary concern of anyone working with electricity. Although most household electrical repairs are simple and straightforward, always use caution and good judgment when working with electrical wiring or devices.

The basic rule of electrical safety is: **Always turn off power to the area or device you are working on.** At the main service panel, remove the fuse or shut off the circuit breaker that controls the circuit you are servicing. Always confirm the power is shut off by testing the circuit with a neon circuit tester. Restore power only when the repair or replacement has been completed.

Electrical improvements and repairs are strictly controlled by local Codes which vary widely from region to region. Always check the Codes before you start.

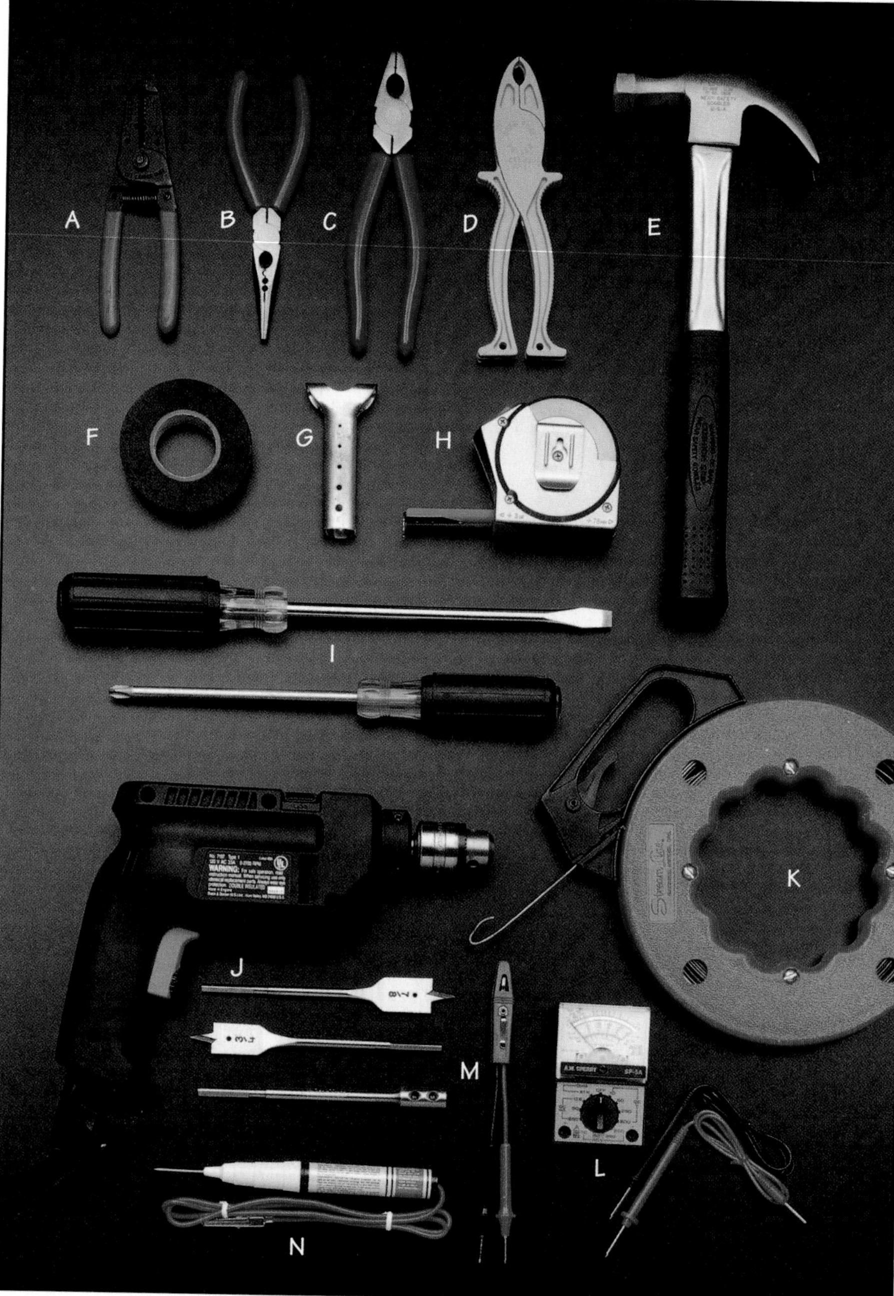

BASIC ELECTRICAL TOOL BOX

A) **Combination Tool:** measures, strips, and cuts wire and cable.
B) **Needlenose Pliers:** bends and shapes wire.
C) **Linesman's Tool:** cuts and twists heavy wire and grips conduit nuts.
D) **Fuse Puller:** removes cartridge-type fuses from fuse box.
E) **Hammer:** attaches wire staples and opens knockouts in metal boxes.
F) **Electrical Tape:** marks wires and attaches cable to fish tape.
G) **Cable Stripper:** removes outer sheathing from NM cables.
H) **Tape Measure:** measures height of new electrical boxes.
I) **Insulated Screwdrivers:** reduce risk of electrical shock.
J) **Drill with Bits and Extension:** bores holes in framing members for cable.
K) **Fish Tape:** installs cable in finished walls and pulls wire through conduit.
L) **Voltage Multi-tester:** optional tool measures voltage from 1 to 1,000 volts.
M) **Neon Circuit Tester:** checks circuit wires for power.
N) **Continuity Tester:** checks switches and receptacles for faults.

BUYER'$ GUIDE

Choosing Wire

Solid copper wires are the best electrical conductors. Buy wires large enough for the amperage rating of the entire circuit. A wire that is too small can become dangerously hot. Wire sizes are categorized by a number where the larger the wire size the smaller the number. To find the size of a wire, check the wire's insulation for writing that indicates the wire size.

If you have aluminum wiring you'll need special connections to install new copper wiring. It's best to call an electrician in this case.

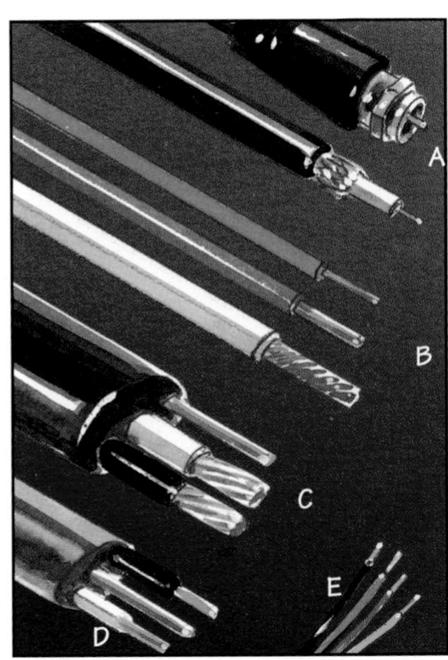

TYPES & SIZES OF WIRE

A) Coaxial Cable: used to connect television jacks. Available with preattached fittings.

B) THHN/THWN Wire: used inside conduit, shown from top to bottom in 14, 12, and 10 gauge.

C) NMB Paper-Filled Sheathed Cable: used for indoor wiring projects in dry locations. Available in "2-wire with ground" or "3-wire with ground" types.

D) UF (Underground Feeder) Cable: used in damp or wet locations. If Code allows its use, bury at least 2 ft. down and protect with a buried board.

E) Low-Voltage Wire: various gauges are used for low-voltage applications such as thermostats.

Not pictured: Metallic Cable (MC): used when durable cable insulation required.

BASIC ELECTRICAL MATERIALS

A) Electrical Boxes: available in metal, plastic, and plastic retrofit types. Metal boxes are used primarily with conduit but can also be used inside finished walls. Plastic boxes have preattached mounting nails and should be used with internal cable clamps inside finished walls. Retrofit boxes are used when adding a switch or receptacle in an existing wall.

B) Receptacles: available in either standard or GFCI (ground-fault circuit-interrupter) types.

C) Switches: available in standard, for a single switch circuit; three-way, for multiple switch circuits; and specialty switches, such as time-delay or programmable.

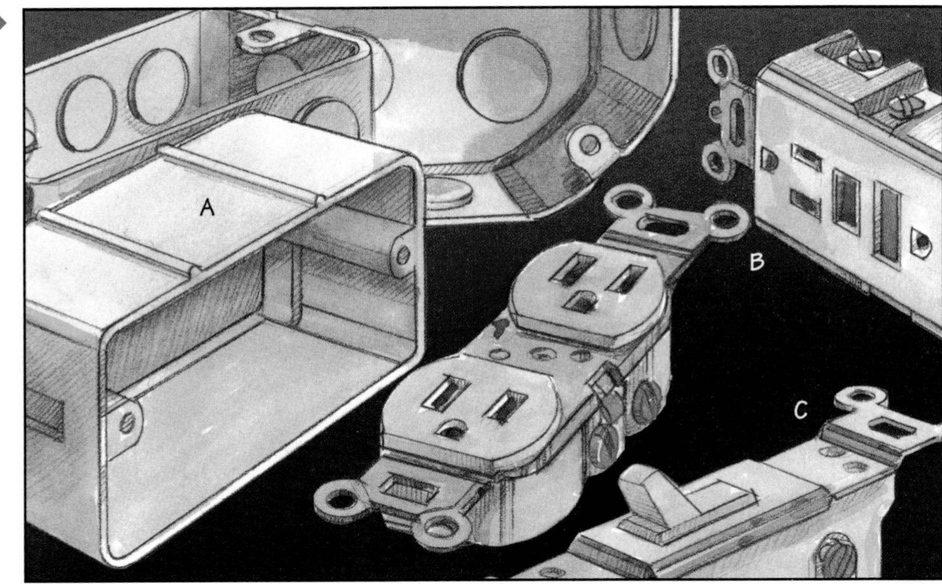

WIRE CONNECTORS

Available in wing flange or regular style, wire connectors are rated for the gauge size and number of wires you are connecting. To ensure safe connections, be sure to follow the manufacturer's rating for minimum and maximum wire capacity. Green wire connectors are used only for connecting grounding wires.

CABLE CLAMPS & STAPLES

Plastic cable staples are used to anchor cables to the sides of framing members and are designed to match the size and quantity of cables to be anchored. Cable clamps are designed for the size of cable to be used and are rated for the opening in the metal electrical box.

Working with Conduit

Electrical wiring that runs in exposed locations must be protected by conduit. For example, conduit is used for wiring that runs across masonry walls in a basement laundry and for exposed outdoor wiring. THHN/THWN wire is normally installed inside conduit.

There are several types of conduit available so be sure to check with your electrical inspector to find out which type meets Code requirements.

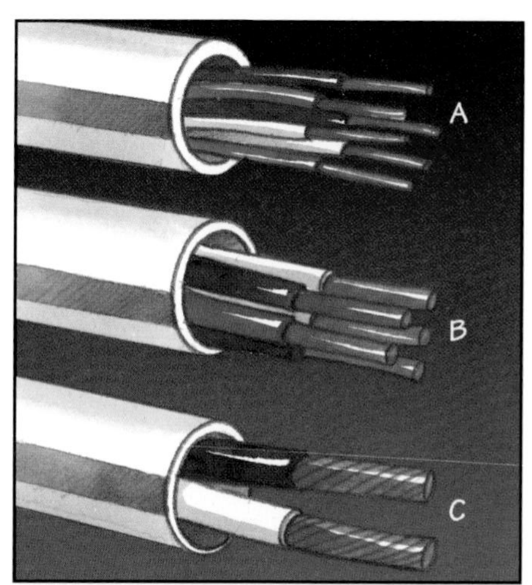

CONDUIT WIRE CAPACITY
When purchasing conduit, keep in mind that conduit capacity is determined by the gauge of wire, conduit size, and local Codes. Usually ½" conduit can fit up to:
A) Six 14-gauge or 12-gauge THHN/THWN wires.
B) Five 10-gauge THHN/THWN wires.
C) Two 8-gauge THHN/THWN wires.
If the number of wires you require exceeds this capacity, you'll need to use ¾" conduit. Always check local Code requirements and plan your conduit and conduit fitting needs before you go to the store.

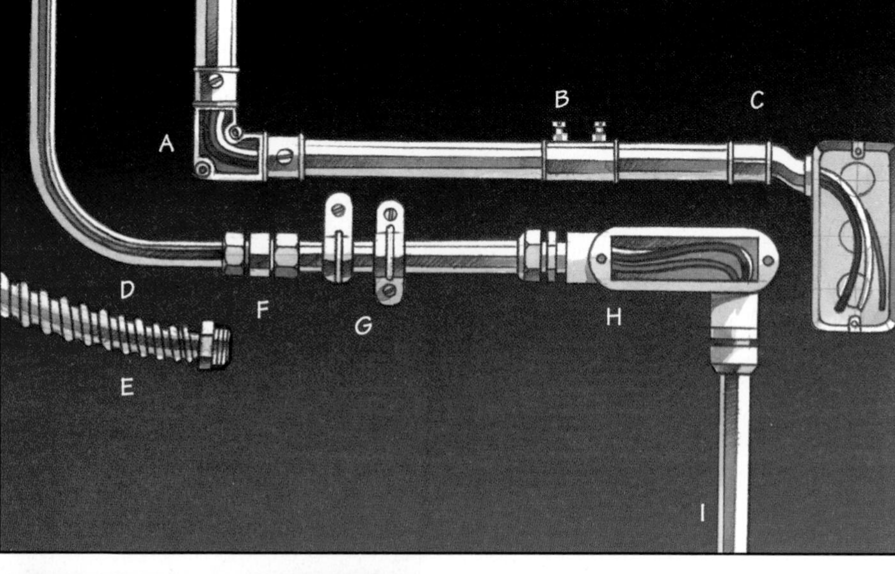

TYPES OF CONDUIT FITTINGS
- **A) Elbow Fitting:** used in tight corners. Elbow cover can be removed to pull wire from separate long wire lengths.
- **B) Setscrew Coupling:** connects separate lengths of metal conduit.
- **C) Offset Fitting:** connects an indoor metal electrical box to a conduit anchored flush against a wall.
- **D) Sweep:** forms a gradual 90° bend for ease in pulling wire.
- **E) Flexible Metal Conduit:** used in exposed locations where rigid conduit is difficult to install.
- **F) Compression Fitting:** watertight coupling for use outdoors.
- **G) Conduit Straps:** hold conduit in place against walls.
- **H) L-Body Fitting:** watertight elbow used in outdoor installations.
- **I) EMT (Electrical Metallic Tubing) Conduit:** used primarily for exposed indoor installations.

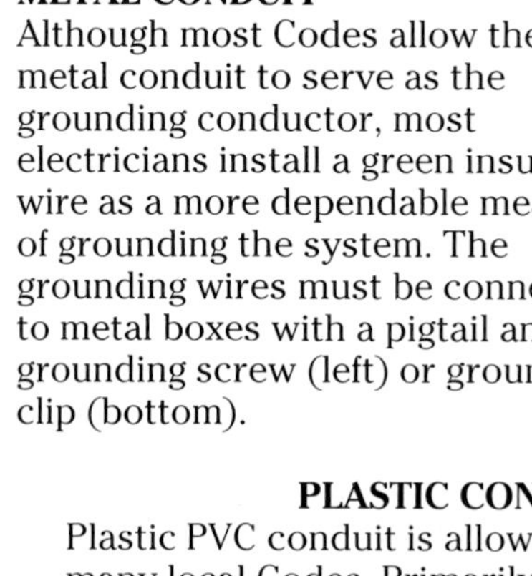

ELECTRICAL GROUNDING IN METAL CONDUIT
Although most Codes allow the metal conduit to serve as the grounding conductor, most electricians install a green insulated wire as a more dependable means of grounding the system. The grounding wires must be connected to metal boxes with a pigtail and grounding screw (left) or grounding clip (bottom).

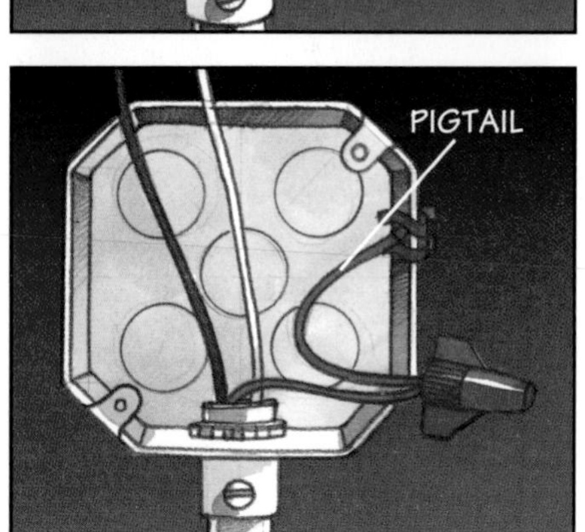

PLASTIC CONDUIT
Plastic PVC conduit is allowed by many local Codes. Primarily used for below-ground applications, it is assembled with solvent glue and PVC fittings that resemble those for metal conduit. Special adapters can be used to attach plastic conduit to metal boxes. When wiring with PVC conduit, always run a green grounding wire for each circuit.

SKILL SCALE

Electrical: Installing metal conduit requires basic electrical skills.

Mechanical: Metal conduit installation requires basic mechanical skills.

HOW LONG WILL IT TAKE?

Installing metal conduit for a standard circuit with three receptacles should take approximately:

EXPERIENCED	60 MIN.
INTERMEDIATE	75 MIN.
BEGINNER	90 MIN.

STUFF YOU'LL NEED:

- ☐**Tools:** Screwdrivers, pliers, fish tape, drill, masonry drill bits, hacksaw.
- ☐**Materials:** Conduit, conduit fittings, cable-pulling lubricant, THHN/THWN wire, masonry screws.

INSTALLING METAL CONDUIT

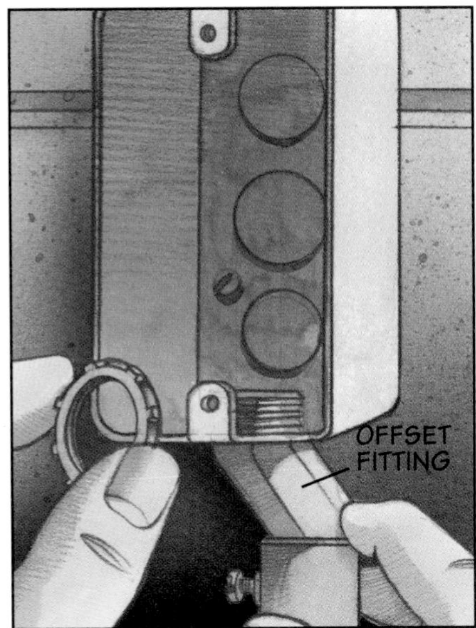

1 Open one knockout for each length of conduit that will be attached to the box. Attach an offset fitting to each knockout using a locknut. Sharp edges of cut conduit can damage wire insulation when you pull the wires through the conduit. Always debur cut conduit before pulling wire.

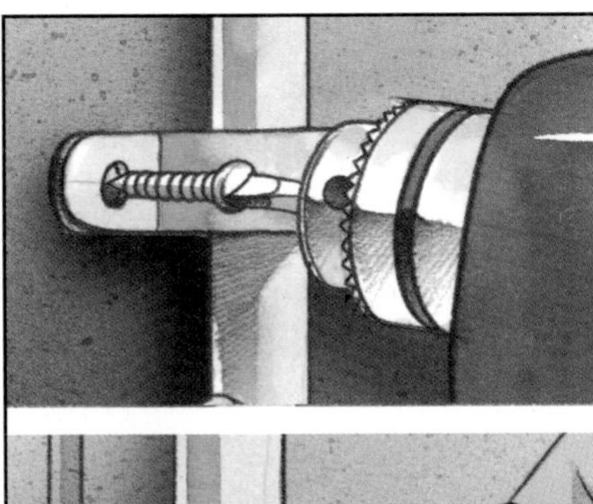

2 Anchor the conduit with pipe straps and masonry anchors. Conduit should be anchored within 3 ft. of each box and fitting, and every 10 ft. thereafter. Continue the conduit run by attaching additional lengths using setscrew or compression fittings.

3 Use an elbow fitting in conduit runs that have many bends, or runs that require very long wires. The cover on the elbow fitting can be removed to make it easier to extend a fish tape and pull wires.

4 At the service breaker panel, open a knockout in the panel. Attach a setscrew fitting and install a length of conduit.

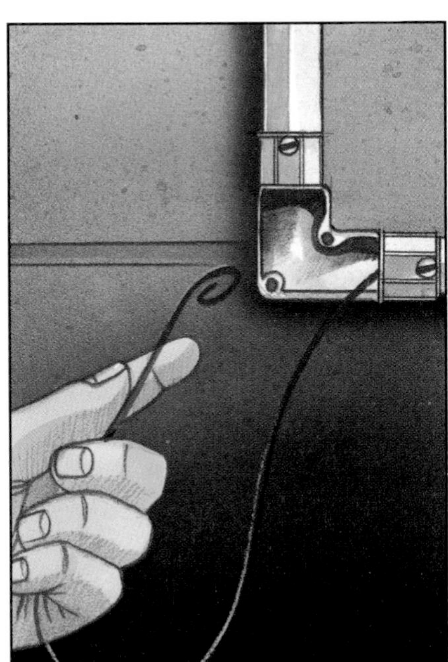

5 Unwind the fish tape and extend it through the conduit from the circuit breaker panel outward. Remove the cover on an elbow fitting when extending the fish tape around tight corners.

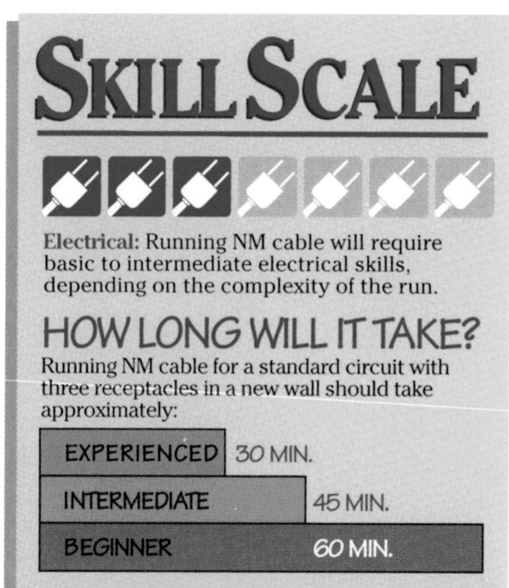

Running Wire for Circuits

NM cable is used for all indoor wiring projects except those requiring conduit. "NM" means non-metallic and refers to the outer sheathing of the cable. It's easy to install when walls and ceilings are unfinished; however, some jobs require that you run cable through finished walls. Running cable in finished walls requires extra planning and often is easier if you work with a helper. Sometimes cables can be run through a finished wall by using gaps around a chimney or plumbing soil stack.

Refer to your wiring plan to make sure each length of cable is correct for the circuit size and configuration. Cable runs are difficult to measure exactly so leave plenty of extra wire when cutting each length. **Cable splices inside walls are not allowed by Code**. Junction boxes where wires are joined must be accessible. Be sure to check with your local electrical inspector when planning a wiring project.

STUFF YOU'LL NEED:

- ☐ **Tools:** Fish tape, drill with drill bits, knife, needlenose pliers.
- ☐ **Materials:** Cable-pulling lubricant, electrical tape, NM cable.

DON'T USE OIL OR PETROLEUM JELLY AS A LUBRICANT FOR PULLING; THEY CAN DAMAGE THE CABLE'S THERMOPLASTIC SHEATHING.

Electrical

RUNNING NM CABLE INSIDE A FINISHED WALL

1 From the space below the wall, look for a reference point like a soil stack, plumbing pipes, or electrical cables that indicates the location of the wall above. Choose a location for the cable that doesn't interfere with existing utilities. Drill a 1" hole into the stud cavity.

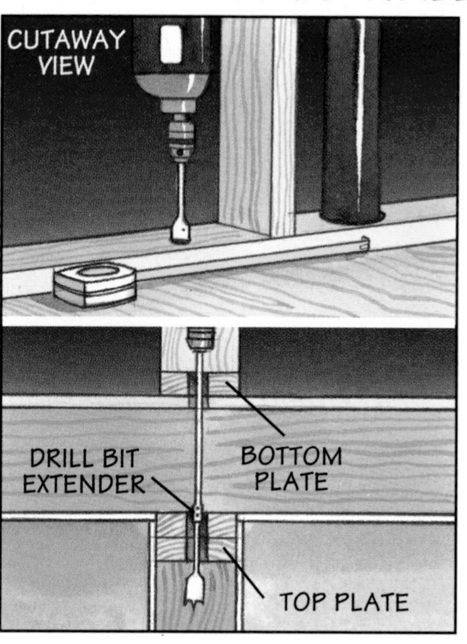

2 From the unfinished space above the finished wall, find the tip of the stud cavity by measuring from the same fixed reference point used in Step 1. Drill a 1" hole down through the top plate and into the stud cavity using a drill bit extender.

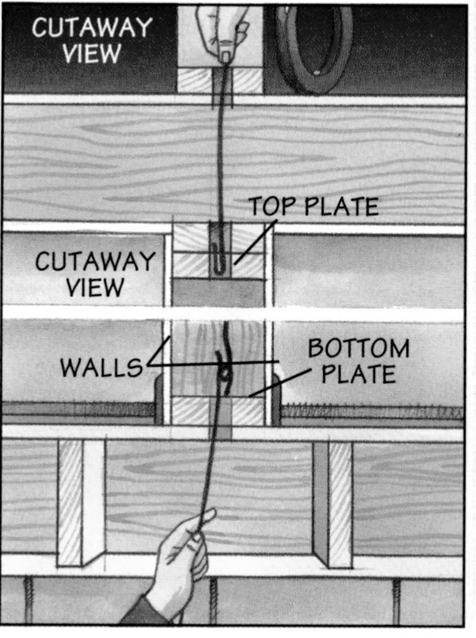

3 Extend a fish tape down through the top plate, twisting the tape until it reaches the bottom of the stud cavity. From the unfinished space below the wall, use a piece of stiff wire with a hook on one end to retrieve the fish tape through the drilled hole in the bottom plate.

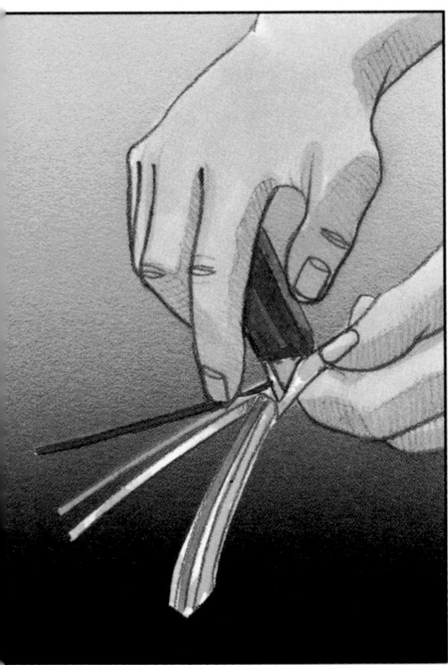

4 Trim back 3" of outer sheathing from the end of the NM cable. Examine the wires to make sure you didn't inadvertently nick or cut the insulation when removing the outer sheathing. Insert the wires through the loop at the tip of the fish tape.

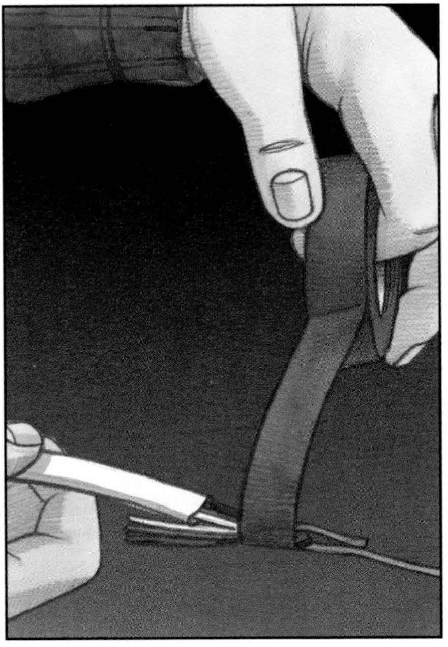

5 Bend the wires against the cable. Use electrical tape to bind them together tightly.

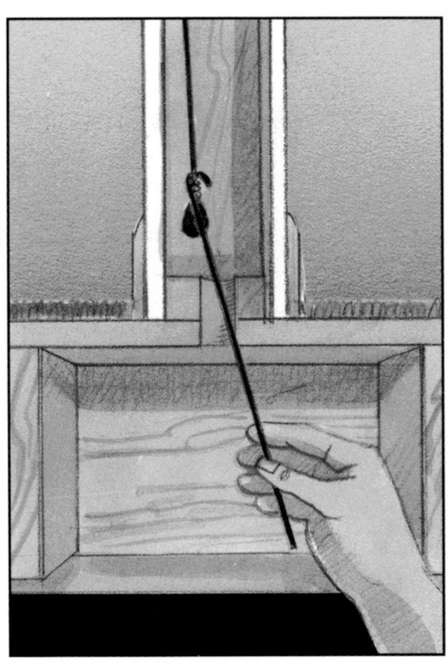

If you do not have a fish tape, use a length of sturdy mason's string and a lead fishing weight or heavy washer to fish down through the stud cavity. Drop the line into the stud cavity from above; then use a piece of stiff wire to hook the line from below.

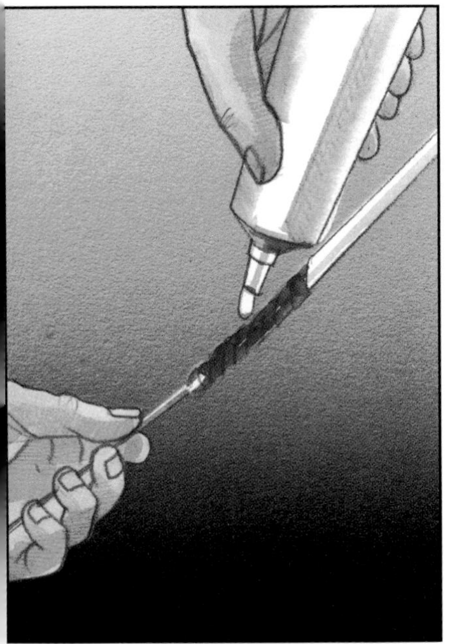

6 If you're having difficulty pulling the cable, apply cable-pulling lubricant to the taped ends of the fish tape. This can be helpful when a cable is pulled through a sharp bend.

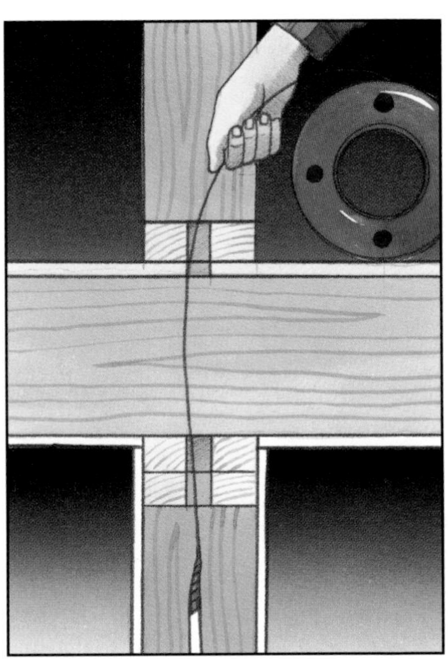

7 From above the finished wall, pull steadily on the fish tape to draw the cable up through the stud cavity. This job will be easier if you have a helper feed the cable from below as you pull.

Depending on the length and the complexity of the run, you may want to get assistance when pulling cable. The cable sometimes can get caught and twisted at the entry point if you're pulling it alone. Having someone help feed the cable into the wall cavity will help keep the cable flowing smoothly and eliminate twisting and bunching up as it is pulled. Twisting and bending the cable too tightly can result in damaged sheathing on the cable.

THE INSIDE STORY ON FISHING CABLES

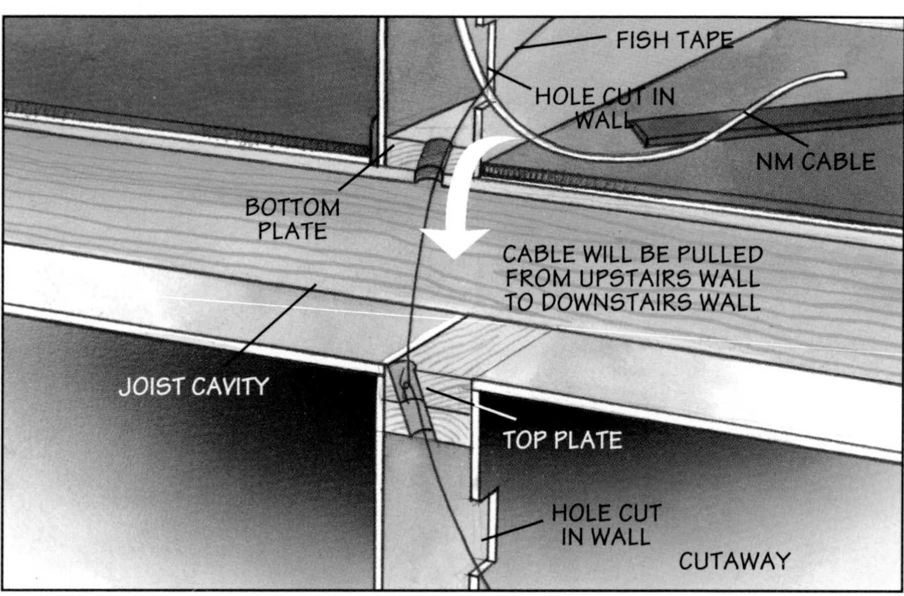

Finished walls that line up: If there's no access space above and below a wall, cut openings in the finished walls to run a cable. This often occurs in two-story homes when a cable is extended from an upstairs wall to a downstairs wall. Cut small openings in the downstairs wall near the top plate and the upstairs wall near the bottom plate, then drill an angled 1" hole through each plate. Extend a fish tape into the joist cavity between the walls and use it to pull the cable from one wall to the next. If the walls line up one over the other, retrieve the fish tape using a piece of stiff wire.

If walls don't line up, use a second fish tape to retrieve the first one. After running the cable, repair the holes in the walls with patching plaster or wallboard scraps and taping compound.

INSTALLING NM CABLE IN NEW WALLS

1 Drill a 5/8" hole in each framing member for the cable run. Holes should be set back at least 1 1/4" from the front face of the framing member. Where cables will turn corners, drill intersecting holes in adjoining faces of studs.

2 Prevent kinks by straightening the cable before pulling it through the studs. Pulling cables through studs is easier if you drill smooth, straight holes at the same height. After running the cable, protect it by attaching nail plates to the face of the studs to protect the cable from nails and screws.

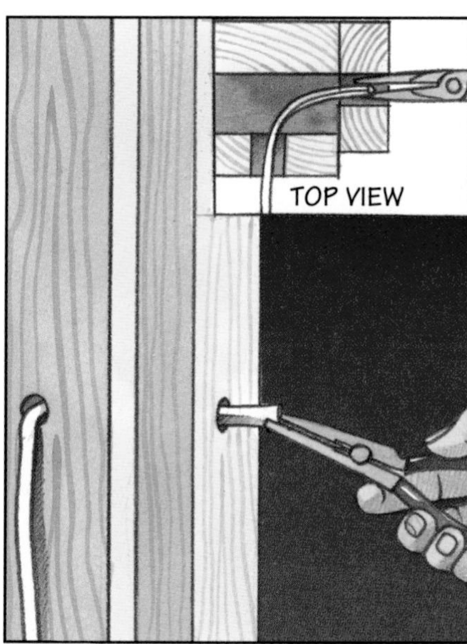

3 At corners, form a slight L-shaped bend in the end of the cable and insert it into one hole. Retrieve the cable through the other hole using needlenose pliers.

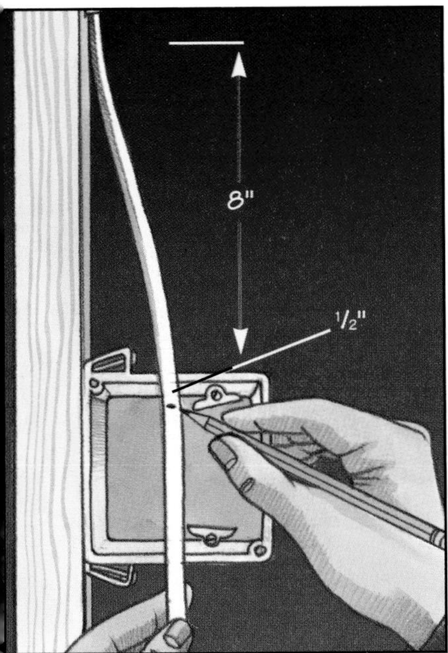

4 At the electrical box, staple the cable to a framing member 8" from the box. Hold the cable taut against the front of the box and mark a point on the cable ½" past the box edge. Cut the cable 12" beyond the marked point. Strip the cable from the marked line to the end and clip away excess sheathing.

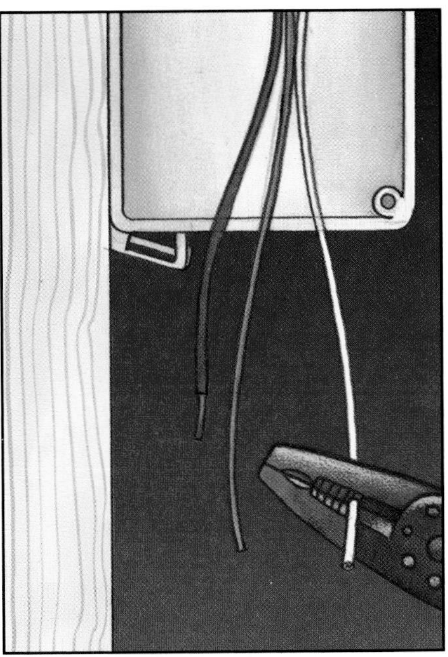

5 Insert the cable through the knockout in the box. Clip back each wire so 8" of workable wire extends past the front edge of the box. Strip ¾" of insulation from each wire in the box. Continue the circuit by running cable between each pair of electrical boxes, leaving 12" of cable at each end.

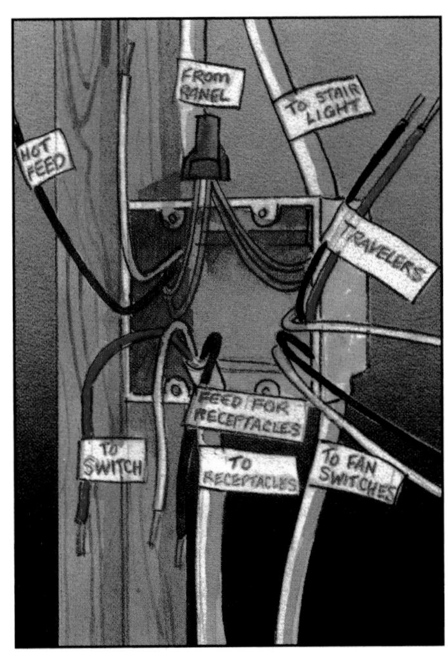

6 Label the cables entering each box to indicate their destinations. In boxes with complex wiring configurations, also tag the individual wires to make final hookups easier. After all cables are installed, your rough-in work is ready to be reviewed by the electrical inspector.

Electrical

AT THE CIRCUIT BREAKER PANEL

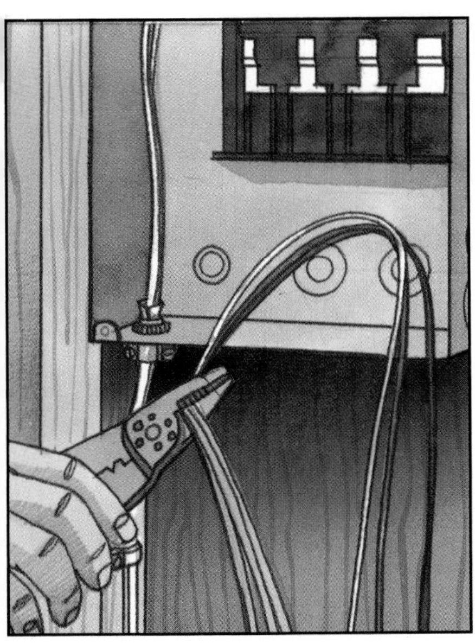

1 Shut off power to the circuit breaker panel. Strip the cable, leaving 1/2" of sheathing to enter the box. Open a knockout in the panel box using a hammer and screw-driver.

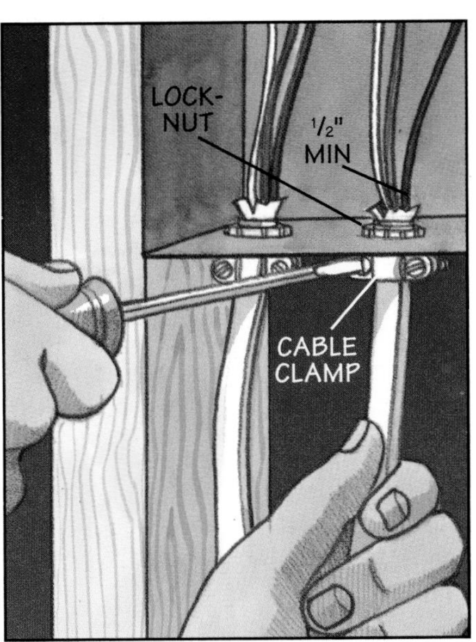

2 Insert a cable clamp into the knockout and secure it with a locknut. Insert the cable through the clamp so that 1/2" of sheathing is exposed. Tighten the mounting screws on the clamp but don't crush the sheathing.

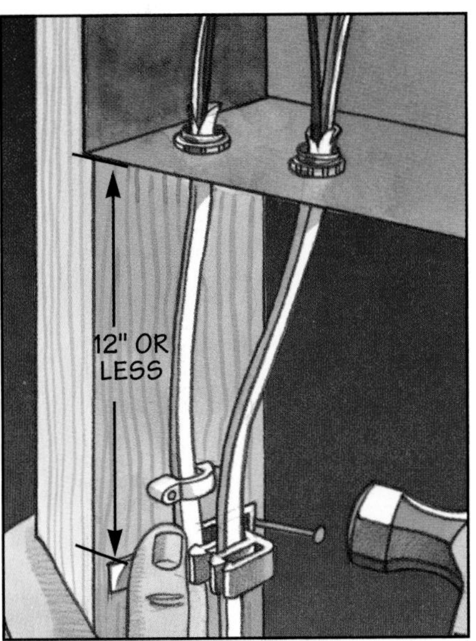

3 Anchor the cable to the center of a framing member within 12" of the panel box using a cable staple. Where two or more cables must be anchored to the same side of a stud, multiple cable staples should be used.

Testing Circuits

An inexpensive neon circuit tester makes it easy to check circuits for power, grounding, and polarity. Remember that the tester only glows when it is part of a complete circuit. If you touch one probe to a hot wire and do not make good contact with the other probe, the tester will not glow even though the hot wire is carrying live power.

When testing for power or grounding, always confirm any negative results by removing the coverplate and examining the receptacle to make sure all wires are intact and properly connected. Do not touch any wires without first turning off the power at the main service panel.

Electrical

SAFETY
Always turn off the power at the main service panel before touching any wires.
ALERT

TESTING A RECEPTACLE FOR POWER

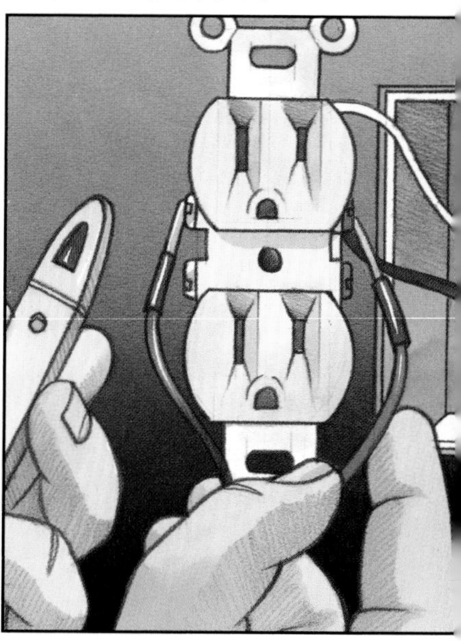

1 Turn off power at the main service panel. Place one probe in each slot of the receptacle. The tester should not glow. If it does glow, double-check the main service panel and turn off the correct circuit. Test both ends of a duplex receptacle. Remember that this is only a preliminary test; you must proceed to Step 2.

2 Remove the coverplate and mounting screws. Gently pull the receptacle out. Don't touch any wires or terminal screws. Touch one probe to a brass terminal and one to a silver terminal. The tester shouldn't glow. If it does, shut off the correct circuit at the service panel. Test both sets of terminals.

TEST FOR GROUNDING

With the power on, place one probe in the short (hot) slot, and the other in the U-shaped grounding hole. The tester should glow. If it does not, place a probe in the long (neutral) slot and one in the grounding hole. If it glows (as shown), the hot and neutral wires are reversed. If tester does not glow in either position, the receptacle is not grounded.

TEST FOR HOT WIRES

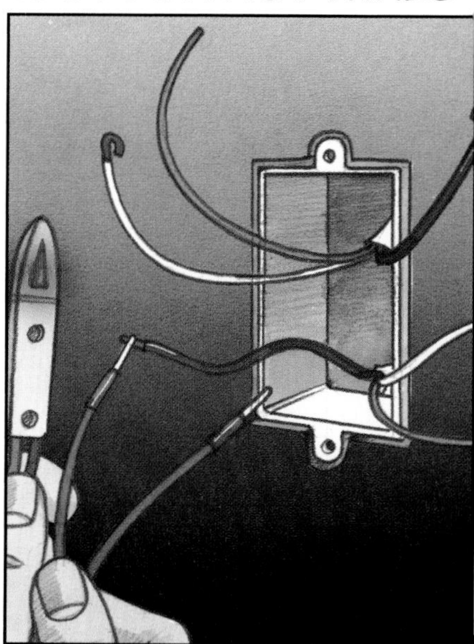

With the power turned off, separate all wires so they don't touch anything else. Restore power. Touch one probe to the bare grounding wire or to the grounded metal box, and the other probe to the ends of each of the wires. Check all wires. If the tester glows, the wire is hot. Turn off power and label the hot wire for identification before continuing work.

TESTING A WALL SWITCH

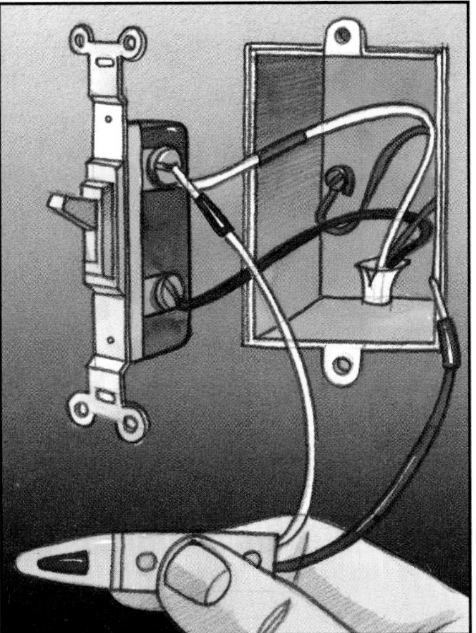

Test for power by touching one probe to the grounded metal box or to the bare copper grounding wire, and touching the other probe to each screw terminal. The tester should not glow. If it does, there is still power entering box. Return to the service panel and turn off power to the correct circuit.

TESTING A TWO-SLOT RECEPTACLE

With the power turned on, place one probe of the tester in each slot. If the tester doesn't glow, there is no power to the receptacle. To test if it's grounded, place one probe in the short (hot) slot, and touch the other to the coverplate screw which must be free of paint. If the tester glows the receptacle is grounded.

HOMER'S HINDSIGHT

Although three prong adapters that fit into two slot holes seem like a good idea, they don't do a thing unless installed properly. The adapter is grounded only if the coverplate screw is grounded to a grounded electrical box. If you use an adapter without grounding it and you plug an electrical motor into the adapter, you're asking for a jolting experience if there's a short in the motor.

TESTING A LIGHT SOCKET

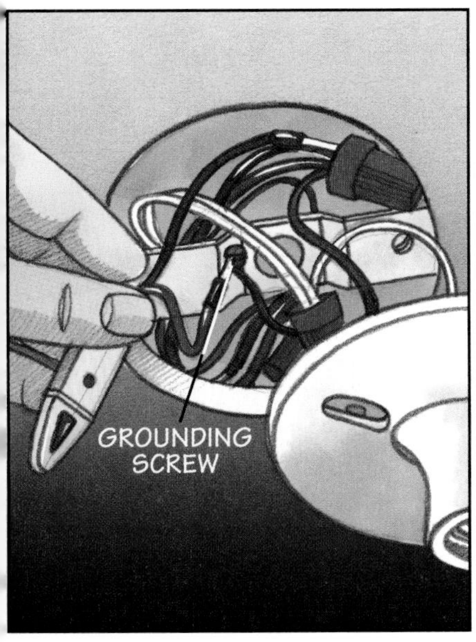

1 To test for current, touch one probe of circuit tester to the screw terminal attached to a black wire. Touch the other probe to the ground screw, bare copper wire, or to the metal box. Repeat test with other screw terminals. If tester does not glow in any position, then there is no power entering the box.

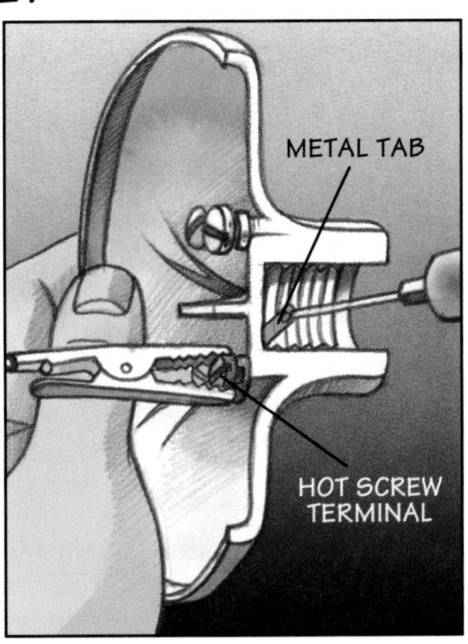

2 Test the socket (shown cut away) with a continuity tester by attaching the clip of a continuity tester to the hot screw terminal (or black wire lead) and touching the probe to the metal tab in the bottom of the socket. The tester should glow; if it doesn't, the socket is faulty and must be replaced.

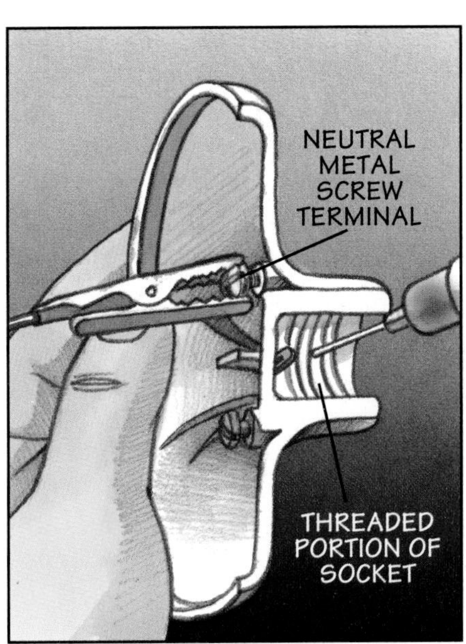

3 Attach the tester clip to the neutral metal screw terminal (or white wire lead) and touch the probe to the threaded portion of the socket. The tester should glow. If it doesn't, the socket is faulty and must be replaced. If the socket is permanently attached, replace the entire fixture.

Making Connections

Connections are easily made with a few simple tools--and can be a real test of character without them. Sliced fingers, punctured hands, and an evaluation of your faith will more than likely result until you opt for these inexpensive, yet "priceless," tools.

When you're stripping insulation and working with copper wire, be careful not to crush the sheathing or not to gouge or damage the copper wire with the tools. This could lead to further problems when power is supplied to the circuit.

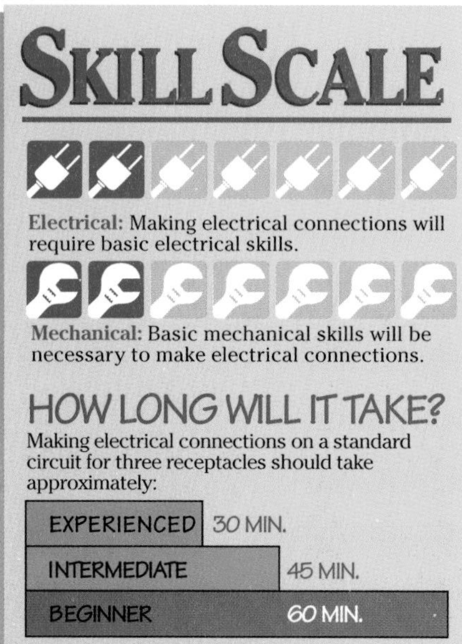

STUFF YOU'LL NEED:

☐**Tools:** Cable ripper, combination tool, lines-man's pliers, screwdriver.

STRIPPING NM CABLE

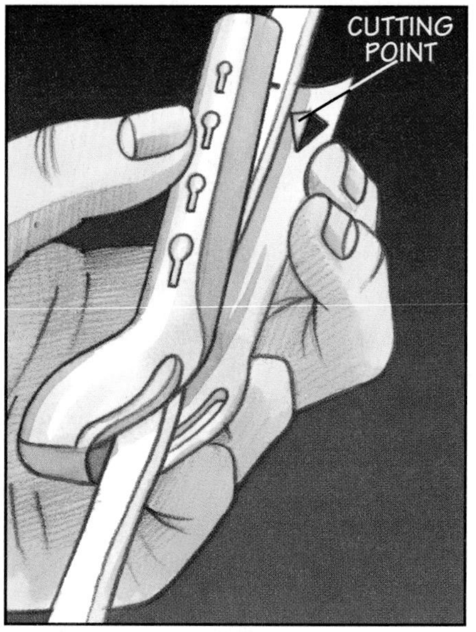

1 Measure and mark the cable 8" to 10" from end. Slide the cable ripper onto the cable and squeeze it firmly to force the cutting point through the plastic sheathing.

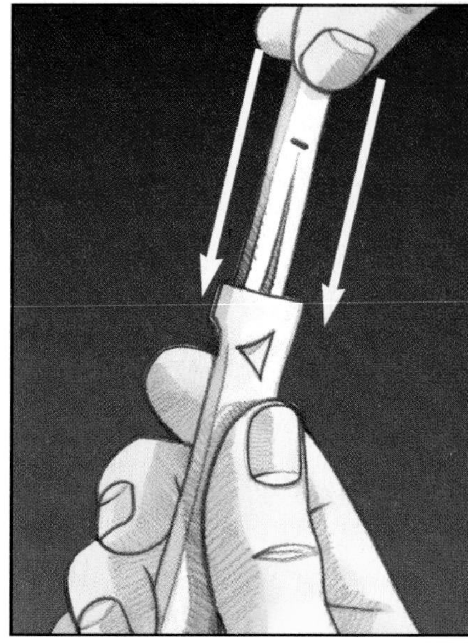

2 Grip the cable tightly with one hand and pull the cable ripper toward the end of the cable to cut open the plastic sheathing.

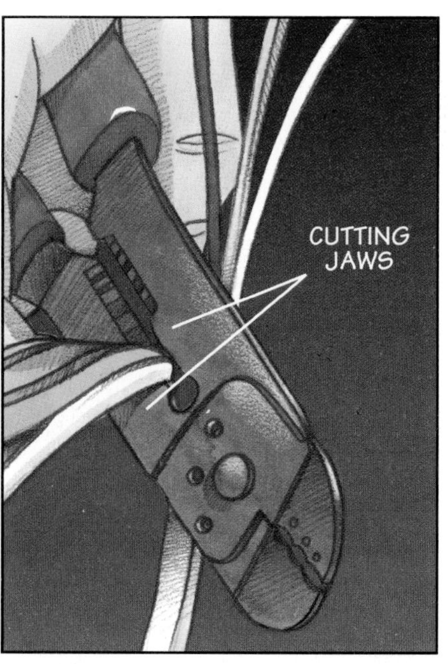

3 Peel back the plastic sheathing and the paper wrapping from the individual wires. Cut away the excess plastic sheathing and paper wrapping using the cutting jaws of a combination tool.

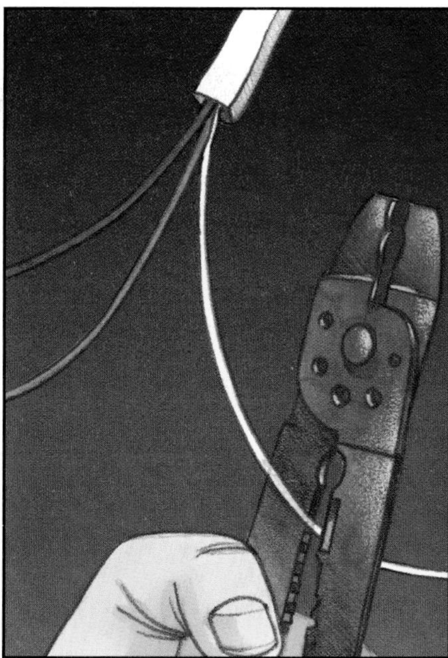

4 If necessary, cut the individual wires using the cutting jaws of the combination tool.

CONNECTING WIRES TO TERMINALS

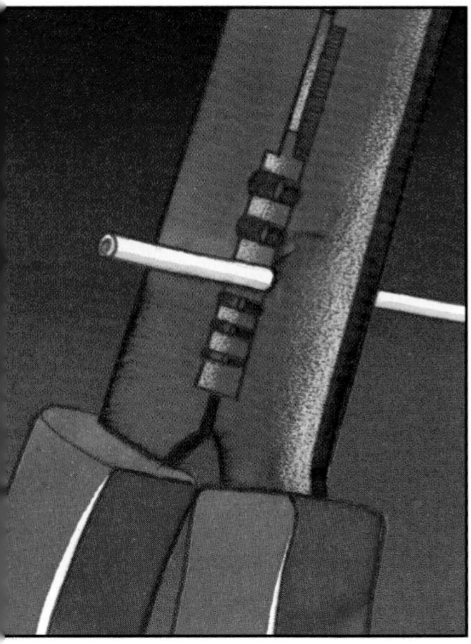

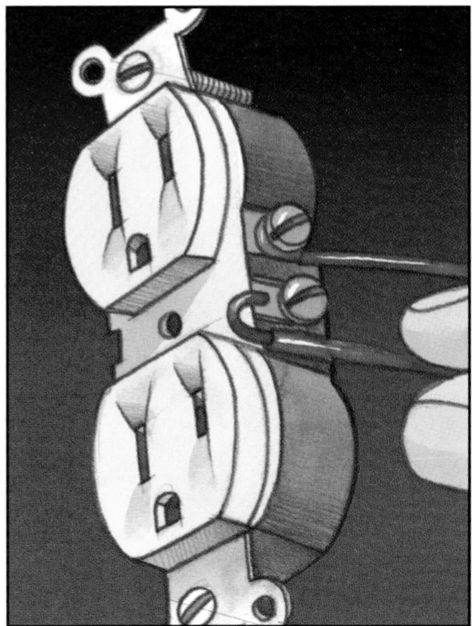

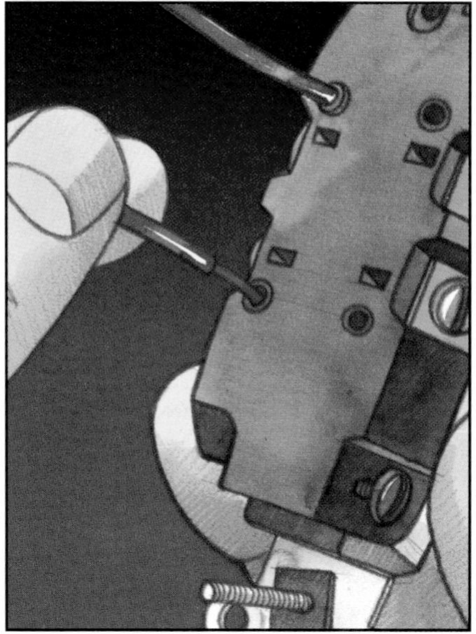

1 Strip about ¾" of insulation from each wire using a combination tool. Choose the stripper opening that matches the gauge of the wire. Clamp the wire in the tool. Pull the wire firmly to remove the plastic insulation.

2 Make a hook on each wire with needlenose pliers. Mount the hook around the screw terminal so it forms a clockwise loop. Tighten the screw firmly. The insulation should just touch the head of the screw. Never place the ends of two wires under a single screw terminal; use a pigtail wire instead.

To use the push-in fittings, insert the bare copper wires firmly into the fittings on the back of the switch or receptacle. When inserted, the wires should have no bare copper exposed. Push-in fittings should be only used with 14-gauge wire.

USING WIRE CONNECTORS

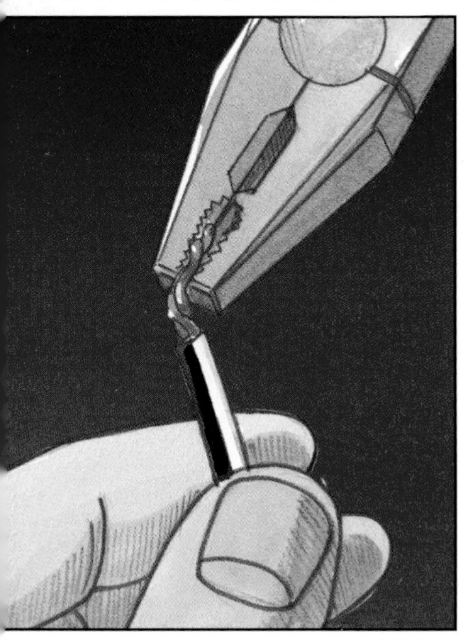

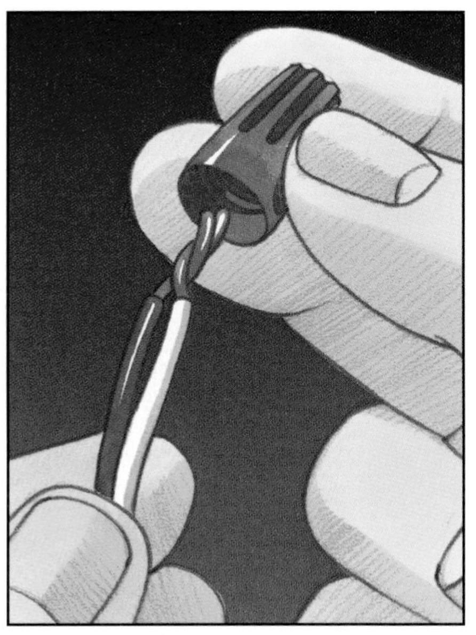

1 Strip about ½" of insulation from each wire with a combination tool. Hold the wires parallel, and twist them together in a clockwise direction using linesman's pliers or combination tool.

2 Screw the wire connector onto the twisted wires. Tug gently on each wire to make sure it is secure. In a proper connection, no bare wire should be exposed past the bottom of the wire connector.

PIGTAILING WIRES

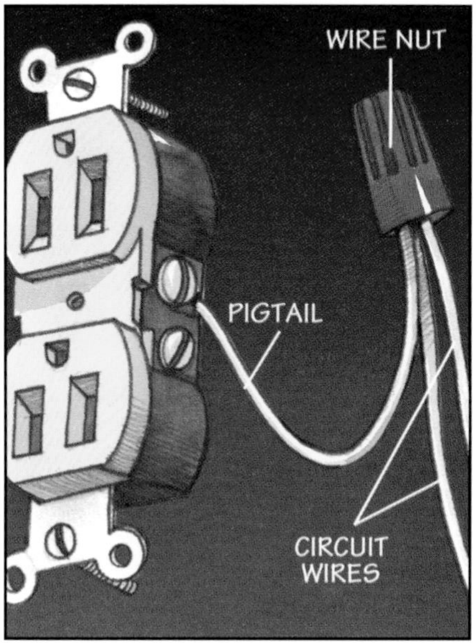

Connect two or more wires to a single screw terminal with a pigtail. A pigtail connects to a screw terminal and to the circuit wires using a wire connector. A pigtail can be used to lengthen circuit wires that are too short and must have the same electrical capacity as the wires you're connecting.

Installing a Junction Box

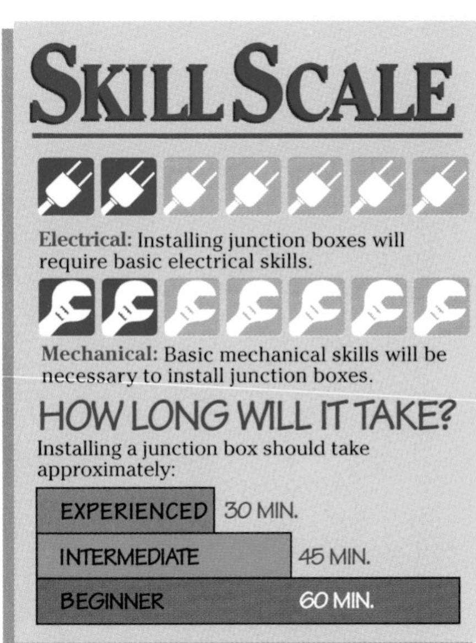

Install an electrical box when you find exposed wire connections or cable splices. Exposed connections are sometimes found where NM cable runs through uncovered joists or wall studs, such as in an unfinished basement or utility room.

When installing a junction box, make sure there is enough cable to provide about 8" of wire inside the box. If the wires are too short, add pigtails to lengthen them as long as all connections fit inside the junction box. If the box is metal, make sure the circuit grounding wires are pigtailed to the box.

STUFF YOU'LL NEED:

- ☐**Tools:** Neon circuit tester, combination tool, screwdrivers, hammer.
- ☐**Materials:** Screws or nails, electrical box, cable connectors, pigtail wire, wire connectors.

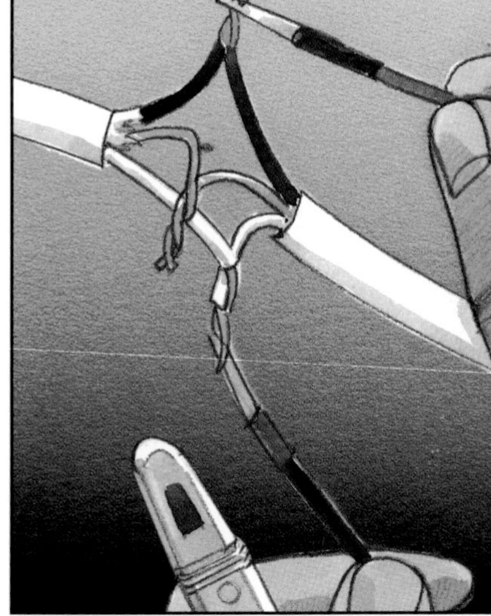

Use a neon tester to check for power. Turn off power to the circuit wires at the main service panel. Carefully remove any tape or wire nuts from the exposed splice. Avoid contact with the bare wire ends until the wires have been tested for power. Once power is off, disconnect the splice wires.

INSTALLING AN ELECTRICAL BOX FOR CABLE SPLICES

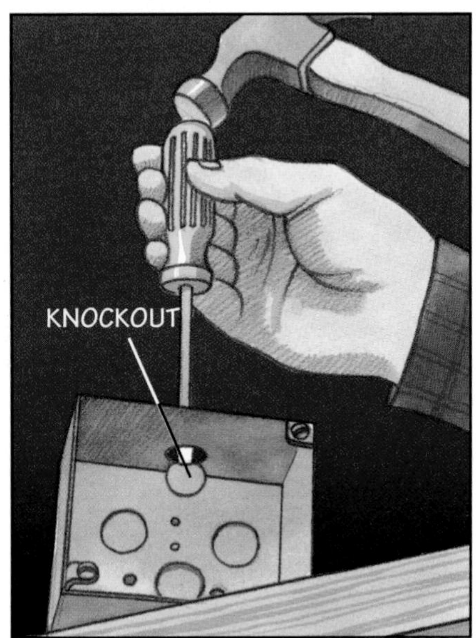

1 Open one knockout for each cable that will enter the box using a hammer and a screwdriver. Any unopened knockouts should remain sealed.

2 Anchor the electrical box to a wooden framing member using screws or nails.

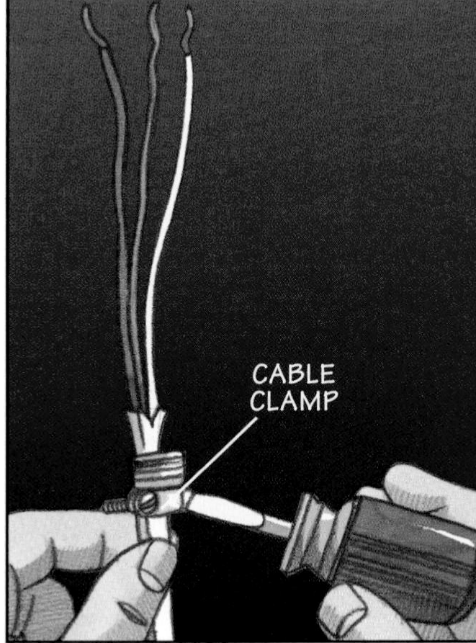

3 Thread each cable through a cable clamp. Tighten the clamp with a screwdriver. Do not over-tighten; overtightening can damage cable sheathing.

INSTALLING AN ELECTRICAL BOX (continued)

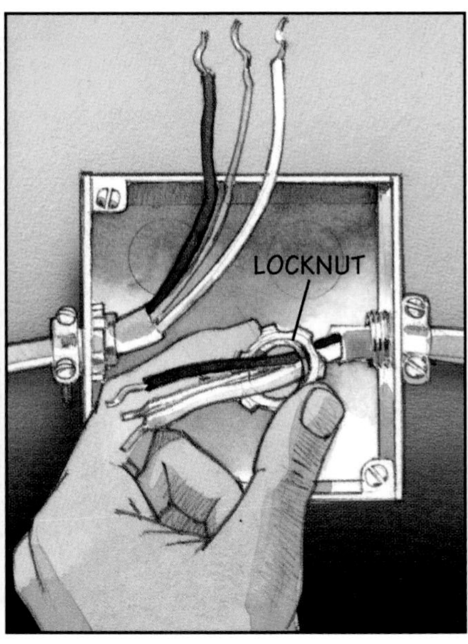

4 Insert the cables into the electrical box and screw a locknut onto each cable clamp.

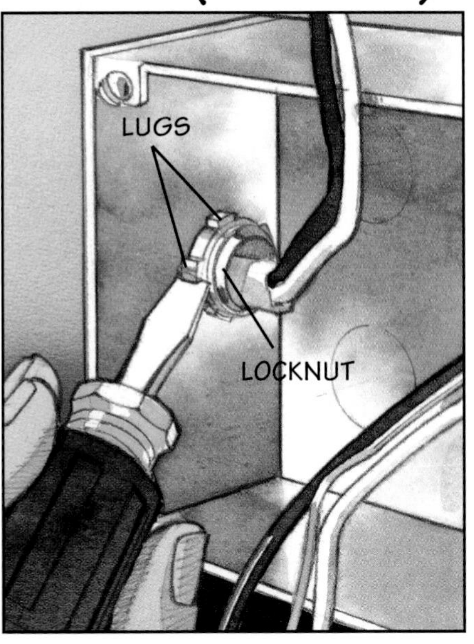

5 Tighten the locknuts by pushing against the lugs with the blade of a screwdriver.

6 Use wire connectors to reconnect the wires. Pigtail the copper grounding wires to the green grounding screw in the back of the box.

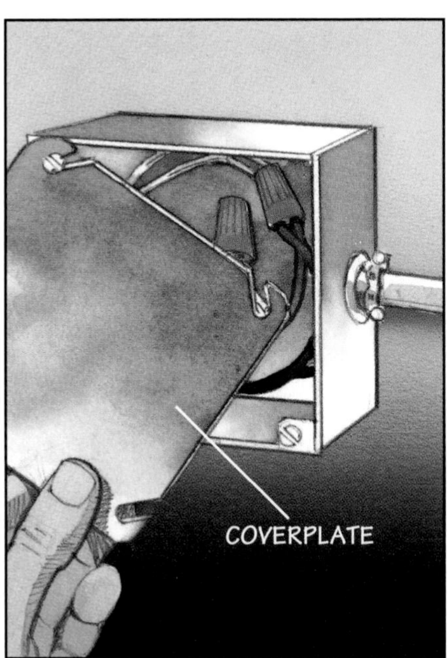

7 Carefully tuck the wires into the box, and attach the coverplate. Turn on the power to the circuit at the main service panel. Make sure the box remains accessible and is not covered with finished walls or ceilings.

Cable entering a metal box must be clamped. A variety of clamps is available, including plastic clamps and threaded metal clamps.

Boxes larger than 2x4", and all retrofit boxes, must have internal cable clamps. After installing cables in the box, tighten the cable clamps over the cables so they are gripped firmly, but not so tightly that the cable sheathing is crushed.

Metal boxes must be grounded to the circuit grounding system. Connect the grounding wires to the box with green insulated pigtail wires and wire nuts.

HOMER'S HINDSIGHT

One of my first electrical projects was truly a "hair-raising" experience. It was a simple task: test a circuit and install a junction box where a taped and twisted connection had been. I removed the tape and used my neon circuit tester which showed the circuit was without power. I went to work removing the wires when I accidentally touched two of them together, and was shocked to find they still had power. Luckily, only my pride was injured this time, thanks to the circuit breaker.

My mistake was in not realizing that the connections had so much residue from the electrical tape that my circuit tester probes couldn't make solid contact with the bare wires. Fortunately, this realization came before any serious Homer-cooking was done.

Installing Boxes for New Walls

For most indoor wiring done with NM cable, use plastic electrical boxes. Plastic boxes are inexpensive, lightweight, and easy to install. Metal boxes also can be used for indoor NM cable installations and are still favored by some electricians, especially for supporting heavy ceiling light fixtures. If you have a choice of box depths, choose the deepest size that fits. Wire connections are easier to make if boxes are roomy.

A square plastic box, 4x4x3" deep, provides extra space for wire connections. It has preattached nails for easy mounting. A variety of adapter plates is available for 4x4" boxes including single-gang, double-gang, and junction box coverplates. Adapter plates come in several thicknesses to match different wall constructions.

STUFF YOU'LL NEED:

- ☐**Tools:** Hammer, screwdrivers, tape measure.
- ☐**Materials:** Fixture boxes, heavy-duty braces.

INSTALLING BOXES FOR RECEPTACLES

1 Position each box against a stud so the front face will be flush with the finished wall. For example, if you will be installing 1/2" wallboard, position the box so it extends 1/2" past the face of the stud. Anchor the box by driving the mounting nails into the stud.

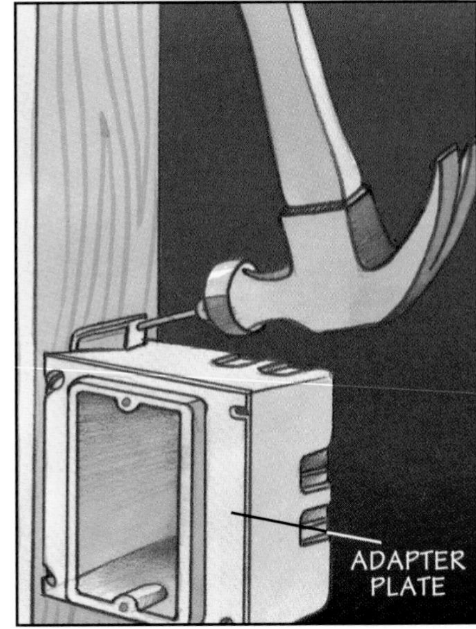

2 If installing 4x4" boxes, attach the adapter plates before positioning the boxes. Use adapter plates that match the thickness of the finished wall. Anchor the box by driving the mounting nails into the stud.

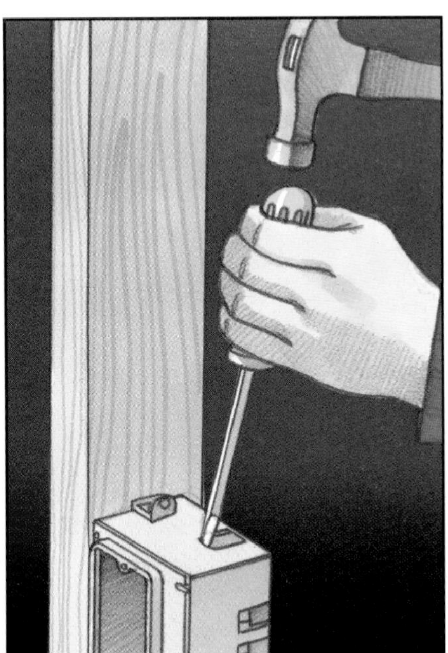

3 Open one knockout for each cable that will enter the box using a hammer and screwdriver.

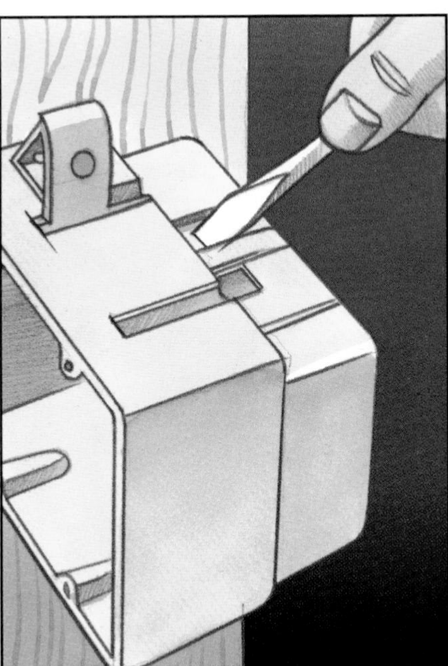

4 Break off any sharp edges that might damage vinyl cable sheathing by rotating a screwdriver in the knockout.

BOXES FOR LIGHT FIXTURES

Position a light fixture box for a vanity light above the frame opening for a mirror or medicine cabinet. Place the box for a ceiling light fixture in the center of the room. Position each box against a framing member so the front face will be flush with the finished wall or ceiling.

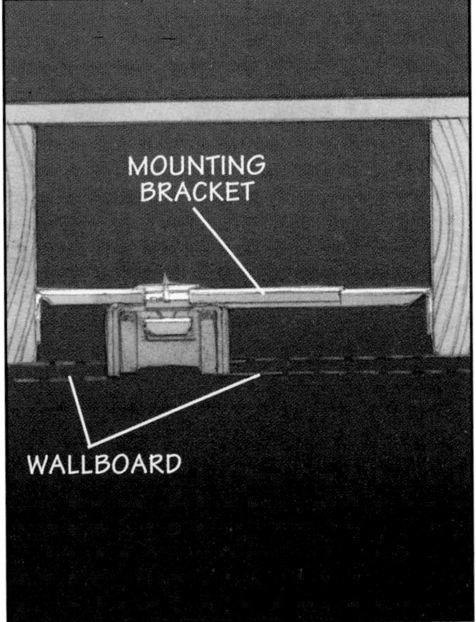

To position a light fixture between joists, attach an electrical box to an adjustable brace bar. Nail the ends of the brace bar to joists so the face of the box will be flush with the finished ceiling surface. Slide the box along the brace bar to the desired position; tighten the mounting screws.

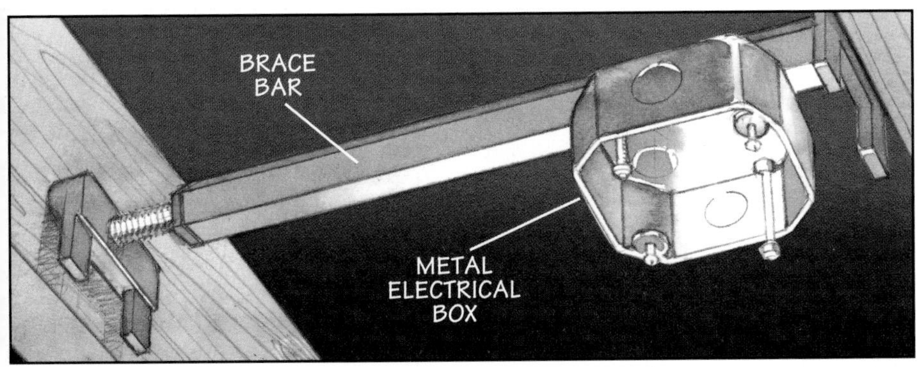

For heavy light fixtures and ceiling fans, use a metal box and a heavy-duty brace bar rated for heavy loads.

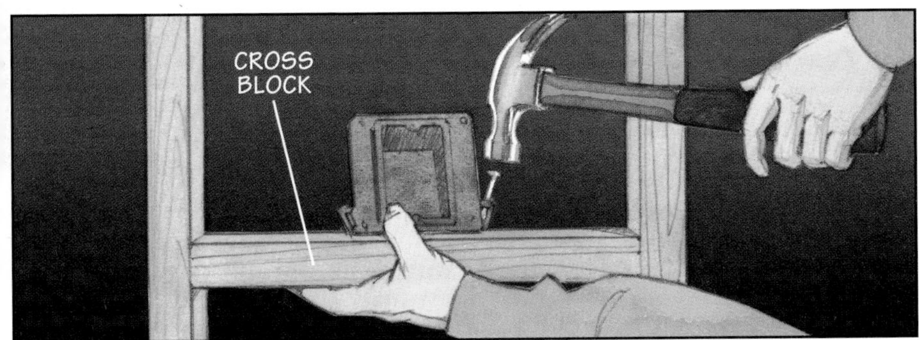

For a switch box between studs, first install a cross block between studs with the top edge 46" above the floor. Position the box on the cross block so the front face will be flush with the finished wall and drive the mounting nails into the cross block.

Install electrical boxes for receptacles, switches, and fixtures only after your wiring project plan has been approved by your inspector. Use your wiring plan as a guide, and follow Electrical Code height and spacing guidelines when laying out box positions. Always use the deepest electrical boxes that are practical for your installation. Using deep boxes ensures that you will meet Code regulations regarding box volume and makes it easier to make the wire connections.

Some electrical fixtures like recessed light fixtures, electric heaters, and exhaust fans have built-in wire connection boxes. Install the frames for these fixtures at the same time you are installing the other electrical boxes.

Electrical boxes in adjacent rooms should be positioned close together when they share a common wall and are controlled by the same circuit. This simplifies the cable installations and also reduces the amount of cable needed. Mark the location of each box on the wall studs. Standard receptacle boxes should be centered 12" above the floor level. GFCI receptacle boxes in bathrooms should be mounted so they will be about 10" above the finished countertop.

Braced octagonal boxes fit between ceiling joists. The metal braces extend to fit any joist spacing, and are nailed or screwed to framing members.

Boxes for Existing Walls & Ceilings

Installing an electrical box in an existing wall or ceiling isn't quite as difficult or "magical" as it may first appear. With a good fish tape, some NM cable, and a plastic retrofit box, you can make your family stand back and admire your "electrical prowess." Just a quick reminder: be sure to check for studs or water pipes before cutting an opening for a retrofit box or you may also have to show off your carpentry and plumbing skills!

Electrical

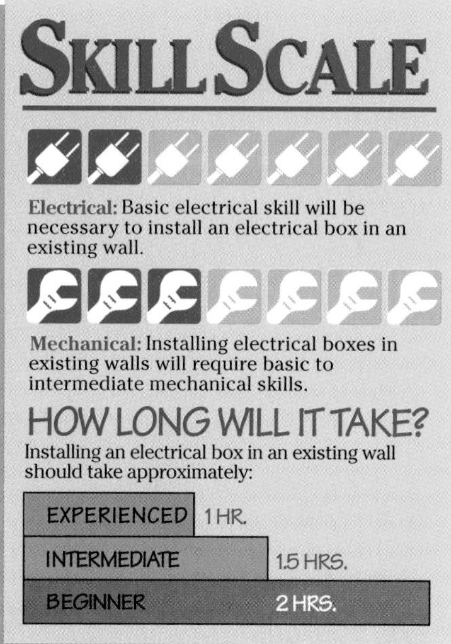

MATERIALS

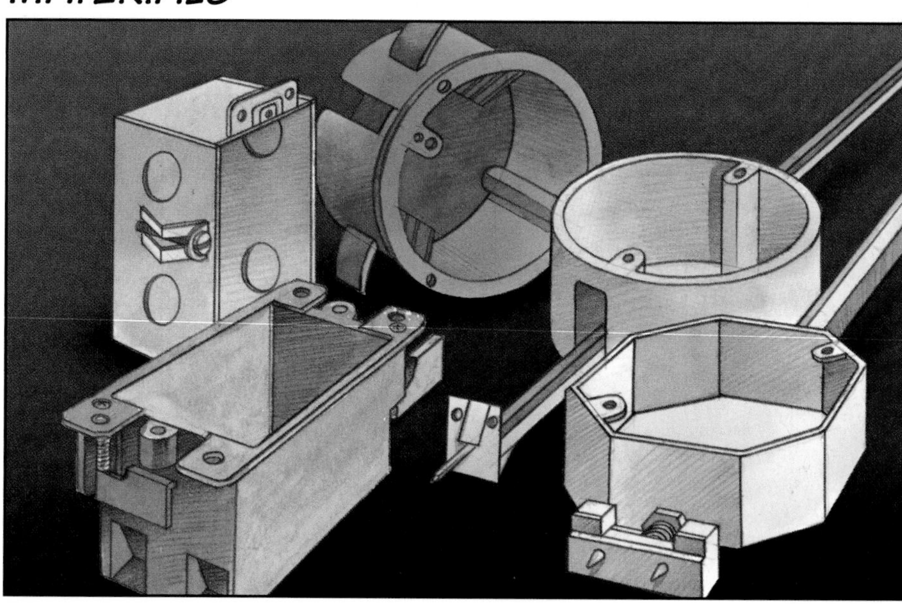

Retrofit electrical boxes are available in a variety of sizes and designs. Braced octagonal boxes fit between ceiling joists, or floor joists if wiring for middle floor or basement areas. The metal braces extend to fit any joist spacing and are nailed or screwed to framing members. Retrofit boxes upgrade older boxes to larger sizes. One type (above) has built-in clamps (or ears) that flip out and tighten against the inside of a wall and hold the box in place. A retrofit box with flexible brackets is shown above.

OUTDOOR BOXES

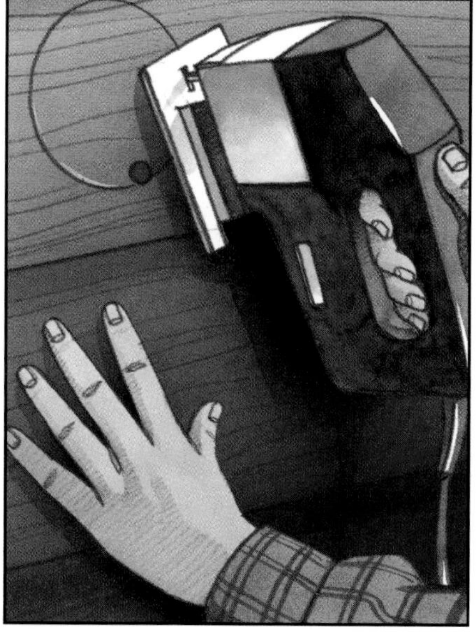

1 On the outside of the house, make the cutout for the new fixture in the same stud cavity with the switch cutout. Outline the fixture box on the wall, then drill a pilot hole and complete the cutout with a wallboard saw or jigsaw.

2 Estimate the distance between the indoor switch box and the outdoor box, and cut a length of NM cable about 2 ft. longer than this distance. Use a fish tape to pull the cable from the switch box to the fixture box.

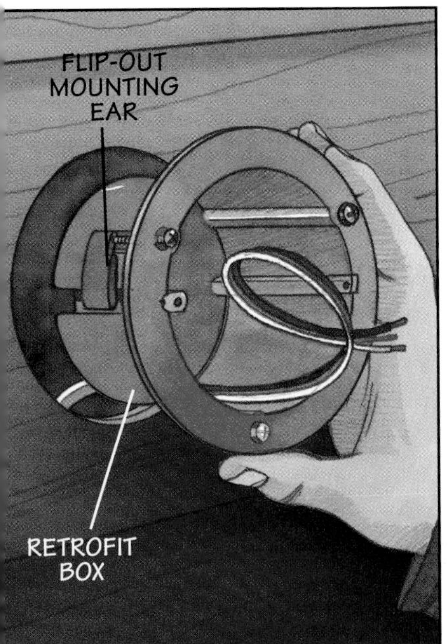

3 Strip about 10" of outer insulation from the end of the cable using a cable ripper. Open a knockout in the retrofit light fixture box with a screwdriver. Insert the cable into the box so that at least 1/4" of outer sheathing reaches into the box.

4 Insert the box into the cutout opening, apply a bead of silicone caulk around the flange, and tighten the mounting screws until the brackets draw the outside flange firmly against the siding.

BUYER'$ GUIDE

Retrofit boxes are designed to upgrade older boxes to larger sizes and also to install switches, receptacles and fixtures in existing walls without requiring total wall reconstruction. Most retrofit boxes have built-in clamps that tighten against the inside of a wall and hold the box in place.

Electrical boxes for an outdoor circuit must be weatherproof. Unless your Code has different requirements, use cast-aluminum electrical boxes with sealed seams for outdoor fixtures and install metal conduit to protect any exposed cables. Standard metal and plastic electrical boxes are not watertight and should never be used outdoors.

A few local Codes require you to install conduit to protect all underground cables, but in most regions this is not necessary. Some local Codes allow you to use boxes and conduit made with PVC plastic.

INDOOR BOXES

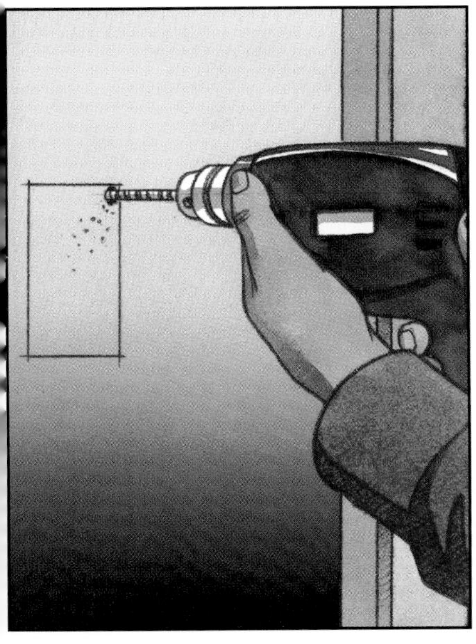

1 Outline the box on the wall. Drill a pilot hole and complete the cutout with a wallboard saw or jigsaw.

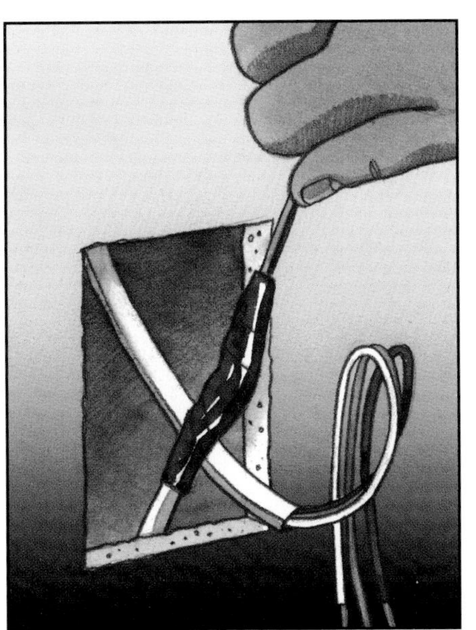

2 Estimate the distance between boxes and cut a length of NM cable about 2 ft. longer than this distance. Use a fish tape to pull the cable from the receptacle cutout to the switch cutout. Strip 10" of outer insulation from both ends of each cable.

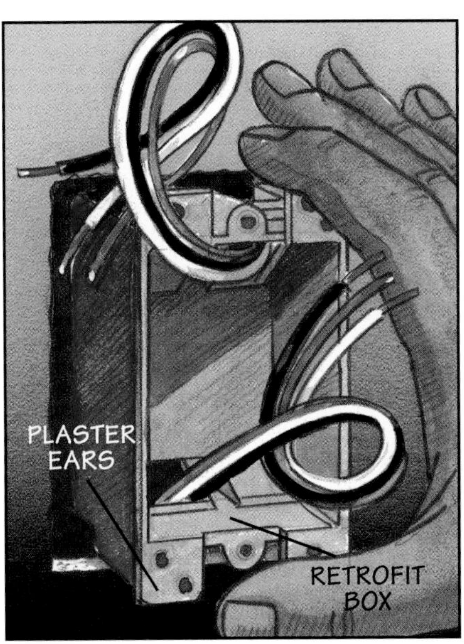

3 Open one knockout for each cable that will enter the box. Insert the cables so at least 1/4" of outer sheathing reaches inside box. Insert the box into the cutout and tighten the mounting screws until the mounting ears flip out and draw the plaster ears against the wall. Tighten internal cable clamps.

STUFF YOU'LL NEED:

- ☐**Tools:** Screwdrivers, needlenose pliers, combination tool.
- ☐**Materials:** Standard or GFCI receptacles, wire connectors.

Installing Standard & GFCI Receptacles

When replacing a receptacle, choose a replacement with the same ratings as the old receptacle. Never install a three-slot receptacle where no grounding exists. Instead, install a two-slot polarized or GFCI receptacle. You can attach the wires to the appropriate terminal screws or simply strip off 3/4" of insulation and use the push-in connectors.

The ground-fault circuit-interrupter (GFCI) receptacle is a safety device that protects against electrical shock caused by a faulty appliance, extension cord, or plug. The GFCI senses small changes in current flow and can shut off power in as little as 1/40 of a second. Because the GFCI is so sensitive, it is most effective when wired to protect a single location. The more receptacles any one GFCI protects, the more susceptible it is to "phantom tripping,"– shutting off power because of tiny, normal fluctuations in current flow.

SAFETY
Always turn off power at the main service panel before attempting receptacle repairs.
ALERT

Receptacles are wired as either end-of-run or middle-of-run. These two basic configurations are easily identified by removing the coverplate and mounting screws and counting the number of cables entering the receptacle box.

End-of-run wiring has only one cable, indicating that the circuit ends. Middle-of-run wiring has two cables, indicating that the circuit continues on to other receptacles, switches or fixtures.

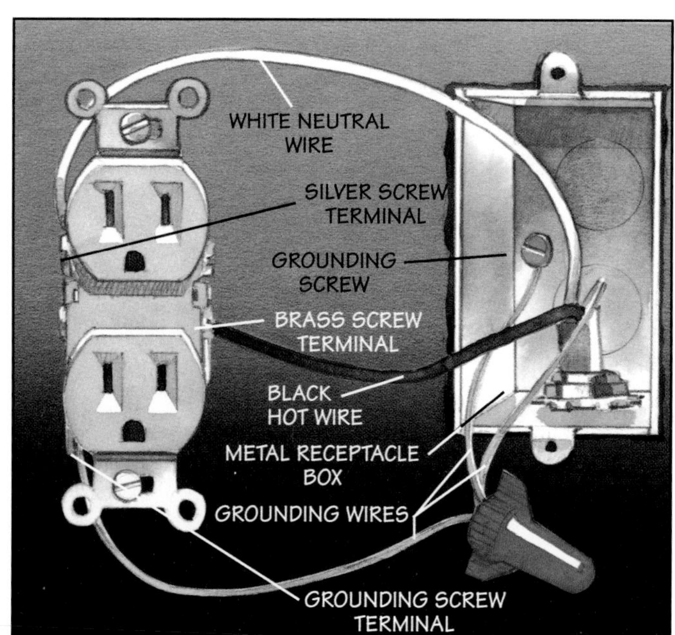

Single cable entering the box indicates end-of-run wiring. The black hot wire is connected to the brass terminal screw and the white neutral wire to the silver terminal screw. In a metal box, the grounding wire is pigtailed to the grounding screws of both the receptacle and the box. In a plastic box, the grounding wire is attached directly to the receptacle terminal.

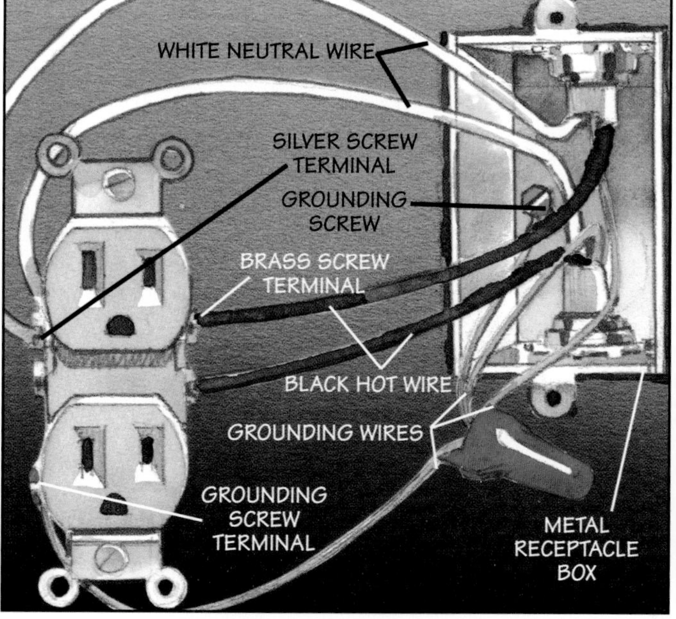

Two cables entering the box indicate middle-of-run wiring. The black hot wires are connected to the brass terminal screws and the white neutral wires to the silver terminal screws. The grounding wire is pigtailed to the grounding screws of the receptacle and the box.

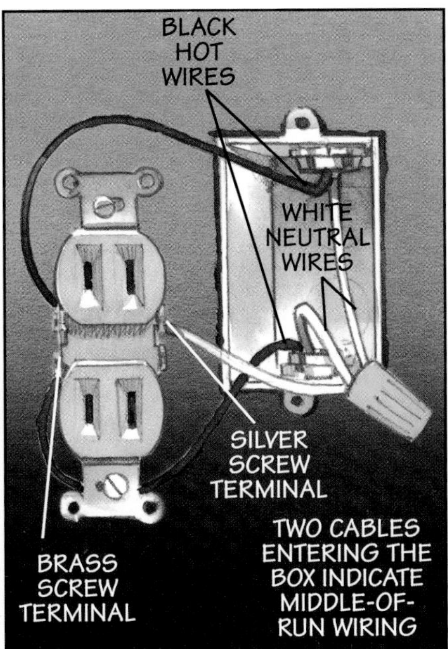

Two-slot receptacles are often found in older homes. The black hot wires connect to the brass terminal screw and the white neutral wires pigtail to the silver terminal. Two-slot receptacles may be replaced with three-slot types but only if a means of grounding exists at the receptacle box.

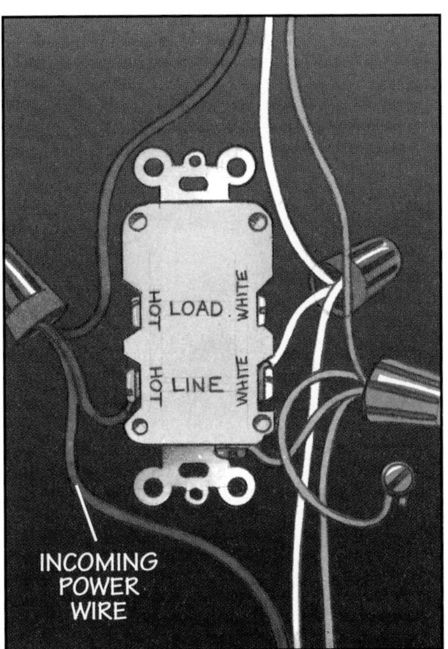

A GFCI wired for single-location protection (shown from the back) has hot and neutral wires connected only to the screw terminals marked LINE. A GFCI may be wired as either an end-of-run or middle-of-run configuration.

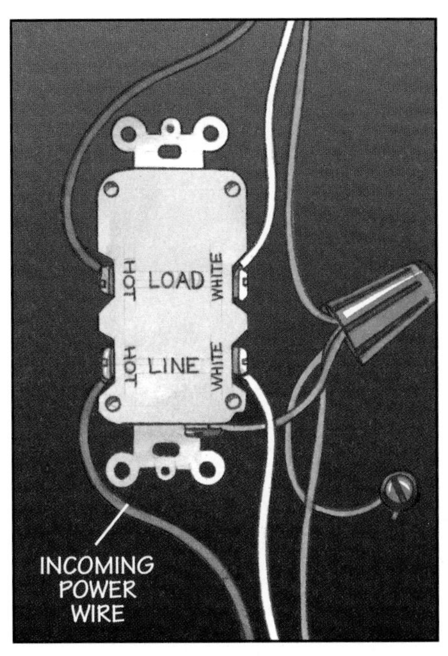

A GFCI wired for multiple-location protection (shown from the back) has one set of hot and neutral wires connected to the LINE pair of screw terminals and the other set connected to the LOAD pair of screw terminals.

Electrical

INSTALLING GFCI SINGLE LOCATION

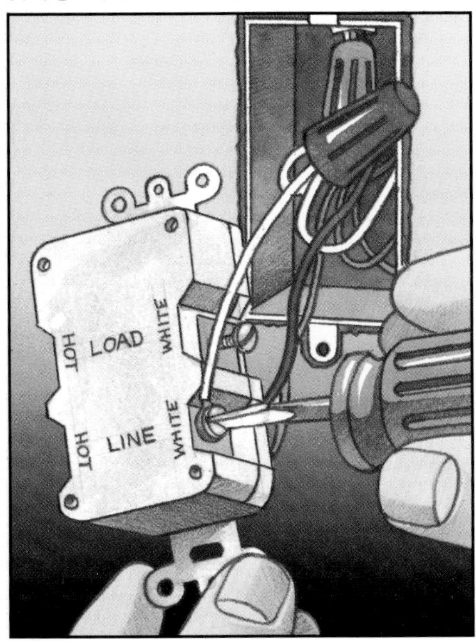

1 Turn off the power at the main service panel and test circuit to be sure. Remove the old receptacle. Pigtail all the white neutral wires together and connect the pigtail to the terminal marked WHITE LINE on the GFCI.

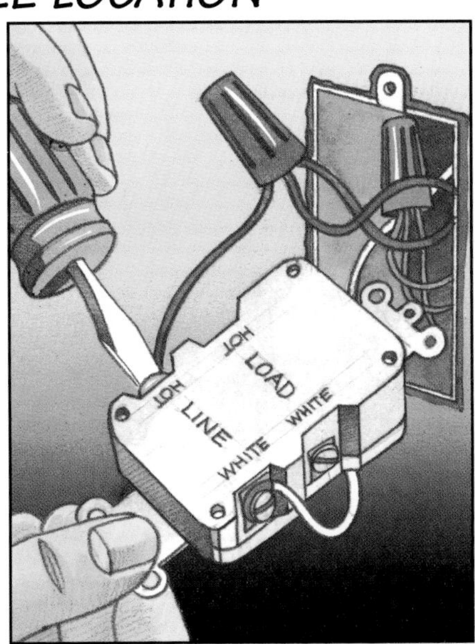

2 Pigtail all the black hot wires together and connect them to the terminal marked HOT LINE on the GFCI.

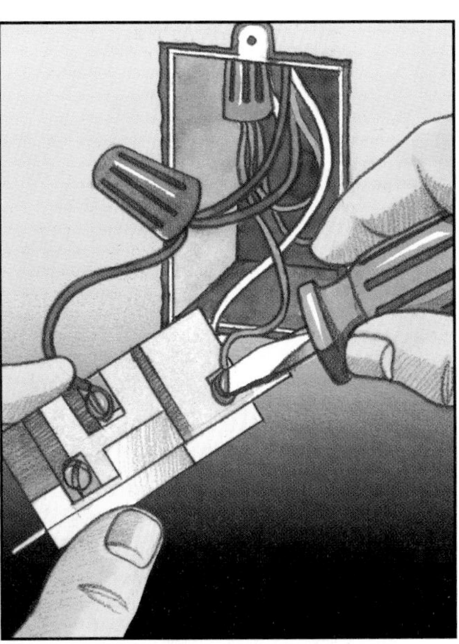

3 Connect the grounding wire to the green grounding screw terminal of the GFCI. Mount the GFCI in the receptacle box and reattach the coverplate. Restore power and test the GFCI according to the manufacturer's instructions.

Replacing & Installing a Standard Wall Switch

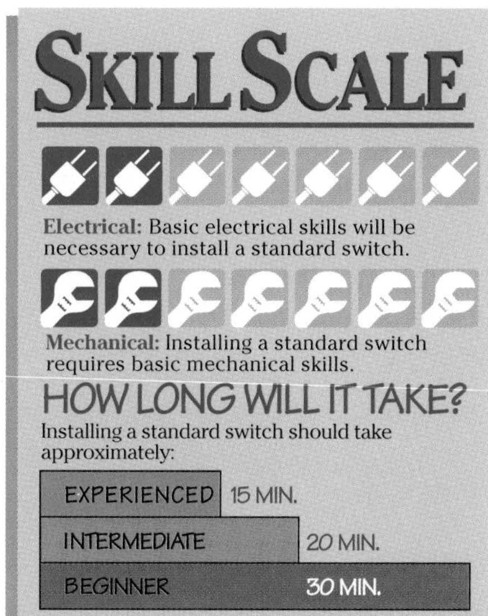

Electrical

STUFF YOU'LL NEED:

- ☐ **Tools:** Screwdrivers, combination tool, neon circuit tester, needle-nose pliers.
- ☐ **Materials:** Standard switch, wire connectors.

BUYER'$ GUIDE

Be sure to buy the appropriate switch for the circuit you are working on. Several rating stamps are found on the strap and on the back of the switch. Switches are stamped with maximum voltage and amperage ratings. Standard wall switches are rated 15A and 125V. Voltage ratings of 100, 120, and 125 are considered to be identical for purposes of identification. The abbreviation UL or UND. LAB. INC. LIST means the switch has been tested and has met approved safety standards of the Underwriters Laboratories.

Most switch problems are caused by loose wire connections. If a fuse blows or a circuit breaker trips when a switch is turned on, a loose wire may be touching the metal box. Loose wires also can cause switches to overheat or buzz. Switches sometimes fail because internal parts wear out. To check for wear, remove the switch entirely and test for continuity. If the continuity test shows the switch is faulty, replace it. A single-pole switch is the most common type of wall switch. It usually has ON-OFF markings on the switch lever and is used to control a set of lights, an appliance or a receptacle from a single location.

A single-pole switch has two screw terminals. Some types also may have a grounding screw. When installing a single-pole switch, check to make sure the ON marking shows when the switch lever is in the up position. In a correctly wired single-pole switch, a hot circuit wire is attached to each screw terminal. However, the color and number of wires inside the switch box will vary depending on the location of the switch along the electrical circuit. If two cables enter the box, then the switch lies in the middle of the circuit. If only one cable enters the box, then the switch lies at the end of the circuit.

SAFETY ALERT

Always turn off power at the main service panel before attempting switch repairs or replacement.

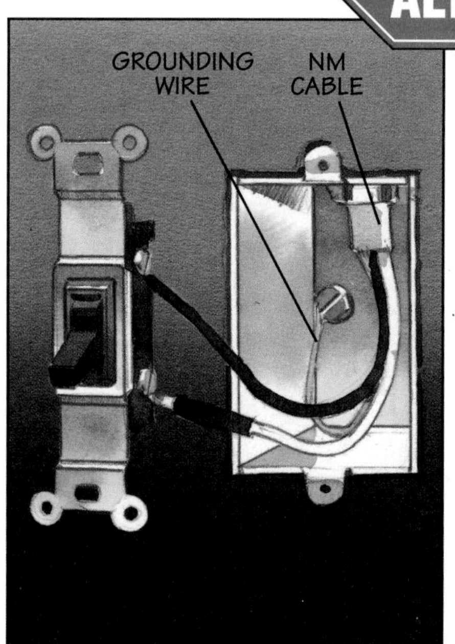

One cable enters the box when a switch is located at the end of a circuit. The cable has a white and a black insulated wire plus a bare copper grounding wire. In this installation, both of the insulated wires are hot. The white wire should be labeled with black tape or paint to identify it as a hot wire.

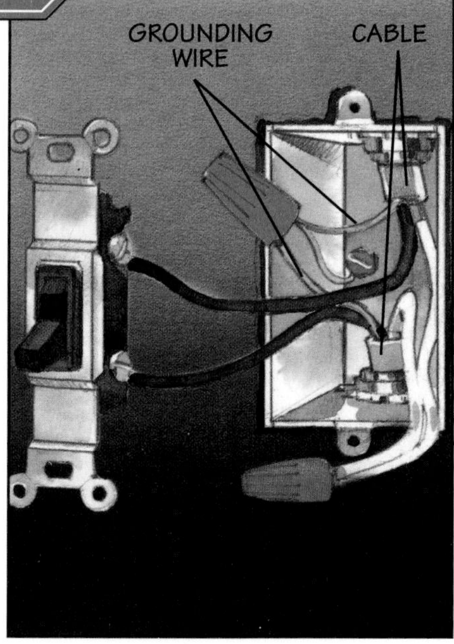

Two cables enter the box when a switch is located in the middle of a circuit. Each cable has a white and a black insulated wire plus a bare copper grounding wire. The black wires are hot and are connected to the screw terminals on the switch. The white wires are neutral and are joined with a wire connector.

REPLACING A STANDARD SWITCH

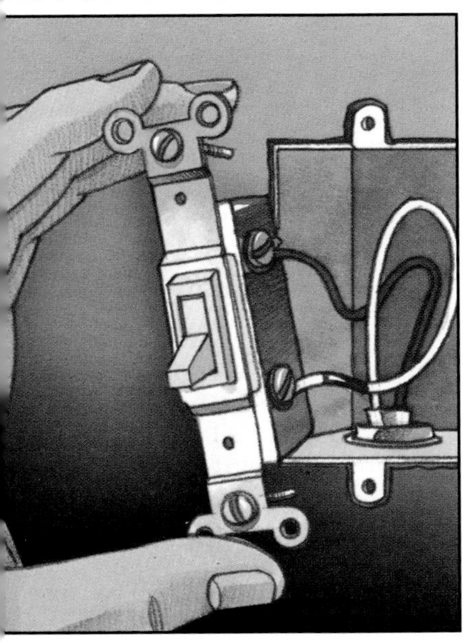

1 Remove the mounting screws holding the switch to the electrical box. Holding the mounting straps carefully, pull the switch from the box. Be careful not to touch any bare wires or screw terminals until the switch has been tested for power.

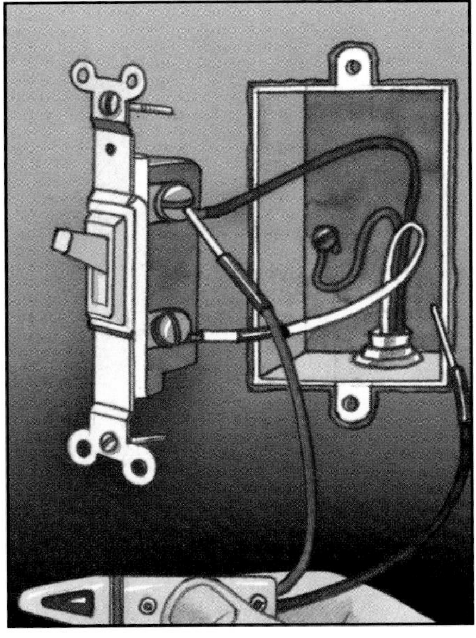

2 Test for power by touching one probe of the circuit tester to the grounded metal box or to the bare grounding wire and touching the other probe to each screw terminal. **If the tester glows, there is still power entering the box.** Turn off the correct circuit at the service panel before proceeding.

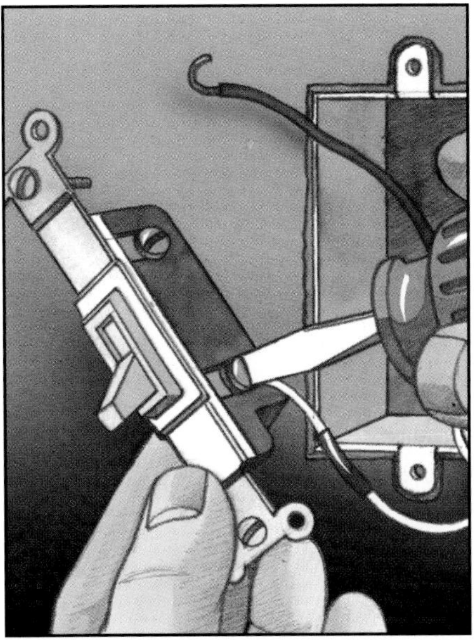

3 Double-check the wire connections. The black wire should be on one brass terminal and the white wire, marked as black, should be on the other. Disconnect the wires from the terminals and remove the switch.

IF THE WIRES ARE BROKEN OR NICKED, CLIP OFF THE DAMAGED PORTION, USING A COMBINATION TOOL. STRIP THE WIRES SO THERE IS ABOUT 3/4" OF BARE WIRE AT THE END OF EACH WIRE.

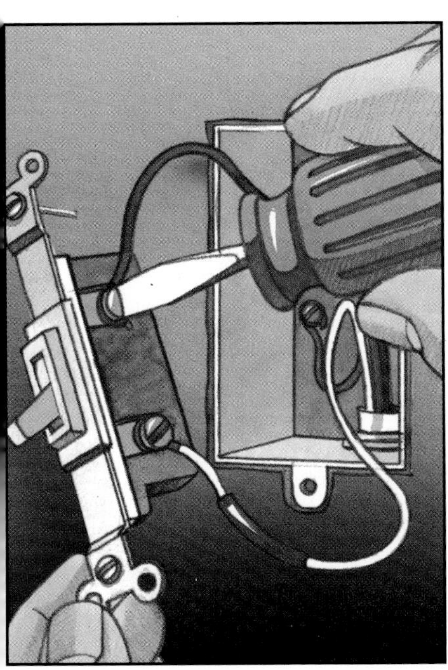

4 Connect the circuit wires to the proper screw terminals on the new switch. Tighten the screws firmly but do not overtighten; overtightening may strip the screw threads. Remember, never screw more than one wire to a terminal, use a pigtail instead (see page 161).

5 Remount the switch, carefully tucking the wires inside the box. Be careful not to break through the protective insulation on the wires when pushing them into the box Reattach the switch coverplate and turn on the power to the switch at the main service panel.

When purchasing a replacement switch, bring along the old one so you can choose an identical new switch that has the same number of screw terminals as the old one. The location of the screws on the switch body varies depending on the manufacturer, but these differences will not affect the switch operation.

Installing a Three-Way Switch

Three-way switches can be a little confusing because, unlike a standard switch, they have three screw terminals and do not have ON-OFF markings. Three-way switches are always installed in pairs and are used to control a set of lights from two separate locations.

One of the screw terminals is darker than the others. This is the common screw terminal. Before disconnecting a three-way switch, always label the wire that is connected to the common screw terminal. It must be reconnected to the common screw terminal on the new switch.

The two lighter-colored screw terminals are called the traveler screw terminals.They are interchangeable so there is no need to label the wires attached to them.

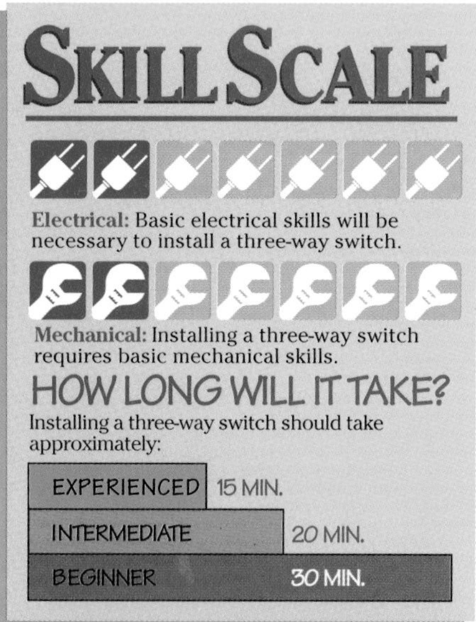

STUFF YOU'LL NEED:

- ☐**Tools:** Screwdrivers, combination tool, neon circuit tester, needle-nose pliers.
- ☐**Materials:** Three-way switch, wire connectors.

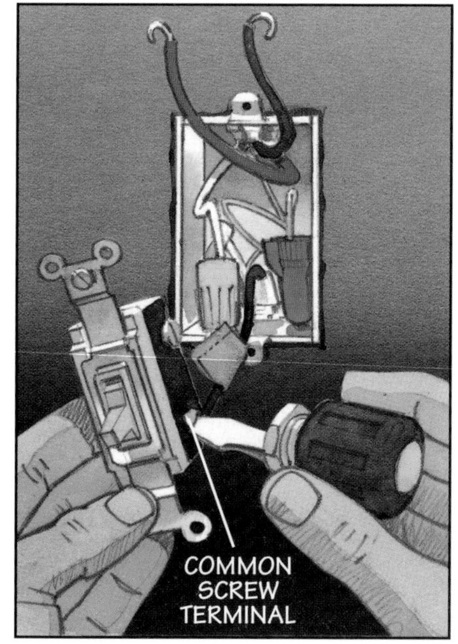

1 Connect the common wire to the dark common screw terminal on the switch. On most three-way switches the common screw terminal is copper or it may be labeled with the word COMMON stamped on the back of the switch.

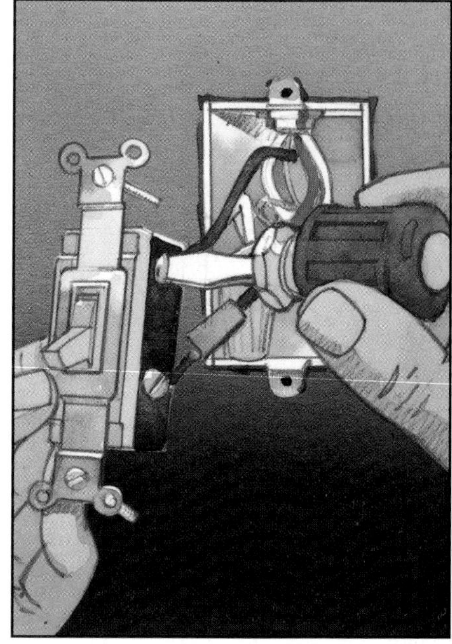

2 Connect the remaining wires to the brass or silver terminals. These wires can be connected to either screw terminal. Carefully tuck the wires into the box. Remount the switch and attach the coverplate. Turn on the power at the main service panel.

TYPICAL THREE-WAY SWITCH INSTALLATIONS

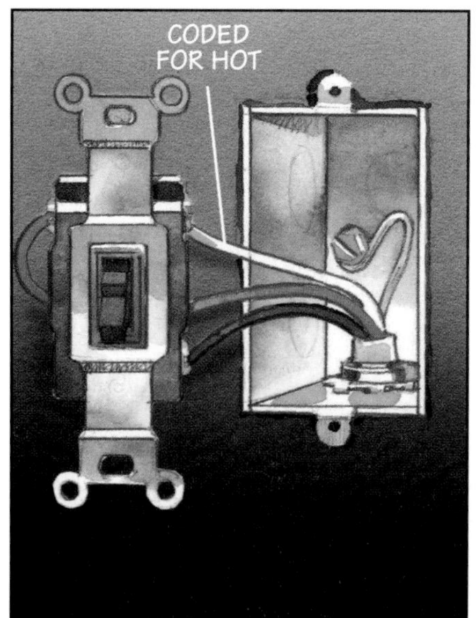

A three-way switch at the end of a circuit has only one cable entering the box. The black wire must be connected to the dark common terminal. The red and white wires are connected to the two silver traveler terminals and the bare copper wire is connected to the grounded box.

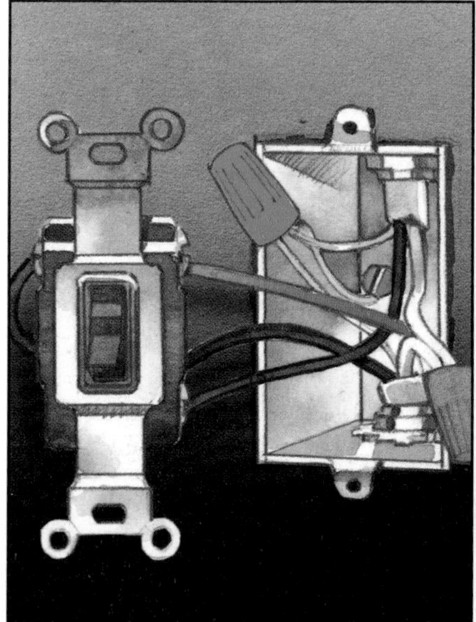

A three-way switch in the middle of a circuit has two cables entering the box, one with two wires and one with three. The black wire from the two-wire cable is connected to the dark, common terminal. The red and black wires from the three-wire cable are connected to the traveler terminals. The white wires are joined and the grounding wires are pigtailed to the box.

FIXTURE BETWEEN SWITCHES

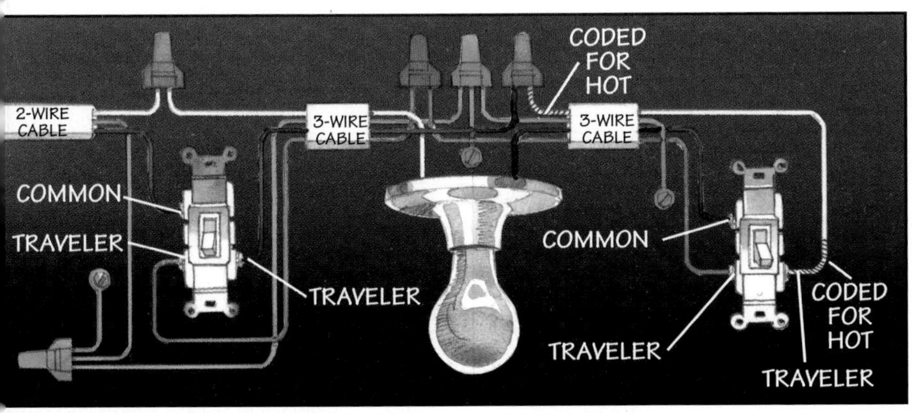

This layout lets you control a light fixture from two separate locations. It requires both two-wire and three-wire cables.

FIXTURE AT START OF CABLE RUN

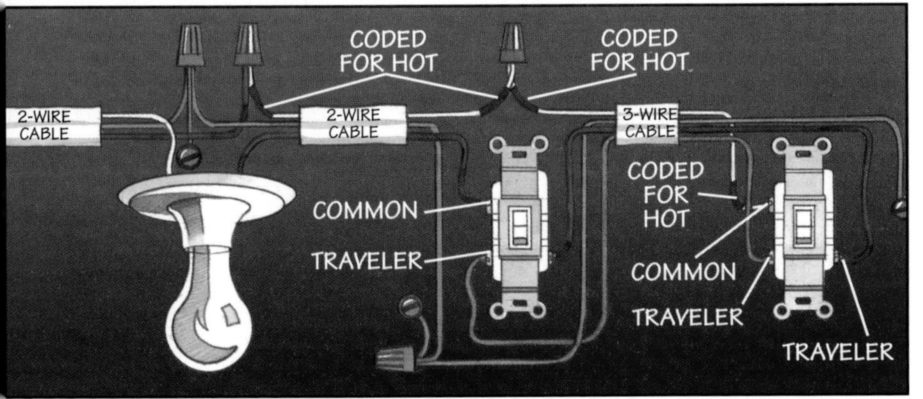

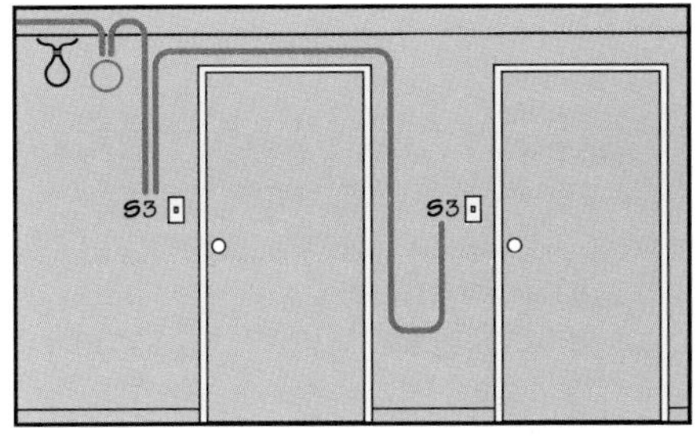

Use this layout where it is more convenient to locate the fixture ahead of the three-way switches in the cable run. It requires both two-wire and three-wire cables.

FIXTURE AT END OF CABLE RUN

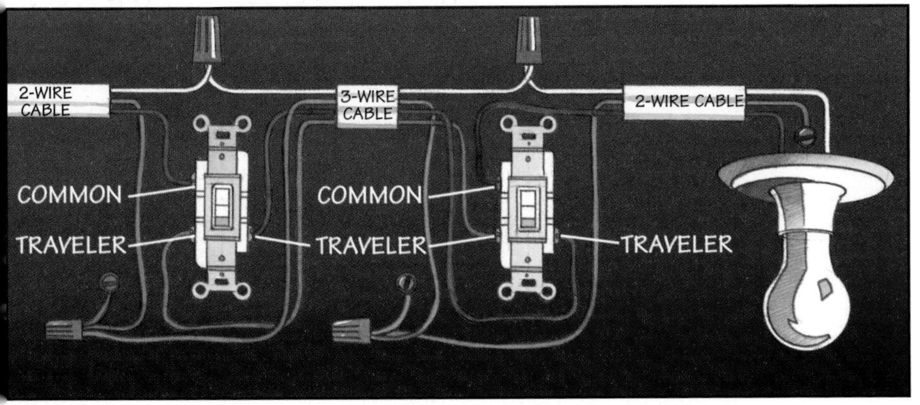

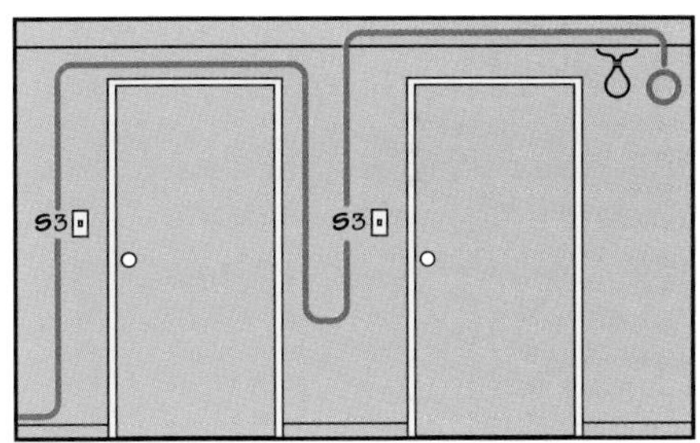

This variation is used where it is more practical to locate the fixture at the end of the cable run. It also requires two-wire and three-wire cables.

TWO FIXTURES BETWEEN SWITCHES

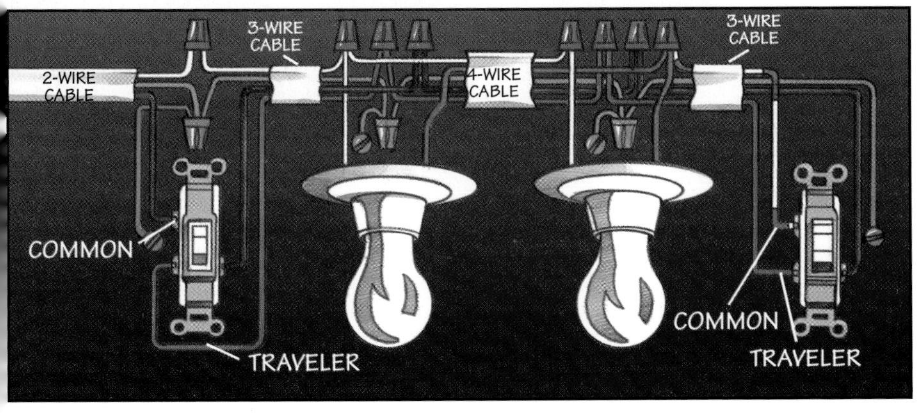

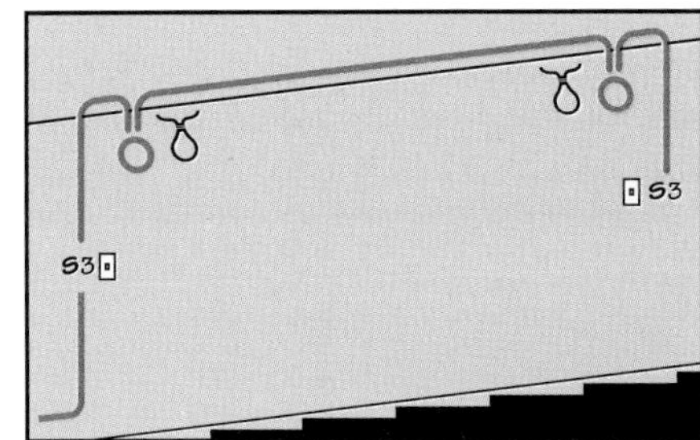

Control two lights from two switches. This layout is typically found in stairways and requires two-wire, three-wire and four-wire cables.

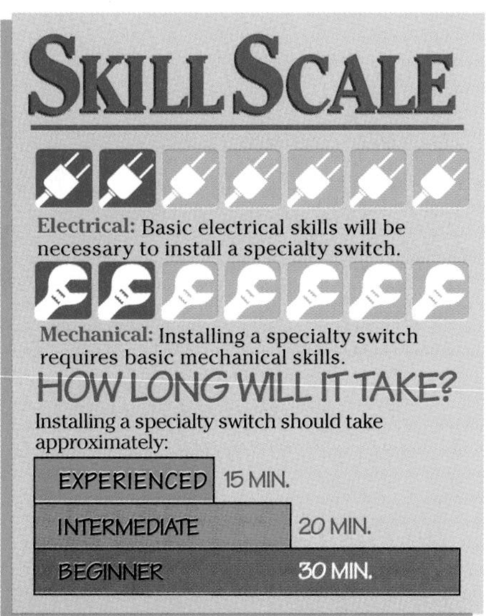

STUFF YOU'LL NEED:

- **Tools:** Screwdrivers, combination tool, neon circuit tester, needle-nose pliers.
- **Materials:** Specialty switch, wire connectors.

Installing Specialty & Dimmer Switches

Specialty switches are available in several types. Timer switches and time-delay switches are used to automatically control light fixtures and exhaust fans. Electronic switches provide added convenience and home security and are easy to install. Electronic switches are durable and they rarely need repair. Most standard single-pole switches can be replaced with a specialty switch.

Specialty switches have pre-attached wire leads instead of screw terminals and are connected to circuit wires with wire nuts.

A timer switch cannot be installed in a box that has no neutral wires. A time-delay switch, however, needs no neutral wire connection so it can be fitted in a switch box that contains either one or two cables. A dimmer switch makes it possible to vary the intensity of light in a fixture. Any standard single-pole switch can be replaced with a dimmer as long as the switch box is of adequate size. Dimmer switches should not be installed in undersized electrical boxes or in boxes that are crowded with circuit wires.

In lighting configurations that use three-way switches, one of the three-way switches can be replaced with a special three-way dimmer. In this arrangement, all switches will turn the light fixture on and off but light intensity will be controlled only from the dimmer switch.

Dimmer switches are available in several styles but all types have wire leads instead of screw terminals. These switches should be connected to the circuit wires using wire nuts. A few styles have green grounding leads that should be connected to the grounded metal box or to the bare copper grounding wires.

TYPES OF SPECIALTY SWITCHES

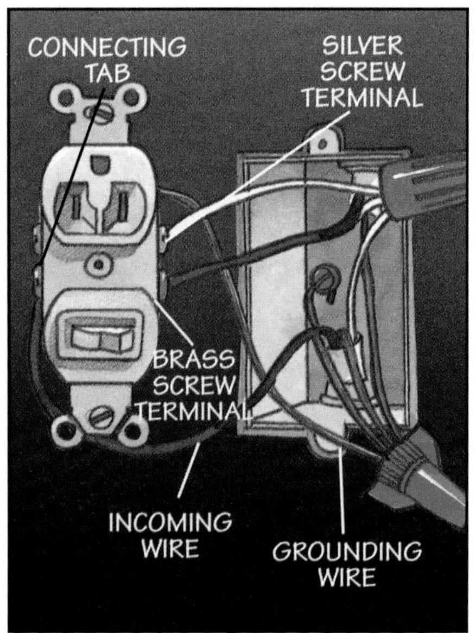

Switch/receptacles require a neutral wire connection. The incoming black wire is connected to the brass terminal on the side that has a connecting tab; the outgoing black wire, to the brass terminal on the other side. The white neutral wire is pigtailed to the silver terminal.

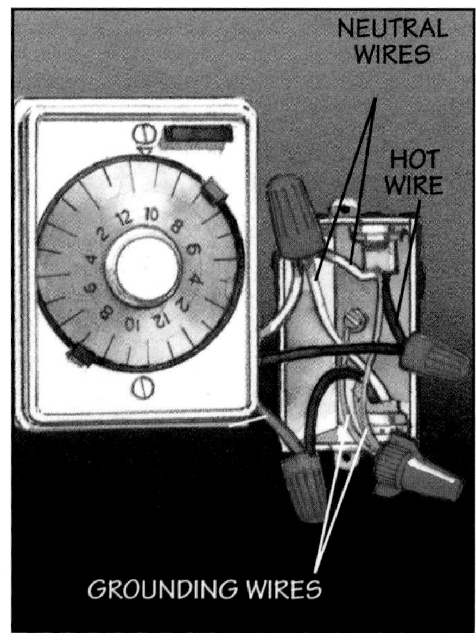

Timer switches have three pre-attached wire leads. The black wire lead is connected to the hot wire and the red lead is connected to the wire carrying power out to the light fixture. The remaining neutral lead is connected to the neutral circuit wires. After a power failure, reset it to the proper time.

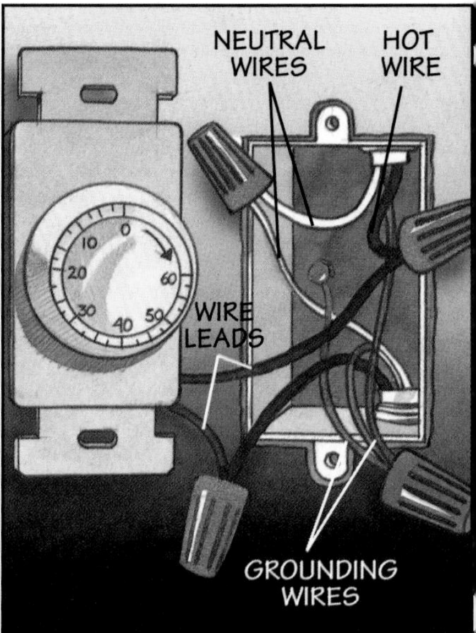

Time-delay switches have black wire leads that are connected to the hot circuit wires. The bare copper grounding wires are pigtailed to the grounded metal box. Connect the white neutral wires together with a wire connector.

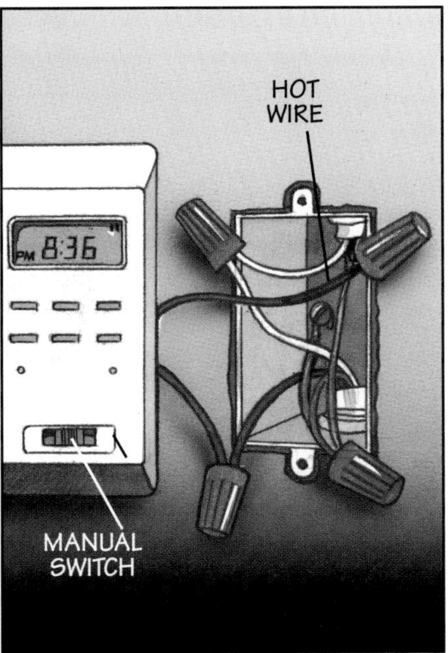

Solid state programmable switches require no neutral wire connections. They can be installed in switch boxes containing either one or two cables. The wire leads on the switch are connected to hot circuit wires with wire connectors. Mechanical analog switches require a neutral wire connection.

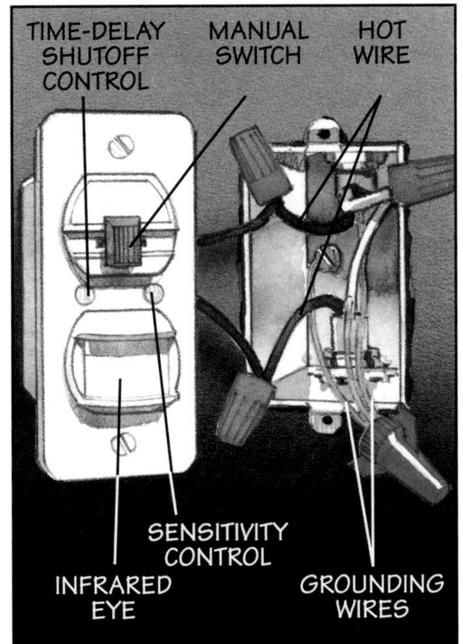

Motion-sensor switches require no neutral wire connections. They can be installed in switch boxes containing either one or two cables. The wire leads on the switch are connected to hot circuit wires with wire connectors.

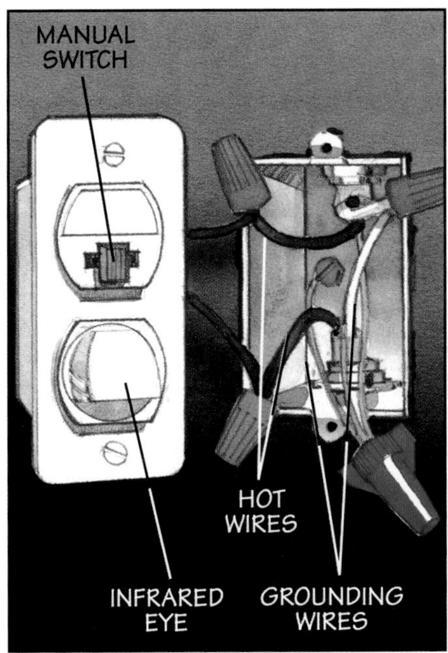

Automatic switches require no neutral wire connections. For this reason, an automatic switch can be installed in a switch box containing either one or two cables. The wire leads on the switch are connected to hot circuit wires with wire connectors.

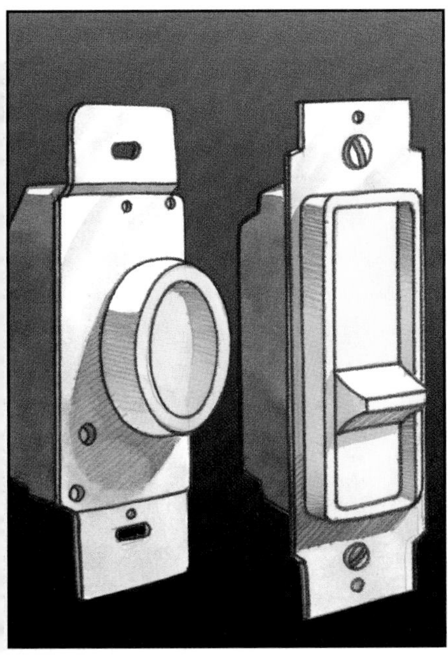

Dimmers are available in different styles. Dial-type dimmers are the most common style. Rotating the dial changes the light intensity from low to high. Slide-action dimmers have an illuminated face that makes the switch easy to locate in the dark. Only use dimmers with incandescent bulbs.

INSTALLING A DIMMER SWITCH

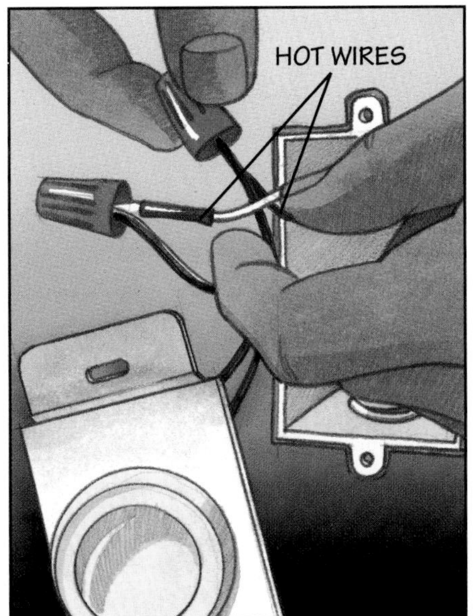

1 Turn off power to the circuit at the main service panel. Use a neon circuit tester to make sure the power is off. Connect the wire leads on the dimmer switch to the circuit wires using wire connectors. The switch leads are interchangeable and can be attached to either of the two circuit wires.

2 A three-way dimmer has an additional wire lead. This "common" lead is connected to the common circuit wire. Remember, the common circuit wire is the one attached to the darkest screw terminal on the old switch. Only one of the three-way switches may be a dimmer switch.

Removing Old Light Fixtures

Removing a ceiling- or wall-mounted light fixture is one of the easiest home electrical repairs and requires only basic tools and some good old common sense. Light fixtures usually have only two wires connected to the circuit wires with twist-on wire connectors. Use a steady ladder when working on ceiling fixtures and be sure to have someone help with heavy fixtures.

Remember to always turn off power to the circuit before attempting any light fixture removal.

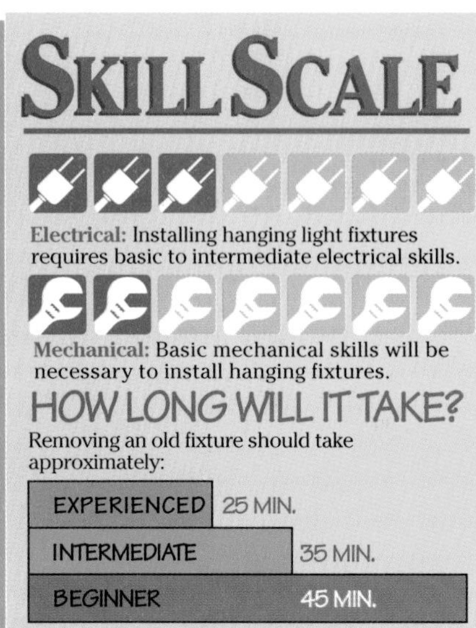

STUFF YOU'LL NEED:

- ☐**Tools:** Phillips and standard screwdrivers, neon circuit tester, regular and needlenose pliers.

REMOVING HANGING FIXTURES

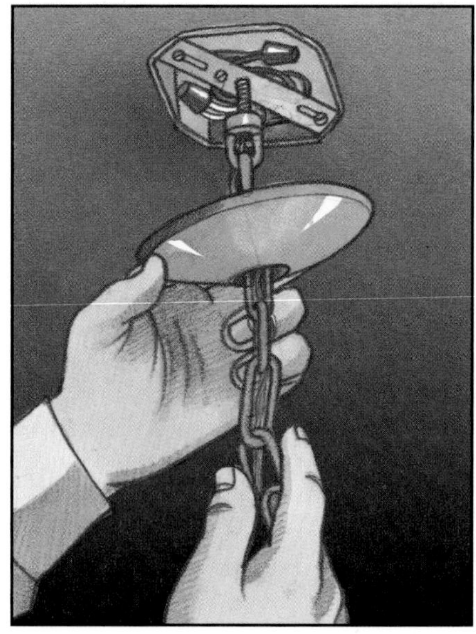

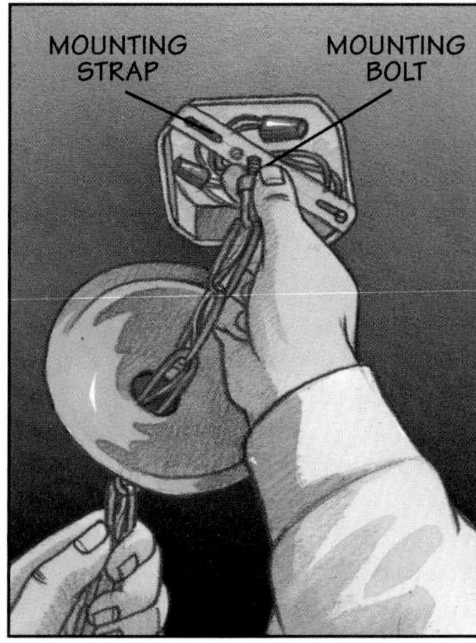

1 Turn off power to the fixture at the main service panel. Remove the coverplate retaining nut and lower the coverplate from the electrical box. Remove the wire connectors to expose the circuit wires. Be careful not to touch the bare wires until you've tested them to make sure the power is off.

2 Test the circuit with a neon tester. Flip the wall switch and test again to be sure the circuit is turned off. Disconnect the circuit wires. Remove the fixture retaining nut and carefully lower the hanging fixture to the floor.

REMOVING GLOBE FIXTURES

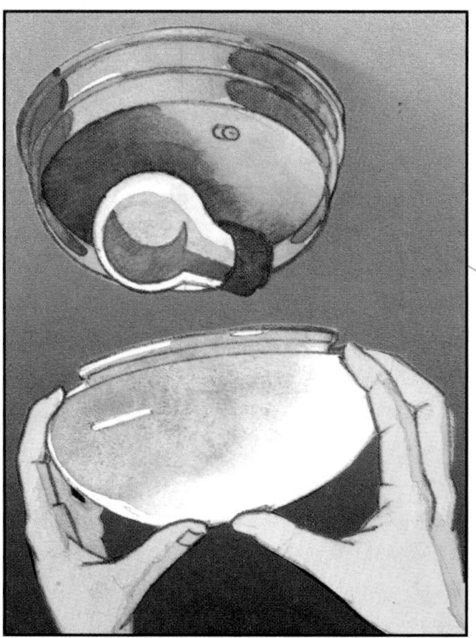

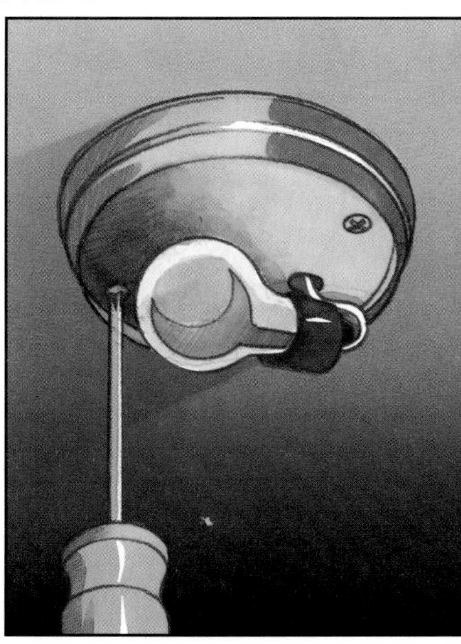

1 Turn off electricity to the light fixture at the main service panel. Remove the globe by loosening the retaining screws.

2 Remove the mounting screws or turn the fixture slightly to free it from the loosened screws.

REMOVING GLOBE FIXTURES (CONTINUED)

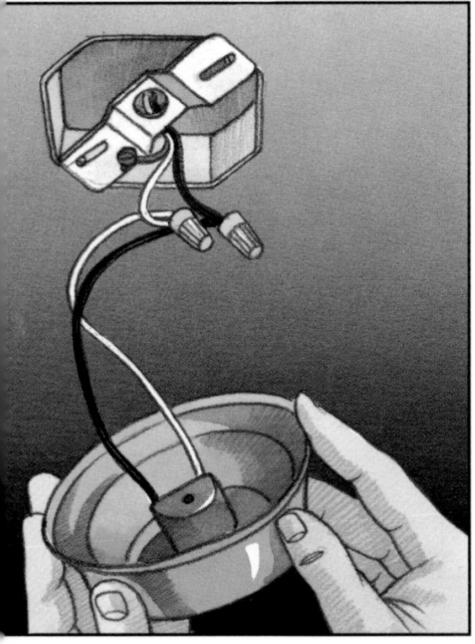

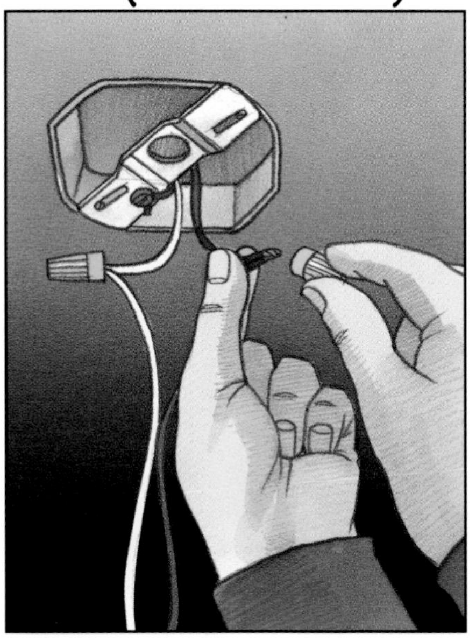

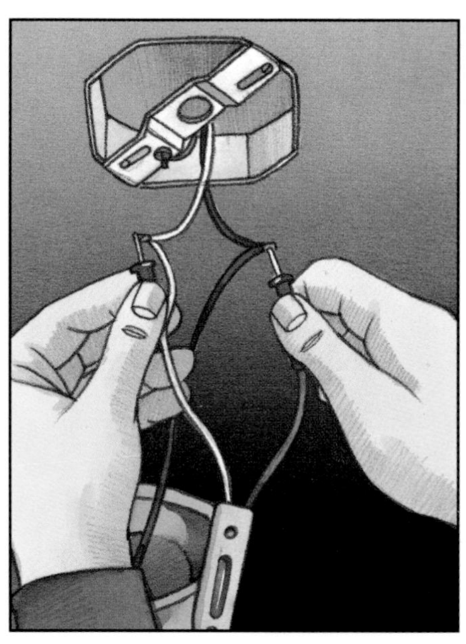

3 Gently pull the fixture away from the box to expose the circuit wires. Be careful not to touch any terminals on the fixture or bare circuit wires until the circuit has been tested for current.

4 Twist off the wire connectors to expose the bare circuit wires, again, being careful not to touch the bare wires.

5 Test the circuit with a neon tester. The tester should not glow. Flip the light switch on the wall and test again. If the tester glows, turn off the correct circuit at the main service panel and test again. If the tester doesn't glow, separate the wires and remove the fixture.

REMOVING RECESSED LIGHT FIXTURES

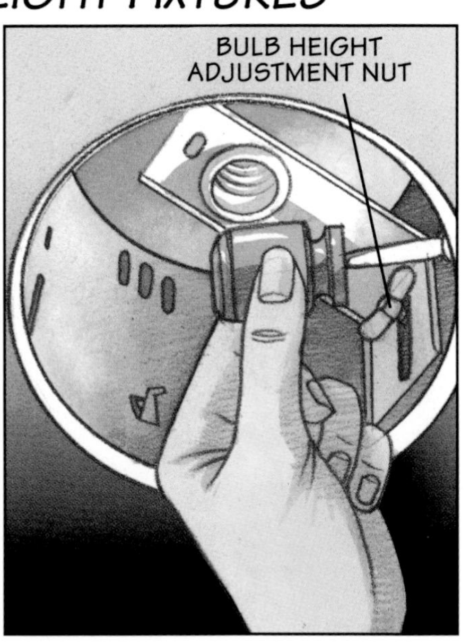

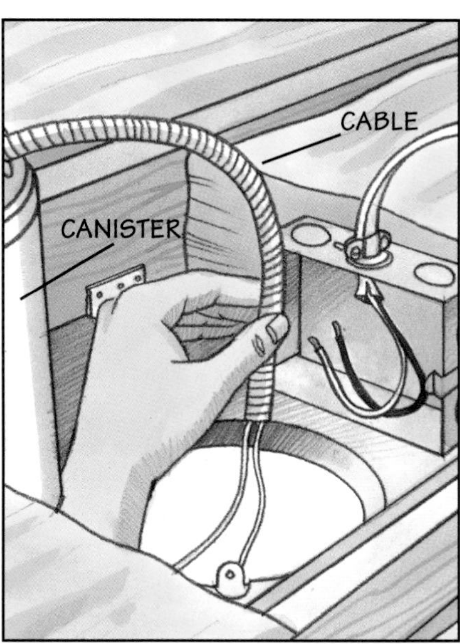

1 Turn off the power to the light fixture at the main service panel. Remove the trim, light bulb, and reflector. The reflector is held onto the canister with small springs or mounting clips.

2 Loosen the screws or clips holding the canister to the mounting frame. Carefully raise the canister and set it away from the opening. Remove the coverplate on the wire box. Test for power with a neon circuit tester. If the power is still on, return to the service panel and turn off the correct circuit.

3 Disconnect the white and black circuit wires by removing the wire connectors. Pull the armored cable from the box and remove the canister through the frame opening.

Installing Hanging Lights

Hanging lights can be a little tricky to install, depending on the style of light fixture and the area of the house where it is being installed. Some styles of hanging light fixtures can be extremely heavy–too heavy for one person to install.

Chandeliers in foyers are not only cumbersome and heavy but the ceiling height at which they are to be installed may require scaffolding in order to provide enough room and support for you and a helper to make the connections.

Most of the time, you can easily install smaller hanging light fixtures by yourself. They are usually in rooms with lower ceiling heights and tend not to be quite so heavy. Be sure to plan your fixture style and location before attempting any installation.

STUFF YOU'LL NEED:

- ☐**Tools:** Phillips and standard screwdrivers, neon circuit tester, regular and needlenose pliers.
- ☐**Materials:** Mounting strap, wire connectors.

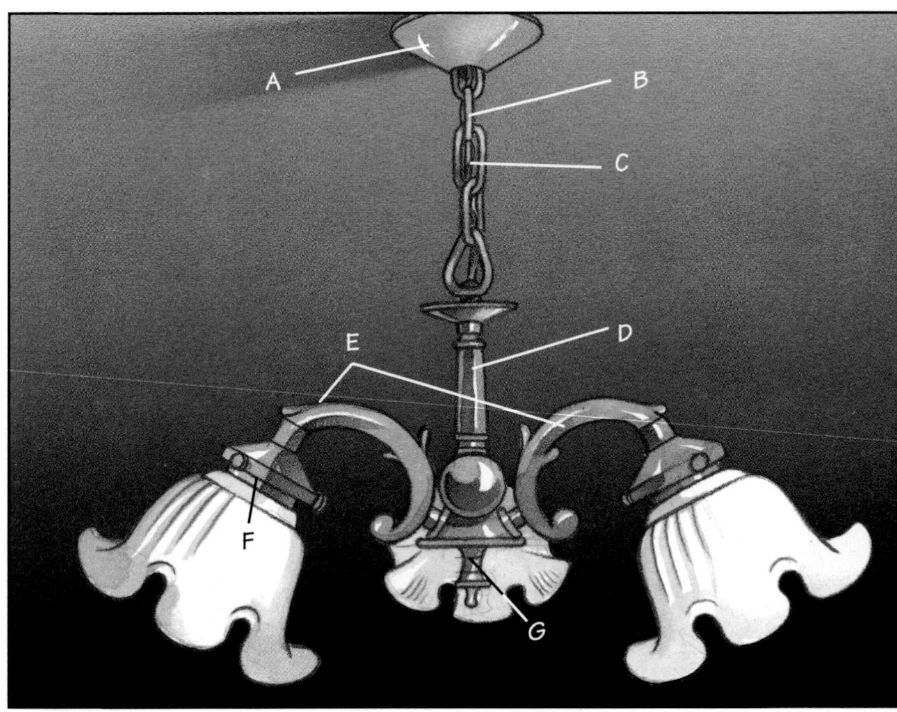

Chandeliers come in a variety of sizes and styles but still have common components. Coverplates (**A**) provide a decorative cover to the circuit wires and electrical box and can be quickly lowered for repair. Support chains (**B**) provide mounting support for the fixture while fixture wires (**C**) bring electricity from the box to the chandelier base (**D**). Some chandeliers have arms (**E**) that provide a pathway for the socket wires and mounts for the globes (**F**). Decorative caps (**G**) conceal socket wire connections.

MOUNTING VARIATIONS FOR CHANDELIERS

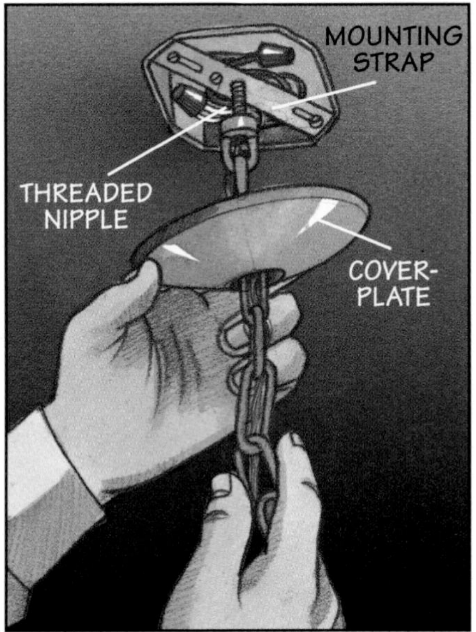

Most chandeliers are supported by a threaded nipple that is attached to an electrical box mounting strap.

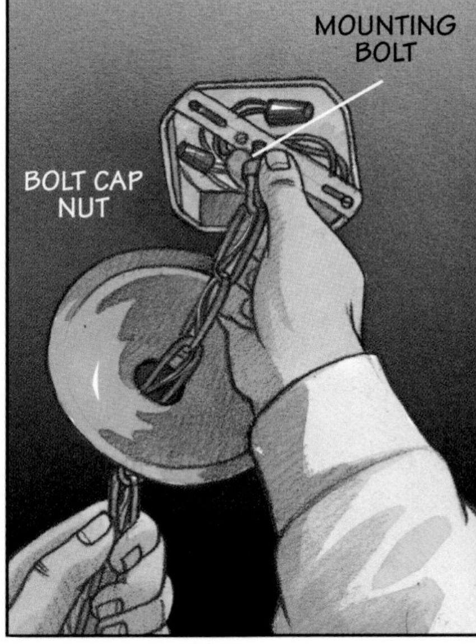

Some chandeliers are supported by bolts threaded into a rotating mounting strap. These fixtures do not use a threaded nipple and are suspended from the coverplate.

MOUNTING THREADED NIPPLE FIXTURES

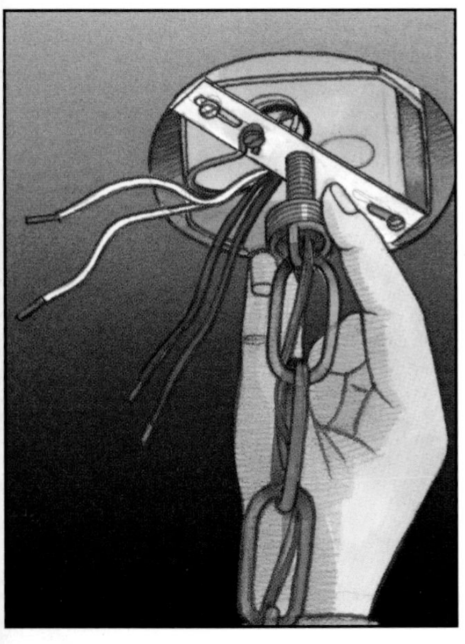

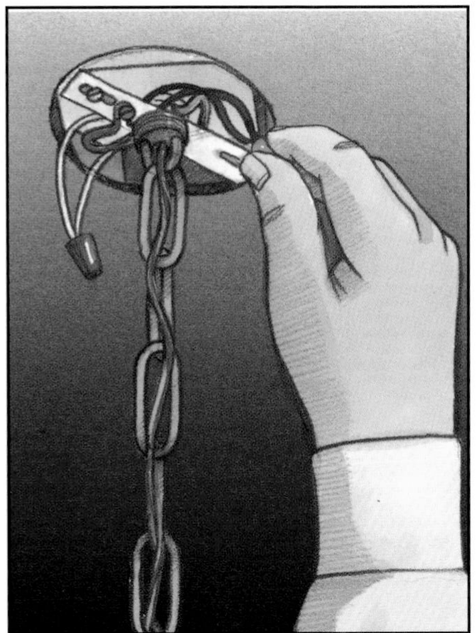

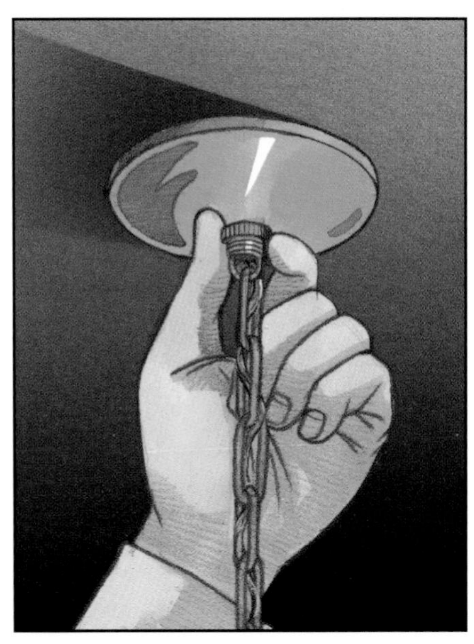

1 With the power turned off at the main service panel, attach the mounting strap to the electrical box and thread the nipple into the strap so that 3/4" of the nipple remains below the strap. Screw the fixture retaining nut onto the threaded nipple.

2 Connect the fixture wires with wire nuts. The marked fixture wire is neutral and should be connected to white circuit wire. The unmarked fixture wire is hot and should be connected to black circuit wire.

3 Tuck the wires into the electrical box. Place the decorative coverplate over the electrical box, and tighten the coverplate retaining nut to hold it in place.

Electrical

MOUNTING STRAP FIXTURES

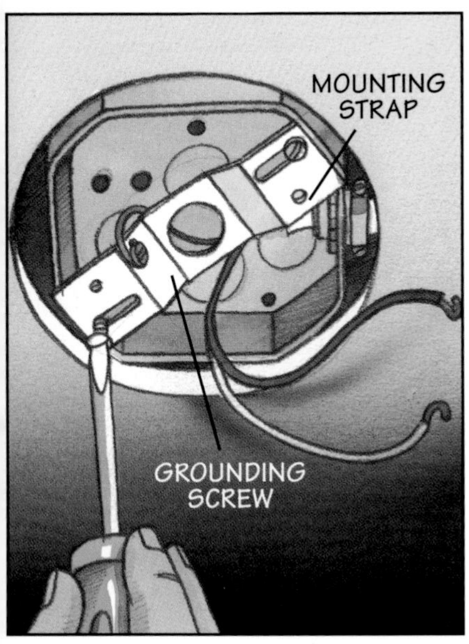

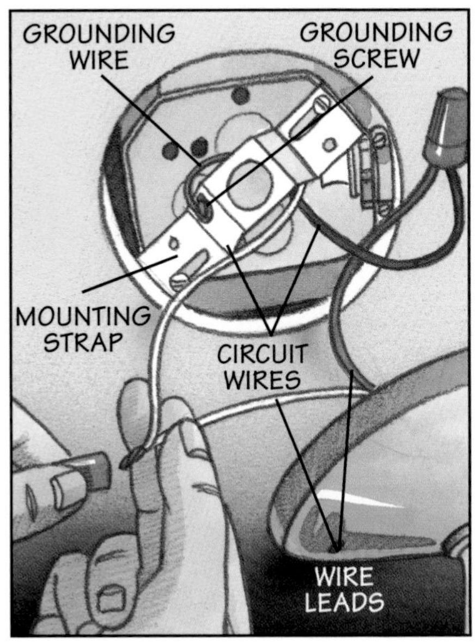

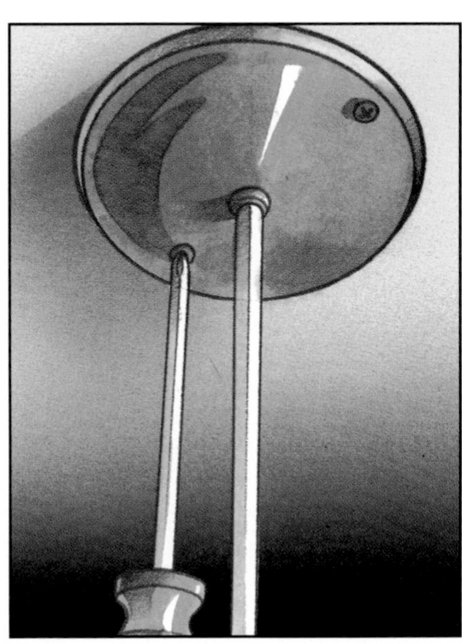

1 With the power turned off at the main service panel, attach a mounting strap to the electrical box, if the box doesn't already have one. The mounting strap has a preinstalled grounding screw.

2 Connect the circuit wires to the base of the new fixture using wire connectors. Connect the white wire lead to the white circuit wire and the black wire lead to the black circuit wire. Attach the bare copper grounding wire to the grounding screw on the mounting strap.

3 Attach the light fixture base to the mounting strap. Install a light bulb with a wattage rating that is the same as or lower than the rating indicated on the fixture. Turn on the power at the main service panel.

Installing Wall-Mounted & Recessed Lights

Whether they are replacing existing fixtures or are new installations, wall-mounted and recessed light fixtures are relatively easy to install once you have determined their locations. If you are replacing an existing fixture, check to see if the mounting strap is suitable for the new fixture mounting holes. If it is not, simply replace it with the proper strap.

When installing a new recessed fixture in an existing ceiling, be careful not to pound too hard when mounting the frame to the ceiling joists. Excessive pressure can crack the joint compound on drywall joints and covered nail and screw holes.

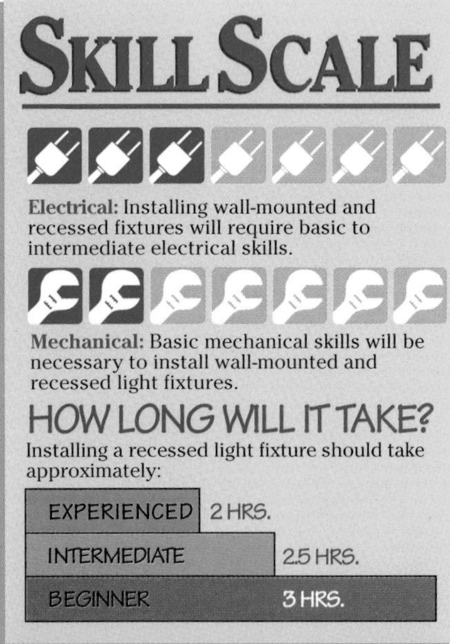

STUFF YOU'LL NEED:

- ☐ **Tools:** Screwdrivers, combination tool, needlenose pliers, wallboard saw, hammer.
- ☐ **Materials:** Electrical box, NM cable, wire connectors.

INSTALLING WALL-MOUNTED LIGHTS

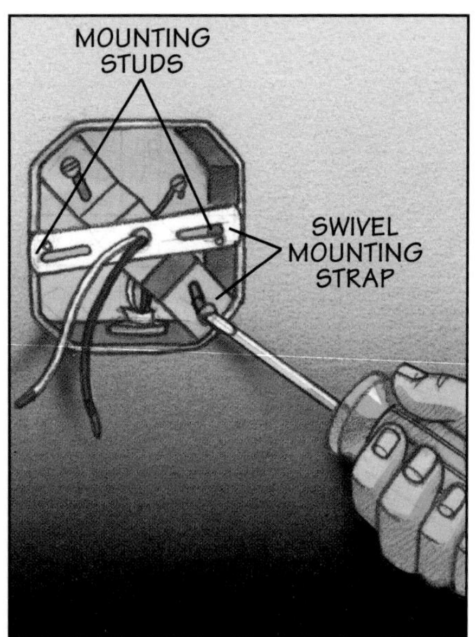

1 With the power turned off at the main service panel, run wire and install an electrical box in the desired location (see pgs. 166 and 178). Attach swivel mounting strap to the electrical box and insert threaded mounting studs.

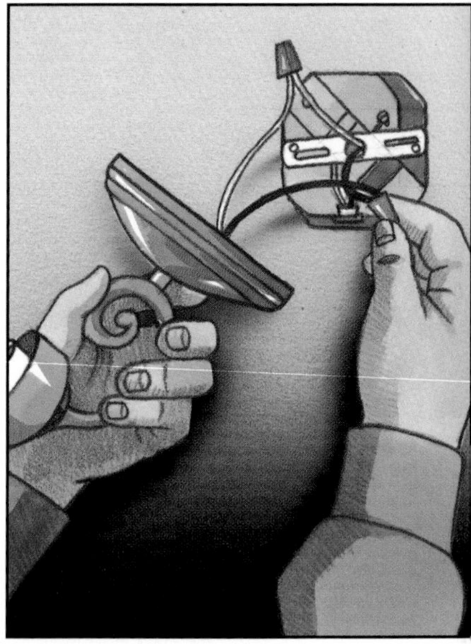

2 Connect the black circuit wire to the black fixture wire and the white circuit wire to the white fixture wire. If the fixture has a green or bare copper grounding wire, connect it to the electrical box.

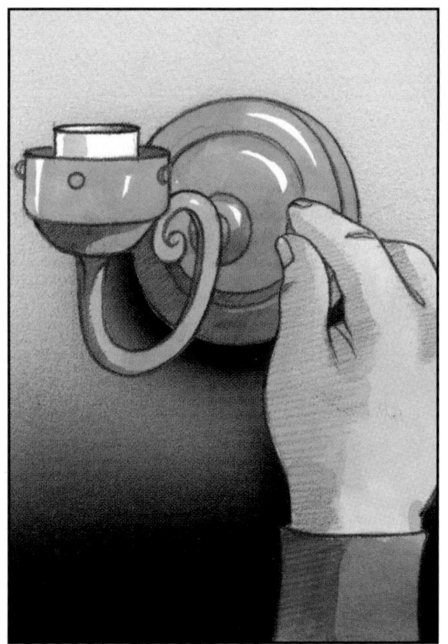

3 Tuck the wires back into the electrical box. Position the swivel mounting strap in a horizontal position. Align the fixture mounting holes with the threaded mounting studs and place the fixture onto the electrical box. Secure the fixture in place with the fixture retaining nuts.

4 Install a light bulb with the proper wattage rating as stated on the fixture. Position the fixture bowl in place and secure with retaining screws. Make the necessary cable and switch connections. Turn on power at the main service panel.

INSTALLING RECESSED LIGHTS

Parts of a recessed light include the mounting frame (**A**); the wire connection box (**B**) and armored cable (**C**); and the socket (**D**), which is housed in the canister (**E**). Springs (**F**) hold the reflector (**G**) in place; the bulb (**H**) illuminates the desired area; and the trim (**I**) covers the fixture hole in the ceiling.

1 Clear away insulation where you will install the recessed light fixture. With the frame in place, trace around the opening with a pencil and cut out the opening. Secure the frame to the joists. Some recessed lights are insulation compatible, "IC," and do not require the insulation to be cleared away.

2 With the power turned off at the main service panel, insert the armored cable from the canister into the wire connection box and secure it in place.

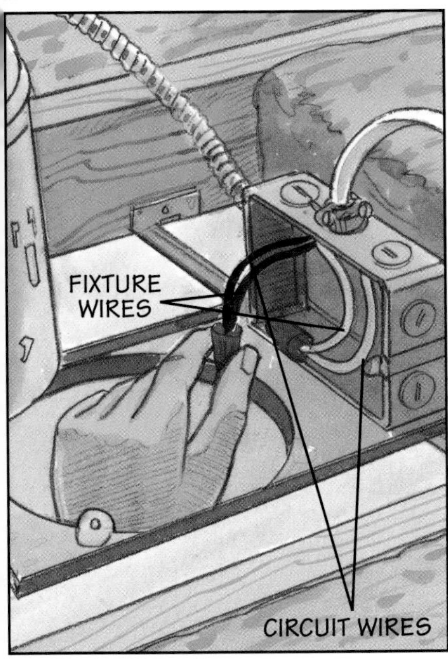

3 Run a length of NM cable from the wall switch to the wire connection box and secure it with cable clamps. Connect the black circuit wire to the black fixture wire and the white circuit wire to the white fixture wire with wire connectors. Screw the coverplate onto the wire connection box.

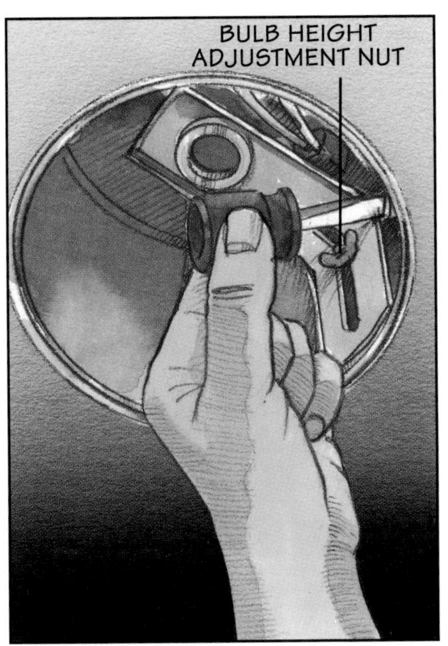

4 Position the canister inside the mounting frame. When replacing attic insulation, be sure to keep insulation 6" away from the canister. Attach the mounting screws or clips to hold the canister in the mounting frame.

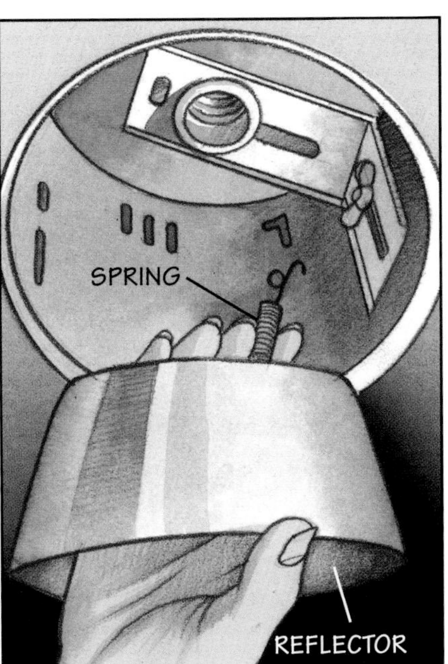

5 Attach the reflector and trim. Canister lights require bulbs with specific wattages. Make sure to follow the manufacturer's instructions when choosing bulbs. Never use bulbs with higher wattage ratings than those suggested. Turn on the power at the main service panel.

Installing Track Lighting

There are two types of track lighting available: one with a power cord that you simply plug into a receptacle and one that must be directly wired into a circuit box.

The first type is fairly simple to install, but you've got to be lucky enough to have a receptacle within close proximity to the track installation. Extension cords running across the ceiling and down the wall probably won't be a style your neighbors will envy!

Track lighting fixtures that are wired directly into a circuit box are the cleanest and most professional-looking. You can use an electrical box from an existing fixture you are replacing. Or, if you're installing track in a new area, you will have to add an electrical box in the existing wall or ceiling and run cable to it.

- ☐ **Tools:** Screwdrivers, combination tool, linesman's pliers.
- ☐ **Materials:** Pigtail wire, wire connectors.

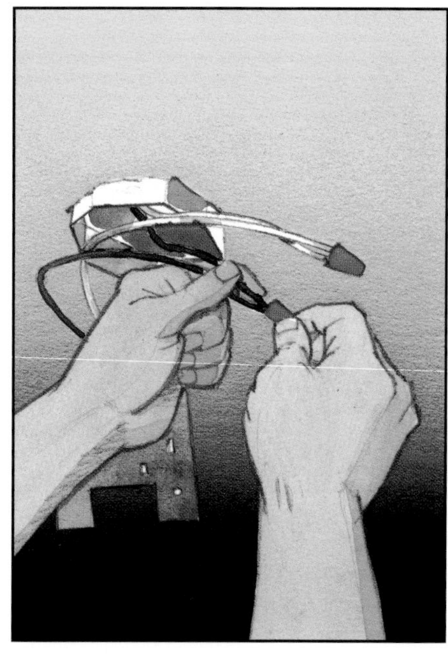

1 With the power turned off at the main service panel, connect the circuit wires to the fixture wires with wire connectors. Connect the white circuit wire to the white fixture wire and the black circuit wire to the black fixture wire. Pigtail the green grounding fixture wire to the bare copper grounding wire and to the metal electrical box.

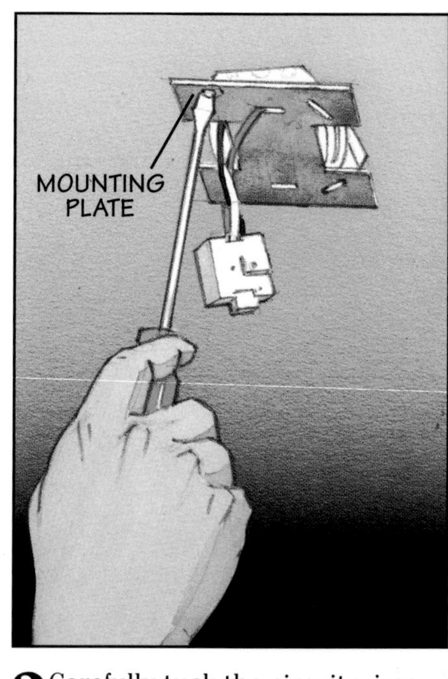

2 Carefully tuck the circuit wires and fixture wires into the electrical box. Attach the mounting plate to the ceiling box.

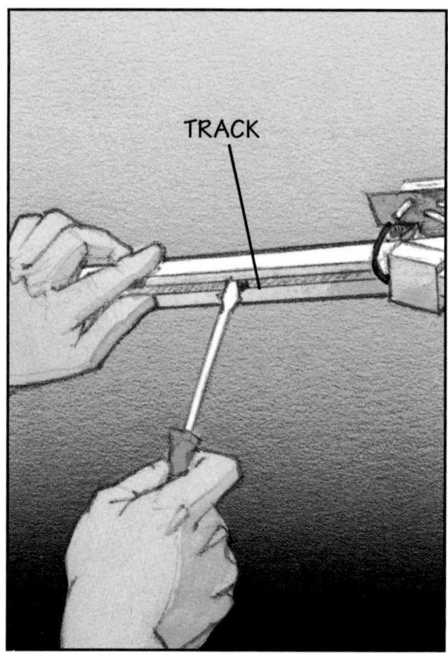

3 Snap the lighting track onto the mounting plate, and position the track as desired. Fasten the track to ceiling with screws and anchors or toggle bolts. It is best to position the tracks underneath the ceiling joists for sturdy installation.

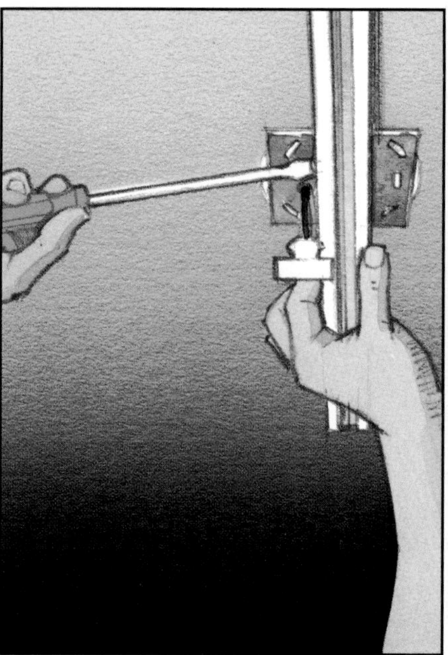

4 Once the track is in position, tighten track locking screws on the mounting plate. Be careful not to overtighten the locking screws; you may damage the track.

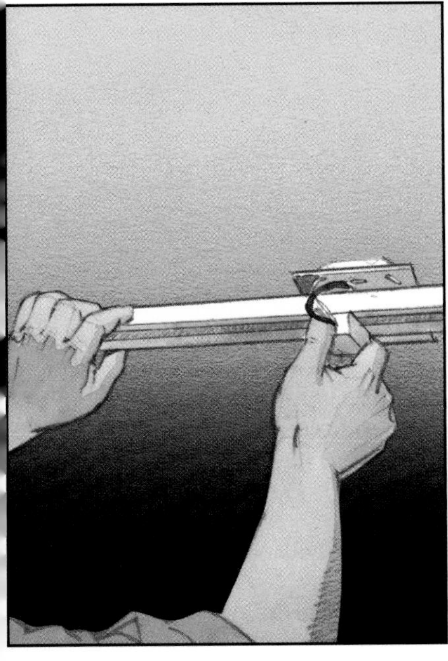

5 Insert the twist-lock connector into the track and rotate 90° to the locked position. Be sure that the contact fingers on the connector seat correctly into the track. Do not force the connector; if it does not snap easily, simply turn it in the opposite direction.

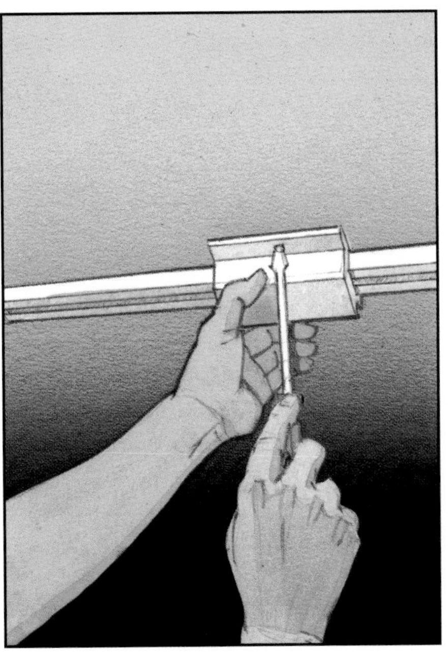

6 Attach the power supply cover over the twist-lock connector, and attach it to the ceiling box. Make certain it completely covers the ceiling box.

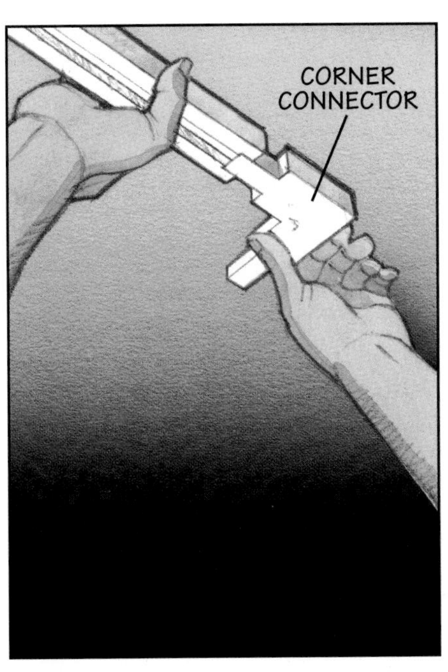

7 Attach track connectors for additional sections of track and corner pieces as necessary for the specific design.

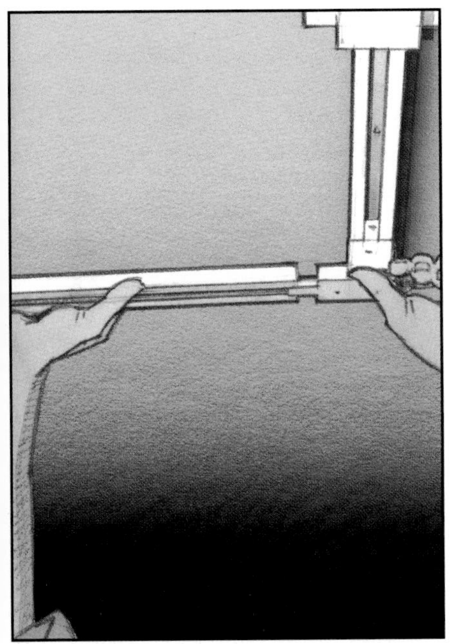

8 Attach additional track sections to ceiling. Close the open ends of track with dead-end pieces.

9 Insert the fixtures into the track and twist-lock the fixtures into place.

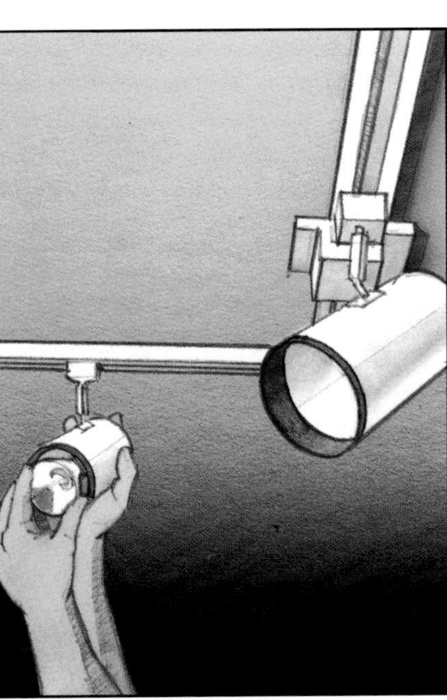

10 Install the appropriate bulbs and turn on the power to the circuit at the main service panel. Turn on power to the fixture at the wall switch and adjust the beams to focus the lighting for the desired effect.

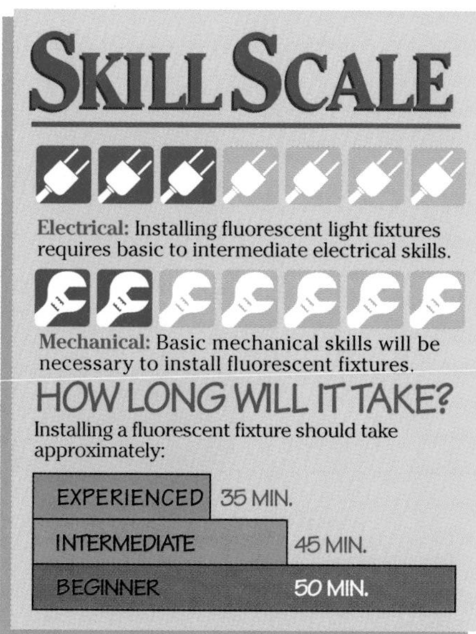

Repairing & Replacing Fluorescent Lights

Fluorescent lights are relatively trouble-free, and use less energy than incandescent lights. A typical fluorescent tube lasts about 20,000 hours and produces two to four times as much light per watt as a standard incandescent light bulb. The most frequent problem with a fluorescent light fixture is a worn-out tube. If a fluorescent light fixture begins to flicker or does not light fully, remove and examine the tube. If the tube has bent or broken pins, or black discoloration near the ends, replace it. Light gray discoloration is normal in working fluorescent tubes.

When replacing an old tube, read the wattage rating printed on the glass surface and buy a new tube with a matching rating. Never dispose of old tubes by breaking them. Fluorescent tubes contain a small amount of hazardous mercury. Check with your local environmental control agency or health department for disposal guidelines.

Fluorescent light fixtures also can malfunction if the sockets are cracked or worn. Inexpensive replacement sockets can be installed in a few minutes. If a fixture doesn't work even after the tube and sockets have been serviced, the ballast is probably defective. Faulty ballasts may leak a black, oily substance, and can cause a fluorescent light fixture to make a loud humming sound.

STUFF YOU'LL NEED:

- ☐ **Tools:** Phillips and standard screwdrivers, neon circuit tester, regular and needlenose pliers.
- ☐ **Materials:** Cable clamps, wire connectors.

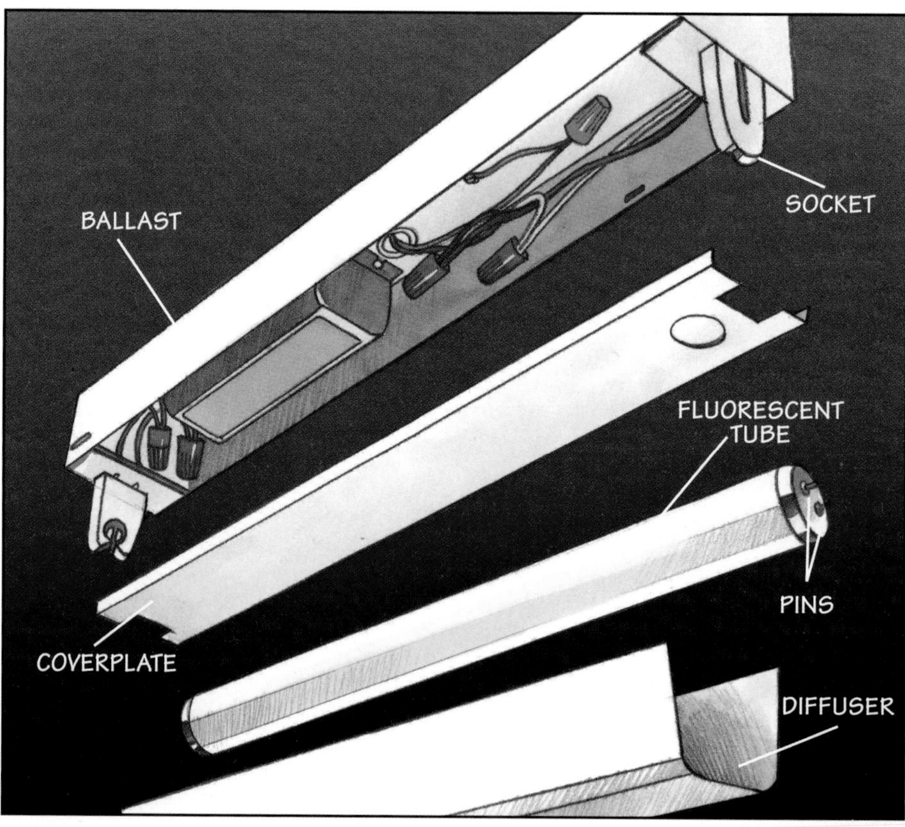

A fluorescent light works by directing electrical current through a special gas-filled tube that glows when energized. A white translucent diffuser protects the fluorescent tube and softens the light. A coverplate protects a special transformer or a "ballast." The ballast regulates the flow of 120-volt household current to the sockets. The sockets transfer power to metal pins that extend into the tube.

New Ballast or New Fixture?

Although ballasts can be easily replaced, it is sometimes more beneficial to check prices before jumping in and buying a new ballast. In many cases, it may be cheaper to purchase and install an entirely new fluorescent fixture than to replace the ballast in an old fixture. Depending on the type of fluorescent fixture, many home stores sell inexpensive fixtures. Sometimes replacement parts seem expensive in comparison.

TROUBLESHOOTING FLUORESCENT LIGHTS

	PROBLEM	REPAIR
	Tube flickers or lights partially.	1. Rotate the tube to make sure it is seated properly in the sockets. 2. Replace the tube and the starter (if present) if the tube is discolored or if the pins are bent or broken. 3. Replace the ballast if the replacement cost is reasonable. Otherwise, replace the entire fixture.
	Tube does not light.	1. Check the wall switch, and repair or replace, if needed. 2. Rotate the tube to make sure it is seated properly in the sockets. 3. Replace the tube and the starter (if present) if the tube is discolored or if the pins are bent or broken. 4. Replace the sockets if they are chipped or if the tube doesn't seat properly. 5. Replace the ballast or the entire fixture.
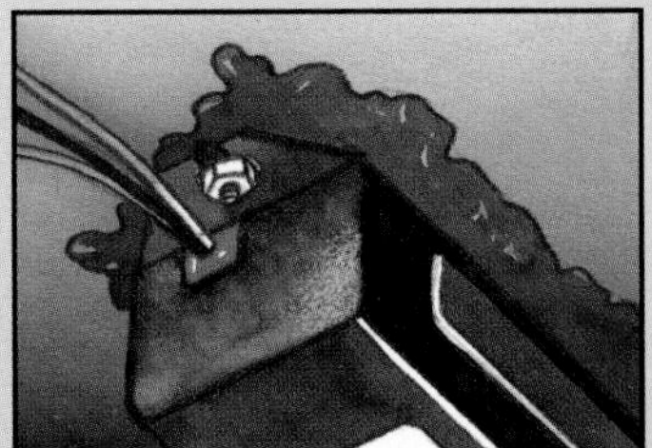	Noticeable black substance around the ballast. Fixture makes a loud humming noise.	1. Replace the ballast if the replacement cost is reasonable. Otherwise, replace the entire fixture. A small amount of humming is normal.

Older fluorescent lights may have a small cylindrical device, called a starter, located near one of the sockets. When a tube begins to flicker, replace both the tube and the starter. Turn off the power. Remove the starter by pushing it slightly and turning counterclockwise. Install a replacement that matches the old starter.

When installing new fluorescent tubes, make sure the new tube has the same wattage rating as the old tube. Insert the tube so that the pins slide fully into the sockets; then twist the tube $1/4$ turn in either direction until it is locked securely.

REPLACING A BALLAST

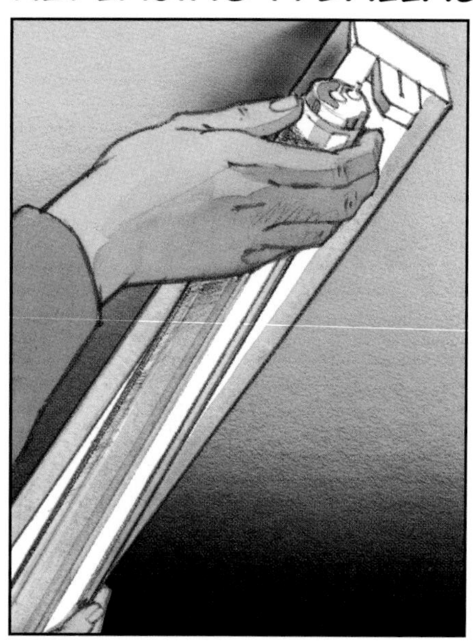

1 Turn off the power at the main service panel. Remove the diffuser, fluorescent tube, and coverplate.

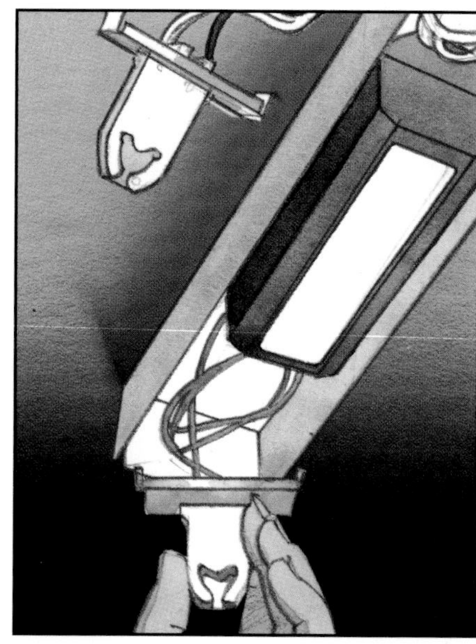

2 Once you have determined that the power is off, remove the sockets from the fixture housing by sliding them out or by removing the mounting screws and lifting the sockets out.

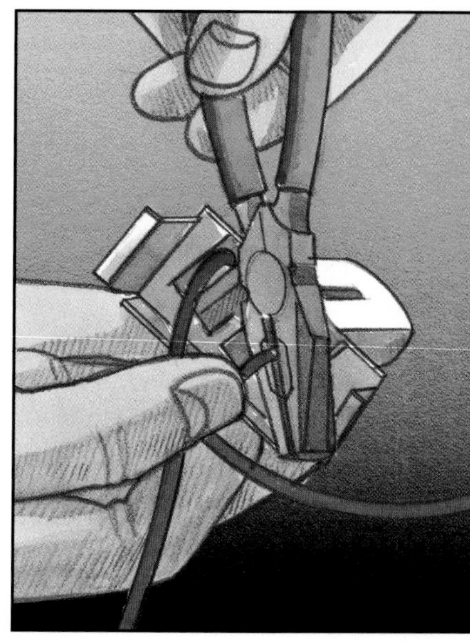

3 Disconnect the wires attached to the sockets by cutting them with a linesman's pliers or combination tool.

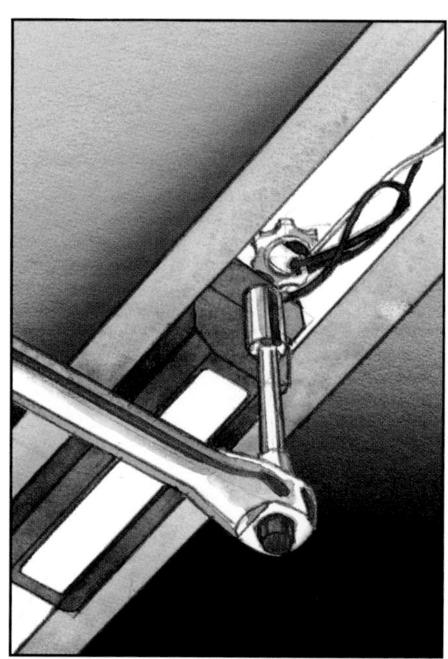

4 Remove the old ballast using a ratchet wrench or screwdriver. Make sure to support the ballast so it does not fall.

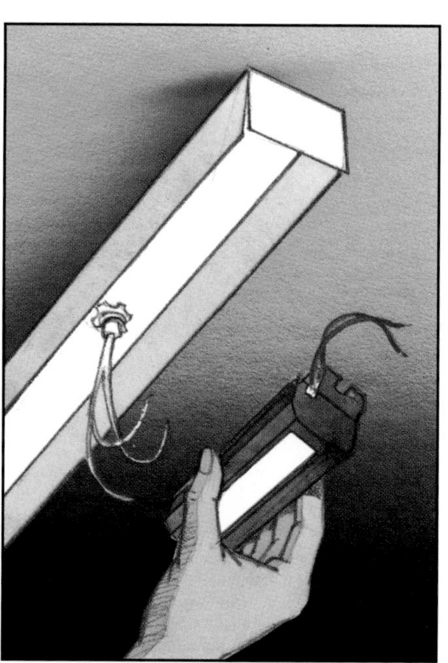

5 Install the new ballast and make sure that it has the same ratings as the old ballast. You may have to drill new holes to accommodate the new ballast.

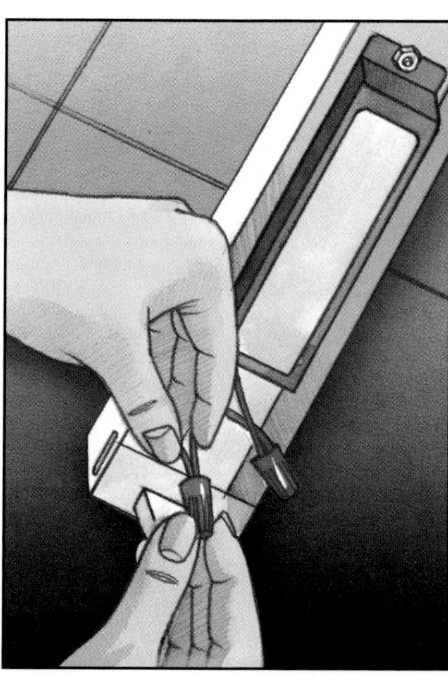

6 Attach ballast wires to socket wires using wire connectors, screw terminal connections, or push-in fittings. Reinstall the coverplate, fluorescent tube, and diffuser. Turn on power to the light fixture at the main service panel.

REPLACING A FLUORESCENT FIXTURE

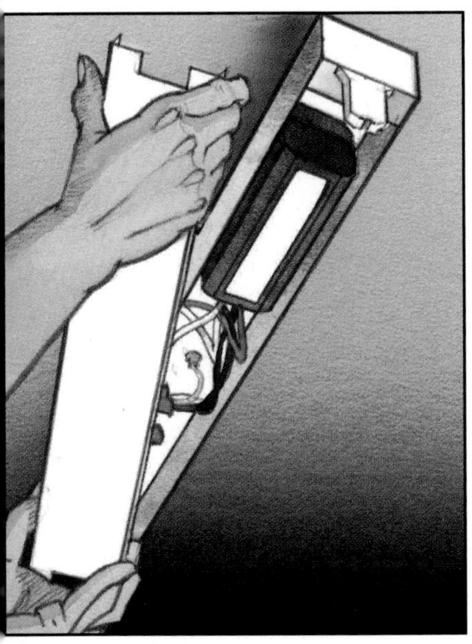

1 Turn off power to the light fixture at the main service panel. Remove the diffuser, bulbs, and coverplate. Test for power using a neon circuit tester.

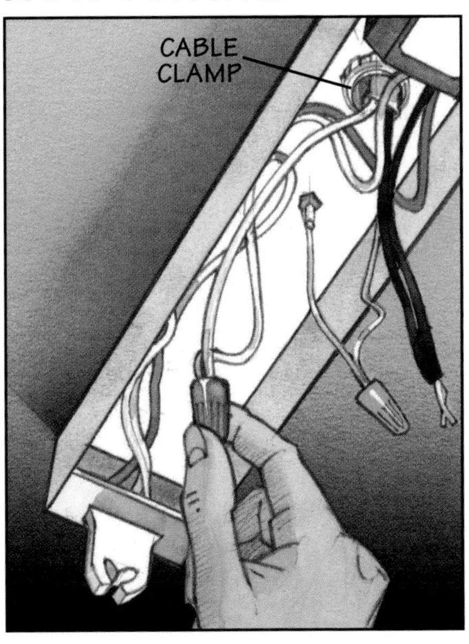

2 Disconnect the insulated circuit wires and the bare copper grounding wire from the light fixture. Loosen the cable clamp that holds the circuit wires.

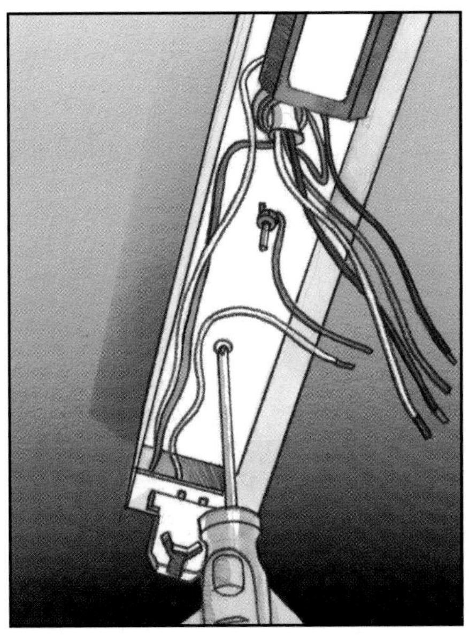

3 Unbolt the fixture from the wall or ceiling and carefully remove it. Make sure to support the fixture so it does not fall.

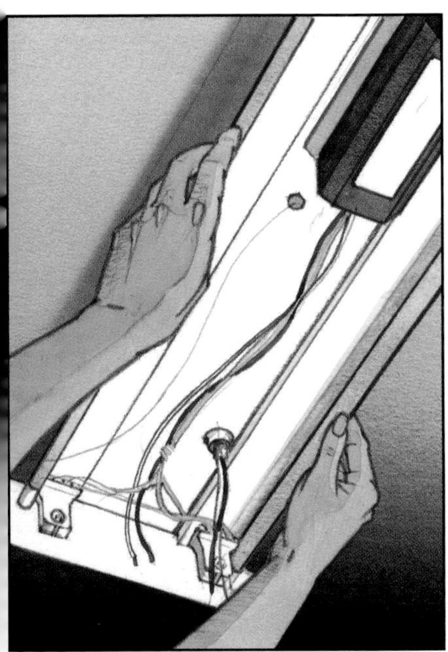

4 Position the new fixture, threading the circuit wires through the knockout opening in the back of the fixture. Bolt the fixture in place so it is firmly anchored to framing members.

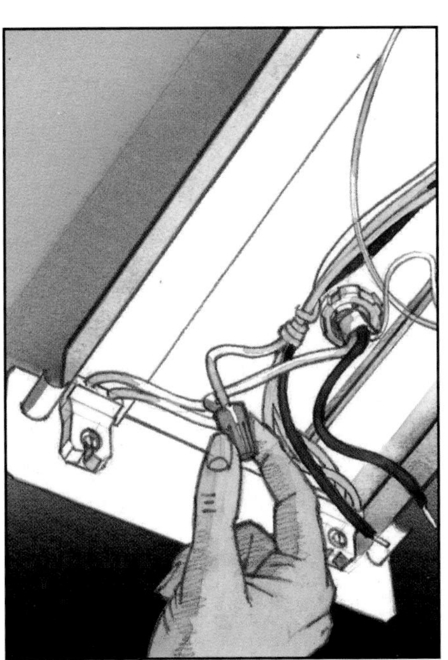

5 Connect the circuit wires to the fixture wires using wire connectors. Follow the wiring diagram included with the new fixture. Tighten the cable clamp holding the circuit wires.

6 Attach the fixture coverplate. Install the fluorescent tubes and attach the diffuser. Turn on power to the fixture at the main service panel.

Installing a Ceiling Fan

Ceiling fans help reduce both heating and cooling costs by circulating air to make room temperatures more comfortable without additional heating or cooling. Fans are available in many different designs and sizes with variable-speed controls and even built-in lights. Installations can range from replacing an existing fixture to a brand-new installation. Ceiling fans are often mounted in place of existing ceiling lights so a built-in light is actually more of a necessity than a luxury. If you replace a light fixture with a fan, you'll need to upgrade the weight carrying capacity of the electrical box. Separate wall switches for the fan and light will require running new wire from the switch to the electrical box. Consult the wiring diagram supplied with the fan.

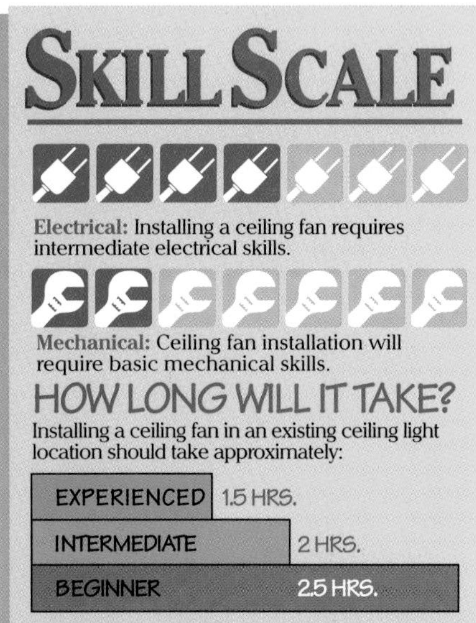

STUFF YOU'LL NEED:

- **Tools:** Screwdrivers, adjustable wrench, nut driver.
- **Materials:** Electrical fixture box, metal brace bar, wire connectors.

Use a metal brace attached to framing members for ceiling fans and large light fixtures that are too heavy to be supported by an electrical box. If you have access to the box in the attic, use a UL approved ceiling mounting box rather than a metal brace.

BUYER'$ GUIDE

Choosing the Right Size Fan

When buying a ceiling fan, be sure to follow these simple guidelines for determining the proper fan size and mounting dimensions according to the room where the fan will be installed.

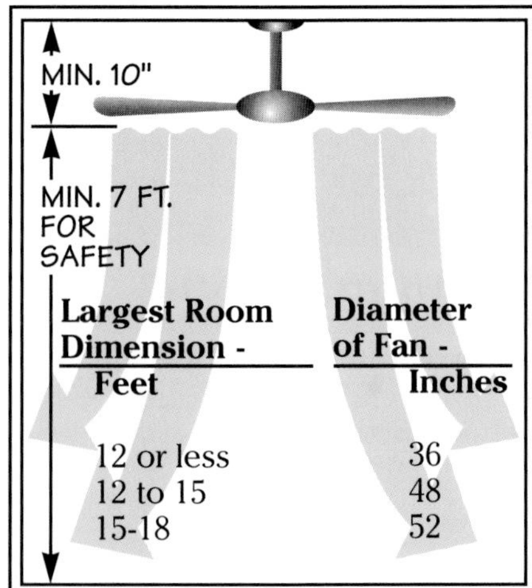

Largest Room Dimension - Feet	Diameter of Fan - Inches
12 or less	36
12 to 15	48
15-18	52

MOUNTING THE FAN

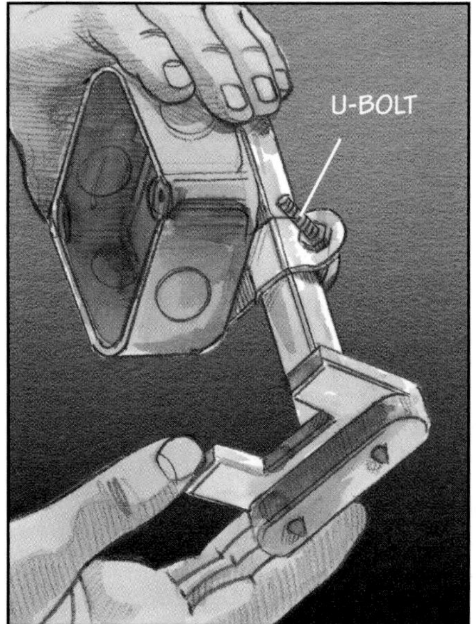

1 Turn off power to the existing light fixture at the main service panel, test for power, and remove the fixture and electrical box. Attach a 1½"-deep metal light fixture box to the brace bar using a U-bolt and two nuts.

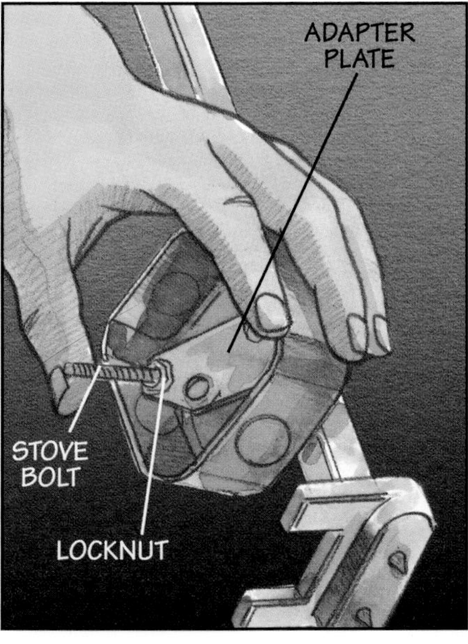

2 Attach the included stove bolts to the adapter plate with locknuts. These bolts will support the fan. Insert the adapter plate into the box so ends of U-bolt fit through the holes on the adapter plate.

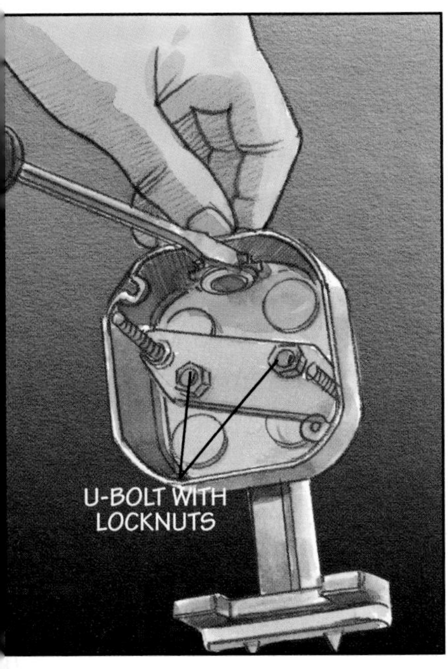

3 Secure the adapter plate by screwing two locknuts onto the U-bolt. Open one knockout for each cable that will enter the electrical box and attach a cable clamp to each knockout.

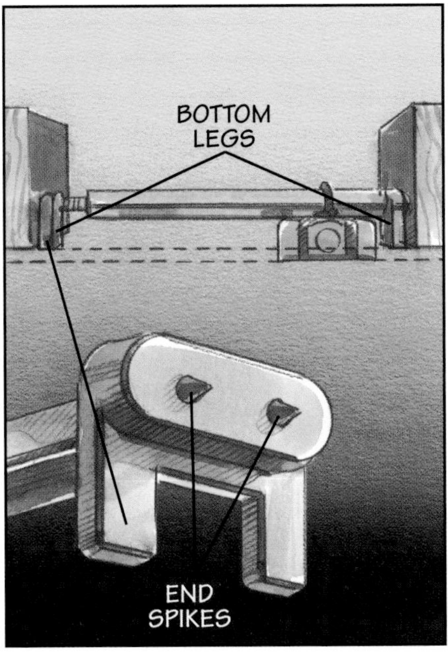

4 From the attic, position the brace between joists so the bottom legs are flush with the bottom of the joists. Rotate the bar by hand to force the end spikes into the joists. The face of the electrical box should be below the joists and be flush with the finished ceiling surface.

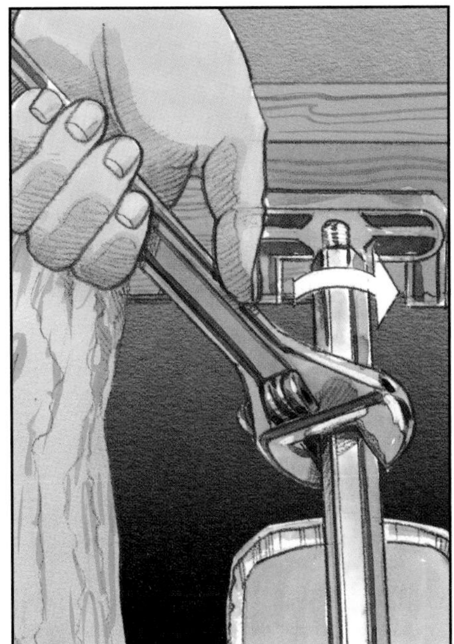

5 Tighten the brace bar one full rotation with a wrench to anchor the brace tightly against the joists. Feed the existing circuit cable into the fixture box and secure with a cable clamp.

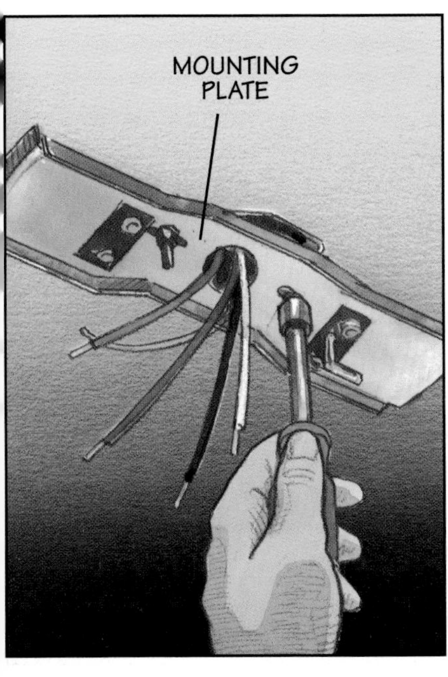

6 Place the ceiling fan mounting plate over the stove bolts extending through the electrical box. Pull the circuit wires through the hole in the center of the mounting plate. Attach the mounting nuts, and tighten them with a nut driver.

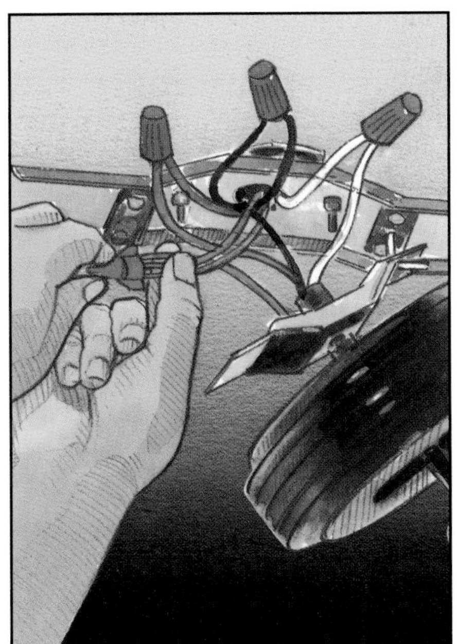

7 Hang the fan motor from mounting hook. Connect the wire leads using wire connectors: black circuit wire to black wire lead from fan; white circuit wire to white lead; and grounding wires to green lead. Complete assembly of fan and light fixture following the manufacturer's directions.

HOMER'S HINDSIGHT

Ceiling fans are great for cooling off on those hot summer days, but installing them for the first time can be a real scorcher!

It was a pretty smooth and simple wiring process since It was replacing an existing light fixture. Most of the installation went fairly quickly until I turned it on for the first time. I thought the darn thing was going to take off for outer space. Naturally, I thought the wobbling problem was due to a manufacturer's defect. I loosened the blades and tried to adjust them, but with no improvement. Finally upon a frustrated trip back to the store, I discovered a novel little package called a ceiling fan balancing kit in the accessory aisle. Since the blades were balanced, I haven't had to touch the fan except when dusting!

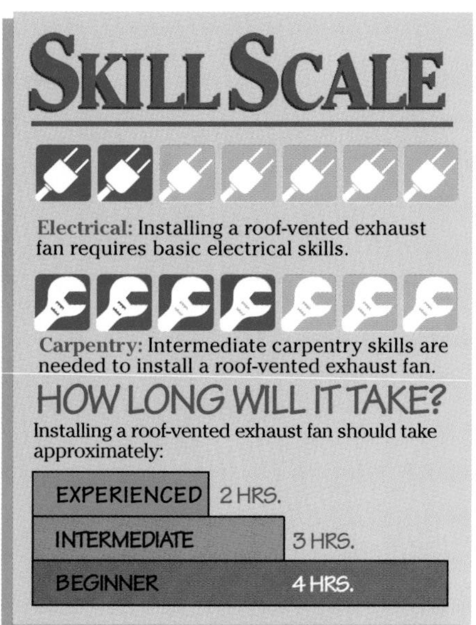

Installing an Exhaust Vent Fan

An exhaust vent fan makes your bathroom more comfortable by removing heat, moisture, and odors. Building Codes usually require that all bathrooms without natural ventilation be equipped with an exhaust vent fan, but even if your bathroom has a window or skylight, installing an exhaust vent fan is a good idea.

Exhaust vent fans are available in several styles. Some have only a fan; some have a light and a fan; and others have a light, fan, and heat lamps or heat blowers. Exhaust vent fans that have only a fan, and those with a fan and light fixture, can usually be wired into your bathroom electrical circuit. Units with built-in heat lamps or heat blowers need a separate electrical circuit.

Most exhaust vent fans are installed in the center of the bathroom ceiling or over the toilet area. They can be vented from the ceiling through the roof or through the outside wall, whichever has the easiest access—depending on the room location inside the house. Be careful not to install a vent fan unit over the tub or shower area unless i is GFCI-protected and rated for use i wet areas. If the exhaust vent fan you choose does not come with a complete mounting kit, purchase on separately.

Exhaust vent fan mounting kits should include: vent hose, vent tailpiece, and exterior vent cover. Vent fans may be installed while wal surfaces are removed or as a retrofi

STUFF YOU'LL NEED:

- ☐ **Tools:** Pencil, drill, jigsaw, hammer, screwdrivers, caulk gun, reciprocating saw, wire stripper, pliers.
- ☐ **Materials:** Screws, 2" dimension lumber, NM cable, wire connectors, hose clamps, roofing cement, pipe insulation, self-sealing roofing nails.

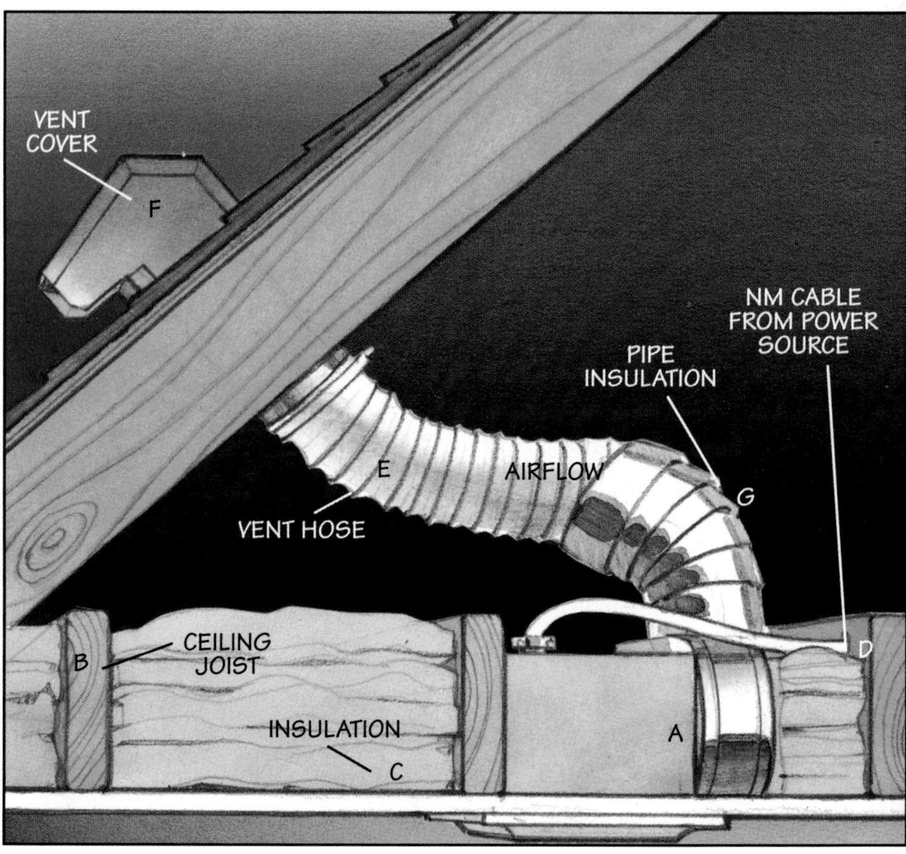

Roof-vented exhaust fans have the vent fan unit (A) mounted between ceiling joists (B) surrounded by insulation (C). NM cable from the power source (D) supplies electricity to the vent fan unit while air is drawn out of the room and exhausted through the vent hose (E) and the vent cover (F). Pipe insulation (G) prevents moist air inside the hose from condensing and dripping down into the fan motor.

Choosing an Exhaust Fan

Check the information label attached to each vent fan unit. Choose a unit with a fan rating at least 5 CFM higher than the square footage of your bathroom.

SONES refer to the relative quietness of the unit, rated on a scale of 1 to 7. (Quieter vent fans have lower SONE ratings.)

PUTTING IN A ROOF-VENTED EXHAUST FAN

1 Position the vent fan unit against a ceiling joist. Outline the unit onto the ceiling from above. Remove the unit, drill pilot holes at the corners of the outline, and cut out the area with a jigsaw or wallboard saw.

Vent fans with heaters or light fixtures require additional framing. Some vent manufacturers recommend using 2" dimension lumber to build dams between the ceiling joists to keep insulation at least 6" away from the vent fan and heater unit.

2 Remove the grille from the vent unit, then attach the vent fan unit to the joist with the unit's edge recessed 1/4" from the finished surface of the ceiling (so the grille can be flush-mounted). Turn off the power before wiring the fan.

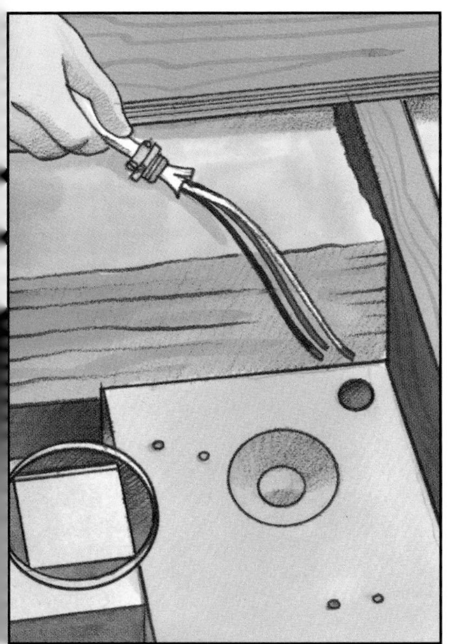

3 Run a length of NM cable from the existing light switch or fixture to the exhaust vent fan unit. Strip 10" of sheathing from the end of the cable at the vent unit, then attach a cable clamp. Insert the cable into the fan unit. From the inside of the unit screw a locknut onto the threaded end of the clamp.

4 Mark the exit location in the roof for the vent hose, next to a rafter. Drill a pilot hole; saw through the sheathing and roofing material with a reciprocating saw to make the cutout for the vent tailpiece.

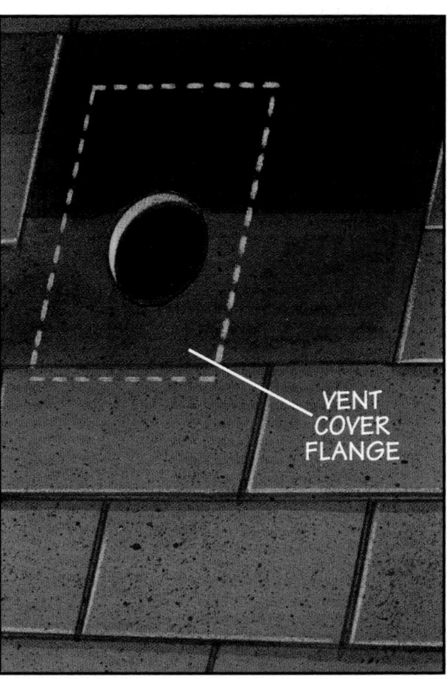

5 From the outside, remove a section of shingles from around the cutout, leaving the roofing paper intact. The removed shingles should create an exposed area the size of the vent cover flange. Always use caution when working on the roof.

PUTTING IN A ROOF-VENTED FAN (continued)

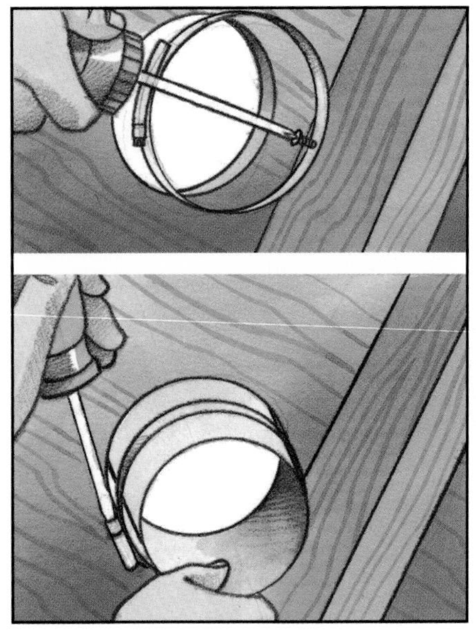

6 Attach a hose clamp to the rafter next to the roof cutout, about 1" below the roof sheathing. Insert the vent tailpiece into the cutout and through the hose clamp. Tighten the clamp screw.

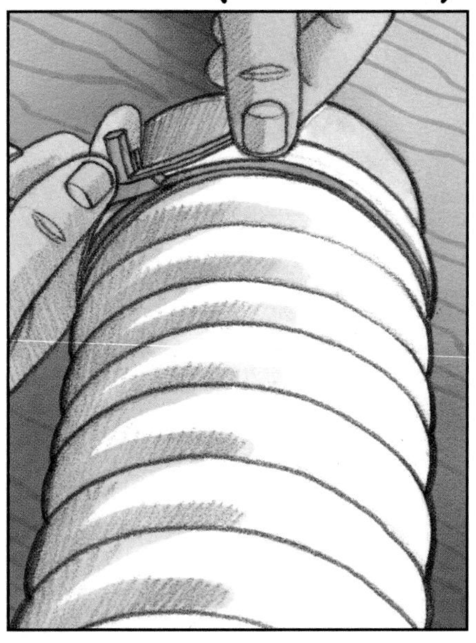

7 Slide one end of vent hose over the tailpiece and slide the other end over the outlet on the fan unit. Slip hose clamps or straps around each end of the vent hose and tighten to secure hose in place.

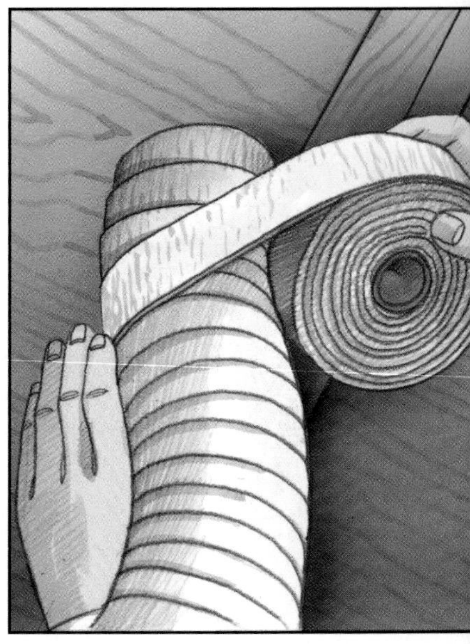

8 Wrap the vent hose with pipe insulation. Insulation prevents moist air inside the hose from condensing and dripping down into the fan motor.

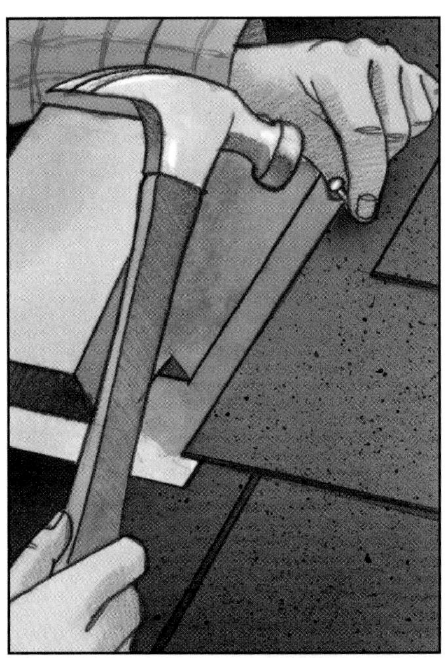

9 Apply roofing cement to the bottom of the vent cover flange, then slide the vent cover over the tailpiece. Nail the vent cover flange in place with self-sealing roofing nails and patch in shingles around the cover.

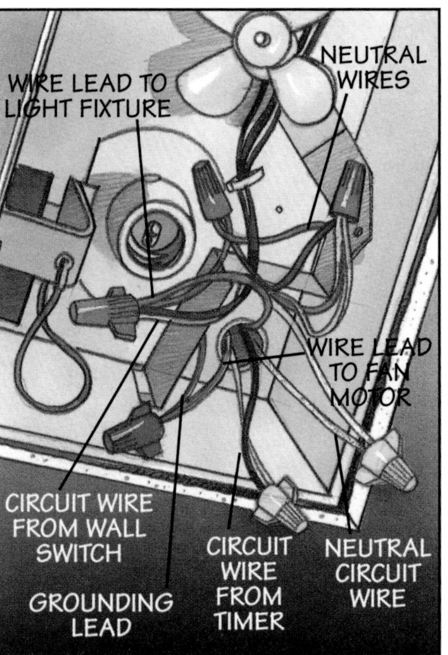

10 Wire the fan as follows: black circuit from timer to wire lead for fan motor; red circuit wire from single-pole switch to wire lead for light fixture; white neutral circuit wire to neutral wire lead; and circuit grounding wire to grounding lead in fan box. Attach coverplate over box when wiring is completed.

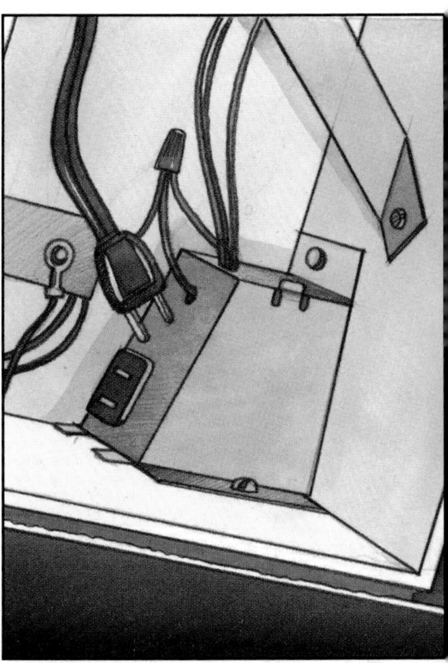

11 Connect the fan motor plug to the built-in receptacle on the wire connection box and attach the fan grille to the frame using the mounting clips included with the fan kit. If wall and ceiling surfaces have been removed for installation, install new surfaces before completing this step.

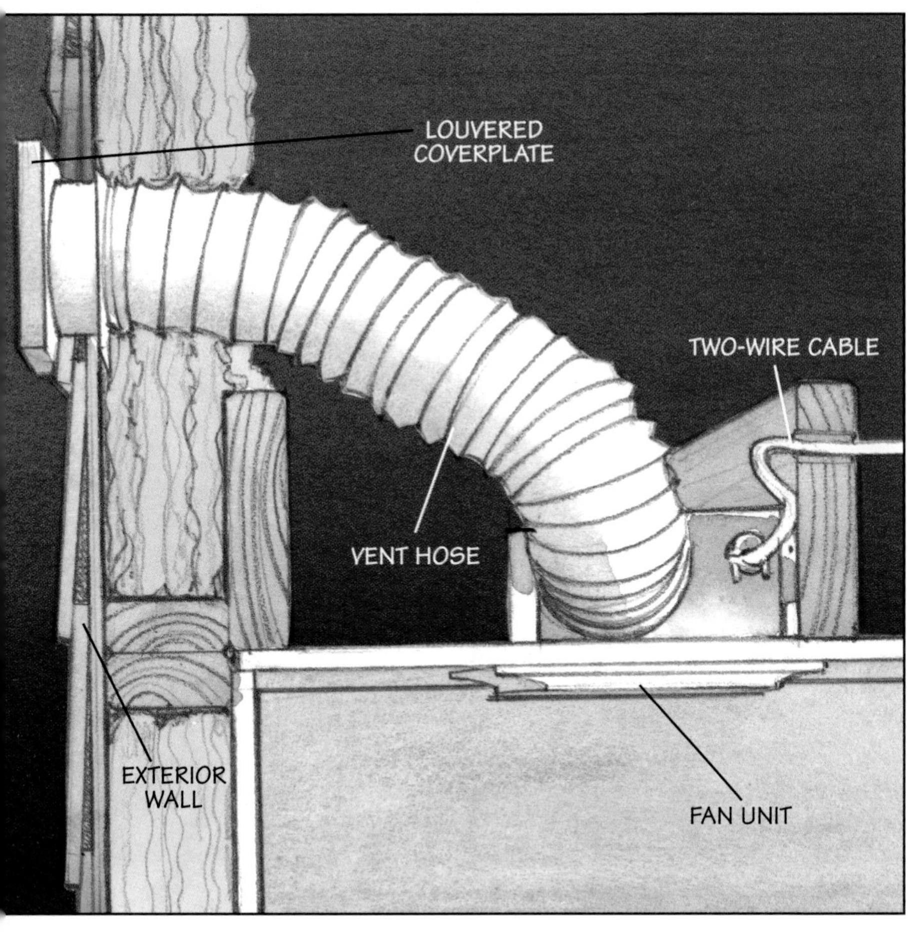

Venting an exhaust fan through a wall is similar to the technique used for roof venting. The fan units are basically the same with a built-in motor and blower that exhausts moisture-laden air from the bathroom to the outdoors through a plastic vent hose. A two-wire cable from a wall-mounted timer or single-pole switch is attached to the fan wire connection box with a cable clamp. A louvered coverplate mounted on the outside wall seals the vent against outdoor air when the motor is stopped.

PUTTING IN A WALL-VENTED FAN

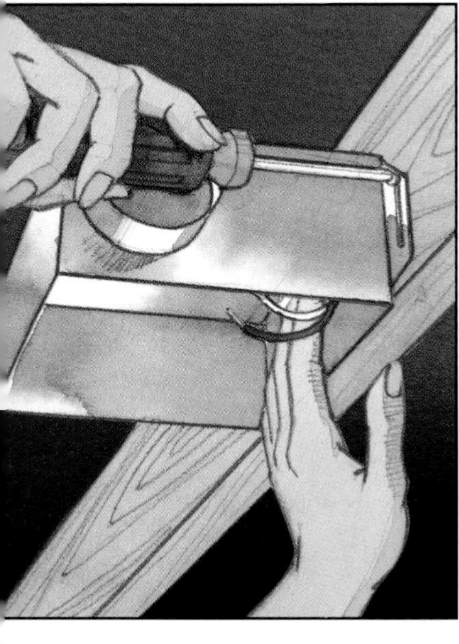

1 Turn off power to the circuit at the main service panel. Position the fan unit frame against a ceiling joist so the edge extends 1/4" below the bottom edge of the joist to provide proper spacing for the grill cover. Anchor the frame with wallboard screws.

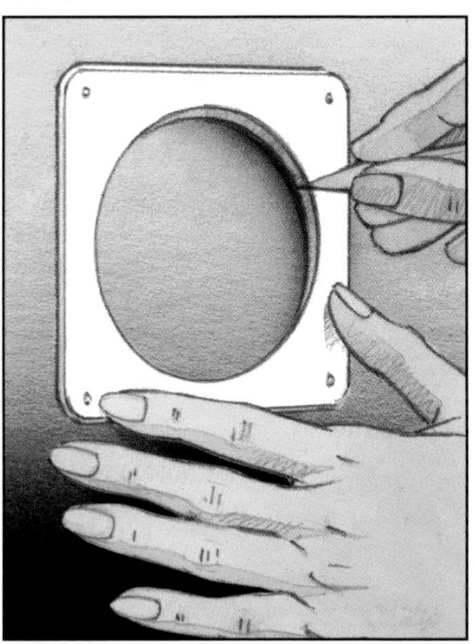

2 Choose the exit location for the vent. Temporarily remove any insulation and draw the outline of the vent flange opening on the wall sheathing.

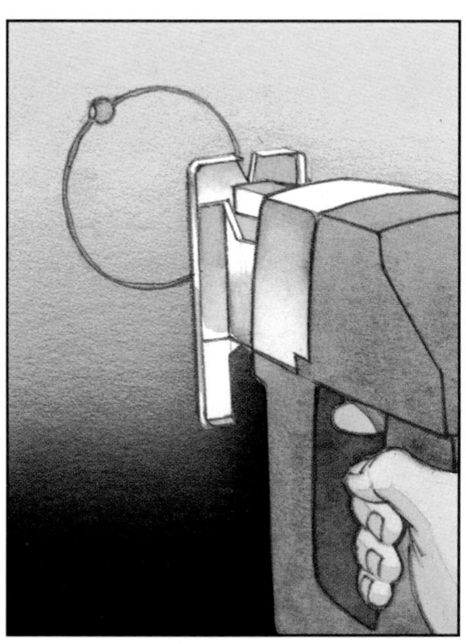

3 Drill a pilot hole, then make the cutout by sawing through the sheathing and siding with a jigsaw. Keep the blade to the outside edge of the guideline.

PUTTING IN A WALL-VENTED FAN (continued)

4 Insert the vent tailpiece into the cutout and attach it to the wall by driving wallboard screws through the flange and into the sheathing.

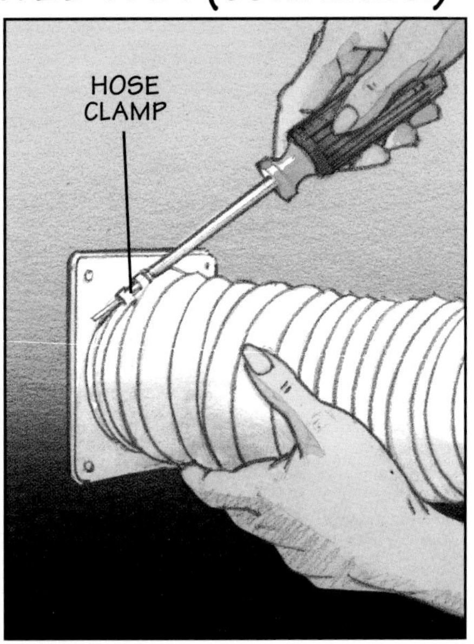

5 Slide one end of vent hose over the tailpiece. Place one of the hose clamps around the end of the vent hose and tighten with a screwdriver. Replace insulation against sheathing.

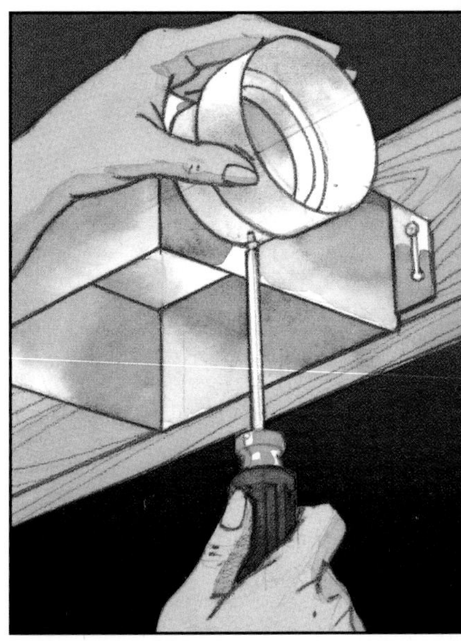

6 Attach a hose adapter to the outlet on the fan frame by driving sheet-metal screws through the adapter and into the outlet flange.

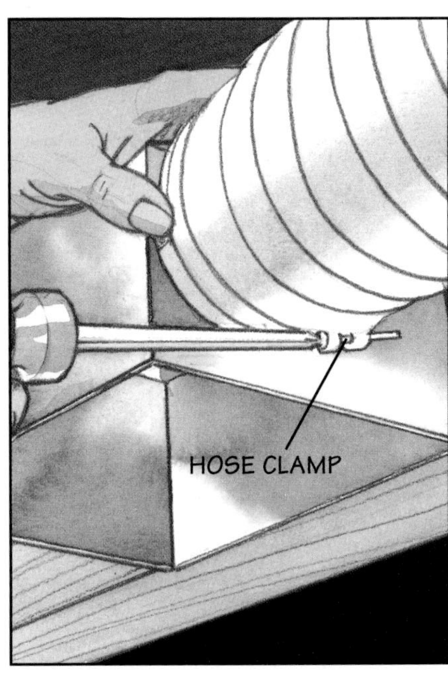

7 Slide the vent hose over the adapter. Place a hose clamp around the end of the hose and tighten it with a screwdriver. Your Building Code may require that you insulate the vent hose to prevent condensation problems.

8 On the outside wall of the house, place the louvered vent cover over the vent tailpiece, making sure the louvers are facing down. Attach the cover to the wall with galvanized screws. Apply a thick bead of caulk around the edge of the cover.

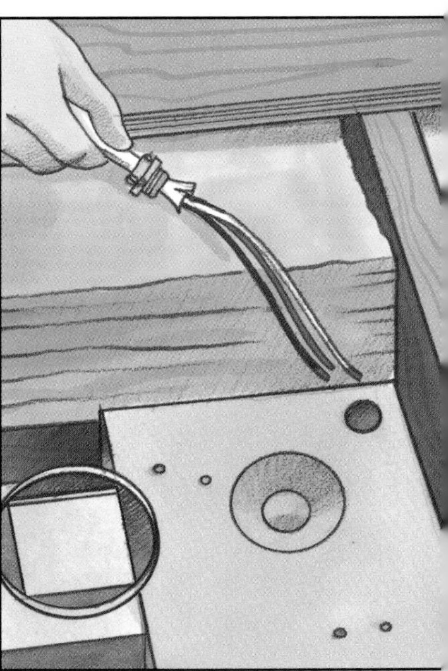

9 Run a length of NM cable from the light switch to the fan unit. Strip sheathing from the end of the cable and attach a cable clamp. Insert the cable into the fan unit and screw a locknut onto the threaded end of the clamp. Complete the installation by making the connections following Steps 10 and 11 on pg. 192.

Installing a Power Exhaust Attic Fan

Although summer is generally a pleasant time of year, summertime in your attic is a different story! Temperatures can easily exceed 150°F and don't change much when left to natural air flow from static louvers and vents. High attic temperatures put an extra load on your home's cooling system and can even cause damage to sheathing and roofing materials.

A simple solution is to install a power exhaust attic fan. A thermostatically controlled attic fan will make your home more comfortable in summer and can save you up to 30 percent on your cooling bill.

SKILL SCALE

Electrical: Installing an attic fan requires basic to intermediate electrical skills.

Mechanical: Attic fan installation will require basic mechanical skills.

HOW LONG WILL IT TAKE?

Installing an attic fan should take approximately:

EXPERIENCED	1.5 HRS.
INTERMEDIATE	2 HRS.
BEGINNER	2.5 HRS.

STUFF YOU'LL NEED:

- ☐ **Tools:** Screwdrivers, combination tool, hammer.
- ☐ **Materials:** NM cable, wire connectors, screws.

MOUNTING OPTIONS

Existing or newly installed static (gravity) roof vents provide quick and easy exhaust for power exhaust attic fans mounted directly below.

Power attic fans mounted directly below static roof vents are easily mounted to roof rafters. Fan mounts are usually spaced for rafters on 16" centers.

Triangular gable louvers provide high volume exhaust for power attic fans.

For stud or rafter mounting, box in the power exhaust attic fan with horizontal 2 x 4" framing members. Mount the unit to the horizontal strips with the mounting flanges in a vertical position.

Rectangular gable louvers can be added to provide high-volume exhaust for power attic fans.

Mount to studs: From inside the attic, anchor the power ventilator to studs behind an existing wall louver. Mounting brackets are usually pre-punched for 16"-center studs.

MOUNTING AN ATTIC FAN

1 Mount the fan over the louver opening. Use screws to attach it to the studs or rafters. If the studs or rafters do not allow the fan to be centered on the opening, add cross-support studs.

2 Remove the regulator cover and fasten the regulator to a stud or rafter within reach of the fan cable.

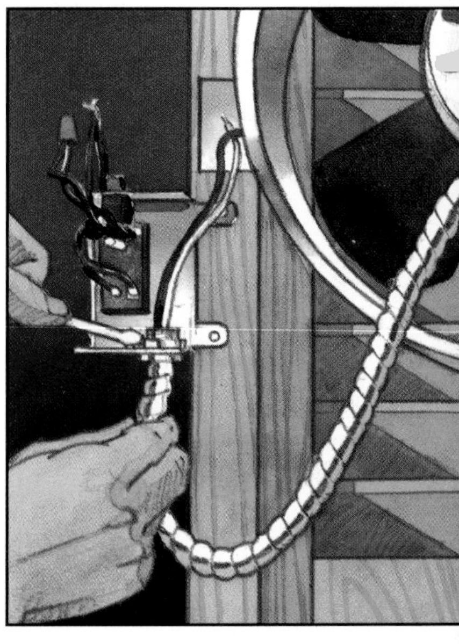

3 Insert the fan cable into the regulator and tighten the clamp or locknut.

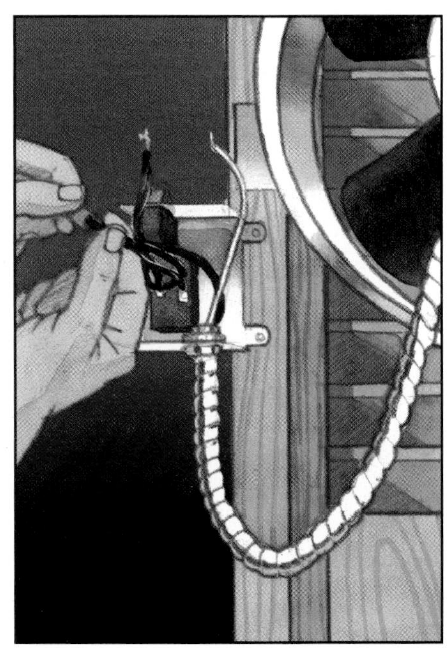

4 Attach the fan wires to the regulator wires according to the manufacturer's wiring diagram. Normally, the black fan wire is connected to the black regulator wire and the white fan wire is connected to the red. If no red wire is present, connect the white fan wire to the white regulator wire.

5 Turn power off and insert the power supply cable into the regulator and tighten the cable clamp. Attach the white supply wire to white regulator wire and the black supply wire to the black regulator wire. Attach grounding wire to the grounding screw.

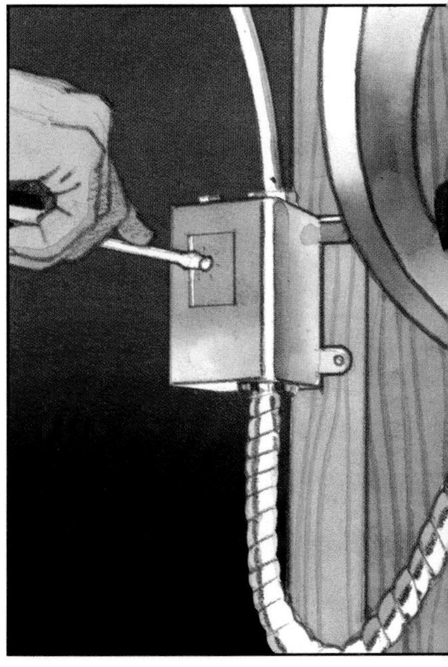

6 Replace the regulator cover and adjust the temperature control. The fan should come on at 95° degrees Fahrenheit and run until the temperature in the attic is lowered to 95° Fahrenheit.

Working with Low-Power Systems

Telephone outlets, television jacks, and thermostat and doorbell wires are easiest to install while wiring new electrical circuits. Install the cables when the framing is exposed, making final connections after the walls are finished.

Telephone lines use four- or six-wire cable–often called "bell wire"–while television lines use a shielded coaxial cable with threaded end fittings called "F-connectors." To splice into an existing television line, use a fitting called a signal splitter. Splitters are available with two, three, or four nipples. Coaxial cable can be difficult to strip. Ask for a demonstration where you buy the cable and connectors.

STUFF YOU'LL NEED:

- ☐ **Tools:** Screwdrivers, wallboard saw, combination tool, needlenose pliers, fish tape, adjustable wrench.
- ☐ **Materials:** Phone and television jack plates, doorbell switch, thermostat, masking tape.

INSTALLING COAXIAL TV CABLE

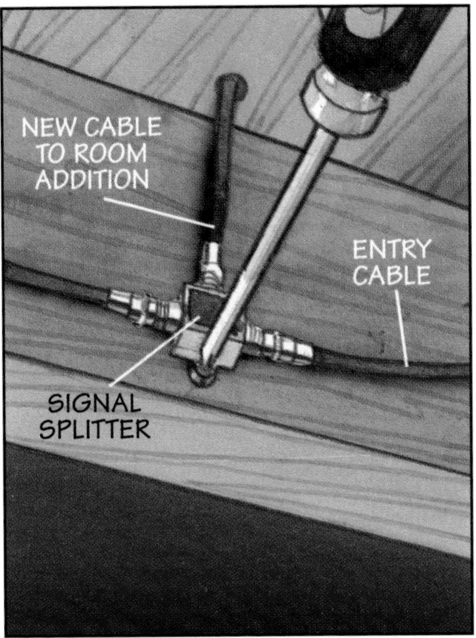

1 Install a signal splitter where the entry cable connects to the indoor TV cables, usually in the basement or another utility area. Attach one end of new coaxial cable to an outlet nipple on the splitter. Anchor the splitter to a framing member with wallboard screws.

2 Run the coaxial cable to the location of the new television jack; use a fish tape, if necessary. Keep the coaxial cable at least 6" away from electrical wiring to avoid electrical interference. In new construction, mark the floor so the cable can be found easily after the walls are finished.

CONNECTING A CABLE TV JACK

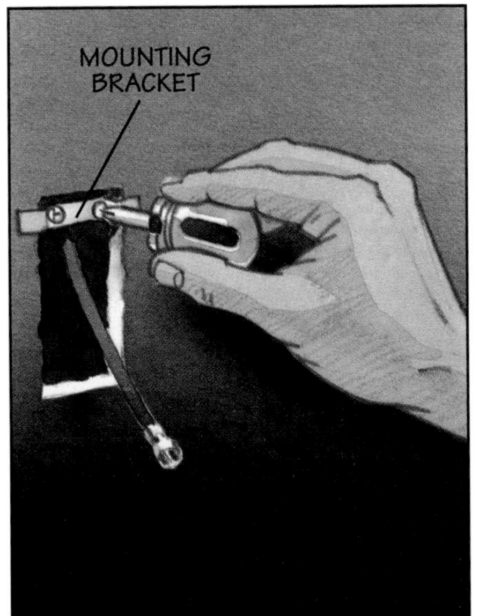

1 Make a cutout opening 1½" wide and 3¾" high at the television jack location. Pull cable through the opening and install two television jack mounting brackets in the cutout. A variety of low voltage mounting plates is available.

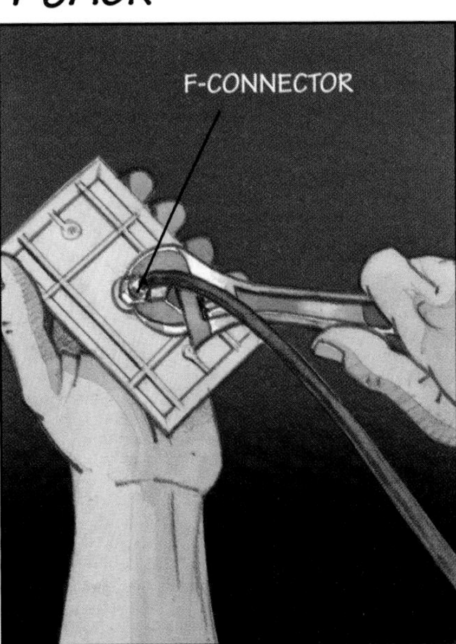

2 Use a wrench to attach the cable F-connector to the back of the television jack. Attach the jack to the wall by screwing it onto the mounting brackets.

ADDING A TELEPHONE EXTENSION

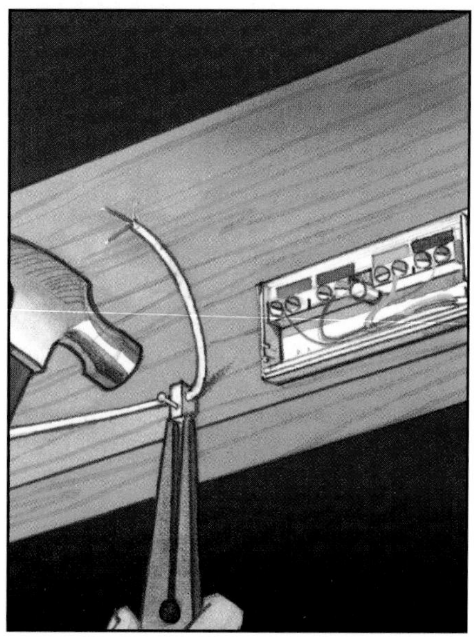

1 Locate a telephone junction in your basement or other utility area. Remove the junction cover. Use cable staples to anchor one end of the cable to a framing member near the junction, leaving 6" to 8" of excess cable.

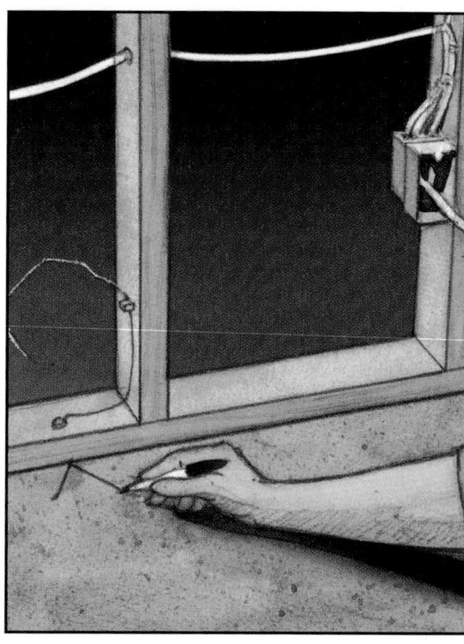

2 Run the cable from the junction to the telephone outlet location. Keep the cable at least 6" away from circuit wiring to avoid electrical interference. Mark the floor so the cable can be located easily.

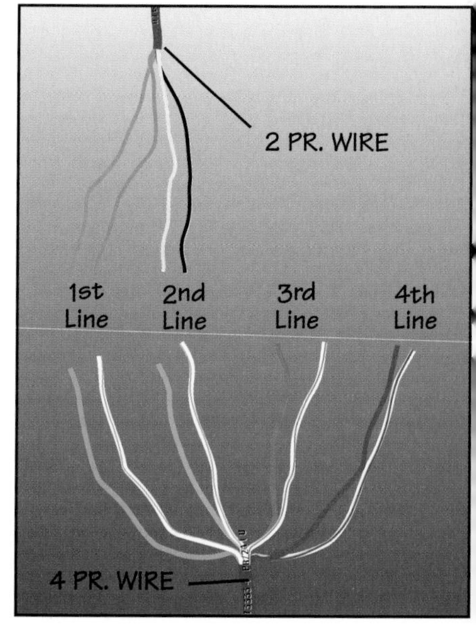

Standard two-pair wire systems use the red and green wires as the first line and the yellow and black wires as the second line. In newer homes, telephone lines are run in four-pair and correspond as shown. These can be used for additional telephones or fax and modem lines.

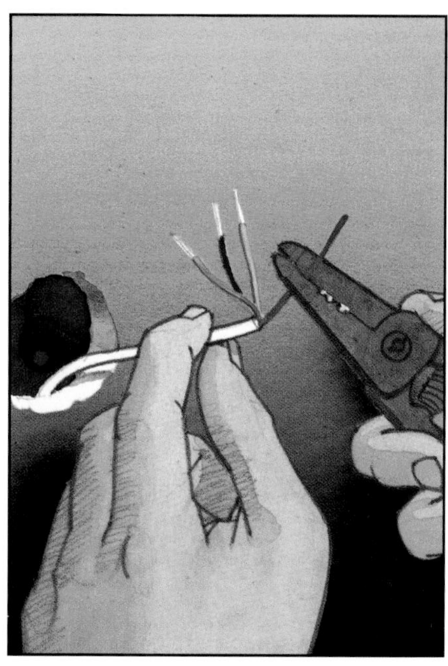

3 At each cable end, remove about 2" of outer sheathing. Remove about 3/4" of insulation from each wire using a combination tool.

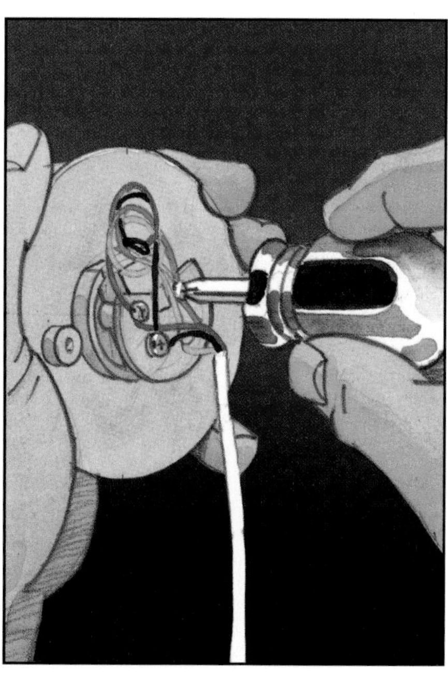

4 Connect wires to similarly colored wire leads in phone outlet. If there are extra wires, tape them to back of outlet. Put the telephone outlet over the wall cutout and attach it to the wallboard.

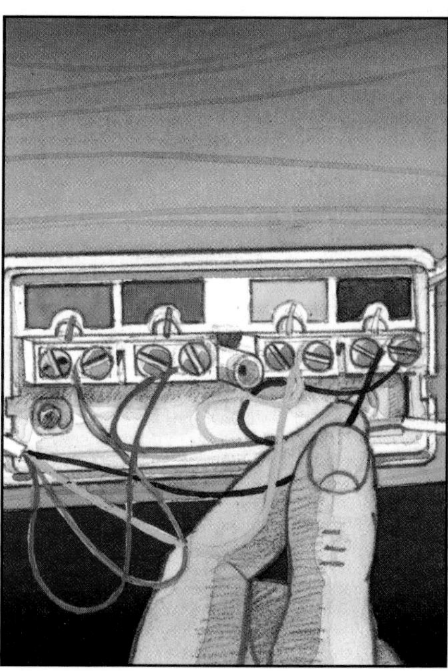

5 At the telephone junction, connect the cable wires to the color-coded screw terminals. If there are extra wires, wrap them with tape and tuck them inside the junction. Reattach the junction cover.

REPLACING A DOORBELL

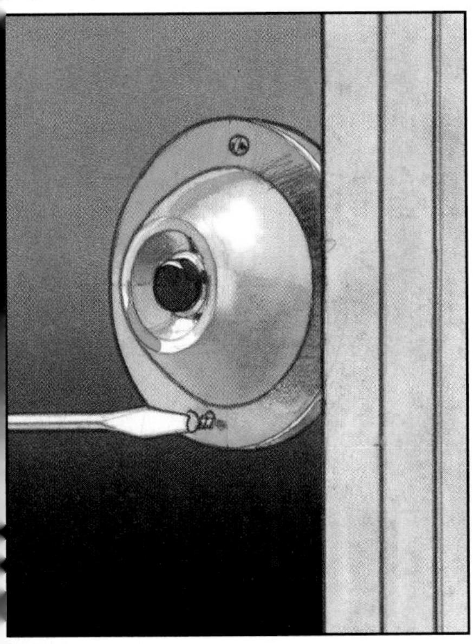

1 Turn off the power to the doorbell system at the main service panel. Remove the doorbell switch mounting screws and carefully pull the switch away from the wall.

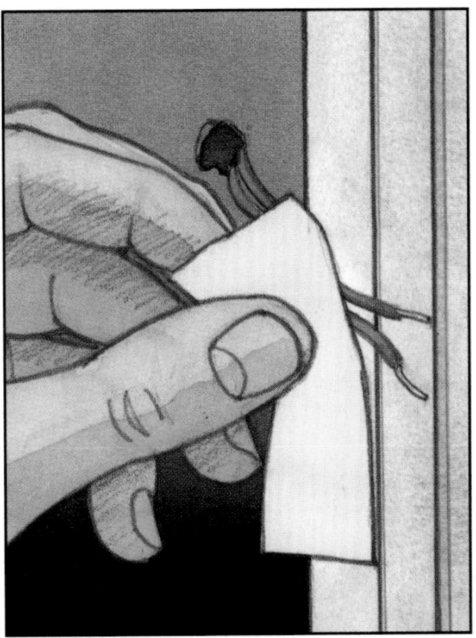

2 Disconnect the wires from the switch and be sure to tape them to the wall to prevent them from slipping into the wall cavity. Connect the wires to the screw terminals on the new switch. Remove the coverplate on the old chime unit inside the house.

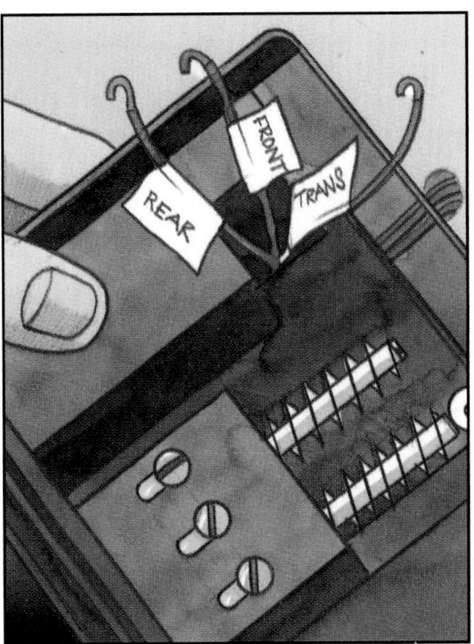

3 Unscrew the mounting screws and remove the old chime unit. Disconnect the wires and label them to identify their screw terminal location again, taping them to the wall to prevent them from falling into the wall cavity. Thread the wires through the base of the new chime unit.

4 Attach the new chime unit to the wall using the mounting screws included in the installation kit.

5 Connect the wires to the appropriate screw terminals on the new chime unit.

6 Attach the coverplate and turn on the power at the main service panel.

BUYER'$GUIDE

Choosing a Thermostat

When buying a new thermostat, make sure the new unit is compatible with your heating/air conditioning system. Take along the brand name and model number of the old thermostat for reference. If you have to replace the transformer, be sure to choose one with amperage ratings that will match the thermostat you will be using.

A low-voltage thermostat controls whole-house heating and air conditioning systems from one central location. It is powered by a transformer that reduces 120-volt current to about 24 volts.

A standard low-voltage thermostat is relatively easy to replace and, as you may have already decided, is usually replaced with a programmable setback thermostat. These programmable thermostats can cut energy costs by up to 35 percent in some areas.

INSTALLING A PROGRAMMABLE THERMOSTAT

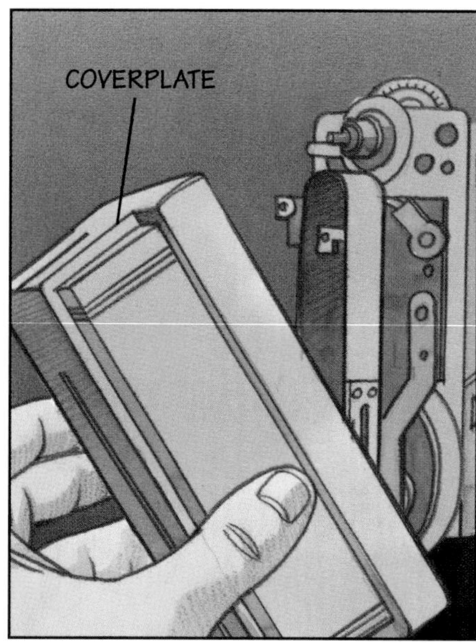

1 Turn off the power to the heating and air-conditioning system at the main service panel. Remove the old thermostat coverplate.

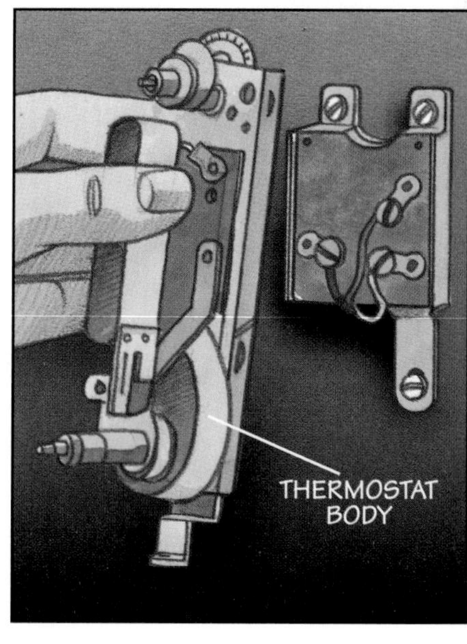

2 Unscrew the thermostat mounting screws and remove the thermostat body.

HEAT PUMPS REQUIRE SPECIAL THERMOSTATS.

3 Label the low-voltage wires to identify their screw terminal locations using masking tape. Disconnect all low-voltage wires.

4 Remove the thermostat base by loosening the mounting screws. Tape the wires against the wall to prevent them from falling into the wall cavity.

5 Thread the low-voltage wires through the base of the new thermostat. Mount the thermostat base on the wall using the screws included with the thermostat.

6 Connect the low-voltage wires to the screw terminals on the thermostat base. Use the manufacturer's connection chart as a guide.

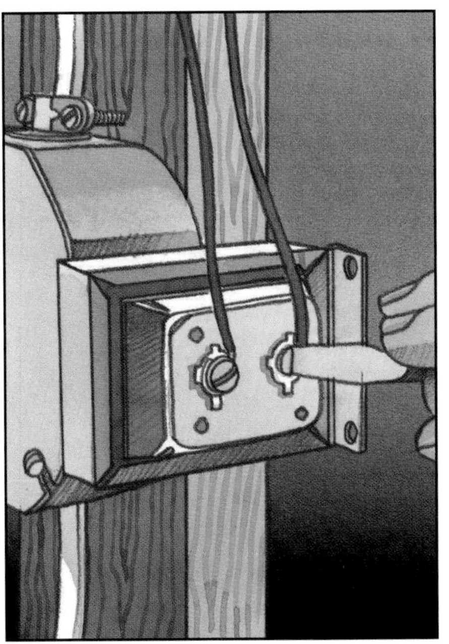

7 Locate the low-voltage transformer that powers the thermostat. This transformer usually is located near the heating/air-conditioning system or inside a furnace access panel. Tighten any loose wire connections and make sure wires and sheathing are in good condition.

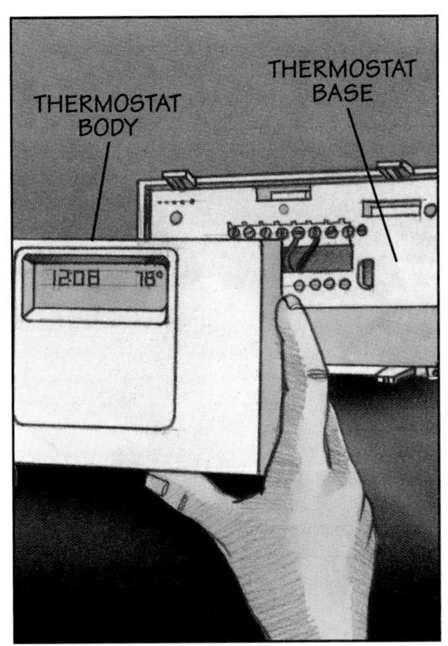

8 Install the batteries in the thermostat body; attach the body to the thermostat base. Turn on the power and program the thermostat as desired.

INSPECTING YOUR THERMOSTAT

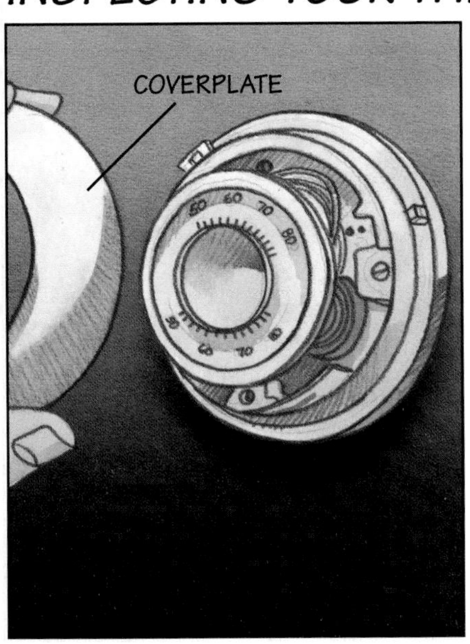

1 Turn off power to the heating/air-conditioning system at the main service panel. Remove the thermostat coverplate.

2 Remove the thermostat body by loosening the mounting screws with a screwdriver.

3 Inspect the wire connections on the thermostat base. Reattach any loose wires. If the wires are broken or corroded, they should be clipped, stripped, and reattached to the screw terminals. Replace the thermostat body and coverplate. Turn on the power at the main service panel.

Lighting Design

Lighting design doesn't start with the selection of light fixtures but with an evaluation of things such as traffic patterns, room usage, and visual preferences of people in the house. Review important factors such as the ability to move quickly and safely from room to room, the need to light people as well as objects and furnishings, flexibility in multi-purpose rooms (kitchens and family rooms), and energy conservation. Like other design elements, light influences the emotional response of people in the illuminated area. The definition and character of areas changes depending on the distribution and pattern of light. You can easily change a functional, well-lit room into a relaxing, softly lit room by adding dimmer switches (page 175).

Light fixtures should not only provide the needed illumination but also enhance the basic architectural and decorative design of the room.

TYPES OF LIGHT

Pendants, which hang and provide general light over an area, include chandeliers and globes.

Accent lights add secondary light to a specific area. Table lamps are often accents.

Task lights provide direct light to areas where specific jobs are performed, such as at desks, work benches, sewing tables, and reading areas. Task lights can be either incandescent or fluorescent. Task lights include desk lamps and under-cabinet lights.

Downlighters cast light down on an area. Recessed and track lights can be downlighters.

Wall washers illuminate walls. Sconces, table lamps, and recessed and track lights may be used. Uplighters that illuminate the ceiling include torchères, table lamps, and pendants. Close-mounted lights for general lighting from the ceiling are common in kitchens and hallways.

CHOICE OF LIGHT SOURCE AFFECTS COLORS

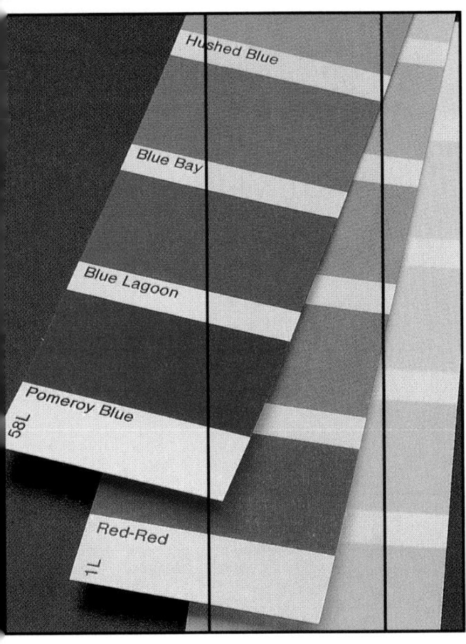

Incandescent light is the most common residential lighting source. It produces warm, soft daylight-colored light that makes skin tones look natural.

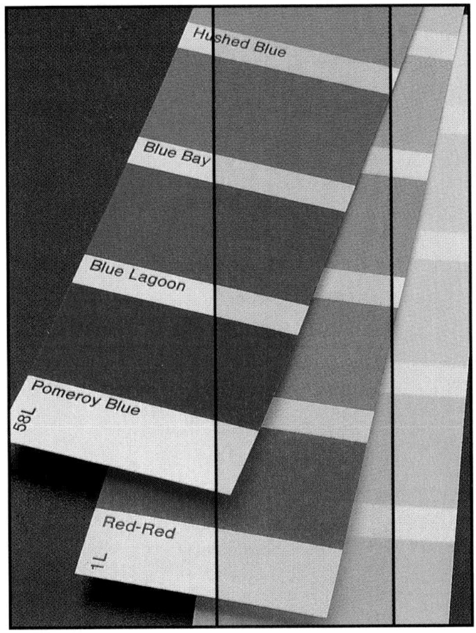

Warm fluorescent light is economical, cool lighting that is often found in commercial settings. Modern fluorescent lighting is colored to produce warm, natural-looking light but the bluish uncolored tubes are often more common because they are cheapest.

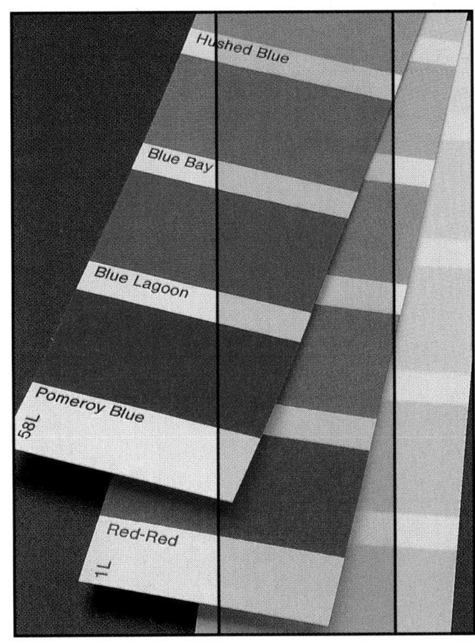

Standard fluorescent lights include the familiar tubes as well as one-piece globes and a variety of bulbs designed for use in conventional lamps. Fluorescent lights cannot be dimmed.

COMMON BULB TYPES AND SHAPES

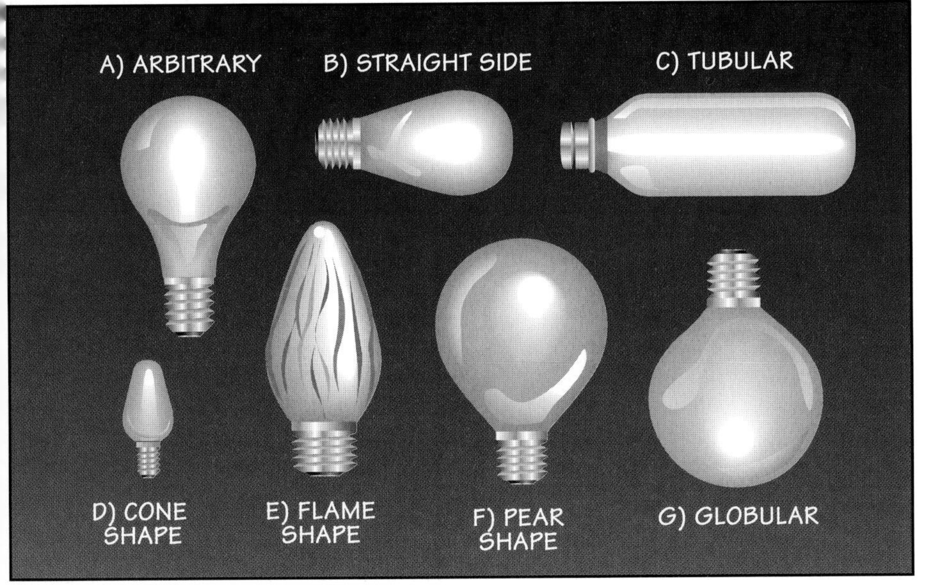

Common shapes for bulbs include: Arbitrary style (**A**), is the standard shape for bulbs found in most residential fixtures. Straight side (**B**), tubular (**C**), and cone shape (**D**) are designed for special use in things such as appliances or special fixtures. Flame shape (**E**), pear shape (**F**), and globular (**G**) are decorative bulbs found in special fixtures.

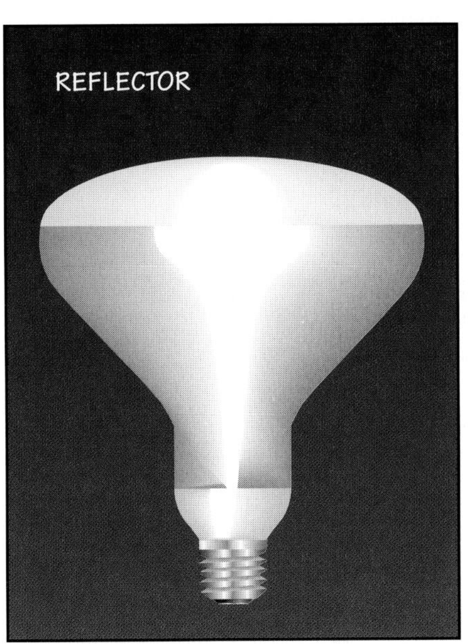

Reflector bulbs have a coating designed to throw light in a desired direction. The bulbs are made with wide (flood) or narrow (spot) beams in many sizes and types.

Lighting for Function & Effect

Several factors will affect the amount of general or local light given off by a light fixture. One factor is placement. If the fixture is high, it will light a wide area; if it's low, it will light a smaller area. A fixture installed behind a baffle will have its light directed to a given area.

Plan your lighting according to the activity that will take place in the room. Provide more light for involved tasks and less for entertaining or relaxing. Decide how much light is needed (brightness), what kind of light is needed (direct or indirect), and which type of light source is best (incandescent or fluorescent).

Direct lighting creates bright spots and hard shadows. Indirect lighting creates a more even brightness and softer shadows. Diffused light eliminates bright spots and hard shadows.

Living Areas

Table and floor lamps furnish adequate general lighting for most living rooms, and fixtures equipped with 3-way bulbs provide more flexibility to the area lighting. Uplights help to brighten and enlarge the room. A 150-watt lamp directed at the ceiling will provide a softer, more evenly distributed light to the room. Wall washers give the room a warm, inviting atmosphere.

Lighting a single wall with a pair of 75-watt lamps will create an entirely different look. Track lighting helps to highlight points of interest such as artwork or sculptures. Mini tracks are available with 40-watt reflector bulbs to show off items such as a smaller wall hanging or a curio shelf.

Downlighting creates concentrated brighter areas for reading, conversing or playing games. This is easily accomplished by using 150-watt recessed lights to provide ample light. You may want to use colored bulbs to bring out a particular color in your design or furnishings.

Dining Areas

Uplight pendants provide general indirect light. A single fixture with 200 to 300 total watts can bounce light off the ceiling for a soft lighting effect. Downlight rise and fall pendants can provide more direct table lighting. Adjustable fixtures will allow you to create bright or intimate effects. Wall washers make the room seem to be more spacious and open. Recessed eyeball fixtures can flood the walls with soft lighting. Accent lights can be arranged to bring intimacy, drama, or even a party atmosphere.

Bulbs that extend above or below the shade will cause a distracting glare. Raise or lower the shade or replace the bulb with a different style to eliminate the problem. Dining and entertaining will normally require less overall brightness depending on the mood desired. One way to provide flexible lighting is to connect the lights to dimmers so the lighting may be varied for effect and function.

Halls & Passageways

Halls and passageways require the least amount of brightness for safe, comfortable use. A close-mounted overhead fixture with 80 to 120 watts will provide good general lighting for a typical entryway. Wall washers will add brightness and warmth to the overall look and atmosphere. Balanced lighting can be easily produced by two sconces, each equipped with a pair of 40-watt bulbs.

Highlights on decorative items in the hallway provide visual interest and can be accomplished by recessed light fixtures. These 75-watt spots can be focused to draw attention to artwork, furniture, or other items of interest. Uplights help to create a feeling of space so that the hallway will appear to be roomier and more spacious. A single lamp with a 100-watt bulb will help to add uplight to a small space.

Reading Areas

The study or reading area must have moderate brightness. Task lighting, such as a 100-watt desk lamp, will put direct light on the subject; downlight from a 150-watt recessed fixture will reduce glare and offer more brightness; track lighting will help to create study zones. Seventy-five-watt lights focused in overlapping pools will shed ample light on the subject. Light coming from several balanced sources makes the best reading light. Glare and shadow are both reduced, and eyestrain is lessened.

Hobby & Recreational Areas

Areas intended for intricate work and recreational activity will require a brighter atmosphere. Task lighting from a 100-watt architect's lamp will concentrate light on a given work area while fluorescent panels provide a bright overall lighted area.

Accent lighting of equal wattage will eliminate shadows and help to even out lighting for the entire area, which helps to increase visibility and reduce eyestrain during activities. A small spotlight can be focused on an area and is a great help for some detail work.

Novelty fixtures can provide both light and character to a room in order to achieve the desired atmosphere.

Kitchen Areas

Kitchen areas should be one of the brightest areas in the entire house. Food preparation requires some of the brightest light in order to effectively perform the tasks and to reduce eyestrain. A single close-mounted light can provide general overall lighting.

Under-cabinet fluorescent lights create bright work areas for the countertops, while incandescent task lighting illuminates the rangetop and cutting board areas. Recessed canisters with reflector bulbs help to spotlight the sink and countertops.

For cooking areas, consider fixtures with removable clear lenses that can be taken off and cleaned in order to keep a bright work area. Fixtures with sealed lenses prevent moisture and cooking residues from penetrating the inside of the fixture, which helps to reduce cleaning time and prolongs the life of fixtures.

Specialty Lighting

Special lights help to create special effects in specific areas. Low-voltage cabinet lights can be used to illuminate a bookcase, while eyeball fixture spotlights can be used to highlight artwork. Canister reflector lights can be used to highlight a corner niche and curios. Sometimes, sconces can be used to create dramatic shadows on architectural features.

Special low-voltage footlights help to lead you up the stairs safely. These 12-volt string lights can also create a theatrical effect.

Task lighting is another form of special lighting.

Marquis-style light fixtures can help to create a more festive and exciting atmosphere in recreational and entertaining areas.

Electrical

Planning the Lighting System

Before you run out and purchase your light fixtures, you should plan out the lighting systems for the entire room and even the adjoining rooms, if they are of an open design and the fixtures will be visible from multiple rooms. Follow these simple steps when planning your lighting system.

1) Draw a graph paper plan like the one at right, showing the configuration of the entire room. Include the location of furniture, architectural elements, and any special features you may have.
2) Assign a probable use to each area of the room.
3) Assign appropriate lighting to each area.
4) Decide which lights should operate together.
5) Determine switch and receptacle placement.

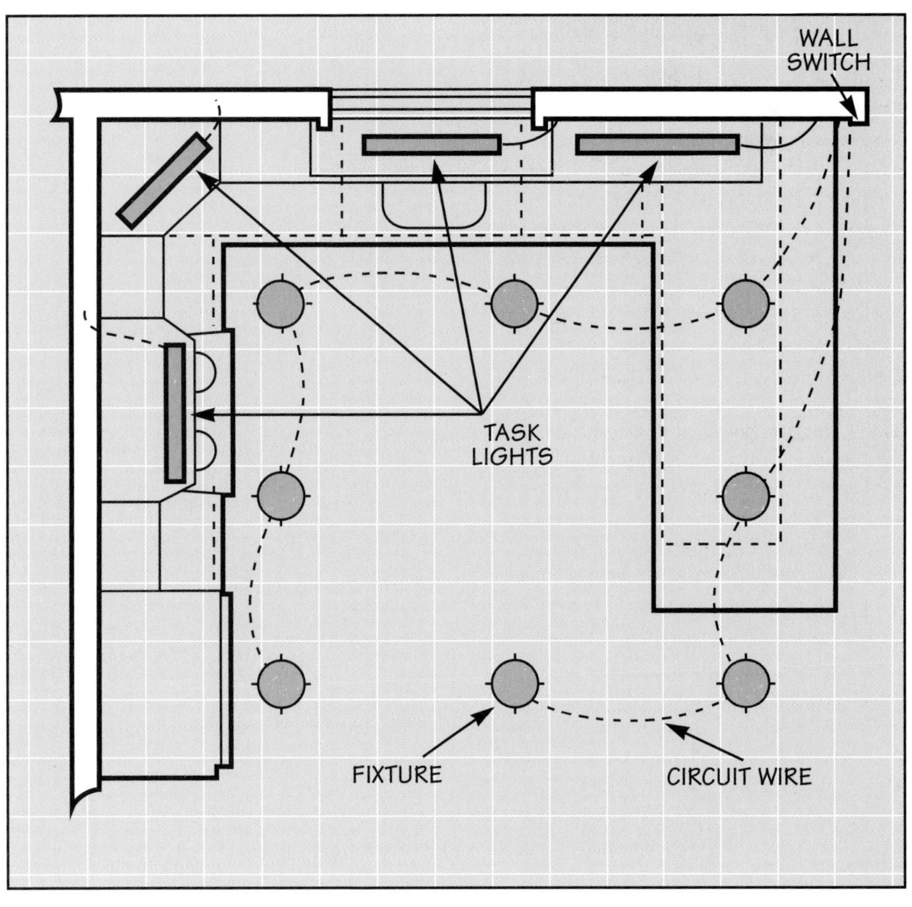

CEILING & WALL BASICS

No one walks into a house and says, "Gee, nice walls." Smooth, well-finished walls are generally not a glamorous project for a home owner to be proud of. Leave a hole or crack in a wall or ceiling though, and people will notice. The good news is that repairing ceilings and walls is a fairly simple, straightforward task.

The type of interior wall construction and finish will depend to a certain extent on the age of the building and on the function of the wall within the structure. Wood framing is by far the most common structural system used for both interior load-bearing and non-load-bearing partitions. Specific structural differences between the two may consist only of a doubled top plate and more extensive cross-bracing in load-bearing walls. In general, wall studs are set 16" on center and nailed to top and toe plates. In some nonstructural walls, wall studs are set 24" on center.

In older houses, thin, closely spaced wood lath strips are nailed to the wall frame to serve as a structural basis for plaster. Plaster is frequently applied in two coats. An undercoat of brown plaster is followed by a finish coat of white finish plaster.

In the vast majority of homes built since World War II, interior walls are wood frame finished with wallboard. The wallboard is nailed to the wall frame in sheets, and seams are finished with wallboard compound.

Common hand tools necessary for ceiling and wall projects include: c-clamps (**A**), caulk gun (**B**), ratchet wrench and sockets (**C**), cold chisels (**D**), pry bars (**E**), hot-melt glue gun (**F**), tin snips (**G**), plumb bob and chalk line (**H**), utility knife (**I**), stapler (**J**), hand plane (**K**), sanding block (**L**), carpenter's level (**M**), framing square (**N**), stud locator (**O**), sliding T-bevel (**P**), hammer (**Q**), wood chisels (**R**), screwdrivers (**S**), nail sets (**T**), combination square (**U**), line level (**V**), coping saw (**W**), tape measure (**X**), and handsaw (**Y**).

Common power tools and safety equipment for ceiling and wall projects include: circular saw (**A**), palm sander (**B**), router with bits (**C**), saber saw (**D**), power driver with bits (**E**), power drill (**F**), cordless drill with bits (**G**), hearing protectors (**H**), dust mask (**I**), safety glasses (**J**), gloves (**K**).

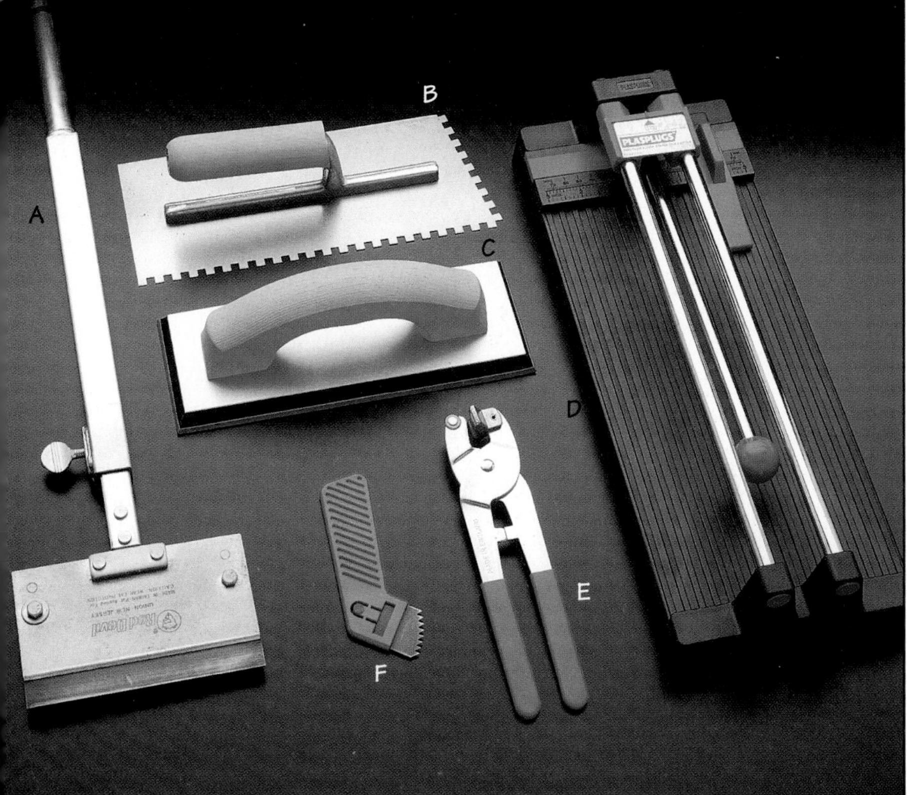

Tools needed for ceramic tile installation include: floor scraper (**A**), notched trowel (**B**), grout float (**C**), sliding tile cutter (**D**) or pliers-type cutter (**E**), and grout scraper (**F**).

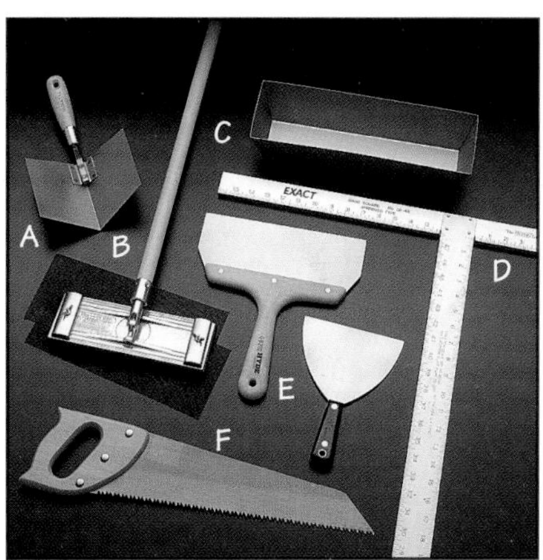

Common wallboard tools include: corner taping trowel (**A**), wallboard sander with sanding screens (**B**), mud tray (**C**), wallboard square (**D**), taping knives (**E**), and wallboard saw (**F**).

Wall materials include: 5/8" wallboard, also referred to as drywall (**A**), 1/2" water-resistant wallboard, or green board (**B**), cementuous backer board, commonly used for tile applications (**C**), corner bead (**D**), wallboard screws (**E**), tongue-and-groove beaded pine wainscoting (**F**), tongue-and-groove beaded oak wainscoting (**G**), beaded oak paneling (**H**), barn-board plank paneling (**I**), and oak plank paneling (**J**). Wallboard is the most common wall and ceiling material used in modern day homes. Its use and location may dictate what type and thickness of wallboard you use. If you're not sure what kind to use, ask where you buy your materials. Paneling comes in different thicknesses which may dictate how it's attached to the wall and what kind of wall it can be hung on. Consult with representatives where you buy the paneling to learn how it should be applied.

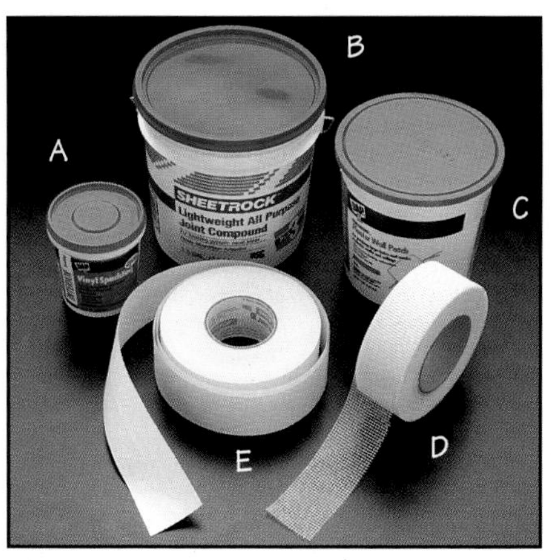

Wallboard joint and taping materials include: vinyl spackling compound (**A**), wallboard joint compound (**B**), plaster wall patch (**C**), adhesive-backed fiberglass mesh joint tape (**D**), and standard paper joint tape (**E**).

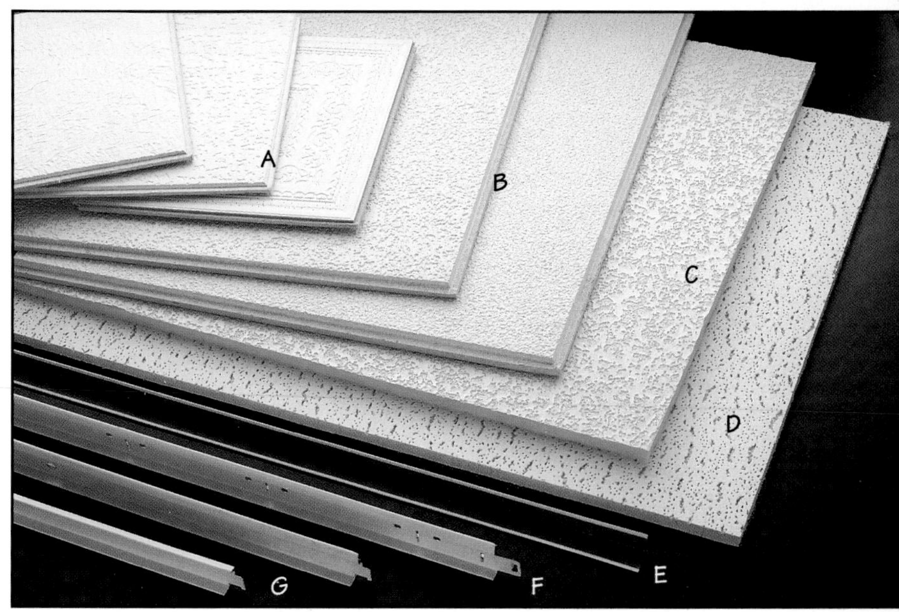

Ceiling materials include: decorative 12" ceiling tiles (**A**), decorative 24" ceiling tiles (**B**), insulated suspended ceiling panel (**C**), acoustical suspended ceiling panels (**D**), wall angle (**E**), suspended ceiling runners (**F**), and 2' and 4' cross tees (**G**).

)ecorative ceramic wall tile is ıvailable in a variety of colors, ;tyles, and sizes, which include: 2½" gloss mosaic tile sheet (A), assorted 3" flat finish wall tile (B), 3½" patterned mosaic tile (C), 4½" flat finish wall tile (D), 6" marble tile (E), 6" natural stone tile (F), 4" gloss tile (G), 8" textured tile (H), border tile (I), 3"x8" natural brick face tile (J), 4" painted tile (K), 4"x8" natural brick face tile (L), and 8" natural marble tile (M). Be sure to use floor tile on floors and wall tile on walls—never use one for the other.

Decorative molding and trim vary in size, shape, and type of wood and include: oak radius corner molding and casing (**A**), oak door and window casing (**B**), oak ranch style casing (**C**), oak colonial casing (**D**), oak sprung cove molding (**E**), fir crown molding (**F**), oak rosette molding (**G**), oak quarter round base shoe molding (**H**), decorative oak outside corner base trim (**I**), decorative oak inside corner base trim (**J**), oak inside corner molding (**K**), pine outside corner molding (**L**), and carved pine trim (**M**).

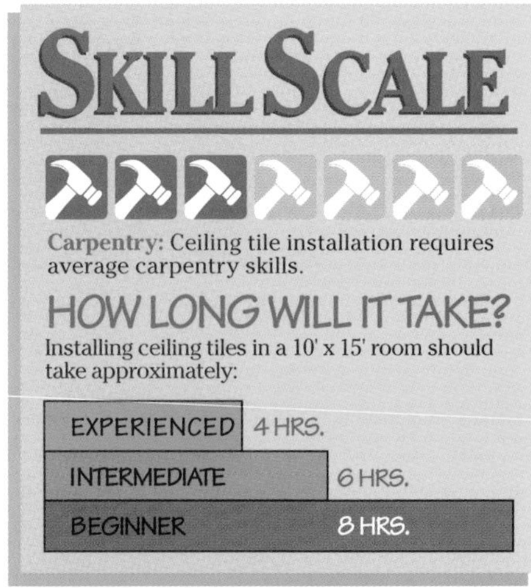

STUFF YOU'LL NEED:

- **Tools:** Chalk line, mason's string, hand stapler, handsaw, hammer, tape measure, carpenter's level, utility knife.
- **Materials:** Furring strips, wood shims, ceiling tiles, staples, cove molding, finish nails.

Installing Ceiling Tile

Ceiling tiles are often used to cover an unsightly ceiling or to reduce noise from the living area above. Ceiling tiles are permanently attached to furring strips with nails, staples, or adhesive. When installing or replacing any portion of your ceiling with tiles, **be sure to wear safety goggles** to protect you from flaking or crumbling tiles. Ceiling tiles are made of a combination of wood or mineral fibers and fiberglass fibers. Some older tiles may even contain asbestos fibers. No matter what type of ceiling tile you are working with, wear a respirator and protective gloves when working with these materials. Always use a sturdy ladder when installing or replacing ceiling tiles, and get some help, whenever possible, for the more difficult and dangerous tasks. Staple length makes a difference, always use manufacturer-specific staples.

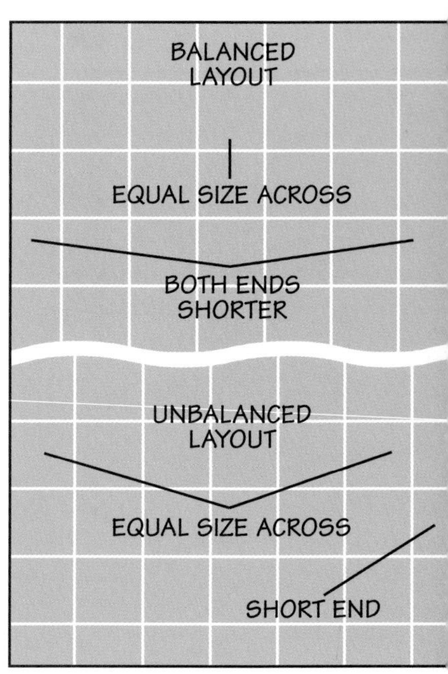

Ceiling tile layout, as in floor tile, should be planned to provide a balanced appearance. Equal sized tiles should be planned on opposite borders if the ceiling is sized so that full tiles can't be used across the entire area. It is best not to leave an unbalanced layout with a short tile only at one end.

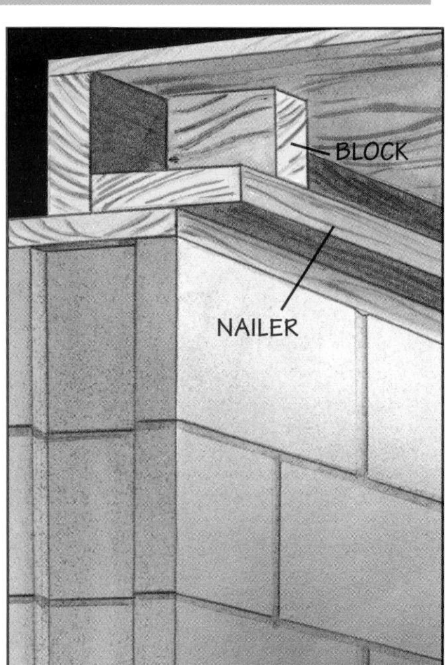

1 Add blocking between joists that sit atop a wall, to provide a nailing base for the furring strips. The blocking can be attached by either straight-nailing or toenailing them to the joists.

2 Measure the distance from the midpoint of the ceiling to the outside walls in 1-foot intervals. For a balanced look adjust the midpoint so equally sized parts of more than half a tile are on each side of the room (see above right).

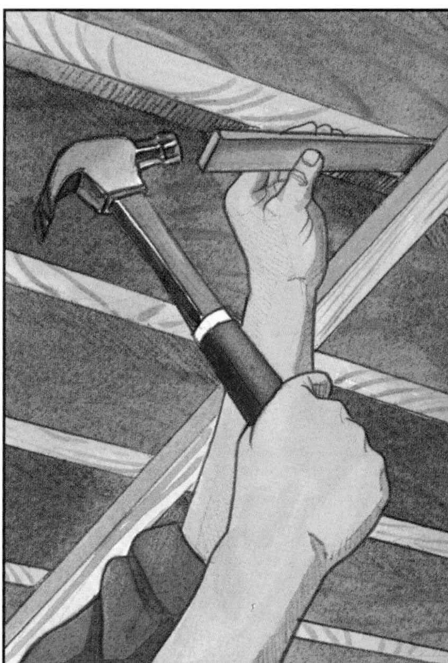

3 Snap chalk lines, perpendicular to the joists, across the bottoms of the joists, and use these marks as guidelines for attaching the furring strips. Attach the first furring strip to the lowest point on the ceiling, and shim the others to that level.

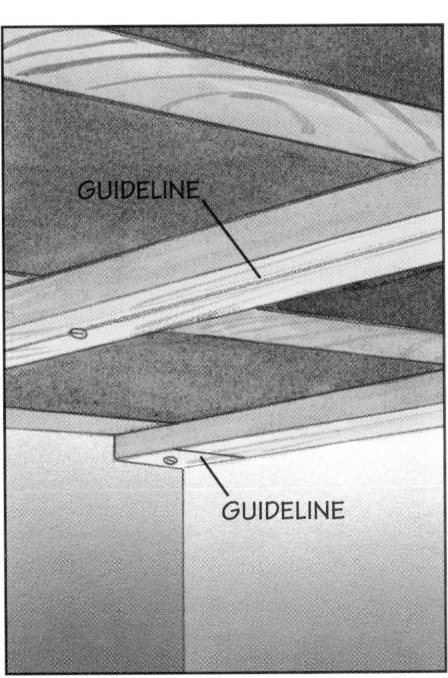

4 Use a carpenter's level to find the proper level for the subsequent furring strips once you have attached and shimmed the first furring strip.

Add a second layer of furring strips, attached perpendicular to the first, or use thicker furring strips if you need to lower a ceiling below protrusions and fixtures.

5 Measure the distance from the adjacent walls that is equal to the trim size of the border tiles as determined in Step 2. Mark these measurements on the furring strips along two adjacent walls. These guidelines will be used to check the alignment of the starter rows of tiles.

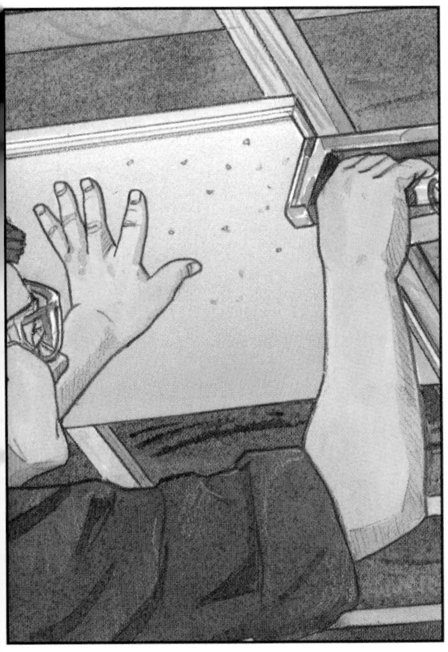

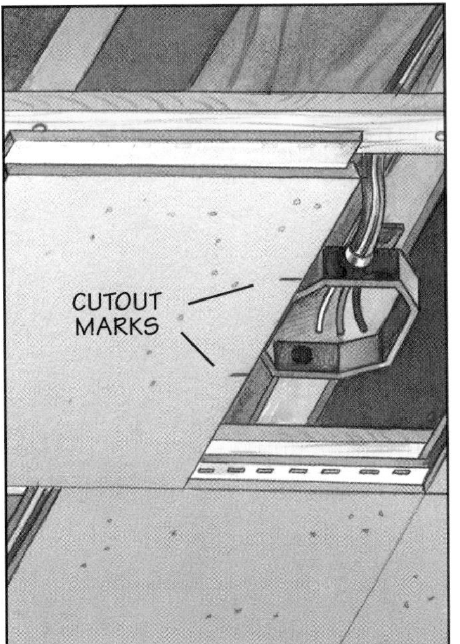

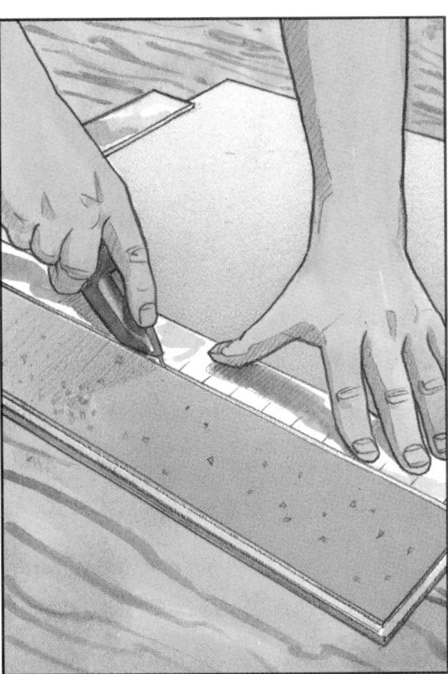

6 Position the first tile in the corner intersection of the layout. If you're cutting tiles for a balanced layout, place the cut edges against the adjacent walls. Staple the tile in place along the grooved edge. Continue until the first row of border tiles is installed, then install full tiles.

7 To make cutouts in a tile, place the tile in position and mark the tile edge lightly at the center of the electrical box. Reposition the tile and do the same on the adjacent tile edge. Mark the intersection of these lines on the back of the tile. Outline the electrical box shape from this center point, and cut out the desired area.

8 Measure and mark the remaining border tiles to size. Cut off the excess on the groove edge. Install the cut edge toward the wall. Face-nail the tiles with panel nails or glue them with panel adhesive. Attach cove molding around the room to conceal gaps between wall and tile.

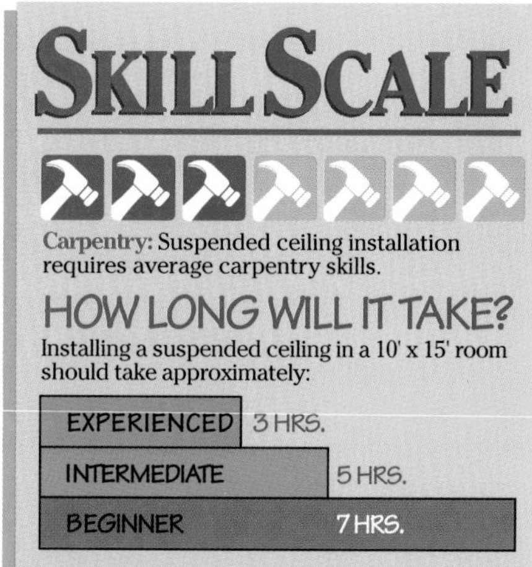

Installing a Suspended Ceiling

Suspended ceilings are made from metal sections, which provide a fairly lightweight structure for acoustic, translucent, or decorative panels. They're usually quite quick and easy to install and require only common household tools.

The lightweight alloy framework is made from three basic components: wall angles, which are fastened to walls; runners, which are similar in function to ceiling joists and are usually installed across a room's longer span; and cross-tees, which are installed between and perpendicular to the runners and tie the entire ceiling grid together. If you decide the runners should not go lengthwise in a room, be aware the job will involve more labor.

The loose ceiling panels sit on the flanges of the framework. They can be easily removed for access to ductwork, plumbing or electrical circuits. Be sure to leave absolutely no less than four inches of space above the framework to provide room to maneuver the panels.

TILE
MIDPOINT
RUNNERS
CROSS TEES
RAFTER

Measure the room and draw a plan showing the layout of the ceiling panels. Plan so that panels of equal size, but larger than a half panel, are left on opposite sides of the room. Orient the runners perpendicular to the existing ceiling joists.

STUFF YOU'LL NEED:

- ☐ **Tools:** Chalk line, mason's string, snips, line level, hammer, tape measure.
- ☐ **Materials:** Wire, runners, cross-tees, wall angle, suspended ceiling tiles, common nails.

Some textured ceilings make it difficult to locate ceiling joists with a stud finder. A quick and easy solution, if you have access, is to simply take a peek into the attic to see in which direction the ceiling joists go. If you're remodeling a basement, keep in mind that floor joists usually run from front and rear outside walls to the center bearing wall.

Joist spacing is either 16" or 24", so once you determine the direction, simply measure from the end wall either 16" or 24" and poke through the ceiling material with a nail, moving either direction in 1/2" increments until you find a ceiling joist. Additional joists can be located by measuring either 16" or 24" from the located joist.

HARDWARE

Wall angle, runners, and cross-tees are the three main lightweight hardware components of a suspended ceiling grid system. Ceiling panels are designed to rest on the flanges of these three pieces.

Runners have slots every few inches into which the ends of the cross-tees lock. Cross-tees that are cut to fit against a wall, rest on top of the wall angle flange.

HANGING A SUSPENDED CEILING

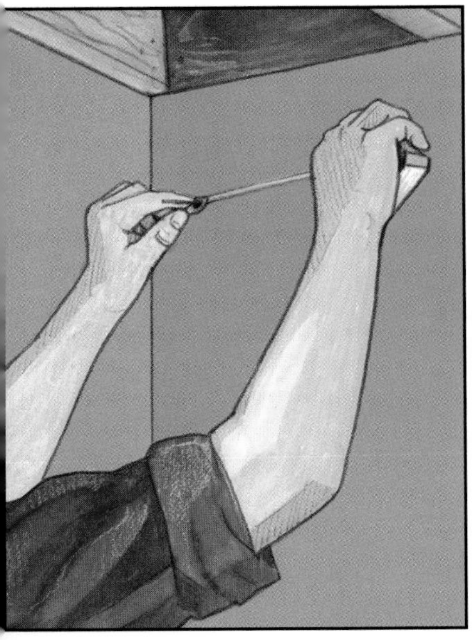

1 Mark the height of the planned ceiling in one corner of the room. Allow 4" as the absolute minimum of clearance height between the new ceiling and the existing ceiling or joists for maneuvering the new panels. Drive a finish nail partway into that mark and fasten one end of a chalk line to the nail.

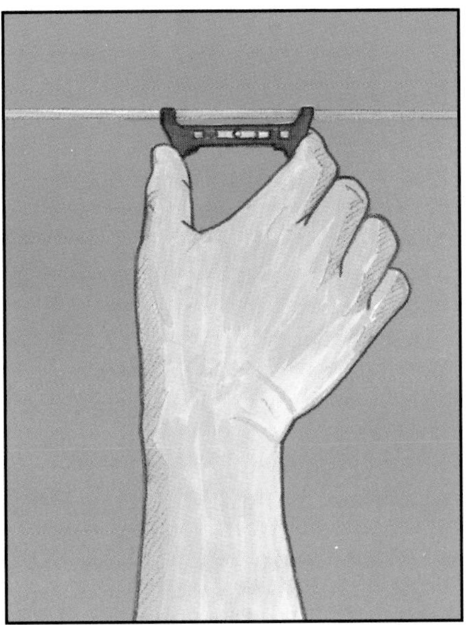

2 Stretch the chalk line to the next corner. Place a line level on the chalk line to locate a level point for the end of the line. Snap a level line across the wall. Using this chalk line for a starting point, snap level lines around the entire room.

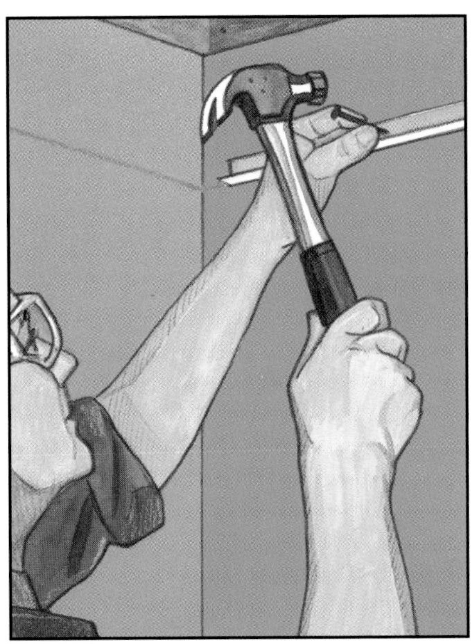

3 Nail or screw the lengths of wall angles to the studs on all walls with the bottom of the angles resting on the chalk line. Miter outside and overlap inside corners.

4 Snap a chalk line across the ceiling where each runner will be located.

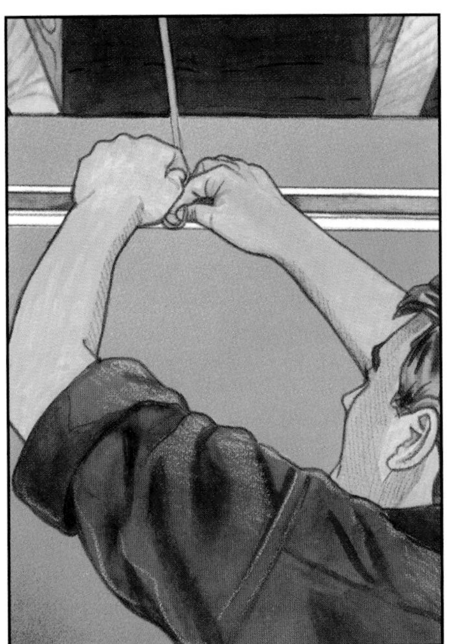

5 Tie a taut mason's string, where the cross-tees are to be located, from nails driven into the wall exactly at the bottom of the wall angle. This will mark location for cross-tee and level of suspended runners. Mason's string must be used because it won't sag once it is pulled taut.

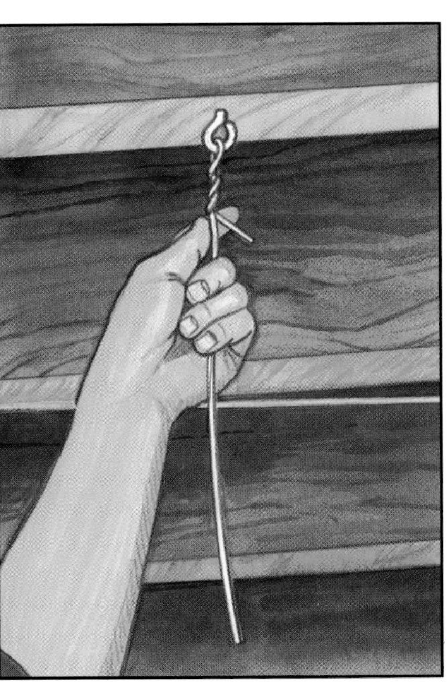

6 Screw eyes should be screwed into the bottom of the joists and be straight up and down. Fasten a wire through each screw eye. Twist the wire to secure it. The wire should hang at least 5" below the cross-tee strings. Place screw eyes into the bottom of ceiling joists where runner and cross-tee lines intersect.

HANGING A SUSPENDED CEILING (continued)

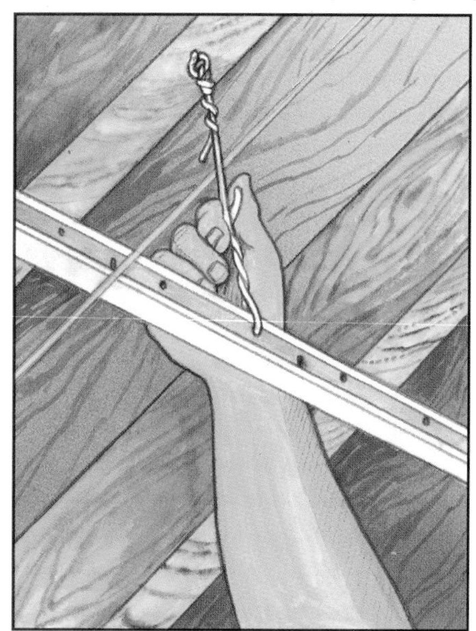

7 Hang the runners. The ends rest on the wall angles. Splice runners together for very long ceilings. Use tin snips to cut them if you have full tiles on one end and partial tiles on the other so the cross-tees fit properly. Fasten the runners with the wires so they are level with the cross-tee strings.

8 Hang the cross-tees. The tees fit into slots in the runners. When cross-tees are cut to fit short edges at the walls, place the cut ends on the wall angles.

9 Install lighting panels or light fixtures (opposite page), then place the ceiling panels in the gridwork.

BOXING OBSTRUCTIONS WITH CEILING PANELS

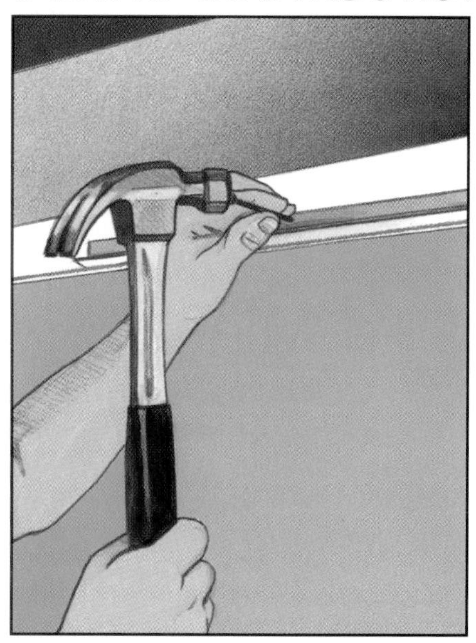

1 Attach wall angle at the desired height below the obstruction. Use a carpenter's level to make sure it is level. Hang runners below the obstruction from wires attached above the edges of the main ceiling.

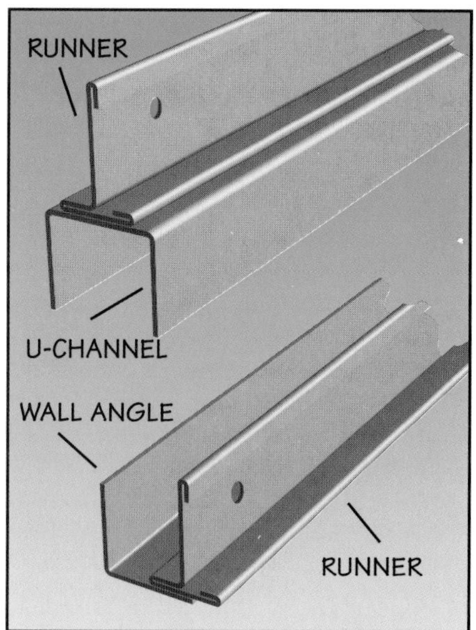

2 Attach channels for vertical panels by riveting U-channels to the runners, on the main ceiling, on either side of the obstruction. Next, rivet wall angle to the runners hanging below the obstruction.

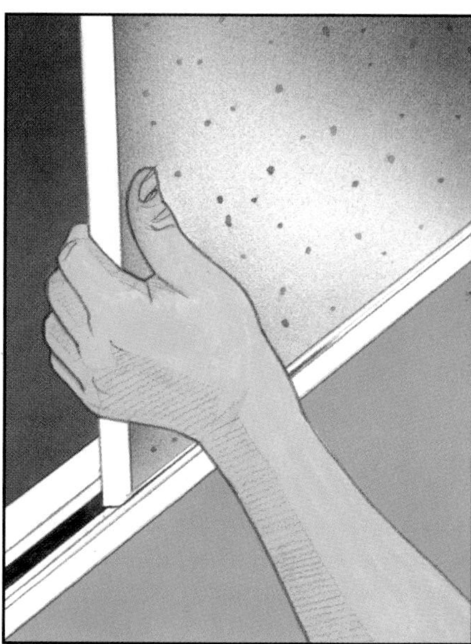

3 Cut ceiling panels to proper size, and insert into the wall angle and U-channel. Cut down cross-tees to fit vertically between U-channel and wall angle. It is a good idea to rivet the cut-down cross-tees to the wall angle and U-channel on the runners. This will help keep the panels and cross-tees secure.

LIGHTING A SUSPENDED CEILING

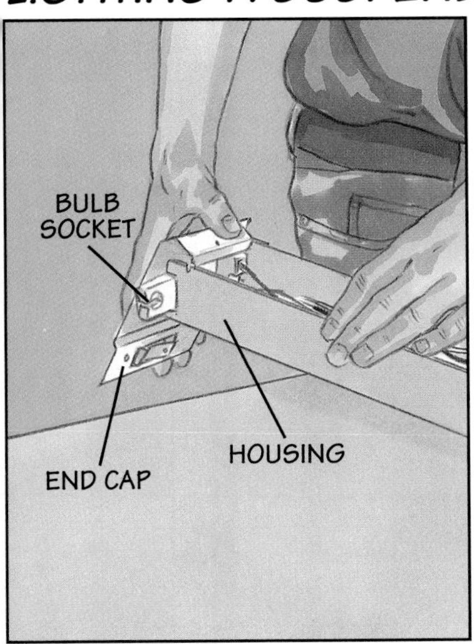

1 Most lights require assembly; follow the manufacturer's directions. Typically, the light comes in several pieces: a reflector, a housing, two bulb sockets per bulb, two end caps, and mounting brackets. Snap the sockets in place, put the end caps on the housing, and screw them in place.

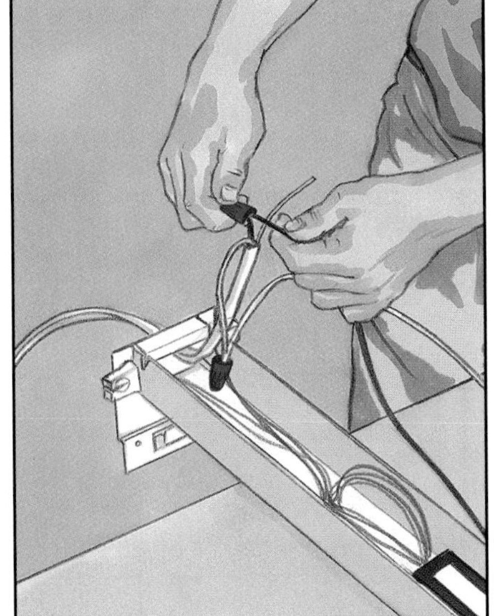

2 You generally need to wire the light before you attach the reflector. First, feed cable through the opening in the fixture. Connect the black wire from the light to the black cable wire, then connect the white cable and light wires. Screw the ground wire to the fixture.

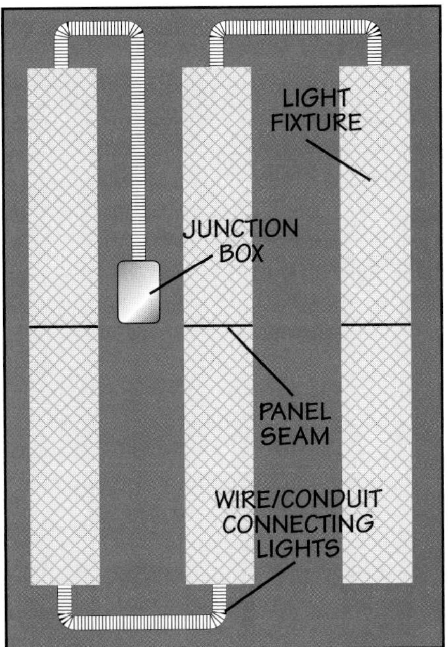

For long runs of fluorescent lighting, you can save time by connecting the fixtures end-to-end with special lock nuts and connectors available where you buy the fixtures. It's more efficient to wire them in sequence than to have individual rows of lights connected to a single junction box.

There are several ways to illuminate a room below a suspended ceiling other than the standard ceiling grid fixtures. You can mount fluorescent fixtures on the ceiling joists and put translucent plastic panels in the ceiling grid directly below the fixtures, or another option is to create a luminous ceiling. This will require fluorescent tubing to be run over the entire area, and then a ceiling composed entirely of translucent panels.

The best fluorescent fixture to use in a luminous ceiling is a 4-foot-long 40-watt rapid-start unit. To determine the number of lamps you need for the entire area, sketch out the dimensions of the ceiling, planning for the lamps to lie in parallel lines between 18 and 24 inches apart. The narrower spacing gives a more even light, but is more expensive. On both ends allow about 8 inches between the ends of the lines and the wall.

3 Fasten the reflector to the end caps. The mounting bracket varies from brand to brand, but the light shown here has a T-bracket that attaches to each end cap. Attach the brackets and then lift the fixture into place and attach.

4 To cover the light, slide a translucent plastic panel into place under the fixture. Angle the piece so you can position first one side and then the other on the grid. If the fit is tight, you can create room by temporarily removing a ceiling panel next to the fixture.

Typical Wall Construction

Wood framing is the most common structural system used for interior load-bearing and non-load-bearing walls. The main difference between the two types of walls is a doubled top plate and, in some cases, cross-bracing in the load-bearing walls. Wall studs are usually set 16" on center and are nailed to the top and sole plates. In some non-load-bearing walls, wall studs are set 24" on center. Gypsum wallboard is fastened to the wall studs with wallboard screws or nails and the seams and fastener holes are covered with wallboard compound. Base molding is applied to the bottom of the wall to provide a decorative transition.

In older houses, thin, closely spaced wood lath strips are nailed to the wall frame to serve as a structural foundation for plaster. Plaster is usually applied in two coats. An undercoat of brown plaster is followed by a finish coat of white plaster. In newer buildings, metal wire is used as the structural foundation for the plaster.

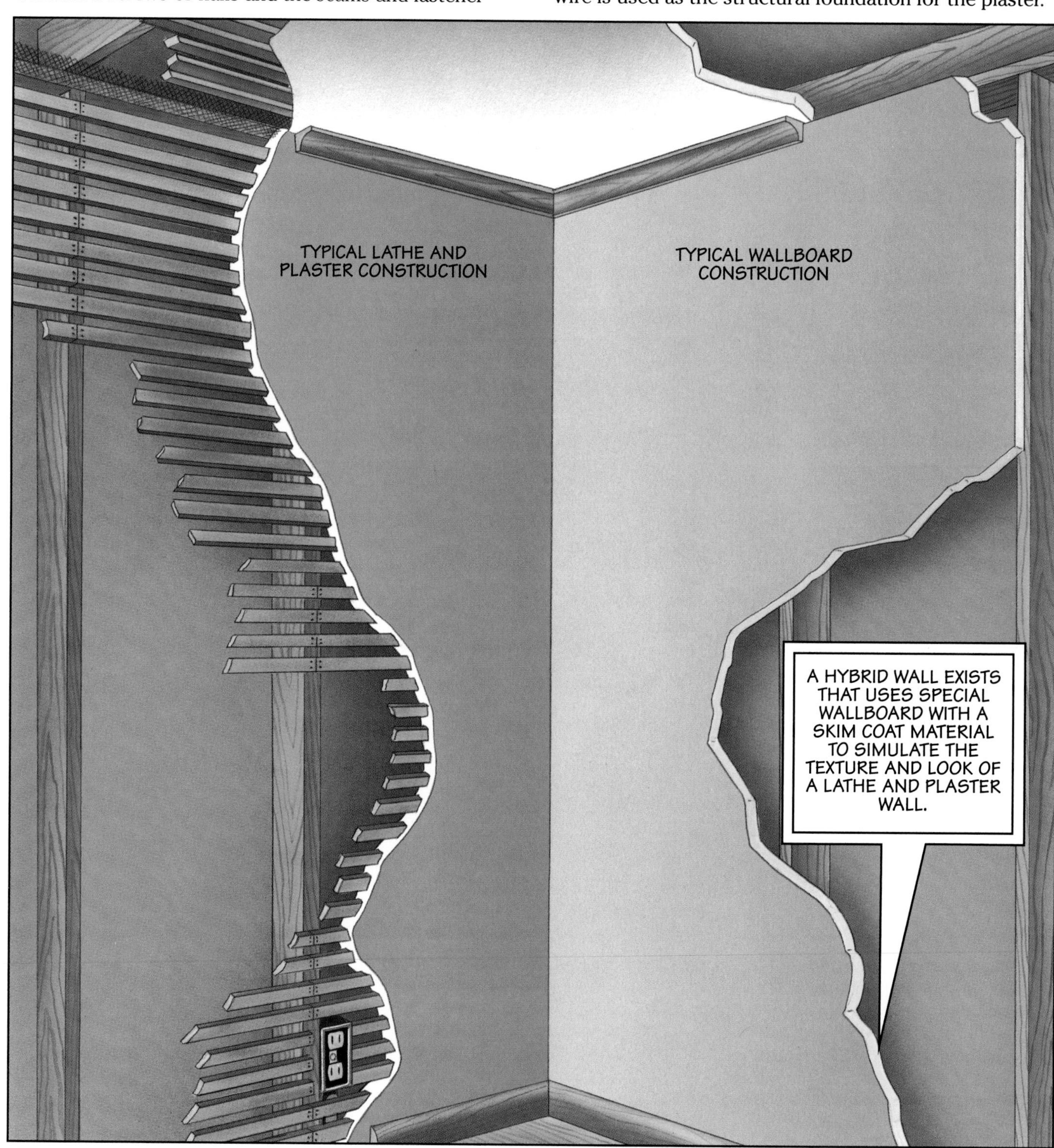

Ceilings, Walls & Floors

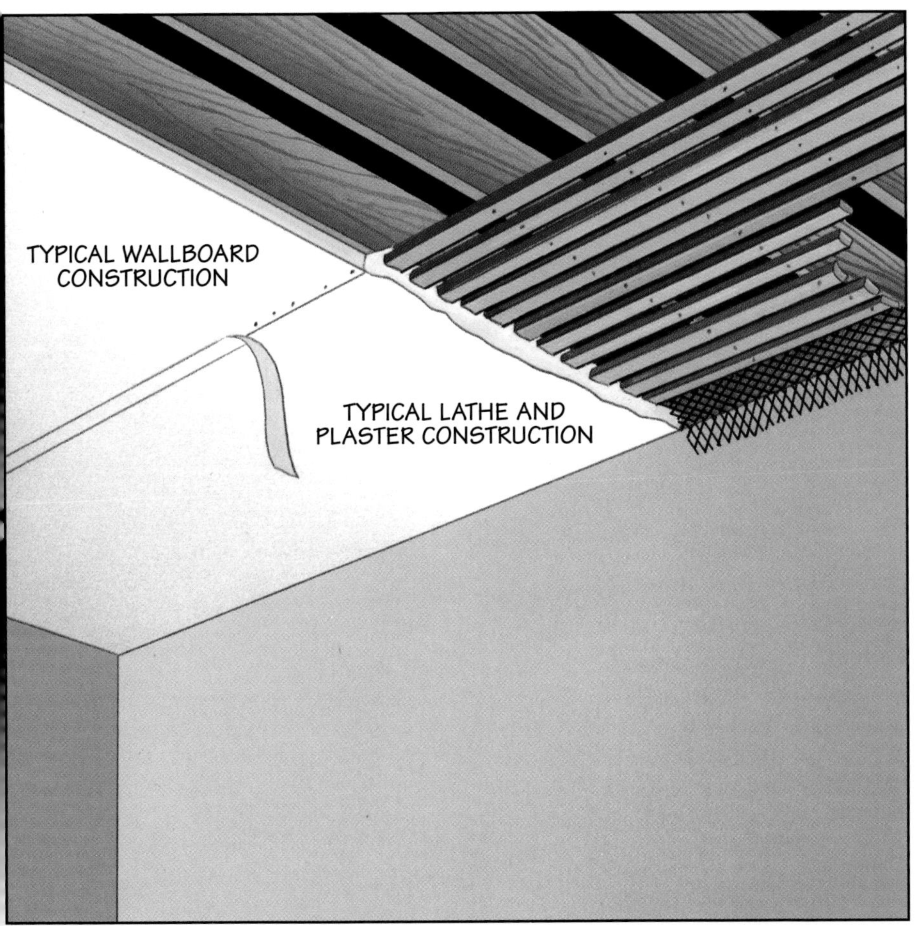

Typical Ceiling Construction

Ceilings are constructed in one of two methods, plaster or gypsum. Plaster ceilings have wood or metal lath fastened to ceiling joists with a base coat and finish coat of plaster applied to the lath and painted. Gypsum ceilings are constructed by fastening gypsum wallboard to the ceiling joists with wallboard screws. The wallboard seams and screw holes are covered with wallboard compound, then the entire surface is either painted or texturized.

Suspended ceilings are constructed by installing a system of runners, cross-tees suspended from ceiling joists and wall angle attached to the sidewalls. These elements provide support for the suspended ceiling tiles, fluorescent light fixtures, and heating and cooling vents. Suspended ceilings are a good way to conceal framing members, plumbing lines, and heating and cooling ductwork while allowing easy access if needed for repair or remodeling.

Repairing Wallboard

Wallboard repairs become necessary for a number of reasons, some preventable while others are totally unavoidable. Careless movers wielding large appliances can cause noticeable damage to walls, while natural settling of the house can cause subtle cracks in tape joints and wallboard panels to loosen and warp. And if there are children in the house, you can count on walls getting damaged from "unknown" causes!

Patching holes and concealing popped nails or screws are the most common wallboard repairs. Unlike plaster, wallboard compounds will stick to painted surfaces. This means that you can patch blemishes, seams, or nails directly over paint, then repaint to blend the patched area into the rest of the wall.

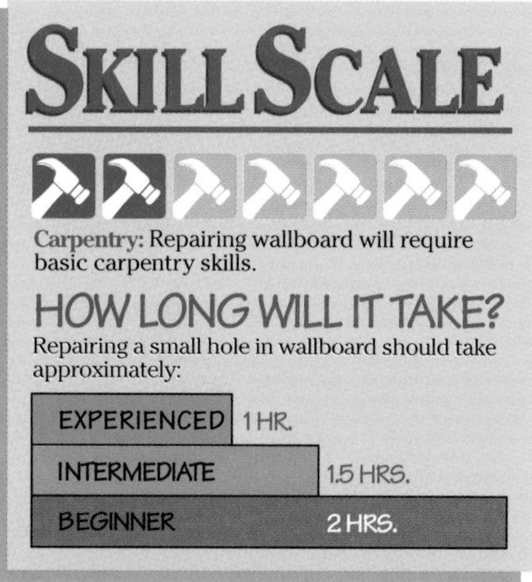

STUFF YOU'LL NEED:

- ☐ **Tools:** Framing square, screwgun, hammer, putty knife, wallboard knife.
- ☐ **Materials:** Wallboard screws, wallboard, joint tape, wallboard compound, spackling, wallboard nails.

PATCHING LARGE HOLES IN WALLBOARD

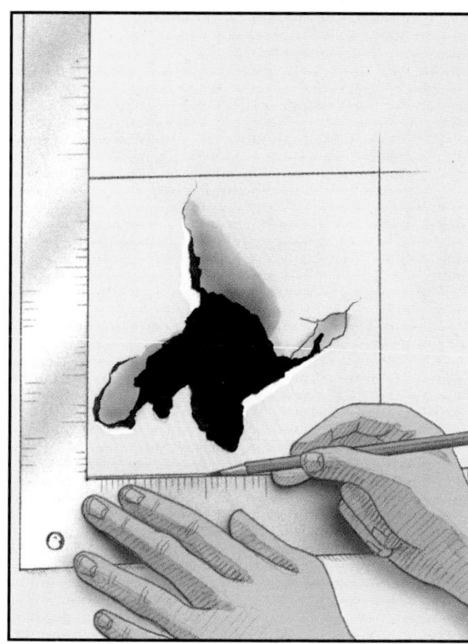

1 Outline the damaged area with a carpenter's square. Use a wallboard saw, jig saw or utility knife to cut away the damaged section.

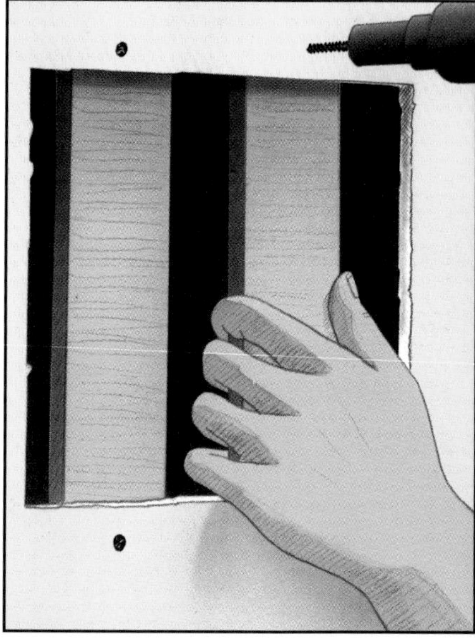

2 Cut wallboard backer strips from $^{3}/_{4}$" plywood or furring strips to the desired length and width depending on the size of the patch area. Install the backer strips using a wallboard screw gun and $1^{1}/_{4}$" wallboard screws to secure the strips in place.

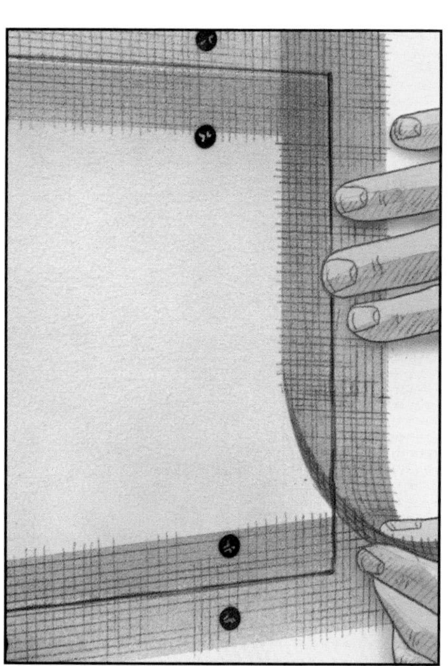

3 Cut a wallboard square to size and screw it to the backer strips. Apply adhesive-backed fiberglass wallboard tape to the cracks, then apply a thin coat of wallboard compound to the joints. Sand the area and apply additional coats of compound as necessary to achieve a smooth finish.

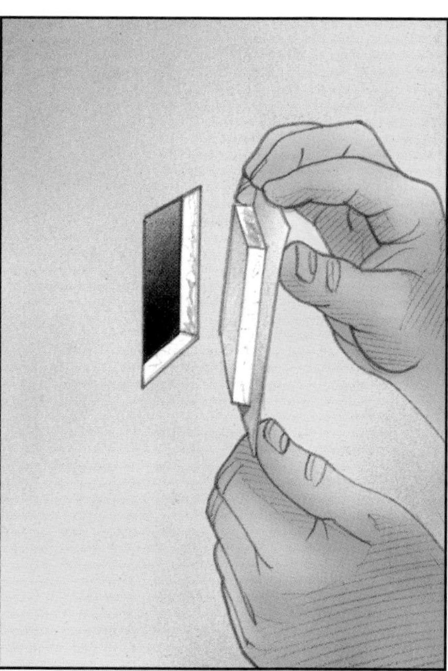

4 On holes no bigger than 3 or 4", make a plug patch by cutting a piece of wallboard, from the back side, to fit the hole. Don't cut all the way through the facing paper. Cut the facing paper $1^{1}/_{2}$ to 2" larger than the hole and pry off the waste with a putty knife. Insert the plug patch and finish with compound.

PATCHING SMALL HOLES IN WALLBOARD

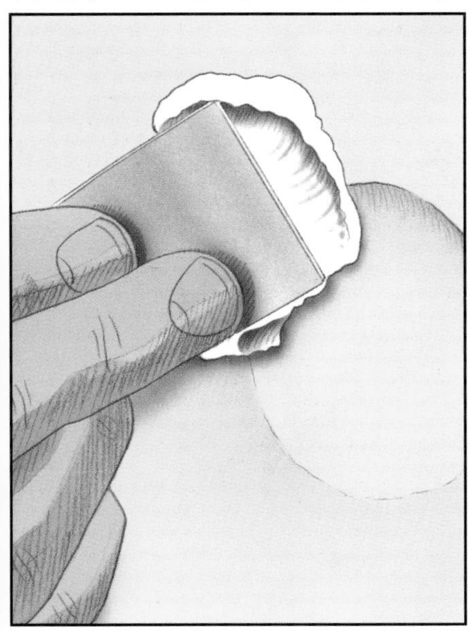

1 Inspect the damaged area. If there are no cracks around the edge of the hole, just fill the hole with spackle, let dry, and sand it smooth.

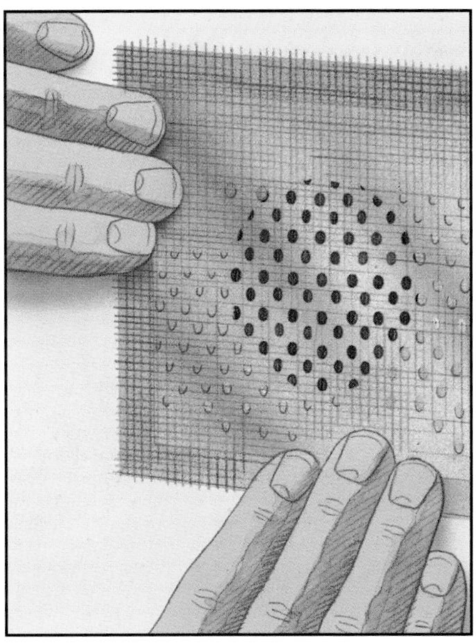

2 If the edges are cracked, cover the hole with a peel-and-stick repair patch. The patch has a metal mesh center for strength. Cut or shape the patch as needed for the specific area.

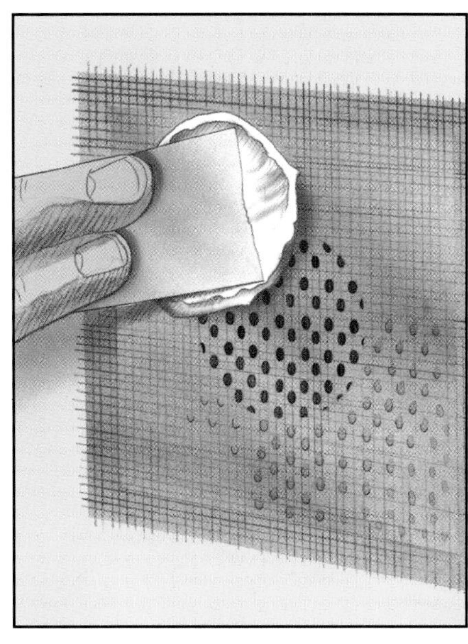

3 Cover the patch with spackle or wallboard compound. Let the patch area set until dry. Use a damp sponge to smooth the repair area. This eliminates dust caused by dry sanding. Apply additional coats of compound, then smooth with a wide blade wallboard knife.

RESETTING POPPED NAILS

Wallboard fasteners pop if they have been improperly applied, or if the framing lumber has dried, causing it to shrink, since the wallboard was applied. Always use wallboard screws when making repairs because the threaded shanks hold wallboard more securely and resist popping.

1 Press the wallboard tightly against the stud or joist. Drive a new screw about two inches from the popped fastener. The screw head should be indented slightly.

2 If possible, remove the nail without damaging the wallboard; or hammer in the popped fastener, leaving a slight indentation. Fill the dents with wallboard compound, let the compound dry, then repaint the patched area.

HOMER'S
HINDSIGHT

One afternoon I noticed a chunk of plaster was about to fall from my ceiling. No big deal, the old homestead was just settling. I decided to get after it before it got worse. Everything I needed was in the basement except a can of latex bonding liquid. A quick trip to the store would have fixed that but I was in a hurry and went to work. This was a mistake because shortly after I'd gone to all the trouble to patch the hole it was cracking and pulling away from the ceiling. I learned that putting on a bonding agent is a necessary step for a good plaster repair. I also learned that being in a hurry usually means doing something twice.

Repairing Plaster Walls

Cracks in plaster walls and ceilings are usually caused by movement in the house structure. To repair them, reinforce these cracks with a fiberglass or peel-and-stick membrane patching tape. In many cases, this is only a temporary fix. Sometimes cracks are due to something you can't do much about, like earthquake tremors—especially if you live in California. More often though, the reason is less exciting, such as the settling of the house. Either way, if the crack keeps coming back, you can decide the crack adds ambience or seek professional advice.

Holes in plaster occur because of impact damage, aging, or exposure to water. If plaster shows brown stains or powdery residue, it has been damaged by water. Check for roof damage or leaky plumbing and fix the problem before repairing the plaster.

REPAIRING SMALL HOLES IN PLASTER

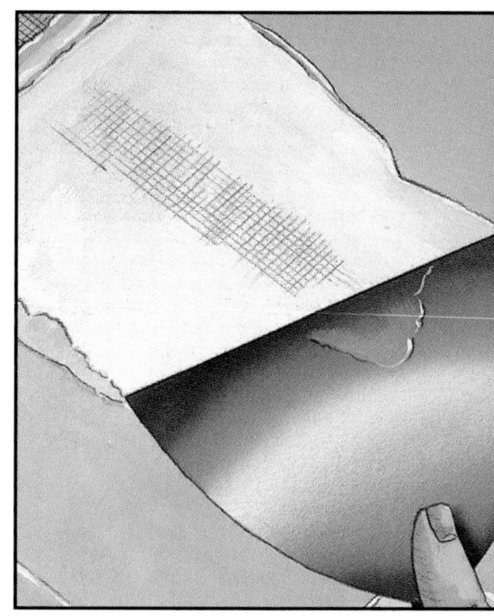

Self-adhesive fiberglass tape is designed to prevent recracking. The tape is applied to the wall and now comes in kits that include a special bonding compound. The material is applied with a paint brush or a putty knife and requires little or no sanding before painting.

SKILL SCALE

Mechanical: Repairing plaster walls will require basic mechanical skills.

HOW LONG WILL IT TAKE?

Repairing a small hole in a plaster wall should take approximately:

EXPERIENCED	1 HR.
INTERMEDIATE	1.5 HRS.
BEGINNER	2 HRS.

STUFF YOU'LL NEED:

- ☐ **Tools:** Putty knife, wallboard knife, paintbrush, paint roller, household can opener.
- ☐ **Materials:** Patching plaster, patching tape, latex bonding liquid, paint.

REPAIRING CRACKS IN PLASTER

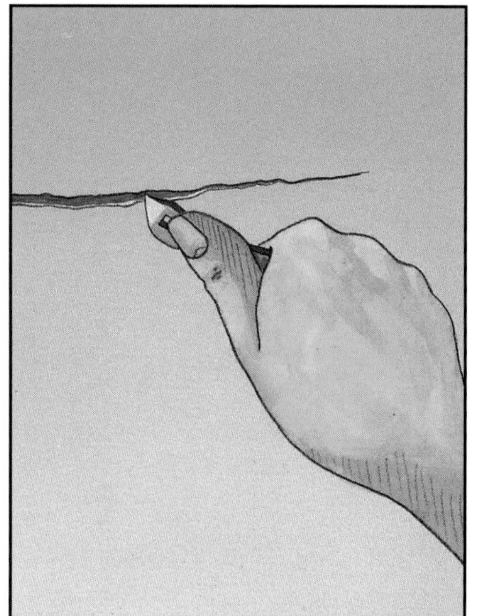

1 With the corner of a scraper or the tip of a can opener, scrape away loose plaster along the edges of the crack and lengthen the crack. Widen the crack slightly, in order to provide a more substantial base for the patching material. If the crack is around a door or window, use mesh tape to prevent recracking.

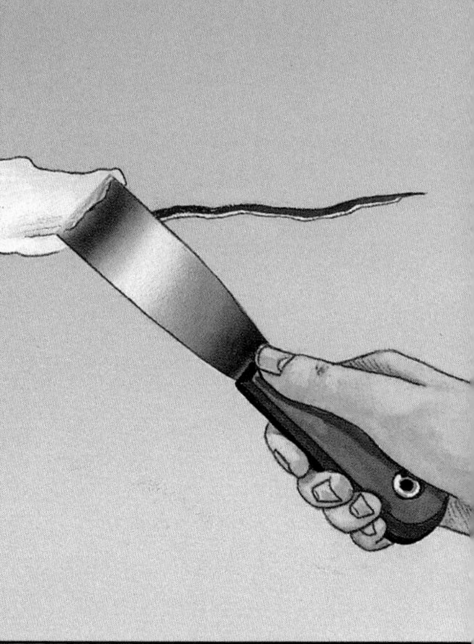

2 Spread wallboard joint compound or vinyl spackling compound along the length of the crack. Overlap the solid plaster along the edges and both ends of the crack. Apply additional coats of patching compound as needed. When the final coat is dry, smooth it with fine sandpaper.

REPAIRING LARGE HOLES IN PLASTER

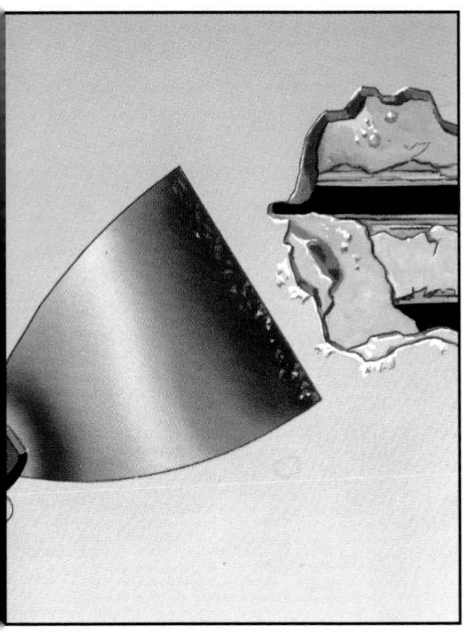

1 Scrape away all loose or scaling plaster to expose the firm base plaster or lath. Make sure that the damaged area does not extend beyond the scraped area.

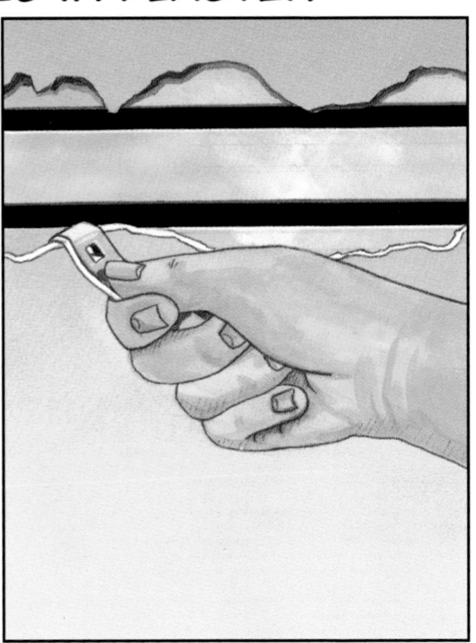

2 Use the corner of a putty knife or the tip of a can opener to undercut the edges of the hole. This will help to lock the patching material into the hole.

3 Brush latex bonding liquid onto the patch area. Fully coat the edges of the old plaster. Do not wet the patch area after coating it. Mix the patching plaster stiff enough to be applied with a trowel.

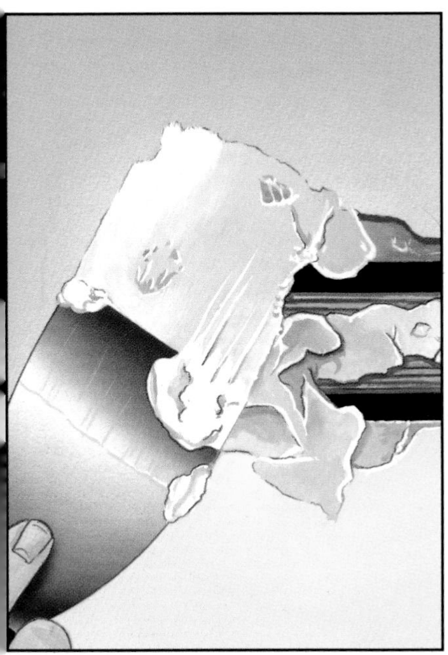

4 Trowel the patching plaster in the hole with a wallboard knife, using a sweeping motion. Work the plaster firmly into the edges of the hole for a good bond. For holes 1/4" deep or less, one coat of patching plaster should be plenty. Let plaster set. In a large area, several layers may be necessary to prevent cracking due to shrinking as the plaster dries.

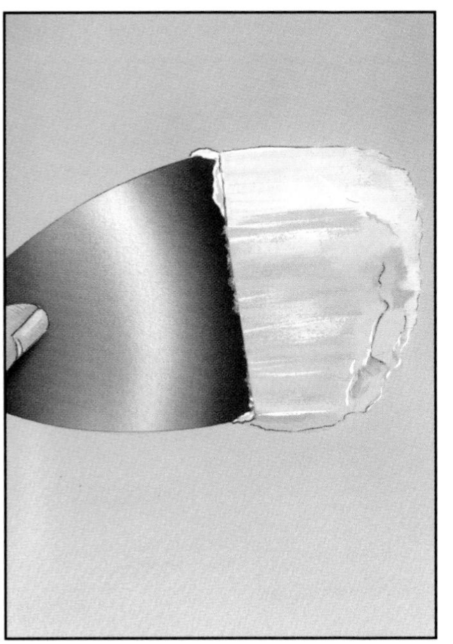

5 For holes deeper than 1/4", apply a second coat of plaster. Use a latex bonding agent between coats and allow at least 24 hours of drying time. Let plaster set, then sand lightly, if needed. Seal the patch area with white shellac, then repaint the area.

Use texture paint or wallboard compound to recreate any surface texture needed to blend in with the surrounding areas.

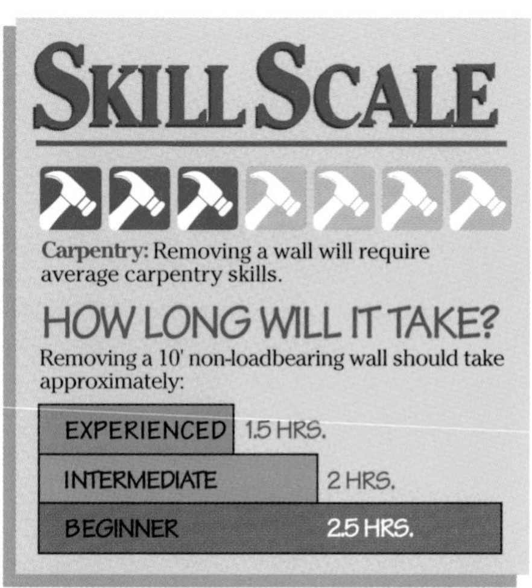

STUFF YOU'LL NEED:

- ☐**Tools:** Hammer, drill, reciprocating saw, prybar, ratchet w/sockets.
- ☐**Materials:** Framing lumber, 16d common nails.

Removing a Wall

Removing a wall can expand your living space considerably and may be the best way to improve access between areas frequently used, such as the dining room and the living room. The job uses similar principles to making a pass-through or a new doorway, although on a much larger scale. Removing a dividing wall, whether it is structural (load-bearing) or simply a partition, is a major undertaking, but it need not be overwhelming. If you follow some basic safety and structural rules, much of the job is straightforward, although it is messy and disruptive. Removing or modifying a load-bearing wall is a serious undertaking. You should consult a professional if attempting to remove or modify a load-bearing wall. Before you start, plan out the entire project and consult your local building inspector for proper code requirements. It is necessary to obtain a building permit before removing a load-bearing wall. In order to obtain a permit, it is necessary to provide the inspector with drawings that include key details of the existing structure and specifications for the installation of the new supporting structure. While a knowledgeable do-it-yourselfer may be able to prepare such drawings, consult with an architect or structural engineer when tackling a project that involves altering structural elements of your home. An interior load-bearing wall generally supports the weight of an upper floor and sometimes, depending on the design, part of the weight of the roof. When a load-bearing wall is removed, provisions must be made to support the loads on that wall. Typically, a horizontal beam is installed in the area where joists of the upper floor rest on the top plate of the wall that is being removed. The beam is supported by vertical columns that transmit the load to the foundation and other structural elements of the house frame.

DETERMINING A LOAD-BEARING OR PARTITION WALL

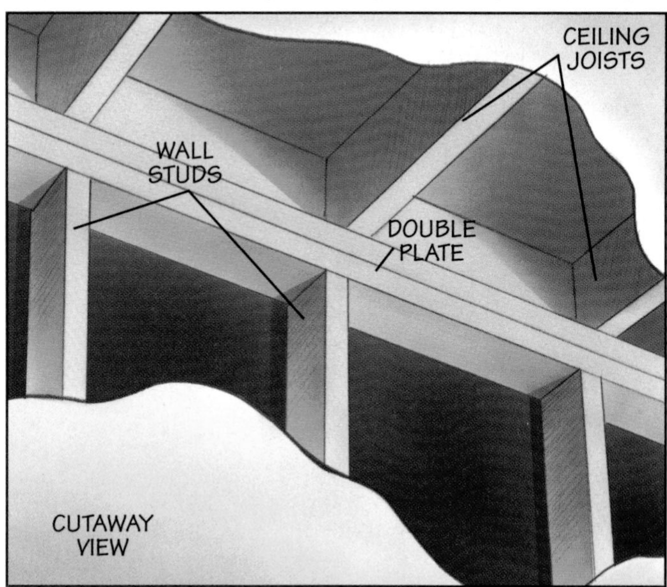

Load-bearing walls carry the structural weight of your home and can be identified by double top plates made from two layers of framing lumber. Load-bearing walls include all exterior walls, and any interior walls that are aligned above support beams or are positioned to support ceiling or floor joist lap joints.

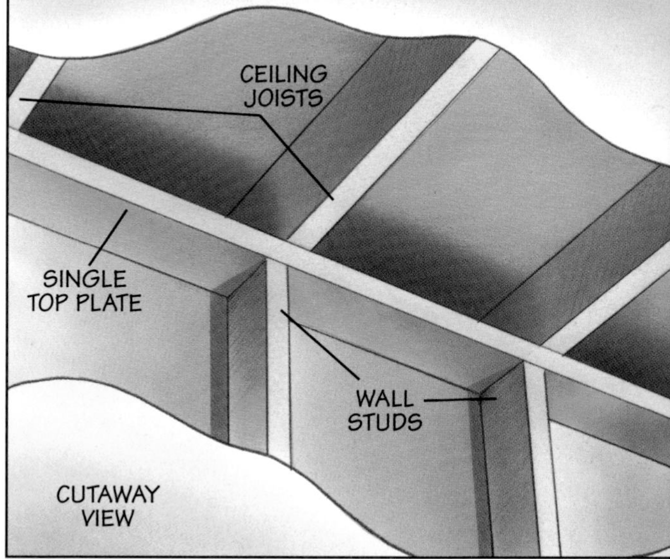

Partition walls are interior walls that are not load-bearing. Any interior wall parallel to floor and ceiling joists is a partition wall. Partition walls have a single top plate and can also be perpendicular to the floor and ceiling joists but are not aligned above support beams. Partition walls perpendicular to the joists may, or may not, be load-bearing. If the wall is perpendicular to the joists, consider it a load-bearing wall until you have a professional determine if it is load-bearing or not.

WESTERN FRAME

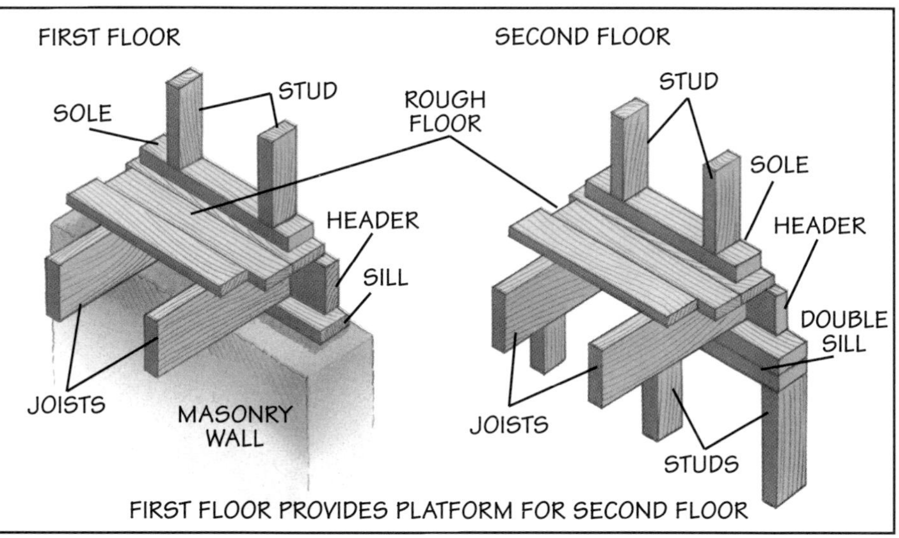

Western frame construction, sometimes referred to as stick or platform construction, is generally the most common system for one-story construction. This particular design is characterized by floor joists, story-height studs spaced 16" or 24" on center, roof trusses spaced up to 4' on center and panel sheathing such as plywood or fiberboard. Unnecessary elements, such as corner-bracing and floor bridging are eliminated. Floor construction provides a work platform permitting efficient tilt-up wall framing.

BALLOON FRAME

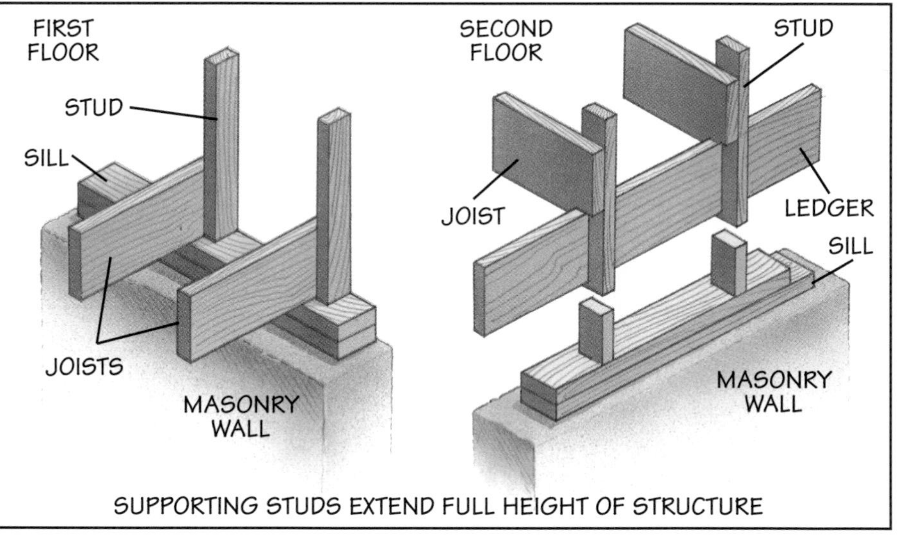

Traditional balloon frame construction, which began around 1850 is characterized by individual joists, rafters and building-height studs spaced 12" to 24" on center, second-floor joists carried on ribbon let-into studs, wood boards for sheathing, subflooring, floor bridging and corner bracing.

POST AND BEAM FRAME

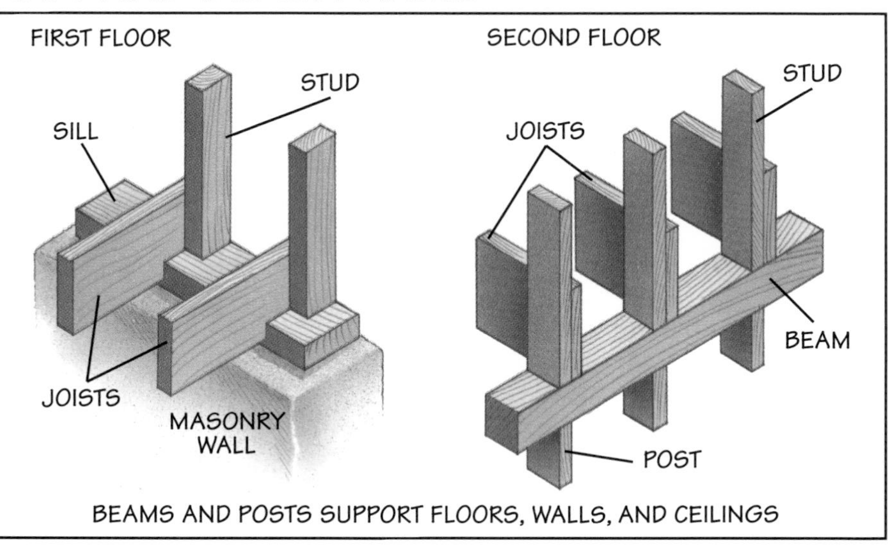

Post and beam construction consists of posts, beams, and planks. Roof and ceiling loads are distributed by planks to beams which transmit their loads directly to posts. Non-load-bearing exterior walls serve only as curtain walls and to brace the frame.

REMOVING A WALL OR WALL SECTION

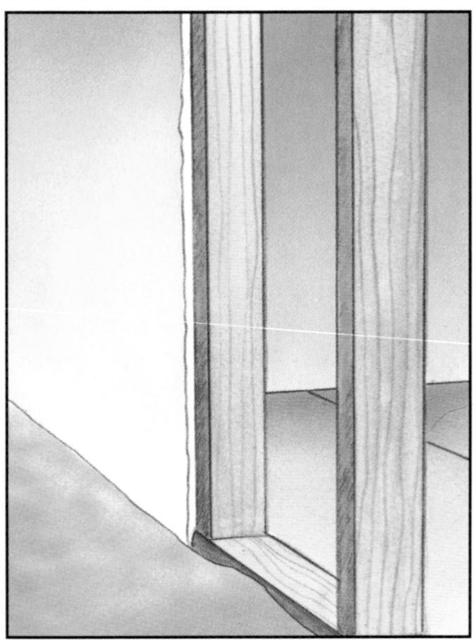

When removing wall surfaces, expose the wall back to the first permanent stud at each side of the opening.

1 Prepare the project site by removing the surfaces from the wall being removed. Remove or reroute any wiring, plumbing lines, or ductwork. Remove the surface of adjoining walls to expose the permanent studs.

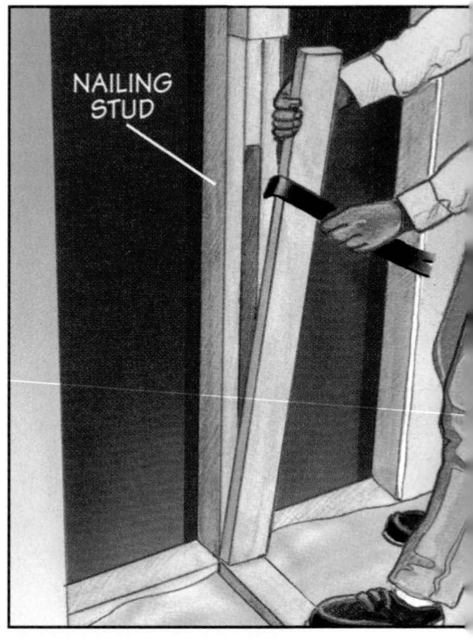

2 Remove studs by cutting them through the middle and prying them away from the sole plate and top plate. Remove the end stud on each end of the wall. If the wall being removed is load-bearing, also remove any nailing studs or blocking in the adjoining walls directly behind the removed wall.

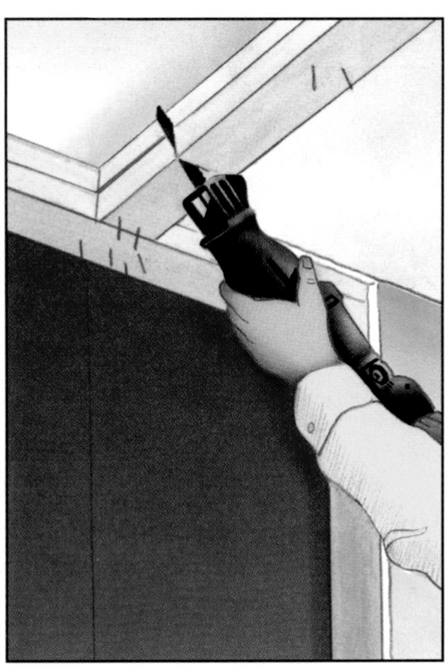

3 Make two cuts through the top plate, at least 3" apart, using a reciprocating saw or handsaw.

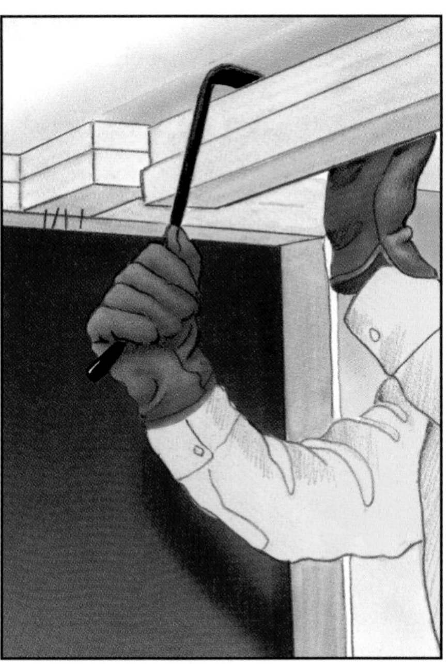

4 Remove the cut section with a pry bar, then remove the remaining sections of the top plate, also using a pry bar.

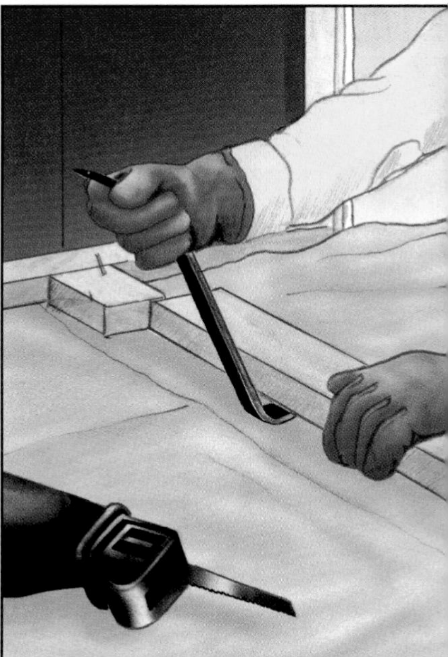

5 Remove a 3"-wide section of sole plate, using a reciprocating saw or handsaw. Pry out the entire sole plate, using a pry bar. If the removed wall was load-bearing, be sure to build and install a header. Check your local building code for size of header (pgs. 305-306).

BUILDING TEMPORARY SUPPORT FOR JOISTS PERPENDICULAR TO WALL

1 Build a 2x4 stud wall that is at least the length of the wall that is being removed and $1^3/_4$" shorter than the distance from the floor to the ceiling.

2 Raise the stud wall up and position it 3'. from the wall, centered on the planned rough opening.

3 Slide a 2x4 top plate between the temporary wall and ceiling. Check to make sure the wall is plumb, then drive shims under the top plate at 12" intervals until the wall is wedged tightly in place.

BUILDING TEMPORARY SUPPORT FOR JOISTS PARALLEL TO WALL

1 Build two 4'-long cross braces, using pairs of 2x4s nailed together. Attach the cross braces to a double top plate, 1 ft. from the ends, using countersunk lag screws. You may want to add carpet or cloth padding to the top of the brace to protect the ceiling.

2 Place the supports directly over a floor joist. Build each post for the support frame $^1/_2$" longer than the floor-to-cross brace distance. Include the carpet or cloth pad in the measurement. Nail the posts to the top plate, 2' from the ends.

3 Adjust the support structure so the posts are almost plumb, then tap the posts inward until the cross braces just begin to lift the ceiling. Do not lift too far, or you may damage the floor or ceiling.

Enlarging a Room Opening

Remodeling a room usually involves several different construction and demolition functions. You can enlarge a door opening or archway, or you can remove the wall entirely. Window openings can be enlarged to give the room more light and make it appear more spacious. No matter how extensive the changes will be, you'll use the basic carpentry practices of demolition, framing, hanging and finishing wallboard, and trim carpentry.

Although the steps involved are relatively simple, enlarging an opening is hard work. The speed with which you finish will depend on your energy level and continued enthusiasm. Sometimes maintaining enthusiasm is hard work too. In the end it'll be worth it.

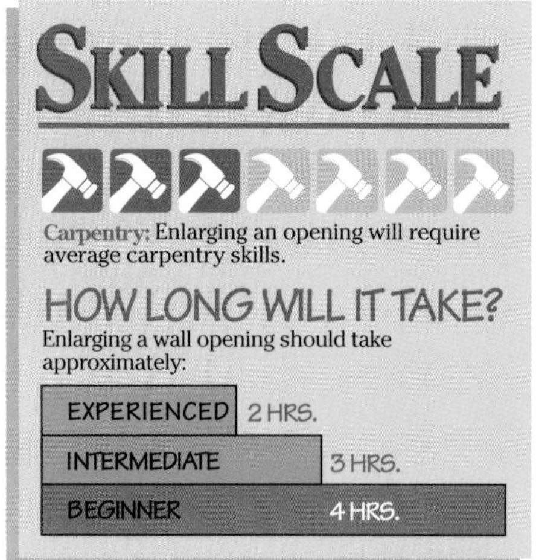

STUFF YOU'LL NEED:

- ☐ **Tools:** Framing square, prybar, reciprocating saw, screwgun, hammer, wallboard knife.
- ☐ **Materials:** Wallboard screws, wallboard, joint tape, wallboard compound.

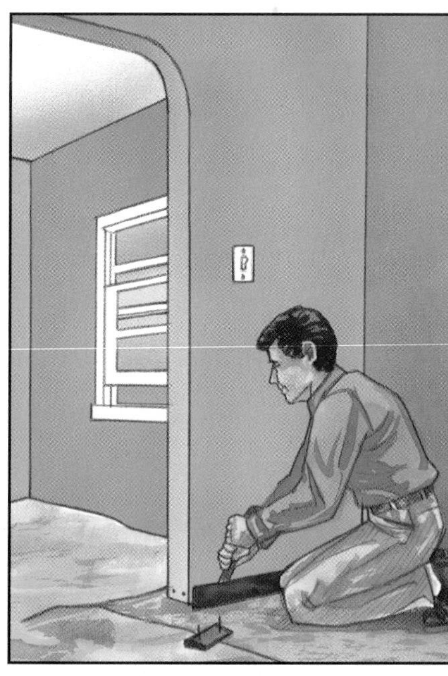

1 Prepare the work area by removing trim moldings. Shut off power and plumbing to the wall areas that will be altered. Remove coverplates from the switches, receptacles, and heating ducts in the project area. Protect the floors with drop cloths, and cover interior doors with plastic to confine dust.

2 Mark rough openings for the new openings, doors or windows, then remove the interior wall surfaces. Be sure to wear safety glasses and a particle mask. Make sure to remove enough wall surface to provide easy access for installing new framing members. After removing the wall surfaces, remove old door and window units (pg. 325), if needed. Clear away all trash before continuing with your project.

3 Make temporary supports (pg. 227) if your project requires you to cut more than one stud in a load-bearing wall. Temporary supports help brace the upper structure of your home until the framing work is done.

4 If you are removing an interior non-load-bearing wall, simply remove the wall surfaces and cut away the studs. However, if you are removing a load-bearing wall, make temporary supports and replace the wall with a sturdy permanent header and posts to support the weight previously carried by the removed wall.

5 Frame the openings for doors (pg. 312) and windows (pg. 326). After the framing work is complete, remove the exterior surfaces.

6 Install the door and window units (pg. 314), then complete any exterior finishing work as soon as possible to protect the wall cavities against moisture.

7 Patch and paint the exterior siding and attach any required exterior moldings. Complete the interior work by installing and finishing the wallboard and painting or wallpapering the walls as desired.

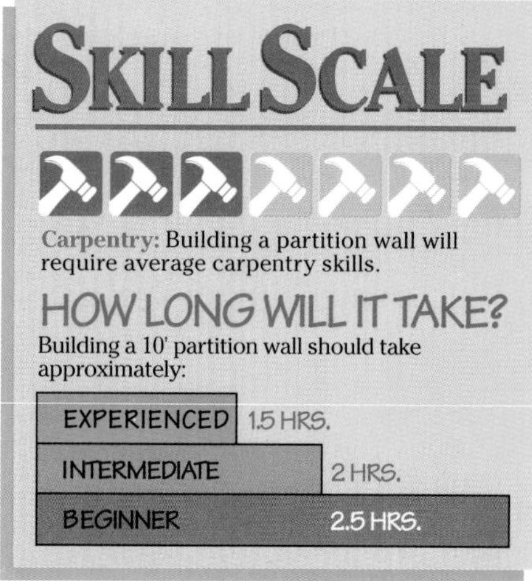

STUFF YOU'LL NEED:

- ☐**Tools:** Framing square, hammer combination square, handsaw, circular saw, tape measure, drill, chalkline.
- ☐**Materials:** Framing lumber, 16d nails.

Building a Partition Wall

Partition walls define new living areas and are often used to create new rooms in unfinished basements. There are two ways to go about building a partition wall–framing the wall in place, or building the framing members on the floor and lifting it into place. The location of the new wall generally dictates which method you use. If you can build the framing first (pg. 233), it's generally the quicker way to go. Once you've planned your layout and constructed the desired partition walls, consult the plumbing and electrical sections of this book if you need to include these utilities. Also, before finishing the walls with wallboard (pg. 235), have the local building inspector review your partition wall construction. The inspector also will check to see that any required plumbing and wiring changes are complete.

Interior partition walls are commonly built with 2x4 framing lumber, but in some situations it is better to frame with 2x6 lumber. Use 2x6 lumber to frame a partition wall that must hold large plumbing pipes, such as waste/drain pipes. In sections where the wall plates must be cut in order to fit pipes and other mechanical fixtures, use metal straps to join the framing members and tie them together.

If the intended use of the new room is a practice room for your teenager's new drum set, you may want to soundproof the new wall. You can easily accomplish this by filling the wall with fiberglass insulation (pg. 232) before applying the wallboard.

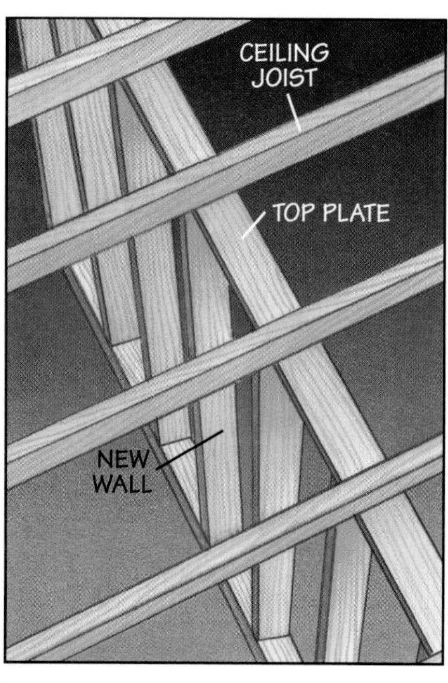

New walls that run perpendicular to joists are attached by fastening the top plate directly to the ceiling joists and the sole plate to the floor joists with 16d nails.

New walls aligned with parallel joists are attached by fastening the top plate directly to the ceiling joist and the sole plate to the floor joists, using 16d nails. It is easiest to modify your design slightly so that you can build the partition directly under a joist.

New walls that run parallel to the joists, but not aligned with the joists need additional blocking. If you have access to the joists above, build cross-bracing. Install 2x4 blocking between the joists, every 2', using 16d nails. The bottom of the blocking should be flush with the edges of joists.

ATTACHING NEW WALLS TO EXISTING JOISTS

1 Mark the location of the new wall on the ceiling, then snap two chalk lines to outline the position of the new top plate. Locate the first ceiling joist or cross block by drilling into the ceiling between the lines, then measure to find and mark the remaining joists.

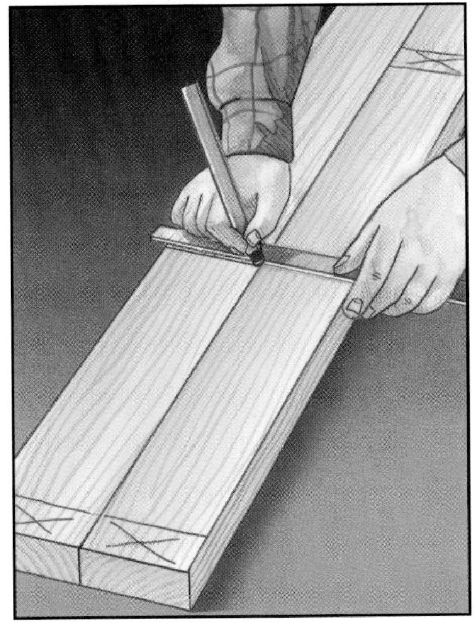

2 Make the top and bottom wall plates by cutting two 2x4s to the wall length. Lay the plates side by side, and use a combination square to outline the stud locations at 16" intervals on center.

3 Use a framing square to make sure the plate is perpendicular to the adjoining walls, but it is more important to make it parallel to the facing wall across the room. Measure equal distance from the facing wall and attach the top plate at the marks. Nail the top plate to the ceiling using 16d nails.

SAFETY ALERT

Always wear safety glasses and hearing protection when using a stud driver.

4 Determine the position of the sole plate by hanging a plumb bob from the edge of the top plate so the plumb bob tip nearly touches the floor. Mark the position on the floor. Repeat at the opposite end of the top plate, then snap a chalk line between the marks to mark the location of the sole plate.

5 On wood floors, anchor the sole plate with 16d nails driven into the floor joists. On concrete floors, attach the sole plate with a stud driver, available at rental centers. A stud driver fires a small gunpowder charge to drive a masonry nail through the framing member and into the concrete.

6 Find the length of the first stud by measuring the distance between the sole plate and the top plate at the first stud mark. Add $^1/_8$" to ensure a snug fit, and cut the stud to length.

ATTACHING NEW WALLS TO EXISTING JOISTS (continued)

7 Position the stud between the top plate and sole plate so the stud markings are covered.

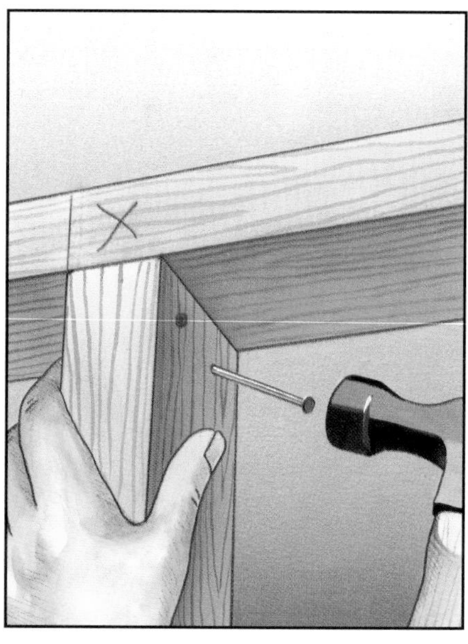

8 Attach the stud by toenailing through the sides of the studs and in the top plate and sole plate. Measure, cut, and install all remaining studs one at a time.

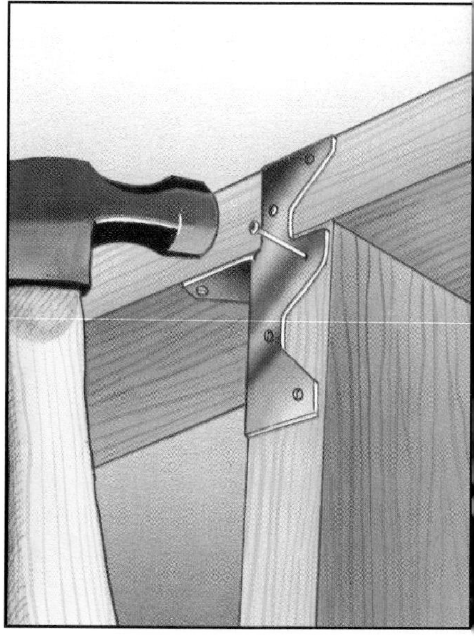

Option: Attach the studs to sole plate and top plate with metal connectors and 4d nails.

9 Install 2x4 blocking between studs, 4ft. from the floor. Blocking, sometimes known as fire blocks, are installed to prevent fire from spreading quickly inside walls. Arrange to have the wiring and any other utility work completed, then have your project inspected. Install wallboard and trim as desired.

SOUNDPROOFING A WALL

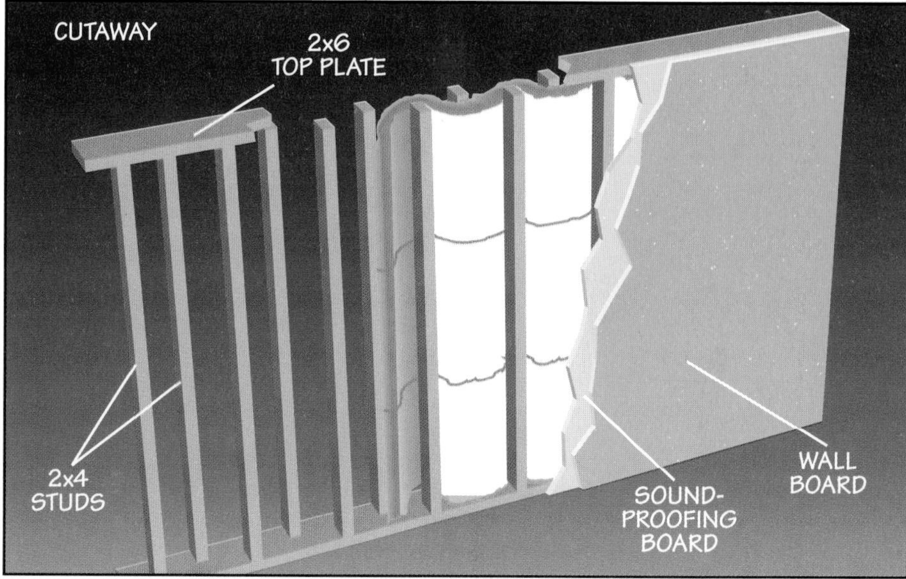

Reducing the sound transmission of a wall can be accomplished quite easily by modifying the typical construction of the new wall. Start by using top and sole plates that are wider than the wall studs. Place the wall studs 8" on center, but stagger the studs so they alternate, each stud lining up on opposite edges of the plate. Weave fiberglass batt insulation in between the studs along the entire wall, the full height of the studs. Complete the soundproofing by applying a layer of soundproofing board to the wall studs, then covering that with gypsum wallboard. If you don't have soundproofing board, a double layer of gypsum wallboard will work.

FRAMING A PARTITION WALL ON THE FLOOR

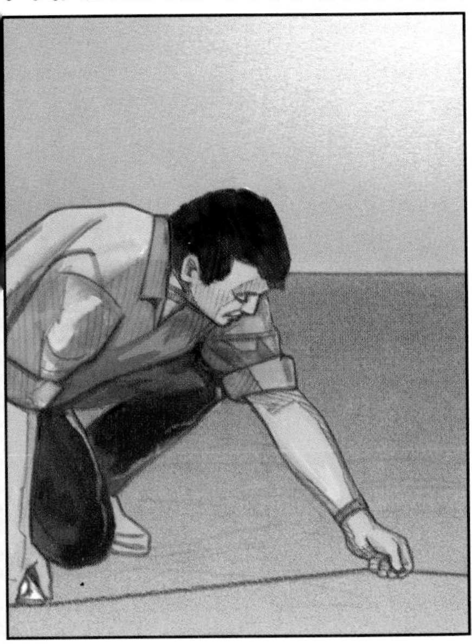

1 Mark the floor line for the bottom plate where the new wall will be installed. Measure away from the opposite wall where the new wall will be installed, place a mark on the floor at each end of the proposed wall and snap a chalk line between the two marks.

2 Mark the ceiling line for the top plate by measuring away from the opposite wall and placing a mark on the ceiling at each end of the proposed wall. Snap a chalk line between the marks.

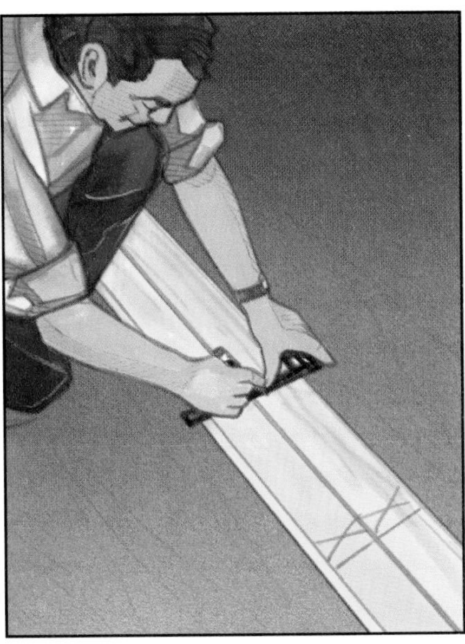

3 Determine the length of the wall and cut 2x4 top and bottom plates to length. Place the 2x4's side by side and lay out the top and bottom plates, spacing the studs 16" on center and marking king and jack stud locations for doorways.

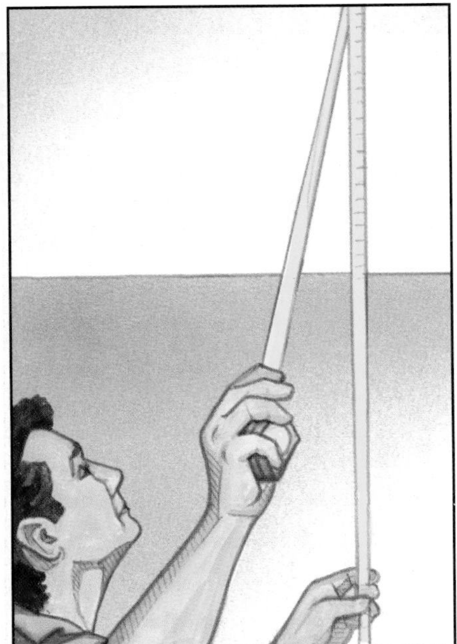

4 Measure the distance between the floor and the ceiling, or the joists, at several locations along where the wall will be constructed. Take the shortest distance and subtract $3^1/_8$" ($1^1/_2$" each for the top and bottom plates and $^1/_8$" for space to maneuver the wall into place). This will be the stud length.

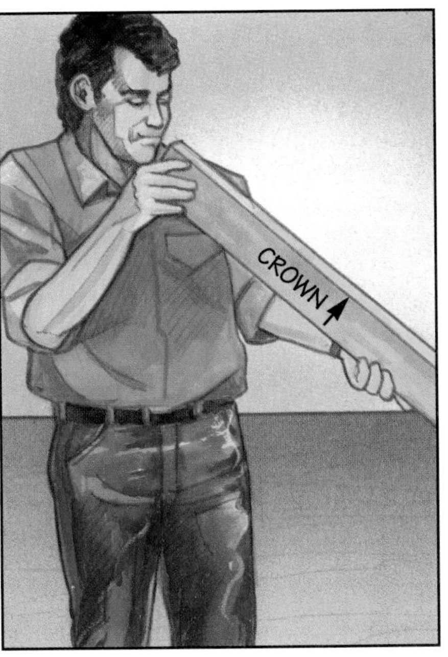

5 Count the number of wall studs you will need according to the laid out plates and cut them to the appropriate length. Inspect each stud to determine if it has a crown and mark on the face of the stud which way the crown goes.

6 Lay the bottom plate on edge along the floor line. Take the first stud and place it on edge with the crown up. Nail the bottom plate and stud together using 16d nails.

FRAMING A PARTITION WALL (continued)

7 Lay the top plate on edge with the layout marks facing the bottom plate and nail to the first stud using 16d nails. Insert the remaining studs, crown up, and nail in place with 16d nails.

8 Once all studs have been attached to the top and bottom plates, raise the wall and position the plates on the floor and ceiling lines.

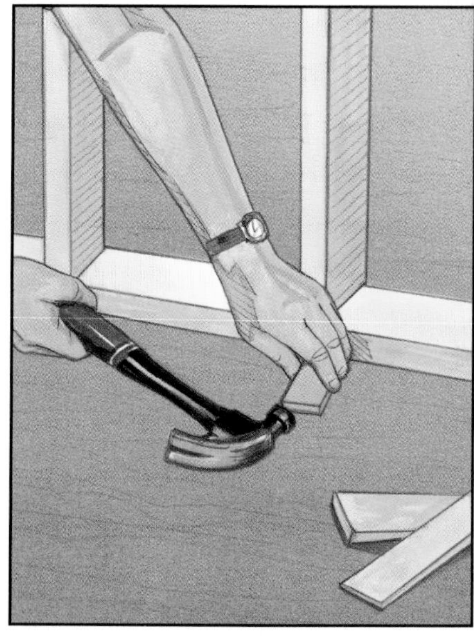

9 If the wall fits too loosely, shim under the bottom plate to tighten the wall in the space. Secure the wall to the floor and ceiling joists using 16d nails.

FRAMING PARTITION WALL CORNERS (cutaway views)

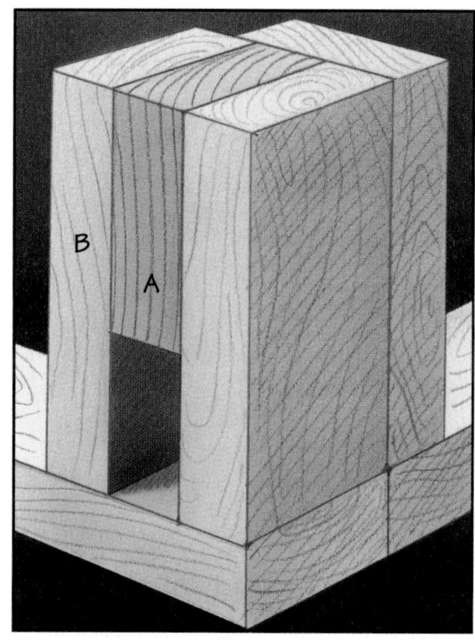

L-corners are constructed by nailing 2x4 spacers (**A**) to the inside of the end stud. Nail an extra stud (**B**) to the spacers to provide a surface for nailing wallboard on the inside corner.

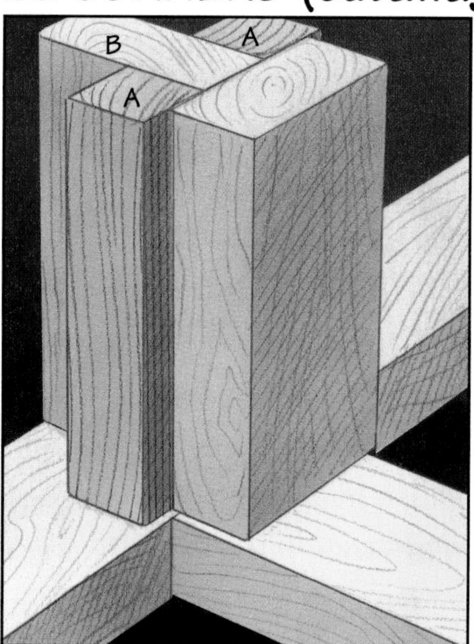

Where a T-corner meets a stud, fasten 2x2 backers (**A**) to each side of the side wall stud (**B**) to provide a nailing surface for wallboard.

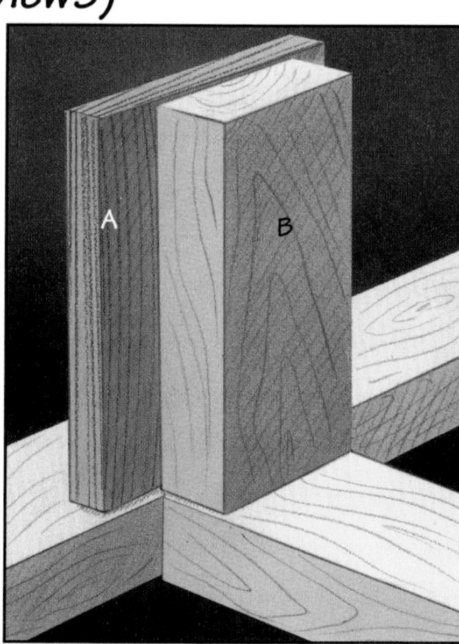

Where a T-corner is between studs, fasten a 1x6 backer (**A**) to the end stud (**B**) with wallboard screws to provide a nailing surface for wallboard.

Installing Wallboard

Wallboard is commonly available n 4x8' and 4x12' sheets, and in hicknesses of 3/8", 1/2", 5/8", and 3/4". or easy handling in most pplications, it is best to use 4x8 heets of 1/2"-thick wallboard. For xtra fire protection where building odes require it, or for soundproofing walls and ceilings, you can use 5/8" or even 3/4" wallboard. Wallboard can be very heavy. Unless you're into pain, avoid a hernia or wrenched back by getting a little assistance for wallboard projects.

Wallboard can be installed with wallboard nails and a hammer. More commonly though, it is installed with wallboard screws and a drill or screwgun outfitted with a magnetic driver bit. Spacing of nails and/or screws varies with local building codes. Wallboard can also be installed with panel adhesive and wallboard screws. Adhesives bridge minor framing voids, and provide the wallboard with a smooth easy-to-finish surface that is not subject to nail or fastener pops.

Wallboard panels are tapered along the long edges, so that the adjoining panels form a slightly recessed seam that can be covered with paper tape and wallboard joint compound. Panels joined end-to-end are more difficult to finish, so it is best to avoid end-butted seams wherever possible.

Before installing wallboard panels, inspect them for broken corners and cracks. Damaged wallboard is difficult to install and causes finishing problems.

Wallboard can be cut with a wallboard saw or sharp utility knife. The sheet must be supported, face side up, on lengths of wood laid across sawhorses. The saw should be held at a shallow angle to the surface of the wallboard. A helper should support large pieces to prevent them from breaking away toward the end of the cut.

STUFF YOU'LL NEED:

- ☐ **Tools:** Hammer, wallboard T-square, utility knife, wallboard saw, screwgun.
- ☐ **Materials:** Nails and screws, panel adhesive, joint compound, wallboard tape.

PREPARING FOR WALLBOARD INSTALLATION

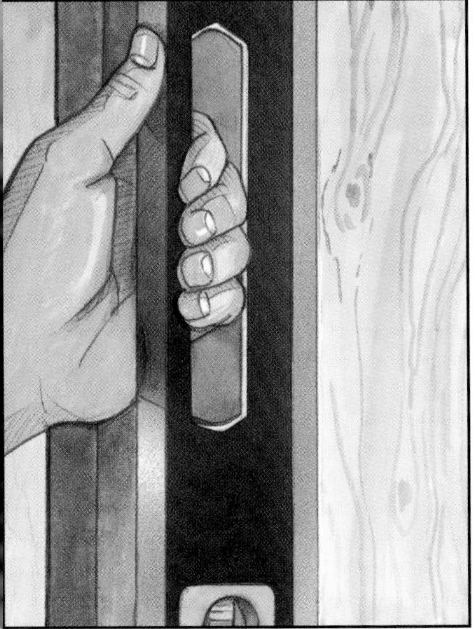

1 Check the stud alignment with a straightedge that is at least 4' long. Remove and replace any warped studs.

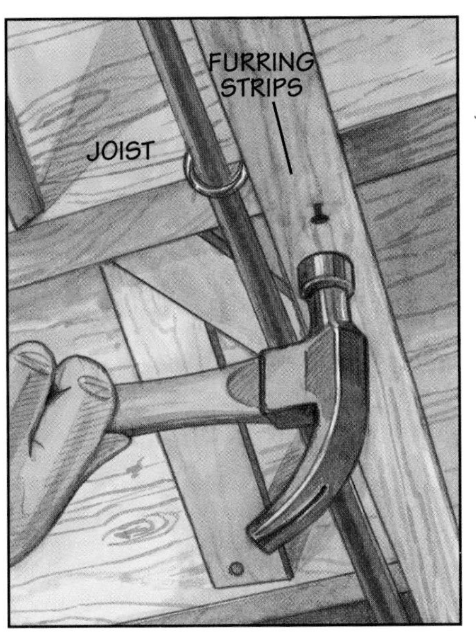

2 Check for obstructions, like water pipes or heating ducts that hang below joists. Nail furring strips to the framing members to extend the wall or ceiling surface, or, if possible, move the obstructions.

3 Mark the locations of studs with a carpenter's pencil or masking tape on the floor. The wallboard will cover the studs, so these marks show where to nail.

INSTALLING WALLBOARD CEILINGS

1 When installing wallboard, the ceiling panels should be installed before the wall panels. Mark the ceiling joist locations on the top plate as a nailing guide for installing the wallboard.

2 You will want to work with a partner when installing a wallboard ceiling. Build a t-shore out of 2x4 framing lumber for your helper to use to hold up the wallboard panel. Build a scaffold out of sawhorses, framing lumber and plywood, tall enough so that when you stand on it, the top of your head just touches the bottom of the ceiling joists. Lift the panel into position running perpendicular to the joists and hold the wallboard tightly against the joists with the top of your head. This frees your hands for fastening the wallboard. Tack the panel in place with wallboard nails and finish securing it with wallboard screws.

Mounting variation: Apply panel adhesive to the bottom of the joists. Place a sponge in your cap to provide a cushion for your head when holding the panel.

RAISING SHEETS SINGLE-HANDED

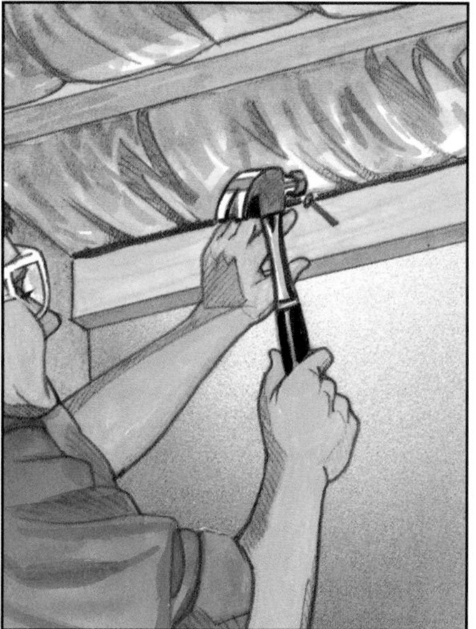

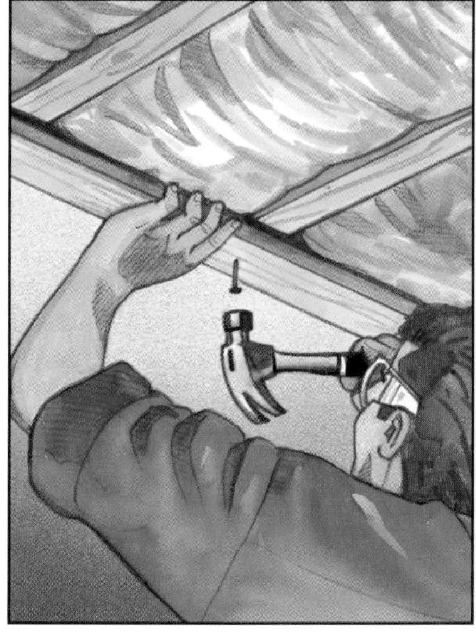

1 Temporarily nail a 1x4 cleat to the wall studs. The cleat should be the thickness of the wallboard below the ceiling joists. This will hold the end of the panel in place as you raise it up to the joists. This may be a good idea even if you're working with someone else.

2 Before you raise the second sheet, tack a 1x4 cleat into the ceiling joists onto the end of the first wallboard panel. Attach the cleat so that it extends half of its width beyond the first panel end. This will hold the end of the next panel in place as it is raised.

TOOL TIPS

There are several tools available at most rental centers that will make wallboard installation a much more enjoyable and much less back-breaking task! One of these items is the panel lift. This simple device lets you lift a full 4x8' sheet of wallboard safely and easily. The lift allows you to load the wallboard and lift the panel up to an 11'-high ceiling. The lifts are on casters so you can roll them into position, set the caster brakes, and safely and securely place the panel into position. Most lifts have a tilting platform feature that lets you easily install wallboard on sloped ceilings and can normally hold up to a full 4x16' sheet of wallboard.

INSTALLING WALLBOARD WALLS

1 Measure the exposed area to find the dimensions for the wallboard panels. Joints should fall over studs or nailing strips, but should not be aligned with corners of windows or doors. Leave a gap of no more than 1/4" between wallboard and jambs.

2 Set the wallboard panel on sawhorses with the smooth side facing up. Mark the panel for cutting according to your measurements.

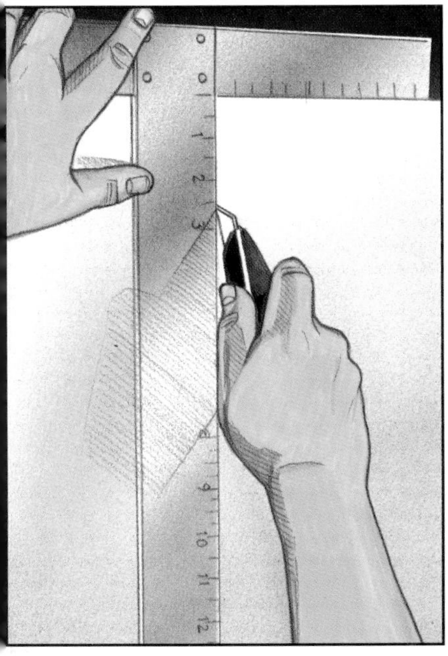

3 To make straight cuts, score the face paper with a sharp utility knife, using a wallboard T-square as a guide, then deepen the cuts into the gypsum with additional passes. As a safety measure, when using a utility knife, cut away from your other hand.

4 Complete straight cuts by bending the panel away from the scored line until it breaks. Cut through the back paper with a sharp utility knife to separate the wallboard pieces.

5 To cut notches, use a wallboard saw to make the parallel cuts. Score the remaining line with a utility knife, then snap the notched piece backward and cut through the back paper.

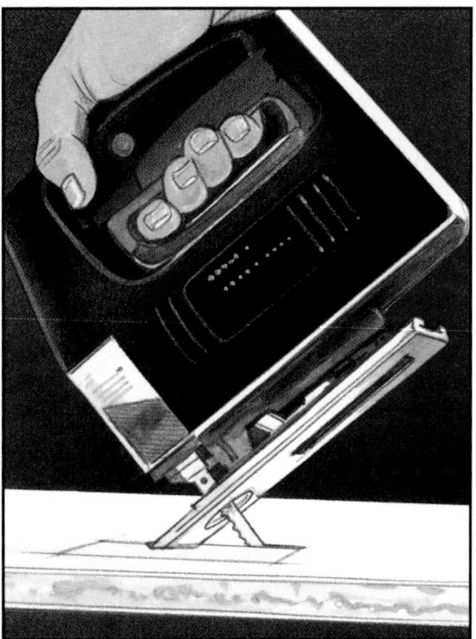

6 To make cutouts for receptacles, circle-top windows, or other odd shapes, rub chalk on the outer edges of the object with the unusual shape. Press the wallboard against the object, transferring the chalk to the back of the panel. Remove the panel and cut just outside the chalk lines with a jigsaw or keyhole saw.

7 If you're using panel adhesive, place a bead of adhesive along each stud. Then position the wallboard panel tightly against the framing members. For large panels, you can use a wallboard lifter or wood shims to raise the wallboard so it fits snugly against the ceiling.

8 Anchor the wallboard panels by driving wallboard screws, spaced every 10", into the framing members. The screw heads should be driven in to a depth just below the wallboard surface but not through the paper.

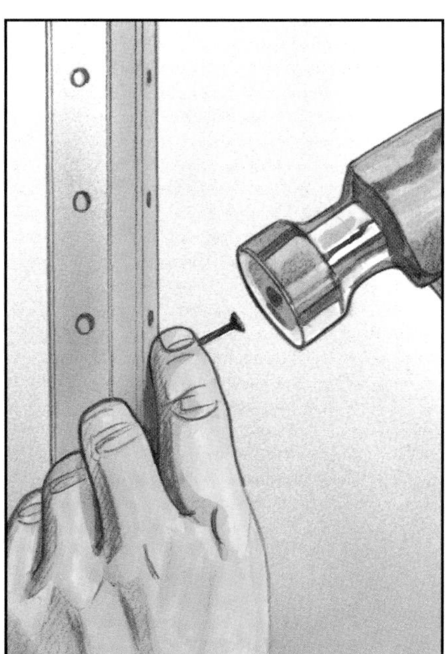

9 At outside corners, cut metal corner bead to length, and attach with wallboard nails, spaced according to local code. Apply a double layer of wallboard compound to each side of the corner, using a 6" wallboard knife.

Panel adhesive bonds the wallboard to the framing members permanently. If y make a mistake, you'll have to cut and remove the wallboard panel and possibly the wall studs too!

TOOLTIPS

Wallboard can be fastened using several tools, each one dependent on the quantity of wallboard to be hung and the tool budget you're working with. The most economical method is to use your common claw hammer with wallboard nails. For most instances, this will work adequately.

The next option is to purchase a special drywall hammer to use with wallboard nails. This hammer has a much broader head than your claw hammer, with a special shape that will set the nails at a proper depth without making too deep of an imprint. It also has a cutting edge, similar to a hatchet, on the other end, to make cutouts without having to mark and take the panel down to cut with a knife or saw. With either hammer, you'll need to double nail to securely hold the panel in place.

A more popular method, and beginning to be the standard, is to use a screwgun with wallboard screws. Screws tend to hold the wallboard more securely and are much quicker to install and easier to finish. The screwgun has an adjustable collar that lets you set the depth of the screw head for whatever material you're using.

Finishing Walls

To finish wallboard, apply wallboard joint compound to all seams, nail and screw holes, and corners. Because wallboard compound shrinks as it dries, three coats are needed to compensate for shrinkage. Apply the first coat with a 4" or 6" taping knife and let it dry thoroughly. Apply the last two coats with a 10" knife to "feather" the compound and smooth out any remaining irregularities. To prevent cracking, all joints must be reinforced. On outside corners, nail metal corner bead over the wallboard before applying the compound. On inside corners and flat joints, apply a thin first layer of compound, then press strips of paper or fiberglass wallboard tape in the damp compound.

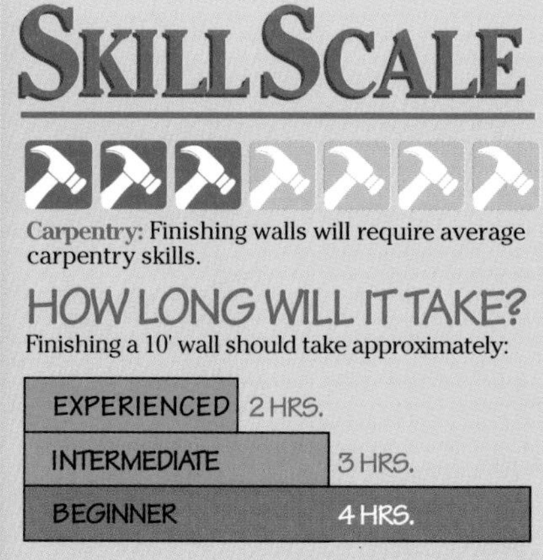

STUFF YOU'LL NEED:

- ☐ **Tools:** Putty knife, wallboard knife, pole sander.
- ☐ **Materials:** Joint tape, wallboard compound, sandpaper or sanding screens.

MATERIALS FOR FINISHING WALLBOARD

Use premixed wallboard compound for most taping and finishing jobs, to eliminate messy mixing. It is available in both base and finish coats. Use paper wallboard tape when using premixed wallboard compound.

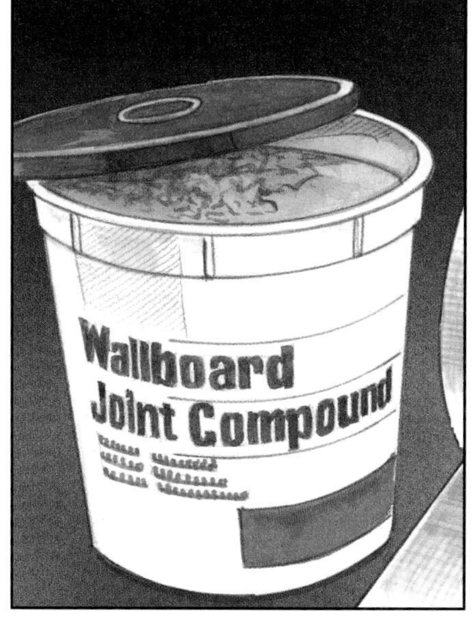

For small projects, use quick-set wallboard compound that is mixed with water. Quick-set compound hardens in 1 to 2 hours. Use fiberglass wallboard tape when using quick-set compound.

TAPING JOINTS

1 Apply a thin layer of wallboard compound over the joint with a 10" or 12" wallboard knife.

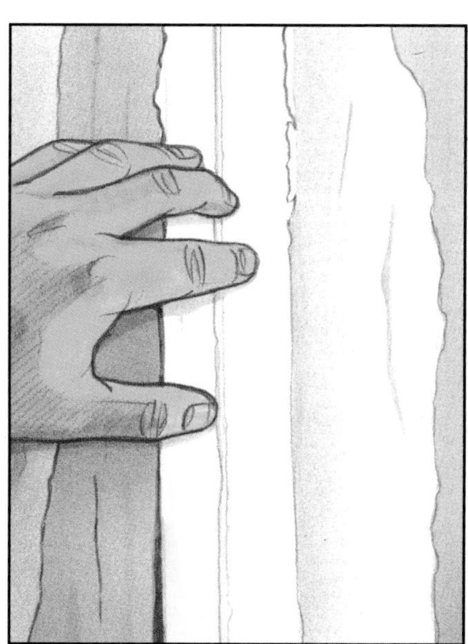

2 Press the wallboard tape into the compound immediately, centering the tape on the joint. Wipe away the excess compound, smooth the joint with a 6" wallboard knife, and let it dry.

TAPING JOINTS (continued)

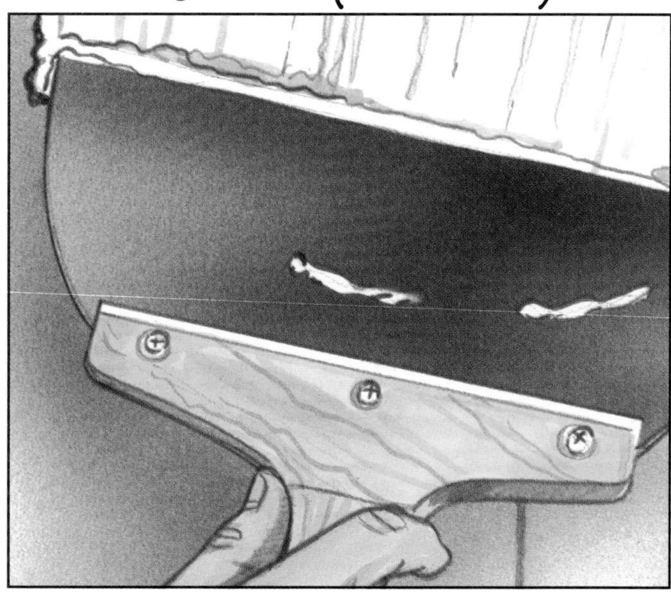

3 Apply a coat of compound with a 10" or 12" wallboard knife. Allow it to dry overnight before applying the finish coat.

4 Apply and sand smooth the finish coat. If dust is a problem (and sanding creates a lot of dust), close off adjacent rooms with plastic sheeting or use a wet sanding sponge.

INSIDE CORNERS

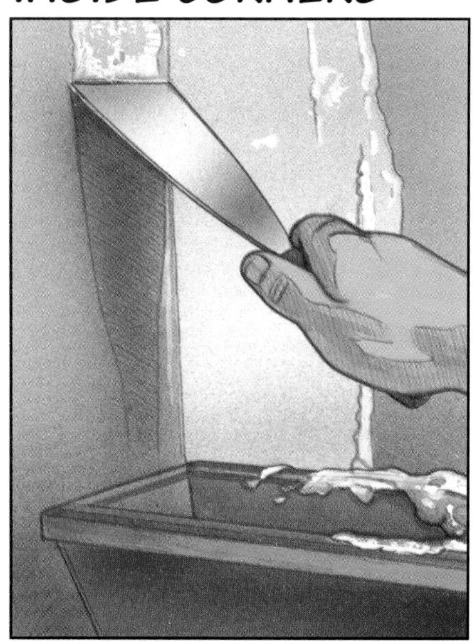

1 Apply a thin layer of premixed wallboard compound to both sides of the inside corner, using a 4" wallboard knife.

2 Fold a strip of paper wallboard tape in half by pinching the strip and pulling it between your thumb and forefinger. Position the end of the folded tape strip at the top of the corner joint. Press the tape into the wet compound with a wallboard knife, and smooth both sides of the corner.

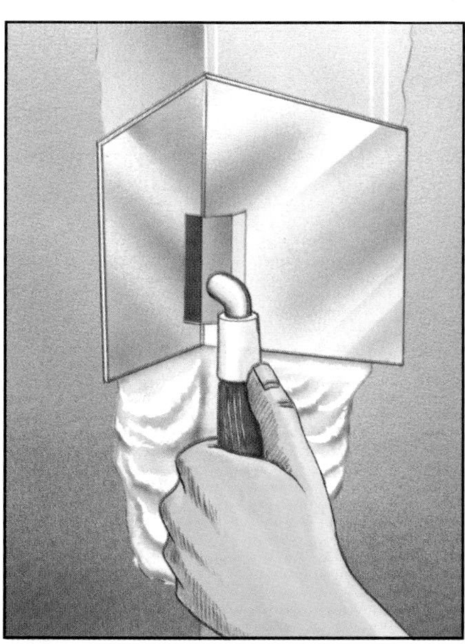

3 Apply a second coat of wallboard compound with a corner trowell. After the second coat dries, apply a final coat of compound. Smooth the final coat with a wet sander.

FINISHING OUTSIDE CORNERS

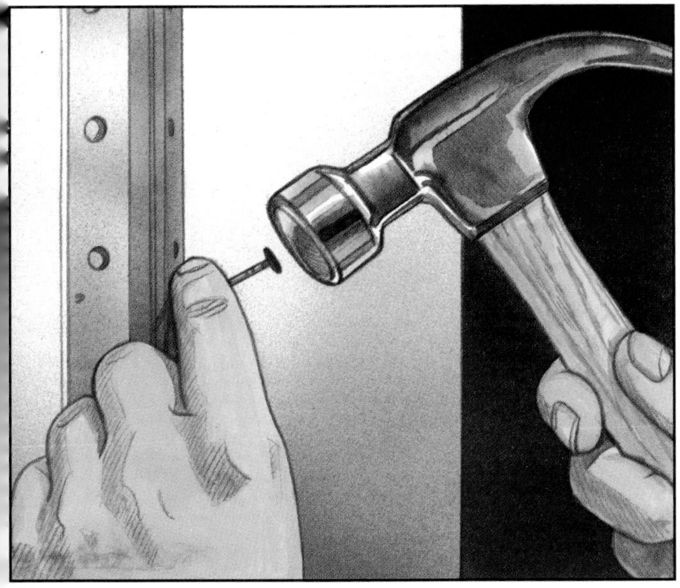

1 Position steel corner bead on the outside corners. Using a level, adjust the bead so the corner is plumb. Nail the corner bead into place with wallboard nails spaced according to your local building codes.

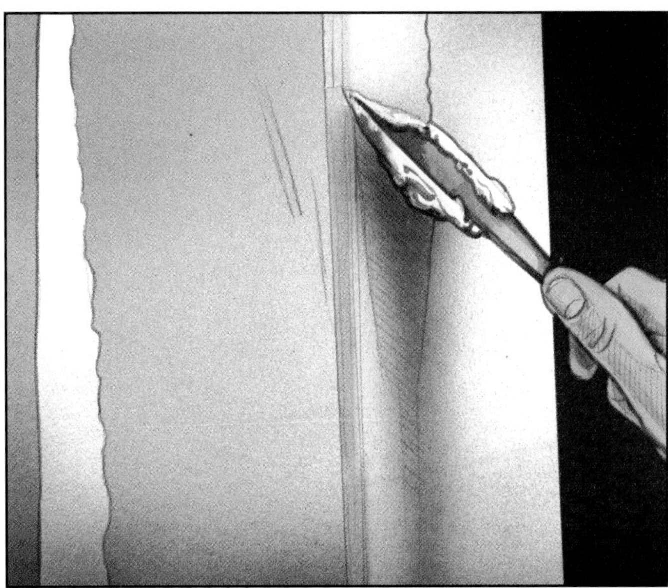

2 Cover the corner bead with three coats of wallboard compound, using a 6" or 10" wallboard knife. Let each coat dry and shrink overnight before applying the next coat. Smooth the final coat with a wet sander.

FINISHING NAILS AND SCREWS

Cover screw or nail heads with three coats of wallboard compound, using a 4" or 6" wallboard knife. Allow each coat to dry overnight before applying next coat. If the nail or screw missed the stud, take it out, don't just cover over it.

SANDING JOINTS

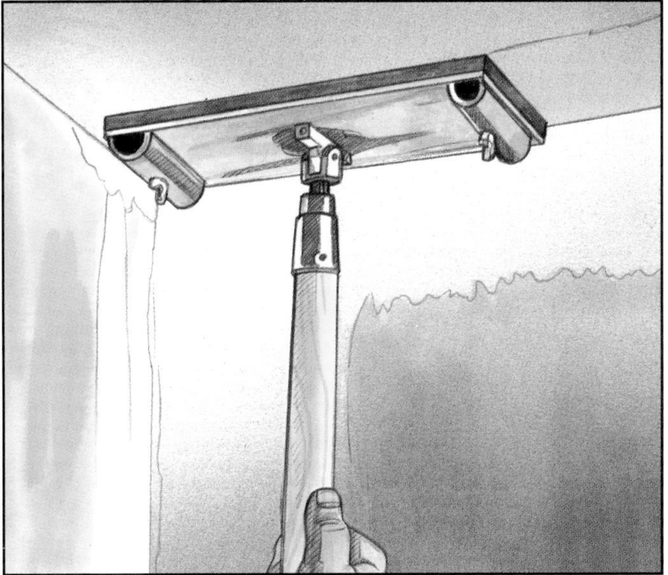

Sand joints lightly after the wallboard compound dries. Use a pole sander to reach high areas without a ladder. Be sure to wear a dust mask when dry-sanding.

Installing Paneling

Walls that are in poor condition can be covered with paneling to provide a decorative surface and "dress up" the room. Paneling can be extremely practical if used in conjunction with insulation, and is a fairly easy way to dress up an unfinished basement. There are various types of decorative paneling for walls, such as solid-wood planking and decorative sheet panels with various patterns.

Solid-wood paneling is made from planks with a tongue-and-groove edging. This provides a way to attach it to the wall and allows movement in the wood, due to humidity changes, preventing splitting. Most solid-wood paneling is made from softwoods like pine, redwood, cedar, and fir.

A wider choice of paneling is available in manufactured sheet paneling. Made with real veneers or printed paper patterns, these panels simulate wood grain, brick, stone, and other types of surfaces.

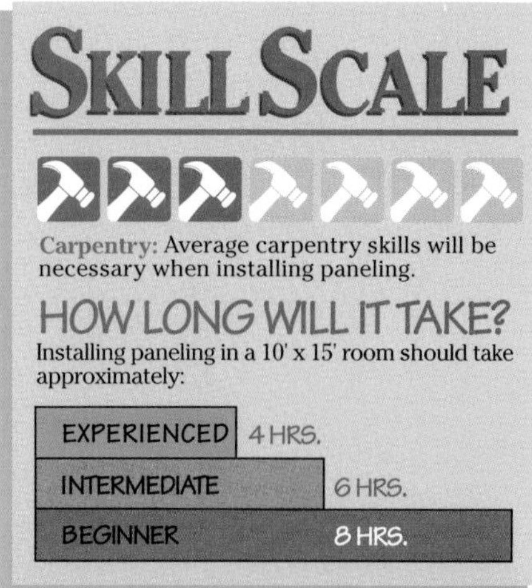

STUFF YOU'LL NEED:

- **Tools:** Hammer, pry bar, jig saw, scribing compass, circular saw, chalk line, electronic stud finder, tape measure.
- **Materials:** Paneling, paneling nails.

Decorative panels should be seasoned for a few days in the room where they will be installed. Stack them so that air can circulate on all sides and support them so they don't warp or get damaged.

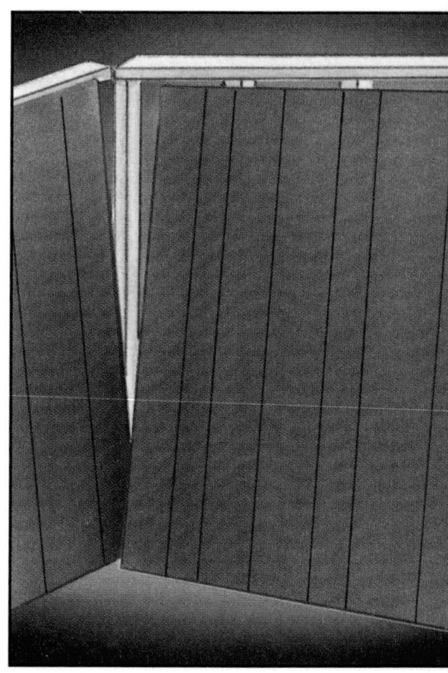

Arrange the panels in place before installation to determine color and grain pattern conditions of the planned panels. Working directly from a stack of sheets may result in undesirable pattern combinations.

CUTTING AND FITTING PANELING

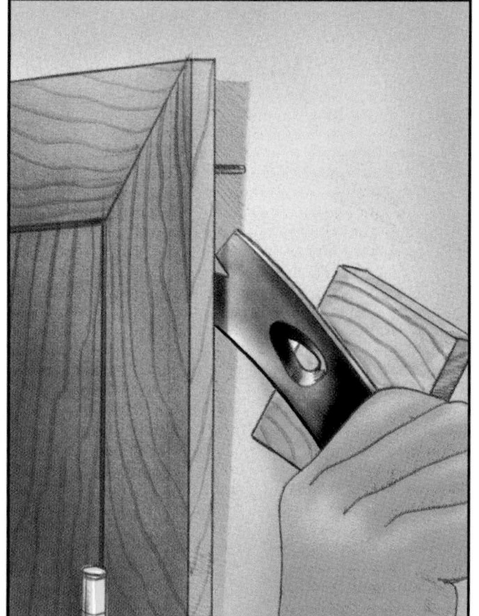

1 Remove all trim and molding from baseboards, windows, doors, and ceilings. Use a wood block under the pry bar to protect the walls from damage. If you want to replace the moldings, now's the time. You can put paneling around existing molding, but you'll have to remove the baseboard.

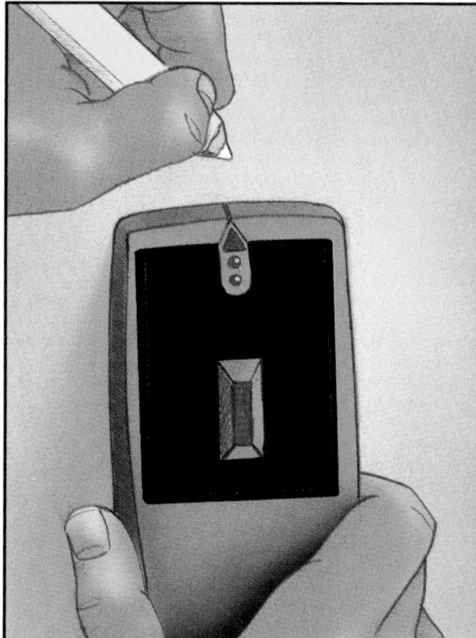

2 Use a stud finder to locate the studs. Start in corner farthest from entry point and find the stud that is closest to, but less than, 48" from corner. Find and mark the studs every 48" from the first marked stud.

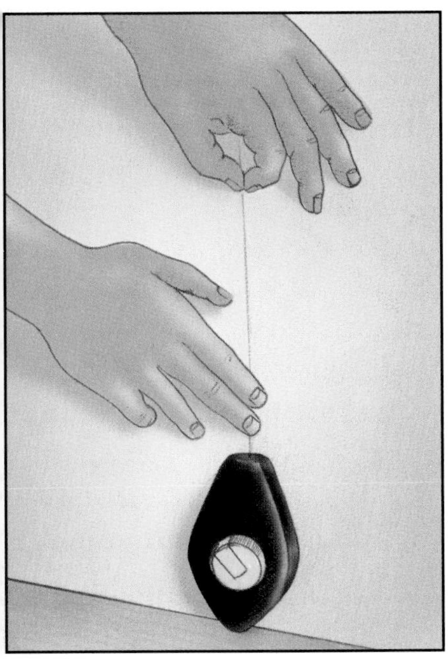

3 Snap a chalk line on the wall to mark plumb lines through the stud marks. Paneling seams should fall along these lines.

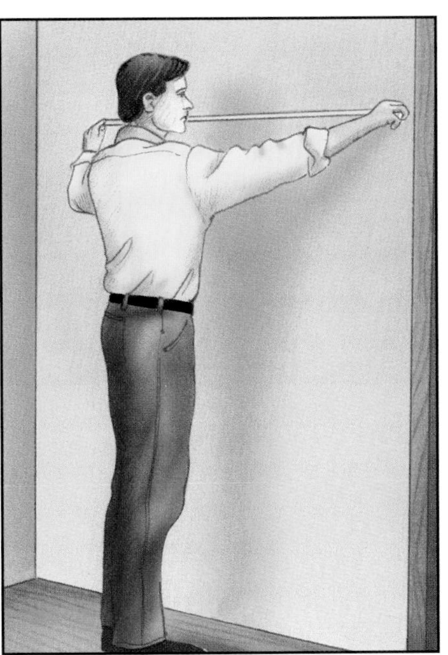

4 Measure the distance from the corner to the first plumb mark and add 1" to allow for scribing.

5 Lay the first paneling sheet face-side down to prevent chipping the decorative face with the saw blade. Use a circular saw and a clamped straightedge to cut the paneling to the desired size.

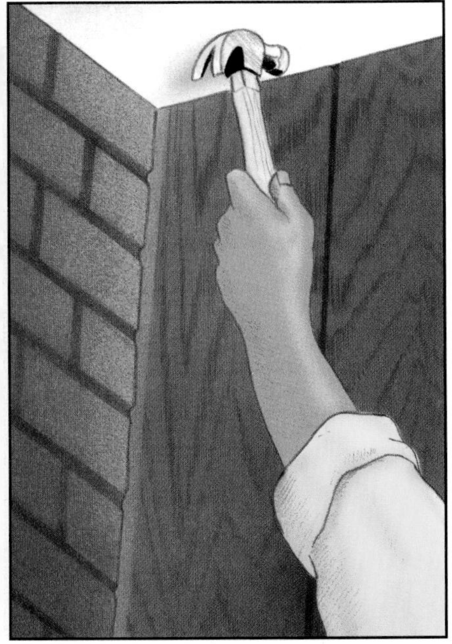

6 Position the first sheet of paneling against the wall so that the cut edge is 1" away from the corner, and the opposite finished edge is plumb. Temporarily tack the top of the paneling to the wall.

7 Spread the legs of a compass to $1^1/_4$". With the point against the wall corner and the pencil against the face of the paneling, run the compass down the full height of the wall. Corner irregularities will be scribed on face of paneling. Remove the paneling from the wall.

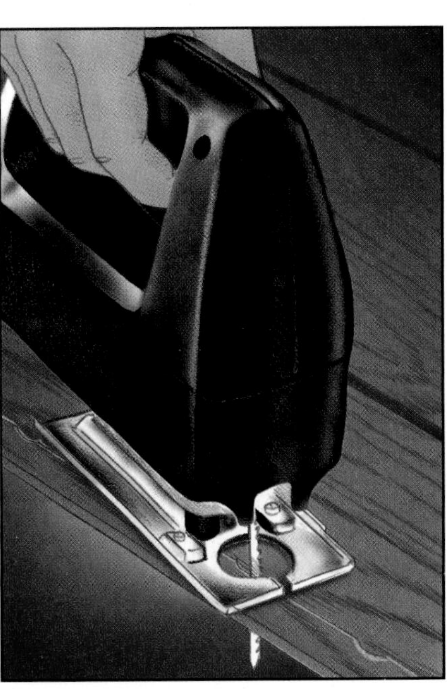

8 Lay the paneling face-side up, and cut along the scribed line with jigsaw. To prevent splintering, use a fine-tooth wood-cutting blade. The scribed edge should fit perfectly against the wall corner.

INSTALLING PANELING

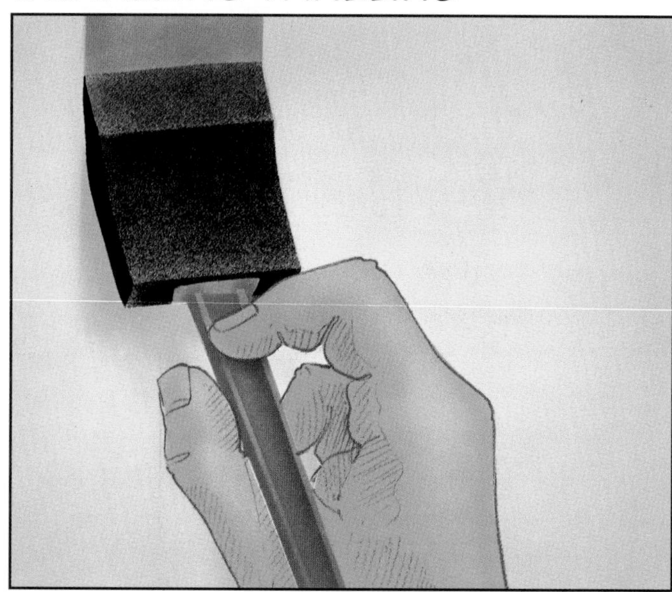

1 Apply stain to the wall along the plumb line so the wall will not show through slight gaps at the joints in the paneling. Select a stain that matches the color of the paneling edges, which may be darker than paneling surface.

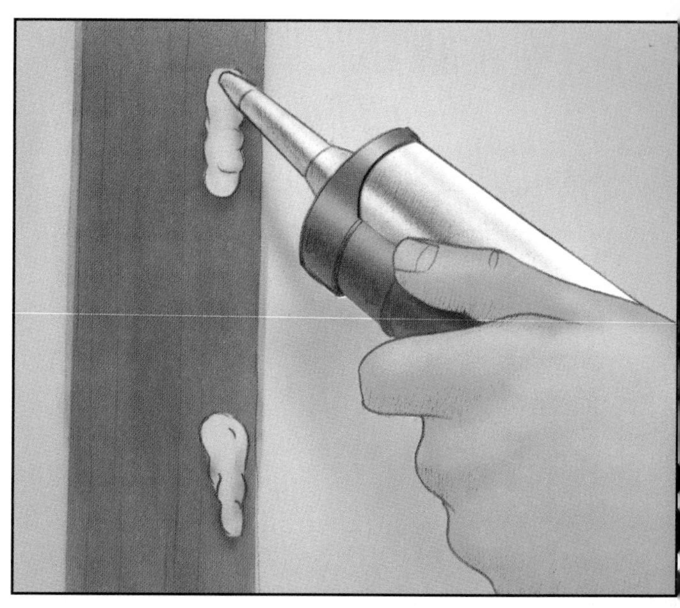

2 Use a caulk gun to apply 1"-long beads of panel adhesive to the wall at 6" intervals. Keep the beads about 1" back from the plumb lines, to prevent adhesive from seeping out through the joints. For new construction, apply adhesive directly to the wall studs.

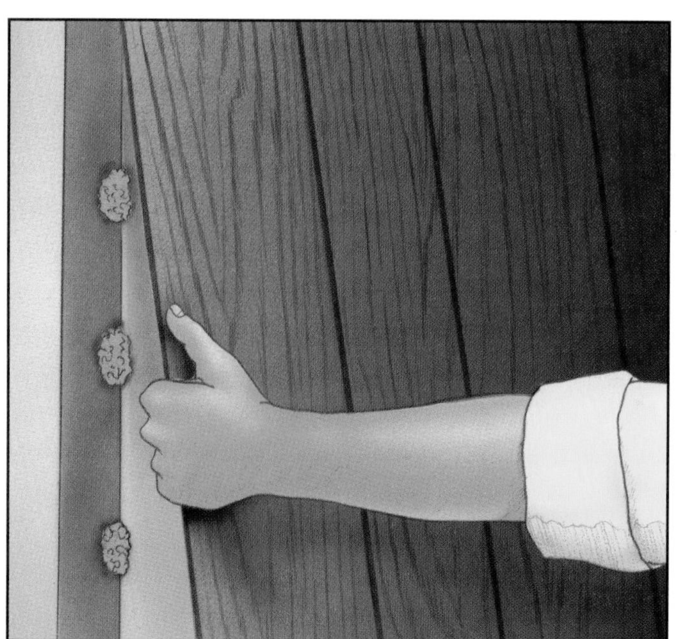

3 Attach paneling to the top of the wall, using 4d finish nails driven every 16". Press the paneling against the adhesive, then pull it away from the wall. Press the paneling back against wall when the adhesive is tacky. This usually takes about 2 minutes.

4 Hang the remaining paneling so that there is a slight space at the joints. This space allows the paneling to expand in damp weather. Use a dime as a spacing gauge.

CUTTING OPENINGS IN PANELING

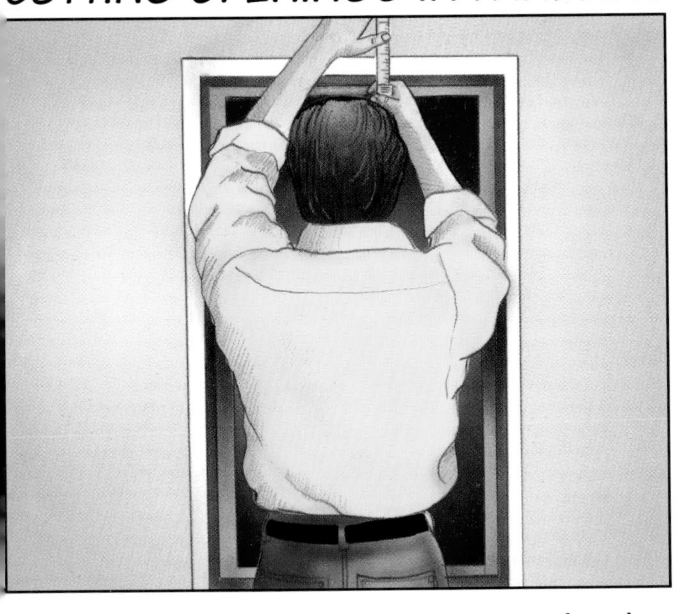

1 Measure the window and door openings, and mark the measurements of the opening outlines on the back side of the paneling.

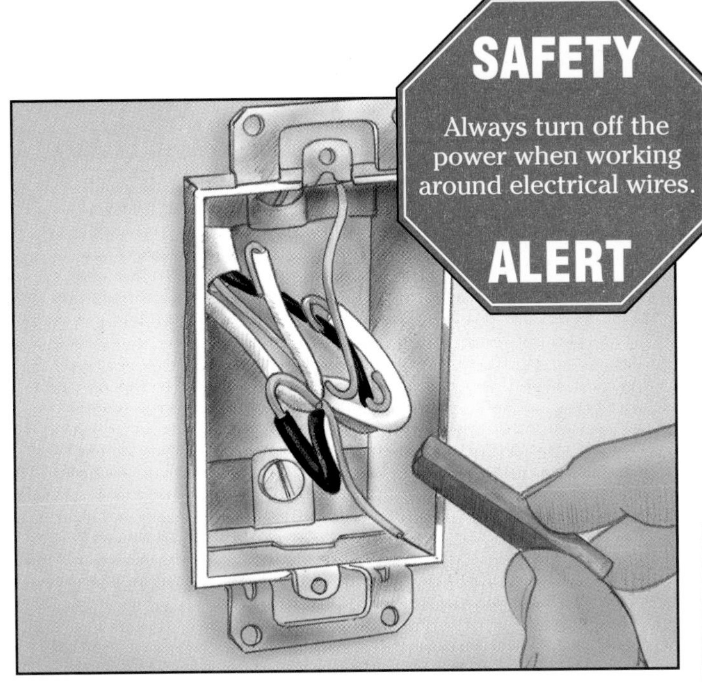

2 Coat the edges of electrical and telephone outlets and heating vents with chalk or lipstick.

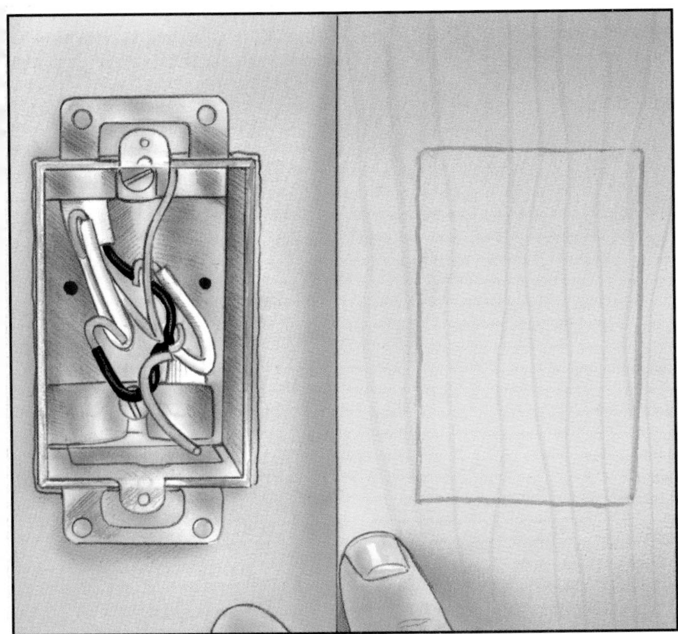

3 Press the back side of the paneling against the wall. Marks from the outlets and vents will be transferred to the paneling.

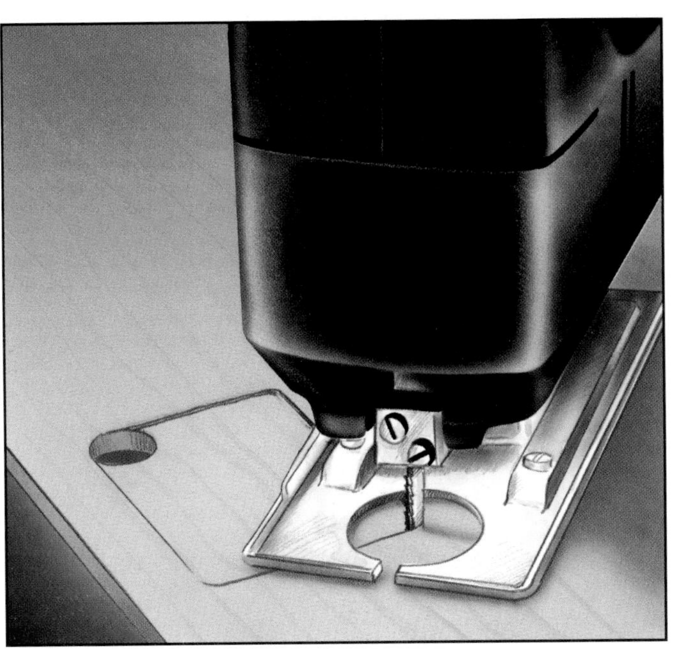

4 Lay the paneling face-side down. Drill pilot holes at one corner of each outline. Use a jigsaw and fine-tooth, wood-cutting blade to make the cutouts.

STUFF YOU'LL NEED:

- ☐ **Tools:** Chalk line, tape measure, tile nibbler, tile cutter, grout float, notched trowel.
- ☐ **Materials:** Ceramic tile, tile adhesive, grout, latex grout additive, silicone sealer.

HOMER'S HINDSIGHT

Moisture resistant wallboard, commonly referred to as greenboard, is specifically designed for use in bathrooms or laundry rooms where it may be exposed to water. Cementuous backer board is another type of wallboard that is designed to be used with ceramic tile. If I had known about these products, I could have saved a lot of time having to replace the wallboard in my basement bathroom. It's really amazing how much damage a little water can cause to regular wallboard. It was a real mess removing the rotted crumbled wallboard. I'm glad I won't have to do that again!

Installing Ceramic Tile

Ceramic tile is frequently used for bathroom walls, shower stalls, laundry room walls and sometimes kitchen walls, above the countertop backsplash and below the upper cabinets. When properly installed, ceramic tile will outlast almost any other commonly used wall material.

For most wall projects, tiles that are 6" in size are the easiest to install because they require less cutting and cover more surface area. Smaller tiles can form more intricate patterns and create striking visual accents and highlights. Of course, the smaller the tiles, the more you'll have to install.

Whatever tiles you plan to use, the walls must be clean, sound, and dry. You can't effectively tile over wallpaper or flaking and powdery paint. Make the surface as flat as possible so the tiles adhere firmly. And remember, use floor tiles for floors, and wall tiles for walls.

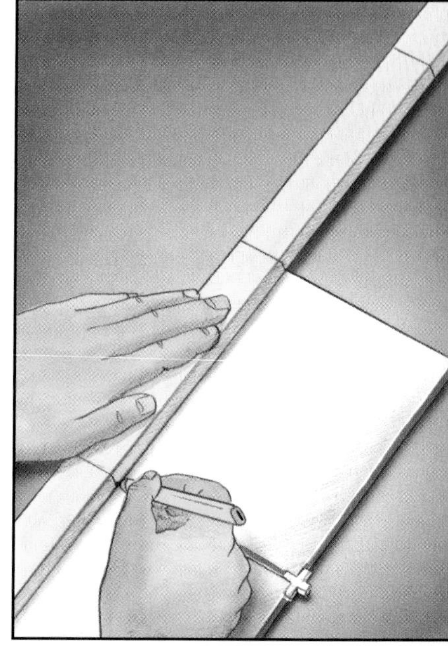

Make a tile stick to mark layout patterns on walls. Set a row of tiles and plastic spacers in the selected patterns on a flat surface. Mark a straight 1x2 to match the tile spacing. If tiles are square, you'll need one stick. For rectangular tiles, make two sticks for horizontal and vertical layouts.

MARKING A LAYOUT FOR WALL TILE

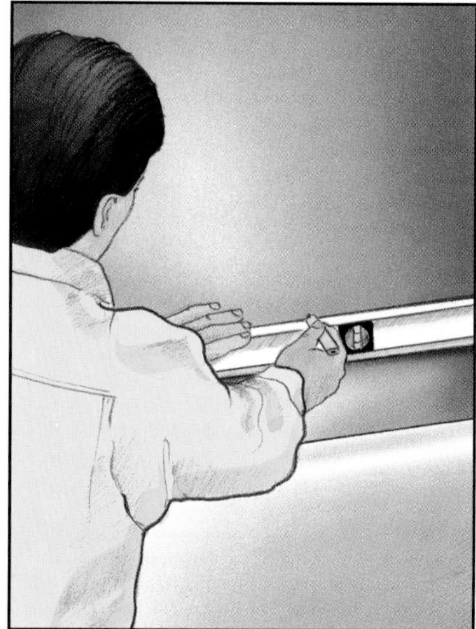

1 Mark the wall to show the planned location of wall cabinets, recessed fixtures, and ceramic wall accessories. Measure and mark a point equal to the height of one ceramic tile above the tub edge. If the edge isn't level, measure up from the lowest spot. Draw a level line at this point around the entire room.

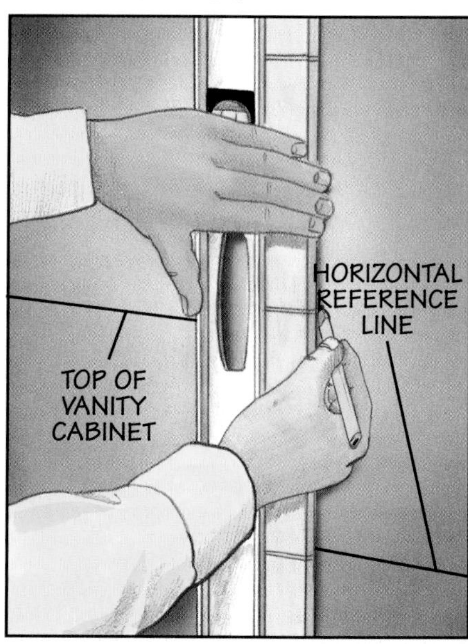

2 Use the tile stick to see how the tile pattern will run in relation to other features in the room, like countertops, window and door frames, and wall cabinets. Hold the tile stick perpendicular to the horizontal reference line, with one joint mark touching the line, and note the location of tile joints.

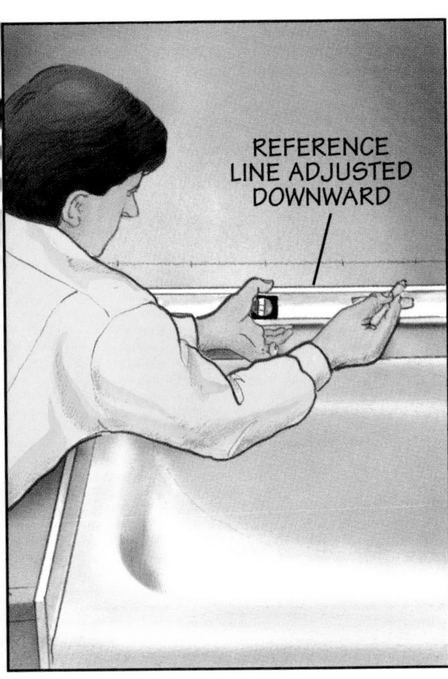

3 Adjust the horizontal reference line if the tile stick shows that tile joints will fall in undesirable spots.

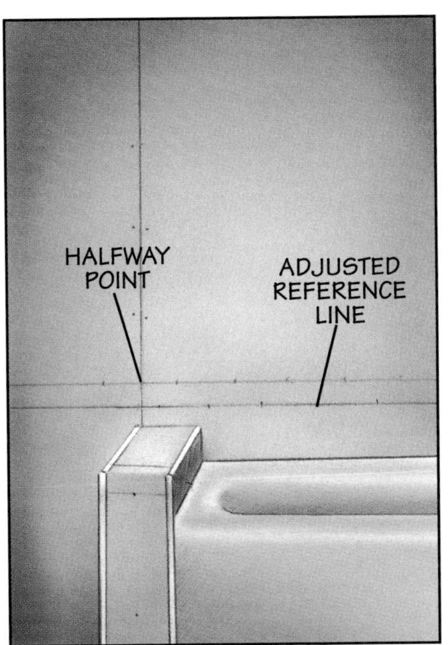

4 On each wall, measure and mark the halfway point along the horizontal reference line. Using the tile stick as a guide, mark lines in each direction from the halfway point to show where the vertical grout joints will be located. If the tile stick shows that corner tiles will be less than 1/2 of a full tile width, adjust the layout as shown in next step.

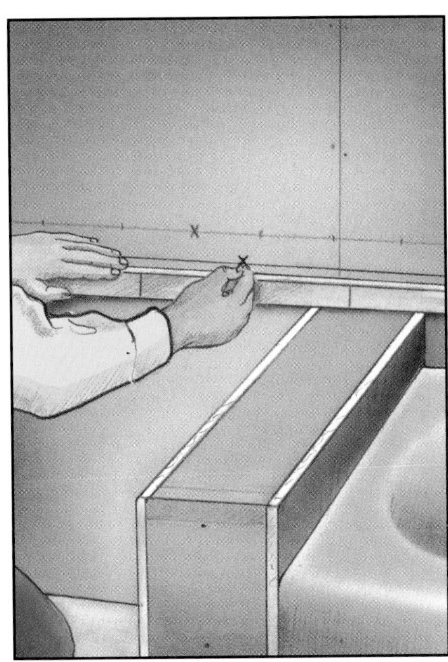

5 Adjust the layout of vertical joints by moving the halfway point 1/2 the width of a tile in either direction. Use a carpenter's level to draw a vertical reference line through this point, from the floor to the top tile row.

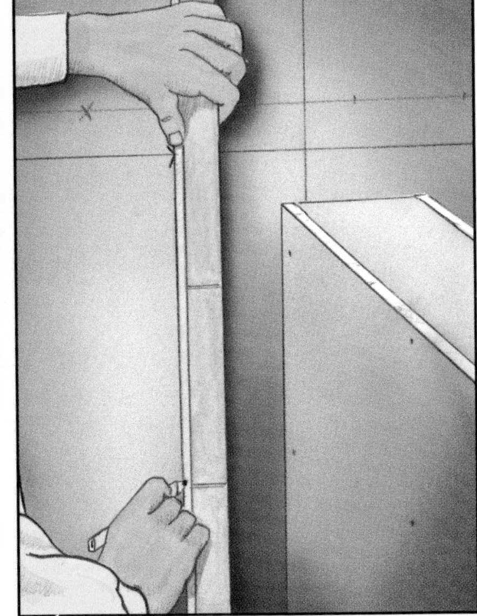

6 Use the tile stick to measure up from the floor along the vertical reference line, a distance equal to the height of one tile plus 1/8", and mark a point on the wall. Draw a level reference line through this point, across the wall.

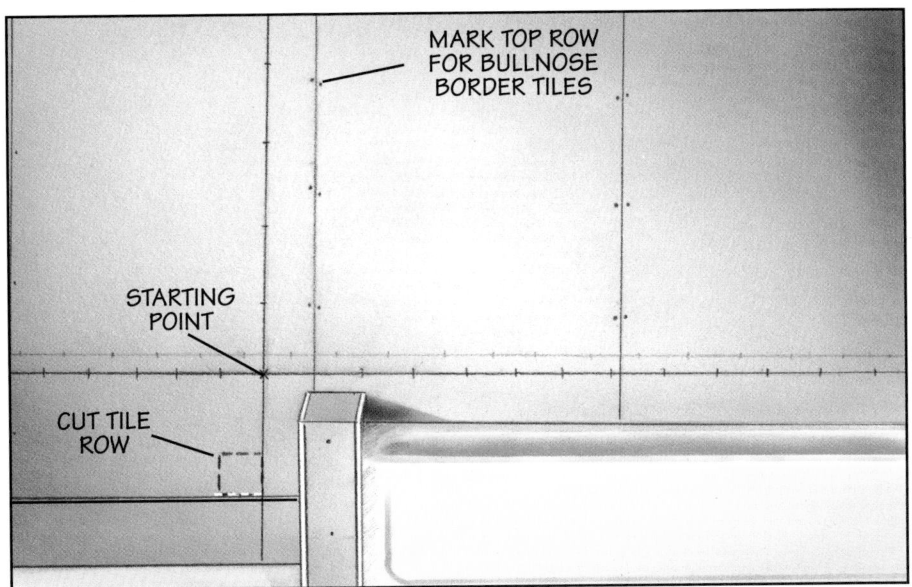

7 Mark reference lines to show where the remaining tile joints will be located, starting at the point where vertical and horizontal reference lines meet. Include any decorative border or accent tiles. If a row of cut tiles is unavoidable, position it near the floor, between the first and third rows, or at the top, near border tiles. Extend all horizontal reference lines onto adjoining walls that will be tiled, then repeat steps 4 to 7 for all other walls being tiled.

INSTALLING CERAMIC WALL TILE

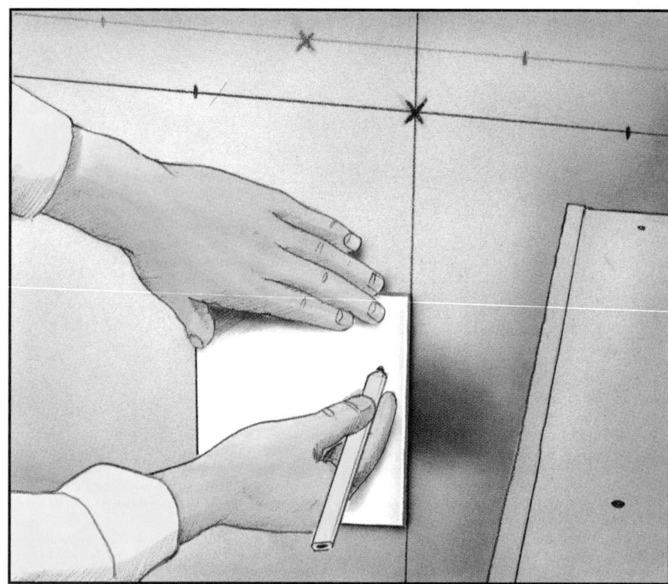

1 Mark the layout pattern, then begin installation with the second row of tiles from the floor. If the layout requires cut tiles for this row, mark and cut tiles for the entire row at one time.

2 Make straight cuts with a tile cutter. Place the tile faceup on the tile cutter with one side flush against the cutting guide. Adjust the cutting tool to the desired width, then score a groove by pulling the cutting wheel firmly across the tile. Snap the tile along the scored line, as directed by the tool manufacturer.

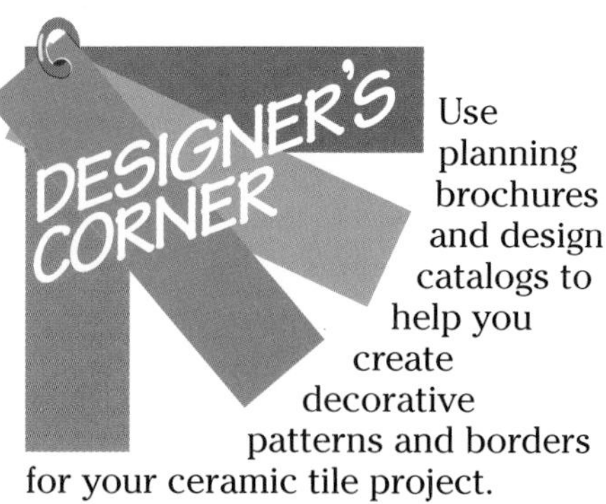

Use planning brochures and design catalogs to help you create decorative patterns and borders for your ceramic tile project. Brochures and catalogs are available free of charge from many tile manufacturers.

Most stores that sell tile have design catalogs and some even have on-staff designers to help with your tiling project. Find out what the tile will look like before you buy it. Take some samples home to see how the color looks in the room.

Because colors appear different depending on the light source, look at the tiles in daylight as well as under the lighting that exists in the room. Remember, too, that once all of the tiles are installed and you have a large area of color, the color may appear different than the small sample you originally tested.

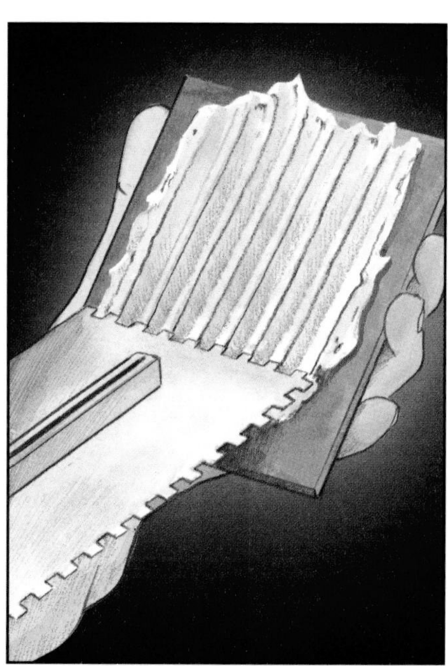

3 Mix a small batch of dry-set mortar containing a latex additive. Some mortar has additive mixed in by the manufacturer, and some mortar must have additive mixed in separately. Cover the back of the first tile with adhesive, using a notched trowel.

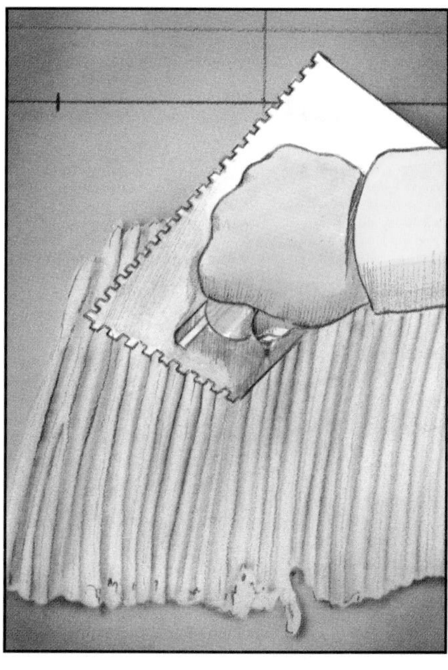

Alternate: Spread adhesive on a small section of the wall, then set the tiles into the adhesive. Dry-set adhesive sets quickly, so work fast if you choose this installation method.

4 Fasten a level support board to the wall under the first row of tiles to carry the weight of the tiles until the adhesive dries sufficiently to hold the tiles. Apply the first tile to the wall with a slight twisting motion to set the tile, aligning it exactly with the horizontal and vertical reference lines.

5 Continue setting tiles, aligning them with the reference lines. Work from the center to the sides in a pyramid pattern. Use plastic spacers inserted in the corner joints to maintain even grout lines (inset). Remove the support board and install the base row as the last row of full tiles.

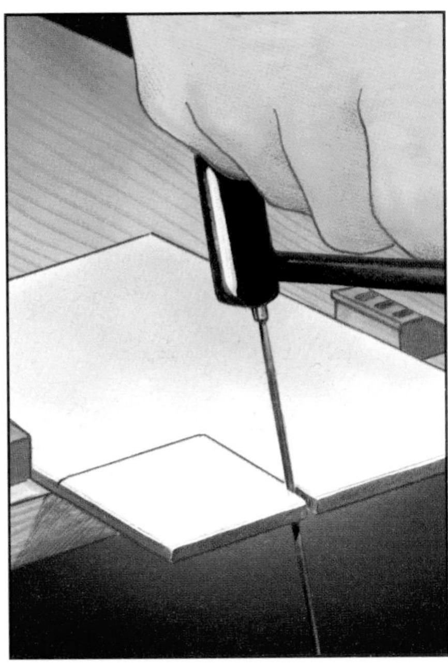

6 Make notches and curved cuts in tile by clamping the tile to a flat surface, then cutting it with a rod saw which has an abrasive blade designed for cutting tile. Cutting tiles by hand takes patience. If you have a lot of tiles to cut get them cut by the store or rent a wet saw cutter.

7 As small sections of tile are completed, set the tile by laying a scrap 2x4, wrapped with carpet or cloth, onto the tile and rapping it lightly with a mallet or hammer. This embeds the tile solidly in the adhesive and creates a flat, even surface.

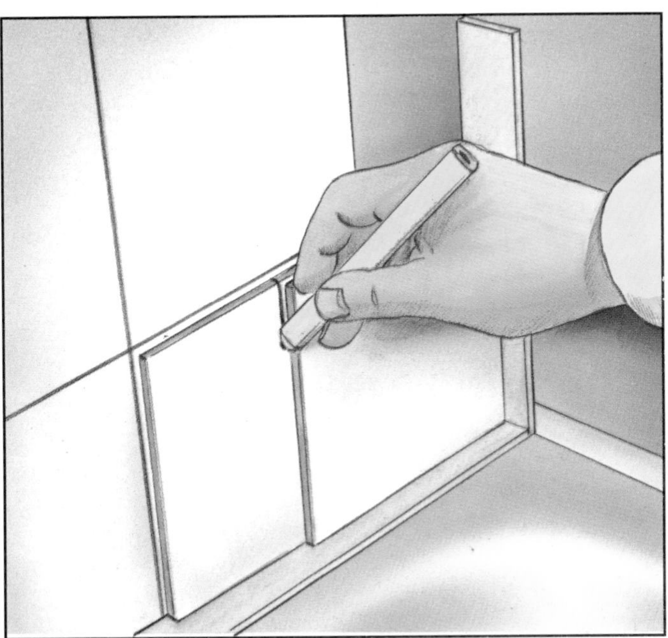

8 To mark lines for straight cuts, begin by taping the side of the tile. Position a tile directly over the last full tile installed, then place a third tile so the edge butts against spacers. Trace the edge of the top tile onto the middle tile to mark it for cutting.

9 Cut holes for plumbing stub-outs by marking the outline of the hole on the tile, then drilling around the edges of the outline, using a ceramic tile bit. Gently knock out the waste material with a hammer. For a little added expense you can buy a hole cutter to make a hole with one cut. The rough edges of the hole will be covered by protective plates (escutcheons) on the fixtures.

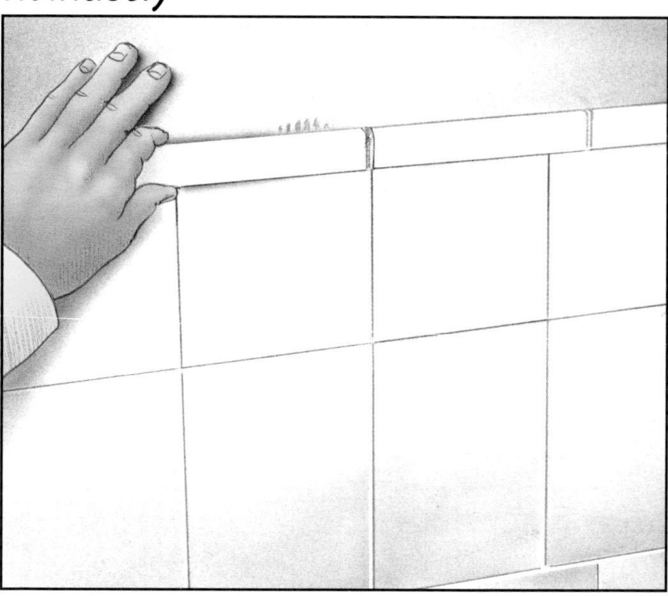

10 Install the trim tiles, such as bullnose edge tiles, at the border areas. Wipe away the excess mortar along the top edge of the tiles.

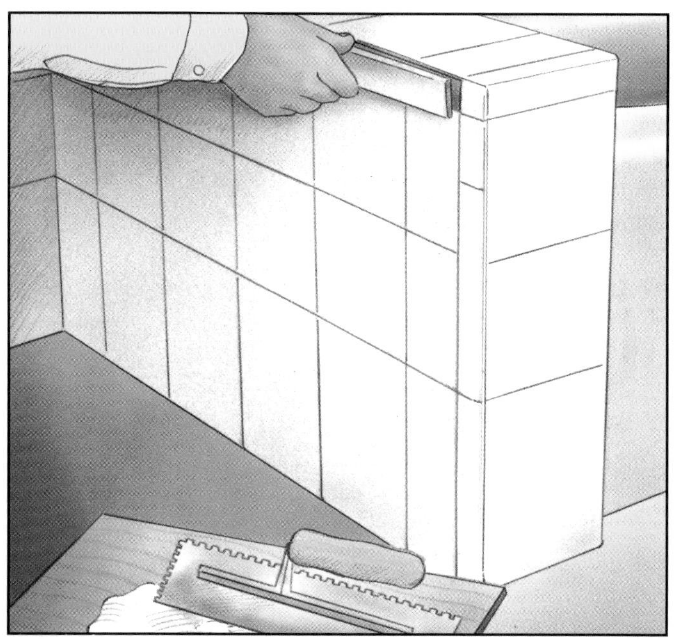

11 Use single bullnose and double bullnose tiles at the outside corners to cover the rough edges of the adjoining tiles.

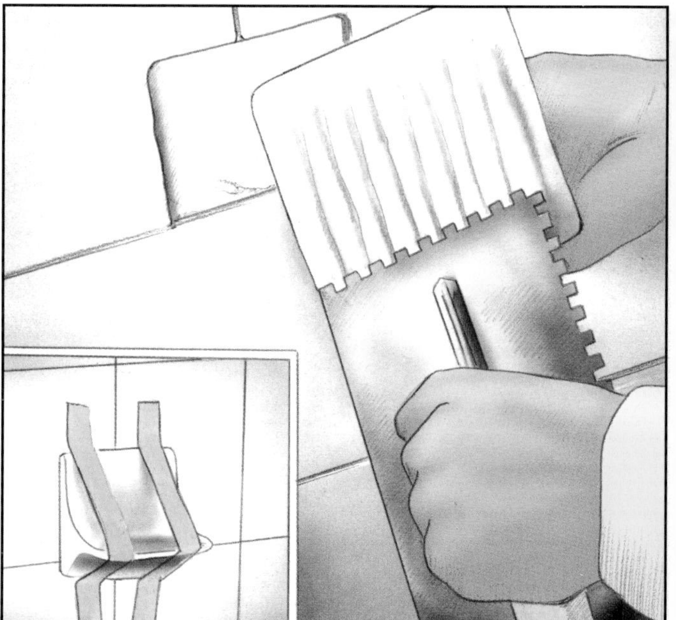

12 Install ceramic accessories by applying dry-set mortar to the back side of the accessory; then press the accessory into place. Use masking tape to hold the accessory in place until the adhesive dries.

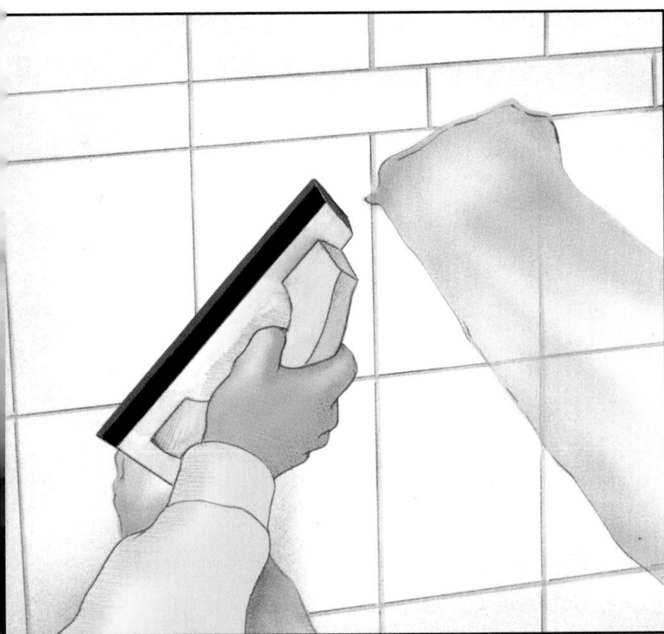

13 Let mortar dry completely according to manufacturer's recommendation, then mix a batch of grout containing the latex additive. Apply the grout with a rubber grout float, using a sweeping motion at a 45° angle to grout lines to force it deep into the joints. Do not grout the joints along the bathtub, floor, and room corners.

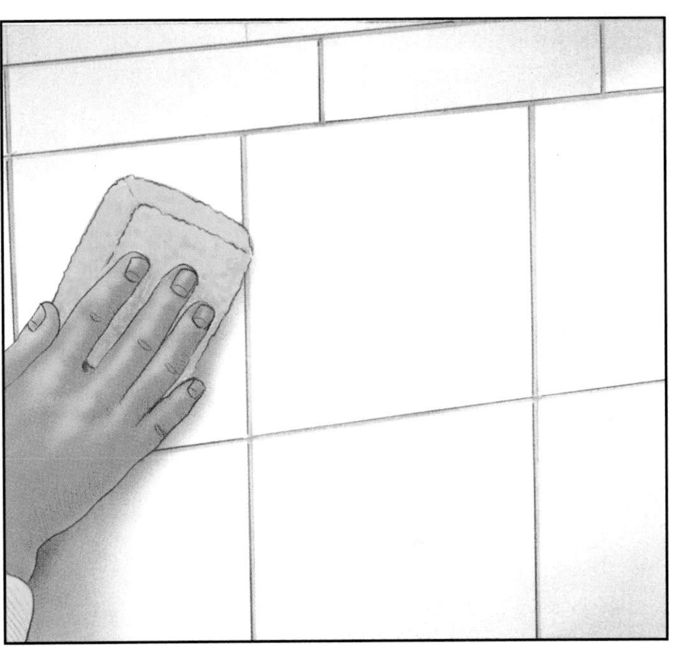

14 After recommended grout drying time, wipe away the excess grout with a damp sponge, then dress the grout lines by dragging a small dowel along all joints.

15 When the grout is completely dried, this may take up to 2 weeks to become bone dry, brush silicone sealer onto the joints with a small paint or foam brush. A grout wheel used to paint grout lines may speed up the process if you have a lot to do. Silicone sealers are helpful in preventing stains and mildew from forming on the grout.

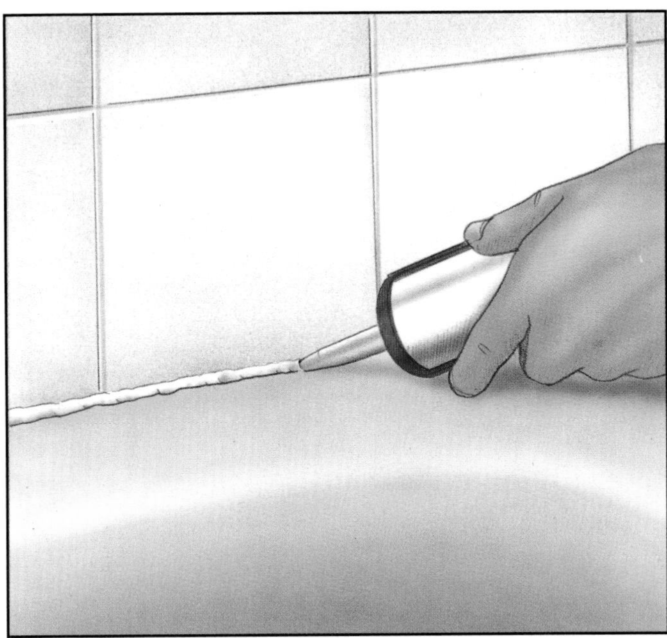

16 Seal expansion joints around the bathtub, floor, and room corners with tub & tile caulk. After the caulk dries, buff the tile with a dry, soft cloth.

FLOOR BASICS

Repairing and installing flooring can be simple and worry-free if you plan carefully, use the proper tools, and take your time. Always use the proper safety equipment and be sure to get assistance whenever possible. Certain types of flooring, such as large carpeting, will definitely be easier if you have a helper, whereas vinyl tile is quite easy to install all by yourself.

Don't be afraid to spend a little money to rent the proper tools for the job. With them, the job will be actually enjoyable, while without them, the project can turn into your worst nightmare and the quality of the finished job will be greatly disappointing. The main thing to remember is to take as much time as you need and don't panic. It's just a floor! You can always correct any mistakes you happen to make without threatening world peace!

Flooring hand tools include: hand miter box and backsaw (**A**), cold chisel (**B**), ball peen hammer (**C**), claw hammer (**D**), nail sets (**E**), pry bar (**F**), flat bar (**G**), chalk line (**H**), combination square (**I**), framing square (**J**), handsaw (**K**), screwdrivers (**L**), tape measure (**M**), wood chisels (**N**), utility knife (**O**), hand stapler (**P**), wallboard knife (**Q**), and putty knife (**R**).

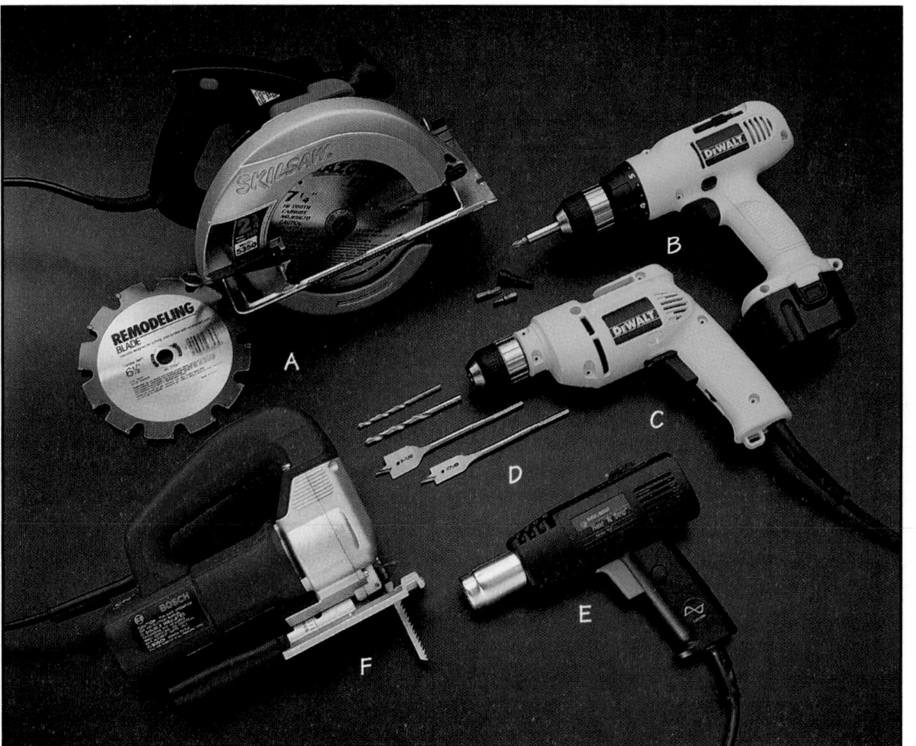

Power tools for flooring projects include: circular saw w/remodeling blade (**A**), cordless driver w/bits (**B**), electric drill (**C**), drill bits (**D**), heat gun (**E**), and jigsaw (**F**).

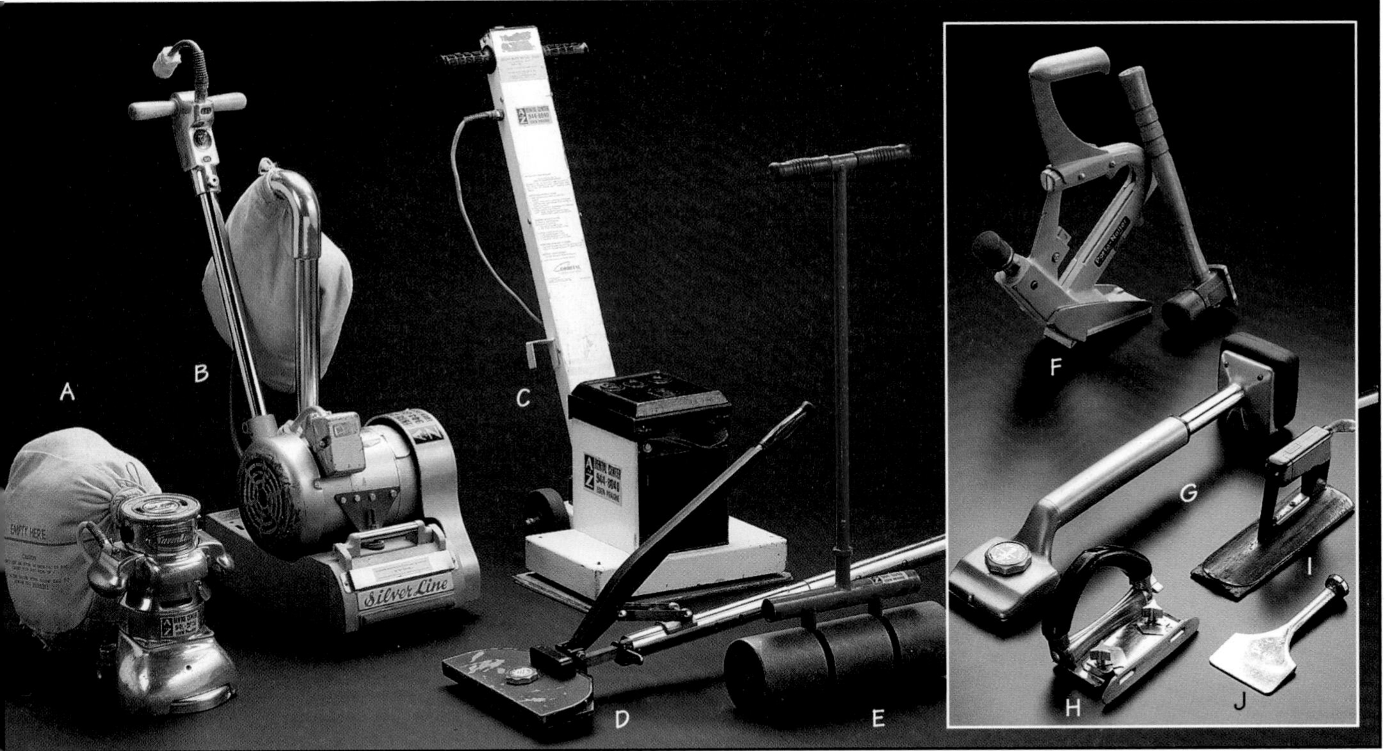

Special flooring tools that can be rented include: **(main photo)** edge sander (**A**), drum sander (**B**), orbital floor sander (**C**), carpet stretcher (**D**), floor roller (**E**), **(inset photo)** special floor nailer (**F**), knee kicker (**G**), wall trimmer (**H**), carpet seamer (**I**), and stair tool (**J**).

SPECIALTY FLOORING TOOLS

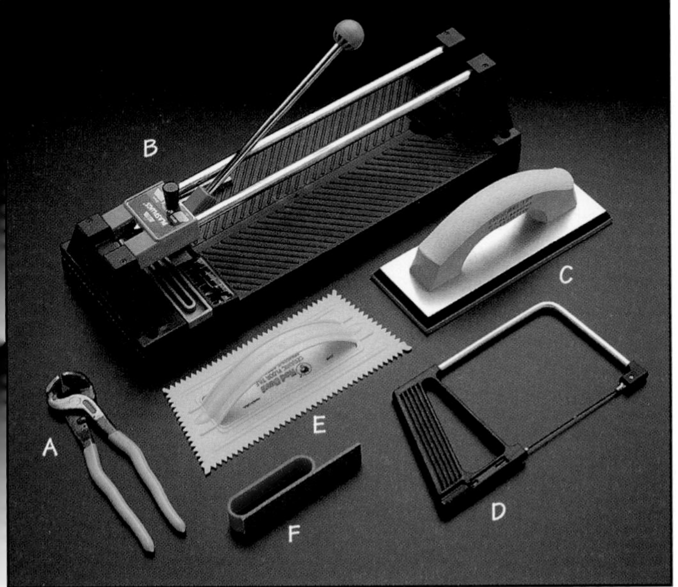

Special ceramic tools include: tile nipper (**A**), tile cutter (**B**), grout float (**C**), tile saw (**D**), notched trowel (**E**), and tile sander (**F**).

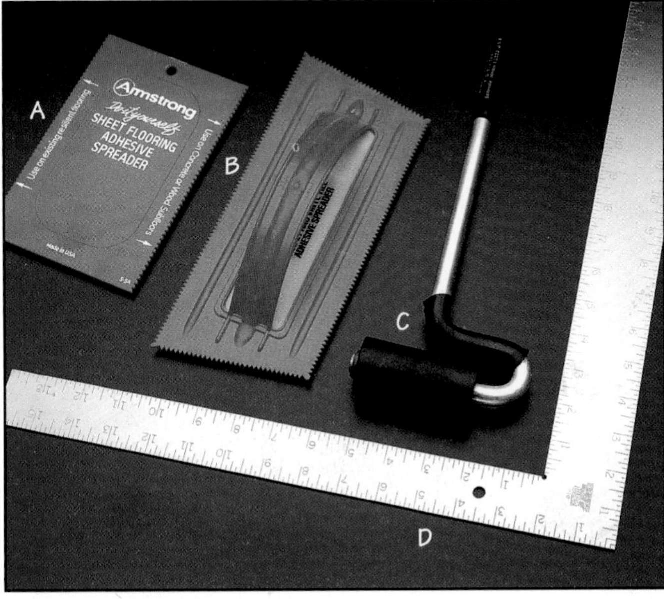

Special vinyl flooring tools include: notched spreader (**A**), notched trowel (**B**), J-roller (**C**), straightedge or framing square (**D**).

Flooring Materials

Flooring materials are available in a wide variety of colors, styles, sizes, and types, with an even broader range of cost differences. Within each type of material, whether it be ceramic floor tile, hardwood strips, vinyl tiles, carpeting, or sheet vinyl, there are varying grades and associated per unit costs which are dependent on the specific quality of construction for each type.

Do your homework before you finally purchase your flooring. The real test of the cost effectiveness of the flooring comes when the flooring is installed and actually in use day after day. Inferior-quality flooring materials will become evident after a fairly short period of constant use; then you'll just have to start the process all over again!

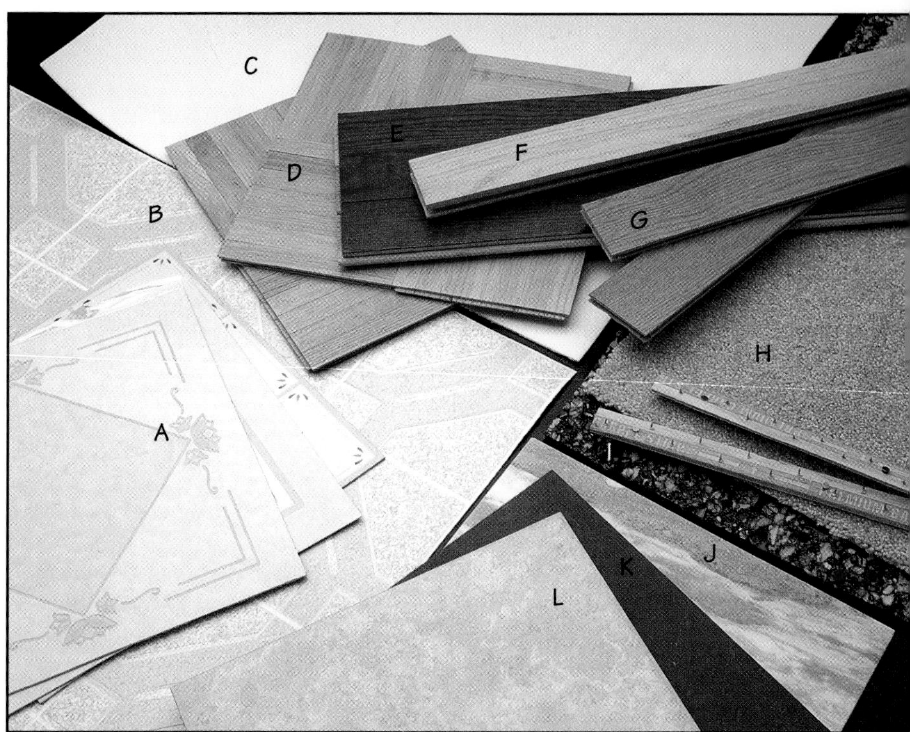

Common flooring materials include: adhesive-backed vinyl floor tiles (**A**), sheet vinyl (**B**), foam underlayment (**C**), parquet wood floor tiles (**D**), prefinished hardwood floor planks (**E**), unfinished hardwood flooring strips (**F**), prefinished hardwood flooring strips (**G**), carpeting (**H**), tackless strips and carpet pad (**I**), ceramic tile (**J**), slate tile (**K**), and marble tile (**L**).

SELECTING THE RIGHT MATERIALS

Material	Ceramic Tile	Carpeting	Vinyl Tiles	Sheet Vinyl	Parquet Tiles	Hardwood
Installation	Easy to handle and install	Somewhat difficult to handle and install	Easy to handle and install	Somewhat difficult to install	Relatively easy to handle and install	Relatively easy to handle and install
Durability	Very durable	Durability depends on grade	Fairly durable	Fairly durable	Fairly durable	Fairly durable
Maintenance	Relatively easy to maintain	More difficult to maintain	Fairly easy to maintain	Easy to maintain	Easy to maintain	Easy to maintain
Water Resistance	Water-resistant			Water-resistant		
Cost	Moderate to highly priced	Moderate to highly priced	Low to moderately priced	Low to moderately priced	Moderate to highly priced	Moderate to highly priced

Measuring Rooms for Flooring

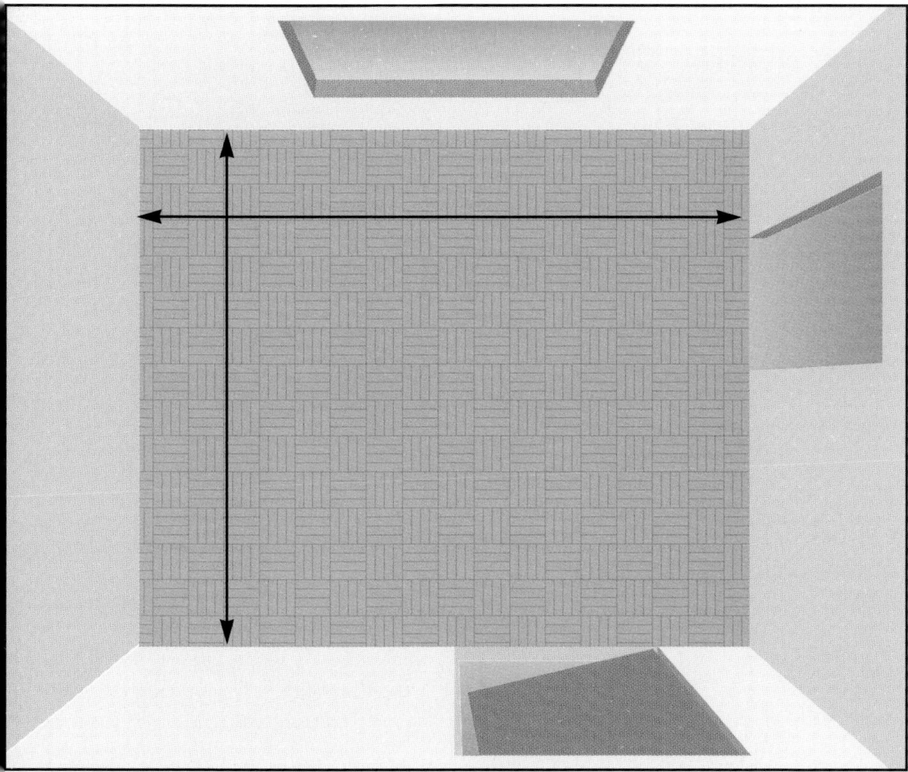

Rooms with no built-in fixtures make it relatively easy to calculate square footage and flooring material requirements. Simply take the width multiplied by the length. For example, a 10'-wide-by-15'-long room will need 150 square feet of flooring material. Add 10% for waste to ensure you have enough material for the job. Some stores will take back unused material.

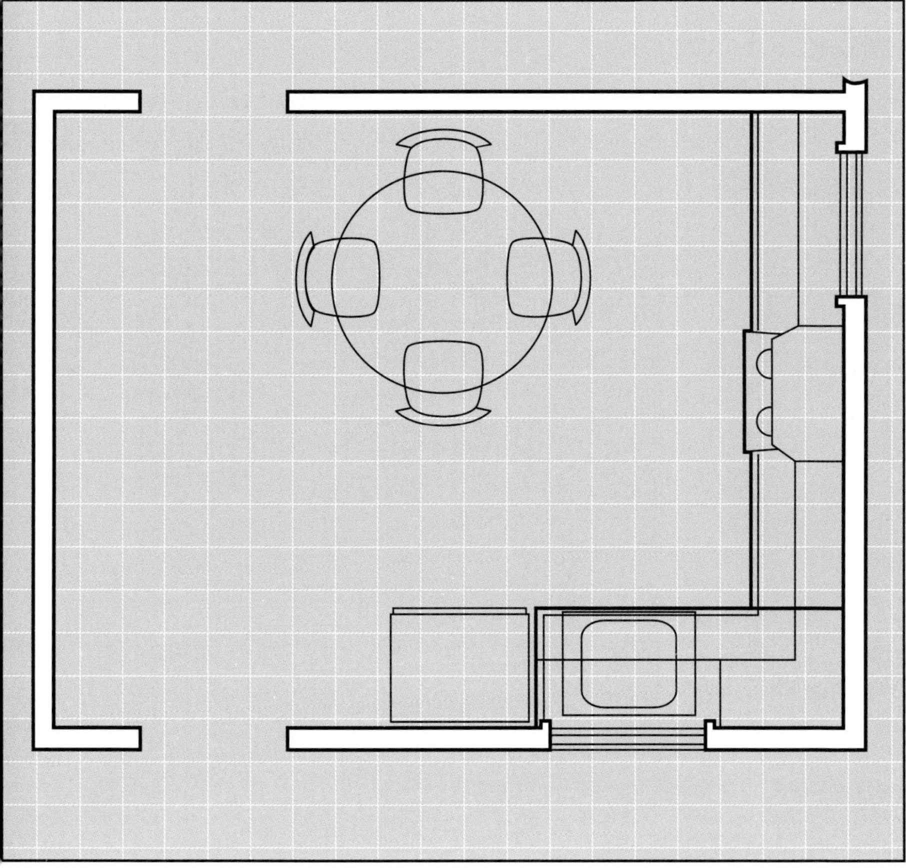

Rooms with built-in fixtures are measured by taking the overall dimensions first. Measure the longest dimension of the room and the widest dimension, then multiply them together to get the square footage. Then measure the length of each permanent fixture at its base and multiply it by its width. Subtract this amount from the basic square footage of the room. Now measure the square footage of each closet, bay, and protrusion where the flooring will be installed in the room and add it to the room's overall square footage. This should give the total square footage of material needed for the room.

The first thing to do before you begin your flooring project is to measure and estimate how much material the project will require. Use these measurements to make a dimensioned drawing of the room. This will be an indispensable tool throughout the planning phase of your project.

Use the drawing as an accurate record of the size and shape of the room. Include closet and door openings and indicate the exact placement of fixed elements, such as built-in cabinets, hearths, chimneys, pipes, and floor furnace registers, plus add 10% for waste. This drawing should serve as a template in planning and layout, to allow you to estimate how much the material will cost and help you to get the most coverage for your investment dollar.

Rooms come in an infinite variety of sizes and shapes. Some consist of four straight walls, while others have lots of nooks and jogs from built-in cabinets and closets. All surface area irregularities must be taken into consideration when planning for flooring material.

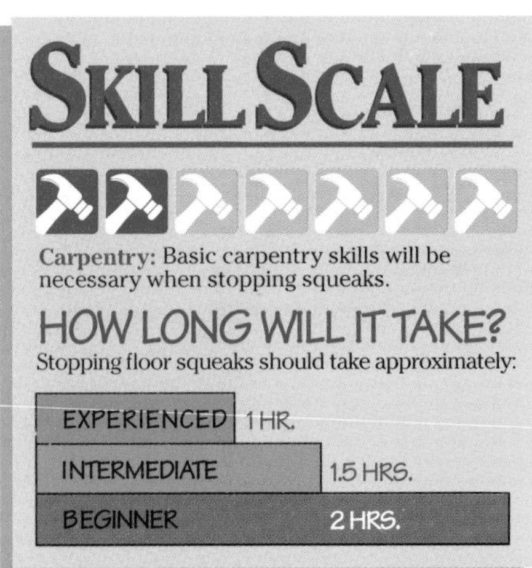

Stopping Squeaks

Floors and stairs squeak when wooden floorboards or structural beams rub against each other. The bridging between the joists can squeak when the floor above flexes under traffic. Floorboards may squeak if they have not been properly nailed to the subfloor. Water pipes or air ducts may also rub against floor joists.

When possible, fix squeaks from underneath the floor or staircase. If the bottom of the floor or staircase is covered by a finished ceiling, work on squeaks from the top side. With hardwood floors, drive finish nails into the seams between planks to silence squeaking. Check pipe hangers, heating ducts, and bridging for rubbing problems. Loosen tight pipe hangers and separate wooden bridging members to eliminate noise problems. Carpeted floors can sometimes be fixed from above if access below is restricted.

STUFF YOU'LL NEED:

- ☐ **Tools:** Hammer, screwdriver.
- ☐ **Materials:** Wood shims, nails, wood screws.

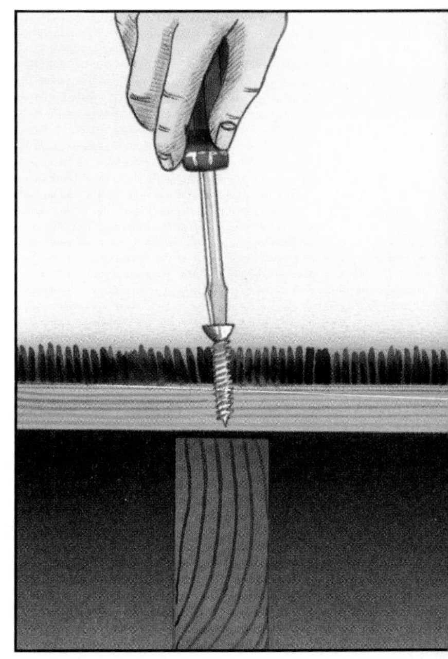

Squeaky floors covered with longer piled carpet can be silenced by driving a wallboard screw through the carpet and pad, into the floor joist. Countersink the screw head in the subfloor. This will release any trapped pad under the screw head and allow the carpet to lie flat.

SHIMMING THE SUBFLOOR

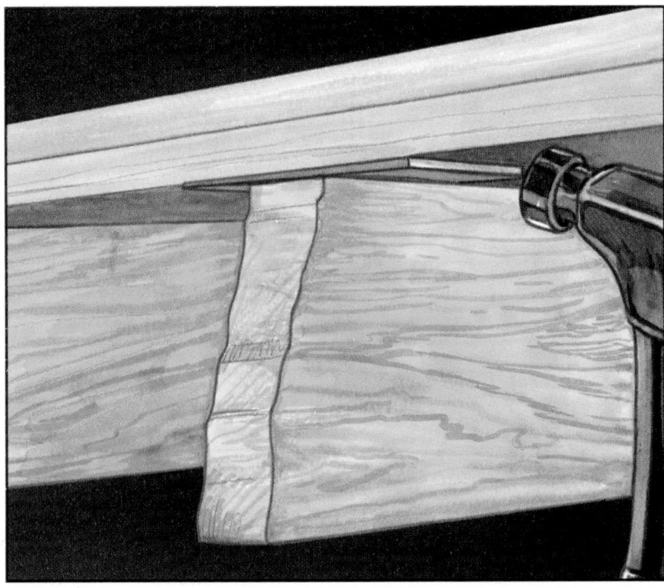

If floor joists are not tight against the subfloor in the area that is squeaking, shimming may solve the problem. Wedge shims between the joist and subfloor and tap them into place. Do not pound the shims into place because this will lift the floor and cause more squeaking.

CLEATING THE SUBFLOOR

Where several boards in the subfloor above a joist are moving, a cleat to hold them is more effective than shimming the boards individually. A piece of 1x4, wedged against the subfloor and nailed to the joist and the flooring will keep the subfloor from moving.

REINFORCING JOISTS

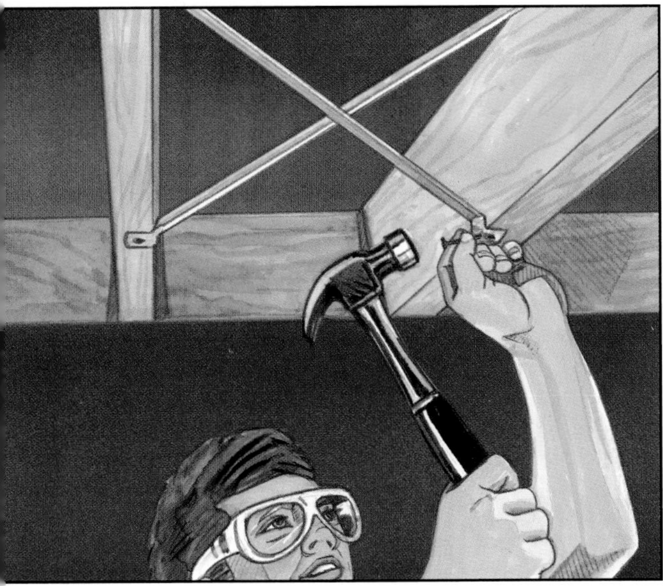

Squeaking over a large area may indicate that the joists beneath the floor are shifting slightly and giving inadequate support to the subfloor. Steel bridging, attached between joists, holds the joists from moving side to side and stabilizes the subfloor.

SCREWS FROM BELOW

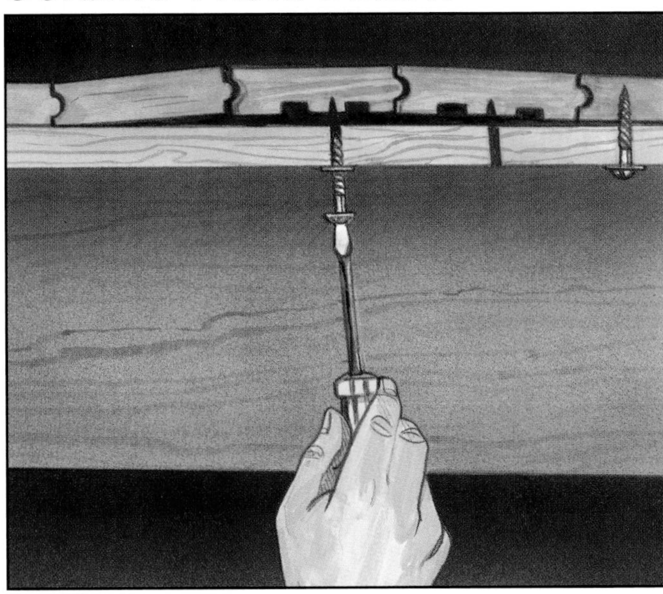

Drill a pilot hole through the subfloor, then a smaller pilot hole into the finished floor. Have someone stand on the raised boards while you pull the loose boards down by tightening with a wood screw.

SURFACE NAILING

Nail down from the top with 8d finish nails when you can't get access to the floor from below. Locate the floor joists and nail directly into them for a more permanent fastening job that won't work loose.

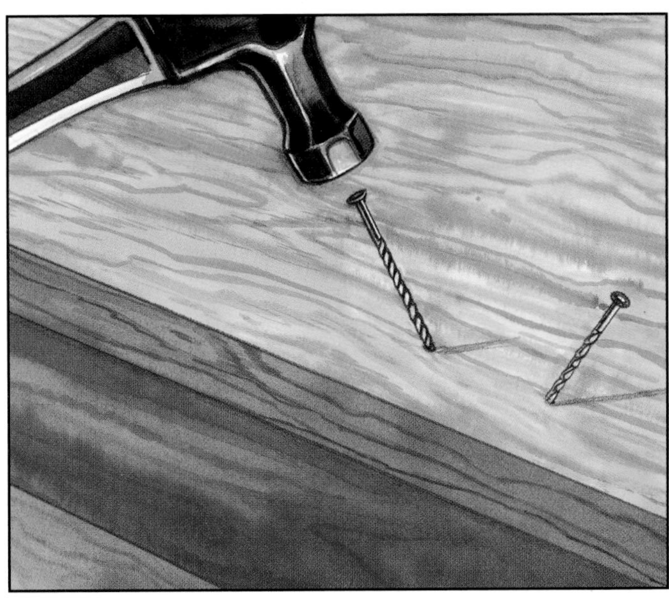

Anchor stair treads to risers by driving flooring nails at opposing angles to prevent loosening. With hardwood treads, drill pilot holes for the finish nails, drive the nails into the risers, and use a nail set to recess the nails. Then use wood putty to fill the nail holes.

Removing Existing Flooring

Old flooring can be removed if the material has been badly damaged or if it is not permanently bonded to the subfloor. Old resilient floor coverings that are embossed or cushioned should be removed or covered with a new layer of plywood underlayment before installing the new flooring material.

Ceramic floor tile that is damaged or loose must be completely removed. It is easiest to break the tiles with a hammer and then pry up the pieces with a cold chisel and hammer. If the ceramic tile was set in mortar, chip the tile away using a masonry hammer and chisel. Then cut the old subfloor into small sections with a circular saw (this will probably ruin the blade) and remove the sections with a pry bar.

Some products are available that provide a level surface to the existing flooring, if you really don't have the energy to remove the entire area of existing flooring. If the condition of the existing floor is such that you can put a new layer of flooring on top of it, you can use an embossing leveler over the old flooring to provide a smooth level surface that can accept the new flooring. If the surface of the existing flooring is too badly damaged, you will more than likely have to install new underlayment over the entire area. Sometimes, it is easier to install new underlayment than it is to remove the existing flooring. Keep in mind that more layers of flooring and underlayment on a floor will increase the height of the floor. Consequently, you'll have to undercut door jambs and door stops to make them fit properly. Also, the kickboard on the cabinets will be shorter if the flooring and underlayment is installed around the cabinets. Be sure to examine the alternatives and their ramifications before proceeding with your flooring project.

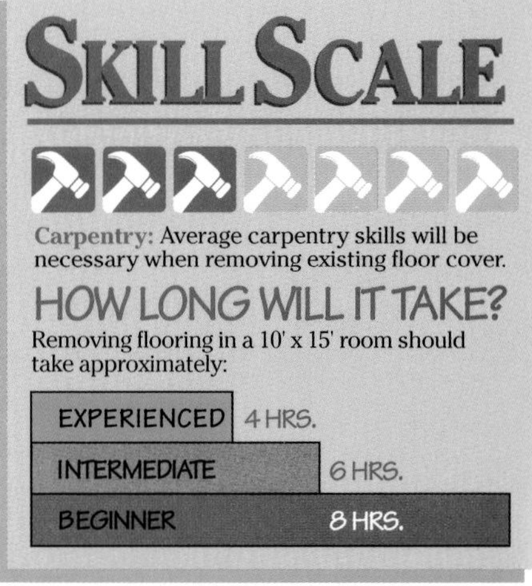

STUFF YOU'LL NEED:

- ☐ **Tools:** Hammer, pry bar, drill, wood chisel, heat gun, wallboard knife, floor scraper, rolling pin, circular saw, hand saw.

THRESHOLDS

Remove thresholds by prying them up from the floor with a metal pry bar. If the floor jambs were undercut to house the threshold, saw the threshold into two pieces and remove each piece separately.

DOOR CASINGS

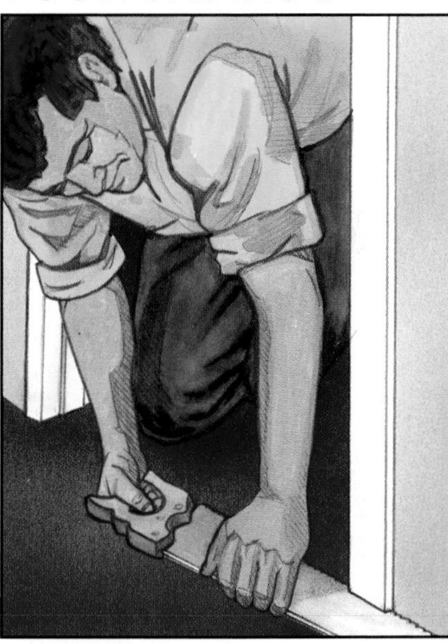

Lay a piece of new flooring next to the casing, and mark the thickness on the casing. Saw away the casing using a fine-tooth handsaw.

VINYL COVE BASE

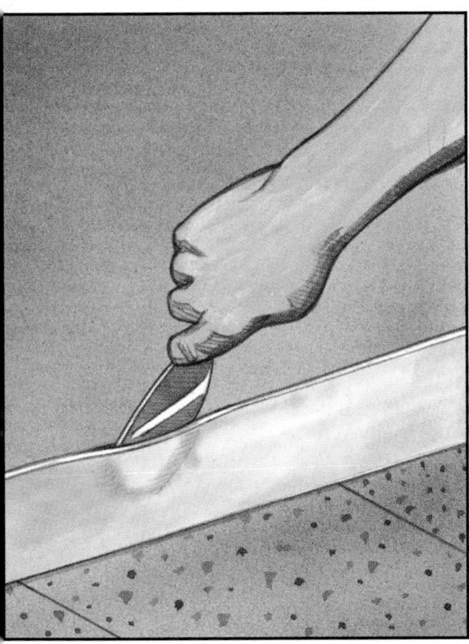

Loosen cove base from the wall with a wide-blade putty knife, and strip it away. Scrape the wall with the putty knife to remove any remaining adhesive.

CERAMIC TILE BASE

Pop each tile loose from the wall using a metal pry bar. If you are concerned about scratching or damaging your wall, place a scrap piece of wood behind the pry bar. Scrape the wall free of any remaining grout or adhesive.

AROUND CABINETS

Remove vinyl flooring around cabinets by cutting with a sharp utility knife along the base of the cabinets. If you have ceramic or hardwood flooring that is underneath the cabinets, you will probably have to remove the cabinets from the wall in order to pry up the flooring.

REMOVING CARPET

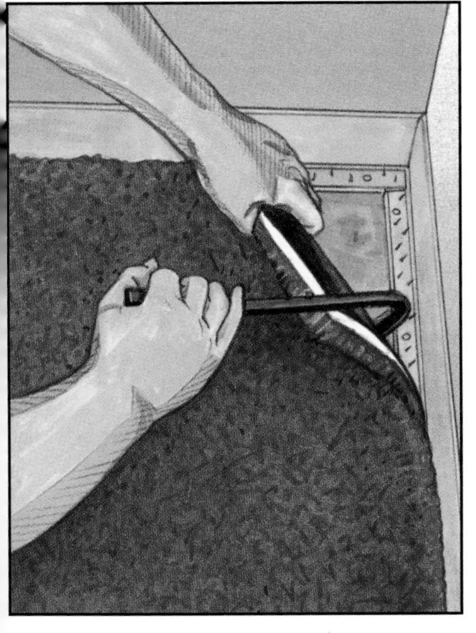

1 To remove carpet installed on a tackless strip, remove all metal edgings and cut the carpet into manageable strips with a utility knife. Pry up on the carpet corner, and pull it free from the strip along both walls. Repeat the process until the entire carpet is released.

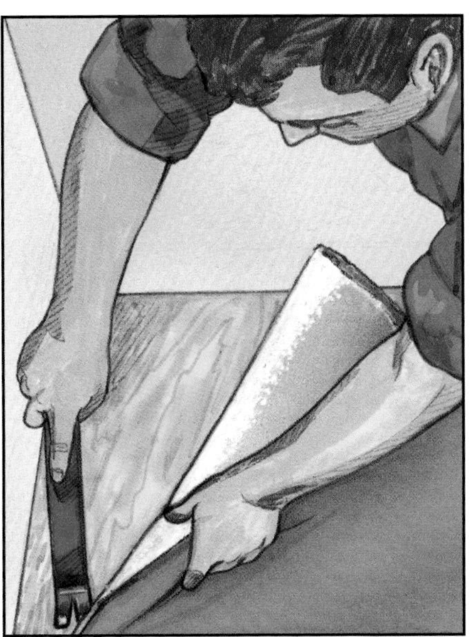

2 To remove carpet installed with carpet tacks, simply slide a flat pry bar under one edge of the carpet and pry up several tacks. Proceed until all tacks are removed.

3 If you want to keep the carpet in one piece, release one corner and work your way along the carpet section. Once it has been released, roll the piece up and haul it away.

REMOVING CERAMIC TILE

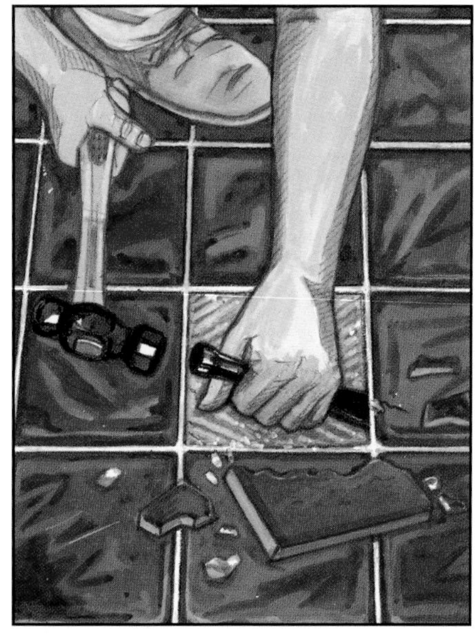

1 Chip out the grout along the grout lines. Use a hammer and cold chisel to tap the pieces free. Use safety glasses when removing ceramic tile. And remember that in some cases the only option in removing ceramic tile is to use heavy equipment such as a jackhammer.

For ceramic tile set in adhesive, chip away the tile using a masonry hammer and cold chisel. Use a long-handled floor scraper to scrape away tile fragments and any old adhesive residue. A floor sander may be used to create a smooth finish on the subfloor.

For ceramic tile set in mortar, chip away tile using a masonry hammer and chisel. Cut the old subfloor into small sections using a circular saw with an old carbide blade. Pry up the sections with a pry bar. If the old tile was laid on underlayment, cut through the underlayment and mortar, but not the subfloor.

REMOVING WOOD FLOORING

1 Before prying up plank flooring, bore out any screw plugs and remove the screws used for additional fastening.

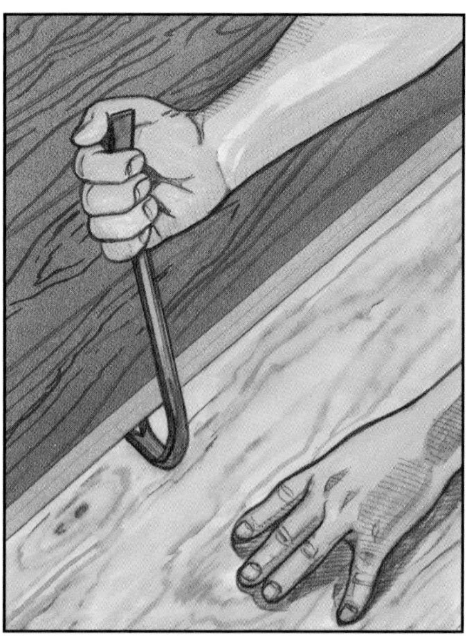

2 Insert a pry bar under the first floorboard and force it up. If there is not enough room for the pry bar, cut out a section of the first board with a circular saw. Remove the cut section, then insert the pry bar into the opening and pry up the rest of the board.

3 Proceed across the floor, prying up one board at a time. Work down the length of each board, placing the bar directly under the blind-nailing positions. If the wood flooring has been glued down, use a chisel to cut through to the bottom of each piece, and tap it loose with a hammer.

HOMER'S HINDSIGHT

Asbestos, which can cause cancer, can be found in some older vinyl flooring materials. When airborne, asbestos isn't a particle at all, it's actually a fiber. Enlarged under a microscope, asbestos fibers resemble tiny swords. The shape of these asbestos fibers allows them entry into deep reaches of the lungs, where they get trapped and enveloped in the lungs. Scar tissue develops around the fiber causing irreversible damage which can lead to cancer.

Now that you're aware of what can happen when you're exposed to asbestos, stay as far away from it as possible! if you have older vinyl flooring material that you are planning to remove, check with your state department of environmental affairs or your local health department. They can tell you how to find a certified professional to test the flooring material and eventually remove and dispose of it, if necessary.

Some states, however, let you legally perform certain asbestos-containing material (ACM) projects yourself. However, if you are allowed to do this, it is not recommended unless you have the proper safety clothing and equipment, and are instructed in the proper usage and cautions. If you just want to do your own testing and not removal, contact your local authority, get protective clothing and be sure to obtain a quality industrial respirator. Test fit the respirator before you use it. The fine asbestos dust can easily get past the edges of an ill-fitted respirator.

WORK SMARTER

You have several options when removing old flooring. Analyze the condition of your existing flooring and determine what course of action should be taken. If the flooring is mildly worn or damaged use an embossing leveler to smooth out the flooring surface to provide a stable base for the new flooring material. Remove the existing flooring if it is too badly damaged to resurface with embosser and is relatively easy to remove. If the surface is too rough for embosser and too difficult to remove, cover the existing flooring material with a new layer of underlayment.

UNDERLAYMENT OPTIONS

Use an embossing leveler to smooth out mildly rough existing flooring. Be sure to check the label to see if the leveler is recommended for use with your particular flooring material.

Apply new underlayment over existing flooring if the flooring material is too difficult to remove and too badly damaged to use an embossing leveler. Make sure you have room with existing cabinets and fixtures to fit the underlayment.

Replacing Underlayment

In order to provide a flat, level surface for your new vinyl or ceramic flooring, you'll want to make sure the floor is covered with a good layer of plywood underlayment. Nail down any loose flooring with 6d ring-shank nails. Set all nail heads below the flooring surface and fill any cracks or holes with plastic wood filler.

Specialty tools and supplies that will be handy when installing and repairing underlayment include ready-mix latex underlayment, plastic wood filler, and a flat trowel.

Use 1/4" lauan plywood when replacing or installing new underlayment. Lauan plywood provides a flat, uniform surface–an ideal underlayment for most flooring materials. However, local codes may dictate another type of underlayment and many tile manufacturers recommend using cementuous backer board for ceramic tile installations.

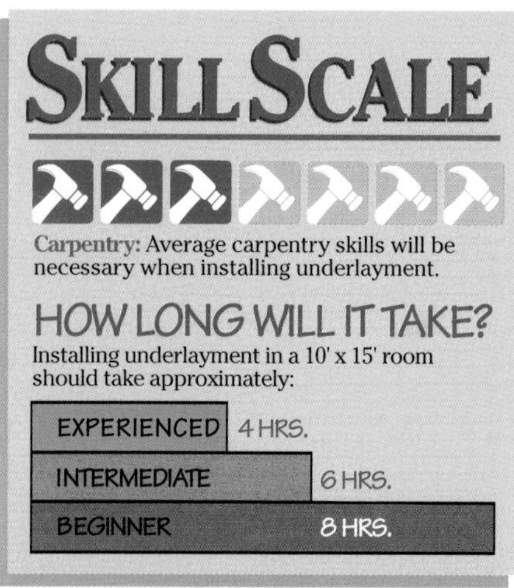

STUFF YOU'LL NEED:

- ☐**Tools:** Hammer, pry bar, jigsaw, tape measure, handsaw, trowel, safety goggles.
- ☐**Materials:** Ready mix latex underlayment, 6d ring shank nails.

INSTALLING UNDERLAYMENT

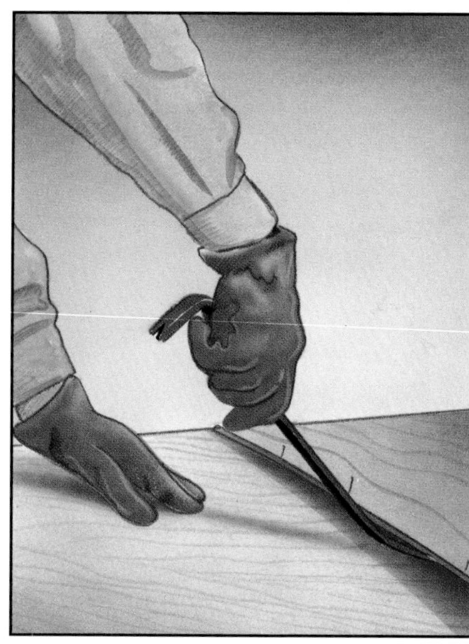

1 Use a flat pry bar to remove the old flooring underlayment.

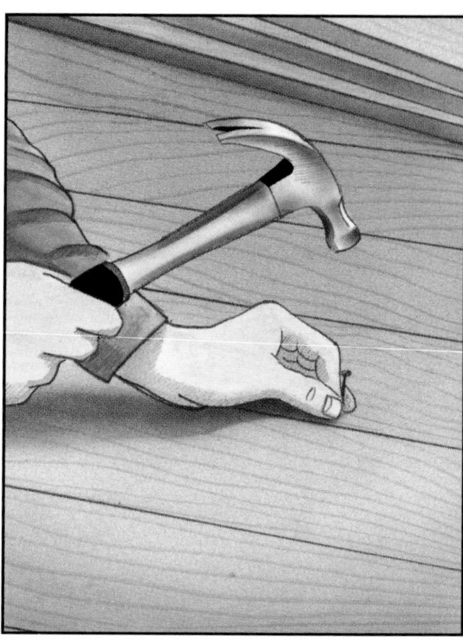

2 Nail down any loose subfloor boards with ring-shank nails. Replace boards that are warped, bowed, or damaged.

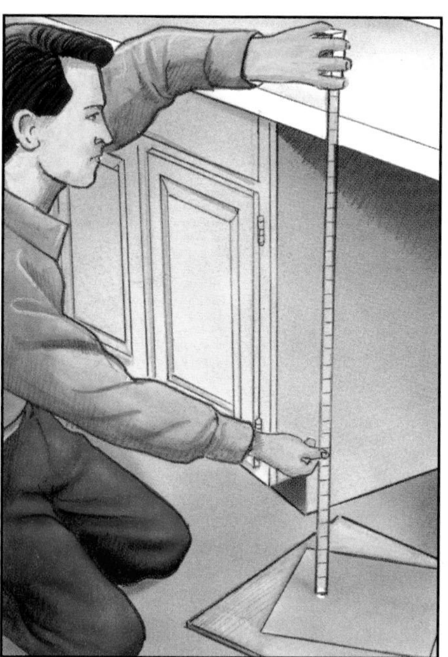

3 Make sure the finished height of the new floor will allow room for the appliances to be replaced. The countertop may need to be shimmed up, or the old flooring removed, to allow appliances to fit.

4 Remove the base molding, then undercut the bottom edges of door casings to make room for the new underlayment and flooring. Use small pieces of underlayment and flooring as a spacing guide, then trim the casings with a handsaw.

5 Inspect the subfloor for low spots. Fill any low areas with ready-mix latex underlayment. Let the underlayment dry, then sand it smooth.

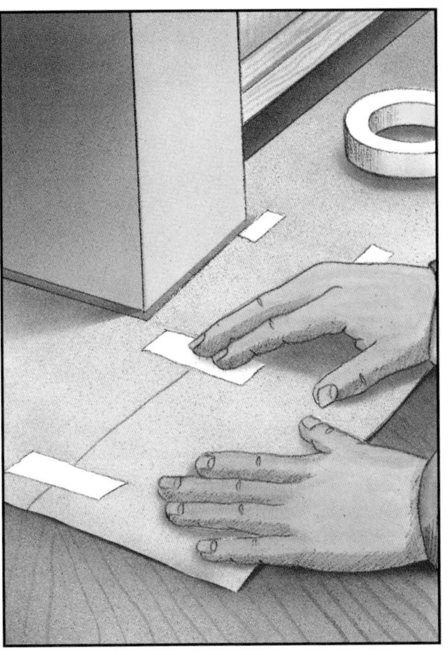

6 Make a template of cardboard or paper for irregular areas, then trace the template outline onto the underlayment.

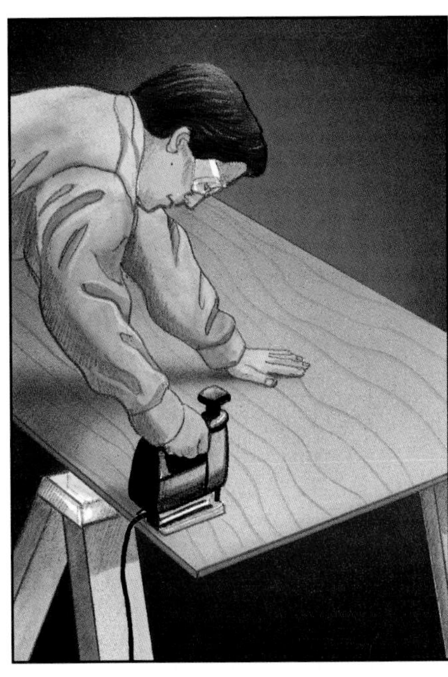

7 Cut the underlayment to fit using a circular saw for long straight cuts and a jigsaw for irregular shaped cuts.

8 Wearing safety goggles, install plywood underlayment along the longest wall. You need to leave a gap between each panel for expansion. The width of the gap varies from manufacturer to manufacturer (between ⅛" to ⅟64") so be sure to check the instructions carefully.

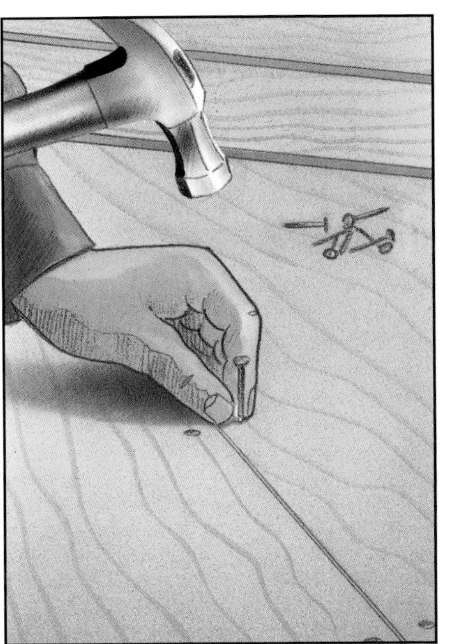

9 Secure the underlayment with 6d ring-shank nails, driven every 6" along the edges of the plywood. Also nail every 6" along the floor joists and every 2" on the perimeter of the floor. Some manufacturers recommend filling the edge gaps with ready-mix underlayment compound. Again check the instructions for specifics.

10 Cover the remaining areas, staggering the plywood seams. Fill any irregularities in the plywood underlayment with ready-mix latex underlayment before installing the flooring material. Let the latex underlayment dry, sand it smooth, then clean the surface thoroughly.

Installing Felt-Back Sheet Vinyl

Sheet vinyl and resilient sheet goods are made of vinyl and are manufactured in 6- or 12-foot widths. Use a floor plan of your kitchen to determine if your sheet goods can be installed without seams. Large areas may require that pieces of flooring be joined together, so try to plan any seams for inconspicuous areas. Sheet vinyl works well for small areas, but is often ungainly in larger rooms.

To eliminate cutting errors, create a template of your kitchen with heavy paper or a template kit offered by some flooring manufacturers. A template allows you to trace an accurate outline of your kitchen onto the new flooring. You'll need to find a large, level area to lay the flooring completely flat to transfer the template markings.

STUFF YOU'LL NEED:

- ☐ **Tools:** J-roller, hand stapler, putty knife, notched spreader, flooring knife, scribing compass, framing square, rolling pin.
- ☐ **Materials:** Flooring adhesive, masking tape, heavy paper, vinyl flooring, seam sealer.

MAKING A FLOORING TEMPLATE

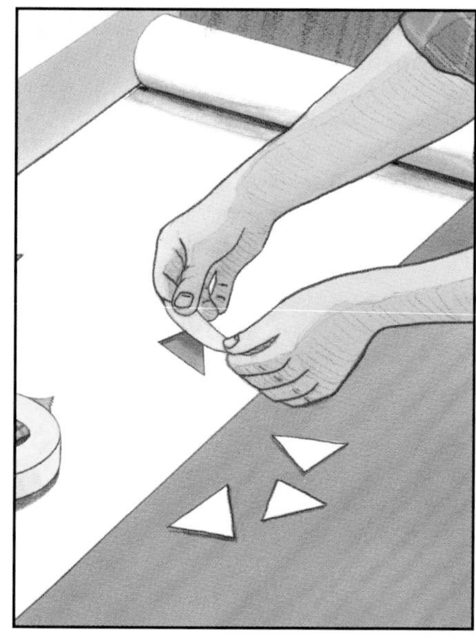

1 Use sheets of heavy butcher's or builder's paper. Place the edges of paper against walls, leaving a 1/8" margin. Cut triangular holes in the paper with a utility knife. Fasten the template to the floor by placing masking tape over the holes.

2 Follow the outline of the room, working with one sheet of paper at a time. Overlap the edges of the adjoining sheets 2" and tape them together.

Resilient flooring adhesive and seam sealer must be specifically made for the particular flooring you're installing. Avoid future adhesion problems by taking a little extra time to get the appropriate materials before installation. Consult your local flooring dealer or store before installing to be certain your materials are compatible with each other.

It is also a good idea to be consistent with brands of supplies for your flooring project. All flooring materials and supplies are not compatible with each other, but if you stick with the same manufacturer for flooring material, adhesive, seam sealer, and cleanup solution, you should have a floor covering that will stay where you put it.

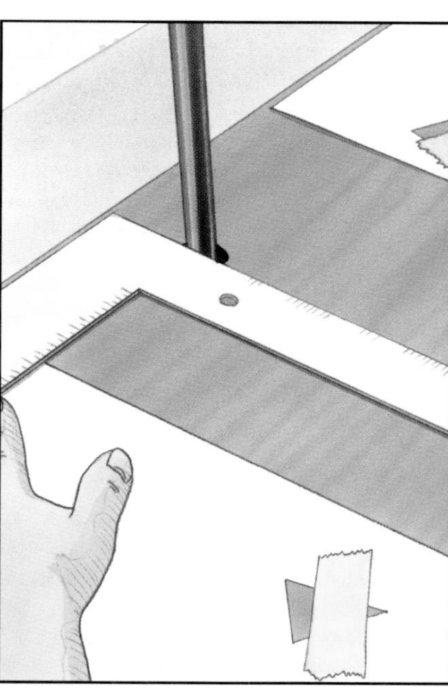

3 To fit the template around pipes, tape sheets of paper on either side. Measure the distance from the wall to the center of the pipe, using a framing or combination square, and subtract 1/8".

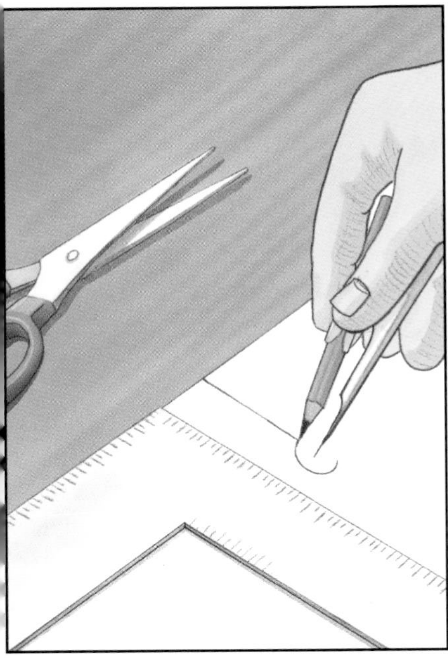

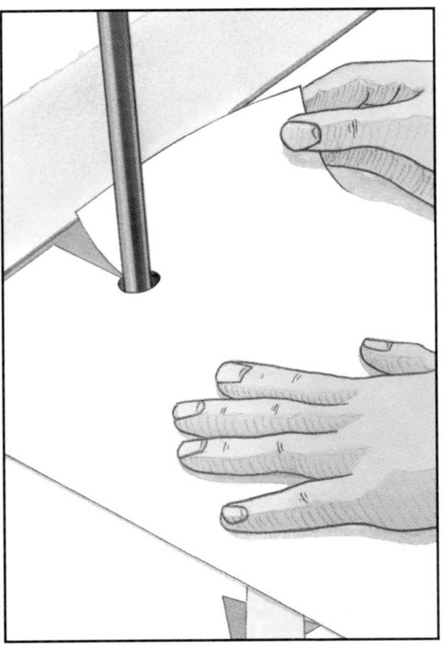

4 Transfer the measurement to a separate piece of paper. Use a compass to draw the pipe diameter onto the paper, and cut a hole with scissors or a utility knife. Cut a slit from the edge of the paper to the hole.

5 Fit the hole cutout around the pipe. Tape the hole template to adjoining sheets.

6 When the template is completed, roll or loosely fold the paper template for carrying. Get a helper to lay the sheet goods out on a flat, level surface.

Ceilings, Walls & Floors

SUPPLIES FOR INSTALLING FELT-BACK SHEET VINYL

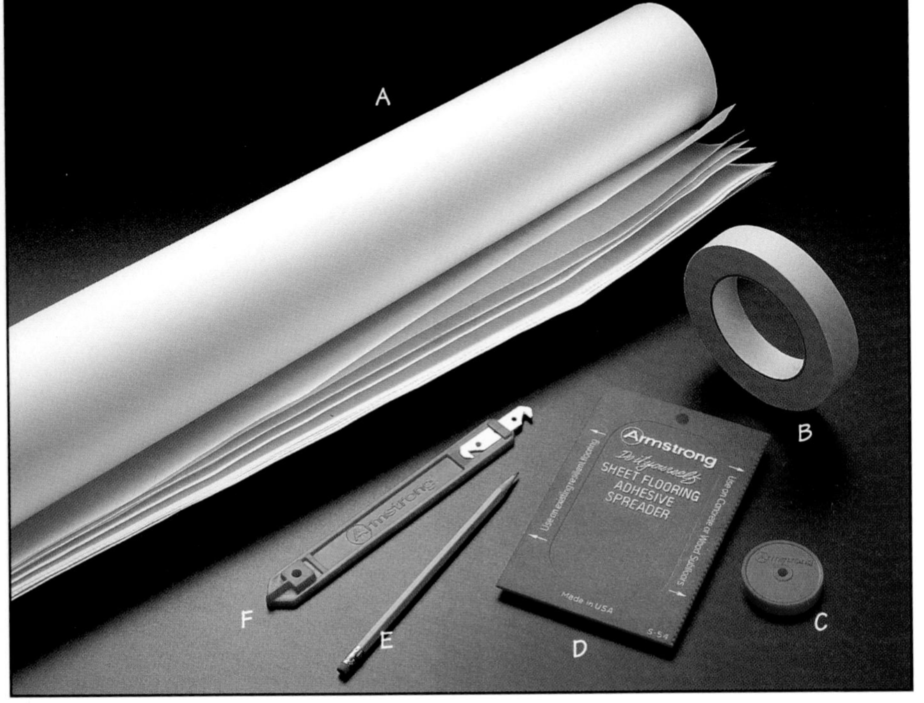

Materials necessary for felt-back sheet vinyl installation include: heavy butcher's paper (**A**), masking tape (**B**), marking guide (**C**), adhesive spreader (**D**), pencil (**E**), and paper template knife (**F**).

Installation Kits

Many vinyl sheet flooring manufacturers provide or sell complete installation template kits which include everything necessary to construct an accurate flooring template. These kits normally include a roll of heavy paper, masking tape, marking guide, trimming knife and a complete set of instructions. The complete installation kits make it relatively easy to lay out the flooring and can even save on your material cost by reducing the chance of ruining a sheet of vinyl due to improper measurements and cutting. In order to assure that costly mistakes aren't made when cutting flooring you must follow the instructions very carefully.

INSTALLING RESILIENT SHEET GOODS

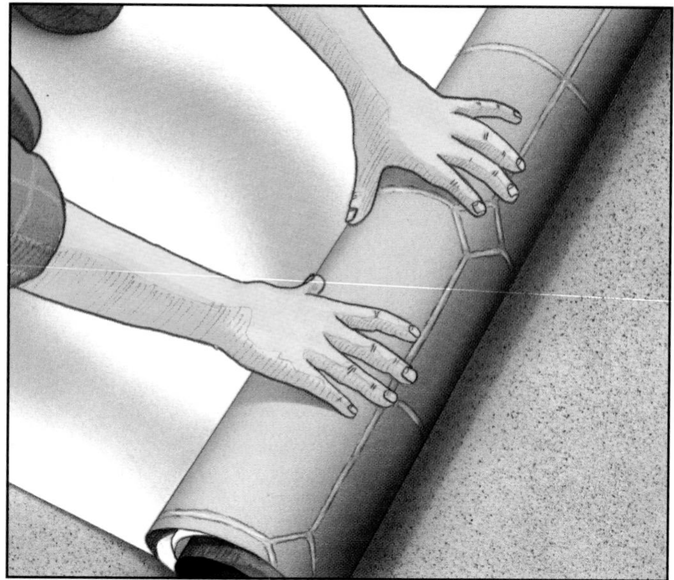

1 Unroll the flooring on any large, flat, clean surface. To prevent wrinkles, sheet goods come from the manufacturer rolled with the pattern side out. Unroll the sheet, and turn it pattern side up for marking.

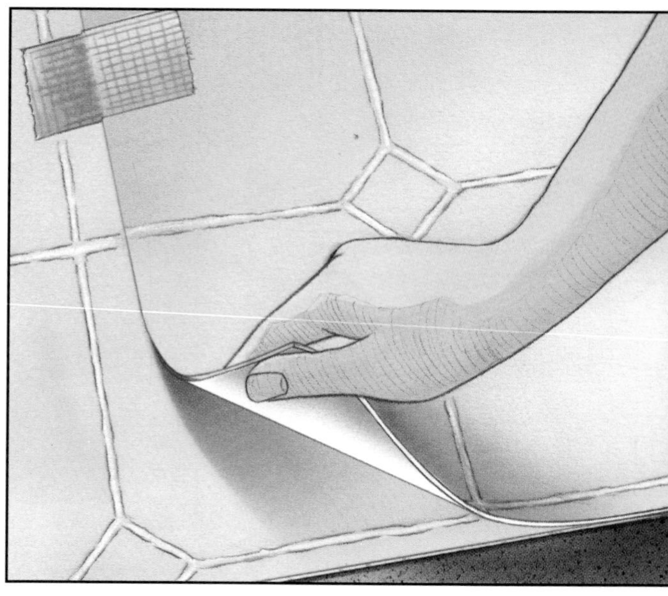

For two-piece installations, overlap the edges of the sheets at least 2". Plan the seams to fall along pattern lines or simulated grout joints. Align the sheets so that the patterns match, and tape the sheets together.

2 Position the paper template on the sheet goods, and tape it into place. Trace the outline of the template onto the flooring with a felt-tipped pen.

3 Remove the template. Cut the sheet goods with a sharp flooring knife, or a utility knife with a new blade, along the template outline marks.

4 Cut holes for pipes or posts using a flooring knife or a utility knife. Then cut a slit from the hole to the nearest edge of the sheet goods. Make cuts along one edge of the pattern lines, if possible. The cut will blend better into the floor's pattern if the cut is on one edge of the pattern line.

5 Roll up the flooring loosely and transfer the roll to the kitchen. Be careful not to fold the flooring. Unroll and position the vinyl carefully. Slide the edges beneath the undercut door casings.

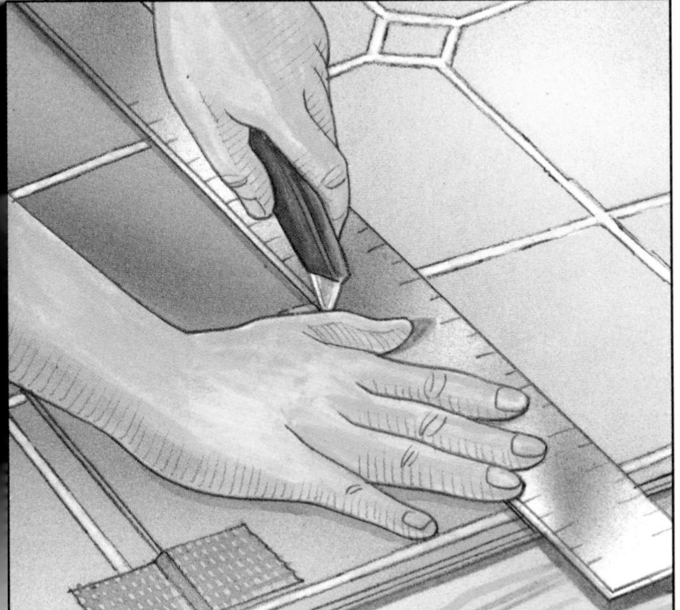

6 If you had to use two pieces of flooring, cut the seams using a straightedge as a guide. Hold the straightedge tightly against the flooring, and cut along the pattern lines through both pieces of vinyl flooring.

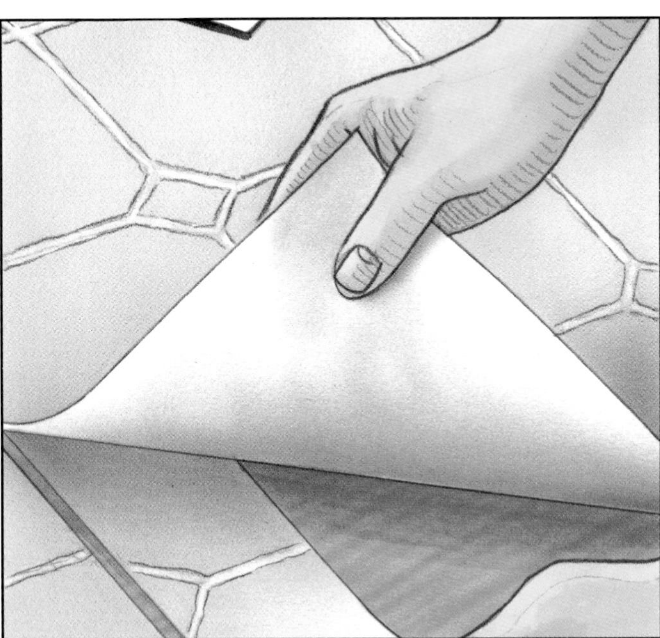

7 Remove both pieces of scrap flooring. The sheet goods now will be pattern-matched.

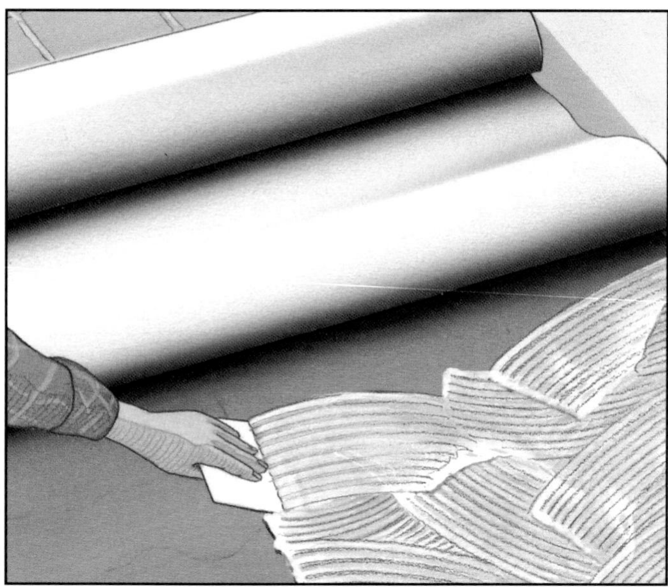

8 Some types of sheet goods require a full spread of adhesive under the flooring. Glue one-half of the sheet at a time. Dry-fit the sheet goods, then fold back half of sheet and apply adhesive to the floor with a notched trowel.

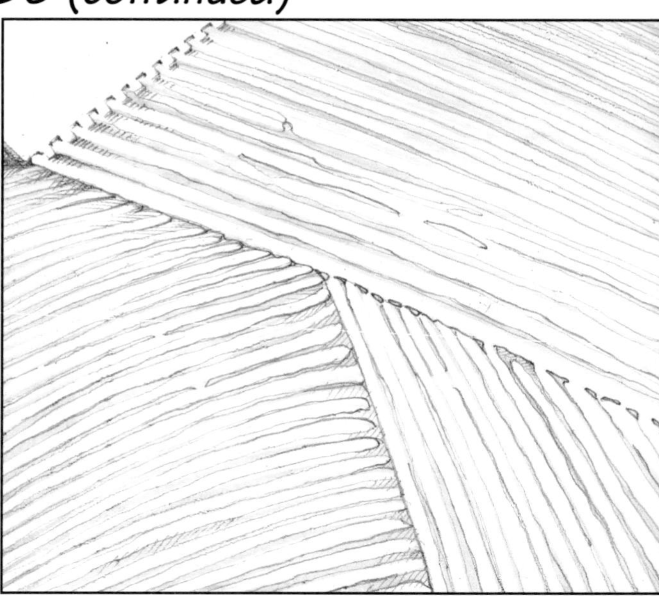

9 Be sure to let the adhesive dry for 10-15 minutes until tacky. Get the adhesive smooth to decrease the chance of bubbles, then fold the flooring over the adhesive.

10 Lay the flooring on the adhesive, then repeat the procedure for the other half of the sheet. Fold the edge back and apply adhesive to the area. Be sure that the adhesive is correct for the type of flooring material and underlayment you're using, or else the flooring material may pull away from the underlayment after a period of time.

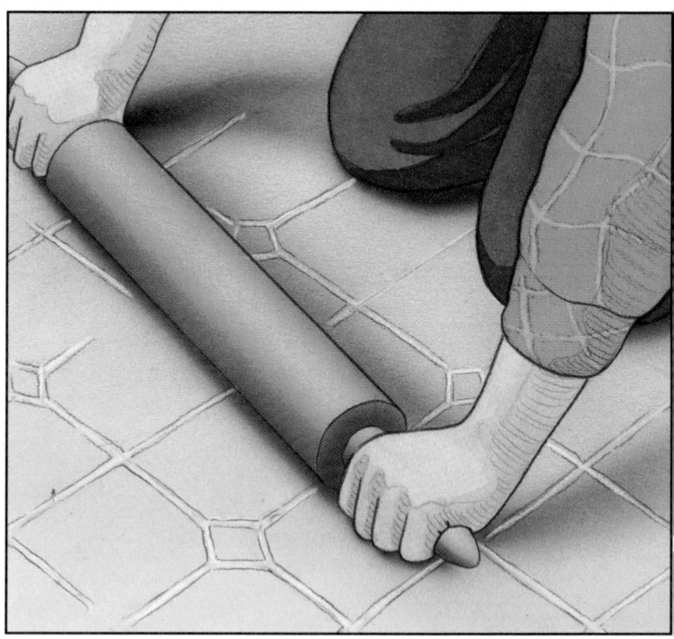

11 Bond the sheet goods with a rolling pin or J-roller. Be sure to smooth from the middle, then work your way out. You can just as easily use a 2x4 with a damp towel around it. This will slide easily and you don't have to annoy the baker in the house by using the rolling pin.

12 If you had to use two pieces of flooring, make sure the flooring along any seams is bonded to the underlayment by rolling with a J-roller.

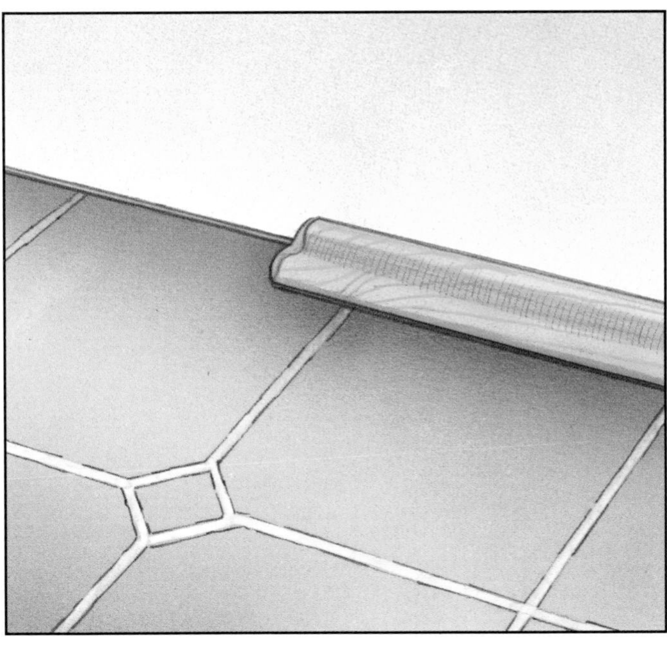

13 Use shoe molding to conceal the expansion gaps against the walls. Keep the molding slightly above the flooring, usually the thickness of the flooring. Remember, the molding is for appearance and not to physically hold the flooring down.

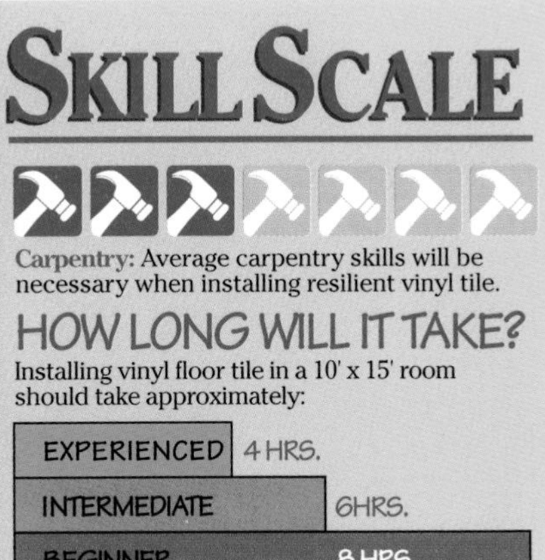

STUFF YOU'LL NEED:

- **Tools:** Chalk line, floor roller, notched trowel, tape measure, framing square, flooring knife.
- **Materials:** Vinyl floor tile, floor tile adhesive.

Installing Resilient Vinyl Tile

Resilient vinyl tiles are relatively easy to install. Many styles are available with self-sticking adhesive backs and are made for do-it-yourself projects. Some resilient tiles, however, should be set in flooring adhesive.

Vinyl tiles are designed with embossed surfaces to help conceal wear marks and also hide seams, floor irregularities, and indentations left by furniture. Carved, textured, and grained surfaces are more than just good-looking. They are easier to maintain because dirt lies in the recesses instead of being walked on and ground into the tile.

Establish perpendicular layout lines to guide your tile installation. The tiles should be "dry-fit" prior to gluing to make sure the finished pattern is pleasing. Begin installation at the center of the room and work toward the walls.

ESTABLISHING LAYOUT LINES

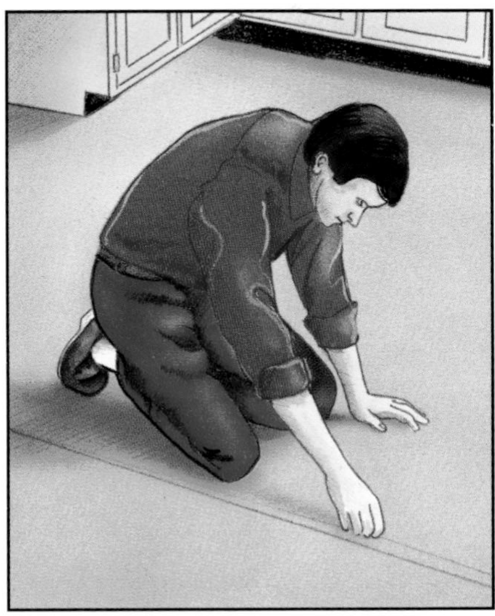

1 Establish a layout line by measuring opposite sides of the room and marking the center of each side. Snap a chalk line between the marks.

ESTABLISHING LAYOUT LINES (continued)

2 Measure and mark the center of the chalk line. From this point, use a framing square to establish a second line perpendicular to the first. Snap a second layout line across the room.

3 Check for squareness with a "carpenter's triangle." Measure and mark one layout line 3' from the center point. Measure and mark the perpendicular layout line 4' from the centerpoint.

4 Measure the distance between the marks. If the layout lines are perpendicular, the distance will be exactly 5'.

TIPS FOR INSTALLING TILES

Make cardboard templates the same size as the tile. Use the templates to test-fit the cuts at wall corners or around pipes and posts. Trace the template outline on the tile for cutting.

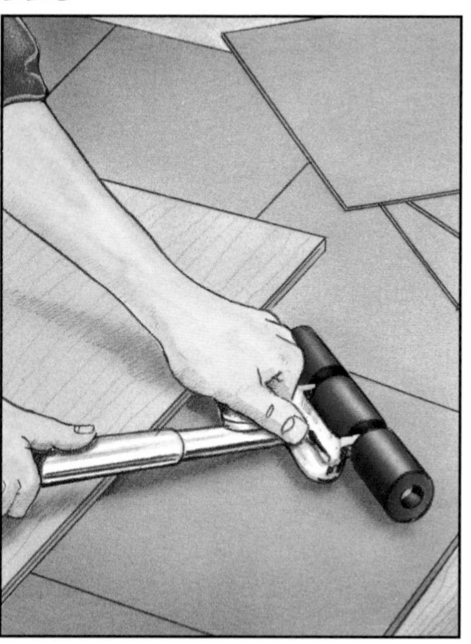

Bond the flooring by applying pressure with a floor roller or rolling pin.

Use scrap plywood pieces for kneeling on set tiles. The plywood distributes the weight to prevent the tiles from shifting.

INSTALLING RESILIENT VINYL TILE

1 Dry-fit the tiles along the layout lines in both directions. Make sure that the finished layout is pleasing to your taste before permanently installing the tiles.

CLEAN, CLEAN, CLEAN! IF THE UNDERLAYMENT ISN'T CLEAN, THE TILES WON'T STICK

2 Adjust the layout, if necessary. Snap a new chalk line parallel to the original line. Dry-fit the tiles to the new layout line.

3 Begin laying tiles at the centerpoint of the layout lines. Apply the tiles to one quadrant of the floor, laying the tiles in the sequence shown. Repeat the process for the remaining quadrants.

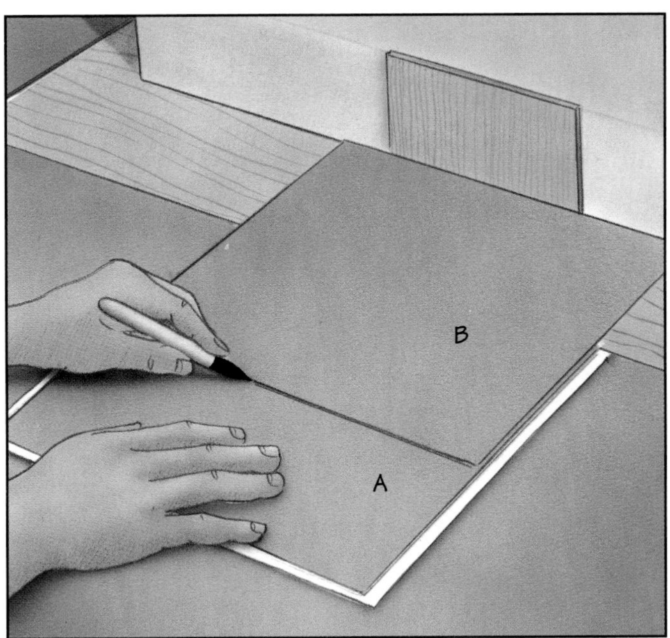

4 Mark the border tiles for cutting. To allow for expansion and contraction of the subfloor, leave a 1/4" gap at the walls. Place a 1/4" spacer upright against the wall. Place a loose tile (A) directly over the last full tile. Place another tile (B) against the spacer, over tile A. Mark the tile A as shown, and cut with a utility knife.

Installing Parquet Tile

Parquet tile flooring is a covering of decorative wood made from hardwoods such as oak, birch, cherry, mahogany, and teak. These are used for their beautiful grain patterns and rich coloring.

The type of parquet flooring you choose is determined only by the types offered by the manufacturer and, of course, the price. Another item to consider is the method of installation, depending on the type of subfloor you'll cover. All parquet tile types compare in ease of application.

Wood parquet floors can also be constructed from tongue-and-groove tiles, milled from solid wood or made from veneered plywood. They can be nailed to a wood floor or left as a floating parquetry.

Parquet tiles normally range in thickness from 1/4" to 7/8". You can set the tiles as either parallel strips or arrange them in various combinations to make herringbone or woven patterns.

STUFF YOU'LL NEED:

- **Tools:** Chalk line, floor roller, notched trowel, tape measure, framing square, flooring knife, handsaw.
- **Materials:** Parquet floor tile, floor tile adhesive.

LAYING A PARQUET TILE FLOOR

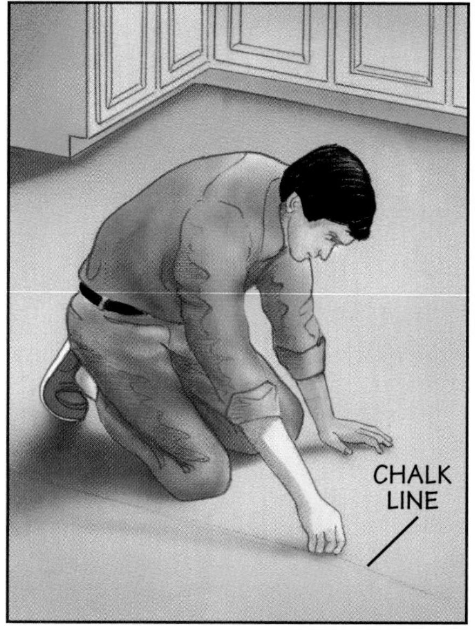

1 Plan the layout of your parquet floor carefully. Precision measurements at this stage are imperative. To find the starting points for laying the tiles, square off the room with chalk lines snapped from opposite corners or the midpoints of opposite walls.

2 Dry-fit the tiles along the layout lines in both directions. Make sure that the finished layout is visually pleasing to you before installing the tiles.

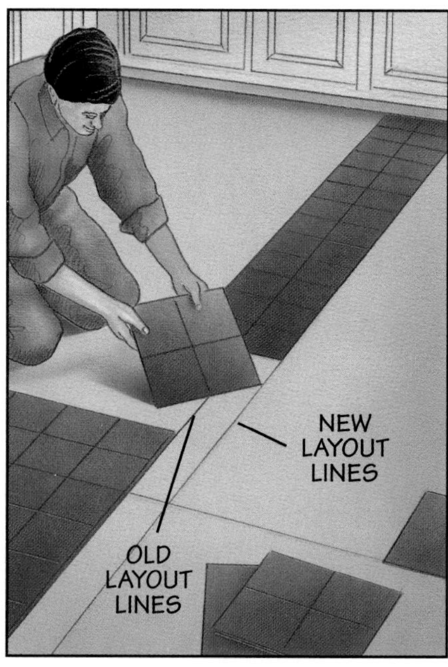

3 Adjust the layout, if necessary. Snap a new line parallel to the original. Dry-fit tiles to new layout line.

4 Use a notched trowel to spread the flooring adhesive according to the manufacturer's directions. Take care not to cover the layout lines with adhesive.

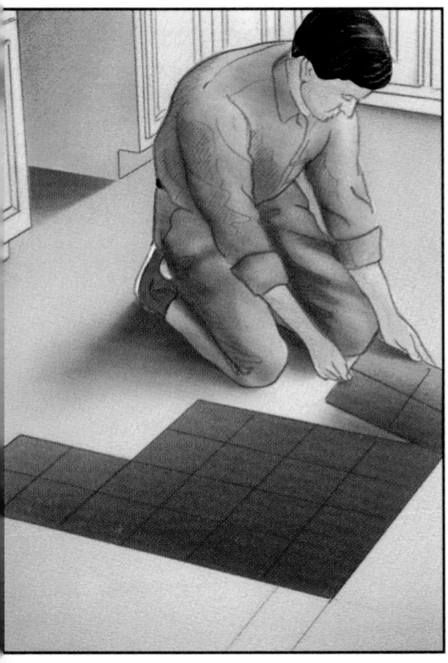

5 Begin laying the tiles at the center point of the layout lines. Apply the tiles to one quadrant of the floor, laying the tiles in the sequence shown. Repeat the procedure for the remaining quadrants.

6 Use scrap plywood pieces for kneeling on set tiles. Plywood distributes the weight to prevent the tiles from shifting.

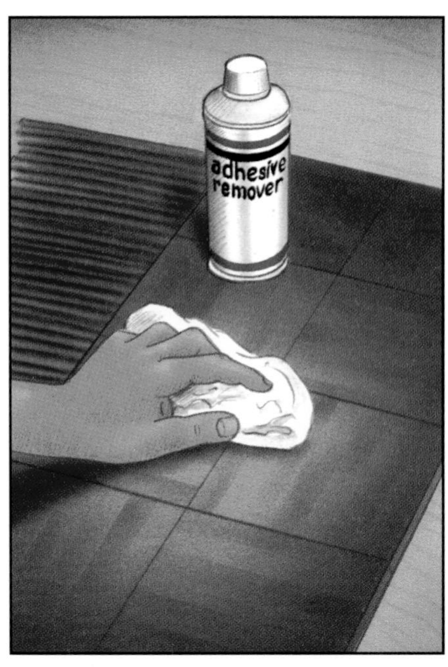

7 Wipe up adhesive that seeps between the joints immediately. Use a solvent recommended by the flooring adhesive manufacturer. Check to make sure the adhesive remover won't harm the parquet tiles' finish.

8 Bond the flooring by applying pressure with a floor roller or rolling pin.

9 Use a cardboard template to fit tiles in irregular areas. Cut the cardboard to match the space, and allow for an expansion gap next to the wall as shown for ceramic tile on page 275. Trace the template outline on the tile, then cut the tile to fit with a jigsaw or coping saw.

10 To cut a door frame, lay a loose tile upside down against the frame, and saw. You can then slide the flooring in under the door frame. Use molding to cover gap between the flooring and the wall.

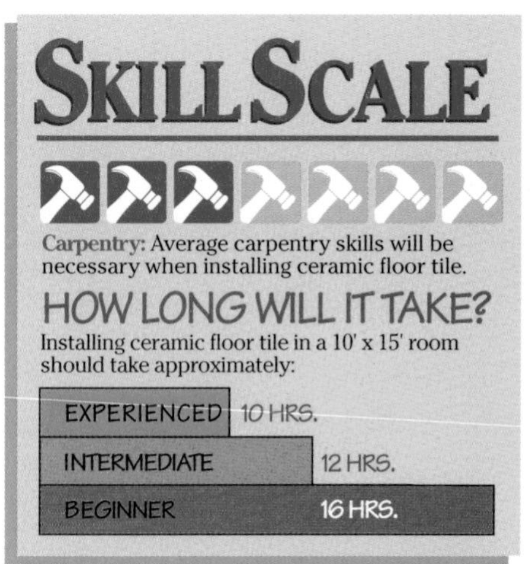

STUFF YOU'LL NEED:

- **Tools:** Chalk line, tape measure, tile nibber, tile cutter, grout float, notched trowel.
- **Materials:** Ceramic tile, tile adhesive, grout, sealer.

Installing Ceramic Floor Tile

Tiling is a universally popular method of decorating a floor, with an almost inexhaustible range of colors, textures, and patterns to choose from, depending on the degree of durability required. Tiles can be cut and fitted into awkward-shaped areas far more easily than sheet materials.

Ceramic tile should be installed over subfloors no less than 1$^{1}/_{8}$" in total thickness. Thinner subfloors may flex, causing the tiles to break or the grout to crack. Most tile manufacturers recommend installing ceramic tile over cementuous backer board rather than another type of underlayment.

If you have a large area to tile, consider buying or renting a mortar tub to mix up big batches of grout. Also, be sure to sweep the subfloor thoroughly before installing tiles.

BUYER'$ GUIDE

Ceramic floor tile is available in many styles, colors, and patterns.

Glazed tile has a hard surface layer of color and may be glossy, matte, or textured. Unglazed tile, often called quarry tile, has color throughout its entire thickness and provides a surer grip than glazed tile in a flooring application.

Quarry tiles are usually thicker and more difficult to cut. It is best to use these tiles in areas where you don't have to fit them against complicated shapes.

Stone or slate tiles are very exquisite looking but also very expensive! Sizes and thicknesses will vary depending on the manufacturer. Some materials are so costly it is best to have a professional install them.

Tile floors have two drawbacks–they can be cold for bare feet and glasses will definitely break if dropped on them.

LAYING A CERAMIC TILE FLOOR

1 Establish layout lines (pg. 269) and dry-fit the ceramic floor tiles along layout lines in both directions. Make sure that the finished layout is pleasing to your taste before installing the tiles permanently.

2 Adjust the layout, if necessary. Snap a new line parallel to the original, and dry-fit the floor tiles to the new layout line.

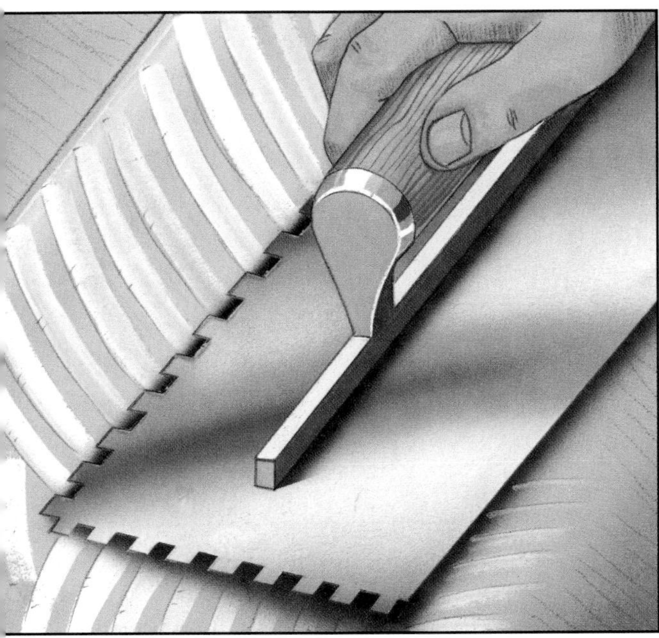

3 Apply adhesive to floor according to manufacturer's directions. Begin at the center point of the layout lines. Use a notched trowel and take care not to cover the layout lines.

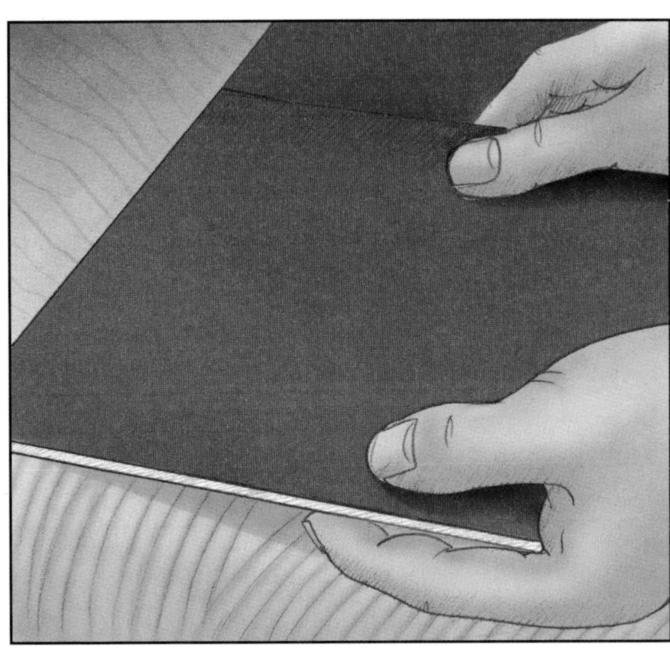

4 Begin laying the tiles at the center point, placing the edges against the layout lines. Use plastic spacers to maintain even grout lines between the tiles.

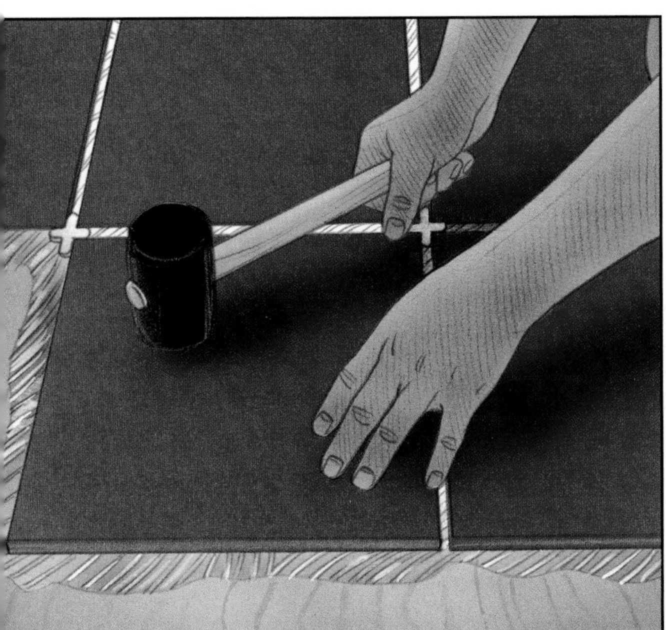

5 Tap the tiles with a rubber mallet to set the tiles, ensure good adhesion, and produce a level floor.

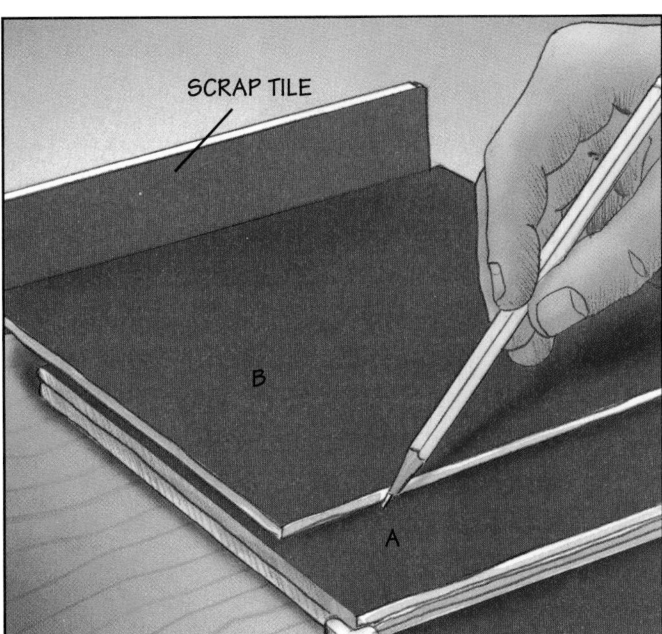

6 Mark the border tiles for cutting. To allow space for grout, place a scrap tile upright against the wall. Place a loose tile (**A**) directly over the last full tile. Place another tile (**B**) against the upright tile, on top of tile A. Mark tile A, and cut it to fit the border space.

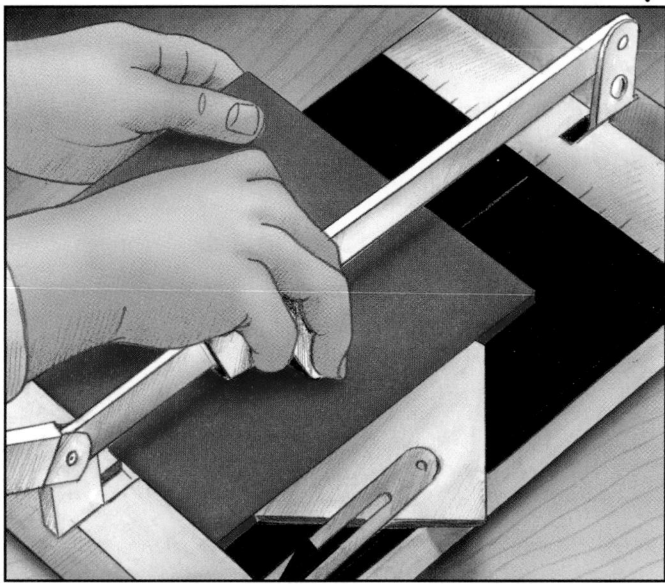

7 To make straight cuts, place the tile faceup in the tile cutter. Adjust the tool to proper width, then score a continuous line by pulling the cutting wheel across the tile's face. Snap the tile along the scored line. Smooth rough edge of cut tile with a tile sander.

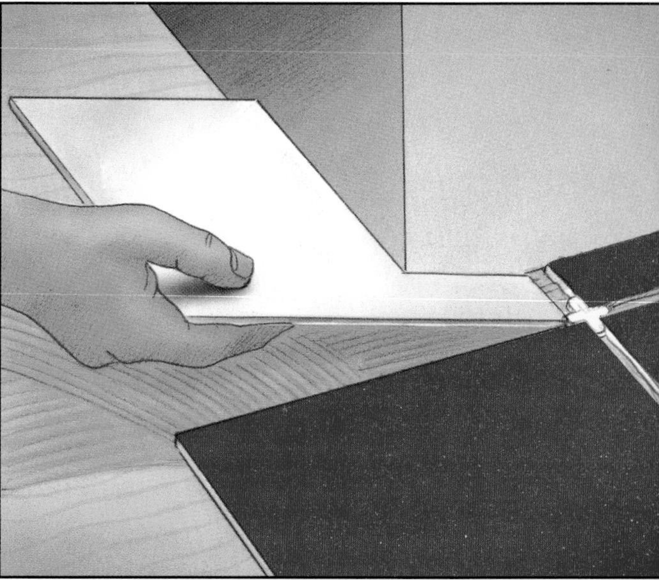

8 Use a cardboard template to fit tiles in irregular areas. Cut cardboard to match area, and allow for grout lines. Trace template outline on tile, then cut to fit.

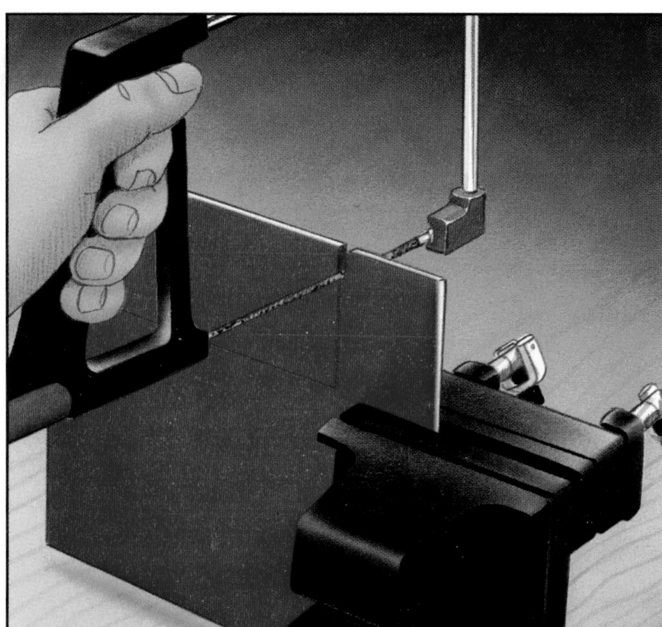

9 Secure tile with vise or clamps for cutting irregular shapes. Jaws of vise should be faced with rubber or wood to prevent scratches. Cut along outline with a tile saw. Smooth rough edges with a tile sander. Cutting tile by hand takes a long time. If you have many tiles to cut, buy or rent a wet saw designed to cut tiles. The extra expense will save you hours of sawing.

10 Mix grout and latex additive according to manufacturer's directions. If you're using colored grout, dry mix all the bags together before adding water. This assures uniform color for all grout. Apply grout to floor with a rubber float. Use a sweeping motion to draw the float across grout lines at a 45° angle to force grout into joints. Teflon grout floats cost more, but will save clean-up time because they wipe grout off the tiles better than standard floats.

11 Wipe away excess grout with a damp, special grout sponge. Let grout dry slightly, then wipe away powdery haze. Let grout cure as directed by manufacturer. You may have to repeat this two or three times to get all the grout off the surface of the tile.

12 Wet mop the floor twice a day for three days then allow grout to cure for seven to ten days. This will result in harder, longer-lasting grout that is less likely to develop hairline cracks. Then apply silicone sealer to floor with a brush. Let dry, then apply a second coat. Only apply sealer to the grout not to the tile.

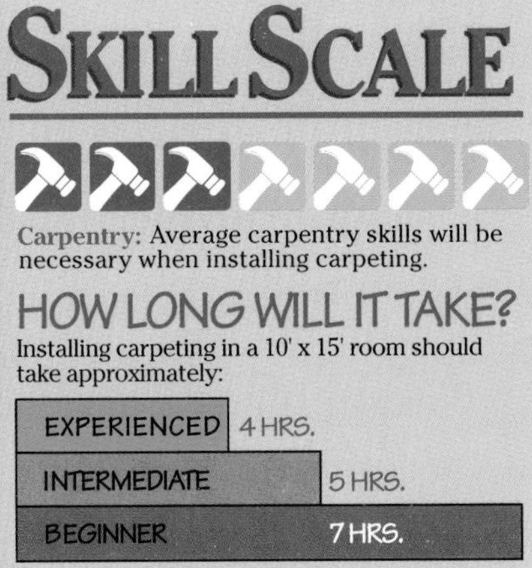

STUFF YOU'LL NEED:

- **Tools:** Tape measure, knee kicker, stair tool, power stretcher, seamer, wall trimmer, hammer.
- **Materials:** Carpeting, pad, tackless strips.

Installing Carpet & Carpet Pad

There are various factors to consider when you're shopping for carpeting and planning to do the installation yourself.

Fiber content, type of pile, and durability are material factors to look at when selecting a particular carpet. The best carpets have been traditionally made from wool or a mixture of wool and a percentage of man-made fiber. Wool carpet is quite expensive, but with blends of nylon, polypropylene, acrylic, rayon, and polyester, modern carpeting has been designed to combat things such as stains, wear, and high costs. If the installation involves seams, consider hiring a professional.

Installing carpeting isn't technically difficult, but can be a challenge on large areas with limited access. Remember, carpeting comes normally in 12'-long rolls and can be quite heavy and difficult to handle. If you have to seam two pieces together, make sure you join the pieces with the "grain" or coloring texture going in the same direction.

BUYER'$ GUIDE

Carpeting is not limited to indoor settings. Indoor/outdoor carpeting, which used to look like bad artificial turf, is now available in many colorful patterns, designs and textures which, by the way, are a lot easier on bare feet!

Indoor/outdoor carpeting is often used in patio settings where durability and water exposure are concerns. Most indoor/outdoor carpeting is made with short pile and is very easy to clean up with a broom or vacuum.

Installation is very similar to felt-backed vinyl flooring except that the adhesive is designed specifically for indoor/outdoor applications. Follow the same steps as required for felt-backed vinyl sheet flooring on pg. 264.

INSTALLING CARPETING AND CARPET PAD

1 Cut the tackless strips to fit the entire perimeter of the room, including the door areas.

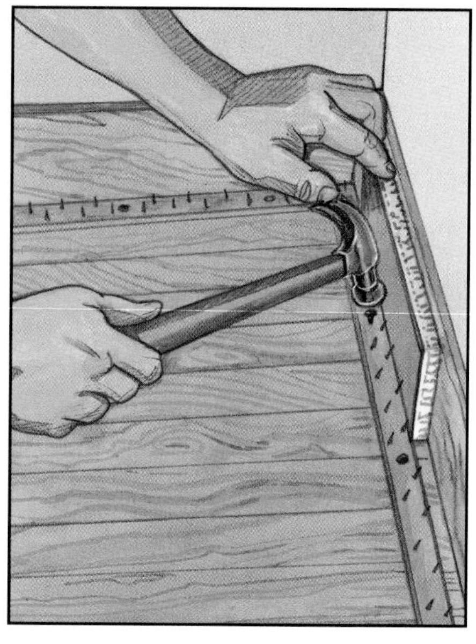

2 Nail the strips to the floor using a hammer. Position the strips with the points facing the wall. Keep a space equal to the thickness of the carpet between the walls and the strips. Use concrete nails if installing on a slab.

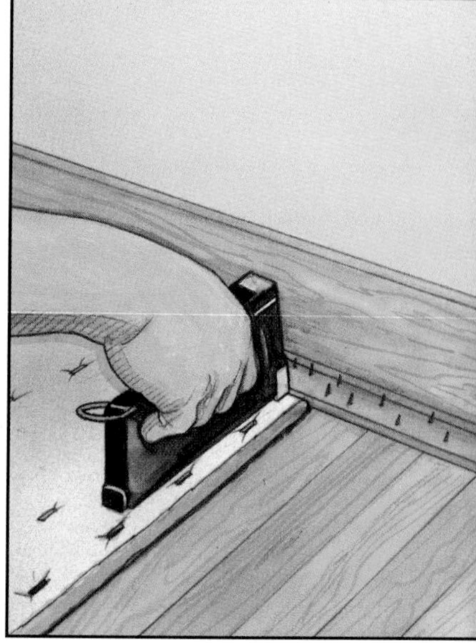

3 Lay the carpet padding over the entire floor inside the strips. Trim excess padding with a utility knife and seal the joints between padding with duct tape. Staple the padding every 10" – 12" to keep the padding in place, or use pad glue if working on a slab.

HOMER'S
HINDSIGHT

Carpet pad generally doesn't receive much admiration since it is not visible below the carpeting, but the consequences of installing an inferior pad is most definitely noticeable.

Due to my short-sighted budget restraints, I elected to install a "bargain" carpet pad and put the money into a high-grade carpet. The installation went smoothly and I was quite impressed with the finished job. Unfortunately, after several months of wear and tear my high grade carpet was looking pretty worn due to the poor support it received from the low grade pad. It was an expensive lesson, but I learned that the quality of the pad is just about as important as the quality of the carpeting!

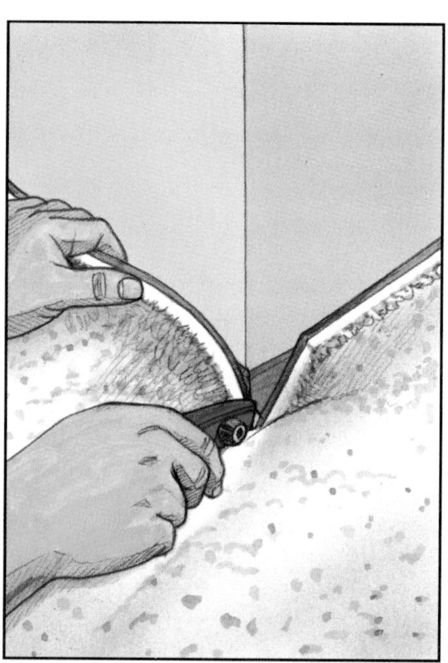

4 Measure and cut the carpet with 3" extra in each direction. Lay the carpet in place and make relief cuts at the corners so the pieces lie flat.

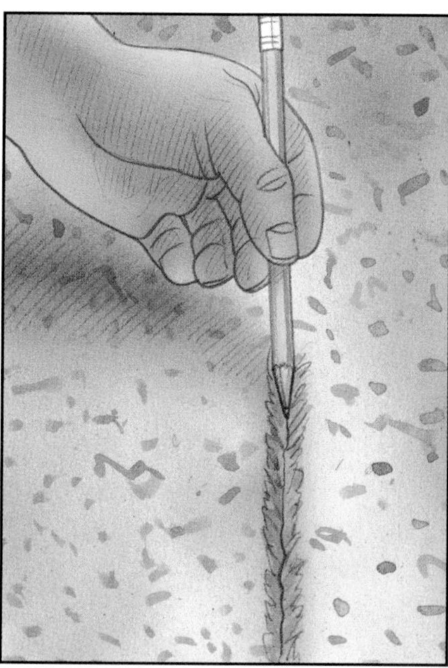

5 Plan for seams to occur in low-traffic and low-visibility areas. Position the seams perpendicular to the largest window or light source in the room. Run a pencil along the proposed seam line to part the carpet pile. This will ensure that only the carpet backing is cut and not the pile.

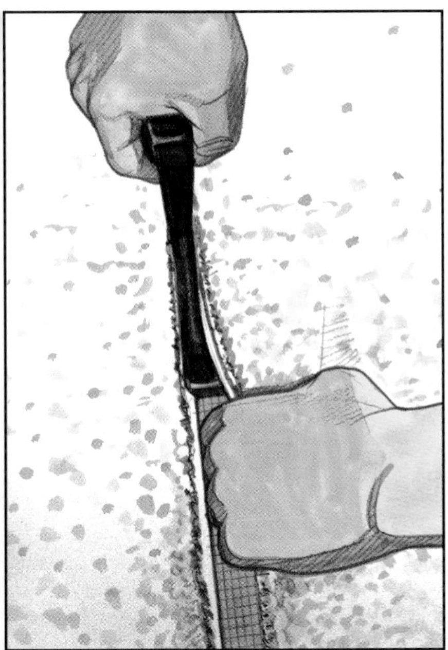

6 Cut a length of seaming tape and lay it between the pieces. Use a seaming iron to melt the adhesive. Move the iron slowly and pinch the seam together behind the iron, pushing the pieces into the adhesive before it cools. Some carpets require special seams. Check with the manufacturer.

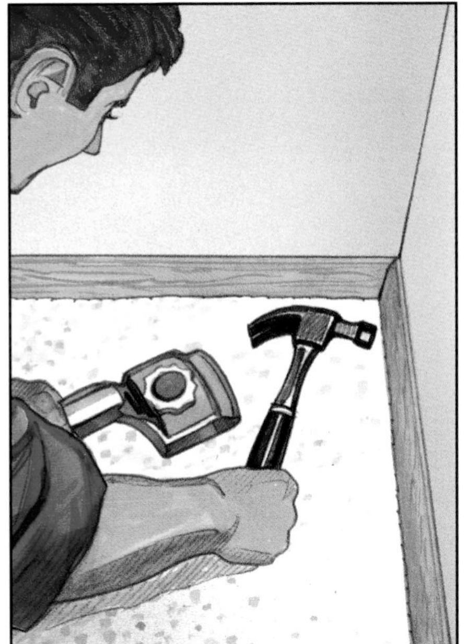

7 Stretch the carpet over the tackless strips. Start in a corner at a narrow end of the room. Use a knee kicker to push the carpet along one wall in the corner onto the strips. Set the carpet on the strips by tapping with the flat side of a hammer. Repeat along the adjacent wall to secure that corner.

8 Use a power stretcher to secure the opposite corners. Place the foot of the stretcher against the first wall you secured and adjust the stretcher so the head is about 6" from the opposite wall. Press the lever into place to stretch the carpet onto the strips. Repeat with the foot against the second wall.

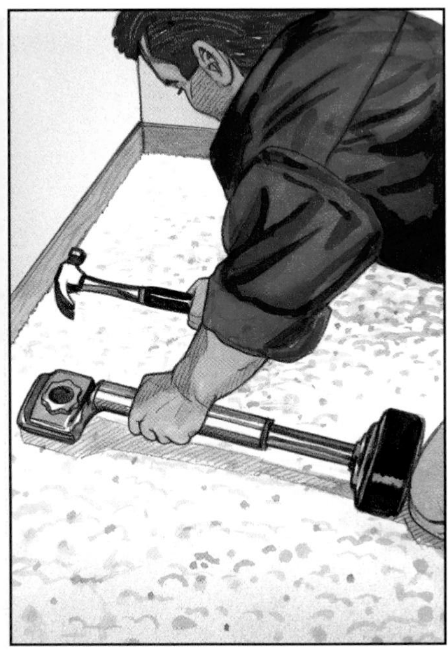

9 Reposition the stretcher to secure the remaining corner, then complete the stretching by kicking the carpet onto the strips from the finished walls to the farthest corner.

10 Trim the edges of the carpet with the wall trimmer, then tuck the edges into the space between the strips and the wall with the stair tool or broad knife.

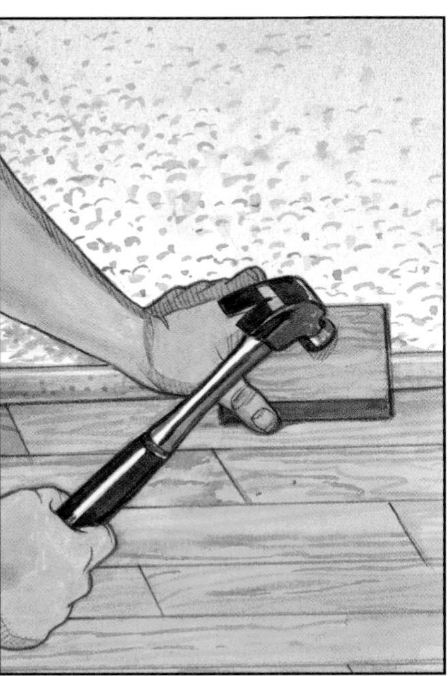

11 Wherever the carpet meets other flooring, install a binder bar. Kick the carpeting to fit over the hooks in the binder bar, then clamp the carpet in place by hammering the metal flange closed. Use a block of wood over the flange to prevent denting the flange.

Installing Hardwood Strip Flooring

Wood flooring has an appeal that is nearly universal. Its warmth and durability evoke the craftsmanship and tradition of an earlier age, yet it lends itself well to the interior design of contemporary homes. Properly installed and well-maintained, wood flooring can last as long as the house itself.

Wood flooring systems have increased in popularity and undergone a technical evolution in the past thirty years. Modern wood flooring is available in the standard 2"-wide unfinished solid hardwood strips, 4"-wide unfinished hardwood strips, and 8"-wide planks with a prefinished hardwood veneer. The planks are composed of 2"-wide thin hardwood strips, which are laminated to a plywood base and prefinished in a variety of stained colors with multiple coats of polyurethane varnish topcoat. The unfinished strips usually are available in random lengths, while the prefinished planks are a standard length of 8' long. All types of strip flooring have tongue-and-groove edges that make joining a relatively simple process.

The wood strip flooring is laid in rows on the subfloor, which is covered with building paper and then fastened with nails. Some types of prefinished plank flooring are glued together and left to float on a thin foam pad without being fastened to the subfloor at all.

The edges are usually fitted with shoe moldings at the walls and thresholds at the doors. The unfinished surfaces are usually coated with stain and then a durable polyurethane topcoat.

If the finish becomes scratched or thin, spot-refinish the small area or put a touch-up coat of finish on the entire floor. If the finish has become so badly worn that the wood surface under it is showing signs of wear and discoloration, you'll have to refinish the entire floor.

Physical damage to your hardwood flooring strips can usually be quite easily repaired without having to replace entire floor sections. Cracks and holes can be patched and splintered edges can be reglued. If the floorboards are badly damaged, you can replace one or more boards to repair the damaged area.

Before you begin any structural repairs on the hardwood strip flooring, make sure you know its design features and exactly how it is fastened together; otherwise, you may find yourself replacing the entire floor!

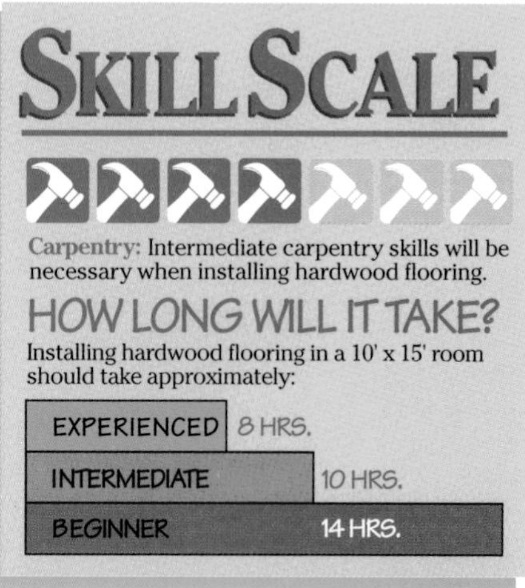

STUFF YOU'LL NEED:

- ☐ **Tools:** Tape measure, handsaw, circular saw, hammer, nailset, flooring nailer, drill w/bits.
- ☐ **Materials:** Hardwood flooring strips, flooring nails, building paper or foam underlayment.

PREPARING THE SURFACE

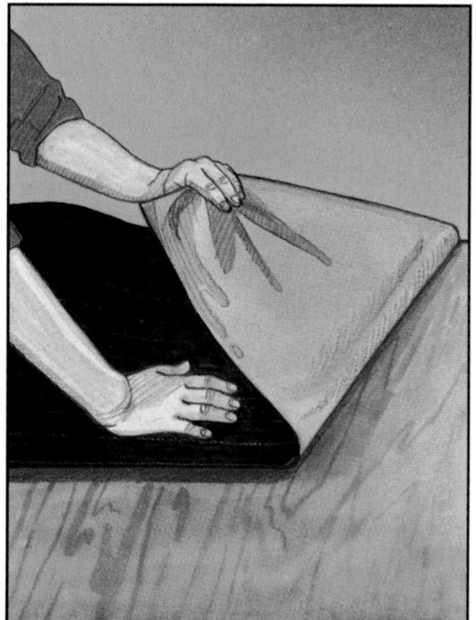

On nailed-down plank flooring, lay building paper over the subfloor lapping it 3" at the seams. Fit the paper closely around obstructions, tack down the sheets, then mark the joist locations on the paper.

On floating floors, roll out the foam backing and cut it to fit the room. Secure the joints with masking tape.

Treat flooring as you would trim molding to border such areas as a fireplace hearth. Miter the boards and rip off the tongues where necessary to fit.

Strips of plank flooring should be delivered at least 4 days before installation, if possible, and stored in the room where it will be installed. The temperature and humidity should be close to levels that will be normal for the room. Untie the bundles and stack the individual boards loosely so air can circulate through the stacks.

The tools necessary for wood flooring installation and repair are readily available at most home improvement stores and building centers. Most small repairs can be made with household carpentry tools, but if you rent tools be sure to know how they work before you leave the rental store. Otherwise, not only will you have to go back for instruction, but you might ruin some expensive flooring if you're not sure how to use the tools properly.

For major repairs and installations, be sure to ask the tool rental agent for a complete demonstration before you bring the tool home. Carefully follow the tool manufacturer's operating instructions and safety tips when using the equipment.

NAILING METHODS

1 Predrill nail holes at the places marked for floor joists. The tongue of the plank is fairly delicate so predrilling is advisable to avoid splitting.

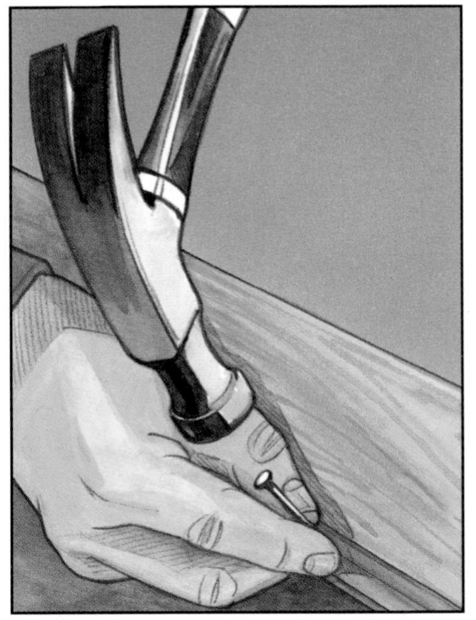

2 Put the nail into the drill hole and drive it almost all the way into the floor strip. Finish driving the nail with a nail set.

A special nailer, which can be rented from most home centers, makes laying hardwood floor strips go much faster than hand nailing every board. When clear of the wall (a few courses of boards), seat the nailer over the edge of the board at a floor joist mark, and strike the head with a mallet.

INSTALLING HARDWOOD STRIP FLOORING

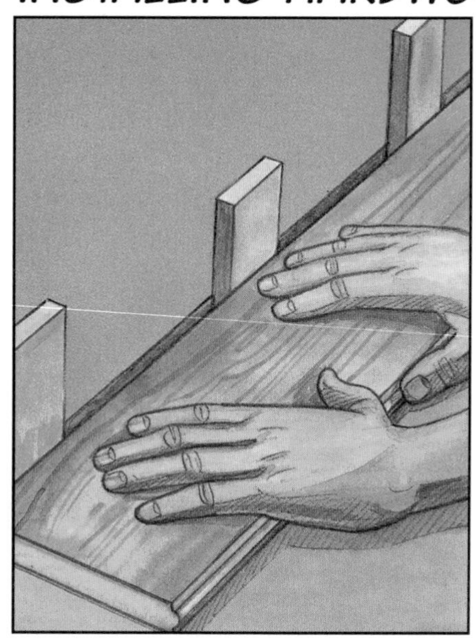

1 Begin the installation at the longest wall. Use 1/2" spacers to provide a gap for seasonal expansion of the flooring. Apply carpenter's glue to grooved end of each piece of flooring just before installing. Glue will help the flooring joints stay tight. On floating floors, glue the tongue and groove sides.

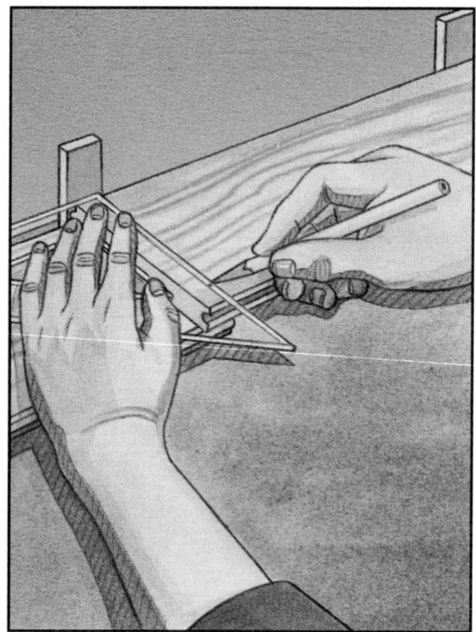

2 Turn the last plank in the row so that the tongue lays against the wall. Mark and cut the plank to length. Turn the plank so that the cut edge is against the wall. If you're using a handsaw, saw with the decorative side up. If an electric saw is used, the decorative side should face downward.

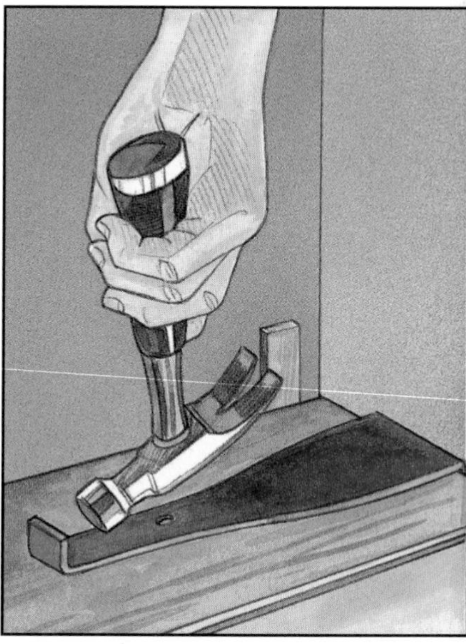

3 Press the last planks together with a pry bar wedged between the end of the plank and the base of the wall. Be careful not to damage the wallboard. Some hardwood flooring manufacturers provide a special pull bar (as shown) that simplifies this procedure.

4 Begin the next row with the leftover piece of the cut plank. If this piece is shorter than 8", you should take a new plank instead, cut it in half, and begin the row with one of the halves. Then continue with a whole plank. Remember that there must always be at least 8" of plank length between the joints.

5 Use a buffer block (a scrap piece of flooring) to tap the boards together into parallel alignments before beginning to nail each successive course. The block protects the tongues from being damaged by a hammer blow.

6 When you must fit a board around an irregular shape, such as a doorway, measure with a combination square, as shown. Scribe the cutout for a perfect fit. For a curve, scribe with a compass.

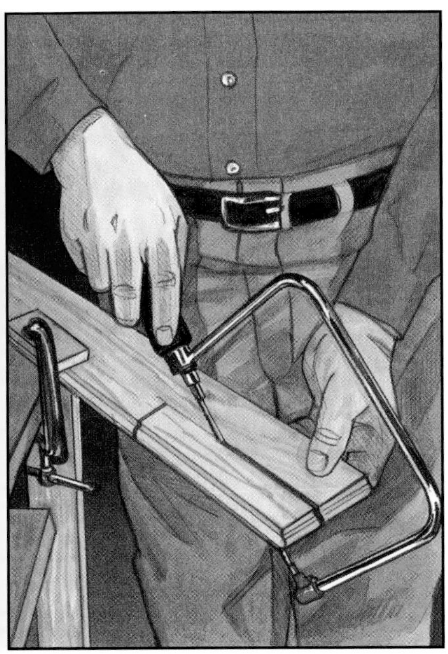

7 Use a coping saw or jigsaw to cut along the scribed lines. Use a C-clamp to help hold the piece steady on a work surface as you make the cut. Protect the face of the strip from the clamp with a small piece of scrap wood.

Use a cardboard template to fit boards in irregular areas. Cut the cardboard to match the space, and allow for an expansion gap next to the wall. Trace the template outline on the board, then cut it to fit with a jigsaw.

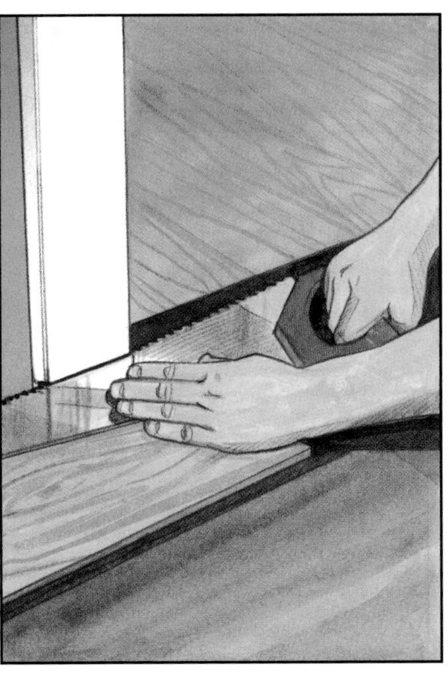

8 To cut a door frame, lay a loose plank upside down against the frame, and saw. Then slide the flooring in under the door frame.

9 The last row of planks must often be sawed lengthwise. Lay the last plank on top of and edge-to-edge with the plank in the next-to-last row. Trace the wall contour on the last plank, using a piece of planking as a guide, and saw the plank to fit.

10 To get this last course tight against the rest of the floor, use a pry bar between the wall and the last course to wedge it into position. This last course of boards most often needs to be face-nailed.

On floating floors, press the sawed plank into place and finish by prying the planks together. Allow the glue to dry for 12 hours before using the floor. Any glue still left may be removed with a little household solvent or acetone.

Refinishing Hardwood Floors

Refinishing hardwood floors is one of the most popular do-it-yourself projects, and for good reason. Few projects offer such a dramatic reward for a relatively small investment of time and money. Scratches and the uneven wear on hardwood floors generally don't leave many options other than refinishing. Many floors, however, do not need sanding because the imperfections are only superficial and not deep into the wood. Sometimes stripping the old topcoat and applying a fresh finish is all that is necessary to resurface the floor.

Refinishing can be a relatively simple task, although you'll need a respirator and goggles to combat the dust when you start sanding.

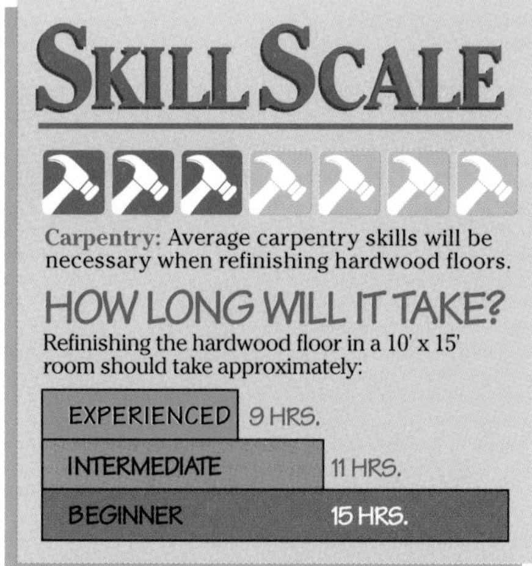

STUFF YOU'LL NEED:

- **Tools:** Floor sander, edge sander, orbital sander, hand scraper, paint pad, hammer, nail set.
- **Materials:** Chemical stripper, sandpaper, polyurethane varnish.

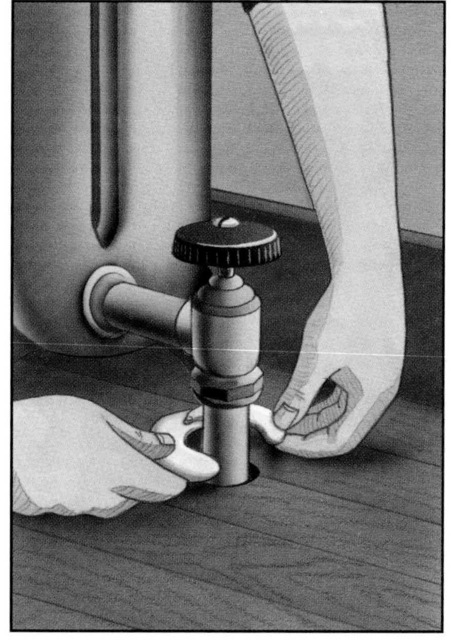

1 Remove heating-register grills, pipe collars, and any other obstructions.

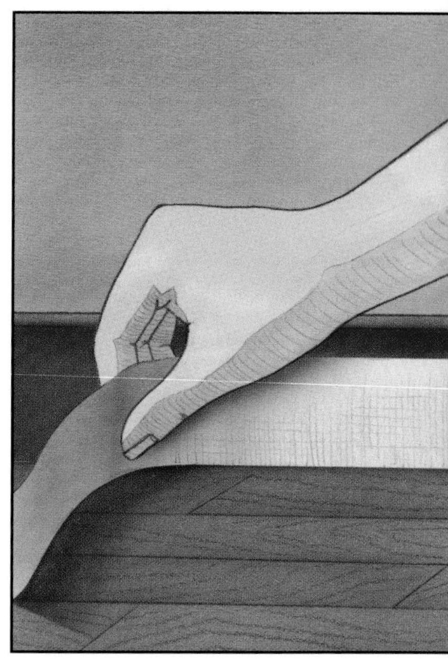

2 Use pregummed paper or wide masking tape to protect wood baseboard moldings.

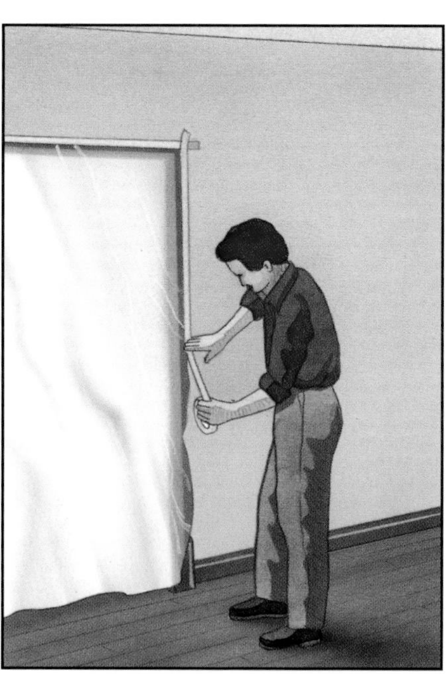

3 Ventilate the work area by opening windows and exterior doors. Close interior doors and cover openings with plastic sheeting.

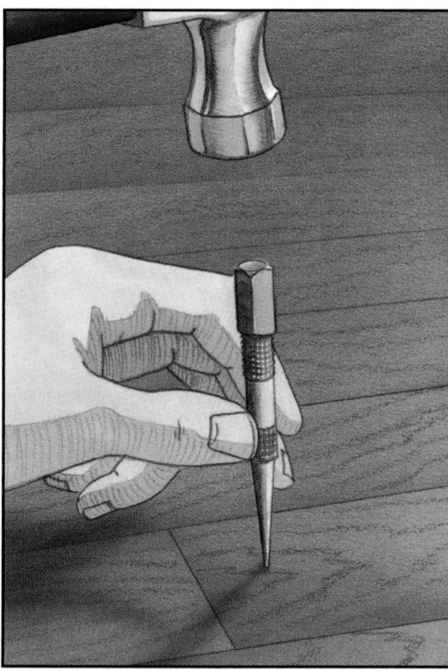

4 Countersink protruding nails and screws so they are about 1/4" below the floor surface.

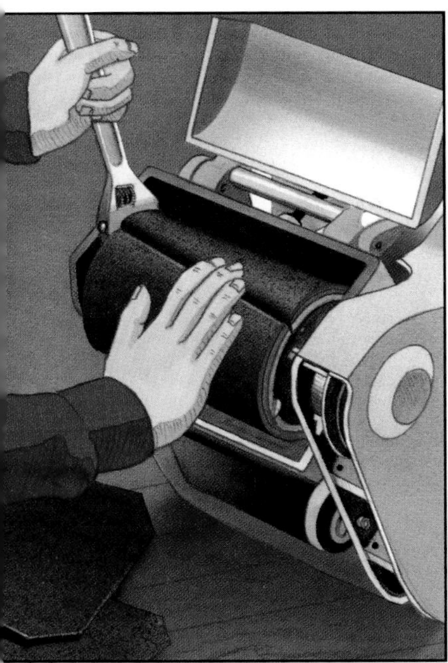

5 Install 80-grit sandpaper on the drum sander. It is a good idea to test the sander on a sheet of scrap plywood until you're comfortable with the sander's operation.

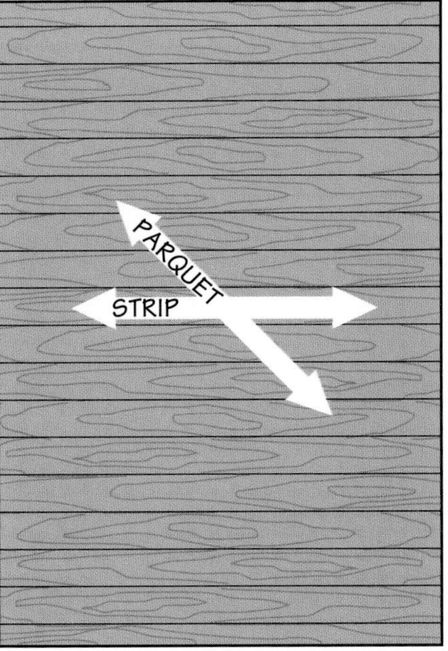

6 Plan your sanding job according to the type of floor and its condition. To sand a floor with little or no surface damage, plan to make one pass using fine sandpaper. For a strip wood floor, sand back and forth along the wood grain. For a parquet tile floor, sand back and forth diagonally across the tiles.

7 For a floor with extensive surface damage, make two passes. The first using very coarse sandpaper, the second using finer grit. On strip wood floors, make the first pass diagonally across the grain and the second along the grain. For parquet tile, make the first pass diagonally across the tiles one way; and the second diagonally the other way.

8 Start sanding the floor by positioning the drum sander in the center of the room, about 6" out from the wall. With the sanding drum in the raised position, turn on the machine and begin moving forward, lowering the drum as the sander moves. Sand a straight path, following the direction of the floorboards, and keep the machine moving constantly.

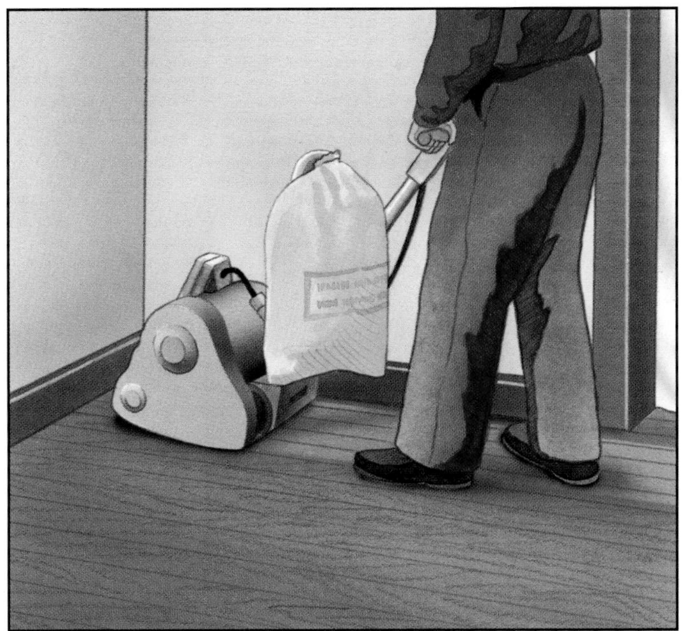

9 Complete the first pass. Sand to within about 1' of the end wall in the first sanding pass, raising the drum as you near the corner. If the sandpaper clogs quickly or leaves quite a bit of finish intact, switch to a coarser grit. As a general rule, use the finest grit that is effective for the job.

REFINISHING HARDWOOD FLOORS (continued)

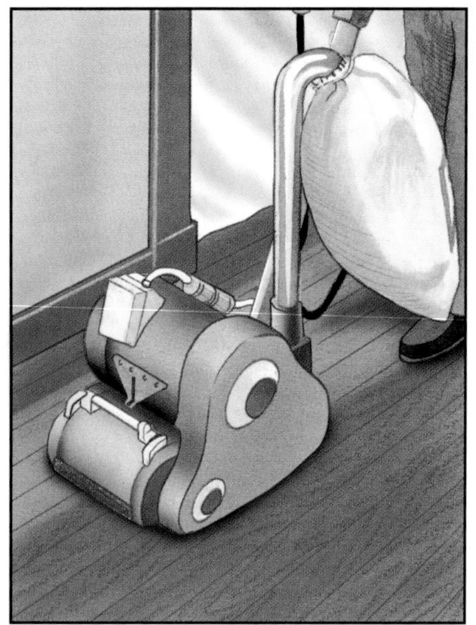

10 Make a second sanding pass. Reposition the sander at the starting point so the next path overlaps the first by ½ its width. Sand a second pass using the same method. Replace the sandpaper as needed, and sand overlapping paths to the other side wall, then sand the other half of the room.

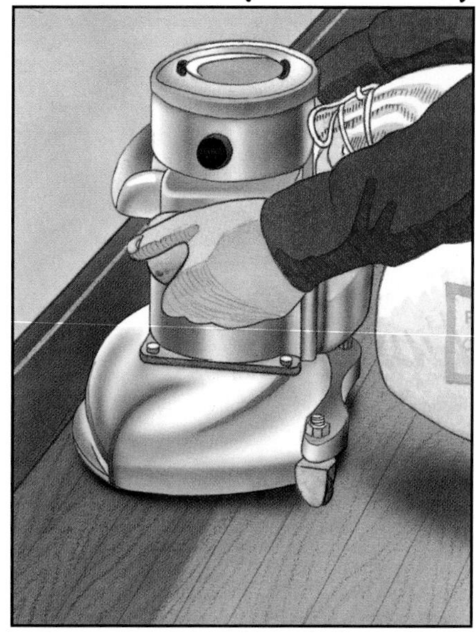

11 Sand the borders with an edger to sand off the finish from the border areas of the floor. When you turn on the edger, make sure the sandpaper is not resting on the floor, and maintain a light, even pressure on the machine as you work. Use the same sandpaper sequence as with the drum sander.

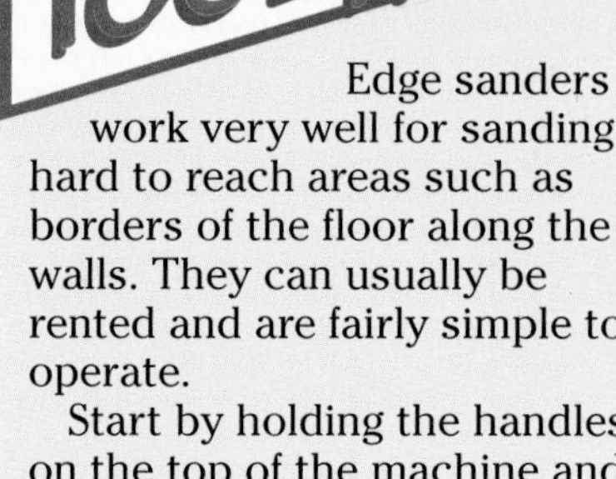

Edge sanders work very well for sanding hard to reach areas such as borders of the floor along the walls. They can usually be rented and are fairly simple to operate.

Start by holding the handles on the top of the machine and drape the power cord over your shoulder to prevent running over it and getting it caught in the sander.

Tilt the sander onto its back caster to lift the disc off the floor. Switch the sander on and lower it to the floor surface. As soon as you contact the boards, sweep the machine in any direction but keep it moving. There is no need to press down on the sander. When you have finished, tilt back the machine and switch it off, letting the motor run down before moving the sander.

12 Scrape or sand the hard-to-reach areas. Use a sharp scraper to resurface the floor in awkward areas that can't be reached with a power sander. Use a finishing sander with 180-grit paper to feather out any remaining uneven areas and sanding ridges.

Orbital finishing sanders, sometimes called jitterbug sanders (once you use them you'll know why they're called that) are available at most rental stores. These sanders get close to the edge of the room and are less likely to damage the floor than drum and edge sanders. Fitted with medium grit sandpaper, they will remove the old finish faster than scraping and will also help to blend in floor areas.

After sanding with 80-grit paper, switch to 120-grit for the second sanding stage. Most of the old finish should be gone before you switch sandpaper grits. Make additional passes with 150-grit and 180-grit sandpaper as necessary.

CHEMICALLY STRIPPING A WOOD FLOOR

1 Apply chemical stripper to the amount of floor area that you can scrape in the active working time of the stripper you're using. Refer to the label on the stripper container for the appropriate active working time. Normally a 2'-wide, 6'-long area is a good working size for active working times of 30 minutes.

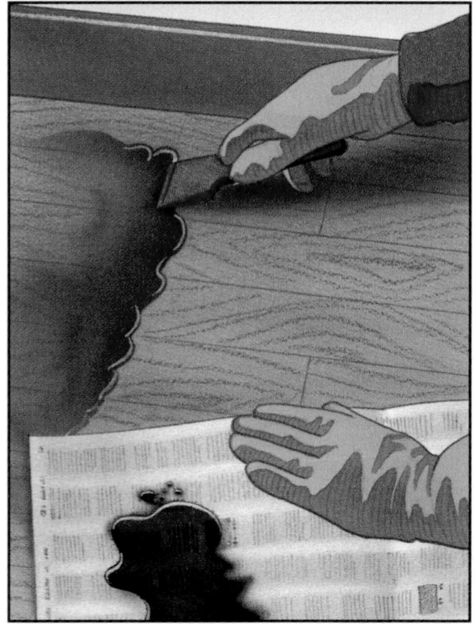

2 Scrape off the stripper and the old finish. Use a nylon stripper knife to remove the sludge, making sure to scrape in the same direction as the grain in the floorboards. Old newspaper is handy for depositing the sludge. Repeat steps 1 and 2 for the rest of the floor.

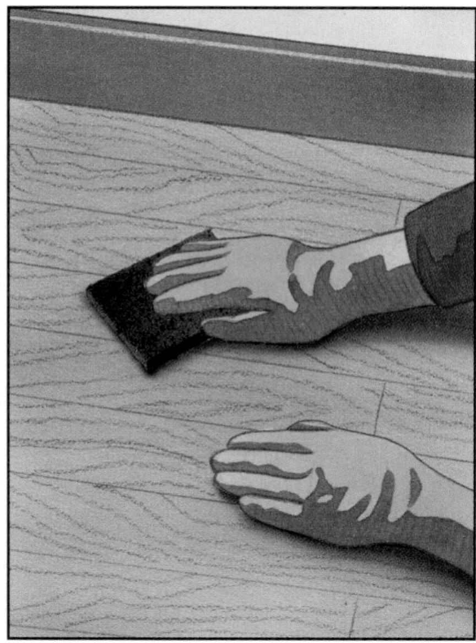

3 Scrub the floor with a medium abrasive pad dipped in mineral spirits. Remove the residue left by the stripper as well as the dissolved topcoat finish.

4 Clean out the gaps between the floorboards. Whenever you chemically strip a floor, the gaps and joints in the floor fill up with stripper and old finish. Left in the gaps, these chemicals can destroy your new topcoat. Simply scrape the old sludge out of the gaps with a putty knife or a palette knife.

5 Sand out stains in the floorboards. Bleach and oxalic acid are effective on some stains. Touch up with stain that matches the old stain color. After the stain dries, apply three coats of polyurethane topcoat.

HOMER'S HINDSIGHT

Paint strippers and solvents are becoming more friendly toward users and the environment, but there are still many available that need to be used with extreme caution and disposed of with great care.

If you have leftover stripper, secure the cover tightly and either save it for future use or contact your sanitation company to find out the proper disposal method for the particular type of solvent or stripper.

APPLYING WATER-BASED POLYURETHANE TO FLOORS

1 Seal the sanded wood floor with a mixture of water-based polyurethane and water, applied with a painting pad and pole extension. Refer to the manufacturer's recommendations for the proper mixture. Let the seal-coat dry, then use a medium abrasive pad to lightly buff the surfaces to remove any raised wood grain caused by the water. Vacuum the surface with a bristle attachment, or wipe with a tack cloth.

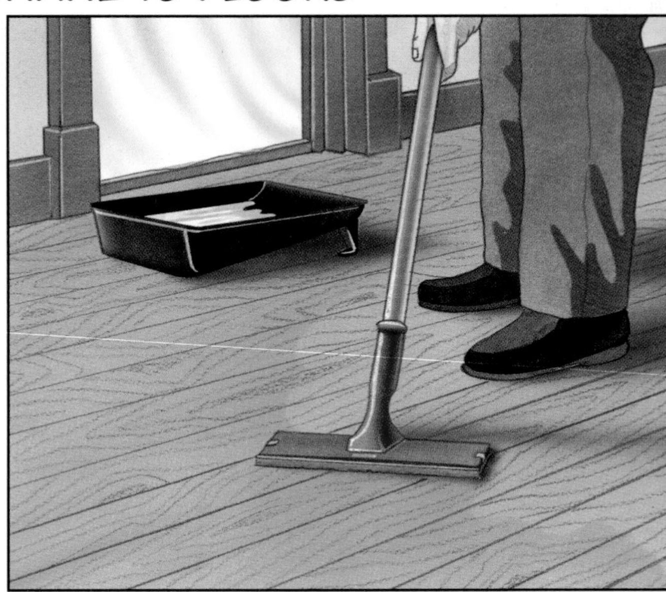

2 Apply a thin coat of undiluted water-based polyurethane, brushing with the grain. Avoid brushing the finish too much by applying it as evenly as possible on the first pass.

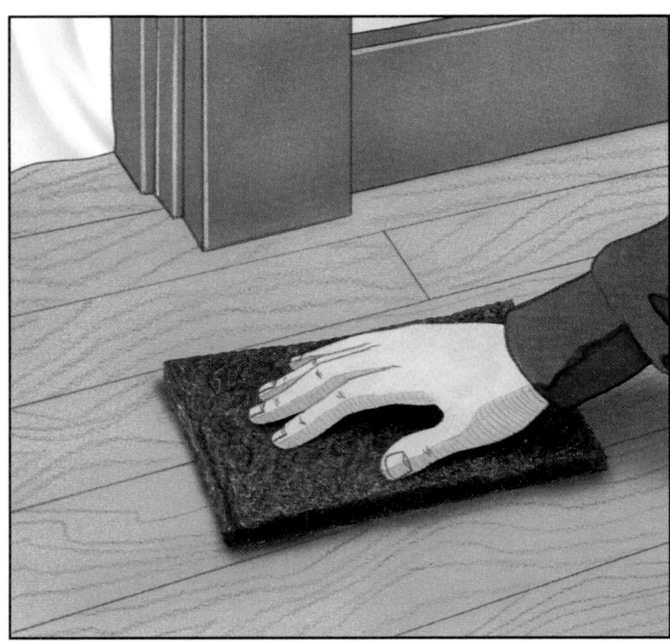

3 Let the finish dry, then buff the floor with an abrasive pad. Vacuum or wipe the floor and apply additional coats of water-based polyurethane as needed to build the finish to the desired thickness, buffing between coats. Most floors require at least three coats of water-based polyurethane for a hard, durable finish.

4 When the final coat of water-based polyurethane is dry, buff the surfaces with water and a fine abrasive pad to remove surface imperfections and diminish the gloss, if so desired.

Thresholds & Floorstrips

Thresholds cover the floorboard edges that end at a door and serve as a transition element to other flooring materials such as carpet, vinyl, ceramic, and hardwood. Thresholds are constructed traditionally of wood, although some modern styles are made of plastic solid-surface materials, similar to the material in solid-surface countertops. No matter what the material is, thresholds serve a decorative as well as a functional purpose in providing a transition from room to room. Removing and installing thresholds can be accomplished quite easily when replacing flooring.

STUFF YOU'LL NEED:

- ☐ **Tools:** Handsaw, tape measure, hammer, pry bar, nailset.
- ☐ **Materials:** Floorstrips, thresholds, nails.

REMOVING THRESHOLDS

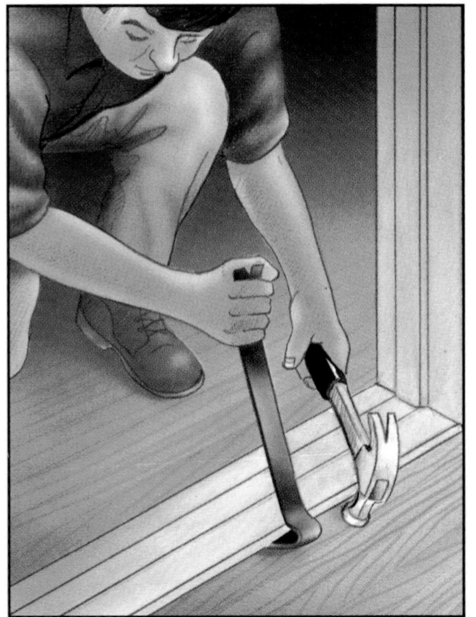

1 Remove the threshold by prying up from the floor with a hammer and metal pry bar if the door stops are not undercut.

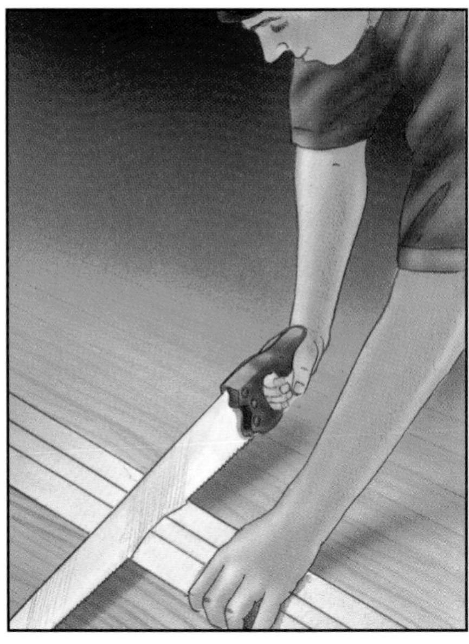

2 If the door jambs were undercut to house the threshold, saw the threshold into two pieces and remove each piece separately, or use a cat's paw to remove the finish nails from the threshold and hammer it out from underneath the door stops.

INSTALLING A NEW THRESHOLD

1 Before installing a new wood threshold, undercut the door stops, if necessary, then cut the threshold to length.

2 Predrill pilot holes and nail the threshold to the floor with 8d finish nails, or, if you choose, counterbore the threshold and fasten it with countersunk wood screws.

CHOOSING THE RIGHT FLOOR STRIP

Seam binders are used to decoratively cover seams of similar flooring materials. Seam binders are available in metal, plastic, wood, and solid-surface styles.

Thresholds are specifically used in doorways to provide a transition between flooring types and rooms. Thresholds are typically made of wood or solid-surface material.

Reducers are used to provide transition between flooring of different heights due to different floor materials or changes from remodeling projects.

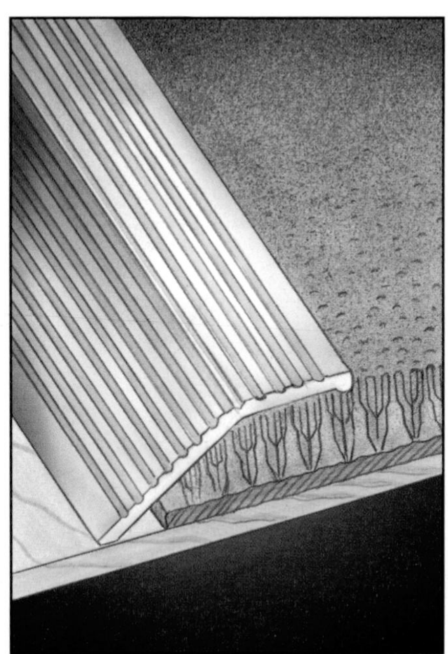

Carpet trim is used to provide a decorative edge on a carpeted surface and to conceal the seam where it meets the adjacent flooring material.

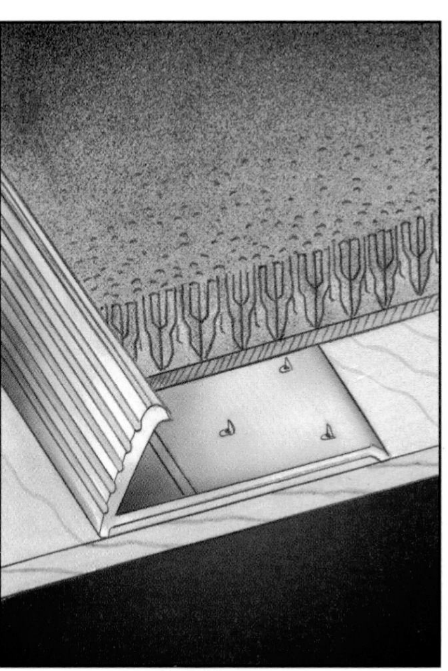

Carpet grippers are used as a combination tackless strip and decorative edge where the carpeted floor meets a noncarpeted adjacent flooring material.

Stair edging helps to protect carpeted and hardwood tread fronts from excessive wear.

Baseboards, Coves & Chair Rails

The most important tools for working with trim and moldings are a sharp pencil and a sharp saw in a quality miter box. These tools let you mark and cut mitered joints accurately. Tight-fitting joints are the primary goal in trim carpentry. These will be quite difficult to accomplish unless you use a quality backsaw and miter box or power miter saw.

Installing trim and moldings isn't too technically difficult if you follow the proper procedures and use the proper tools. A simple method of making decorative trim styles is to combine two or more molding shapes to create custom moldings.

STUFF YOU'LL NEED:

- ☐ **Tools:** Tape measure, hand or power miter box, hammer, nail set, coping saw.
- ☐ **Materials:** Molding, finish nails.

IDENTIFYING TRIM TYPES

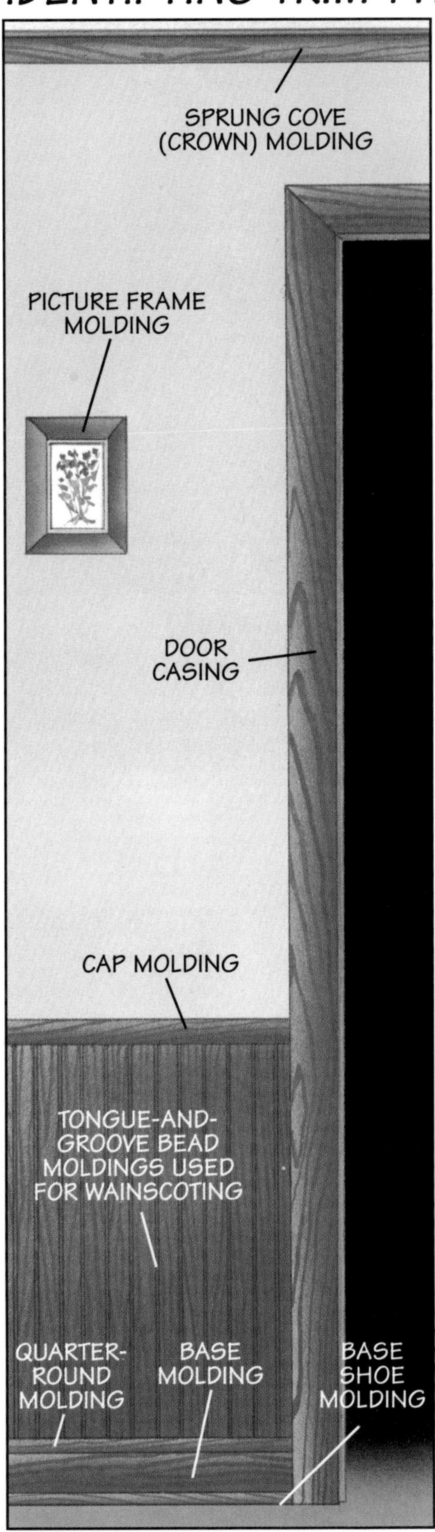

Standard moldings and trims, when installed properly, provide a professionally finished appearance for any room.

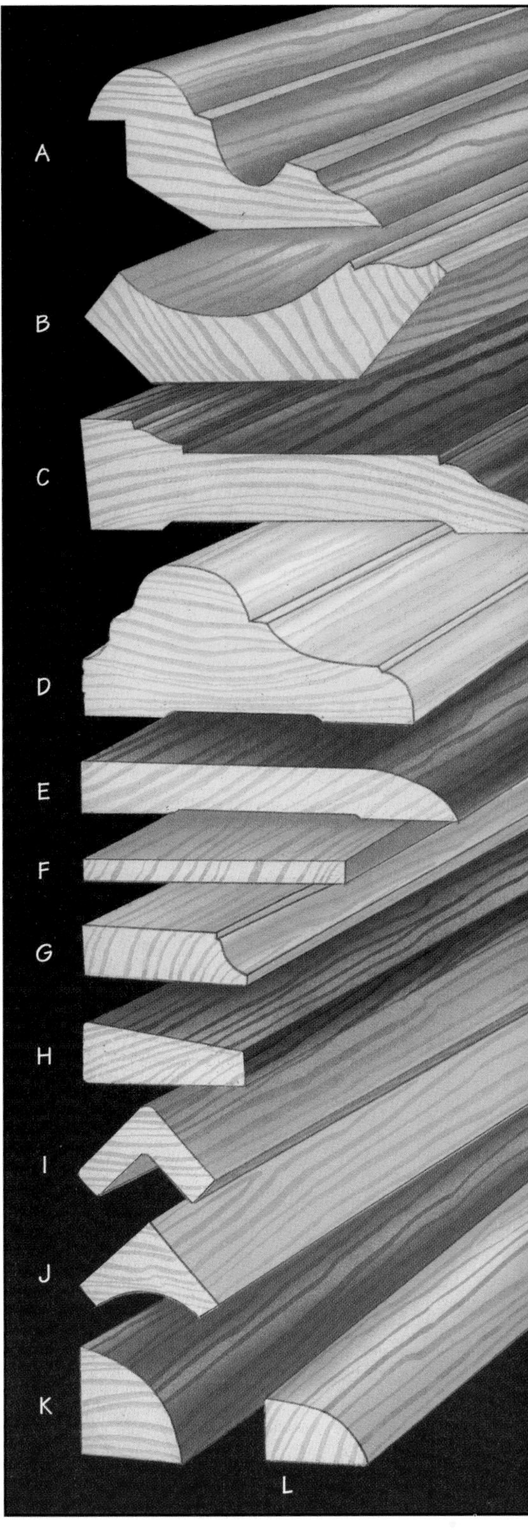

Common trim and molding styles include: cap molding (**A**), crown molding (**B**), base molding (**C**), chair rail (**D**), ranch baseboard (**E**), lattice (**F**), colonial strip (**G**), bifold door stop (**H**), outside corner (**I**), inside corner (**J**), quarter round (**K**), and base shoe (**L**).

COMBINE MOLDINGS

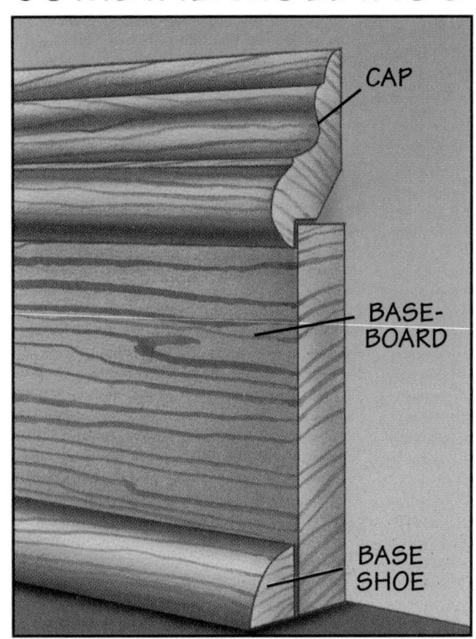

Ornamental trim styles can be created by combining two or more types of standard trim. Molding styles that are no longer produced can be duplicated with this method.

Decorative crown molding can be created by combining two sprung cove moldings. The square nailing strip in the corner provides a nailing surface for both moldings.

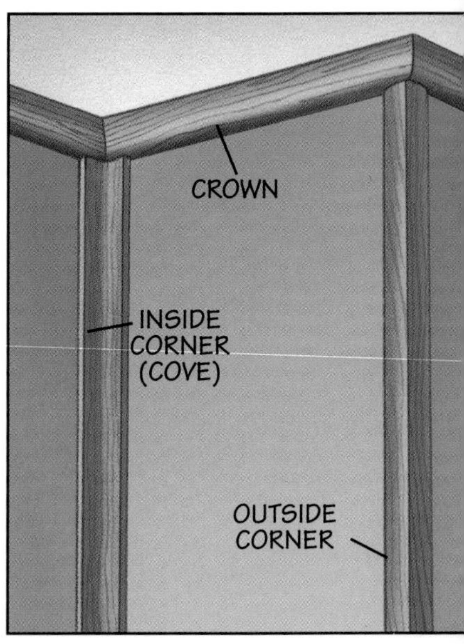

Inside and outside corner moldings add elegance to a room. Corner moldings on walls are often used with a cove or crown molding along the ceiling lines.

Edge molding or chair rail can be used to form a decorative border on wainscoted and partially paneled walls.

CUTTING MITERS IN MOLDINGS

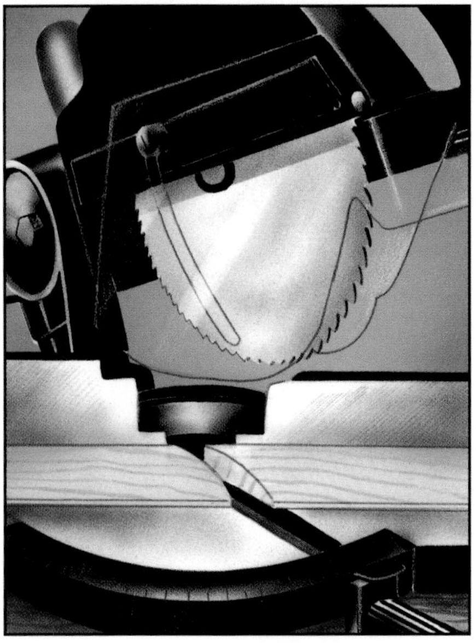

1 Cut casings at a 45° angle with the flat back edge tight against the bottom base of the miter box. Baseboard miters are cut with the flat back edge tight against the vertical rear base of miter box.

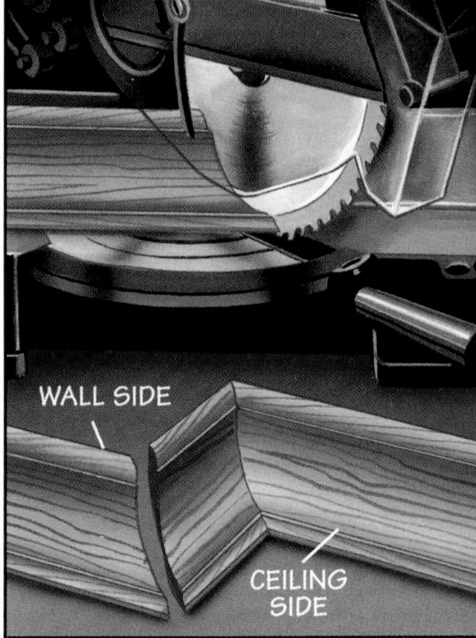

2 Sprung cove molding is cut by positioning the ceiling side of the molding tight against the bottom base of the miter box. The wall side of the molding should be tight against the vertical rear base of the miter box.

CUTTING AND FITTING BASEBOARDS

1 At inside corners, butt one end of the baseboard into the corner. On the back side of the adjacent baseboard, outline the profile of the baseboard with a pencil.

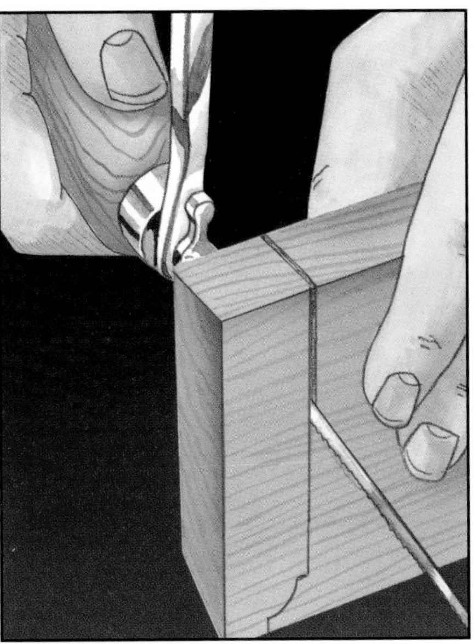

2 With a coping saw, trim the baseboard along the marked profile. Clamp the baseboard in a vise when cutting, and keep the blade perpendicular to the baseboard face.

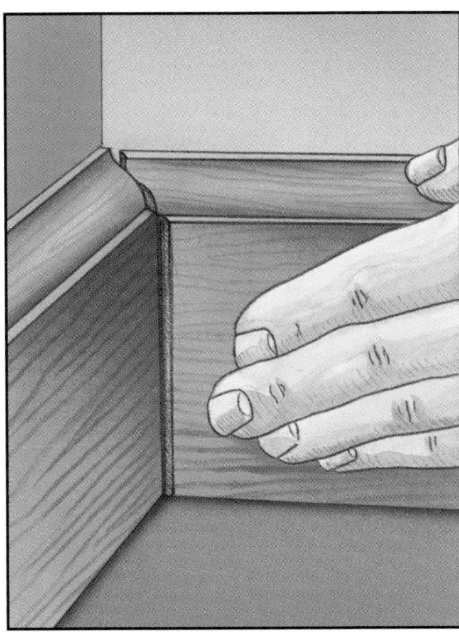

3 Fit the baseboard pieces into the corner. The baseboard with the coped edge fits tightly over the adjoining square-cut baseboard molding.

4 Fit outside corners by cutting the ends of the baseboards at opposite 45° miters. Attach the trim with finish nails and recess the nail heads with a nail set.

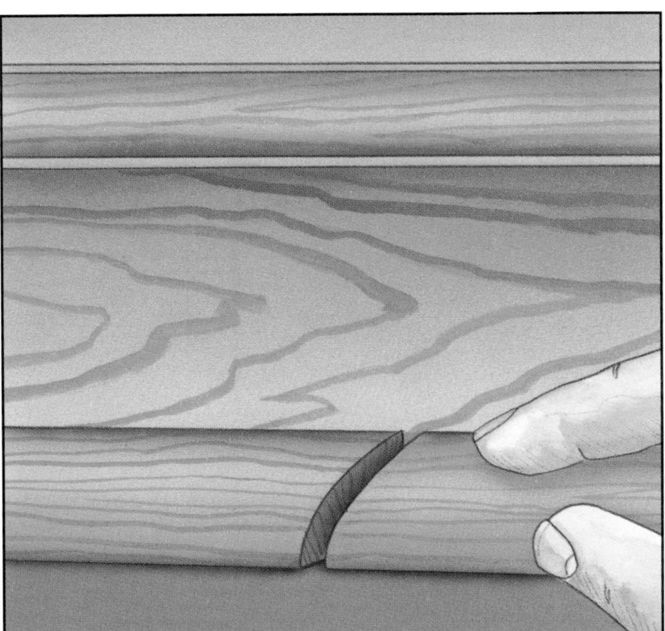

5 For long spans of molding, join shorter pieces by mitering the ends at parallel 45° angles. This way, the mitered joint will not reveal a gap if the wood shrinks. Be sure to pre-drill hardwoods before nailing so you don't split the wood.

INSTALLING CROWN MOLDING

BUTT COPE 1 BUTT COPE

2 4

BUTT COPE 3 COPE BUTT

Plan your crown molding layout for a typical room by starting with the piece opposite the door (1). The coped joints butting in to both ends of that piece will show their best side to anyone entering the room. This is difficult because the last piece you install (4), will have to be coped on both ends.

1 The first piece of molding is cut square and run into the corner. The second piece is cut to the shape of the molding's profile (coped) and will butt neatly into the face of the other piece. The paper-thin point on the bottom of the coped piece will make the finished joint look like a miter.

2 Before the crown molding can be coped, the end must be mitered to expose the profile. Positioned accordingly in the miter box (pg. 292), the molding rests tightly against the horizontal bottom base and the vertical rear base of the miter box.

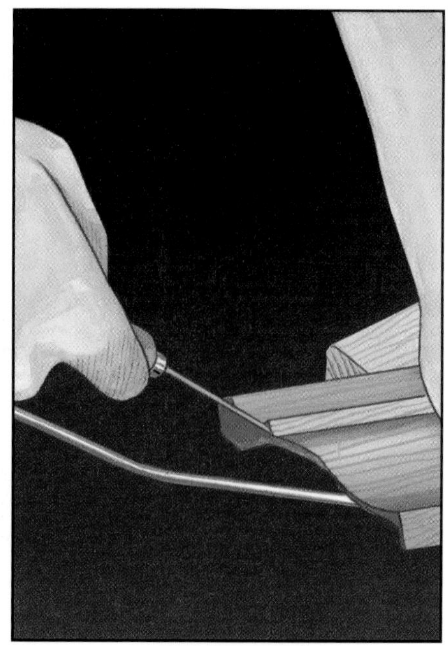

3 After exposing the profile of the crown molding, the back part of the stock is cut away with a coping saw, which must be held at a severe angle or the coped joint will not fit tight.

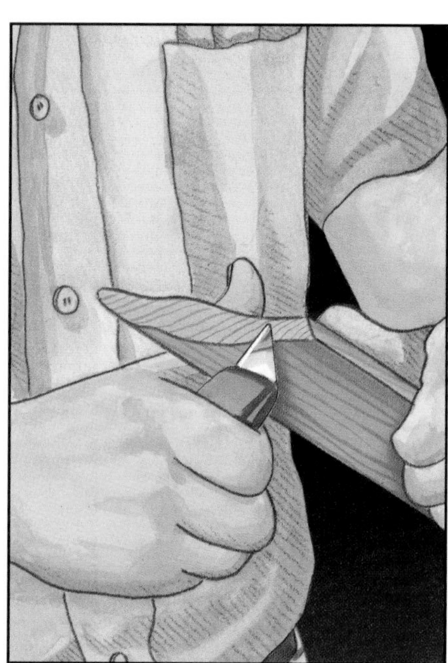

4 Even with the coping saw at a severe angle, it's tough to remove enough wood through the S-curve in the crown molding. Additional stock often has to be pared away with a utility knife.

When you install the first piece of crown molding by cutting both ends square, the last piece will have to be coped on both sides. To avoid this, you can put up a short piece temporarily and cope the first piece of crown molding into it. This coped joint needs to be accurate or else it will be immediately noticed.

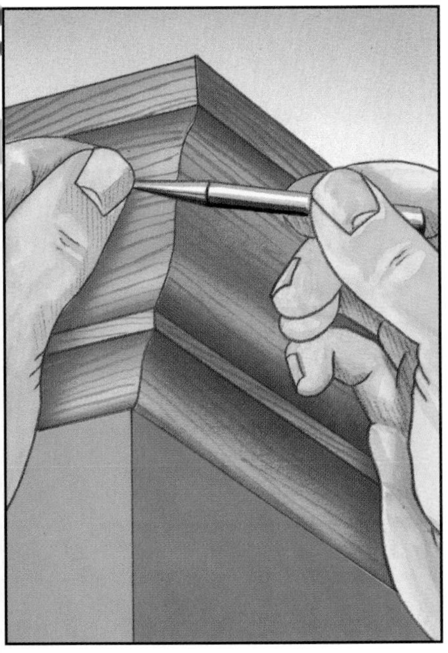

5 Molding on outside corners should be mitered to fit. If an outside miter is open just slightly, sometimes you can close it by burnishing the corner with a nail set.

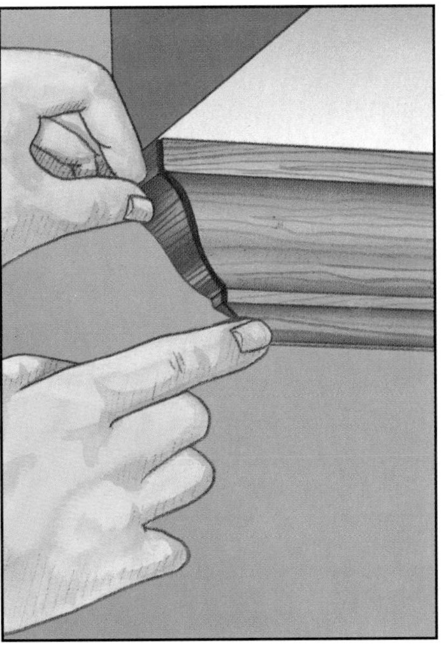

6 When a line of crown molding has to be neatly terminated on an open wall, the end should be mitered and "returned" into the wall with a small piece of molding. To avoid splitting such a delicate piece, simply glue it in place.

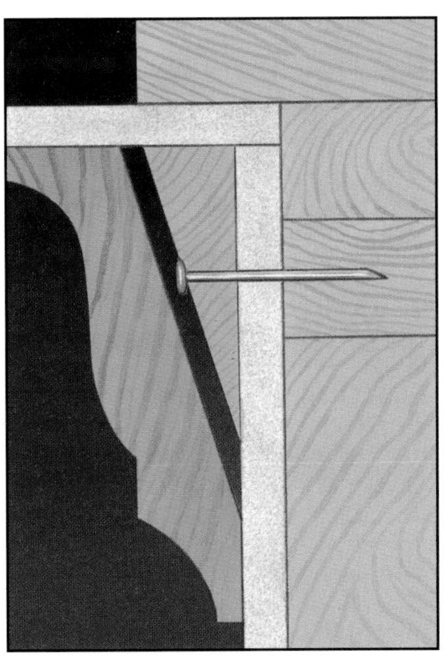

When nailing crown molding, walls parallel with the ceiling joists can be a problem. Cut a length of 2x4 to fill the space behind and to provide a nailing surface for the crown molding.

INSTALLING CHAIR RAIL

Install blocking to provide a stable fastening structure for the chair rail. Remove the wallboard and install the blocking at the desired height, usually 32" above the finished floor. If you're installing wainscoting, you'll also need blocking halfway between the floor and the chair rail blocking.

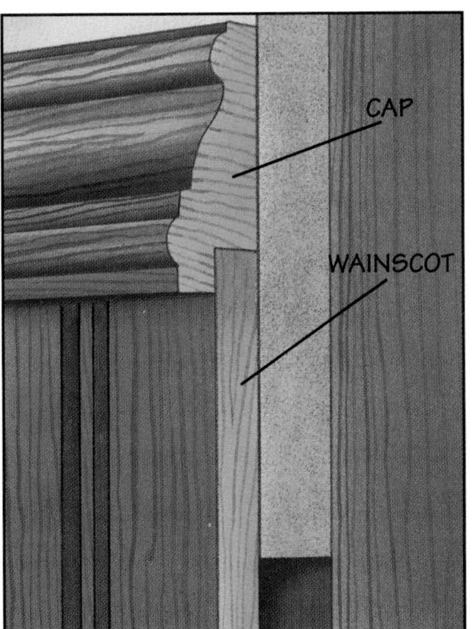

With the blocking installed and the wallboard replaced, fasten the chair rail through the wallboard and into the blocking with finish nails spaced 8" apart. Use cap molding to finish off the top edge of the wainscoting and to provide a substantial chair rail.

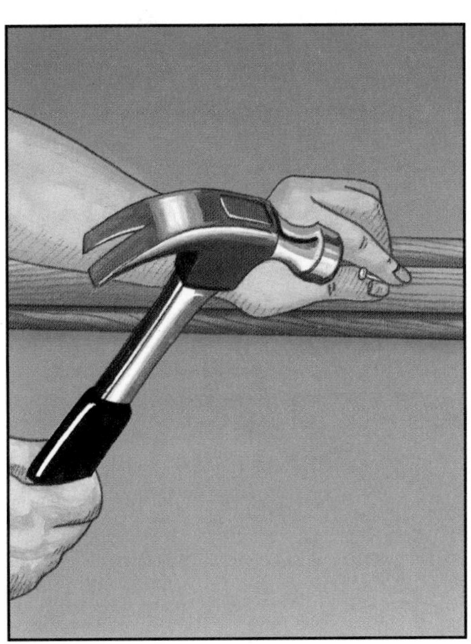

Use chair rail without wainscoting to give a more subtle visual break on the wall while still providing protection to the wall surface.

DOOR & WINDOW BASICS

Doors are, of course, subject to daily use and suffer ultimately from normal wear. Windows are exposed to the destructive effects of weather and use. Periodic maintenance will keep your doors and windows smoothly functional, but eventually the accumulated deterioration will lead you to consider replacement.

Replacing a door or window is not only critical to the energy efficiency, comfort and convenience of your home, it's also an opportunity to make a dramatic change in your home's appearance.

The best news of all is that putting in a door or window can be a relatively easy, one-day project, especially if you aren't changing the size of the opening!

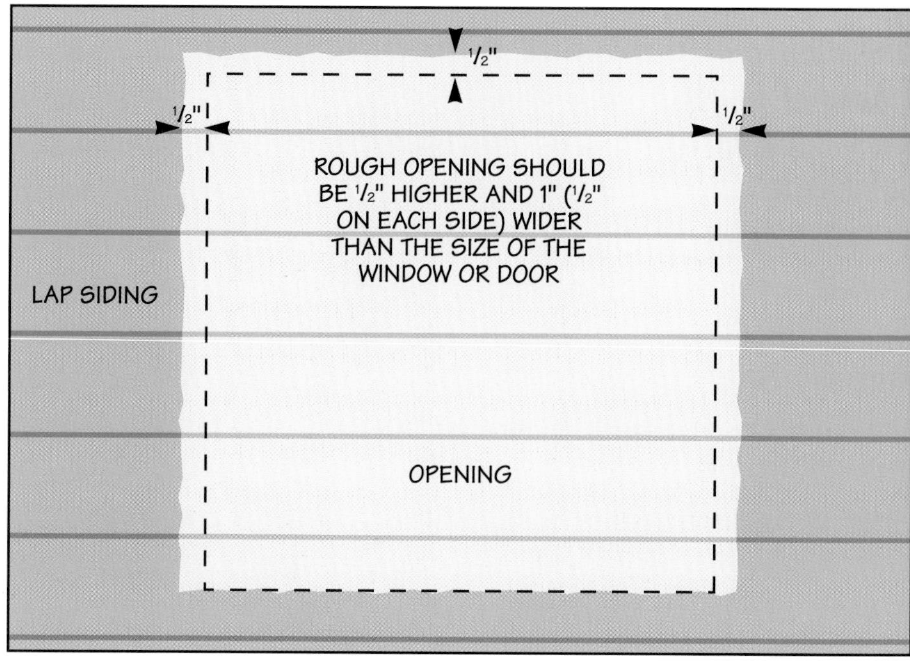

Measure the rough opening once the old door or window has been removed, or if it is new construction, once the framing has been completed. Measure from side to side and from top to bottom of the opening and choose door or window units to fit. Keep in mind that the rough opening should be slightly larger than the door or window unit to allow room for plumb and level adjustments and for insulation and weatherproofing.

TOOLS AND MATERIALS FOR DOORS AND WINDOWS

Hand Tools include: caulk gun (**A**), flat bar (**B**), miter box w/backsaw (**C**), hacksaw (**D**), wood chisels (**E**), screwdrivers (**F**), pliers (**G**), locking pliers (**H**), metal snips (**I**), chalk line (**J**), spline roller (**K**), nail set (**L**), stapler (**M**), utility knife (**N**), ratchet wrench w/sockets (**O**), hammer (**P**), framing square (**Q**), handsaw (**R**), combination square (**S**), tape measure (**T**), and a carpenter's level (**U**).

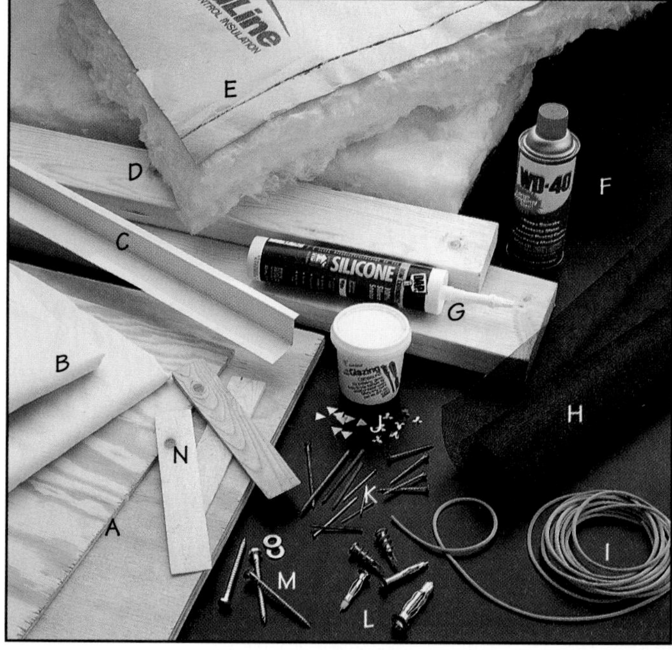

Materials include: plywood (**A**), drop cloth (**B**), drip cap (**C**), framing lumber (**D**), fiberglass insulation (**E**), spray lubricant (**F**), silicone caulk (**G**), screen material (**H**), screen spline (**I**), glazing compound and points (**J**), wood screws, common nails, casing nails and finish nails (**K**), hollow wall anchors (**L**), lag screws (**M**), and wood shims (**N**).

Anatomy of Doors & Windows

Doors and windows cause a breech in the integral structure of your home, a weak point that requires reinforcement to carry the load above. Exterior doors require framing on the sides of the opening substantial enough to support the heavy door without distorting and to provide the mass necessary to secure deadbolt locks.

If you aren't changing the size of the opening when you replace a door or window, can you assume that the structural support is adequate? It depends. Look at the current opening for signs that might indicate problems. If the existing door or window operated properly, chances are the structural support is fine. If you have been experiencing problems, now is the time to correct the structural problems before you proceed to the new window or door installation.

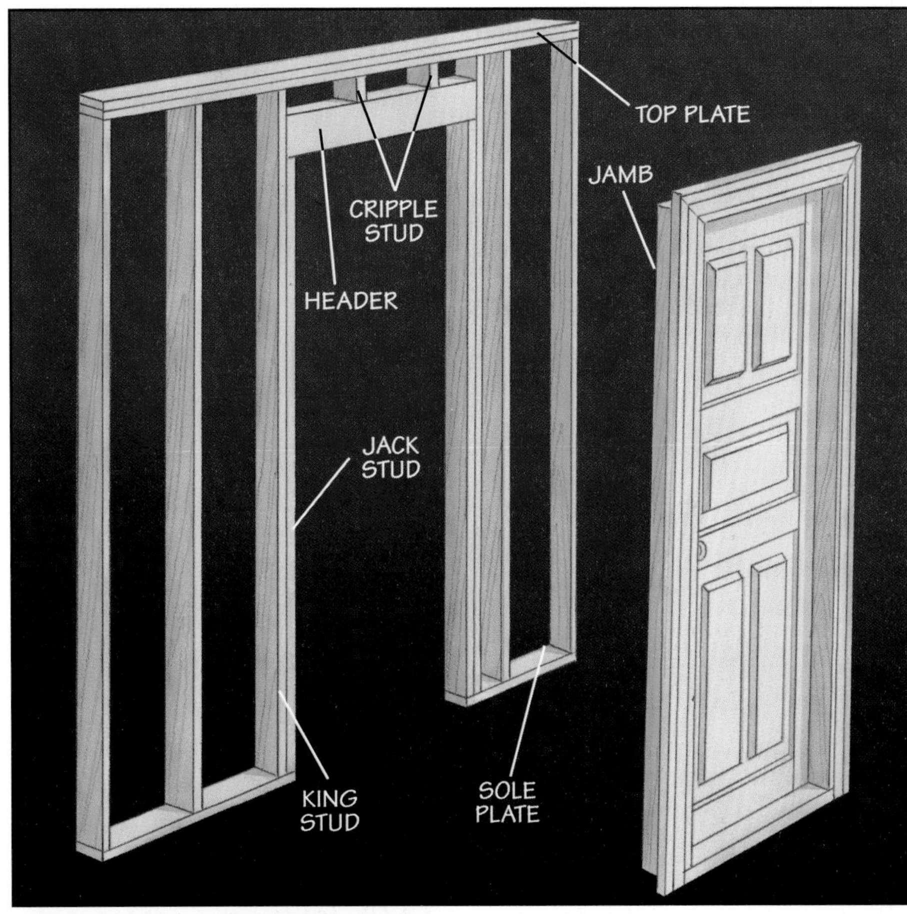

Door openings are designed so the structural load above the door is carried by cripple studs that rest on a header. The ends of the header are supported by king studs (sometimes called trimmer studs), and jack studs, which transfer the load to the sole plate and the foundation of the home.

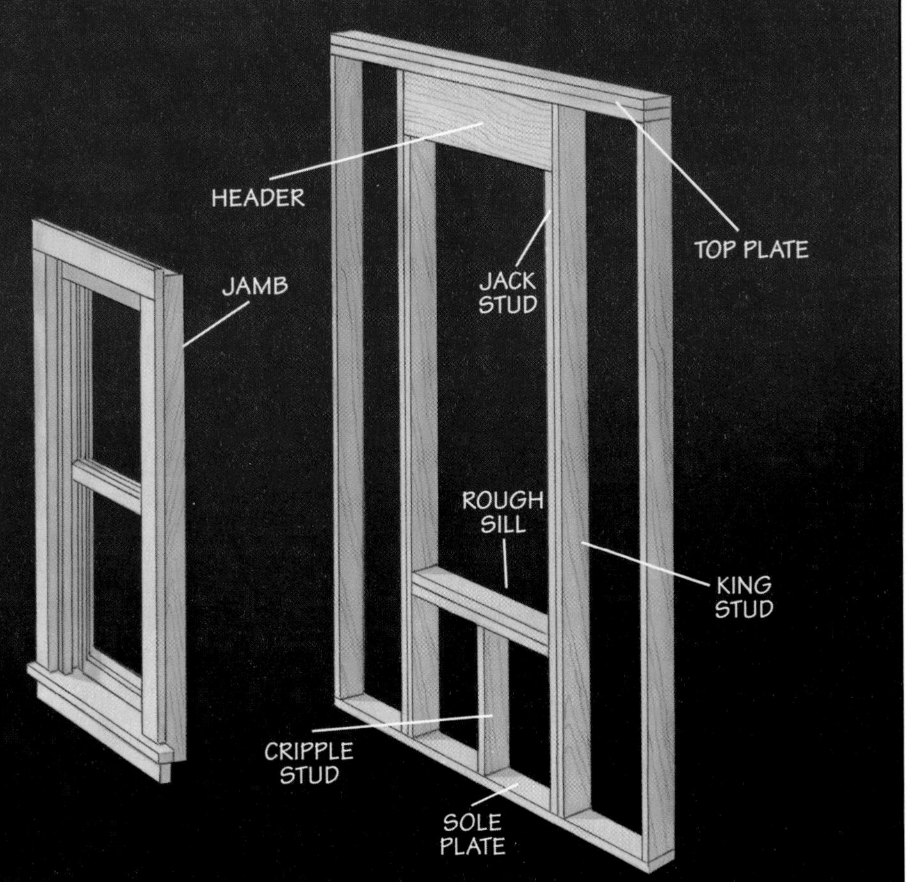

Window openings are similar in that the structural load above the window is carried by cripple studs resting on a header. The ends of the header are supported by king studs and jack studs, which transfer the load to the sole plate and the foundation of the home. The rough sill, which helps anchor the window unit but carries no structural weight, is supported by cripple studs.

To provide room for adjustments during installation, the rough opening for doors and windows should be 1" wider and $^{1}/_{2}$" taller than the unit, including the jambs.

BUYER'$ GUIDE

Choosing the Right Doors & Windows

Wood frames are a good choice for windows and patio doors used in remodeling projects. Their preattached exterior brick moldings blend well with the look of existing windows. Replacement sashes are also available and can improve existing windows. Clad-frame windows and doors feature an aluminum or vinyl shell. They are used most frequently in new construction and are attached with nailing flanges that fit underneath the siding material. Vinyl clad windows come in a variety of colors and don't need painting.

Several types of glass are available from window and door manufacturers. Single-pane glass is outdated in most situations and suitable only in very mild climates or in outbuildings. Double-pane windows have a sealed air space between the layers of glass to reduce heat loss. They are available in several variations with improved insulating ability, including "low-E" glass with an invisible coating of metal on one surface and windows containing an inert gas like argon. In southern climates, double-glazed tinted glass reduces heat build-up. Tempered glass has extra strength for use in patio doors and large picture windows. R-values of windows and doors, listed in manufacturers' catalogs, indicate the energy efficiency of the unit. Higher R-values indicate better insulating properties. Top quality windows can have an R-value as high as 4.0. Exterior doors with R-values above 10 are considered energy efficient. Low-E glass helps to prevent sun damage to interior surfaces such as upholstery fabric, drapery and carpet by blocking harmful sunlight.

Be sure to check the wall thickness before ordering doors and windows. Manufacturers will customize the frame jambs to match whatever wall construction you have. Find your wall thickness by measuring the jamb width on an existing door or window.

COMMON WINDOW STYLES

Casement windows pivot on hinges mounted on the side of the frame. They are available in many sizes, and in multi-window units that combine as many as five separate windows. Casement windows offer a more contemporary look and provide an unobstructed view with good ventilation.

Double-hung windows slide up and down, and have a more traditional appearance. New double-hung windows have a spring-mounted operating mechanism instead of the troublesome sash weights found on older windows.

Sliding windows are relatively inexpensive and require little maintenance but don't provide as much open ventilation as casement windows since only half of the window can be open at one time. They do, however, provide a clear, unobstructed view.

Bay windows, sometimes known as bow windows or garden windows, make a house feel larger without expensive structural changes. They are available in dozens of sizes and styles.

COMMON DOOR STYLES

Interior panel doors have an elegant, traditional look. They are very durable and provide good soundproofing.

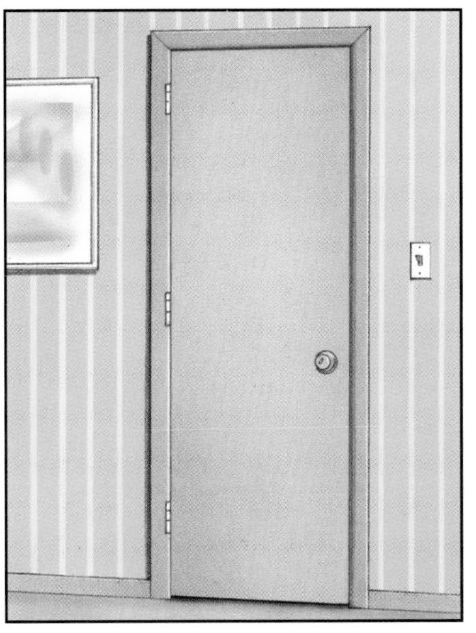

Interior hollow-core prehung doors have a contemporary look and are available in many stock sizes. Hollow-core doors are lightweight and inexpensive.

Decorative storm doors can improve the security, energy efficiency and appearance of your entry. A storm door prolongs the life of an expensive entry door by protecting it from the elements.

Entry doors with sidelights brighten a dark entry hall, and give an inviting formal look to your home. In better models, sidelights contain tempered, double-pane glass for better security and energy efficiency.

Sliding patio doors offer good visibility and lighting. Because they slide on tracks and require no floor space for operation, sliding doors are a good choice for cramped spaces where swinging doors do not fit.

Hinged patio doors have an elegant appearance. Weathertight models are used to join indoor and outdoor living areas, while indoor models are used to link two rooms. Because these doors open on hinges, your room design must allow space for them to swing.

Locksets & Latches

Locksets and latches fall into three basic types: passage locksets, which may or may not include a lock but which principally serve as a mechanism to hold the door shut; entry locksets, which also perform a latching function, but include a keyed security lock; and security or deadbolt locks, which offer a more secure barrier to unauthorized entry, but do not include a knob or latch mechanism.

While most modern locksets are more or less interchangeable within their basic types, older passage locksets employ an incompatible method of mortised installation. That means you'll probably have to replace the whole door if you can't repair an older lockset.

Backset is the distance from the center of the doorknob spindle to the edge of the door. When you select a replacement lockset, be sure to buy one with the same backset as the previous unit.

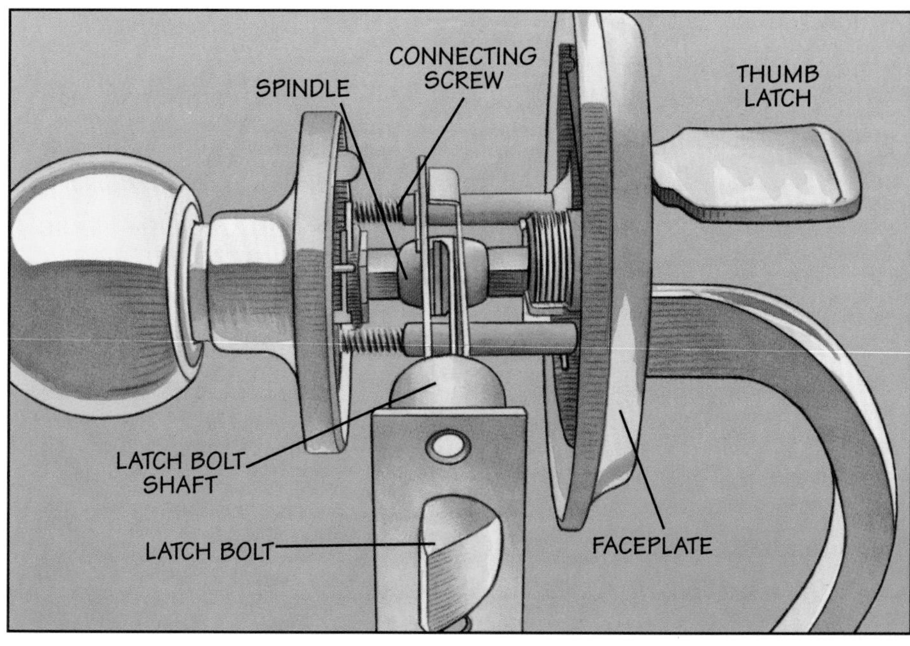

Locksets operate by extending the latch bolt into a strike plate (see facing page) set in the door frame. The latch bolt is moved back and forth by the spindle or connecting rod operated by a thumb latch, handle, or a keyed cylinder. If the doorknob or key binds when turned, the problem usually lies in the spindle and latch bolt mechanism. Cleaning and lubricating the moving parts will correct most problems.

TYPES OF LOCKSETS

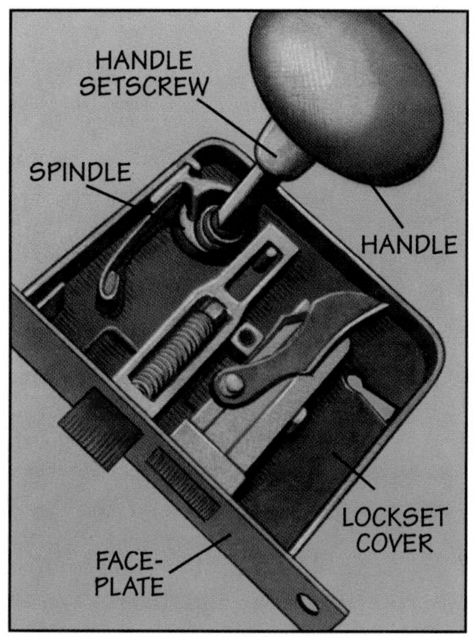

Older passage locksets are easily cleaned and lubricated by loosening the handle setscrew and removing the handles and spindle. Loosen the faceplate screws and pry the lockset from the door. Remove the lockset cover, lubricate the parts and then reassemble it.

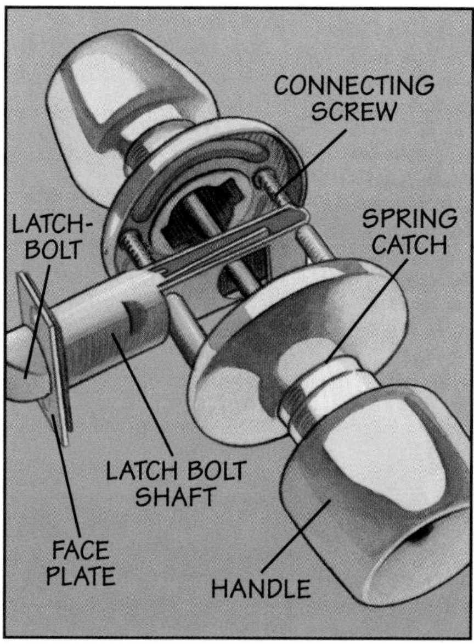

Modern passage locksets usually don't need much maintenance. If they do they're cleaned and lubricated by releasing the spring catch and connecting screws, and removing the handles. Remove the faceplate and latch bolt, lubricate the parts and reassemble.

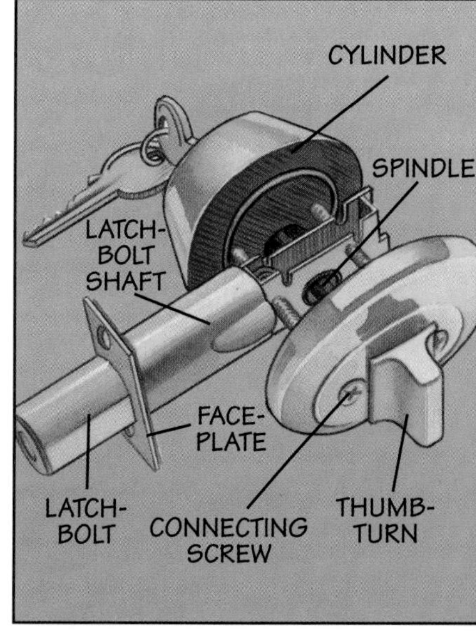

Security locks, like passage locksets, should be relatively trouble free. If they need maintenance, remove the connecting screws and cylinders. Remove the faceplate and latch bolt. Lubricate the components and reassemble.

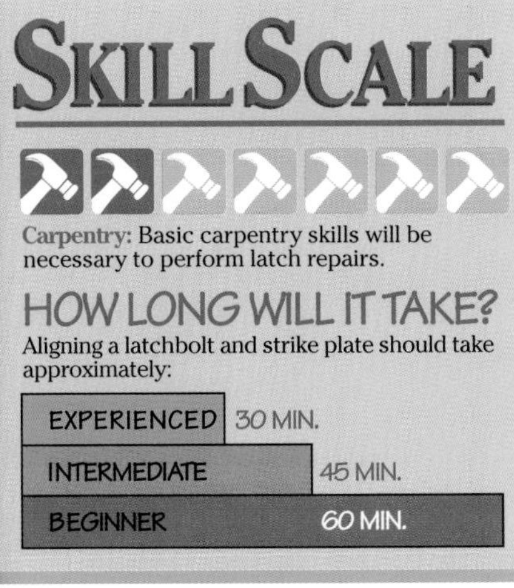

STUFF YOU'LL NEED:

- ☐ **Tools:** File, combination square, screwdrivers.
- ☐ **Materials:** Penetrating oil, shims.

Solving Door Latch Problems

When a door fails to latch, the problem is usually one of alignment. The latch bolt, for some reason, is not dropping smoothly into the center of the strike plate.

Determine in which direction the latch bolt is off center. If it meets the strike plate above or below center, the problem can be corrected by shimming a hinge to change the angle at which the door hangs. The shim may solve the problem, but it also may make the door bind with the jamb. If the alignment seems fine, but the door won't latch or must be pushed firmly to latch, the door is probably warped. A warped door may indicate a moisture problem. Check the edges of the door to make sure they're properly sealed. Suspending the door between two sawhorses and weighing down the center may counteract the warp, but you should think about buying a replacement door.

Misalignment with the strike plate will prevent the latch bolt from extending into the strike plate opening. Check for loose hinges and align the strike plate and the latch bolt to operate properly. It may be enough to slightly enlarge the strike plate opening with a file.

ALIGNING THE LATCH BOLT AND STRIKE PLATE

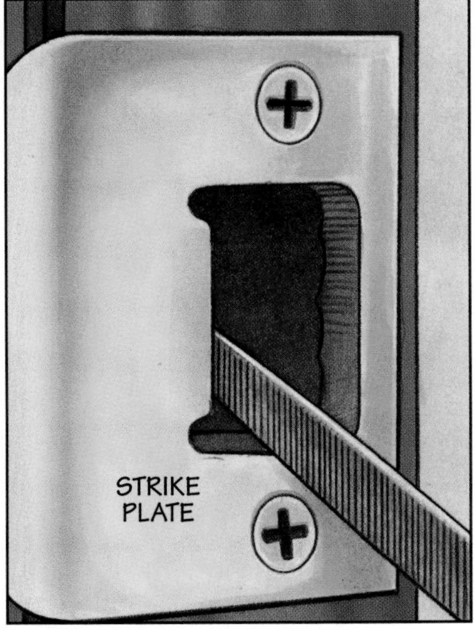

1 Fix and tighten any loose hinges and test the door. If the latch bolt still doesn't catch, you can fix any minor alignment problems by filing the strike plate until the latch bolt fits.

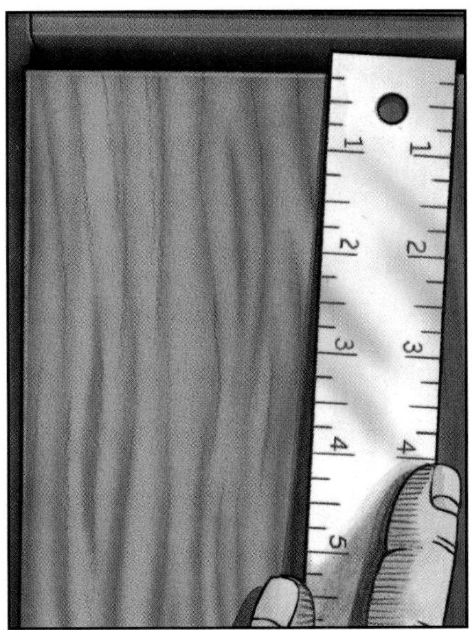

2 Check the door for a square fit. If the door is badly tilted, then remove the door and shim either the top or bottom hinge to correct the problem.

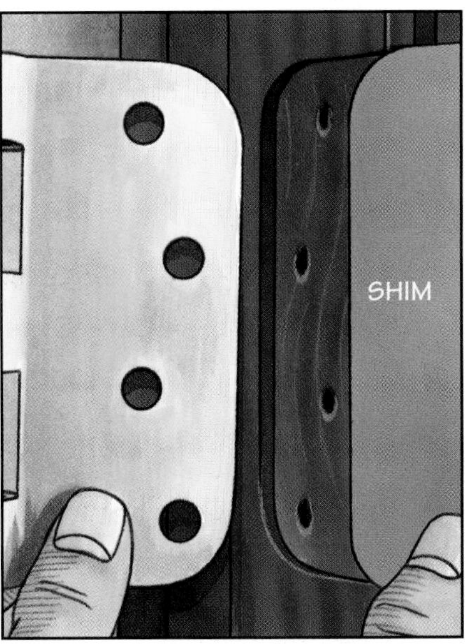

3 If necessary, you can raise the position of latch bolt by inserting a thin cardboard shim behind the bottom hinge. To lower the latch bolt, shim behind the top hinge.

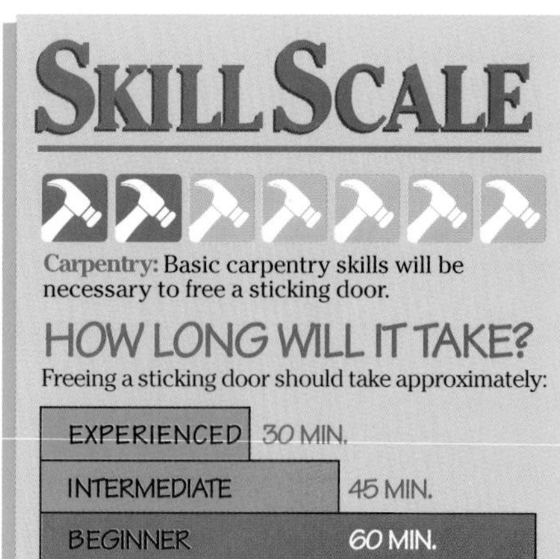

Freeing a Sticking Door

Doors stick when the hinges sag, when the door frame shifts, or when humidity causes the door and door frame to swell.

If the door seems to be sagging within the frame, make sure the hinge screws are tight. Once you have tightened the hinge screws, if a door continues to stick, you will need to sand or plane the door edge at the sticking point. Don't attempt this during a period of high humidity – you may remove too much! Wait for dry weather, test to affirm that the door is still sticking, then have at it! Seal the edges of the newly unstuck door to minimize the effects of humidity in the future.

STUFF YOU'LL NEED:

- ☐ **Tools:** Screwdrivers, drill w/bits, utility knife.
- ☐ **Materials:** Wood glue, wood dowels or golf tees.

BE CAREFUL NOT TO DAMAGE THE HINGE FINISH.

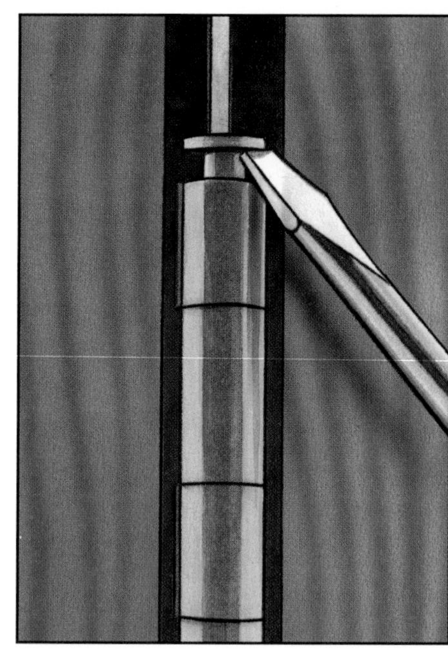

1 Drive the lower hinge pin out with a screwdriver and hammer. Hold the door in place and drive out the upper hinge pin. Some hinges have an access hole in the bottom. To avoid marring the hinge finish, you can insert a nail or small Phillips screwdriver and drive the pin upward.

2 Once the door is removed from its hinges, tighten any loose screws. If the wood behind the hinge will not hold the screws tightly, remove the hinges completely.

3 Coat wooden golf tees or dowels with wood glue and then drive them into the worn screw holes. Let the glue dry completely and cut off the excess wooden tee.

4 Drill pilot holes in the new wood and rehang the hinge with the new wood as a base for the screws.

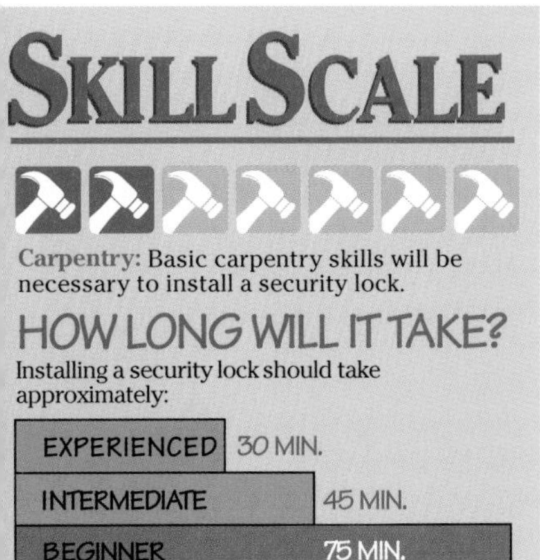

Installing a Security Lock

When selecting a deadbolt lock for your entry door, you need to choose whether you prefer a single or double cylinder style. Both are equally available in selected styles.

Single cylinder locks can be opened from the inside with a thumbturn, while double cylinder locks require a key from either side.

STUFF YOU'LL NEED:

- ☐**Tools:** Screwdrivers, drill w/bits, hole saw.
- ☐**Materials:** Lock template, security lock.

Deadbolt or security locks provide an additional barrier to unwanted intruders and are relatively easy to install.

INSTALLING A SECURITY LOCK

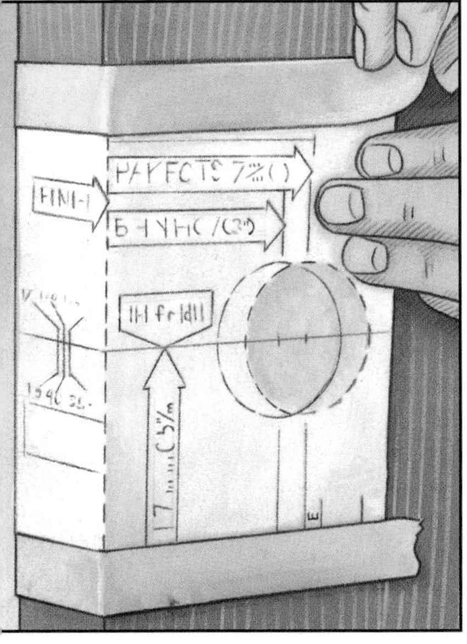

1 Measure to find the lock location. Tape the cardboard emplate, supplied with the lockset, ɔnto door. Use a nail or awl to mark he centerpoints of the cylinder and he latch bolt on the door.

2 Bore a cylinder hole with a hole saw and drill. To avoid splintering the door, drill through one side until hole saw pilot (mandrel) just starts to come out the other side. Remove the hole saw and then complete the hole from the opposite side of the door.

3 Use a spade bit and drill to bore the latch bolt hole from the edge of the door into the cylinder hole. Make sure to keep the drill perpendicular to the door edge while drilling.

INSTALLING A SECURITY LOCK (continued)

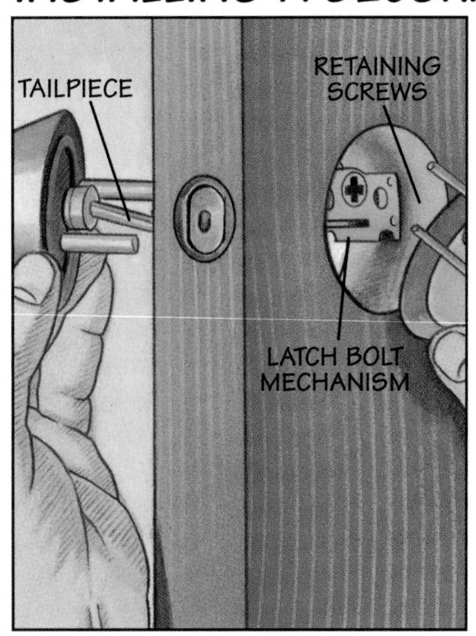

4 Insert the latch bolt into the edge hole. Insert the lock tailpiece and connecting screws through the latch bolt mechanism, and screw the cylinders together. Close the door to find the point where the latch bolt meets the door jamb.

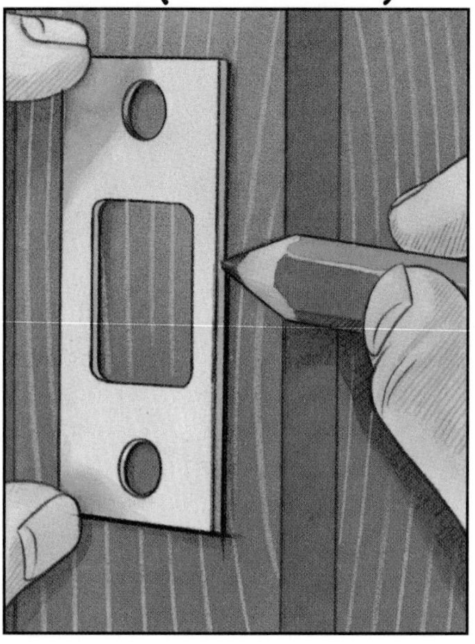

5 Mark the outline of the mortise with a pencil. Use the hardware as a marking template when drawing the outline for strike plate mortises and hinge mortises.

6 Cut the outline of the mortise by holding a chisel with the bevel-side in and tap the butt end lightly with a mallet or hammer until the cut is at the proper depth.

7 Make a series of parallel depth cuts 1/4" apart across the mortise with the chisel held at a 45° angle. Drive the chisel with light mallet blows to the butt end of the chisel.

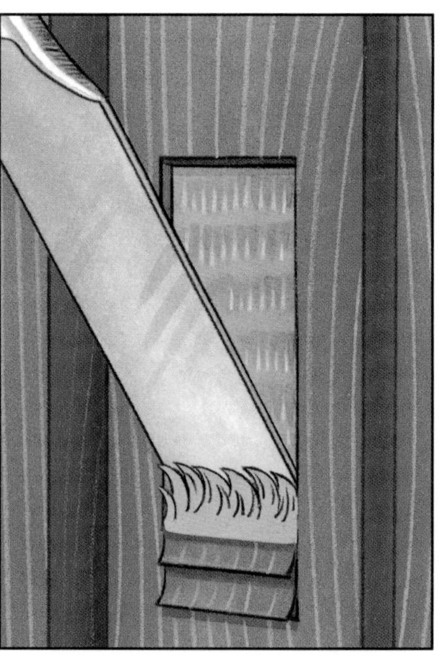

8 Pry out the waste chips by holding the chisel at a low angle with the bevel-side toward the work surface. Drive the chisel by light hand pressure.

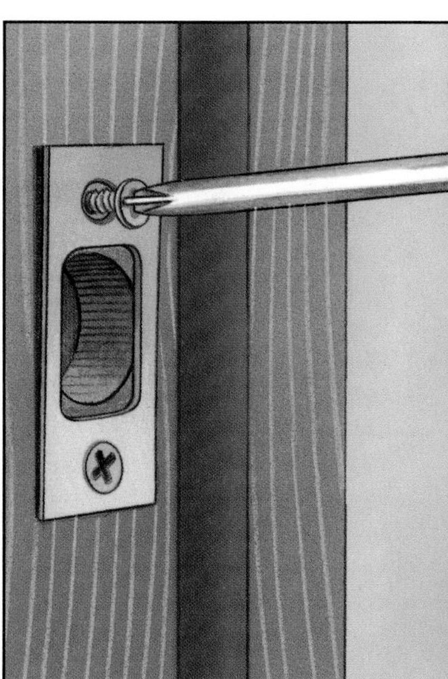

9 Bore the latch bolt hole in the center of the mortise with a spade bit. Install the strike plate using the retaining screws provided with the lockset.

Making an Opening

Depending on the size of the window or door unit you're planning to install, you may have to enlarge or create a new rough opening in order to accommodate the new unit's frame. Making a bigger opening is not a particularly complicated process. Depending on the type of wall, load-bearing or non-load-bearing, the opening can usually be enlarged without too much hair-pulling and name-calling!

If the opening is in a load-bearing wall you'll need temporary supports (pg. 227) to brace the overhead joists until your permanent framing is done. Use existing studs as king studs wherever possible. Once the old unit is removed and the temporary supports are in place, the project involves moving a few studs, making a new header and removing a bit of extra siding. It all sounds simple, but if you're enlarging an exterior opening, check the weather forecast, just in case!

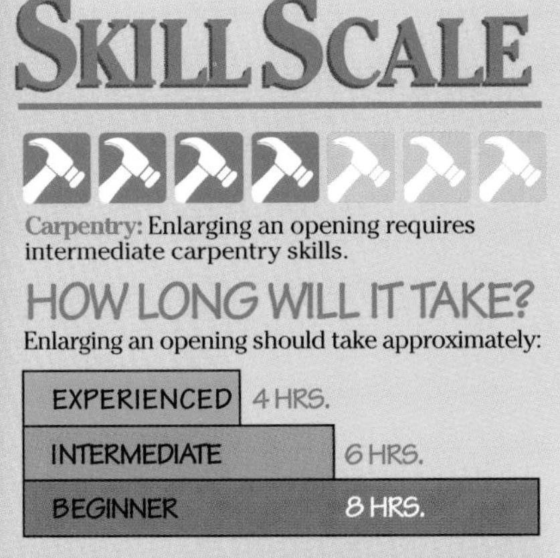

STUFF YOU'LL NEED:

- ☐ **Tools:** Hammer, carpenter's level, pry bar, tape measure, pencil, combination square, circular saw or reciprocating saw.
- ☐ **Materials:** Framing lumber, 16d nails.

1 Prepare the project site and remove the interior wall surfaces. Measure and mark the rough opening width on the sole plate. Mark the locations of the jack studs and king studs on the sole plate. Where possible, use existing studs as king studs.

2 Measure and cut the king studs to fit between the sole plate and the top plate. Position the king studs and toenail them to the sole plate with 16d nails.

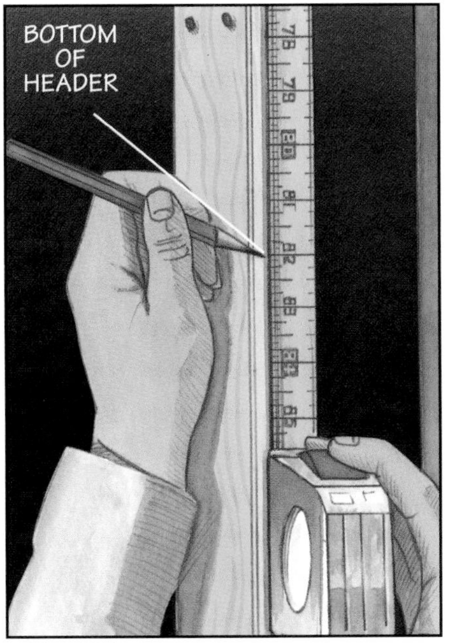

3 Measure down from the ceiling to position the header the same height as the other windows in the room; mark the rough opening height on one of the king studs. For most windows, the recommended rough opening is ½" taller than the height of the window frame. This line marks the bottom of the window header.

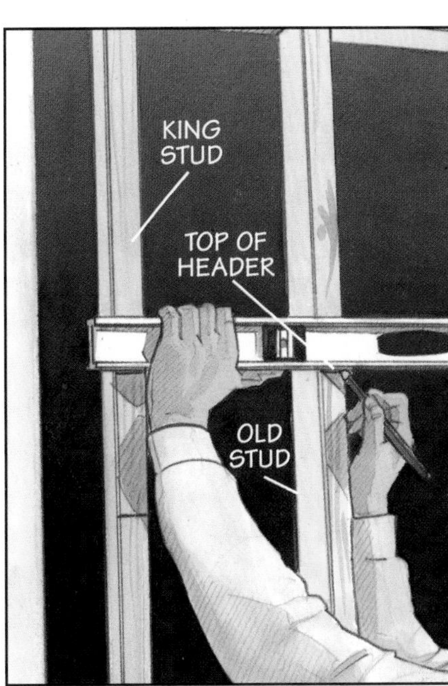

4 Measure and mark where the top of the window header will fit against the king stud. Use a carpenter's level to extend the lines across the old studs to the opposite king stud.

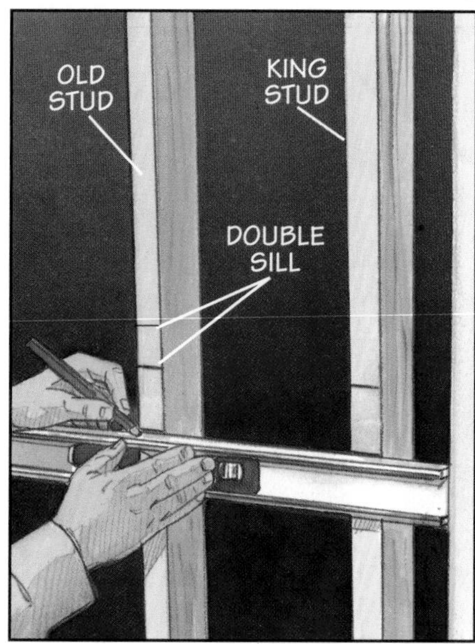

5 Measure down from the header line and outline the double rough sill on the king stud. Use a carpenter's level to extend the lines across the old studs to the opposite king stud. Make temporary supports if you will be removing more than one stud.

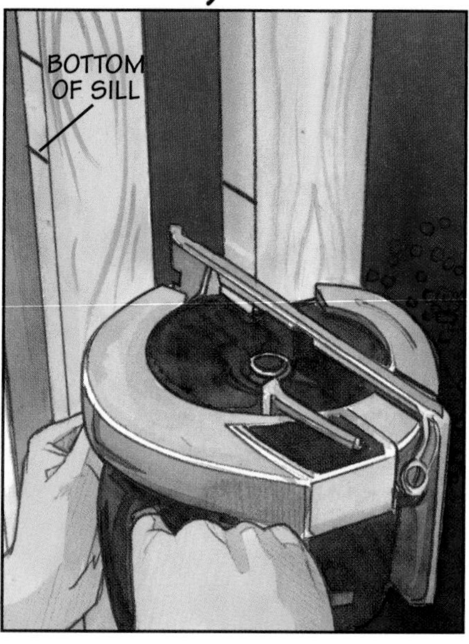

6 Use a circular saw set to maximum blade depth to cut through the studs along the lines marking the bottom of the rough sill and along the lines marking the top of the header. Don't cut the king studs. Be careful when cutting to avoid any kickback. If necessary, finish the cuts with a handsaw.

7 Tear out the old studs inside the rough opening using a pry bar. Build a header to fit between the king studs on top of the jack studs using two pieces of 2" dimension lumber sandwiched around 3/8" plywood.

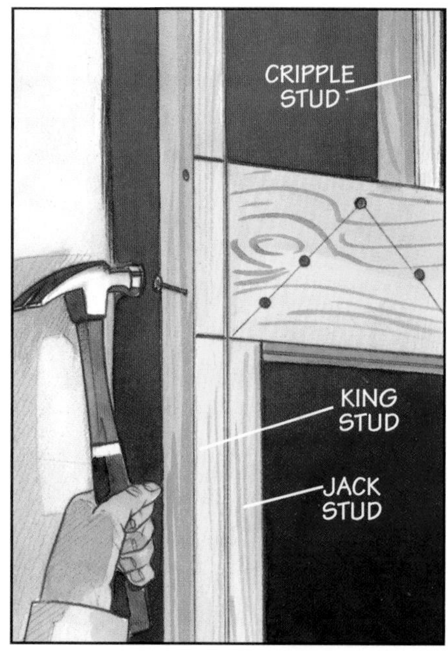

8 Cut two jack studs to reach from the top of the sole plate to the bottom header lines on the king studs. Nail the jack studs to the king studs with 16d nails driven every 12". Position the header on the jack studs and attach it to the king, jack and cripple studs, using 16d nails.

9 Build the rough sill to reach between the jack studs by nailing a pair of 2x4s together. Position the rough sill on the cripple studs and nail it to jack studs and cripple studs with 16d nails.

10 Use a reciprocating saw or a circular saw to cut away the siding and sheathing covering the new rough opening. Install new wallboard on interior surfaces (pg. 236). Be careful to watch out for wiring inside the wall.

Removing an Entry Door

Before you can install your new entry door unit, you must clear away the old door and frame. This is a fairly easy task, requiring more muscle than skill, and not too much muscle either, if you take your time and proceed systematically.

Since, other than the interior trim, you probably don't intend to salvage any of the old pieces, you don't need to be too concerned about damaging any of them. Make the removal process as easy on yourself as you can. If you have a reciprocating saw and metal-cutting blade, use it to cut through any nails that can't be readily pulled out, then hammer the remaining nail shanks flush with the rough opening. You can also saw the door frame and pry it out in pieces if you have to, or maybe you just happen to feel a little destructive!

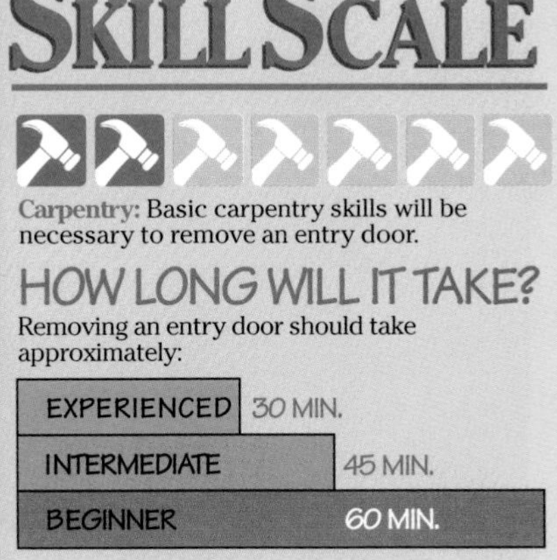

STUFF YOU'LL NEED:

- ☐**Tools:** Pry bar, utility knife, hammer, reciprocating saw.
- ☐**Materials:** Scrap wood.

REMOVING AN ENTRY DOOR

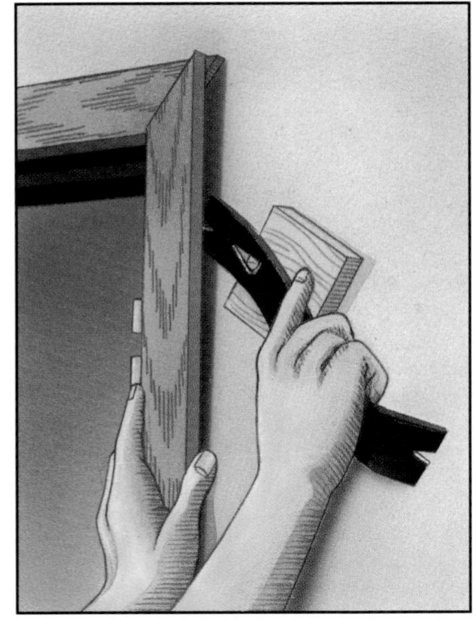

1 First use a utility knife to score between the moulding and the wall then use a pry bar and hammer to gently remove the interior door trim. Protect the wallboard or plaster by using a thin piece of scrap wood under the pry bar. Save the trim to reapply after the new door is installed.

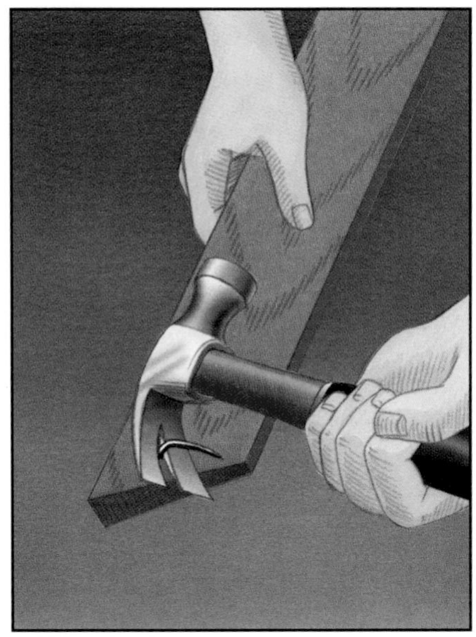

2 To prevent the face of the trim from splintering, remove any remaining finish nails by pulling them from the back with a hammer.

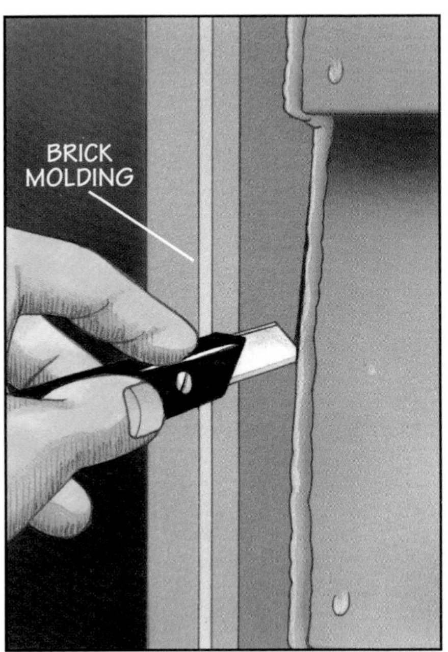

3 Use a utility knife to cut away the old caulk between the exterior siding and the brick molding on the door frame.

4 Pry away and discard the old door jamb and threshold. Stubborn nails can be cut with a reciprocating saw.

Installing a Prehung Entry Door

With energy-efficient insulation and weather stripping, easy-to-maintain baked enamel primer coat and a wide variety of styles, a new steel entry door can greatly enhance the comfort, security and appearance of your home.

Because replacement steel entry doors are prehung with jambs, brick molding, and hardware (except locksets), installing them need not be a difficult project. Insulated steel entry doors can be heavy, though, so you may want to line up a helper before you begin.

Entry doors are also made of wood or fiberglass. Talk to your door supplier about the door most appropriate to your situation.

STUFF YOU'LL NEED:

- ☐**Tools:** Metal snips, hammer, carpenter's level, pencil, circular saw, wood chisel, nail set, caulk gun.
- ☐**Materials:** Building paper, drip edge, wood shims, fiberglass insulation, casing nails, silicone caulk.

1 With the rough opening prepared, remove the new door unit from its packing. Be sure not to remove the retaining brackets that hold the door closed. These need to be in place in order to safely maneuver the door unit.

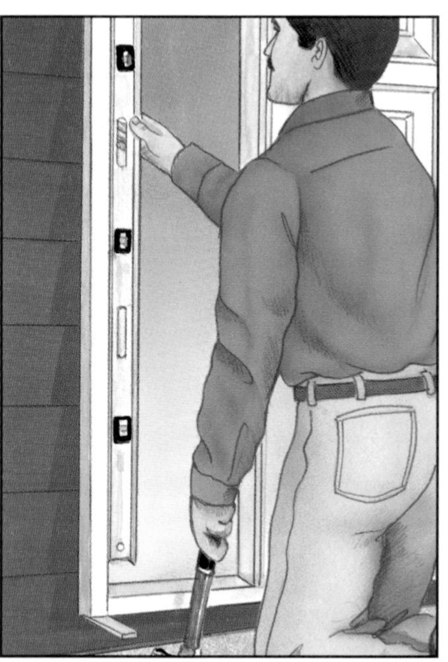

2 Test-fit the door unit, centering it in the rough opening. Make sure the door is plumb. If necessary, shim under the lower side jamb until the door is plumb and level. Maintain consistent spacing between door and jamb but strive for a plumb and level door as well.

BUYER'$ GUIDE

Selecting a Door

When buying a door, you'll need to specify a left- or right-hand swing as well as an inswing or outswing door. A good way to determine which version you need is to imagine yourself standing in the doorway with the door opening toward you. In that position, a left-hand door would have the knob on the left and a right-hand door would have the knob on the right.

Another critical factor is the size of the door. If you're replacing an existing door, be sure to purchase a replacement with the same size requirements as the old one. Sidelights are not included in the door size but need to be considered when determining the rough opening size. Make sure of the opening's rough measurements and check them with the measurements of the door being purchased.

Steel doors prove to be the most durable and offer the best security.

3 Trace the outline of the brick molding onto the siding. If you have vinyl or metal siding, be sure to enlarge the outline to make room for the extra trim moldings required by these sidings. Remove the door unit after finishing the outline.

4 Cut the siding along the outline, just down to but not into the sheathing, using a circular saw. Stop just short of the corners to prevent damage to the siding that will remain. Finish the cuts at the corners with a sharp wood chisel. Be cautious of kickback, nails and wiring. Wear safety goggles.

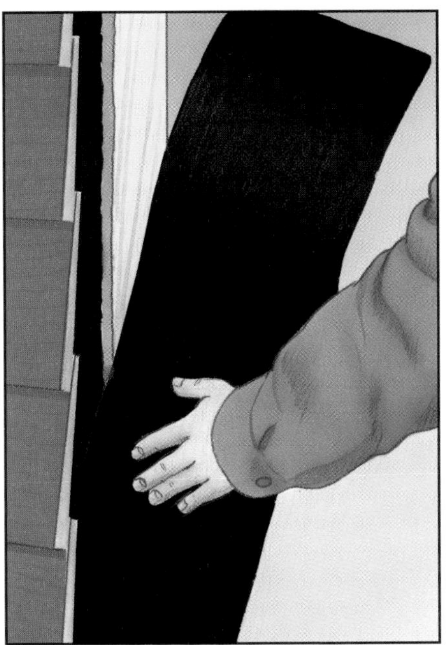

5 Cut 8"-wide strips of building paper and slide them between the siding and sheathing at the top and sides of the opening to shield framing members from moisture. Bend the paper around the framing members and staple it in place.

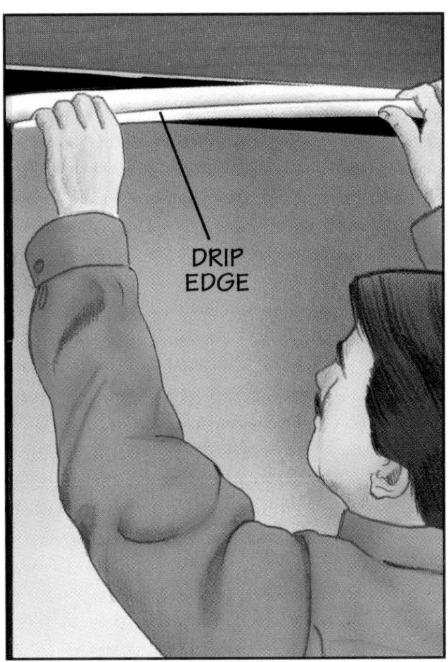

6 To provide an added moisture barrier, cut a piece of drip edge to fit the width of the rough opening, then slide it between the siding and the building paper at the top of the opening. Do not nail the drip edge.

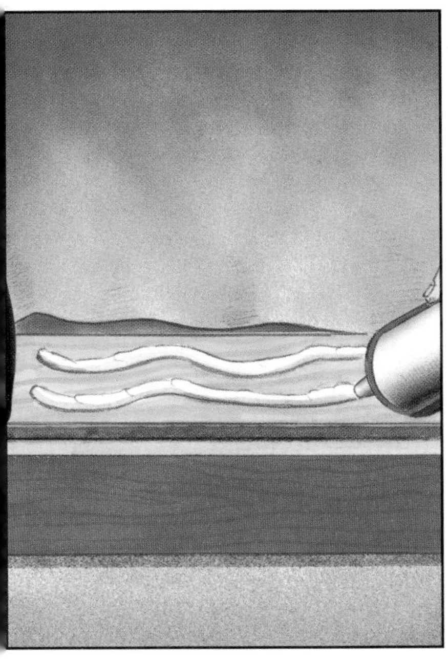

7 Apply several thick beads of silicone caulk to the subfloor at the bottom of the door opening. Also apply silicone caulk over the building paper on the front edges of the jack studs and header.

8 Center the door unit in the rough opening and push the brick molding tight against the sheathing. Have a helper hold the door unit in place until it is nailed.

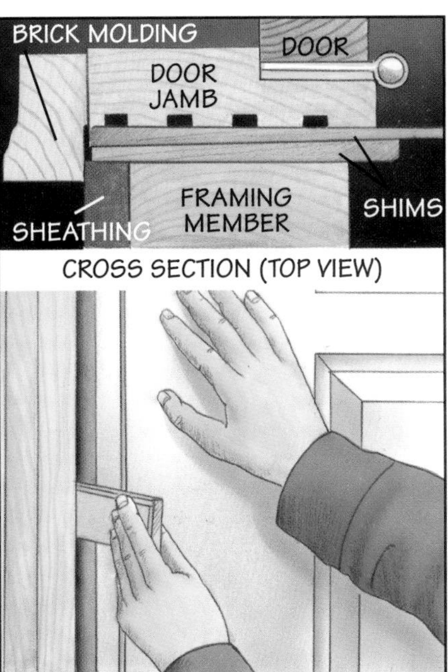

9 From inside, place pairs of wood wedge shims together to form flat shims (bottom), and insert shims into the gaps between the door jambs and framing members. Insert shims at the lockset and hinge locations, and every 12" thereafter.

Doors & Windows

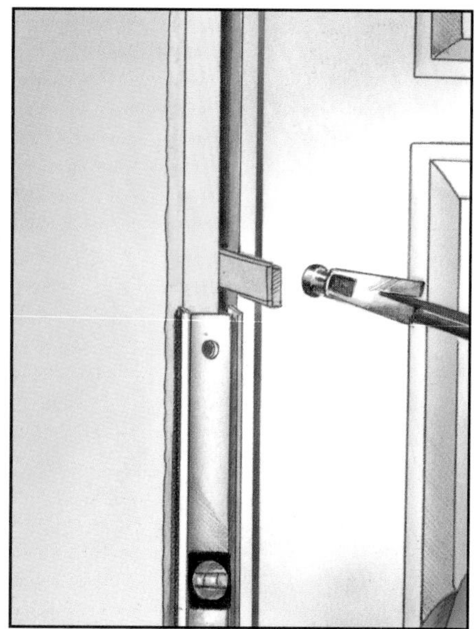

10 Using a carpenter's level, make sure the door unit is plumb. Adjust the shims, if necessary, until the door is plumb and level. Fill the gaps between the jambs and the framing members with loosely packed fiberglass insulation.

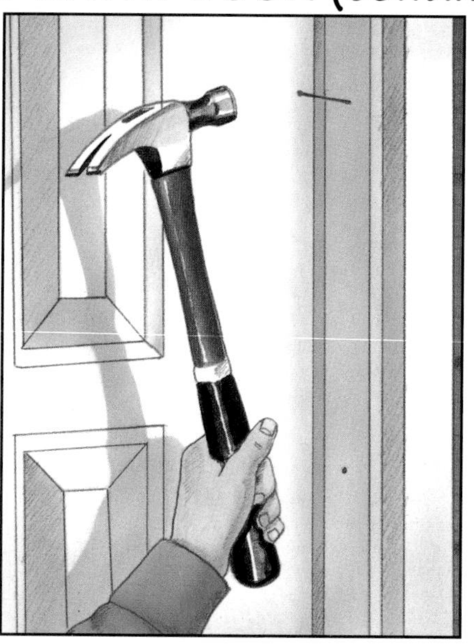

11 From outside, drive 10d casing nails partway through the door jambs and into the framing members at each shim location. Before driving the nails all the way in, check to see if the door works smoothly. Adjust if necessary, then use a nail set to drive the nail heads below the surface of the wood.

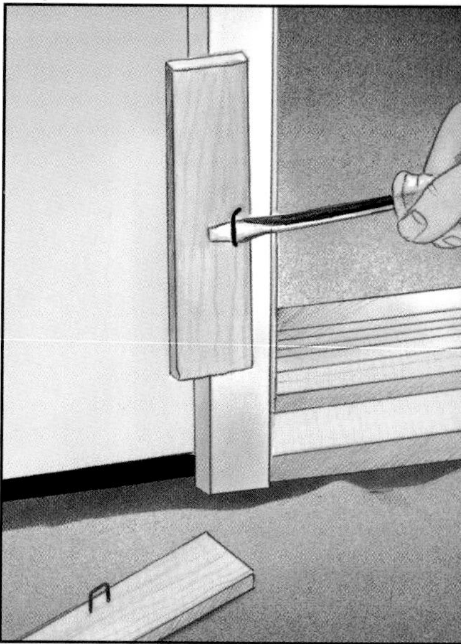

12 Remove the retaining brackets installed by the manufacturer; open and close the door to make sure it works properly.

13 Remove two of the screws on the top hinge and replace them with long anchor screws (usually included with the unit). These anchor screws will penetrate into the framing members to strengthen the installation.

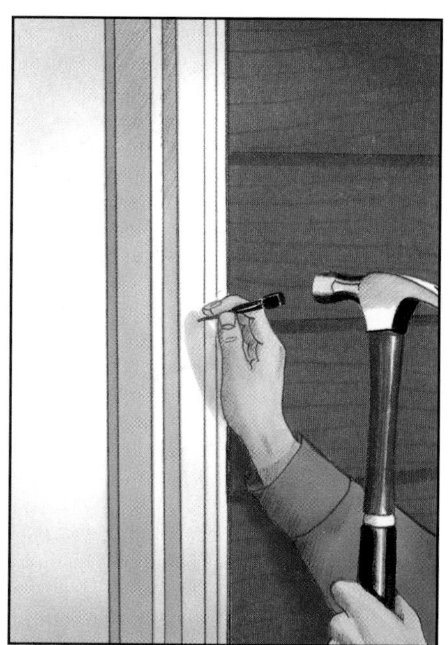

14 Anchor the brick molding to the framing members with 10d galvanized casing nails driven every 12". Use a nail set to drive the nail heads below the surface of the wood.

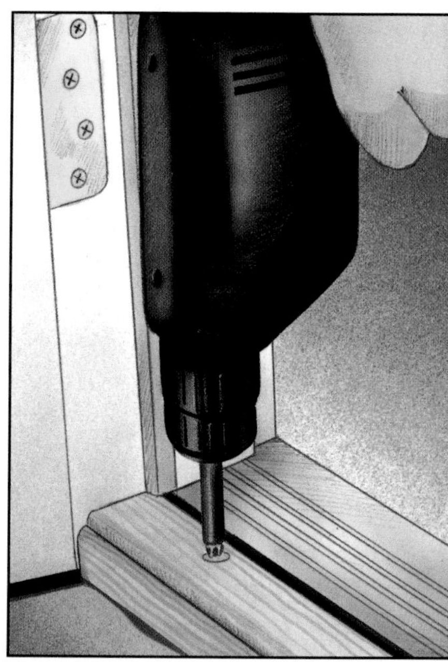

15 Adjust the door threshold to create a tight seal, following manufacturer's recommendations. Don't make it too high or it will make the door difficult to open and will prematurely wear the bottom of the door.

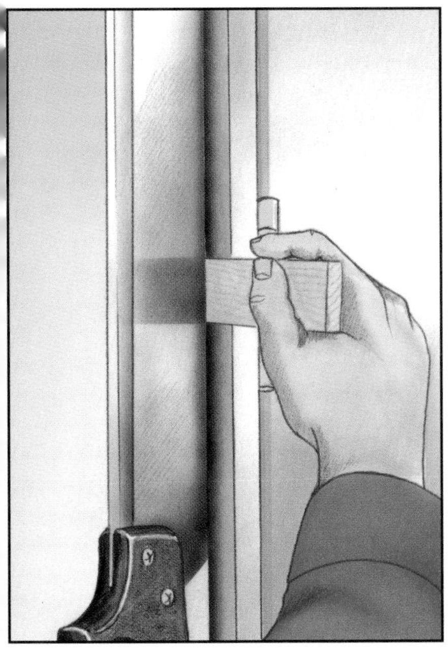

16 Cut off the shims flush with the framing members using a handsaw.

17 Apply paintable silicone caulk around the entire door unit. Fill nail holes with caulk. Finish the door and install the lockset as directed by the manufacturer.

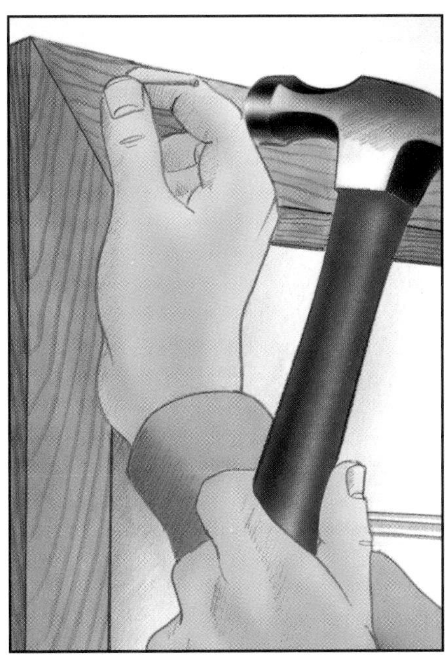

18 Replace the casing on the inside of the door jamb. If the trim was damaged during removal, cut and install new casing.

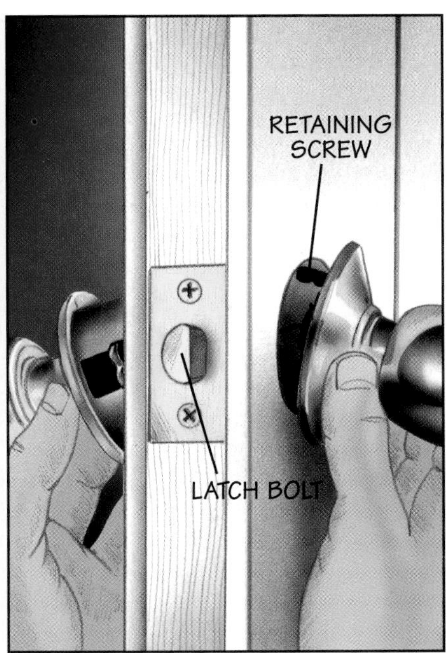

19 Install a new door lock. First, insert the latch bolt mechanism through latch bolt hole. Then insert the lockset tailpieces through the latch bolt and screw the handles together by tightening retaining screws.

20 Screw the strike plate to the door jamb and adjust the plate position to fit the latch bolt. Caulk any gaps between the siding and new door molding.

21 If you wish, install additional weather stripping and door sweeps as necessary.

Framing a Prehung Interior Door

A properly constructed door opening reinforces the wall above and on either side of the door. In a load-bearing wall, this is essential compensation for the wall studs eliminated by the door opening. Even in a partition wall, it is important that the structure surrounding the door frame be solid and stable in order to prevent wallboard tape joints from cracking due to excessive door operation.

You can save yourself some potential headaches by purchasing the prehung door unit you plan to install before beginning framing. The opening you build should be about 3/4" wider than the measured width of the door frame to be installed. This makes it easy to slip the prehung door unit in place and allows enough room to make the necessary adjustments.

In basement applications with a high moisture content, use pressure treated wood for the sole plate.

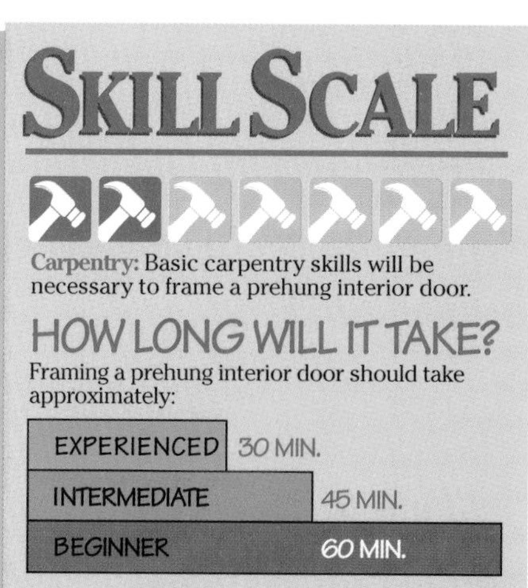

STUFF YOU'LL NEED:

- **Tools:** Hammer, framing square, tape measure, plumb bob, pencil.
- **Materials:** Nails, framing lumber.

1 Mark the ceiling and snap a chalk line to mark where the top plate will be installed. Nail the top plate through the ceiling into the ceiling joists or blocking, angling the nail to provide greater holding strength.

2 Using a plumb bob, mark the floor where the sole plate will be installed. Nail the sole plate to the floor, angling the nails into the floor joists or blocking. Do not nail the sole plate to the floor between the jack stud locations because this portion of the plate will be removed before door installation.

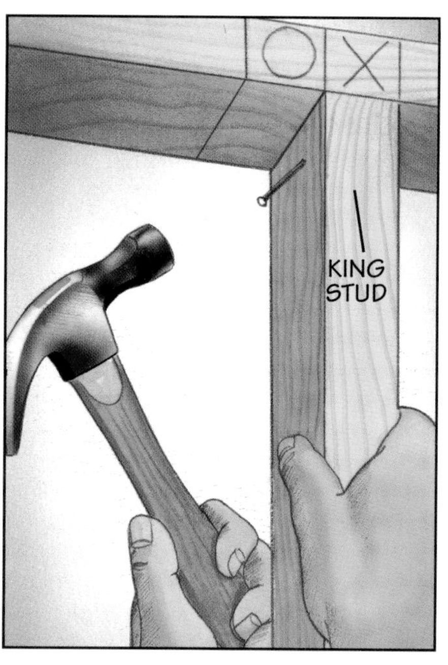

3 Measure and cut the king studs and position at the markings. Drive nails at a 45° angle for the toenailed joint or attach the studs with metal connectors.

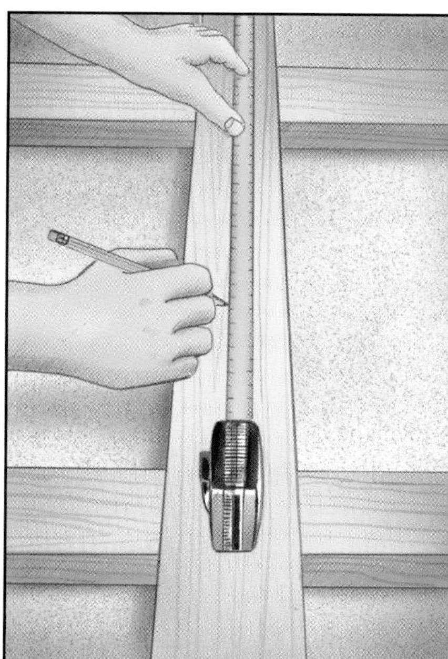

4 Measure the length of the jack studs to 80 7/8", mark and cut them to size.

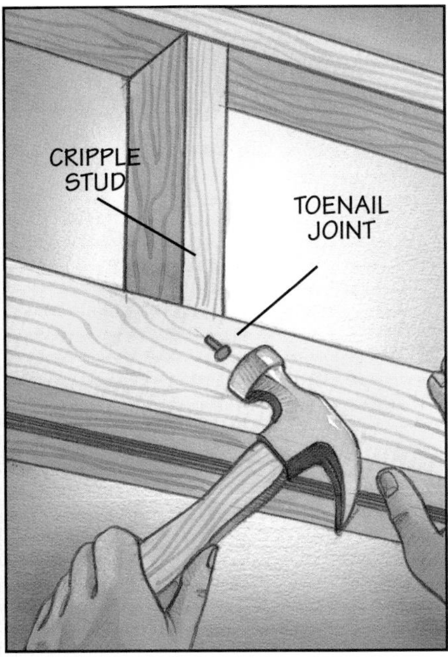

5 Install a cripple stud halfway between the king studs. Toenail the cripple stud to the top plate and through the side of the header into the cripple stud. Headers should be made from two 2x4s sandwiching a ¾ inch piece of plywood.

6 Position the jack studs against the inside of the king studs, and nail them in place. Nail through the king studs into the header.

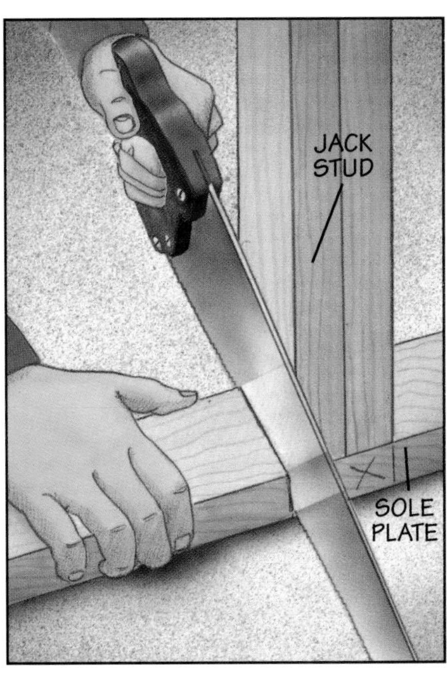

7 Saw through the 2x4 sole plate at the inside edges of the jack studs. Remove the cut portion of the plate.

Doors & Windows

CUTTING OFF AN INTERIOR DOOR

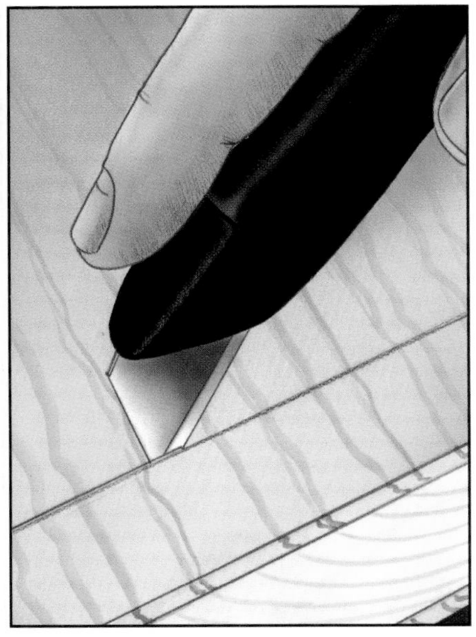

1 With the door in place, measure ³/₈" up from top of the floor and mark the door. Remove the door from the hinges and mark the entire cutting line. Cut through the door veneer with a sharp utility knife to prevent it from chipping when the door is sawed.

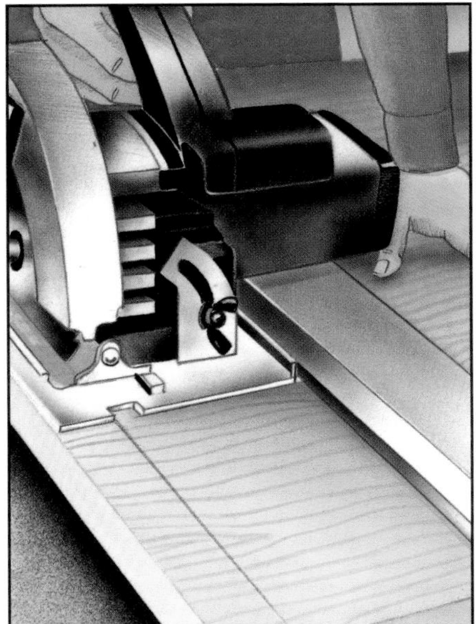

2 You may also apply masking tape to the cut line to prevent the wood from splitting when sawing. Lay the door on sawhorses. Clamp a straightedge to the door as a cutting guide and saw off the bottom of the door. The hollow core of the door may be exposed.

3 To replace a cut-off frame in the bottom of the door, chisel the veneer from both sides of the removed portion. Apply wood glue to the cut-off frame, spread with a brush and insert the frame into the opening. Clamp the frame, wipe away the excess glue and let it dry overnight.

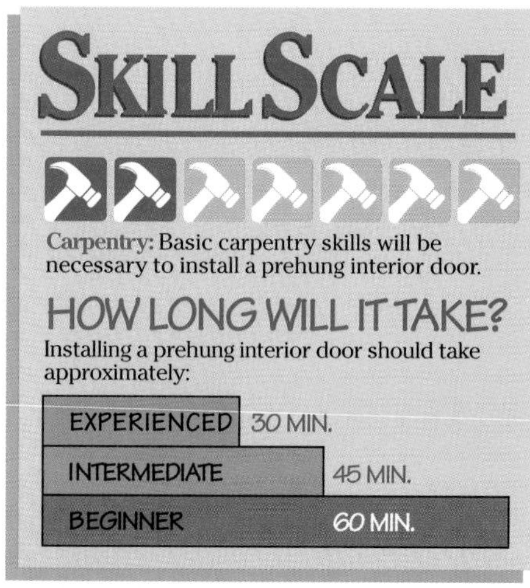

STUFF YOU'LL NEED:

- ☐ **Tools:** Hammer, handsaw, carpenter's level, pry bar, circular saw, utility knife.
- ☐ **Materials:** Wood glue, wood shims, casing nails.

Installing a Prehung Interior Door

Prehung doors greatly simplify the task of installing or replacing an interior door. Once the framed opening is complete, the prehung door can be slipped into position, shimmed square and plumb, and nailed in place. The hinges are already mortised and attached, and holes are bored and ready for lock and bolt hardware!

If you're planning to paint or stain the door or trim, apply the finish before you install the unit. That way, you avoid the dripping or running problems you would encounter when finishing upright surfaces.

Most standard doors are sized to fit walls with 2x4 construction. If you have thicker walls you can order a door to match, or you can add jamb extensions to the standard size door.

Standard prehung doors have $4^{9}/_{16}$" wide jambs and are designed for 2x4 wall construction with $^{1}/_{2}$" wallboard. If your walls are thicker, you'll need to attach jamb extensions to the edge of the door frame unless using a split jamb door. For example, if your walls are built with 2x6 studs, extend the jambs by attaching wood strips to the jamb edges.

INSTALLING A FLAT JAMB INTERIOR DOOR

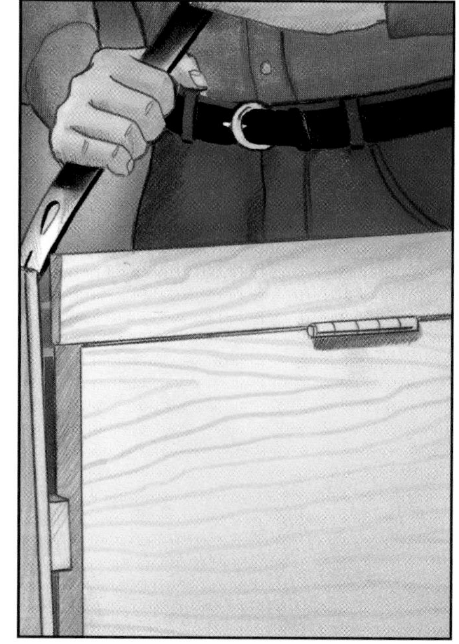

1 Remove the shipping carton and inspect the unit for damage. The door unit should have casing attached to one side of frame, and include premitered casing for the other side of the frame.

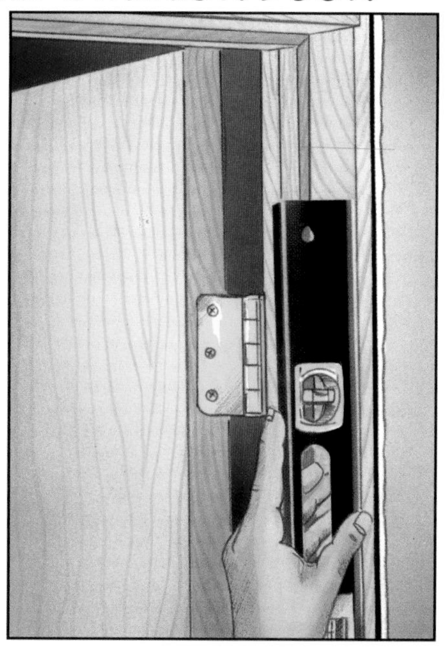

2 Set the door unit into the framed opening and check it for plumb with a carpenter's level.

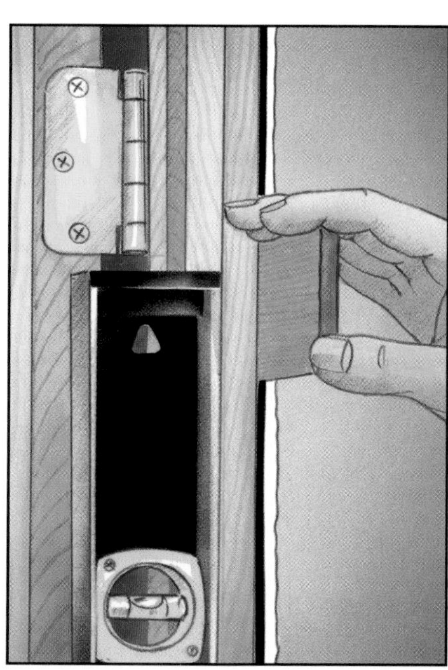

3 To plumb door unit, insert wood shims between the door jamb and the frame on the hinged side of the door. Tap the shims with a hammer until the level shows that the jamb is plumb.

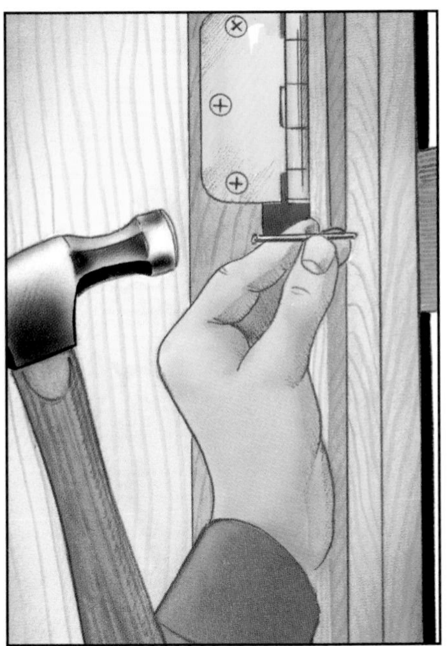

4 Gaps between the jamb and framing at the hinge and lock locations should be filled with shim material. Nail the jamb to the frame with 6d finish nails driven through the shims.

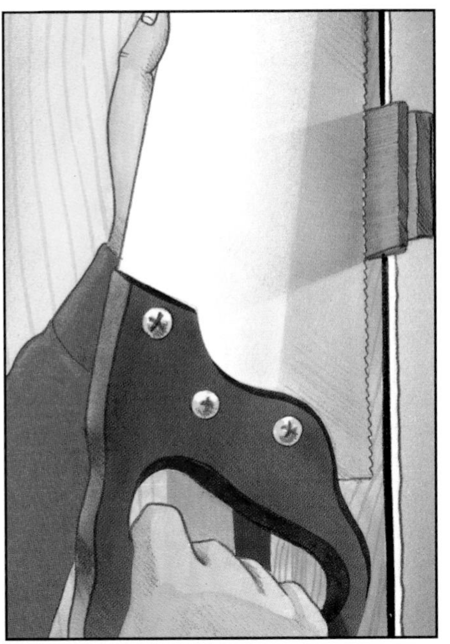

5 Cut off the shims with a handsaw. Hold the saw vertically to avoid damaging the door jamb or the wall.

6 Nail the premitered trim to the jambs, using 4d finish nails driven at 16" intervals. Recess nailheads with a nail set.

INSTALLING SPLIT-JAMB INTERIOR DOORS

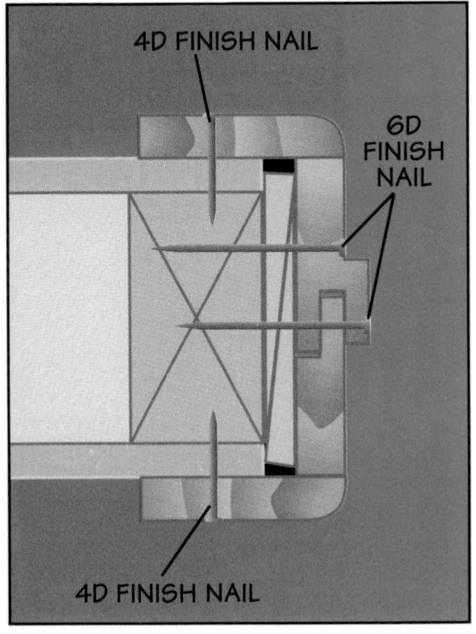

Split-jamb prehung doors have a two-piece jamb that sandwiches the wall. One added advantage of a split-jamb door is that the casing is already attached. You don't have to be able to cut accurate miter cuts to wind up with a professional looking job.

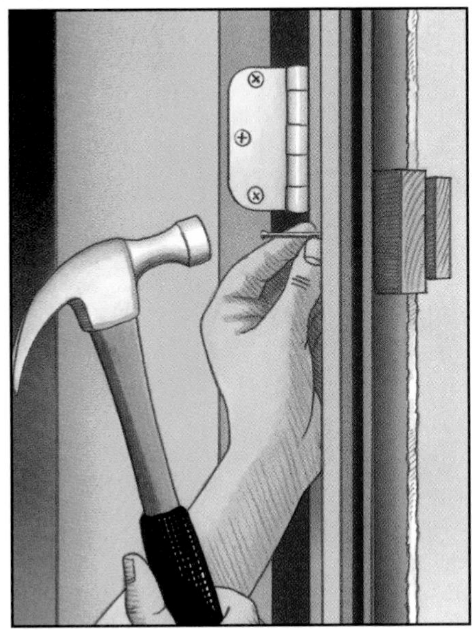

1 Separate the two halves of the jamb, set the door stop side in the opening and tack through the casing about 12" from the top. Block and shim at the hinge locations, on both jambs, and above the jamb. Plumb and square the unit. Nail through the jamb (not the stop), and into the frame with 6d finish nails.

2 Cut the shims flush with the first half of the jamb. Inset the other half of the split-jamb into the first half and gently push it into place until the casing reaches the wall. Use 6d finish nails to nail through both halves of the jamb right in the center of the stop. Nail the casing to the wall with 4d finish nails.

Installing Moldings for Interior Doors

Prehung interior door units usually include mitered trim molding as part of the package. As long as you are careful to square up the door frame when you install it, the mitered corners should fit perfectly!

If, however, you are replacing existing molding or prefer a style of molding different from that supplied with the door unit, you'll have to measure and cut your own.

The standard 45° miter presumes the door frame is perfectly square. In older homes, this is more often the exception than the rule. If a framing square set into the corner of the frame indicates the frame is not square, you'll need to adjust the miter in order to make a tight fit. At each corner, cut one of the trim molding pieces at a 45° miter. Then cut a piece of scrap molding to make test cuts to determine the proper adjoining angle.

SKILL SCALE

Carpentry: Basic carpentry skills will be necessary to install door molding.

HOW LONG WILL IT TAKE?

Installing door molding should take approximately:

EXPERIENCED	30 MIN.
INTERMEDIATE	45 MIN.
BEGINNER	60 MIN.

STUFF YOU'LL NEED:

- ☐ **Tools:** Miter box, back saw, tape measure, pencil, framing square, hammer, nail set.
- ☐ **Materials:** Wood trim, casing nails, wood filler.

CUTTING MITERS IN MOLDING

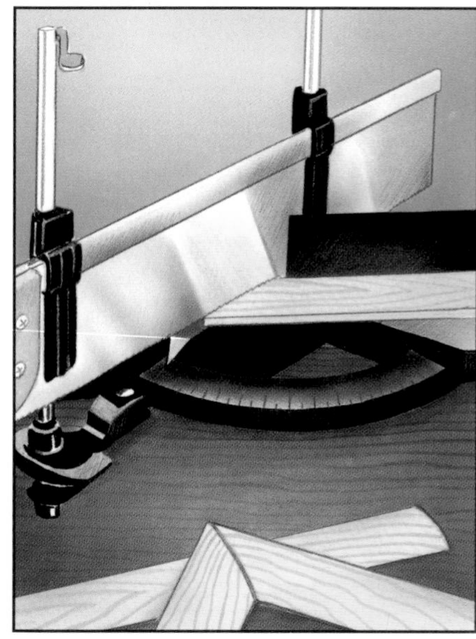

A hand miter box and backsaw are used to cut precise angles on mitered moldings for window and door casings. Hand miter boxes are good for small trimming projects.

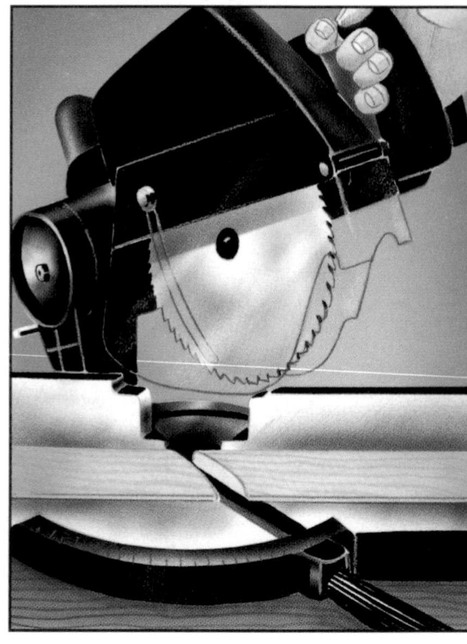

A power miter box is used to cut straight and compound angles for moldings and door casings. Power miter boxes make quick work of large trimming projects.

INSTALLING INTERIOR DOOR MOLDINGS

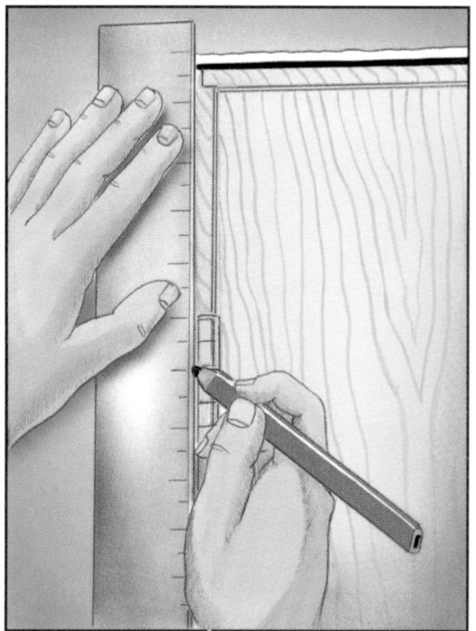

1 On each the top and side jambs, mark a setback line ⅛" to ¼" from the inside edge. Moldings will be installed flush with these lines.

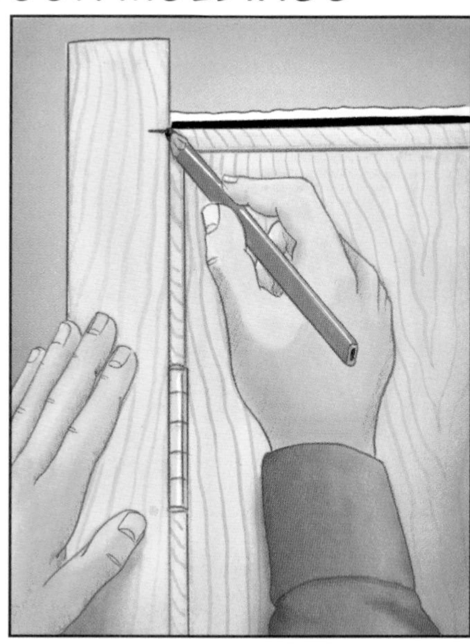

2 Place a length of molding along one side jamb, flush with the setback line. At the top of the molding, mark the points where the horizontal and vertical setback lines meet.

Doors & Windows

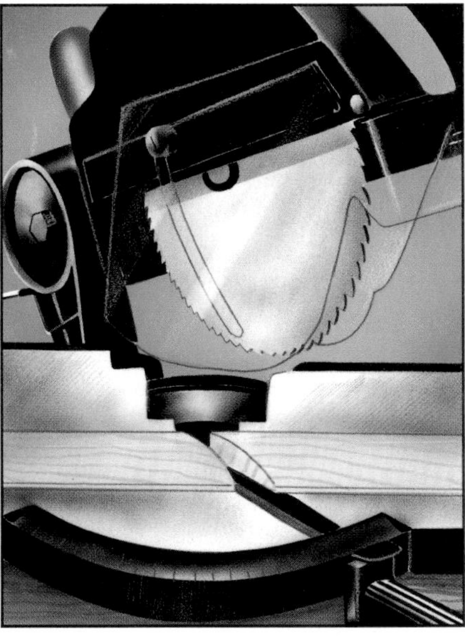

3 Cut the ends of the molding at 45° angles using a miter saw. Measure and cut the other vertical molding piece using the same method.

4 Attach the vertical moldings with 4d finish nails driven through the moldings and into the jambs, and with 6d finish nails driven into the framing members near the outside edge of the molding. Drill pilot holes to prevent splitting and space the nails every 12".

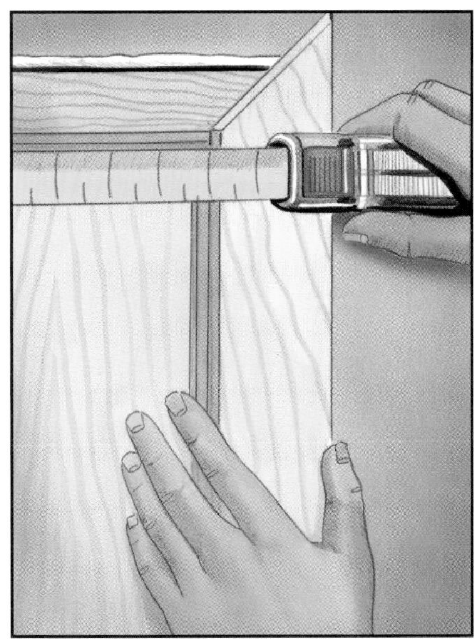

5 Measure between the installed moldings on the setback lines and cut the top and bottom moldings with the ends mitered at 45°.

6 If the door unit is not perfectly square, make test cuts on scrap pieces to find the correct angle for the joints. Drill pilot holes and attach with 4d and 6d finish nails.

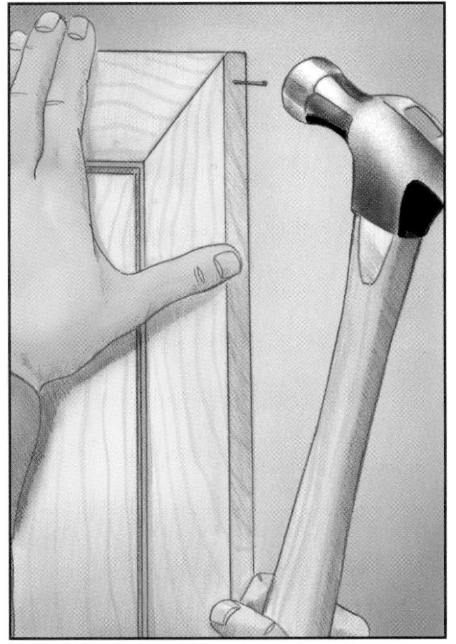

7 Lock-nail the corner joints by drilling pilot holes and driving a 4d finish nail through each corner.

8 Drive all nail heads below the wood surface using a nail set; fill the nail holes with wood putty.

STUFF YOU'LL NEED:

- ☐ **Tools:** Hacksaw, hammer, tape measure, pencil, drill and bits, screwdrivers.
- ☐ **Materials:** Storm door unit, wood spacer strips, casing nails.

Installing a Storm Door

A storm door, as simple as it is, provides many benefits to your home. It can add years to the exterior finish and surface of your entry door; it helps to insulate and weatherproof your entry door; and it provides additional security and improves the appearance of your house, all at the same time.

You can find a storm door to complement just about any house style. It is best to look for models that feature a solid inner core, low-maintenance finish and a seamless outer shell.

Storm door frames allow for a small degree of accommodation to your existing door opening, but it is important to measure the opening carefully. Find the dimensions from the inside edges of the entry door's brick molding. Subtract approximately 1/4" from the width of the opening to arrive at a suitable storm door size. Any difference in opening size can easily be adjusted and compensated for when you install the storm door frame.

When you select or order a storm door, remember to specify one that has a door handle on the same side as your entry door. This will make passage through the storm and entry doors much less cumbersome than if the handles are on opposite sides.

Storm doors, because of the large amount of glass exposure and the tight weatherseal they provide, can cause sunlight to produce considerable heat build-up in the space between the storm door and the entry door. In the winter, this additional heat can be a good thing, but in the middle of summer, the heat build-up can actually be hot enough to damage the plastic trim on entry doors. For this reason, some entry door manufacturers do not recommend installing a storm door with their products.

It's a good idea to check the manufacturer's recommendations and restrictions of your existing entry door before buying a storm door unit.

FITTING A STORM DOOR FRAME TO THE DOOR OPENING

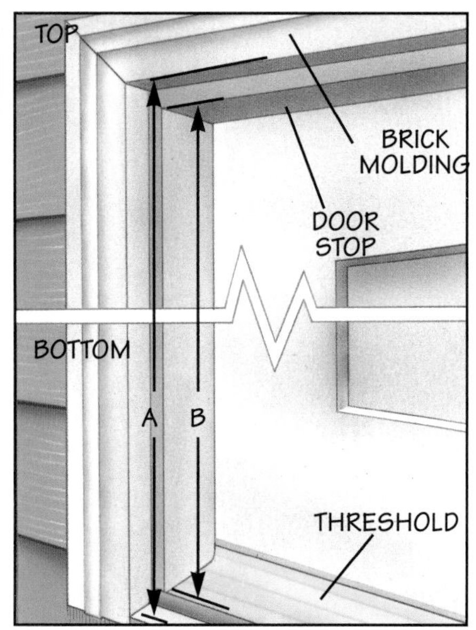

1 Measure from the threshold to the top of the door opening along the corner of brick molding (**A**), and along the front edge of entry door stop (**B**). Subtract 1/8" from the measurements to allow for small adjustments when the door is installed.

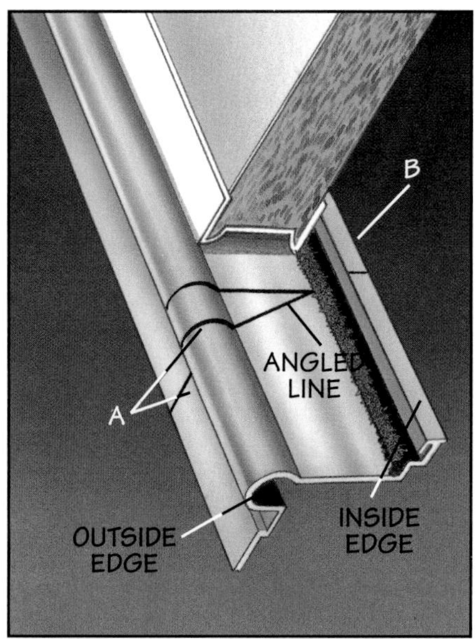

2 Measuring from the top of the storm door frame, mark the adjusted points on the corner bead. Draw a line from point A to the outside edge of the frame and from point B to the inside edge. Draw an angled line from point A on the corner bead to point B on the inside edge.

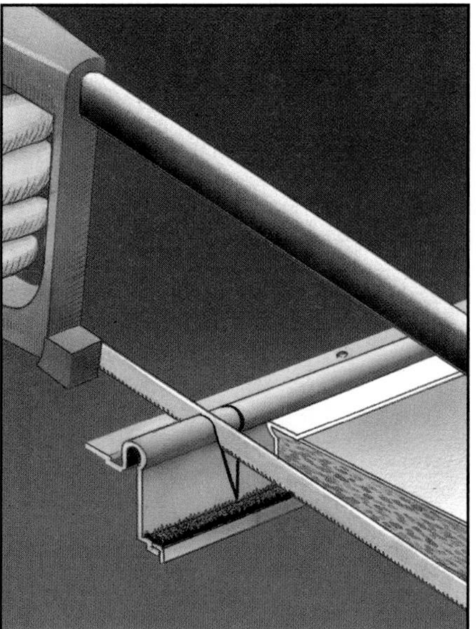

3 Use a hacksaw to cut down through the bottom of the storm door frame, following the angled line. Make sure to hold the hacksaw at the same slant as the angled line to ensure that the cut will be smooth and straight.

FITTING AND INSTALLING A STORM DOOR

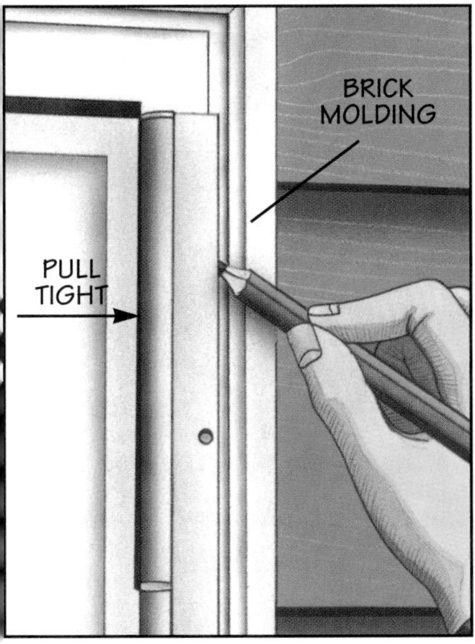

1 Position the storm door in the opening and pull the frame tight against the brick molding on the hinge side of the storm door. Then draw a reference line onto the brick molding, following the edge of the storm door frame.

2 Push the storm door tight against the brick molding on the latch side, then measure the gap between the reference line and the hinge side of the door frame. If the distance is greater than $^3/_8$", spacer strips must be installed to ensure that the door will fit snugly.

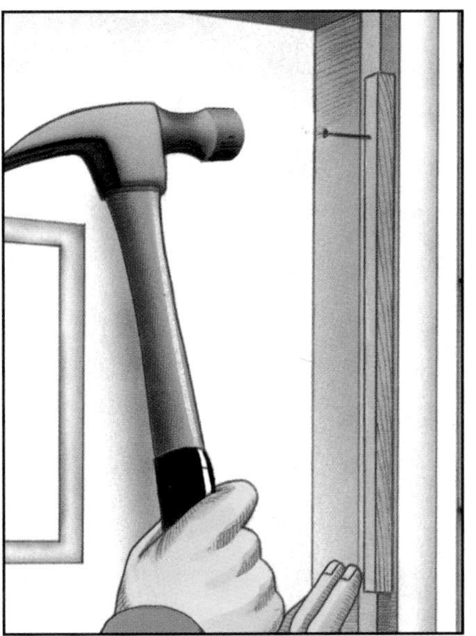

3 To install spacers, remove the door, predrill and nail thin strips of wood to the inside of the brick molding at storm door hinge locations. The wood strips should be $^1/_8$" thinner than the gap measured in step 2. If you have a sidelight, be careful of the nail length so as not to cause damage.

4 Replace the storm door and push it tightly against the brick molding on the hinge side. Drill pilot holes into the brick molding through the pre-drilled holes in the hinge side frame of the storm door. Then attach the frame with mounting screws spaced every 12".

5 Remove any spacer clips holding the frame to the storm door. With the storm door closed, drill pilot holes and attach the latch side frame to the brick molding. Use a coin to keep an even gap between the storm door and the storm door frame.

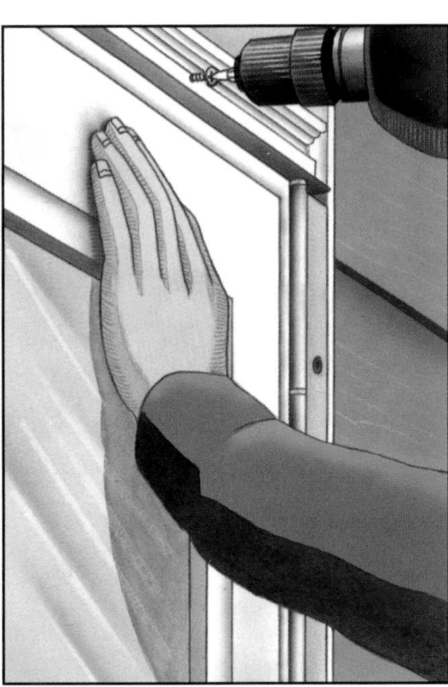

6 Center the top piece of the storm door frame on top of the frame sides. Drill pilot holes and screw the top piece to the brick molding. Adjust the bottom sweep and attach locks and latch hardware as directed by the manufacturer.

Installing a Patio Door

Patio doors dramatically incorporate an outdoor deck or patio into your living space, fostering an easy flow of traffic into and out of your house. To simplify installation, buy a patio door with the door panels already mounted in preassembled frames. Patio doors have very long bottom sills and top jambs and are susceptible to bowing and warping. Install the patio door so it is level and plumb, and anchor the unit securely to framing members to prevent the possibility of bowing and warping. Yearly caulking and touch-up painting help prevent moisture from warping the jambs.

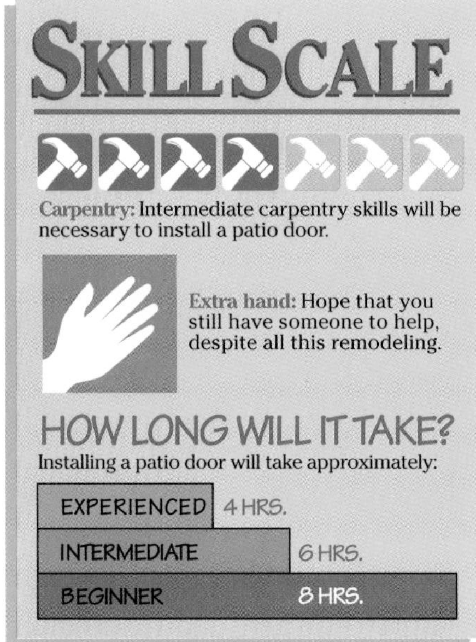

STUFF YOU'LL NEED:

- ☐**Tools:** Hammer, circular saw, wood chisel, stapler, caulk gun, pry bar, pencil, carpenter's level, cordless screwdriver, handsaw, power drill w/drill bits.
- ☐**Materials:** Shims, drip edge, building paper, silicone caulk, casing nails, wood screws, sill nosing.

INSTALLATION TIPS

Heavy glass panels may be removed if you must install the door without help. Reinstall the panels after the frame has been placed in the rough opening and nailed at opposite corners. To remove and install the panels, remove the stop rail, found on the top jamb of the door unit.

Adjust the bottom rollers after installation is complete. Remove the coverplate on the adjusting screw, found on the inside edge of the bottom rail. Turn the screw in small increments until the door rolls smoothly along the track without binding as it is opened and closed.

TIPS FOR INSTALLING HINGED PATIO DOORS

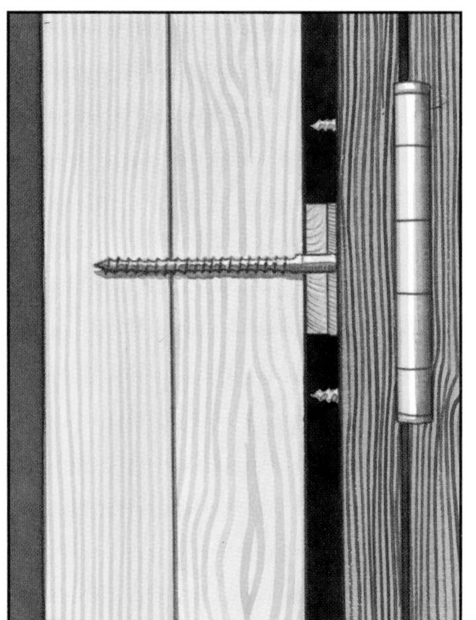

Provide extra support for door hinges by replacing the center mounting screw on each hinge with a 3" wood screw.

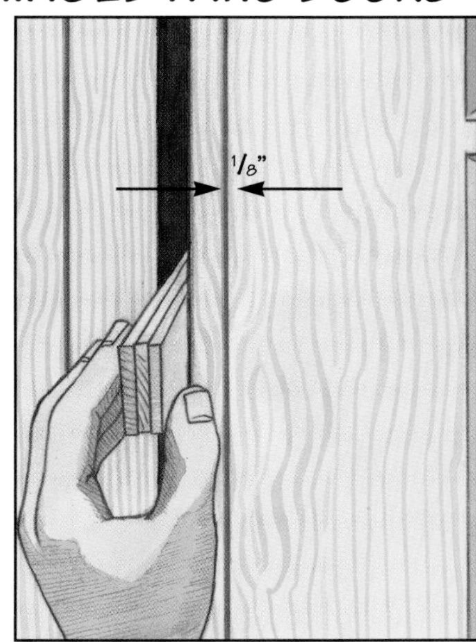

Keep a uniform 1/8" gap between the door, and the top and side parts of the jamb to ensure that the door will swing freely without binding. Check this gap frequently as you shim around the door unit.

INSTALLING A PATIO DOOR

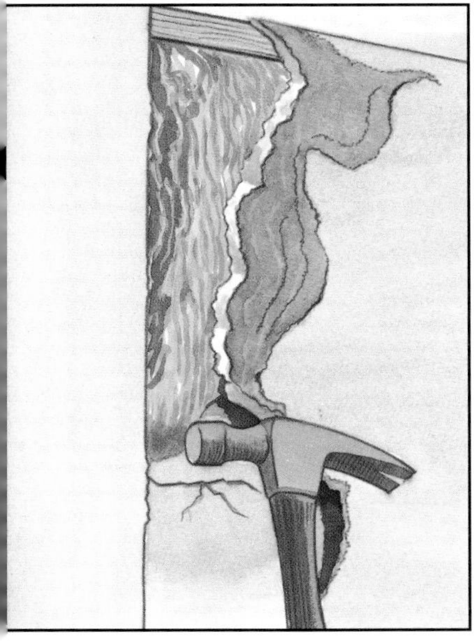

1 Prepare the work area and remove the interior wall surfaces, then frame the rough opening for the patio door. Remove the exterior surfaces inside the framed opening.

2 Test-fit the door unit, centering it in the rough opening. Check to make sure door is plumb. If necessary, shim under the lower side jamb until the door is plumb and level. Have a helper hold the door in place while it is unattached.

YOU CAN BUY HINGED END-SWING DOORS MADE TO FIT THE OPENING OF OLDER SLIDING DOORS.

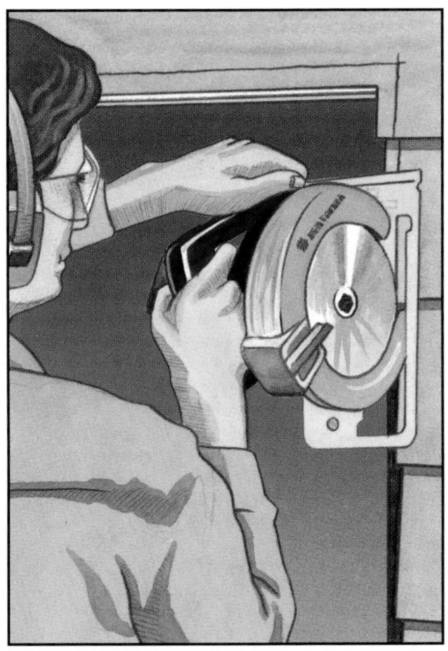

3 Trace the outline of the brick molding onto the siding, then remove the door unit. If you have vinyl or metal siding, enlarge the outline to make room for the extra trim moldings required by these sidings.

4 Using a circular saw, cut the siding along the outline, just down to the sheathing. Stop just short of the corners to prevent damage to the siding that will remain. Finish the cuts at the corners with a sharp wood chisel. Be careful of kickback and wiring inside the wall cavity.

5 To provide an added moisture barrier, cut a piece of drip edge to fit the width of the rough opening, then slide it between the siding and the existing building paper at the top of the opening. Do not nail the drip edge.

6 Cut 8"-wide strips of building paper and slide them between the siding and the sheathing. Bend the paper around the framing members and staple it in place.

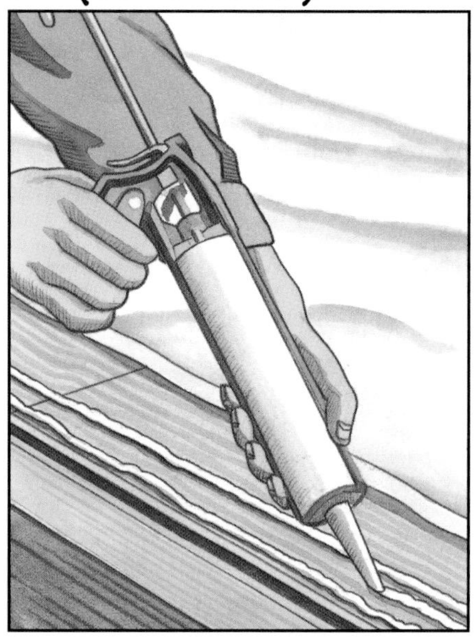

7 Apply several thick beads of silicone caulk to the subfloor at the bottom of the opening.

8 Apply silicone caulk around the front edge of the framing members where the siding meets the building paper.

9 Center the patio door unit in the rough opening so the brick molding is tight against the sheathing. Have a helper hold the door unit from outside until it is shimmed and nailed in place.

10 Check the door threshold to make sure it is level. If necessary, shim under the lower side jamb until the patio door unit is level.

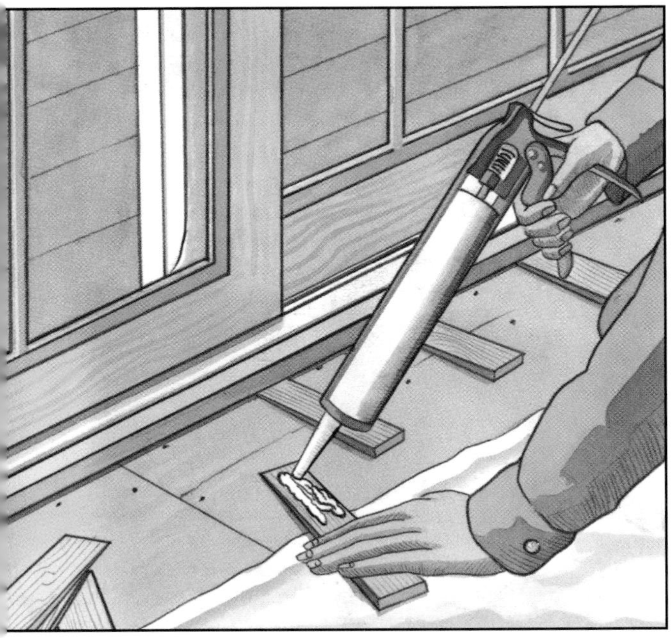

11 If there are gaps between the threshold and the subfloor, insert shims coated with caulk into the gaps, spaced every 6". Shims should be snug, but not so tight that they cause the threshold to bow. Clear off the excess caulk immediately.

12 Place pairs of wood shims together to form flat shims. Insert the shims into gaps between the side jambs and the jack studs, spaced every 12". For sliding doors, shim behind the strike plate for the door latch.

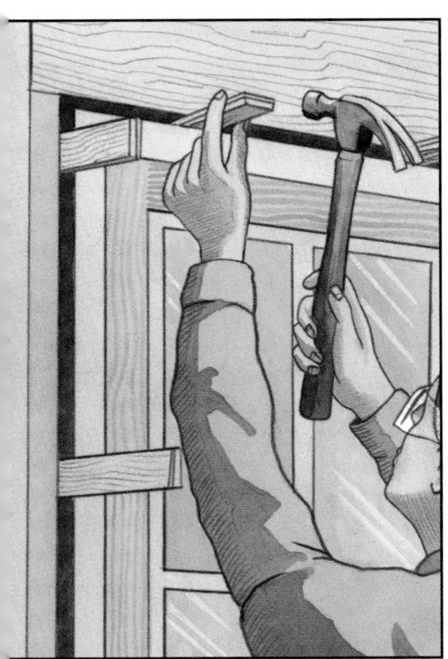

13 Insert shims into the gap between the top jamb and the header, spaced every 12".

14 From outside, drive 10d casing nails, spaced every 12", through the brick molding and into the framing members. Use a nail set to drive the nail heads below the surface of the wood.

15 From inside, drive 10d casing nails through the door jambs and into the framing members at each shim location. Use a nail set to drive the nail heads below the surface of the wood.

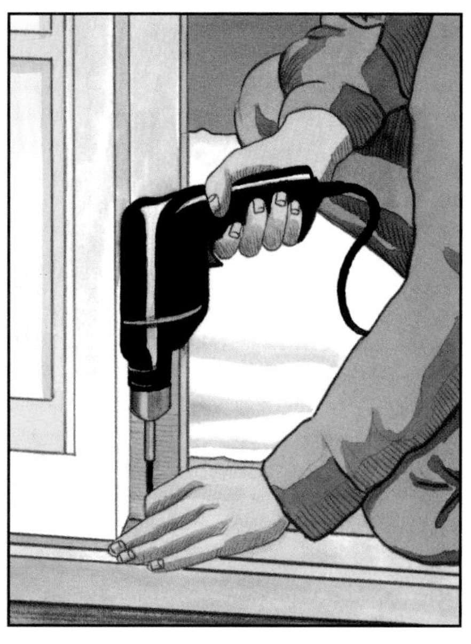

16 Remove one of the screws on the stop block found in the center of the threshold. Replace the screw with a 3" wood screw driven into the subfloor as an anchor.

17 Cut off the shims flush with the face of the framing members using a handsaw. Wearing gloves, fill gaps around the door jambs and beneath the threshold with loosely packed fiberglass insulation.

18 Reinforce and seal the edge of the threshold by installing sill nosing under the threshold and against the wall. Drill pilot holes and attach the sill nosing with 10d casing nails.

19 Make sure the drip edge is tight against the top brick molding; apply paintable silicone caulk along the top of the drip edge and along the outside edge of the side brick moldings. Fill all exterior nail holes with silicone caulk.

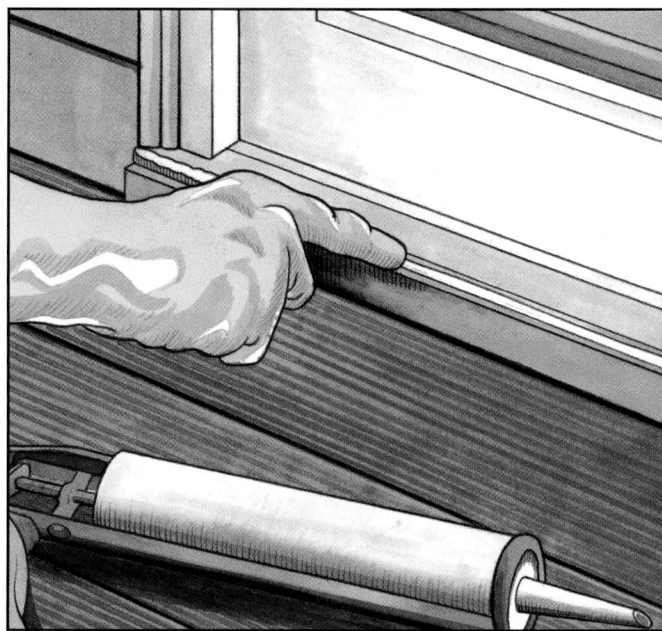

20 Caulk completely around the sill nosing. To press the caulk into cracks, use your finger or an inexpensive caulking tool. As soon as the caulk is dry, paint the sill nosing. Finish the door and install the lockset as directed by the manufacturer.

Removing Windows

Over time, a window may become o deteriorated or inefficient that eplacement of the entire unit is the asiest and most economical repair.)r else, if you want to upgrade the ppearance and the energy fficiency of your home, you will nost likely end up replacing older vindows with contemporary rehung units. But, before you can nstall the new windows you have o remove the old ones.

This may seem complicated, but ctually, removing windows is a ery simple process. The most lifficult factor will be if the vindows are located on upper evels of your home. If this is the ase, you'll need to rent scaffolding r get a good sturdy ladder in order o safely complete this project.

Window units can be umbersome and awkward to andle, so be sure to get assistance efore attempting window removal, specially at elevated locations.

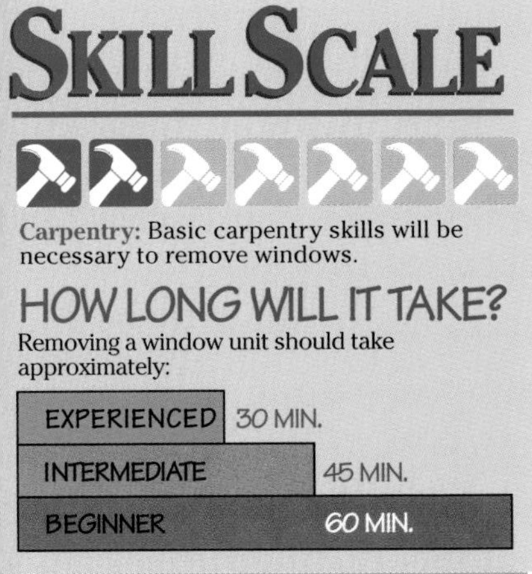

STUFF YOU'LL NEED:

- **Tools:** Pry bar, utility knife, reciprocating saw, hammer.
- **Materials:** Scrap wood.

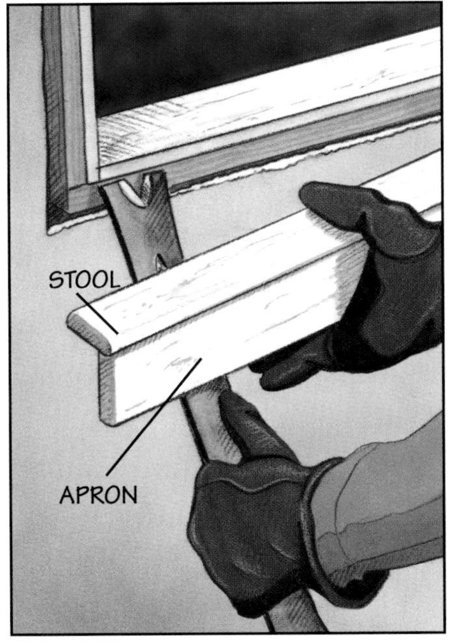

1 Pry off the window aprons and stools, using a pry bar. Use a piece of scrap wood under the pry bar to keep from damaging the wallboard surrounding the window.

2 For double-hung windows with sash weights, remove the weights by cutting the cords and pulling the weights from the pockets.

3 Cut through the nails holding the window frames to the framing members, using a reciprocating saw. For windows attached with nailing fins, cut or pry loose the siding material or brick moldings, then remove the mounting nails holding the unit to the sheathing.

4 Pry the outside brick moldings free from the framing members, using a pry bar. Pull the unit from the rough opening, using a pry bar.

Installing a Window

Replacement windows are available in various shapes, styles, colors and construction types. They are most commonly made of wood, aluminum, or vinyl. Each manufacturer's product has its own specific installation instructions but as a whole, window units are installed in the same manner.

Prehung windows come complete with finish frames and can be inserted in one piece into the rough opening left by the old window. Once the old window has been removed, measure the rough opening size and be sure to purchase a new window unit to fit the rough opening.

Most good windows must be custom ordered several weeks in advance. Don't be overconfident about the delivery schedule of the windows you order. It's very risky to remove the existing windows prior to the delivery of the new windows. Because of sudden weather changes, shipment delays and improper order fulfillment, you could wind up with a big hole in the side of your house and nothing to cover it with. Ideally, it's best to keep the old windows in place until the new ones have arrived, been inspected for damage, and verified for size.

As important as the windows are to the security, appearance and energy efficiency of your home, you'll be pleasantly surprised by the simplicity of installing them. If the windows are located on upper levels of the home, you'll need to rent scaffolding or have a good sturdy ladder to safely install windows at these elevations. Because windows are quite awkward to handle, it's generally a good idea to get assistance and even have two ladders, one person on each, to safely and easily install upper-level windows.

STUFF YOU'LL NEED:

- ☐ **Tools:** Hammer, pencil, carpenter's level, handsaw, reciprocating saw, stapler, nail set, caulk gun.
- ☐ **Materials:** Wood shims, building paper, drip edge, casing nails, fiberglass insulation, silicone caulk.

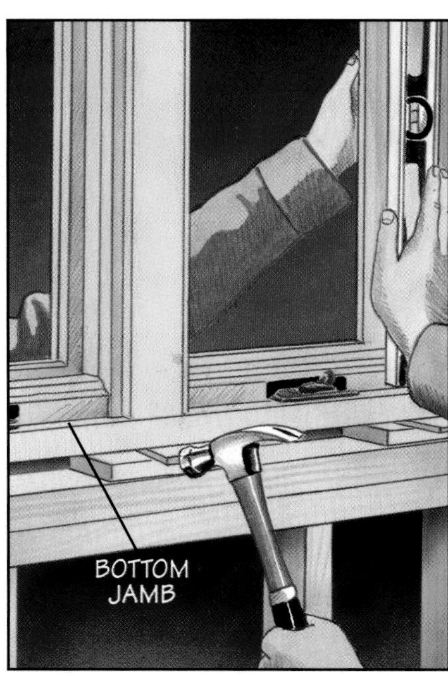

1 Remove the interior wall surface and then test-fit the window, centering it in the rough opening. Support the window with wood blocks and shims placed under the bottom jamb. Check to make sure the window is plumb and level, and adjust the shims, if necessary.

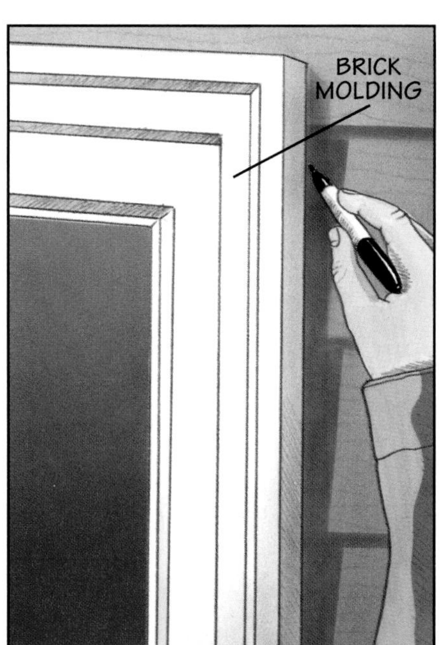

2 Trace the outline of the brick molding on the siding. If you have vinyl or metal siding, enlarge the outline to make room for the extra J-channel moldings required by these sidings. Remove the window after finishing the outline.

3 Cut the siding along the outline just down to the sheathing. Use a reciprocating saw held at a shallow angle or a circular saw adjusted so blade depth equals the thickness of the siding. Then use a sharp chisel to complete the cuts at the corners.

4 Cut 8"-wide strips of building paper and slide them between the siding and sheathing around the entire window opening. Bend the paper around the framing members and staple it in place.

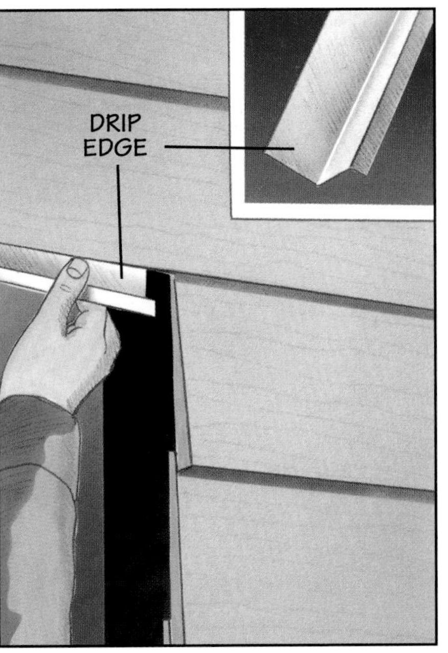

5 Cut a length of drip edge to fit over the top of the window and then slide it between the siding and building paper.

6 Insert the window into the opening, and push the brick molding tight against the sheathing.

7 Check to see how much adjustment will be necessary to level and plumb the window unit.

8 If the window is perfectly level, predrill and nail both bottom corners of the brick molding with 16d casing nails. If the window is not perfectly level, nail only at the higher of the two bottom corners.

9 If necessary, have a helper adjust the shim under the lower corner of the window, from inside, until the window is level.

INSTALLING A WINDOW (continued)

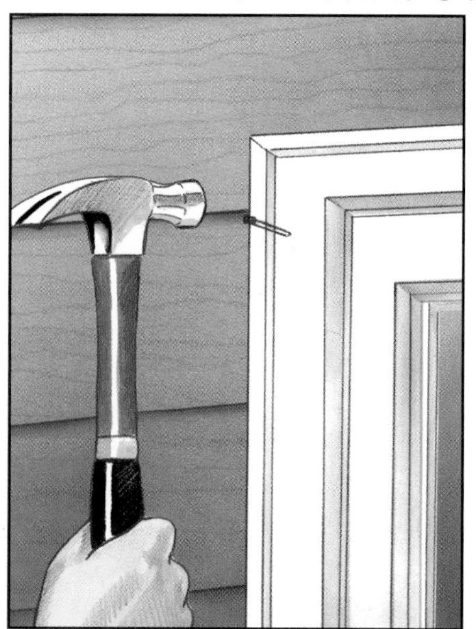

10 From the outside, drive 16d casing nails into pre-drilled holes through the brick molding and into the framing members near the remaining corners of the window. If the window is a vinyl-clad window, nail through the nailing flange into the framing members to hold the window in place.

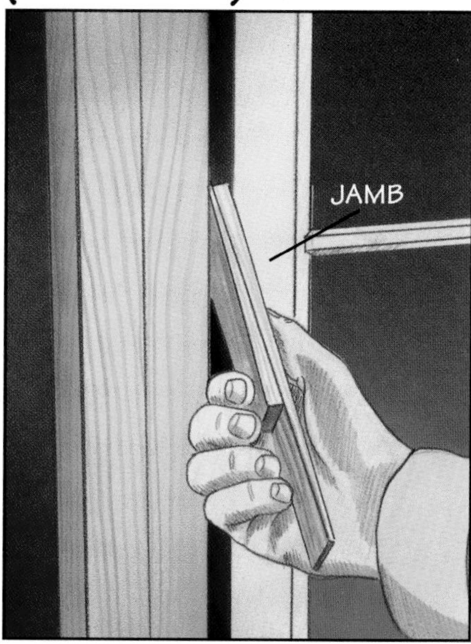

11 Place pairs of shims together to form flat shims. From inside, insert the shims into the gaps between the jambs and framing members, spaced every 12".

12 Adjust the shims so they are snug, but not so tight that they cause the jambs to bow. On multiple-unit windows, make sure the shims under the mull posts are tight.

13 Use a straightedge to check the side jambs to make sure they do not bow. Adjust the shims, if necessary, until the jambs are flat. Open and close the window to make sure it works properly.

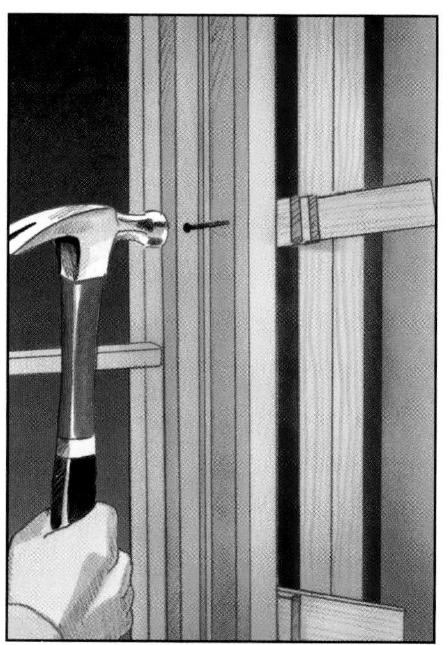

14 At each shim location, drill a pilot hole, then drive an 8d casing nail through the jamb, shims, and into the framing member. Drive the nail heads below the wood surface with a nail set.

15 Fill the gaps between the window jambs and the framing members with loosely packed fiberglass insulation. Be sure to wear work gloves when handling insulation.

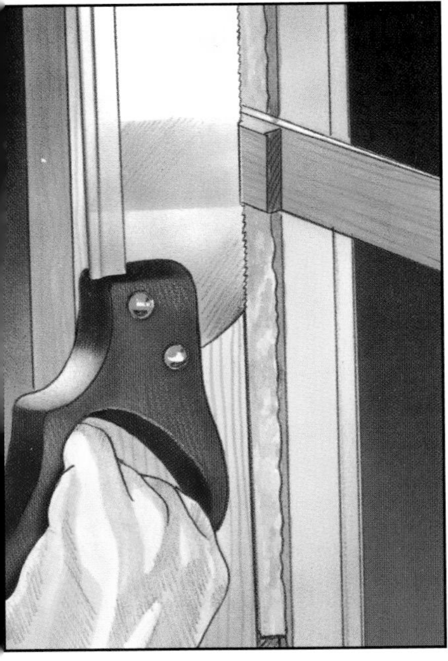

16 Trim the shims flush with the framing members using a handsaw.

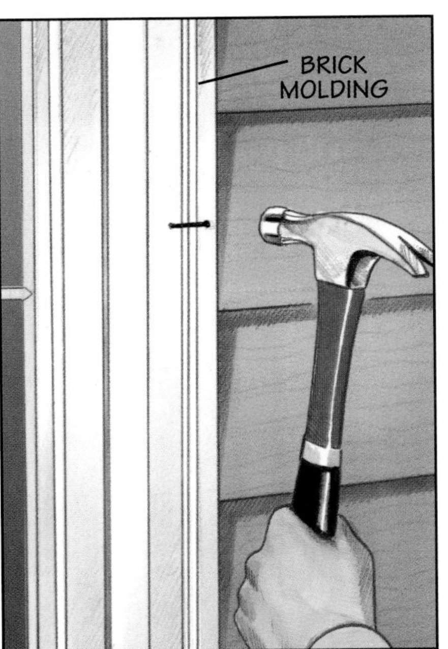

17 From the outside, drive 16d galvanized casing nails, spaced every 12", through predrilled holes in the brick moldings and into the framing members. Drive all nail heads below the wood surface with a nail set.

18 Apply paintable silicone caulk around the entire window unit and fill the nail holes with caulk.

Doors & Windows

INSTALLATION VARIATION: MASONRY CLIPS

Use metal masonry clips when brick molding on a window can't be nailed because it rests against a masonry or brick surface. The masonry clips hook into precut grooves in the window jambs and are attached to the jambs with utility screws. After the window unit is positioned in the rough opening, the masonry clips are bent around the framing members.

Anchor the masonry clips with utility screws. Masonry clips also can be used in ordinary lap siding installations if you want to avoid making nail holes in the smooth surface of the brick moldings. For example, windows that are precoated with polymer-based paint can be installed with masonry clips so that the brick moldings are not punctured with nails.

Installing Vinyl-Clad Windows

Vinyl-clad windows have a durable vinyl coating that fully encases the exterior window frame. To simplify installation and provide a weather-proof seal, vinyl-clad windows have an installation fin molded into the vinyl coating. The fin is pre-drilled with mounting holes spaced evenly around the perimeter of the window unit. Galvanized roofing nails, usually 2" long, are used to nail through the fin into the framing members. The large round head of the roofing nail holds the fin securely to the exterior sheathing.

Installing vinyl-clad windows is fairly quick and easy. Depending on the size of the window unit and the elevation at which it is being installed, they can usually be installed by one person.

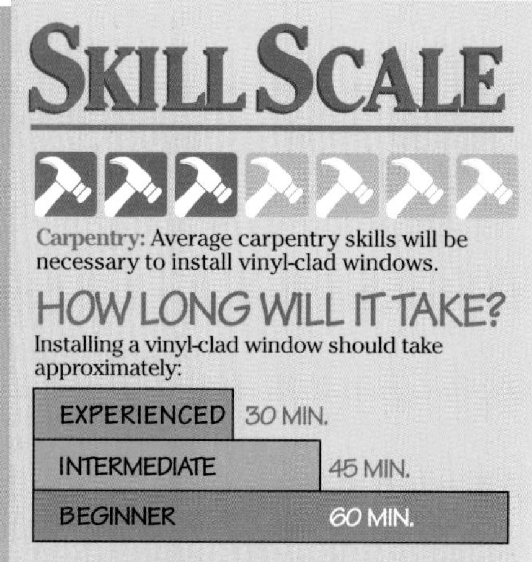

STUFF YOU'LL NEED:

- ☐ **Tools:** Carpenter's level, hammer, caulk gun.
- ☐ **Materials:** Wood shims, 2" galvanized roofing nails, silicone caulk.

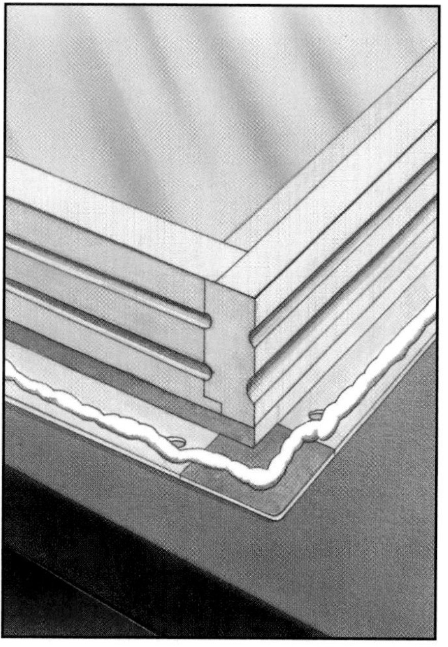

1 After framing the rough opening (pages 305 to 306) or removing the old window, apply a continuous bead of silicone caulk to the back of the installation fin around the full perimeter of the window.

2 Place 1/4" blocks under the sill corners to provide clearance and set the window unit into the rough opening.

3 Level the window unit across the head using a carpenter's level. Place shims under the sill at the jambs to level the unit.

4 Plumb the window unit using a carpenter's level on the exterior frame jambs.

5 Secure the window unit by nailing the installation fin with 2" galvanized roofing nails in both upper corners.

6 Shim as necessary at the jambs for equal width at the sill, head and center.

7 Check the diagonal measurement of the window unit, corner to corner, to ensure a square installation. Reshim the window unit if necessary.

8 Finish securing the unit in the opening by nailing through the installation fin in all prepunched holes with 2" galvanized roofing nails. Seal the installation fin to the exterior sheathing with silicone caulk. Install the siding allowing 1/4" to 3/8" space for perimeter sealant. Seal the perimeter of the window unit with a quality silicone caulk.

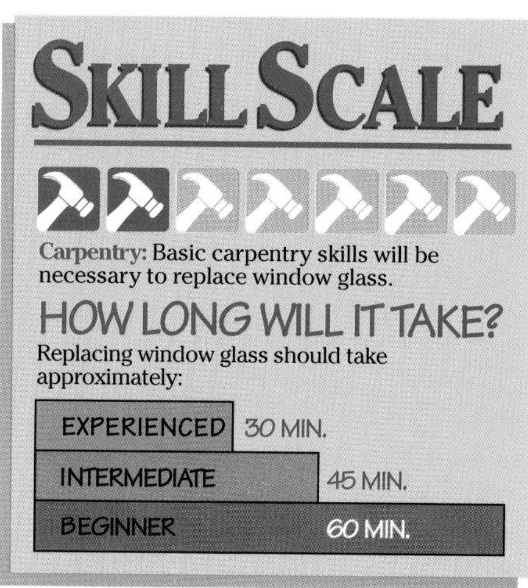

Replacing Glass

The age-old problem with window panes remains the same today – they break! Antique leaded-glass panes often loosen and rattle. Modern panes exhibit some modern problems as well. A double pane may tend to fog if moisture gets between its layers, and a plastic pane will yellow and craze over time. Whatever the problem, the tools you need to work on windows are few and simple!

The National Glazing Code (yes, there is such a thing), requires that shatter-resistant panes be used in certain applications such as doors and sidelights. Be sure to check with a professional glazier or window dealer before replacing a pane. If you plan to install a double or triple pane, order the unit in advance because it may have to be built to size.

You can cut your own glass or plastic single pane. When cutting glass, always wear work gloves and safety goggles. Practice cutting a scrap piece first and work on a level surface padded with layers of newspaper or a piece of thin carpet. Cutting a plastic pane is much safer, but be careful not to scratch its relatively soft surface.

STUFF YOU'LL NEED:

- **Tools:** Putty knife, heat gun, sandpaper, caulk gun, paintbrush.
- **Materials:** Glazing points, glazing compound, glass, paint.

BUYER'S GUIDE

Choosing Glass Replacement

When repairing a broken window, you can use either glass or clear acrylic as a replacement material. Glass will provide the clearest and most scratch-resistant view, but if durability is a concern, clear acrylic can be substituted. Clear acrylic is extremely durable but very susceptible to scratches and marring. Tempered glass may be an option to provide both strength and durability with a clear view; however, you can't cut tempered glass yourself. It must be precut to the size you need it.

INSTALLING NEW GLASS

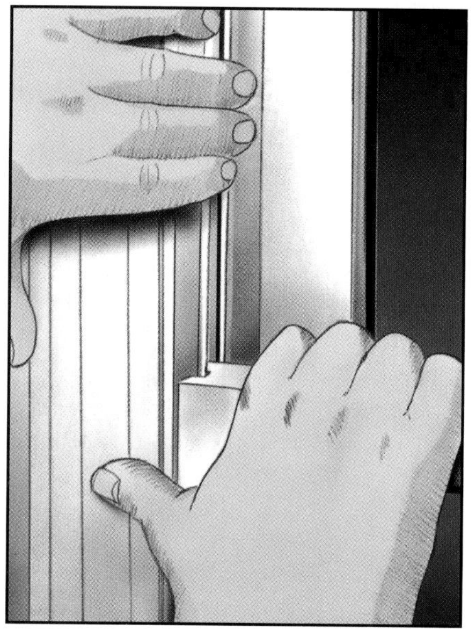

1 Remove the spring-loaded double-hung windows by pushing against the flexible vinyl channels to release the channel pins. Older double-hung windows can be repaired while the window remains in the frame.

2 With traditional glazing, soften the old putty with a heat gun or torch, being careful not to scorch the wood. Scrape away the soft putty with a putty knife. On newer windows, simply pry out the vinyl glazing strips.

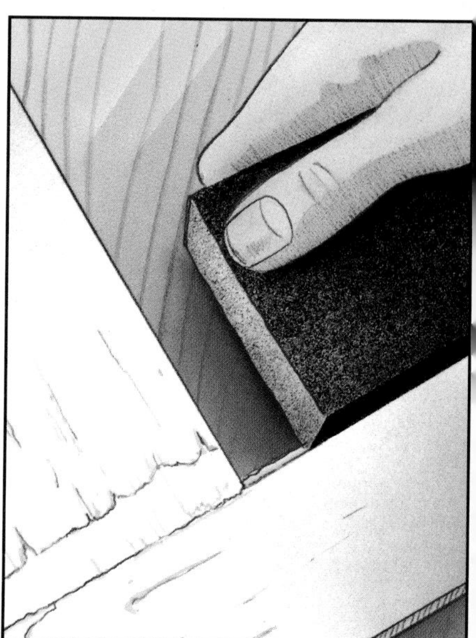

3 Remove the broken glass and metal glazing points from the frame; then sand the L-shaped grooves to clean away the old paint and putty. Coat the bare wood with a sealer and let dry.

4 Apply a thin layer of glazing compound in the primed grooves. Press the glass lightly to bed it. Press in new glazing points every 10" with the tip of a putty knife. Do not put any downward pressure on the glazing points when inserting or they could break the glass.

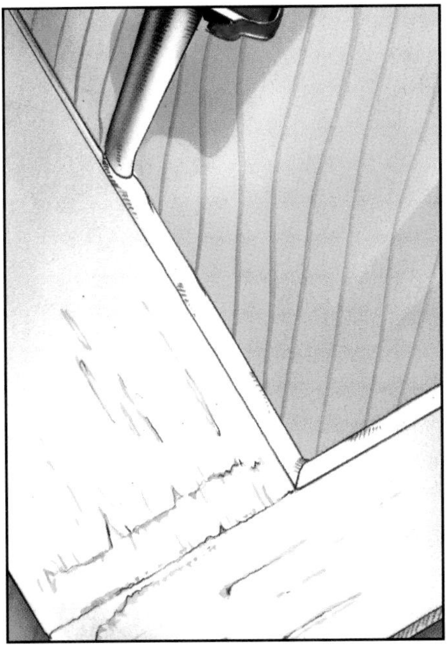

5 Apply glazing compound. Move the tube tip along the edge of the glass while steadily squeezing the trigger. Smooth the glazing with a wet finger or cloth.

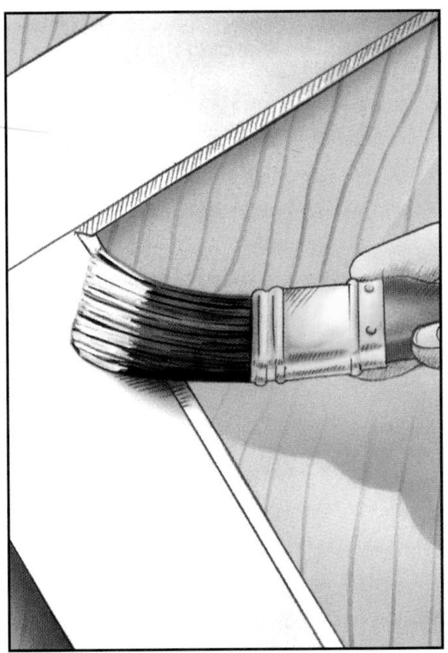

6 Latex glazing can usually be painted the same day. Overlap the paint onto the glass by 1/16" to improve its weather seal.

Doors & Windows

Replacing Screens

Window screens are relatively easy to repair and replace. Fiberglass screening is easy to install, but tends to sag. Aluminum screening is more expensive but stronger, though it eventually oxidizes in humid climates. Both types of screening are replaced the same way.

Of the two screening materials, aluminum is less likely to tear or sag while fiberglass will not corrode or oxidize. Whatever material your screens are made of, match the repair method to the nature and extent of the damage.

Oxidized or dirt-encrusted aluminum screening, for example, needs only rubbing with a wire brush and once-over cleaning with a vacuum cleaner. Loose joints on wooden frames can easily be reinforced with fasteners, angle plates or screws. Holes in screening can be fixed in several ways with glue, an awl, metal thread and pre-manufactured patches.

SKILL SCALE

Carpentry: Basic carpentry skills will be necessary to replace window screen.

HOW LONG WILL IT TAKE?

Replacing window screen should take approximately:

EXPERIENCED	30 MIN.
INTERMEDIATE	45 MIN.
BEGINNER	60 MIN.

STUFF YOU'LL NEED:

- ☐ **Tools:** Utility knife, hammer, spline roller, stapler, hacksaw, awl, screwdrivers.
- ☐ **Materials:** Screen material, spline material.

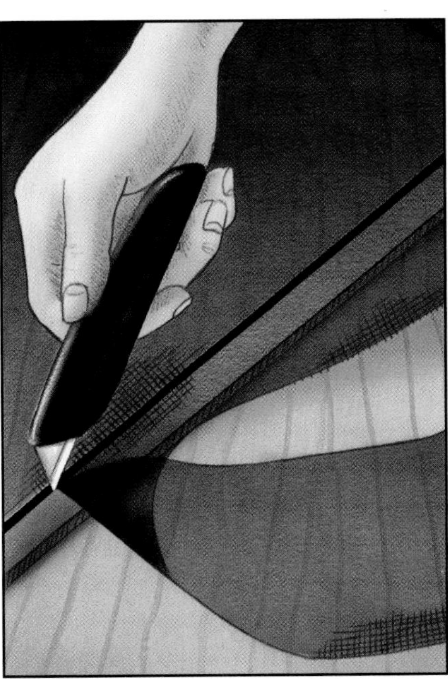

For easy handling, cut the screen fabric an inch or two larger than the opening on both sides so you can pull it tight, then trim the fabric after the screen molding or spline is reinstalled.

REPLACING SCREEN IN A WOODEN FRAME

1 Pry up the screen molding with a small chisel or screwdriver. If the molding is sealed with paint, use a utility knife to cut the paint film and free the molding.

2 Stretch the new screen fabric tightly across the frame and hold it in place with staples or thumbtacks. It usually works well to leave extra screen overhang the frame so you can pull it tightly before stapling. Then simply trim the overhang once it is secured.

3 Nail the screen molding back in place with wire brads. Cut away the excess screen fabric with a utility knife.

REPLACING SCREEN IN AN ALUMINUM FRAME

1 Pry the vinyl spline from the grooves around the edge of the frame with a screwdriver. Retain the old spline, if it is still flexible, or replace it with new spline.

2 Stretch the new screen fabric tightly over the frame so that it overlaps the retaining grooves.

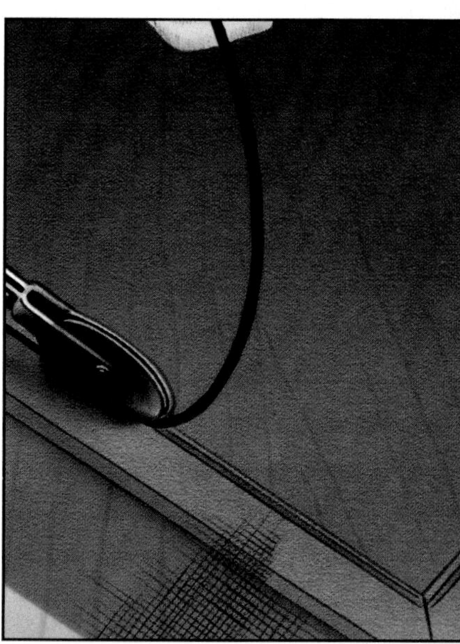

3 Use a spline roller to press the spline and screen into the grooves. Cut away the excess screen fabric with a utility knife.

REPLACING A METAL-FRAME SCREEN

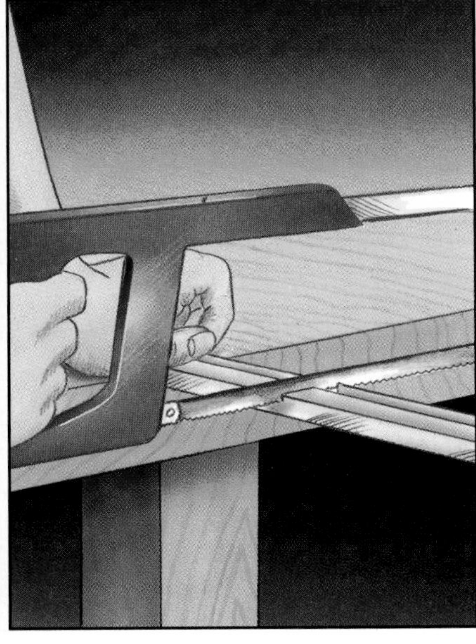

1 With a hacksaw, cut the framing pieces to length, leaving the ends square. Remember to subtract the length of the two corner brackets (see right) from the measurements.

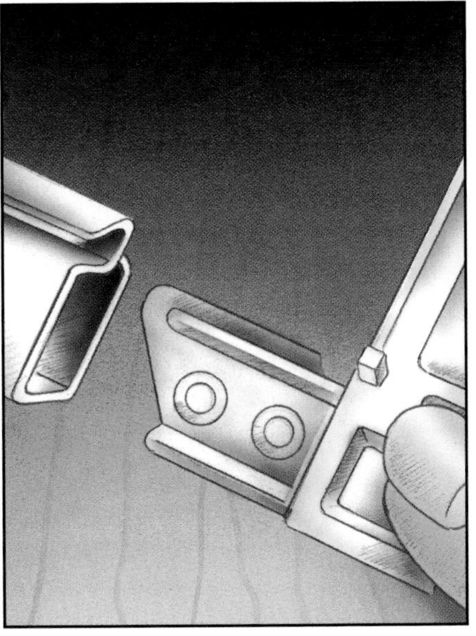

2 To assemble frame, push the corner brackets into the framing pieces. If sawing pinched the framing pieces closed, pry them open with an old screwdriver.

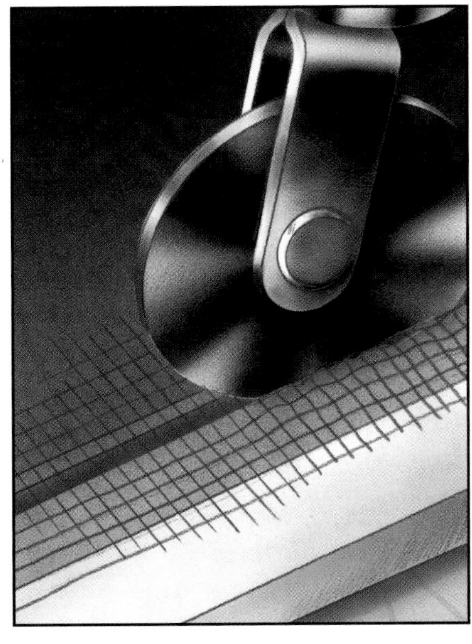

3 Cut the screen material $^1/_2$" larger than the frame and trim the corners diagonally. Push the screening into the groove with the convex roller of a splining tool or a stiff-bladed putty knife.

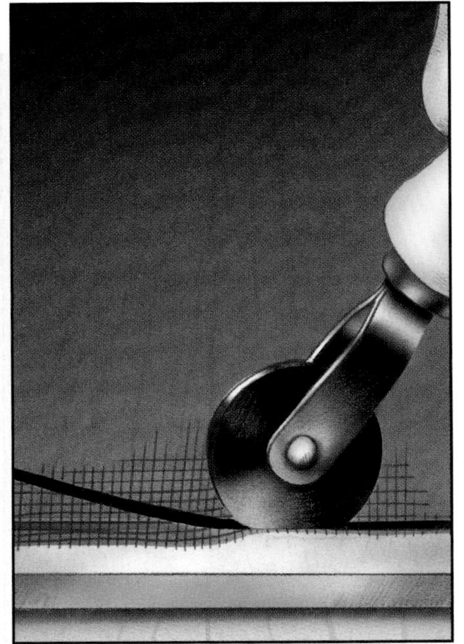

4 With the concave roller of the splining tool, force the spline and screening into the groove. Use short, firm strokes. Cut off the excess spline and screen material.

PATCHING A SCREEN

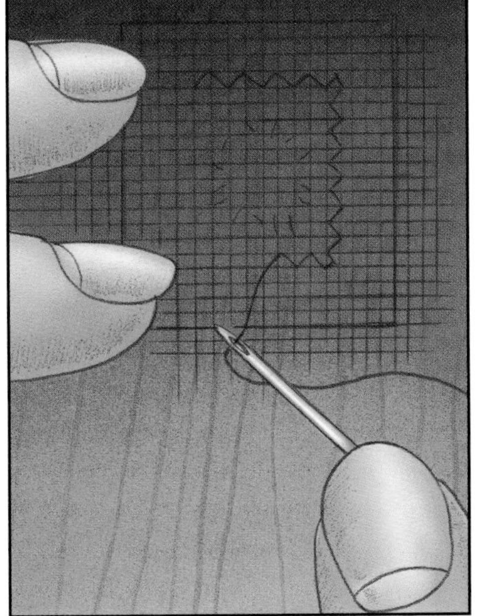

Repair holes in plastic or fiberglass screens by sewing a screen patch over the hole. Pull "threads" from the patch material. Small holes can sometimes be closed with waterproof glue. Use it sparingly and wipe away any drips before the glue hardens.

For holes in metal mesh, pull cross threads from the patch's edges. Bend the wires and push them through the mesh around the hole and crimp the ends. Smaller holes can often be fixed by reshaping the mesh with a toothpick or straightened paper clip.

Window Security

To delay, and hopefully deter thieves, it is good practice to install locks on your windows. You really can't rely on the clamshell (or butterfly) latch often found on double-hung windows. It's not really a lock. Its purpose is to draw the sashes together to reduce drafts and rattling.

You can improvise a lock by drilling a hole through the interior sash and partway into the exterior sash, then inserting a bolt, dowel, or large nail into the hole. You'll want to use a peg that is slightly narrower than the hole so you can remove it easily when you want to open the window. The ready-made locks shown in this section are variations on this idea. If possible, get keyed locks from a single manufacturer so that one key will fit them all. To ensure your family's safety, keep a key near each window, hidden from outside view, so that the window can be opened quickly in an emergency.

If the local fire code permits it, additional security can be provided by replacing single glazing with polycarbonate or wire-embedded glass. More drastic measures include installing security shutters, a grille, or a security gate.

Window security can be as expensive, or inexpensive, as you want. Although specific security bolts are designed for windows (see facing page), regular bolts, while a little less convenient, work just as well to keep the windows shut.

Also, on sliding patio doors, you can block the sliding door by wedging a board between the inside door panel and the jamb to lock the door closed.

GLIDING WINDOW LOCKS

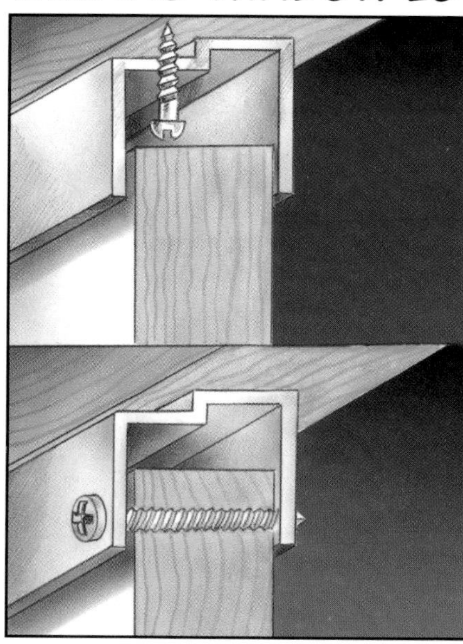

A screw stop can be made simply by installing a screw vertically in the top channel to prevent the sash from being lifted out (top). A horizontal screw (bottom) will keep the sash from sliding.

A track stop attaches to the window track to prevent the window panel from sliding open. Simply rotate the handle counterclockwise to loosen the bolt. Slip the stop over the window track and turn the handle clockwise to tighten the bolt.

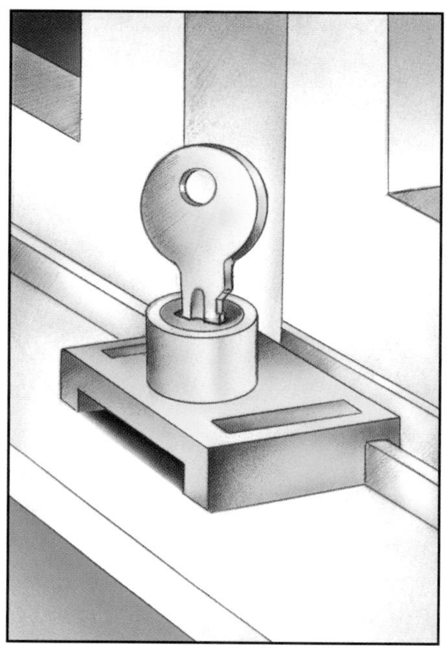

A key track stop is a locking track stop that can be attached to the window track whether the window is open or shut. Simply turn the key to anchor the lock.

CASEMENT LOCK

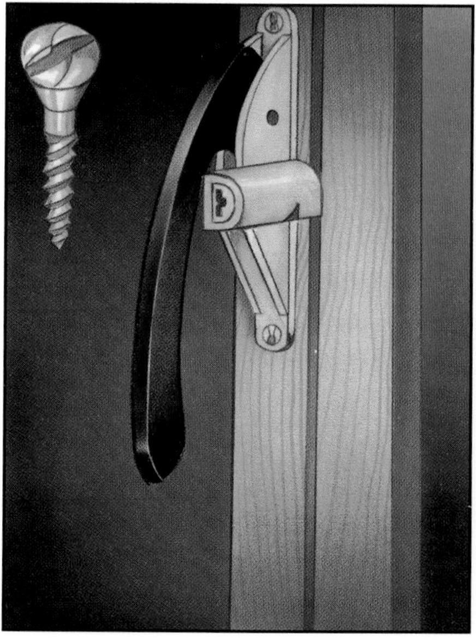

A locking key latch can be used to replace the standard manual latch on a casement window. Key latches are usually mounted with one-way screws. When buying this lock, you must specify whether it is for the right or left side of the sash.

DOUBLE-HUNG WINDOW LOCKS

Locking pins are usually installed on each side of the sash. Simply drill the proper-size hole through the top corner of the lower sash into the bottom of the upper sash and mount the cap and pin holder. Make sure the sashes are aligned properly before you drill.

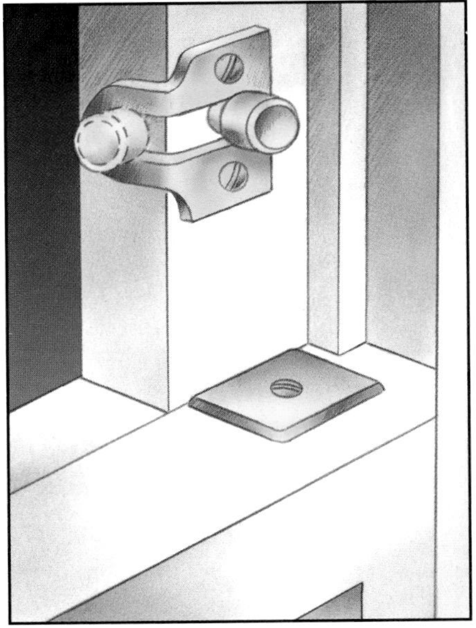

Ventilating locks are screwed to the side of top sash 1" or more above the meeting rail. The strike plate is screwed to the top rail of the lower sash directly below the lock. It usually works best to use one or more on each side to regulate the window opening.

Security bolts are drilled through the top of the lower sash, partway into the bottom of upper sash. The washer and bolt are inserted into the hole and tightened with a nut driver.

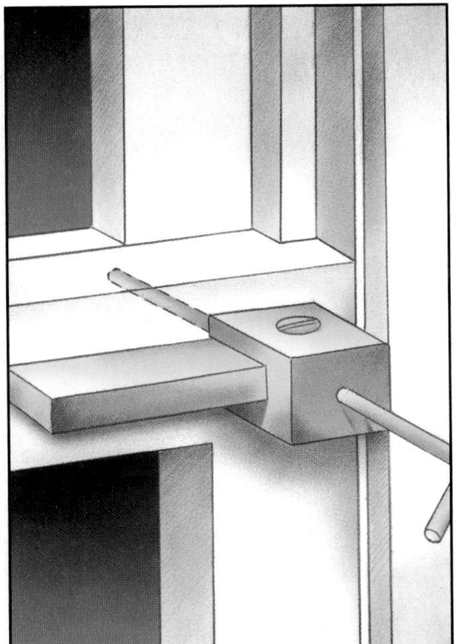

Rod locks are a modified locking pin. They are installed in much the same way as the locking pin. Simply hold the lock against the top rail of the lower sash and use it as a template to mark the holes. Drill the rod hole through the lower sash and partially into the top sash and mount the lock in place.

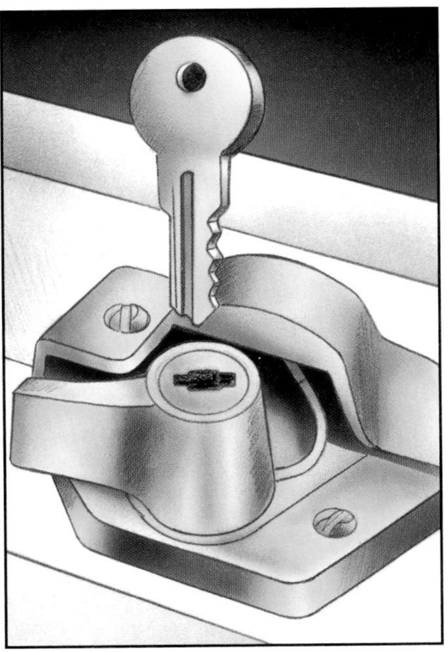

A key turnbuckle replaces the clamshell latch and should be mounted with one-way screws. If the new screw holes align with the existing screw holes, fill them with wood putty or wood matchsticks in order to provide a more solid mount. Then redrill the pilot holes and attach the turnbuckle.

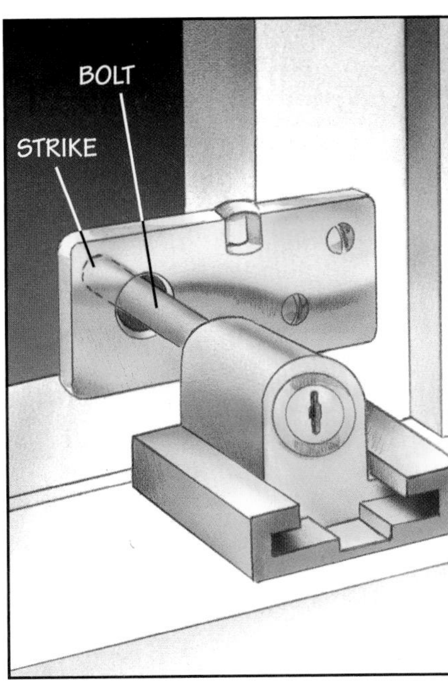

Key bolts use a locking bolt and strike plate to secure the window sashes. They are mounted at the top corner of the lower sash and the strike plate is screwed to the side rail of the top sash.

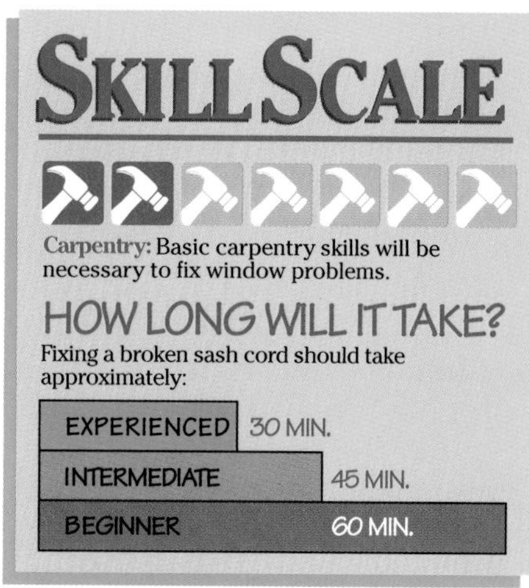

Fixing Window Problems

A wood double-hung window suffers from the problems typical of any wood window. The wood shrinks, rots or warps, window joints loosen, and paint buildup makes the sashes stick shut. In addition, the balance system can wear out or break. A broken sash cord is a very common problem.

To maintain the seemingly effortless motion made by windows that swing and slide, you must regularly clean and lubricate a variety of mechanical parts. Dust and grease accumulate in the operators and clog the splines of the gears. Periodically lubricating the operator in place with silicone spray is a good practice.

A thorough cleaning once a year requires careful disassembly of the operator from the window. Dirt also builds up in the tracks and around the window. Vacuum the tracks and scrub the sashes and frames with a mild detergent. Steel surfaces frequently rust and should be scraped and repainted with rustproof exterior paint.

In many ways you can treat a casement window as you would a double-hung window. If the sash binds against the jamb or sill, perhaps it is swollen with moisture, or the hinges are loose, making the window sag. Either sand the edge of the sash where it rubs, or inspect and then fix or replace the hinges. Repositioning a casement window stop as you would a door stop may help to quiet a rattling window.

Even the best maintenance practices can't prevent parts from breaking down. Luckily, most breakdowns can be repaired. For each type of window and door, there are numerous models with their own distinctive parts. Save broken parts to help you find matching replacements. If your local store doesn't stock the items you need, take the part to a window specialist or call the manufacturer.

Before doing any repairs, make sure the window is sound enough to make the repair worthwhile.

STUFF YOU'LL NEED:

- □ **Tools:** Pry bar, utility knife, scissors, paint zipper, hammer, screwdrivers, vacuum cleaner.
- □ **Materials:** String, cleaners, lubricants.

CLEANING AND LUBRICATING TIPS

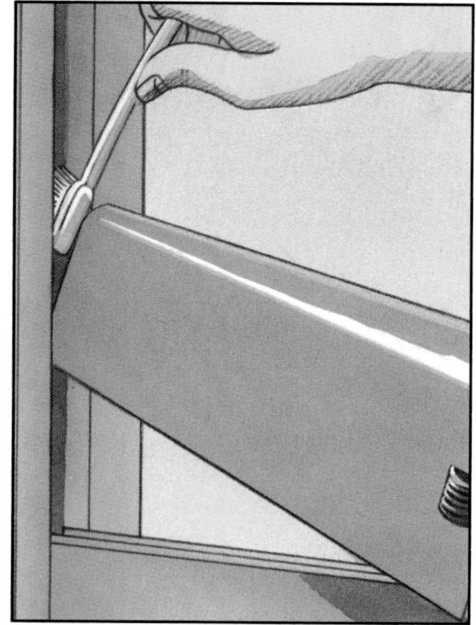

Clean the tracks on sliding windows and doors with a hand vacuum and a toothbrush to keep them operating smoothly. Dirt buildup is common on storm window tracks.

A variety of cleaners and lubricants, such as spray solvents and lubricants, penetrating oils, silicone sprays, and powdered graphite, are available for window maintenance. An ordinary bar of soap will also do the trick.

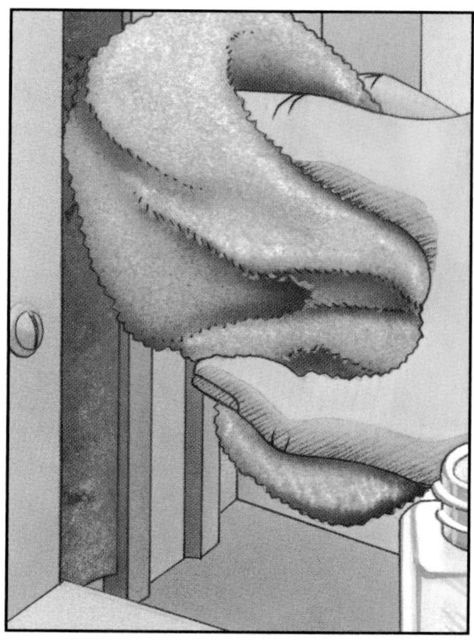

Clean weather stripping by spraying with cleaner and wiping away the dirt. Use paint solvent to remove paint that may bind windows; then apply a small amount of lubricant to prevent sticking. Solvents may damage vinyl clad windows. Test the paint solvent on a hidden part of the window first.

FREEING A STUCK WINDOW SASH

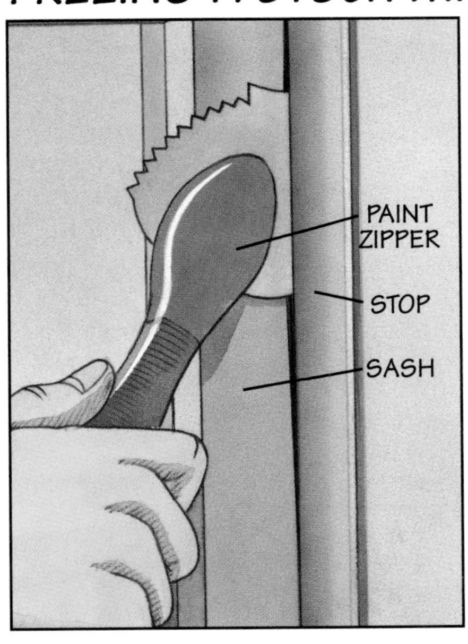

Cut the paint film if the window is painted shut. Insert a paint zipper or utility knife into the crack between the window stop and sash.

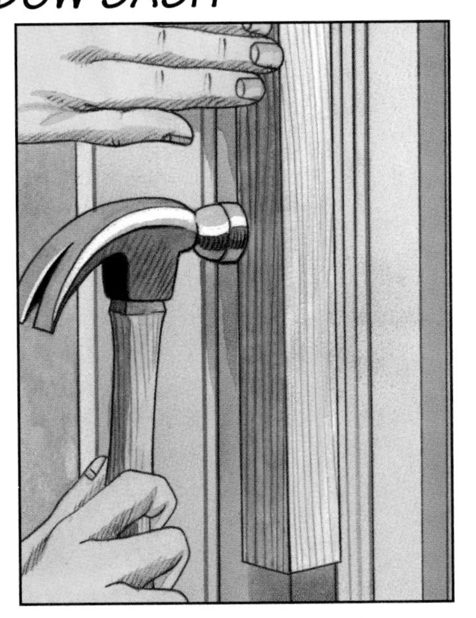

Place a block of scrap wood along the window sash. Tap lightly with a hammer to free window.

ADJUSTING SPRINGS

Adjust the screws found on the track insert. Turn each screw until the window is properly balanced.

YOU CAN BUY REPLACEMENTS FOR SASH CORDS THAT COMBINE SPRING BALANCES AND WEATHER STRIPPING.

REPLACING BROKEN SASH CORDS

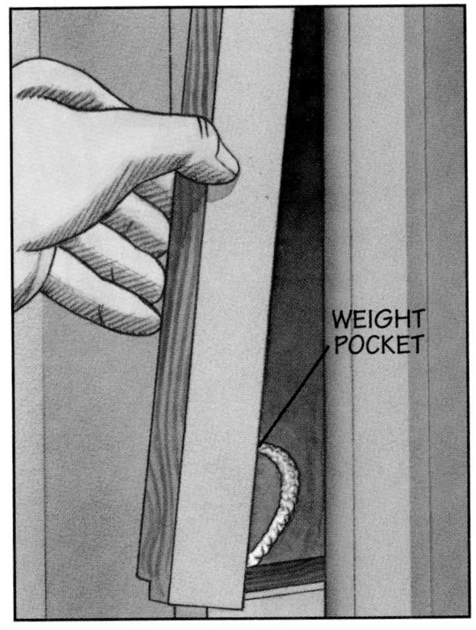

1 After removing the window by prying the window stops and weather stripping from the frame, cut the old sash cord and then pry out or unscrew the cover of the weight pocket found in the lower end of the window channel. Remove the weight and cut the old sash cord off it.

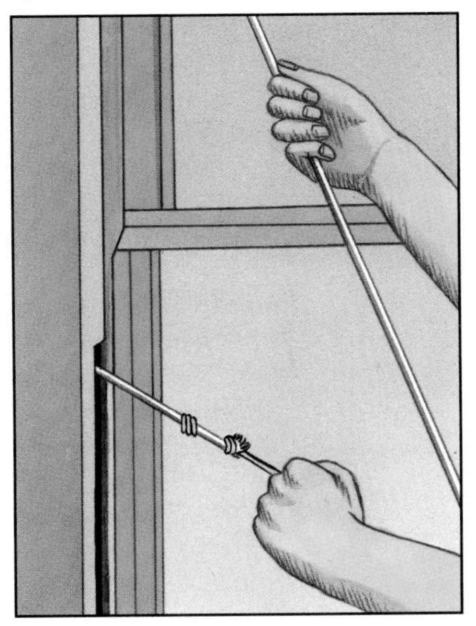

2 Tie a piece of string to a small nail and the other end to the new sash cord. Drop the nail over the pulley and let it drop into the weight pocket. Pull the new sash cord through and tie it to the weight with a strong knot. Return the weight to the pocket and pull the cord to raise the weight up against the pulley.

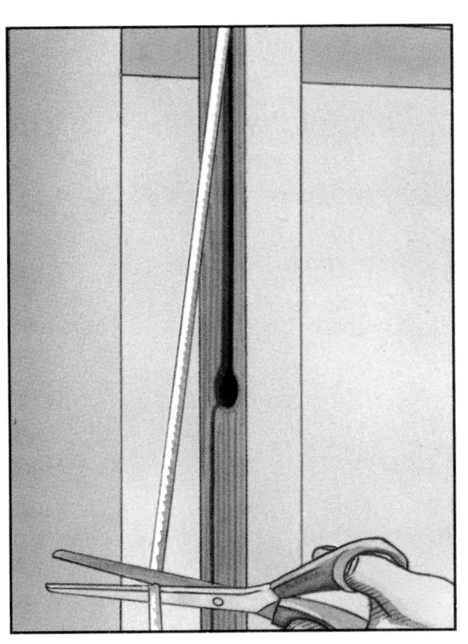

3 Rest the bottom window on the sill. While holding the sash cord firmly against the side of the window, cut the cord 3" beyond the hole in the window sash. Knot the sash cord and wedge the knot in the hole. Replace the pocket cover, slide the window in place, and reattach stripping and stops.

Maintaining Roll-up Garage Doors

Like the cars behind them, garage doors need the occasional tune-up. They need it for much the same reasons: Parts get dirty, they wear, they come out of alignment.

Because this happens slowly, you're liable not to notice it until the problem is out of hand. It may be a minor nuisance, like a door that locks you out of the garage. Or it may be a major problem—a door out of alignment can seriously injure someone.

The best insurance is to check the door periodically. Start with the easy stuff: Is the latch catching on both sides of the door? Are the hinges bolted firmly in place? Are the rollers in working condition?

Once you're sure the door is mechanically sound, make sure it opens and closes gently. If not, start looking for problems. Clean the tracks, but don't lubricate them, and don't lubricate the surfaces of the rollers. The oil will only trap dirt and cause more problems. Save your oil for the other moving parts—apply light machine oil to the hinges, roller shafts, latches, and the fitting that holds the cable to the door.

Look to see if the door is rubbing or binding somewhere or if it's rubbing against the door trim. Check to make sure the rollers aren't binding in the track. In either case, you need to adjust the track brackets, as explained on the next page.

If the door still doesn't close correctly, it's probably out of balance, and could hit someone or something as you open and close it. It's a problem that's simple enough to fix, as explained on page 342.

SAFETY ALERT
Torsion springs are dangerous and should be adjusted only by a garage-door professional.

Torsion springs counterbalance the weight of the garage door and help to raise the door as it is opening and restrain it as it is closing. The springs are always under tension and are extremely powerful and dangerous.

STUFF YOU'LL NEED:

- ☐ **Tools:** Wrenches, C-clamp, screwdriver, hammer, ladder, paintbrush, locking pliers.
- ☐ **Materials:** Lubricant, paint, masking tape.

PARTS OF A TYPICAL ROLL-UP DOOR

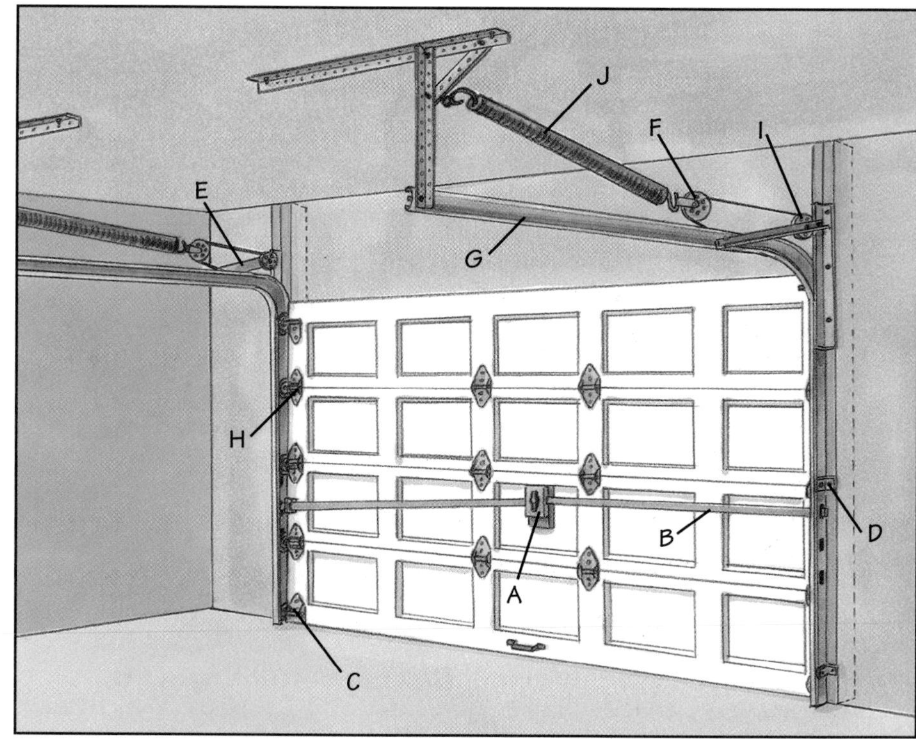

Roll-up garage-door components include: door lock (**A**), lock bar (**B**), cable anchor (**C**), track bracket (**D**), front track brace (**E**), clevis pulley (**F**), track (**G**), roller hinge (**H**), stud pulley (**I**), and tension spring (**J**).

ROLL-UP DOOR MAINTENANCE TIPS

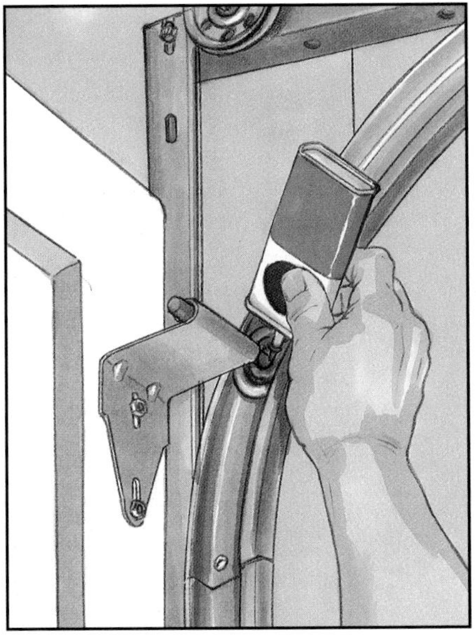

Lubricate your garage door two to three times a year. You'll want to put oil on any moving part, except for the garage track and roller surfaces. Oil on either will catch dirt, and actually make it harder to operate the door.

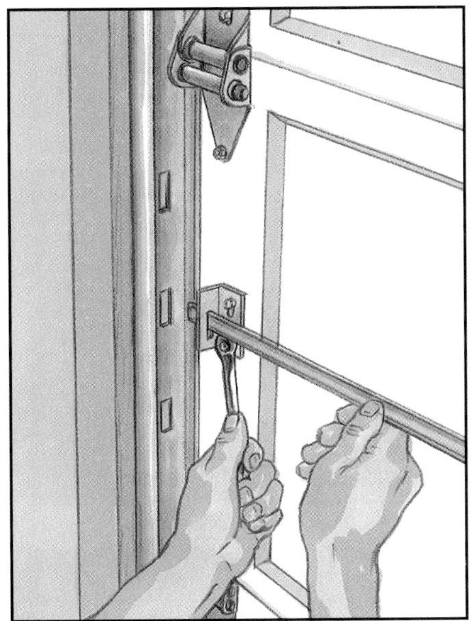

A latch that doesn't lock is as good as no lock at all. Check to make sure the lock bar slides smoothly into the lock hole. If not, loosen the bracket that holds the bar in place, slide the bracket into the proper position, and retighten.

Vibration can cause screws and bolts to come loose. A loose hinge can seriously damage the door. Check to make sure all screws and bolts are tight. Don't forget the screws that hold the handle in place. If the handle slips out of the latch, you could find yourself locked out of the garage.

Look to see if the door binds on the door frame. Stop the binding by moving the door track. Loosen the mounting brackets and slide the track (and door) away from the door frame. Retighten brackets. Add shims under the bracket mount if you can't move the track enough.

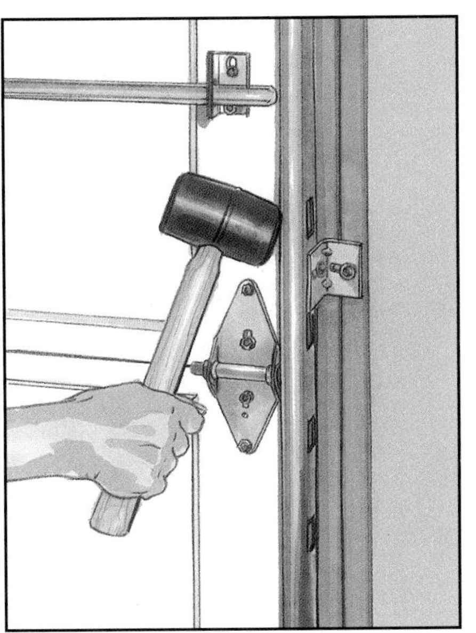

Position the door and track so there is ⅝ to ⅞ of an inch between the edge of the door and the track. Check along the entire track. Adjust the mounting brackets by loosening them and tapping gently with a hammer. Retighten the brackets before using the door.

Prevent rot or rust by painting a badly scratched door. Choose a paint that will adhere to the door. To check if the paint will adhere to the door, paint a spot, and put masking tape over it after it's dry. If removing the tape removes paint, you need another type of paint or you didn't do enough prep work.

ADJUSTING AN OUT-OF-BALANCE DOOR

With time, the cables and springs on a garage door stretch, and the door can come dangerously out of balance. The usual problem is a door that closes too quickly—endangering your feet, your children, or anything else in its path. The door can also open too quickly, which can damage the door or your shoulder. A properly balanced door remains stationary when it's opened 3 to 4 feet. When you open or close it, it should come to a gentle stop. If it slams down, or closes and then reopens slightly, you'll need to adjust the spring tension.

1 Begin with the door about 3 feet above the ground. Move it up and down until you find the point where the door remains stationary when you let go. If that point is more than 4 feet or less than 3 feet above the ground, you need to balance the door.

2 Make all adjustments with the door open. This takes the pressure off the door springs. Prop the door open with a ladder to make sure the door won't close accidentally while you're working on it. If your ladder isn't tall enough, clamp c-clamps in the door track to hold the door in place.

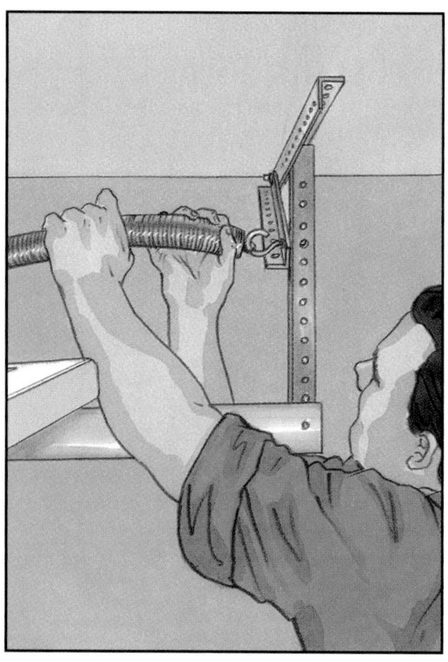

3 Make sure the spring is compressed completely, and then remove it from the track hanger. If the door was closing too quickly, move the spring to the next higher hole on the bracket. If it was opening too quickly, move it to the next lower hole. Move both springs, and retest the balance.

4 Close the door and check with a level to make sure the door comes down evenly on both sides. If it isn't, adjust the spring tension on each side of the door until it is.

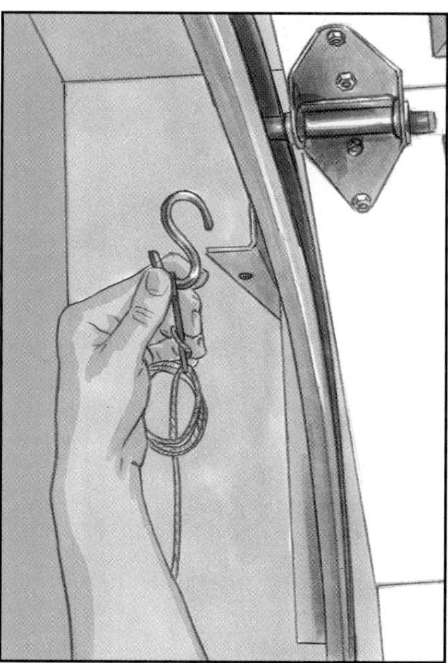

5 If you need to make fine adjustments, you can adjust the lifting cable instead of the spring. The cable is attached to the door, and runs to an s-hook that attaches to the track support. With the door propped open, take the s-hook out of the support, and tighten or loosen the cable as needed.

Maintaining Garage-Door Openers

One garage-door opener looks pretty much like the next. Trust what your eyes are telling you—they are pretty much the same. Some have large motors, some have small ones. Some have chain drive and some have direct drive.

Take motor size. Garage-door openers are typically available with ¼-, ⅓-, or ½-horsepower (hp) motors. Not surprisingly, the size you choose has a lot to do with the price you pay. What is a surprise is that a ¼-hp motor can open a door up to 18 feet wide, and 8 feet high—the largest residential door available.

Some openers use a chain-and-sprocket arrangement to open the door. Others open doors with a screw drive and a "traveler" that moves along the drive.

While either arrangement is more than strong enough, the more substantial looking screw drive is usually the weaker of the two. The traveler is its weak point—it's usually made of plastic.

Manufacturers say you will do equally well with either drive. They do, however, recommend a chain drive in Northern climates. The screw drive requires grease, which may freeze in winter and keep the door from opening.

Infrared safety sensors are mandatory for garage-door openers. The sensor monitors an invisible beam of light across the doorway, and stops the door from closing if a car—or a child—happens to be in the way. Several companies make sensors that can be added to existing systems. Inspect the opener periodically, as explained on page 345.

The one thing that varies from brand to brand is the warranty. Look for a good one from a well-known company and you'll have bought the best opener for the job.

Each garage-door opener comes with its own instructions, and you should follow the manufacturer's directions carefully. While specifics vary, all openers have some things in common.

You'll need a power source. Code, common sense, and the plug on the end of the cord all dictate a grounded (three-prong) outlet.

All doors have a button that mounts inside the garage and opens and closes the door. Put the button at least 5 feet above floor level, so that children cannot operate it.

Resist the urge to push the remote button before the opener is completely installed. Operating the opener beforehand will knock it out of whack, and you'll have to spend time getting everything back in alignment.

COMPONENTS OF A TYPICAL GARAGE-DOOR OPENER

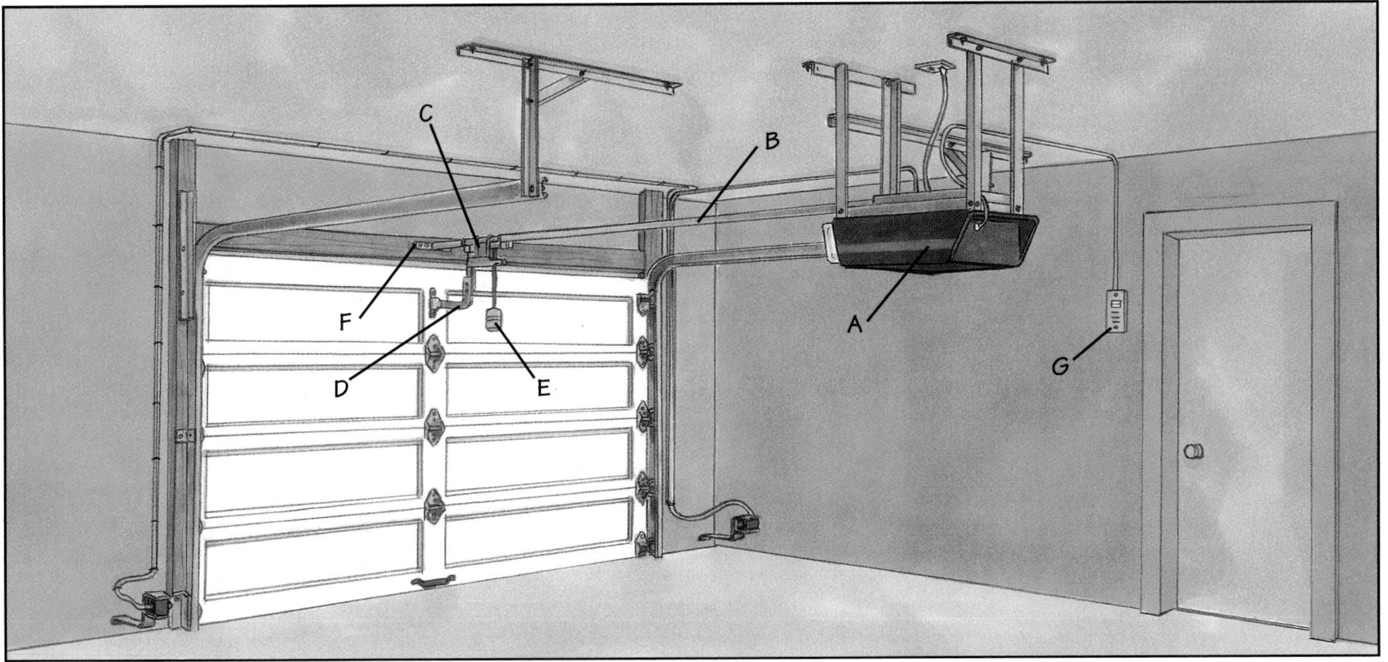

Garage-door opener components include: the power unit (**A**) activated by a transmitter, key, or auxiliary switch. The rail (**B**) guides and supports the traveler (**C**), which connects the door-opener chain to the support arm (**D**), which is attached to the garage door. The manual safety release (**E**) disengages the trolley from the garage-door arm and allows manual operation of the door in the event of a power failure. The header bracket (**F**) secures the rail above the door and supports the idler assembly and pulley that guides the chain drive. The interior auxiliary switch (**G**) allows garage-door opener operation from inside the garage.

ADJUSTING AND MAINTAINING GARAGE DOOR OPENERS

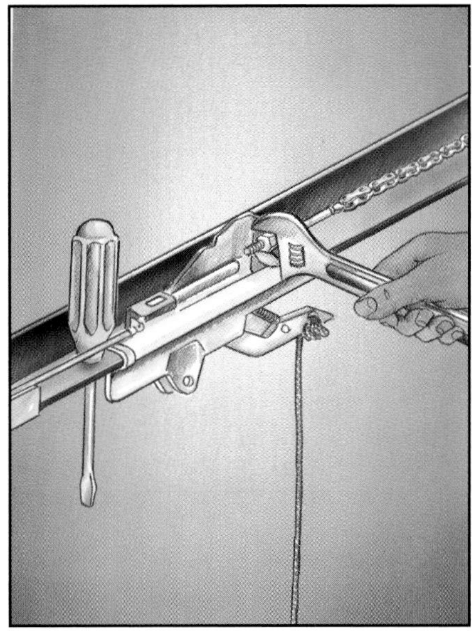

Adjust the chain tension to eliminate a sagging chain. If the chain sags more than 1/2" below the rail, it may bang against the rail and cause undue wear on the drive sprocket. Tighten the chain until it rests 1/2" above the base of the rail, but be careful not to overtighten.

Adjust the limit screws if the garage door opens more than 5' but fails to open completely. Unplug the opener and locate the up-limit adjustment screw on the power unit. Turn the screw clockwise. Plug in the opener, run it through a cycle and adjust as necessary to open the desired amount.

CHECK THE WIRE TERMINALS FOR LOOSE AND BROKEN CONNECTIONS.

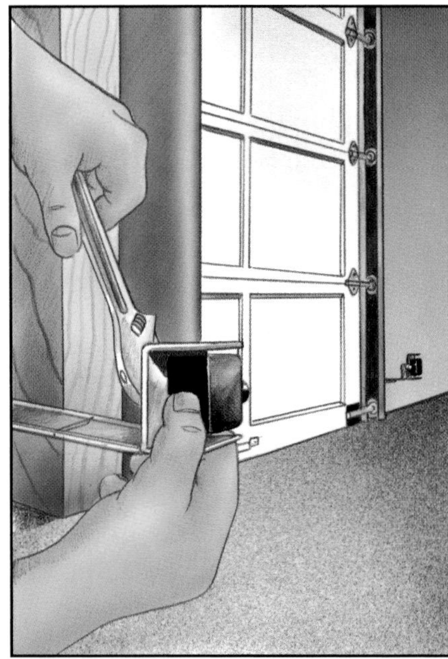

Periodically check the alignment of the safety reversing sensors and adjust as necessary to maintain proper operation. The sensors should face each other across the garage door opening in order to function properly.

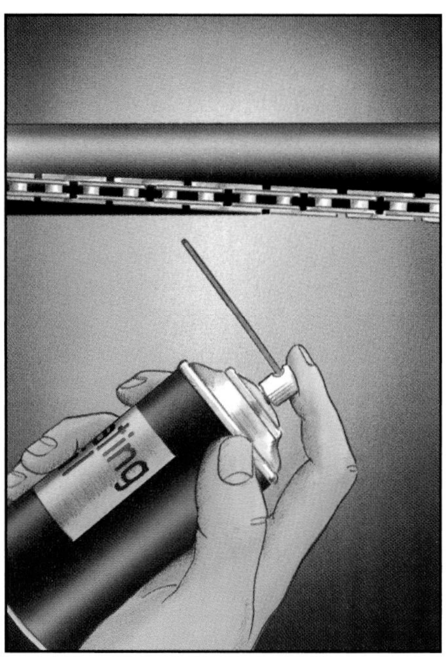

Clean and lubricate the drive chain and track of the automatic door opener. Use a light penetrating oil instead of grease to keep from collecting dirt and grit.

Changing Frequencies

Some automatic garage door openers are available with programmable remote switches. These switches allow you to change the frequency at which the transmitter operates to activate the garage door opener. This is a useful feature to get around the nuisance if someone else on your block just happens to have an opener that operates on the same frequency as your opener. For additional security, you can change your frequency setting if you happen to lose one of your transmitters.

The setting changes are relatively easy to make by finding the rocker switches in the power unit. To create a transmission code to activate your opener, use a sharpened pencil to set switches in a random off-on pattern. Open the transmitter and find the rocker switches. Set the switches to the identical off-on pattern used in the power unit. The door will respond exclusively to the signal from your preset transmitter.

SAFETY TESTING GARAGE DOOR OPENERS

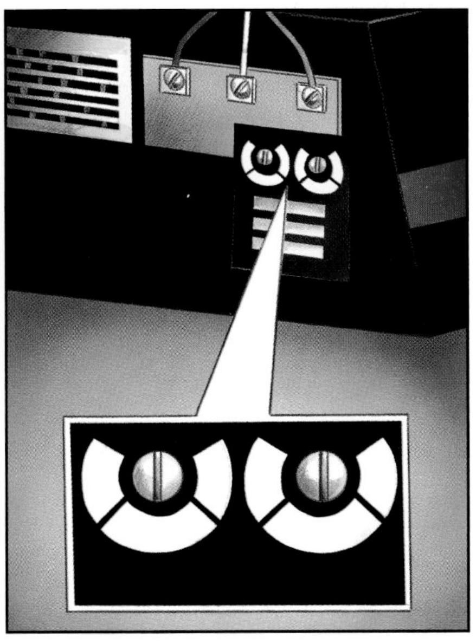

Adjust the down-force sensitivity if the opener is either auto-reversing too easily or too hard. Unplug the power unit and adjust the down-force screw, depending on which solution is required.

Periodically test the down-force sensitivity setting of the garage door opener. Place a board, 1" or thicker, on the garage floor in the center of the doorway, and trigger the opener to close the door. When the door comes in contact with the board, the opener should strain slightly; then reverse and open the door. If the pressure is too great or too slight, make adjustments as necessary, then test the pressure by hand.

Test the down-force sensitivity by hand after you have used the board method mentioned above. This will allow you to physically determine the amount of pressure the opener is exerting in case the door comes in contact with children or other individuals. Stand in the center of the doorway and trigger the opener to close the door. As the door is closing, hold the bottom of the door in your hands and exert pressure to stop the door. Determine if the auto-reversing pressure is too much or too little and make the necessary adjustments on the down-force sensitivity screws.

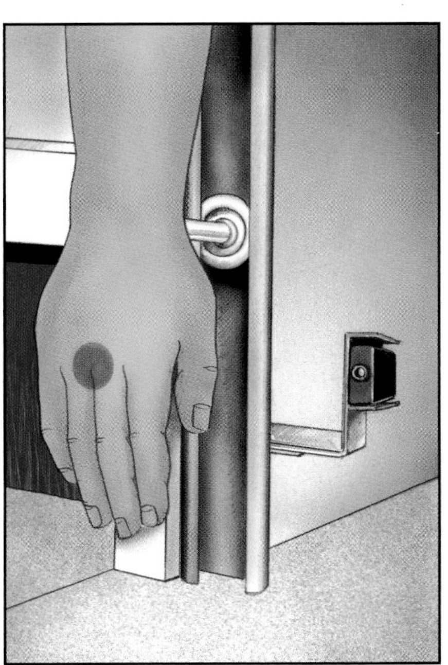

Test the safety reversing sensors by placing your hand in the sensor beam as the garage door is closing. The garage door opener should automatically reverse and bring the door back to an open position. If it doesn't, check the wire connections and the sensor alignment, and clean the sensor lenses.

CABINET & COUNTERTOP BASICS

Cabinets come in a wide variety of shapes, finishes, and styles and, whether they are traditional framed or contemporary frameless cabinets, their basic construction is similar. They all have a back and sides with either adjustable or fixed shelving, and a drawer or a door. Different styles of doors, drawer fronts, and hardware will give your cabinets their individual character and personality.

As important as looks and style are to a room's atmosphere, keep in mind that the main purpose of cabinets is to provide adequate storage for foodstuffs and cooking utensils. Don't sacrifice convenience, efficiency, and utility in your cabinet design just for a cosmetic difference, because the beauty will take a back seat to function after you've had to work around a cumbersome cabinet layout.

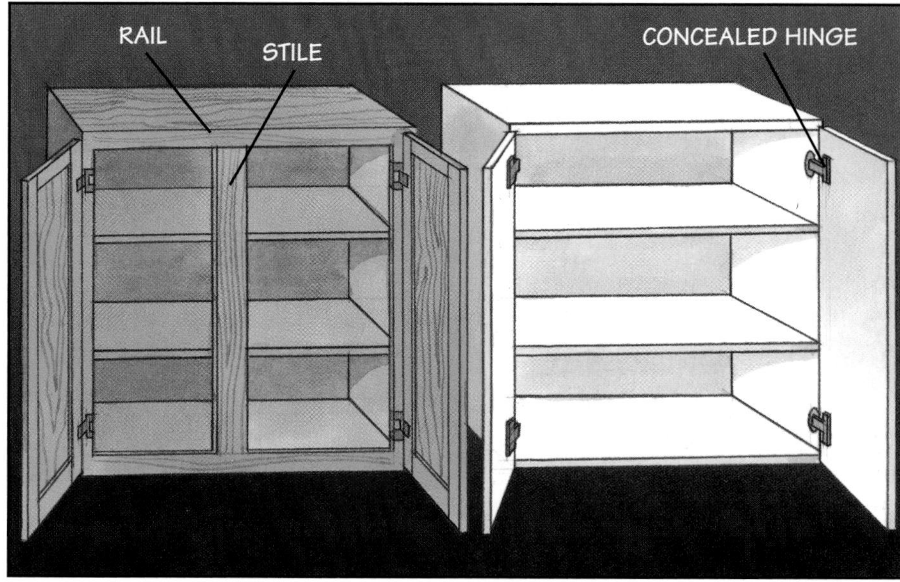

Framed cabinets have openings that are completely surrounded by face frames made of vertical stiles and horizontal rails. Door hinges are attached directly to these frames. Framed cabinets give a traditional look.

Frameless cabinets, sometimes called "European-style," have a more contemporary styling than traditional framed cabinets. Frameless cabinets use special concealed hinges that are attached to the inside walls of the cabinet.

ESSENTIAL TOOLS

Power tools for cabinet and countertop construction include: circular saw (**A**), router/bits (**B**), belt sander (**C**), palm sander (**D**), jigsaw (**E**), reciprocating saw (**F**), cordless driver (**G**), and power drill/bits (**H**).

Hand tools for cabinet and countertop construction include: framing square (**A**), carpenter's level (**B**), hand saw (**C**), nail set (**D**), chalk line (**E**), ball peen hammer (**F**), claw hammer (**G**), cold chisel (**H**), putty knife (**I**), tape measure (**J**), screwdrivers (**K**), C-clamps (**L**), combination square (**M**), electronic stud finder (**N**), utility knife (**O**), scribing compass (**P**), flat bar (**Q**), caulk gun (**R**), handscrew clamp (**S**), and a 4' straight edge (not pictured).

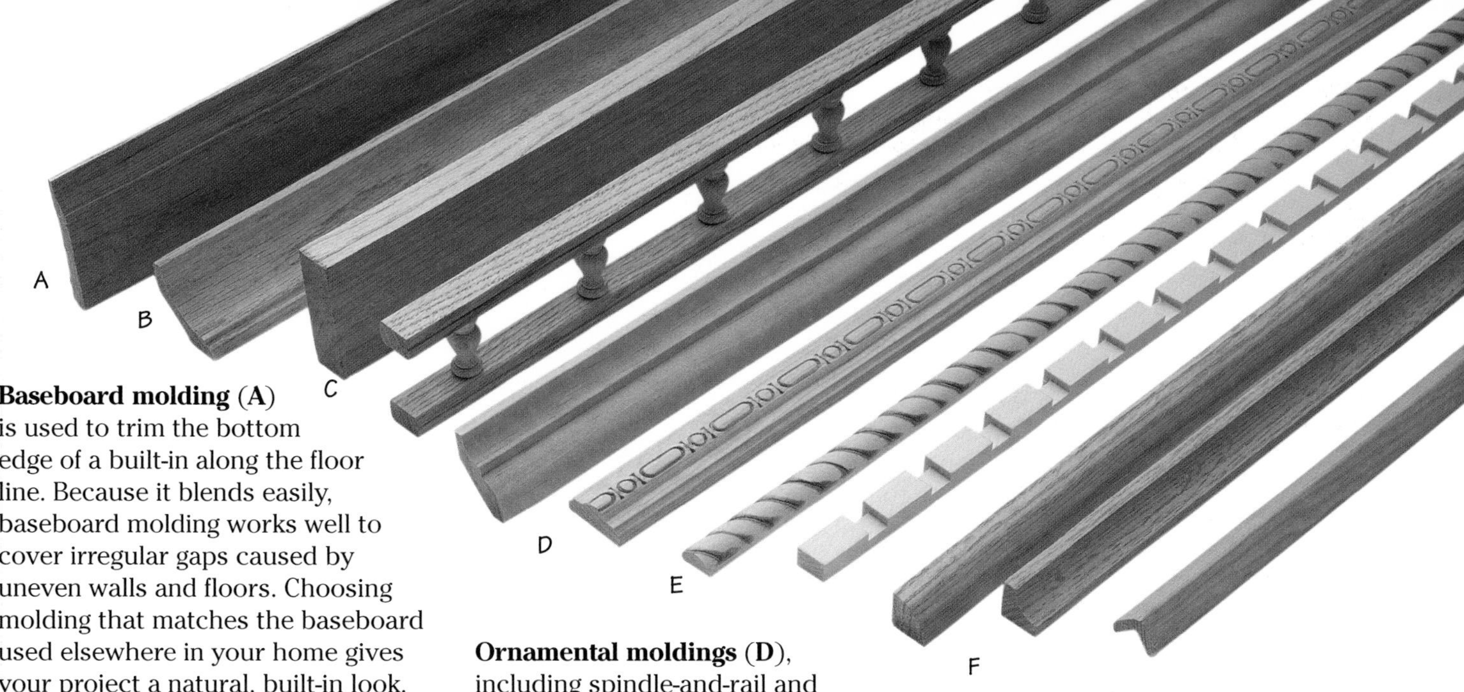

Baseboard molding (A) is used to trim the bottom edge of a built-in along the floor line. Because it blends easily, baseboard molding works well to cover irregular gaps caused by uneven walls and floors. Choosing molding that matches the baseboard used elsewhere in your home gives your project a natural, built-in look.

Crown molding (B) is a simple unobtrusive trim for covering gaps between a built-in project and a wall or ceiling and also adds a decorative accent to a built-in.

Hardwood strips (C) are used to construct face frames for a built-in cabinet, cover unfinished edges of plywood shelves, and as filler strips between cabinets. Maple, oak, and poplar strips are widely available in 1x2, 1x3, and 1x4 sizes.

Ornamental moldings (D), including spindle-and-rail and embossed moldings, give a distinctive decorative appearance.

Shelf-edge molding (E) gives a decorative edge to plywood, particleboard and hardwood shelves. It can also be used with finish-grade plywood to create panel-style doors and drawer faces.

Trim or cove moldings (F) are both decorative and functional. They can be used to cover gaps around the base and sides of a built-in, to hide the edges of plywood surfaces, or simply to add visual interest to the project. Moldings are available in dozens of styles and are available at most home improvement centers. Synthetic trim moldings, available in many styles, are less expensive than hardwood moldings. Synthetic moldings are made of wood composites or rigid foam covered with a layer of melamine.

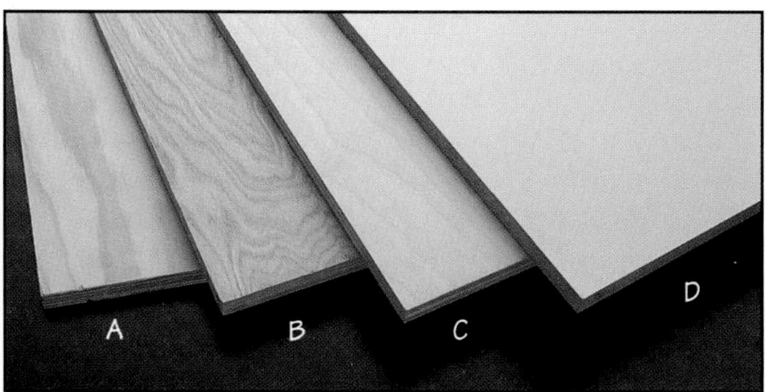

Finish-grade plywoods are used for exposed areas of a cabinet and usually are edged with hardwood strips or moldings. Sanded pine plywood (**A**) is commonly used for cabinets that will be painted or for hidden areas. Most sheet goods are sold in 4x8' sheets and $^1/_4$", $^1/_2$", or $^3/_4$" thicknesses; some types also are sold in 2x4' sheets. Oak plywood (**B**) is usually finished with tinted oils or stains. Birch plywood (**C**) is frequently used for surfaces that will be painted or clear-coated for a natural finish. Particleboard (**D**), coated with a plastic resin called melamine, is used for making contemporary-style cabinets.

Common lumber used in cabinet construction includes: Pine (**A**) which is an easy-to-cut softwood often used for built-ins that will be painted. Walnut (**B**) is an expensive, richly-colored wood sometimes used for built-in bookcases. Maple (**C**) and oak (**D**) are heavy, strong hardwoods with attractive grain patterns. They usually are finished with tinted oils or stains. Cedar (**E**) is a warm-colored softwood used for exposed surfaces of a built-in. Because of its attractive color and grain, it usually is left unfinished or coated with a clear finish. Poplar (**F**) and Birch (not pictured) are light-colored hardwoods with very straight grain and are excellent woods for fine painted surfaces.

Planning & Preparing for Cabinet Installation

When you consider all its built-in features, the kitchen is the most complicated room in the house to design. Start your design process by locating the three most-used elements in a kitchen: the sink, stove, and refrigerator. It's best to situate these components so they form a working triangle with a perimeter of 12 to 24 feet. Be sure to have a lighted and vented hood above the stove or cooktop.

A peninsula cabinet with a counter provides a convenient preparation area and helps to separate the kitchen from the adjacent dining area. The dishwasher usually should be located near the sink and below the dish cabinet in order to minimize the motions when loading and unloading the dishwasher. If your plan allows, locate your sink below a window to provide plenty of natural light when cleaning up.

It's a good idea to select your major kitchen appliances as well as your sink before you design your cabinet system. Each major appliance will come with a specification and installation guide that gives dimensions needed for rough openings in the cabinets.

Where possible, avoid floor plans that encourage people to use the working part of the kitchen as a through passage to other parts of the house. When planning storage layout, make sure every item is within easy reach and that there is room to open drawers and doors without backing into a wall or injuring others.

Use a planning system to help you visualize the placement of new cabinets and appliances. Modular reusable design kits help you determine the shape of your kitchen and help you plan your dream kitchen. Experiment with different arrangements and determine how they affect the optimum kitchen work triangle.

Shelf Shopping

A variety of shelves and pullouts makes the best use of a cabinet's interior space. Adjustable shelves provide more flexibility because they allow you to change shelf spacing to accommodate different-size items. Racks, lazy Susans, and special pull-outs provide simple solutions to storage problems of trash bags, bulky kitchen utensils, bottles, cans, and pots and pans.

PLANNING THE CABINET LAYOUT

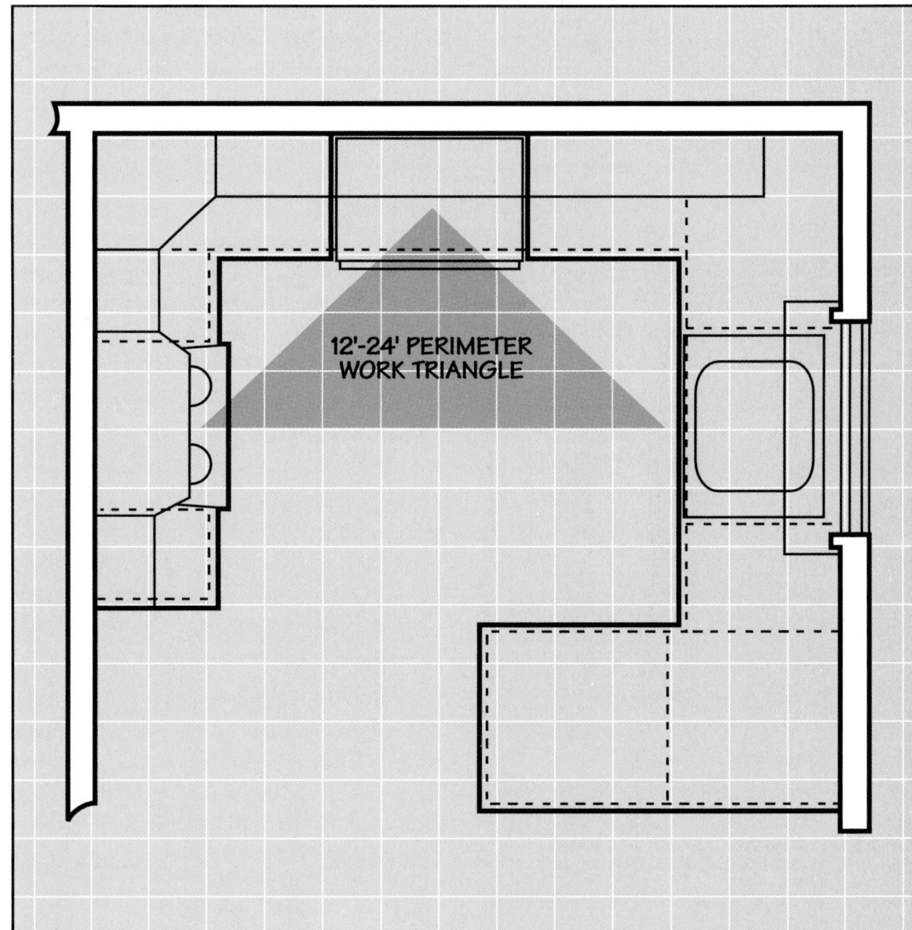

Before you order cabinets, take the time to lay out your kitchen on paper and plan it according to your traffic flow and storage requirements. Avoid unnecessary movement by creating a work triangle with a perimeter of 12 to 24 feet. The refrigerator and foodstuffs should be close to where the meals are prepared with ample work surface area for preparation. Group appliances requiring plumbing together, with the sink on an outside wall.

PREPARING FOR INSTALLATION

1 Sand down any rough spots and holes, cleaning up the wall patch repairs by applying wallboard taping compound with a trowel. Let the compound dry and then sand lightly. Locate and mark wall studs using an electronic stud finder.

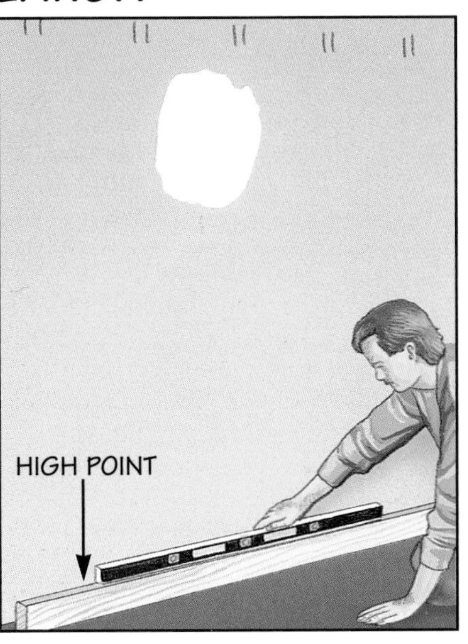

2 Find the high point along the floor area that will be covered by the base cabinets. Place a level on a long, straight 2x4, and move the board across the floor to determine if the floor is uneven. Mark the wall at the high point of the floor.

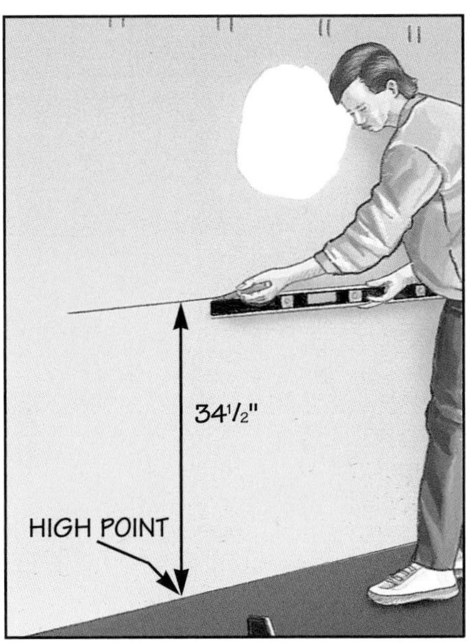

3 Measure up 34½" from the floor at the high-point mark. Use a level to mark a base cabinet reference line on the walls. The base cabinets will be installed with their top edges flush against this line. This line must be level or you'll never finish with a level countertop.

HOMER'S HINDSIGHT

My first cabinet project was a real eye-opener. With the excitement of the project coupled with my youthful eagerness, I was more intent on completing the project than in getting level reference lines. Well, it wasn't until I had installed the countertop that I noticed something wasn't quite right. The countertop and cabinets were so off-kilter that when you spilled water on one end, you'd have a "raging river" running the entire length of the countertop. Needless to say, I had to go back and remount the cabinets and countertop, this time on a level reference line!

4 Measure up 19½" from the 34½" base cabinet reference line and mark a ledger board reference line. Install 1x3 temporary ledgers with the top edge flush against the ledger reference line.

5 Attach the ledgers with 2½" wallboard screws driven into every other wall stud. Mark the stud locations on the ledgers. The cabinets will rest temporarily on the ledgers during installation.

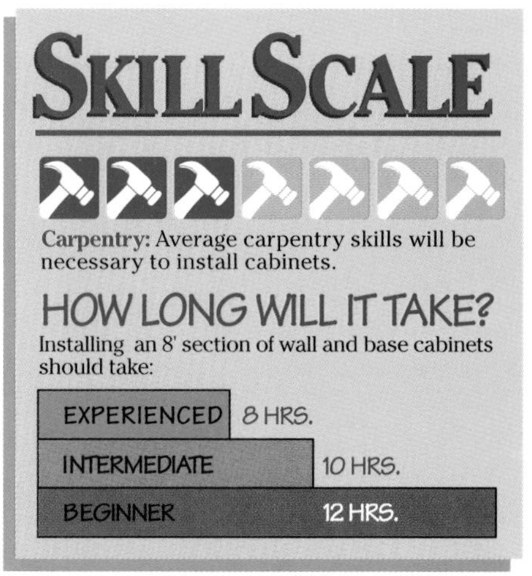

Installing Cabinets

When installing cabinets, you must firmly anchor them to the wall studs. Hollow wall anchors won't provide adequate support for cabinets loaded with the weight of plates, groceries, etc.

The cabinets must be hung exactly plumb and level so that the doors and drawers operate smoothly and don't creep open after closing. It helps to number each cabinet and mark its position on the wall prior to hanging. For ease of installation, remove the cabinet doors and drawers, and number them appropriately for the cabinet so they can be easily replaced after all of the cabinets are installed.

Always begin with the corner cabinets, also referred to as "blind cabinets," making sure they are plumb and level.

STUFF YOU'LL NEED:

- □ **Tools:** Combination square, screwdriver, drill.
- □ **Materials:** Doors, hinges, drawer pulls, door pulls, screws.

HOMER'S HINDSIGHT

Sometimes with certain projects, it just doesn't matter how much experience you have or how smart you think you are, you still need a good plan in order to have a successful installation. Cabinets are one of those projects! A detailed cabinet design is essential prior to ordering and installing the cabinets. It takes a little more time up front, but it will save you loads of time and frustration later when you're fitting all of the components together.

FITTING A BLIND CORNER CABINET

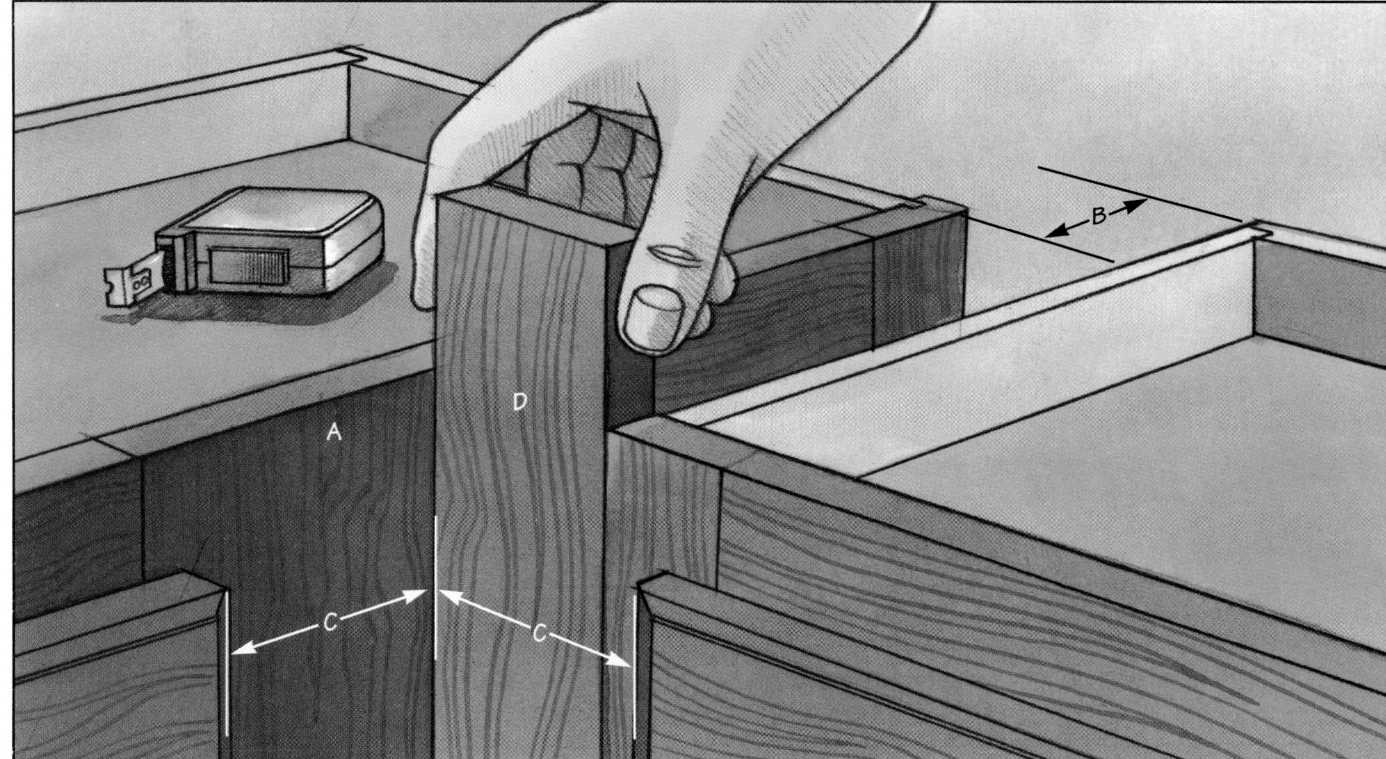

Before installing cabinets, test-fit the corner (blind) cabinet (**A**) and the adjoining cabinets to make sure that the doors and handles don't interfere with each other. If necessary, increase the clearance by pulling the blind cabinet out according to the distance (**B**) on your planned layout. To maintain even spacing between the edges of the doors and the cabinet corner (**C**), cut a filler strip (**D**) and attach it to the adjoining cabinet.

INSTALLING WALL CABINETS

1 Position the corner cabinet on the ledger and drill 3/16" pilot holes through the hanging strips in the top and bottom of the cabinet back. Use screws long enough to extend 1" to 1 1/2" into the stud. Snug up the screws. Loosen them if adjustments are necessary.

2 If needed, attach a filler strip to the adjoining cabinet. Clamp the filler in place and drill pilot holes through the cabinet face frame near the hinge locations. Use a counterbore bit to recess the screw in the face frame. Attach the filler strip to the cabinet using either wood or wallboard screws.

3 Position the adjoining cabinet on the ledger, tight against the blind corner cabinet. Check the face frame for plumb, then drill 3/16" pilot holes through the cabinet hanging strips. Attach the cabinet to the wall and snug up the screws. Loosen them if adjustments are necessary.

4 Clamp the corner cabinet and the adjoining cabinet together at the top and bottom. Handscrew clamps should be used because they will not damage the wood face frames.

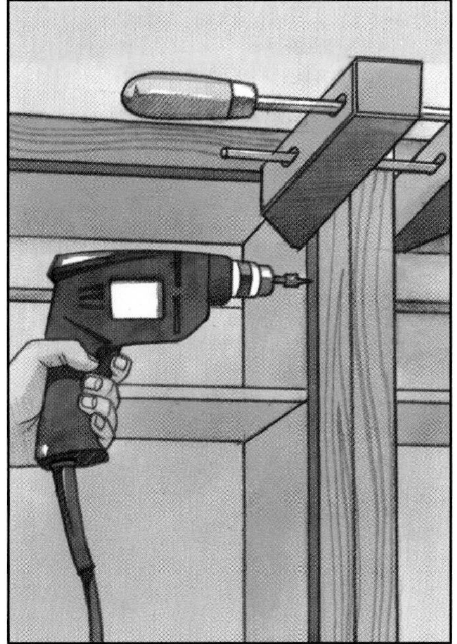

5 Position and attach each additional cabinet. Clamp the face frames together and drill counterbored pilot holes through the side of the face frame. Join the cabinets, then drill 3/16" pilot holes in the hanging strips and attach the cabinets to the wall studs.

6 Fill small spaces between a cabinet and a wall or appliance with a filler strip. Cut the filler to fit the space, then wedge the filler into place with wood shims. Drill counterbored pilot holes through the side of the cabinet face frame, and attach the filler strip with wood or wallboard screws.

7 Remove the temporary ledger. Check the cabinet run for plumb and adjust if necessary by placing wood shims behind the cabinet on the stud locations. Tighten the wall screws completely, then cut off the shims with a utility knife.

8 Use trim moldings to cover any gaps between the cabinets and walls. Stain the moldings to match the cabinet finish.

9 Attach a decorative valance above the sink. Clamp the valance to the edge of the cabinet frames and drill counterbored pilot holes through the cabinet face frames into the end of valance. Attach the valance with wood or wallboard screws.

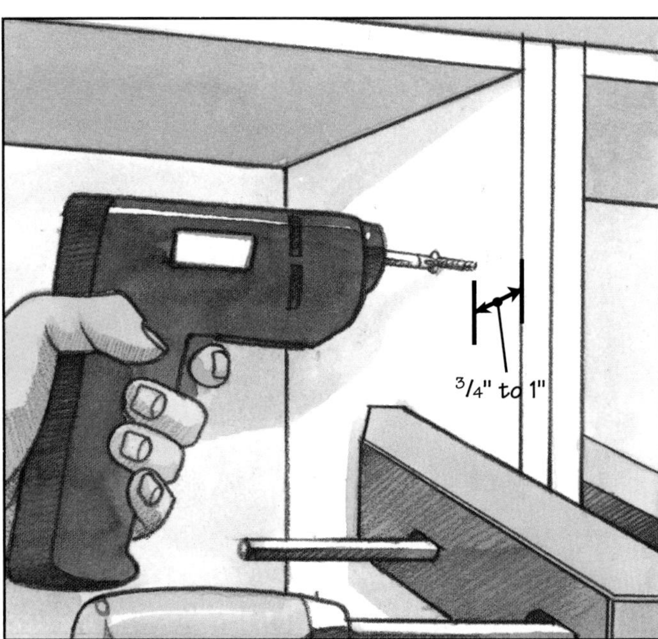

Join frameless cabinets with cabinet connector screws or wood screws just shorter than the thickness of the two cabinet sides. Each pair of cabinets should be joined by at least four screws placed 3/4" to 1" in from the front edge of the cabinet.

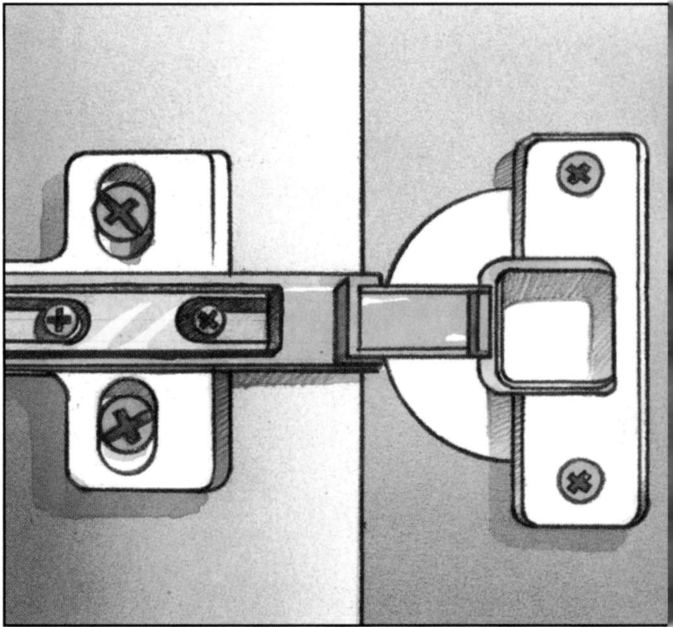

Hinges on frameless cabinets are screwed directly to the inside of the cabinet, eliminating the need for face frames. The hinges are hidden, providing a cleaner look, and usually have a full range of adjustments for almost every cabinet installation. Each hinge has adjustments for door angle, overlay, elevation, and gap spacing. These adjustments are made simply with a Phillips screwdriver by adjusting the appropriate screw for the desired correction.

INSTALLING BASE CABINETS

1 Position the corner cabinet so the top is flush with the reference line. Insert wood shims under the cabinet base to get it plumb and level. Because some cabinet frames are not perfectly square, it's important to make sure the top of the frame is level. That way you'll get a level countertop.

2 If necessary, attach a filler strip to the adjoining cabinet. Clamp the filler in place and drill counterbored pilot holes through the side of the face frame. Attach the appropriate fill strip according to your cabinet layout plan with wood or wallboard screws.

3 Clamp the adjoining cabinet to the corner cabinet. Make sure the cabinet is plumb, then drill counterbored pilot holes through the corner cabinet face frame into the filler strip. Join the cabinets, then drill 3/16" pilot holes through the hanging strips and attach the cabinet loosely to the wall.

4 Use a jigsaw to cut any cabinet openings needed for plumbing, wiring, or heating ducts. If you don't have a jig saw, consider buying a hole saw for this step, especially if you have many holes to cut. Although they cost a bit, they make cutting holes a snap.

5 Position and attach additional cabinets, making sure the frames are aligned. Clamp the cabinets together, then drill counterbored pilot holes through side of face frame and join the cabinets. Be sure to join frameless cabinets with 1¼" screws and finish washers. Use at least four screws per joint.

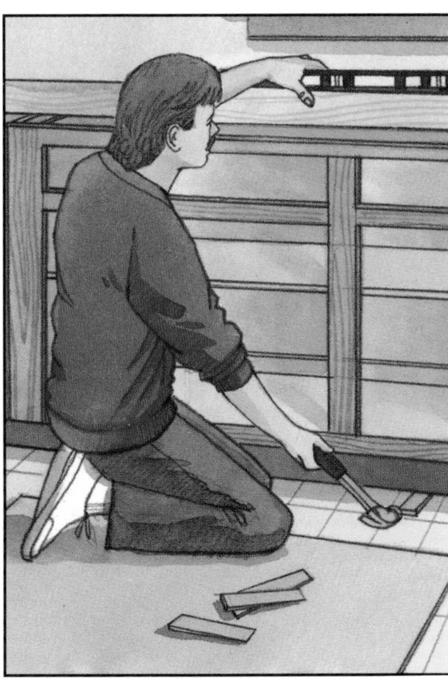

6 Make sure all cabinets are level. If necessary, adjust by driving wood shims underneath the cabinets. Place wood shims behind the cabinets on the stud locations wherever there is a gap. Tighten the wall screws and cut off the shims with a utility knife.

INSTALLING BASE CABINETS (continued)

Specially shaped cabinets and accessories are available for maximizing cabinet room. Lazy Susans are the most common cabinet accessory used to get more usable space from corner cabinets.

7 If the corner has a void area not filled by the cabinets, screw 1x3 cleats to the wall, flush with the reference line. The cleats will help support countertop. Anchor all cabinets securely to the wall through the hanging strips on the cabinets.

8 Use decorative trim moldings to cover gaps between the cabinets and the wall and to give the installation a professional, finished look. Install the the toe-kick area with a strip of hardwood or hardwood plywood finished to match the cabinets.

INSTALLING A BASE ISLAND CABINET

1 Set the base cabinet in position, and trace the cabinet outline on the flooring. Remove the cabinet and attach 2x4 cleats to the floor at the opposite corners of the cabinet outline using the appropriate length screws. Position the cleats $^3/_4$" inside the cabinet outline.

2 Lower the base cabinet over the cleats. Be sure to check the cabinet for level, and shim under the base if necessary.

3 Attach the cabinet to the floor cleats using 6d finish nails. Drill pilot holes for the nails and recess the nail heads with a nail set. You can use finish screws, too, in case you need to move the cabinet later.

WORK SMARTER

To avoid injury to yourself and damage to your existing electrical, plumbing, and heating/air-conditioning systems, always check for wiring, pipes, and duct work before cutting into any wall. Also, always determine if the wall is load bearing before you start cutting into it.

Load-bearing walls can be modified but will need to be structurally reinforced before any modifications can be attempted (see pg. 227).

If possible, select another wall, preferably nonbearing, for the location of your recessed cabinet or other fixture.

INSTALLING RECESSED MEDICINE CABINETS

1 Locate the first stud beyond either side of the planned cabinet location, then remove the wall surface between these studs. Removing the wall surface all the way to the ceiling simplifies the patching work. Cut along the center of the studs using a circular saw with the blade set to cut at a depth equal to the thickness of the wall surface.

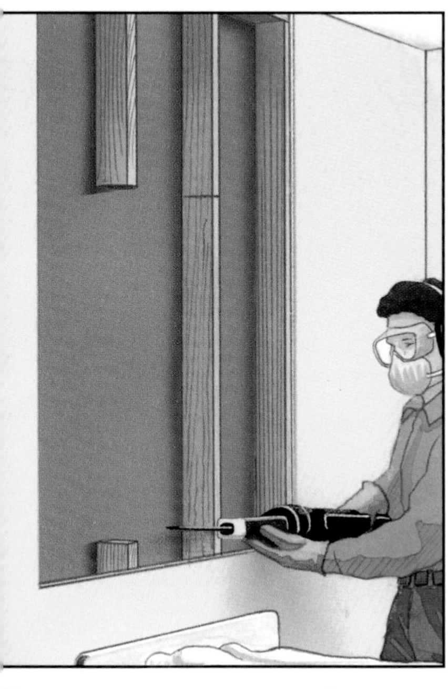

2 Mark a rough opening 1/2" taller than the cabinet frame on the xposed wall studs. Add 1 1/2" for ach header and sill plate, then cut ut studs in the rough opening rea. Frame out the top and bottom f the rough opening by installing a eader and a sill plate between the ut wall studs.

3 Make sure the header and sill plate are level, then nail them in place with 16d common nails. Mark the rough opening width on the header and sill plates, centering the opening over the sink. Cut and nail the jack studs between the header and the sill plate just outside the rough opening marks.

4 Wire for light fixtures and install new wall surface. Position the cabinet in the opening. Check it for level, then attach the cabinet by drilling pilot holes and driving wood screws through the top and bottom of the cabinet sides into the framing members. Attach the doors, shelves, and hardware.

Replacing Cabinet Hardware

An easy and relatively inexpensive way to dress up your kitchen or bathroom is to replace the existing cabinet hardware. Door knobs, drawer pulls, and hinges are available in such a wide variety of styles and shapes that you can change the entire mood of a room by making these simple alterations.

You can increase the formality of a room by adding polished brass (or ceramic) knobs and pulls and polished brass hinges. Or, give the room a more casual "feel" by using hardwood pulls with concealed hinges. Depending on your specific tastes and design ideas, the selection of hardware is virtually unlimited.

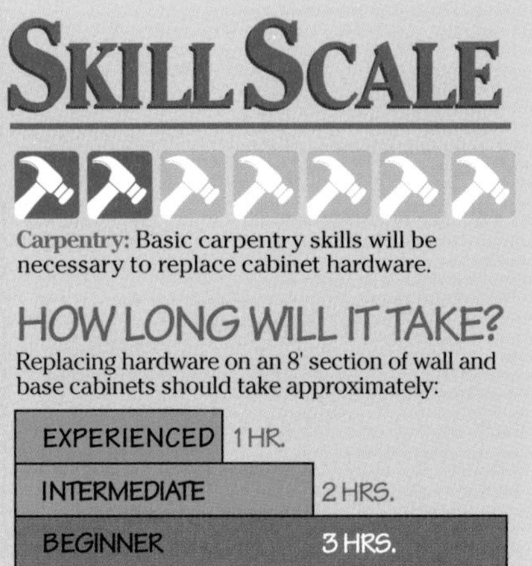

- ☐ **Tools:** combination square, screwdriver, drill.
- ☐ **Materials:** Hinges, drawer pulls, door pulls, screws.

Door and drawer pulls and knobs are available in a wide variety of styles, colors, and finishes. Plastic knobs (**A**), porcelain and antique brass decorative pulls (**B**), polished brass pulls (**C**), antique brass pulls (**D**), wrought iron pulls (**E**), painted porcelain knobs (**F**), decorative gothic pulls (**G**), antique brass knobs (**H**), wooden knobs (**I**), plastic pulls (**J**), and polished brass knobs (**K**) are just a small sampling of the cabinet door and drawer hardware available for customizing your cabinetry.

REPLACING DOOR PULLS

1 Take the existing door pull off by removing the fastening screw. If you will not be using the same screw hole, be sure to use a wood filler that matches the finish of the cabinet door to fill the hole. Use a combination square to make consistent layout marks on the doors for the new door knobs.

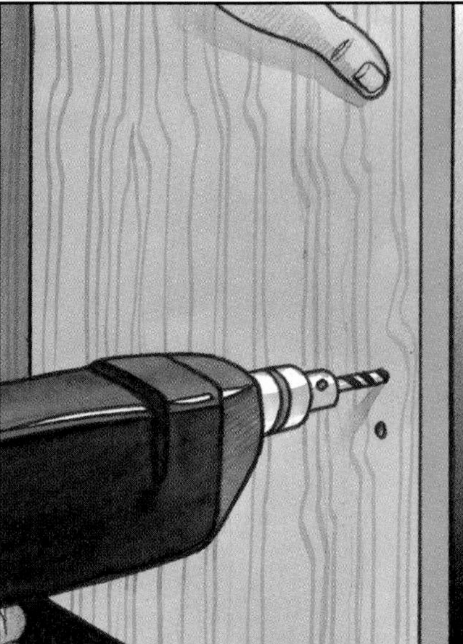

2 From the face of the door, drill holes for the new door knobs, being careful not to press so hard as to splinter the back side of the door. Insert a fastening screw into the hole and attach the knob by tightening it to the door. Some fastening screws are made of soft metal; be careful not to strip the threads.

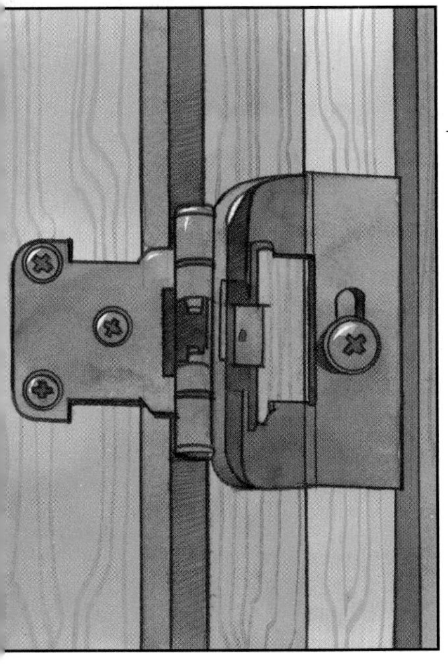

Hinges on framed cabinets are screwed directly to the face frames. Better-quality cabinets have adjustable hinges that allow door realignment.

TRIP SAVER

Concealed hinges are not as forgiving and flexible as other types of hinges. They have to exactly match the door you plan on using. If you're planning to replace doors and use concealed hinges, take along an old door, an old hinge, and the precise measurements of the cabinet frame and opening on which you'll be installing the hinges.

Get the correct style of concealed hinge for the type of door you have. Older concealed hinges screw directly to the door back and have to be precisely located. Many newer style concealed hinges have an adjustable plate that will adjust for gap spacing, elevation, and door angle. However, if you update to the newer style, you'll need to rout a special groove in the door edge to accommodate the adjustment plate.

REPLACING HINGES

1 Remove the old doors, hinges, catches, and other hardware with a screwdriver or power screwdriver.

2 Using a combination square, set the lock at the 2" mark and position the hinges an equal distance from the top and bottom of the door. Use a finish nail or awl to mark the screw locations.

3 Drill pilot holes and attach the hinges with screws. Mount the knobs, handles, and catches. A power screwdriver will speed up this job, but be careful not to strip the threads or break the screw.

4 Attach the cabinet doors to the frames. Make sure the doors overlap the openings by an equal amount on all sides. Allow a $^{1}/_{8}$" gap between doors that cover a single opening.

Replacing Cabinet Doors And Drawer Fronts

A time- and money-saving way to upgrade the look and style of your kitchen is to simply replace the cabinet doors. This may be a better alternative than replacing your entire cabinet system.

The first thing you'll need to do is accurately measure the door openings where you plan to replace doors. Check for the squareness of the opening and measure the opening size to 1/16" accuracy. Most custom doors are built to your exacting specifications but can take several weeks to be custom built. If you get anxious and remove all of the old doors while you're waiting for the new ones, you may have a few weeks without any doors at all. Be sure not to plan any dinner parties until the new doors are completely installed!

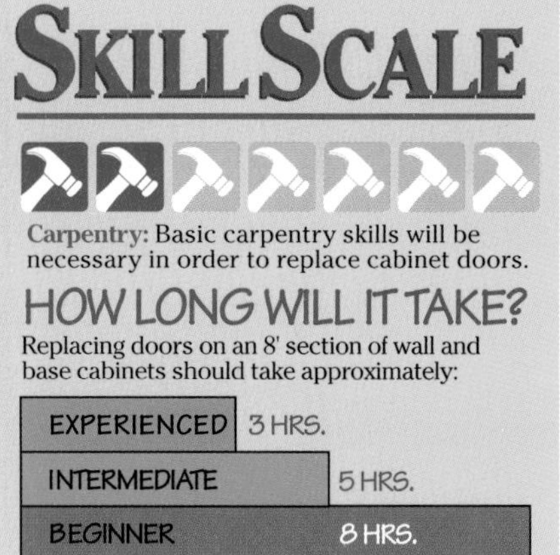

- **Tools:** Tape measure, handsaw, screwdriver.
- **Materials:** Cabinet doors and drawer fronts, hinges, screws.

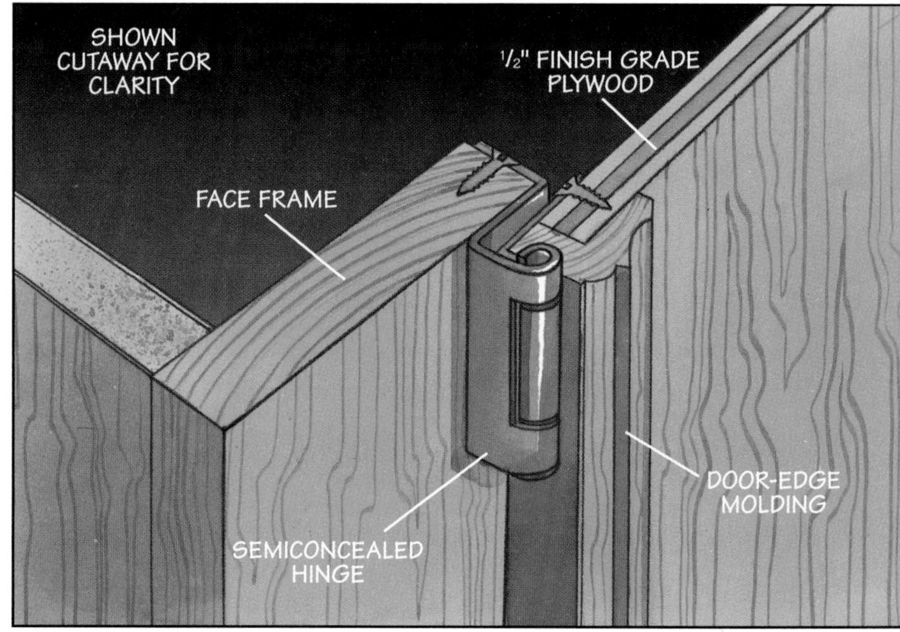

Anatomy of an overlay door: Overlay doors are made with 1/2" finish-grade plywood panels framed with door-edge moldings. They're designed to overhang the face frame by about 3/8" on each side. Semiconcealed overlay hinges are attached to the back of the door and to the edge of the face frame. This door style is also used to make folding doors.

INSTALLING CABINET DOORS

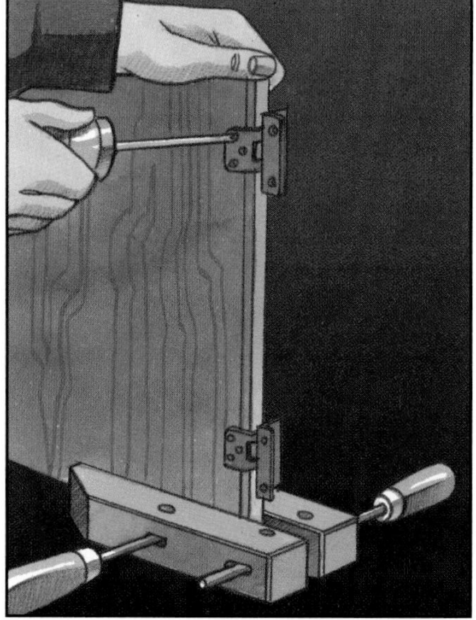

1 Mount the hinges to the back of the new door, 2" from the top and bottom. Use three hinges, evenly spaced, if the door is taller than 30".

2 Use masking tape to mark a reference line on the top face frame rail; the proper distance depends on the door size and hinge you're using. The door should be centered over the door opening.

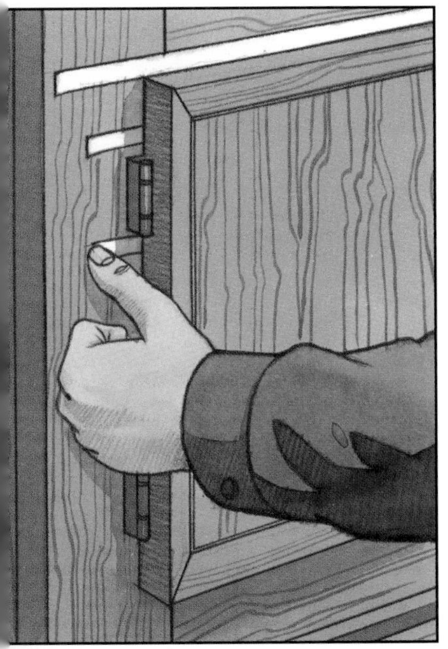

3 Position the door over the opening, aligning the top edge with the tape reference line. Mark one hinge location on the face frame with masking tape.

4 Open the hinges and position the door against the edge of the face frame so the hinges are aligned with the tape marking the hinge locations. Drill pilot holes in the face frame and anchor the hinges to the face frame with the mounting screws. Remove the masking tape.

5 Attach door handles or knobs and any door catch hardware. Follow the manufacturer's directions to install the hardware.

INSTALLING CABINET DRAWER FRONTS

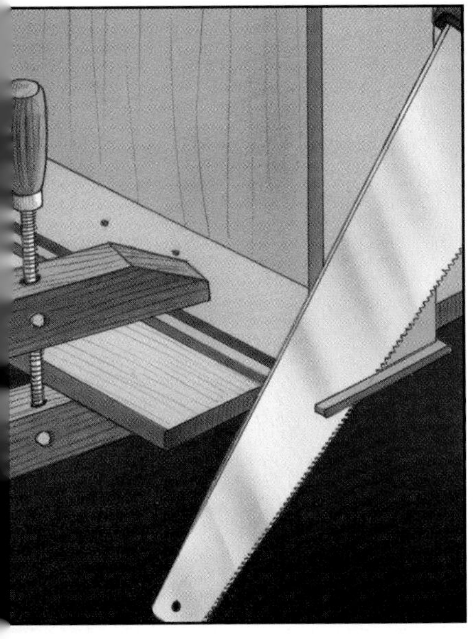

1 Saw off all overhanging edges of existing solid drawer fronts. If the drawer fronts are two-piece, remove the screws and discard the decorative face panel.

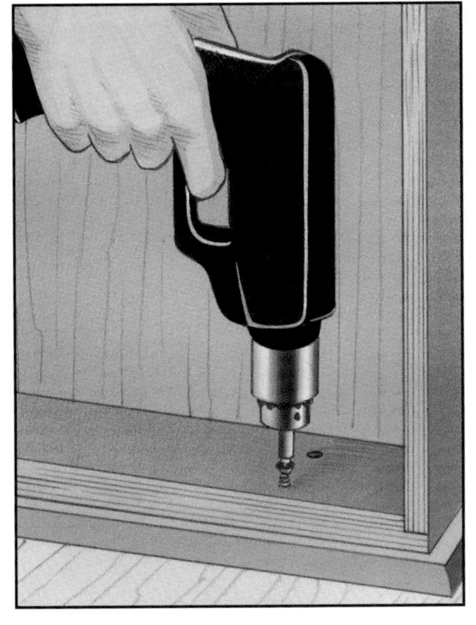

2 Attach the new fronts by drilling pilot holes and driving screws through the inside of the drawers into the new fronts. Make sure the drawer fronts overlap the drawers by an equal margin on all sides.

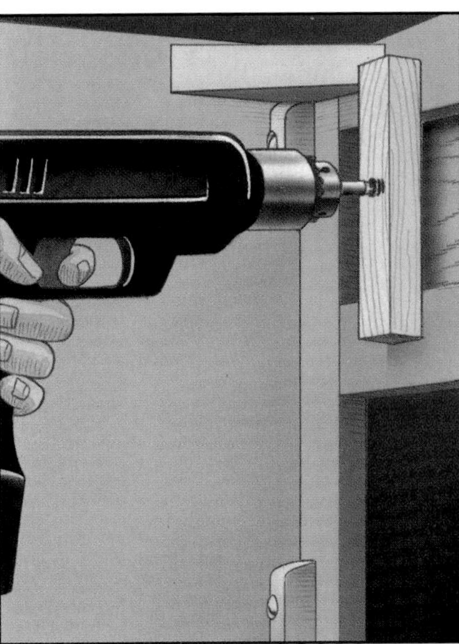

3 Attach false drawer fronts on sink and cooktop cabinets by cutting wood blocks to span the drawer openings. Place the blocks across the openings on the inside of the cabinets. Fasten by driving screws through the wood blocks into the false drawer fronts.

Countertops

Countertops provide the main work-surface area in a kitchen, so they must be made from durable materials. Because of germ and bacteria concerns, they must also be easy to clean. Many different types of materials are used in countertop construction, such as decorative laminate, ceramic tile, marble, granite, stainless steel, and, more recently, synthetic solid-surface material.

Countertops are often used to add color, pattern, texture, and shape to kitchens, but most importantly, they provide a stable work surface for food preparation, serving, and, ultimately, kitchen cleanup. The style and construction of your countertop will vary depending on your use and design preferences.

Post-form countertops are made by machines that apply a great deal of heat and pressure to sheet laminates as they are glued to particleboard. As a result, the counter can be formed with rounded corners and edges. Laminates are available in hundreds of colors and patterns to match any kitchen decorating scheme. Many post-form countertops can be purchased as stock items at home improvement stores and require only a minimal amount of trimming before installation.

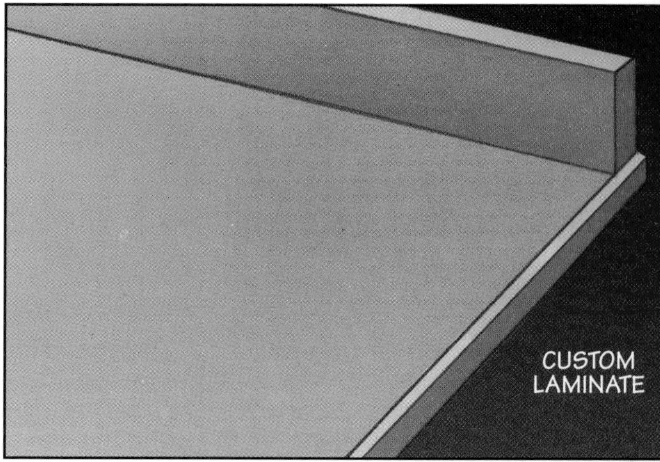

Custom laminate countertops can be hand-built fairly easily on site; their special edge treatments allow you to customize them for your particular design preferences. These special edge treatments can range from solid wood, synthetic solid surface material, decorative laminate, and rubber edging, to ceramic tile, stainless steel, and decorative inlay material.

Ceramic tile is especially durable and creates a beautiful surface that resists spills and stains. It is more expensive than decorative laminate and can sometimes crack if a heavy object is dropped on the counter. Tile is available in a wide variety of sizes, colors, styles, and prices. Most special tools needed for tile construction can be rented.

Synthetic solid-surface materials are manufactured from acrylic or polyester resins mixed with additives and made into sheets that are 1/4", 1/2", or 3/4" thick. Solid-surface materials are some of the most expensive countertop materials, but they are the most durable and easy to clean and maintain.

Removing Old Countertops

Removing old countertops will utilize not only your carpentry and demolition skills, but also a minimal amount of your plumbing skills. If you have a cast-iron sink, you'll probably want some help removing it to avoid breaking something or hurting yourself.

It might seem scary at first, but once you make that first cut and start prying up the old counter, your apprehensions will disappear and you'll find that demolition can be a good tension reliever!

SKILL SCALE

Plumbing: Basic plumbing skills will be necessary in order to remove an old countertop.

Carpentry: Basic carpentry skills will usually be necessary in order to remove an old countertop.

HOW LONG WILL IT TAKE?

Removing the countertop on an 8' section of base cabinets should take approximately:

EXPERIENCED	1 HR.
INTERMEDIATE	1.5 HRS
BEGINNER	2 HRS.

STUFF YOU'LL NEED:

☐**Tools:** Adjustable wrench, screwdriver, pry bar, reciprocating saw, cold chisel, ball peen hammer, utility knife.

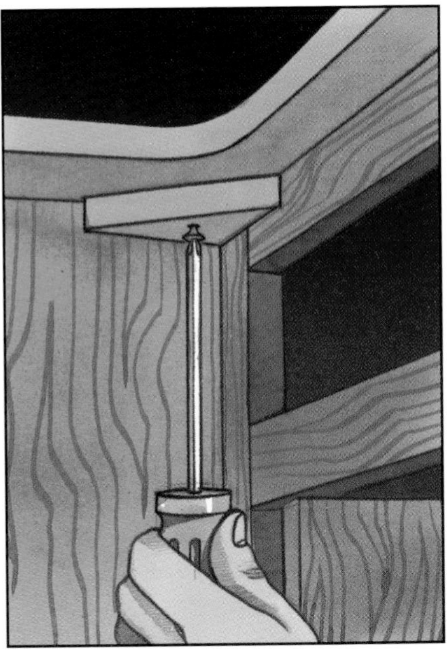

1 Turn off the water at the shutoff valves. Disconnect and remove the plumbing fixtures and appliances. Remove any brackets or screws holding the countertop to the cabinets. Unscrew the take-up bolts on mitered countertops.

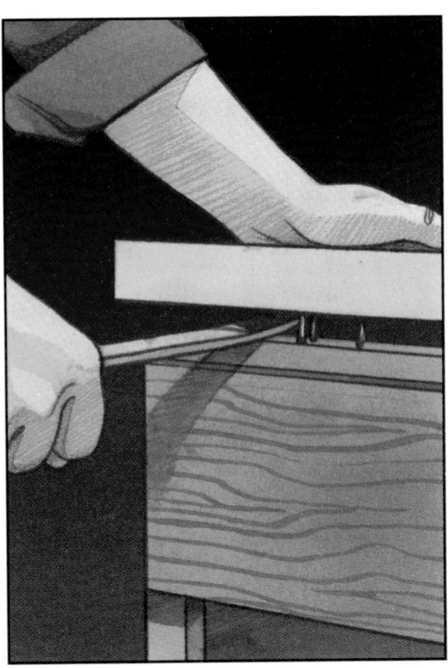

2 Use a utility knife to cut caulk beads along the backsplash and the edge of the countertop. Remove any trim, then, using a flat pry bar, try to lift the countertop away from the base cabinets.

3 If the countertop can't be pried up, use a reciprocating saw or jigsaw with a coarse wood-cutting blade to cut the countertop into pieces for removal. Be careful not to cut into the base cabinets.

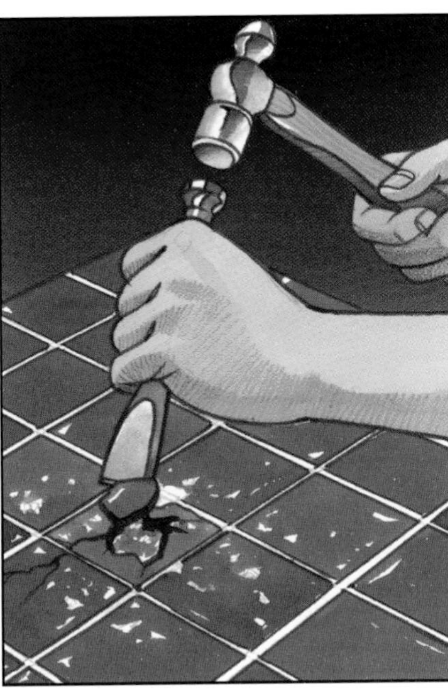

When removing ceramic tile countertops, wear eye protection to protect you from flying ceramic chips. Chisel the tile away from the base with a masonry chisel and a ball peen hammer. A tile countertop that has a mortar bed can be cut into pieces with a circular saw and an abrasive masonry-cutting blade.

Installing Post-Form Countertops

Of all the counter types available, pre-manufactured post-form countertops are the most readily available for the home do-it-youselfer and are probably the easiest to install. Most home improvement stores carry a wide variety of color selections and all of the necessary components to complete the job.

You will definitely want to get some help in handling and maneuvering the countertop to avoid damaging walls, doors, and ceilings and injuring innocent onlookers.

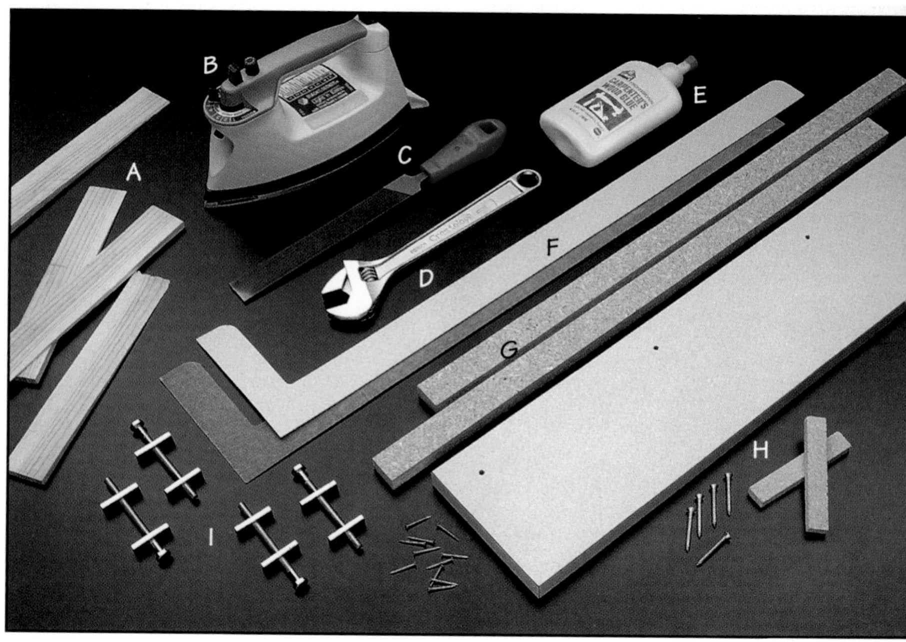

Special tools and materials for post-form countertop installation include: wood shims (**A**), household iron (**B**), file (**C**), adjustable wrench (**D**), wood glue (**E**), endcap laminate (**F**), endcap battens (**G**), endsplash kit (**H**), and joint fastener bolts (**I**).

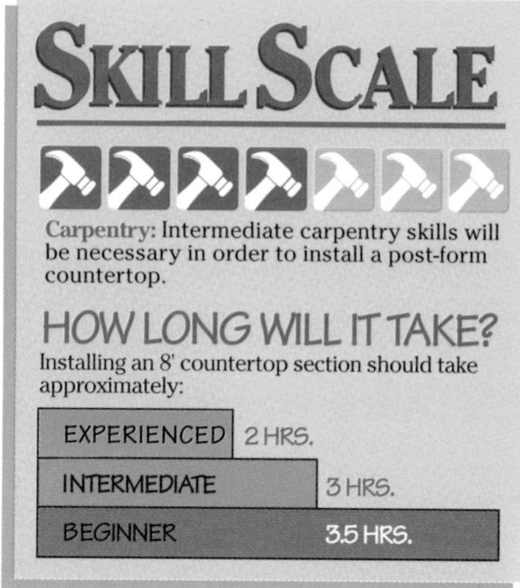

- ☐ **Tools:** Jigsaw, belt sander, household iron, file, carpenter's level, scribing compass, caulk gun, C-clamps.
- ☐ **Materials:** Joint fastener bolts, endcap laminate, endcap battens, wood shims, screws, siliconized latex caulk, wood glue.

INSTALLING POST-FORM COUNTERTOPS

1 Measure the span of base cabinets, from corner to the outside edge of the cabinet. Add 1" of overhang if the end will be exposed. If an end will butt against an appliance, subtract $^{1}/_{16}$" to prevent scratching the appliance.

2 Use a framing square to mark a cutting line on the bottom surface of the countertop. Cut off the countertop with a jigsaw using a clamped straightedge as a guide. Smooth with a belt sander after cutting.

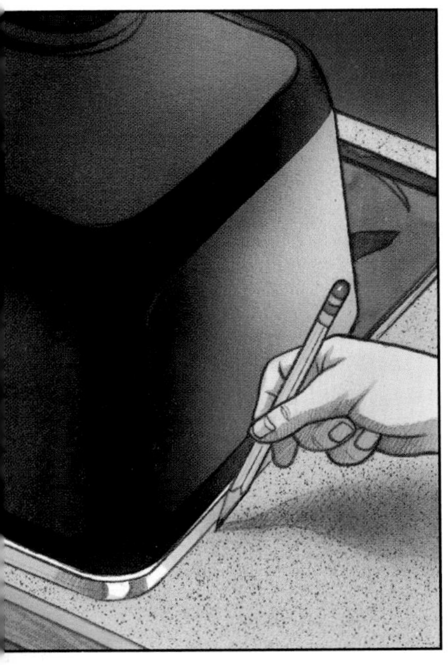

3 With the countertop upside down, mark the cutout for the self-rimming sink. Position the sink and trace an outline. Remove the sink and draw a cutting line using the manufacturer's recommended length inside the sink outline. If the manufacturer supplies a template, use it to draw the cutting line.

4 If you're installing a cooktop, mark the cutout using the manufacturer's recommended cutout shape. Position the metal frame on the upside down countertop, and trace the cutting line around the edge of the vertical flange. Remove the frame.

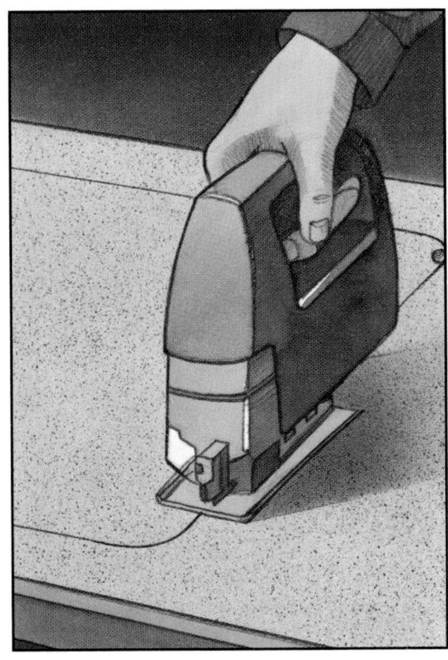

5 With the countertop still upside down, drill a pilot hole just inside the cutting line. Make the cutouts with a jig saw. Support the cutout area from below so it doesn't fall though.

6 Turn the countertop over and attach battens from the endcap kit to the edge of the countertop using carpenter's glue and small brads. Sand out any unevenness in the edge with a belt sander.

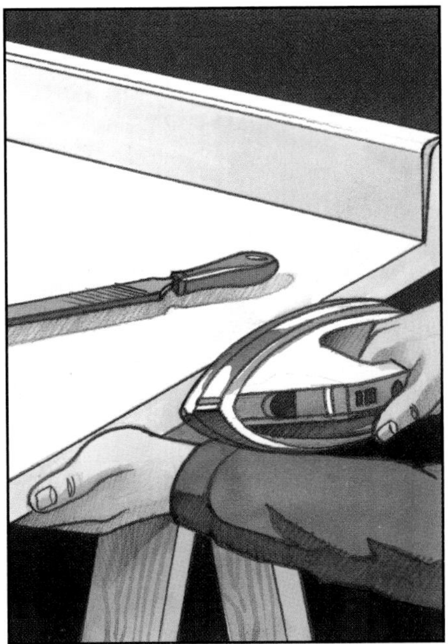

7 Hold the endcap laminate against the end, slightly overlapping edges. Activate the adhesive by pressing an iron, set at the medium heat setting, against the endcap. Cool with a wet cloth. File the endcap edges flush by filing toward the countertop to avoid pulling it away from the countertop.

8 Position the countertop on the base cabinets. Make sure the front edge of the countertop is parallel to the cabinet face. Check the countertop for level. Make sure that drawers and doors open and close freely. If needed, adjust the countertop with wood shims.

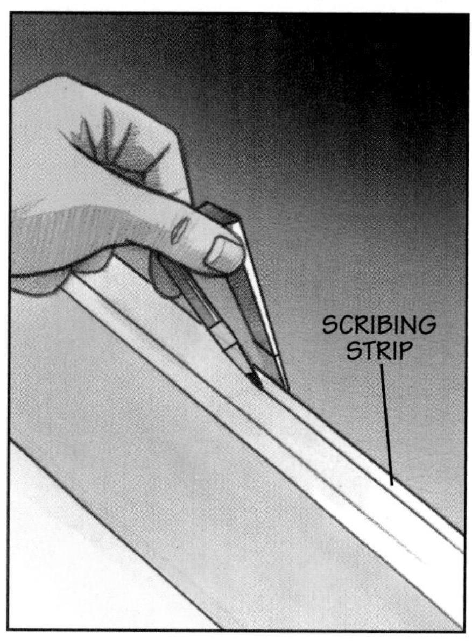

9 Because walls are usually uneven, use a compass to trace the wall outline onto the backsplash scribing strip. Set the compass arms to match widest gap, then move the compass along the length of the wall to transfer the outline to the scribing strip.

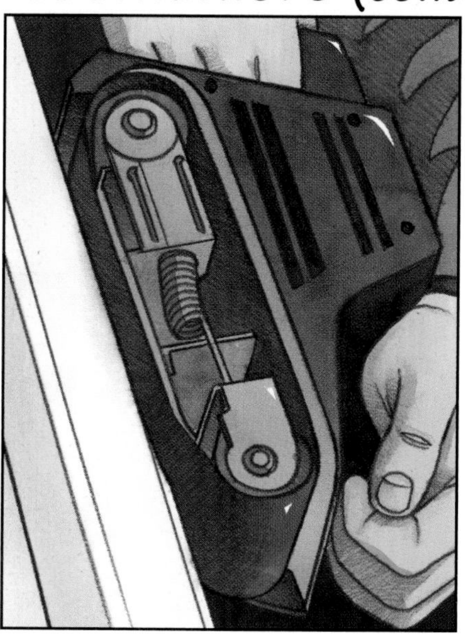

10 Remove the countertop. Use a belt sander to grind the backsplash to the scribe line.

11 Apply a bead of siliconized latex caulk on the edges of the mitered countertop sections. Force the countertop pieces tightly together.

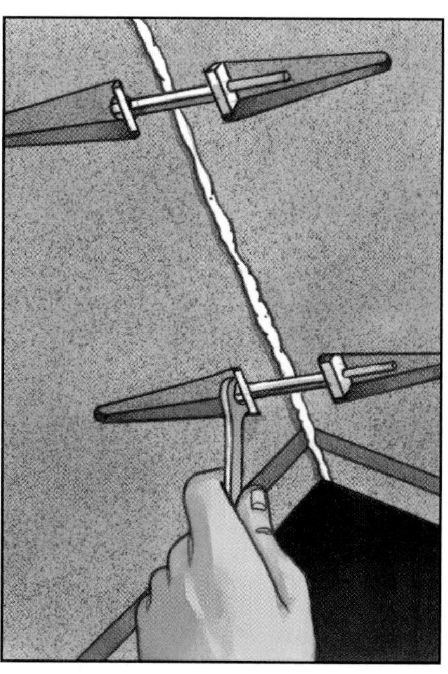

12 From underneath the countertop, install and tighten joint fastening bolts to keep the miter from shifting and spreading. Tap the seam with a rubber mallet until surfaces of adjoining countertop are even.

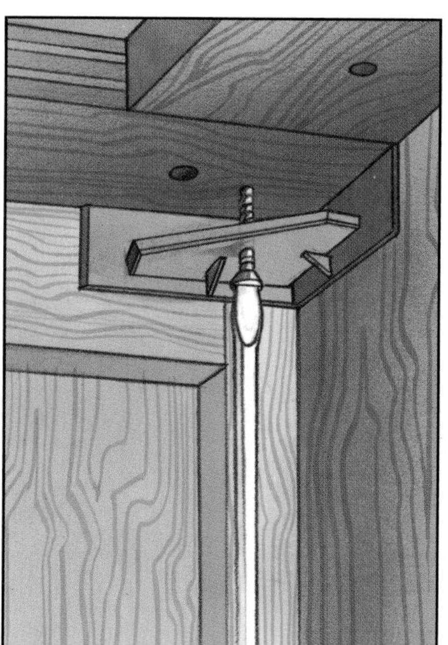

13 Position the countertop on the cabinets and attach with wallboard screws driven up through corner brackets inside the cabinets. The screws should be long enough to secure the countertop, but not so long that they would bubble or puncture the top surface.

14 Seal the seam between the backsplash and the wall with a quality siliconized latex caulk. Smooth the bead with a wet fingertip and wipe away the excess caulk.

Custom Laminate Countertops

A countertop made with laminate can be tailored to fit any space, and can be customized with a decorative edge treatment of hardwood, laminate, inlayed metallic laminate, or ceramic. Laminates are available in lengths from 4 to 12 feet and widths from 18 to 60 inches. Another type of laminate has consistent color through the thickness of the sheet. Solid-color laminate countertops do not show the dark lines at the trimmed edges and give a smoother look to countertops. Solid-color laminate is more expensive than regular laminate.

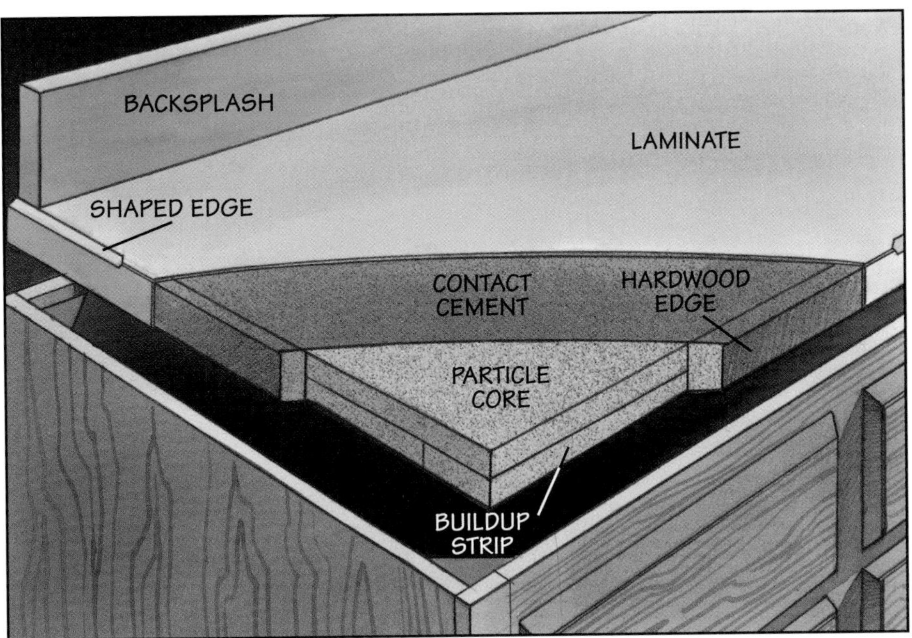

Custom laminate countertops use a core of $^3/_4$" particleboard and a perimeter built up with strips of particleboard glued and screwed to the bottom of the core. The edge can be laminate-covered particleboard or hardwood and shaped with a router to your individual design preference. The laminate pieces are bonded to the particleboard or hardwood with brush-on, roll-on, or spray-on contact cement. The laminate is then trimmed with a router and finally filed flush with adjoining laminate edges.

Solid-Surface Countertops

Solid-surface materials, marketed under trade names such as Corian®, Avonite®, and Gibraltar®, are manufactured from plastic resins blended with additives and then are formed into sheets and normally installed by licensed professionals. They are made in solid colors or patterns that resemble marble, granite, or other natural and synthetic materials and designs.

Solid-surface materials can be shaped and cut with common woodworking tools equipped with carbide-tipped blades. Normally, the standard sheets are available in $^1/_2$" and $^1/_4$" thicknesses and sizes ranging up to 31" wide and 145" long. The sheets of solid-surface material can be welded together with color-matched joint adhesive for applications that require longer or wider sheets and to form corners and built-up edges. Once the seams are welded with the joint adhesive and machined, they become virtually invisible, giving the impression of one continuous sheet.

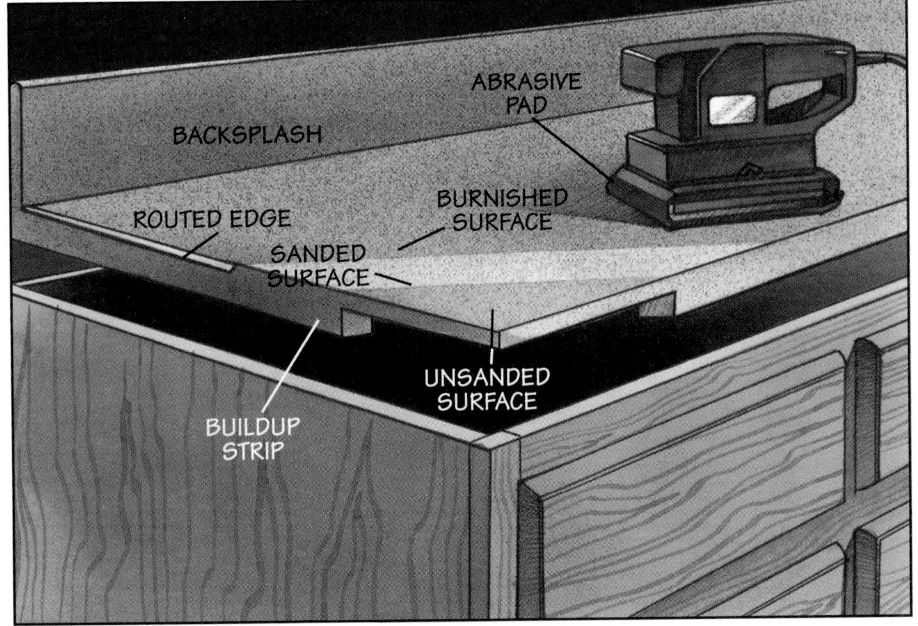

Solid-surface countertops are normally made from $^1/_2$"-thick material with built-up edges of $^3/_4$"-thick solid-surface strips attached with special joint adhesive. The edges are then shaped with a router. The surface is smoothed with sandpaper and is burnished with a scouring pad attached to the bottom of an orbital sander. Depending on the type of abrasive used, you can produce a range of finishes from matte to glossy. The backsplash, made from $^1/_2$"-thick material, is attached to the wall with panel adhesive and sealed with siliconized latex caulk.

Building a Ceramic Tile Countertop

Because countertop surfaces are exposed to water, it is advisable to use moisture-resistant adhesive or mortar and glazed tiles. The tiles may be sold individually or in mosaic sheets attached to mesh backing. Some tiles have edge lugs that automatically set the width of grout joints. For smooth-edged tiles, use plastic spacers to maintain even grout joints.

A successful tile job requires a solid, flat base and careful planning. Dry-fit the tile job to make sure the finished layout is pleasing to the eye. After installation, seal the grout with a quality silicone sealer to prevent water damage.

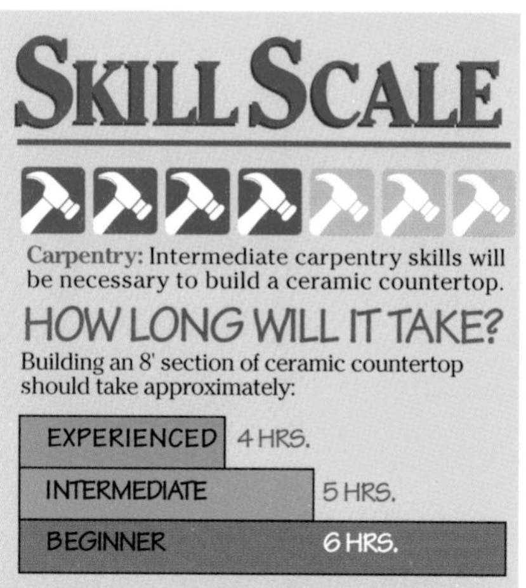

STUFF YOU'LL NEED:

- ☐ **Tools:** Tile cutter, putty knife, screwdriver, tile nippers, notched trowel, caulk gun, hammer, grout float, sponge, small brush, framing square, tape measure.
- ☐ **Materials:** Latex grout additive, grout, siliconized latex caulk, tile adhesive or mortar, latex underlayment, denatured alcohol.

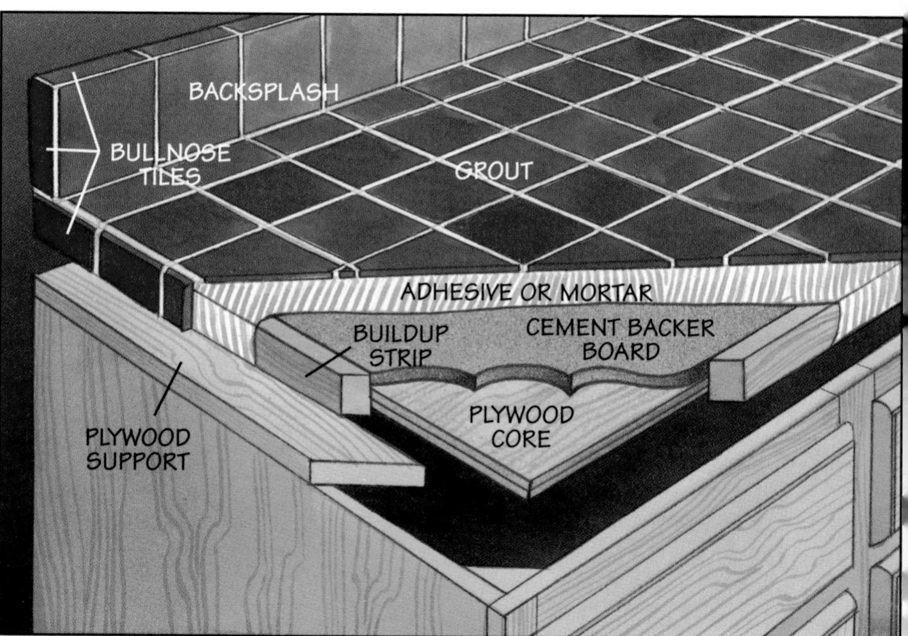

Ceramic tile countertop: The countertop core is exterior plywood and cement backer board cut to the same size as the cabinet. Edges are built up with wood strips attached to the outer edges of core. Tiles are set into place with adhesive. Grout fills the gaps between the tiles. Bullnose tiles, which have rounded edges, are used to cover the edges of the countertop and backsplash. Backsplash tiles can be installed over a separate plywood core or directly to the wall behind the countertop. Use $^3/_4$x3" plywood supports, attached every 2 feet across the base cabinet and around the edges of the cabinet.

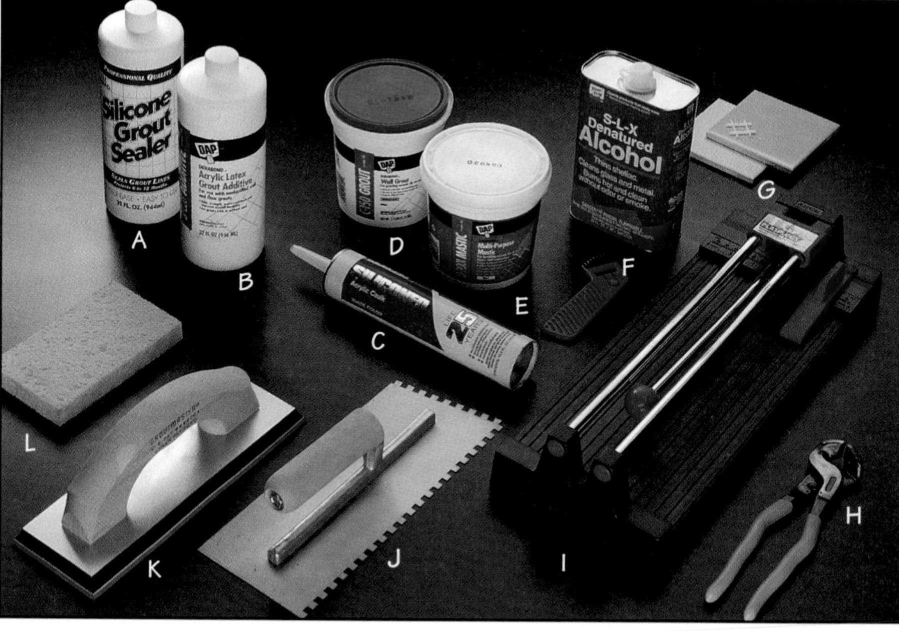

Special tools and materials needed to build a ceramic tile countertop include: penetrating silicone grout sealer (**A**), latex grout additive (**B**), siliconized latex caulk (**C**), tile grout (**D**), tile adhesive (**E**), denatured alcohol (**F**), ceramic tile (**G**), tile nippers (**H**), tile cutter (**I**), notched trowel (**J**), grout float (**K**), and cellulose sponge (**L**).

BUILDING A CERAMIC TILE COUNTERTOP

1 Cut 3" wide frame supports from 3/4" exterior plywood. Use 1 1/4" wallboard screws or 4d common nails to attach the supports every 24" across the cabinet, around the perimeter, and next to the cutout locations. From exterior plywood and cement backer board, cut a countertop core to the same size as the cabinet unit (AxB) using a circular saw.

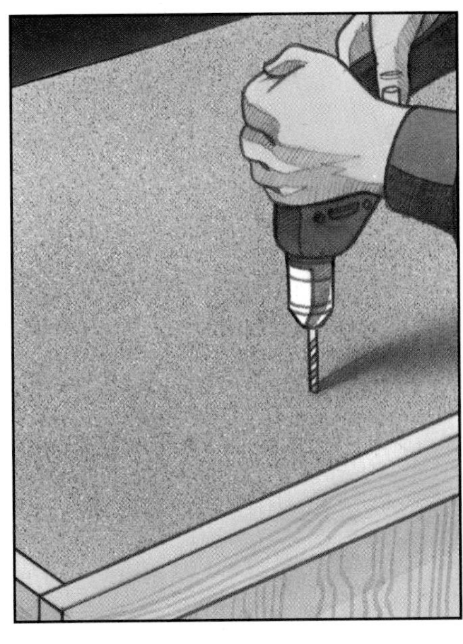

2 Position the countertop core tightly against the wall and fasten it to the cabinets by driving wallboard screws down into the frame supports.

3 Use latex underlayment to fill any low spots, cracks, and screw holes in the countertop core. Let the underlayment dry, then sand it smooth.

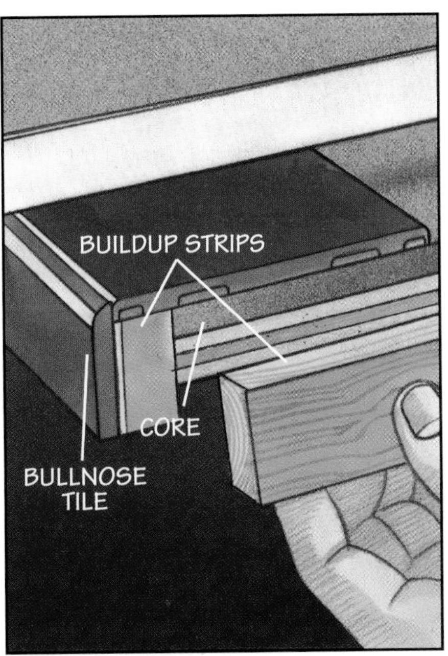

4 If the countertop will have bullnose edge tiles, attach 1x2 buildup strips of pine or exterior plywood to the exposed edges of the countertop core using carpenter's glue and 6d finish nails. The top of the strip should be flush with the top of the core.

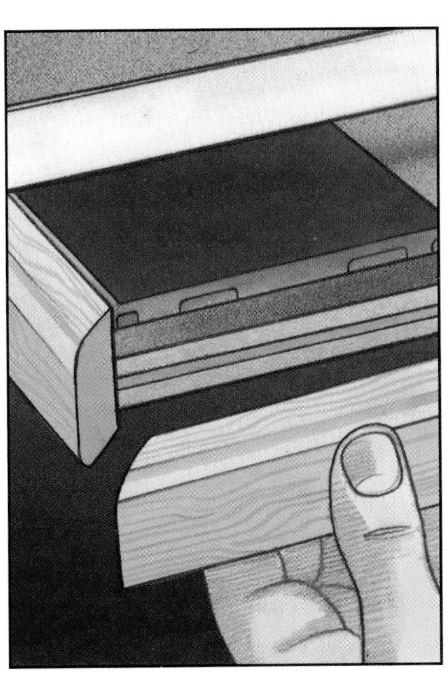

For a decorative wood edge, attach stained and sealed 1x2 hardwood strips to the edge of the core with carpenter's glue and finish nails. The top edge of the strip should be flush with the top surface of the tile. Determine if you'll be using mortar or adhesive before sizing the decorative strip.

5 To create a symmetrical tile layout, measure and mark the middle of the countertop core. Use a framing square to draw a layout line perpendicular to the front edge of the core. From the front edge of the core, measure along line A the length of one full tile and mark it on the core. Use the framing square to draw a second layout line perpendicular to line A at the mark.

6 Dry-fit rows of tiles along the layout lines. Use plastic spacers if tiles do not have self-spacing lugs. If the dry fit shows that the layout is not pleasing, line A may be adjusted in either direction. Dry-fit all of the tiles, and mark the cutting lines on any tiles that must be trimmed.

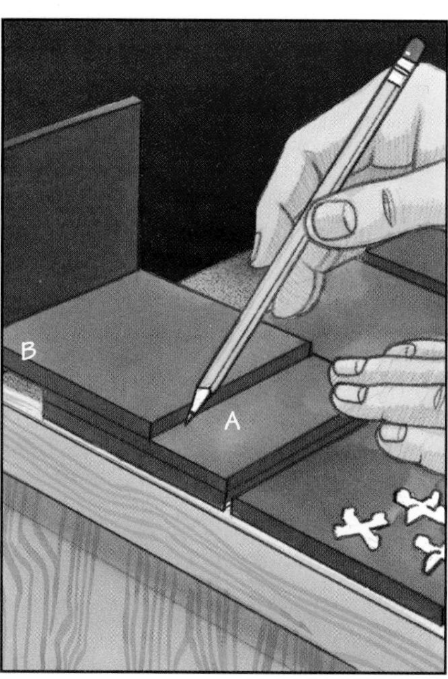

7 Mark the border tiles for cutting. To allow for grout lines, put a tile upright against the wall. Place a loose tile (**A**) over the last full tile, then butt a full tile (**B**) against the upright tile. Mark tile A and cut it to fit the border space.

8 To make straight cuts, place the tile faceup in the tile cutter. Adjust the tool to the proper width, then score a continuous line by pulling the cutting wheel firmly across the face of the tile.

9 Snap the tile along the scored line, as directed by the tool manufacturer. Smooth the cut edges of the tile with a tile sander.

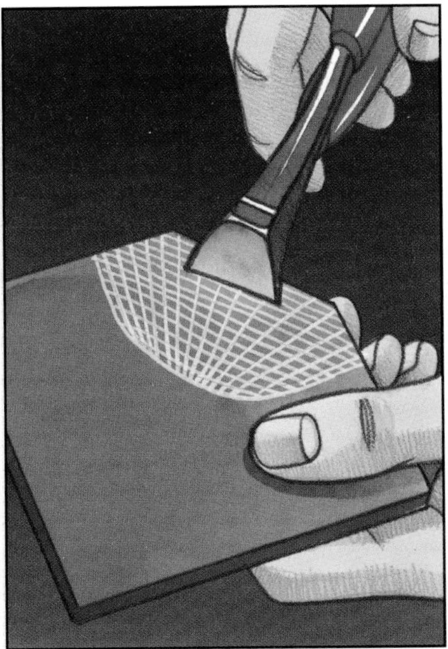

10 For curved cuts, score a crosshatch outline of the cut with the tile scoring tool. Use tile nippers to gradually break away small portions of tile until the cutout is complete.

11 Apply a thin layer of adhesive to the edge of the countertop and the back of the tile, using a notched trowel. Press the tiles into place with a slight twist. Insert plastic spacers between the tiles. Self-spacing tiles require no plastic spacers.

12 Spread adhesive along the layout lines and install the perpendicular rows of tiles. You should use mortar instead of adhesive if the countertop will be in a high moisture area. Use plastic spacers to maintain even spacing. Check the alignment frequently with a framing square.

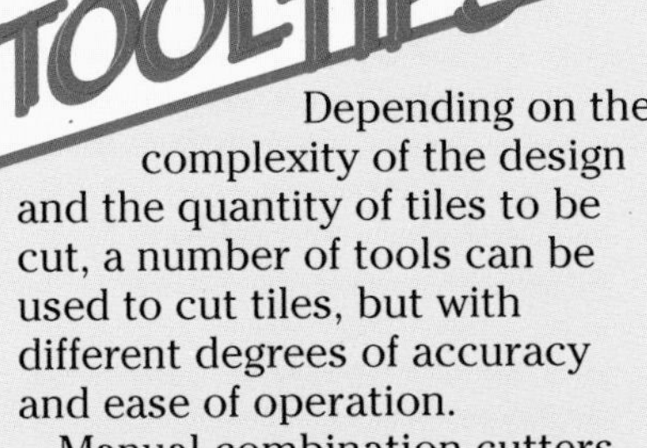

Depending on the complexity of the design and the quantity of tiles to be cut, a number of tools can be used to cut tiles, but with different degrees of accuracy and ease of operation.

Manual combination cutters are pliers-type tools and have cutting wheels on one side and breakers on the other. These are the least accurate and most difficult tools to use.

Tile cutters lay flat on the floor or benchtop and hold the tile in place at the desired size markings. Pull the cutter along the parallel slide bars to score the tile, then press the lever to break the tile along the cut. This is the most commonly used type of cutting tool because it is moderately priced and easy to use.

13 Install the remaining tiles, working from the layout line outward to the ends. Work in small areas, about 18" square. Use denatured alcohol to remove any adhesive from the face of the tiles before it dries. For the backsplash, install a single row of bullnose tiles directly to the wall, or use sink rail tiles if putting cement reinforced backer board on the wall for a backsplash.

14 After each small area is installed, "set" the tiles. Wrap a short piece of 2x4 in scrap carpeting or a towel. Lay the block against the tiles and tap it lightly with a mallet or hammer. Remove the plastic spacers with a toothpick.

15 Mix the grout and latex additive. Apply the grout with a rubber grout float. Use a sweeping motion to force the grout into the joints.

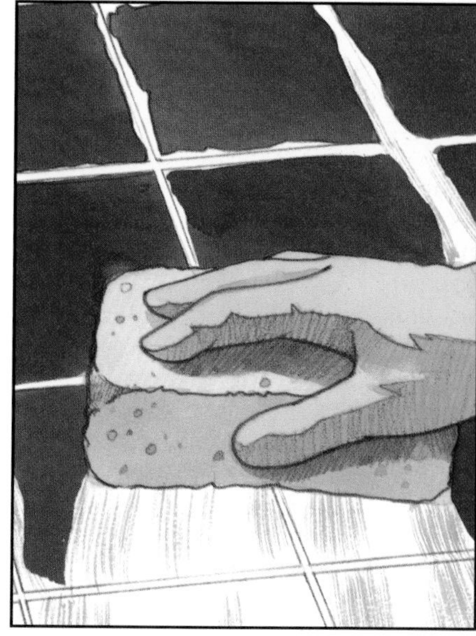

16 Wipe away the excess grout with a damp sponge, let it dry for 1 hour, then wipe away the powdery haze. Let the grout cure as directed by the manufacturer before caulking and sealing.

17 Seal the joints around the backsplash with silicone caulk. Smooth the bead with a wet finger, then wipe away the excess caulk. Let the caulk dry completely.

18 After the grout has dried, apply penetrating silicone sealer to the grout with a brush. Let it dry, then apply second coat. Once it has dried completely, buff with soft cloth.

Edge treatments include rounded bullnose tiles cut to fit the edge, and a hardwood edge shaped with a router. Hardwood edges should be attached and finished before the tile is installed. Protect hardwood edges with masking tape when grouting and sealing the tile job.

SHELVING & STORAGE

Shelves are a great way to store items like books, records, and videocassettes, but keep in mind that the weight the shelf will carry is a critical factor in the overall design. A set of encyclopedias puts a far greater strain on a shelf than a dozen paperbacks. An overloaded shelf is not likely to break, but it will sag and destroy the aesthetics of the shelving unit, giving it an appearance of instability.

You can increase the load-bearing capacity of a shelf in any one of a number of ways. Use solid wood; it's more rigid than plywood, and particleboard can actually snap under too much weight. Trim the edges of the shelf with continuous strips of hardwood lumber to reinforce the shelf, or simply make the shelf out of thicker material. You can also make the shelf shorter. The greater the span of the shelf, the weaker it will be. Even a strong shelf will tend to sag under the weight of a full load of books if it is over 30" long.

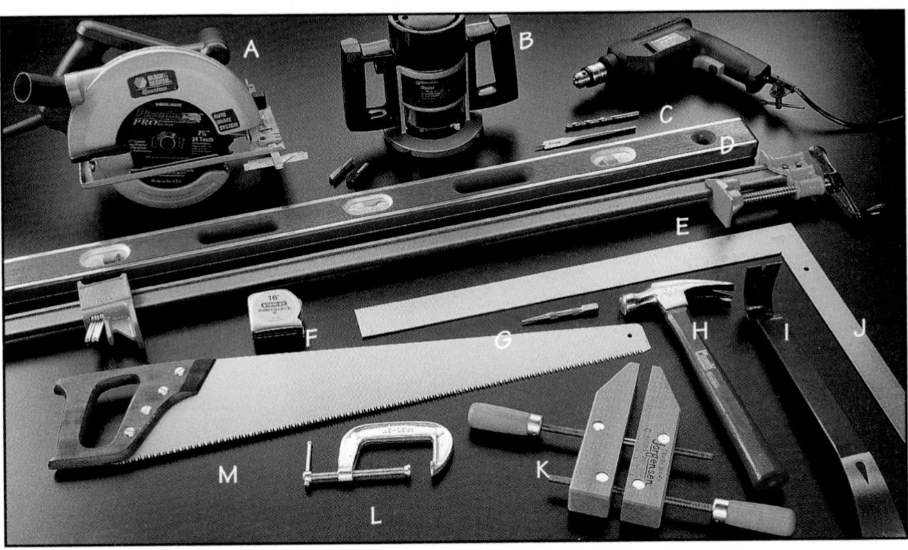

Basic tools for building and installing shelves include: circular saw (**A**), router w/bits (**B**), power drill w/bits (**C**), carpenter's level (**D**), bar clamp (**E**), tape measure (**F**), nail set (**G**), claw hammer (**H**), pry bar (**I**), framing square (**J**), handscrew clamp (**K**), C-clamps (**L**), and hand saw (**M**).

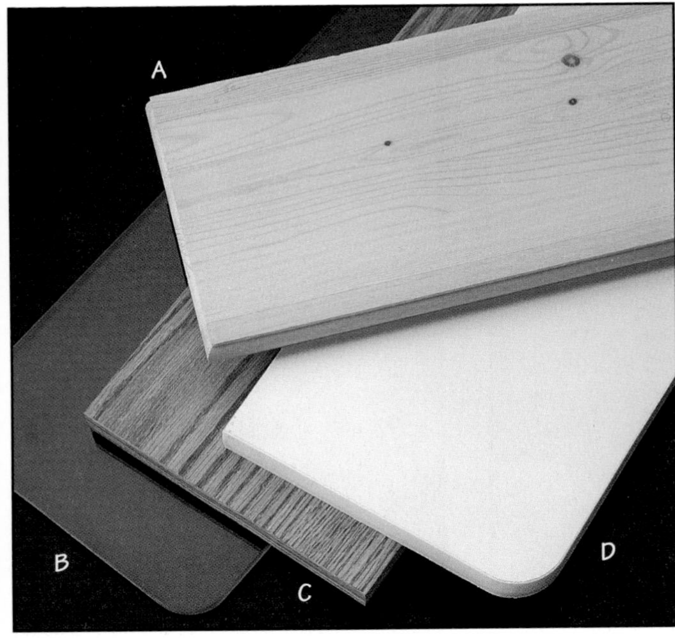

Shelving material includes: hardwood board cut to size with routed edge (**A**), decorative glass (**B**), woodgrain plastic laminate over particleboard (**C**), and white melamine over particleboard with plastic edging (**D**).

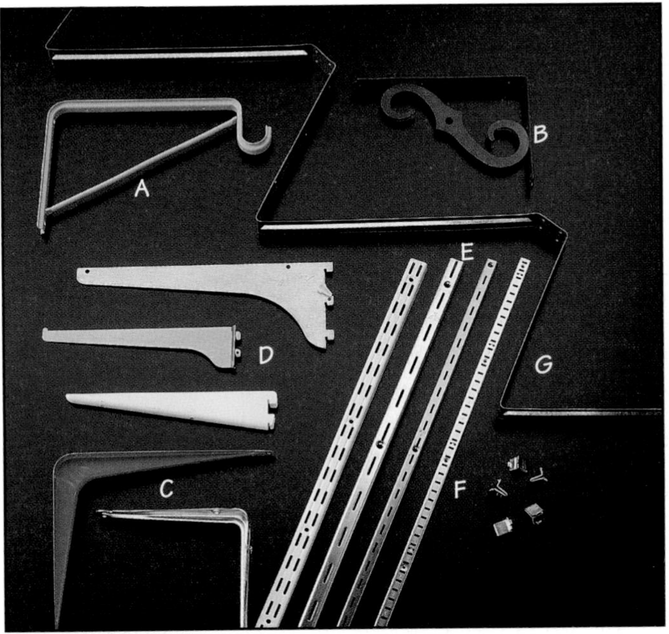

Shelving standards include: stationary brackets which are available in closet style with rod bracket (**A**), decorative style (**B**), and utility style (**C**) and come in a wide range of sizes. Horizontal cantilevered brackets (**D**) and arm-bracket standards (**E**), are used to create adjustable shelving. End-clip standards with clips (**F**) also create adjustable shelving while Z-standards (**G**) are used for utility shelves.

Hanging Stationary & Adjustable Shelving

Sturdy wall shelving can be installed quickly and easily using metal arm brackets. Stationary brackets are available in both decorative and utility styles, and come in a wide range of sizes.

For greatest strength, choose brackets with diagonal supports. In most applications, attach the longer bracket arm to the wall, and the shorter arm to the shelf. It is best to use a stud finder to locate the wall studs. This will save on potential wallboard repair and patching. Whenever possible, attach the shelving standards directly to the studs for the greatest strength.

Long wall shelves should be supported by standards a minimum of every 48 inches. Increase the size of brackets and spacing of support depending on the shelving load.

Adjustable shelving uses a system of metal standards and arm brackets to provide a more flexible storage solution than stationary brackets. For more decorative shelving, you can mortise the metal standards into strips of prefinished hardwood, giving the entire shelving unit a professional look. Simply use an electric router to cut grooves into the hardwood strips, then insert the metal standards inside the grooves and attach them to the wall. A router can also be used to mold a decorative edge on the shelves if you so desire.

Shelves are sturdiest when their standards are anchored directly to wall studs, but if you must anchor between studs, be sure to use hollow wall anchor bolts, and follow the manufacturer's weight limits.

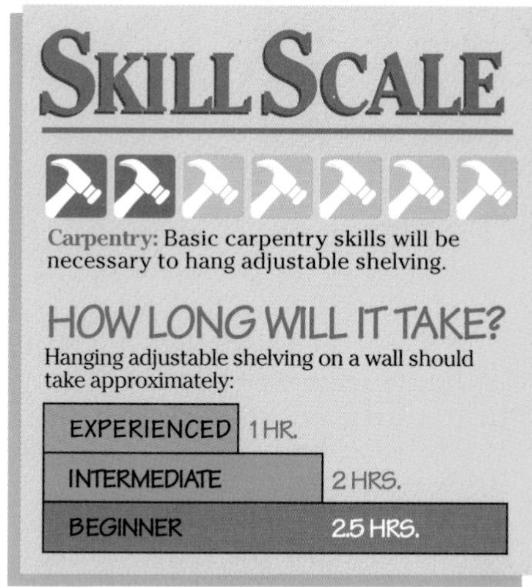

STUFF YOU'LL NEED:

- ☐ **Tools:** Router, saw, screwdriver, drill.
- ☐ **Materials:** Standards, arm brackets, hardwood strips, screws.

STATIONARY BRACKETS

1 Attach hardware to studs whenever possible. Save time by using an electronic stud finder to locate the studs. For heavy loads, attach a standard to every stud along the span of shelving.

2 If you're attaching shelf brackets to masonry walls, use plastic concrete anchors and screws. Attach one shelf bracket for every 16" to 24" of shelf span, depending on the intended load weight.

3 Level the shelf brackets and standards using a carpenter's level. If necessary, hold the level on a straight 2x4 for long spans.

ADJUSTABLE BRACKETS

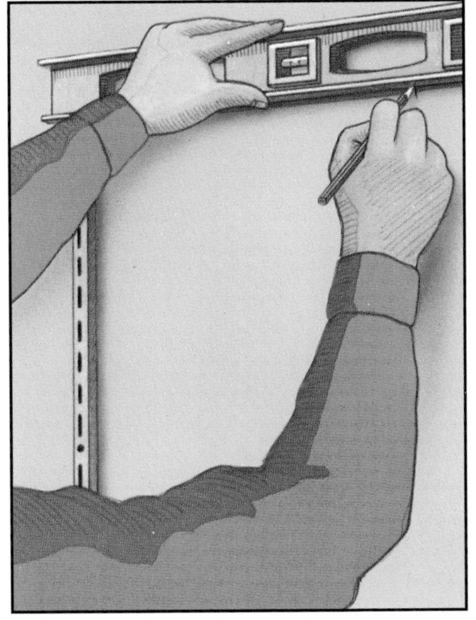

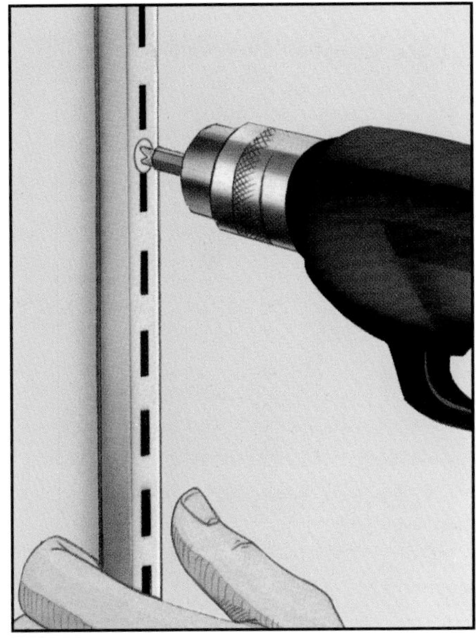

1 Using an electronic stud finder, locate the wall studs where the shelf standards will be mounted. Position the standards so the top ends are pointing towards the ceiling. The top ends are usually the ones that start out with a countersunk screw hole first, and then slots for the wall bracket.

2 Mount the first standard at the desired location using 3" wallboard screws. Use a carpenter's level to make sure the standard is plumb. Place the level on the top of the mounted standard and make a level mark at the stud location where the next standard will be.

3 Attach the next shelf standard to the wall using 3" wallboard screws. Again, use a carpenter's level to make sure the standards are plumb. Attach the arm brackets and hang the shelves.

WALL ANCHORS

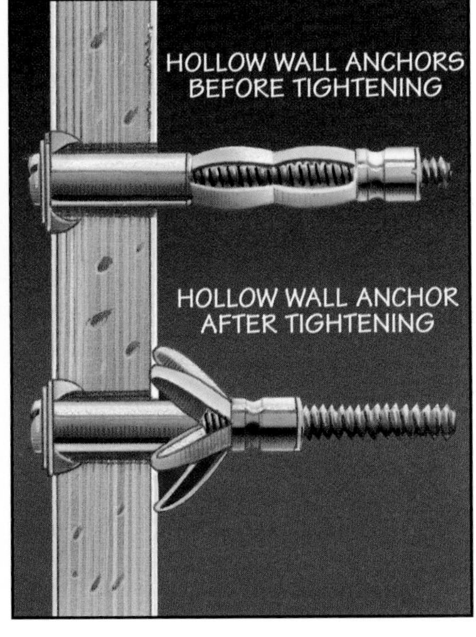

Attach hardware between studs using hollow wall anchor bolts. Do not exceed the manufacturer's recommended load limits for between-stud installations.

DECORATIVE TRIM

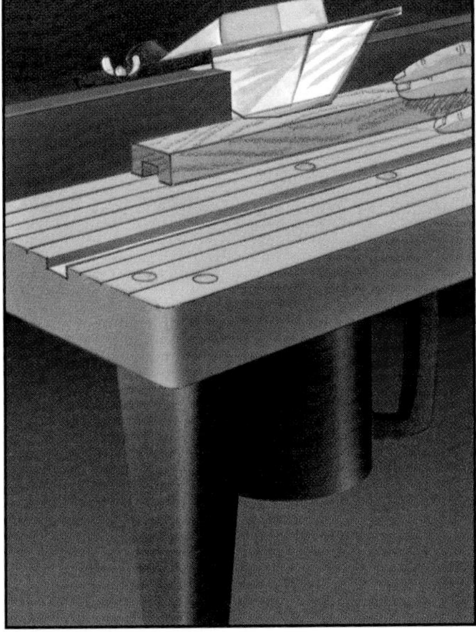

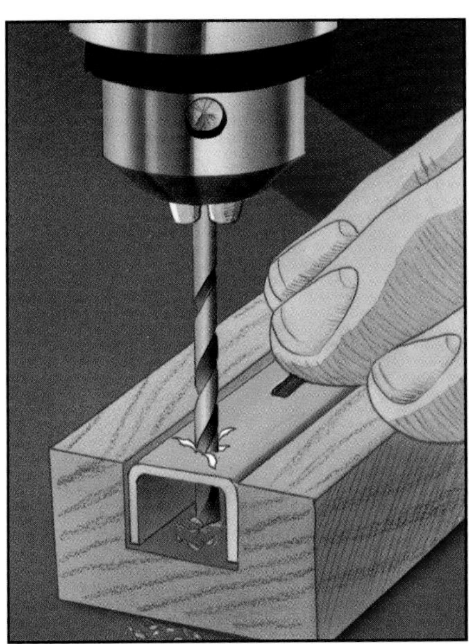

1 Cut 1x2 hardwood strips the same lengths as the shelving standards. Cut a groove along the center of each strip using a router table. Make several passes until the groove is equal to the depth and width of the metal standard.

2 Insert the standards into the routed grooves, drill pilot holes through the hardwood strips at each screw opening, and attach to the wall studs. Use a carpenter's level to plumb the shelf standards.

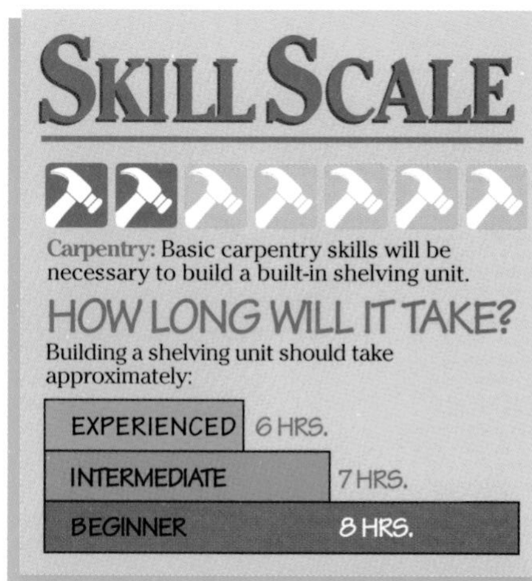

STUFF YOU'LL NEED:

- ☐ **Tools:** Tape measure, circular saw, drill, hammer, nail set, screwgun.
- ☐ **Materials:** Finish nails, common nails, hardwood lumber, 2x2 material, paint or wood stain and varnish, trim molding, 3" wallboard screws.

Built-in Shelving

Permanent shelves can be built into virtually any space where storage is needed. The space between a door or window and an adjacent wall corner is often a good location for built-in shelving.

A shelving unit can be built out of any 1" lumber except particleboard, which has a tendency to sag when subjected to heavy weights. For heavy loads, like books, a shelving unit should be built from 1x10 or 1x12 hardwood boards and should span no more than 48". Shelves can be supported from the ends by pegs or end clips, and if additional support is needed, hardwood support strips can be attached to the underside of the shelf.

Shelving units can be used for storing frequently used items or displaying collectibles. The size and construction of the shelving unit will vary depending on the weight of the objects to be stored or displayed.

CONSTRUCTING A BUILT-IN SHELVING UNIT

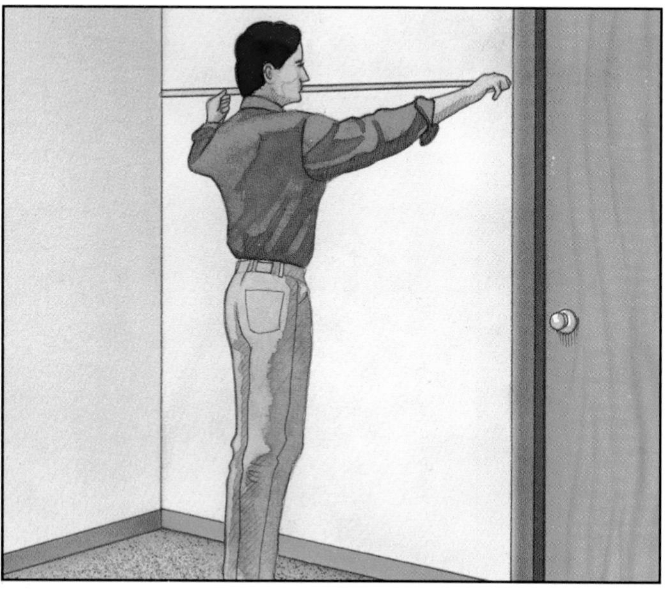

1 Measure the height and width of the available space. For easy installation, the basic unit is built 1" shorter than the ceiling height. Remove the baseboards and cut them to fit around the shelving unit. Replace the baseboards after shelving unit has been nailed in place.

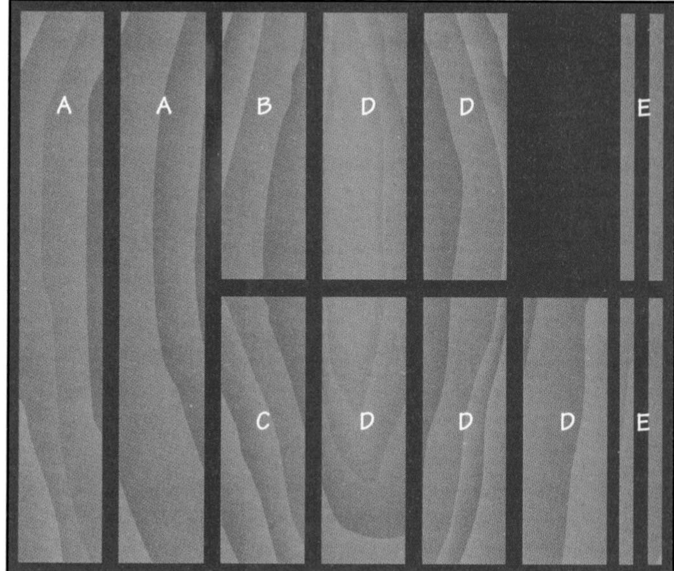

2 Mark and cut two side panels 1" shorter than the floor-to-ceiling measurement. Cut the shelving unit top, bottom, and shelves $1^1/_2$" shorter than the unit width measurement. Measure and cut four 2x2 frame supports $1^1/_2$" shorter than the unit width measurement.

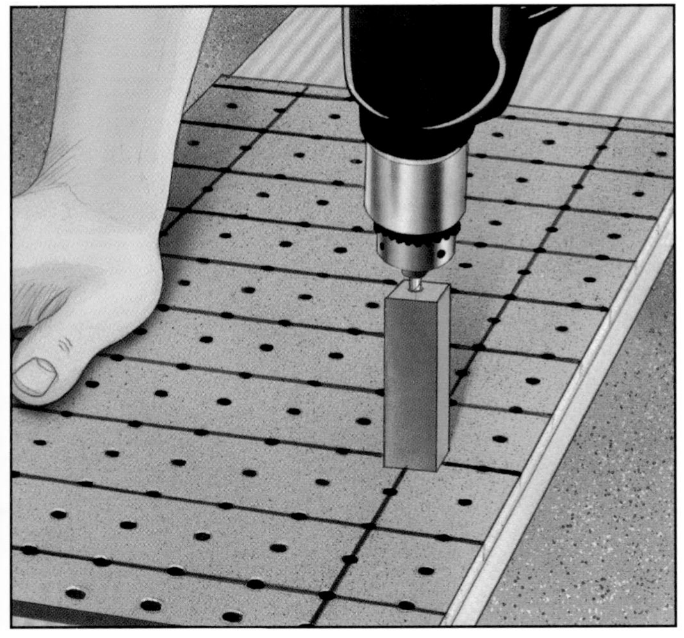

3 Using scrap pegboard as a guide, drill pairs of 1/4" holes along inside of each side, spaced every 9" horizontally and every 2" vertically. Holes should be 3/8" deep. Use a scrap piece of wood or a bit attachment as a depth guide.

4 Paint or stain the wood as desired before assembling the unit. Attach the sides to the ends of the frame supports. Drive 6d finish nails through the sides and into the end grain of the frame supports.

5 Tilt the unit into position flush against the wall. Screw through the top rear frame support into the wall studs, and through the bottom frame supports into the floor, using 3" wallboard screws.

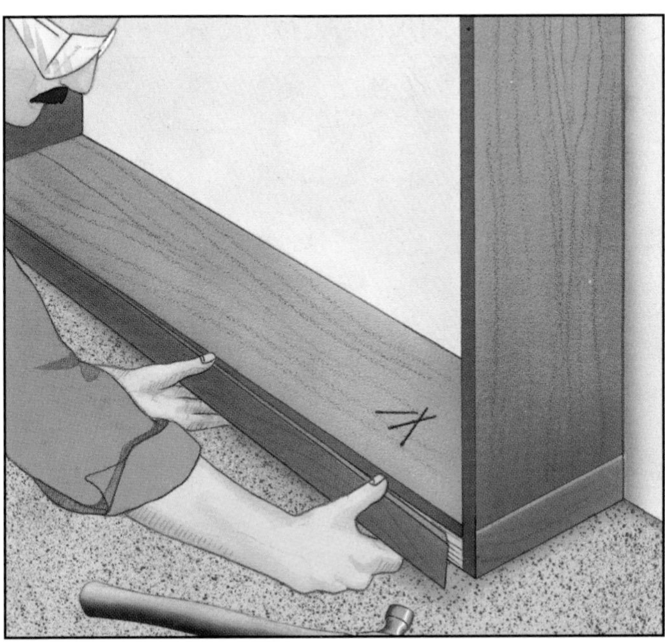

6 Attach the shelving unit bottom and top by driving 6d finish nails through the sides into the end grain of the top and bottom. Replace the baseboards around the bottom of the shelving unit. Use a nail set to recess the nail heads. Install the shelf pins in the desired holes and place the shelves in on the pins.

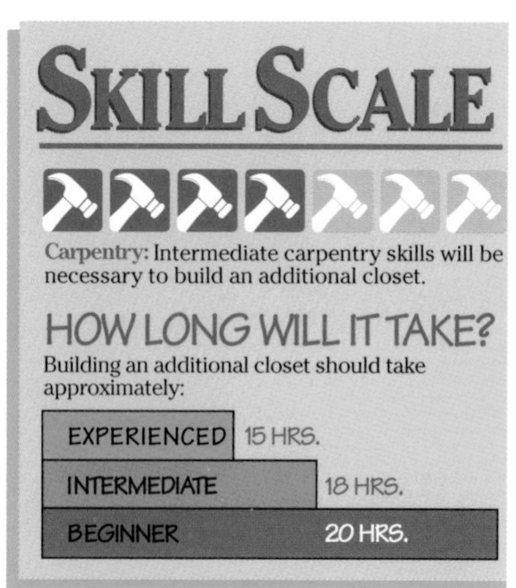

Adding a New Closet

Building a closet is a great way to add a permanent storage area to your home. It's cost-effective too. You'll get more storage volume for your dollar than from any other project, and you'll add value to your home.

Closets can be added or built on just about any wall in your house. Walls along stairways or entryways provide ideal locations for closets, and if you have an available inside corner, you can actually save material by only needing to build two walls for the closet instead of three! Building a closet can also be the perfect first-time carpentry project, because it entails framing, drywall hanging and taping, door hanging, and trim carpentry–all on a small scale. It requires just enough planning and construction to give you a good taste without overwhelming you with a long frustrating project.

Buy your door before you begin framing so you can follow the manufacturer's directions regarding the rough and finished opening sizes specific to the individual door.

STUFF YOU'LL NEED:

- ☐ **Tools:** Tape measure, framing square, plumb bob, pry bar, utility knife, hammer, carpenter's level, circular saw, drill, power driver, nail set, back saw.
- ☐ **Materials:** 2x4 material, wallboard material, trim molding, wallboard joint compound, wallboard tape, prehung door.

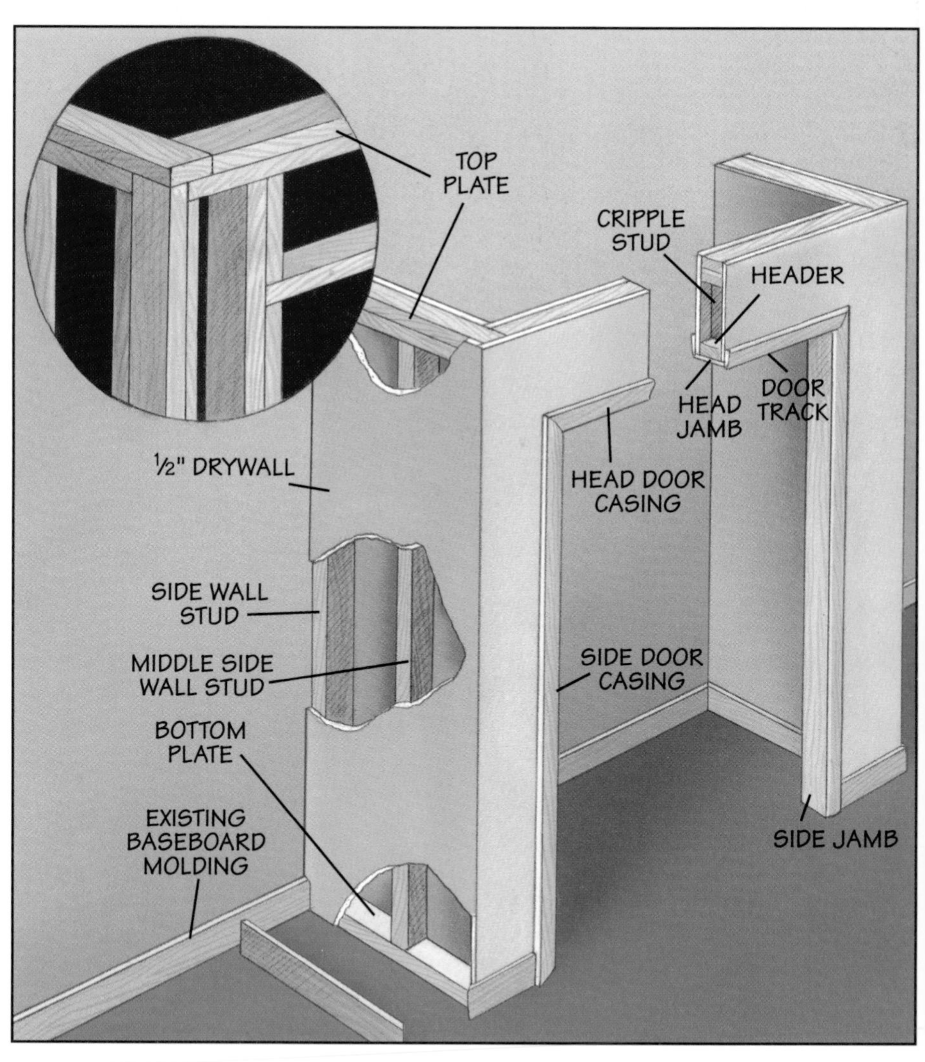

By overlapping the top plate corners, you can anchor the plates to the ceiling regardless of which way the ceiling joists run. If the ceiling joists run perpendicular to the wall, install the upper front plate first. Then toenail each upper side wall plate to the front plate and to a side wall stud. If the ceiling joists run parallel to the wall, reverse the plate installation order. Install the top side wall plates first, nailing them to the ceiling joist and the side wall studs. When installing the lower three pieces of the double top plate, note that each end of the lower front piece ends 1½" from the corner. The corner studs are built into the plates to make a strong corner joint.

BUYER'$ GUIDE

Choosing Trim Types

If you're planning to paint your closet's trim you can save money by ordering finger-jointed trim instead of clear trim. Finger-jointed trim is made of small pieces of solid wood joined into long strips. They are usually available in hardwood and softwood types. The joints are so tight that they are invisible under paint, but are noticeable under a clear or stained finish. So, there is no need to spend the extra money required for clear stock unless you plan to stain and varnish your trim.

LAYING OUT THE PLATES

1 Using a tape measure and a framing square, mark the outside edges of the top plate on the ceiling. Make sure the front layout line is parallel to the wall and the closet ends are at right angles to the front wall. Use a level to mark a plumb line down the wall and across the baseboard trim.

2 Drop a plumb bob to the floor from the outside corners of the ceiling plate lines. Drive a nail partway into the floor where the point of the plumb bob touches the floor. These two points mark the outside front corners of the bottom plate and correspond to the plate corners on the ceiling.

3 Mark the baseboard cut line 1/2" outside the side wall lines marked in Step 1 to allow room for drywall on the closet wall. Score the cut lines with a utility knife to avoid splintering, then cut with back saw. Remove the cutout section with a pry bar.

FRAMING THE CLOSET

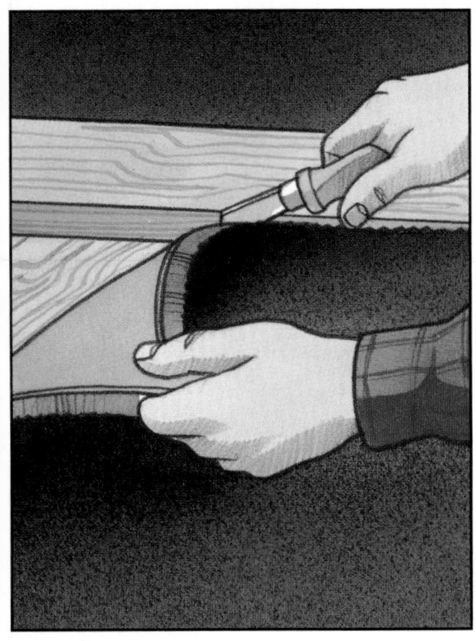

1 On carpeted floors, cut back and remove the carpet so the bottom of each wall stud and bottom plate can fit directly on the floor. Cut the two wall studs to length and align them with the vertical layout lines. Nail the wall studs directly into the top and bottom plates, and the studs, if they line up, of the existing wall.

2 Install the double top plate so the corners of the plates overlap (inset pg. 376). Cut all of the plate members to size, then fasten the three upper plates to the ceiling according to which way the ceiling joists run.

3 Fasten the three lower top plates to the upper top plates. Be sure to leave space on the ends of the lower top plates for the corner wall studs to fit in place.

FRAMING THE CLOSET (continued)

4 On the floor surface (sheathing, vinyl, or wood) lay out the outside edge of the bottom plate, marking a right-angled corner at each nail point. Also mark where the rough opening will begin in the front of the closet wall. Cut and install the bottom plate members, nailing them into the floor.

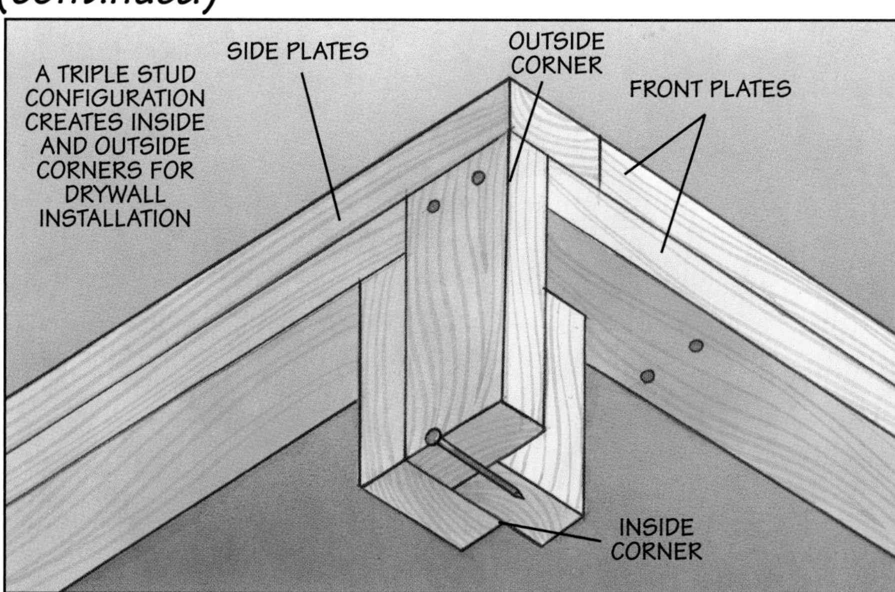

5 Each corner requires three studs to create inside and outside edges where drywall can be fastened. Cut and install the outermost stud first, driving nails into the top and bottom plates. Secure the top of each corner stud by driving two nails through the stud and into the end of the lower front top plate. Then install the remaining corner studs. Toenail these studs to the plates and nail the corner studs to each other.

6 Cut and install the remaining wall studs. Use a level to plumb up each side wall stud. Draw lines on the plates, marking where each side of each stud should be. Keep the studs on these lines as you toenail them to the top and bottom plates.

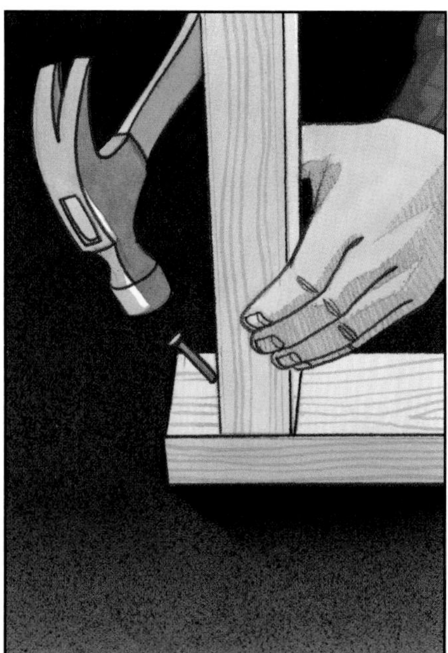

7 Cut and install the trimmer studs, sometimes called king studs, next. Toenail each trimmer to the bottom plate first, keeping it $1\frac{1}{2}$" back from the end of the bottom plate. Then use the level to plumb up each stud before toenailing it to the top plate.

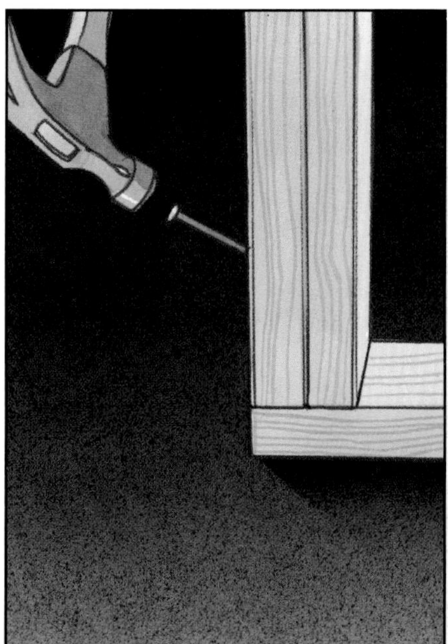

8 The jack studs are the shortened studs that form the sides of the rough opening and support the ends of the header. Cut the jack studs to the rough opening height, nail them to the trimmer studs, and toenail them to the plates.

9 Cut the header to fit between the trimmer studs. Hold the header down against the tops of the jack studs and drive a pair of 16d nails through each trimmer stud into each end of the header.

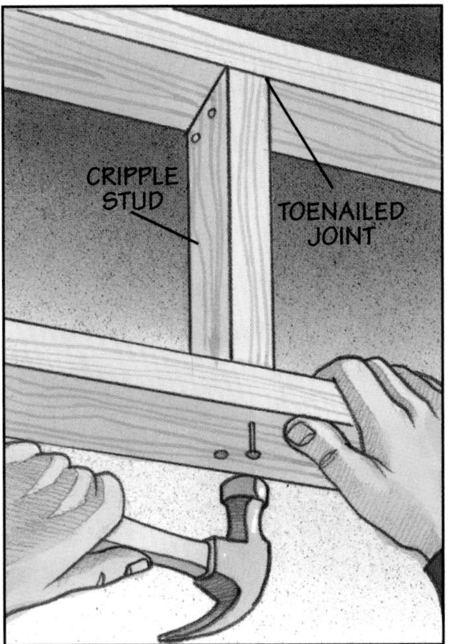

10 Cut the cripple studs to fit between the header and the top plate. Drive a pair of nails through the bottom of the header and into the bottom end of the cripple stud. Then toenail the top of the jack stud to the top plate.

WORK SMARTER

With the closet framed in, you'll be able to see what electrical fixtures (switches, receptacles, door chimes, etc.) will need to be relocated for safety and convenience. Replacing a standard switch or receptacle plate with a solid outlet box cover lets you convert a receptacle box to a junction box.

Now you can run wire from the old box to a new box that will be installed in the new closet wall or elsewhere. See pages 162 through 170 for information on junction boxes, wiring, and switch and receptacle installation. Always use extreme caution when making electrical repairs and be sure to check with your local building inspector before starting any electrical projects.

INSTALLING WALLBOARD AND TRIM

1 Measure and cut your wallboard panels to cover the framing members in the closet walls. If possible, use full sheets on the exterior side walls to minimize the number of joints that require taping and compounding.

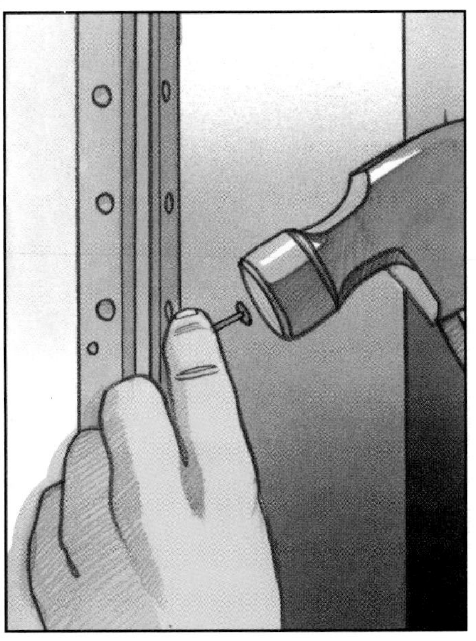

2 Install corner beads on the exterior corners to provide straight and durable outside corners and a guide for applying joint compound. See page 235 for more information on installing and finishing wallboard.

3 Finally, install the door, door trim, and molding. See page 312 for information on installing prehung doors, door molding, and trim.

Building a Closet Organizer

Closet organizers make efficient use of space and can easily double your closet storage capacity. There are many manufacturers selling many different styles of premanufactured organizers, and depending on the type of system you look at, it can actually cost hundreds of dollars to buy a custom-made organizer. The funny thing is that they are all designed similarly, with places to hang your clothes, store your clothes, and organize your shoes!

On the other hand, if you're willing to do it yourself, you can build an organizer for a standard 5' closet for the low cost of a single sheet of plywood, a clothes pole, and a few feet of 1x3 lumber. Your low-cost organizer will perform the same function as an expensive unit.

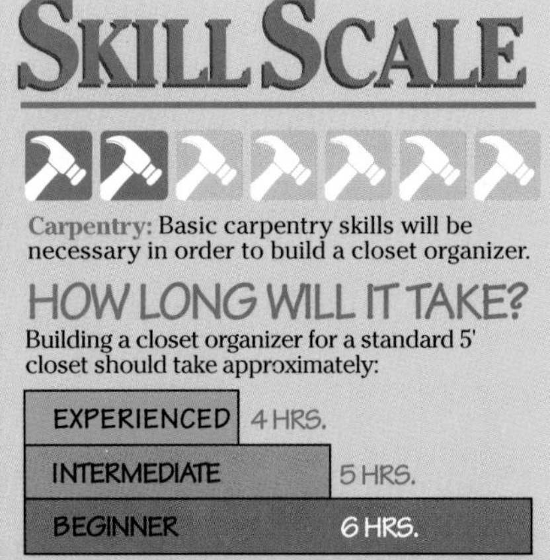

STUFF YOU'LL NEED:

- ☐ **Tools:** Hammer, tape measure, framing square, circular saw, screwdriver.
- ☐ **Materials:** Finish nails (6d and 8d), 1x3 lumber, one 4'x8' sheet of $^{3}/_{4}$"-thick plywood, clothes pole, 6' clothes pole, brackets, paint or wood stain.

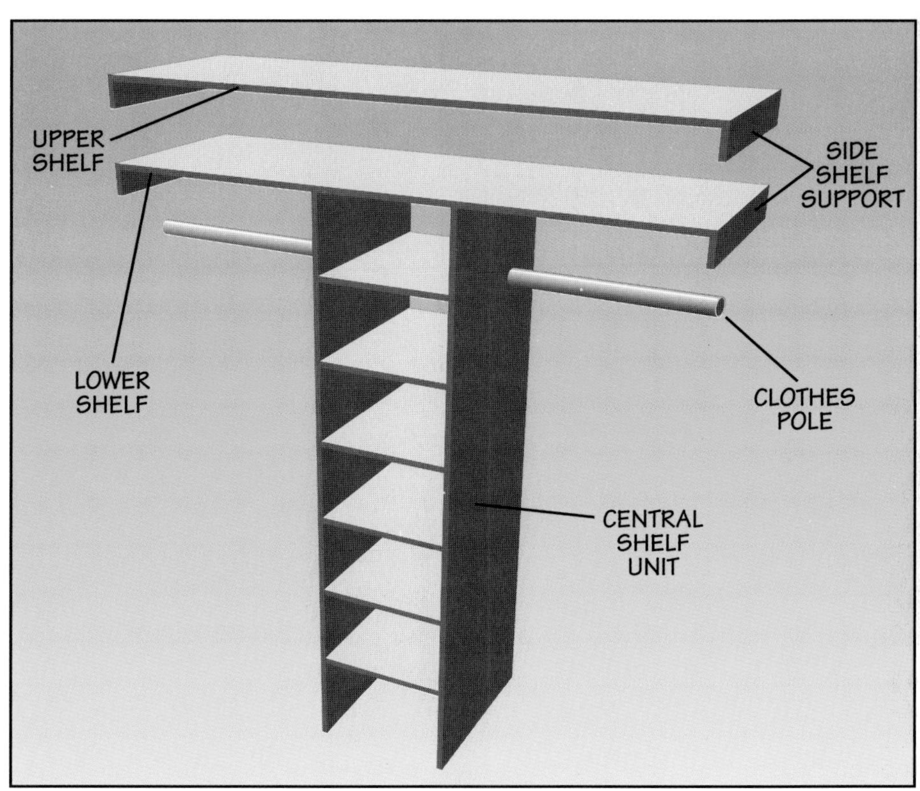

Closet organizers can be purchased in a variety of styles and configurations, or, with basic tools and minimal material, you can build a custom unit specifically designed for your individual needs.

BUILDING A CLOSET ORGANIZER

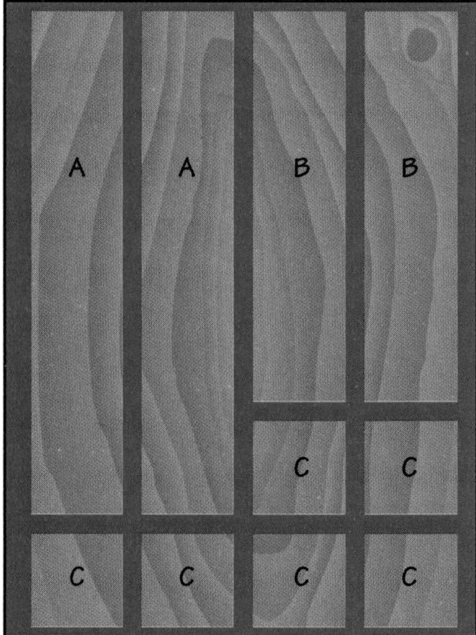

A single sheet of plywood yields two $11^{7}/_{8}$"-wide sides, two long $11^{7}/_{8}$"-wide shelves and six $11^{7}/_{8}$"-wide square shelves.

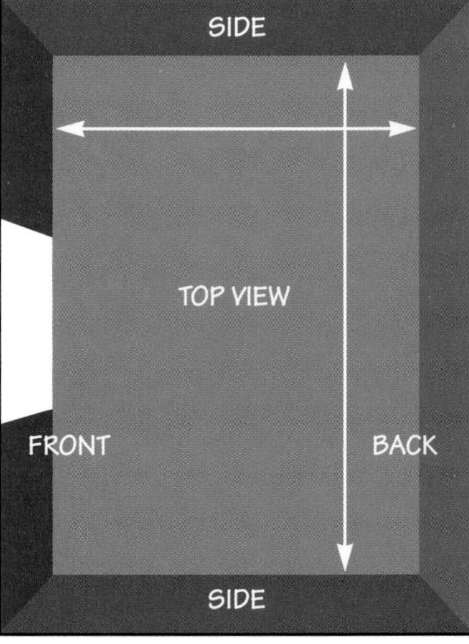

1 Measure the back and side walls to determine the length of shelf supports. Be sure to deduct $1^{1}/_{2}$" from the length of the back wall shelf support measurement ($^{3}/_{4}$" thickness for each end support).

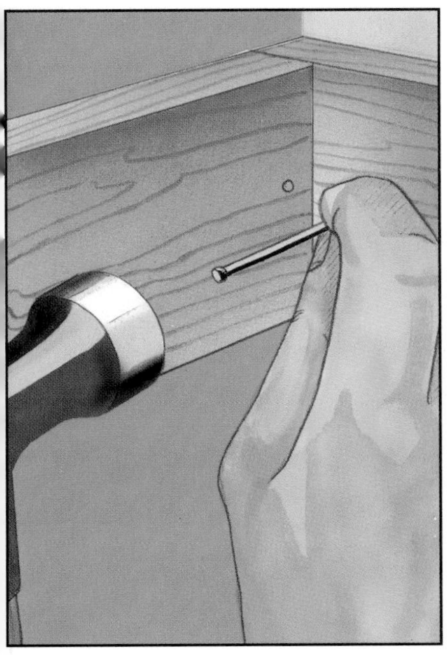

2 Cut 1x3 shelf supports to fit the back and end walls of the closet. Attach supports to the wall with the top edges 84" above the floor using 8d finish nails driven into the wall studs.

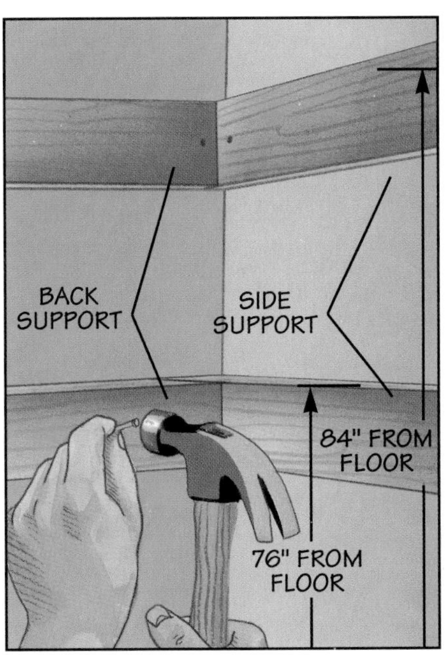

3 Cut the additional shelf supports and attach them to the wall with the top edges 76" above floor using 8d finishing nails driven into the wall studs.

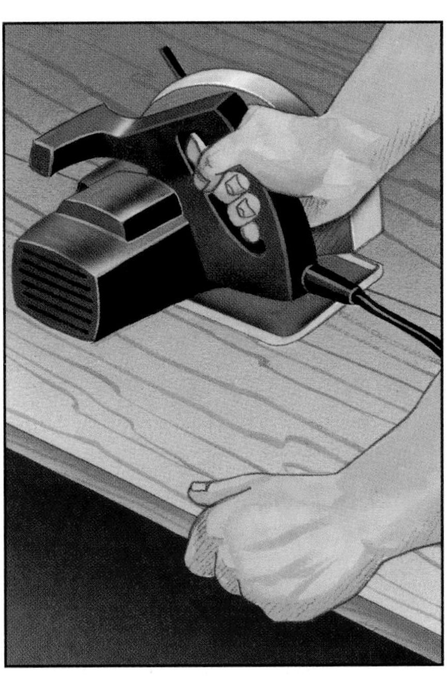

4 Cut two 11⅞"-wide shelves from ¾" plywood, then cut their length to fit the closet width.

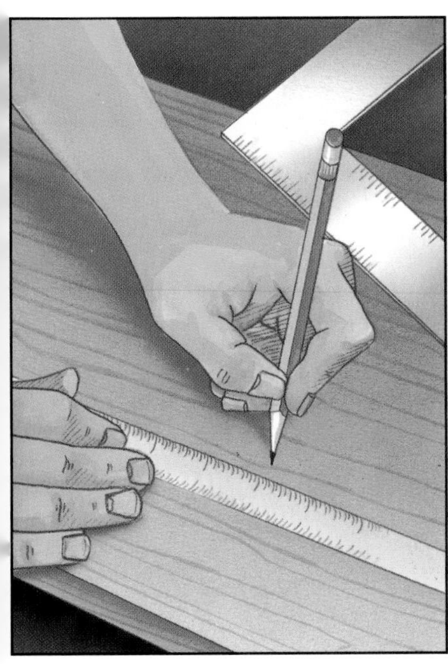

5 Measure and cut two 11⅞x76" shelf unit sides from ¾" plywood.

6 Measure and cut six 11⅞"-square shelves from ¾" plywood.

7 Assemble the central shelf unit using 6d finish nails. Space the shelves evenly or according to height of items to be stored. Leave the top of the unit open.

BUILDING A CLOSET ORGANIZER (continued)

8 Position the central shelf unit in the middle of the closet.

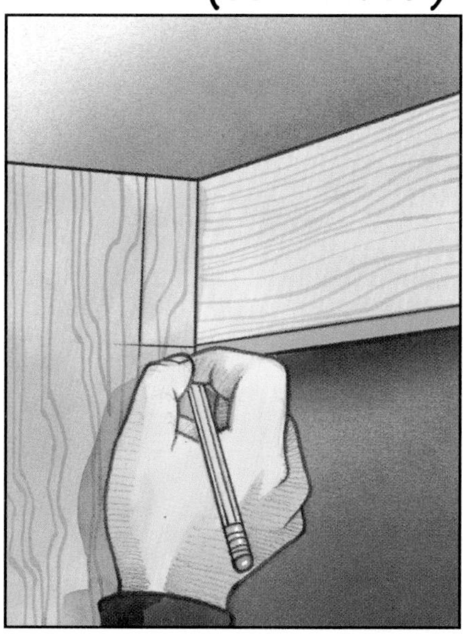

9 Mark and notch the shelf unit sides to fit around the lower shelf support.

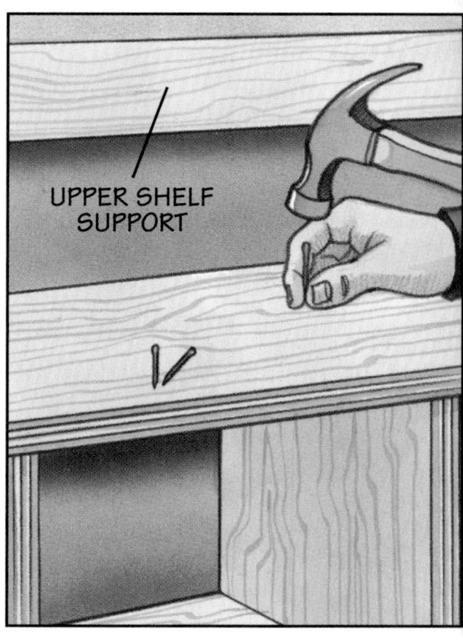

10 Lay the long shelf on the lower shelf supports and on top of the central shelf unit sides. Attach it with 6d finish nails.

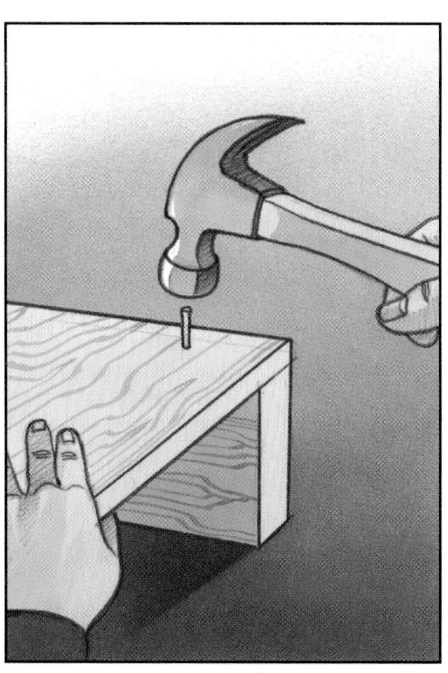

11 Lay the remaining long shelf on the upper shelf supports and attach with 6d finish nails.

12 Attach the pole brackets to the shelf unit sides, 11" from the rear wall and 3" below the long shelf. Attach the opposite bracket directly to the wall stud with a screw or to wallboard using a hollow wall anchor. If so desired, install brackets for a lower clothes pole 38" above the floor.

The finished closet organizer allows easy access to stored items. Shoes, blankets and other bulky articles can be easily stored in the central shelf unit.

Building Utility Shelves

Utility shelves are something that every home needs and are available in many premanufactured styles, sizes, and, of course, prices. But if you're willing to invest some effort and a little raw material, a good-quality shelving unit can be built quite affordably and easily. With some 2x4 material and 3/4" plywood you can build a simple, yet flexible storage center in just a single afternoon.

Depending on your need, the utility shelves can be built for the garage, basement, or maybe both locations. If you want to get fancy, you can put side panels and a face frame on the shelf unit to create a finished look. The possibilities seem almost endless!

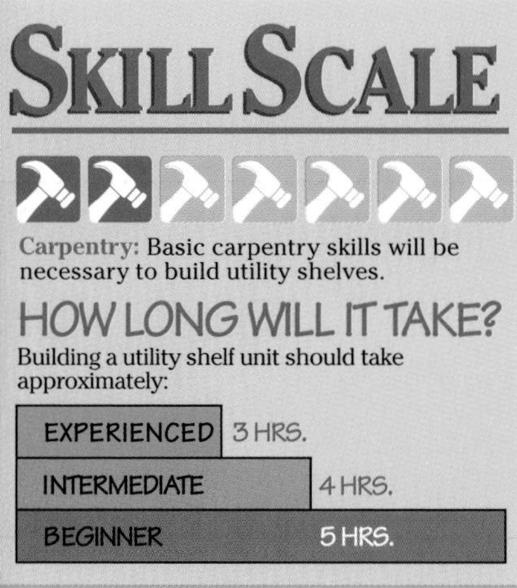

STUFF YOU'LL NEED:

- ☐ **Tools:** Power screwdriver, drill, circular saw, bar clamps, C-clamps, handscrew clamps, router.
- ☐ **Materials:** 2x4 material, 3/4" plywood, wood screws, wood glue.

Adjustable utility shelves are an ideal method of storing many differently shaped tools, equipment, and miscellaneous items. Shelving can be easily built for basements, storage rooms, and garages.

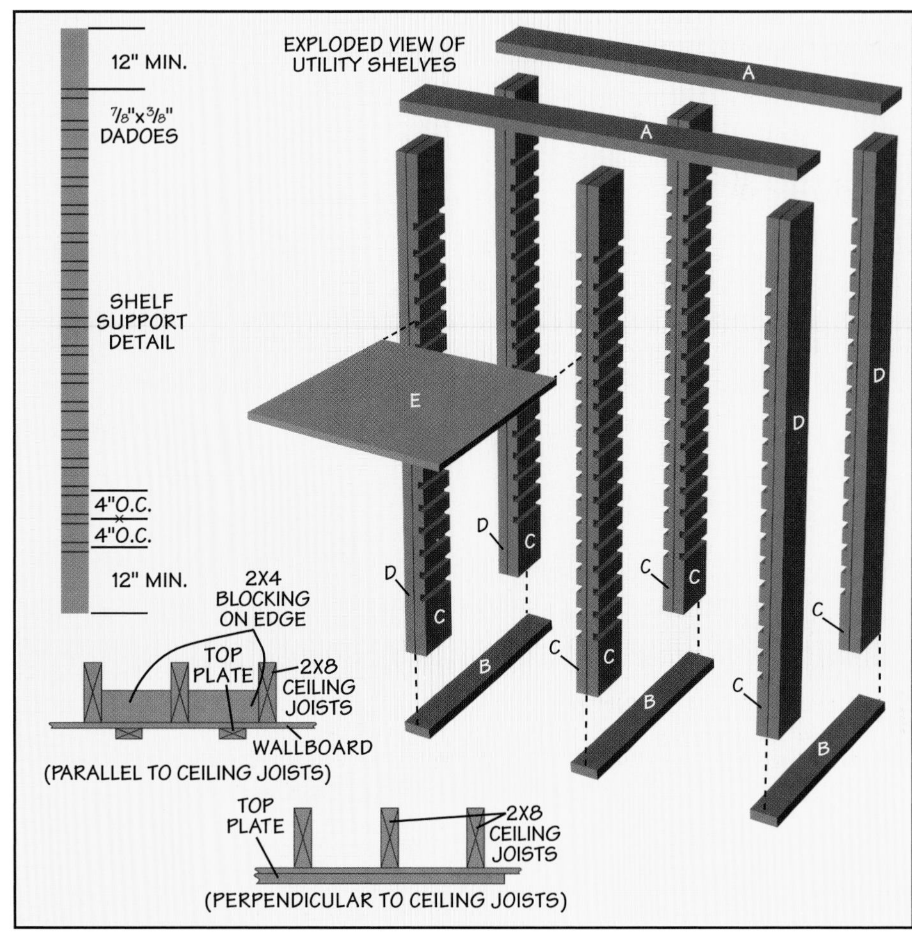

BUILDING UTILITY SHELVES

1 Mark the location of the top plates on the ceiling. One plate should be flush against the wall, and the other should be parallel to the first plate with the front edge 24" from the wall. Cut the 2x4 top plates to full length of the utility shelves, then attach them to the ceiling joists using 3" screws.

2 Using a plumb bob as a guide, mark points directly beneath the outside corners of the top plates to find the outer sole plate locations. Mark the sole plate locations by drawing lines perpendicular to the wall, connecting each pair of points.

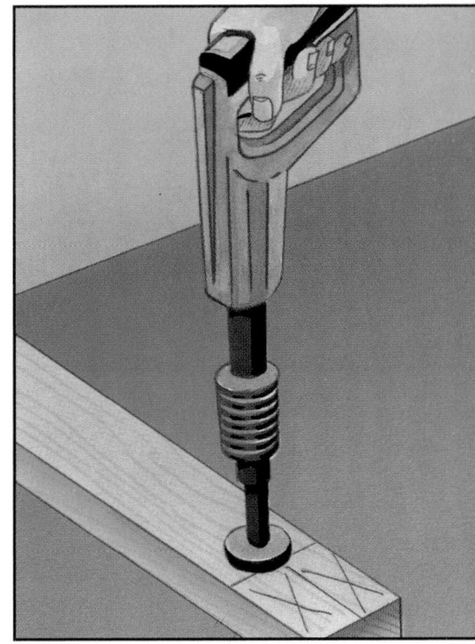

3 Cut outer 2x4 sole plates, and position them perpendicular to the wall, just inside the outlines. Shim the plates to level if needed, then attach them to the floor with a stud gun or screws. Attach a center sole plate midway between the outer sole plates.

4 Prepare the shelf risers by cutting 7/8"-wide, 3/4"-deep dado grooves with a router. Cut dadoes every 4" along the inside face of each 2x4 riser with the top and bottom dadoes cut about 12" from the ends of the 2x4. Gang-cut the risers by laying them flat and clamping them together, then attaching a straightedge guide to align the dado cuts. For each cut, make several passes with the router, gradually extending the bit depth until the dadoes are 3/4" deep.

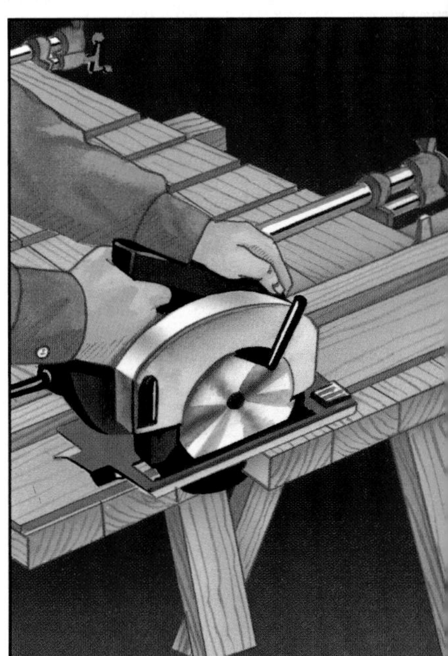

5 Using a circular saw and a straightedge guide, trim the shelf risers to a uniform length before unclamping them.

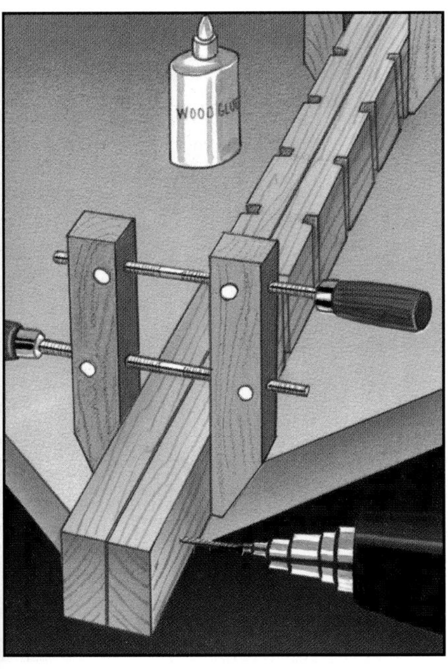

6 Build two center shelf supports by positioning pairs of shelf risers back-to-back and joining them with wood glue and 2 1/2" screws.

7 Build four end shelf supports by positioning the back of a dadoed shelf riser against a 2x4 of the same length, then joining the 2x4 and the riser with glue and 2 1/2" screws.

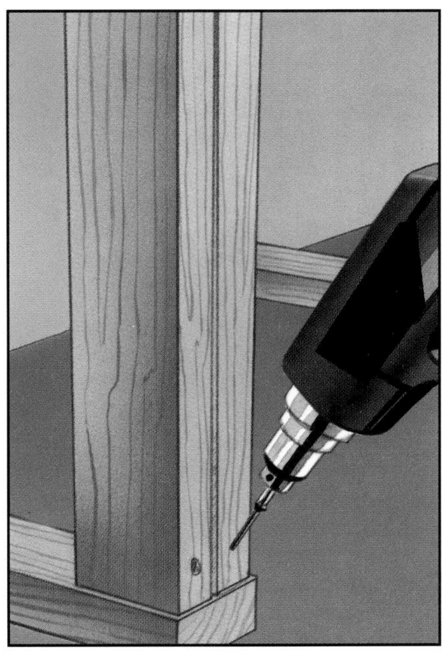

8 Position an end shelf support at each corner of the shelving unit between top and sole plates. Attach the supports by driving 3" screws at an angle into the top plate and sole plates.

9 Position a center shelf support (both faces dadoed) at each end of the center sole plate, then anchor shelf supports to the sole plate using 3" screws driven at an angle. Use a framing square to align the center shelf supports perpendicular to the top plates, then anchor to top plates.

10 Measure the distance between the facing dado grooves, subtract 1/4", then cut plywood shelves to fit. Slide the shelves into the grooves.

If you're building a utility shelving unit for the garage, you may want to use exterior-grade, pressure-treated lumber for the sole plates and even the shelf supports. If you have rainwater, melted snow, or the occasional floor washing with a garden hose, it would be a wise choice to use lumber that is designed to stand up to this type of moisture. Even in some basements that have a high humidity factor, it would be wise to use treated lumber.

Improving Existing Storage

There are several options available to maximize closet and cupboard space. Organizers are made of either a laminate covered particleboard material called melamine, or of vinyl-coated steel wire.

The melamine product provides a clean, bright professional appearance with the impression of a custom-built, built-in cabinet.

Vinyl-coated steel wire organizers provide flexible storage options with a clean, bright appearance. Wire organizers are available in pre-manufactured units that fit a wide variety of locations and uses.

Melamine units are generally more expensive than wire units. Both are easy to install.

Pre-manufactured closet organizers are an economical and efficient way to utilize closet space for clothing, which is by nature, somewhat oddly shaped and difficult to store. Organizers can be entirely made of either melamine or vinyl-coated wire, while a combination of the two systems can make for a truly functional and flexible storage area.

Shelves & Storage

When buying premanufactured wire storage baskets, bins, and trays for use behind doors, be sure to accurately measure the depth of the space between the back of the door and the front edge of the shelf unit. If the baskets are too large, the door will not close properly.

You may want to leave a little bit of space as a safety cushion to compensate for some oddly shaped items that you may be storing in the wire units. If the storage unit is adequately sized for the space, but the items being stored hang out beyond the storage unit, you may run into problems with adequate storage space.

Wire storage units come in a wide variety of sizes, shapes, and styles for just about every storage need you may have. Wire baskets, trays, shelf units, and completely self-contained rolling units can be used in almost any configuration you need.

Sliding wire baskets and trays provide easily accessible storage solutions for under-counter cabinet space utilization.

HOMER'S HINDSIGHT

Wire storage units are an efficient and economical way to improve your storage space, but installing them can be a test of character if not done properly.

I learned on my first installation that if you can't get the exact size of shelf unit you need, have the store where you purchased the unit cut it to the appropriate length. I thought I could cut it myself with my trusty old hacksaw, but unfortunately when I finished, it looked like it was in a train wreck and didn't survive!

BUYER'$ GUIDE

With the wide variety of manufacturers making storage organizers and shelving units, you should research the various brands carefully. When you finally decide to purchase, be sure to get all of the material that you'll need for the particular installation from the same manufacturer. Be careful not to mix components from the various makers because they don't use standardized mounting procedures or hardware. Mounting clips used on some brands of organizers may not fit on different brands of shelf units or baskets.

You can mix brands of organizers on different closet applications, but within individual spaces, use the same brand.

Pre-manufactured and pre-assembled melamine cabinets can be purchased for virtually any storage need. Melamine is a good choice for areas where durability and ease of cleaning is a consideration such as in a garage, laundry room or mud room area.

Many cabinet manufacturers are incorporating wire storage baskets and trays as standard equipment on their cabinets. You can upgrade older cabinets by purchasing sliding or stationary wire units and installing them yourself by simply following the manufacturers' directions.

Some cabinet manufacturers offer wood-grain alternatives to sliding trays and drawers typically made of white or other colored melamine.

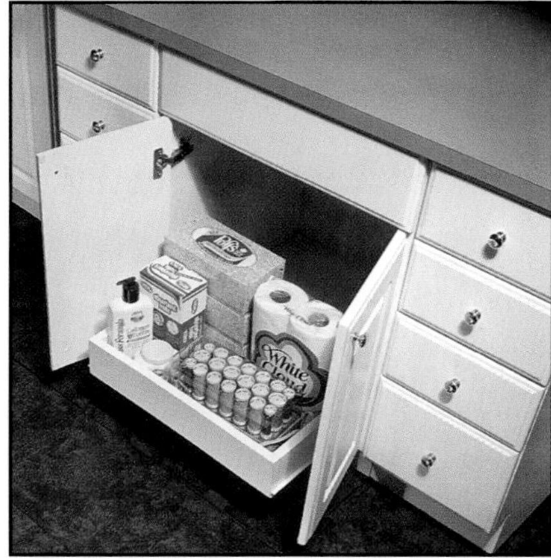

Sliding drawer trays make efficient use of lower cabinet space and make it a lot easier to get to those things in the back of the cabinet.

Off-the-Shelf Storage Solutions

Many storage and organizing systems are available from various manufacturers. They are normally available in vinyl-coated wire or melamine styles.

Depending on the manufacturer, there are design and installation differences that should be determined before you choose a style. Usually, wire shelf units have support clips every 12", but that may vary with the manufacturer. One important factor to consider is that within the same installation, closet, or storage area, you need to keep the same brand of components in order to properly install the system. Some manufacturers fasteners are not compatible with others, so do a little investigating first to find out what fasteners you should use..

Wire shelving and storage units are available in a variety of styles and designs. Shelf units can have hanger bars with individual spacing (**A**), segmented spacing (**B**), or continuous free-flow (**C**).

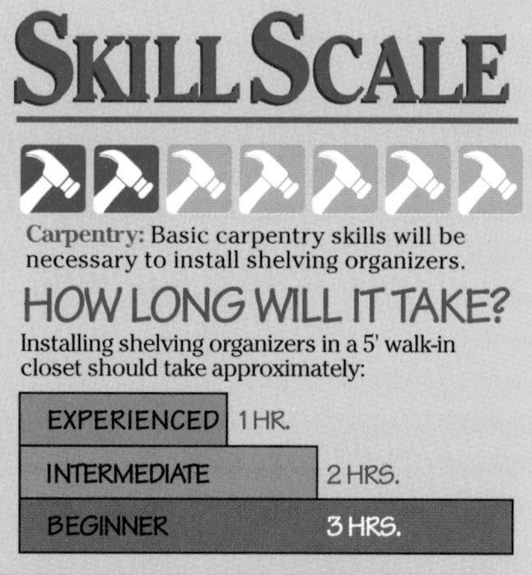

1 Measure up from the floor for the desired shelf height and mark the wall with a pencil. Use a carpenter's level to mark a horizontal reference line around the closet.

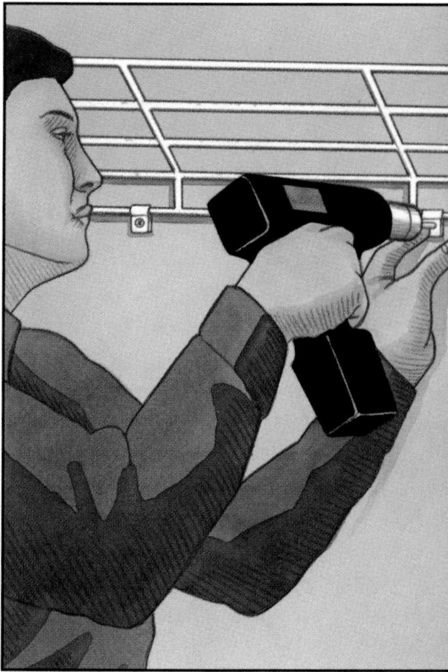

2 Mount the shelf unit by attaching the mounting clips with screws driven into the wall studs. Refer to the manufacturer's directions regarding spacing of mounting hardware. If necessary, use hollow wall anchors to fasten between wall studs. Attach diagonal supports, as necessary, according to the manufacturer's directions.

Before you purchase your closet organizing system, draw a rough sketch of your desired plan. Take into consideration the space required for the clothing and items that you'll be storing. Determine if you'll want a combination of wire and melamine components, or if you'll stay with one particular style. This plan will be helpful in shopping and comparing various brands of shelving and organizing systems.

TOOLTIPS

LEVEL LINE

Drawing a level reference line seems simple enough, but can actually be rather difficult when attempting to do accurately around a walk-in closet. The length of walls will have a direct relation to the difficulty of getting the lines to match up.

Using a standard carpenter's level is the most obvious choice but, once you use it, will seem like the most ridiculous tool you could have selected. The problem lies in the fact that most levels are 3' or 4' in length and most walls are much longer than that. As you move around the closet, trying to level from your original reference marks, you'll discover that although you may be only a fraction of a bubble off from line to line, when you get to the end you're off by a sizeable distance. One way to simplify this whole process is to purchase, borrow, or rent a water level.

Water levels are available in manual or electronic models and can be used in various locations and projects including fences, decks, drop ceilings, landscaping, concrete footings, and closet shelving. Manual and electronic versions work under the basic physical principal that water will flow away from a source that is at a higher elevation and will stabilize at an elevation that is level with the source. Manual versions require close monitoring while electronic models, which run off a 9-volt battery, will sound an alarm when the level point is reached. Then all you do is mark the positions and scribe a reference line, confident that you have an accurate level line.

INSULATING & WEATHER-PROOFING BASICS

Whether you live in a warm or cold climate, adequately weatherizing and insulating your house has many benefits. Most importantly it saves money. Even in homes with average insulation, heating and cooling costs account for over half of the total energy bill. And because most insulating and weatherstripping products are relatively inexpensive, an investment in them can be recovered through energy savings in a short period of time.

A well-insulated house not only saves money, but is also easier on the environment because it uses less energy. By reducing energy use, you help reduce pollution and slow the depletion of irreplaceable natural resources. In an average home in a cold climate, it is estimated, reducing energy usage by only 15% can save the equivalent of 500 pounds of coal each year. And finally, a tightly sealed, well-insulated house eliminates drafts and cold spots, creating a more comfortable home for your family to enjoy.

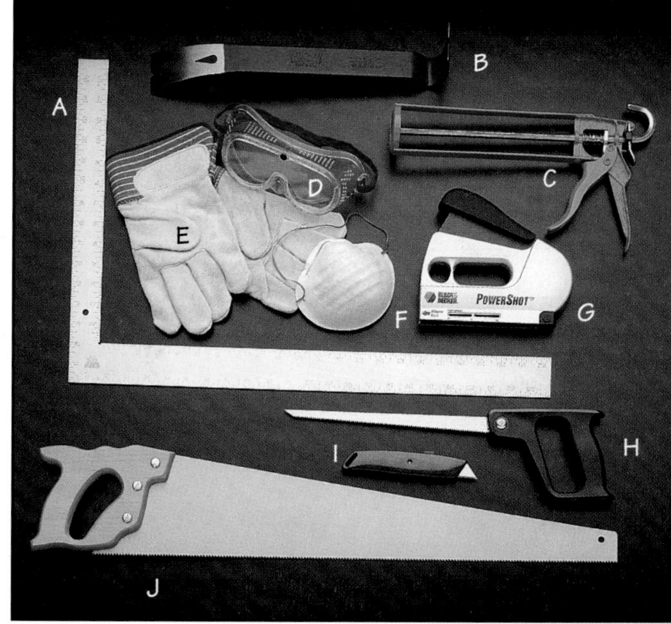

Basic insulating tools include: framing square or straightedge (**A**), flat pry bar (for pushing insulation into tight spaces) (**B**), caulk gun (**C**), safety glasses (**D**), work gloves (**E**), dust mask (**F**), hand stapler (**G**), keyhole saw (**H**), utility knife (**I**), and handsaw (**J**).

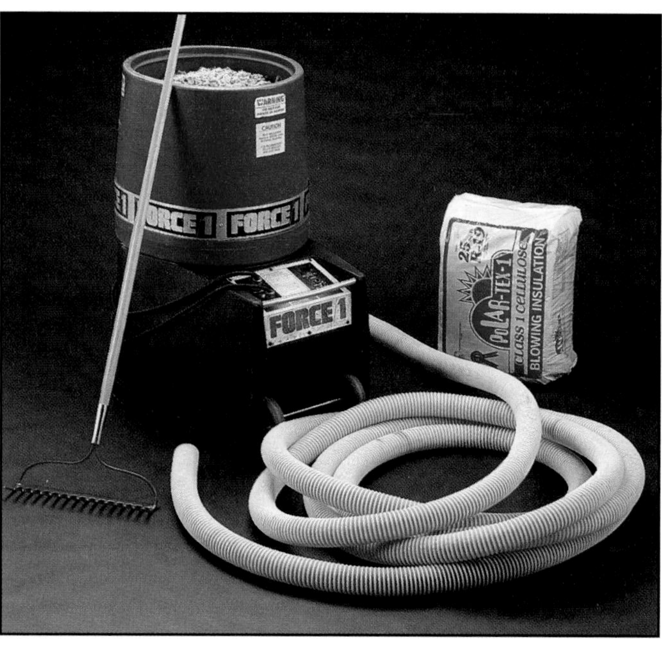

Loose-fill insulation tools include a loose-fill insulation blower (available at most rental centers) and a common garden rake.

Fiberglass insulation includes: friction-fit batts (**A**), kraft paper faced rolls (**B**), and attic blankets (**C**). Insulation manufacturers are moving away from roll insulation and going towards batt insulation only. Be sure to ask, where you buy the insulation, what the appropriate form is for your application.

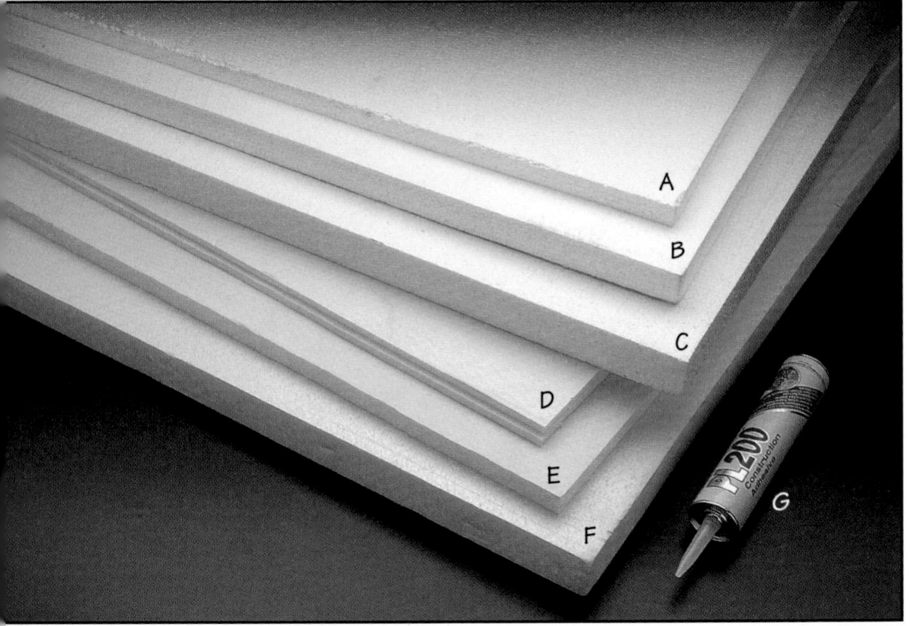

Rigid insulation boards and materials include: 3/4" thick foam (**A**), 1 1/2" thick foam (**B**), 2" thick foam (**C**), 3/4" thick styrene (**D**), 1 1/2" thick styrene (**E**), 2" thick styrene (**F**), and panel adhesive (**G**).

INSULATION GUIDE

Cold Climate	
Attic or roof: R38	
Wall: R19	Floor: R22
Moderate Climate	
Attic or roof: R26	
Wall: R19	Floor: R11
Thickness chart:	
Fiberglass:	
R13	3 1/2"
R21	5 1/4"
R25	7 1/4"
R30	10"
Open-cell polystyrene:	
R4	1"
R6	1 1/2"
R8	2"
Extruded polystyrene:	
R5	1"
R10	2"

SAFETY ALERT

Wear safety glasses, work gloves, particle mask and long sleeves when insulating.

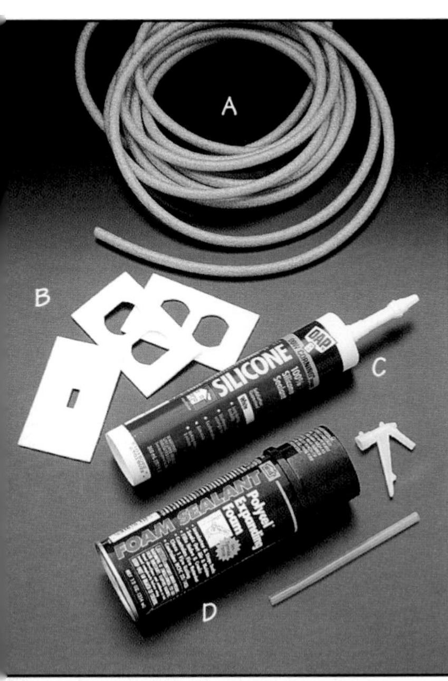

Weatherproofing materials include: caulking backer rope (**A**), switch and receptacle sealers (**B**), silicone caulk (**C**), and sprayable expanding insulating foam (**D**).

Weatherproofing materials for doors include: rubber and aluminum weather strips (**A**), metal v-channel (**B**), door sweep (**C**), threshold insert (**D**), and adhesive backed plastic v-channel (**E**).

Insulation materials and loose-fill include: attic insulation baffles (**A**), cellulose loose-fill insulation (**B**), and 6 mil plastic sheeting vapor barrier (**C**).

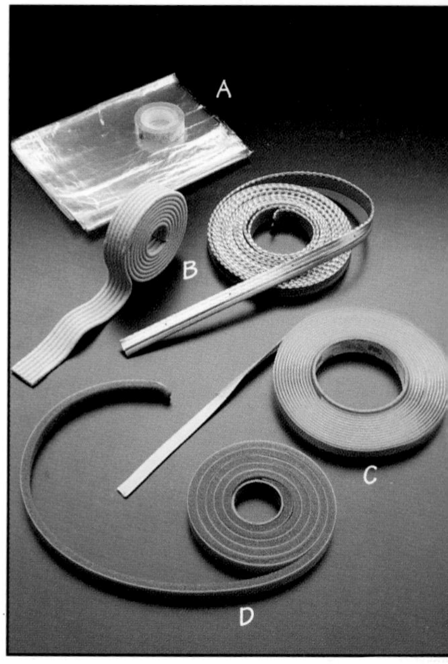

Weatherproofing materials for windows include: shrink-wrap window insulating kit (**A**), roll caulking (**B**), adhesive-backed caulk tape (**C**), and self-adhesive foam strips (**D**).

EVALUATING YOUR HOME'S ENERGY EFFICIENCY

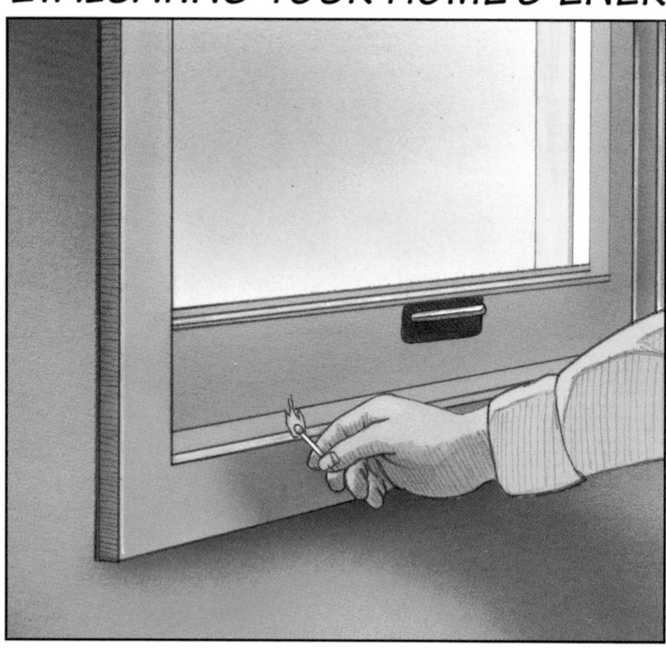

Check for drafts around windows and doors by holding a lit match to gaps at the door or window on a windy day. The flame will move or blow out, then hold the smoldering match to the area to see how the draft affects the smoke. Fluttering indicates weather stripping is inadequate, and it should be replaced or upgraded.

Measure the temperature in different parts of a room. Differences of more than one or two degrees indicate that the room is poorly sealed or air movement inside the house is restricted. Update weatherstripping around doors and windows, then measure temperatures again. If the differences still exist, you may have an air flow problem with your heating system. Often, your public utility company provides information about air flow problems and how to correct them.

Make a visual inspection of existing weather stripping and insulation. Look for signs of deterioration, such as crumbling foam or rubber; hardening of flexible products, such as felt or foam rubber; or damaged or torn metal stripping. Replace the products as needed. Most weatherstripping products will last only a few years so expect this to be a seasonal chore.

Conduct an energy audit on your home with the assistance of your local public utility company. Most power companies will provide either an energy audit kit, or conduct the audit for you—sometimes free of charge. The audit will help you identify any energy loss areas, and recommend solutions.

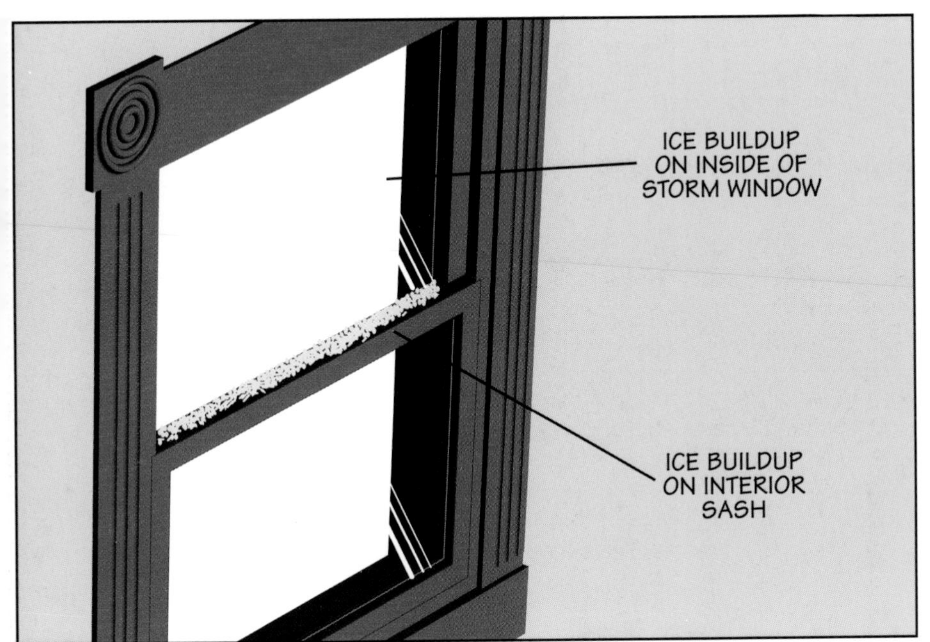

Look for condensation, frost, or ice buildup on the inside surfaces of interior window sashes. Moisture buildup indicates that interior windows are not properly protected from the colder air outside. Check the seal around storm windows. If you find gaps, fill them with foam backer rope or peelable caulk. Check for condensation, frost, or ice buildup on storm windows or the outside surface of interior windows. Condensation indicates that warm, moist air is escaping, and that the seal between the interior window and the storm window needs attention. Fill any voids with peelable caulk or install clear plastic over the exterior of the storm window.

VAPOR BARRIERS

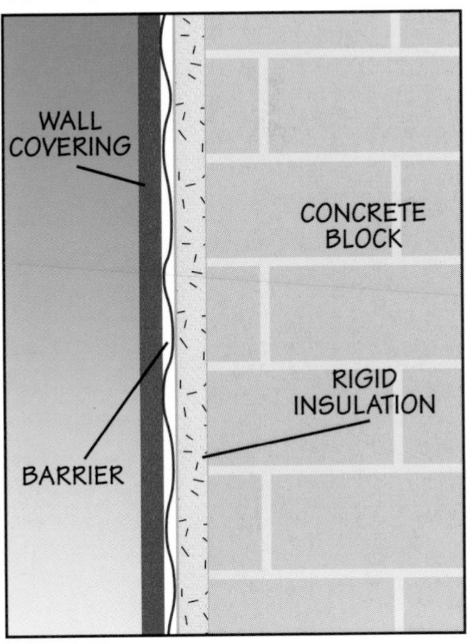

Install vapor barriers made of 4 mil or 6 mil poly on the warm-in-winter side of the insulation. Vapor barriers protect the structural members of your house from condensation that can occur where warm, humid air meets cold air.

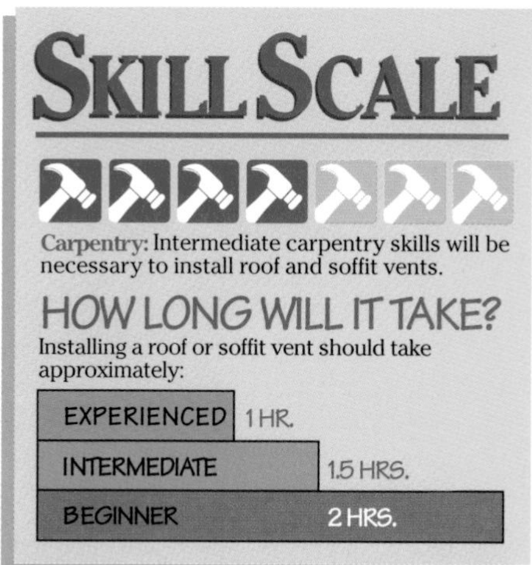

STUFF YOU'LL NEED:

- ☐ **Tools:** Hammer, reciprocating saw, drill w/bits, roofing knife, jigsaw.
- ☐ **Materials:** Roof vents, soffit vents, roof cement.

Installing Soffit & Roof Vents

Proper air circulation is an important part of a healthy roof and soffit system. If you have inadequate venting, you risk wood rot, mildew, and water damage in your attic from trapped moisture. You can also have exterior roofing problems along with higher cooling costs in the summer.

A balanced circulation system will have one square foot of venting for every 300 cubic feet of free air in an attic. Use this ratio to find how many vents you need.

You should have an equal distribution of intake (soffit) and outtake (roof) vents for the circulation to be effective. Check for blockages of airflow in your attic vents, baffles and roof vents. Also check for improperly installed attic insulation, which is a common contributor to poor ventilation.

Vents can range from static open units and turbine style to thermostatically controlled electric fan units. The type of vent you purchase will depend on the amount of air you need to move, the size of your attic, the scope of the project you wish to undertake and, of course, your budget!

HOMER'S HINDSIGHT

Soffit and roof vents are designed to provide circulation for the attic space. Installing them can also be a refresher course in common sense. My first vent project went so quickly that I forgot to install baffles before insulating. When my vents didn't work, I had to crawl back through the attic and all that insulation just to install the baffles that should have gone in first!

EFFECTIVE INSULATION REQUIRES VENTILATION

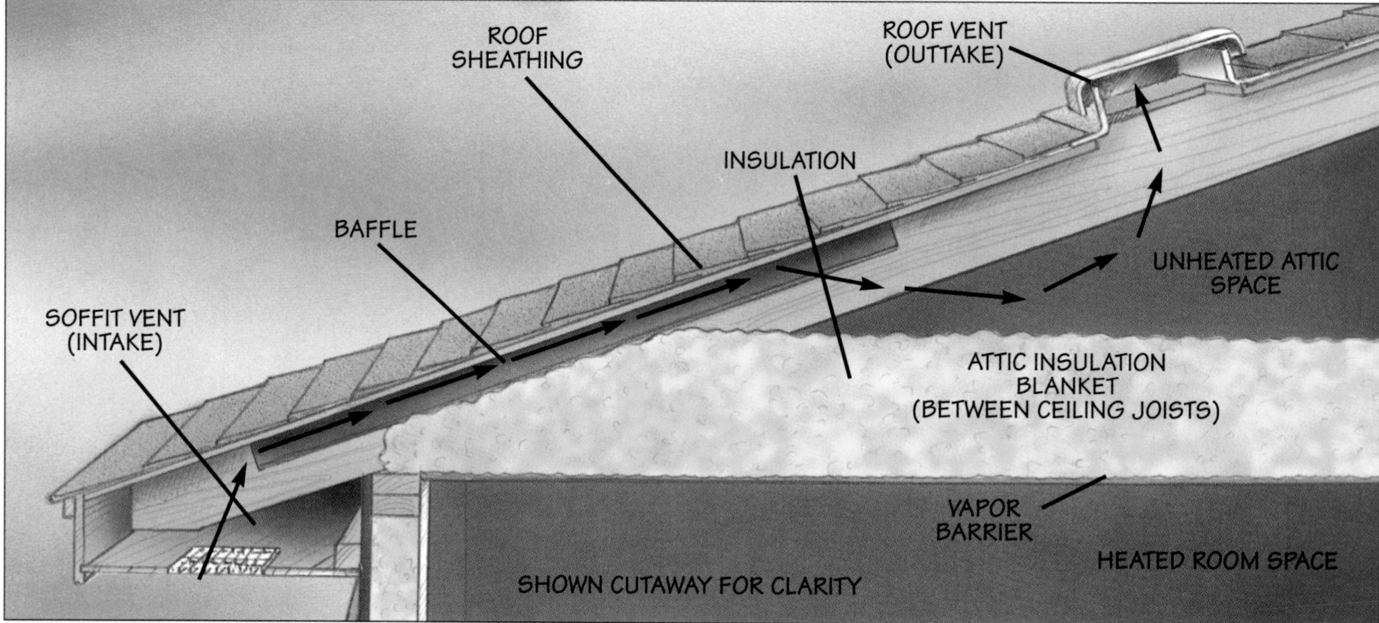

Sufficient airflow is critical to proper roof system ventilation. Airflow prevents heat build-up in your attic, and helps protect your roof from damage caused by condensation or ice. A typical ventilation system has vents in the soffits to admit fresh air, which flows upward beneath the roof sheathing and exits through roof vents.

Measure attic space to determine amount of vents per cubic foot. You should have 1 square foot of unblocked vent for every 300 cubic feet of free attic space. Distribute intake and outtake vents evenly throughout your attic. For adequate air circulation, vents must draw and release air through multiple sources. An easy way to approximate the volume of air in the attic is to multiply the floor space in the attic by the height of the attic at the peak, then divide by two.

SOFFIT VENT OPTIONS

Soffit vents can be added to increase air flow into attics on houses with a closed soffit system. Make sure there is an unobstructed air passage from the soffit area to the roof before you install new soffit vents.

Continuous soffit vents provide even air flow into attics. They are usually installed during new construction, but they can be added as retrofits to unvented soffit panels.

ROOF VENT OPTIONS

Install roof vents when you simply need to add more outtake vents. Installation is fairly simple. You can install a powered vent fan to increase air circulation without adding several more vents.

Install gable vents in the ends of gables. These vents function the same as other roof vents, but are less conspicuous in nature.

Install continuous ridge vents as a solution to inadequate attic ventilation. Because ridge vents span the entire length of the ridge, they provide more consistent air circulation than other vents. Ridge vents are best installed during roof construction, but can be retrofitted during a reroofing job.

INSTALLING SOFFIT VENTS

1 From inside the attic, locate and mark a place for the soffit vent that allows the air to flow freely. Drill through the soffit to enable you to spot the location from outside.

2 Outline the vent on the soffit. Be sure the vent will fall between rafter ends or nailer strips.

SAFETY
Use a secure platform (ladder or scaffolding) when working at above ground elevations.
ALERT

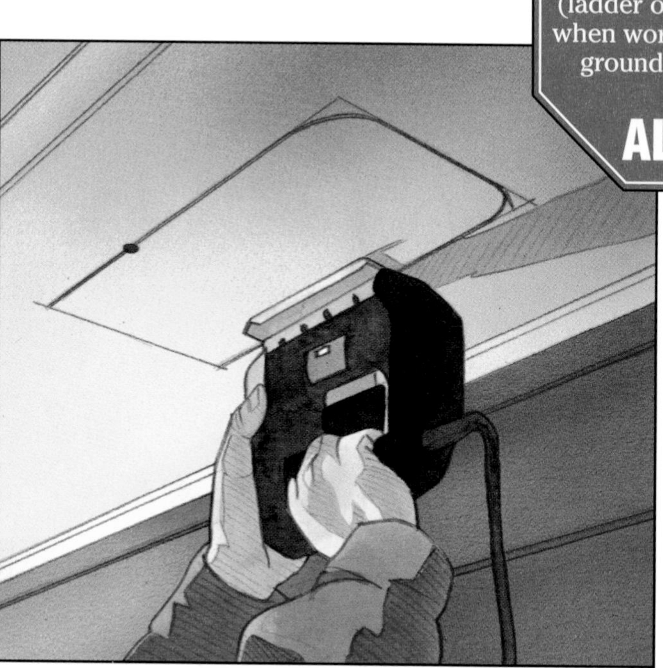

3 Cut vent openings $^1/_4$" inside the marked lines to leave room for fastening the vent covers.

4 Install the soffit vents and fasten them with stainless steel or galvanized wood screws.

INSTALLING A ROOF VENT

1 Drive a nail through the roof from inside to mark the position of the vent hole. Locate roof vents high on the roof, but below the ridge line, and on the least visible slope of the house. Place the vent between rafters, so you do not cut through a rafter. Locate turbine vents close to the ridge, with a minimum clearance of 8" above the ridge line. Use the nail as a centerpoint and mark a circle with a diameter equal to opening on the vent.

2 Remove the shingles just above and to the side of the cutout area that will be covered by the flange base of the vent. Do not remove shingles below the vent location. The base flange will overlap the shingles below. Drive the centering nail back through the roof. Drill a pilot hole and use a reciprocating saw to cut the vent hole.

3 Apply roofing cement to the underside of the base flange, and center the vent over the hole. Nail the base flange at the top and side edges. Cover the nail holes and edges of the flange with roofing cement.

4 Reattach the surrounding shingles. Cut the shingles to fit around the flange, similar to shingling around a vent pipe.

Installing Fiberglass Insulation

Adding fiberglass insulation to attics or basement walls is a quick, easy do-it-yourself project that will provide you with immediate payback in energy savings.

Most local building codes require minimum amounts of insulation for new construction. Check with your building inspector–these minimum requirements make good guidelines for owners of older homes as well.

The ability of an insulation type to resist the flow of heat is measured by its "R-value."

In this section you'll learn how to install a fiberglass attic blanket. You may also want to consider blowing in loose insulation for attics (pg. 400) if your existing level of insulation is low. Once you have an adequate amount of blown insulation, fiberglass attic blankets work well to provide additional coverage over the blown insulation.

You'll also learn how to attach rigid insulation boards to the inside walls of your basement. As an alternative, you can install fiberglass batts between 2x4 furring by simply stapling them to the wall studs.

Regardless of what type of insulation you use in your attic, be sure you have adequate air flow (pg. 394) to avoid condensation problems. Adequate air flow requires proper baffling and venting and should be done prior to any additional insulating.

Fiberglass insulation is fairly easy to work with and handle, but has one major drawback. The fine fibers in the fiberglass tend to get airborne as you work with it. These fibers get itchy and scratchy when they come in contact with exposed skin and also, can eventually cause respiratory problems if inhaled over a period of time. Protect yourself by wearing a particle mask or respirator, safety glasses or goggles, long-sleeve shirt, work gloves and cap when working with fiberglass insulation. This outfit will be hot, especially in the attic!

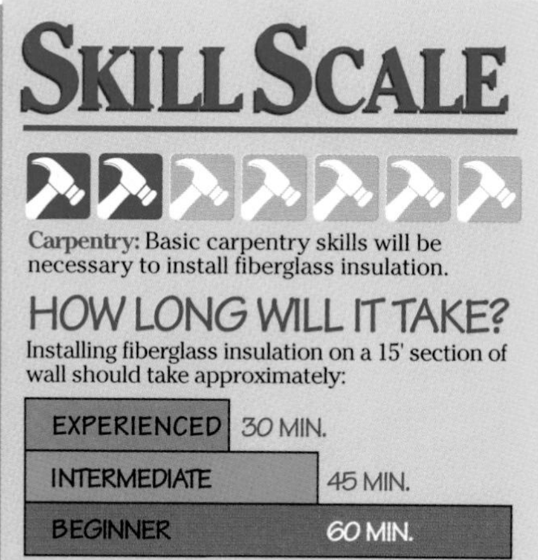

USING BAFFLES TO PROMOTE VENTILATION

Install baffles to keep new attic insulation from blocking the flow of air through your attic. You can purchase and install ready-made baffles, or make your own from plywood or rigid insulation board.

STUFF YOU'LL NEED:

- ☐ **Tools:** Utility knife, hand stapler, work gloves, goggles, particle mask.
- ☐ **Materials:** Insulation, baffles, chicken wire.

INSULATING ADDITIONAL ENERGY LOSS AREAS

Install fiberglass insulation between floor joists over crawl spaces or unheated basements. Make sure the vapor barrier faces up, and install chicken wire or insulation stays to hold the insulation in place.

Insulate the rim joist at the top of your foundation walls by filling it loosely with fiberglass insulation. Pack the insulation just tightly enough that it does not fall out.

Insulate garage walls in attached garages. Use faced fiberglass insulation with the vapor barrier facing into the garage. Cover with wallboard in areas that are vulnerable to damage.

TIPS FOR WORKING WITH INSULATION

Build dams to keep attic insulation away from recessed ceiling lights, vent fans, and other electrical fixtures that generate heat and are not rated for contact with insulation.

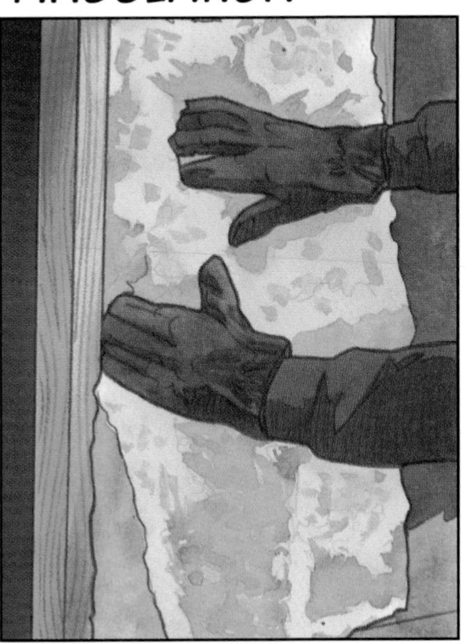

Don't compress insulation to fit a spot. Insulation needs air space within the material to be effective in resisting heat transfer. If the insulation you want to install is too thick, trim or tear it to match the depth of the wall, ceiling or floor cavity.

Attach fiberglass insulation with pre-attached vapor barriers by folding over the paper flap and stapling to wall studs.

Installing Loose-Fill Insulation

If your house has already been built but needs insulation (most do), consider cellulose. It's inexpensive, has a high R-value, and you can apply it behind existing walls and ceilings.

To install cellulose, drill holes and blow it in place with a machine that is like a shop vacuum run in reverse. The holes are easily camouflaged—drill them behind a piece of siding you've temporarily removed. Most stores that sell cellulose rent blowers and show you how to use them.

STUFF YOU'LL NEED:

- ☐ **Tools:** Tape measure, hand stapler, drill w/bits, insulation blower, ladder, hammer, pry bar.
- ☐ **Materials:** Cellulose insulation, staples, foam baffles, fiberglass insulation, anils.

INSULATING THE ATTIC

1 Block off areas where you don't want the cellulose. You don't want to block ventilation so install a baffle above each soffit vent to provide an air passage. (If you have a continuous soffit vent, install a baffle in every third space between rafters.)

2 Once the baffles are in, block off the soffit, so it won't fill with cellulose and cause moisture problems. Block the soffit by cutting sections of fiberglass insulation and stuffing them between the joists just before the soffit.

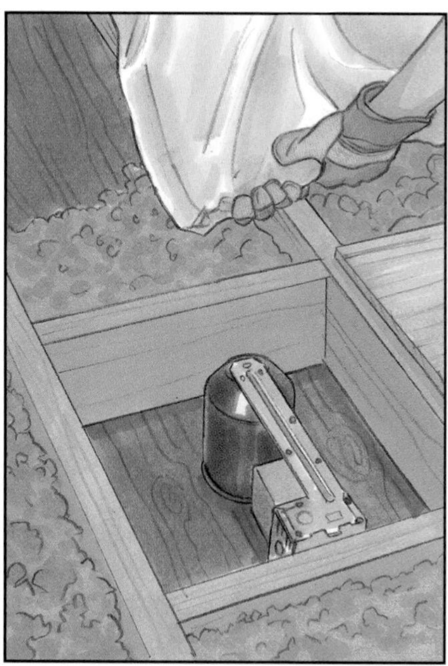

3 The National Electrical Code (and common sense) require that you keep insulation at least 3 inches from heat-producing fixtures like recessed ceiling lights. Nail 2-bys between the joists, positioning them to keep the cellulose away from the fixture.

4 If the attic has a floor, remove a board to give you access to the bays between the joists. Insert the blower hose the entire length of the bay and back it out as the space in front of it fills with insulation. If there's no floor, put down pieces of plywood, and walk along them as you spray the insulation in place.

BLOWING LOOSE-FILL INTO A WALL

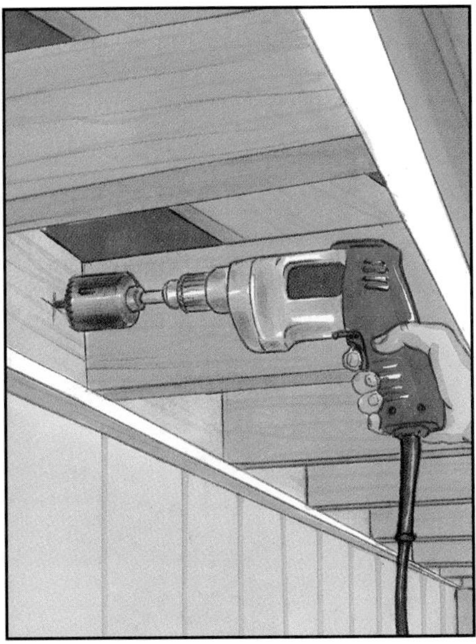

1 Drill access holes that are the diameter of the blower's filler hose. If you drill the holes from outdoors, remove a piece of siding first. Pick a piece slightly above the interior floor level and drill holes through the sheathing. On the top floor, you can remove the fascia or soffit instead of the siding.

2 You also can insulate from inside the house. Remove the baseboard and drill holes in the wall behind it. Drill the holes at least 1½ inches off the floor in order to avoid the interior framing. On the second floor, it may be easier to hide the holes by drilling down into the wall from the attic.

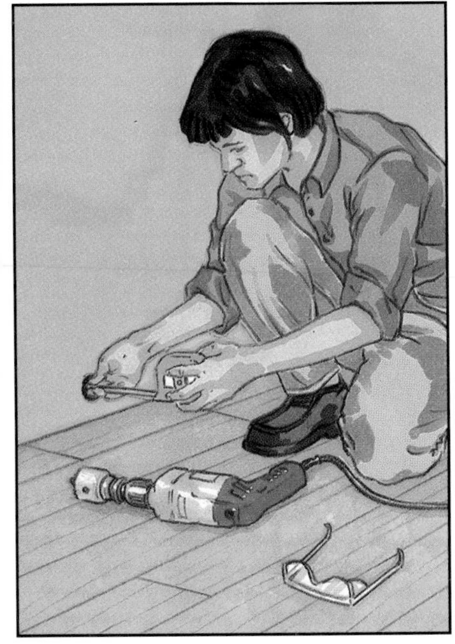

3 Check with your tape measure for obstructions that might block the insulation. If the tape hits an obstruction, drill an access hole above it. When you insulate, fill the bay from both the original hole and the new one.

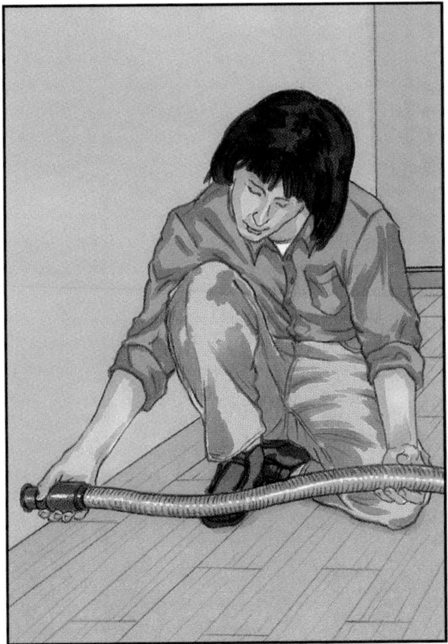

4 Once the holes are drilled, insert the filler tube and push it to within 18 inches of the top of the wall. Blow in the insulation, retracting the tube as the bay fills. When you've insulated the entire wall, cover the holes by replacing the trim or siding you removed.

Most insulation requires a vapor barrier on the side that is warm in winter. With cellulose, however, you may not need one. You won't need a vapor barrier in the attic—as long as you have one square foot of ventilation for every 150 square feet of insulation. If you have less ventilation than that, paint the ceiling below the insulated area with special vapor-retarding paint. You won't need to paint the walls, unless the winter temperature typically drops below -15 F°. Before you insulate, look closely for peeling paint that may be a sign of existing moisture trouble. If the problem seems to get worse after you insulate—or if you see signs of trouble elsewhere—a coat of vapor-retarding paint on the inside wall should solve the problem.

Insulation blowers are usually available at the store where you buy the insulation and sometimes are included for use at no additional charge when certain quantities of insulation are purchased. Regardless how or where you get the blowing equipment, be sure to have the clerk or salesperson give you a complete demonstration of how the blower works before you take it home. Most blowers are similar in operation, but may have subtle differences that can cause injury, or just aggravation, if you're not made aware of them. Also check to make sure you have all of the fittings, attachments, and hoses before you leave, or else you may have a tough time finishing your specific application.

Insulating an Unfinished Attic

The insulation you put in your attic does more than keep your house from losing heat in the winter, it also keeps your house from gaining heat in the summer. And when your home's warmth escapes through your roof, it not only inflates your heating bills, it also causes ice build-up that can ruin your roof.

Having enough insulation is only part of the solution, though. You need to provide for adequate ventilation in your attic space as well.

Your first order of business before adding insulation will be to check your attic's ventilation. Make certain that the insulation you add doesn't interfere with the vents. Installing baffles at the eaves will preserve the free flow of fresh air.

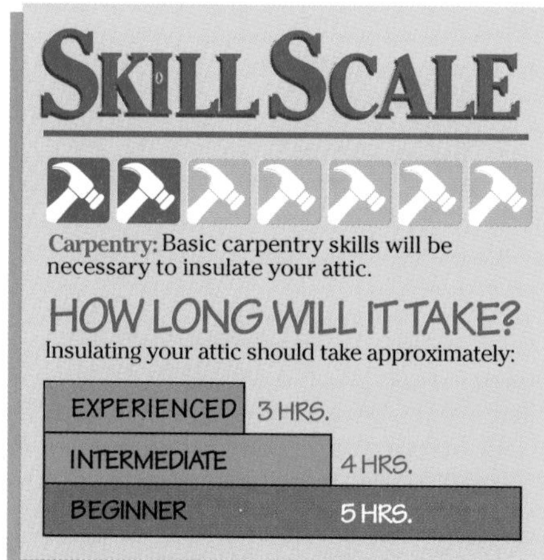

STUFF YOU'LL NEED:

- ☐ **Tools:** Utility knife, straightedge, dust mask, safety goggles.
- ☐ **Materials:** 6 mil poly, insulation blankets, baffles.

ADDING ATTIC INSULATION

1 Inspect your existing insulation by measuring the depth and evaluating the condition of the vapor barrier. Patch any damage to the vapor barrier (if the attic is completely uninsulated, lay strips of 6 mil poly between the ceiling joists and staple to the joist tops).

2 Install baffles at the eave areas of the attic to keep the new insulation from restricting the air flow along the roof sheathing.

USE A PLANK OR PLYWOOD TO STAND ABOVE THE JOISTS

3 Measure the insulation runs between joists from top sill plate to top sill plate. Cut rolls to length in a well-ventilated work area. Use a straightedge and a sharp utility knife.

4 Roll out the blanket starting at the outside and working toward the access point. Overlap slightly when butting seams. For maximum insulation, roll out a second blanket layer perpendicular to the first layer. Don't use backed insulation or another layer of vapor barrier.

Insulating Basement Walls

An insulated basement makes that space more comfortable and helps keep the upstairs floors warmer, too. One of the easiest, most effective, and commonly used forms of insulation for masonry walls is rigid foam.

Rigid foam is available in both urethane and polystyrene, in thicknesses from ½" to 2". Of the two varieties, urethane is the more expensive, but also the easier to work with and the better insulator.

Rigid foam panels are cut with a knife or an insulation saw so that they fit snugly between preinstalled furring strips, then glued to the masonry with panel adhesive.

A vapor barrier should be stapled over the insulation. This prevents dampness emanating from the masonry wall from damaging the wallboard sheath, which should be applied over the foam insulation as a fire-protective measure.

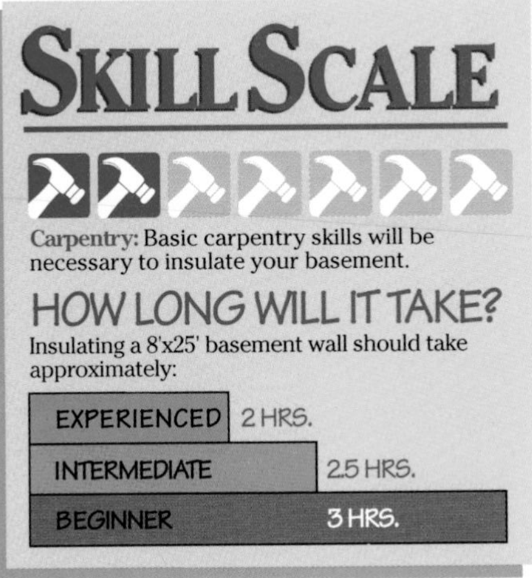

STUFF YOU'LL NEED:

- ☐ **Tools:** Utility knife, caulk gun, insulation or keyhole saw, straightedge, tape measure.
- ☐ **Materials:** 6 mil poly, rigid insulation, panel adhesive.

WORKING WITH RIGID FOAM INSULATION

1 Attach furring strips to wall spaced to fit the width of rigid foam board insulation. Align the strips with a plumb line and use masonry anchors to attach them to the wall.

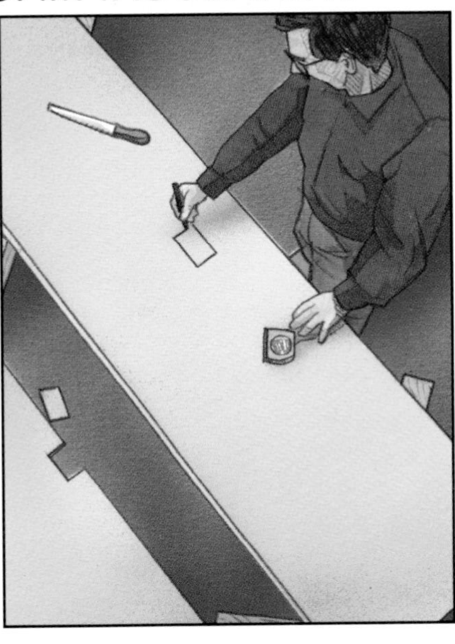

2 Cut the rigid panels to fit between furring strips, from sill plate to cap plate, using an insulation board saw (looks like a keyhole saw). Mark cutouts for windows, jacks and other obstructions.

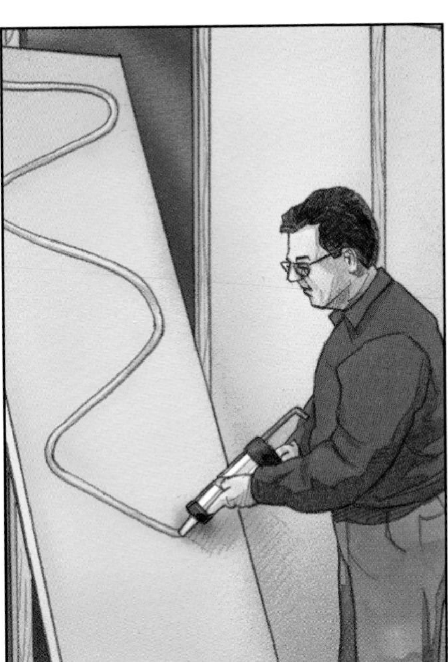

3 Attach the boards to the wall and plates (make sure they're clean and dry) with panel adhesive that will not dissolve the insulation.

4 Staple a plastic vapor barrier to the furring strips, then attach the wall covering of your choice to protect the insulation and vapor barrier, and provide a more attractive look.

Weatherproofing Your House

Most weatherproofing projects involve windows and doors, because these are the primary heat-loss areas in most homes. Caulk and weatherstripping are the principal tools used to weatherize windows and doors. Storm windows and storm doors also play an important role in weatherproofing your home. Similar products like plastic window-well covers can make a significant contribution.

There are many types of weatherstripping materials available and most are designed for specific applications. Generally metal or metal reinforced weatherstripping is more durable than products made solely from plastic, rubber, or foam.

Weatherproofing your house is an ideal project for homeowners because it can be done a little at a time, according to your schedule.

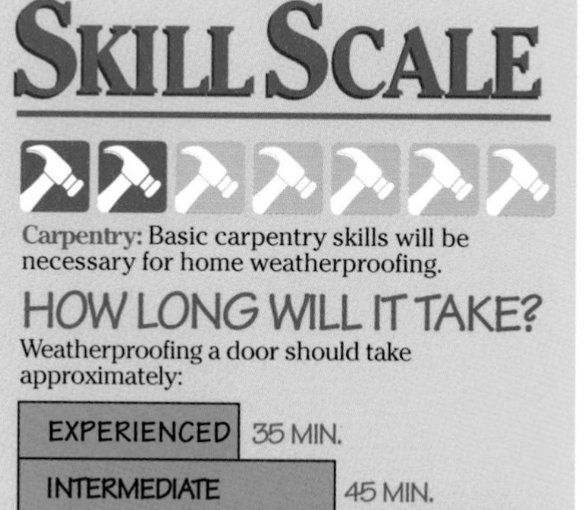

STUFF YOU'LL NEED:

- ☐ **Tools:** Hammer, putty knife, screwdrivers, pry bar, wood chisel, stapler, caulk gun.
- ☐ **Materials:** Silicone caulk, expandable insulating foam, weatherstripping, wood filler.

Cover window wells with preformed window-well covers to minimize heat loss through your basement windows. Most window-well covers have an upper flange designed to slip under the siding. Fasten them to foundation walls with masonry anchors, and weight down the bottom flange with stones or gravel. Caulk around the edges for extra weather protection.

Before purchasing the window-well covers, measure the widest point of your window well, and be sure to note whether it is rectangular or semicircular in design.

WEATHERPROOFING TIPS

Caulk around dryer vents, exhaust vents from vent fans, and any other fittings mounted to the side of your house.

Seal between baseboards and floorboards. Remove the base shoe and spray in expandable foam. While preventing drafts, this also stops insects from entering your living areas. Be aware that a little foam goes a long way. Don't overuse or it will expand too much.

Insulate around spigots, television cable jacks, telephone lines, and other entry points to your house with expanding foam insulation. Be careful when working around power service cables.

WEATHERPROOFING AN ENTRY DOOR

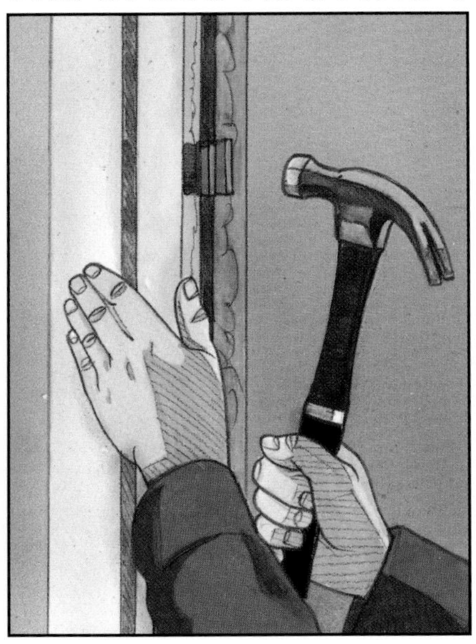

Adjust the door if it has fallen out of alignment. Evening out gaps around doors will save a lot of time and weatherstripping material. Reset and shim hinges to even out gaps and adjust strike plates and latches to keep doors snug in their frames.

1 Install metal tension strips next to the door stops, at the point where the door contacts the stops when closed. Pry out the tension strips with a putty knife to create a good seal. Lever out the half of the strip that contacts the door with a putty knife to create a good seal when the door is closed.

2 Add reinforced felt seal stripping to the edge of the door stop on the exterior side.

3 Attach a new bristle sweep to the bottom of the door.

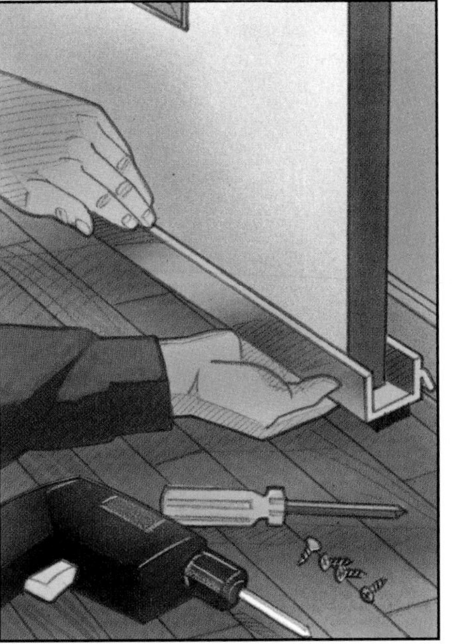

Option: Attach a new door bottom with an integral sweep on the inside and drip edge on the outside. This may require that you adjust your threshold height, or plane the bottom of the door slightly. If you plane the door, make sure to seal the wood.

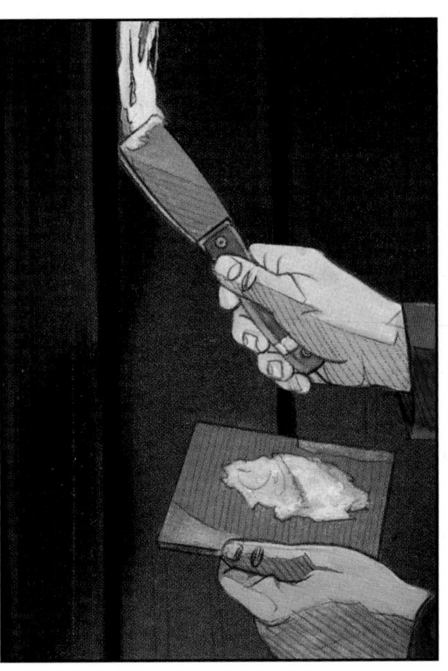

4 Fix any cracks in door panels or around light panels with wood filler or caulk.

REPLACING A THRESHOLD

1 Cut the old threshold with a back saw, then pry out the pieces. Clean area below threshold.

2 Measure the opening for the new threshold and cut to fit. Lay a bead of caulk then position and attach the new threshold. Make sure the angle is sloping slightly away from the house so water does not build up or enter through the new threshold.

3 Cut and install the threshold. Insert screws in the slot in the top of the threshold. Test the fit. If it is too tight, plane down your door or lower the threshold.

WEATHERPROOFING OTHER DOOR TYPES

Use rubber compression strips to seal the channels in patio door jambs, where the movable panels fit when closed. Also install a patio door insulator kit, which is plastic sheeting installed on the interior side of the door.

Attach a new rubber sweep to the bottom, outside edge of the garage door if the old sweep has deteriorated. Also check the door jambs for drafts, and add weatherstripping, if needed.

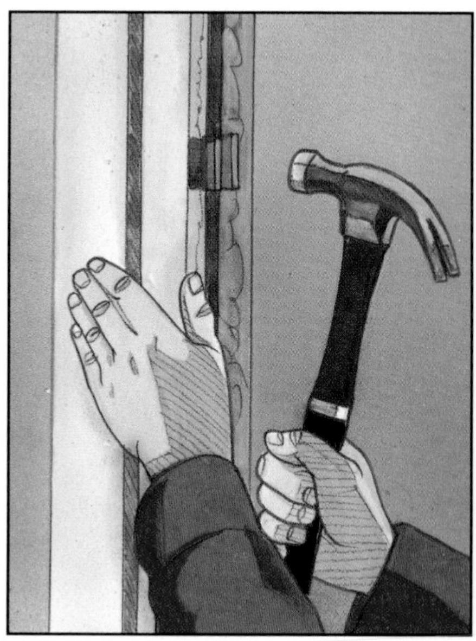

Adjust the door frame to eliminate large gaps between the door and the jamb. Remove the interior case molding and drive new shims between the jamb and the framing member on the hinge side. Close the door to test the fit, and adjust as needed before insulating and reattaching the case molding.

TIPS FOR MAINTAINING STORM DOORS

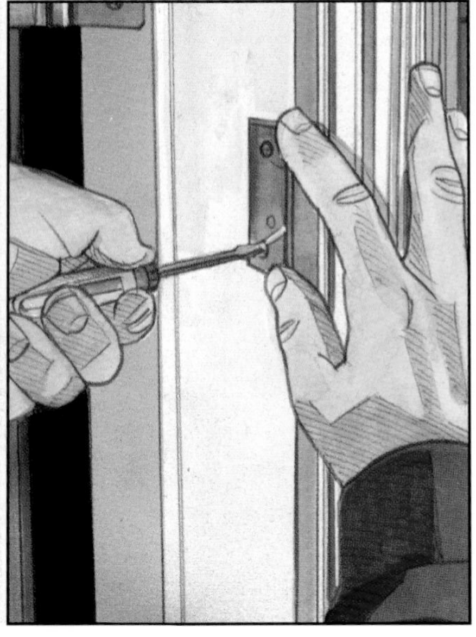

Test latches and adjust as needed. A properly functioning storm door latch draws the door tightly and securely into the frame, and holds it in place. Latch failure makes the door vulnerable to wind.

Add a wind chain if your storm door does not have one. Wind chains prevent doors from blowing open and off the hinges. Set the chain so the door will not open more than 90°.

Adjust door-closer tension to close the door securely, without slamming. Most closers have tension adjustment screws at one end of the cylinder. Closers usually will lock in place to hold doors open, but using them in this manner can lead to bent closing rods.

WEATHERPROOFING WINDOWS

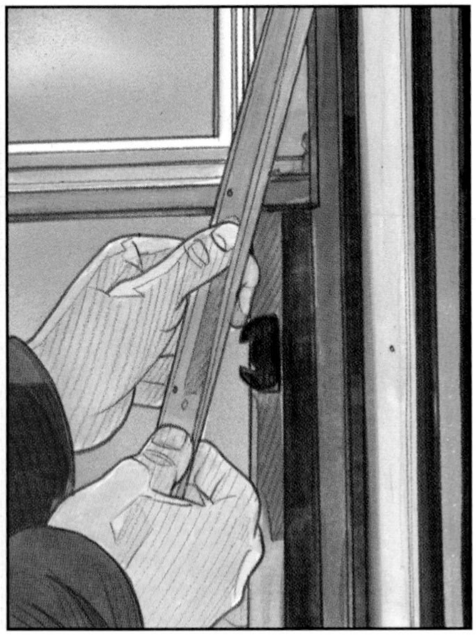

1 Cut and install metal v-channels in the sash channels. The v-channels should extend at least 2" beyond the sash ends when closed. Attach the v-channels with a tack hammer and the fasteners provided with the material.

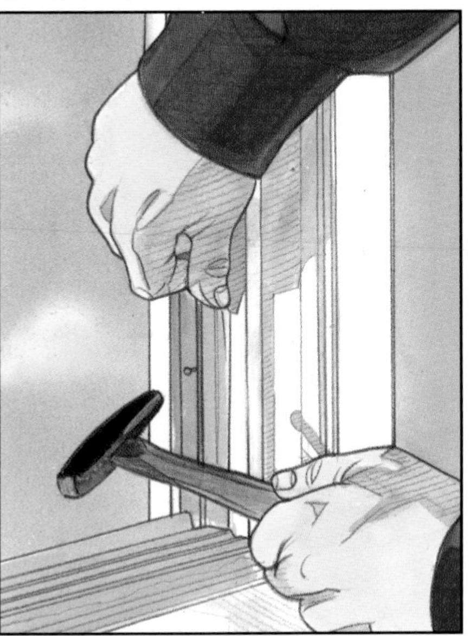

2 Drive the fasteners flush against the stripping so the window sash will not snag them. Flare out the open ends of the v-channels with a putty knife to create a tight seal with the sash.

3 Wipe down the underside of the bottom sash with a damp rag and wait for it to dry, then attach self-adhesive compressible foam to the outside edge of the sash underside. Use high-quality hollow neoprene strips. Self-adhesive strips won't stick if the surface is too cold (about 50 degrees F).

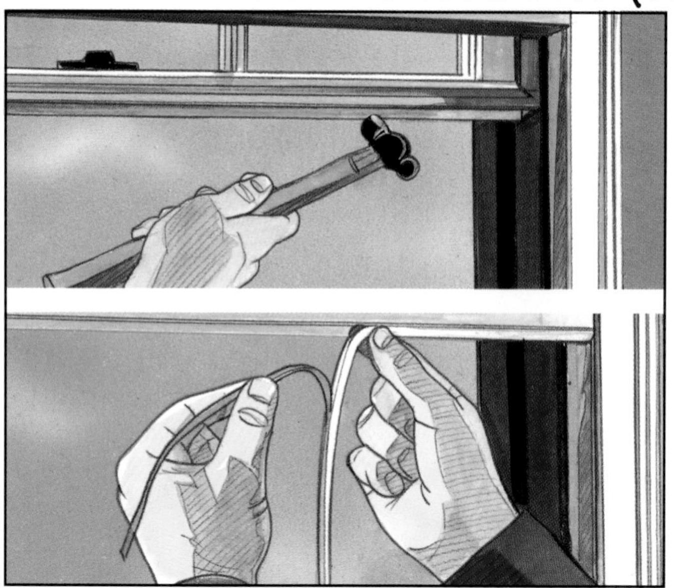

4 Seal the gap where the top sash meets the bottom sash. For double-hung windows, lift the bottom sash and lower the top sash to create access to the bottom rail of the top sash, and tack a metal tension strip to the inside face. For single-hung windows with a stationary top sash tack tubular gasket or reinforced felt to the outside face of the top rail on the bottom sash. Position the strip so it compresses slightly against the top sash when the window is locked shut.

5 Apply caulk around the interior window casing with clear silicone caulk. For added protection, lock the window in the closed position and caulk the gaps around the interior edges of the sash with clear, peelable caulk, which can be removed easily when the heating season is over.

Add plastic sheeting, or a shrink-wrap product, to the window interior to block drafts and keep moisture away from the window surfaces. Follow the manufacturer's installation directions, which often include using a hair dryer to tighten the plastic and remove wrinkles, making it almost invisible.

Install exterior plastic sheeting on the outside of your window, following the manufacturer's directions. Rolls of tacking or stapling strips are often included with the product.

WEATHERPROOFING OTHER WINDOW TYPES

Attach metal v-channels to sliding windows where the sash fits. Also attach reinforced felt around the remaining three sides of the sash. Use a tubular gasket to seal the gap where the sashes meet.

Attach self-adhesive, foam compression strips to casement windows around the window stops on all four sides of the sash. Self-adhesive strips won't stick if the surface is too cold (about 50 degrees F).

Use the same strategy on metal-and vinyl-clad windows as with wood-frame windows, but use only self-adhesive weather stripping products that will not puncture the cladding.

TIPS FOR WEATHERPROOFING STORM WINDOWS

Create a tight seal by attaching foam compression strips to the outside of the storm window stops. Fill any gaps between the exterior window trim and the storm window with caulk backer rope.

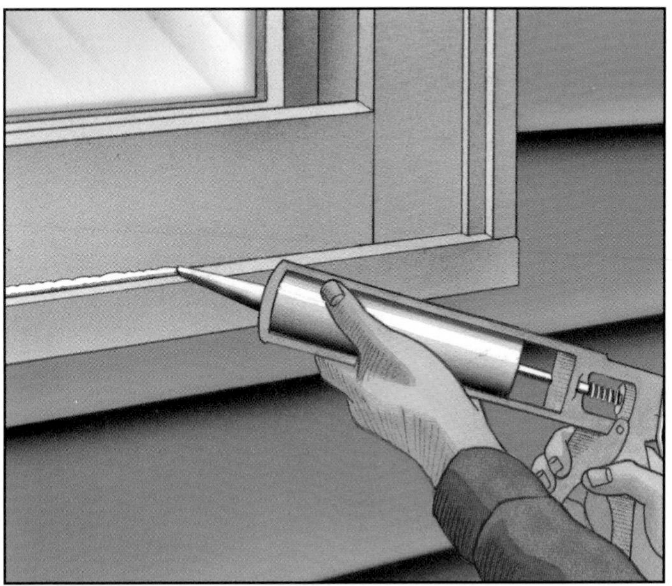

When using peelable caulk around the storm windows, be careful not to seal the weep holes. These allow moisture to escape.

EXTERIOR MAINTENANCE BASICS

Every hour of every day, paint is peeling, shingles are curling, gutters are sagging and decks are rotting all over America. It's called entropy–the natural tendency of things to break down over time–and it's hard at work on the exterior of your house.

When entropy visits the outside of your house, its effects are right out there for everyone to see. Without regular maintenance, the appearance of your house can quickly slide into shabby.

But don't despair, while the demands of exterior maintenance are persistent, the skills required are, happily, basic. When the exterior of your house is well maintained, it's safe, it looks good, it works the way it should, and it's right out there for everyone to see...and admire.

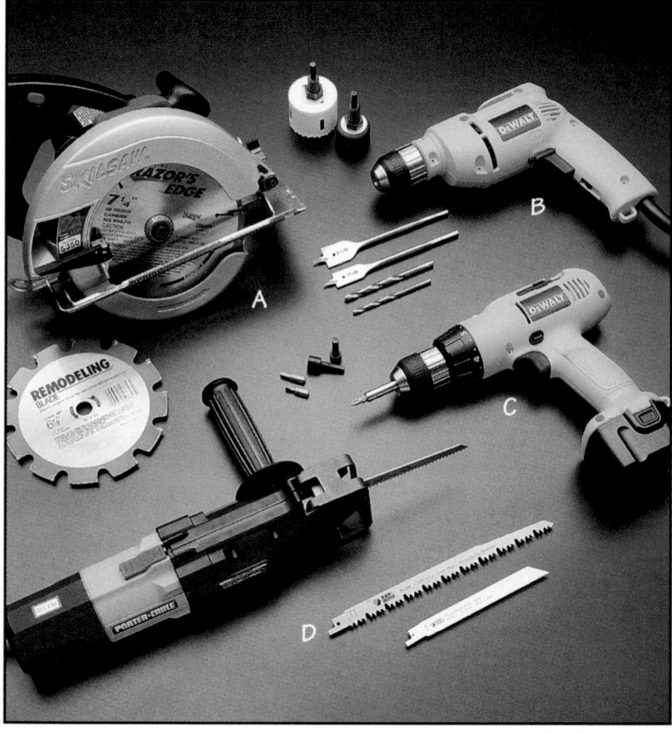

Exterior power tools include: circular saw (**A**), power drill w/bits (**B**), cordless drill/driver (**C**), reciprocating saw (**D**), and GFI extension cord (not pictured).

Exterior hand tools include: carpenter's level (**A**), caulk gun (**B**), putty knife (**C**), wire brush (**D**), hammer (**E**), combination square (**F**), tape measure (**G**), wood chisels (**H**), screwdrivers (**I**), flat bar (**J**), tin snips (**K**), locking pliers (**L**), pliers (**M**), hammer stapler (**N**), rivet gun (**O**), nail set (**P**), hack saw (**Q**), siding zip tool (**R**), ratchet wrench w/sockets (**S**), utility knife (**T**), hand saw (**U**), and framing square (**V**).

TOOL TIPS

Many tools are available from rental stores to make exterior home repair easier, but don't forget about the variety of equipment that makes it safer and more enjoyable too!

Depending on the type of work to be performed, you can find virtually any number of different pieces of equipment that will make the job safer and the work go more smoothly.

Working at elevations can be accomplished by simply using a stepladder or extension ladder. Be sure to use fiberglass ladders if you're working around power lines or performing electrical repair.

Ladder stabilizers can be added to provide more stability on extension ladders used at high elevations. They also prevent damaging the gutters by putting the ladder out away from the gutter system.

Ladder jacks are used with two or more extension ladders to allow you to work from a plank without having to use scaffolding. Either wooden or aluminum planks can be used with ladder jacks.

Big projects may require the use of scaffolding. This takes a little longer to set up, but makes a much more secure and stable platform to work from. You may want to use aluminum planking to provide a more "bounce-free" work platform than with conventional wooden planks.

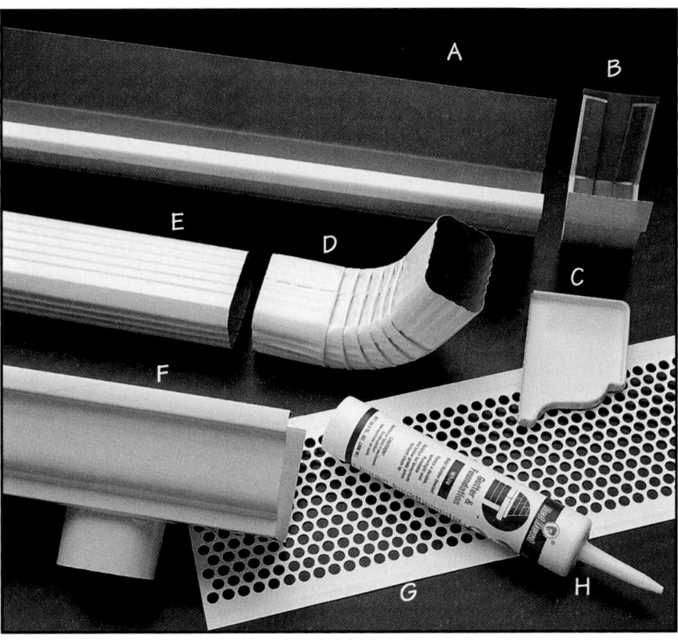

Exterior materials include: gutter section (**A**), gutter seam (**B**), gutter end cap (**C**), downspout elbow (**D**), downspout (**E**), downspout outlet (**F**), gutter screen (**G**), and silicone gutter caulk (**H**).

PREVENTING WATER INFILTRATION PROBLEMS

Proper grading will keep water away from the foundation and out of the basement. Slope all surface areas around the perimeter of your home away from the foundation.

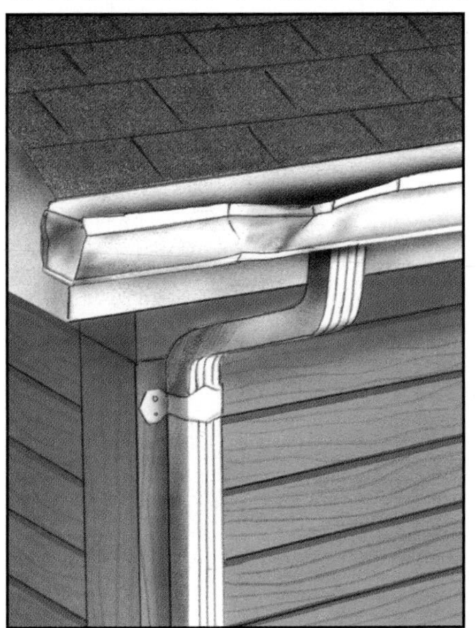

Improperly maintained gutters will not be effective in channeling rain water. They will back up and allow water to possibly infiltrate the roof system or build up at the foundation.

Downspout extensions direct gutter water away from the foundation and help to dissipate runoff along the grade.

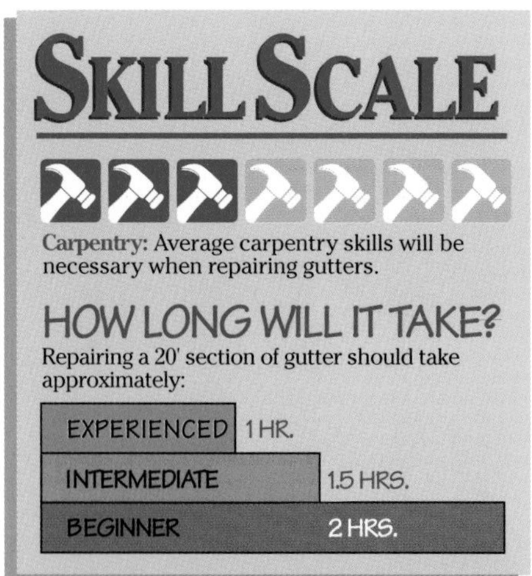

STUFF YOU'LL NEED:

- ☐**Tools:** Wire brush, paintbrush, rivet gun, pry bar, hacksaw, hammer, putty knife, scissors, caulk gun, screwdriver.
- ☐**Material:** Gutter liner, gutter adhesive/caulk, sheet metal screws, rivets, plastic roofing cement.

BUYER'$ GUIDE

Evaluating Gutters

Gutters are predominantly available in one of four different types, wood, galvanized steel, aluminum, and vinyl.

Wood gutters are usually made of fir, redwood or red cedar which are decay resistant and add a natural elegance to the exterior of a home.

Galvanized steel gutters are often the lowest priced of all systems and usually have an enamel finish. Unless frequently painted, galvanized gutters will have a shorter life than alternative gutters.

Aluminum gutters are available in several enamel colors and are lightweight and corrosion-resistant.

Vinyl gutters are becoming more popular because they are durable and easy to install. Sections and fittings are pre-colored and come in standard sizes that basically snap together.

Repairing Gutters

Gutters keep the water that falls on your roof from collecting near your foundation. Houses without gutters usually have a distinct "drip line," where the water that has fallen from the roof edge has eroded the soil beneath. Where entrances or walkways pass under a roof edge, gutters prevent the nuisance of water sheeting off the roof and directly onto passersby below.

Because gutters are a focal point for some of the harshest natural elements of deterioration–wind, water, ice and sunlight–damage from corrosion and physical stress is almost inevitable. When that happens leaks and resultant water damage can quickly follow.

Corrosion in a gutter system typically occurs from the inside out. If yours are beginning to leak as a result of corrosion having eaten its way through, your gutters' prognosis is not good. Patching (pg. 413) may provide a temporary solution, but this would be an excellent time to start shopping for a new gutter system.

Sometimes, even when the gutter system itself is sound, the gutter supports have failed in some fashion. If the gutters are sagging, water that would normally flow smoothly toward one of the downspouts pools instead at the low spot and then spills over the side of the gutter.

Sagging gutters may also be evidence that your fascia boards have deteriorated. Before remounting a sagging gutter, inspect the underlying fascia to determine its soundness.

USE CAUTION WHEN WORKING ON ELEVATED SURFACES!

INSTALLING GUTTER LINERS

1 Cut a section of gutter liner material to the desired length (cut it long enough to fill the entire run, if possible). For narrow gutters, trim the liner to the width as well. Slip the liner below the hangers, forming a continuous trough.

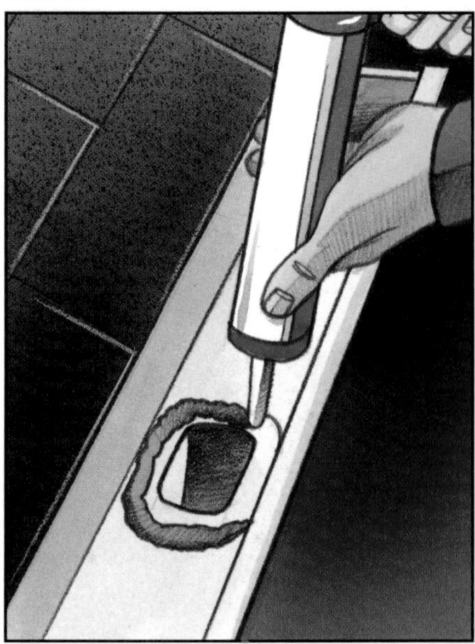

2 Attach downspout adapters and end caps or corner pieces, following the manufacturer's instructions. Connections are usually made with a special adhesive/caulk provided by the manufacturer with the liner.

REPAIRING LEAKY METAL GUTTERS

1 Clean the area around the leak with a wire brush and water, then once the area has dried, scrub it with an abrasive pad.

2 Apply plastic roofing cement over the leak and feather it out on the surrounding area to flatten any steep edges in the repair.

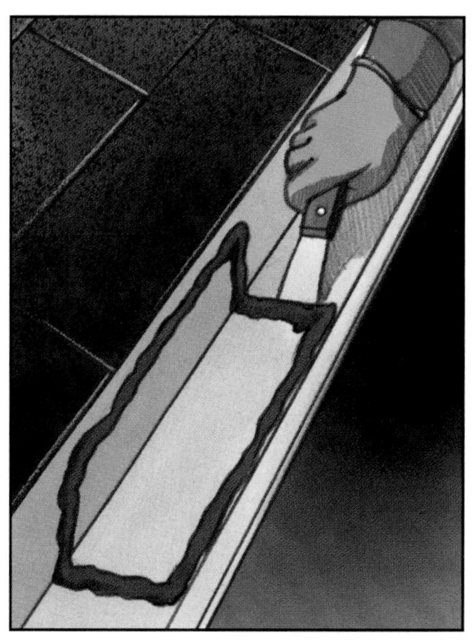

If the leaks are larger than nail holes, use tin snips to cut a strip of flashing (the same material as the gutter) wide enough to fill the area. Bend the strip to fit and imbed the flashing in the cement. Feather out the cement around the edges of the repair.

REPAIRING LEAKY JOINTS

1 Remove screws or connecting hardware at the joint and disassemble. You may need to remove other gutter or downspout sections near the leaky joint first.

2 Clean any caulk or adhesive from both parts of the joint using a stiff wire brush. Replace rubber gaskets on vinyl or PVC gutters.

3 Apply silicone caulk to one of the parts, at the joint area, then reassemble the gutter system. Resecure fasteners or connectors.

REPLACING A SECTION OF METAL GUTTER

1 Remove the screws and connectors from the entire section of gutter that contains the damaged area.

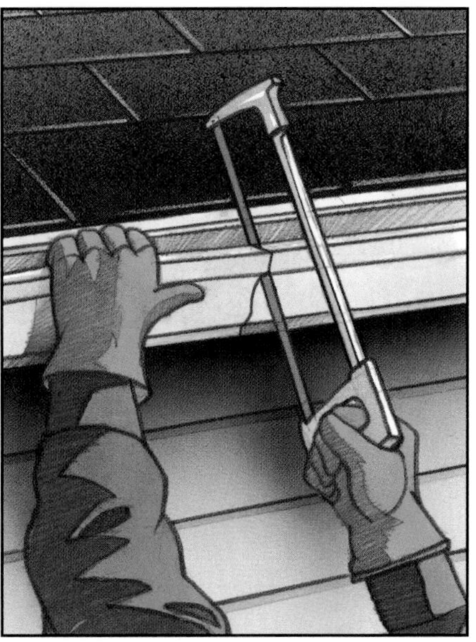

2 Remove the gutter section from the gutter hangers. For spike-and-ferrule fasteners, set a 2x4 spacer block in the gutter below the ferrule to protect the gutter and provide leverage, then pull out the spike.

3 Cut the replacement section of gutter so it is 2" longer than the removed section, using a hacksaw. Keep the spacer block in place to keep the gutter from bending while you cut.

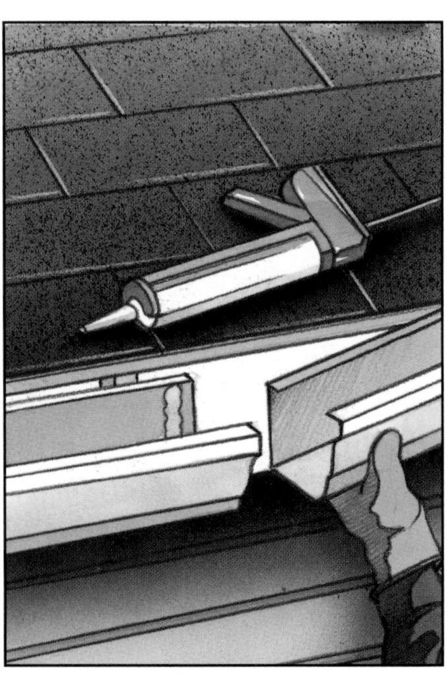

4 Apply plastic roof cement or special gutter repair compound to the overlap areas on the original gutters, and set the new section in place. Be sure to lap the upslope section of gutter on top of the downslope section to prevent undue wear on the sealed joint.

5 Drill pilot holes for rivets, then fasten the joints between the old and new gutter sections.

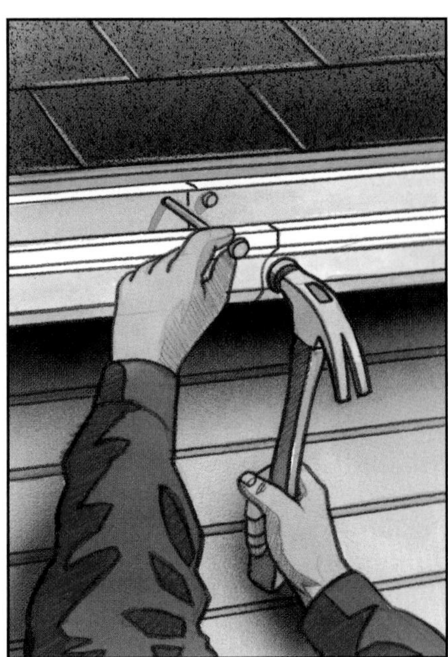

6 Drill pilot holes for spike-and-ferrule fasteners through gutters, with spacer blocks in place. Insert spikes in the front of the gutter, slip on the ferrules, then drive the spikes into the fascia until the heads are flush with the gutter.

Installing a Vinyl Gutter System

If you are faced with complete replacement of your gutter system, or would like to add a gutter system to your home, vinyl gutters can be a cost-effective choice that you can install yourself.

Though somewhat susceptible to extremes of heat and cold, they are, on the whole, extremely durable. Because vinyl gutters are corrosion free and permanently colored, they normally require very little maintenance.

Vinyl gutter systems are designed for homeowner and do-it-yourself installation, with modular components that easily snap together and also utilize a system of easy-to-install hanging brackets.

Snap-together gutter systems are assembled from preformed parts and connectors. Most systems use straight lengths, inside corners, outside corners, outlets, downspout offset, straight connectors, end caps, hanging brackets, and a splashblock or outlet.

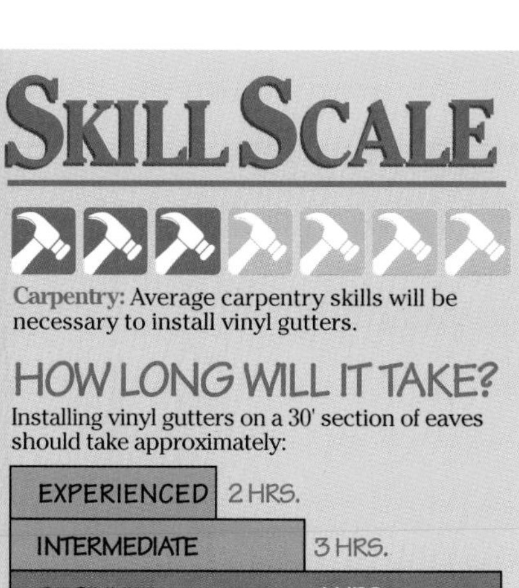

STUFF YOU'LL NEED:

- **Tools:** Hacksaw, chalk line, ladder, tape measure, hammer, cordless drill/driver, level.
- **Material:** Vinyl gutter system, screws.

ASSEMBLING AND HANGING VINYL GUTTERS

1 Start at the end opposite the downspout location, or in the middle on runs longer than 35'. Lay out a slope line for the gutters beginning 1" down from the eaves' overhang. Measure a slope of 1/4" per ten feet toward the downspout, then snap a chalkline.

2 Tack the downspout outlets and corners in position as a measuring aid. Make sure the tops are flush with the slope line. Follow the manufacturer's directions for recommended setback distances from the ends of the fascia.

ASSEMBLING AND HANGING VINYL GUTTERS (continued)

3 Install hanging brackets for the entire run, following the manufacturer's directions. Hangers should be attached every 24" to 30" on the fascia, with the tops flush with the slope line.

4 Begin hanging lengths of gutter at the downspout outlet. Lubricate the gaskets at the outlets and corners according to the manufacturer's directions. Hang gutter sections for the entire run, leaving space for connectors, if needed. Trim the pieces to fit with a hacksaw.

5 Join the sections together with the appropriate connectors, adjusting for expansion as needed according to the manufacturer's directions. Also apply lubricant to the connector seals, if required.

6 Attach gutter lengths and corners, then secure corners and downspout outlets in place. Also attach end caps to outlets and any exposed ends.

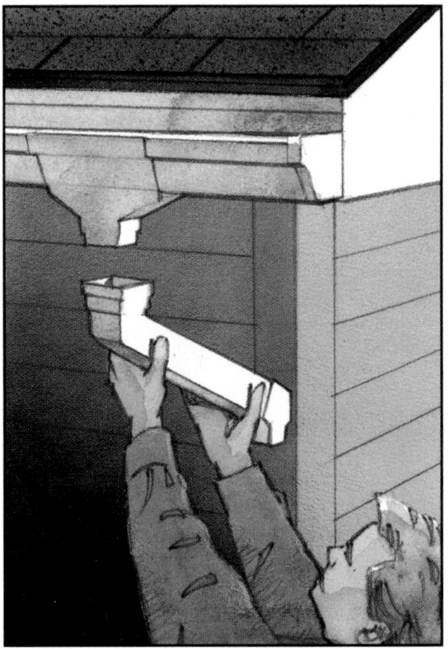

7 Tape a downspout elbow into the downspout outlet, with the lead end facing toward the wall. Attach a downspout hanger to the siding so it will hold another elbow in line with the elbow at the outlet. Cut a piece of drain pipe to fit between the elbows.

8 Install another hanger and elbow at the base of the siding, in line with the elbow mounted at the wall. Cut drain pipe to fit between the elbows, then assemble the downspout, starting at the bottom. Add an outlet pipe, splash block and strainers.

Repairing Siding

Although the number of siding materials available today is great, the repair procedures are fortunately far fewer, and your choices more basic. Many types of siding, including horizontal lap, board-and-batten and tongue-and-groove are repaired similarly.

For most types of siding, you'll be able to make minor patch repairs, as well as more major repairs that call for replacement of sections of damaged siding. Some siding repairs or replacement, however, may require the expertise or assistance of a professional contractor.

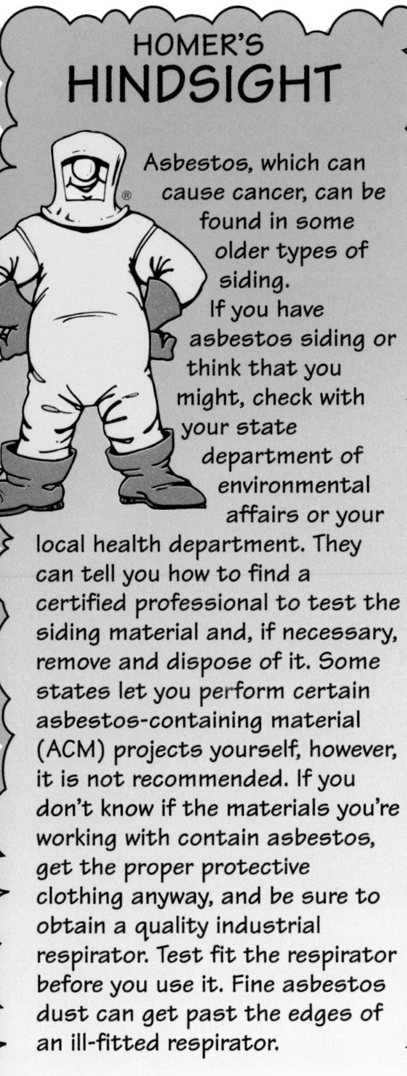

HOMER'S

HINDSIGHT

Asbestos, which can cause cancer, can be found in some older types of siding.

If you have asbestos siding or think that you might, check with your state department of environmental affairs or your local health department. They can tell you how to find a certified professional to test the siding material and, if necessary, remove and dispose of it. Some states let you perform certain asbestos-containing material (ACM) projects yourself, however, it is not recommended. If you don't know if the materials you're working with contain asbestos, get the proper protective clothing anyway, and be sure to obtain a quality industrial respirator. Test fit the respirator before you use it. Fine asbestos dust can get past the edges of an ill-fitted respirator.

COMMON SIDING TYPES AND PROBLEMS

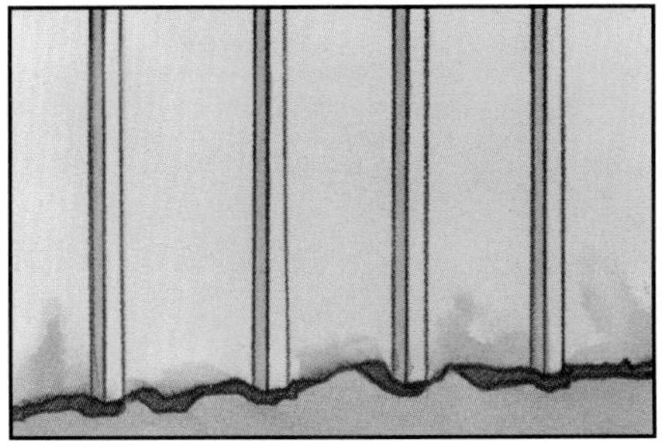

Wood board-and-batten siding will require repair mainly due to weathering or water damage and is also relatively easy to repair.

Cedar shakes are traditionally single, hand-split tapered boards that vary in length and are rough in texture. Cedar shingles are similar, but are machine-sawn. Both are fairly easy to repair.

Wood lap siding is the likeliest siding to need repairs due to splitting, weathering and water damage. Luckily, it is also one of the easiest to repair.

Aluminum and metal siding is somewhat susceptible to damage from weather and the occasional foul ball, but repairs can be made quite easily with the proper tools.

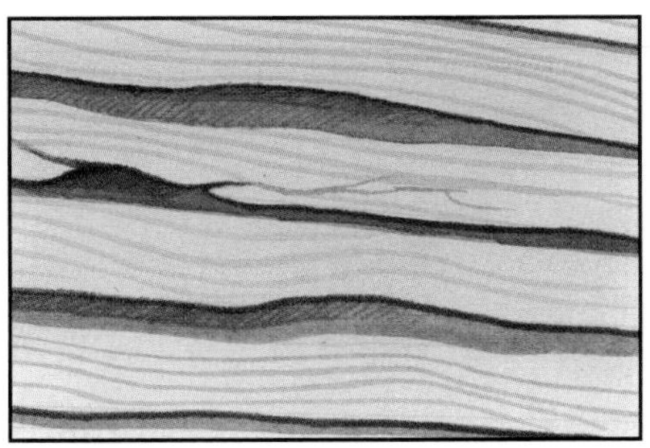

Vinyl siding has limited repairability, depending on the repair area. Always check your warranty information before making any repairs, so you do not inadvertently void the manufacturer's warranty.

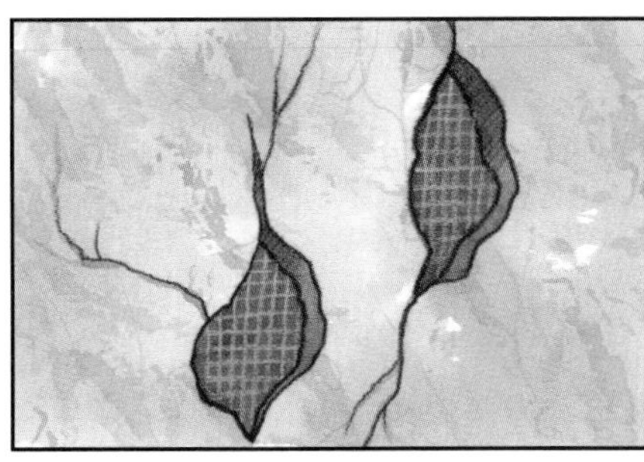

Stucco siding repairs can usually be handled by the homeowner with a little practice and the proper tools and materials.

Repairing Wood Siding

Wood siding is subject to wood's tendency to deteriorate from the effects of weather. Some varieties of wood, cedar and redwood for example, are less susceptible to rot and are therefore more desirable as siding. Composite materials, such as hardboard, resist rot but are vulnerable to moisture penetration unless treated and sealed.

Siding standards have varied over the years. If you're replacing siding on an older house, you may find it difficult to locate a suitable match. Contact your usual supplier of building materials. He may be able to special order replacement siding or to suggest a source of specialty siding in your area.

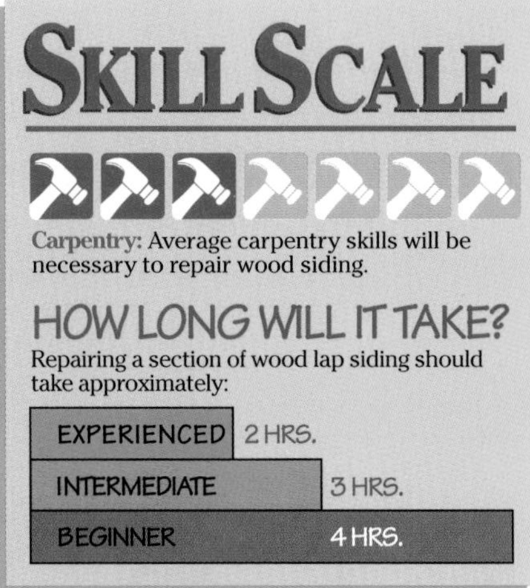

STUFF YOU'LL NEED:

- **Tools:** Putty knife, flat bar, hammer, hacksaw, circular saw, keyhole saw, jigsaw, hand stapler.
- **Material:** Epoxy wood filler, wood spacers, siding material, siding nails, building paper.

TIPS FOR REPAIRING WOOD SIDING

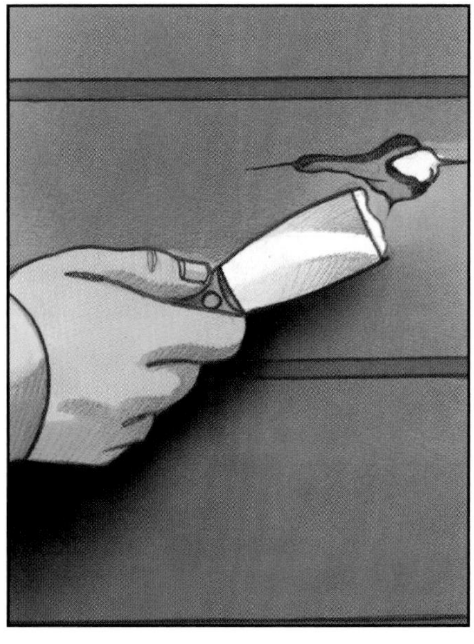

Fill small holes in wood siding by cleaning the repair area thoroughly with a chisel. Use a putty knife to fill the area with an epoxy wood filler and then paint it accordingly.

Use spacers to hold overlapping siding clear of your work area during repairs. Work gradually, and pry a wide area on either side of the immediate repair area to avoid splitting or cracking the old wood.

Label the siding pieces as you remove each piece. Keeping track makes it easier to reinstall siding or use the original pieces as templates for replacement siding.

Stagger vertical joints when you replace siding to maintain a well-balanced appearance. For best results, cut out the old siding at the framing member locations.

Leave expansion gaps between wood siding materials, including wood lap, shakes and shingles, and panel siding. The siding material must have room to expand and contract with the weather and shifting of the house, or it may buckle.

REPLACING SHINGLES OR SHAKES

Replace shingles and shakes: first, pull the nails securing the damaged materials, using a shingle puller. Alternate: split damaged shingles with a hammer and chisel, then remove nails. Next, split new shingles or shakes to fit, allowing a 1/4"-wide expansion gap. Starting with the lowest row, fit the replacement shingles in position, overlapping to follow the pattern. Slip the tops of the highest new row under the shingles in the row above. Nail shingles near the top, with aluminum or zinc-coated nails.

REPLACING DAMAGED WOOD LAP SIDING

1 Locate the nearest wall framing member on each side of the damaged area and mark cutting lines next to the studs. Also mark the repair area well beyond the damaged area, into solid wood. Remove any trim or obstructions necessary for access to the repair area.

2 Cut the siding at wall studs, using a circular saw set to a depth equal to the thickness of the siding. Stagger vertical cuts. Cut siding nails on the top course by sliding a hacksaw blade between the damaged board and the overlapping board.

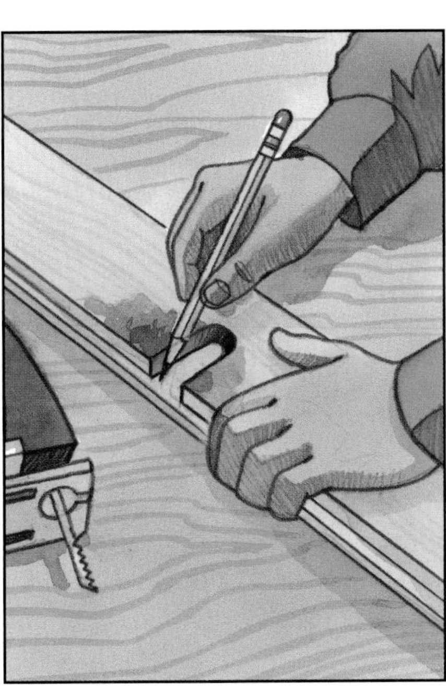

3 Use old siding as a pattern for tracing cutouts around wall openings, fixtures, or obstructions.

REPLACING DAMAGED WOOD LAP SIDING (continued)

4 Cut replacement siding boards to fit, leaving an expansion gap of 1/16" on each end. Treat the cut ends of the siding boards with a primer or sealant before installation. Also inspect building paper and wall sheathing in the repair area.

5 Replace damaged building paper before attaching the new siding. Cut the replacement paper so it overlaps the repair area by at least 4". Tuck the top edge of the patch under the course of paper directly above the repair area and attach with staples.

6 Nail new siding boards in place, using the same nailing as was used on the original boards. If you are replacing more than one board, begin with the lowest boards and work up, maintaining the proper overlap.

7 Use paintable siliconized acrylic caulk to fill all vertical joints between boards, and to cover any exposed nail heads. When the caulk is dry, prime and paint the new siding to match the original boards.

REPLACING BOARD-AND-BATTEN SIDING

1 Remove the battens on each side of the damaged panel. Remove the damaged panel and check the underlayment, then cut a replacement panel from matching material.

2 Prime the edges and backside of the new boards or panels, then insert the new board, maintaining a 1/8" expansion gap at the joints, and secure with nails. Caulk the joints between the new and old boards, then reattach the battens. Stain or prime and paint to match.

Repairing Vinyl & Metal Siding

Repairs for vinyl and aluminum iding are more restricted than most ther siding. Your resources for epair material are limited to naterials you may have left over rom the original installation. Some ome supply stores carry these iding materials, but your specific iding material may be proprietary o the contractor. Many contractors ell individual replacement parts, so you don't have any leftover naterial, contact the original nanufacturer to obtain replacement arts.

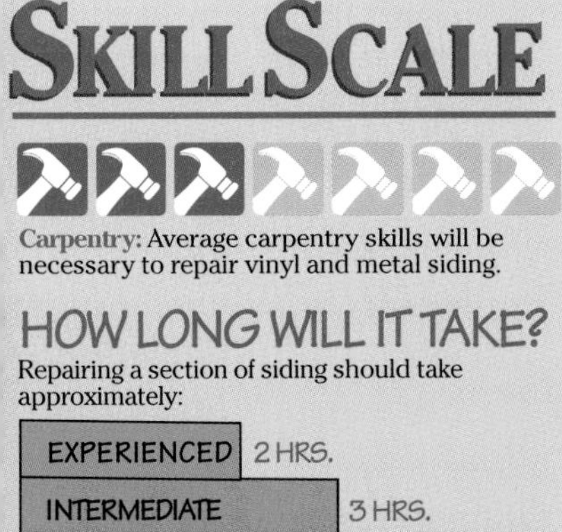

Carpentry: Average carpentry skills will be necessary to repair vinyl and metal siding.

HOW LONG WILL IT TAKE?

Repairing a section of siding should take approximately:

EXPERIENCED	2 HRS.
INTERMEDIATE	3 HRS.
BEGINNER	4 HRS.

STUFF YOU'LL NEED:

- ☐ **Tools:** Flat bar, hammer, tin snips, combination square, caulk gun, zip tool.
- ☐ **Material:** Siding material, panel adhesive, end caps.

PATCHING VINYL SIDING

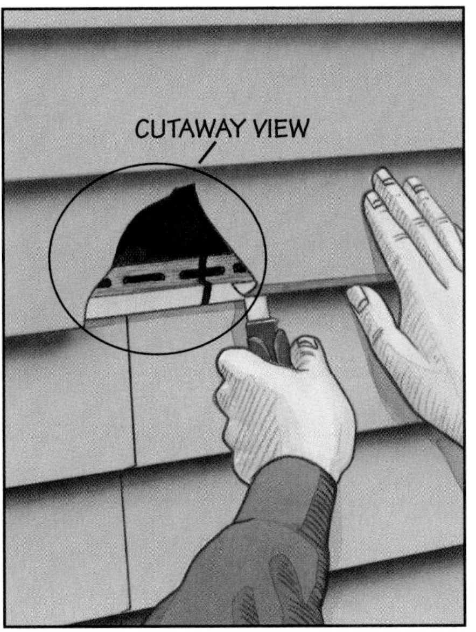

Use a zip tool to separate vinyl siding panels. Insert the zip tool at an end joint, under the bottom lap of the panel above the repair area. Slide the zip tool along the bottom lap, pulling out and downward slightly. Zip tools can be purchased at most building centers.

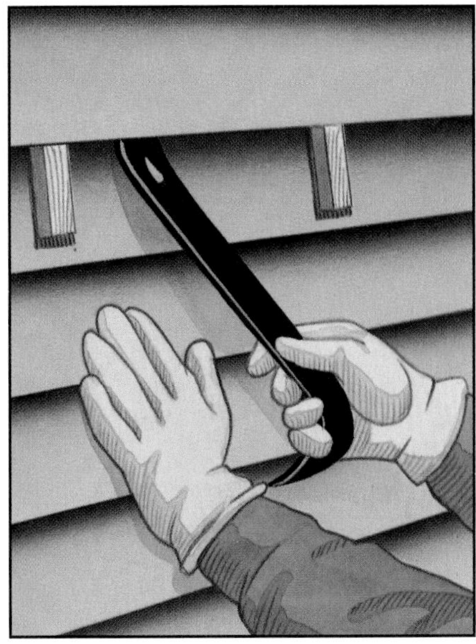

1 Separate panels in the repair area, using a zip tool. Insert spacers between the panel above the repair area and the sheathing, then use a pry bar to loosen and remove nails securing the damaged panel or panels.

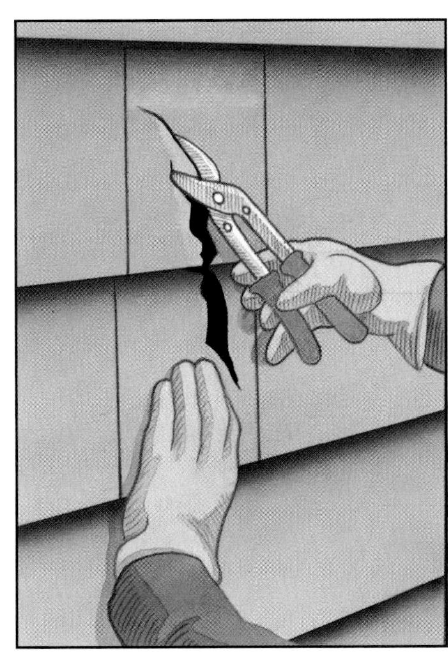

2 Make vertical end cuts through the damaged panel, using tin snips or a utility knife and straightedge. Cut a replacement panel 2" longer than the original from matching material.

3 Insert replacement panel or panels in the repair area, starting at the bottom. Secure panels with the same fasteners used originally. For the last panel, force the fastener in with a pry bar slipped under the lap above. Use a zip tool to lock the panels together.

REPAIRING ALUMINUM SIDING

1 Cut out the damaged section, using a roofing knife and tin snips. For best results, do not make vertical cuts in line with a seam on adjoining courses. Also make a horizontal cut near the top of the reveal area on the damaged panel. Do not remove fasteners.

2 From matching stock, cut replacement pieces 2" longer than the exposed area. Trim off the fastener channel on the top piece. Deburr all exposed siding edges with a file. If replacing more than one piece, attach the lower replacement panels with fasteners.

3 Apply panel adhesive to the back of the top replacement piece. Insert the new piece over the repair area, so the bottom flange interlocks with the panel below. Press the new panel in place to seat it in the adhesive, then caulk the ends of new panels.

REPLACING ALUMINUM END CAPS

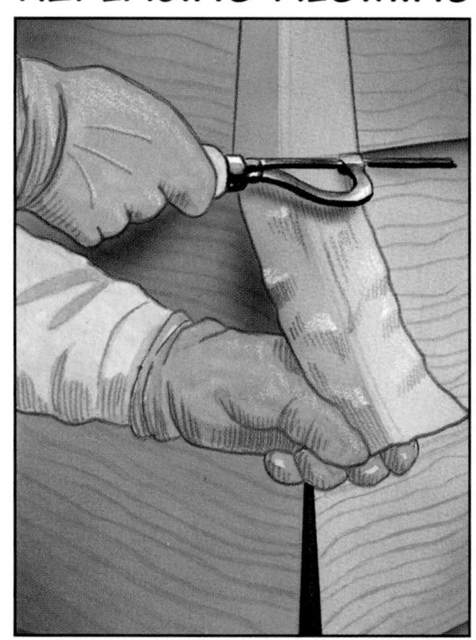

1 Remove damaged corner caps. Loose caps may come off easily. If a cap is pinned tightly under the overlapping cap above, pry out the bottom of the damaged cap, then cut along the top of the cap.

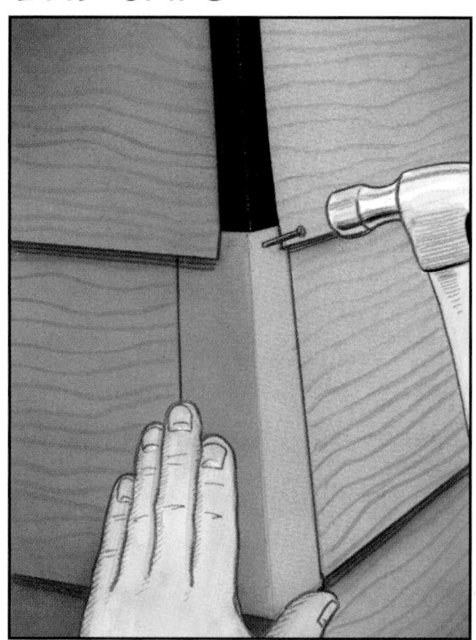

2 Locate matching replacement caps, then attach the lower caps using aluminum nails, starting at the bottom, if replacing more than one cap.

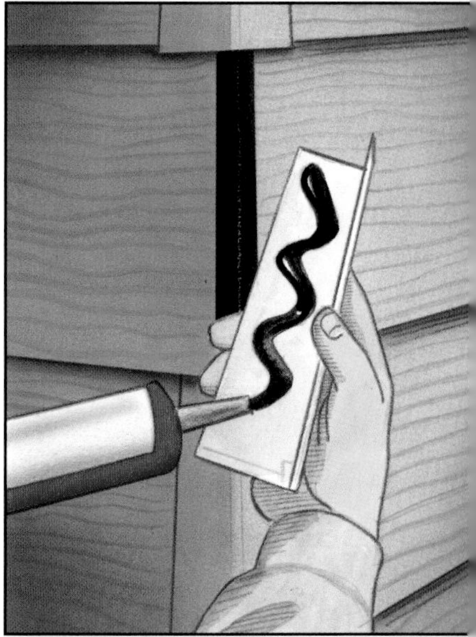

3 Trim the nailing tab off the top replacement cap, then apply panel adhesive to the back. Snap the cap over bottom lips of joining siding courses, then seat the cap in the roofing cement, making sure it is properly aligned.

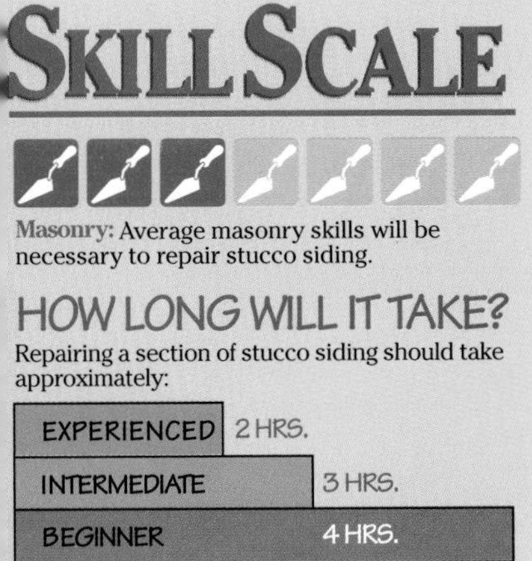

STUFF YOU'LL NEED:

- ☐**Tools:** Putty knife, wire brush, caulk gun, trowel, whisk broom.
- ☐**Material:** Stucco caulk, stucco patch, coloring pigment.

Repairing Stucco

Patching damaged stucco can be tricky business. If the repair is to be satisfactory, you must match both the texture and the color of the surrounding wall.

Prior experience with masonry tools will give you a distinct advantage when attempting to match a particular stucco texture. Stucco pigments can be obtained at masonry supply stores and are meant to be mixed in with the final coat. When pigmenting stucco, keep in mind that the color is likely to change as the stucco dries. For the best match, take the time to experiment with stucco and pigment proportions until you find a tint that matches the existing stucco wall when dry.

Make necessary repairs to the underlying structure before you begin. Plan on building up your repair in layers over several days with adequate time between layers to permit the stucco to cure.

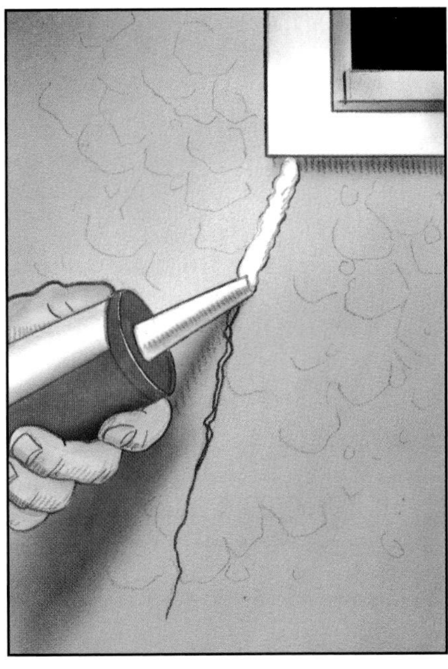

Fill minor cracks with specialty stucco caulk products. These caulks do not harden fully, and will maintain a flexible bond between cracks. Stucco caulks are not available in colors, so the repair area will be plainly visible. You can, however, paint over caulk strip to match the color of your stucco.

REPAIRING DAMAGED STUCCO

1 Clean out old, loose stucco from repair area. Inspect the areas surrounding the visible damage o the stucco, pressing gently on he sides until you find solid wall. A loose wall that gives under hand pressure indicates a more serious repair.

2 Fill the hole with premixed stucco patch using a trowel. For best results, apply the stucco in two or three layers, letting each layer dry completely between applications.

3 Smooth out the final coat to match the surrounding texture, using a trowel, then dab with the end of a whisk broom to blend in texture of repair.

Repairing Fascia & Soffits

Fascia and soffits are an evolutionary improvement on the more traditional exposed rafters and open eaves. Fascia boards are intended to protect the cut ends of the rafters and to prevent water from being drawn back along the overhang and down inside the walls. Fascia boards also provide an even surface to which gutters may be evenly attached.

Soffits prevent birds and other pests from nesting under your eaves or from easy access into your attic. When properly vented, they provide the ideal weather-protected site for fresh air intake for optimum ventilation and insulation.

Proper maintenance is essential to the soundness of your fascia and soffits. Gaps or deterioration can allow moisture to seep into the soffits, causing them to rot or buckle.

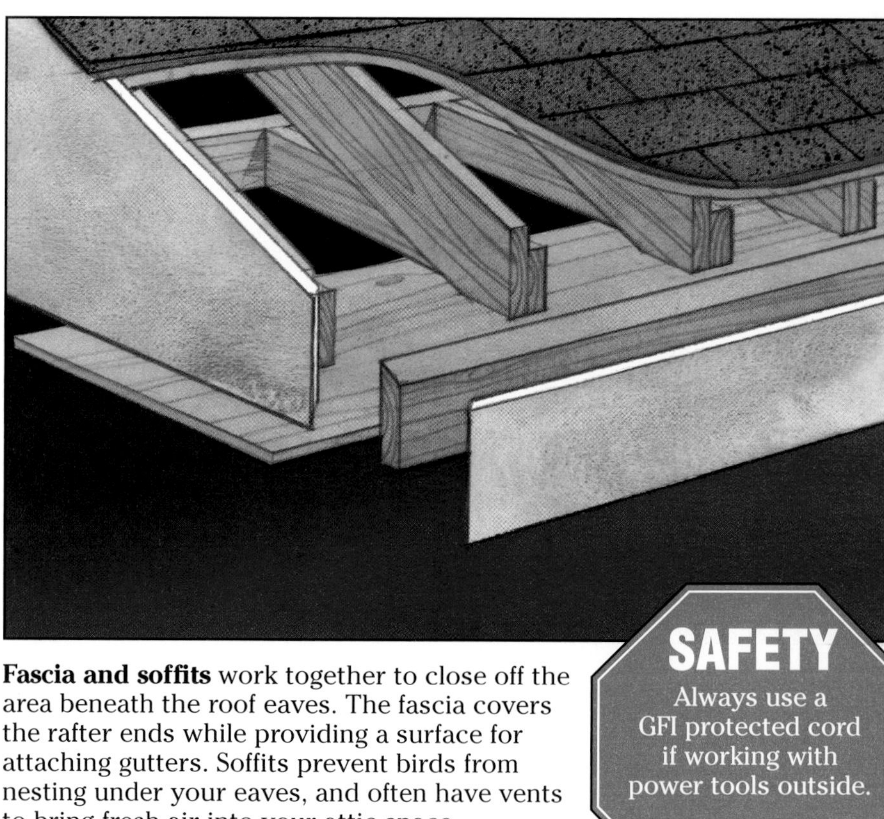

Fascia and soffits work together to close off the area beneath the roof eaves. The fascia covers the rafter ends while providing a surface for attaching gutters. Soffits prevent birds from nesting under your eaves, and often have vents to bring fresh air into your attic space.

SAFETY ALERT

Always use a GFI protected cord if working with power tools outside.

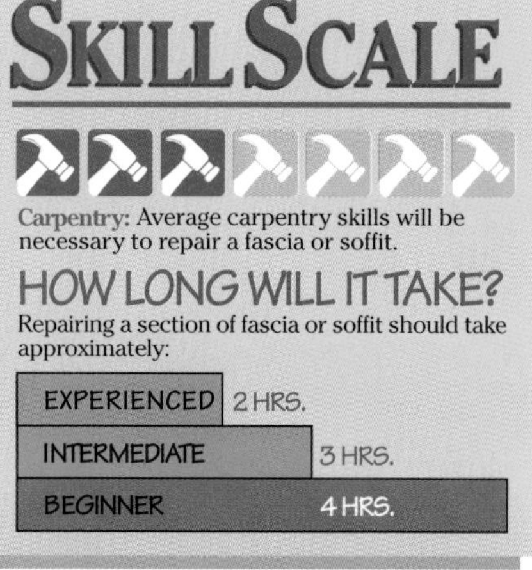

STUFF YOU'LL NEED:

- ☐ **Tools:** Flat bar, hammer, ladder, jigsaw, caulk gun, drill/driver, circular saw.
- ☐ **Material:** Galvanized nails or screws, fascia material, soffit material.

INSTALLING FASCIA COVERS

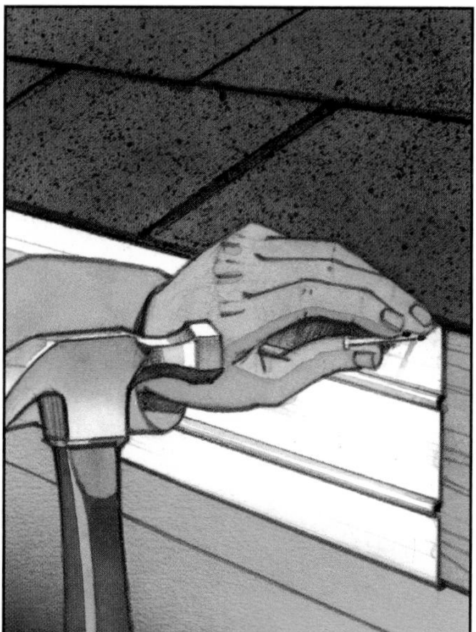

Conceal worn fascia boards with metal or vinyl fascia covers. Most metal covers have factory-applied finishes that can be painted to match your trim. Vinyl covers, sold in a variety of colors, are not designed to be painted.

Use fascia covers to hang new soffits. Fascia covers with metal or vinyl F-channels are designed to hold matching soffit panels. J-channels mounted to the side of your house suspend the other side of the soffit panels.

REPLACING A SECTION OF FASCIA

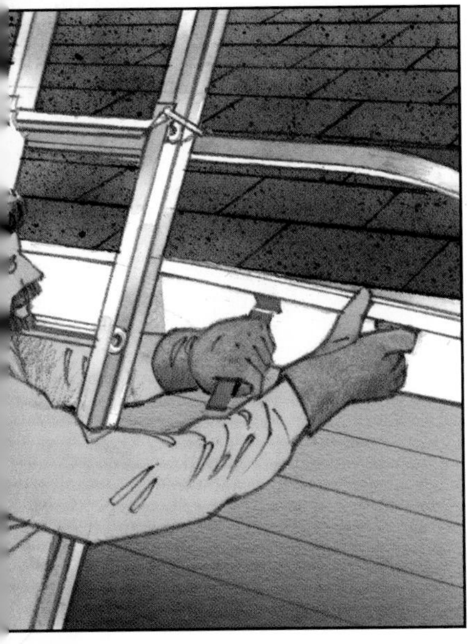

1 Remove gutters or trim, exposing the entire section of fascia board containing the damaged area.

2 Pry the fascia loose with a flat pry bar, then remove. Fascia usually is nailed at every rafter end, except when it is attached directly to a fascia header.

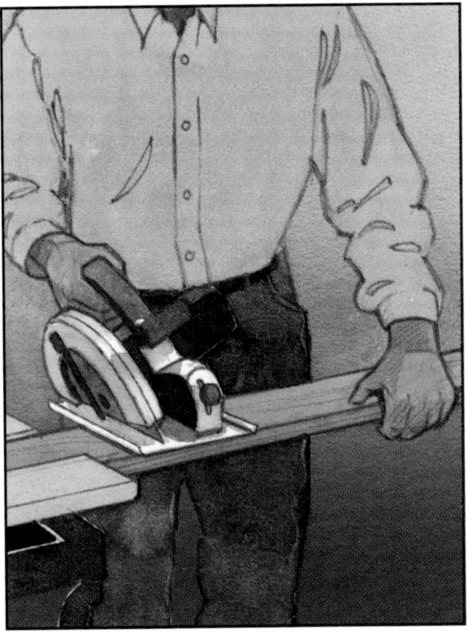

3 On your worksurface, mark off the damaged area of fascia so the cutting lines fall at rafter locations. Miter-cut the fascia board at the cutting lines to remove the damaged section.

4 Nail or screw the original piece or pieces of fascia back in place, leaving open the area for the replacement board. Measure the open area, then cut a replacement board to fit. Cut the new board at a matching miter, and allow for a 1/8" expansion gap at each end.

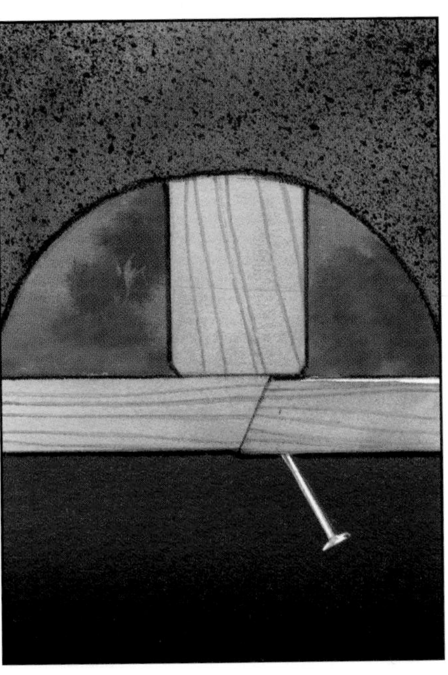

5 Position the replacement board with equal expansion gaps at each end, then nail it at the rafter end. Lock-nail the joint through the miters.

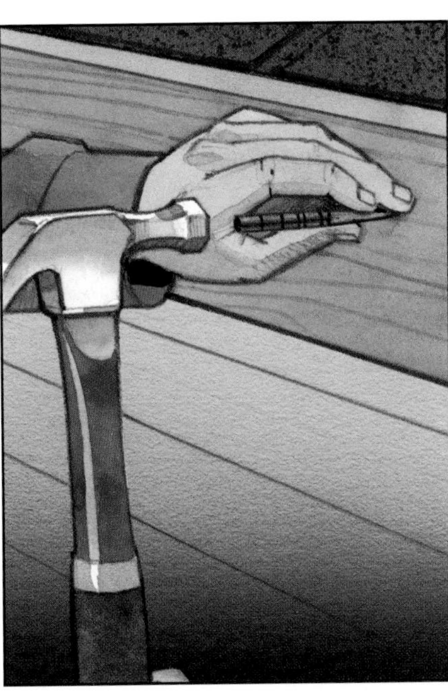

6 Replace fascia moldings, then set the nail heads and fill the nail holes with caulk. Prime and paint or stain to match the existing fascia.

REPAIRING PLYWOOD SOFFITS

1 Remove molding suspending the panel, then locate the closest rafter lookout or rafter end on either side of the damaged area. Drill entry holes for a jigsaw then cut out the damaged section, cutting as close as possible to the rafter lookout or rafter end.

2 Remove fasteners, then pry out the damaged panel with a flat pry bar. Measure the opening. Attach nailing strips to the rafter lookout or rafter end at the edges of the opening.

3 Cut a replacement soffit panel to fit the opening, using exterior-grade plywood the same thickness as the original panel, usually ¼". Make cutouts to accommodate soffit vents if they were present in the damaged section.

4 Position the replacement panel over the opening, then attach it to the nailing strips with 1¼" galvanized deck screws.

5 Replace any moldings that help hold the panel in place.

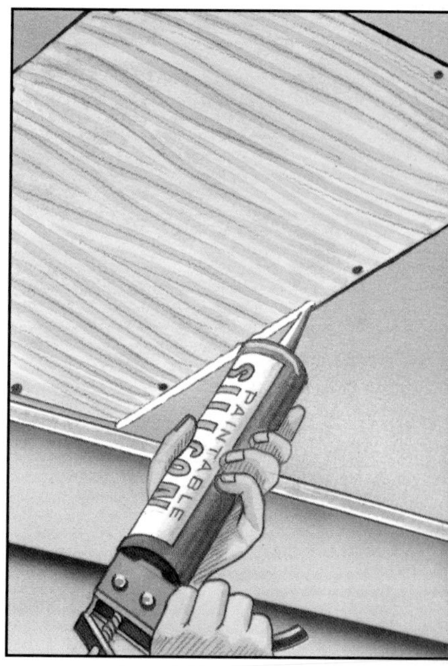

6 Fill nail holes, screw holes and joints with paintable siliconized caulk. Paint the replacement panel soffit to match the rest of the soffit. Install any vent covers.

REPAIRING LENGTH-RUN TONGUE-AND-GROOVE SOFFITS

1 Remove any molding suspending the boards, then locate the closest rafter lookout or rafter end on either side of the damaged area. Drill entry holes for a jigsaw, then cut across the damaged section as close as possible to the rafter lookout or rafter end. Pry the damaged section loose. Remove fasteners.

2 Cut and install a 2x2 nailing strip at each edge of the opening in the soffit. Fasten the nailing strips to the rafter lookouts or rafter tails with 2" galvanized deck screws.

3 Cut replacement tongue-and-groove boards the same thickness as the original boards. Begin installing the new boards next to the siding, nailing to the nailing strips.

4 Trim one lip from the last board, then position it in the opening (see inset). Nail in place, fill holes and joints, then paint the replacement boards to match the soffit. Replace soffit vents, if necessary.

REPAIRING WIDTH-RUN SOFFITS

1 Cut along the fascia with a jigsaw to free the damaged section (width-run soffit is usually inserted into grooves in the fascia). Remove support moldings, then pry out the damaged soffit boards.

2 Cut replacement boards to length and insert the strips into the groove in the fascia, trimming a lip from the last board. Reattach support molding, caulk holes and gaps, then paint to match.

Deck Maintenance

Decks are exposed year-round to alternating rain and baking sun and, in northern climates, the freeze-thaw cycle as well. This exposure dries the wood out, making it susceptible to water retention and rot unless treated annually with sealer-preservative.

In damp climates, decks can develop a mossy patina. This can be removed by scrubbing the deck surface with a mild bleach solution.

Restore an old weathered deck to its original wood color with a deck brightening solution. Deck brighteners are available at home improvement stores.

The stresses of foot traffic and weather will cause some deck nails to pop up. If driving them back down does not solve the problem, remove the nails and replace with corrosion-resistant deck screws.

Drive new fasteners to secure loose decking to joists. If using the old nail or screw holes, new fasteners should be slightly longer than the originals.

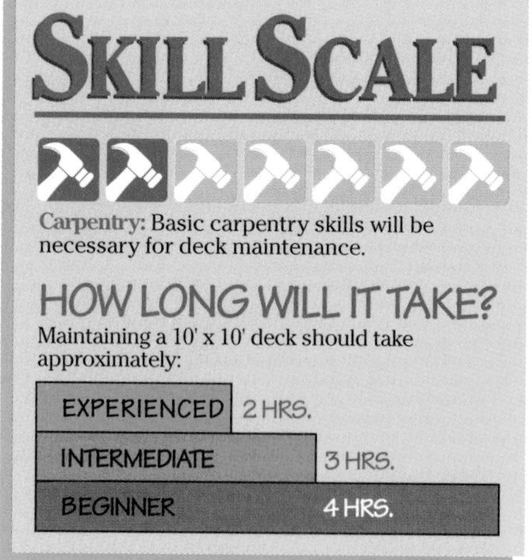

STUFF YOU'LL NEED:

- ☐**Tools:** Screwgun, sprayer, scrub brush, finishing sander, paintbrush.
- ☐**Material:** Deck brightener, deck sealer, deck screws.

RENEWING A DECK

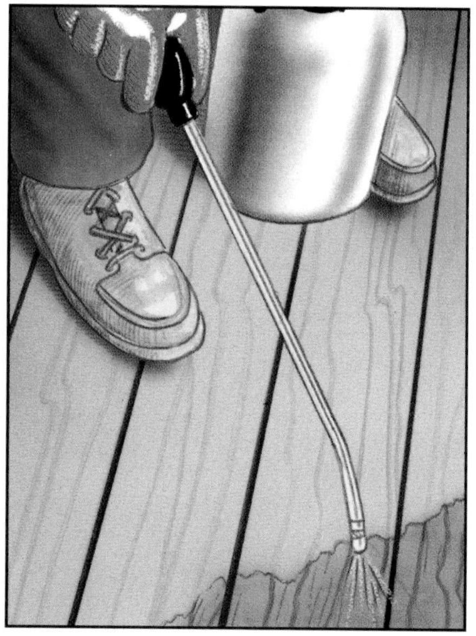

1 Mix deck–brightening solution as directed by manufacturer. Apply solution with pressure sprayer. Let solution set for 10 minutes.

2 Scrub deck thoroughly with a stiff scrub brush. Wear rubber gloves and eye protection.

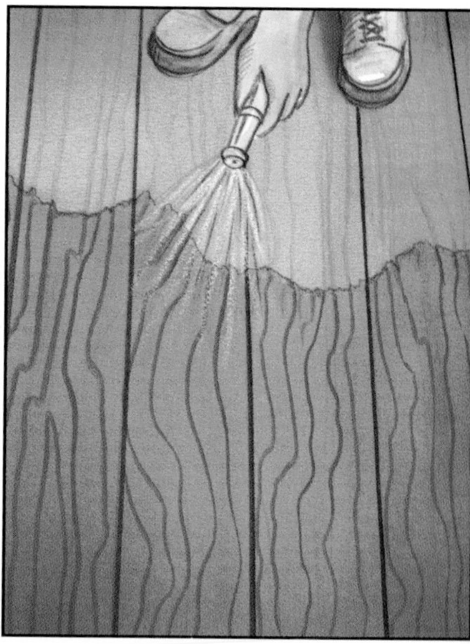

3 Rinse deck with clear water. If necessary, apply a second coat of brightener to extremely dirty or stained areas. Rinse and let dry. Apply a fresh coat of sealer or stain.

Use an orbital sander to smooth out any rough areas before applying finish to decking boards, railing, or stair treads.

FINISHING A PRESSURE-TREATED DECK

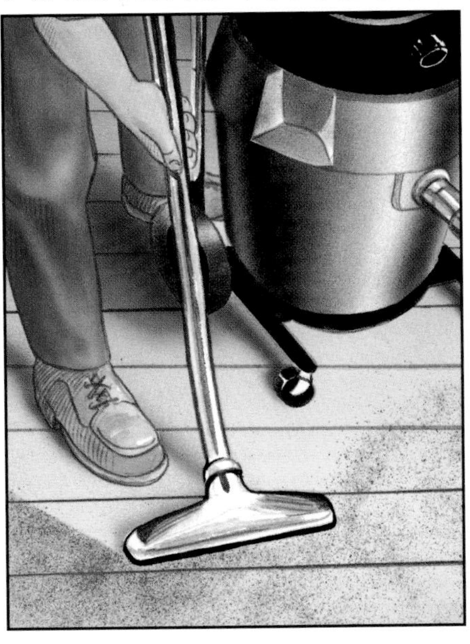

1 Sand rough areas and vacuum the deck. Apply a staining sealer to all deck wood, using a pressure sprayer.

2 Use a paintbrush to smooth out drips and runs. Porous wood may require a second coat of staining sealer for even coverage.

FINISHING A REDWOOD OR CEDAR DECK

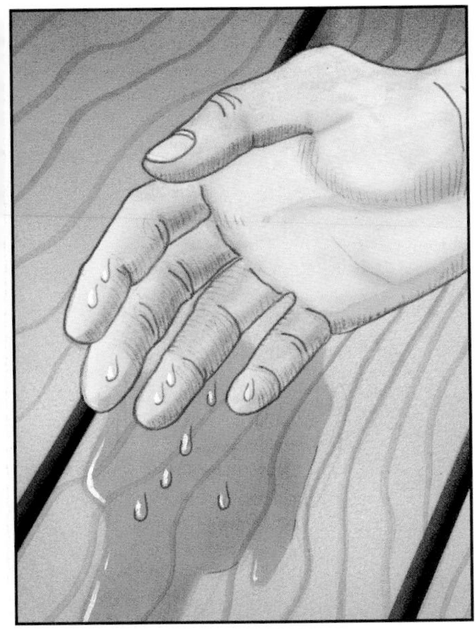

1 Test wood surface by sprinkling water on it. If the wood absorbs water quickly, it is ready to be sealed. If wood does not absorb water, let it dry for several weeks before sealing.

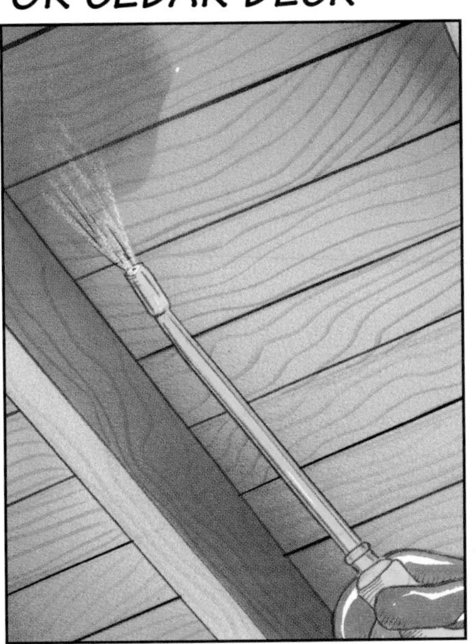

2 Sand rough areas and vacuum deck. Apply clear sealer to all wood surfaces, using a pressure sprayer. If possible, apply sealer to underside of decking and to joists, beams, and posts.

3 Use a paintbrush to work sealer into cracks and narrow areas that could trap water.

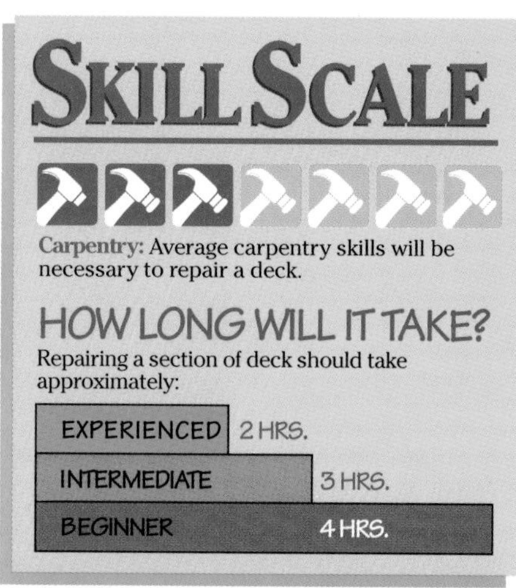

STUFF YOU'LL NEED:

- **Tools:** Pry bar, wood chisel, hammer, sprayer, scrub brush, paintbrush, screwgun.
- **Material:** Treated decking lumber, galvanized nails or screws, baking soda, sealer.

Repairing a Deck

Damaged decking is both unsightly and dangerous. Wood rot, if untended, can spread and affect otherwise good wood nearby. The occurrence of deterioration at one site strongly suggests the possibility of rot elsewhere, as well. When repairing deck boards, watch for signs of damage to the underlying structure. If necessary, use a flashlight to examine support posts and joists for indications of rot or infestation.

When removing deteriorated deck wood, there's no sense being delicate about it–you're going to discard the old decking anyway. If fastening screws are difficult to remove, cut the board in pieces with a chisel or saw, then pry up the pieces. If you need to remove decking to reach a damaged joist, pry up enough so you can work comfortably. Don't make the job more difficult than it needs to be. Before cutting completely through any damaged joist, make sure the deck is well supported on either side of the cut. You don't want to make the problem bigger by collapsing the deck! If you have to replace structural members, use treated lumber unless the members are visible. Then match the existing support members with either redwood or cedar.

After replacing rotted decking, the new parts are not going to match the older parts. If that bothers you, you have three choices: wait a few years, until the new wood weathers too; "weather" the new wood with a solution of baking soda (1 cup) and water (1 gallon); or clean the entire deck with deck brightener so that the old wood is as bright as the new, and then let the whole thing mellow out together. In any case, this is an ideal time to apply another coat of sealer-preservative.

REPAIRING DAMAGED DECKING & JOISTS

1 Remove nails or screws from the damaged decking board, using a cat's paw or screwgun. Remove the damaged board.

2 Inspect the underlying joists for signs of rotted wood. Joists with discolored, soft areas should be repaired and reinforced.

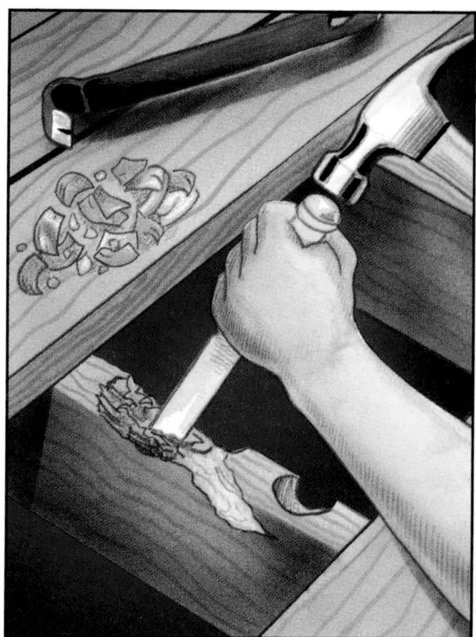

3 Use a hammer and chisel to remove any rotted portions of joist.

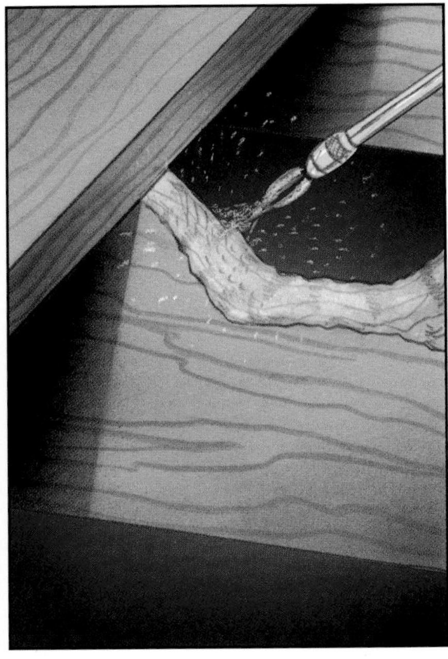

4 Apply a thick coat of sealer-preservative to the damaged joist. Let dry, then apply a second coat of sealer. Cut a reinforcing joist from pressure-treated lumber.

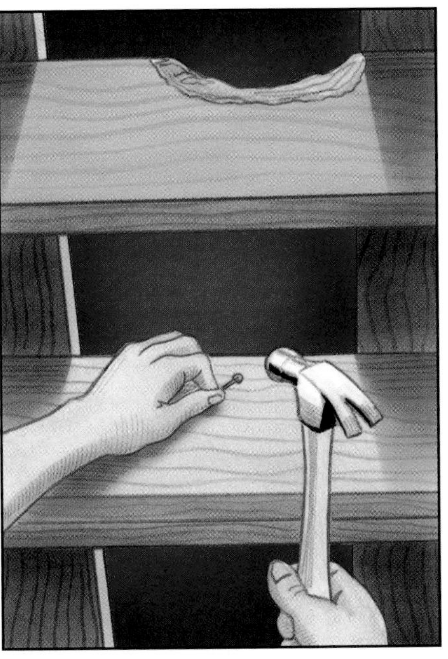

5 Treat all sides of the reinforcing joist with clear sealer-preservative, and let dry. Position the reinforcing joist tightly against the damaged joist, and attach with 16d galvanized nails driven every two feet.

6 Attach the reinforcing joist to the ledger and header joist by toenailing with 16d galvanized nails. Cut replacement decking boards from matching lumber, using a circular saw.

7 If the existing decking is gray, "weather" the new decking by scrubbing with a solution made from 1 cup of baking soda and 1 gallon of warm water. Rinse and let dry.

8 Apply a coat of sealer-preservative or staining sealer to all sides of the new decking board.

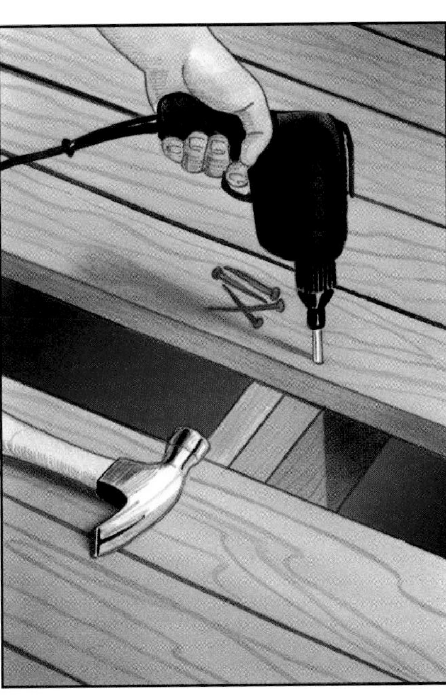

9 Position the new decking and attach to joists with galvanized deck screws or nails. Make sure the space between the deck boards matches that of existing decking.

Replacing a Step

Steps receive more traffic and wear out sooner than any other portion of your deck. For safety's sake, any steps that show signs of deterioration or have been seriously damaged should be immediately replaced.

Remove a damaged step by first cutting it in half. You should then be able to use a pry bar to pull the halves away from the nails. If your steps are fastened with screws, your task should be even simpler: remove the screws, then remove the steps.

For the replacement steps, use treated deck lumber or cedar or redwood decking that closely matches the existing steps. Seal the new steps thoroughly to inhibit future deterioration.

1 Remove the damaged steps and measure the width of the stair treads and mark the tread outline on the stringers. Cut two 2x6's for each tread, using a circular saw.

2 Position the front 2x6 on the tread cleat or notched stringer, so that the front edge is flush with the tread outline on the stringers.

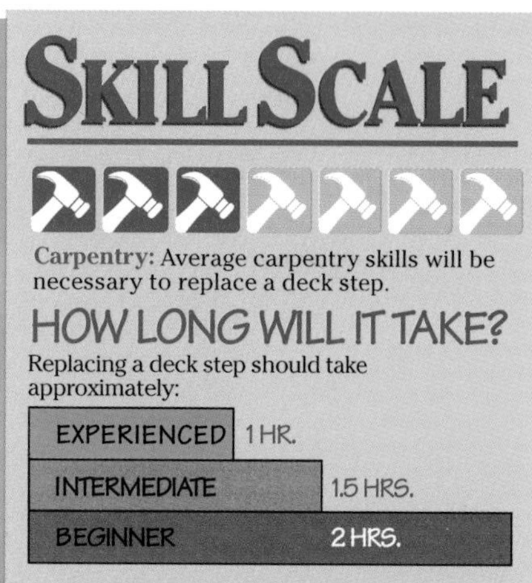

STUFF YOU'LL NEED:

- ☐ **Tools:** Pry bar, hammer, ratchet wrench w/sockets, circular saw, tape measure.
- ☐ **Material:** Treated decking lumber, galvanized nails or screws.

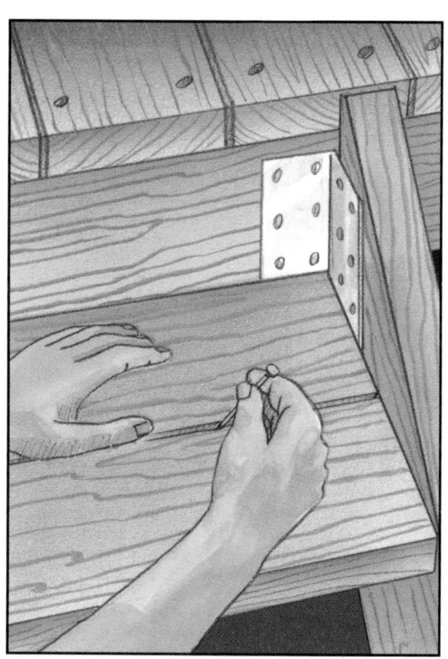

3 Position the rear 2x6 on the cleat or notched stringer, allowing a small space between the two treads and between the rear tread and the riser. Use a 16d nail as a spacing guide between boards and between the back board and the riser. Drill 1/8" pilot holes and attach the 2x6's to the cleats or stringers with lag screws.

Metal step brackets can be attached to the tops of the stringers. This method will allow the treads to overhang the sides of the stringers.

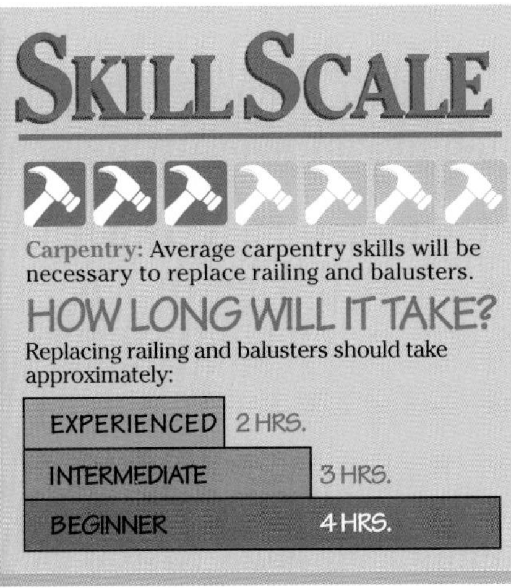

STUFF YOU'LL NEED:

- ☐ **Tools:** Hammer, jigsaw, screwgun, drill, torpedo level, tape measure, circular saw.
- ☐ **Material:** Decking material, galvanized nails and screws.

Replacing Railing & Balusters

Sturdy railings are important preventers of deck mishaps and are essential if your deck is elevated more than one step above the ground. To assure structural integrity, the railing posts must be securely attached to the outside framing members of the deck with lag screws.

If your deck railing, or any part of it, is wobbly or damaged, replace it at once. If you suspect that your deck railings or balusters might not meet the minimum standards established by your local building codes, find out what those standards are and plan to bring your deck up to code.

Be certain your balusters are uniformly sound and solidly attached. Vertical balusters should be spaced less than 6" apart. This is especially critical if you have young children who could slip through a wider space.

There are many ways to construct railings and balusters. It is always best to replicate replacement railing and balusters with the same construction as the originals.

Decorator Rails

Replacing your deck railing and balusters can also be a cost– effective and dramatic way to transform the appearance of your deck. Preshaped railings and turned posts and balusters can be purchased in a variety of styles that make it easy to build highly decorative and distinctive railings.

REPLACING A STAIR RAILING

1 Mark the rail position on the posts and remove the damaged railing. Position the new 2x4 rail against the inside of the stairway posts. Align the rail with the top rear corner of the top post, and with the pencil mark on the lower post. Have a helper attach the rail temporarily with deck screws.

2 Mark the outline of the post and the deck rail on the back side of the stairway rail.

3 Use a level to mark a plumb cutoff line at the bottom end of the stairway rail, then remove the rail.

REPLACING A STAIR RAILING (continued)

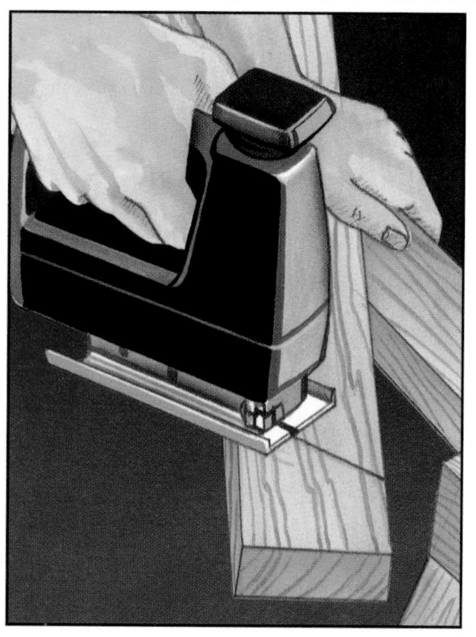

4 Cut along the marked outlines using a jigsaw or circular saw.

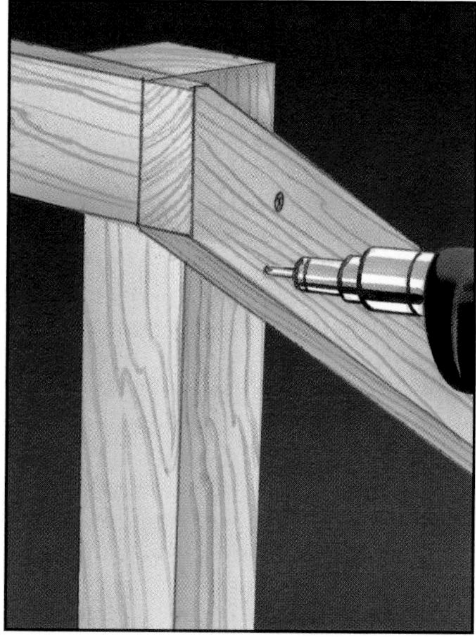

5 Position the stairway rail flush against the top edge of the posts. Drill 1/8" pilot holes, then attach the rail to the posts with 2 1/2" deck screws.

If the deck railing has a cap, measure and cut a cap for the stairway rail. Mark the outline of the post on the side of the cap, and bevel-cut the ends. Position the cap over the stairway rail so that the edge of the cap is flush with the inside edge of the rail. Predrill and fasten with deck screws.

REPLACING A BALUSTER

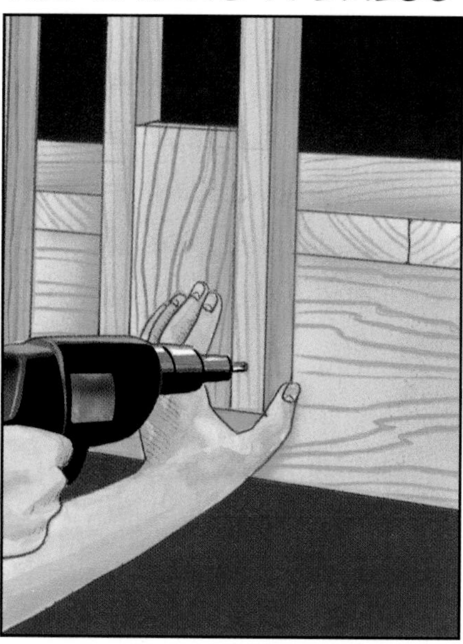

1 Remove the damaged baluster. Measure and cut a replacement baluster to the proper length. Use a spacer block to ensure equal spacing between the balusters. Position the baluster tight against the spacer block, and attach it to the deck and railing with the top flush with the top of the rail.

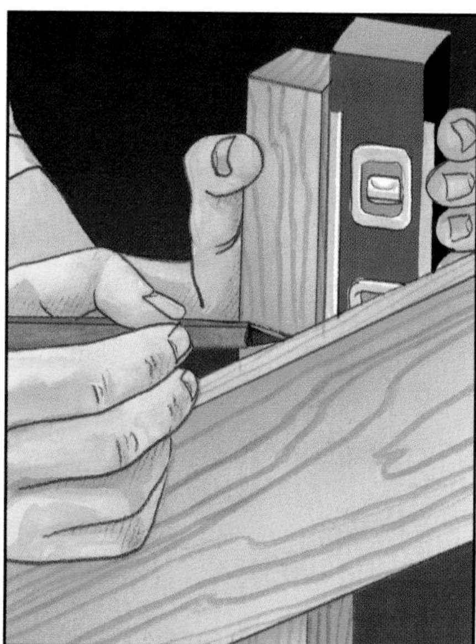

2 For stairways, position the baluster against the stringer and the rail, and adjust for plumb. Draw a diagonal cutoff line on the top of the baluster, using the top of the stair rail as a guide. Cut the baluster on the marked line. Seal the ends with clear sealer-preservative.

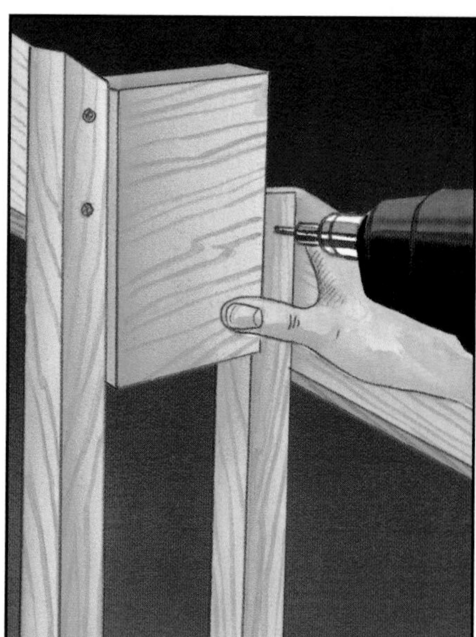

3 Position the baluster tight against the spacer block, with the top flush to the top of the stair rail and attach it with 2 1/2" deck screws.

REPLACING A DECK RAILING

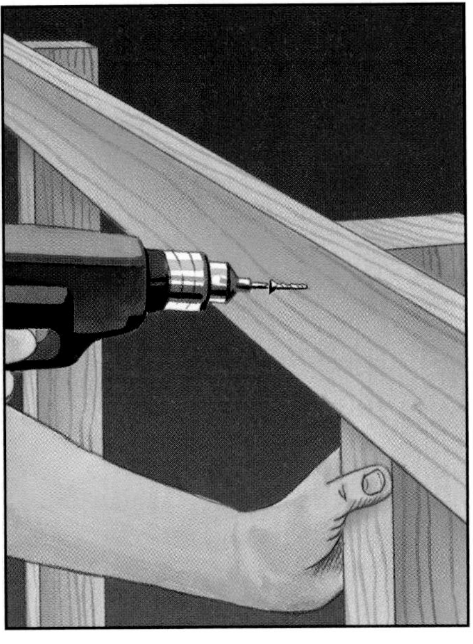

1 Remove the damaged railing. Measure and cut 2x4 replacement side rails. Position the rails with the edges flush to the tops of the posts, and attach to the posts using 2½" deck screws.

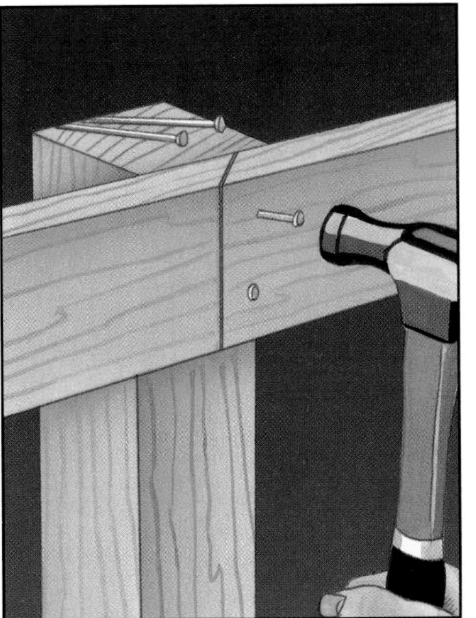

2 Join 2x4s for long rails by cutting the ends at 45° angles. Drill 1/16" pilot holes to prevent the nails from splitting the end grain, and attach the rails with 16d galvanized nails (screws may split the mitered ends).

3 Attach the ends of the rails to stairway posts, flush with the edges of the posts. Drill 1/8" pilot holes and attach the rails with 2½" deck screws. Decorative post caps are readily available.

4 Position the 2x6 cap so the edge is flush with the inside edge of the rail. Drill 1/8" pilot holes and attach the cap to the rail with 2½" deck screws driven every 12". Also drive the screws into each post. Bevel the ends at 45° angles. Drill 1/16" pilot holes and attach to the post using 16d galvanized nails.

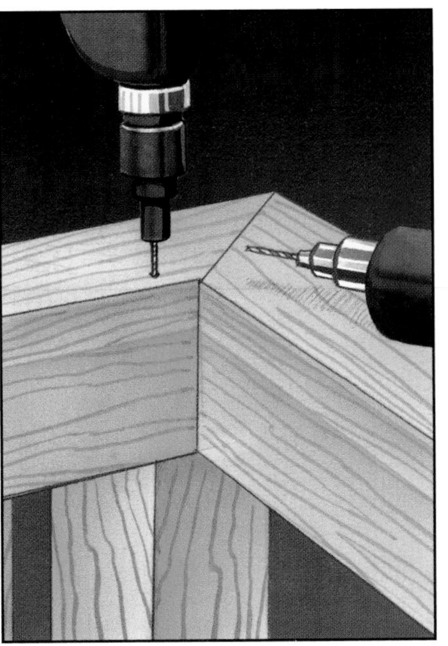

5 At corners, miter the ends of the railing cap at 45° angles. Drill 1/8" pilot holes, and attach the cap to the post with 2 ½" deck screws.

6 At the top of stairs, cut the cap so that it is flush with the stairway rail. Drill 1/8" pilot holes and attach the cap with 2 ½" deck screws.

ROOFING BASICS

Fixing or replacing your roof is not the most exciting way to spend your time and money. It's just a notch above buying gravel, but way short of buying a boat. Still, it's a whole lot better and cheaper to fix your roof before it leaks than to procrastinate and then have to fix your roof and your ceiling as well.

The best way to assure that you won't have to go back up on the roof anytime soon is to buy the best quality roofing materials you can afford.

Top-notch asphalt shingles are guaranteed for up to 20 years. They're thicker than cheap shingles, so they resist curling and cupping and generally withstand more abuse from extremes of weather. If you happen to have asbestos roof shingles, it's best to hire a professional to do the removal and repair.

If you're comfortable working with sheet metal, you can buy galvanized steel or aluminum in bulk rolls and custom cut it to fit. Otherwise, you'll have to spend a little more for flashing in prefabricated form.

TOOLS AND EQUIPMENT FOR ROOFING

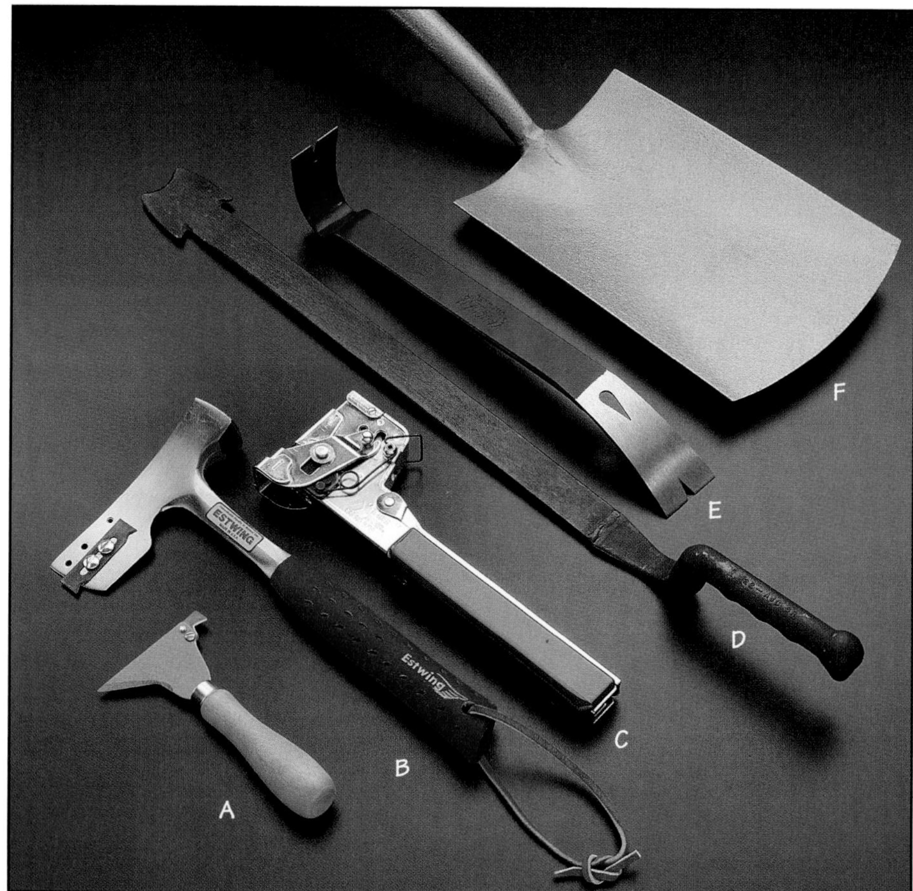

Basic Roofing Tools: roofing knife (**A**), roofing hammer (**B**), hammer stapler (**C**), slate ripper or shingle puller (**D**), flat bar (**E**), and roofing shovel (**F**).

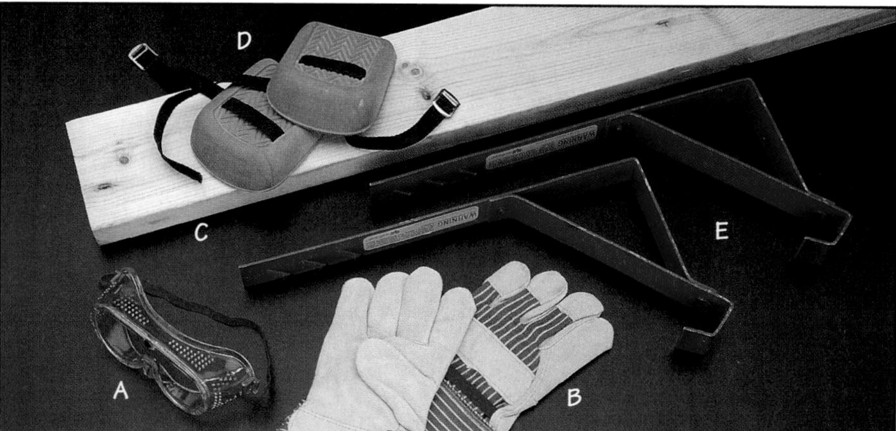

Roofing safety equipment includes: safety glasses (**A**), work gloves (**B**), 2x6 plank (**C**), knee pads (**D**), and roofing jacks (**E**).

Common roofing materials include: plastic roofing cement (**A**), roofing caulk (**B**), cedar shake shingles (**C**), three-tab asphalt shingles (**D**), roll roofing (**E**), building paper (**F**), and ice guard underlayment (**G**).

Common roof flashing includes: valley flashing (**A**), roll flashing material (**B**), vent stacks (**C**), and roof edge (**D**).

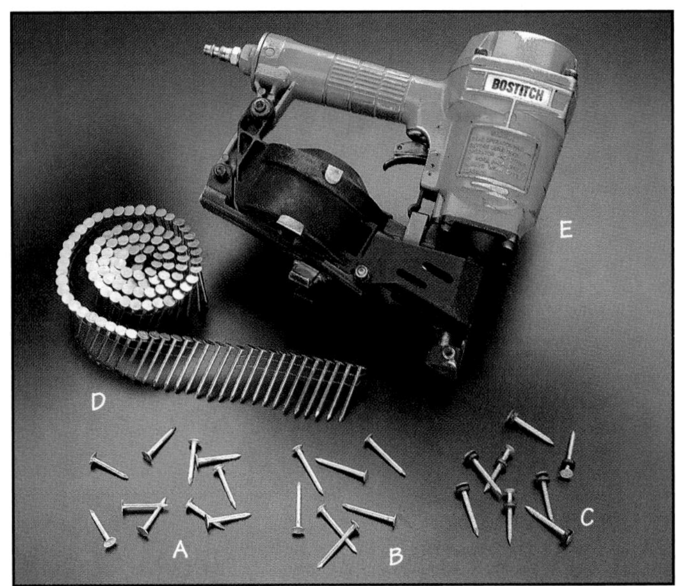

Common roofing fasteners include: aluminum nails for aluminum flashing (**A**), galvanized roofing nails for asphalt shingling and wood shakes (**B**), rubber gasket nails for flashing materials (**C**), and nail cartridges (**D**) for pneumatic nailer (**E**).

SAFETY

If you have asbestos shingles, hire a professional to remove them.

ALERT

COMMON ROOFING TYPES

Asphalt shingles are the most common roofing material. They're easy to apply, economical, and come in a variety of colors and textures. Traditional asphalt shingles have a mineral base coated with asphalt. Fiberglass shingles are also coated with asphalt, but have a base made of glass fibers.

Wood shakes or shingles have an attractive natural appearance, and are very durable. Maintenance is minimal, but installation is more labor intensive than for asphalt shingles.

Some types of roofing are extremely difficult and even dangerous to work on if you're not familiar with the material. If you have clay tile, slate, or asbestos shingles, and you're not a pro at dealing with roofing, it's probably worth your while to hire a professional to do the job and save yourself time, aggravation, and broken bones!

Identifying Roofing Problems

A working roof and gutter system usually goes unnoticed. If they are working properly, they provide adequate air circulation and venting, protection against the elements, and proper drainage of rain and snow.

If you find problems with the roof, such as leaks, worn sections, missing shingle parts, or cupped or bowed shingles, replacing your roof may be a better idea than trying to repair it. You may be able to reroof over the existing roof layer, but at some point you will need to strip away the old roof and start over, especially if you already have more than one layer on the roof.

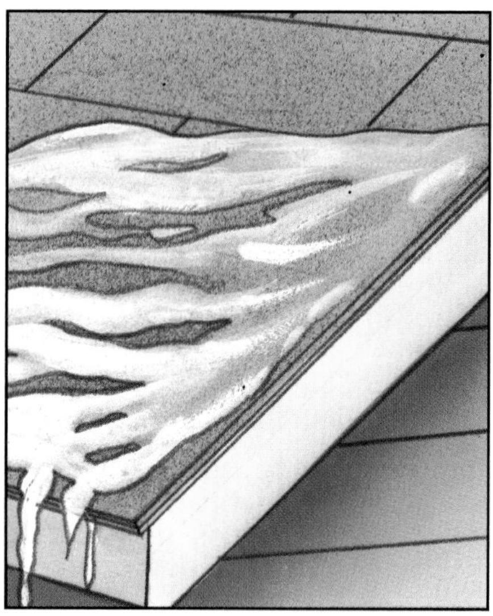

Ice dams usually indicate inadequate ventilation. The air on the inside of the roof is warmer than the outside, causing snow to melt, then dam up when it refreezes. The ice can work its way under shingles and cause damage.

Buckled and cupped shingles generally indicate a moisture problem. Your best solution is to tear off the old shingles, repair the problem, and reroof.

Wear occurs as shingles age. If the majority of shingles are damaged or worn, tear off and replace the old shingles.

Damaged or deteriorated shingles are a main cause of roof leaks. Replace the damaged shingles, or apply a new layer of shingles over the old roof.

Detached or loose flashing often can be replaced or reattached by cleaning out the old caulk or roof cement, and replacing it with fresh material.

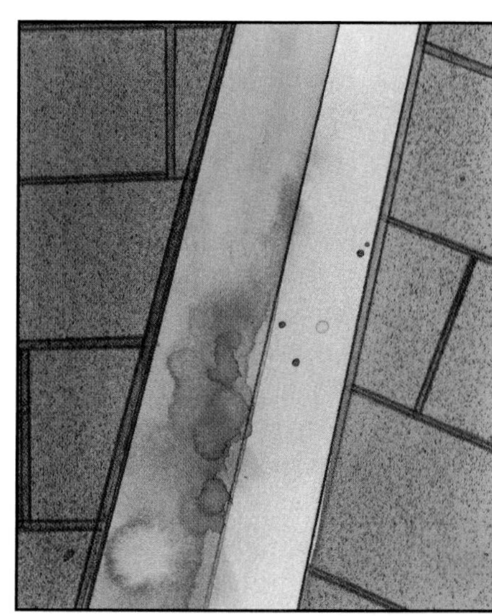

Damaged or deteriorated flashing usually occurs as a result of extensive weathering and oxidation. Old flashing often can be replaced and recaulked without too much difficulty.

Getting Ready for a Roofing Project

When you're up on the roof, prying up roofing materials and then stray nails, under pressure to work quickly and continuously, tensed against losing your balance, the temptation will be to pitch the torn-up roofing material off the nearest edge. Don't do it. Falling shingles can rain destruction on your house and gardens unless you take care to protect them with plywood shields and heavy tarps. If your situation allows it, you may find it convenient to set up two discard areas–one on each side of the house. The more you can keep tear-off debris together, the less work you'll have picking it up later.

Protect your house against damage from discarded roofing materials. Hang large tarps over the side of the house. Also, protect your landscape against falling debris by setting up plywood sheets against the house and over gardens and yard elements.

USE ROOF JACKS

1 Nail roof jacks on a steep roof after shingling the first four courses. Locate the jacks so you are nailing in the section of a shingle that will be covered, and does not interfere with the standard nailing pattern of three-tab shingles.

2 Shingle normally over the tops of the roof jacks, then insert a board across the two jacks to form a safe support for yourself and your tools. Continue your work at the new level. You may want to use more than one set of roof jacks.

3 Detach the roofing jacks by hitting the bottom of the jacks toward the ridge, and sliding the jacks upward, off the nails. Slip a pry bar under a shingle, and use it to finish driving in the hidden nails left from the roof jacks.

Repairing Leaky Roofs

If damage to your roofing is limited to one or more localized areas, you may be able to fix the problem for the immediate future by replacing a few shingles and liberally applying roofing cement.

Damaged or missing shingles are obvious. Cracks or separated joints in the flashing can be harder to locate. When tracking the source of a leak, keep in mind that water, having penetrated the roofing, often flows down the sheathing or, once through the sheathing, often runs down a joist before finally dripping onto the ceiling below. If you can get into the attic or crawl space and if the roof joists are exposed, try to locate the actual entry point from below before going up on the roof. Use reference points, like chimneys, ventilation pipes, windows or valleys to help you pinpoint the site once you're back up on the roof.

While you're up there patching shingles that have already leaked, survey the roof for other problem areas that may develop.

SKILL SCALE

Carpentry: Average carpentry skills will be necessary to repair a leaky roof.

HOW LONG WILL IT TAKE?

Repairing a leaky roof should take approximately:

EXPERIENCED	3 HRS.
INTERMEDIATE	4 HRS.
BEGINNER	5 HRS.

STUFF YOU'LL NEED:

- ☐ **Tools:** Ladder, claw hammer, caulk gun, flat pry bar, wood chisel, shingle puller.
- ☐ **Material:** Roofing cement, roofing nails, shingle material.

MAKING REPAIRS WITH ROOFING CEMENT

Reattach buckled shingles with roofing cement. Also use roofing cement to patch any cracks or other minor shingle problems.

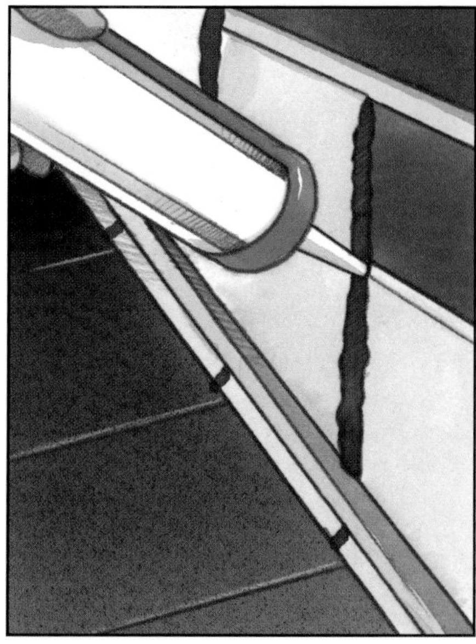

Refresh deteriorated roofing cement around flashing if the seal is bad. Joints around flashing are one of the most common places where leaks can occur.

REPLACING ASPHALT SHINGLES

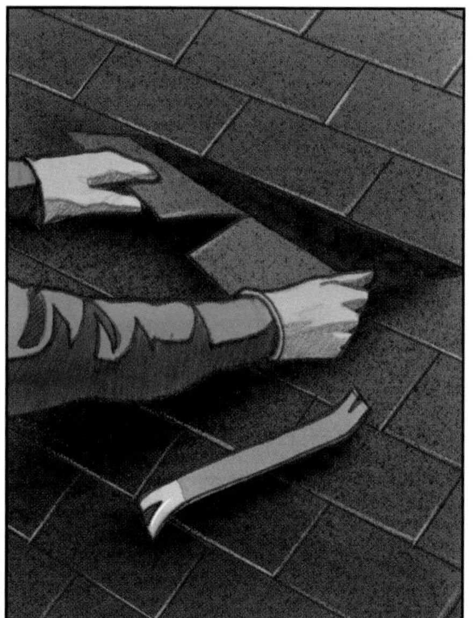

1 Tear off the uppermost shingle needing repair by grasping the sides and wriggling it loose. If you are replacing multiple shingles, start with the highest shingle. Remove all damaged shingles this way. Be careful not to damage surrounding shingles that are in good condition.

2 Remove old nails with a pry bar. If you cannot pry them out, drive the nails flat into the sheathing, using a hammer. Patch any holes in the building paper with roofing cement.

3 Install new shingles on lower courses following the normal shingle installation procedure as shown on the bundle wrapper.

4 Coat the top of the last shingle above the seal line with roofing cement.

5 Slip the last shingle into place under the overlapping shingle. Depending on the arrangement of the shingles, you may be able to drive a couple of nails into the shingle by gently lifting overlapping tabs of other shingles. If not, press shingle down firmly to seat roofing cement.

REPLACING WOODEN SHAKES

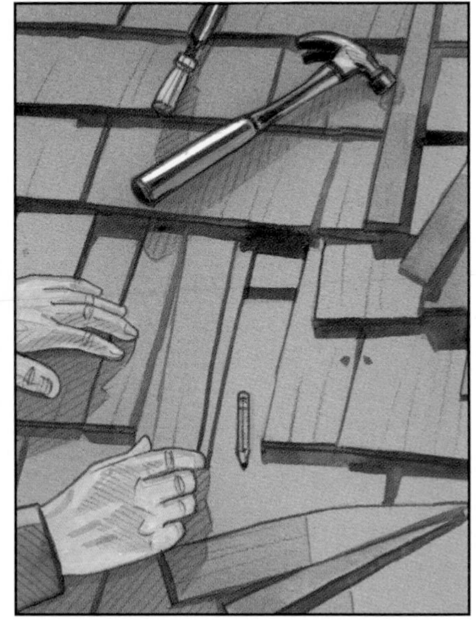

1 Split the damaged shingle with a hammer and chisel and remove the shingle pieces. Use a shingle puller to remove hidden nails. Slip shingle puller under the shingle above, catch a nail, and hammer on the flat part of the handle to pull or cut the nail. Check building paper and repair or replace as necessary.

2 Before installing new shingles, seal them with waterproof stain, if necessary, to match the existing shingles. Insert a new shingle. Trim to fit as necessary, leaving about ⅜" clearance on either side of the piece for expansion.

3 Secure shingle with roofing cement on the backside, or nail it in place.

Installing Flashing

If you have experience working with sheet metal and the equipment necessary to do so, you can cut and form your own flashing. Bulk flashing is available in aluminum or galvanized steel in rolls of various widths. Because it's softer, aluminum is easier to work with than galvanized sheet metal. Because it's harder, galvanized steel is more durable.

Prefabricated flashing components, in already creased and shaped lengths, need only be trimmed to fit. If your roof is fairly conventional in design, suitable ready-made parts should be available.

If you prefer, a custom sheet-metal fabricator can cut and form your flashing to fit. Carefully measure chimneys, dormers and roof slope to assure a good, watertight seal.

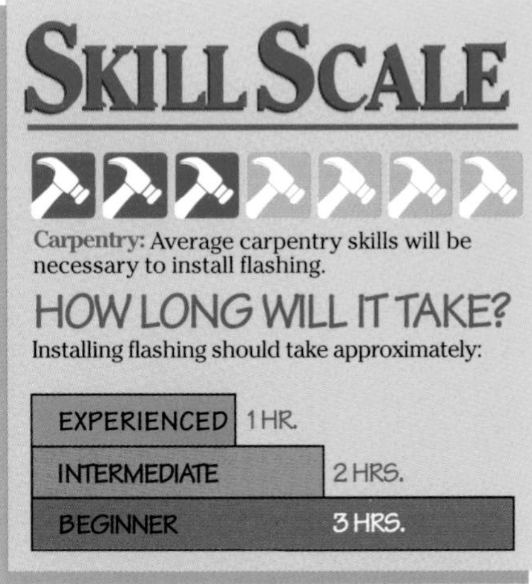

STUFF YOU'LL NEED:

- ☐**Tools:** Flat bar, hammer, roofing hammer, tin snips, caulk gun, wire brush.
- ☐**Material:** Flashing material, roof cement.

BENDING & SHAPING FLASHING

Cut and bend your own flashing. Use a surface with a straight edge as a bending jig for flashing to make fast, uniform bends. A sawhorse or workbench works well.

Use old flashing as a template for replacement flashing, using matching flashing material. This is especially useful for reproducing complicated flashing, like chimney flashing.

PATCHING FLASHING

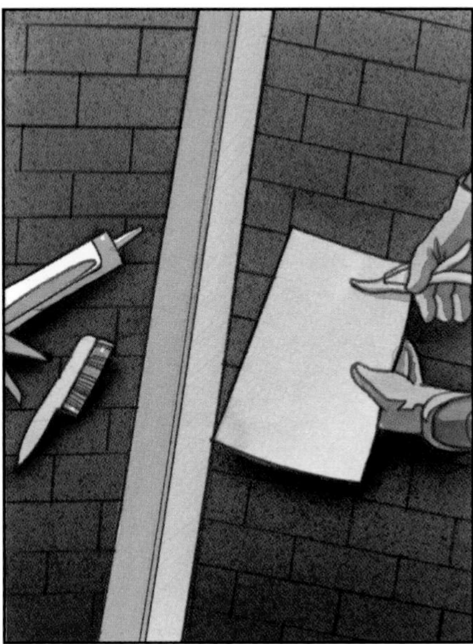

1 Cut a patch from flashing material wide enough to slip under the shingles at each side of the repair area. Break the seal between the valley flashing and the shingles around the damaged area. Scrub the damaged flashing with a wire brush, and wipe it clean.

2 Apply a bed of roof cement to the back side of the patch. Slip the patch under the shingles on each side of the repair area. Press the patch securely into the roof cement. Add cement at the seams and the shingle joints. Feather out the cement to prevent water from damming up in the flashing.

INSTALLING VALLEY FLASHING

1 Fit galvanized sheet metal valley flashing so the crease is flush against the valley. Nail the flashing at the edges and cover the nail holes with plastic roofing cement. Overlap successive pieces at least 8". Trim the edge of the flashing at the eaves to parallel the roof edge.

2 Add overlapping pieces as you work upwards. Overlap and seal the seams with roofing cement. At the peak, bend the flashing over the top or trim at the ridge.

In warmer climates, make valley flashing out of mineral roll roofing. Install an 18" wide strip face down in the valley center and nail the edges of the flashing at 12" intervals. Seal the edges and nail heads with roofing cement. If you can't use single strips, allow a 12" overlap sealed with roof cement.

INSTALLING FLASHING AROUND PIPES

1 Shingle all the way up to the bottom of the pipe. Buy replacement flashing that matches your vent stack diameter and roof pitch. Apply roofing cement to underside flange of pipe flashing.

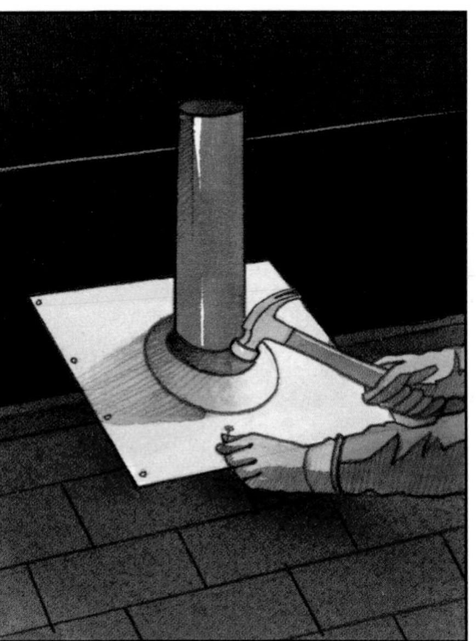

2 When the flange is flush against the roof, anchor it with roofing or rubber gasket nails. Slip the rubber gasket over the pipe.

3 Lay shingles around the stack and trim them to fit around pipe.

INSTALLING STEP FLASHING AROUND A DORMER

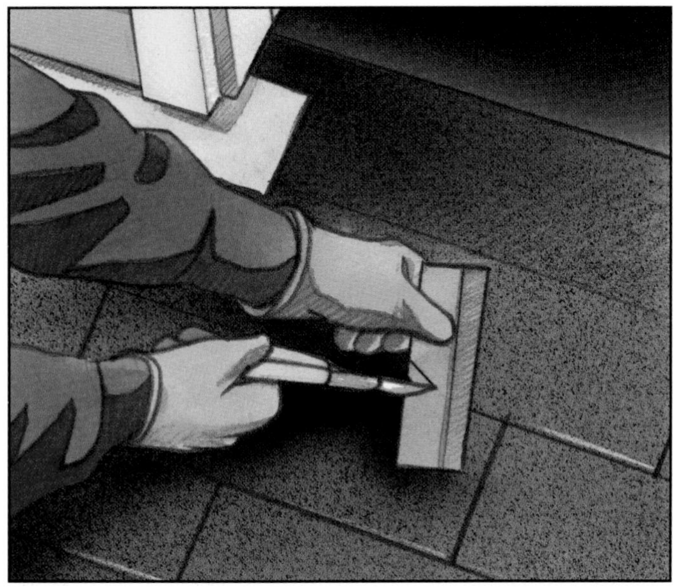

1 Attach base flashing to the front of the dormer. Pry up the lower courses of dormer siding. Tuck the step flashing under the siding to test-fit it. You will probably need to trim the edges but be careful to trim no shorter than 2".

2 Apply roofing cement to the roof deck next to the dormer. Tuck the first course of 8" step flashing under the siding, then press it firmly against the cement on the roof. Secure each piece of flashing to the roof, not to the dormer, with one nail.

3 Apply roofing cement to the face of the step flashing to be covered by shingles. Lay a shingle over the first course of the step flashing. Press the end of the shingle firmly to seat the overlapping portion in the roofing cement.

4 Repeat steps 2 and 3, overlapping step flashing and shingles by 2", until flashing is complete. Trim the last piece of step flashing at top of dormer valley. Reattach the siding. You can cover the front of the base flashing cosmetically by cutting shingles and applying to the flashing with roofing cement.

INSTALLING CHIMNEY FLASHING

1 Apply masonry primer to the chimney where the base flashing will go. Apply plastic roofing cement to the underside of the base flashing and attach flashing around the low side of the chimney, over the shingles. Secure the base flashing to chimney with mortar nails.

2 Apply step flashing around chimney as you would around a dormer.

3 Install saddle flashing around the base of chimney at the high side of chimney the same way you installed the base flashing.

If you have a plywood cricket and the saddle flashing for the cricket that needs replacing, you may have to custom make the flashing for the cricket. To install, nail base of saddle flashing only. Seal edges with roofing cement.

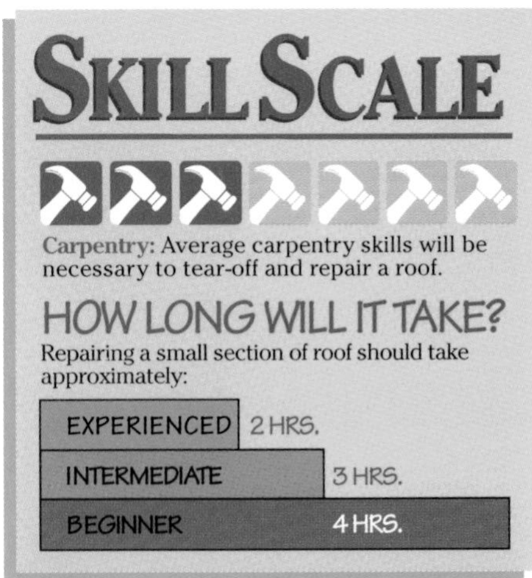

STUFF YOU'LL NEED:

- ☐**Tools:** Claw hammer, roofing knife, roofing shovel, flat pry bar, reciprocating saw, drill/driver.
- ☐**Material:** Sheathing material, screws.

Roof Tear-off and Repair

Tearing off an old roof is hard work. You may have as many as two layers of shingles to pry up and discard. Roofing materials start out heavy and seem to gain weight as the day goes on. The elevation makes it important that you keep your balance and the pitch of the roof makes it more difficult to do so. You must work as quickly as possible, because your roof is vulnerable to the weather while it is exposed.

Get helpers if you can. This would be an excellent time to call in old favors. Before you let anybody on your roof, though, check your insurance coverage. And if the pitch of your roof is steep, make certain that each worker is secured by roofing jacks or a safety harness.

Unless you have enough skilled assistance that you can tear off and reroof the entire house in a day or two, try to break the project into segments and only tear off as much as you can realistically replace before proceeding to the next segment. Never leave an exposed roof unprotected overnight. If darkness falls on unfinished work, cover unshingled areas with tarps weighed down by shingle bundles.

HOMER'S HINDSIGHT

When I was getting ready to tear off my old roof, I planned it all out very carefully. I gathered the equipment I needed, rounded up a couple of friends, even rented a dumpster. If I'd remembered to check the weather forecast, everything would have been perfect . . .

REMOVING THE OLD ROOF

1 Cut the seals around the flashing, and remove any flashing that needs to come off. If you have custom-made chimney flashing still in good shape, remove it carefully and save it for reuse.

2 Remove the ridge cap, using a flat pry bar.

3 Remove the old shingles in large rolled sections, if possible, using a flat-tined pitchfork or roofing shovel. Keeping the tear-off material in large chunks will make the tear-off job easier to manage and less messy. If you are saving your gutters, be careful not to ruin them during tear-off.

4 Pry out any remaining old nails, some roofing shovels have a notched edge specifically for this. The sheathing surface must be completely flat. Sweep the roof completely to prepare for building paper. You may want to clean up stray nails from the yard, using a release magnet available at most rental centers.

REPLACING DAMAGED SHEATHING

1 Remove damaged sections of roof boards, using a pry bar and claw hammer. Cut out an area well beyond the damaged material to ensure you have only solid material remaining.

2 If the rafter is splintered or deteriorated beneath the sheathing, add nailing strips as necessary. Use a 2x4 cleat for nailing support.

3 Cut new sheathing from exterior-grade plywood, be sure to match the thickness of the old sheathing. Position the sheathing seams over rafters, with an expansion gap no greater than ⅛", then attach with nails or screws. To replace damaged one-inch-thick stock, cut plywood to size.

Applying Underlayment

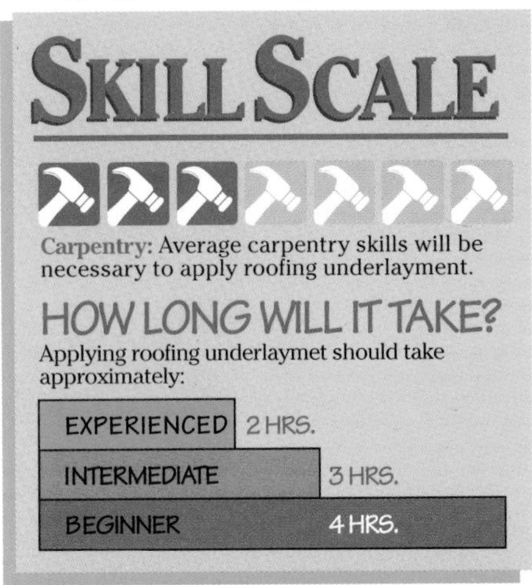

STUFF YOU'LL NEED:

- □**Tools:** Claw hammer, flat pry bar, hammer stapler, utility knife, chalk line.
- □**Material:** Building paper, ice guard underlayment.

Everything your mother told you about your underwear is true of underlayment as well. Holes are to be avoided. Attention to the little details indicates refinement and quality.

While the outer roofing layer does the basic job of shedding and channeling rain, the underlayment adds protection as a final barrier to moisture penetration.

The general idea with roofing materials is that water will most commonly flow downward from the peak or ridge to the eaves, so overlaps of the materials should be arranged to prevent this downward flowing water from seeping under an edge. On shingles, this downward-oriented overlap is obvious but the principle sometimes eludes the appliers of underlayment.

If you are conscientious about its application, underlayment will offer a degree of protection to your roof, should it rain before the shingles are applied. And if your house gets in an accident, you'll have peace of mind that comes from knowing its underlayment is nice.

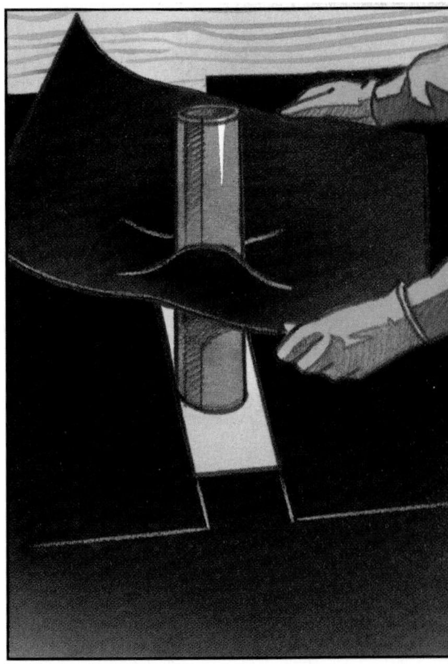

Fit a building paper patch over obstructions. Leave about 12" of paper on either side of the obstruction, and run felting courses right up to each edge of the obstruction.

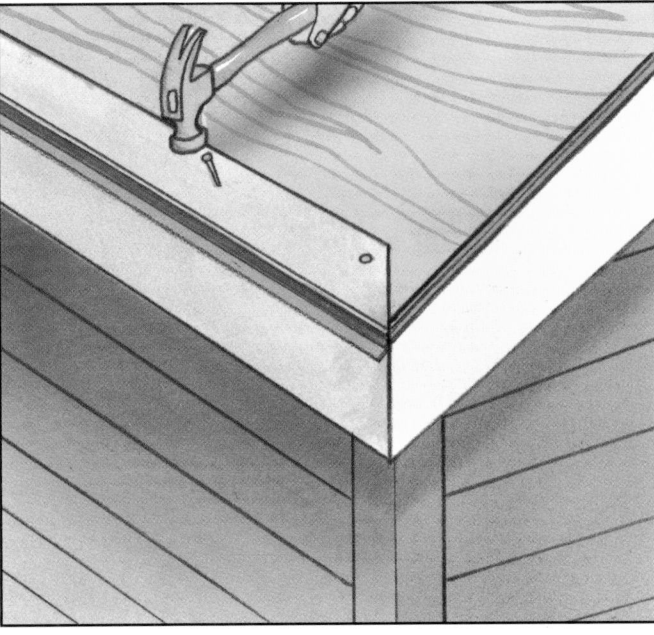

1 Nail a strip of roof edge flashing along the edge of the eaves. Overlap strips by 2". Trim ends flush with rake ends and miter end of drip edge at rake ends where it will butt against the drip edge covering the raker.

2 Snap a chalk line 35 ⅝" up from the eaves, so the first course of the 36"-wide ice guard membrane overhangs the eaves by ⅜". Also apply the ice guard membrane in the valleys of the roof. Apply enough ice guard up the roof to extend inside the wall line by at least 24". If possible, have someone help you install the ice guard, to make the job more manageable. In warm climates, ice guard may not be necessary, so check your local codes.

3 Measure up from eaves to a point 32" above top of ice guard, and snap a new chalk line. Roll out the first course of building paper, and overlap ice guard 4". Fasten building paper every 12" with a hammer stapler, then cut paper flush at rake ends.

4 Work your way up the roof deck with building paper courses, allowing 4" horizontal overlaps and 12" vertical overlaps. Run felt up to obstacles, patch them, and resume course on other side of obstacle. Roll building paper across valleys from both sides, overlapping 36", then cut off.

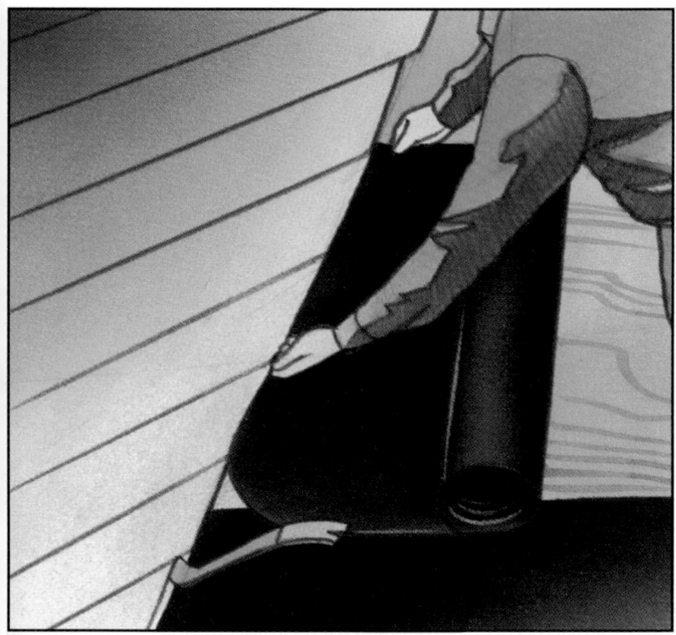

5 Install building paper at a dormer or sidewalls, starting at sidewall. Carefully pry up the siding, and tuck at least 2" of paper under the siding to create an unbroken seal at the roof and wall joint. Also, run paper course at least 6" over each side of a hip.

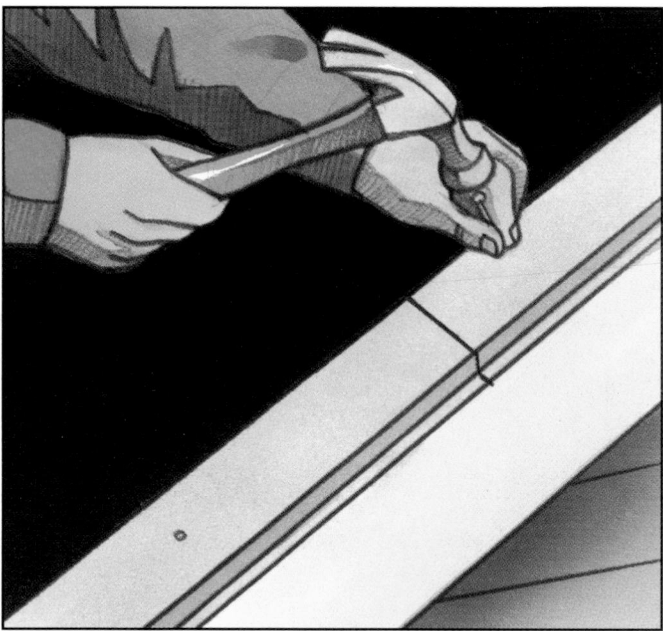

6 Nail a strip of roof edge over the rakers, starting at the bottom and working toward the ridge. Overlap joining strips of drip edge by 2". Miter the ends of drip edge where it meets drip edge at eaves.

Shingling

Think of shingling as your well-earned reward for the conscientious work you did with the underlayment and flashing. Shingling proceeds quickly. The notches in each shingle help you keep each course aligned properly to maintain even rows with the eaves and rake edges (the sloped ends of the roof edge that go to the peak). You have the satisfaction of knowing that, once shingled, the project will be complete and it will look good – just like a real roof!

First you'll have to tote those heavy bundles of shingles onto your roof and distribute them, of course. And, unless you have a power nailer, your arm is going to get very tired swinging that hammer. And there are only about five days a year when it's actually pleasant to be up on your roof all day. On second thought, forget that part about shingling being a big reward. Your reward for a job well done will be the fact that rain doesn't come through your ceiling.

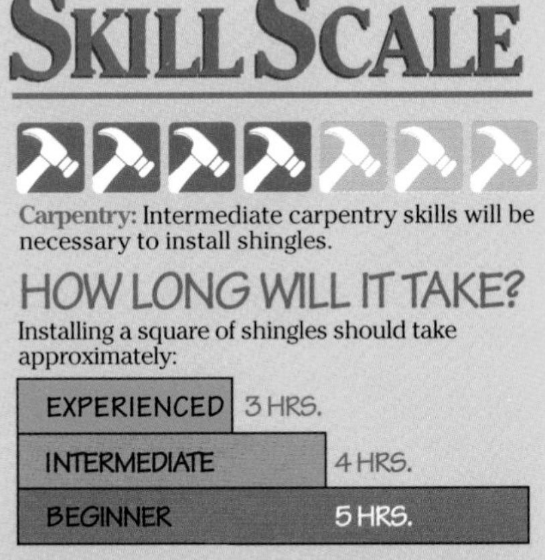

STUFF YOU'LL NEED:

- ☐ **Tools:** Claw hammer, roofing hammer, roofing knife, framing square, caulk gun, tape measure, chalk line, and pneumatic nailer.
- ☐ **Material:** Shingles, roofing nails, roof cement.

ROOFING WITH ASPHALT SHINGLES

1 Snap a horizontal chalk line 11½" up from the eaves onto the ice guard sheathing, to create an alignment line for the starter course of shingles. Do not use red chalk, because red pigment will stain roofing materials.

2 Starting at the rake edge, install a starter strip of shingles, rotated upside-down. Trim off 6" of first shingle so the vertical seams will be offset from this course. Overhang the eaves by ½". Attach shingles using galvanized roofing nails. Place nails about every 12", so each shingle has four nails.

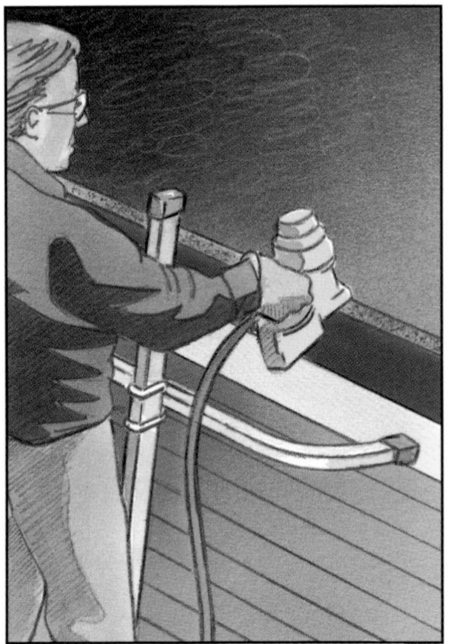

An alternative starter course, is to cut off the tabs on the shingles and install them right side up. This way, the adhesive on the shingle will help seal the eave edge.

3 Apply the first full course over the starter strip. Begin at rake edge, and start with a full shingle. Overhang the eaves by ½" and keep first course shingles flush with starter strip.

4 Snap a chalk line to create a vertical centerline, in the general area of the roof center. Choose a seam between two shingles on the first course, and place centerline so it does not intersect with any obstructions. Use a framing square at the eaves or ridge to ensure a perpendicular line.

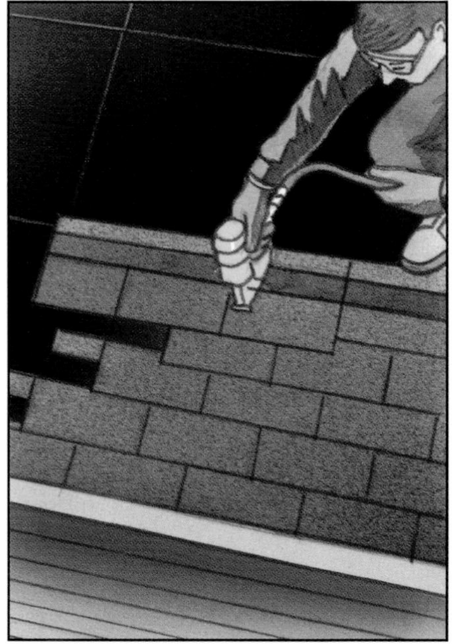

5 Butt two shingles of next course at centerline, revealing a 5" exposure of first course. Attach shingles with roofing nails placed ⅝" above each tab slot. Install three more courses of shingles next to centerline, working toward ridge. Stagger each course horizontally by 6".

6 Shingle to the rakers on either side of the second course. Use the tab cutouts of the previous course to align new shingles. Butt the shingle against the last shingle, then adjust the bottom edge of the shingle so it barely covers the top of the tab slot. Before starting the fifth course, install roofing jacks.

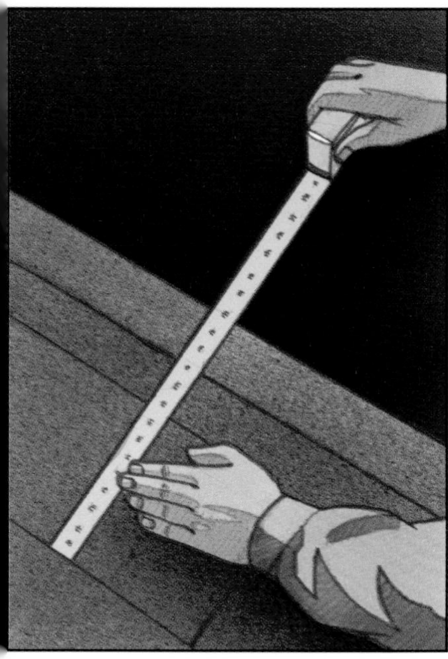

Periodically check the alignment of the shingles to make sure the rows are running straight. In several places along roof, measure up from the bottom of the last course to the building paper line. Do not try to correct misalignments by shifting just one shingle. Gradually adjust over the course of a row or two until the alignment is corrected.

7 Finish shingling all the way up to the ridge, flashing as needed. Fill out shingles sideways to finish a section of shingles. Shingle up enough so the ridge caps will fully cover dead area of shingle. On first side, trim flush. On second side, overlap ridge and tack down shingle to protect open ridge.

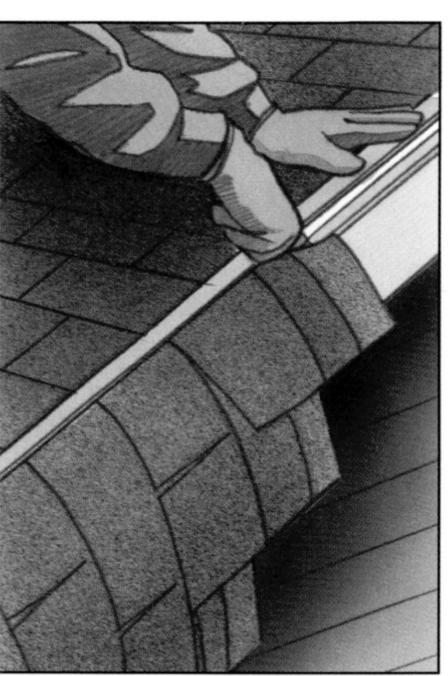

8 When all the shingling is completed, trim the shingles at the rakers to overhang raker by ⅜". Use a straightedge to keep your cutting line straight.

SHINGLE VALLEYS WITH A WEAVE CUT

1 Shingle the main roof up to the eaves of the dormer. Shingle the entire dormer roof, overlapping the valley and main roof with the dormer shingles.

2 Shingle the remaining main roof, slightly overlapping the valley and dormer roof.

3 Use a scrap piece of material as a protective backer and place under the ends of the main roof shingles that overlap the valley and dormer. Use a straightedge and utility knife to cut through the main roof shingles along the valley. Pull out the scrap material. This will give you a quick and easy weave appearance for the valley.

SHINGLING VALLEYS WITH VALLEY FLASHING

1 Lay out shingles carefully around dormers or other obstructions. Shingle completely up first side of dormer, including step flashing, according to shingle pattern. Shingle across the top until one seam clears width of dormer. Snap a vertical chalk line at seam down to eaves or up to the ridge.

2 Shingle upward from eaves on second side of dormer, filling in shingles between dormer and chalk line, until you tie into course across top of dormer. Make sure first full shingle at eaves aligns or overlaps chalk line to match the original shingle pattern.

3 Shingle dormer roofs starting at bottom of gable end. Use the normal shingling pattern, and work back toward main roof. Run shingle courses far enough to overlap the center of valley between dormer and main roof.

4 Trim dormer shingles at valley flashing where dormer and main roof meet, 3" from center of valley, using tin snips. Add the ridge cap.

SHINGLING HIPS AND RIDGES

1 Cut 12" square ridge, or hip, caps from regular shingles. Trim ends of the lap portion to taper 1". Snap a chalk line 6" parallel to the hip on either side. Attach each side of a cap with one roofing nail, 1" from the edge, just above the sealing tab. Leave a 5" exposure on the overlap. Shingle all hips before ridge.

2 Cap joining hips with a hip shingle split 4" up the middle. Nail in place and cover the nail heads with roofing cement. Shingle ridges as you would hips, working from each end toward the middle.

3 At the midpoint of ridge, butt joining ridge caps. Cut off the lap portion of the last cap shingle and nail over butted caps. Cover nail heads with roofing cement.

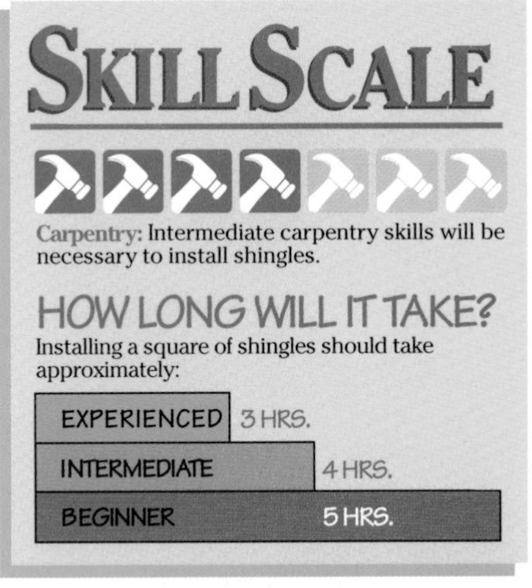

Reroofing over an Existing Roof

STUFF YOU'LL NEED:

- **Tools:** Claw hammer, roofing hammer, roofing knife, framing square, caulk gun, tape measure, chalk line, and pneumatic nailer.
- **Material:** Shingles, roofing nails, roof cement.

Lucky you. If you're reading this, your roof currently has only one layer of shingles and those, though worn out, are basically sound and in good repair. As a candidate for reroofing (in this case we're talking about your house, not you personally) you'll be able to proceed almost directly to shingling. That means no tear-off, no big dumpster for the torn-off roofing, and no frenzied rush to beat an approaching rainstorm–unless you have three layers of shingles on the roof. You can only have three layers on your roof at one time. If you have three layers before you put the new layer on, you'll have to tear off the old shingles first, then put on the new layer of shingles.

If you can simply put another layer of shingles on the roof, the main problem you must overcome when reroofing over a first layer of shingles is that the underlying surface is not smooth. It is, in fact, shingled. The successive courses of shingles are stacked like flat little stairs. Another course directly on top would not be good.

Fortunately, the solution to this problem is not a big deal. You split a course of shingles, width-wise, so that they just match the exposure of the bottom row of shingles on the old roof. Once you've filled that in, every course of the new roof will have a nice flat base. Easy!

BE CAREFUL WHEN WORKING ON THE ROOF. IT'S EASY TO LOSE YOUR BALANCE, ESPECIALLY WHEN WORKING DOWNHILL!

1 For the starter course, cut each shingle in lengthwise strips to fit over the "exposure" of the existing first course (usually about 5"). If you need to install drip edge, and can install one without damaging shingles, do so. Start your first course so the tab slots are offset from those of the existing course. Use 1¼"-long roofing nails.

2 Trim the width of each shingle in the next course so shingles will butt against the bottom of the existing third course and match the existing overhang. Offset the course from the existing vertical seam.

3 Butt successive courses against the bottom of existing courses. Apply remaining shingles as you normally would for new installation.

4 Remove damaged and old flashing as you install shingles, and replace with new flashing. Add a spacer shingle underneath old flashing around obstructions, to bring new flashing up to new shingle level.

5 Shingle around obstructions using normal shingling procedure. Leave any existing flashing in good condition in place. Seal new seams well with roofing cement and trim new shingles to fit around obstructions.

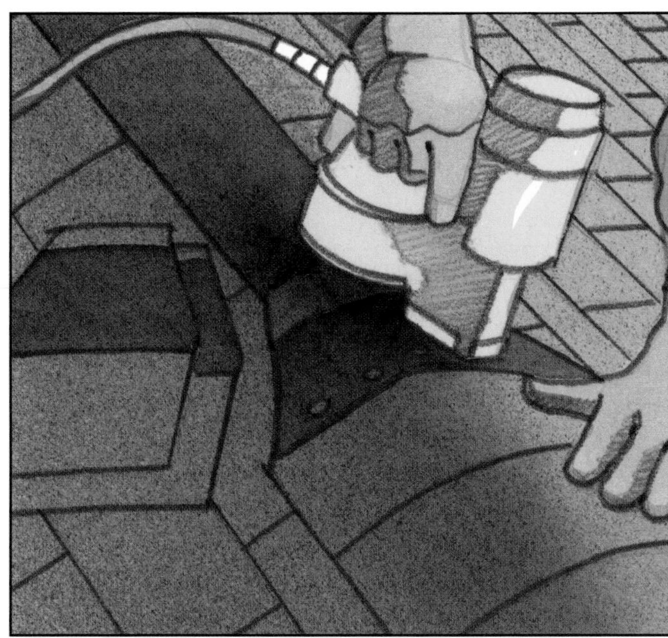

6 Tear off old hip and ridge caps before applying last courses of shingles up to a ridge. Replace hips and ridge caps with new shingles after all other shingling has been completed.

Installing Roll Roofing

Roll roofing is an alternative to individual asphalt shingles and is commonly used for outbuildings, garages, storage sheds and lean-tos that usually have more gradual roof pitches. It is normally sold in rolls and when allowed to flatten out in pre-cut strips of 18' or less, is fairly easy to install single-handed.

Roll roofing is generally made of the same material as asphalt shingles, and in the same thicknesses, except it comes in wider widths and you can cut it into strips according to your needs.

One way to install roll roofing is to overlap half of each preceding course with each subsequent course, nail the top edge of each course, and cement the remaining edges. This results in a more appealing roof because there are no exposed nails covered with roof cement, but depending on wind conditions, can be less durable. The steps on these pages show the more wind resistant installation.

STUFF YOU'LL NEED:

- ☐**Tools:** Roofing hammer, roofing knife, framing square, caulk gun, tape measure, chalk line.
- ☐**Materials:** Roofing material, roofing nails, roof cement.

1 Sweep the roof deck clean and install drip edge and underlayment (pg. 448). Once the roofing material has been unrolled and allowed to flatten, apply the first course, the full width of the sheet, so that the lower edge and end will extend over the eaves and rake edges about 3/8".

2 Nail the top edge of the first course along a line 1/2" to 3/4" parallel to the top edge of the sheet, spacing the nails 18" apart. This holds the sheet in place until the second course is laid.

3 Nail along the eaves and rake edges on a line approximately 1" in from the edge of the roofing, the nails should be placed on 2" centers and slightly staggered along the eaves to avoid splitting the roof board.

4 Apply the second course of roofing material so that it will overlap the first course by 2". Nail the top edge with nails spaced approximately 18" apart.

5 Lift the lower edge of the overlapping sheet and apply lap cement evenly over the upper 2" of the lower course. Use enough lap cement to achieve a good bond, the thickness of the cement should be no more than $^1/_8$". Excessive use of cement can cause softening of the asphalt in the roofing

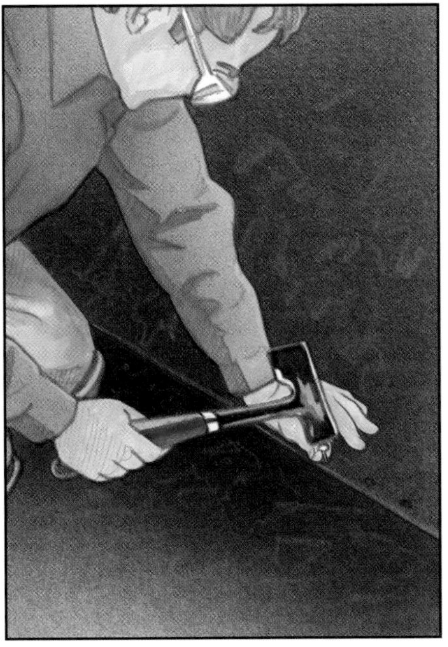

6 Embed the overlapping sheet in the cement and nail through the lap on 2" centers. Stagger the nails slightly to avoid splitting the roof boards, placing them not less than $^3/_4$" up from the exposed edge of the sheet.

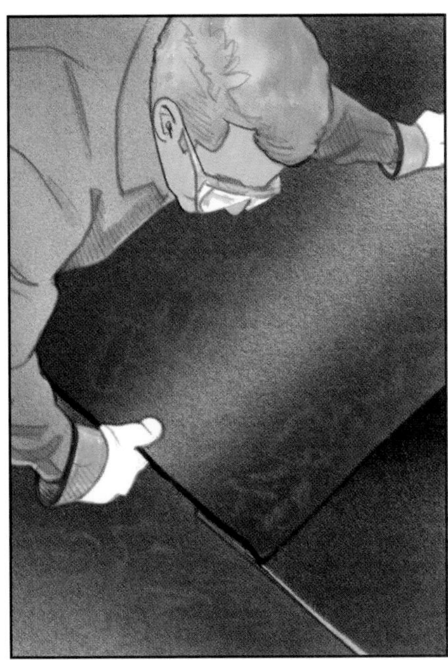

7 Overlap the ends of rolls by 6" and cement them the full wid'h of the lap. Stagger the nails in rows 1" and 5" from the end of the lap and space nails on 4" centers in each row. Stagger all laps so that in no case is an end lap adjacent to an end lap in the preceding course.

8 Cut strips of roofing 12" wide and bend them through their centers. Snap a chalk line parallel to the ridge 5$^1/_2$" down on each side of the roof. Spread lap cement on each side of the ridge even with the chalk line. Embed the bent strip in the cement over the ridge. Nail the strip in place so the nails penetrate the cement and the sheathing.

COVER ALL NAILS WITH ROOF CEMENT TO PREVENT LEAKS

REPAIRING A ROLLED ROOF

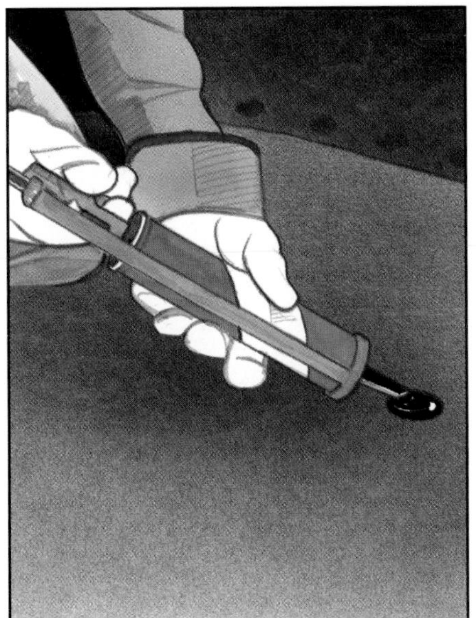

For small holes or punctures, clean out the damaged area and fill with roof sealer or roof tar.

For larger holes, cut out the damaged area and replace it with a section of roofing material. Replace the roof paper if it is damaged also. Be sure to lap borders of the new section of roofing material accordingly and cement and nail as in applying new roofing material.

CONCRETE BASICS

The most common paving material for driveways and sidewalks is concrete. The decision to use concrete should take into consideration its price and appearance, but also climatological factors and intended use.

Concrete is a very hard material, but its rigidity makes it susceptible to cracking as a result of frost heaving. And salts in chemicals used to melt ice in northern climates often wreak havoc with the composition of concrete.

One way to get an idea of whether or not concrete is suitable for the project and your area is to survey your neighborhood. See if your neighbors' concrete has lasted and ask them how it was installed.

Many problems of concrete–cracking, chipping, crumbling, and pop-outs–are due to improper installation. It is very important to have the proper water-to-concrete mix, and a slower drying process is almost always advisable. You can slow the drying process by covering new concrete with plastic.

If you handle the water-to-concrete ratio and the drying time well, the only problems you'll have are watching out for mischievous children, and dogs who might leave a paw print in your work.

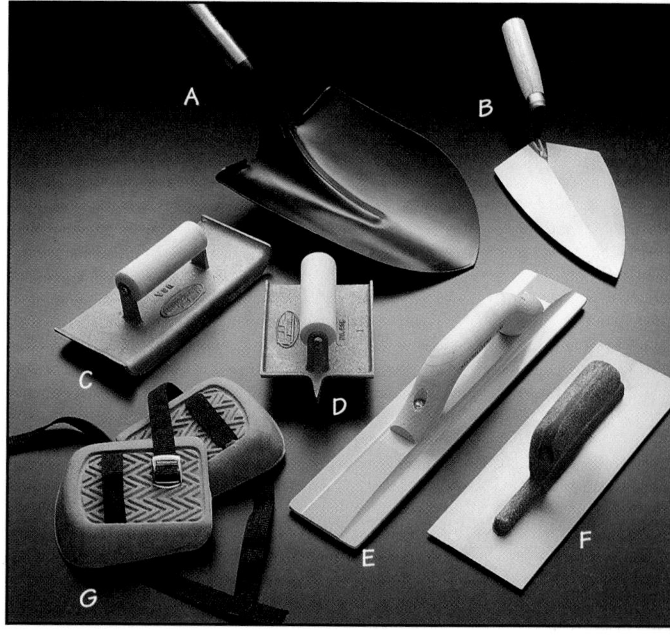

Basic hand tools for concrete repair include: shovel (**A**), pointed trowel (**B**), hand edger (**C**), hand jointer (**D**) magnesium float (**E**), finishing trowel (**F**), and knee-pads (**G**).

Common concrete rental equipment includes: wheelbarrow (**A**), hand tamper (**B**) or power tamper, bull float with handle extensions(**C**), and concrete mixer (**D**).

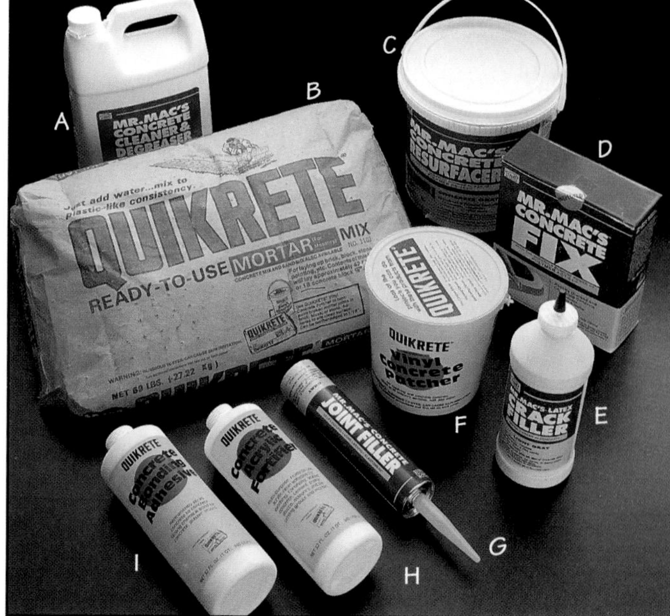

Common premixed products for repairing concrete include: concrete cleaner (**A**), ready-to-use mortar mix (**B**), concrete resurfacer (**C**), concrete repair mix (**D**), latex crack filler (**E**), vinyl concrete patch (**F**), concrete joint filler (**G**), concrete acrylic fortifier (**H**), concrete bonding adhesive (**I**).

COMMON CONCRETE PROBLEMS

Concrete heave is common in colder climates. Frost in the ground forces concrete slabs upward and, if control joints are missing or inadequate, sections of the slab pop up. The best solution is to break off the affected section, repair the subbase, and pour a new section set off by isolation joints.

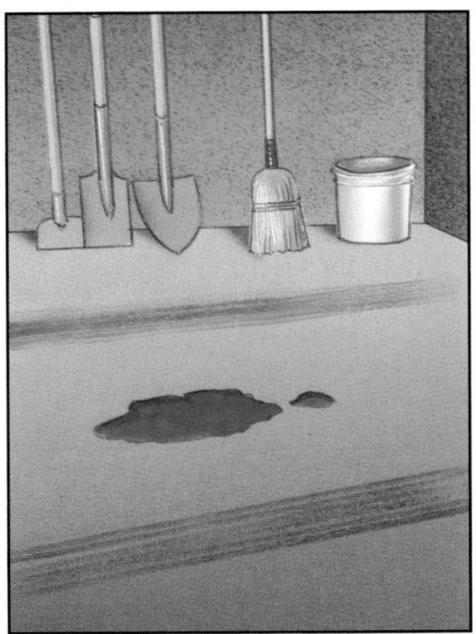

Staining and discoloration can ruin the appearance of an otherwise sturdy concrete surface or structure. Commercial concrete cleaners can be used for cleaning. Extra tough stains may be removed with muriatic acid. For long-term protection, seal surfaces with clear masonry sealant.

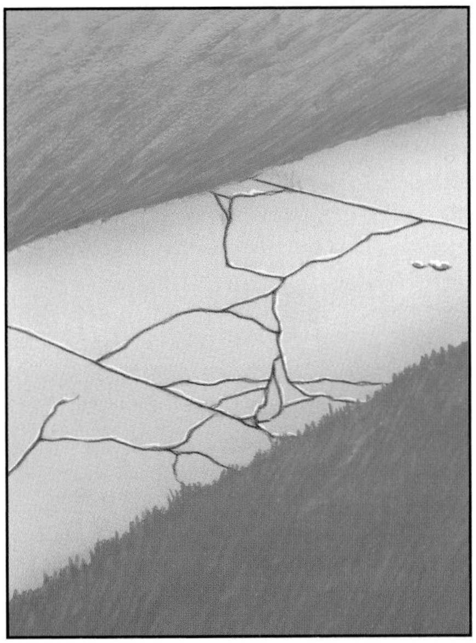

Cracking is inevitable with most concrete projects. By adding control joints, you can keep the cracking to a minimum. Fill small cracks with concrete repair products and patch large cracks with vinyl-reinforced patching material.

Chipping and pop-outs occur as a result of moisture, stress, or if the concrete surface was improperly floated or cured. Localized chipping or pop-outs can be cleaned out and patched.

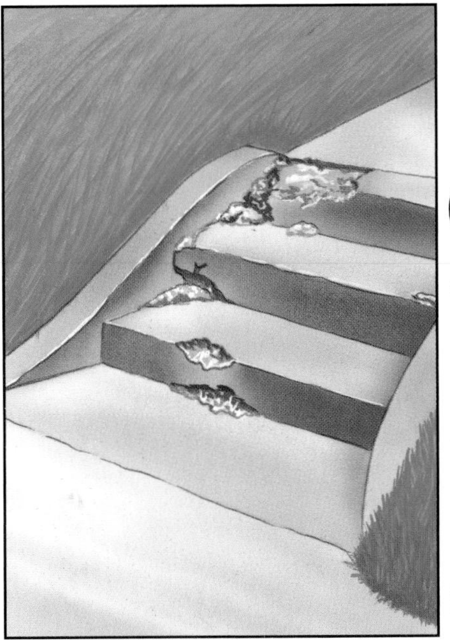

Crumbling is a general degeneration that occurs as a concrete surface or structure ages. Other than patching crumbled areas, there is very little that can be done to remedy the problem. Interpret it as a warning sign that the structure or surface will require replacement in the near future.

HOMER'S HINDSIGHT

My first concrete project was a lesson in cleanliness. I had finished the job and was so impressed with my performance that I thought I'd reward myself with a nice cold glass of lemonade. One thing led to another and by the time I got back to clean up my tools, the cement was already dried and crusted on. I thought I'd be able to simply wash off the cement but was sadly mistaken when it couldn't be removed. Needless to say, I had to replace the tools because they rusted so badly from the cement that they just couldn't be used. That was an expensive lesson!

Mixing Concrete

When cement, sand, gravel, and water are combined in the correct proportion, the mixture produces a chemical reaction that binds those materials into a uniform, dense compound–concrete.

For small jobs–post anchors, limited repair work, cement overshoes–cement blended with water in a wheelbarrow or mixing tub may be perfectly adequate.

For larger projects, you'll want to rent a gasoline or electric power mixer. Machine-mixed concrete is likely to be more consistent than hand-mixed.

If your concrete requirements are large and your time is limited, consider ordering ready-mix concrete from a local source. Plan ahead, have all your forms ready and, unless you are experienced yourself, get a knowledgeable friend to help you. Once the concrete is delivered, you will have two hours to finish it.

Concrete is made from the same basic ingredients, whether it is purchased as ready-mix, or is mixed from scratch. Portland cement is the key ingredient, along with sand and mixed aggregate to provide the structure of concrete. Water causes the ingredients to hydrate and then dry into a solid mass.

ESTIMATING CONCRETE

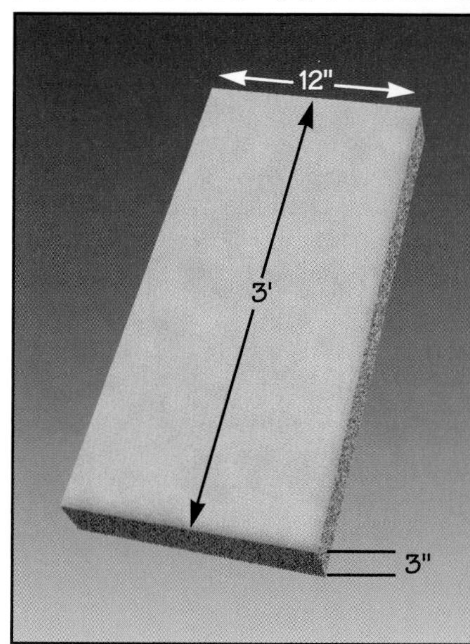

Measure the width and length of the project in feet, then multiply the dimensions to get the square footage. Measure the thickness in feet, 4" equals 1/3 foot, then multiply the square footage times the thickness to get the cubic footage. Twenty-seven cubic feet equal one cubic yard.

JUDGING CONCRETE CONSISTENCY

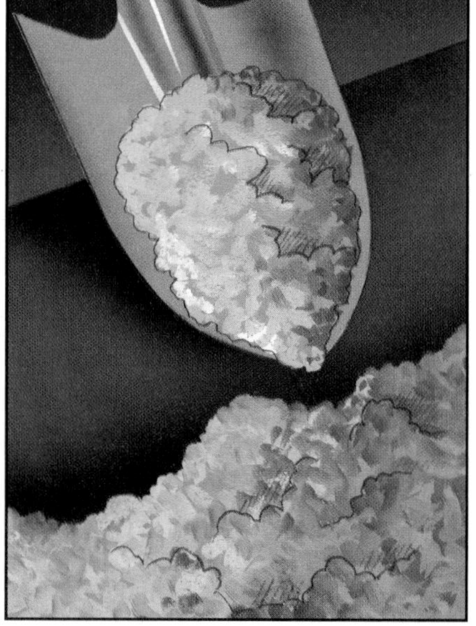

Concrete that is mixed too dry will not screed, float, or trowel properly and will result in a pour that will be impossible to finish. Dry chunks of portland cement and aggregate will not be worked and mixed properly into the concrete.

Concrete that is mixed too wet will be too loose to properly screed and float, and will take too long to set up and trowel. Wet mix has a greater tendency to surface peel, once it has cured, due to the excessive surface moisture.

Concrete that is mixed correctly will pour and flow smoothly and will screed off in a nice even screed. It also will float quite easily, allowing you to work the aggregate down without too much effort and without raising too much water. Troweling will go much smoother and will result in a premium finish.

MIXING CONCRETE BY HAND

1 Empty the contents of the premixed concrete bags into a wheelbarrow or mixing trough. Read the directions on the bag and measure the amount of water required into a bucket, then add to the dry mix.

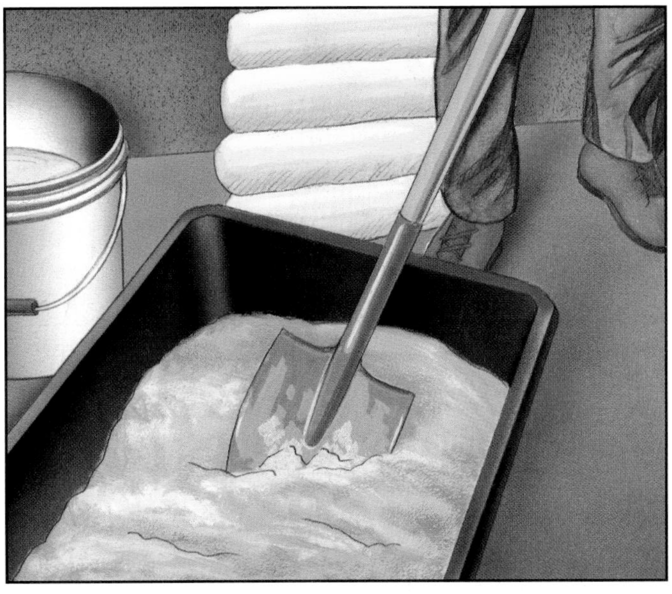

2 Work with a hoe or shovel until the proper consistency is achieved. Be careful not to overwork the mixture.

MIXING CONCRETE WITH A POWER MIXER

1 Add half the required amount of water to the mixer, turn it on, then let it run for a minute.

2 Add all of the dry, premixed concrete, then the rest of the water. Mix for about three minutes. Transfer the mix to a wheelbarrow or buckets as soon as you are done mixing.

Repairing Concrete

Most concrete repairs can usually be made in a few short hours, on a mild day, and with absolutely no rain in the forecast! Although concrete repairs are normally quite simple, keep in mind that the material is rather heavy to carry (normally about 60 pounds per bag of concrete mix), and can be somewhat back-breaking to mix together if you have a lot of it to do and don't have a power mixer. This might be a good time to call in a few favors from your friends and neighbors, just to make the job smooth and enjoyable.

Be sure to use bonding liquid to provide proper adhesion on concrete patch work.

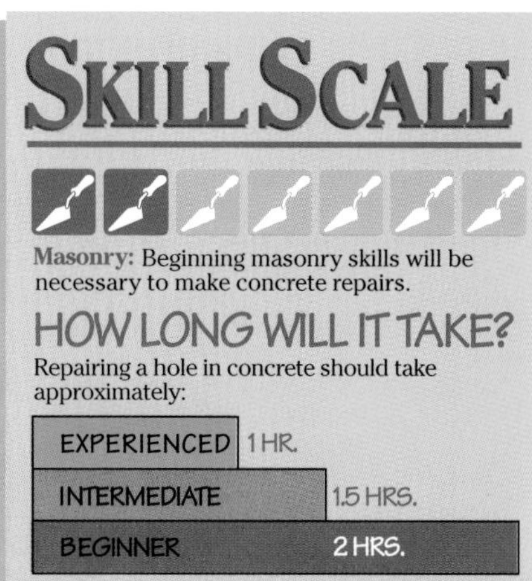

STUFF YOU'LL NEED:

- ☐ **Tools:** Wire brush, masonry chisel, ball-peen hammer, trowel, wallboard knife, vacuum, sledge hammer, tamper, screed board, hand float, shovel.
- ☐ **Material:** Portland cement, vinyl-reinforced concrete, latex bonding liquid, ready-mix or premix concrete mix.

PREPARING CRACKED CONCRETE FOR REPAIR

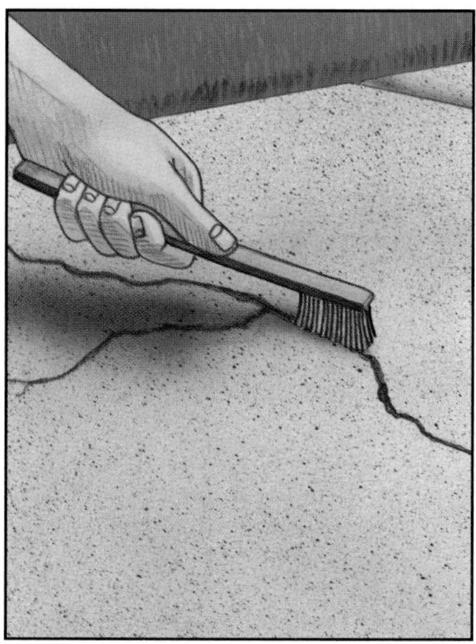

1 Remove loose material from the crack using a wire brush, chisel, or a wire wheel attachment to a portable drill. Apply bonding liquid. Loose or semi-loose material left in the crack will result in an ineffective repair.

2 Chisel out the base of the crack to create a dovetail surface, using a cold chisel and ball-peen hammer. The dovetail shape prevents the repair material from pushing out of the crack.

FIXING SMALL CRACKS IN CONCRETE

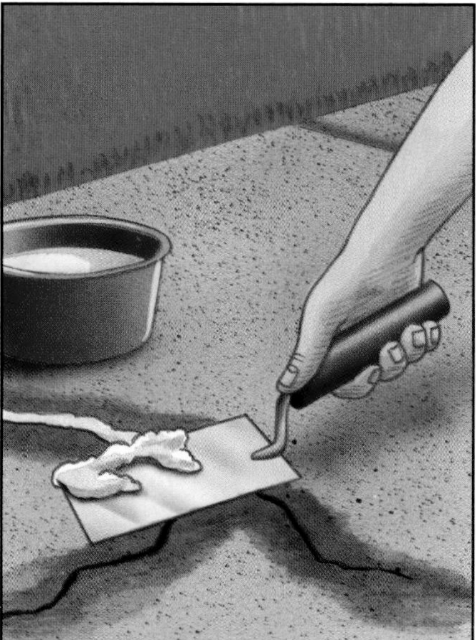

1 Prepare the crack, then dampen the area. Mix a thick paste of portland cement and water, then trowel it into the crack, overfilling the crack slightly.

2 Feather out the repair compound so it is level with the surface. Let the repair cure.

FIXING HORIZONTAL CRACKS

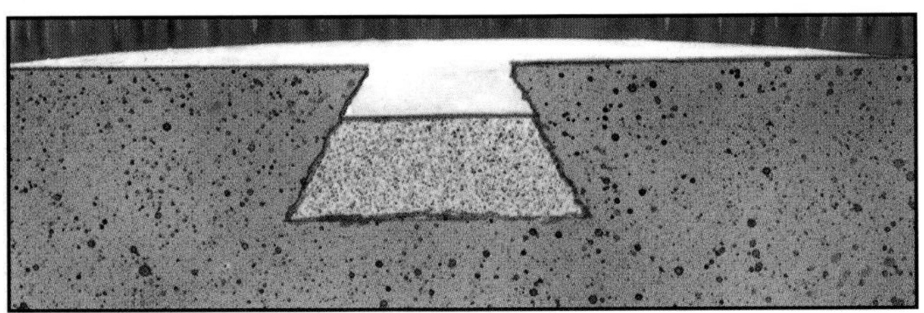

Prepare the crack, then pour sand into the crack within $^1/_2$" of the surface. Mix vinyl-reinforced concrete, or prepare a portland cement/water paste, with enough sand added to make the mixture gritty. Trowel the mixture into the crack, overfilling it slightly, then feather it out even with the surface.

FIXING VERTICAL CRACKS

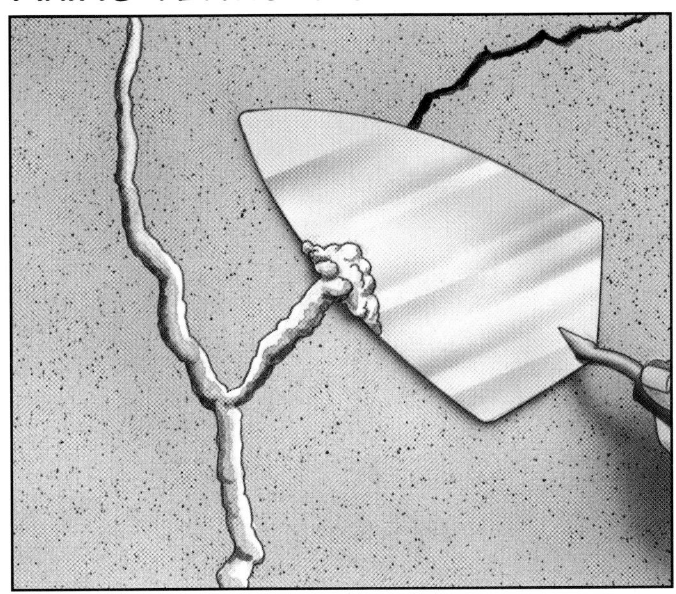

Prepare the crack, then pour sand into the crack within $^1/_2$" of the surface. Mix vinyl-reinforced concrete, or prepare a portland cement/water paste, with enough sand added to make the mixture gritty. Trowel a $^1/_4$"- to $^1/_2$"-thick layer into the crack, and let it dry. Continue adding $^1/_4$"- to $^1/_2$"-thick layers until the crack is slightly overfilled. Feather it out even with the surface.

PATCHING POP-UPS IN CONCRETE

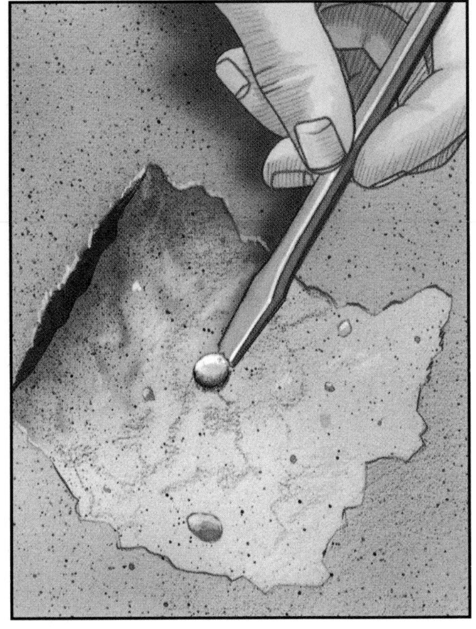

1 Chip out rocks at the bottom of the pop-up hole with a masonry chisel and a ball-peen hammer. Wear goggles to avoid eye injury.

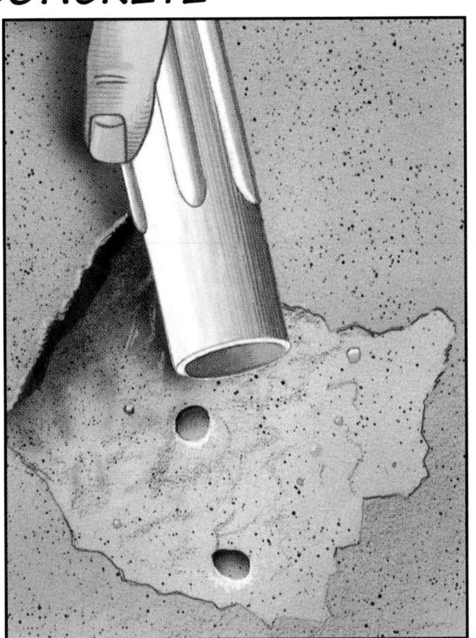

2 Remove dirt and debris from the hole with a shop vacuum. If the hole contains oil or grease, wash with a detergent, then rinse with water.

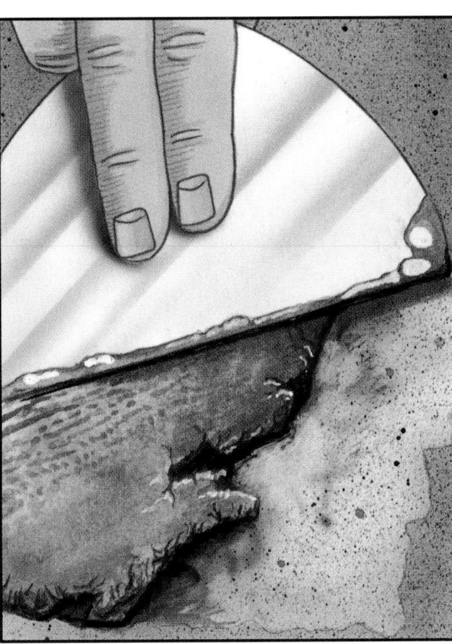

3 Coat the edges of the hole with a latex bonding liquid. Mix concrete with water, then stir in bonding liquid. Pour in the mixture and smooth with a flexible knife or trowel.

REPAIRING CHIPPED STEPS

1 Clean the chipped concrete with a wire brush. Brush the patch area with a latex bonding liquid, using a paintbrush.

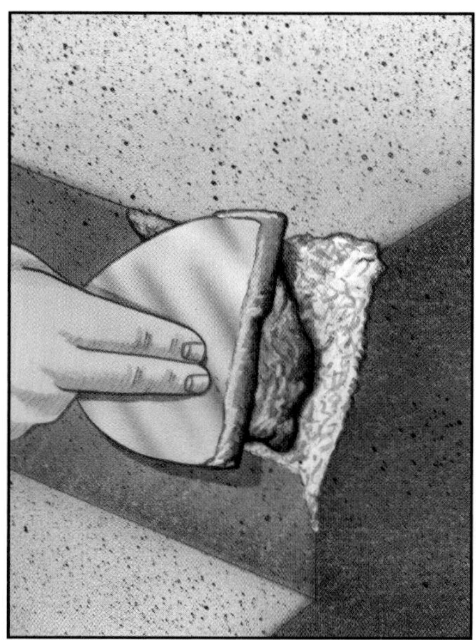

2 Mix the concrete patcher with water, then stir in the bonding liquid, as directed by the manufacturer. Apply to the patch area with a flexible knife or trowel.

3 Tape scrap lumber pieces around the corner of the step to hold the patch until it hardens.

CLEANING AND SEALING CONCRETE

1 Clean the concrete with a brush and a 5% solution of muriatic acid and water. Wear gloves, goggles, and protective clothes when working with acid.

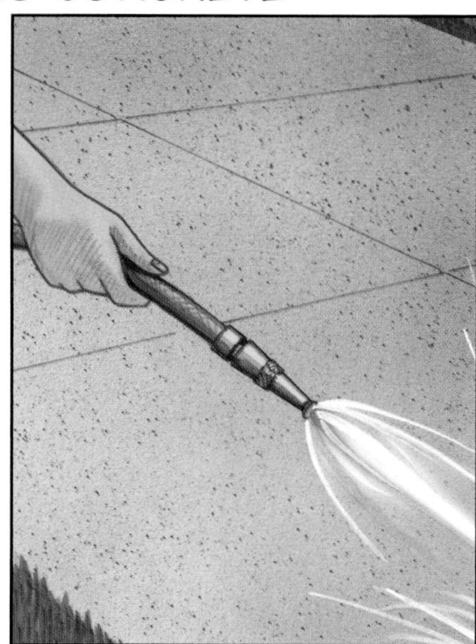

2 Flush the surface with a trisodium phosphate solution, then rinse with a garden hose or high-pressure washer.

3 Apply concrete sealer with a paint roller, squeegee, or garden sprayer.

REPAIRING A BROKEN SLAB

1 Dig a 6"-wide trench on each side of the slab to create room for the forms. Using a sledge hammer, break up the damaged slab and remove the pieces from the work site. Always wear safety glasses and work gloves for this.

2 Prepare the subbase by leveling and smoothing out with sand or gravel as is necessary. Tamp the entire subbase to prevent settling.

3 Stake 2x4 forms flush against the sides of the existing slabs, even with their top surfaces. Make sure to follow the grade of the slabs.

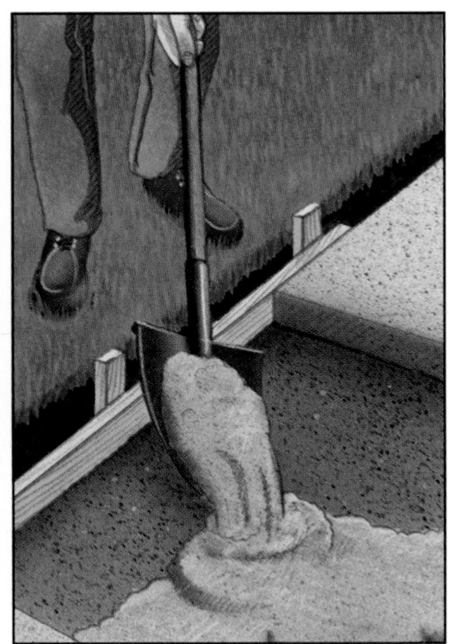

4 Mix the concrete according to the manufacturer's directions and pour the concrete into the forms.

5 Screed the concrete along the forms then float it to work the aggregate down and to bring the cement and water to the surface. Let it cure, checking it regularly. Once the mixture has set up enough to trowel, work the surface with a trowel to bring up the water, then smooth out the finish.

6 Once the finish has dried and cured, apply several coats of concrete sealer, allowing it to dry fully between coats. You can use a plastic covering to slow the drying process and ensure well-cured concrete if you're repairing on a hot summer day.

INDEX

Index

C

E

Index

M

N

Z

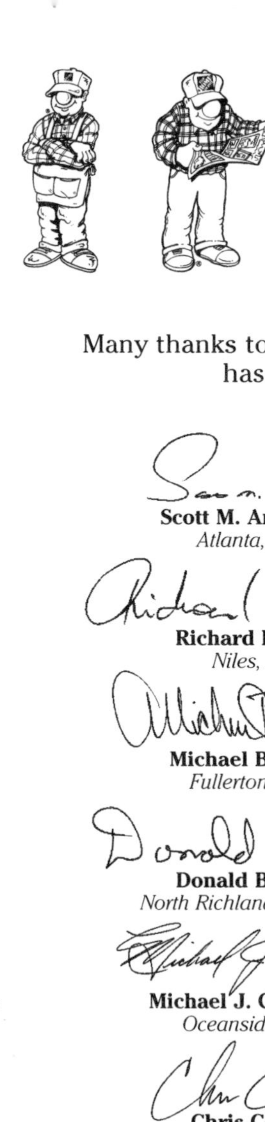

Many thanks to the following employees of The Home Depot whose "wisdom of the aisles" has made *Home Improvement 1-2-3* the most useful book of its kind.

Scott M. Andrews
Atlanta, GA

Richard Baran
Niles, IL

Michael Baugus
Fullerton, CA

Donald Bittick
North Richland Hills, TX

Michael J. Carnegie
Oceanside, CA

Chris Coats
Niles, IL

Jack Crowley A.S.I.D.
South Plainfield, NJ

Kimberly Curtin
Fullerton, CA

Dave Davies
Canoga Park, CA

Nancy A. Dee
Commack, NY

Patrick Diamond
Selden, NY

Jim Dionian
Patchogue, NY

Antonio Domecq
Hawthorne, CA

Dennis Donelan
East Meadow, NY

Ollie Elder Jr.
Alhambra, CA

Andy Etkind
Atlanta, GA

Byron C. Fitzgerald
Woodstock, GA

Marty Gallagher
S. Plainfield, NJ

Gordon Gammon
Calumet City, IL

Chuck Garrett
Duluth, GA

Michael Grant
Atlanta, GA

Bill Gronenthal
Roswell, GA

Rob Hallam
Atlanta, GA

Jim Handelin
Burbank, CA

Mark E. Harris
Atlanta, GA

Ronald Hickman
Commack, NY

James Hojnicki
Orland Park, IL

John S. Hollerorth
Decatur, GA

Debora Hubbard
Atlanta, GA

Richard Hutchinson
Murrieta, CA

Steve Jepsen
Arlington, TX

Mac Kennedy
Austell, GA

Barbara Koller
Atlanta, GA